# A POLITICAL HISTORY OF THE ARAMEANS

# ARCHAEOLOGY AND BIBLICAL STUDIES



Number 13

SBL PRESS

# A POLITICAL HISTORY OF THE ARAMEANS

## From Their Origins to the End of Their Polities

K. Lawson Younger Jr.

SBL PRESS

SBL PRESS

Atlanta



Library of Congress Cataloging-in-Publication Data

Younger, K. Lawson.
A political history of the Arameans : from their origins to the end of their polities / K. Lawson Younger, Jr.
p. cm. — (Society of Biblical literature archaeology and Biblical studies ; number 13)
Includes bibliographical references and index.
ISBN 978-1-58983-128-5 (paper binding : alk. paper) — ISBN 978-1-62837-080-5 (hardcover binding : alk. paper) — ISBN 978-1-62837-084-3 (electronic format)
1. Arameans—History. 2. Arameans—Politics and government. 3. Middle East—Politics and government. I. Title.
DS59.A7Y68 2015
939.4'3402—dc23 2015004298

Printed on acid-free paper.

To Alan Millard,

a pursuer of a knowledge and understanding of אֲרַמִּי אֹבֵד

# CONTENTS

# PREFACE

When I began this project, there were two recent full-length monographs devoted to the study of the Arameans: P.-E. Dion, *Les Araméens à l'âge du fer: Histoire politique et structures sociales* (Paris: Gabalda, 1997); and E. Lipiński, *The Aramaeans: Their Ancient History, Culture, Religion* (Leuven: Peeters, 2000). Both of these works were devoted more or less to all aspects of the study of this people group (history, culture, religion, etc.).

Archaeological discoveries have brought much new information to light. New discoveries and advances in the understanding of the Middle Assyrian and Luwian text sources, and, to a lesser extent, the archaeology connected to these, have greatly improved our comprehension of the history of the Arameans. Various excavations have brought clarity to some of the crucial questions. Renewed excavations of long-known sites (e.g., Zincirli, Tell Taʿyinat, Tell Ḥalaf, Tell Fakhariya) and the publication of materials found at excavated sites since the two monographs mentioned above have all contributed to a much richer knowledge. Recent anthropological studies in tribal structures and in nomadism, including important archaeological work at Jebel Bišri, have created more nuanced perspectives.

Consequently, this volume is devoted only to the political history of the Aramean entities, in so far as such is possible. The nature of the sources, whether textual or archaeological, make such a project quite challenging yet highly rewarding. There is much that we still do not know, but what we do know generates an exciting new synthesis. The impacts of all the Aramean tribal entities on the history of the ancient Near East cannot be overestimated.

A great boon to the writing of this volume was the wonderful opportunity to hold the Seymour Gitin Distinguished Professorship at the W. F. Albright Institute of Archaeological Research in 2012–13. This led to an initial draft of the manuscript. I must also voice my deepest appreciation to Trinity Evangelical Divinity School's generous sabbatical policy, which led to this volume's production.

It is impossible to write a study of this sort without the support of numerous scholars, some of whom I know only through their important scholarly publications. While it is impossible to thank everyone here, I have received over the years very particular help and encouragement from the following: B. T. Arnold, P. Bordreuil, P.-E. Dion, F. M. Fales, S. Fassberg, D. E. Fleming, S. Gitin, T. P. Harrison, J. D. Hawkins, R. S. Hess, S. W. Holloway, W. G. Lambert, A. Lemaire, J. Llop-Raduà, D. Pardee, J. D. Schloen, B. B. Schmidt, W. M. Schniedewind, J.-A. Scurlock, A. G. Vaughn, and A. R. Millard, to whom this volume is dedicated.

I must also express my deep thanks and appreciation to B. J. Collins and Bob Buller, who have been both patient and helpful at every turn in the production of this volume. Special thanks go to three of my students: A. D. Riddle (who graciously and adeptly created the maps for this volume), S. W. Booth (who brought many archaeological and bibliographic data to my attention), and N. A. Huddleston (who helped me with indexing and other proofreading issues). Any errors lie solely with me.

Finally, in every way I must give thanks to my wife, Patti. Without her innumerable, great sacrifices and support, this work could never have come to completion.

Vernon Hills, Illinois
2 February 2015

# Figures and Tables

Figures

TABLES

# Abbreviations

| | |
|---|---|
| *AAA* | *Annals of Archaeology and Anthropology* |
| *AAAS* | *Annales archéologiques arabes syriennes* |
| *AASOR* | *Annual of the American Schools of Oriental Research* |
| ÄAT | Ägypten und Altes Testament |
| AB | Anchor Bible |
| *ABD* | *Anchor Bible Dictionary*. Edited by David Noel Freedman. 6 vols. New York: Doubleday, 1992. |
| *ABL* | *Assyrian and Babylonian Letters Belonging to the Kouyunjik Collections of the British Museum*. Edited by Robert F. Harper. 14 vols. Chicago: University of Chicago Press, 1892–1914. |
| *AbrN* | *Abr-Nahrain* |
| AbrNSup | Abr-Nahrain Supplements |
| ABS | Archaeology and Biblical Studies |
| *ActSum* | *Acta Sumerologica* |
| ActSumSup | Acta Sumerologica Supplementary Series |
| *ADD* | *Assyrian Deeds and Documents Recording the Transfer of Property, Including the So-Called Private Contracts, Legal Decisions and Proclamations Preserved in the Kouyunjik Collections of the British Museum, Chiefly of the 7th Century B.C.* C. H. W. Johns. 4 vols. Cambridge: Deighton, Bell, 1898–1923. |
| ADPV | Abhandlungen des Deutschen Palästina-Vereins |
| *AfO* | *Archiv für Orientforschung* |
| AfOB | Archiv für Orientforschung: Beiheft |
| ÄgAbh | Ägyptologische Abhandlungen |
| *AHw* | *Akkadisches Handwörterbuch*. Wolfram von Soden. 3 vols. Wiesbaden: Harrassowitz, 1965–1981. |
| *AION* | *Annali dell'Istituto Orientale di Napoli* |
| *AiS* 1 | *Einleitung und Inschriften*. Vol. 1 of *Ausgrabungen in Sendschirli*. Mitteilungen aus den orientalischen Sammlungen der königlichen Museen zu Berlin 2. Berlin: Spemann, 1893. |
| *AiS* 2 | *Ausgrabungsbericht und Architektur*. Vol. 2 of *Ausgrabungen in Sendschirli*. II. Mitteilungen aus den orientalischen Sammlun- |

| | |
|---|---|
| | gen der königlichen Museen zu Berlin 12. Berlin: Spemann, 1898. |
| *AiS* 3 | *Thorskulpturen von Sendschirli.* Vol. 3 of *Ausgrabungen in Sendschirli.* Mitteilungen aus den Orientalischen Sammlungen der königlichen Museen zu Berlin 13. Berlin: Reimer, 1902. |
| *AiS* 4 | *Bericht über die fünfte Grabung, 1902.* Vol. 4 of *Ausgrabungen in Sendschirli.* Mitteilungen aus den orientalischen Sammlungen der königlichen Museen zu Berlin 14. Berlin: Reimer, 1911. |
| *AiS* 5 | *Die Kleinfunde von Sendschirli.* Vol. 5 of *Ausgrabungen in Sendschirli.* Mitteilungen aus den Orientalischen Sammlungen der königlichen Museen zu Berlin 15. Berlin: de Gruyter, 1943. |
| *AJA* | *American Journal of Archaeology* |
| *AJBI* | *Annual of the Japanese Biblical Institute* |
| *AJSL* | *American Journal of Semitic Languages and Literatures* |
| ALASP | Abhandlungen zur Literatur Alt-Syrien-Palästinas und Mesopotamiens |
| *AnAnt* | *Anatolia Antiqua* |
| ANEM | Ancient Near East Monographs/Monografías sobre el Antiguo Cercano Oriente |
| *ANEP* | *The Ancient Near East in Pictures Relating to the Old Testament.* 2nd ed. Edited by James B. Pritchard. Princeton: Princeton University Press, 1994. |
| *ANES* | *Ancient Near Eastern Studies* |
| ANESSup | Ancient Near Eastern Studies Supplement Series |
| *ANET* | *Ancient Near Eastern Texts Relating to the Old Testament.* 3rd ed. Edited by James B. Pritchard. Princeton: Princeton University Press, 1969. |
| AnOr | Analecta Orientalia |
| *AnSt* | *Anatolian Studies* |
| AO | Collection of Antiquités Orientales of the Musée du Louvre, Paris |
| AOAT | Alter Orient und Altes Testament |
| *AoF* | *Altorientalische Forschungen* |
| ARM | Archives royales de Mari |
| *ArOr* | *Archív orientální* |
| ARU | *Assyrische Rechtsurkunden in Umschrift und Uebersetzung nebst einem Index der Personen-namen und Rechtserläuterungen.* J. Kohler and A. Ungnad. Leipzig: Pfeiffer, 1913. |
| AS | Assyriological Studies |

| | |
|---|---|
| ASORDS | American Schools of Oriental Research Dissertation Series |
| *AuOr* | *Aula Orientalis* |
| AuOrSup | Aula Orientalis Supplementa |
| *AUSS* | *Andrews University Seminary Studies* |
| *BA* | *Biblical Archaeologist* |
| BaF | Baghdader Forschungen |
| BAH | Bibliothèque archéologique et historique |
| *BAIAS* | *Bulletin of the Anglo-Israel Archaeological Society* |
| *BaM* | *Baghdader Mitteilungen* |
| *BAR* | *Biblical Archaeology Review* |
| BARI | BAR International Series |
| *BASOR* | *Bulletin of the American Schools of Oriental Research* |
| BATSH | Berichte der Ausgrabung Tall Šēḫ Ḥamad/Dūr-Katlimmu |
| BBB | Bonner biblische Beiträge |
| BBVO | Berliner Beiträge zum Vorderer Orient Texte |
| *BCSMS* | *Bulletin of the Canadian Society for Mesopotamian Studies* |
| BDAG | Danker, Frederick W., Walter Bauer, William F. Arndt, and F. Wilbur Gingrich. *Greek-English Lexicon of the New Testament and Other Early Christian Literature*. 3rd ed. Chicago: University of Chicago Press, 2000. |
| BE | The Babylonian Expedition of the University of Pennsylvania, Series A, Cuneiform Texts |
| *Bib* | *Biblica* |
| BibInt | Biblical Interpretation Series |
| BibOr | Biblica et Orientalia |
| *BIN* | *Babylonian Inscriptions in the Collection of James B. Nies*. New Haven: Yale University Press, 1917–. |
| BKAT | Biblischer Kommentar, Altes Testament |
| BM | tablets in the collections of the British Museum |
| *BN* | *Biblische Notizen* |
| *BNP* | *Brill's New Pauly: Encyclopaedia of the Ancient World*. Edited by Hubert Cancik. 22 vols. Leiden: Brill, 2002–2011. |
| *BO* | *Bibliotheca Orientalis* |
| *BSOAS* | *Bulletin of the School of Oriental and African Studies* |
| BTAVO | Beihefte zum Tübinger Atlas des Vorderen Orients |
| BWANT | Beiträge zur Wissenschaft vom Alten und Neuen Testament |
| BZAW | Beihefte zur Zeitschrift für die alttestamentliche Wissenschaft |
| *CAD* | Ignace J., et al. Gelb, *The Assyrian Dictionary of the Oriental Institute of the University of Chicago*. 21 vols. Chicago: The Oriental Institute of the University of Chicago, 1956–2010. |
| CAH | Cambridge Ancient History |

| | |
|---|---|
| CahRB | Cahiers de la Revue Biblique |
| *CAI* | *A Corpus of Ammonite Inscriptions*. W. E. Auffrecht. Ancient Near Eastern Studies 4. Lewiston, NY: Mellen, 1989. |
| CAL | Comprehensive Aramaic Lexicon (www.cal1.cn.huc.edu) |
| *CANE* | *Civilizations of the Ancient Near East*. Edited by Jack M. Sasson. 4 vols. New York, 1995. Repr. in 2 vols. Peabody, MA: Hendrickson, 2006. |
| *CBQ* | *Catholic Biblical Quarterly* |
| CDA | *A Concise Dictionary of Akkadian*. J. Black, A. George, and N. Postgate., 2nd ed. Wiesbaden: Harrassowitz, 2000. |
| CHANE | Culture and History of the Ancient Near East |
| *CHD* | *The Hittite Dictionary of the Oriental Institute of the University of Chicago*. Edited by Hans G. Güterbock, Harry A. Hoffner Jr., and Theo P. J. van den Hout. Chicago: The Oriental Institute of the University of Chicago, 1980–. |
| *CIS* 2.1 | Part 1 of vol. 2 of *Corpus inscriptionum Semiticarum*. Paris: Reipublicæ Typographeo, 1889. |
| CM | Cuneiform Monographs |
| ConBOT | Coniectanea Biblica: Old Testament Series |
| *COS* | *The Context of Scripture*. Edited by William W. Hallo. 3 vols. Leiden: Brill, 1997–2002. |
| *CRAI* | *Comptes rendus des séances de l'Académie des Inscriptions et Belles-Lettres* |
| CT | Cuneiform Texts from Babylonian Tablets in the British Museum |
| CTN | Cuneiform Texts from Nimrud |
| *CTU* | *The Cuneiform Alphabetic Texts from Ugarit, Ras Ibn Hani, and Other Places*. Edited by Manfried Dietrich, Oswald Loretz, and Joaquín Sanmartín. Münster: Ugarit-Verlag, 1995 |
| DaF | Damaszener Forschungen |
| *DaM* | *Damaszener Mitteilungen* |
| *DCH* | *Dictionary of Classical Hebrew*. Edited by David J. A. Clines. 9 vols. Sheffield: Sheffield Phoenix Press, 1993–2014 |
| DMOA | Documenta et Monumenta Orientis Antiqui |
| *DNP* | *Der neue Pauly: Enzyklopädie der Antike*. Edited by Hubert Cancik and Helmuth Schneider. Stuttgart: Metzler, 1996–. |
| *DNWSI* | J. Hoftijzer and K. Jongeling, *Dictionary of the North-West Semitic Inscriptions*. HdO 1/21. Leiden: Brill, 1995. |
| *DOTT* | *Documents from Old Testament Times*. Edited by D. Winton Thomas. London: Nelson, 1958. |
| EA | El-Amarna tablets. According to the edition of Jørgen A. |

| | |
|---|---|
| | Knudtzon. *Die el-Amarna-Tafeln*. Leipzig: Hinrichs, 1908–15. Repr., Aalen: Zeller, 1964. Continued in Anson F. Rainey, *El-Amarna Tablets, 359–379*. 2nd ed. Kevelaer: Butzon & Bercker, 1978. |
| *EAK* | *Einleitung in die assyrischen Königsinschriften*. Rykle Borger and Wolfgang Schramm. 2 vols. Leiden: Brill, 1964–1973. |
| EBib | Études bibliques |
| *EDB* | *Eerdmans Dictionary of the Bible*. Edited by David Noel Freedman. Grand Rapids: Eerdmans, 2000. |
| EHAT | Exegetisches Handbuch zum Alten Testament |
| ErIsr | Eretz-Israel |
| *EVO* | *Egitto e Vicinte Oriente* |
| FOTL | Forms of the Old Testament Literature |
| HACL | History, Archaeology, and Culture of the Levant |
| *HALOT* | *The Hebrew and Aramaic Lexicon of the Old Testament*. Ludwig Koehler, Walter Baumgartner, and Johann J. Stamm. Translated and edited under the supervision of Mervyn E. J. Richardson. 4 vols. Leiden: Brill, 1994–1999. |
| HANEM | History of the Ancient Near East Monographs |
| HCCT | Hirayama Collection of Cuneiform Tablets from Emar |
| HdO | Handbuch der Orientalistik |
| HSAO | Heidelberger Studien zum Alten Orient |
| HSM | Harvard Semitic Monographs |
| *HTR* | *Harvard Theological Review* |
| *HUCA* | *Hebrew Union College Annual* |
| ICC | International Critical Commentary |
| *IEJ* | *Israel Exploration Journal* |
| *IOS* | *Israel Oriental Studies* |
| *JA* | *Journal asiatique* |
| *JAEI* | *Journal of Ancient Egyptian Interconnections* |
| *JANESCU* | *Journal of the Ancient Near Eastern Society of Columbia University* |
| *JAOS* | *Journal of the American Oriental Society* |
| *JBL* | *Journal of Biblical Literature* |
| *JCS* | *Journal of Cuneiform Studies* |
| *JESHO* | *Journal of the Economic and Social History of the Orient* |
| *JJS* | *Journal of Jewish Studies* |
| *JNES* | *Journal of Near Eastern Studies* |
| *JNSL* | *Journal of Northwest Semitic Languages* |
| *JPOS* | *Journal of the Palestine Oriental Society* |
| *JSOT* | *Journal for the Study of the Old Testament* |

| | |
|---|---|
| JSOTSup | Journal for the Study of the Old Testament Supplement Series |
| *JSS* | *Journal of Semitic Studies* |
| K | tablets in the Kouyunjik collection of the British Museum |
| *KAI* | *Kanaanäische und aramäische Inschriften*. H. Donner and W. Röllig. 3 vols. Wiesbaden: Harrassowitz, 1962–64. |
| *KAJ* | Keilschrifttexte aus Assur juristischen inhalts. E Ebeling. Leipzig, Hinrichs, 1927. |
| KAT | Kommentar zum Alten Testament |
| *KAV* | *Keilschrifttexte aus Assur verschiedenen Inhalts*. O. Schroeder. WVDOG 35. Leipzig: Hinrichs, 1920. |
| *KBo* | *Keilschrifttexte aus Boghazköi*. Leipzig: Hinrichs, 1916–23; Berlin: Mann, 1954–. |
| Koya | tablets in the Museum of the Directorate of Antiquities in Koya |
| *KTU* | *Die keilalphabetischen Texte aus Ugarit*. Edited by Manfried Dietrich, Oswald Loretz, and Joaquín Sanmartín. Münster: Ugarit-Verlag, 2013. |
| *KUB* | *Keilschrifturkunden aus Boghazköi*. Berlin: Akademie, 1921–. |
| LAPO | Littératures anciennes du Proche-Orient |
| LHBOTS | Library of Hebrew Bible/Old Testament Studies |
| *MARI* | *Mari: Annales de recherches interdisciplinaires* |
| MARV 1 | *Mittelassyrische Rechtsurkunden und Verwaltungstexte*. H. Freydank. VAS 19. Berlin: Akademie Verlag, 1976. |
| MARV 2 | *Mittelassyrische Rechtsurkunden und Verwaltungstexte II*. H. Freydank. VAS 21. Berlin: Akademie, 1982. |
| MARV 4 | *Tafeln aus Kār-Tukultī-Ninurta*. Vol. 4 of *Mittelassyrische Rechtsurkunden und Verwaltungstexte*. H. Freydank and C. Fischer. Ausgrabungen der Deutschen Orient-Gesellschaft in Assur. E, Inschriften 7. Keilschrifttexte aus mittelassyrischer Zeit 2. WVDOG 99. Berlin: Saarbrücker, 2001. |
| MARV 5 | *Mittelassyrische Rechtsurkunden und Verwaltungstexte V*. H. Freydank and B. Feller. Ausgrabungen der Deutschen Orient-Gesellschaft in Assur. E, Inschriften 7. Keilschrifttexte aus mittelassyrischer Zeit 3. WVDOG 106. Saarbrücken: Saarbrücker, 2004. |
| MARV 6 | *Mittelassyrische Rechtsurkunden und Verwaltungstexte VI*. H. Freydank and B. Feller. WVDOG 109. Saarbrücken: Saarbrücker, 2005. |
| MARV 7 | *Mittelassyrische Rechtsurkunden und Verwaltungstexte VII*. H. Freydank and B. Feller. Ausgrabungen der Deutschen Orient-Gesellschaft in Assur, E. Inschriften 7. Keilschrifttexte aus |

| | |
|---|---|
| | mittelassyrischer Zeit 5. WVDOG 111. Saarwellingen: Saarländische, 2006. |
| MARV 10 | *Mittelassyrische Rechtsurkunden und Verwaltungstexte X.* D. Prechel, H. Freydank, and B. Feller. Ausgrabungen der Deutschen Orient-Gesellschaft in Assur. E, Inschriften 7. Keilschrifttexte aus mittelassyrischer Zeit 9. WVDOG 134. Wiesbaden: Harrassowitz, 2011. |
| MC | Mesopotamian Civilizations |
| *MDAI* | *Mitteilungen des Deutschen archäologischen Instituts* |
| *MDOG* | *Mitteilungen der Deutschen Orient-Gesellschaft* |
| MT | Masoretic Text |
| *NABU* | *Nouvelles assyriologiques brèves et utilitaires* |
| *NBL* | *Neues Bibel-Lexikon.* Edited by M. Görg and B. Lang. 3 vols. Zürich: Benziger, 1991–2001. |
| NCBC | New Century Bible Commentary |
| ND | field numbers of tablets excavated at Nimrud (Kalḫu) |
| *NEA* | *Near Eastern Archaeology* |
| *NEAEHL* | *The New Encyclopedia of Archaeological Excavations in the Holy Land.* Edited by Ephraim Stern. 5 vols. Jerusalem: Israel Exploration Society & Carta; New York: Simon & Schuster; Washington, DC: Biblical Archaeology Society, 1993–2008. |
| NIBC | New International Biblical Commentary |
| NIV | New International Version |
| NRSV | New Revised Standard Version |
| OBO | Orbis Biblicus et Orientalis |
| *OEANE* | *The Oxford Encyclopedia of Archaeology in the Near East.* Edited by Eric M. Meyers. 5 vols. New York: Oxford University Press, 1997. |
| *OEBA* | *The Oxford Encyclopedia of the Bible and Archaeology.* Edited by B. Alpert Nakhai. Oxford: Oxford University Press, 2013. |
| OECT | Oxford Editions of Cuneiform Texts |
| OG | Old Greek |
| OIP | Oriental Institute Publications |
| OIS | Oriental Institute Seminars |
| OLA | Orientalia Lovaniensia Analecta |
| *OLP* | *Orientalia Lovaniensia Periodica* |
| *Or* | *Orientalia* (NS) |
| *OrAnt* | *Oriens Antiquus* |
| OTG | Old Testament Guides |
| OTL | Old Testament Library |
| OTS | Old Testament Studies |

| | |
|---|---|
| *OtSt* | *Oudtestamentische Studiën* |
| *PEQ* | *Palestine Exploration Quarterly* |
| PIHANS | Publications de l'Institut historique-archéologique néerlandais de Stamboul |
| *PNA* | *The Prosopography of the Neo-Assyrian Empire*. Edited by Simo Parpola. 3 vols. in 6. Helsinki: Neo-Assyrian Text Corpus Project, 1998–2011. |
| *PRU* | *Le palais royal d'Ugarit*. Edited by C. Schaeffer, Mission de Ras Shamra, Paris: Imprimerie Nationale, 1956–. |
| PW | *Paulys Real-Encyclopädie der classischen Altertumswissenschaft*. New ed. by Georg Wissowa and Wilhelm Kroll. 50 vols. in 84 parts. Stuttgart: Metzler and Druckenmüller, 1894–1980. |
| *Qad* | *Qadmoniot* |
| *RA* | *Revue d'assyriologie et d'archéologie orientale* |
| RAI | Rencontre assyriologique internationale |
| *RB* | *Revue biblique* |
| *REA* | *Revue des études anciennes* |
| RGTC | Répertoire géographique des textes cunéiformes |
| *RHA* | *Revue hittite et asianique* |
| RIMA | The Royal Inscriptions of Mesopotamia, Assyrian Periods |
| RIMA 1 | A. K. Grayson, *Assyrian Rulers of the Third and Second Millennia BC (To 1115 BC)*. RIMA 1. Toronto: University of Toronto Press, 1987. |
| RIMA 2 | A. K. Grayson, *Assyrian Rulers of the Early First Millennium BC (1114-859 BC)*. RIMA 2. Toronto: University of Toronto Press, 1991. |
| RIMA 3 | A. K. Grayson, *Assyrian Rulers of the Early First Millennium BC II (858-745 BC)*. RIMA 3. Toronto: University of Toronto Press, 1996. |
| RIMB 2 | G. Frame, *Rulers of Babylonia: from the Second Dynasty of Isin to the End of Assyrian Domination (1157-612 BC)*. The Royal Inscriptions of Mesopotamia, Babylonian Periods 2. Toronto: University of Toronto Press, 1995. |
| RIME 2 | D. Frayne, *Sargonic and Gutian Periods (2334-2113 BC)*. Royal Inscriptions of Mesopotamia, Early Periods 2: Toronto: University of Toronto Press, 1993. |
| RINAP | Royal Inscriptions of the Neo-Assyrian Period |
| RINAP 1 | H. Tadmor and S. Yamada, *The Royal Inscriptions of Tiglath-pileser III (744-727 BC), and Shalmaneser V (726-722 BC), Kings of Assyria*. RINAP 1. Winona Lake, IN: Eisenbrauns, 2011. |

| | |
|---|---|
| RINAP 3.1 | A. K. Grayson and J. Novotny, *The Royal Inscriptions of Sennacherib, King of Assyria (704-681 BC), Part 1*. RINAP 3/1. Winona Lake, IN: Eisenbrauns, 2012. |
| RINAP 3.2 | A. K. Grayson and J. Novotny. *The Royal Inscriptions of Sennacherib, King of Assyria (704-681 BC), Part 2*. RINAP 3/2. Winona Lake, IN: Eisenbrauns, 2014. |
| RINAP 4 | E. Leichty, *The Royal Inscriptions of Esarhaddon, King of Assyria (680-669 BC)*. RINAP 4. Winona Lake, IN: Eisenbrauns, 2011. |
| *RlA* | *Reallexikon der Assyriologie*. Edited by Erich Ebeling et al. Berlin: de Gruyter, 1928–. |
| Rm | tablets in the collections of the British Museum |
| RS | Ras Shamra |
| *RSO* | *Rivista degli studi orientali* |
| RSOu | Ras Shamra-Ougarit |
| *RSF* | *Rivista di Studi Fenici* |
| SAA | State Archives of Assyria |
| SAA 1 | S. Parpola, *The Correspondence of Sargon II, Part I. Letters from Assyria and the West*. SAA 1. Helsinki: Helsinki University Press, 1987. |
| SAA 2 | S. Parpola and K. Watanabe, *Neo-Assyrian Treaties and Loyalty Oaths*. SAA 2. Helsinki: Helsinki University Press, 1988. |
| SAA 4 | I. Starr, *Queries to the Sungod: Divination and Politics in Sargonid Assyria*. SAA 4. Helsinki: Helsinki University Press, 1990. |
| SAA 5 | G. B. Lanfranchi and S. Parpola, *The Correspondence of Sargon II, Part II. Letters from the Northeastern Provinces*. SAA 5. Helsinki: Helsinki University Press, 1990. |
| SAA 6 | T. Kwasman and S. Parpola, *Legal Transactions of the Royal Court of Nineveh, Part I: Tiglath-Pileser III through Esarhaddon*. SAA 6. Helsinki: Helsinki University Press, 1991. |
| SAA 7 | F. M. Fales and J. N. Postgate, *Imperial Administrative Records, Part I. Palace and Temple Administration*. SAA 7. Helsinki: Helsinki University Press, 1992. |
| SAA 8 | H. Hunger, *Astrological Reports to Assyrian Kings*. SAA 8. Helsinki: Helsinki University Press, 1992. |
| SAA 10 | S. Parpola, *Letters from Assyrian and Babylonian Scholars*. SAA 10. Helsinki: Helsinki University Press, 1993. |
| SAA 11 | F. M. Fales and J. N. Postgate, *Imperial Administrative Records, Part II. Provincial and Military Administration*. SAA 11. Helsinki: Helsinki University Press, 1995. |

| | |
|---|---|
| SAA 12 | L. Kataja and R. Whiting, *Grants, Decrees and Gifts of the Neo-Assyrian Period*. SAA 12. Helsinki: Helsinki University Press, 1995. |
| SAA 13 | S. W. Cole and P. Machinist, *Letters from Priests to the Kings Esarhaddon and Assurbanipal*. SAA 13. Helsinki: Helsinki University Press, 1998. |
| SAA 14 | R. Mattila, *Legal Transactions of the Royal Court of Nineveh, Part II: Assurbanipal through Sin-šarru-iškun*. SAA 14. Helsinki: Helsinki University Press, 2002. |
| SAA 15 | A. Fuchs and S. Parpola, *The Correspondence of Sargon II, Part III: Letters from Babylonia and the Eastern Provinces*. SAA 15. Helsinki: Helsinki University Press, 2001. |
| SAA 16 | M. Luukko and G. Van Buylaere, *The Political Correspondence of Esarhaddon*. SAA 16. Helsinki: Helsinki University Press, 2002. |
| SAA 17 | M. Dietrich, *The Babylonian Correspondence of Sargon and Sennacherib*. SAA 17. Helsinki: Helsinki University Press, 2003. |
| SAA 18 | F. Reynolds, *The Babylonian Correspondence of Esarhaddon*. SAA 18. Helsinki: Helsinki University Press, 2003. |
| SAA 19 | M. Luukko, *The Correspondence of Tiglath-pileser III and Sargon II from Calah/Nimrud*. SAA 19. Helsinki: The Neo-Assyrian Text Corpus Project, 2012. |
| *SAAB* | *State Archives of Assyria Bulletin* |
| SAAS | State Archives of Assyria Studies |
| SAOC | Studies in Ancient Oriental Civilizations |
| SBLDS | Society of Biblical Literature Dissertation Series |
| SBLRBS | Society of Biblical Literature Reources for Biblical Study |
| SBLWAW | Society of Biblical Literature |
| SCCNH | Studies on the Civilization and Culture of Nuzi and the Hurrians |
| ScrHier | Scripta Hierosolymitana |
| *SEL* | *Studi epigrafici e linguistici sul Vicino Oriente antico* |
| SemeiaSt | Semeia Studies |
| SHANE | Studies in the History (and Culture) of the Ancient Near East |
| *SJOT* | *Scandinavian Journal of the Old Testament* |
| SM | tablets in the Suleimaniya Museum |
| *SMEA* | *Studi Micenei ed Egeo-Anatolici* |
| SMNIA | Tel Aviv University Sonia and Marco Nadler Institute of Archaeology Monograph Series |
| SQ | Tell Satu Qala |

| | |
|---|---|
| *SSI* | *Textbook of Syrian Semitic Inscriptions*. J. C. L. Gibson. 3 vols. Oxford: Oxford University Press, 1973–79. |
| SSN | Studia Semitica Neerlandica |
| StBoT | Studien zu den Boğazköy-Texten |
| StOr | Studia Orientalia |
| StPohl | Studia Pohl |
| StPohlSM | Studia Pohl Series Maior |
| StSem | Studi Semitici |
| *STT* | *The Sultantepe Tablets*. O. R. Gurney, J. J. Finkelstein, and P. Hulin. 2 vols. London: British Institute of Archaeology at Ankara, 1957–64. |
| *TA* | *Tel Aviv* |
| THeth | Texte der Hethiter |
| TOTC | Tyndale Old Testament Commentaries |
| TR | Tell al-Rimah |
| *Transeu* | *Transeuphratène* |
| TSO | Texte und Studien zur Orientalistik |
| *TUAT* | *Texte aus der Umwelt des Alten Testaments*. Edited by Otto Kaiser. Gütersloh: Mohn, 1984–. |
| *TynBul* | *Tyndale Bulletin* |
| *UF* | *Ugarit-Forschungen* |
| VA | Vorderasiatisches Museum |
| VAS | Vorderasiatische Schriftdenkmäler der staatlichen Museen zu Berlin |
| *VT* | *Vetus Testamentum* |
| VTSup | Supplements to Vetus Testamentum |
| *WO* | *Die Welt des Orients* |
| WVDOG | Wissenschaftliche Veröffentlichungen der deutschen Orient-Gesellschaft |
| *ZA* | *Zeitschrift für Assyriologie* |
| *ZAH* | *Zeitschrift für Althebräistik* |
| *ZAW* | *Zeitschrift für die alttestamentliche Wissenschaft* |
| *ZDMG* | *Zeitschrift der deutschen morgenländischen Gesellschaft* |
| ZDMGSup | Zeitschrift der deutschen morgenländischen Gesellschaft Supplementbände |
| *ZDPV* | *Zeitschrift des deutschen Palästina-Vereins* |
| *ZK* | *Zeitschrift für Keilschriftforschung* |

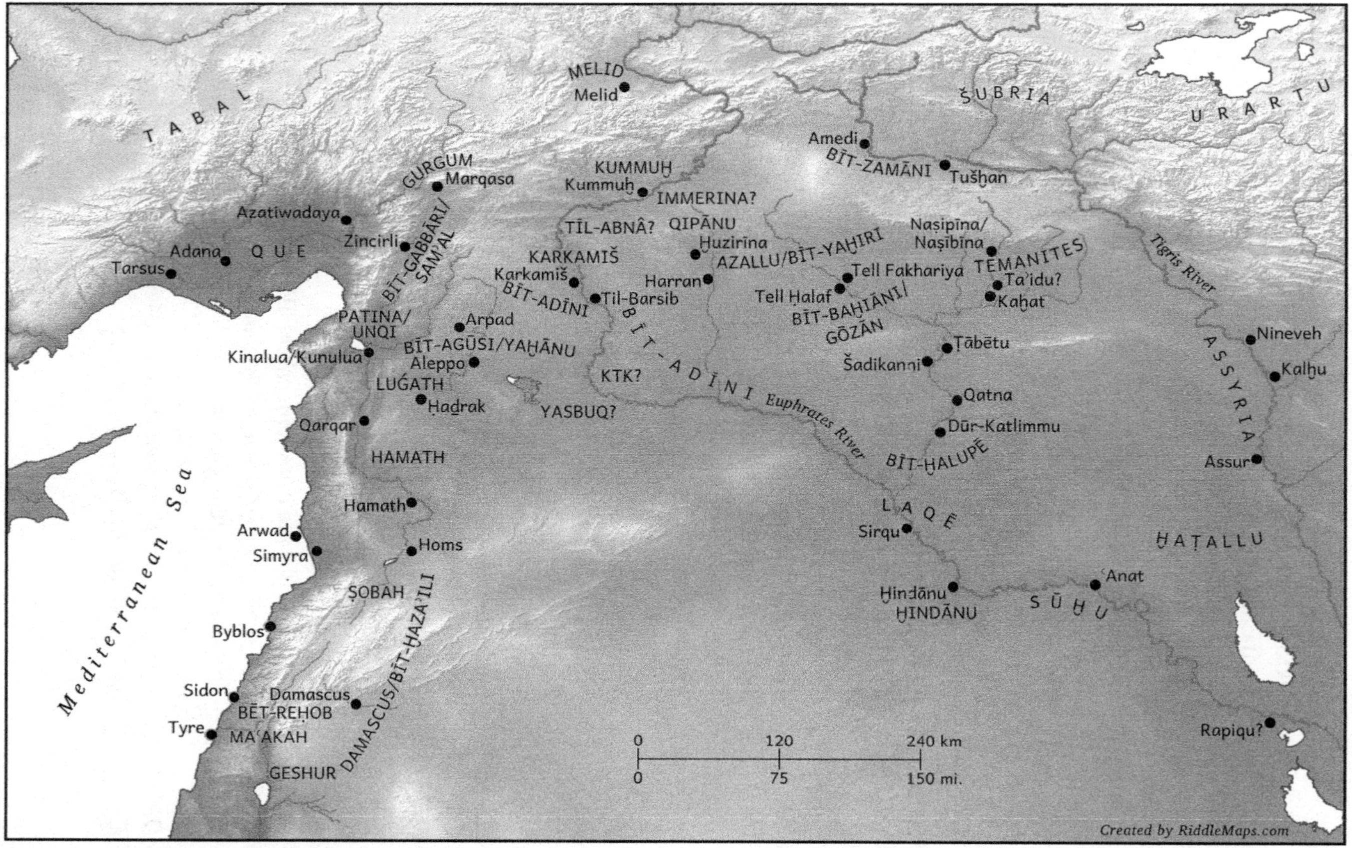

The Aramean polities of the Levant and Jezirah

# 1
# PRELIMINARY ISSUES

## 1.1. Geography

Aramean history unfolded in the regions of the northern Levant and Upper Mesopotamia (the Jezirah), an area that corresponds roughly to the modern state of Syria, although a part of modern southeastern Turkey would also be included.[1] This area has been called a "crossroads of civilization" because numerous major trade routes of the eastern Mediterranean and Near East intersect here.[2] Caravans and military expeditions moved between the economic and political poles of the ancient Near Eastern world, from Egypt to Anatolia (Asia Minor), from the Mediterranean to Mesopotamia.

### 1.1.1. Geographic Integrity: Agricultural Production

This region shares a physical environment that distinguishes it from other large geographic units around it, giving it integrity as a geographic unit. In the ancient Near East, agricultural production provided the foundation for the development and maintenance of state-level societies during the Bronze and Iron Ages (3400–550 BCE). The rain-fed farming plains of this region provide a stark contrast to the artificially irrigated plains of southern Mesopotamia and the rain-fed highland plateaus of Anatolia, distinguishing it from them as geographic units.

---

1. The term *Levant* is used here as a descriptor for the eastern seaboard of the Mediterranean Sea. *Jezirah* is the Arabic word meaning "island," identifying the area lying between the Tigris and Euphrates Rivers.

For Maraş as the northern boundary of the area and Tell Ḥalaf as its eastern boundary, see Bunnens 2000b, 18. Klengel (2000, 21 n. 1) cites the territory south of the Taurus Range as part of the area of "Syria."

2. Akkermans and Schwartz 2003, 2.

Moreover, while a general geographic unity produced a similar agricultural system for all of the Levant,[3] the northern Levant has larger plains than its southern counterpart; Lebanon and Palestine have agricultural valleys of limited size. Thus, the Levantine north supported larger populations and political units than did the south. In contrast, the northern Levantine plains are not easily distinguished geographically from the Jezirah (upper Mesopotamia). An additional distinction between the northern and southern Levant is that the best harbors are all in the north, whereas the south is marked by an overall absence of good harbors.

Rainfall and soil were the main factors in the agricultural environment. Syria has a climate characterized by hot, dry summers and cool, rainy winters, with regional variations (depending largely on elevation). In antiquity, dry farming (that is, rain-fed agriculture) was predominant. The limit for rain-fed arable farming is roughly the 200 mm (8 inch) per annum level (fig. 1.1); however, it is only beyond the 300 mm (12 inch) per annum level that farming was generally secure and profitable. Available moisture is the prime determinant in plant and animal variation.[4] The precipitation gradient regulates distribution. Excavations of sites that lie in the relatively high rainfall zones yield evidence of a heavier emphasis on cropping than do drier areas. They also demonstrate pig domestication, whereas drier zones do not (Smith and Munro 2009, 931).

The agricultural cycle began with the autumn rains, which softened the ground sufficiently for plowing and sowing. The success of these crops was completely dependent on the quality and timing of the following winter rains. Rains usually ended in the spring. The grain harvests generally fell in April or May (depending on elevation). Other harvests followed until the vine harvests in the late summer months. Barley and wheat were the leading grain crops (Eyre 1995, 175–89).

Relatively extensive farming methods in a fairly mixed rural economy meant that dry farming could often tolerate a high proportion of poor and even failed grain harvests. But with no rainfall from late spring to early autumn, any year that saw a low rainfall in the winter could anticipate drought and the consequent famine soon to follow.

Soil and commercial considerations were also determining factors. For example, the olive flourishes in much of Palestine and western Syria in well-drained, sandy, and rocky soil and has a low rainfall requirement. Thus, by

---

3. "Similarities include mixed cropping of wheat, barley, legumes, and horticulture as well as the presence of flax (Linum spp.), donkeys (*Equus asinus*), and onagers (*E. hemionus*)" (Smith and Munro 2009, 931).

4. Smith and Munro conclude that "environment has a stronger influence on the range of plants and animals present at a site than chronology" (2009, 931).

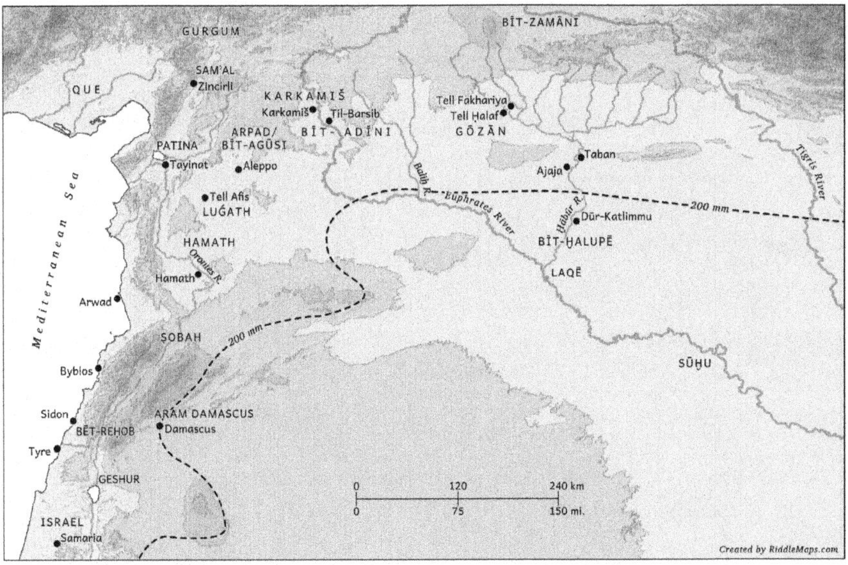


Fig. 1.1. Rainfall map showing 200 mm per annum line

the Iron Age, olive-oil production was a major commercial activity in lands that were unprofitable for grain. Grape and fig cultivation were also possible.

While farming was virtually impossible on land that received less than 200 mm, often this "steppe" was ideal for sheep grazing and thus important for the development of mobile pastoralism in the regions just to the south or east of the so-called Fertile Crescent. Steppes are often favored grazing locations for sheep and goats because these animals can easily tolerate the dry conditions and do not have to compete with agricultural fields for land. Wild animal taxa also fit this pattern: more arid-adapted species, such as gazelle, equids, and hare, are found in greater relative abundances at sites in dry areas, while forest-adapted species, such as red deer and fallow deer, are more common in wet areas (Smith and Munro 2009, 934).

### 1.1.2. The Delimitation of the Regions

One quick, convenient way to envision the makeup of the region is to divide it into three main zones, not of equal size, based on rainfall. First, in the west, a narrow coastal plain is bounded on the east by a north–south mountain range and receives abundant rainfall. Second, there is an arc-shaped zone of valleys and plateaus, fabled for its fertility (the Fertile Crescent),

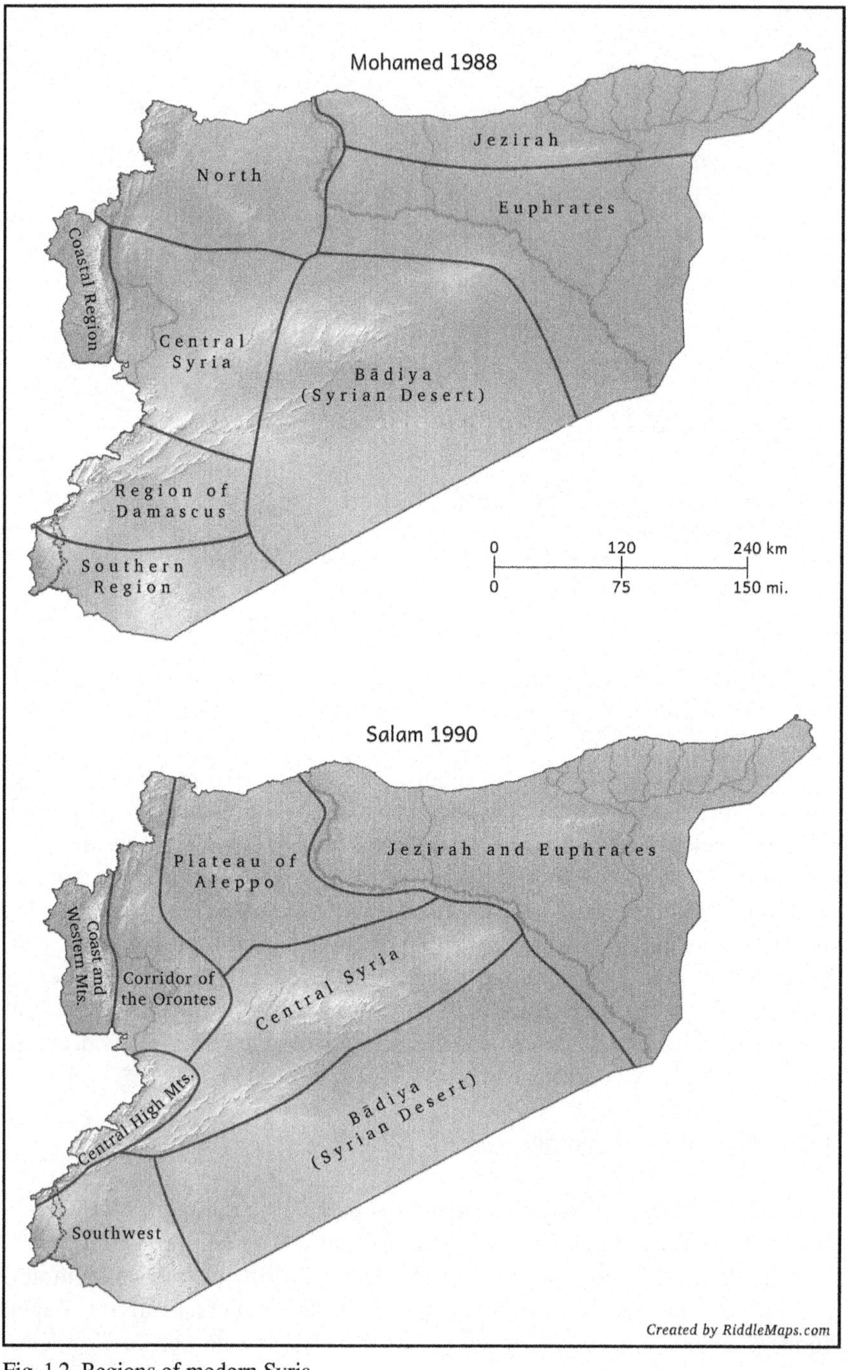


Fig. 1.2. Regions of modern Syria

that receives sufficient rainfall (200–400 mm; 8–16 in) for agriculture. Third, there is a large semiarid steppe zone that receives less than 200 mm of rainfall, ideal for mobile pastoralism.

However, there is another way of envisioning Syria that follows the characteristics of the natural environments and is more helpful for understanding its historical developments. This method divides Syria into two major divisions: western and eastern Syria, each having a number of regions. The Euphrates is the rough dividing point. In this method of analysis, a longitudinal line extending south from the bend in the Euphrates serves as a general delimitation between west and east (fig. 1.2, Mohamed 1988). Modern Syrian social scientists have analyzed the delimitations of these regions.[5] How different scholars have analyzed the regions is helpful for seeing both distinctions and interconnections.

### 1.1.2.1. Western Syria

#### 1.1.2.1.1. Overview

A common way of dividing western Syria is to see two geographic units: (1) a complex of four parallel coastal mountain–valley systems and (2) an inland composite of plateaus, plains, or steppes (fig. 1.3). The major geographic feature that characterizes western Syria is a system of four parallel mountain ranges extending north to south with valleys running in between. The valleys in this complex are all part of the Great Rift (that continues southward down through Palestine and into Africa). The Orontes River flows northward through parts of this complex. The gaps between the mountain ranges are strategic and agriculturally significant zones allowing access between regions. To the west of the western mountain ranges is the coastal plain. If one compares the divisional maps of Salam and Mohamed (see n. 5), it is clear that both scholars divide the western mountains and coastal plain from valley and eastern mountains (see fig. 1.2). This is an important division that is reflected in the history of the geographic unit. The western mountains–coastal plain unit was, in general, separate politically from the valleys and inland regions. The heights of the western ranges created political and cultural divisions that are still reflected in modern contexts. The coastal plain was the area where the Phoenician city-states developed without any real Aramean penetrations.

Inland western Syria is comprised primarily of plateaus, plains, or steppes. This composite is wider in the north and narrower in the south. Over-

5. In the introduction to his work on Ḥoms and Ḥama, M. al-Dbiyat (1995, 13–18) discusses the regional divisions of two scholars: A. A. Salam (1990) and B. Mohamed (1988).

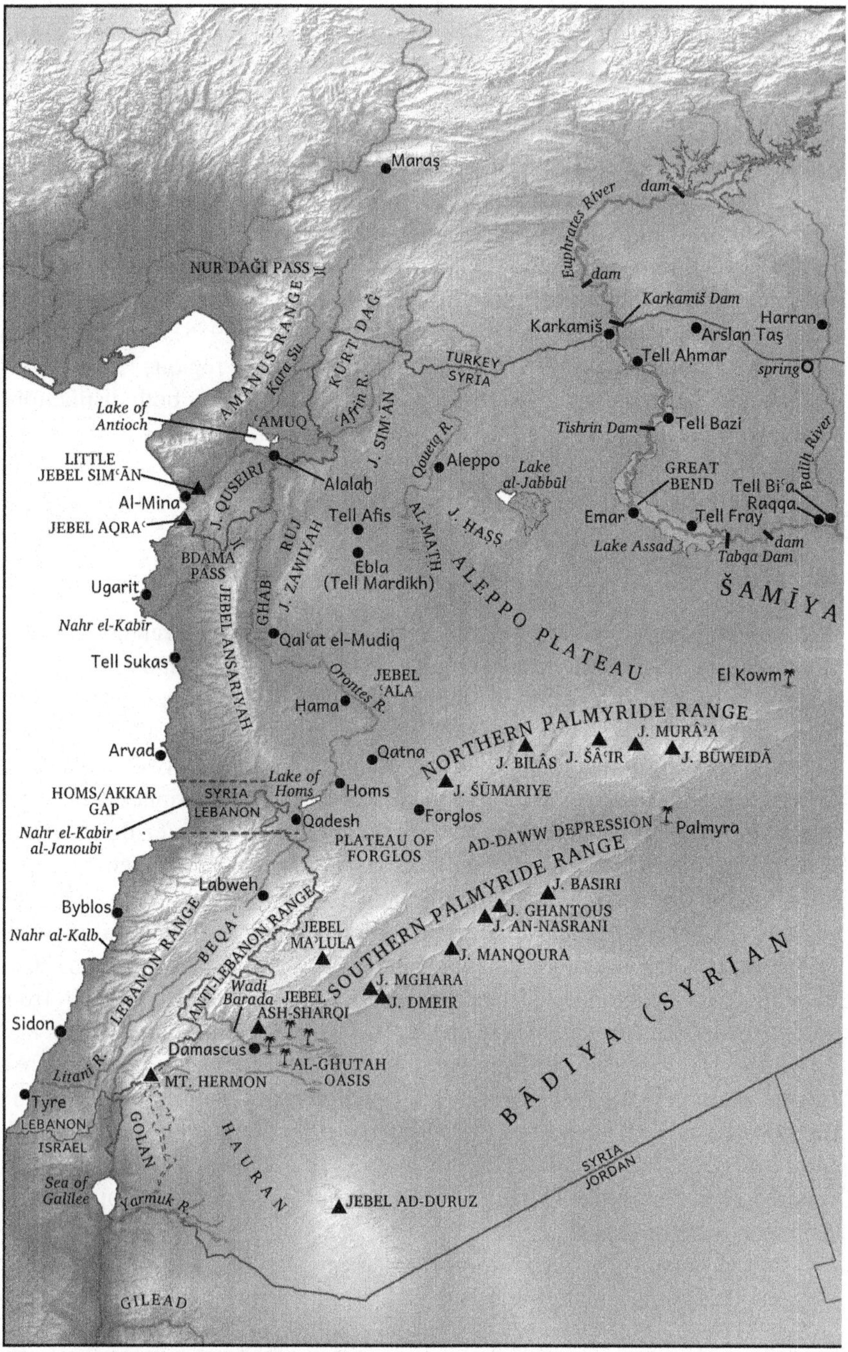


Fig. 1.3. Physical map of Syria

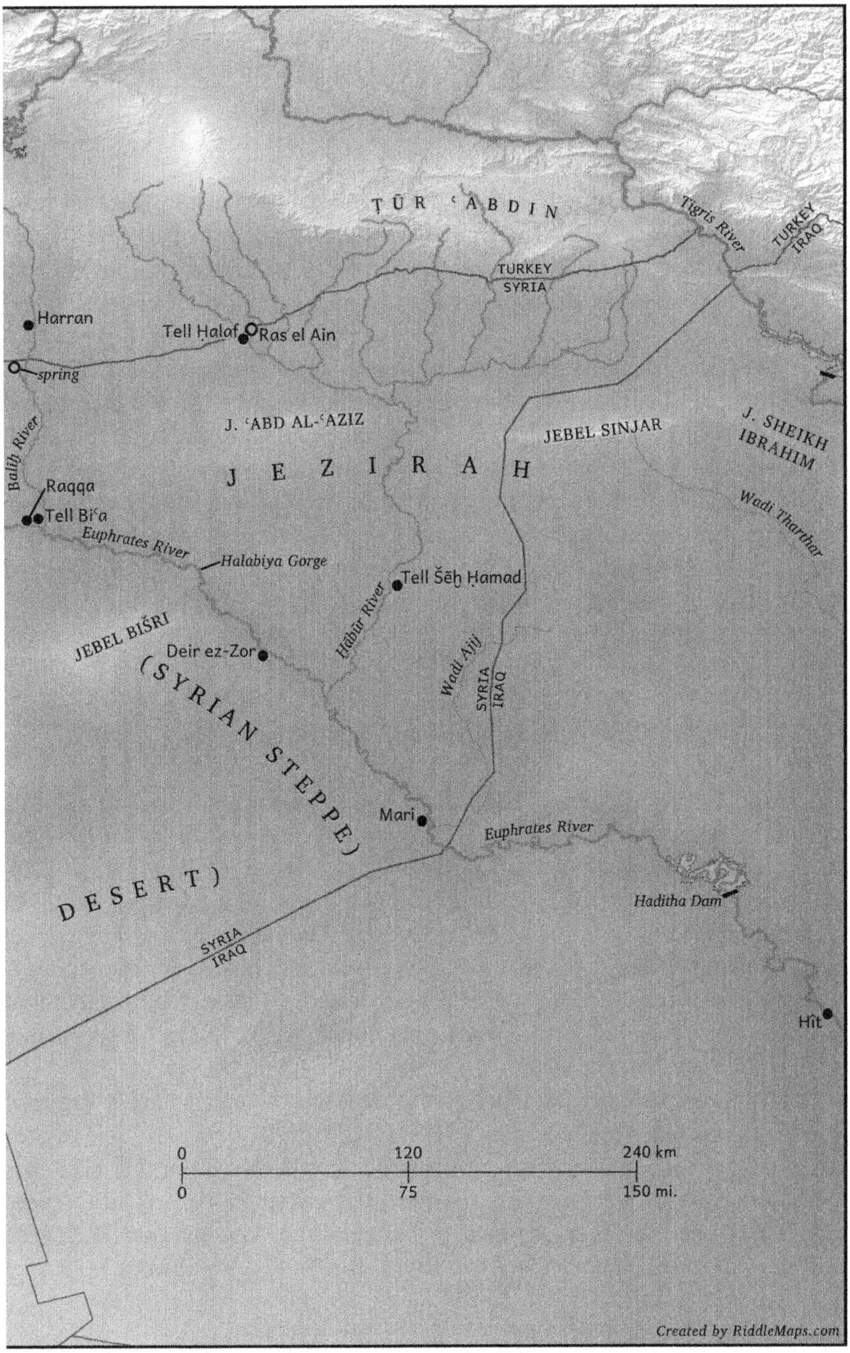
ṬŪR ʿABDIN
Tigris River
TURKEY
IRAQ
TURKEY
SYRIA
Harran
Tell Ḥalaf
Ras el Ain
spring
J. ʿABD AL-ʿAZIZ
JEBEL SINJAR
J. SHEIKH IBRAHIM
Baliḫ River
J E Z I R A H
Raqqa
Tell Biʿa
Wadi Tharthar
Euphrates River
Halabiya Gorge
Tell Šēḫ Ḥamad
JEBEL BIŠRI
Ḫābūr River
Wadi Ajij
Deir ez-Zor
SYRIA
IRAQ
(SYRIAN STEPPE)
Mari
Euphrates River
DESERT)
Haditha Dam
SYRIA
IRAQ
Hît
0
120
240 km
0
75
150 mi.
Created by RiddleMaps.com

all, it receives less rain than the parallel mountain valley systems. Yet in parts of it, especially in the north, dry farming is possible.

1.1.2.1.2. The Coastal Plain

To the west of the parallel system of mountains is a coastal plain that runs, for the most part, the full length of the eastern seaboard of the Mediterranean (fig. 1.3). In Syria, this littoral is generally quite narrow, roughly 5 to 10 km (3 to 6 miles) wide. It has a "Mediterranean climate," being relatively humid and receiving around 600–1,000 mm of annual rainfall. It includes a number of good seaports that in antiquity spawned a number of small Phoenician city-states that had maritime connections throughout the Mediterranean, some of the more important of which, in a north-to-south order, were Arvad, Byblos (Gubla), Sidon, and Tyre. The coastal mountains receive over 1,000 mm of annual rainfall. In antiquity, both the coastal plain and mountains were forested. Both areas are characterized by Mediterranean terra rossa soils and are conducive to cultivation of Mediterranean crops such as olives, figs, and grapes. Due to their height, the coastal mountains greatly impede the movement of precipitation from the west so that the regions to the east are much drier than the coast (Wirth 1971, 41–67).

1.1.2.1.3. The Four Parallel Mountain and Valley Systems

The four parallel mountain and valley systems from north to south can be seen in table 1.1 and figure 1.3 (p. 6). The northernmost of the western ranges is the Amanus Range (Nur Dağları), between 1,830 to 2,224 m (6,002 to 7,295 ft) in height. Today this range makes up the Turkish province of Hatay. In antiquity it was famous for its cedar forests.[6] The height of the range poses a significant challenge to east–west travel, which accounts for the strategic importance of the Nur Dağı Pass at Fevzipaşa for the east–west piedmont highway, the so-called saddle route, that connected northern Mesopotamia with southeastern Anatolia.[7]

To the east, roughly parallel to the Amanus, is the much smaller range of Kurt Dağ (ancient Mount Atalur) (800–1,201 m; 2,624–3,939 ft). This rugged upland limestone massif is part of a larger northern system that stretches eastward. One of the Orontes's northern tributaries, the Kara Su (ancient Saluara River), flows southward in between the Amanus and Kurt Dağ Ranges. Another tributary, the ʿAfrin River, also flowing southward, is located

6. They are prominent, for example, in the Gilgamesh Epic.

7. For more on the piedmont "saddle route," see Comfort, Abadie-Reynal, and Ergeç 2000; and Comfort and Ergeç 2001.

Table 1.1. Four Parallel Mountain Valley Systems[a]

| | | WEST | CENTER | EAST |
|---|---|---|---|---|
| | 1 | Amanus Range and Little Jebel Sim'ān | the 'Amuq (the plain of Antioch) | Kurt Dağ and Jebel Sim'ān |
| N | 2 | Jebel Aqra' (Mount Casius)–Jebel Quseiri, and Jebel Ansariyah | the Ghab | Jebel Dweili–Jebel 'Ala–Jebel Bariša, Jebel Zawiyah |
| S | 3 | Jebel Ansariyah | the Ḥoms and Ḥama Plateau[b] | Jebel 'Ala |
| | 4 | the Lebanon Range | the Beqa' | the Anti-Lebanon Range |

a. Jebel and Dağ (pronounced Dā) are respectively the Arabic and Turkish words for mountain/mount.

b. This plateau is very open on the east with only Jebel 'Ala creating a slight eastern limit. Nevertheless, the Ansariyah Range creates a clear western limit.

to the east of Kurt Dağ and to the west of Jebel Sim'ān (870 m; 2,854 ft). The 'Afrin's total length is 139 km. These rivers flow into the 'Amuq (the Antioch Plain), where they met in antiquity in the Lake of Antioch (no longer extant); then they flow into the lower Orontes River as it turns southwestward and enters the sea. As it flows to the sea, the Orontes runs through a gorge that is bordered on the north by Little Jebel Sim'ān. While the plain narrows at this point,[8] there is still an access to the seacoast, and thus it provided a route for the movement of people and goods between the coast and inland Syria. This plain enjoys high annual rainfall averages, creating a highly fertile environment capable of intensive agricultural production.

In between the Amanus and Jebel Ansariyah Ranges is the singular mountain, Jebel Aqra' (1,729 m; 5,671 ft). It was known in antiquity as Ṣaphon (Mount Casius to the Greeks). Jebel Quseiri is just to the east of Jebel Aqra' and helps form a mountainous terrain around which the Orontes makes its circuitous turn. Parallel to Jebel Quseiri is the mountainous complex with the triad Jebel Dweili, Jebel 'Ala, and Jebel Barisha (west to east order, highest point 847 m), plus the narrow range known as Jebel Wastini just to the south of Jebel Dweili (see fig. 7.1).

To the south of Jebel Quseiri is the Jebel Ansariyah (Nuseiriyeh) Range (height: 1,220 to 1,640 m; 4,002 to 5,379 ft). Parallel to the Jebel Ansariyah

8. This part of the plain is often associated with the so-called Cyprus-Antioch depression.

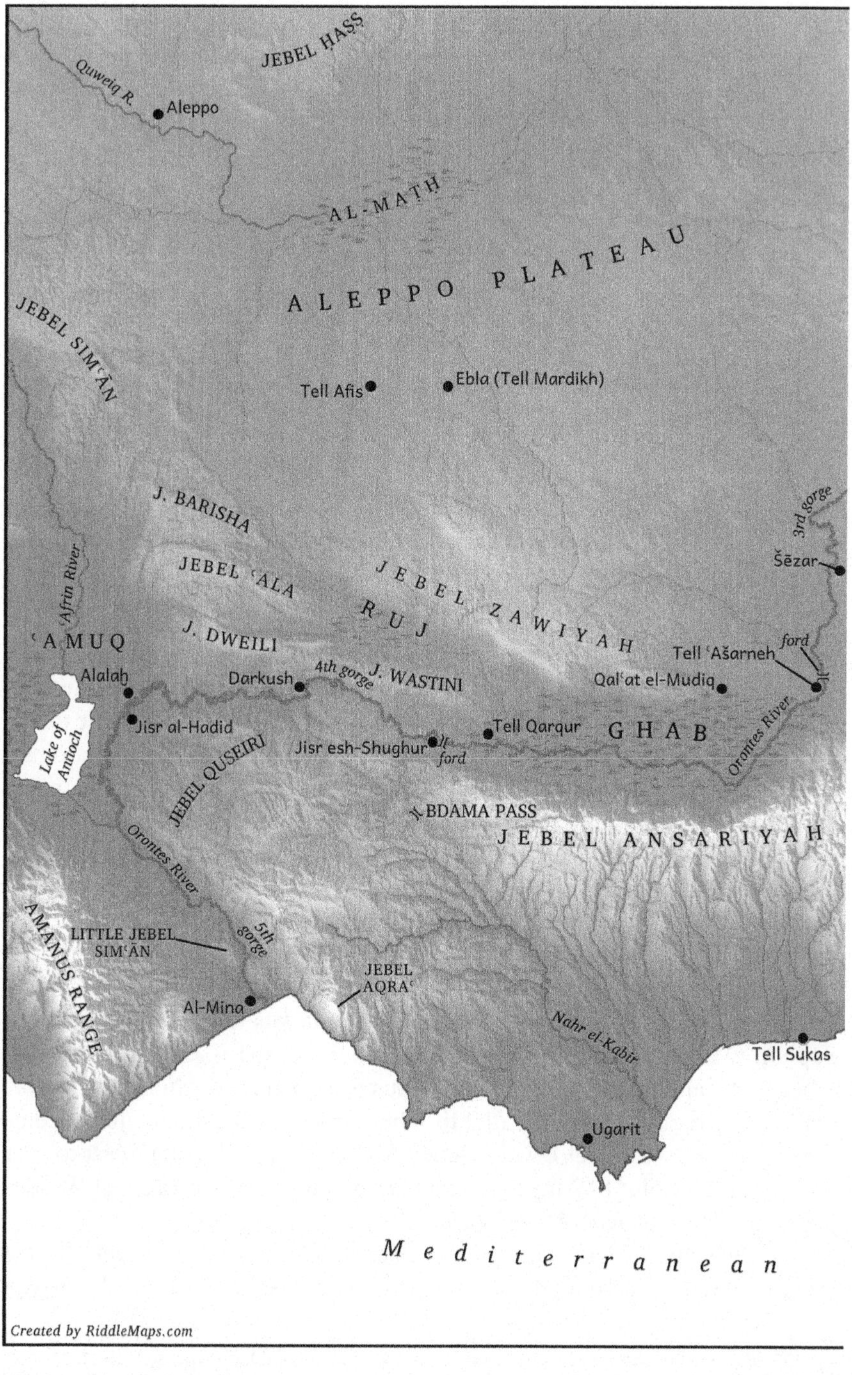


Fig. 1.4. The Orontes River

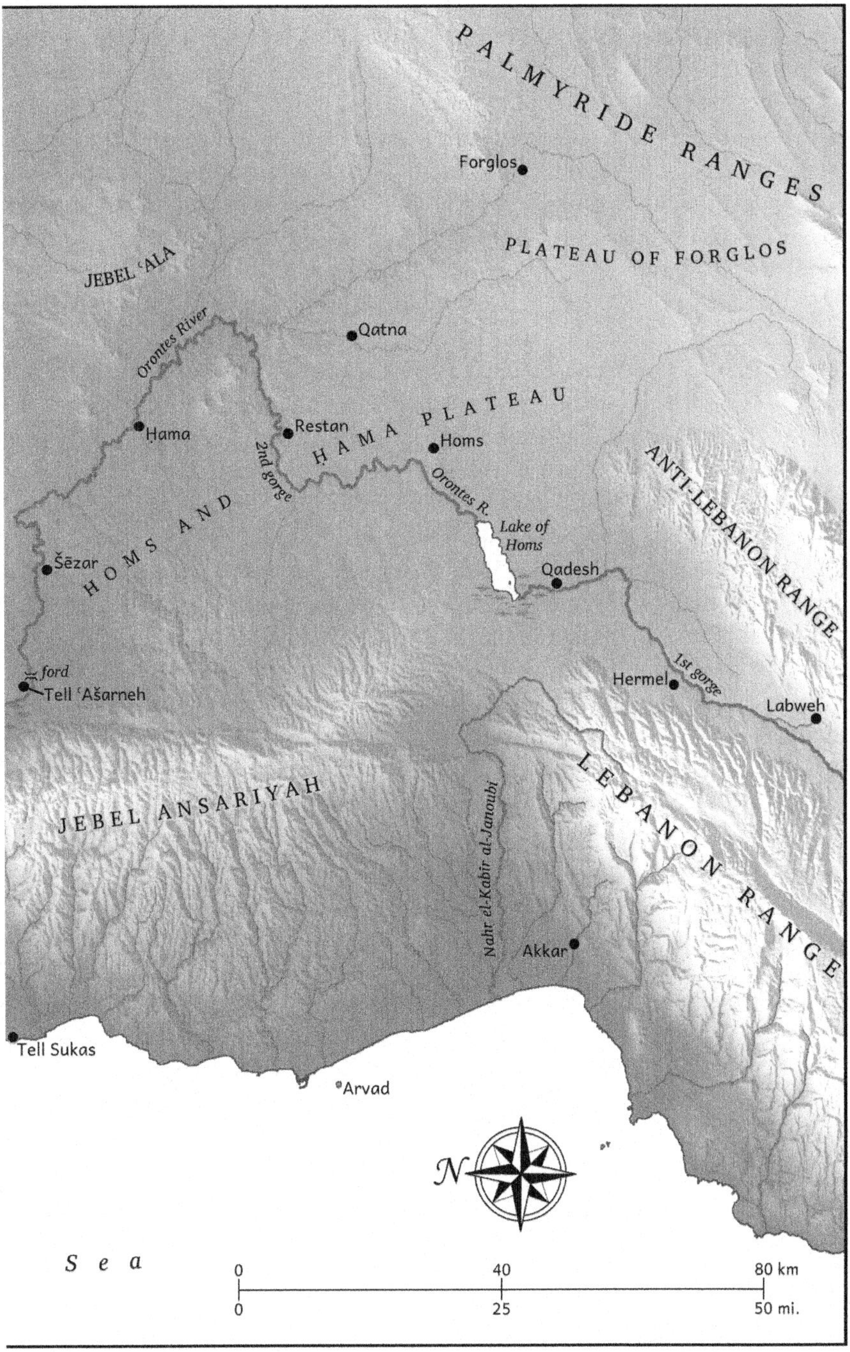
PALMYRIDE RANGES
Forglos
PLATEAU OF FORGLOS
JEBEL ʿALA
Orontes River
Qatna
HOMS AND HAMA PLATEAU
Restan
Ḥama
Homs
2nd gorge
Orontes R.
Lake of Homs
ANTI-LEBANON RANGE
Šēzar
Qadesh
ford
Tell ʿAšarneh
Hermel
1st gorge
Labweh
JEBEL ANSARIYAH
Nahr el-Kabir al-Janoubi
LEBANON RANGE
Akkar
Tell Sukas
Arvad
N
Sea
0
40
80 km
0
25
50 mi.

Range is the Jebel Zawiyah Range (940 m; 3,083 ft). The Ghab depression is situated between them. The Jebel Ansariyah receives an average rainfall of around 1,500 mm, due to the fact that it serves as a barrier to the frontal systems coming from the Mediterranean. It also stores large quantities of water because of its geological structure, namely, a limestone karst system (an underground chamber of water) that provides perennial springs at the range's base (Vannesse 2011, 287). In contrast, the Jebel Zawiyah is much drier, receiving only 500 mm of rainfall per annum.

Just north of the Ghab, between Jebel Quseiri and the Jebel Ansariyah Range, is the Bdama Pass. The Nahr el-Kabīr (also known as En Nahr el-Kebīr; the ancient Raḫbānu River) begins near the upper reaches of this pass and flows southwestward into the Mediterranean near Latakia.[9] Between Jebel Wastini and Jebel Zawiyah there is a valley basin known as the Ruj. The Bdama Pass and the Ruj Valley provided a route west to east across the Orontes (with a ford at Jisr esh-Shughur), permitting communication and trade between the Mediterranean and inland Syria.

In the Ghab (roughly 10–15 km wide), the Orontes meanders very slowly for approximately 62 km as a broad and shallow expanse, much impeded by reeds and amounting in antiquity to a vast, insalubrious swamp (Dion 2006, 45). The plain is quite flat, with the altitude ranging between 176 and 180 m above sea level. It was here that the Egyptian Eighteenth Dynasty pharaohs hunted elephants (no longer extant in the region today). On its west side, the space between the marshes and the Jebel Ansariyah Mountains is very small. Therefore, armies and caravans used a route on higher ground on the east side of the Ghab, where most of the important settlements were located, such as Tell Qarqur, and Qal'at el-Mudîq (Apamaea). On the southern end of the Ghab, a ford was located at Tell 'Ašarneh (the site of the city of Tunip in the second millennium BCE). This was an important strategic site in the early history of the region.

South of the Ghab lies the Ḥoms and Ḥama Plateau, with the Ansariyah Range defining the western limit. The eastern limit near Ḥama (ancient Hamath) is Jebel 'Ala (642 m; 2,106 ft), but much of the eastern side of the plateau is open to the Plateau of Aleppo to the north and east; near Ḥoms the eastern side is open to the Plateau of Forglos.

There is a significant gap between the Ansariyah Range on the north and the Lebanon Range to the south. This is known as the Ḥoms/Akkar Gap.[10] Because of its considerable size, it provides the easiest access between the Mediterranean coast and the Syrian interior (with access east to Tadmor/

9. See Effendi 1854, 54, for a romantic description of the terrain.

10. Also known as the Emesenian Gap.

Palmyra, see below) and allows some humid air into the Syrian interior. The gap provides the setting for the entrance of the river, Nahr el-Kabīr (al-Janoubi), "the (southern) great river," into the Mediterranean Sea (creating the modern border between Syria and Lebanon). In late antiquity this river was known as the Eleutherus River (1 Macc 11:7; 12:30). The gap also provides the topographical basis for the lake/marsh area to the southwest of Ḥoms on the Orontes River. Some of the towns that dotted the Ḥoms and Ḥama Plateau were particularly important in the second millennium during the Bronze Age, such as Qatna (El-Mishrifeh, northeast of Ḥoms) and Qadesh (Tell Nebi Mend, southeast of Ḥoms). The history of this region during the Iron Age is still unclear due to the lack of textual documentation.[11]

The Lebanon and Anti-Lebanon Ranges comprise the fourth and southernmost section of the parallel systems. The Lebanon Range has heights over 3,000 m, with the highest point being 3,083 m (10,112 ft). The range is about 160 km (100 miles) in length and receives over 1,000 mm (40 in) of rainfall annually. Like Mount Amanus, forested in antiquity, it was famous for the "cedars of Lebanon." On the west side are many deep V-shaped wadis or gorges that run down the mountains into the sea and make north–south travel difficult. Perhaps the best known of these is the Nahr al-Kalb ("the Dog River").

On the east side of the Lebanon Range is a steep escarpment that drops off into the Beqa‘ Valley. The Beqa‘ is a long, narrow valley that stretches 140 km (85 miles) up to the area just south of Ḥoms. It is an uplifted valley most of which is above 900 m (2,953 ft). The northern end of the valley is blocked by swamps and lakes that form behind a basalt outflow near Qadesh. The southern end is a jumble of ridges and valleys. The Litani River flows southward through the southern end of the valley and then turns west and empties into the Mediterranean. Travel east–west is difficult because of the lack of good passes through the Lebanon and Anti-Lebanon Mountains; travel north–south is difficult because of various ridges in the valley and the blockages at either end of the Beqa‘.

Consequently, the main trade route in antiquity went to the east of the Anti-Lebanon (Jebel aš-Šarqī) Range, through Damascus. This range stretches from Mount Hermon (Jebel esh-Sheikh) (2,814 m; 9,230 ft) on the southern end to approximately 85 miles north overlooking the Ḥoms/Akkar gap. The Wadi Barada separates Mount Hermon from the northeastern continuation of the Anti-Lebanon. The range (2,629 m; 8,623 ft) gradually declines in height as it extends northeast. The mountain range receives around 1,000

11. In terms of the archaeological record, however, the situation is improving. M. Al-Maqdissi reopened the excavation of El-Mishrifeh (Qatna), revealing important remains from the Iron age (Al-Maqdissi 1996, 1997).

mm (40 in) of rain annually. To its north are the Ḥoms and Hamath Plateau and the Plateau of Forglos.

1.1.2.1.4. The Orontes River

The major river within this series of valleys is the Orontes (modern Nahr al-Āṣī; fig. 1.4). It was known in Assyrian sources as the Arantu (Greek Ὀρόντης; Streck 2003–5). It originates in Lebanon at the great springs of Labweh,[12] located in the Beqa‘ Valley (i.e., the western side of the Anti-Lebanon Range).[13] This is not far from the source of the Litani River, which flows southward before turning into the sea. The Orontes River is, in fact, fed by a huge karst system, with Ain ez-Zarka being one of its permanent springs (its large recharge is up to 27 billion $m^3$ of water for the system; El Hakim and Bakalowicz 2007). The Orontes flows northward within the system of parallel mountain ranges.

The Orontes River is unnavigable, its flow irregular. This is due, in part, to two alternating watercourses: abrupt gorges and embanked plains (Weullersse 1940, 20). In the gorges, the river runs swiftly, and there is generally limited contact with human life. In the plains, the flow of the river slows to a meander, and the riverbed is generally higher than the plain so that the river embankments serve as natural dams, though in some cases there are no real embankments, and the surrounding plain is transformed into marsh or swamp (this occurs in the Ghab and to a lesser degree in the ‘Amuq). Two abnormal traits also characterize the Orontes, namely, the relative weakness in its tributaries in supplying water (only in the winter) and, in contrast, the enormous number of subterranean sources in its bed or near its course so that the river is, so to speak, "born from itself."[14] Thus the river is reinvigorated along its course, not so much from its tributaries (which are seasonal, and even then limited), but from the subterranean water sources. This feature ensured in antiquity that there was a constancy to the water flow in the Ghab, making this region a draw for humans for millennia.

As it flows northward, the Orontes passes through five gorges on its way to the Mediterranean Sea (fig. 1.4; see Weulersse 1940, 16, fig. 5). Initially, the upper Orontes flows through a deep gorge near Hermel. It then enters into the Lake of Ḥoms (at the southern end of the vast plain of the modern district of Ḥoms). Next, the Orontes passes through a second gorge just

12. This is Lebo-Hamath of the Old Testament (לבוא חמת/לבא חמת); see Num 13:21, 34:8, Josh 13:5, Judg 3:3, 1 Kgs 8:65, 2 Kgs 14:25, 1 Chr 13:5, 2 Chr 7:8, Ezek 47:20, 48:1, and Amos 6:14.

13. Numerous wadis contribute to the river's origins (Weulersse 1940, 15).

14. Weullersse 1940, 21. This is the karst system; see above.

before Restan. It now turns to the northeast, passing through the plain that is today the region of Ḥama (ancient Hamath). Here the land is in need of irrigation (Dion 2006, 45), so the ancients may have developed some type of device that anticipated the large water wheels that are admired even today in Ḥama. Agriculture played a decisive role in the economy of the ancient kingdom of Hamath, since it was landlocked and quite poor in mineral resources. At this point the river turns abruptly westward for roughly 25 km, flowing through a third narrow gorge. In this stretch, the river is very different. Since the riverbed is narrow, between high banks, even cliffs, the river's flow is fast. Flowing out of this gorge into a plain, the Orontes turns northward at Tell 'Ašarneh and flows into the broad swamps and marshlands of the Ghab (see above). The Ghab's northern end is near Tell Qarqur (ancient Qarqar). North of the Ghab, the river continues through a fourth gorge that ends near the town of Darkūš. As with other cases where the Orontes exits a gorge, the current slows dramatically. The current is slowest at the rocky barrier of Jisr al Hadid, where the river turns to the west and then southwest for approximately 45 km. Here it flows through the 'Amuq (Antioch) Plain before entering the fifth and final gorge at Little Jebel Sim'ān (about 6 km from the sea). It then empties quickly into the Mediterranean Sea.

#### 1.1.2.1.5. Western Inland Syria

Western inland Syria is basically a composite of plateaus and plains or steppes (fig. 1.3, p. 6). The four parallel mountain and valley systems described above inhibit the movement of rainfall from west to east. Thus western Inland Syria is much drier than the coast, although the north still receives sufficient rainfall for dry farming. In the north, there are fertile agricultural plains known as the Aleppo Plateau. In the midst of this plateau (midway between the Mediterranean and the Euphrates) is the north-to-south-flowing Quweiq River, which terminates in the morphologic depression of Al Maṭḥ (Matthers and Collon 1981). The important city of Aleppo (ancient Ḫalab) is located in the midst of the plateau. Winter wheat, olives, and grapes are all grown in this region.

In southern inland Syria, the Anti-Lebanon Mountains greatly impede the movement of precipitation to the east, resulting in the dry steppe north of Damascus. Since Damascus itself receives less than 200 mm (8 inches) of rain annually, its existence is dependent on the Wadi Barada, which flows down from the Anti-Lebanon Range, terminating in the al-Ghutah Oasis in the Damascus Plain. If there were no Barada River, there could be no Damascus (Burns 2007, xvii). The city was of great importance because of its location on the Mari-Tadmor-Damascus trade route.

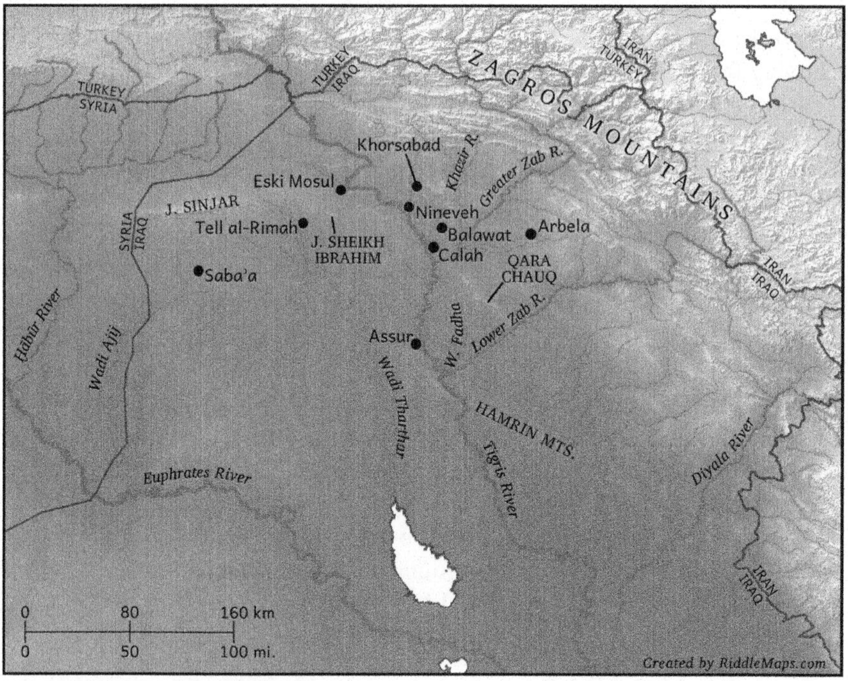


Fig. 1.5. The Assyrian heartland

South of Damascus is the Ḥawran (Ḥauran) basalt plateau (average elevation 610 m; 2,001 ft), a region of substantial fertility owing to the decomposition of its volcanic rock, though there are also barren lava fields. The Jebel ad-Duruz (Druze Mountains, 1,800 m; 5,904 ft) is located here. To the west of the Ḥawran, on the eastern side of the Sea of Galilee, is the Golan region (where the Aramean polity of Geshur was located). The Yarmuk River Valley forms its southern boundary, separating it from the area known in biblical sources as Gilead, a plateau in the northern part of the modern state of Jordan.

### 1.1.2.2. Eastern Syria

The region of eastern Syria is larger than western Syria (fig. 1.3, p. 7). It can be envisioned as two major geographic subregions, with the Euphrates River as the dividing line from roughly the Great Bend eastward. The first subregion is the Jezirah. It is the area defined by the left bank of the Euphrates[15]

15. Throughout this volume, the "left" bank is oriented by the flow of the river southward and eastward.

and hence is "inside." The second subregion is the Syrian Steppe and Desert (the right bank of the Euphrates, the "outside" area).

Alternatively, the region can be envisioned with the 300 mm rainfall line as a dividing line that creates two different agricultural subregions. The northern agricultural subregion is rain-fed farming, while the southern is a zone primarily for mobile pastoralism (except for the rivers cutting through it, where irrigation is possible).

1.1.2.2.1. The Jezirah

The Jezirah is a largely semiarid steppe that topographically is a basin; its surface is flat and smooth with gentle slopes. As a result, movement across the region was easy and convenient. Its elevation is roughly between 150 to 300 m (492 to 984 ft), though this is interrupted by two moderately elevated mountain ranges oriented east–west: to the east of the Ḫābūr River, Jebel Sinjar (Assyrian Singāra), which is 1,480 m (4,854 ft) in elevation, 43 km long, and 8 km wide; and to the west, Jebel 'Abd al-'Aziz (Assyrian Dibar), which is 920 m (3,018 ft) in elevation, 40 km long, and 5 km wide (Wirth 1971, 53; Edgell 2006, 23, 458–59). The Ṭūr 'Abdīn mountain range (ancient Kašiyāri) is a limestone formation with an elevation between 900 to 1,400 m (2,952 to 4,592 ft). It forms the northern edge of the Jezirah. However, while the Ṭūr 'Abdīn Range looks rather imposing from a southern approach, it is important to consider the Ṭūr 'Abdīn as an integral part of the Mesopotamian topography, not as a frontier zone, since the upper Tigris region is not reached by the Tigris itself but is most directly and easily reached by crossing over the Ṭūr 'Abdīn mountain range (Radner 2006, 274–75).[16] Besides the two rivers that delimit it, the Tigris and Euphrates, the Jezirah is traversed by two other significant rivers, the Balīḫ in the west and the Ḫābūr in the east. Both rivers flow south and are tributaries of the Euphrates.

The Jezirah receives 200–600 mm (8–24 in) of average annual rainfall,[17] and on this basis it can be divided into two areas (fig. 1.1). The first area is in the north and receives the more significant rainfall totals (over 300 mm and above annually). The area is roughly located north of a line from Jebel Sinjar

16. Radner states: "The Upper Tigris region is never accessed by water, as the Tigris cuts deeply through the mountains north of Cizre/Jazirat ibn 'ūmar (at the border between Iraq and Turkey) and cannot be navigated upstream; also going downstream is extremely dangerous and usually avoided."

17. This description is mainly concerned with the Syrian Jezirah; there are great similarities with the Iraqi Jezirah, but some differences. One difference can be seen in toponymy: geographical names with the word *bīr* ("well" in Arabic) abound in Syria, but not Iraq. See Oates and Oates 1976, 114.

(just on the other side of the modern border with Iraq) to Harran (on the Balīḫ River) to Karkamiš/Carchemish (on the Euphrates River at the Turkish border). The broad plains of the upper Balīḫ and the upper Ḫābūr are important as a source of winter wheat (currently serving as the "breadbasket" for the nation of Syria). Thus in antiquity, the upper Ḫābūr "triangle" (i.e., all the area of the tributaries that comprise the Ḫābūr) was supportive of a large population. In a sense, the Jebel Sinjar and Jebel 'Abd al-'Aziz form a type of "funnel" for all the tributaries of the Ḫābūr, creating the upper Ḫābūr triangle.

The second area, the larger part of the Jezirah, is south of this Jebel Sinjar-Harran-Karkamiš line and sees the rainfall drop off, with the flat steppe being given over mainly to grazing. However, along the Euphrates and Ḫābūr Rivers irrigation farming was possible at some sites. Tell Šēḫ Ḥamad on the Ḫābūr is one example. The site is located in an area on the Ḫābūr River that receives less than 200 mm of rainfall per annum, but in ancient times a series of irrigation canals were used at the site, elevating its moisture availability (Fales 2008). Another example on the Euphrates River would be the site of Mari. In addition, there are indications that canal irrigation within Assyria along the Tigris might have increased production there by as much as one and a half to two times preirrigation levels.[18]

Another way of envisioning the Jezirah is by its three river systems. The Balīḫ and Ḫābūr Rivers create two west–east districts within the Jezirah. Yet the Euphrates, due to the magnitude of its water flow and its fertile alluvial valley, where artificial irrigation is possible, creates its own zone. Hence, one can envision the Jezirah as three zones: the northwest (Balīḫ) zone, the northeast (Ḫābūr) zone, and the south (Euphrates) zone.[19]

The Balīḫ is a minor tributary of the Euphrates with an average flow of 6 $m^3/s$ (maximum 12 $m^3/s$; minimum 5 $m^3/s$). The small valleys that comprise the headwaters of the Balīḫ are located in Turkey, some 30 to 50 km north of the modern Syrian–Turkish border. A major source for the Balīḫ, however, is located in Syrian territory close to the border where a number of productive karst springs ensure a fairly uniform flow of water. This is the Tell Abyad aquifer, which, like the Ras el Ain, is also a karst aquifer (Wirth 1971, 421–22; Wagner 2011, 160; Fales 2014, 227–29).

The Ḫābūr is the main internal river of the Jezirah. It has a length of 486 km and an average flow of 50 $m^3/s$ (maximum 300 $m^3/s$; minimum 35 $m^3/s$; see Wirth 1971, 110). It takes most of its flow from karst springs emerging at

18. Wilkinson et al. 2005; Ur 2005; Bagg 2000.

19. The modern administrative districts of Raqqa (Balīḫ), Hassakeh (Ḫābūr), and Deir ez-Zor (Euphrates) reflect these three natural divisions.

Ras el Ain,[20] while the rest of its flow comes from the Ṭūr ʿAbdīn mountain range.

Before modern dams, the Euphrates (whose water sources derive from what is today Turkey) yielded an average water flow of 840 $m^3/s$, with the highest water flow being in April and May and the lowest in autumn (August–December) with a flow of only 250 $m^3/s$.[21] In the spring with the melting of the snows in Anatolia, the spring flood flow can be 5,000 $m^3/s$.[22]

In ancient times, north of Karkamiš the Euphrates flowed through a series of valleys and gorges (today dams have changed this). South of Karkamiš, down the river just beyond Tell Bazi (roughly from the dam of Karkamiš to the dam of Tishrin), was an important zone for agriculture, trade, and communication. After a roughly 100 km north–south stretch, the river course turns east into the Neogene Euphrates depression (Wagner 2011, 142). This is known as the Great Bend of the Euphrates (sometimes referred to as the "Elbow"). This area, being located in the zone receiving less than 200 mm rainfall, did not contain a large number of ancient sites, though some important sites such as Tell Meskene (Emar) and Tell Fray were located here (now covered by Lake Assad). The area at the confluence of the Balīḫ River with the Euphrates is the location of Tell Bi'a (ancient Tuttul), not far from the modern city of Raqqa.

Further down the river one encounters the region of the Middle Euphrates, where the river has cut its path through the plateau of the Syrian Steppe, forming an alternation of gorges and valley expansions 2 to 12 km wide. The region's landscape is characterized by a deep valley where the irrigable land is quite a bit below the surface of the surrounding steppe. Thus a steep escarpment some 80 to 250 m high at the edge of the irrigated area creates a sharp boundary and limits the area available for agricultural purposes.[23] In modern geographical terms, this area is a "river oasis." The local Arabic name for it is the Zor (reflected in the modern provincial capital's name, Deir ez-Zor). Satellite views of the region show well the sharp demarcation line of the terrain and the narrowness of the valley (as narrow as 12 km at points). On both sides of the river is a buffer zone at the edge of the steppe overlooking the valley that extends some 30 to 50 km inland from the river without any natural boundaries but extends roughly to the line of the first wells in the

20. See Wagner 2011, 142. For the Ras el Ain aquifer, see p. 160.

21. See Ionides 1937, 38, table 18; Wirth 1971, 109–10.

22. Wirth 1971, 109–10. In 1954 the flood measured 7,000 m3/s, and the catastrophic flood of May 1967 measured 8,500 m3/s (p. 110).

23. The contemporary inhabitants of the Zor refer to the escarpment ridge and steppe beyond it as *jebel* "mountain," even though it averages only some 61 m or 200 feet in height.

steppe (Buccellati 1990a, 95). Nevertheless, the steppe on the left bank of the Euphrates (on the north and east bank, i.e. the Jezirah) is, in the minds of both ancient and modern inhabitants, perceptually different from the steppe on the right bank (on the south and west bank, the so-called Šamīya). On both sides of the Euphrates, wells are an important part of the landscape,[24] as also are foggaras.[25]

The river enters the basaltic gorge of Ḥalabiya (in the modern province of Deir ez Zor). This area served as a natural and political border throughout history.[26] The region extends in many senses as far south down river as the modern city of Ḥît, which had large bitumen reserves, whose exploitation is clearly attested in the written sources, mainly from the second millennium BCE onward. Bitumen was used frequently, as attested in the ceramics excavated in the region, where it was utilized to line storage jars, waterproof pavements, and draw patterns on ceramics.

The geographic constraints (the narrowness of the cultivable strip, the enclosed valley, the proximity of the Euphrates and of its floods) have always limited the possibilities for human settlement (Buccellati 1990a; Kepinski, Lecomte and Tenu 2006a, 10). Thus what made the Middle Euphrates vital was neither its agricultural potential nor its raw material resources but its strategic position on international trade routes and on the routes of the pastoralists.

On the one hand, the region supplied open access to Babylonia to the southeast via the Euphrates, and to north Syria and Anatolia on the northwest. On the other hand, it was a crossroads of international trade routes between the region of the Diyala and Iran to the northeast and the Levant to the southwest. It was the means of contact between Assyria and the world of the steppe (Kepinski 2009, 150).

To the east of the Ḫābūr, south of Jebel Sinjar, and east of the Tigris was an area dominated by nomadic pastoralism. Wadi Ajij and Wadi Tharthar run through this zone from north to south, terminating in the marshes before

---

24. In the Sūḫu texts (Texts 2 and 4; see RIMB 2:288–89), a cluster of three wells is mentioned, all apparently in reasonable distance from one another.

25. A foggara is an underground conduit for water in desert country. Specifically, it is an artificial underground tunnel dug into the cliff, escarpment or base of a mountainous area, so as to bring water out to the surface. These tunnels are straight and horizontal with sloping sections, so as to allow the water to drain out into an oasis or an irrigation system. Such foggaras are located on the southwestern spur of Mount Bišri. See Pappi 2006, 243.

26. This area is roughly from Tell Humeida at the entrance (6 km to the north of the gorge) to Tell Abu Fahd at the exit (6 km to the south of the defile). Tell Qabr Abu al 'Atiq, located on the left bank, also had the same strategic importance and consequently, historical importance of the region of the basaltic gorge of Ḥalabiya.

reaching the Euphrates. Again the importance of wells, especially along the routes, can be seen.

Geographically, the Jezirah is the steppe area that formed the natural hinterland to Assyria farther to the east (today, northern Iraq). The nucleus of Assyria (fig. 1.5) was but a small entity and had the basic shape of a heart or triangle with Assur, the initial capital, being located near its bottom point.[27] In the north and the northeast, the Zagros Mountains form a natural boundary; in the southeast, toward Babylonia, the Ḥamrīn Mountains and the Lower Zab River form natural barriers. To the west, the heartland of Assyria flanks the flat tableland of the steppe (i.e., the Jezirah); in the northwest, it touches the slopes of the Sinjar mountain chain. The western borderline of the heartland does not have a natural boundary that would have prevented the Assyrians from penetrating into the dry farming belt of the Ḫābūr region. Thus the Jezirah was Assyria's hinterland steppe and caused Assyria to be "essentially a steppe-bound empire" (Kühne 1995, 69). The geo-climatic position of Assyria and the Jezirah is responsible for its economic potential and thereby its historical disposition throughout its existence. This explains why, during the Neo-Assyrian period, provincial centers lying rather far away were liable for grain rations to the deity Aššur. The need for dry-farming land was one of the motives for the constant Assyrian drive to the west,[28] with the result that the Jezirah, especially the northern and central Ḫābūr area, became part of "Assyria proper" (Postgate 1992a). The Arameans of the Jezirah were the victims of this Assyrian imperial expansion.

1.1.2.2.2. The Syrian Steppe and Desert

The Syrian Steppe and Desert receive less than 200 mm (8 inches) of rainfall annually (fig. 1.1). Agriculture is largely impossible, except for some irrigation farming at oases such as Palmyra (ancient Tadmor) and El Kowm and to a limited extent on Jebel Bišri (fig. 1.3, p. 7). An important portion of the area, however, supports mobile pastoralists, particularly in the area on the right bank of the Euphrates known as the Šamīya. The inner steppe region is

27. This area is commonly referred to as the "Assyrian Triangle," comprising about 13,000 $km^2$ between ancient Assur, Nineveh, and Arbela. In his study, M. Altaweel (2004, 4) demarcates the heartland of Assyria as the 150 × 79 km area having a north–south axis from the Lower Zab to Eski Mosul and an east–west axis from Wadi Tharthar and Jebel Sheikh Ibrahim to Wadi Fadha, Qara Chauq, and the Khazir River. This area formed the nucleus of the Assyrian Empire and included the capital cities.

28. "The other being the lack of natural resources, especially metal" (Kühne 1995, 72).

known in Arabic as the Bādiya "Syrian Desert." The Syrian Desert covers an area of approximately 250,000 $km^2$ (Edgell 2006, 427).

On a northwest to southeast line, this area has three geographic zones (fig. 1.3). The first is the northern Syrian Steppe (also sometimes designated the Aleppo Plateau). It is generally comprised of flat to hilly landscapes at topographic elevations around 400 m, although Jebel al-Ḥaṣṣ rises to 580 m. In addition, there are two salt flats in the morphologic depressions of al-Maṭḥ (the terminus of the Quweiq River) and Jabbūl.

The second zone is essentially a series of fold mountains formed by transpression to the anticlockwise rotation of the Arabian Plate as the Red Sea opened, with individual folds draped over faults (Edgell 2006, 24). These are the Palmyrides or Palmyrene Ranges that comprise a 400 km–long and 100 km–wide belt, rising 200–500 m above the surrounding plain and stretching northeast from the southern end of the Anti-Lebanon Mountains to the Euphrates Plain (Edgell 2006, 456). The Palmyrides are arid, with sparse vegetation, receiving less than 200 mm of annual rainfall. They are comprised of two mountain chains—the northern Palmyrides (also known as the Jebel Abu Rujmayn) and a southern Palmyride Range (sometimes collectively referred to as the Jebel ar Ruwayq)—extending from the southwest to the northeast, with altitudes between 1,000 and 1,300 m. The northern Palmyrides are broad brachyanticlines with gentle slopes and broad watersheds, while the southern Palmyrides are trending anticlines causing steep slopes and narrow watersheds (Wagner 2011, 140–41). The northern Palmyride Range extends more in an east–northeastward direction from the Ḥoms depression and to the Palmyra (Tadmor) area, while the southern Palmyride Range follows a purer northeastward line. Thus the two ranges converge into one chain in the area of Palmyra, with this single range continuing northeastward into Jebel Bišri. However, the northern Palmyride Range is, in fact, distinguished from Jebel Bišri by the Bišri Fault, which geologically separates the Bilâs Block from the Bišri Block (Brew et al. 2003). The oasis of El Kowm, comprised of dozens of artesian springs, is located here.

Individual mountain massifs of the northern Palmyrides are Jebel Šūmariye (Choumariye) (1,075 m high, 20 km long), Jebel Bilâs (1,098 m high, 30 km long), Jebel Šâ'ir (Chaar) (1,279 m high, 15 km long), Jebel Murâ'a, and Jebel Būweidā (Bouaida) (1,390 m high, 45 km long).

The main mountain massifs of the southern Palmyrides are Jebel Ma'lula (1,910 m, 30 long), Jebel an Nasrani (1,405 m high, 30 km long), Jebel ash Sharqi (500–1,000 high, 60 km long), as well as other mountains (Jebel Dmeir, Jebel Mghara, Jebel Manqoura, Jebel Ghantous, Jebel Basiri) reaching peak altitudes of 1,100–1,390 m.

In between the Palmyrides runs the Jhar Fault, forming the lengthy southwest–northeast aligned, broad transpressional basin called Ad Daww depression (roughly 600 m in altitude). It is an elongated area of 1,178 $km^2$ that extends toward Palmyra (Tadmor). It provides a corridor to Damascus from the Euphrates region, as well as a link with the Ḥoms depression that creates a corridor to the coast. These corridors became important routes for trade and communication for both central and southern Syria with the Middle Euphrates region. Consequently, the oasis of Palmyra (ancient Tadmor), located in the depression at the point that the southern and northern Palmyrides merge, served a vital role in this zone.

Approximately 50 km west of the modern city of Deir ez-Zor, south of the Euphrates at the entry point of the Balīḫ River, is the table mountain known as Jebel Bišri (867 m; 2,844 ft).[29] Mount Bišri is, in fact, "a northeastern plunging formation in the Palmyrides and has been connected to the formation of this mountain belt and the cultures surrounding it" (Lönnqvist, Törnä, Lönnqvist, and Nuñez 2011, 77). It is about 30 × 60 km in area and is generally semiarid with steppe-type vegetation lying between the 100 mm and 150 mm isohyets. Sporadically in the area of Jebel Bišri, including the southern, western, and eastern piedmonts, are oases that are fed by springs and wells.[30] It is part of a border region between mobile pastoralist groups and sedentary agriculturalists. Jebel Bišri is important for its early connections with the Arameans (see chs. 2 and 3).

The third zone, which lies to the southeast of the southern Palmyride Range, is the region formed by the Hamad and Rutbah Uplifts. It is known today as the Bādiyat aš Šām or Syrian Desert.

## 1.2. Chronological Issues

For discussions of relative chronology, scholars have tended to utilize the chronological terms or periods used in Mesopotamian archaeology (e.g., Uruk, Early Dynastic I–III, etc.) or Palestinian archaeology (e.g., Early Bronze I–IV, Middle Bronze I–III, etc.).[31] However, recent archaeological work in Syria has permitted the development of a periodization based more on local sequences (see table 1.2). One period that this work has especially clarified is the Iron Age (1200–550 BCE).[32] This is the time period with

29. Lönnqvist et al. 2011, 53–82.

30. For detailed discussions, see Pappi 2006; Lönnqvist et al. 2011, 64, map.

31. For an evaluation of this tendency in periodization, see Akkermans and Schwartz 2003, 13.

32. Mazzoni 1984, 1990a, 1990b, 1991–92, 1995, 2000a, 2000b; Lehmann 1996, 1998. For some balancing comments, note Whincop 2007, 2009, 2010.

Table 1.2. Periodization of Iron Age Syria. (Adapted from Akkermans and Schwartz 2003, 364 with changes based on Mazzoni 2005, 12–14.)

| Date | **Western Syria** | | | | |
|---|---|---|---|---|---|
| 1200 | | | | | |
| 1100 | Iron I | | | | Afis VII |
| 1000 | | Sukas H2 | | | |
| 900 | | Sukas H1 | | | |
| 800 | Iron II | | | | Afis VIII |
| 700 | | | Al Mina 6–10 | | |
| 600 | Iron III | Sukas G3 | Al Mina 5 | | Afis IX |
| 500 | | Sukas G2<br>Sukas G1 | | | |
| 400 | Achaemenid Persian period | | Al Mina 3–4 | Mardikh VI palazzetto | Afis X |
| 300 | | Sukas F | | | |

| **Middle Euphrates** | | **Ḫābūr** | **Mesopotamia** |
|---|---|---|---|
| | Local kingdom at Karkamiš | Local ruler Aššur-ketta-lēšir | Middle Assyrian period |
| Neo-Assyrian occupation at Tell Aḥmar and Arslan Tash | | Dūr-Katlimmu Neo-Assyrian levels | Neo-Assyrian period |
| | | Dūr-Katlimmu Red House | Neo-Babylonian period |
| | | | Achaemenid Persian period |

which this book is primarily concerned, although the end of the Late Bronze Age (i.e., LBA II, 1400–1200 BCE) will be important in the discussion of the origins of the Arameans.

The Iron Age in Syria saw many new political and economic developments. In the first part of the period, the larger political entities of the Late Bronze Age were replaced by various local states. The monumental art and architecture of these new political entities assumed a vital new style that is one of the most significant aesthetic contributions of ancient Syrian civilization (Akkermans and Schwartz 2003, 360). In the later part of the period, Syria was melded into the Neo-Assyrian, Neo-Babylonian, and Achaemenid Persian Empires. Although the conquest of Syria by Alexander the Great did not bring about an immediate change in material culture, the establishment of the Macedonian Seleucid dynasty with its Hellenization policy (ca. 300 BCE) was a significant change and is consequently considered the end of the Iron Age in Syria.

Significant economic and technological developments took place during the Iron Age. By the end of the second millennium, iron had emerged as an important metal for the manufacture of weapons and tools throughout the Near East (Waldbaum 1999). With the disruption of trade at the end of the Late Bronze Age, the supply of tin was curtailed (tin is necessary for the production of bronze, being alloyed with copper). In contrast to tin and copper, sources of iron were abundant. In addition, iron can produce a harder and more durable product than bronze. Finally, iron, unlike bronze, does not require elaborate installations for its production. Thus, the manufacture of this "democratic metal" was not dependent on wealthy institutions and could be conducted at all social levels.[33]

The Iron Age in Syria is typically divided into three parts (see table 1.2): Iron I (1200–900), Iron II (900–700), and Iron III (700–550), followed by the Persian period (550–330). Other periodizations have been used, and a consensus has not yet been reached. The Iron I period is the most poorly documented phase, with material attested from Tell Afis, Tell Ḥama F, and most recently Aleppo. In fact, the best-documented sequence from the Late Bronze Age into the early Iron Age has been obtained from Tell Afis.

Thus principally based on evidence from Tell Afis, Mazzoni has suggested a subdivision of the period into Iron IA (1200–1075), Iron IB

33. Akkermans and Schwartz 2003, 360. Sherratt (2003, 43–44) notes the economic stimulus to iron's rise: the devaluation of bronze as a result of its increased quantity contrasted with the higher value of iron in the late-second-millennium context, driving its demand. Note Josh 6:19, 24.

(1075–1000), and Iron IC (1000–900).[34] Iron IA can be characterized as "the beginnings: between instability and recovery," with the first half of twelfth century being primarily a time of instability and the second half of the century being the beginning of reurbanization. Iron IB saw the emergence of significant new urbanization. It was a period of greater stability, political increase, and steady urbanization. Finally, Iron IC, the flourishing of the Iron I, saw general political and economic prosperity throughout the Levant, with Phoenician cultural diffusion playing an important role.

In the Iron II period (900–700), the diagnostic Red-Slipped Burnished Ware characteristic of the great regional capitals in Syria was introduced (Mazzoni 2013), apparently from the Levantine coast. Cypriot painted imports occur with some frequency. Mazzoni (2013) subdivides the Iron II period into two subdivisions: the Iron IIA (900–800) and the Iron IIB (800–700). The Iron IIA was a time of new trends. The effects of Phoenician, Aramean, and Assyrian material culture were significant (e.g., Phoenician Red-Slipped Burnished Ware and Assyrian influence in art). The period experienced an intensification of trade (both land and sea), which stimulated economic development and cultural interconnections. Syria became a "manufacturing zone" for bronze and ivory. The Iron IIB was characterized by initial flourishing and then collapse. The roles of Assyrian provincial capitals such as Kār-Shalmaneser (Tell Aḥmar) and other outposts such as Ḫadattu (Arslan Taş) increased the Assyrianization process and contributed to a decrease in regionalization.

Iron III (ca. 700–539 BCE) finds a decrease in Cypriot imports and an increase in Greek imports on the coast, Neo-Assyrian imitations, and a continuing use of Red-Slipped Burnished pottery. During this period Syria experienced a deculturation due to the decline in local patrons; on account of the Assyrian imperial administration, it experienced an emulation of Assyrian culture, resulting in the Assyrian koinė of the period (Mazzoni 2013). This deculturation continued during Neo-Babylonian domination.

The Persian period saw an even greater popularity of Greek pottery, mortaria with high ring bases and ridged sides, "torpedo" amphoras, and a new cooking pot with a short neck and everted rim (Akkermans and Schwartz 2003, 366). Ceramic standardization increased during this last period of the Iron Age, perhaps due to the inclusion of Syria in a large-scale empire with broader economic networks.

34. The following is based principally on Mazzoni 2000a, 2005, 2013. See also Harrison 2009a, 181–83 and the table on p. 177.

## 1.3. Linguistic Issues

The end of the Late Bronze Age and beginning of the Iron Age in Syria was a period of great change. There is considerable debate about the nature of the transition between the two periods, not only in Syria, but elsewhere. This debate will be discussed in more detail in the next chapter. Here it is only necessary to note the linguistic impact. With the demise of great urban centers of the Late Bronze Age such as Ugarit, Alalaḫ, and Emar with their palace-centered economies, their different languages/dialects and cuneiform writing systems disappeared. The use of the Hurrian language, once so significant in Late Bronze Age Syria, began to wane and then vanished. In the northern regions of Syria and Anatolia, the Hittite language (also written in cuneiform) disappeared. However, there is not a complete disconnect with the preceding period. This can be demonstrated by the continuity of occupation at some large centers such as Hamath and Karkamiš, as also with some inland parts of western Syria.[35]

Nonetheless, the Iron Age in Syria manifested a range of languages playing significant roles.[36] These included Luwian (sometimes referred to as Neo-Hittite), Phoenician, Aramaic, and Akkadian (especially, but not exclusively, the Assyrian dialect). For the sake of completeness, it should also be noted that there were some Arabic involvements in the region, mainly on the eastern fringes,[37] with the survival of some Dispersed Oasis North Arabian[38] inscriptions that have been found throughout Mesopotamia and the Levant,[39] though these inscriptions do not appear until the Iron II period.

In the first part of the Iron Age, before the Neo-Assyrian, Neo-Babylonian, and Medo-Persian Empires, three languages (Luwian, Phoenician, and Akkadian) are attested, mainly in particular geographic regions. Aramaic was not so limited, being found in most regions.

---

35. E.g., Tell Afis. See Mazzoni 1997a.

36. Greenfield 1998; Lipiński 2000b; Dion 2001; Lemaire 2001a.

37. These involvements are documented mainly in the Assyrian inscriptions. At the battle of Qarqar (853), one of the allies listed by Shalmaneser III is Gindibu' (= Jindub, an Arabic name for "locust") (RIMA 3:23, A.0.102.2, ii.94; Fabritius 1999). An Aramaic seal of unknown provenance from the ninth century BCE (Bordreuil 1986, 75) honors ʿAttār-šamayn, a name that is much later associated with a federation of Arabian tribes in the inscriptions of Aššurbanipal (Weippert 1973–74, 44–45). The Sūḫu annals of Ninurta-kudurrī-uṣur record his confiscation of the goods from an Arabian caravan originating from Saba and Teima (RIMB 2:100). Note also the fragments in a South Arabic script (or Dispersed Oasis North Arabian?) discovered in excavations from Ḥama (ancient Hamath).

38. For the terminology, see Macdonald 2000.

39. Sass 1991, 38–102, figs. 8–41.

### 1.3.1. Luwian

Luwian speakers comprised a large part of the population in central and southern Anatolia during the third through the first millennia BCE. The Luwian language was recorded in two different scripts: (1) the cuneiform script of Mesopotamian origin written on clay tablets discovered among the royal archives of the Hittite imperial capital, Ḫattuša (modern Boğazköy) and dating to the period of the Hittite kingdom (ca. 1650–1200 BCE); and (2) the hieroglyphic script dating also to the Hittite kingdom but much more common for the period of the Neo-Hittite states (ca. 1150–700 BCE).[40] Located in southeastern Anatolia and northern Syria, these Neo-Hittite states[41] utilized the hieroglyphic script to write all sorts of texts, from monumental inscriptions to everyday texts.[42] J. D. Hawkins observes:

> Each [Neo-Hittite] state seems to have developed its own tradition of monumental inscriptions. The evidence of a handful of letters and economic documents written on strips of lead suggests that by this period the Hieroglyphic script had been developed for writing such every-day administrative documents which would normally have been written on perishable material, wood, leather or papyrus, and thus that the Neo-Hittite states practised a high degree of literacy, most of which has been lost for ever. They probably wrote in this way all the types of text that the Hittite Empire wrote in cuneiform on clay, and we should remember that references in the cuneiform clay documents of Hattuša to wooden documents and "scribes on wood" suggest the existence of a parallel lost corpus of literacy during the Empire period.[43]

Thus cuneiform Luwian ceased to be written after the fall of the Hittite Empire (early twelfth century), but the hieroglyphic Luwian script continued as the autochthonous/indigenous writing system in all of the Neo-Hittite states, and only in these states. The Luwian language was not the same as the language termed in modern vernacular as *Hittite* (termed by the Hittites

40. Hawkins 2000, 2; 2003, 128; Melchert 2004; Payne 2006, 2008.

41. For some of the biblical connections with these states, see Cancik 2002; Collins 2007, 197–218.

42. Payne 2010; Hawkins 1995a, 1297.

43. Hawkins 2000, 2–3. See also Symington 1991, who discusses this issue in the context of the publication of the writing board recovered from the Ulu Burun (Kaş) shipwreck off the southern coast of Turkey. Starke (2003, 117; 1999) notes that since the cuneiform Luwian script was used for everyday type documents, its abandonment meant that hieroglyphic Luwian replaced it for these sorts of texts. These were written on perishable or otherwise reusable media (e.g., wooden boards) and hence few survive. On the other hand, see the remarks concerning the genres of its use by van den Hout 2006, 220–22.

themselves as "Nesite") but was closely related to it. Both are Indo-European languages.[44]

It is likely that the hieroglyphic Luwian script functioned in the various Hittite successor states as an identity marker, as it linked them with the glorious past of the mighty Hittite Empire (Payne 2006, 125). Such a link with the past may even have been felt to be more important than the more practical advantages offered by the linear alphabetic script (Phoenician and later Aramaic scripts). The fact remains that all Hittite successor (Neo-Hittite) states continued to write in hieroglyphic script until their demise, despite it being not only a more complicated and archaic writing system but also not even particularly well suited to the language it recorded, as its syllabary cannot record consonantal clusters, a frequent feature of Indo-European languages (Payne 2006, 125).

Some of the important Neo-Hittite states on the eastern side of the Taurus Mountains where hieroglyphic Luwian inscriptions have been discovered include Melid (modern Malatya), Kummuḫ (classical Commagene), Gurgum, Karkamiš, Masuwari (Til-Barsib, modern Tel Aḥmar), Patina (also known as Unqi/ʿUmq, modern ʿAmuq), Samʾal (Yādiya/Bīt-Gabbāri, modern Zincirli), and Hamath.

### 1.3.2. Phoenician

Phoenician was a West Semitic language written in the so-called linear alphabetic script (Segert 1997). This script may have been known in ancient times as Tyrian (Younger 2014b). Phoenician was the language of city-states such as Tyre, Sidon, and Byblos, but it was also the language farther north along the Syrian coast at sites such as Arqâ (Tell ʿArqa), Ṣimirra (Tell al-Kāzil), Arwad (Arvad)—along with continental dependencies Ṭarṭūs and ʿAmrīt, Usnu (Tel Dārūk), Siannu (Tel Siyannu), and Gabala (Gabla).

There are Phoenician inscriptions from inland and farther north, but these are not necessarily indicative of a Phoenician societal component in these places. These include the Hassan-Beyli Inscription, the Kulamuwa Inscription (from Zincirli), and the Cebel Ires Dağı Inscription. There are a number of bilinguals and trilinguals in which Luwian is placed alongside the Phoenician, including the Karatepe (Röllig 1999), Ivriz,[45] Incirli (Kaufman 2007), and Çineköy Inscriptions (Tekoğlu and Lemaire 2000).

44. Concerning the use of hieroglyphic Luwian in the earlier Hittite Empire period and its relationship to Hittite, especially during the fourteenth and thirteenth centuries, see van den Hout 2006.

45. For a preliminary report, see Dinçol 1992; Röllig 1992, 98.

### 1.3.3. Akkadian

Akkadian was an East Semitic language written in the Mesopotamian cuneiform script. The Ḫābūr River area had been in the possession of Assyria before the advent of the Aramean states there. For a time in this period, some local Akkadian dialects survived (e.g., in Šadikanni).[46] This area was later reconquered in the early Neo-Assyrian period. The Tell Fakhariya (Hadadyiṯʿî) Inscription (written in Aramaic and Akkadian) demonstrates the bilingual nature of this region after the Aramean penetration and the reassertion of Assyrian power. Due to the establishment of an efficient Assyrian administration in this region, the Assyrian language continued to be used, even after the destruction of the Neo-Assyrian Empire, throughout the first part of the Neo-Babylonian period.

### 1.3.4. Aramaic

#### 1.3.4.1. The Script

The Arameans were a large group of linguistically related peoples who spoke dialects of a West Semitic language known as Aramaic[47] that was initially written in the twenty-two letter linear alphabetic script. Early on, this script was utilized for the writing of Phoenician, Hebrew, and Aramaic texts.[48] The earliest Aramaic language texts date from the ninth century, although the script cannot be clearly differentiated as Aramaic script at this point (fig. 1.6).[49]

---

46. See chapter 3.

47. Kaufman 1997; Cook 1997; Aufrecht 2001; Dion 2001; Huehnergard 1995; Lipiński 2000b; Fales 1996a; 2011c; Greenspahn 2002; Creason 2004; Schniedewind 2006; and Beyer 1986; Folmer 1995, 2012; Kottsieper 2009; Martínez Borobio 2003.

48. Phoenician scribalism had a programmatic effect on the character of alphabetic literacy in the Levant in the early part of the first millennium BCE. In the coastal Phoenician script, the Old Canaanite sign inventory was reduced to the twenty-two necessary to represent the Phoenician consonantal phonemes. This twenty-two-letter alphabet was adopted into the Levantine interior regardless of the number of consonantal phonemes the individual languages needed to represent. Thus it was adopted for Hebrew, even though it could not represent all its phonemes (ש being used for both *śin* and *šin*) and for Aramaic, even though its twenty-seven phonemes were inadequately represented by the same twenty-two letter signs. See McCarter 2008, 47.

49. One of the oldest Old Aramaic inscriptions is the Tel Ḥalaf Pedestal Inscription (mid-ninth century). See Dankwarth and Müller 1988. The Tel Fakhariya Inscription is certainly the earliest full-length Old Aramaic inscription (ca. 850–830 BCE). See *COS* 2.34:153–54.

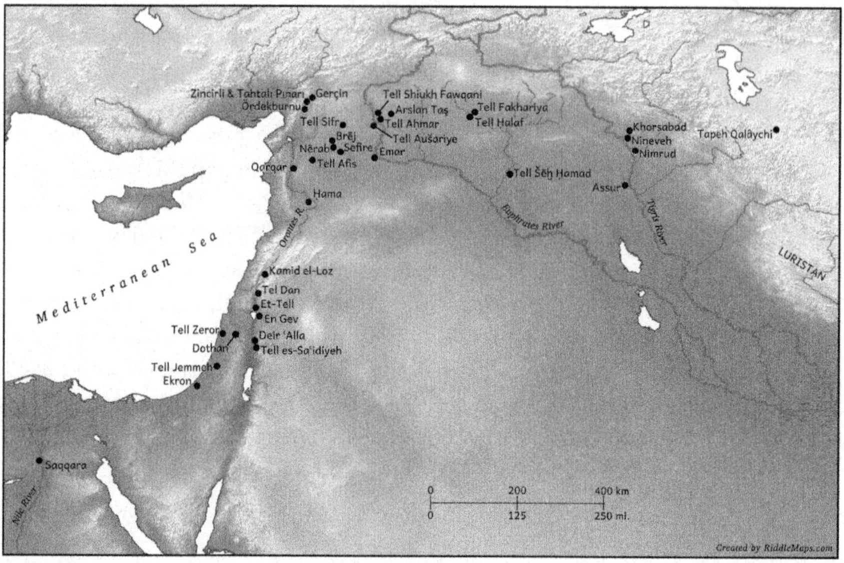


Fig. 1.6. Map showing locations of Old Aramaic inscriptions

The development of the script in which the Aramaic language was written in the first millennium can be divided into four periods (Lemaire 2006, 50):

1. Old Aramaic (ninth–eighth centuries BCE). This was the early linear alphabetic script that developed into the Aramaic script. By roughly the eighth century, the Aramaic language was being written in a script that can be called specifically Aramaic. This was used primarily by peoples speaking Aramaic in the Levant, as well as Mesopotamia, even in some cases by people who did not speak Aramaic (e.g., the Manneans, Tapeh Qâlaychi near Bukān).
2. Early Imperial Aramaic (seventh through the first part of the sixth centuries BCE). This was a distinctively Aramaic script that was used as a type of second official script of the Neo-Assyrian and Neo-Babylonian Empires.[51]
3. Imperial Aramaic of the Achaemenid Empire (ca. 540–330 BCE). During this period the Aramaic language reached its zenith,

50. Lemaire is writing specifically on the Old Aramaic script, but these divisions are nonetheless functional.

51. For Aramaic in the Assyrian, Babylonian and Persian Empires, see Schniedewind 2006; Beaulieu 2006; Millard 2003; Fales 2000b, 2007a, 2010a.

extending from Upper Egypt (Elephantine) to the border between Afghanistan and Uzbakistan and from Daskyleion to the Indus. Although not the only official language and script of this empire, Aramaic could be used everywhere in the Achaemenid administration.

4. Hellenistic period (330 BCE–first century CE). The Aramaic language was used less and less and only in Semitic-speaking contexts. The Aramaic script, however, gave birth to a number of other local scripts, some of which were used for non-Semitic languages.

This use of the Aramaic script corresponds somewhat to the development of the Aramaic language, though not precisely.

1.3.4.2. The Language

The Arameans' greatest contribution to the history and culture of the ancient Near East was the Aramaic language.[52] It became the lingua franca of the ancient Near East. In fact, Aramaic continues to be spoken by a small population even today.[53] In general, a fivefold periodization can be envisioned:

1. Old Aramaic (from the earliest inscriptions to the end of the Neo-Assyrian Empire: ca. 870–612 BCE),
2. Imperial Aramaic/Official Aramaic (612–200 BCE),
3. Middle Aramaic (200 BCE–250 CE),
4. Late Aramaic (250–1200 CE)
5. Modern Aramaic (1200–present).

Old Aramaic is the main concern for this study.

As for the origin of the Aramaic language in itself, a specialist in the language has recently pointed out that Aramaic cannot be directly connected to any of the Bronze Age manifestations of Northwest Semitic and that one may assume that, while it took "its distinctive shape at some point in the Bronze Age, it remained unwritten, and hence invisible, for several centuries" (Gzella 2014, 71–72). This "invisible" period must be at least four and a half centuries, perhaps more.

52. While Aramaic was one of the major languages of antiquity, many times more important as a literary Semitic language than Hebrew, it has usually been treated like Hebrew's ugly step sister (Kaufman 1996, 279–80).

53. See the forthcoming volume being produced by the Modern Aramaic Project of the Advanced Studies Institute of the Hebrew University (2012–2013) led by S. Fassberg.

The various polities where the Aramaic language was spoken before the Neo-Assyrian expansion were Bīt-Zamāni, Laqē, Bīt-Ḫalupē, Bīt-Baḫiāni, Bīt-Adīni, Bīt-Agūsi (Bēt-Gūš/Arpad), Bīt-Gabbāri (Sam'al/Y'dy, modern Zincirli), Lu'ash (the modern district of Idlib), Hamath, Zobah (Ṣobah), Bēt-Reḥob, Damascus (Ša-Imērīšu/Bīt-Haza'ili), Geshur, and Ma'akah. There were also a number of Aramean and Chaldean groups that used Aramaic: Utū', Puqūdu, Gubulu, Ḫaṭallu, Bīt-Yabiri, Bīt-Dakkūri, Bīt-Amukāni, Bīt-Ša'alli, and others.[54]

Aramaic continued to be spoken even as these polities were absorbed into the Neo-Assyrian Empire. In fact, due to early Aramean penetrations as well as the various Assyrian deportations, Aramaic became increasingly used in the late Neo-Assyrian period, with mutual influences occurring between both Aramaic and Neo-Assyrian.

However, Old Aramaic did not consist of a uniform dialect, no doubt due to the various tribal groups that gave rise to the different polities, as well as various different regional influences.[55] Thus Old Aramaic can generally be divided into six early dialects (Kaufman 1997):

1. Standard (Syrian) Aramaic (or western Old Aramaic)—the language of inscriptions from the mid-ninth to the end of the eighth century with a geographic spread within a 100 km radius of Aleppo;
2. Sam'alian Aramaic—inscriptions found at modern Zincirli in Turkey;
3. Eastern Aramaic—found in the Tell Fakhariya Inscription;
4. Mesopotamian Aramaic—economic and legal texts exhibiting Akkadian influence.
5. Levantine Aramaic—found in the Tell Dan Inscription and Hazael's booty inscriptions;
6. Southern Aramaic—probably attested in the texts from Tell Deir 'Alla.

These dialects began to disappear with the rise of Early Imperial Aramaic during the Assyrian Empire. They had largely vanished by the time that Imperial Aramaic (or Official Aramaic) became the standard (ca. 612 BCE). The processes involved in this are not fully known, though the role of the Neo-Assyrian Empire was a substantial reason.

54. See chapter 10.
55. See the discussion in chapter 2.

# 2
# THE ORIGINS OF THE ARAMEANS

It is important to separate the discussion of the questions concerning the ultimate origins of the Arameans from the issues surrounding the rise of the polities as encountered in the earliest documents. Thus, this chapter is particularly geared to engagement with questions related to sources and definitions, matters of fundamental importance to understanding the political composition of the various Aramean entities. In the next chapter, the discussion will focus on the regional factors that were at work in bringing about these entities.

## 2.1. The Word "Aram" in the Earliest Sources

### 2.1.1. Earliest Occurrences

Scholars have cited various alleged occurrences of "Aram" from many earlier third and second millennium texts.[1] However, most of these cannot definitely be linked with the Arameans.[2] Possible exceptions have been suggested in texts from Egypt and Ugarit.

An Egyptian list of place names from the reign of Amenhotep III (r. ca. 1391–1353 BCE) mentions *pꜣ-ꜣrm(w)* "the one of Aram" (see fig. 2.1).[3] The list seems to locate this "Aram" in north-central Syria (close to Amurru?). In Papyrus Anastasi III (from the time of Merenptah, r. 1213–1203), a report from an officer on the eastern frontier of the Nile Delta about 1210 BCE

1. For a discussion and assessment, see Lipiński 2000a, 26–35.

2. For example, a place name *A-ra-mu*$^{ki}$ occurs in the third-millennium Ebla tablets, along with similar place names such as *Arimu*$^{ki}$ and *Arramu*$^{ki}$. However, these cannot at present be linked with any certainty with the Arameans.

3. For Amenhotep's list, see Edel 1966, 28–29, pl. II (register 7). Edel notes the nomadic tribal nature of the designations in registers 7–11 and concludes, "Das kann wohl nichts anderes als 'das (Land) Aram' heissen."

tells of a colleague arriving from a town "in the district of Aram."[4] This papyrus is more difficult and unhelpful than the toponymic list of Amenhotep III. M. Görg has argued that both of these are early references to the Arameans in Egyptian texts.[5] The Amenhotep list seems to be a genuine reference; however, in my assessment, the papyrus is uncertain.

Fig. 2.1. *pꜣ-ꜣrm(w)* "the one of Aram." The restoration of *m* instead of *ayin* is very likely (Edel 1966, 28).

Some scholars have suggested that "Arameans" are mentioned in thirteenth-century texts from Ugarit.[6] However, in the case of the Ugaritic alphabetic cuneiform inscriptions, it is clear that all of the occurrences of *ʾrm* are, in fact, personal names of individuals, not gentilics.[7] The same is true in the case of the syllabic cuneiform texts from Ugarit.[8] In sum, the Egyptian text of Amenhotep III seems to attest to a region called *ʾrm* possibly located in north-central Syria as early as the fourteenth century BCE, but little else can be gleaned from this attestation. In the Ugaritic texts, however, Aram is not attested.

2.1.2. Later Occurrences

The term "Aram" is utilized in other ancient Near Eastern texts. The first indisputable occurrence of "Arameans" is found in Tiglath-pileser I's inscriptions (1114–1076), where this group, on every occasion, is termed the "Aramean Aḫlamû" (*aḫ-la-mì-i* KUR *ar-ma-ia*.MEŠ),[9] with "Aramean" as a gentilic/ethnicon/*nisbe* (*aḫlamî*/*aḫlamê armāya*, attested thus far only in the genitive; see discussion under Aḫlamû below). It has also been suggested that KUR.*Ar-ma-ia*, when attached to the designation *Aḫlamû* may represent "something more than a simple, topical, marker of ethnicity, and in point of fact refer to a somewhat more specific spatial notion, a 'mental-map'-type construct evoking an actual 'land of the Arameans' " (Fales forthcoming, 5). In this particular case, it would reference the region of the western (right)

4. For Papyrus Anastasi III, see Gardiner 1937, 31–32; *ANET*, 258–59.

5. Görg 1976, 499–500; 1979, 7–10; reprinted in Görg 1989, 157–60. See also Pitard 1987, 82. However, Lipiński (2000a, 32–33) argues against these texts referring to the Arameans. See now Edel and Görg 2005, 122–24, 143–44.

6. See, e.g., Reinhold 1989, 27.

7. Olmo Lete and Sanmartín 2003, 103–4. In one case, *ʾarm* is a toponym (a village, not a gentilic).

8. RS 15.37 (line 13); RS 20.176 (line 25); RS 16.178 (line 10).

9. RIMA 2:23, A.0.87.1, v.46–47, etc.

bank of the Euphrates between the Balīḫ and Ḫābūr Rivers.[10] This usage, however, is germane only to the context of Tiglath-pileser I and should not be universalized for the Arameans as a whole. In Aššur-bēl-kala's inscriptions (r. 1073–1056 BCE), they are referred to as the Arameans (a collective noun in the singular: *arumu*, most commonly in the genitive for KUR.*a-re-me*), while the *aḫlamû* are a distinct group.[11] The term *aḫlamû* dies out, except in archaic usage, after the reign of Adad-nērārī II (r. 911–891 BCE; see further below). Later from the mid-eighth century, one encounters the intriguing designation LÚ É *a-⌜ram⌝* "the people of Bīt-Aram" in a letter from the governor's archive from Nippur.[12] In the Neo-Assyrian royal inscriptions and the "everyday" documentation of the empire, the *nisbe* is *Ar(a)mayyu/Ar(a)māyu*, which is normally written *Ar-ma-a-a*, more rarely *Ar-ma-a-ia*, fem. *Armi/etu* (Fales forthcoming). In these sources the "land of Aram" can be used, along with "the land of Ḫatti," to designate the area west of the Euphrates River,[13] but it is also used in later Assyrian texts for a location in southern Mesopotamia. The Assyrian sources never use "Aram" to designate Damascus. Instead, this kingdom is designated Ša-imērīšu (lit. "of his asses"), Damascus, or Bīt-Ḫazā'ili ("House of Hazael").

In contrast, in the Aramaic inscriptions, "Aram" is used to designate both the kingdom of Damascus,[14] and the kingdom of Arpad/Bīt-Agūsi/Bēt-Gūš ("all Aram" and "Upper and Lower Aram").[15] Scholars have been divided over the occurrence of "Aram" in the Melqart Stela.[16] Some have understood this as an attribution to Damascus;[17] others see its use as an attribution to Arpad, which is the more likely (see Lipiński 2000a, 215–16). In their edition of the Ördekburnu Stela, Lemaire and Sass (2013, 122) suggest understanding *kbb .ʾ⌜r⌝m* in line 6 as "Kubaba *of Aram.*"[18] This occurrence,

10. Sader 1987, 271; Schniedewind 2002, 277–79.

11. Brinkman 1997, 11 n. 11. In Assyrian, the short second syllable is affected by vowel harmony: *Arumu*, *Areme*, *Arama*, gentilic: *Aramāya*.

12. Cole 1996a, 214, no. 104:5. Cole states: "Whether this graph represents 'Aram' or 'Arameans,' or whether it stands for a specific tribe or settlement of Arameans called Bīt-Aram is uncertain."

13. For example, see the Iran Stela of Tiglath-pileser III: RINAP 1:86, 35, iii.1: MAN.MEŠ *šá* KUR.*ḫat-ti* KUR.*a-ri-me* "the kings of the land of Ḫatti (and) the land of Aram."

14. Zakkur Inscription (ca. 796 BCE). See *KAI* 202; *COS* 2.35:155.

15. *ʾrm klh* and *ʾly ʾrm wtḥth*. See Sefire I A4–6a (ca. 760 BCE). *KAI* 222–24; Fitzmyer, 1995, 29. Compare LÚ *a-ram*.MEŠ [*ga*]*b-bi-šú-nu* in Cole 1996a, 65, no. 15:8. For detailed discussion, see chapter 8.

16. *KAI* 201; *COS* 2.33:152–53.

17. Most recently, Mykytiuk 2009.

18. Even if this is the correct understanding of the word division in the inscription, it yields a hitherto unknown and unusual appellation for this well-known goddess of Karkamiš.

if correctly read, would perhaps designate a similar nuance to the Assyrian usage for the area west of the Euphrates. For a discussion of the biblical textual occurrences, see below.

2.1.3. Etymology

Regarding the etymology and meaning of *ʾAram*, there is no consensus. One early proposal was to derive it from the root *rwm*, "to be high, exalted" and posit a meaning of "highland."[19] This hypothesis requires a prothetic *aleph*.[20] Part of the difficulty is the uncertainty whether *ʾAram* is a geographical name,[21] a divine name[22] or a personal name.[23]

The most recent proposal for the etymology of *ʾAram* has been put forth by Lipiński.[24] He argues that "*ʾArām* is an internal ('broken') plural of *riʾm*, 'wild bull,' 'buffalo,'"[25] and that the term describes the people as "wild bulls." He suggests that this may derive from the use of the wild bull as a totem, which may explain the numerous Syro-Hittite images of the storm god Hadad striding atop a wild bull:

> If the true etymology of *ʾārām* is "wild bulls," such an appellation of a people or a tribe implies a totemic social and religious structure, an essential peculiarity of which is the association of groups of persons or clans with

19. See Kraeling 1918, 22. Apparently Grimme was the first to suggest deriving "Aram" from *rûm*, "to be high," and he suggested the highland Najd in northern Saudi Arabia as its possible location. See Grimme 1904, 15.

20. While a prothetic *aleph* does occur in Old Aramaic, it tends to be found before sibilants or interdentals. Prothesis of an initial *aleph* /ʾi/ can occur: (1) *ʾšm* /ʾišm/ < *šim "name" (Hadad 16, 21; Sefire C 25); the form without the prothetic *aleph* occurs frequently in Old Aramaic (*šm*); (2) *ʾzh* /ʾiḏā/ < *ḏā < *ḏāt "who" (fem. rel. pronoun) (only in Samʾalian, Panamuwa 2). See Segert 1975, 210 (§5.3.9.10.3: "Formen mit Alef protheticum, das den Vorsatzvokal andeutet [vlg. arab. *ism*]: Sg. abs. אשם S I C 25; cstr. אשם H 16,21; mit Suff. 3. Pl. m. אשמהם S II B7"). See also Tropper 1993, 185 (§41.218).

21. It has also been proposed that the term was a geographical name that was associated with a tribe and eventually became the designation of a confederation of tribes. See O'Callaghan 1948, 95–96; M. F. Unger 1957, 41; *HALOT*, 89: "originally probably from *māt Arimi*, the Syrian steppe."

22. Streck (1906a, 197) thought that the term might derive from a divine name.

23. The biblical evidence seems to point to a personal name, an eponymous ancestor, but this is problematic since the evidence occurs in passages that scholars have typically dated late.

24. Lipiński 2000a, 51–54. See a fuller discussion of broken or internal plurals in Aramaic, see Lipiński 2003, 2008.

25. Lipiński 2008, 35. Lipiński (2000a, 52) states: "Now, the word *ʾārām* is identical with the Arabic 'broken' plural *ʾārām*, 'white antelopes,' in older languages 'wild bulls' or 'buffalos.'"

> groups of animals belonging to the same species and constituting the totem species.[26]

Lipiński utilizes two lines of argument. First, he considers the nominal formation pattern *qutūl* to be evidence of "broken plurals" in a number of the tribal names.[27] He feels that this form represents the "broken" plural of *qātil* (Lipiński 2003, 338). Second, he argues that "broken" plurals existed in Old Aramaic as attested in the Tell Fakhariya Inscription.[28]

However, the existence for "broken" plurals in Aramaic is dubious. Regarding the first line of argument, Lipiński's postulated broken plurals are understood by Zadok (2013, 273) as examples of a well-documented West Semitic nominal formation pattern: "the nominal pattern *qutūl* is a byform of *qatūl* by vowel assimilation."[29] In the case of the second argument, there is, in fact, no clear, convincing evidence of "broken" plurals in Old Aramaic. While the Tell Fakhariya Inscription is the cornerstone to Lipiński's argument for their existence in the language, ultimately none of the possible examples is convincing (Kaufman 1982, 148–49).

There are three instances in this inscription where an apparently singular form occurs in a plural context *mt kln*, (lines 3, 5); *nhr klm* (line 4); *mʾh swr* (line 20). From the parallels at Sefire and Bukān,[30] it is clear that *swr* in the Tell Fakhariya Inscription is not a broken plural, whatever the precise explanation.[31] The term *mt* is a loanword and most certainly is not a broken plural. It must be a collective. The word *nhr* is also likely a collective (Fassberg 2007, 426–34). Methodologically Lipiński has taken very doubtful examples from this one inscription—examples that have a more viable explanation than that of "broken" plurals—and used it as the foundation for

---

26. Lipiński 2000a, 52. Concerning the problem of the medial *aleph* in *riʾm*, Lipiński argues that "The medial *aleph* disappeared, just like *hamza* staying between a consonant and a vowel. Its elision causes no change except the displacement of the syllabic boundary, as in *'A-rām* for *'Ar-'ām*." See also Lipiński 2008, 35.

27. Lipiński (2008, 36) puts it this way: "As conclusion, one may say confidently, I believe, that Aramaic once had a broken plural, even if exact patterns cannot always be established. The vocalized forms of Aramaic tribal names in cuneiform texts of the 8th century B.C. provide, at least, some patterns of broken plural used in Southern Babylonia."

28. Lipiński (2003, 348) states: "The existence of Aramaic 'broken' plurals can hardly be denied in the inscription of Tell Faḫarīya." See also Lipiński 2000a, 52.

29. Zadok (2013, 273) remarks: "An especially pertinent case is Biblical Hebrew *gedûd*, whose Aramaic counterpart is extant in the Akkadian (early Neo-Babylonian) transcriptions *gudūd*, plural *gudūdāni*."

30. Sefire: [*wšbʿ* .] *šwrh* . *yhynqn* . *ʿgl*; Bukān Inscription: *šbʿ* . *šwrh* . *yhynqn* . *ʿgl* . *ḥd*; Tell Fakhariya: *mʾh* . *swr* . *lhynqn* . *ʿgl*.

31. Fassberg 2007; Brugnatelli 1991; Sima 2002, 119–20; Tropper 1998; Gropp and Lewis 1985, 53; and Kaufman 1982, 148–49.

positing "broken" plurals on a massive scale in the explanations of the etymologies of various terms throughout the Aramean world. Even if "broken" plurals occurred in Old Aramaic—and there is no real actual evidence that they did—this surely was a less common phenomenon than Lipiński's nearly default explanation throughout his volume. If "broken" plurals were a feature in Old Aramaic, no vestiges of this phenomenon have survived into the later stages of the language.[32] Usually limited vestiges of early phenomena survive in the later stages and attest to their existence in the earlier stages. This is not the case with "broken" plurals.[33]

As part of a more comprehensive study of the phenomenon of postpositional *kl* in Aramaic, Stadel (2011) investigates the usage of *kl* in the Tell Fakhariya Inscription.[34] There are four occurrences of *kl*, all of which are postpositional: *wntn . rʿy . wmšqy . lmt . kln* "and gives pasture and watered ground to all the lands" (lines 2b–3a); *wntn . šlh . wʾdqwr lʾlhyn . klm . ʾḥwh* "and gives prosperity and offering to all the gods, his brothers" (lines 3b–4a); *gwgl . nhr . klm* "the controller of all the rivers" (line 4); and *mʿdn mt . kln* "who makes all the lands luxuriant" (lines 4–5a). He notes that in all four cases the antecedent is always formally indeterminate.[35] Except in the second occurrence, they are all morphologically singular. Of course, at this early stage, Old Aramaic has not developed the definite article to mark determinacy. Stadel suggests that the postpositional *kl* with the suffix marks the singular forms as logically plural and determined.[36] This is the most likely explanation for the Tell Fakhariya Inscription's usage.

Thus, there is no actual evidence to support Lipiński's theory of "broken plurals" in Aramaic. Regarding the etymology and meaning of "Aram," it is better to admit that this still remains unknown. Obviously, this has ramifications for Lipiński's highly speculative ideas about bulls and totems being connected with the tribal Arameans.

---

32. I thank Steven Fassberg for kindly drawing my attention to this very significant point.

33. Obviously, Northwest Semitic regularly shows a *combination* internal-external plural type for segholates (e.g., מַלְכִין/מֶלֶךְ).

34. This is an important discussion given that all Lipiński's proposed examples of broken plurals, other than *mʾh swr* in line 20, have postpositional *kl*.

35. *ʾlhyn* is obviously plural and may be inherently determined (Stadel 2011, 39).

36. Only the first occurrence has the equivalent to *kl* in the Akkadian: *kal dadmē* (written DÙ URU.URU). The other occurrences of *kl* do not have the equivalent in the Akkadian, just plural forms. Of course, the Akkadian has no definite article.

## 2.2. The Question of Qir/Kir[37]

In Amos 9:7, Yahweh is said to have brought the Arameans (in this context referring specifically to the Arameans of Damascus) to their present homeland from a place called Qir or Kir (קיר), and he is about to reverse their history by sending them back to their place of origin (Amos 1:5) (see Paul 1991, 55). Malamat (1973, 139) remarked:

> The passages in Amos imply that, after almost half a millennium of Aramean settlement in Syria, there still circulated a national account of Aramean migration, much like the chronicle of the Israelite exodus from Egypt or that of the Philistines from Caphtor. They further point to the historical consequences of Aramean "misbehavior," leading to their return to their ancestral homeland—reminiscent of the threat to a disobedient Israel of being sent back to Egypt (cf. Deut 28:68; Hos 8:13).

Two other passages mention Qir/Kir. Second Kings 16:9 describes the fulfillment of Amos's threat when Tiglath-pileser III captured Damascus (732 BCE) and deported its inhabitants to Qir/Kir.[38] Unfortunately, the section of Tiglath-pileser's capture of Damascus in 732 is missing from his annals. Finally, Qir/Kir is mentioned in Isa 22:6 along with Elam as areas from which troops are mustered.

The exact location of Qir/Kir is still uncertain. Some scholars, on the basis of Isa 22:6, have sought its location in the vicinity of Elam (Malamat 1973, 139; Gehman 1970, 57, 540). However, the poetic parallelism of this verse does not demand an immediate geographical proximity. Other scholars have associated Qir/Kir with Jebel Bišri. Although this is possible, there is at present no direct evidence to confirm this.

With the publication of a tablet from Emar (Emar VI 42), some scholars noted that there seemed to be support for a place named Qir or Kir.[39] Since Arnaud originally read the signs of the place name as *ki-ri*, the text appeared to read: "Pilsu-Dagan, son of Baal-kabar, king of Emar, king of the people of the land of Kiri" (Arnaud 1985–86, no. 42, 8–9). This seemed to locate Qir/

---

37. For the first part of this section, see Younger 2007a, 137–38.

38. Most Old Greek manuscripts do not refer to Kir in 2 Kgs 16:9, perhaps suggesting that this is a scribal gloss based on the reference in Amos. See Rollston 2000. However, the Lucianic recension of 2 Kgs 16:9 has απωκισεν την πολιν, which is understanding *qîr* as "city." Furthermore, in the LXX all of the references to Kir (2 Kgs 16:9, Amos 1:5, 9:7, Isa 22:6) are corrupted, which may hint at some type of late-scribal redactional work. See also Thompson 1992.

39. E.g., Zadok 1991, 114; Rollston 2000; and esp. Lipiński 1989, 39; 2000a, 41 n. 101.

Kir along the course of the Middle Euphrates, not all that far from Mount Bišri. However, no sooner was the tablet formally published than Arnaud himself raised doubts about the reading (Arnaud 1987, 11 n. 4). A number of other scholars have proposed reading the toponym as Ḫurri (*Ḫur-ri*, instead of *ki-ri* or *qí-ri*).[40] The confirmation of the reading "Ḫurri" came with the publication of another tablet from Emar.[41]

In a recent article, Elitzur (2012) has noted the place name *Durmasqanīn* located in Bēn haNeharot ("Between the Rivers") according to the Babylonian Talmud (Eruvin 19a). The name *Durmasqanīn* seems to hint at the place to which the Assyrians may have exiled the people of Damascus. The spelling of *Durmasqanīn* is probably derived from the late dissimilated spelling of Damascus seen in Chronicles: *Darmeśeq* and *Darmāśeq*. Bēn haNeharot was the designation of the northern part of Mesopotamia—later the Jezirah. The Rabbinic sources also mentioned a town *Ihi-Deqira* in this region, which may be the same place as Ιδικαρα/Δακιρα/Diacira of some classical sources. Two of the classical writers mentioned the environs of this town as a source of bitumen and salt. In Akkadian, *qīru* means "bitumen." Thus Elitzur suggests that *Ihi-Deqira*, perhaps not far from *Durmasqanīn*, preserved the element *Qīr* (= "bitumen"), which had also been the earlier geographical name of this region or of a particular spot in it.

This is an interesting proposal that has the advantage of a place name reflective of Damascus and an etymology for Qir that could explain the geographic name (see Fales forthcoming n. 33). However, the sources are late; the location of *Durmasqanīn* is not certain and could be some distance in the Jezirah from *Ihi-Deqira*; and importantly, *Ihi-Deqira* itself may not be a toponym original to the Late Bronze Age/Iron Age (at present no evidence that it goes back earlier than the classical sources). Thus, there is still no real evidence for the location of Qir/Kir.

Finally, it is important to note that based on Amos 1:5 and 9:7, Qir/Kir was the place where the Arameans of Damascus originated. These texts are not claiming that this was the place from which "all" the Aramean tribal entities derived, as it is sometimes interpreted.[42]

---

40. Durand 1989a, 34–35; 1989b, 183; Arnaud 1987, 21; Zaccagnini 1990; Dietrich 1990; Fales 1991a. In spite of this evidence, Lipiński (2000a, 41 n. 101) insists on reading *Qí-ri*. He proposes to locate Qir at the ancient Roman fortress of Qraya, but the textual evidence does not support this.

41. Tsukimoto 1990, 191–92 (HCCT no. 7, lines 28–36). See also Astour 1996, 31–32; and Adamthwaite 2001, 262–65.

42. This is similar to Jebel Bišri mentioned in Tiglath-pileser I's inscriptions. See chapter 3's discussion.

## 2.3. Socially Constructed Groups

There is much that is still unknown about the Arameans' socially constructed groups.[43] The following is an attempt to discuss the known terminology and to describe its usage within the various contexts.

### 2.3.1. The Ethnicon Nomenclature

The ancient Near Eastern texts designated entity identification through grammatical markers. This section will discuss these with special attention to their use with reference to the Aramean entities. There are two main ways that ethnicon marking occurs in most of the texts in our study.[44]

One of the ways that the Aramean entities are so marked, as seen in the Assyrian documents, is what can be called the *bītu*-formulation. An entity can be defined by reference to a "personal name" (possibly an ancestor) (PN)[45] or a "group name" (GrN),[46] yielding the terminology of the *bītu* in the forms: *bīt*-PN/GrN (lit. "house of PN/GrN") and *mār* PN/GrN (lit. "son" of PN/GrN).[47] While it is possible to form an ethnicon with the use of the gentilic ending *-a-a* on a *bīt*-PN/GrN form (very rare), the much more common way is with the form *mār* PN/GrN.[48]

While the *bītu* has principally a political meaning, it also carries a geographical connotation. Postgate (1974, 234) puts it this way: "The *bītu* is more than a mere tribe, which might move at any time from one district to another, but its association with a personal name brings home the fact that the political and geographical entity is founded on a tribal system." Thus the ethnicon marking of *mār* PN/GrN associates that person so designated as a "member" of the "polity of constructed relatedness," that is, the *bītu*.[49]

---

43. For a discussion of the vocabulary and concept of "socially constructed groups," see A. Porter 2009, 218; 2012, 37–61.

44. For overview of the terminology, see Nuccetelli 2004.

45. In the Levant, most of the entities appear to be named after persons, though not necessarily an ancestor, e.g., Bīt-Ḫaza'ili, Bīt-Ḫumrî, Bīt-(A)gūsi, etc.

46. I have chosen not to use "tribal name" because a number of the entities so designated are clans or confederations. I am using GrN as the abbreviation for "group name" so that there is no confusion with the fairly common abbreviation GN "geographic name."

47. Cf. the Aramaic forms: *br* PN (singular); *bny* PN (plural).

48. This is an idiomatic usage found in earlier texts denoting a citizen or native of a city or country or tribe. See *CAD* 10.1:315–16. The use of the sign DUMU is the more common writing, but the sign A can also be used.

49. Perhaps a type of ancestralization was involved. For Hebrew, see *HALOT*, 137–38 s.v. בֵּן, esp. number 5.

Studying the use of the term *bītu* to describe the Aramean entities in the Jezirah and the Levant reveals that it is generally used as a designation for the highest socially constructed group: perhaps a confederation of tribes, but most often, a tribal kingdom that has, at least from the Assyrian perspective, a definable geographic territory. An example of a tribal confederation receiving the *bītu*-formulation is Bīt-Ḫalupē located on the Lower Ḫābūr.[50] In addition, there are a few examples of the *bītu*-designation being used for a confederation or perhaps a tribe: Bīt-Yaḫiri in the Jezirah and Bīt-Šabāya[51] in the Middle Euphrates. These groups may have been on the decline, though very little is known about them. However, while the *bītu*-formula was used most often of a tribal kingdom throughout the Jezirah and the Levant, it was never used in southern Mesopotamia to describe Aramean polities (see further below).

Other socially constructed groups—like clans, tribal groups or confederations[52]—were usually designated LÚ.GrN or KUR.GrN.[53] Thus the second way of ethnicon marking was the use of the gentilic ending *-a-a* added to the entity's name: LÚ.PN/GrN-*a-a* or KUR.PN/GrN-*a-a*.[54] The earliest marking of an individual Aramean tribal entity occurs in the inscriptions of Aššur-dān II using this formulation KUR.*ia-ú-sa-a-ia*. A list in one of Tiglath-pileser III's Summary Inscriptions[55] and the narrative of the Aramean episode in the Inscriptions of Ninurta-kudurrī-uṣur[56] demonstrate that the majority of clans, subtribes, tribes, and confederations do not receive the *bītu*-PN/GrN designation, but are simply designated LÚ.PN/GrN, e.g., LÚ.*ḫi-ra-a-nu* "the Ḫīrānu" or LÚ.*ḫa-ṭal-lu* "the Ḫaṭallu" (clearly a confederation).

---

50. RIMA 2:153, A.099.2, line 114. On this tribe name, see below.

51. Aššurnaṣirpal II (RIMA 2:213, A.0.101.1, iii.14–15). Only attested in this passage, Bīt-Šabaya was located downstream from Ḫindānu, on the left bank, a designation (tribal in origin) of the land in front of Haridu (see Liverani 1992a, 66). The name is written É-mŠÁ-*ba-a-ia*. The sign ŠÁ can also be read *níg* or *gar*. Scholars have understood the reading as Bīt-Šabaya or Bīt-Garbaya. See Liverani 1992a, 66 n. 300.

52. There is much anthropological baggage with the use of "tribe," "clan," etc. However, for practical reasons, the terminology is used with full recognition of the problems. I will use "socially constructed group" as often as possible, but this is not always reasonable.

53. Often the name of any ancestor, but not always (see the data in the chapter on southern Mesopotamian tribes below).

54. See Hämeen-Anttila 2000, 84 (§3.10.b); GAG §56, p–q (von Soden notes the use is possibly of West Semitic origin). The form LÚ.PN-*a-a* appears to be used more often than KUR.PN-*a-a*.

55. RINAP 1:118, 47, lines 5–10a; Tadmor 1994, 158–61 (Summary Inscription 7:5–10). For full discussion, see chapter 10.

56. See Cavigneaux and Ismail 1990; reedited by RIMB 2:294–300 (texts will be cited with the numbering from this edition).

In fact, the *bītu*-formulation is never used to designate any Aramean tribal entity in southern Mesopotamia;[57] however, it is used to designate Chaldean polities. Thus, the *mār*-PN/GrN formulation of the ethnicon is almost rarely used for Aramean entities in the region.[58] This does not appear to be random, but a deliberate distinction made by the Assyrians,[59] since apparently none of the Aramean entities fit their definition of *bītu*, as they use it for entities in the Jezirah and the Levant.[60] The most complex that any of these southern Mesopotamian entities becomes is a confederation.

No doubt the fluidity inherent in tribal structures within this region was a contributing factor. These Aramean groups—even through the distorted lens of the Assyrian and Babylonian writers—yield the overall picture of a society in the midst of various procedures of coalescence or fragmentation, stimulating new identifications. Some tribes may have achieved an equilibrium; but many others were still in the processes of coalescence or accretion (e.g., the case of the Rupū' who were incorporating the smaller group of Gāmu).[61] The vaster and geographically more dispersed tribal complexes, such as the Puqūdu and the Gambūlu, while still retaining their distinctive self-identification, had developed a number of inner clanic subdivisions, represented by different "sheikhs," who united their military and political efforts or took individual courses of action, according to the circumstances. For the Jezirah, an example can be seen in the case of the Laqē confederation. It is attested for a period of about fifty years in the Neo-Assyrian royal inscriptions, located on both banks of the Middle Euphrates, between the confluence of the Euphrates in the region of Abu Kemal and the Ḫābūr. It was perhaps united through an actual "covenant/treaty (*'dy*)."[62]

Not only was coalescence possible; fragmentation too was always a potential. Thus a family or clan could separate itself from the tribe in accordance with its needs. The Ḫaṭallu confederation is a good example. A number of its clans listed in the inscriptions of Ninurta-kudurrī-uṣur become indi-

57. This is also true for a large number of the "tribal" entities in the Jezirah and certainly some of those encountered in north Syria.

58. Only two possible exceptions are known to me: "PN, the Lītawean" (*mār* ᵐ*Li-ta-me*) (Brinkman 1989, 38–40 = BM 40548); and "PN, the Yašumean" (*mār* ᵐ*ia-a-šu-mu*) (SAA 17:25, 22.r.6–8). See chapter 10.

59. Streck 2014, 299. In southern Mesopotamia, Chaldean personal names have the ethnicon form: PN *mār* GrN, e.g., *Ea-zēra-qīša mār Awkāni*; Aramean personal names have PN + GrN + gentilic (*-a-a*), e.g., ᵐ*i-ḫi-ru* LÚ.*gam-bu-la-a-a*.

60. This seems to affirm Postgate's articulation of the definition of a *bītu* quoted above.

61. See chapter 10.

62. Clearly tribal entities could enter into treaties with other polities, e.g., the Rupū' tribe and the city of Nippur (*adê*). See Cole 1996a, 48, no. 6:4–7a, esp. line 4.

vidual tribes in later Assyrian and Babylonian sources: Li/uḫuātu, the Amatu, the the Minū', and so on (see further below).[63]

What becomes clear is that the *bītu*, while it might be associated with an ancestor, was a "construction of relatedness," not necessarily based on actual descent (though descent could obviously be a factor in the construct). Since in many instances the "ancestor" was a powerful person or king, and was associated with a geographic location, the designation was a *functional descriptor* of those who were "members" of that *bītu* (hence the terminology *mār* PN/GrN, etc). However, the members of that *bītu* were, in many cases, not biologically related; in other words, such groups were not a unity of descent per se, but a unity of constructed relatedness. One might say the higher the social unit, the more common the constructed relatedness. Fales (2011a, 213) posits that the original roots of self-designation may lie in the necessity of self-protection and social cohesion as well as the desire for new self-identification, for which there was a growing need as a result of the collapse of the system of regional states at the end of the second millennium. Furthermore, the *bītu* does not seem to be exclusively linked to a preexisting nomadic or seminomadic group. In brief, the *bītu* could—and often did—include both nomadic and sedentary components (see fig. 2.5 below).

The Assyrian designations[64] have their roots in the actual socially constructed terms used by the various different peoples of the ancient Near East (i.e., the use of the terminology is not unique to the Aramean entities, but was common throughout the West Semitic world and beyond). For example, the use of expressions like *byt*-PN/GrN and *br*/*bny* PN/GrN with reference to the kingdom of Arpad has long been known (Dion 1997, 225–26). In the stelae from Sefire, one finds *byt gš*[65] (Assyrian: Bīt-Agūsi); and in the Zakkur Inscription, its accompanying *brgš* (one word), used as the title of the king of Arpad (*KAI* 202:A5). The plural form also occurs: *bny gš* (*KAI* 222:B3). The Hebrew Bible utilizes this terminology extensively (e.g., *bny 'mn* "Ammonites").[66] Other tribal/clan based entities that may be given the

63. Note also *ABL* 896:15 relates that a family/clan was "uprooted" from the Puqūdu tribe: PN S[AL].ME-*šú u qi-in-nu-šu issu libbi ša* LÚ.*puquddi ittasaḫ* "PN has taken his wives and his family/clan (*qinnu*) out of the Puqūdu tribe." For a discussion of the *qinnu* unit, see Nielsen 2011, 255–59.

64. The earliest occurrence of this terminology for the Arameans is found in the Assyrian Chronicle, line 3 (1082–1081 BCE): *bītāt māt Aramāya* "the houses of the Arameans" or "the Aramean houses (tribes)." See below.

65. *KAI* 222:A16, B3, 11; 223:B10. *l*[xxxx]*bytgš* "Belonging to [ ] of Bēt Gūš." See Puech 1978, 165; Mitchell 1996.

66. For further discussion, see Couturier 2001; Dion 1997, 225–32.

Table 2.1. The Designations for Ḫayānu

| Stone Slab Inscription RIMA 3:9 (53′–54′) | Kurkh Monolith RIMA 3:16 (i.42) | Kurkh Monolith RIMA 3:18 (ii.24) | Kurkh Monolith RIMA 3:23 (ii.83) |
|---|---|---|---|
| [ᵐ*ḫa*]-*a-a-ni* KUR *sa-am-ʾa-la-a-a* | ᵐ*ḫa-a-ni* KUR *sa-am-ʾa-la-a-a* | ᵐ*ḫa-ia-a-nu* DUMU *gab-ba-ri* | ᵐ*ḫa-ia-ni* DUMU *ga-ba-ri* |
| Ḫayānu, the Samʾalian | Ḫayānu, the Samʾalian | Ḫayānu, the man of Bīt-Gabbāri (i.e., the Bīt-Gabbārite) | Ḫayānu, the man of Bīt-Gabbāri (i.e., the Bīt-Gabbārite) |

*bītu*-formulation can also be designated in this fashion: Chaldean groups, Kassite groups, and so on.[67]

Some scholars have thought that the Assyrians typically referred to a nation by the name of the ruling dynasty when they first encountered them so that in the form *bīt*-PN, the PN is the name of the dynasty at the time of the first encounter with the polity (Sader 1987, 272–3; Lamb 2007, 30). This is not quite right. The Assyrians gave names that were connected to a personal name (often not an ancestor) that, in their opinion, merited the name for the tribal entity. One example of this can be seen in the small north Syrian polity known in its own earliest inscriptions as *Yʾdy* (likely vocalized Yādiya) (see the Kulamuwa inscription[68]). Its ruler at the time of first contact with Assyria is known by different designations in Shalmaneser III's inscriptions (see table 2.1).

Ḫayānu is referred to in the Kulamuwa inscription in line 3 (*ḥyʾ*). Gabbar (*gbr*) is mentioned in line 2 of that inscription. There is a real possibility that there was no biological connection between the former and the latter (Tropper 1993, 21). In the initial contacts with this polity, its king Ḫayānu is referred to as the Samʾalian; later the same king is referred to as the Bīt-Gabbārite (DUMU(*mār*) *gab-ba-ri*) (in the same inscription!).

That the choice of the PN used in the *bīt*-formula has absolutely nothing to do with initial contact can be seen in the fact that before, during, and for a time after the reign of Hazael, the city-state of Aram-Damascus was referred to as Ša-imērīšu (KUR (*šá*)-ANŠE-*šú* / *i-me-ri-šú*, lit. "of his asses"), or as simply "Damascus"; but later, after Hazael's reign, it was referred to as Bīt-

67. Brinkman 1968, 249–56 and n. 1595; Dion 1997, 232.

68. *KAI* 24; Tropper 1993, 27–46; *COS* 2.30:147–48. See chapter 6 below.

Ḫaza'ili ("House of Hazael").[69] Thus the *bīt*-PN was used as a designation after—sometimes long after—the entity came into existence. The same holds true for the polity of Arpad, called Bīt-(A)gūsi. Thus, in a number of cases, these were all-powerful, later leaders of their tribal polity, not the ancestors, and the Assyrians knew of these entities before giving the particular *bīt*-PN designation to them. Interestingly, in at least one instance, the PN of the *bītu* is feminine: ᵐ*ba-ar-a-ta-ra* DUMU ᶠ*ḫa-lu-pé-e*, "Baratara (Bar-ʿAttār), a man of Bīt-Ḫalupe."[70] The PN of this *bīt*-PN construction is written with the feminine determinative and likely denotes an entity based on a tribal matriarchal leader, perhaps an ancestress.[71]

### 2.3.2. The Different Levels of Socially Constructed Groups

This section will discuss the different levels of the socially constructed groups as observed in the textual sources. It will also investigate the power structures within these levels. Thus it will lay the groundwork for the discussion in chapter 3, giving the reader an orientation to the vocabulary.

In fundamental distinction from other political entities, such as city-states,[72] tribal polities and social organizations were not clearly distinguished, and communal identity rested upon a perception of shared kinship rather than political affiliation. Many of the terms, no doubt, expressed vertical and horizontal relatedness (not necessarily real descent). The flexibility of their usage complicates efforts at understanding them. Certainly, one can sympathize with one scholar's comment: "The nomenclature of nomadic groups is always confusing and shifting" (Postgate 1994, 85).

Table 2.2 is an attempt at representing this discussion graphically, though due to the flexibility and, in some instances, the uncertainties, it should not be taken as authoritative. Table 2.3 has been included in order to enable the reader to compare and contrast the Aramean socially constructed groups with the earlier Amurrite socially constructed groups. The original roots for the different levels of these groups seem to lie, at the minimum, in the necessity for self-protection, social cohesion, and the desire for self-identification. One of the origins of the terminology appears to be rooted in "family" metaphors that were applied to the political organization of the tribe.[73] Thus the

69. For a good, brief summation of this usage, see Kuan 1995, 30 n. 78.

70. RIMA 2:153, A.099.2, line 114.

71. See further discussion in §4.5 on Laqē.

72. This applies especially in the southern Mesopotamian context. See Barjamovic 2004, 89.

73. Barjamovic (2004, 89 n. 96) cites SAA 18:134, text 162, as an example of this. Although the letter has been understood as being from an official, rather than a tribal

community was led by a chieftain, along with his "brothers" and the tribal "elders."

There appear to be at least four levels that can be differentiated. As in the other West Semitic groups, the smallest social unit among the Arameans was the *byt ʾb* "the house of the father" (Schloen 2001; Bendor 1996). The term *byt ʾb* is now attested with this particular nuance in an Aramaic document from the period, specifically in the Aramaic version of the bilingual inscription of Ninurta-bēlu-uṣur, the governor of Kār-Shalmaneser and eunuch of Šamšī-ilu, from Ḫadattu (Arslan Taş).[74] This would be, at the minimum, the literal "house of the father," the nuclear family; but it is clear from usage elsewhere that this represented, in many instances, the extended nuclear family, perhaps even in some cases, a small lineage or descent group. However, it was not *entirely* biological in its connections. Marriages brought in those from another *byt ʾb* that required the groups to devise ways of inclusion, and these ways were not necessarily uniform. The *byt ʾb* becomes a social reality only because the participants ascribe to a set of common symbolizations.[75] Thus, it was the basic familial relationship (vertical and horizontal) that was constituted within the *byt ʾb*. The leader of such a group was the "father" (*ʾab*). There is some evidence for the conceptional unit of the *byt ʾm* "the house of the mother" and matriarchal structures, even at the clan and tribal level (in the ancient Near Eastern and biblical sources).[76] Obviously, at this level lineage was the most clear factor in social identity.

The second level of social units was what will be termed here the "clan."[77] This is more difficult to conceptualize, and the fact that the Old Aramaic term for this level is as yet unattested adds to the difficulty.[78] The Hebrew term *mšpḥh* "clan" seems to describe a type of maximal lineage,

leader, Barjamovic believes that the vocabulary points to a tribal context. Thus a chieftain named Kabtiya writes the Assyrian king and reports that because he had gone on patrol with his "brothers" (*aḫḫē*) to keep an eye on the land of Rāši (KUR.*a-ra-ši*), he arrived too late for the loyalty-oath ceremony for the treaty (*adê*). Later, he took the loyally oath for the treaty before the gods of the king both in Nippur and Uruk. Kabtiya then said: "(My) men (ERIM.MEŠ), their sons and their wives, together with their gods, should (also) enter the treaty of the king, my lord!" A comparison with the wording of the Sefire treaty (Fitzmyer 1995), in my opinion, makes this interpretation very likely.

74. See Röllig 2009, 272–78 (*byt ʾb* in lines a6′ and b5). The Akkadian version confirms the usage.

75. Like in Babylonian society where *salātu* "kinship by marriage" was utilized, see van der Toorn 1996, 42.

76. Note Bīt-Ḫalupē (see discussion in §4.5) and Judg 9.

77. It is realized that the term "clan" is anthropologically problematic, but it is used here as a pragmatic.

78. Perhaps *yhlʾ* "clan" as in Syriac. Nöldeke (1915–16, 167) suggested that *gwʾ* (*gawā*) "clan" was the Old Aramaic term. The term *mšpḥh* (which is found, e.g., in Hebrew

Table 2.2. Aramean Socially Constructed Groups and Institutions

<table>
<tr><td colspan="12">mlk/šarru “king”; rb(ʾ)/rabû/LÚ.GAL “chief”; rʾš/raʾasu “chief”; nsyk/nasīku “sheikh”; śr(?)/NUN “prince/chief”; sbʾ “elder/chief”<br>ālik pāni “the military commander” (lit. “the one who goes before”)</td></tr>
<tr><td colspan="12">byt PN/GrN/bīt PN/GrN / šbṭ(?) // LÚ.PN/GrN<br>“house of PN/GrN” = “tribal polity” / “tribal confederation” // “tribe”</td></tr>
<tr><td colspan="12">ʿdh/puḫru “the (great plenary) assembly”</td></tr>
<tr><td colspan="8">rʾš “chief” / rēš karāši “chief of a tribe or confederation”;<br>nsyk/nasīku “sheikh”; rb(ʾ)/rabû “chief”; ngr/nāgiru “herald/chief”</td><td colspan="4">rʾš “chief” / rēš karāši “chief of a tribe or confederation”; nsyk/nasīku “sheikh”; rb(ʾ)/rabû “chief”; ngr/nāgiru “herald/chief”</td></tr>
<tr><td colspan="8">sbʾ “elder” / šībūtu “elders”; ʾbwt “fathers”</td><td colspan="4">sbʾ “elder” / šībūtu “elders”; ʾbwt “fathers”</td></tr>
<tr><td colspan="8">ʿdh/puḫru “assembly”</td><td colspan="4">ʿdh/puḫru “assembly”</td></tr>
<tr><td colspan="4">karāšu “camp”<br>šbṭ(?) “tribe /tribal confederation”<br>bty PN/GrN/bītāti PN/GrN “houses of PN/GrN”</td><td colspan="4">karāšu “camp”<br>šbṭ(?) “tribe /tribal confederation”<br>bty PN/GrN/bītāti PN/GrN “houses of PN/GrN”</td><td colspan="4">karāšu “camp”<br>šbṭ(?) “tribe /tribal confederation”<br>bty PN/GrN/bītāti PN/GrN “houses of PN/GrN”</td></tr>
<tr><td colspan="2">rʾš / rēšu / raʾasu “chief”; nsyk/nasīku “sheikh”</td><td colspan="2">rʾš / rēšu / raʾasu “chief”; nsyk/nasīku “sheikh”</td><td colspan="2">rʾš / rēšu / raʾasu “chief”; nsyk/nasīku “sheikh”</td><td colspan="2">rʾš / rēšu / raʾasu “chief”; nsyk/nasīku “sheikh”</td><td colspan="2">rʾš / rēšu / raʾasu “chief”; nsyk/nasīku “sheikh”</td><td colspan="2">rʾš / rēšu / raʾasu “chief”; nsyk/nasīku “sheikh”</td></tr>
<tr><td colspan="2">sbʾ “elder” / šībūtu “elders”; ʾbwt “fathers”</td><td colspan="2">sbʾ “elder” / šībūtu “elders”; ʾbwt “fathers”</td><td colspan="2">sbʾ “elder” / šībūtu “elders”; ʾbwt “fathers”</td><td colspan="2">sbʾ “elder” / šībūtu “elders”; ʾbwt “fathers”</td><td colspan="2">sbʾ “elder” / šībūtu “elders”; ʾbwt “fathers”</td><td colspan="2">sbʾ “elder” / šībūtu “elders”; ʾbwt “fathers”</td></tr>
<tr><td colspan="2">ʿdh/puḫru “assembly”</td><td colspan="2">ʿdh/puḫru “assembly”</td><td colspan="2">ʿdh/puḫru “assembly”</td><td colspan="2">ʿdh/puḫru “assembly”</td><td colspan="2">ʿdh/puḫru “assembly”</td><td colspan="2">ʿdh/puḫru “assembly”</td></tr>
<tr><td colspan="2">LÚ.PN/GrN / (Aram. ?) “clan”</td><td colspan="2">LÚ.PN/GrN / (Aram. ?) “clan”</td><td colspan="2">LÚ.PN/GrN / (Aram. ?) “clan”</td><td colspan="2">LÚ.PN/GrN / (Aram. ?) “clan”</td><td colspan="2">LÚ.PN/GrN / (Aram. ?) “clan”</td><td colspan="2">LÚ.PN/GrN / (Aram. ?) “clan”</td></tr>
<tr><td>ʾb “father”</td><td>ʾb “father”</td><td>ʾb “father”</td><td>ʾb “father”</td><td>ʾb “father”</td><td>ʾb “father”</td><td>ʾb “father”</td><td>ʾb “father”</td><td>ʾb “father”</td><td>ʾb “father”</td><td>ʾm “mother”</td><td>ʾm “mother”</td></tr>
<tr><td>byt ʾb extended family</td><td>byt ʾb extended family</td><td>byt ʾb extended family</td><td>byt ʾb extended family</td><td>byt ʾb extended family</td><td>byt ʾb extended family</td><td>byt ʾb extended family</td><td>byt ʾb extended family</td><td>byt ʾb extended family</td><td>byt ʾb extended family</td><td>byt ʾm extended family</td><td>byt ʾm extended family</td></tr>
</table>

Table 2.3. Streck's Table of Amurrite Tribal Structures and Institutions with Adaptions from Fleming and Kärger and Minx. See Streck 2002, 180; Fleming 2004a, 26–103; 2004b; Kärger and Minx 2011–13.

<table>
<tr><td colspan="6">Sheikh (sugāgum) = "king" (šarrum)</td></tr>
<tr><td colspan="6">"Tribe" / "Tribal Confederation"<br>Sim'alite: gayum / Yaminite: li'mum</td></tr>
<tr><td colspan="6">Assembly (puḫrum) / (riḫṣum)</td></tr>
<tr><td colspan="2">Sheikh (sugāgum)<br>"Chief of Pasture" (merḫûm)</td><td colspan="2">Sheikh (sugāgum)<br>"Chief of Pasture" (merḫûm)</td><td colspan="2">Sheikh (sugāgum)<br>"Chief of Pasture" (merḫûm)</td></tr>
<tr><td colspan="2">Subtribe or Clan<br>Sim'alite: gayum; Yaminite: li'mum;<br>Amurrite: palgu</td><td colspan="2">Subtribe or Clan<br>Sim'alite: gayum; Yaminite: li'mum;<br>Amurrite: palgu</td><td colspan="2">Subtribe or Clan<br>Sim'alite: gayum; Yaminite: li'mum;<br>Amurrite: palgu</td></tr>
<tr><td colspan="2"></td><td colspan="2">Elders (šībūtum)</td><td colspan="2"></td></tr>
<tr><td>Head (qaqqadum)</td><td>Head (qaqqadum)</td><td>Head (qaqqadum)</td><td>Head (qaqqadum)</td><td>Head (qaqqadum)</td><td>Head (qaqqadum)</td></tr>
<tr><td>(extended) family</td><td>(extended) family</td><td>(extended) family</td><td>(extended) family</td><td>(extended) family</td><td>(extended) family</td></tr>
</table>

that is, a descent group which established ties of kinship between a group of families (*byt ʾb*) through a common ancestor who was no longer living;[79] thus adding a level of protection and social function.[80] It established vertical kinship solidarity. Perhaps, similar to the *gayum* in the Sim'alite tribal structure at ancient Mari,[81] these "clans" might be of varying size and relationship. However, like "tribe" below, this was a socially constructed group that included those without actual descent, and its flexibility was undoubtedly greater than what most modern westerners might envision. Consequently, this is sometimes referred to in the literature as a subtribe. In the Assyrian texts, it seems to be referenced by the simple ethnicon marking LÚ.PN/GrN(*-a-a*).[82]

The leadership of the "clan" was centered, first of all, in an individual, frequently designated "the head" or "chief" (*rʾš/rēšu/raʾasu*).[83] While this term is also used for the leader of a tribe or tribal confederation, it is clear that it could specify the leader of a tribal subgroup, a clan.[84] This level of leadership could also be designated by the terms: *rbʾ/rabû* "chief" or *nsyk/nasīku* "sheikh." However, there is clear semantic overlap of the *rʾš* and the *sbʾ* "elder" (usually plural).[85] These "elders" (Assyrian designation: *šībūtu*) were the group wherein the collective rulership of the clan resided, with the *rʾš*, in fact, being one of these elders (in a sense one among "brothers"). Nevertheless, the elders (*sbʾ*) invariably defer to the chief/sheikh (*rʾš/rbʾ/nsyk*), especially in contexts where singular leadership is demanded. In turn, the elders were the "fathers" (*ʾbwt*), that is, the leaders of the various "houses of the fathers." They (with perhaps additional members) formed the *ʿdh* "the assembly" (Assyrian: *puḫru*). All of these leadership terms were also used on the tribal level, a fact that complicates the interpretation of the evidence.

---

and Phoenician) is not attested in Aramaic, though see 4QpapTob ar 2.9 and CTLevi ar b B.16. Kärger and Minx (2011–13, 367–68) note the root $plg_5$ "clan" (*DNWSI*, 913).

79. A component that is perhaps more important in the ancient Near Eastern context than might be thought.

80. See Schloen (2001, 150–65), esp. for his discussion of the military function of the Israelite *mšpḥh*.

81. Fleming 2004b, 206; 2004a, 44–47.

82. It is also possible that another Hebrew equivalent might be the *bty ʾbwt* (Reviv 1989, 16).

83. The Akkadian term *raʾsāni* "chiefs" (Neo-Assyrian < West Semitic **raʾš* with the Akk. plural) is used in first-millennium texts to designate Aramean and Chaldean tribal leaders, as well as Sutean leaders in Upper Mesopotamia in the second millennium.

84. See Reviv 1989, 16. Cf. Exod 6:14; Num 36:1 and 1 Chr 5:15, 24; 7:2–3, 7–11, 40; 8:6, 10, 13, 27; 9:9; 2 Chr 19:8; 23:2; 28:12.

85. The Hebrew term is *zqn*.

Furthermore, it is very important to remember that such groups can divide (or fragment) to form new "clans," who will bear different names. Over time, some of these socially constructed groups could grow and develop into tribes; or tribes could diminish and become simple clanic-type groups.

The third level was the "tribe." One of the odd coincidences of the sources is that the actual Old Aramaic word for "tribe" is unattested. It might possibly have been the word *šbṭ*, though this word is only attested in later Aramaic. The Aramaic terms *mḥnh/mḥnt*ʾ or *mšry/mšry*ʾ may also have been used. In the Assyrian texts, the term LÚ.PN/GrN is the most common way of designating a "tribe"; but this term can also be used to designate a clan.[86] It is also possible that the Assyrian designation *karāšu* "camp"[87] was used to denote a tribe (see the discussion of the *rēš karāšī* below). It appears that the Assyrians rarely used the *bīt*-PN/GrN formula to designate a tribe, though this was, of course, a possibility.

Any discussion of the very important level of the "tribe" enters immediately into various problems and issues, in part because the term "tribe" has had such a difficult time in the anthropological literature, and in a number of cases for good reason (Porter 2012, 37–61). Porter's recent discussion captures the issue well:

> The tribe, if one were to retain this term, should be defined as a set of *social* relationships based on idioms and/or practices of kinship and descent as the means through which people understand their place in society and the nature of their relationships with others. No necessary nature to that place, no necessary nature to those relationships, should be assigned, however, for each group may define both the rules that create their social relationships and the various ways in which they practice them as they wish. One may obviously therefore belong to a tribe and a state at the same time (Porter 2012, 59).

Thus the concept of tribe is a very fluid one, with structures that are adapted to specific ecological and political niches.[88] LaBianca (1997) stresses that it is the important aspects of tribal continuity that define a tribe: flexibil-

86. It is clear from the southern Mesopotamian evidence that GrN was not uncommon, though PN (perhaps an ancestor) was a major usage.

87. The first term, *mḥnh*, occurs in the Zakkur inscription (*KAI* 202:A5, 6), though it refers there to "army." Nevertheless, it may have served as the Aramaic term. See n. 112 below: *rwš hmḥnyh*.

88. The definition of "tribe" is problematic. The very fact that there are so many definitions in the anthropological literature indicates the inherent fluidity of the term (van der Steen 2006, 28). See also the discussion in Fleming 2004a, 24–35; 2004b.

ity, in-group loyalty, and *notions* of common lineal descent.[89] Political and economic organization can be contributing factors to the group construct. Although the group structure is based on a kinship affiliation, and there is a degree to which this affiliation is real, it is often adaptable and manipulated in order to admit new members to the group or to make permanent or temporary alliances (van der Steen 2006, 28).

Thus the tribe is primarily a social term, not primarily an economic one, although it does include economic aspects, and has a social framework. It can therefore include both nomadic and settled populations (Bienkowski 2009, 16). Older scholarship on tribes tended to focus more on the genealogical, developmental, and nomadic pastoralist aspects, based on tightly defined definitions of descent and kinship and lists of essential traits (the so-called segmentary model). But more recent study has shown that a relational model is more consistent with the data, because it is capable of explaining the creation, recreation, and negotiation of relationships that are not necessarily connected by lines of descent linking successive generations. These relationships can be real or fictional—they can be manipulated or generated if it is useful to do so.

Thus the tribe derives its unity not from a fixed territorial identity per se, but from a sense (that is a constructed perception) of extended kinship. What this means is that a tribe, which typically has both sedentary and mobile components, may inhabit a core territory, but it can move about, contract, and expand depending on circumstances. Consequently, "despite their frequent mobility, tribes do forge a strong bond with the territory they control, both functionally in terms of their control of its resources but also in an emotional, ideological sense, whereby the territory is their homeland, where their ancestors and roots are" (Bienkowski 2009, 18). The land does not make the tribe; the tribe is made by relationships that denote a particular form of social identity.[90]

By means of manipulation of claimed ancestors, individuals and households are able to affiliate with other tribes. This permits individuals and households, as well as larger social units, to split, subdivide, or coalesce, depending on economic opportunities or conflicts with a given social unit. Given sufficient external threat, it also permits the coalescing of tribes into

89. The issue of real descent may be emphasized more in certain groups, yet flexibility is always present to some degree.

90. This leads Bienkowski (2009, 17) to posit the following definition for a tribe as a "sociopolitical system which enables effective negotiations within a constantly shifting network of relationships with people *portrayed* as interrelated and with territory, creating a sense of belonging and identity" (emphasis added).

confederations and to form kingdoms (Bienkowski 2009, 18). Porter (2012, 42) has recently summed it up this way:

> Kinship could be, and very often was, *created* for social, economic, and political reasons, and it was done through duplicating idioms of blood—sacrifice and incorporation into the ancestral (familial) group through the assumption of responsibility for funerary and post-funerary mortuary traditions, sometimes executed together.

Therefore, to be incorporated into a familial, clannish, or tribal community meant the embracing of numerous generations, not just the living (i.e., three or four generations), but many prior generations now deceased. The dead were included in the community of the living. Hence, implicitly there was a need to maintain the social group's wholeness, whether artificially or in reality through a cult of the ancestors. The pronouncing of the name (Aram. *zkr šm*; Akk: *šumam zakāru*) of deceased ancestors was a very important means of the maintenance of familial, clannish, or tribal wholeness.[91]

This process of artificial construction with remote ancestors—in many cases, tied to an ancestor cult ritual (*kispu*[*m*])—is attested in the ancient Near Eastern king lists. There appears to be a common "Amurrite link" in the traditions of the Assyrian King List,[92] the Genealogy of the Hammurapi Dynasty, the Ugaritic king list,[93] and Mari materials. The evidence from Mari demonstrates a clear connection of these lists with the notion of the *kispu*(*m*).[94] Such genealogical constructions serve as socially accurate in terms of their function.[95]

---

91. Compare the biblical notion of restoring clan wholeness through the *gōʾēl*, who, among many potential functions, may redeem the dead by continuing his line, i.e., "raising up the name of the deceased upon his property" by means of acquiring "the wife of the deceased." See Brichto 1973, 21.

92. Summed up there: *napḫar* 17 *šarrāni āšibūtu kultari* "altogether seventeen kings, tent dwellers."

93. Grayson 1980–83, 102–3 (A I 12; B I 10; C I 9); Lambert 1968; M. S. Smith 2002, 96–98. Brinkman (1989, 46) notes: "we must keep in mind that genealogical statements were often reflections of contemporary political or economic configurations rather than faithful records of blood descent."

94. Charpin and Durand 1986, 161 and n. 92. The evidence from Ugarit is suggestive of such a link.

95. While "socially constructed," with fragmentations and coalescences occurring, it would be a mistake to "understate" the important part lineage does play in such groups. Clan and tribal relationships were not simply a web of fictions; real lineages did exist. Perhaps a good way to express it is lineage does play a role, but it is not simply about "real" lineage. The importance of real elements of lineage is reflected in the conception of "descendant" (*yldt*, cf. Heb. *mwldt*) derived from root *yld*.

In sum, the key to understanding the vocabulary for these socially constructed groups is a realization of the fluidity and flexibility that is inherent in the usage. Consequently, in table 2.2 the possible vocabulary and designation "tribe" is found in a number of places in order to indicate the flexibility in its usage. Certainly group size has impact on this. But in the case of the ancient documents, there is precious little information that enables discernment.

Flexibility is also reflected in the leadership terminology as seen in table 2.2. This fluidity in the designations for the leadership and the power invested in them is due in good measure to the nature of such communities.

In numerous Assyrian and Babylonian documents, the term *nasīku* "chieftain, sheikh"[96] was used as the designation of Aramean tribal chieftains,[97] especially from the time of Sargon II onward. This term was used most often to designate a tribal leader in central and southern Mesopotamia. However, it is found as early as Aššurnaṣirpal II where he describes the Laqē confederation leaders (e.g., Ilâ is designated as a *nasīku* of Laqē).[98] Other terms were also commonly used like *rb(ʾ)/rabû*/LÚ.GAL or *rʾš/raʾasu*.

Gellner has pointed out that in highly self-policing and self-administering groups, there is a resultant weakness or absence of central agency. This means that a vital aspect of socially constructed groups, especially at the level of the tribe, becomes the action of "nesting":

> Groups contain subgroups, which in turn contain other subgroups, whose relationship to each other is once again similar. There is no preeminent or crucial level of social organization. The balance of power operates inside groups as much as it does between them.[99]

Tribal confederations, tribes, clans or the smallest segments (the *bēt ʾab*) all function in roughly the same way. In such cases, there are multiple possible ways for the nesting of various groups, which dictate many different "nestings" of power. Many coalescences and fragmentations, no doubt, were frequently tied to the various configurations of the nestings of power within such socially constructed groups.

Because of the artificial construction of kinship affiliation through "shared ancestry," which was based on the perception of the tribe as a

---

96. The term *nasīku* is recorded for the first time at Late Bronze Emar. See Sigrist 1982, 246–47.

97. One can compare Hebrew נָסִיךְ (Josh 12:21; Ezek 32:10; Mic 5:4; Ps 83:12). The reading of *nsyky* in Aḥiqar 119 may, in fact, be *ksyky*. See *DNWSI*, 735, s.v. *nsyk*; and Porten and Yardeni 1986–99, C1.1.167.

98. RIMA 2:215, A.0.101.1, iii.45–46.

99. Gellner 1990, 109–10. Although his discussion is about modern tribal communities, the explanatory power for the ancient Near Eastern contexts is clear.

"family," one of the obvious ways of "nesting," both internally and externally, was through marriage alliances. These were a logical means of promoting political and economic integration (see Barjamovic 2004, 89 n. 96). Evidence for this among the Arameans can be seen, for example, in two letters. In the first,[100] an official writes the Assyrian king informing him that Bēl-iqīša, the chief of the Aramean tribe of the Gambūlu had been systematically creating marriage alliances by wedding his daughters with some of the prominent families in Babylon, Borsippa, and Bīt-Dakkūri.[101] The second letter attests to the Aramean tribal practice of intermarriage among three of the tribes in southern Babylonia and the resultant complications that these marriages brought forth.[102]

The tribal confederation was an even larger "political unit." This is the fourth level of structure. Tribes could be aggregated into temporary or permanent, higher-order clusters, often prompted by strong individual leadership. This is what Eickelman has designated "the power of persuasion" as opposed to "the power of force." Thus "learning how to be persuasive, one becomes a man of honor in tribal societies, and persuasion is more central to the workings of tribal society than the use of force" (Eickelman 2002, 125). The historically and psychologically contingent emergence of strong, charismatic leaders is central to the process of the coalescing of tribes into confederations, as well as kingdoms (Cribb 1991, 53; van der Steen 2006).

Certainly, the *bīt*-PN/GrN could be used to designate such an entity, though as discussed above, it is used most often to designate a tribal kingdom in the contexts of the Jezirah and Levant. The confederation was most often simply designated by LÚ.PN/GrN(*-a-a*). In some cases, there might be a leading tribe, but in other cases all tribes within the confederation cooperated on the basis of equality. Tribes of a confederation would help and support each other in times of stress, but they remained nonetheless autonomous. The leader of such a unit could receive various designations: *mlk/šarru*; *rb(ʾ)/rabû*/LÚ.GAL; *rʾš/raʾasu*; *nsyk/nasīku*; *sbʾ* (all of these terms are used at various times in different contexts and geographic regions).[103] There were a number of known Aramean confederations. Interestingly, most of these were located in the Jezirah and/or southern Mesopotamia.

An important text that has not been fully integrated into the discussion of Aramean tribal structures is the text of Ninurta-kudurrī-uṣur from Sūḫu (the

---

100. SAA 18:41–46, 56.14–r.5. See chapter 10.

101. Note the parallel actions of Ibzan (Judg 12:8) who arranged marriages for his "thirty" sons and "thirty" daughters "outside" his clan. Note the use of חוץ.

102. SAA 18:90–91, 113.r.2′–12′, esp. r.4′, 9′. See the explication in chapter 10, 27. Damūnu.

103. See also the discussion of the *ālik pāni*, "military commander/chieftain" below.

so-called Sūḫu Annals).[104] A small portion will be presented here in order to make important observations about the socially constructed groups and their leadership.

> Barely three months had passed at the beginning of my governorship, when I sat on the throne of my father. 2,000 men of the Ḫaṭallu tribe—from (*ultu*) the Sarūgu (clan) to (*adi*) the Luḫūya (clan)—with their archers and their heads of camps—gathered together (*ipḫurū-ma*); and they imparted a command to each other (i.e., came to an agreement). Šama'gamni, the herald (LÚ.NIMGIR/*nāgiru*) of the Sarūgu, who is thoroughly confused by falsehood, was their commander/chieftain (*ālik pānīšunu*). They came up for a raid against the land of Laqē. And while in the steppe they advised themselves, saying: "The governor of Sūḫu is hostile to us. How will we go pass and conduct a raid on the land of Laqē?" (S.0.1002.2, i.7b–16a)

> Šama'gamni, the herald (*nāgiru*) of the Sarūgu, and Yā'e, the son of Balammu, of the Amatu, their heads of camps (*rēš karāši*), said the following to them: "Among the governors of the land of Sūḫu, his ancestors, none dared to go to war against 1,000 Arameans. Now he must go to war against 2,000 Arameans! If he does attack us, we will go to war against him and gain possession of the land of Sūḫu. But if he does not attack, we will bring down the booty (of Laqē); and we will add (more) troops, i.e., (more) troops will join us; and we will go and attack the houses (i.e., clans) of the land of Sūḫu; we will seize his cities of the steppe; and we will cut down their fruit trees." (S.0.1002.2, i.16b–27a)

A number of comments can be made. First, there was a confederation called the Ḫaṭallu.[105] The text's wording "from (*ultu*) the Sarūgu clan to (*adi*) the Luḫūya clan" indicates only the basic parameters of the confederation. In parallel texts, one reads "to (*adi*) the Minū' clan."[106] Thus, the Ḫaṭallu confederation was comprised of, at least, four clans or subtribes: the Sarūgu, the Luḫūya, Minū', and the Amatu, and perhaps others. It is clear from the mention of some of these groups in later Assyrian texts that they could act independently of the confederation.

Second, the Ḫaṭallu … gathered together (*ipḫurū-ma*). Although this is a verbal form, it is a clear reference to the confederation's (great plenary) assembly (*puḫru*; Aramaic *ʿdh*). It is not known exactly who composed this assembly, but it seems likely that the tribal heads (*r'š*)[107] and elders (*sb'*),

104. RIMB 2:295–96, S.0.1002.2, i.7b–27a. For a discussion, see Younger 2015a.

105. For a full discussion of this tribe and the clans/tribes mentioned here, see chapter 10.

106. RIMB 2:292, S.0.1002.1, line 20. See Zadok 1985, 63–70.

107. These could sometimes be referred to as "brothers."

along with perhaps a representative of every *byt ʾb*, the leaders of clans (*rʾš lbt ʾbwt*), and any other people that the confederation leadership considered essential to such an assembly would be included. Of course, due to the inexactitude of the terms, some of these "titles" could be represented in the same person. Certainly, the tribal heads or elders might be "brothers," and hence also "chieftains" in their own right.

From two letters (*ABL* 915 and *ABL* 293) documenting activities among the Gambūlu tribe in southern Mesopotamia, it is clear that there was an assembly of "the Gambūlu—the elders and the young" (LÚ.*gam-bu-lu* LÚ.AB.BA.MEŠ *ù* LÚ.TUR.MEŠ)[108] that had authority to appoint a leader of the tribe (or in this specific case, request the Assyrian king to appoint a leader).[109] Hence, this "great plenary assembly" was certainly convened for the very important matter of the nomination of a new chief (*rʾš*, *nasīku*, *rbʾ*) or of a military commander (*ālik pāni*). While the smaller assembly/council of elders (or "brothers") was certainly empowered for such decisions, there were times when the great plenary assembly (*ʿdh*/*puḫru*) would be involved in the decision. In such circumstances—and this could also be true on lower levels like the clan—the assembly must be persuaded to take the action that was being suggested and that any questions or objections to the action would need to be convincingly answered. So while the chieftain was technically "in command," he was in charge only in so far as the assembly was willing to join in the action.[110] Thus the political authority of a chieftain rested upon the loyalty of the assembly without whose consent he held little executive

108. *ABL* 915, lines 2–3. See the discussion of Barjamovic 2004, 92. Note the wording of SAA 17:132, 150.3–4: DUMU.MEŠ–DÙ.MEŠ(*mārē banî*) *ši-bu-tu u ṣe-ḫe-ru-tu* "the noblemen/citizens, the elders and young men."

109. One should compare the assembly [*qhl*] of *zqnym* and *yldym* in the Rehoboam/Jeroboam narrative of 1 Kgs 12:1–20.

110. This was similar to what one sees in Old Babylonian Mari where the *puḫrum* convened to nominate the tribal and local leaders (*sugāgum*). See Anbar 1991, 135–40. A letter from Yasim-el to Zimri-Lim of Mari (Charpin 1988, 412:6–10, 16–22) provides an interesting parallel. Note particularly the second half of the quotation: "On the 5th of Lilliatum, (as the day) was getting on, the Numḫâ army began to assemble in the midst of Qaṭṭarâ. [When] the army had assembled, Kukkutanum (the general [*rab amurri*] of Asqur-Addu) [left] his town of Nunasaru, showed up at the assembly (*puḫrum*) of the army, and laid his complaint [before] the army as follows … (The rebellion is not my fault.) Kukkutanum said [this and] many other things to the assembly of the army, and he both put the army in a craze and moved the consensus of the *muškênum* to revolt against Ḫaqba-ḫammu their [lord]. [So Ḫaqba]-ḫammu unknowingly sent Kakiya to the assembly of the army [at] Qaṭṭarâ [in order to] carry out deliberations and to launch a military expedition(?). They then killed [that man], while the *muškênum* went over to the side of Kukkutanum, and they (all) began to make an assault on Qaṭṭarâ." See esp. Fleming 2004a, 207 and comments there.

power. The inability of a single individual to decide the policies and the fate of the community and its members can be seen in a number of instances.[111] Even though social and political organization of the tribal communities was not always clearly differentiated, the sources indicate that a large measure of political power in a tribe was shared between a number of the prominent figures, undoubtedly through various "nestings" of relationships. The "brothers" (or elders) had a broad political authority, presumably representing the policy of their clans or tribes, in case of tribal confederations.

Third, the text reveals the leadership structures for this particular confederation: "Šama'gamni, the herald (*nāgiru/ngr*) of the Sarūgu, and Yā'e, the son of Balammu, of the Amatu (LÚ.*a-mat-a-a*), their heads of camps (*rēš karāšī*).[112] Thus Šama'gamni served in three capacities: as "commander" (*ālik pānīšunu*, lit. "the one who goes before them") of the confederation, and as "the herald" (*nāgiru/ngr*) and as "the head of camp(s)" (*rēš karāši*) for the Sarūgu clan! In another text, he is given the designation LÚ.GAL (*rabû*)[113] "the chief" (= Aramaic *rb*ʾ).[114]

Šama'gamni's offices have interesting correspondences with those of another Iron Age tribal leader, Jephthah, who in Judg 11:11 is described as the ראשׁ and קָצִין of the Gileadites. While ראשׁ is the exact equivalent to *rēšu*, interestingly, the Old Greek translates קָצִין with ἡγούμενος,"[115] lit. "one who goes before" which corresponds exactly to *ālik pāni*.[116] The *ālik pāni* seems to have been primarily a military designation, perhaps a shortened form of *ālik pāni ummāni*, "the one who goes before the army," or *ālik pāni ṣābim*, "the one who goes before the troops."[117] Many of the latter phrase's usages

111. In SAA 15:109, 159.4–11, a member of a tribal community (probably the chieftain) conveys an imperial offer of cooperation for his people and his brothers to contemplate. In other words, he could not simply take action himself. In SAA 15:144, 221.2–r.2, an imperial request for the extradition of criminals appears to have had to pass through the "brothers." Again, the decision did not simply rest with the chieftain.

112. Cf. the much later phrase *rwš hmḥnyh* "the head of the camp" in *DJD* ii 42[2].

113. RIMB 2:302, S.0.1002.3, ii.3′.

114. See also the Sefire Stelae: *KAI* 222:A39, 40, 41; 223:B3 and C15–16; and the *tamītu* text (Lambert 2007, no. 5) discussed below.

115. Judges A: εἰς κεφαλὴν καὶ εἰς ἡγούμενον. Judges B: εἰς κεφαλὴν καὶ εἰς ἀρχηγόν. The Judges B variant can be explained as a simple glossing for "leader"; whereas the Judges A variant is more difficult to explain. In my opinion, it is clearly an attempt on the part of the translator to capture an important nuance in the Hebrew term קָצִין, a nuance of which the translator of Judges B was perhaps unaware.

116. For those who are overly sensitive to biblical historicity issues, let me say that my point here is simply to observe the interesting commonality in the vocabulary—vocabulary that was used over a very long period.

117. Sometimes written syllabically IGI.DU or DU.IGI. Note the majority of occurrences are in a military context, even for the usage with deities. See *CAD* 1.1:344–46.

occur in texts from Mari where a tribal "military" leader designation seems apparent. The designation appears to be used for other Aramean tribal leaders.[118]

The term "herald" (LÚ.NIMGIR/*nāgiru*) brings up again a problem in the reading of several Old Aramaic texts, namely *ngr* versus *ngd*. In Sefire Stela III, line 10, Fitzmyer (1995, 138–39, 151–52) has read *ngdy* "my officials," while Lemaire and Durand (1984, 119, 129, 145) have read *ngry* "mes préfects."[119] The same problem is found in the Adon Papyrus,[120] and in the recently discovered Katumuwa Inscription.[121] Although Dion (1997, 278 n. 31) took Ninurta-kudurrī-uṣur text's use of *nāgiru* to be possible evidence in favor of *ngr*, Lipiński (2000a, 500–503) argued that "the use of this title in the document from Sūḫu simply reflects a particular Neo-Assyrian terminology." A certain parallel usage is found in Sennacherib's Annals where the Assyrian monarch claims to have defeated "Ḫumban-undaša, the herald of the king of the land of Elam" (^md^*ḫu-um-ban-un-da-šá* LÚ.NÍMGIR *ša* LUGAL KUR.ELAM.MA.KI).[122] In this text, *nāgiru* has clearly a military role. However, these cuneiform examples cannot solve an epigraphic problem. At the present time, there is simply not an unambiguous use of the word *ngr* in an Old Aramaic text.

Sassmannhausen (1995, 153–58) argued that the term *nāgiru* may have served as the title of a tribal chief. In the case of Šama'gamni, this term seems to designate only his authority within his own clan or subtribe, the Sarūgu. But it is possible that this office was used to designate a leader of a tribe.[123]

It would seem from the narrative that the phrase "their heads of camps" (*rēš karāšīšunu*, actually written: LÚ.SAG KAL×BAD.MEŠ-*šú-nu*) is used to designate a leadership position above that of *nāgiru*/*ngr*; but again, because of the fluidity in these terms, there may have been contexts when it was vice versa. Furthermore, the term *rēšu*/*r'š*, as pointed out above, might be used to designate simply the "head" of a clan or extended family, or perhaps with ellipsis of *karāšī*, "the head (of camps)."

As already noted, another place where some kind of power resided was in the clan or tribal elders (Akk. *šībūtu*; Aram. sing. *sb'*[124]). The sheikh or chief needed to consult the "elders." In one sense he governed with their con-

---

118. SAA 17:18, 15.8′; 17:88, 96.13. See discussion in chapter 10.

119. *KAI* 224:10: *ng*⌈*r*⌉*y*.

120. *KAI* 266:8. Date 604 BCE.

121. Pardee 2009, 53–54, 56, lines 3–4: *ngd*/*r*. See the comments of Lemaire 2013, 147.

122. RINAP 3.1:183, 22, v.82 (with variant: LÚ.*na-gi-ru*).

123. Compare the usage of the biblical Hebrew term נשיא (*HALOT*, 727).

124. *DNWSI*, 1099, s.v. *šb*; note *sb*, *sb'*.

sent; they were his witnesses (*šību* is often used with this specific meaning). In some texts of Ninurta-kudurrī-uṣur, this group is mentioned:

> Anyone in the future who comes forward and should ask the elders of his land and the elders of the land of Laqē (*šībūt mātīšu u šīb*[*ū*]*tu ša māt Laqē*): "Is it true that Ninurta-kudurrī-uṣur, governor of the land of Sūḫu and the land of Mari, inflicted this [defeat] at the command of the god Apla-Adad, the great lord, his lord?"[125]

Philologically, this reference to the elders might simply be to older people (Lipiński 2000a, 492). However, the fact that the term *šībūtu* is in a genitive relationship with *mātīšu* and with *ša māt Laqē* seems to specify the leaders of Sūḫu and Laqē as witnesses. Hence it is, in fact, most likely a reference to this leadership group. Certainly, Ninurta-kudurrī-uṣur is not saying "just go talk to some old men" and they will confirm my victory, particularly since his inscriptions were written perhaps no more than a decade or two after the event.

The reference to *šībūtu* in an Assyrian administrative text from Tell Ḥalaf (Gūzānu) that belonged to Mannu-kī-Aššur may also refer to this leadership group.[126] Lipiński (2000a, 492) rightly points out that this probably refers to the city elders who were, in fact, tribal and sedentary.[127]

All of this demonstrates a range of flexibility in the leadership vocabulary that no doubt reflects the reality of the flexibility of the Aramean socially constructed groups. Such groups were very dynamic, with considerable adaptation.

Regarding the origins of the Aramean tribal system, a final word must be said. Bunnens (2000b, 13–14) has argued that

> The origin of the tribal system must be looked for in the ruins of the interregional system of the Late Bronze Age. The collapse of the Late Bronze Age meant not only the removal of the exploitation system of that age, it also meant the removal of protection from war waged by regional powers. The local communities, therefore, turned to another form of collective organization, and the most obvious choice was a system based on kinship. This contributed to giving unprecedented importance to tribal organization. This may have resulted in a resurgence of nomadism, but not necessarily.

---

125. RIMB 2:293, S.0.1002.1, lines 46b–48. See also RIMB 2:297, S.0.1002.2, line 34; and RIMB 2:314, S.0.1002.8, lines 19′–20′.

126. Weidner, Ungnad, and Friedrich 1940, no. 20.

127. Cf. the use of the biblical term *zqn*.

However, the fact that many of the socially constructed group structures that can be found in the texts of the second millennium can also be found in the first millennium (howbeit with some differences in vocabulary) argues that it is far more likely that structures of the socially constructed groups of the second millennium continued into the first (with the typical transformations that occur with such groups: i.e., coalescence or fragmentation).

## 2.4. Nomadism

### 2.4.1. Models and the Issues of Nomadism

Scholars have proposed a number of different models to explain the origins of the Arameans. These models have been developed in conjunction with underlying fundamental presuppositions concerning the nature of "pastoral nomadism" (or better "mobile pastoralism") in its relationship to sedentary societies. Hence, the models are reflections of the anthropological views popular at the time of their geneses, namely: (1) that a basic hostility exists between the two, or (2) there is a basic symbiotic relationship between them.

In addition, major paradigm shifts in the discipline of archaeology during the twentieth century (e.g., traditional, processual, postprocessual, etc.) have impacted the types of explanations of the data. It is beyond the scope of this volume to give a detailed account of all the systemic issues; rather what follows is a general outline with particular focus on the issues germane to the Arameans.

The earliest model that became the scholarly consensus was an "invasion model" (see fig. 2.2). This model portrayed the Arameans as "waves" of wild barbaric nomads flowing out from the fringe of the desert steppe, from the south and east of the fertile crescent, and overwhelming the agricultural zones, often wiping out the settled populations and bringing urban civilization to an abrupt end. These nomadic hoards quickly Aramaized the areas that they conquered. As part of an evolutionary process, these nomads would see the advantages of sedentary life and would settle into villages and towns, their place on the steppe taken by other nomadic groups, which in turn would eventually follow the same process. Thus the Arameans invaded the Fertile Crescent from the Syrian desert, and by the late twelfth century BCE, were threatening the very existence of Assyria. One of the more influential supporters of this hypothesis was W. F. Albright (1975, 532) who proposed that the Arameans were "camel nomads" whose use of the camel was an integral part of their mercantile and military success.[128] Thus, according to this

128. Lambert (2004b, 353) put it in these words "the Aramaeans flooded into Meso-

model, the Arameans were considered simply another wave among many of nomadic Semites that periodically emerged from the desert to overwhelm and destroy the civilized communities of Mesopotamia.

A second, more subtle view was a "migration model" that pictured the nomadic migrations as a river rather than waves (see fig. 2.3).[129] Like the Amurrites, the Arameans were a group that had migrated in several stages from the Syrian desert (Briquel-Chatonnet 2004, 7–10). They were seen as nomads who filled in the areas around the urban landscape and over time sedentarized. There were four great Semitic migrations (the Aramean wave being the third): the first was the Akkadian wave at some unknown early date; the second was the Amurrite wave at the beginning of the Old Babylonian period; and the fourth was Arab invasion after the advent of Islam.[130]

Both of these models were based on a traditional model of migration and/or invasion (invasion being a type of migration).[131] And importantly, both of them were driven by a fundamentally negative attitude toward nomads. Szuchman has recently summed this up:

> By the 1950s researchers continued to assume that the primary role of nomads throughout history was as agents of destabilization ... Kupper, for example, was convinced that "une conflit permanent" existed between sedentary and nomadic societies, a clash which resulted in waves of nomadic invasions from the Syrian desert into the otherwise bucolic rural and urban centers of Mesopotamia and the Levant.[132]

Thus, both the first and second models were heavily dependent on a late nineteenth– and early twentieth–century notion of nomadism that assumed an underlying basic hostility between nomadic and sedentary communities. But another part of the problem lay in the simplistic interpretation of cer-

potamia and north Syria in a massive migration, disrupting everything." See also Winckler 1905, 2; Tadmor 1979, 11–14; Postgate 1974, 234–37; and Hawkins 1982, 380–82.

129. Kupper (1957, 1959) presented a peaceful migration view, describing the spread of the Amorites like a river from the steppe of Syria. Kupper saw a permanent hostility between the sedentary and nomadic communities. "Insérée entre des étendues désertiques et des chaînes abruptes, la Mésopotamie devait être le théâtre d'un conflit permanent entre le sédentaire et ceux qui convoitent ses richesses, le nomade et le montagnard" (p. xi). See also Dossin 1959.

130. Moscati nuanced this arguing that violent invasions occurred from time to time on a background of continuous and mainly peaceful penetration. See Moscati 1959b, 72.

131. Moreover, "an invasion theory is technically a sub-class of migrationist theories." See Lönnqvist 2008, 197.

132. Szuchman 2007, 119. I would like to thank Dr. Szuchman for kindly providing me with a copy of his dissertation. There are many important observations in it and it has proven to be a very valuable contribution to scholarship.

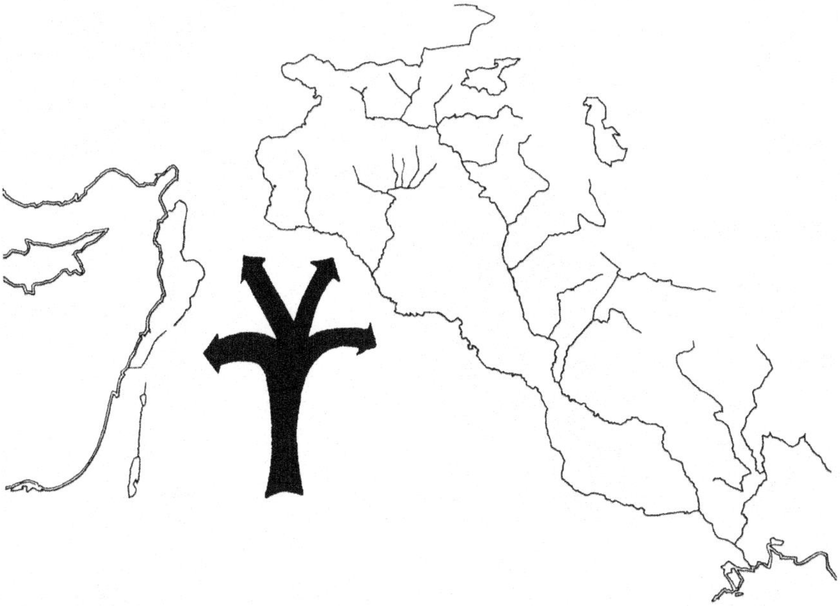

Fig. 2.2. The invasion model (based on Buccellati 1990a, 101)

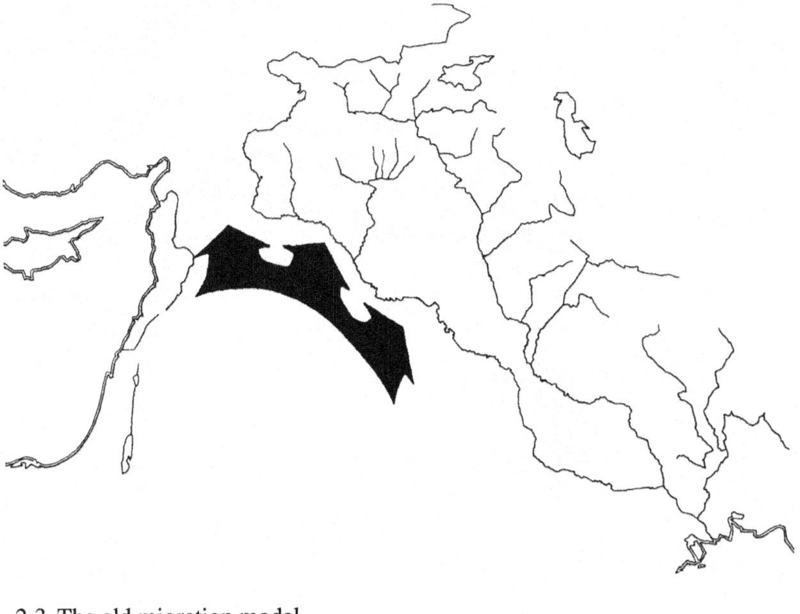

Fig. 2.3. The old migration model

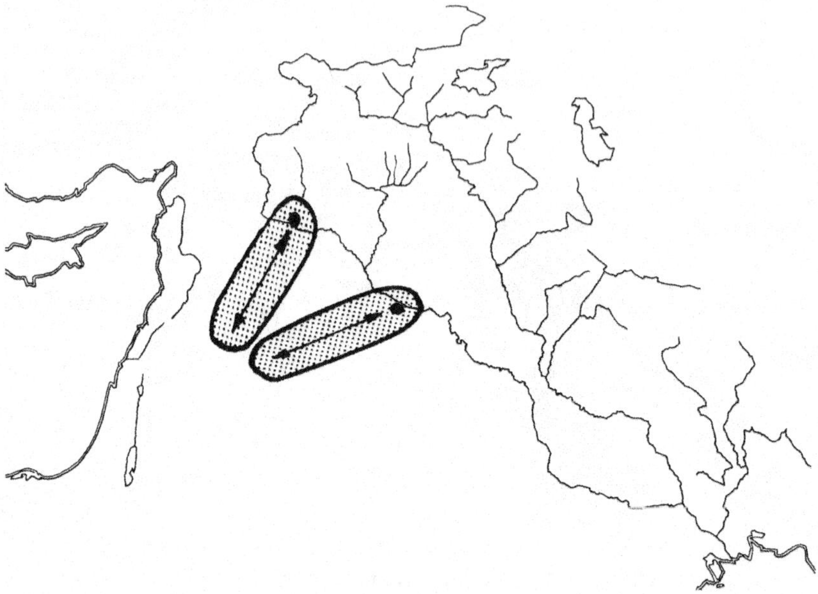

Fig. 2.4. Symbiotic relationship (enclosed nomadism) model

tain ancient Near Eastern textual materials that manifested biases against sheep- and goat-herding nomads portraying them as a constant threat to the sedentary agricultural, "civilized" peoples (Szuchman 2007, 119).

In the explanations for the origin of the Arameans (and for that matter the Amurrites), these theories of invasion or migration went out of vogue in the 1980s, particularly in English-speaking scholarship. They were replaced with largely indigenous explanations for the Arameans' origins, sometimes linked to a rise in environmental causal theories as the major ways of explanation for cultural transitions, often without any particular role of human interventions (Lönnqvist 2008, 195).

Yet at this same time, in the 1980s, anthropology and archaeology provided additional methodological means to advance the study, and further significant work developed in the study of nomads in the 1990s.[133] A number of ethnographic studies provided important insights into the variety and complexity of mobile pastoralism (e.g., D'Hont 1994). Nevertheless, issues of propinquity always loomed as a barrier to firm conclusions.[134]

133. Zarins 1992; Bar-Yosef and Khazanov 1992; Cribb 1991; LaBianca 1990.

134. See the recent critique by Porter 2012. For my own development of the assessment of propinquity, see Younger 2002c.

Also during the period (actually starting slightly before in the 1960s and 1970s), migration and invasion models were being discarded as explanations by many anthropologists and archaeologists. Chapman and Hamerow (1997, 1) have put it this way:

> archaeologists downplayed the significance of migrations and invasions over a period of almost 30 years. All manner of local processes were invoked to explain the most important cultural changes, creating a strong bias towards local, "indigenist" or "immobilist" theorizing.

Consequently, there was a divide between the traditional approach of "diffusionists" or "migrationists" on one side, and the processual approach of "indigenists" or "immobilists" on the other, with a significant number of scholars opting for the latter approach.[135]

Thus a third model emerged, which I am designating the "symbiotic relationship model"[136] (see fig. 2.4). With this model, there was also a shift from an understanding of basic hostility between sedentary and nomadic groups, to a fundamentally symbiotic relationship. Based on the study of modern nomadic groups, it was posited that while there is often confrontation between pastoral nomadism and sedentary agriculture, the two are fundamentally complementary—a nomad-sedentary symbiosis. It is important to note that Rowton, one of the early theorists of this model, did not deny conflict between the two groups, but argued that the basic relationship was not permanent hostility, but symbiotic. Rowton[137] used the terms "enclosed nomadism" and "dimorphic chiefdom" to describe a type of social organization "which represents a curious blend of city-state, tribe, and nomadism" (Rowton 1973b, 201). Tribes migrated within an area controlled by a central urban authority, but were not subject to that authority. The tribes themselves had some sedentary and some mobile members who interacted with the various levels of sedentary society. Rowton's work led to further research that produced a more integrated view of the processes of nomadic and sedentary adaptations in the ancient world (Schwartz 1995). By the 1980s, the work of Rowton and his successors on the integration of the pastoral and agricultural sectors was beginning to be applied to the emergence of Aramean nomadism.[138] G. Schwartz (1989, 281) emphasizes that "the nomads, rather than keeping to the fringes of sedentary society, moved well within the borders of

135. For a survey, see Killebrew 2005, 197–201.

136. The fundamental notion of a symbiotic relationship is what is in common among the scholars who hold the position as described here. It goes without saying that there are many variations and nuances among these scholars.

137. Rowton 1967, 1973a, 1973b, 1976a, 1976b, 1977.

138. For example, Schwartz 1989; Pitard 1996.

the settled zone, where nomad and sedentist existed in a mutually dependent symbiotic relationship."

Some recent reviews of the Mari texts and archaeological evidence argue that the division between nomad and sedentary was perhaps even more porous than Rowton had claimed for the early second millennium (Fleming 2004a; McClellan 2004; Porter 2002, 2004; and Lyonnet 2004). Although Rowton had succeeded in integrating the two elements of the tribe-state dichotomy that featured in work prior to the 1960s, according to Fleming (2004a, 71), the tribe and the state at Mari were one and the same. The use of the term *ḫana* in the Mari texts is not the name of a separate tribe, but means "tent-dweller" (Durand 1992, 113 and n. 138; 1998, 417–18); thus Mari was "a fully integrated tribal kingdom," rather than an urban kingdom ruling over integrated sedentary and tribal elements (Fleming 2004a, 71). In a very real sense it was a tribal kingdom (Porter 2012, 59–64). Thus, in the 1990s and early 2000s, the symbiotic relationship model[139] became the most preferred model to explain Amurrite mobile pastoralism among Assyriologists.[140] Naturally, it also became the model for explaining mobile pastoralism in the context of Aramean origins.

Moreover, during the late 1980s and the two decades following, Rowton's model was integrated with the collapse model as an explanation for the transition from Late Bronze Age to Iron Age. Liverani was the first to meld Rowton's model to the consequences of the collapse of the Late Bronze Age palace economy.[141] In his understanding, during the Late Bronze Age, the apparatus for economy exchange was in the hands of the palaces in urban centers who controlled the populations in the hinterlands. When these palace economies collapsed (due to internal factors), new processes of exchange and new social structures took their place. Urban settlements became smaller, more diffuse, and more numerous, and the nomads of the steppe responded

139. A fourth model, proposed by Buccellati (1990a, 98–102), is the "nomadization model." Buccellati puts it forth this way: "the steppe is the place whereto one hides from the valley, rather than the irrepressible gene pool from which nomadic waves originate. Rather than seeing only occasional evidence for a sedentary life, I see in the texts pervasive evidence for a peasant settled population that takes to the steppe for economic and to some extent for political reasons. Instead of sedentarization of nomads, I think we must speak of nomadization of the peasants" (p. 100). See also Buccellati 1992. While there can be no doubt that there are times when sedentary folk turn to mobile pastoralism, a nomadization process, this model has not gained many adherents as an explanation for the origins of the Amurrites or the Arameans so far as I can discern.

140. Streck 1998–2001c, 2002. While he presents this model, it is perhaps not accurate to place Streck completely within this group of theorists.

141. Liverani 1987, 69. For the issues concerning collapse, see Yoffee and Cowgill 1988; Schwartz and Nichols 2006; and McAnany and Yoffee 2010.

to these changes by becoming sedentary. The villages that had been tributary to the palaces were transformed into clans or subgroups of pastoral tribes. The Early Iron Age saw a shift from the administrative system at the heart of the Bronze Age palace states to a kinship system. A transition from a city-state to a kin-based state was characteristic of the Syro-Levantine area.[142] In the wake of the collapse of the Late Bronze kingdoms, these Aramean tribes filled the vacuum left by the collapse of these kingdoms. In this, they followed a well-established settlement pattern in the ancient Near East.

Thus internal factors of socioeconomic dynamics were preeminent, and the external or migratory factors were rather limited. Sader stated it in direct terms: "the primary, if not only, cause for the collapse [of the Late Bronze Age] is to be looked for in the social and economic crisis of the city-state ... The emergence of the Arameans is to be understood not as the cause but rather as the result of the collapse of the urban system" (Sader 1992, 158, 162; 2000; 2010). Along similar lines, Pitard (1994a, 209–10) stated:

> It seems quite unlikely that the Arameans were immigrants into Syria and Upper Mesopotamia at all, but rather that they were the West Semitic-speaking peoples who had lived in that area throughout the second millennium, some as pastoralists and some in villages, towns, and cities. During the period following the collapse of the Hittite empire, this West Semitic element of the population slowly became politically dominant in several areas, and it is this element, then, that begins to appear in the sources in the late twelfth century.[143]

While the "collapse" explanation in combination with an indigenous model was an important attempt to nuance the understanding of the rise of the Arameans, it is clear that such a *mono-causal* explanation is insufficient for all the data (McClellan 1992; Younger 2007a). In a number of respects, it was reductionist,[144] and thus insensitive to other factors. For example E. van der Steen has pointed out that there is never simply one explanation for why nomads settle, or why they take to nomadism and pastoralism again. She notes:

142. Liverani 2014, 396–97. Actual documentation for this transition of village to clan is lacking for the Arameans. In addition, in my opinion, Liverani overstates the Bronze Age/Iron Age distinction. There is plenty of evidence for tribal structures tied to villages in the second millennium.

143. He adds: "There is simply no evidence that the population of Upper Mesopotamia and northeast Syria were displaced by large groups of Aramean tribes that had been living previously in the desert" (210 n. 6). See also Pitard 1996; Schniedewind 2002.

144. It is clear that a number of proponents of this model were heavily influenced by the French Annalistes.

> Factors like climate, disease, population pressure, economic decline or its opposite economic revival and international political circumstances have all been used as possible explanations, but not one of them can claim to provide the final answer and which of these, or which combination of these, is valid may differ with every event (van der Steen 1999, 171).

In addition, as mentioned above, "the retreat from migrationism" (Adams, Van Gerven, and Levy 1978)—in other words, the abandonment of migration as having any explanatory place in the models of the rise of the Aramean polities, at least among a significant number of scholars—has had a particular limiting effect on recent reconstructions. However, it is interesting to note that the only two full-length monographs in recent years devoted specifically to the history of the Arameans utilize a "migration" explanation in their reconstructions; yet they really do not draw from the wealth of studies devoted to mobile pastoralism (Dion 1997; Lipiński 2000a).[145]

### 2.4.2. Some Further Recent Developments

It perhaps goes without saying that there is a rich, continually flowing stream of new literature on mobile pastoralism, both in general, and in specific, addressing ancient Near Eastern studies. Thus the following are developments and contributions that seem especially important to the discussion of Aramean origins.

First, it is important to understand that while the basic trade relationship between mobile pastoralists and sedentary communities is symbiotic, it is an unequal relationship: "nomads are much more dependent on agricultural products from sedentary farmers than are farmers on pastoral nomadic products."[146] Thus this nomadic-sedentary symbiosis can be unstable because of the competition between village and nomadic groups for limited resources (Szuchman 2007, 137; 2009a; 2009c). Furthermore, various forms of interactions between nomadic and sedentary societies can lead to the subjugation of the latter by the former. Raiding and demands of tribute are two ways in which the economic adaptations of the nomadic lifestyle (i.e., mobility and military strength) are used as political adaptations to the sedentary

145. I do not mean to imply that either scholar had no awareness of the issues, but that they have not engaged this issue in a full manner. Lipiński seems particularly to emphasize a basic hostility between the Aramean nomads and the sedentary population (characterizing them on more than one occasion as "roaming bands"). But to his credit he does not rule out *a priori* migration as an explanation.

146. Cribb 1991, 10–15; Khazanov 1994, 203. While based on studies of twentieth-century models, this seems very consistent with what is seen in the ancient Near Eastern texts.

world (Khazanov 1994, 222–27). Interactions that involve subjugation by nomads of sedentary communities exist alongside the necessary mutualism of nomadic–sedentary interactions (Szuchman 2007, 137).

The fact is the economic, social, and political relationships between nomadic and sedentary communities are highly complex and multifaceted. They can be symbiotic and competitive at the same time (Szuchman 2007, 137). Undoubtedly, over an extended period of time and with different groups in different geographic/environmental contexts, a wide spectrum of relationships can and should be envisioned. Add to this, a mix of different leaders with various different personalities, goals, etc. and the spectrum is even a deeper variety of relationships over time. If climate change is introduced as a variable, this might add another dimension to the complexity. To envision the relationship between mobile pastoralists and sedentary communities as basically hostile or basically symbiotic is posing the issue wrongly. As scholars, there is a need to express the complexity of relationship more adequately, not juxtapose polar opposites which are not adequate to explaining all the data.

Second, it is important to understand that there is a variability to tribal nomadic adaptations along the lines of mode of subsistence and extent of mobility. This can be envisioned along two axes: a mode of subsistence axis (ranging from agriculture to pastoralism) and a mobility axis (ranging from sedentary to fully nomadic).[147] Aramean socially constructed groups (see above) are not all the same! In fact, they fit on a very wide spectrum. Hence, there were tribes that were more or less sedentary (e.g., Bīt-Gabbāri/Sam'al) with some pastoralist elements; others were more or less nomadic (apparently like the Ḫaṭallu confederation) with small elements that were sedentary;[148] and others with great variation in between (like the Laqē confederation; see fig. 2.5). This is, in fact, attested in the textual records.[149] So while tribes like the Tu'mānu and Ḫaṭallu may appear in the Sūḫu texts (Younger 2015a) to be very mobile—raiding sedentary regions,[150] they could have some sedentary elements. For instance, a group like the Lītawu (Li'tā'u)[151] had some sedentary elements as a text like BM 40548 indicates where these Arameans were

147. See Cribb 1991, 15–22 and fig. 2.1; Fleming 2004a, 34–36; Szuchman 2007, 135–38; Lönnqvist 2008, 200; and for Luwian nomadism, see Simon 2010.

148. Szuchman's study only addresses the more sedentary entities (e.g. Bīt-Zamāni). He does not address the Aramean tribal groups that appear to be less sedentary (e.g., the Ḫaṭallu).

149. Our present knowledge is, of course, partial and incomplete, but in a number of instances it is possible to evaluate where roughly certain groups would be placed on these axes.

150. Yet, the Ḫaṭallu have a small sedentary element.

151. For the vocalization of this tribe, see Zadok 2013.

engaged in agricultural work owning their own fields and orchards.[152] From Tiglath-pileser III's Summary Inscription 7, it is very apparent that numerous groups out of the thirty-five Aramean tribal groups listed were, in fact, settled in cities and forts, even though many of these were undoubtedly small.[153] The Laqē confederation is an example of a tribal entity that had capital cities (e.g. Sūru, the capital city of the Bīt-Ḫalupē tribe; Sirqu, perhaps the main capital city) along with other cities, yet was composed of many villages and hamlets. In the inscriptions of Ninurta-kudurrī-uṣur, a large number of *adurû* (É.DURU$_5$.MEŠ) of Laqē are mentioned as being raided by the Ḫaṭallu confederation.[154] This term refers to a small rural settlement with a permanent water supply (corresponding roughly with *kapru* "village," though it can be as small as a simple farmstead).[155] Importantly, an *adurû* is also equated with an *ālu*, which speaks to the diminutiveness contained in the semantic range of the latter term, *ālu(m)*.[156] In fact, Fadhil and Radner (1996, 423 n. 21) have noted that the distinction between *ālu* "city/town" and *kapru* "village" is not clear-cut in Assyrian usage. Van Driel (2001, 109) noted that "for the Mesopotamians the congregated tents of the non-sedentaries also constituted an URU.' "[157] Therefore, many of these settlements in Laqē were nothing more than small villages. The point is that the Laqē confederation had a clear sedentary component; nevertheless, due in large measure to the nature of its territory, it had a very sizeable pastoralist component.

On the middle Tigris, the Utū'/Itū' tribe had both mobile and sedentary components as a text of Tukulti-Ninurta II recording his campaign of 885 BCE demonstrates:

> I approached the Tigris; and I captured the encampments (*maškanāte*) of the land of the Utū'/Itū' together with their villages (*kaprānīšunu*), which were situated on the Tigris. I massacred them (and) I carried off much booty from them.[158]

In this context, the term *maškanāte* clearly indicates encampments of tents for seasonal pastoralism, while the term *kaprāni* signifies actual agricultural vil-

152. BM 40548, lines 8–12 as cited by Lipiński 200a, 423–24; Brinkman 1968, 270–71 n. 1738. Dated to the ninth year of King Erība-Marduk (ca. 765).

153. See RINAP 1:118, 47, lines 8–9; Tadmor 1994, 158–61, summary 7, lines 8–9.

154. See RIMB 2:296, S.0.1002.2, i.28.

155. See *CAD* 4:39, s.v. *edurû*; *AHw* 14, s.v. *adurtu*, *adurû*.

156. Thus [*a-d*]*u-ru-ú* = *ālum* (OEC 4, 150 iii.55; *a-du-ur-tum* = *ālānu* (British Museum 1904, 10.iii.53). The term *adurû* is also combined with other terms to create toponyms (*adur* X; *adurû ša* X).

157. See the discussion of the inscriptions of Tiglath-pileser I in chapter 3.

158. RIMA 2:173, A.0.100.5, lines 49–50a.

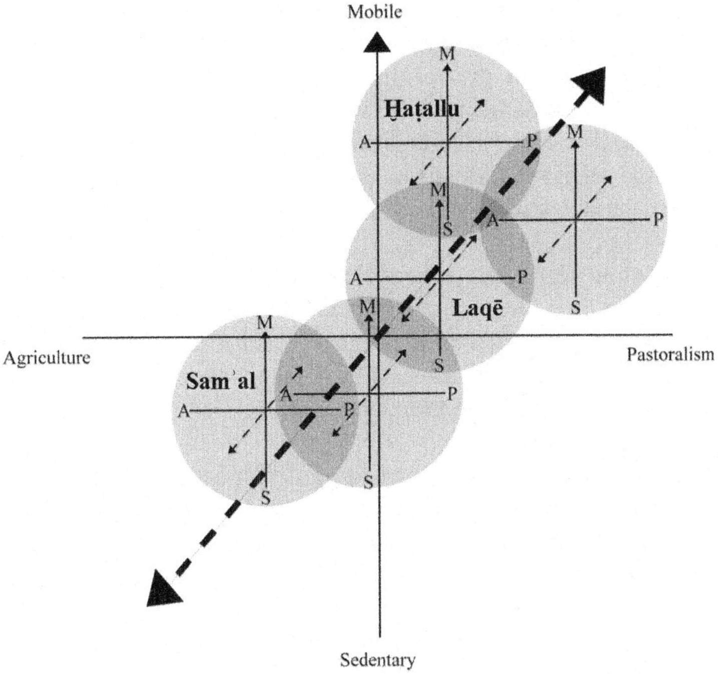


Fig. 2.5. Aramean tribal variation in modes of subsistence and mobility (based on Cribb 1991, fig. 2.1; and Szuchman 2007, fig. 15)

lages (see Fales 2007b, 293). Particularly interesting in the Aramean context is the treaty between Aššur-nērārī V and Matiʿ-ʾEl of Arpad which contains these curses: "may one thousand houses (É.MEŠ) decrease to one house (É); may one thousand tents (TÚG.*maš-ku-nu*) decrease to one tent (TÚG.*maš-ki-ni*)."[159] Clearly, the sense of *maškanu* in this text is "tent" versus "house," and is a curse on Matiʿ-ʾEl's encampments that they will be diminished.

Consequently, contrary to previous interpretations, scholars now tend to agree that tribes could control a well-defined territory,[160] and that certain components of the tribal communities could be permanently settled in towns and villages (Barjamovic 2004, 89). Yet, in contrast to the city-states, socially constructed group identity was not geographically fixed; segments of the tribe could therefore remain spatially separate for extended periods without loosing their sense of belonging.

159. SAA 2:13, 2.vi.3–4.

160. Some tribal communities were certainly formed as territorial polities. The power of a tribal community to police its territory and defend its borders is also commonly attested. See, for example, SAA 18:70–71, text 87.

While the scholarly literature attempts to address why some groups settle, it often neglects the question of why some groups did not settle. Cribb (1991, 16) notes that the greater the degree of pastoralism, the stronger the tendency toward nomadism.[161] However, even when members of a tribal community settled in a city-state in southern Mesopotamia that was not part of their tribal territory, they always retained their tribal identity.[162] In any case, many variables were often involved, and so tribes fit on a very wide spectrum.

Third, while very often ancient Near Eastern scholars divide the ancient population into the sedentary and nomadic categories, W. G. Lambert noted that there was in antiquity a third category: "displaced persons" (my designation; his was "exiles and deportees").[163] This is linked to the next point (i.e., this has connections with the issue of migration), but it deserves mention as a separate point.

Lambert provides a number of examples, mostly from second-millennium Syria to document this category. One particular example that he notes is found in the inscription of Idrimi.[164] While there is an issue of genre which I will not enter into,[165] nevertheless the inscription is valuable for its description of "displaced persons."

In brief, Idrimi grew up in Aleppo with his family, but "something nasty" (*masiktu*) happened that caused them to leave Aleppo, settling in Emar (his mother's hometown). Idrimi soon realized that he could not remain in Emar as a subject to the king of Emar, and so he left with his horse and chariot and a retainer. He spent the night with Sutean warriors (other displaced persons?); and then moved to the Canaanite city of Ammiya where he found other people of Aleppo as well as other people from Mukiš, Niya, and Amae. The text states: "(When) they saw that I was their lord's son, they gathered around me. 'I have become chief; I have been appointed.' I dwelt in the midst of the Ḫapiru warriors for seven years" (*COS* 1.148:479). After living among this group of displaced people from his homeland, Idrimi returned and became ruler of Alalaḫ (as a vassal to the Mittanian ruler Parattarna).

---

161. Thus, "the more animals you have, the further you have to move."

162. This is seen from both the Assyrian royal inscriptions and the imperial letters. E.g., an Assyrian letter of Nabû-ušallim (SAA 17:121, text 140) reports on Arameans who were living in Uruk, yet did not pay allegiance to that city, but rather remained loyal to the tribal chieftain Merodach-Baladan, a Chaldean!

163. Lambert 2004a; See also Bunnens 2009, 72.

164. In many ways, Idrimi fits into the category of a *kaltum*. The word *kaltum* was used as a designation for individuals who were part of a sociopolitical group that were political refugees actively competing to be kings based on royal familial ties. For a discussion of the term in its Amurrite context, see Miglio 2014a, 441–44; 2014b, 131–33.

165. See Lambert's discussion of this issue (2004a, 214 n. 2).

The point to be made is not so much about Idrimi as it is about these other displaced persons. It appears that they too had come to Ammiya in Canaan either being compelled by political factors to leave or having chosen to seek a better (safer?) place. It seems that one group had successfully settled in Ammiya and others having heard the news followed in their path (see the discussion of chain migration below) (Lambert 2004a, 215).

Thus in the region of Syria and the Upper Euphrates, there was a significant category of "displaced persons" who sought refuge wherever they could find it, a population that was undoubtedly quite mixed in all respects. They were a mobile population group, but not like typical mobile pastoralists/nomads. As Bunnens (2009, 72) puts it, they "were a people living on the fringe to escape the constraints—especially corvée labour and taxation—imposed on inhabitants of sedentary settlements." Some of these functioned as armed bands of outlaws and brigands; others adapted as best they could. The term *ʿapiru* was undoubtedly one of the terms commonly used in the period to designate such uprooted people; another term was *Sutû*, although this appears to have been a more generic term for "steppe person" (see below). But they were a third category that must be considered, particularly since their ranks increased significantly in times of weak government and social disorder.

A very interesting illustration of this comes from a later period, but the vocabulary is particularly interesting in light of this category. Sargon II states:

> VII (57) *i-na* KUR *ma-ad-bar šá-a-tú* LÚ.*a-ra-me* (58) LÚ.*su-ti-í a-ši-bu-ut kuš-ta-ri* (59) *mun-nab-tu sa-ar-ru* DUMU *ḫab-ba-ti* (60) *šu-bat-sun id-du-ma uš-har-ri-ru me-ti-iq-šú*
>
> In the land of that steppe, the Arameans and Suteans who dwell in tents (*ašibūt kuštari*)—fugitives, criminals, (and) plunderers (*munnabtū sarrū mār ḫabbāti*)—had pitched their settlements, and had made its way desolate.

Idrimi, having come to power, related that "I made them settle down; those who did not want to live in settled abodes, I made to do so; and so I brought security to my country."[166] The very security of some of the polities near to the steppe was at risk because of these "displaced persons."

Fourth, it is important to include migration (and invasion) back into the range of explanation for the rise of the Aramean polities, at least in the ways that present scholarship is developing the theoretical conceptions.[167] As

166. Idrimi 85: KI.TUŠ *šu-ub-tam ušēšibšunu ša* KI.TUŠ *lā uššabū anāku ušēšibušunu u mātīya ukinnu.*

167. Migration theorists identify differing types of migration (Manning 2013; Harzig and Hoerder 2009). The current approaches are no longer tied to the once-for-all mass

noted above, in the models for the rise of the Aramean polities, the last two decades have seen a tendency to downplay migration as an explanation in historical reconstruction.[168] This has happened to the point that the Arameans are presented in the literature as simply the same mobile pastoralists that were always "there" throughout the centuries.[169] In this view, the interaction between the Assyrians and Arameans "would simply have produced a modification of the social structures of the local populations and the takeover of power by one part of them."[170] It is quite an irony that in the very decades when many theorists have opted for an immobilist model of explanation for the origins of the Arameans, some of the greatest migrations in human history have been happening!

But there is clear textual evidence of actual tribal migrations among the Arameans. One example can be seen in the migration of the Yaḫānu tribe from the central Tigris to a location west of the Euphrates around Arpad (see next chapter). As already pointed out, some tribes were quite mobile. They move not just between seasonal areas, but to entirely new locations. The Ḫaṭallu group is another example: from the Upper Euphrates region (south of Til-Barsib, in the great bend of the Euphrates, and perhaps in confederation at an earlier stage with Bīt-Adīni?) to the Wadi Tharthar area; then later they migrated (or a portion of the group did) to southern Mesopotamia.[171] Another example is the tribe of Rupū'. Around the end of the eighth century the Assyrian *turtānu* Šamšī-ilu, who was based in Til-Barsib (Kār Shalmaneser), fought them in the area of Upper Euphrates. Early in his reign Tiglath-pileser III fought them in central Mesopotamia. Later, during his reign, Sargon II faced them on the Tigris, near the border of the Elamite state (Cole 1996a, 49). Throughout the history of the ancient Near East, there have been many tribal group migrations.[172] Even an important modern example

---

migration of the traditional migration models. See Yasur-Landau 2007, 609; and Faust and Lev-Tov 2011, 16–18.

168. It is interesting that in contrast to Anglo-American intellectual traditions, most of Western European scholarship continued to employ migrations and invasions as explanatory models (an exception to this trend is Denmark and Norway, where processual theory influenced archaeological practice). See Chapman 1997, 12–13.

169. See Sader 2000; Pitard 1994; Schniedewind 2002. The model can be conceptually very evolutionary.

170. Kepinski's description of the view. See Kepinski 2009, 150.

171. Fales gives some excellent examples of the variability in mobility of some of the Aramean tribes in southern Mesopotamian. See Fales 2007b, 293–95.

172. Charpin and Ziegler (2003, 29) have suggested that Amorites were part of large migrations in the twenty-first century BCE and consequently sedantarized widely. They use the concept of "*toponyms in mirror,*" the repeated spread of the same Amurrite toponyms to reflect the sedentarization process in the third millennium BCE onwards. See

can be cited from the the early nineteenth century. The Shammar nomads *drove* tribes like the ʿUbaid, once the lords of the Jezirah, across the Tigris into Iraq (Cole 1996b, 24 n. 4). This demonstrates that tribal displacement or forced migration sometimes took place. Of course, climate can sometimes be a factor.[173]

Lönnqvist has made important contributions to this discussion. Her insightful critique of the symbiotic model is worthy of quotation:

> Clearly it has been important to restrict the explanations stressing migrations and invasions to appropriate fields of inquiries. However, in the same time the total abandonment of the migrationist or invasionist hypotheses and models does not conform with the archaeological evidence of stratigraphic discontinuities in every instance. "The retreat from migrationism" has taken some archaeologists too far beyond the data itself. The epigraphic sources originating from archaeological contexts cannot simply be ignored as they form an integrated part of the evidence from the past.[174]

Most demographers and geographers attribute the decision to migrate to an interplay between "push" factors and "pull" factors, in conjunction with the availability and cost of transportation.[175] "Push" factors are perceived as negative conditions in the home region; and "pull" factors are perceived as positive conditions in the destination region. How the "push" and "pull" factors are perceived is also a function of access to information about potential destinations. Thus an important variable is that of information flow.

It is also significant that population density is not the most crucial "push" factor. Powerful "push" factors can be social and cultural considerations, lineage fragmentation, political, religious, or social oppression, climate, economic considerations, or a combination of these. Anthony (1997, 23) has pointed out that the density-dependence view of migration routinely ignores the effects of these other "push" factors, as well as "pull" factors, "transportation costs," and "information flows."

---

Charpin 2003b and the discussion in chapter 10 on the Arameans of southern Mesopotamia. For the migration of the Mušku, see Malatya in chapter 3 below.

173. In a letter from the time of Sargon II (SAA 1:74, text 82), the correspondence reveals the (unwelcome, but unavoidable) presence of Arabs in the Jezirah (who apparently have crossed the Euphrates at Ḫind/zānu) in search of pasture during a drought, though their grazing area is to be restricted by a eunuch appointed by the governor of Kalḫu. See also the Neo-Assyrian letter (possibly from the time of Sargon II), where Šarru-dūrī writes to the king, informing him among other things that the Arabs have crossed the Euphrates at Ḫindānu (ND 2626, Saggs 2001, 87 = SAA 19:16–17, text 12).

174. Lönnqvist 2008, 199–200. For further discussion about "the retreat from migrationism," see Chapman and Hamerow 1997; and Lönnqvist 2000, 112–13.

175. Anthony 1997, 22. See also Trilsbach 1987; Tilly 1978.

For many modern demographic geographers, the "pull" factors are among the most critical components in successful migration models (Anthony 1997, 24). Thus, the probability that *x* will migrate to *y* at time *t* is partially determined by *x*'s knowledge about place *y*; this in turn is largely determined by the prior history of migration between *x* and *y*. Earlier migrants return home recounting information about optimal routes to the destination, and as a result these same routes to the destination are utilized by later migrants. This type of "chain" migration concentrates on the specific routes, destinations, and social settings that are attractive to the home region. Anthony (1997, 24) has emphasized that

> Migration, particularly long-distance migration, is channeled by access to information about a limited number of attractive routes and destinations. Migration therefore proceeds in streams toward known targets, not in broad waves that wash heedlessly over entire landscapes.

Thus "information flows" are an important issue. Finally, migration is more likely to occur between place *x* and place *y* when travel costs are low. In the case of mobile pastoralists who make seasonal migrations, travel costs are not a major factor, if the routes are available and the "pull" and/or "push" factors are great.

In summary, the decision to migrate is a function of "pushes," "pulls," the structure of "information flows," and perceived "transportation costs." All of these are mediated through family and household needs, decision-making customs, and local economic structures. Although population densities clearly have important effects on migration, demographers would find it impossible to investigate migration without incorporating data on "pushes," "pulls," "information flows," and "transport costs." None of these need be causally related to population density in the migrants' place of origin (Anthony 1997, 26).

At this point, it is important to stress that the treatment of migrations as simply the products of "push" and "pull" factors is insufficient to understand migrants in their complexity of culture, gender, class, identification, and intent, and in their moves between complex societies (Harzig and Hoerder 2009, 4). Thus there is a need, where possible, to look at both ends of mobility in migration events, understanding the manifold complexity in multiple events.[176]

176. Harzig and Hoerder (2009, 2) give an interesting datum that illustrates this. Men and women of Chinese culture arriving in Canada between 1980 and 2000 hailed from 132 different countries of prior settlement! Therefore, to assume that all the Arameans moved simply from one spot is to miss the complexity in the historical record.

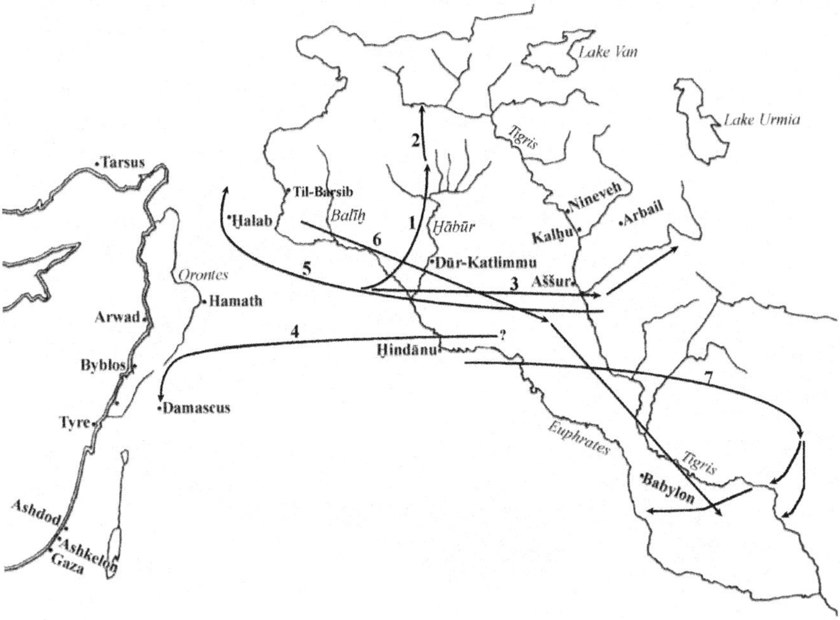


Fig. 2.6. Some select known Aramean tribal migrations

1. Migrations into the Upper Ḫābūr region (chapter 3)
2. Migration into the Upper Tigris region (Bīt-Zamāni) (chapters 3 and 4)
3. Migrations into the Lower Zab region; penetration into the area of Īdu (chapter 3)
4. Migration into the Damascus area (chapters 3 and 9)
5. Migration of the Yaḫānu tribe into the Arpad region (chapter 4)
6. Migration of the Ḫaṭallu and other tribes into the Wadi Tharthar area; migration of the Ḫaṭallu into southern Mesopotamia (chapter 10).
7. Migrations into southern Mesopotamia (chapter 10)

From the late second millennium to well into the first three or four centuries in the first millennium, Aramean socially constructed groups migrated throughout Mesopotamia (see fig. 2.6). No doubt, in such a far-flung region, there were many "push" and "pull" factors. Certainly, in the first millennium, the Assyrians were a major "push" factor for a number of these groups: Tiglath-pileser III and Sargon II were perhaps the greatest "push" factors of them all. While ancestral ties were a major potential "staying" factor, with mobile groups this is less of a problem since they must cope with distance-identity issues through "distanciation," that is the stretching/shrinking of time and space through a mesh of social, ideological, and various practices to bind disparate and distant components of a sociopolitical entity into one (A. Porter 2009, 202; 2012, 61).

Therefore, it would seem that the best model is the one that allows for complexity and flexibility in its explanations. In other words, it is a more comprehensive model that (1) draws on the richness of mobile pastoralism and its various interactions with the sedentary and other mobile pastoralists (note again the example of the Shammar versus ʿUbaid above); (2) draws on the recognition of a third category of "displaced persons"; (3) draws on the wealth of historical and archaeological data; and (4) draws on a sensitivity to a range of explanatory models that have awareness of geographic, environmental issues (including a more sophisticated understanding of migrations).

## 2.5. Links with the Aḫlamû and Sutû

The early history of the Arameans is tied to that of the Aḫlamû and Sutû, groups already known in the Late Bronze Age who seem to have played a role in that period's demise (Brinkman 1968, 277–78 n. 1799). In ancient Mesopotamia, certain terms (Aḫlamû, Sutû, Umman-manda, etc.) were applied as "monikers" that belonged more to an ideological (often pejorative) tradition than to a concrete reality.[177]

### 2.5.1. The Aḫlamû

The first proposed etymology for the term *aḫlamû* was given by M. Streck (1906a, 193) deriving it from an Arabic root *ḫilm* (plural *aḫlām*) meaning "confederates, allies, fighting companions." Moscati demonstrated that this was quite faulty, not the least of which because of the actual meaning of the Arabic root (Moscati 1959a; see also Pitard 1987, 84–85).

On the other hand, Moscati (1959a, 304–5, 307) proposed that *aḫlamû* was an ethnonym, a proper name of a particular group that was separate from the Arameans. However, Brinkman rightly pointed out the difficulty with understanding *aḫlamû* as a proper name.[178] He suggested that the term might be a designation of "a certain type of semi-nomad, whatever his ethno-linguistic affiliation, somewhat as Sutû and Ḫapiru were used at various times."

Another etymological proposal is that of Lipiński (2008, 35; 2000a, 37–38; 1989, 32) who argues that the term derives from the root *ġlm* (cf. Heb. *ʿlm*) "boy, lad"; hence the *aḫlamû* (which he normalizes as *aḫlāmu*) must be a "broken plural" (i.e., *ʾaġlām*) with the original meaning of "boys,

177. Fales 2013, 53, and n. 16.

178. Brinkman 1968, 277 n. 1799; also Lipiński 2000a, 38.

lads, bands of lads."[179] Lipiński appeals to von Soden for support.[180] However, as pointed out by Bulakh (2012, 547), "for von Soden this etymon is a hypothetical (not actually attested) Arabic form." Thus this etymology is not problem free. M. P. Streck argues that the internal plural "cannot readily be assumed for Amurrite."[181] See the discussion above on the broken plural in Old Aramaic (§2.1.3 above).

Streck (2000, 334–35) has offered another alternative etymology and morphological understanding. He understands the form *aḫlamû* as an *ʾaQTal* adjective form (possibly elative)—which he documents in the Amurrite onomastics. Thus this form should be an adjective, perhaps an elative, of the root *ḥlm* "to be strong."[182]

While I would favor this explanation, it seems apparent that the etymology of the word is insufficient in the determination of its meaning. Instead, it is the word's usage in various contexts that reveals its meaning. Its usage was clearly not as an ethnicon.[183] Rather, the contexts seem to indicate that it was a collective term used with some type of social nuance. This usage certainly changed in the ninth century when there was a semantic shift to using it as a synonym for Aramean[184] (see further discussion below).

Interestingly, while the term *aḫlamû* occurs in Assyrian and non-Assyrian texts, the attestations in Assyrian texts are primarily found in royal inscriptions, while non-Assyrian occurrences are mostly in letters.[185] Both corpora are informative. In the non-Assyrian usage, there are a few references from the first half of the second millennium, but many occur in the second half.

---

179. See also Lipiński 1981, 279 ("the pattern *ʾaqtāl* is used in Semitic languages as the plural of collective nouns designating persons").

180. Lipiński 2008, 35: "see *AHw* 21a, s.v. *aḫlamû*. Von Soden posits that it is a foreign word from the hypothetical root **ʾaġlām* 'Jungmannschaft?' "

181. Streck 2000, 335. He states: "Als Nominalform für letzteres schlägt Lipiński 1981, 279, 'aQTaL vor, doch handelt es sich dabei um einen typisch südsemitischen inneren Plural, der nicht ohne weiteres für das Amurritische vorausgesetzt werden kann."

182. He states: "Als Wurzel wurde (the root) 'stark sein' (Gelb 1980) und *ġlm* (arabisch *ġulām*, hebräisch *ʿalm* 'Jüngling') vorgeschlagen. Weil letzteres vermutlich Primärnomen ist, ist *ḥlm* zu bevorzugen. Also *ʾaḥlam*? 'stark.' "

183. Although most Aḫlamû were probably of Semitic stock, it would be a mistake to assume that all were. Some were undoubtedly displaced persons.

184. Fales 2002a, 182 and n. 13; forthcoming, 16–17.

185. Herles 2007b, 320. For other later references not in Herles, see SAA vols. 3, 4, 8, 10, and 18 and OIP 114, 109.

2.5.1.1. Non-Assyrian Occurrences

The following are some of the more important non-Assyrian attestations:

1. The earliest known occurrence of *aḫlamû* comes from the Old Babylonian period. Aḫlamû are attested in an Old Babylonian letter; possibly written to Hammurapi, ca. 1728–1686 (low chronology) 1696–1654 (ultra-low chronology) concerning events in Sūḫum (van Soldt 1994, 54–55, text 60, line 32). According to M. P. Streck, the *aḫlamû* in this letter appear to be Amurrites (Streck 2000, 28; Brinkman 2004).
2. Aḫlamāyu messengers (DUMU.MEŠ LÚ.KIN.$GI_4$.A *aḫ-la-ma-iu*) at Uruk during the time of Rīm-Anum, who is considered a contemporary of Samsu-iluna, ca. 1686–1648 (low chronology) 1654–1616 (ultra-low chronology). This is a so-called *asīru*-text 7.[186]
3. The reign of Ammiṣaduqa of Babylon (ca. 1582–1562 (low chronology) 1550–1530 (ultra-low chronology)—a tribe of Aḫlamû was living near Sippar (Nashef 1982: 5; Groneberg, Kupper, Leemans and Stol 1980: 5; van Lerberghe 1982).
4. Aḫlamû are attested at Sippar in the letter of Ur-Utu where the *Aḫ-la-mu-ú* were expected to bring barley (in late sixteenth century BCE).[187] From this letter, it is important to note that some Aḫlamû were sedentary agriculturalists.
5. Aḫlamû raid and plunder Dilmun dates mentioned in a letter from Dilmun, found in Nippur (ca. late 1400s).[188]
6. Men on guard duty at Nippur are described as Ḫīrānu, while later in the text they are designated Aḫlamû (first half of the fourteenth century) (Clay 1912b, 114:10 and 16, pl. 53).[189]
7. Other instances of Aḫlamû receiving rations at Nippur (Kassite period, fourteenth century) (Sassmannhausen 2001, 131):
   a. "an *aḫlamû* gets 1 sutu of flour" (BE 15, 44:11)
   b. "an *aḫlamû* gets 2 sutu of barley" (BE 15, 154:26)
   c. "an *aḫlamû* is mentioned in connection with the "Palace slave" (ARAD É.GAL)[190] and "Slave of the King" (ARAD LUGAL)" (Clay 1912b, 18:18)

---

186. Loretz 1978, 129, 149, no. 20 (= BM 14078); see also Lipiński 2000a, 37.
187. Lerberghe and Voet 1991, no. 87 (Di 227), lines 16–22.
188. Ni 615:14–17. See A. Goetze in Cornwall 1952, 144.
189. See the discussion of this tribe in chapter 10.
190. Or "construction worker." See the discussion of Brinkman 2004, 294–95.

d. "several *aḫlamû* are named as recipients of bread" (Clay 1912b, 118:58)

8. Gold caravans between Babylonia and Egypt (ca. 1400 BCE) (EA 200) were being raided by Aḫlamû (middle of the fourteenth century; Moran 1992, 277).
9. A letter of the Hittite king Ḫattušili III to the Babylonian ruler Kadašman-Enlil II (mid-thirteenth century) is intercepted by Aḫlamû (Faist 2001, 231–33)
10. Aḫlamû gate-guards at Nippur (ca. 1300 BCE) (Clay 1912b, 56:3, pl. 24)
11. Two Aḫlamû arrive at Emar from Sūḫu bringing a report (ca. 1235?)[191]
12. Other occurrences at Emar in contracts (Adamthwaite 1996, 93).
13. Around 1181 BCE (period of Meli-šiḫu), a female slave is designated *Aḫlamītu* in a deed (Pedersén 2005, 92).[192]
14. Around 1050 BCE, during the reign of Adad-apla-iddina, according to an inscription of Simbar-Šipak (Simbar-Šiḫu) (RIMB 2:73, B.3.1.1, lines 10, 14) and Babylonian Chronicle 25,[193] Arameans and Sutû/Suteans sacked temples of Sippar, Nippur, and other cult centers.

There are some important points that can be gleaned from these non-Assyrian passages, as Herles (2007b, 325–26) has pointed out. First, they attest to some Aḫlamû being sedentary agriculturalists, and hence they witness to the importance that agriculture plays in the so-called dimorphic zone together with pastoralism. Second, only numbers 5, 8, and 14 mention raiding (an important survival factor for nomads). Otherwise, the Aḫlamû are often presented as in the service of the state. Third, these texts evince that the nomads had significant control of the trade routes. Nomads might serve as messengers or caravan leaders, but in many instances they had control of the caravan routes.

Some of the non-Assyrian texts locate the Aḫlamû in the Šamīya, that is, the steppe east of Jebel Bišri. The area of Sūḫu is noticeable in a few texts.

191. Durand and Marti 2005, 123–24. In line 18 which reads 2 LÚ *aḫ-la-mu-ú*, they translate "deux Araméens." However, this is based on their interpretation of the etymology of *māt Mar(r)i*, namely, that it is possibly derived from Aramaic. The designation KUR.*ar-ma-ia*.MEŠ "Arameans" does not occur. This is, at best, indirect evidence.

192. For the date, see Cavigneaux and Beyer 2006.

193. Walker 1982, 414–15, 399–402 (lines 29–34), 416 (lines 8–11); Glassner 2004, 282–90.

It likely served as the point at which the Aḫlamû made their migrations to places like Sippar, Nippur, and Uruk. This Middle Euphrates region provided the route from Babylonia to Egypt and thus the area where the caravans were being intercepted (Beaulieu 2011–13).

Finally, it is also noteworthy that the non-Assyrian texts never speak of the Aramean-*aḫlamû*, but only of the *aḫlamû*. Therefore, this combined form, and hence the connection (i.e., Aramean-*aḫlamû*) is an Assyrian phenomenon, as observed by Brinkman (1968, 277 n. 1799).

### 2.5.1.2. The Assyrian Textual Occurrences

The following are some of the more important Assyrian attestations:

1. The first mention of the *aḫlamû* in the Middle Assyrian inscriptions is in a campaign of Adad-nērārī I (r. 1295–1264 BCE) in the area of Katmuḫu in northern Mesopotamia: (22) (…) *ka-ši-id* KUR *ku-ut-mu-ḫì ù na-gab re-si-šu* (23) *gu-un-nu aḫ-la-mì-i su-ti-i ia-ú-ri* (24) *ù* KUR.KUR-*šu-nu mu-ra-piš mì-iṣ-ri ù ku-du-ri* "(...) the conqueror of the land Kutmuḫu and all its allies, the hordes of Aḫlamû (and) Yaurian Sutû and their lands, the expander of borders and boundaries."[194]
2. Shalmaneser I mentions the *aḫlamû* in his campaign against Hanigalbat and its ruler, Šattuara, who is supported by Hittites and Aḫlamû. The Assyrian king proceeds with extreme brutality, he "slaughtered the armies of the Hittite and Aḫlamû like sheep."[195]
3. In a Foundation Deposit written on alabaster stone from the ziqqurrat in Kār-Tukulti-Ninurta, Tukulti-Ninurta I claims that "I brought under one command the lands[196] Mari, Ḫana, Rapiqu, and the hills or mountains of the Aḫlamû (*ù ša-da-an aḫ-la-mi-i : šadān Aḫlamî*) … (and many other defeated lands)."[197] With the mentioning of Mari, Ḫana, and Rapiqu, a location in the Middle Euphrates region is immediately in view. Masetti-Rouault has suggested that "the hills or mountains of the Aḫlamû" refer to Jebel Bišri, particularly since Jebel Bišri is actually not a single massive mountain, but a conglomeration of many hills forming a coherent plateau (Masetti-Rouault 2001, 69; Pappi 2006) (see below).
4. It is almost one hundred years later that the Assyrian inscriptions once again mention the Aḫlamû, namely, in the time of Aššur-rēša-

194. RIMA 1:132, A.0.76.1, lines 22–24.
195. RIMA 1:184, A.0.77.1, lines 78–80.
196. RIMA 1:273, A.0.78.23, line 83: 1-*en lu ul-taš-kín-šu-nu*.
197. RIMA 1:273, A.0.78.23, line 70.

išI I (r. 1132–1115 BCE). This king boasts of his victory, but boasts besides of his cruelty, with which he proceeded against this group: *ša-giš* ERÍN.MEŠ-*at* *aḫ-la-mi-i* DAGAL.MEŠ *mu-pár-ri-ir el-la-te-šú-nu* "slaughterer of the extensive army of the Aḫlamû (and) scatterer of their confederated clans."[198] Herles (2007b, 329) argues that the clear emphasis on brutality indicates that the Aḫlamû are such an extensive opponent that an Assyrian victory could no longer be regarded as natural. The Aḫlamû are not just a horde (*gunnu*), but were now a real, serious threat to the Assyrian kingdom, "an extensive army (ERÍN.MEŠ-*at* … DAGAL.MEŠ). The second word in Aššur-rēš-iši I's second epithet *ellātešunu* is important since Assyrian *ellutu*'s base meaning is "kinship group, clan," which can also connote confederate or cohort, hence the translation "confederated clans."[199] In any case, the term is emphasizing the socially constructed composition of these Aḫlamû groups.

5. With the inscriptions of the Tiglath-pileser I (r. 1114–1076 BCE), the Aḫlamû are mentioned for the first time in connection with the Arameans; and conversely the Arameans are mentioned for the first time in the Assyrian texts. Hence, this group, on every occasion, is termed the Aramean Aḫlamû, with "Aramean" as a gentilic/ethnicon (*aḫlamî/aḫlamê armāyya*, attested thus far only in the genitive; Brinkman 1997, 11 n. 11; 1968, 277 n. 1799). The two denominations *aḫlamu* and KUR.*aramāya* should be viewed as forming a single unit, and the final MEŠ "usually suffices for the two names." This text of Tiglath-pileser I will be discussed in detail in chapter 3.
6. In Aššur-bēl-kala's inscriptions (1073–1056 BCE), they are referred to as the Arameans (a collective noun in the singular: **arumu/*aramu*?, most commonly in the genitive for KUR *a-re-me*) and the *aḫlamû* are a distinct group (Brinkman 1997, 11 n. 11). See the Assyrian texts below for all of the contexts.

The Assyrian texts seem to indicate contacts with the Aḫlamû primarily in two locations: (1) the area east of Jebel Bišri to the Euphrates (i.e., the same basic area as the non-Assyrian texts) and (2) a region in the north Jezirah, north of the two mountains Jebel ʿAbd al-ʿAziz (Assyrian Mount Dibar) and Jebel Sinjar (Assyrian Mount Singāra; see ch. 1, p. 17). The earliest Assyrian sources report of conflicts with the Aḫlamû in this region during

198. RIMA 1:310, A.0.86.1, line 6.

199. See *CAD* 7:82–85, s.v. *illatu* A. I realize that the term can mean army, troops, etc., but I think in this passage where the Aḫlamû are the focus, the translation that I have opted for is closer to the intention of the text.

the westward expansion of the early Middle Assyrian kings and include in particular mention of the area of Katmuḫu.

Herles (2007b, 338) has also noted that two "routes" of migration may be postulated from this geographic data, namely, a south–north (Jebel Bišri to the area north of the two Jezirah mountains) and another east–west (Katmuḫu to Harran). The first route may reflect the appropriate areas for winter and summer pasturage.

Beside the fact that the scribes of Tiglath-pileser I qualify the Arameans as *aḫlamû*, there are other important connections between the terms *aḫlamû* and *arumu/aramu*.[200] Although the precise relationship of the Aḫlamû to the Arameans is not entirely clear, the Assyrians saw it as very close. Thus a scribe of the ninth century might have termed "Aramean" the people whom his predecessor in the thirteenth century would have termed "Aḫlamû." That the two groups were related can be seen by the fact that the tribe of Ḫīrānu are identified as Aḫlamû in the Kassite period around 1150 BCE,[201] and as Arameans in the inscriptions of Tiglath-pileser III[202] (see further ch. 10 below). The situation can be understood if the Aḫlamû were the section or group of the Arameans whom the Babylonians first encountered (Millard 1992a, 348).

Based on the usage of the term, Fales (2011b) has recently suggested that the Assyrians may have differentiated between the Aramean-*aḫlamû* (i.e., mobile nomads) and Arameans without the *aḫlamû* designation who they saw as more sedentary who had fortified urban areas. He has suggested that the term *aḫlamû* meant "nomad, barbarian or something similar,"[203] or even "drifter" (Fales forthcoming, 15).

It seems to me to have served as a broad generic designation for "steppe person": one who might be Semitic, but not necessarily; one that may be tribally linked, but not exclusively; one that is likely a mobile pastoralist/nomad, but in some cases, a sedentary farmer.[204] Thus, while there was overlap with the term Sutû (see below), *aḫlamû* was the broadest term that might be used.

After the texts of Tiglath-pileser I and Aššur-bēl-kala, the word *aḫlamû* generally disappears from the Assyrian royal inscriptions. After the reign of Adad-nērārī II (911–891), the term dies out, except for a few clearly anach-

---

200. Brinkman 1968, 277–78 n. 1799: Assyrian *Arumu*; Babylonian *Aramu*.

201. Clay 1912b, 114:10, 16, and pl. 53.

202. RINAP 1:118, 47, lines 5–8; Tadmor 1994, 158–60, summary 7. This is a point emphasized by Cole 1996b, 24 n. 2.

203. Fales 2011b, 36; see also Herles 2007b, 337–39.

204. In this sense, it is not very different from *Sutû*, though the Sutû derive from an actual tribal group; see below. Aḫlamû may have more philological similarity to *ḫapiru*; Fales 2002a.

ronistic occurrences. Babylonian scribes continue its usage for a time, but by around 1000 BCE, the term *aḫlamû* underwent a semantic shift, becoming an accepted archaism for "Aramean" (being included in the lexical texts and other materials where Aḫlamû meant "Aramaic" or "Aramean," that is, someone or something "with/in the Aramaic language."[205]

As many scholars have observed, the appearance of the Aramean tribes in Upper Mesopotamia and their expansion into Babylonia is comparable with the spread of the Amurrites a millennium earlier. Some type of kinship of Arameans and Amurrites is possible, but the attempt by M. Noth (1928, 41–48; 1961a, 41–48) to prove that the Amurrite language can be understood as "protoaramäisch" was disproved by D. O. Edzard.[206] A. R. Millard (1992a, 348) rightly remarks:

> Certainly there are a few similarities, such as names beginning with *ya* or ending with *-an*, and although when the only distinctive Aramean feature, the language, can be analyzed—and none survives from before ca. 850 BC—it has some markedly different characteristics, no more can be said at present than that both stem from a common NW Semitic ancestor.[207]

Zadok (1985b, 81–82) observed that none of the West Semitic names of individuals who are described as either Aḫlamû or Sutû is typically Aramaic, though some names are of "a clear Amorite type."

Yet, the terms *Aḫlamû* and *Amurrû* are at least occasionally used as synonyms for the same people and designate the same descent groups.[208] Brinkman gives the following examples: persons connected with the four most common pertinent patronyms or ancestral names—Ḫanānu, Ḫīrānu, Irību, and Qunanibu—are sometimes labeled *Amurrû* (MAR.TU)[209] and sometimes *Aḫlamû* (written syllabically);[210] and in Ni. 918:1–3 and UM 29-13-702:2–4, three descendants of Ḫanānu (Arik-Sukkal, Mandidaya, and

205. See Brinkman 1968, 277; Fales 2002a; *CAD* 1.1:193 s.v. *aḫlamû*: adj. "Aramaic (language)."

206. Edzard 1964; Malamat 1973, 140.

207. Aramaic may have developed from one of the Amorite dialects spoken in Upper Mesopotamia. Aramaic was certainly influenced by an Amorite substratum. See Zadok 1991, 107; and Kaufman 1974, 23.

208. As opposed to distinguishing groups *Aḫlamû* and *Amurrû* from separate regions on the Middle Euphrates and in western Syria respectively. See Brinkman 2004, 296.

209. UM 29-13-443 ii 17–18, 20–21 (total in ii 23: LÚ.MAR.TU.M[EŠ]); FLP 1313 I 4–7 (total in I. 8: MAR.TU.ME); BE 15 198: 49–50, 52–53 (total in line 55: LÚ.MA[R.TU ...]). Brinkman 2004, 296 n. 65.

210. Clay 1912b, 114, lists descendants of Irību, Qunanibu, and Ḫīrānu as *Aḫlamû* (lines 9–10, 16); UM 19-13-702 has descendants of Ḫanānu, Ḫīrānu, Irību, and Qunanibu as *Aḫlamû*. The fifth, known ancestral name, *Namru, is thus far attested only as a

Qīšat-Sukkal) are labeled *Aḫlamû*; in Ni. 1068 ii 19′, 21′–22′, the same three men with the same ancestral name, are labeled *Amurrû* (MAR.TU.MEŠ). There is the possibility that some of these usages are anachronistic.

As mobile pastoralists, the Arameans' association with the *Aḫlamû* seems to indicate that the Jebel Bišri region was a particular area where the Arameans originate, or at least a particular group that is active in the Middle Euphrates region (Zadok 1991, 109). This seems to be confirmed by the equation Yaḥmadiu(m) = Aḫlamû.[211] The Bišri Range is a good place for pasture, has many wells near its southeastern section and sustained a continuous and important concentration of Amurrite and later of Aramean nomads.[212] It stands to reason that the "Aḫlamites' mountains" are to be identified with Jebel Bišri (see above), or with a wider mountainous territory west and south of Ḫana which included Jebel Bišri, seeing that the sources usually specify the mountain's name (see Assyrian Occurrences, number 3 above). King Šar-kali-šarrī (ca. 2200 BCE) of Akkad boasts about his defeat of the MAR.TU in "Basar." Mount Basar (modern Jebel Bišri) was known in this period as "the mountain of Amurrum" (RIME 2:90–94, E2.1.4.2; Lönnqvist 2011, 197).

### 2.5.2. The Sutû

The Sutû/Suteans were also a group of tribes known from early sources.[213] They are attested as early as the Mari correspondence of the eighteenth–seventeenth centuries as the name of a type of tribal confederation of nomadic tribes, active over the Syrian steppe to the west of the Middle Euphrates.[214] They are also mentioned in Old Syrian and Egyptian sources as nomadic tribes of the Levant, as well as groups encountered in Old Babylonian sources (Heltzer 1981, 79–98). In a sense, the term, like *aḫlamû*, is used as a broad generic designation of a "steppe person," so that while a *sutû* might be a pastoralist, he might be simply a person of the steppe who fit into the third category "displaced persons."[215] While the Sutû and Aḫlamû were

---

MAR.TU group (UM 29-13-443 ii 16; FLP 1313 I 3; BE 15 198: 48) and only in the phrase DUMU [I]*nam-ri*. Brinkman 2004, 296 n. 66.

211. Or MAR.TU = Yaḥmadiu(m) = Aḫlamû. This description of the area in which the Aḫlamû were found matches the posited area for the location of the city-state of Yaḥmadiu and the tribal area associated with it. See D. Owen 1993, 182 n. 6.

212. Saggs (1984, 62) speculates that the reason for the Aramean thrust into the Euphrates area beginning at this time was due to the great deforestation of the Jebel Bišri.

213. See Kärger and Minx 2011–13; Streck 2014, 303–5.

214. Anbar 1991, 88–89, 97, 110, 115–17, 133–34, 205–7.

215. See the discussion of this third category above. Also note Zadok's comments on the difficulties in distinguishing between *sutû* and *aḫlamû*. See Zadok 1991, 105–6.

identical with certain—if not all of the—mobile segments of the Amurrites (Zadok 1991, 105), they were not all the same.

In the Neo-Assyrian texts, the Sutû are rarely mentioned. However, in the Middle Assyrian texts there is a growing number of attestations. Some of the more important occurrences come from the site of Tell Ṣābi Abyad, which was an Assyrian *dunnu* ("fortified agricultural center") in the Balīḫ River region (Wiggermann 2000, 172–74). The Middle Assyrian occupation at Tell Ṣābi Abyad dates from the late thirteenth and twelfth centuries BCE. The Assyrian Ilī-padâ, the grand vizier (*sukkallu rabi'u*), formalized a treaty (TSA T04-37) with the local Sutû (specifically designated as the Niḫsānu tribe). The treaty likely dates sometime between 1200–1180 BCE.[216] This treaty has not yet been published (Wiggermann forthcoming), but the Tell Ṣābi Abyad website gave the following for tablets discovered in 2004:

> The treaty is probably an "office copy" for local administrative use; the real, official document was not kept at the fortress of Tell Ṣābi Abyad, but at Ilīpadâ's chief residence (in Assur?). Such office copies were also found at other places, for example at the "ministerial departments" of Ugarit on the Mediterranean coast.
>
> We come across the Suteans elsewhere in our texts as well. They pass information on to the Assyrians and appear to be acting as spies—a function for which they were well suited, considering the fact that they were travelling nomads and that they were therefore well informed about many matters all over the country.[217]

In the treaty, the Assyrians were represented by Ilī-padâ, while the Niḫsānu tribe was represented by its chiefs/sheikhs (GAL.MEŠ [*rabû*]) (Wiggermann 2008, 561). The treaty appears to stipulate that the Suteans will not aid the enemies of Assyria (Llop-Raduà 2012a, 214; Fales 2011b, 30). Two of the six paragraphs "regulate" the Suteans' "drinking habits"—"clearly a source of interethnic tension: Suteans are not allowed to buy beer on tick, and they are not allowed to drink the beer that they bought in the pub ("at the brewer's," *pāni sirāšê*), but have to take it back to their camp."[218]

---

216. Ilī-padâ died during the reign of Enlil-kudurrī-uṣur (1187–1183 BCE) so the treaty may date from the early part of his reign or possibly from the reign of Aššur-nērārī III (1193–1188 BCE). Ilī-padâ's death may be the reason for the decline in the *dunnu* (end of level 5 being ca. 1180 BCE). See Duistermaat 2008, 95; Akkermans 2006.

217. See www.sabi-abyad.nl.

218. Wiggermann 2008, 563. Fales (2014a, 234) gives the following translation of §§5–6 of the treaty (based on Wiggermann 2010, 28): "(§5) When a Sutean goes to an (Assyrian) settlement, he may not drink his beer in the tavern (there), (but) he must take the beer, and return to (his own) camp; (only then) may he drink the beer. Beer should be sold, he may not take it for free. (§6) When a Sutean wants to drink on credit then he

J. Llop-Raduà (2012, 214) points out two highly unusual things about this treaty: (1) normally, agreements could only be sanctioned by the Assyrian king (who did not appear here),[219] (2) Assyria usually concluded treaties when in a position of superiority. The full publication hopefully will help solve the issues.

While no earlier treaty is extant, it is interesting that another text (T93-3) may imply the possibility of one, either written or oral, between the Sutû and the Assyrians (Wiggermann 2008, 561–63). T93-3 is a letter from Mudammeq-Aššur, a regional functionary in the service of the grand vizier Aššur-iddin to Mannu-kî-Adad, the steward of the *dunnu* of Tell Ṣābi Abyad (reign of Tukulti-Ninurta I). Mudammeq-Aššur is to organize a dinner for representatives of the Assyrian administration and the local Sutû pastoralists, an occasion at which the two parties could confirm their good relations and discuss current affairs. The dinner was to take place in Dunni-Aššur, an Assyrian center somewhere north of Tell Ṣābi Abyad and Saḫlala.[220]

In addition, Duistermaat (2008, 563) points out that: "In the administrative texts T98-58 and T96-34 from Ṣābi Abyad a number of persons (among them Suteans) receive bronze *kappu*-bowls, perhaps distributed at a dinner party (such as the one of T93-3) as honorary gifts."

Sutû are mentioned in other Middle Assyrian documents. A personal name *Su-ti-ú* appears in a deed about giving bread to an individual dated to the eponymy of Aššur-šallimšunu (i.e., the accession year of Tiglath-pileser I, 1114 BCE), probably from the archive of the Assur temple.[221] *Suti'u* seem to be mentioned in texts from Kār-Tukulti-Ninurta, but they are all damaged (Freydank and Fischer 2001, 26–28). In an acquisition text from Assur, a two-year old cow was bought from a Sutean (*su-ti-e*).[222]

Oil was given to the Sutû of the land of Qatni (*Su-ti-e* KUR.*Qa-at-n*[*i*? ] who brought the news about the Sutû of the land of Nešḫa[ ] (KUR. *Né-eš-ḫa*-[…]) to the king (Ninurta-apil-Ekur, 1181–1169 BCE).[223] Perhaps, the KUR.*Qa-at-ni* should be identified with the site on the Ḫābūr.

should (first) issue some sort of deposit, and one may give him the beer. The innkeeper (/brewer) may charge an interest for the beer, but no other Sutean (at random) should attempt to recover it, one may burden the interest (only) on the Sutean who has been given the beer, when he encounters him."

219. One wonders if the powers apparently exercised by the later Šamšī-ilu parallels and informs the earlier situation.

220. Saḫlālu is also mentioned in a text from Tell Šēḫ Ḥamad. See Cancik-Kirschbaum 1996, 96–97, text number 2, line 43.

221. See Freydank 1991, 122–24; MARV 6.81:9.

222. Assur 3/1, 36 (AO 20.157): 1–8 (Eponym Ittabsi-dēn-Aššur). See Jakob 2003, 171 n. 12.

223. MARV 2.22:10–13. See Jakob 2003, 102.

In another text a ewe is acquired from a Sutean who is designated *su-ti-e I-ia-ú-ra-ie* "the Yaurian Sutû."[224] A tablet from Tell al-Rimah (ancient Qatara) describes the receipt of customs duty payable on a donkey which a government agent bought from another *su-ti-e Ia-ú-ra-ie-e* "Yaurian Sutû."[225] These attestations inform the royal inscription of Adad-nērārī I where the king claimed to have defeated "the hordes of Aḫlamû (and) Yaurian Sutû" (*gu-un-nu aḫ-la-mì-i su-ti-i ia-ú-ri*).[226] Clearly, the double designation *su-ti-i ia-ú-ri* is a single entity. It would appear that the designation "Yaurian" is perhaps a tribal or clan designation,[227] although alternatively it could represent a toponymic designation referring to a place or region where the Sutû reside.[228] However, the evidence from Tell Ṣābi Abyad (cited above) may support the notion of a clanic or tribal designation.[229]

The Sutû are also mentioned in the Middle Assyrian texts from Tell Šēḫ Ḥamad. A few examples will illustrate. In one letter, an official reports to his lord that "In the land/mountains of [ ] there are no Sutû (*Su-ti-ú*)" and further "A single Sutû (1 LÚ *Su-ti-ú*) [...] is in the city of Saḫlala."[230] Interestingly, in another letter, a group of "Sutû (*Su-ti-e*) brought grain to Ḫanigalbat," which seems to indicate their role in trade.[231] In yet another letter, it states "Two Qairanian Sutû (2 *Su-ti-[ú] Qa-i-ra-na-iu-*⸢*ú*⸣) have roamed about in the desert around the city of Sab'u."[232] Texts from Tell Chuēra,[233] located in the Jezirah between the Ḫābūr and Balīḫ Rivers, mention the Sutû in connection with horses and sheep.[234] The mention of horses is particularly interesting. Are the Sutû capturing and breaking in wild horses that are being purchased? Or are the Sutû breeding horses to sell? Unfortunately, we cannot say for cer-

224. Assur 3/1, 44 (AO 21.382):1–5, esp. lines 3–4 (Eponym Usāt-Marduk). See Jakob 2003, 171 n. 10; Zadok 2012, 570.

225. TR 2059, lines 3–4. See now Postgate 2013, 267.

226. RIMA 1:132, A.0.76.1, line 23.

227. See Lipiński 2000a, 39; Szuchman 2007, 14.

228. See some of the examples listed by Fales forthcoming, 12.

229. Fales (forthcoming, 13 and n. 54) suggests that *gu-un-nu aḫ-la-mì-i su-ti-i ia-ú-ri* of Adad-nērārī I text might be understood as "the hordes of semi-nomad Yaurian Sutians," taking the term *aḫlamû* as a purely social designation.

230. Cancik-Kirschbaum 1996, 96–97, Nr. 2:41–42.

231. Ibid., 133, Nr. 8:1″.

232. Ibid., Nr. 13:19–20. For additional occurrences, see Nr. 3:18; Nr. 8:61′; Nr. 15:20; Nr. 18:23; Nr. 21:6.

233. All the texts appear to date (based on eponym dates) to the reign of Tukulti-Ninurta I. Interestingly, there is an important individual who is the addressee in a number of letters with the personal named Sutī'u (ᵐ*su-ti-e*).

234. Jakob and Janisch Jakob 2009, 48, text 9, line 4; and esp. p. 54, text 15, line 18: "the horses are from the Sutû (*su-ti-e*) and mules from the Hurrians"; and line 25–27: "The horses of the Sutû (*su-ti-e*) have been brought out with me."

tain, but the fact that some Sutû are dealing with horses would imply that at least a few were more mobile than simple pastoralists.

Recently, R. Zadok (2012, 572) has made the important observation that the Sutû were very marginal in the administration and political life of the Jezirah during the Middle Assyrian rule.[235] He notes that "none of the individuals engaged in raising and breeding of livestock (shepherds, cowherds, ass drivers, etc.) at Dūr-Katlimmu, Duara, Dūr-Adad, Naḫur and Tuttul was a Sutean, although one would expect a certain demand for them by the palatial system, as semi-nomads specializing in livestock."[236] Furthermore, he observes that "no Suteans or bearers of West Semitic names are recorded among the recipients of garments from Dūr-Katlimmu and its region, who were employed by the Assyrian state" (Zadok 2012, 572; Röllig 2002). Finally, Sutû are absent in the documentation about Duara (Röllig 2008b, 190, 192).

In the inscriptions of Aššur-bēl-kala (1073–1056 BCE), the Sutû (*su-te*$_9$-*e*.MEŠ) are mentioned in two texts in connection with the location "at the foot of Mount Lebanon," where Aššur-bēl-kala claimed to engage them (for the texts, see below). Unfortunately, the other entities listed along with the Sutû are only partially preserved.[237]

In the Babylonian texts of the same time period, the distribution of occurrences of Sutû in time and place roughly matches the distribution of the contemporary Arameans. In other words, wherever Sutû are mentioned, Arameans may generally be linked with them, but not vice versa. The two groups are apparently distinguished in an inscription of Simbar-Šiḫu (Simbar-Šipak) (1025–1008 BCE) which describes an attack of "hostile Arameans and Sutû" during the reign of Adad-apla-iddina (1068–1047).[238] But "Suteans" and "Arameans" are not always distinguishable groups in Babylonian texts.[239]

The main pastoral tribes mentioned in the Amarna letters are the Sutû.[240] In these letters, on the one hand, Sutû tribes were active in international

235. Zadok states: "The marginality of the Suteans in the administration and political life of the Jazira shows a continuity from the Mitannian into the Middle Assyrian rule of that region."

236. Zadok 2012, 572. See Tsukimoto 1992; and W. Röllig 2008a, 5–7.

237. RIMA 2:98; A.0.89.6, lines 6′–15′; RIMA 2:107; A.0.89.9, lines 3′–10′.

238. RIMB 2:71–73, B.3.1.1, line 10. While earlier scholars thought that Adad-apla-iddina was an Aramean usurper, it has been demonstrated that this is not the case. See Walker 1982, 414–15, 399–402 (lines 29–34), 416 (lines 8–11). See also Babylonian Chronicle 25, Glassner 2004, 282–90.

239. See chapter 10 on the Arameans in southern Mesopotamia.

240. EA 16:38 (LÚ.MEŠ *su-tu*$_4$-*ú*) and 40 (LÚ.MEŠ *su-ti-i*), EA 122:34 (LÚ.MEŠ KUR *su-te*), EA 123:14 ([LÚ.M]EŠ KUR *su-te*), EA 169:25 (LÚ.MEŠ ERÍN.MEŠ *sú-u-*

trade, escorting caravans and protecting them when they crossed dangerous areas.[241] On the other hand, Sutû were the very ones plundering the caravans, as is well attested in the Amarna archives (Liverani 2001, 73). Such military actions certainly took the form of irregular warfare (Vidal 2010). In addition, Sutû are seen on occasion as mercenaries in regular armies, though their precise roles are not entirely clear since they would not have the weaponry or training that the regular army had. Vidal (2010, 96–99) suggests that they served as skirmishers. Their experience in brigandage (kidnapping, assault, robbery)[242] meant that guerilla warfare was their area of expertise.

It has been suggested that the Hittites used the lexeme "Sutean" as a generic term to refer to a well-attested ethnic group, namely, the Kaška tribes from the north of Anatolia.[243] However, the Hittite usage is clearly one adapted for their particular context and is unlikely to be informative with respect to the term's original use in Mesopotamian or Levantine texts.[244]

Heimpel (2003, 25–28) has argued that the Sutean language was, in fact, Aramaic. But this seems to be going beyond what the evidence would allow. However, like the term *aḫlamû*, the term *sutû* was certainly used in later times anachronistically to refer to Arameans.

The Sutû, along with the Aḫlamû, are mentioned in a *tamītu* text from a Babylonian king (identified only as *annanna* "so-and-so") dating from the period 1100 to 900.[245] Two things are worth noting. First, they are described

*tù*) and 29 (LÚ.MEŠ *sú-u-tù*), EA 195:29 (LÚ.MEŠ *su-te-ia*), EA 246:r.8 (LÚ.MEŠ KUR *s*[*u-ti*]), EA 297:16 (LÚ.MEŠ KUR ⌜*su*⌝*-ti* 7.MEŠ), EA 318:13 (LÚ.MEŠ *su*!*-ti-i*).

241. EA 16. See Liverani 2004a; Vidal 2006.

242. Note EA 318:12: LÚ.MEŠ *ḫa-ba-ti* "plunderers, robbers" is the description given to the Suteans. Vidal, 2010, 101.

243. Van de Mieroop 2007, 54; and Vidal 2010, 95–96.

244. It is not necessary to rehearse in full the discussion of the usage of ŠUTI/SUTE by Hittitologists. The writing *ŠUTU* is likely an Akkadogram for Hittite *latti-*, "tribal troop(s), tribe?." *CHD* L, 48–49 s.v. *latti-* states: "In military contexts *latti* and its logogram denote groups of fighting men characteristic of the Kaška. The logogram through its relationship to the Sutaeans suggests that these bands were made up of nomads … It is probable that *lalli* or the logogram denoted not just troops, but also the tribe itself. This cannot be established from our limited evidence. As a kind of shorthand, however, we have used the term 'tribe' in our translations." However, the Hittites, Arzawaeans, and Kaškaeans all utilize ERÍN.MEŠ *ŠUTI*, which may indicate that the term refers to soldiers of a particular type of arms, mode of fighting, or dress; see Beal 1992, 107–8. In other words, there was something in the warfare of the Mesopotamian/Levantine Suteans that is reflected in the Hittite usage. Beal (personal communication) suggests the possible parallels with "hussars" or "zouaves." While the "zouave" is an Algerian tribe, there were "zouaves" in the US army during the civil war, who were not Algerians! I thank Richard Beal for discussing this issue with me.

245. Lambert 2007, no. 5; for a discussion of *tamītu* texts, see his introduction. I thank the late Prof. Lambert for providing a prepublication copy of this text. The Aramaic

as tent dwellers living within this king's land by the edge of the sea, implying that they were still nomads with no sedentary component. Second, the earliest use of the term *rabannātu* "sheikhs" occurs in this *tamītu* (line 6), apparently referring to the Sutean leaders. This is significant because the term is derived from the Aramaic word *rb*(') and thus may imply that this group of Sutû had Aramean affinities.

In sum, the Sutû and Aḫlamû were "steppe people." They were not exclusively mobile and pastoralist, but a majority were. Some Sutû and Aḫlamû were, in fact, Arameans; but not all Sutû and Aḫlamû were Arameans. On the one hand, the Sutû and Aḫlamû provide glimpses into the world out of which the Aramean socially constructed groups emerged; on the other hand, the lack of clarity in the terms obscures and forestalls any attempt at getting at the origins of the Arameans. While the terms Sutû and Aḫlamû overlap in meaning, they must at times be differentiated from one another. It would seem that the term Aḫlamû was a broader term than Sutû (see above). Fales (forthcoming, 16) notes that this group was not entirely kinship-based, and was portrayed in the Assyrian texts as hostile, rarely amicable. However, the Sutû were kinship-based and were mainly amicable and only sometimes hostile.

While it is possible to trace the movements of certain Aramean tribes over a period of time, such tracings do not yield an ultimate place of origin. The problem is that the Arameans (and their predecessors, the Sutû and Aḫlamû) were mobile; they migrated—and more than once. Their clans, tribes and confederations reconfigured—and more than once. So it may be, to the disappointment of scholars who are driven to try and solve problems, that the ultimate origin of the Arameans may never be answered.

## 2.6. Aram in the Biblical Texts

In addition to the ancient Near Eastern textual data, the biblical texts contain usages of the term "Aram" as well as "Aramean." However, it must be said at the outset of this discussion that a number of these uses occur in texts that are difficult and debated among biblical scholars, especially those in the Pentateuch. Moreover, because the biblical texts' interests are concerned with Israel and its God, their usefulness for historical reconstruction of the history of the Arameans is at certain points minimal.[246] However, there are instances

term *rb* occurs in the Sefire Stelae: *KAI* 222:A39–41, 223:B3 and C15–16; and in the Sūḫu Annals (see above).

246. Either because they do not provide any real data or their ideological position renders their usefulness marginal.

where they provide a major source, even the only source, for our knowledge and so must be utilized with the same due caution as the other ancient Near Eastern sources. Consequently, where this is the case, the discussions will be found in the appropriate chapters. Here, I will present some very basic data, and will also discuss the biblical texts that might be relevant to question of Aramean origins, primarily in the Pentateuch.

### 2.6.1. Basic Data

In the Hebrew Bible, the word "Aram" is used four ways. First, "Aram" is most frequently a designation of the Aramean city-state of Damascus. The gentilic form ארמי is also used most often to describe the Arameans of Damascus. From roughly 1000–732 BCE, the city of Damascus rose to become one of the most important Aramean states in the Levant, and from the biblical perspective, it was "the Aram" (Younger 2013). This usage is mostly in the books of Kings, Chronicles and Isaiah. It is erroneously translated in a number of English translations as "Syria." This has created much confusion among modern readers because of the tendency to associate this term with the modern political entity, which did not exist in any period of biblical history and which does not reflect in any way the geographic domains of any ancient polity.[247]

Second, Aram seems to be used in a few instances as a personal name, perhaps a tribal name (Zadok 1988, 97, 217). Genesis 10:22 states that Aram is a son of Shem; verse 23 that Aram's sons were Uz, Hul, Gether,[248] and Mash. Although the name Aram might not be simply a personal name, but is being used to denote the eponymous ancestor of the Arameans, other than the ascription of these supposed genealogical connections, it is impossible to understand what that tradition was.[249] In Gen 22:20–24, Bethuel was one of the sons of Nahor, the brother of Abraham. Verse 21 states that Nahor was also the father of Kemuel (קמואל), the father of Aram (אבי ארם) (hence, Aram was on the same generational level as Jacob and Laban).

Third, "Aram" is used to refer to all the Aramean kingdoms or tribes as a whole (1 Kgs 10:29 = 2 Chr 1:17; Judg 10:6). In Jer 35:11, the term is used to refer to the Aramean tribes of southern Mesopotamia that are in Nebuchadnezzar's army.

---

247. Even Aram-Damascus at its greatest extent did not control the Jezirah that is part of modern Syria.

248. See §3.3.2.1.

249. Genesis 10 is generally understood to be the work of P. See Pitard 1994a, 207–8.

Fourth, the term "Aram" can be compounded with other toponyms where the Arameans were a major people group during the Iron Age: Aram-Beth-Reḥob, Aram-Damascus, Aram-Ma'akah, Aram-Naharaim, Aram-Ṣobah, and "Paddan"-Aram (note this is the only instance where Aram is the second component). This compounding of "Aram" with other toponyms is unique to the Bible. Aram is occasionally used alone to label Aram-Naharaim (Num 23:7; Judg 3:10) and Aram-Ṣobah (2 Sam 10 = 1 Chr 19).[250] However, both of these can occur with simply the "Aram" component. Only Aram-Naharaim and Paddan-Aram occur in the pentateuchal materials. Since the other compounds listed above were political entities, they will be discussed in the appropriate chapters throughout the volume.

In the biblical texts, Aram-Naharaim is a geographical name for an area in upper Mesopotamia, specifically the great bend of the Euphrates River (Pitard 1992a; on the geographic extent, see further below). The name occurs five times in the Bible, twice in the pentateuchal sources. It was the area where the patriarchal family of Terah settled after the move from Ur. In Gen 24:10, Abraham's servant went "to Aram Naharaim, to the city of Nahor" (אֶל־אֲרַם נַהֲרַיִם אֶל־עִיר נָחוֹר). This same area seems to be designated Paddan-Aram (see below). It is also named as the homeland of Balaam, the son of Beor (Deut 23:5).[251] It was the country of Cushan-rishathaim, the first oppressor of Israel in the book of Judges (Judg 3:8). David is said to have fought with troops from this area during his war with Ammon and its Aramean allies (1 Chr 19:6; cf. Ps 60:2 [Eng. superscription]).[252] There are three instances where the Naharaim designation has been dropped with only Aram remaining (Num 23:7; Judg 3:10; and Hos 12:13).

A number of extrabiblical sources make reference to this land during the last half of the second millennium BCE, designating it with simply the second component.[253] Several Egyptian pharaohs fought with or had dealings with a state called in the Egyptian sources, *Naharin(a)*, clearly derived from the West Semitic word *nhr* (Gardiner 1947, 1:173*–80*). Attestations of this name are found in the inscriptions of Thutmose I (1493–1481), Thutmose III (1479–1425 BCE, sole reign: 1457–1425 BCE),[254] Amenhotep III, and all the way to the reign of Ramesses III (1184–1153 BCE; Helck 1971,

250. Although not aside from the presence of the full writing of the region or the entity.

251. Note that Balaam is the subject of the Aramaic inscription from Deir 'Alla.

252. Old Greek translates the pentateuchal passages with simply Μεσοποταμία; 1 Chr 19:6 and Ps 60:2 it combines this with Συρία. Judges 3:8 is unique having (twice): Χουσαρσαθωμ βασιλέως Συρίας ποταμῶν "Cushan-rishathaim, king of Syria of the rivers."

253. See O'Callaghan 1948, 131–33; J. J. Finkelstein 1962, 73–75.

254. See, for example, *COS* 2.2B:14–18, lines 8b–16a.

277; Edel 1966, 2–3). The first occurrence refers to the Hurrian kingdom of Mittani, although mainly to the area of the Euphrates bend (or elbow), without being defined more precisely. The later Egyptian occurrences demonstrate clearly that *Naharin(a)* was used as a synonym for the land of Mittani (also known as Ḫanigalbat), including land to the west of the Euphrates that was under Hurrian control. The Mittani region is also the focus in the use of the term in the Amarna Letters (fourteenth century) in the forms *na-aḫ-ri-ma* (*Naḫrima*) and *na-ri-ma* (*Nārima*).[255] The /m/ in these spellings reflects the Canaanite spelling.[256]

Lipiński (2000a, 251–52) argues that the term "Naharima" is also found in one of the hieroglyphic Luwian inscriptions of Uratami, king of Hamath (specifically HAMA 2 §4, where he is apparently reading the last word of the inscription as the word *Naharima*). He concludes that the etymology of *Naharima/Naharăyim* is not the dual of *nhr*, but rather means "riverland."[257] However, his understanding is based on Laroche's identification of the second sign of the last word as *har*, a value discarded today by scholars of hieroglyphic Luwian.[258] The correct reading is *ni-ki-ma-sa*(REGIO) (Hawkins 2000, 413), which has the wrong vowels and the wrong determinative for it to represent Semitic *naharima*.[259] As for the dual, the Masoretic Hebrew pointing of נַהֲרַיִם as a dual may reflect a late understanding of the toponym.[260] Hence, the word may have originally been a Semitic plural yielding the meaning of "riverine land," the hieroglyphic Luwian having nothing to do with this.

The toponym, *Naharin(a)*, is never prefixed with "Aram"; this only occurs in the biblical texts. However, this is also true of a number of other entities in the Hebrew Bible (e.g., Aram-Ṣobah, Aram-Beth-Reḥob, Aram-Damascus, Aram-Ma'akah). Where the term appears in connection with the patriarchs (and probably the other attestations as well), its use may be functionally anachronistic (Malamat 1973, 140), since the area was not under

255. EA 75:39: KUR *na-aḫ-<ri->ma*; EA 140:32 KUR *na-ri-ma*; EA 194:23 KUR [*n*]*a-*[*a*]*ḫ-ri-mi*; EA 288:35 KUR *na-aḫ-ri-ma*.KI; and on a docket on EA 27, it is written in Hieratic.

256. Later, in Hebrew too. See Rainey 1996, 145.

257. See Lipiński 2001, §29.54 and §67.16.

258. Hawkins (2000, 414) states: "Laroche's identification of the second sign (*ki*) as *HH*, no. 24 (LIS), and his attribution of a value *har*, and his ensuing recognition of the place-name *Naharaim* should all be discarded. The sign is certainly *ki*, as seen by Meriggi, but as a place-name *Nikima* suggests no parallels."

259. REGIO "land" is a different determinative than FLUMEN.REGIO (*hapatai-*) "river land."

260. See J. J. Finkelstein 1962, 84–86. It may reflect a learned or unlearned folk etymology (85 n. 41).

Aramean control prior to the time of Tiglath-pileser I, so far as we know. On the other hand, the tendency in the Hebrew Bible to prefix "Aram" to known political entities may indicate that the biblical scribes are glossing the geographic entity for their later readers.[261] The name *Naharin(a)/Naharaim* does not occur in first millennium extrabiblical texts. While earlier sources may have been utilized, the Hebrew Bible is undoubtedly the product of the Iron Age and geographic designations from this period should be expected to dominate.[262] Thus it is best to understand this usage as a functional anachronism common with geographic entities (see further discussion below).

Towns included in the land of Naharin(a)/Naharaim (Finkelstein 1962, 84–86) are Harran, Nahor, Pethor/Pitru, and Tunip.[263] Also a town with the

---

261. Zadok (1985b, 83) states: "It should not be forgotten that a large section of the Jezireh was designated as *Aramu* in late MA sources (this is the origin of the biblical name *'Aram Nahărayim*)."

262. Perhaps a good parallel can be seen in the use of the term "Mittani" in the Egyptian inscription of Sheshonq I (Bubastite Portal at Karnak). See Ritner 2009, 204, and 211 n. 18, where he states: "Despite frequent remarks on the anachronism of this reference to the defunct political entity of Mitanni (e.g., Breasted 1906–1907, 4:349 §710), the term may well have survived as a general geographic reference (for remote Asia), paralleling common contemporary preference for the anachronyms Ceylon, Burma, Congo, and so forth. There is no justification for dismissing his records as 'vague' or 'unhistorical,' and a narrative of the conquest—albeit fragmentary (Karnak Stela)—does exist; contra J. Wilson in Pritchard 1969 (*ANET*³), 263–64."

263. For Nahor, see Kupper 1998–2001. A town in Upper Mesopotamia located not far from the source of the Ḫābūr River (see map in Heimpel 2003, xxii), mentioned in the texts from Mari (Kupper 1998, 112:16, 14′; usually written: *Na-ḫu-ur* or *Na-ḫur*, once *Na-aḫ-ḫu-ur*). The town is mentioned in Gen 24:10 (if this is the same place in view). It is found upstream from the kingdom of Ašlakkâ and borders on the land of Yapṭurum. The earliest mention of this town is in an itinerary from the Sargonic period (Foster 1992) (= station 12 on the road to Kaniš). At the time of the Mari archives, it was never the capital of a kingdom. Zimri-Lim conquered it in his second regnal year (cf. Charpin 1988, text 118); he installed his representative there (Kupper 1998, 115:34–36) and a garrison (cf. Charpin 1988, text 348; Kupper 1998, text 70). But he attached it to Ibâl-Addu of Ašlakkâ (cf. Kupper 1998, texts 51, 62), who banished momentarily his wife Inib-šarri, daughter of Zimri-Lim, there (Jean 1950, text 113; Dossin 1967, texts 76, 79); then he assigned it to Ḫāya-Sumû of Ilān-ṣurâ (Charpin 1988, texts 305, 306; Kupper 1998, text 81). The town seems to have played a particular role because the kings of Idamara chose to meet there (Charpin 1988, texts 347, 352). Charpin (1992, 102 n. 28) has suggested the idea that the city was a kind of sanctuary for the tribal confederation (Charpin 1988, 117). It was on the road heading toward Cappadocia taken by Assyrian merchants (see Charpin 1992), and its name also appears in the archives of Kaniš (Groneberg 1980, 86). Naḫur still existed in the time of the kingdom of Mitanni, before being annexed by Assyria. It was plundered by the troops of Adad-nērārī I (VAS 19, 14: 24). Texts dating from Shalmaneser I allude to governors (*bēl pāḫete*) of Naḫur (*KAJ* nos. 109, 113) and a deportation from the city (*KAJ* nos. 113, 121). These texts are Middle Assyrian dating roughly from the Iron I period. Pethor/Pitru is likely Tell Aušariye on the Euphrates River, opposite Tel

name of Teraḥ as an element was located on the Balīḫ River, Tīl-ša-turaḫi. These indicate that the designation Naharin(a)/Naharaim covered areas on both the east and west sides of the Euphrates, as well as the Balīḫ River Valley and perhaps the western part of the Ḫābūr triangle.

Paddan-Aram is another name for the homeland of the patriarchs. This is the only instance where "Aram" is the second component in compound toponyms. It occurs eleven times (all in Genesis, primarily in the account of Jacob).[264] There are two possible etymologies: (1) Akkadian: *padānu* "track, way" (≈ Akk. *ḫarrānu*) or (2) "plain, field." The latter meaning is derived from analogy with Hos 12:13 [Eng. 12] which states "Then Jacob had to flee to the land of Aram (*śdh ʾrm*)"; hence perhaps *pdn ʾrm* means "the plain of Aram."[265] The term as used in the Bible appears to be more restrictive than (Aram)-Naharaim, referring chiefly to the area of the upper Balīḫ River around the city of Harran where the family was located.[266]

### 2.6.2. Pentateuchal Materials

At this point I will present a brief survey of the possibly relevant texts in the patriarchal narratives of the book of Genesis.[267] These narratives describe the presence of Arameans in upper Mesopotamia in the second millennium BCE. Abraham's servant went to Aram-Naharaim to find a wife for Isaac (24:10),[268] and Rebekah and her relatives are designated Arameans: "Isaac

---

Aḫmar/Til-Barsib. Tunip is located at Tell ʿAcharneh on the Orontes River. See Fortin 2001a; Fortin and Cooper 2013.

264. Gen 25:20 (Isaac married Rebekah, daughter of Bethuel the Aramean from Paddan-Aram); Gen 28:2 (Isaac told Jacob: "go to Paddan Aram to the house of your mother's father Bethuel"); Gen 28:5 ("Jacob went to Paddan Aram to Laban the son of Bethuel the Aramean the brother of Rebekah"); Gen 28:6 (Isaac had sent Jacob to Paddan-Aram); Gen 28:7 (Jacob had gone to Paddan-Aram); Gen 31:18 (Jacob took all his possessions accumulated in Paddan Aram); Gen 33:18 (Jacob came from Paddan Aram); Gen 35:9 (after Jacob returned from Paddan Aram); Gen 35:26 (these were the sons of Jacob who were born to him in Paddan Aram); Gen 46:15 (These were the sons of Leah bore to Jacob in Paddan Aram); "Paddan" without Aram in Gen 48:7 ("As I (Jacob) was returning from Paddan"). In these texts, the Old Greek has translated Paddan-Aram as Μεσοποταμία, with or without Συρία.

265. *HALOT*, 913. According to *HALOT*, *paddān* occurs only in P.

266. Because this is a different pattern than all the other compounds and because of the possible parallel in Hos 12:13, one wonders if it is not a uniquely coined designation for the patriarchal homeland. It seems that it should be treated like similar phrases such as שְׂדֵה־מוֹאָב, שְׂדֵה־אֱדוֹם, שְׂדֵה־פְלִשְׁתִּים, or שְׂדֵה־צֹעַן.

267. For a recent full interaction with the biblical passages, see Rom-Shiloni 2012.

268. Genesis 24 has been dated to the Persian period based on linguistic, literary, and ideological arguments (Rofé 1990, 27–39). But Rendsburg (2002, 23–35) challenges Rofé's reliance on the linguistic data for dating the story as late. He finds Gen 24's unique

was forty years old when he married Rebekah, the daughter of Bethuel, the Aramean of Paddan-Aram, the sister of Laban, the Aramean" (Gen 25:20). As noted above, according to the genealogy of Gen 22:20–24, Bethuel was one of the sons of Nahor, the brother of Abraham. One of Nahor's other sons was Kemuel, the father of Aram (see above). In Gen 28:5, Isaac sent Jacob "to Paddan-Aram to Laban, the son of Bethuel, the Aramean." The "Haran" account (Gen 29–31) that follows is the core of the Jacob cycle.[269] Laban is also referred to as "the Aramean" in Gen 31:20–24, and in 31:47, as a witness to the treaty established between them, Laban and Jacob name the heap of stones: Laban giving it an Aramaic name (יְגַר שָׂהֲדוּתָא)[270] and Jacob a Hebrew name (גַּלְעֵד). Moreover, this tradition concerning the patriarchal family's origins can be seen in Hosea 12:13 [Eng 12]: "Jacob fled to the land of Aram (שְׂדֵה אֲרָם), there Israel served for a wife." Today, many biblical scholars do not accept the historicity of the patriarchal narratives.[271]

From this survey of the patriarchal narratives, it is very evident that there was a tradition of connectedness between the ancestors of ancient Israel (particularly within the Jacob cycle) and ancient Arameans. This tradition of connectedness—though it is a less specific version of the same tradition—culminates in the dedication oath that the Israelites were to pronounce at the time of the offering of the firstfruits recorded in Deut 26:5: *ʾᵃrammî ʾōbēd ʾābî*, most commonly translated into English as "my father was a wandering Aramean."

These words have puzzled exegetes since ancient times. What is the subject and what is the predicate of the clause? Who is *ʾābî* "my father?" What is the meaning of *ʾᵃrammî ʾōbēd*? How is the clause connected to the clauses that follow it: "He went down to Egypt and lived there as a foreigner, few in number, and there he became a great nation, mighty, and populous?"

---

language to be an intentional Aramaic favor given to the story to validate its geographical setting in Haran (pp. 24, 31–32).

269. Traditionally understood to be a mixture of J and E, in which several traces of P are discernible. Frankena (1972, 53), following Eissfeldt (1964, 264–72), felt that "the greater part of these chapters" belongs to an older source than J, the so-called "Laienquelle," because they contain many old elements that "show familiarity of the author(s) not only with customs prevailing in Harran in the second half of the 2nd millennium," but an acquaintance with Babylonian expressions.

270. The postpositive (i.e., suffixed) definite article was a later development in Aramaic and is an indicator of the date of this form in this text.

271. From the total lack of any substantial archaeological evidence, such a conclusion is perhaps understandable. Yet, expecting evidence for a couple of families (*bēt ʾab*) in the Upper Mesopotamian and Levantine sources of either the second or the first millennium BCE is, in any case, unrealistic. The arguments become centered on the probability of setting (see Van Seters and Lipiński below), which is rarely convincing, no matter what dates are being advocated. The role of memory is another factor that is difficult to trace.

Unfortunately, the precise meaning of the sentence remains uncertain.[272] There are four possibilities in the interpretation of "my father" (*’abî*). It could refer to Jacob;[273] it could refer to Abraham;[274] it could be a collective, referring to Jacob's entire family that went with him (note the very similar passage in Num 20:15–16, which begins "our ancestors went down to Egypt"); or it could even refer to all the ancestors, Abraham and Jacob as well as his sons. Concerning the first two options, Steiner (1997, 129) observes:

> Neither of these identifications is without its problems. Abraham "went down to Egypt" (Gen 12:10) but did not become a great nation there; he spent time in Aram, but it is not clear that his birthplace, Ur of the Chaldees, was located there. Jacob lived in Aram twenty years, but Genesis seems to go out of its way to stress that he was not an Aramean (see Gen 31:20, 47).

He suggests *’abî*, as a singular noun, may refer generically to Abraham, Jacob and Jacob's sons, that is, the "ancestry, father(s)."[275] "Aramean" probably refers to the fact that the ancestors of Israel came from the region known as "Aram Naharaim" and "Paddan Aram" (Gen 24:4, 10; 25:20). Thus Steiner (1997, 130) concludes:

> All but one of the latter [Jacob's sons] were born in Aram of Aramean mothers; Aramaic was presumably their native tongue. All of them were emigrés or fugitives from Aram, and all of them went down to Egypt rather than perish from hunger.

The real crux of the passage, however, is the meaning of the term *’ōbēd*. First, it has been understood to mean "perishing."[276] For example, R. Judah Ibn Bal‘am understood the sentence to mean "a perishing Aramean was my father," which he took to refer to Jacob's wretched condition in Aram during the twenty years that he was there, citing Jer 50:6 and Ps 119:176 in support

---

272. The present consensus considers *’ābî* to be the subject and *’ᵃrammî ’ōbēd* to be a predicate noun phrase. Targum Onqelos translates ארמי אבד אבי with the interpretive לבן ארמאה בעא לאובדא ית אבא, "Laban the Aramean sought to destroy my father (i.e. Jacob)." See Steiner's study and assessment (1997). Norin has argued that Targum Onqelos's understanding reflects the original sense of the confession. See Norin 1994.

273. See, e.g., R. Judah Ibn Bal‘am (quoted by Steiner 1997, 128); Van Seters 1975, 33; Janzen 1994.

274. See, e.g., Rashbam (as quoted by Steiner 1997, 128) and Shor 1994, 366. This is argued on the basis of Gen 12:1, 20:13, Jer 50:6, and Ps 119:176.

275. Steiner, 1997, 129–30. Nelson (2002, 309) argues that words like ירד and גור, often connected to Abraham (Gen 12:10, 18:18) were connected to Jacob, and thus configure Jacob as the collective representative of all the forefathers.

276. For this meaning of *’bd*, see Prov 31:6–7: "give intoxicating drink to him who is perishing (*l’wbd*)…, let him drink and forget his poverty (*ryšw*)."

of this interpretation. Van Seters (1975, 33) states "a 'wandering Aramean' could mean no more than 'a perishing nomad' and could refer to Jacob's forced descent to Egypt because of famine." Janzen (1994, 359–75) argues that *'ōbēd* means "perishing" with the specific connotation in this context of starvation (*'ōbēd* refers to perishing from starvation in Job 4:10). He asserts that the confession focuses specifically on the fruitfulness of the land now as compared with its frequent inability to sustain life in the ancestral period. The words *'ᵃrammî 'ōbēd 'ābî* should be translated: "A starving Aramean was my father."[277]

Second, it has been understood to mean "straying," hence "wandering." S. R. Driver (1902, 289) argued that *'ōbēd*

> when applied to animals, especially sheep, suggests the idea of lost (and so in danger of perishing) by straying … and as such an idea would be applicable to Jacob, with his many wanderings, it is not improbable that it may have been felt to be associated with the word here.

Otzen (1974) explains its use "because it encompasses the entire patriarchal history and in this way emphasizes the relationship of the early Israelite tribes with the Arameans, who lived a nomadic life." Thus, it refers to the unsettled, migratory life of Jacob or of all the patriarchs, or to their expatriate status (cf. Gen 20:13 and Ps 105:13). McConville (2002, 376) notes that "wandering" is "preferable to dying or starving as the translation of *'ōbēd*, because the idea of homelessness is further developed in the verse." Lipiński (2000a, 55–59) feels that the meaning of "wandering" fits well the context of Deut 26:5. But he notes that the qualification *'ōbēd* applied to *'Arammî* does not refer to primitive nomads, wandering aimlessly. Rather, it alludes to "pastoralists who depend on domesticated livestock for a livelihood and migrate in order to find pasturage for their animals, but also establish rights over the territory within which they migrate." Hence, he prefers translating *'ᵃrammî 'ōbēd 'ābî* as "my father was a roaming Aramaean."

Third, Luckenbill (1920) compared the phrase *'ᵃrammî 'ōbēd* with the Akkadian phrase *arame ḫalqu munnabtu* and argued that it is "nothing more than a general term for 'fugitive' " (*munnabtu* is a noun derived from the Akkadian verb *abātu* B,[278] a cognate to Hebrew *'ābad*). Discussing the Akkadian evidence, Millard (1980a) clarified this possibility arguing that when Jacob left Laban, his position was analogous to a *munnabtu* "a person

277. For earlier advocates of the meaning "perishing, destitute," see Beek 1950, 199–200, 211.

278. *CAD* 1.1:45–47, s.v. *abātu* B. The other lexeme *abātu* A means "to destroy, lay waste, ruin."

seeking political asylum," "a refugee"; hence, he was a man seeking political asylum where Laban could not touch him. Thus "Jacob's action made him a political fugitive; he was an *ʾōbēd* from *ʾarām*, as many persons in cuneiform texts were described as *munnabtūtu* of particular cities or countries" (Millard 1980a, 155). In connection with the confession at the first fruits, Millard notes that the expression *ʾarammî ʾōbēd ʾābî* had a special nuance. "To the Israelite settled in his Promised Land, who came with his firstfruits to God, the contrast of his 'confession' would be all the greater. His ancestor was a political refugee and a social misfit; he, the descendant, was cultivating his own land as a citizen of an established nation" (1980a, 155). In the Genesis account of Jacob's departure from Aram with his family, the verb "flee" is used four times (Gen 31:20–22, 27).[279]

Although the subject of the nominal clause has mostly been understood as *ʾābî* and the predicate as *ʾarammî ʾōbēd*, the history of interpretation has yielded some different understandings. The Old Greek rendered: Συρίαν ἀπέβαλεν ὁ πατήρ μου, "my father has abandoned Syria/Aram";[280] while the Peshitta poses the opposite: *ʾby ʿtdbr lʾrm*, "my father was taken to Aram." In both versions the gentilic *ʾarammî* has been understood to refer to a place name, Syria/Aram, and an ideological translation produced.[281]

Whichever of these interpretations is correct (discounting the versions!), it is clear that the "Confession" means to contrast the homeless, landless beginnings of the Israelites with their present possession of a fertile land.[282] The Hebrew *ʾarammî ʾōbēd ʾābî* is alliterative, which would facilitate memorization of this phrase. At the yearly celebration of the Firstfruits, Israel's landless beginnings would be kept fresh in the nation's collective memory.

Importantly, Tigay notes that "this clause is probably very ancient, for it is unlikely that Israelite tradition would have chosen to describe Israel's ancestors as 'Arameans' once the Arameans of Damascus became aggressive toward Israel in the ninth century BCE."[283] The same consideration, Tigay

279. Levine has argued that the semantic range of Biblical Hebrew *ʾābad* encompasses the meanings of two Akkadian cognates, *abātu* A "to destroy, ruin" and *abātu* B, a stative verb connoting absence and flight. See Levine 1995, 149–57; and 2008.

280. For the variant, see Rom-Shiloni 2012, 226 n. 61.

281. As pointed out by Rom-Shiloni 2012, 226–27, later Jewish tradition analyzed the phrase in such a way that Jacob was not Aramean at all!

282. Tigay 1996, 240. The land element of the pentateuchal theme is especially emphasized in Deuteronomy. See Clines 1997.

283. Tigay 1996, 240. Pitard (1987, 86) speaking about the designation of some of the patriarchs as "Aramean" states: "Perhaps the description is not precise, but the feeling of relationship between Israel and the Aramaeans must certainly have had some basis, especially since from the time of David, the Aramaean states were viewed as enemies of Israel. It would be strange for an artificial relationship to be invented at such a time …

notes, may underlie "the fanciful [targumic] interpretation of the clause as '[Laban the] Aramean sought to destroy my father.' This interpretation … is due, perhaps, to a disbelief that the Bible would describe one of Israel's ancestors as an Aramean."

### 2.6.3. The Issue of Cultural Memory

As is well known there is considerable disagreement among biblical scholars as to how to evaluate the narratives of Genesis and Deut 26:5. The dating of the patriarchal narratives typically range from the late monarchy to the postexilic period.[284] For example, Van Seters (1975, 39–64) has argued that the nomadic lifestyle of the biblical patriarchal traditions fits better and more accurately reflects the time of the late Neo-Assyrian or even the time of the Neo-Babylonian period, that is, the seventh and sixth centuries BCE. On the other hand, Lipiński argues that the biblical patriarchal traditions in the book of Genesis reflect the time corresponding with the tenth century BCE, stating (2000a, 59–76, esp. 59): "The historical circumstances of that time form thus, as it seems, the background of the biblical episodes referring to the relations between the biblical patriarchs and the Arameans of the Balīḫ and Ḫābūr valleys."

At this point mention should be made of another important aspect that may advance the discussion, namely, the issue of cultural memory.[285] In the narratives there is a deep attachment to the region of Haran as the place of patriarchal origins, the ancestral homeland.[286] Why should this be so? Hendel (2010, 40) suggests that this question leads to the domain of mnemohistory. The interconnections between the remembered past and the historical past are the focus of this type of inquiry.

He suggests that in the case of the biblical memory of the patriarchal homeland, we may be able to trace a chain of memory and cultural tradition that long predates the biblical text. Haran (Akk. *Ḫarrānu*) was a strategically located site on the Upper Balīḫ River on important trade routes. Fleming

---

numerous tribal groups which are lumped together as the Amorites of the early second millennium appear in documents from various centuries, sometimes connected with other groups, sometimes alone. The Aramaeans could well have been some of the tribes which took part in migrations through Syria during those years. There is no reason why there could not have been some relation between the ancestors of Israel and ancestors of the Aramaean tribes who set up the states in Syria at the end of the second millennium." See also Charpin 2003a; Daniels 1990, 241–42.

284. For example, Heard 2001; de Pury 2006.

285. Hendel 2005, 2010; Fleming 1998, 2002, 2004a.

286. On this narrative complex, see esp. the studies of Fishbane 1975 and Rendsburg 1986, 63–65.

(1998, 67–68) notes that the city of Haran was in the heart of Yaminite territory and, as a prominent site with a famous temple, it functioned as a tribal center, even a place of treaty renewal within the tribal confederation. The Genesis tradition of a north Syrian origin for Abraham and his family is both central to the narrative and difficult to explain in terms of peoples and regional political relations during the lives of the Israelite states, the exiles, or early Judaism. Moreover, it preserves a memory that is very different from the familiar Aram centered at Damascus. Haran has no personal interest to Israel outside of Genesis, and the city does not have any persuasive connection to exilic or postexilic communities that would explain either the region or the town as the ultimate point of reference for Israelite ancestry (Fleming 1998, 68). Thus Hendel believes that the references to Haran as the patriarchal homeland are not late, invented memories, but preserve traces of archaic tribal memories that reach back to the Amurrite tribal culture of the early- to mid-second millennium BCE.[287]

The patriarchal narratives, of course, did not reach their present form until long after the events they describe. Consequently, the term "Aram" and the gentilic "Aramean" are anachronistic. However, there is a complexity to this. "Aramean" is used as an ethnicon and reflects an Iron Age designation of a Bronze Age descriptor. In this respect it is analogous to the usage of Aḫlamû or Sutû (see above). But this designation "Aramean" must have some antiquity (see Tigay 1996, 240; Pitard 1987, 86). Obviously, the Arameans did not come into being the year that Tiglath-pileser I used this descriptor. They certainly existed as a people for some centuries prior to this Assyrian contact. Furthermore, the contact with Tiglath-pileser was likely only one tribal group or a confederation in that area (Jebel Bišri, the Šamīya, lower Jezirah).[288] Very likely, there were many other "Aramean" tribes scattered already throughout a broad region.

Thus the use of "Aram" as a prefix to other toponyms and the use of "Aramean" as an ethnicon may be attributable to later scribal glossing of geographic names or to a proleptic usage, a functional anachronistic usage. This would be similar to using the term *China* or *Chinese* to designate the various ancient dynastic empires of that region prior to the Chin dynasty. Neither *Naharin* nor *Aram* is used in the extrabiblical texts of the seventh–sixth century to designate the specific area that is in view in the patriarchal narratives. The fact is functional anachronisms are found in many geographic descrip-

287. Hendel 2010, 42. He adds: "However, the task of mnemohistory does not end with isolating the historical background of cultural memory. We need to trace the back-and-forth, the *Wanderstrassen,* of historical and cultural changes in the subsequent reception of these cultural memories."

288. For a full discussion, see chapter 3.

tors: the usage of "Indian," "Native American," "Hispanic,"[289] "Eskimo,"[290] "the precolonial United States," and the like. All of these are utterly anachronistic, but they are highly functional in practical communication. In spite of being technically wrong, these "functional anachronisms" are very effective, because they are economical. To get these technically "right" might require many words with no assurance that there would be an intelligible communication.[291]

If the patriarchal narratives come from the Neo-Assyrian or Neo-Babylonian periods, their portrayal of a specific region "Aram" in upper Mesopotamia at a time when all independent states had been absorbed into provinces of the Assyrian, Babylonian, or Persian Empires reflects knowledge of either the older political situation, or an ethnic or geographic rather than political terminology, otherwise unknown to us. After the mainly hostile relations between the nations of Israel, Judah, and Aram-Damascus during the monarchic period, it would be truly startling to find Israel asserting that their ancestors were Arameans without any qualification, so claiming kinship with a different people, and jeopardizing their national distinctiveness. In fact, this flies in the face of the communities in Ezra and Nehemiah. Certainly, the postexilic scribes were looking to posit difference, not common origin.

If, on the other hand, the reference to Aram is understood as a functional anachronism, then it was used to describe a people from the late second millennium BCE living in upper Mesopotamia. If one accepts the Egyptian list of Amenhotep III (ca. 1390–1352 BCE) as evidence, this pushes the initial attestation for the term back almost three centuries. If, however, difference is found in the designations Aḫlamû and Sutû versus Aramean, it is not impossible that a group that eventually gains the designation "Aramean" existed for many centuries under the descriptor Aḫlamû and/or Sutû. In fact, it is very interesting that there were Sutû located in the Balīḫ in the Middle Assyrian period according to the texts from Tell Ṣābi Abyad (see above). Another interesting example is the Ḫīrānu tribe who are designated as Aḫlamû in the second millennium, yet are Aramean in the first millennium (see ch. 10). What Hendel and Fleming have suggested regarding cultural memory seems to be an important contribution to the discussion.

---

289. Hispania was a former Roman territory in what is now Spain and Portugal.

290. The term *Eskimo* (in vernacular, "eaters of raw meat") was introduced by Algonkian Indians to refer disparagingly to their neighbors.

291. Although Nuccetelli (2004) is not addressing this particular usage, her discussion is nevertheless quite helpful in sorting out the intersection of ethnic-group terms and their references.

In the end, all of this is a discussion more germane to biblical studies than to a political history of the Arameans! Even if the biblical texts preserve a correct memory of a connection of the Israelite and Aramean tribes, this does not aid significantly in understanding the question of Aramean origins.

# 3
# THE RISE OF THE ARAMEAN POLITIES IN IRON I

THE ARAMEAN ENTITIES EMERGED OVER A WIDE, GEOGRAPHICALLY DIVERSE area. The complexity of the geographic setting in which these polities sprang up means that there were many different factors involved in their development. The very designation "Arameans" masks the fact they were not a unified group, except in general terms of language; and in this, the very diversity of the Aramean tribes is reflected in the diversity of the Aramaic dialects that are encountered in the earliest Old Aramaic inscriptions. It is clear that there were numerous dynamics at work in the creation of the different Aramean polities.

In addition, recent excavations have begun to clarify the period of the Late Bronze Age to Iron Age transition, casting new light on the so-called dark age, which "was perhaps not so dark but only dusky" (Muhly 2003, 26). These excavations have provided new data, both archaeological and textual, that allow a more nuanced understanding. For example, the discovery and publication of many Middle Assyrian texts have greatly enhanced the apprehension of the history of this period and the issues surrounding the Aramean entities of the Jezirah. The same can be said for the hieroglyphic Luwian texts discovered in northern Syria. These recent excavations have also introduced new interpretive issues that must be integrated with prior knowledge.

As a result, it is apparent that a regional approach to the question of the rise of the Aramean polities is a necessity.[1] While this has been advocated previously,[2] recent discoveries have confirmed that such an approach is correct.

1. The stimulus for this approach is McClellan 1992.

2. Younger 2007a, 2014b. For a similar approach to the Arameans in southern Mesopotamia, see Arnold 2011.

We may distinguish at least four major distinct geographic spheres[3] in which the Aramean entities are encountered: a Hittite sphere (northern Syria), an Assyrian sphere (the Jezirah), a Levantine sphere (central and southern Syria), and a southern Mesopotamian sphere (Babylonia). The geographical extent of these spheres are as follows:

1. The Hittite sphere. In the south, Hamath (more precisely Restan on the Orontes); in the east, the Euphrates River basin, more or less north of the Great Bend; in the north, the Amanus Range; in the west, the coast of the Mediterranean Sea.
2. The Assyrian sphere. The boundaries correspond to those of the Jezirah, namely, the Euphrates River in the west and south and the the Tigris River in the north and east.
3. The Levantine sphere. In the north, the area south of Hamath (south of Restan); in the south, the Sea of Galilee; in the east, the Syrian desert; in the west, the Lebanon Mountains.
4. The southern Mesopotamian sphere. The boundaries correspond to the area of Babylonia. This sphere will be dealt with in chapter 10. Here only spheres 1–3 will be investigated in full (see fig. 3.1).

The Šamīya[4] (including Jebel Bišri) was another zone where Aramean entities were present. However, we do not know the names of any of these "socially constructed groups." Later it appears that Arab groups began to make an appearance here during the last part of the Iron Age.

At the time of the Late Bronze/Iron Age transition, when the Arameans first appear in written sources, there was no unified, homogenous population in any of these spheres. The populations in each were comprised of different substrates, the product of many centuries of civilization. The Hittite sphere include Amurrite and Hurrian substrates. Over the course of the last half of the second millennium, the Amurrite group dissipated. Hurrian personal names are encountered in some of the names of the rulers of the first-millennium north Syrian states (e.g., Patina, Hamath, Masuwari). It is difficult to discern, however, whether this substrate derives from the time of Mittanian dominance, or whether those who bore Hurrian personal names were part of the Hittite period of dominance—that is, possibly coming from

---

3. The western coastal Mediterranean sphere is quite different and no Aramean entities are found here. Thus the concern is with inland Syria. See McClellan (1992, 165–66) for clarification of the differences between the coastal and inland regions.

4. This is the name for the steppe on the right bank of the Euphrates. See §1.1.2.2.2.

the former territory of Kizzuwatna[5] or being "Hittite," but bearing a Hurrian name. Alongside these substrates was the Anatolian (Hittite/Luwian) population, the dominant group at the time of the Aramean groups' ascendence (more on this below). The density of these population groups appears to have varied, with certain segments being denser in the north of the sphere, and others in the south.

In the Assyrian sphere, the Amurrite and Hurrian substrates both dissipated over the course of the Middle Assyrian period. The Assyrians, of course, dominated the region, but with the death of Tukulti-Ninurta I, they progressively lost their control over western areas of the Jezirah to the Aramean groups.

In the Levantine sphere, both Amurrite and Hurrian substrates were present, along with other West Semitic groups. While the Egyptians had, in ways, controlled this region, they retained no real presence after the demise of the empire. It must be acknowledged that there is much that is still unknown about this sphere and the rise of the Aramean groups in it.

While this division into three different spheres yields numerous insights, it is important to note that it also obscures some things. For example, Matthiae has recently demonstrated that the architecture of the citadel of Luwian–Aramean Hamath (modern Ḥama)—which has posed a very significant challenge to archaeological interpretation—reflects an earlier south-central Syrian tradition that goes back to late third-millennium Ebla, rather than the north Syrian or Jezirah traditions (Matthiae 2008, 210–12). While Ḥama's tradition has links with these, Matthiae's explanation is a very real possible solution to the challenge of the citadel's interpretation. Thus, while Hamath may be included in my regional approach in the "Hittite" sphere, it may have some important connections with older Syrian traditions preserved in the Levantine sphere (central and southern Syria).

For another example of obfuscation, one could note that there is some evidence for "Hittite" or perhaps better, "Anatolian," influences on the east side of the Euphrates—not simply along the bank, which could be expected, but further east. The discovery of an Akkadian, Aramaic, and Luwian trilingual at Arslan Taş (ancient Ḫadattu), some 30 km east of Til-Barsib (Tell Aḥmar on the Euphrates) dating to around 780 BCE, demonstrates that the Luwian language still had some value in this area seventy-six years after the conquest of Til-Barsib by Shalmaneser III, thus highlighting the multilinguistic, multicultural complexity of this region.[6] In addition, Tell Ḥalaf (Guzāna), a place far to the east of the Euphrates, evinces possible Anatolian

5. Note the connection between Kizzuwatna and Tell Afis in the newly discovered correspondence at Tell Afis (Archi and Venturi 2012, esp. 32–55).

6. See §5.3.

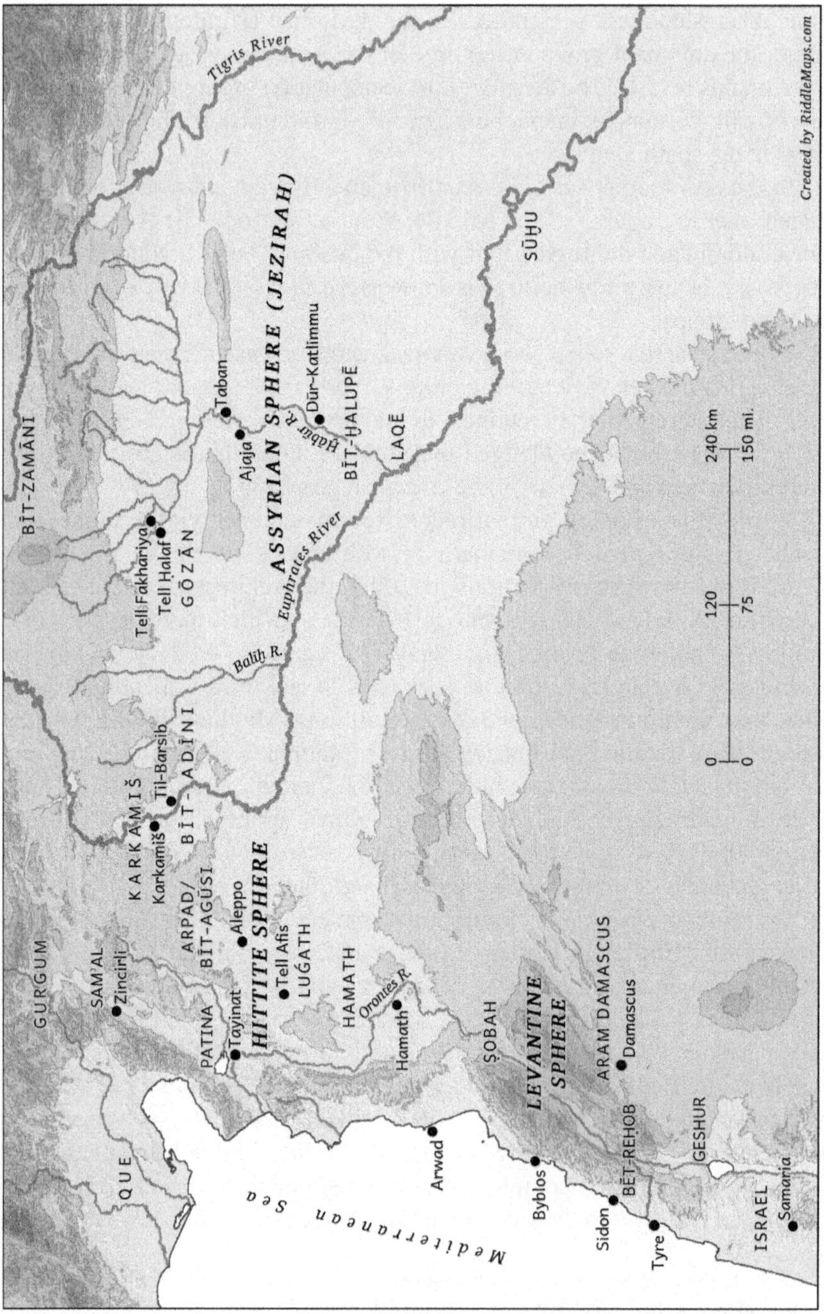


Fig. 3.1. The Hittite, Assyrian, and Levantine spheres in which Aramean entitites are encountered

influences. Finally, according to the inscriptions of TEL AHMAR 1 and 2, the polity of Masuwari had possible political interests in the Middle Euphrates at 'Ana.

In spite of these obfuscations, the separation between the Hittite, Assyrian, and Levantine spheres proves useful for conceptualizing the different geographic regions where the Aramean entities arose and allows for a more comprehensive explanation of the complex processes in their developments.

## 3.1. The Hittite Sphere

The Hittite sphere during the Iron I period (1200–900) is characterized by a significant degree of general political and cultural continuity with the previous Hittite Empire (Younger 2014b). This does not mean that there were no pressures in the region,[7] but in general it did not seem to experience the same upheavals that characterized other zones. The political continuity can be seen especially in the dynastic line in Karkamiš that survived the demise of Ḫattuša[8] and the development of the Neo-Hittite (or Hittite successor) states,[9] which, while lacking a dynastic connection to the Hittite royal house, nevertheless demonstrate a clear attempt to maintain the image of such a political connection.

Since the time of the Hittite king Suppiluliuma I (r. ca. 1344–1322), northern Syria and the Upper Euphrates had been key areas in the organization of the Late Bronze Age Hittite Empire. Karkamiš became the seat of a Hittite vice-royalty based on a lineage from Suppiluliuma himself. Recent evidence has shown that as the Hittite Empire ruled from Ḫattuša declined, the importance of Tarḫuntašša (Cilicia) and Karkamiš (northern Syria) rose to the point where, after the collapse of the Hittite Empire, both their rulers claimed the vacant title "Great King" (Hawkins 1988).

Such a privileged title had been the right of the Hittite king in Ḫattuša alone. In fact, the geographical reference of the label "Hittite" shifted from central Anatolia to northern Syria. Thus while there was a collapse and

7. For example, the evidence now seen for foreign intrusions in the 'Amuq (Tell Ta'yinat) and at Arslantepe (Malatya). See discussion below.

8. The archaeological evidence from excavations at Boğazköy (Ḫattuša) initially pointed to a violent end to the city accompanied by sacking and burning; but recently it has been argued that the traces suggest rather an emptying of the city prior to withdrawal and abandonment; Seeher 2001, 623–34. Other contemporary sites provide evidence for destruction by fire ca. 1200 BCE: Maşat, Kuşaklı, Troy VIIa, Beycesultan Level II, and Ras Shamra (Ugarit). See Hawkins 2009, 164; Genz 2013.

9. Hittite successor (Neo-Hittite) states also developed west of the Amanus Range on the southeastern plateau (Tabal) and in Cilicia (Que, Tuwana, and Hilakku).

destruction of the Hittite Empire, there was a "type" of political and cultural continuity that developed into the Neo-Hittite polities and culture. With its natural geographic connections with southeastern Anatolia, cultural continuity of the Hittite culture is manifested in the developed urban planning with its monumental architecture with portal figures, relief orthostats, and hieroglyphic Luwian inscriptions.[10] The emulation of Hittite artistic conventions and motifs is most effectively seen in the monumental architecture and sculpture, particularly the use of guardian figures like lions and sphinxes at gateways, carved orthostats lining the base of walls, and iconographic details (Aro 2003, 281–337; Winter 1983). This monumental architecture and its reliefs are part of the new foundations and refoundations that characterize the new urbanization of the region.[11]

Furthermore, the choice of the Luwian language was very important. As pointed out in chapter 1, it is likely that the hieroglyphic Luwian script functioned in the various Hittite successor states as an identity marker, linking them with the glorious past of the mighty Hittite Empire (Payne 2006, 125), even though the linear alphabetic script was a far-simpler system. All of the Hittite successor states used the hieroglyphic script until their demise in spite of its inherent disadvantages. As Giusfredi (2010, 36) rightly notes, "First Millennium Luwian definitely behaves as a living language (evolution of rhotacism, differentiated specification of sign values)."[12]

The presence of Luwian population groups in Early Iron Age northern Syria has been explained either by a migration after the breakdown of the Hittite central power (Hawkins 1995, 1297; Wartke 2005, 57), or by gradual migration into the area already during the Late Bronze Age. Klengel has proposed that the Luwians arrived in northern Syria during both periods (Klengel 2000, 25), which makes good sense.[13]

One of the factors that complicates the historical reconstructions is that the differentiation between Luwians and Hittites is not always possible. It has become clear that even the linguistic situation in Ḫattuša itself was more complex (van den Hout 2006, 234). The number of "Luwianisms" that are manifest in the Hittite language during the Late Bronze Age means that Luwian speakers coexisted in central Anatolia among the Hittite communi-

---

10. Aro 2003; Blum and Faist 2002; and Orthmann 1971, 469–71. See also Novák 2002, 2005; Akkermans and Schwartz 2003, 366–77.

11. Winter 1983, 177–97; Mazzoni 1994, 1995; Orthmann 1971, 469–71; Akkermans and Schwartz 2003, 366–77; Novák 2002, 2005. Note the suggestion of Aro (2013, 255) that Karkamiš may evince "a true re-foundation by the Suhi-Katuwa dynasty."

12. In this light, it is intriguing to speculate on the cessation of the cuneiform writing system; see the comments of Aro 2013, 255–60.

13. Aro 2010, 1–9 makes a good case for migrations both before and after the collapse of the empire.

ties (Melchert 2005). Thus Ḫattuša was "a largely bilingual Hittite-Luwian society for the 13th century BCE where Hittites politically and militarily dominated an increasingly Luwian-speaking population" (van den Hout 2006, 234). Hittite, Luwian, and Hurrian names are found among the late Hittite royal family.[14] Consequently, the Luwians and the Luwian language were integral to the Hittite Empire. With the demise of the Hittite Empire, many Luwian-speaking Hittite "citizens" who found themselves in northern Syria naturally continued their "ties" to the late empire simply by the use of Luwian and the co-option of certain imperial traditions. Aro suggests that "the introduction of the Indo-European/Anatolian custom of cremation burials to Syria could be connected to the arrival of the Luwians."[15] Moreover, even in areas of this sphere that might not seem to manifest Hittite/Luwian connections, new evidence is being uncovered. At Tell Afis, three Hittite diplomatic texts were recently found, along with material culture remains that can be linked to the Anatolian tradition. These necessitate a reconsideration of the role played by the Hittites in inner Syria even as late as the reign of Ḫattušili III in the mid-thirteenth century BCE, since the tablets appear to date to this king's reign (Archi and Venturi 2012).

Despite the evidence for continuity in northern Syria, some recent archaeological evidence would indicate that the transition from the empire to the Neo-Hittite successor states was perhaps not as smooth as envisioned. The evidence from Arslantepe in particular may be cited as indicating a transition that was marked at some places by destruction with a subsequent reconstruction (see the discussion of Malatya/Melid below). The destruction of Emar would be another example that the period was less than smooth. One could also cite the presence of "intrusive" material culture, as at Tell Ta'yinat (see discussion below). Nonetheless, that this sphere enjoyed some level of continuity is still a good general characterization.

At some point later, a shift of power from the Luwian dynasties to Aramean rulership seems to have taken place in a number of these polities, though the exact date and circumstances are not known. While a number of these Neo-Hittite states maintained their independence (e.g., Karkamiš retained the name "Ḫatti" and never became an Aramean kingdom), several Neo-Hittite territories eventually came under Aramean control. The kingdom of Hamath, which controlled the middle course of the Orontes River, may

14. Hoffner (1992, 47) states that the Hittite royal family was of an ethnically Hurrian background.

15. Aro 2010, 3. This was pointed out by Singer (2006, 440), where he makes reference to the cremation burials from Ḥama and Karkamiš. Cremation burials have been found in Tell Shiukh Fawqani. See Tenu and Bachelot 2005; Luciani 2000; Tenu 2009. Also Tel Ḥalaf (Guzāna; Niehr 2010).

serve as an example. While it may have been under the control of Taita I, it was most certainly under the dominance of Taita II (eleventh–early tenth centuries BCE; see below). It continued to be a kingdom ruled by a Neo-Hittite dynasty well into the second half of the ninth century. These rulers used non-Semitic names, and their monuments bore hieroglyphic Luwian inscriptions until the Aramean Zakkur (probably from the middle Euphrates city of ʿAna) seized power at the end of the ninth century, and his Aramaic inscription is followed by others in the same language (Dion 1995, 1283).

Another example may be seen in the cultural mutations that took place at Til-Barsib (modern Tell Aḥmar) on the upper Euphrates (just 20 km south of Karkamiš). Known as Masuwari, this small Neo-Hittite kingdom, through a complicated process, became a fortified city under Aḫuni, the leader of the nearby Aramean entity of Bīt-Adīni. Interestingly, a number of Luwian inscriptions have been discovered at Til-Barsib, but none in Aramaic dating to the pre-Assyrian period (Bunnens 1999, 613; see the detailed discussion below).

It is important to remember here that there is a complexity in dealing with the textual and archaeological sources where two "layers" are extant: the layer represented by the culture of the occupying or elite/power forces and the layer represented by the substrates. For example, in the tribal state of Sam'al, the Kulamuwa Inscription distinguishes between the *muškābîm* and the *baʿrīrīm*. This stratification has been interpreted in terms of ethnicity; and a consciousness of ethnic duality certainly existed in other states where Arameans are eventually attested.[16]

In what follows, the individual polities of this sphere will be investigated. While the Arameans are not found in some of these polities—Karkamiš for example—they have been included because they are important to their history. Karkamiš was the main impetus for the survival of the Neo-Hittite states and the center for the dissemination of Neo-Hittite culture in many respects. In short, it is impossible to understand fully what was transpiring in these entities where the Arameans arose without knowledge of the larger picture.

### 3.1.1. Karkamiš

Around 1340 BCE, the famous Hittite emperor Suppiluliuma I installed his son Piyaššili on the throne of Karkamiš under the throne name Šarri-Kušuḫ. Karkamiš controlled the system of vassal states that was set up in

16. See chapter 6 for a full discussion.

1340 Šarri-Kušuḫ (also known as Piyassili) - son of Suppiluliuma I
|
Sahurunuwa
|
1250 Ini-Tešub
|
Talmi-Tešub
|
1200 Kuzi-Tešub (the fall of Ḫattuša) *this ruler has links with future dynastic lines*

Fig. 3.2. Rulers of Karkamiš prior to the fall of the Hittite Empire

Syria by Suppiluliuma.[17] This vice-royalty grew in strength over the next five generations of kings of Karkamiš (all direct descendants of Suppiluliuma) culminating in the reign of Kuzi-Tešub (fig. 3.2; Hawkins 2009). It was during the latter's reign that Ḫattuša fell and the imperial dynasty came to an end (ca. 1180 BCE; Hawkins 2002, 147).

The city-state of Karkamiš survived as the principal representative of the Neo-Hittite states. It is perhaps important to stress the word "survived." It is most likely that Karkamiš did not go through this transition without being impacted. In recent years, scholars have discounted the testimony of the Twentieth Dynasty pharaoh[18] Ramesses III (1184–1153 BCE), in his Medinet Habu Inscription because of the obvious hyperbole that it contains:

> Year 8 (1176) under the majesty of (Ramesses III) … The foreign countries made a conspiracy in their islands. All at once the lands were removed and scattered in the fray. No land could stand before their arms, from Hatti on—Qode (Cilicia), Karkamiš, Arzawa, and Alashiya (Cyprus)—being cut off at [one time]. A camp was set up in one place in Amurru; they devastated its people and its land was like what had never existed. They came on towards Egypt although the fire was prepared before them (i.e. the Egyptian defence was ready). Their alliance was the Peleset, Tjeckker, Shakalusha, Danuna, and Washash … [19]

17. On Karkamiš, see Bryce 2012, 83–98; Weeden 2013, 6–10.

18. Strobel (2013, 521) argues that Ramesses III heavily plagiarized from Ramesses II's and Merenptah's inscriptions. He states: "We can assume with good reason that Hatti, Arzawa and Karkemish are mentioned because they are prominent enemies in the Qadesh-records of Ramses II. It is not possible to use this propagandistic formulation as real historical evidence, neither for Karkemish or Hatti nor for the contemporary states in Western Anatolia, Mira-Kuwalija or Seha-Riverland. The only historical information is given for Amurru in a combination of both inscriptions. Amurru, i.e., the rich coastal plain north of today Lebanon with the capital at Ṣumur, probably Tell Kazel, was invaded and conquered, the royal dynasty vanished and a lot of fugitives fled to the south into the territory under Egyptian control."

19. Kitchen 2008, 32–36. See also Edgerton and Wilson 1936, 49–58.

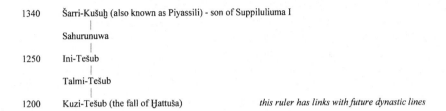

This need not be taken to mean that the city of Karkamiš itself was destroyed, but that the raiding of these lands had an impact on the region as a whole. It is very possible that Ramesses III was referring to the loss of some territory by Karkamiš as a result of such raiding. The destruction layer at Arslantepe would seem to suggest that some places were attacked, suggesting that there were consequences for the wider region. While it appears that Karkamiš itself survived with its architecture and royal house intact after the demise of Ḫattuša,[20] it would be a mistake to think that Karkamiš went through this period without any problems or challenges. Karkamiš "survived."[21]

Nevertheless, it is clear that Karkamiš's status in antiquity was recognized by its neighbors in that "Karkamiš" and "Ḫatti" are often used interchangeably in the Assyrian sources. This is likely a reflection of a claim by the kings of Karkamiš to the position and titles of the Great King of Ḫatti. With the elimination of Ḫattuša, Karkamiš was left holding the line of the Euphrates from Malatya to Emar.[22] Subsequently, and probably quite rapidly, even this rump state dissolved into the independent kingdoms of Malatya, Kummuḫ, Gurgum, Palistin/Walistin and Masuwari.

Excavations at the site of Karkamiš have produced sculpture and inscriptions dating from 1000 to 700 BCE, but nothing substantial and recognizable earlier, perhaps the result of a lack of adequate investigation.[23] Malatya's sculptures and associated inscriptions preserve a continuity of civilization not yet observed at Karkamiš.[24]

Around 1100 BCE, Tiglath-pileser I crossed the Euphrates and encountered Ini-Tešub "king of the land of Ḫatti" (which must refer to the king of Karkamiš; see fig. 3.3).[25] The king's name recalls the famous Ini-Tešub of the Hittite Empire dynasty, and reinforces the impression of dynastic continuity (Hawkins 2000, 74).

A new basalt stela of Suhi I was discovered on the southern slope of the acropolis at the beginning of the 2011 season (Dinçol, Dinçol, Hawkins, Marchetti and Peker 2012). It is now the earliest inscription from Karkamiš

20. At present, this is more of an inference rather than a product of direct evidence. For the architecture, see now Gilibert 2011.

21. See Weeden 2013, 10.

22. Singer suggested that Emar fell to the Arameans. See Singer 2000, 25; 1987, 418–19.

23. See Marchetti et al. 2012. Aro (2013, 251) suggests that the earlier Hittite administrative and cultic center was located somewhere else than where excavations have concentrated.

24. Hawkins 2009, 165. Perhaps with renewed excavation at Karkamiš, this gap will be filled. An Iron I dating for the Malatya sculptures is now accepted; see Hawkins, 2000.

25. RIMA 2:37, A.0.87.3, lines 26–28; 2:42, A.0.87.4, lines, 28–30; 2:53, A.0.87.10, lines 33–35.

itself (ca. 1000–980) and provides some important information regarding its history.[26] The name of one of the kings of Karkamiš that the stela preserves is Šapaziti. The stela also points to a certain equilibrium of power, in itself surprising, between the "Great Kings" and the "Country Lords" of Karkamiš. Finally, it mentions a "dispute with the land of Sura" (the land of Assyria) during the reign of the "Great King Ura-Tarḫunza, son of the Great King Šapaziti," which Ura-Tarḫunza was able to resolve in his favor (Hawkins, Marchesi, and Peker, 2012, 146).[27] Ura-Tarḫunza was "Great King" of Karkamiš sometime in the first half of the tenth century. After this encounter between Karkamiš and Assyria, there are no other references in the Assyrian sources to any far-western states until Aššurnaṣirpal II undertook his campaign around 870 BCE. Fortunately, some of the history of Karkamiš is preserved in hieroglyphic Luwian inscriptions. These do not supply an abundance of information concerning events, but they do allow for a tentative reconstruction of part of the rulership of the city-state (see fig. 3.3).

Kuzi-Tešub was "Great King" until some time in the first quarter of the twelfth century (ca. 1180), after which there is a lacuna in our knowledge of the rulers of Karkamiš. Now, with the new stela of Suhi I, three-generations of "Great Kings" can be traced between 1000 and 900 BCE: Šapaziti, Ura-Tarḫunza, and Tudḫaliya. These were followed by the grandsons of Ura-Tarḫunza (Hawkins 1995b). Roughly contemporary with these "Great Kings" was a four-generation dynasty of "Country Lords" (the so-called House of Suhi): Suhi I, Astuwatamanza, Suhi II, and Katuwa. The present evidence does not demonstrate how the two dynasties, one with titles "Great King, King of Karkamiš" and the other with "Ruler, Country Lord of Karkamiš," might have related to each other (Hawkins 2000, 78), but in some fashion this worked out.[28]

### 3.1.2. Malatya/Melid[29]

The first systematic excavations at the site of Malatya/Melid (modern Arslantepe) on the upper Euphrates from 1930–1968 concentrated on the

26. The text of the new stela is nearly identical to that of KARKAMIŠ A4b, except in the last two lines. See Younger, 2014b, 167, table 1. See also Weeden 2013, 10.

27. Simon's (2012) assertion that this Sura refers instead to the area of Cappadocia in central Anatolia, where the central Hittite power would have continued its existence, seems doubtful, both on the grounds of the orthography and the lack of supporting evidence.

28. For an alternative reconstruction, see Giusfredi 2010, 47–50, but without the benefit of the Suhi I Stela.

29. On Malatya/Melid, see Bryce 2012, 98–110.

Neo-Hittite levels.[30] The excavations from 1968 to 2007 concentrated on the Late Chalcolithic and Late Uruk periods (Frangipane and Palmieri 1983; Frangipane 2004). In 2008, excavations returned to the late levels and have begun to clarify some of the important issues of this period at the site.

Malatya/Melid[31] has produced a group of sculptures with associated hieroglyphic Luwian inscriptions. Hawkins has noted that, surprisingly, not only was Kuzi-Tešub the "king of the land of Karkamiš, son of Talmi-Tešub, king of the land of Karkamiš," he was also the ancestor of the dynasty of Malatya/Melid, being found in the genealogies of two kings of Malatya, where he is called "Great King, Hero of Karkamiš" (Hawkins 1988, 1995b, 2002). The title "Great King" was not borne by any of Kuzi-Tešub's predecessors at Karkamiš, and demonstrates the assumption of the Hittite title after the demise of the line of Suppiluliuma II in Ḫattuša. Hawkins has argued that the hieroglyphic Luwian inscriptions allow a reconstruction of the Malatyan royal lineage, in which two genealogies can be discerned (Hawkins 2000, 287) covering the years ca. 1180–1070 BCE (fig. 3.3).

The renewed excavations at the site have begun to add significant details and nuances to Hawkins's work.[32] Known as Malitiya/Maldiya in the Hittite texts of the Empire period, the site was a fortified center on the Euphrates frontier, facing the area of the Išuwa and Alše polities. This period at Arslantepe is characterized by a city wall and city gate (the "Imperial Gate") and the use of pottery of a "peripheral Hittite" horizon (Manuelli 2009, 2013). This period of occupation was ended by "an event of destruction important enough to leave a deep layer of burnt debris, and to require not just a repair of the old wall, but the building of a new wall and a new gate (at a higher elevation and inner location)" (Liverani 2012, 336). Liverani suggests that this destruction layer may roughly be correlated with the migration of the Mušku, "the vanguard of the Phrygian incomers" (336). Although the identification of the Mušku and Phrygians and their responsibility in the collapse of the Hittite Empire have been questioned in recent historiography,[33] Liverani argues that Assyrian inscriptions may shed light on this.

30. Delaporte 1939, 1940; Schaeffer 1948; Weidner 1952–53, 151–52; Puglisi and Meriggi 1964; Pecorella 1975. For historical and archaeological syntheses, see Hawkins 1993–97, 35–41; Frangipane 1993–97.

31. The native designation for the place is Malizi, which may be compared with the sole attested Aramaic consonantal writing *mlz* (Zakkur Inscription). The Assyrians refer to the country and city as Melid. All these designations refer to the site of Arslantepe and its surrounding plain as far as the west bank of the Euphrates. See Hawkins 2000, 284.

32. Liverani 2012.

33. See Neumann and Strobel 2003–5, 546–47.

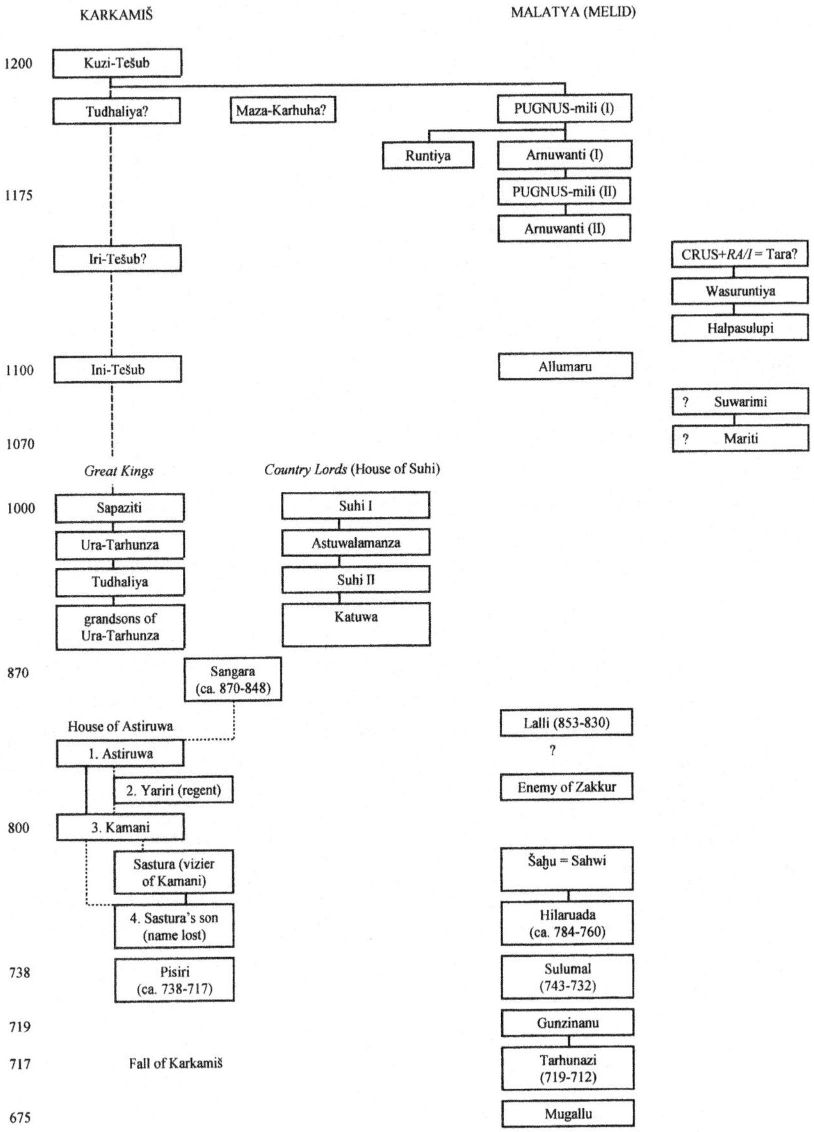


Fig. 3.3. Rulers of Karkamiš and Malatya (Melid) after the fall of Ḫattuša (Hawkins 1988)

Tiglath-pileser I (1114–1076 BCE), in celebrating his victory over 20,000 Mušku,[34] notes that they had previously occupied the lands of Alzu and Purulumzu for fifty years before moving southwards to capture the land of Katmuḫu.[35] This campaign took place in Tiglath-pileser's first year (1114 BCE), which implies that the Mušku had occupied these lands around 1170/1165 BCE (obviously "fifty years" is a round figure). In Liverani's estimation, this date coincides very closely to the traditional reconstruction of a Mušku (Phrygian) migration/invasion[36] from west to east, culminating in the destruction of the Hittite capital city around 1180 BCE, and reaching its easternmost extent (on the Upper Euphrates basin) some ten or fifteen years later (Liverani 2012, 337). Since Alzi (the Alše of the Hittite texts) was certainly located in the Elaziğ area, an invading force would likely have passed through Malatya/Melid. Liverani admits that this is hypothetical, but it fits the destruction layer and the Assyrian textual evidence.

Whether the Mušku were responsible for the destruction or not, the fact that there is a significant destruction layer dating to ca. 1180 BCE at Malatya/Melid means that the transition from the empire to Karkamišean rule was neither simple nor smooth. Some kind of raiding or warfare marked the end of the Hittite imperial period at Arslantepe.

It seems that a new city wall was built, most probably twice in the course of one century (mid-twelfth to mid-eleventh centuries BCE in the site's tentative chronology). Also some important buildings, such as the "Green Building" A1271, were founded inside the citadel. Malatya/Melid remained an important, fortified city and kingdom, with a lower town extending some 200 m (or more) outside the citadel (Liverani 2012, 337). This was the period of the dynastic connections with Karkamiš through Kuzi-Tešub as Hawkins has outlined it (see above).[37]

In 1110 BCE, Tiglath-pileser I campaigned in the area of Malatya/Melid; though he did not attack the city, he did exact tribute.[38] Later, on another campaign, he marched to "Malatya of the great land of Ḫatti" (URU.*mi-li-di-a šá*

34. Organized under five "kings," which may indicate that they were a tribal society. See Zadok 2008, 325, and his comments on the Mušku migration; Wittke 2004, 26–34.

35. RIMA 2:14, A.0.87.1, i.62–88; 2:33, A.0.87.2, lines 18–20; 2:42, A.0.87.4, lines 18–19; 2:53, A.0.87.10, lines 21–23.

36. For the Mušku and Phrygians, see Wittke 2004, 26–55, 82–106, 175–84.

37. It is important to note that the twelfth-century kings of Malatya, the grandsons of Kuzi-Tešub, Runtiya, and Arnuwanti, are attested in inscriptions found on stelae erected around the Tohma Su basin and on its upper course (Kötükale, İspekçür, Darende, Gürün), and not at Arslantepe; see Hawkins 2000, 283.

38. RIMA 2:22–23, A.0.87.1, v.33–41. As noted by Grayson and many others, the text reads "Milidia of the land of Ḫanigalbat," though this (Ḫanigalbat) must be an error for "the great land of Ḫatti."

KUR.*ḫa-at-te* GAL-*te*) and received the tribute of a man named Allumaru (*al-lu-ma-ri*).[39] Nothing is known about this person, though he may have been the ruler of Malatya at the same time that Ini-Tešub ruled in Karkamiš. Around 1070, the city was destroyed by a huge fire. Liverani (2012, 338–39) suggests that this destruction may have been the work of Aššur-bēl-kala.[40] In any case, it ended this phase of occupation at the site and perhaps with it this Malatyan dynasty, which could trace its lineage back to Kuzi-Tešub. If so, the particular phase to which this dynasty seems to belong began and ended with huge fires.

The next period, from roughly 1070–850 BCE, saw "squatters" occupying the Arslantepe mound.[41] But certainly by the time of Aššurnaṣirpal II, the city seems to have been thoroughly rebuilt and serving once again as the capital.

### 3.1.3. Palistin/Walistin/Patina/'Umq

Excavations in the late 1990s on the citadel of Aleppo uncovered the temple of the Storm God of Aleppo (Kohlmeyer 2009). The gradual process of excavation revealed a "pedestal wall" on the north side of the temple complex, which contained twenty-six basalt orthostats with reliefs.[42] An inscription was found on one of these reliefs, which portrayed the Storm God himself in his iconic eagle-chariot drawn by bulls and his supporter the Stag God. The inscription designated ALEPPO 4 simply reads: "God.Mace" (DEUS. MATTEA) (Hawkins 2011, 36–40; 2013, 496).

In 2003, the very well-preserved reliefs of the Storm God of Aleppo and a king were uncovered as a centered focal point of the east wall. The Storm God is to the left, the king to the right. Both reliefs contained inscriptions: the Storm God of Aleppo being identified by an epigraph in raised script (ALEPPO 5), and the king by an eleven-line incised inscription identifying him as Taita, Palistinean king, and recording his dedication to the temple of the Storm God of Aleppo (ALEPPO 6). It reads:

---

39. RIMA 2:43, A.0.87.4, lines 31–33 (A.0.87.3, line 28), 42–43 (A.0.87.4, lines 30 and 31).

40. See RIMA 2:97, A.0.89.5, 12′. Liverani suggests the restoration: KUR *mi-il-d*[*i-a*]. See also Frangipane and Liverani 2013, 358.

41. Liverani 2012, 339–40; Frangipane and Liverani 2013, 352, 357; Manuelli 2013, 382.

42. For the initial publication, see Kohlmeyer 2000. Eleven basalt orthostats were published in this volume. Twenty-six were discovered as of 2004. See also Gonnella, Khayyata, and Kohlmeyer 2005, 90–115.

§1 King Taita (am) I, the Hero, Palistinean king.
§2 For my lord, the Halabean Tarḫunza, I honored (his) desire (lit. "soul/image");
§3 and for me the Halabean Tarḫunza did (my) desire (lit. "soul/image").
§4 Whoever comes to this temple to celebrate the Deity:
§5 if, on the one hand, he (is) a king,
§6 let him sacrifice an ox and a sheep;
§7 if, on the other hand, he is a . . . king's son,
§8 or if he (is) a country lord,
§9 or if he (is) a river-country lord,
§10 let him also sacrifice a sheep;
§11 if, on the other hand, he (is) a lesser man,
§12 (there shall be) bread, oblation and ....[43]

In the following excavation seasons, the south entrance of the cella was cleared, revealing portal figures on its preserved west side: a fish-man and a lion protome in situ, then fragments of a sphinx protome and a lion figure facing outwards bearing between them parts of a broken inscription, ALEPPO 7 (Hawkins 2011, 48–49; 2013, 497–500). This is also an inscription of this same Taita. Unfortunately, this text is very fragmentary, though tantalizingly it mentions Karkamiš and Egypt.[44]

The excavations have revealed a number of different phases of the temple's construction (Kohlmeyer 2008, 2009). In summary, the axially aligned Middle Bronze Age temple (the period of the kingdom of Yamḫad) was destroyed by fire and rebuilt during the Late Bronze Age (Hittite period). Following the Hittite style, this temple was realigned to a bent-axis approach by the placing of the figure of the Storm God of Aleppo as the central focus of the eastern wall flanked on either side by two false windows separated by a bull-man. On stylistic grounds, Kohlmeyer (2009, 195) identified the image of the Storm God of Aleppo as belonging to the period of the Hittite Empire.[45] Hawkins has confirmed this dating based on the fact that the writing of the relief's raised script epigraph (ALEPPO 5), "Halabean Storm God," is an orthography only attested in the Empire period (Hawkins 2011,

43. My translation. See Hawkins 2011, 40–45; 2013, 496–97. For the possible translation "desire" (Luwian: COR-na) in §§2–3, see van den Hout 2002.

44. For discussion of the possible meanings and ramifications of the mention of these entities, see Weeden 2013, 17–18. Note that the text states (if the Luwian is rightly understood): "... he/they brought (an) equid(s) of the land of Egypt [to me?]." Cf. 1 Kgs 10:28–29.

45. Some of the other orthostats also date to this period.

38; 2013, 496–97). This phase of the temple was also destroyed by fire. It appears to have been restored by King Taita some time in the eleventh century BCE, at which time he inserted his own figure to face the Storm-God of Aleppo in the middle of the eastern wall, along with his dedicatory inscription ALEPPO 6. Kohlmeyer believes that Taita's reconstruction returned to the original straight-axis orientation of the cella. He dates the final reorganization of the sculptures of the "pedestal (north) wall" to ca. 900 BCE, which resulted in the figure of the Storm God in his chariot with the supporting Stag God being in the axial position.[46] A final destruction occurred before this reorganization was complete, which led to the site's abandonment. Since later textual sources mention the temple of the Storm God of Aleppo, it is likely that the temple was rebuilt somewhere nearby. However, its archaeological recovery is unlikely, since it is probably underneath the important and recently restored Ayyubid structures.

Hieroglyphic Luwian inscriptions of a king named Taita[47] were known before the discovery of this new inscription at Aleppo (MEHARDE and SHEIZAR; Hawkins 2000, 416–17). Hawkins had initially tied these together, assuming that Taita, the author of ALEPPO 6, was the same individual as the author of the MEHARDE Stela and the husband of the woman commemorated on the SHEIZAR Stela.[48] However, he has recently changed his mind and argued for a Taita I as the author of ALEPPO 6, and a Taita II as the author of the MEHARDE and SHEIZAR Stelae (Hawkins 2011, 41; 2013, 500). The main reason for this is the use of the hieroglyphic sign $VIR_2$ in the ALEPPO 6 text as a determinative rather than a word divider (as it is used in

46. Kohlmeyer 2009, 196. This relief and most of the other sculptures on the "pedestal wall" date to this latest period.

47. Hawkins states (2011, 52): "The name Taita is hardly distinctive: the nearest available comparandum is the name of *Tette* King of Nuḫašše and contemporary of Suppiluliuma I, but though his dynasty shows Hurrian connections, his own name is as unidentifiable as that of Taita." Steitler (2010) has suggested that the name Taita may be of Hurrian origin based on a comparison with the name To'î as recorded in the Hebrew Bible (2 Sam 8:9–10). To'î has been analyzed as a Hurrian name, *Tah'e*, "man," attested as a personal name at Meskene; see Hawkins 2000, 400 n. 30. However, there is a difficulty. There is a *ta* element in Taita's name that does not appear in the name To'î, and Steitler is not able to give a definitive explanation for the significance of this element, or, if it was dropped out of the name To'î, why this occurred. See Weeden 2013, 18 and below.

48. Hawkins 2009, 169–73. He writes: "If Taita's kingdom were in the Amuq Plain, his range of operations attested by his monuments would be large. Though not king of Aleppo, he controlled the city as shown by his dedication of that particular phase of its ancient and famous cult center. In this context too we should consider the great temple of 'Ain Dara, the connections of which with the Aleppo Temple are unmistakable. Even if this were not the work of Taita himself, it certainly belongs in the same tradition" (169).

the MEHARDE and SHEIZAR stelae).[49] Hawkins had dated the ALEPPO 6 inscription of Taita on palaeographic and historical grounds to the eleventh century (Hawkins 2011, 41). This corresponds with the radiocarbon dating of the site (Kohlmeyer 2008, 122). Thus Hawkins puts it this way:

> The modification of the picture demanded by the recognition of two Taitas would be: a kingdom of perhaps three generations, 11th to early tenth century BC, ruled from the Amuq by Taita I controlling Aleppo and Karkamiš(?); and by Taita II controlling (additionally?) as far south as Meharde-Sheizar. As things now stand, this looks perhaps the most probable scenario.[50]

The center of this eleventh-century entity was probably the early Iron Age levels (Amuq, Phase O) of Tell Ta'yinat (ancient Kunulu(w)a/Kinalu(y)a,[51] the later royal city of Patina/'Umq), specifically in the massive remains of Buildings XIII and XIV (Building Period 1), lying below the *ḫilāni* citadel Buildings I, VI, and IV (Building Period 2; Hawkins 2009, 172; Harrison 2013, 74).

An inscription from Tell Ta'yinat discovered in the University of Chicago excavations of the site (designated TAYINAT 1) mentions the land of Walistin. This text, however, does not appear to belong to either Taita. Instead, it mentions an individual named Halparuntiya.[52] It was originally thought that this Halparuntiya was to be identified with Qalparunda of Unqi found in the inscriptions of Shalmaneser III in the accounts for years 857 and 853 (thus the inscription was dated to the mid-ninth century BCE). However,

---

49. Hawkins 2011, 51. He writes: "Examining MEHARDE and SHEIZAR with this in mind, we note that they have advanced quite far in generalising L.386 as the word-divider in marked contrast to the ALEPPO 6 and 7 usage as the $VIR_2$ determinative. This forces us to consider whether this marks MEHARDE and SHEIZAR as significantly later than ALEPPO 6 and 7, and thus to recognise two Taitas, Taita I King of Palistin and Taita II King of Walistin. On the other hand, the shared personal name and title, as well as the epigraphic peculiarities common to the two pairs of inscriptions (see above, ALEPPO 6 and 7, Description), suggests that they can hardly be too widely separated. The degree of separation to be envisaged might best arise from Taita II being, for example, grandson of Taita I."

50. Hawkins 2011, 51. In ALEPPO 6 the name is written: $^{I}$*tá-i-tá-sa;* in MEHARDE: *ta-i-ta-sa*; and in SHEIZAR: $^{I}$*ta-i-ta-si*. In light of Hawkins proposal to distinguish Taita I from Taita II, I would suggest that the orthography of the name (the use of *ta* instead of *tá*) may be an additional factor.

51. The mention of the "Governor of Kunaliya" in the Esarhaddon Loyalty Oath found at Tell Ta'yinat has secured the site's identification; see Lauinger 2012, 91.

52. Hawkins 2000, 365–67. The ethnicon, *wa/i-lá/í-sá-ti-ni-⌜za-sa⌝*(REGIO) "Walistinean," is found in TELL TAYINAT 1, frag. 3–5; the name Halparuntiya occurs in frag. 6). Interestingly, Meriggi (1975, 225) suggested that the "Wadasatini" (earlier reading) was the Luwian designation of the Amuq Plain.

on the basis of style and orthography, it is now dated earlier (tenth to early ninth centuries). Although the ethnicon *walistiniza-* occurs, it is not clearly linked with Halparuntiya. Weeden (2013, 15), nevertheless, tentatively assigns the text to Halparuntiya I.[53]

In addition, there are now two hieroglyphic Luwian stelae recently discovered near the resort town of Arsuz, south of İskenderun and west of the Amanus Mountains. The Arsuz inscriptions are parallel text inscriptions of a Suppilulimma, "the Hero, Walistinean ruler, and son of King Manana." On the basis of palaeography and style, the two stelae appear to date to the tenth century, being comparable with the tenth-century inscriptions from Karkamiš.[54] They also make reference to the city/land of Adana, and to a campaign against the "land of Hiyawa" (ancient Que/Cilicia; Weeden 2013, 19).

In 2012, a large statue, containing an incomplete hieroglyphic Luwian inscription of a king named Suppiluliuma, was discovered in excavations at Tell Ta'yinat.[55] Based on its palaeography, the text likely dates from the ninth century, making it possible that this Suppiluliuma II is none other than the Patinean "Sapalulme" encountered by the Assyrian king Shalmaneser III. Unfortunately, the name of the polity that this Suppiluliuma II ruled is not preserved.

It seems evident that Suppiluliuma I of Walistin and his father Manana, dating to the tenth century, and Halparuntiya I, dating to the late tenth century, easily predate the earliest previously known Patinean king, Lubarna, mentioned in the inscriptions of Aššurnaṣirpal II (ca. 870).[56] Table 3.1 presents the tentative list of the rulers of Palistin/Walistin/Patina/'Umq.

### 3.1.3.1. The Name of the Kingdom

Initially Aleppo 6 was read as "Taita, King of Padasatini (*pa-ta/i*$_5$*-sà-ti-*[*ní*]*-za-sa*) (variant: Wadasatini)" (Hawkins 2005). The second syllable is written with a sign that in the past was read as *da* (L.172, *ta/i*$_5$), but should in fact be read with the value *lá/í* (Rieken and Yakubovich 2010).[57] This has led

53. See also Singer (2012, 465) who has proposed that this Halparuntiya was a ruler "who must have been one of the successors of Taita."

54. According to J. D. Hawkins, as noted by Weeden (2013, 13).

55. See Weeden 2013, 12 and photo on p. 16, fig. 4.

56. Lubarna may be a use of the Late Bronze Age Hittite title, Labarna, though the Assyrians usually use personal names, not titles. See §5.2.1.

57. The value of this sign had been in some doubt, and so the discovery of ALEPPO 6 was not the cause of its reassessment. This has now become the accepted reading for the sign.

Table 3.1. Early Rulers of Palistin/Walistin/Patina/ʻUmq. Adapted from Weeden 2013, 15, table 2.

| Date | Known from HL | Known from Assyrian Texts |
|---|---|---|
| eleventh century ca. 1025? | Taita I (ALEPPO 6–7) | |
| eleventh–tenth century ca. 1000? | — | |
| tenth century ca. 980? | Taita II (MEHARDE + SHEIZAR) | |
| tenth century ca. 960? | Manana (ARSUZ 1+2) | |
| tenth century ca. 940? | Suppiluliuma I (ARSUZ 1+2) | |
| tenth century 920? | Halparuntiya I (TELL TAYINAT 1) | |
| ca. 870, 858 | | Lubarna I (?) (RIMA 2:217, A.0.101.1, iii.71) |
| 858 | Suppiluliuma II (New Tell Taʻyinat Statue) | Sapalulme (II) (+ Lubarna I?) (RIMA 3:16, A.0.102.2, i.42, 52) |
| 858 | | Lubarna I/II (?)* (RIMA 3:25, A.0.102.3, 95) |
| 857 | | Qalparunda II / Halparuntiya II (RIMA 3) |
| 829 | | Lubarna II/III (?)* (RIMA 3:69, A.0.102.14, 148) |

Hawkins to posit the reading *palistiniza-* "Palistinean." With removal of the Luwian ethnic suffix *-iza-* (i.e., the "-ean" ending), the resultant root is *Palistin-*, yielding the toponym as *Palistin/Walistin.*[58] Apparently, the ethnicon "Walistinean" occurs in the pair of near-duplicate stelae from the region of İskenderun, on the coastal side of the Amanus Range (ARSUZ 1 and 2; see above).[59] Hawkins links this form *Palistin-* with the biblical "Philistines."[60]

In the ancient Near Eastern sources, the earliest occurrences of the term Philistine are in Egyptian documents where it is written *prst, prsṯ*.[61] Egyptian *r* can stand for *l*. The Assyrian texts attest the spellings *palaštu* (earlier) *pilištu* (later) (with gentilic forms).[62] The Hebrew Bible has *plšt* "Philistia," and *plšty* "Philistine," with the plural *plštym* "Philistines."

The Septuagint renders the Hebrew as Φυλιστιμ (in the Pentateuch and Joshua), and as Αλλόφυλοι "strangers, foreigners" (in the Prophets and Writings; Elitzur 2004, 28–32). A Greek suffix *inē* (-ινη) first appears in Herodotus's writing ἡ Συρίη ἡ Παλαιστίνη, "the Philistine Syria," referring to the former area of Philistia (Herodotus III, 91).[63] This later became the name of the Roman province, giving us "Palestine."

None of the Iron Age sources have a final *n* in the root of the name of this people who occupy the southern coastal plain of the Levant. This is a major issue in linking the *Palistin/Walistin* of north Syria with the Philis-

---

58. Hawkins 2011, 41. Beside the reading of *lá/í* (L.172), there has also been a reassessment of the usage of the sign *sà* (L.104). See Rieken 2010.

59. Hawkins 2011, 51; 2013, 499. ARSUZ 1 and 2 found at that place (near İskenderun), which supports the ʿAmuq location.

60. Hawkins 2009, 171; 2011, 52. Bryce (2012, 128–29) designates this "A Kingdom of the Philistines?"

61. *p-r-s-t* are mentioned as invaders in the Great Harris Papyrus (Grandet 1994–99; *ANET*, 260–62); in the inscriptions of Ramesses III, Medinet Habu (written: *pw-r-sꜣ-t*) (Kitchen 1983, 25, l. 5; 40, ll. 3–4; 2008, 22, 34; Simons 1937, 176, diagram XXXI, 7; *ANET*, 262–63); and in the Onomasticon of Amenope (twelfth or beginning of the eleventh century), which mentions the areas settled by the Sea Peoples in Palestine (Gardiner 1947, 1:200*, no. 270). *P-r-s-ṯ* is the only reference to "the land of Philistia" in Egyptian documents; it is written on a pillar supporting a statuette. It is an inscription of the Twenty-Second or Twenty-Sixth Dynasties. See Aḥituv 1984, 36 and 155.

62. Adad-nērārī III (810–783 BCE) and a letter of Tiglath-pileser III (745–727 BCE): KUR.*pa-la-áš-*[*tú*], KUR.*pa-la-áš-ta-a-a*, KUR.*pa-la-as-tú*. A list from the time of Tiglath-pileser III and Sargonid kings (722–669): KUR.*pi-liš-ta*, KUR.*pi-liš-ta-a-a*, KUR.*pi-liš-te*, KUR.*pi-liš-ti*, KUR.*pi-*[*liš-t*]*a-a-a*.

63. Herodotus's term, Παλαιστίνη, is a substantivized adjective with the Greek suffix *inē* (-ινη). See Zadok 2009, 669. The stem form is apparently due to popular etymology (common in ancient Greek renderings of foreign names, cf. Schmitt 2007) inspired by Greek παλαι- and παλαιστής rather than reflecting an Aramaic form as argued by Noth 1939, 137.

tines of the southern Levant. Recognizing this problem, Hawkins has most recently argued (I have compiled different quotes):

> But if our *Palistin/Walistin* is to be linked to Philistia, its *in* ending, which can hardly be connected with the Greek *inē*, must find another explanation. One possibility is that the Luwian *iza* ethnicon was formed on the base of the plural *plštym*, 'Philistines', and Luwian being a language without final *m* adapted the form to its own morphology as *plštyn*. (Hawkins 2009, 171)

> The Hebrew masculine plural -*īm* corresponds to Aramaic -*īn*, and we may perhaps envisage an intrusive group of Sea People settlers in the north Levant and their territory being designated by a form of *Palistīn*. A king composing a Luwian language dedication for the Aleppo Temple might then form an ethnicon in -*iza*- to describe himself, thus the "Palistīn-ean King." (Hawkins 2009, 171)

> As to the alternation of initial *pa* and *wa*, we could suppose that it reflects a hesitation in rendering an initial *f*, where Egyptian, Hebrew and Akkadian all opted for *p*. We may also note that if we are to think in terms of two Taitas, the form *Palistin* would be the older by a clear margin. (Hawkins, 2011, 52)

The issue of *pa-/wa-* is not a significant problem (the *w* could be indicating a fricative *f*). But is this suggestion of a double ethnicon the answer to the problem of the presence of the *n*? Singer has suggested that this is a double ethnicon, though he contended in favor of the Greek -*inē* suffix instead of a Semitic -*in* suffix: "In view of the Aegean origin of the Philistines, I think that the origin of the -*in* suffix must rather be sought in the Aegean region, and the appearance of a double ethnicon in *Palist-in-iza* should not pose a difficulty" (Singer 2012, 464). In making this assertion, though, he presupposes a link between the Philistines and the Aegean.

Granting that double ethnicons are possible,[64] caution should still be applied, since it is far from certain that this is, in fact, a double ethnicon: whether a Semitic plural -*īn* or a Greek -*inē* plus Luwian -*iza*-.[65] One must admit that this is highly unusual. Furthermore, the Iron Age evidence for the spelling of the name of the people in the coastal plain of the southern Levant lacks a /n/ *in all of the renderings from the period*. It is just as possible that there is simple similitude in the names (*plšt/plst // plstn*), and that these

64. See Singer 2012, 464 n. 56, where H. C. Melchert and N. Oettinger are cited as supporting this possibility.

65. There is absolutely no evidence before Herodotus of the Greek -*inē* suffix being applied to this root (see n. 63 above). Hence, in my opinion, it is unlikely that this is a Greek -*inē* suffix plus Luwian -*iza*-.

are different entities.[66] See further comments about the gentilic *Palistiniza-/ Walistiniza-* below.

The existence of Aegean material culture at Tell Ta'yinat is an additional factor in making the linguistic link. Hawkins feels that the Aegean-style ceramic assemblages, that is, the late Helladic IIIC pottery (Pruß 2002; Venturi 2007) discovered at Tell Ta'yinat, is evidence of the arrival of a Sea People group (specifically the Philistines) in the 'Amuq Plain (Hawkins 2009, 172). Among the finds at Ta'yinat are Aegean-type cooking jugs,[67] clay figures, and large quantities of cylindrical loom weights (Janeway 2008, 138–39; Rahmstorf 2003). The Mycenaean IIIC:1 pottery is the dominant potting tradition during the Early Iron I levels (FP 6[68] through 3 sequence) at Tell Ta'yinat (Harrison 2010, 88; Janeway 2008, 129–38). In addition, the Mycenaean IIIC:1 tradition pottery[69] has been found at eighteen other sites in the Amuq Valley (Verstraete and Wilkinson 2000, 188–89), demonstrating its spread in the area during the Iron I, Amuq Phase N (usually understood as ca. 1200–1000 BCE; Venturi 2010, 5–11).[70] In addition, there is clear evidence of an increase in site density during the period.[71] Harrison sums up the Iron I at Tell Ta'yinat:

> Somewhat unexpectedly, however, the Early Iron I levels at Ta'yinat have also revealed a material cultural signature that betrays an intrusive Aegean influence, if not direct evidence for the presence of foreign settlers. Superimposed over these distinctive remains, in turn, are the monumental structures of the First Building Period, with their Hittite stylistic features

66. This is why Hawkins (2011, 53) gives the guarded conclusion that a connection between the ethnonym "Philistines" and Palistin/Walistin is "not implausible."

67. A distinctive cooking ware has been found that closely resembles the so-called Philistine Cooking Jugs found in contemporary levels in the southern Levant. See Janeway 2008, 134–36.

68. Interestingly, a clay bulla derives from the earliest Iron I phase in Field 1 (FP 6c) which is inscribed with hieroglyphic Luwian signs (Harrison 2013, 72).

69. The earliest Philistine pottery in the southern Levant is precisely that locally manufactured Mycenaean IIICl , which suggests an origin from the Aegean via Cyprus and Cilicia. See Maeir 2005.

70. Mycenaean IIIC-type pottery is also found at Tell Afis, though in limited quantities.

71. Some scholars (e.g., Sherratt 2003, 2013) see the spread of Mycenaean-style pottery across southern Turkey and the Levant as a phenomenon of "elite imitation" and "cultural diffusion" facilitated by the emergence of a vigorous, multiethnic, and mobile mercantile class centred on Cyprus toward the end of the Late Bronze Age. They see no unidirectional migration: it was the pottery styles that moved, not the peoples associated with them. The "peoples" mentioned in the Egyptian sources are understood to be ethnic constructs inspired by the repertoire of enemies otherwise found in Egyptian royal inscriptions (Strobel 2013, 193–96). See the balanced discussion of Weeden 2013, 4–6. It seems to me that "elite imitation" is totally inadequate as an explanation.

> and rich Luwian epigraphic record, followed by the late-ninth to eighth century *bīt ḫilāni* complex of the Second Building Period.[72]

Thus the Aegean-type pottery of the Early Iron I levels gave way in the Iron II period to the Red Slipped Burnished Ware, a development that can be found at other sites in the region.[73] From this period, Harrison (2010, 91) has demonstrated that the very large Building XIV complex had associated with it a number of monumental column bases, carved orthostats, and many fragments of a hieroglyphic Luwian inscription (TELL TAYINAT 1, see above) recovered in the earlier excavations of Tell Ta'yinat. Evidence now indicates that this building was likely constructed as part of the elite residential area of the rulers of the Land of Palistin (Harrison 2013, 74). How should the archaeological material be interpreted? Harrison suggests:

> While the specific historical circumstances remain elusive, the accumulating archaeological and textual evidence point to the existence of a powerful regional kingdom, associated with the "Land of Palistin," which emerged in the aftermath of the Hittite Empire's collapse, ruled by a line of kings with Hittite names and very possibly with direct ancestral links to the royal dynasty. Intriguingly, this Early Iron Age polity also exhibits strong Aegean cultural ties, both in its material culture and now also epigraphically (sic). Moreover, it appears to have eclipsed Aleppo as the dominant regional power, shifting the locus of power west to the North Orontes Valley. Centered at Tell Ta'yinat, the cultural character and wealth of this Early Iron Age kingdom are reflected in the impressive buildings and standing monuments that once crowned the upper mound and formed its ancient citadel. (Harrison 2009, 187)

Thus for Harrison, there is a continuity between the Aegean-type settlement and the First Building Phase as well as a continuity with the former Hittite Empire. This powerful kingdom of the "Land of Palistin" was a Hittite successor state with strong Hittite royal ties that nevertheless had intriguing strong cultural ties with the Aegean (Harrison 2010, 91). Thus his understanding of the pottery sequence is that of "the gradual eclipse of Mycenaean IIIC:1 pottery, and its eventual replacement in the Late Iron I/Early Iron II by the Red Slipped Burnished Ware tradition" (Harrison 2010, 89).

---

72. Harrison 2009a, 187. In addition, a metal workshop has been uncovered in Field 4 whose dating is based on the associated pottery, most notably the presence of Late Helladic IIIC (Harrison 2013, 74).

73. Janeway 2008, 136–38; Venturi 2007, 297–300. For a full analysis of the pottery at Tell Ta'yinat, see Harrison 2013, 66–68.

Hawkins follows this interpretation of the archaeological material and concludes that in the eleventh century (i.e., sometime between 1095 and 1000 BCE) the kingdom of Palistin/Walistin was likely centered at Tell Ta'yinat. Similarities between the Aleppo temple and the temple at 'Ain Dara show that under king Taita I this kingdom included Aleppo and 'Ain Dara in its realm (Hawkins 2011, 53; Kohlmeyer 2008, 2011). Either under Taita I, or perhaps under the later Taita II, the kingdom extended as far south as the environs of Hamath, at the latest date, sometime in the early tenth century (i.e., 1000–980 BCE).[74] Such a kingdom at this date may plausibly be associated with the archaeological evidence of the intrusion of Mycenaean IIIC pottery through the 'Amuq into inland Syria (Hawkins 2011, 53).

For Singer, there were two separate distinct stages (Singer 2012, 466 and 469). The first was a rudimentary farming settlement of an intrusive population of Aegean origin that was not a Hittite successor state like Karkamiš. The second stage was a Neo-Hittite royal city with large monumental structures with hieroglyphic Luwian inscriptions that may well have been the capital of Taita, king of Palistin. Its people used "the Red Slipped Burnished Ware, totally different from the Aegean-type pottery (Late Helladic IIIC) of the earlier inhabitants." Singer concludes: "There is nothing in this typical Neo-Hittite city that would qualify it as the capital of a 'powerful Philistine kingdom,' i.e., if we understand 'Philistine' in the usual ethnic or cultural sense as one of the Sea Peoples." In his assessment, the Neo-Hittites who erected the monumental structures inherited the name or the designation of the land from the previous inhabitants, that is, Palistin. Later they shortened or distorted the toponym into Patin(a), either by the local population or by the Neo-Assyrian chroniclers (Singer 2012, 468). However, Singer's characterization of the first stage as a rudimentary farming settlement of an intrusive Aegean population is not accurate. According to Harrison,[75] the site was hardly a small farming village since it was at least 20 ha in size.

There seems to be an assumption that the Neo-Hittite state's name was based on the people connected with the Aegean pottery. But there is actually no textual evidence of the identity of these people; nor is there any evidence that they provided the name Palistin/Walistin to the Luwian entity. Why would the Neo-Hittite state that built the monumental structures in Phase I, a polity in which Luwian was the language of its inscriptions want to assume

74. Sass (2010a, 2010b) argues for lowering the date of Taita's reign to 950–900 BCE; but in this case, the arguments are largely speculative without firm evidence. Kohlmeyer (2011, 267 n. 13) rejects this attempt to date the Taita down to 900.

75. Harrison, personal communication.

the name of an intrusive earlier settlement?[76] There seems to be nothing "Philistine" or its equivalent (i.e., Aegean) in the Luwian inscriptions or the later material culture of Palistin/Walistin.[77]

In fact, it may be more likely that the gentilic *Palistiniza-*/*Walistiniza-* has an Anatolian derivation that is separate from the *plšt* of the southern Levant.[78] There may be an important analogy. In the past, some scholars (e.g., Arbeitman and Rendsburg 1981) have attempted to tie the "Danunians" (*dnn*) mentioned in the Egyptian texts, and later in the Adana Plain (Que), to the "Danites" (*dn*) of the Hebrew Bible. But in this case, there are significant disconnections—not the least of which is language![79] In the case of Palistin/Walistin, there is no real assurance of an Aegean linguistic connection.[80]

---

76. Actually there is no evidence that the ancient city (modern Tell Ta'yinat) was named Palistin/Walistin. Later, it will be called Kunulua/Kinalua, a name that might be etymologically Luwian.

77. Kohlmeyer (2011) argues the temples at 'Ain Dara and Aleppo are contemporary, the result of the activity of Taita (I) (likewise suggested by Aro 2003, 304, 313). Kohlmeyer (2011, 263) states: "As far as we can see from his temples, his (Taita's) cultic revival evidently followed traditional lines, both in his visual representation and in his use of the Luwian language for his inscriptions."

78. Kahn (2011, 5) envisions the establishment of a "Land of Palestine" already in the early twelfth century BCE in the 'Amuq and this was the *peleset* enemy fought by Ramesses III. Weeden (2013, 19 n. 93) states: "It is difficult to argue with D. Kahn ..." However, the arguments are ultimately based on the similitude of the Egyptian *plst* and the Luwian "Palistin," ignoring the problem of the *n*. Moreover, there are many interpretive assumptions made by Kahn concerning the inscriptions of Ramesses III that are problematic, especially given the nature of this pharaoh's inscriptions. In addition, at present, the earliest radiocarbon dates for the Iron Age at Tell Ta'yinat come from Field 1, Field Phase 5, yielding a calibrated date of 1115 ± 50 BCE. See Harrison 2013, 65. Kahn (2011, 3–4) makes much of the occurrence of *ḫꜣstw pwrsty* "the foreign lands of peleset" (Kitchen 1983, 102, l. 8) and especially of *tꜣ pwrsty* "the land of peleset" (Kitchen 1983, 73, l. 9), interpreting these as references to the "land of Palistin" in north Syria. However, all of Ramesses III's opponents come from a "land" (*tꜣ*): "Their alliance was (of): the Philistines (*pwrsṯ*), Sikilu (Tjekkeru), Shakalsha, Danu<na>, (and) Washash, lands (*tꜣw*) united" (Kitchen 1983, 40, ll. 3–5). In my opinion, none of these passages must be understood as clear Egyptian references to a land of Palistin in north Syria.

79. The root is *dnn*. This can be seen in the Egyptian transcription *dꜣnwnꜣ* (the earliest attestation of the people group) where it is highly doubtful that a Semitic *-īn* or a Greek *-inē* have been added. Note also the Phoenician ethnicon *dnnym* "the Danunians." It appears that with the addition of the prothetic *aleph*, the second *n* was lost, yielding *'dn* "Adana"; HL á-TANA-wa :: Danunians = Adanaweans. For the Egyptian transcription see Edel 1983, 96; Grandet 1994–99, 1:336; 2:309. Later, there was an Aramean tribe known as the Dunānu in southern Mesopotamia (see ch. 10). It would be foolhardy just because of a similarity between *dn* and *dnn* to assume connections with the Egyptian *dnn*.

80. The later evidence from the area demonstrates this. Lipiński (2000a, 388 n. 222) insists that Patina remained Neo-Hittite until its annexation by Tiglath-pileser III.

There are no personal names that suggest such a connection. Therefore, caution is necessary, since there is no reason that the archaeological evidence of Aegeans must be connected with the Luwian linguistic evidence.

### 3.1.4. Masuwari/Til-Barsib

The modern site of Tell Aḥmar (ancient Til-Barsib[81]) is located on the east bank of the Euphrates, 20 km downstream from Karkamiš. Initial excavations of the site were carried out in 1927–28 and 1929–31 by Thureau-Dangin (Thureau-Dangin and Dunand 1936). Further excavations were carried out from 1988 until the outbreak of the Syrian civil war (Bunnens 1992, 2014). Tell Aḥmar was occupied from the Late Chalcolithic period until the end of the Neo-Assyrian Empire.

Til-Barsib is an example of a Neo-Hittite dynastic seat being taken over by an Aramean polity, and then becoming an Assyrian administrative center. Excavations have uncovered three Early Iron Age levels (Strata A+S 7-6-5). Strata A+S 7-6 contained Middle Assyrian pottery, as well as a Middle Assyrian seal, and correspond to the period of Tiglath-pileser I and Aššur-bēl-kala. Stratum A+S 5 shows a complete reorganization of the area with the erection of a large building that was probably the continuation of the "Bâtiment est" of Thureau-Dangin and Dunand's "niveau araméen" (Bunnens 2014–16, 39). From this period a number of Syro-Hittite reliefs and Luwian

However, Harrison (2001a, 2001b) has argued for an Aramean takeover in the late ninth century, on the basis of archaeology. In any case, there is no Aegean linguistic evidence.

81. The name Til-Barsib is first attested in the ninth century BCE. Obviously the first component "Til" means "mound." But the origin and meaning of the remainder of the place name is still uncertain. Different proposals have been made: (1) Bunnens (1999, 610–11) has attempted to derive it from Aramaic, seeing *br* "well or son" and *syb/šyb* "old man, sheikh," hence "the mound of the well (or the son) of the sheikh." Alternatively, since there is a form *Tarbusiba*, he suggests *ṭwr* "rock," "hill" + *bu* "water" + *syb/šyb* "old man, sheikh," hence "the rock/hill of the water of the sheikh." (2) Fales (1996b, 107–8) argued that *Tarbusiba* is a corrupt form of Til-Barsip. (3) However, Fales reversed his view due to the occurrence of another writing attested at Tell Shiukh Fawqani URU.*Tur-ba-*⸢*si-ba*⸣. KI (no. 9, rev. 4), feeling that this toponym of unknown origin probably was "subjected by the Assyrians to a secondary etymologization as Til-Barsib/p." See Fales 2005a, 660 and n. 221. (4) Saggs (2001, 184) sees Tarbusiba as the native (Aramaic) name (*trbšyb*) and Til-Barsip as the Assyrian version (a folk etymology). (5) Bagg (2007, 255) has pointed out, however, that it is conspicuous that Til-Barsip is attested from Shalmaneser III, whereas Tarbusiba is only attested from the time of Sargon. (6) Finally, according to Zadok 1995, 278, Til-Barsip would be a non-Semitic name with Barsip as potentially an older place name. See also Lipiński 2000a, 65 n. 16. Perhaps, Barsib is the original and Barsip the Neo-Assyrian pronunciation. Compare Ṣobah and Ṣupite with the *b/p* interchange. See now Fales 2014–16b, 35.

inscriptions have been discovered, although not in their original contexts (including the Tell Aḥmar/Qubbah Stela found in the Euphrates River; Bunnens 2006).

In the Neo-Hittite period, the site was known by the Luwian name Masuwari.[82] While Luwian inscriptions have been discovered at Tell Aḥmar and its vicinity, none in Aramaic dating to the pre-Assyrian period have been found (Bunnens 1999, 613). The evidence from these Luwian monuments establishes the existence of a four-generation Hittite dynasty, which ruled for about a century (ca. 975–875 BCE)[83] during the period just before the Aramean occupation of the site (whether by Aḫuni or a predecessor).

Two great inscribed stelae (TELL AHMAR 1 and 2) were found at the site outside of any significant archaeological contexts. TELL AHMAR 1 (Hawkins 2000, 227–30, 239–43), inscribed by Ariyahina's son (own name lost), contains an interesting dynastic narrative tracing the political power from his great-grandfather Hapatila to the succession of his father Ariyahina as a minor, and his displacement by a kinsman(?), who was succeeded by his own son Hamiyata (Hawkins 2000, 225). The latter restored Ariyahina's son to a position of power, but Hamiyata's son, on his own accession, reversed this friendly policy. The text breaks off with the seizure of power by the author, Ariyahina's son, himself, who thus restored the kingship to his own branch of the family (Hawkins 2000, 226). The narrative thus describes the alternation of power between two apparently related families or two sides of the same family:

82. Hawkins (1983) identified the name with the site. The ethnicon form is written with the URBS determinative. Hawkins (2000, 226) has suggested that the name of the site may be reflected in the Hittite toponym Mazuwati (Masuwari being the rhotacized form, i.e., a shift from *t* > *r*, a tendency of hieroglyphic Luwian). This place appears as one of the possessions of Suppiluliuma I's son Piyaššili (alias Šarri-Kušuḫ) in the land of Aštata in the treaty with the Mittanian king Šattiwaza. The city of Mazuwati appears before the city of Šurun (probably modern Širin on the Euphrates). See Beckman 1996, 38–44, esp. 41. However, it is doubtful that the toponym is reflective of Semitic *mṣr*, as suggested by Makinson (2002–5). This would require a shift from Semitic /r/ to Hittite /t/, a most unlikely shift. Moreover, Semitic /ṣ/ appears to be transcribed in Luwian with /z/ (Younger 2014a, 165–67). Makinson conflates many references without concern for the contexts, and pays no attention to the fact that the Hittite toponym in this treaty predates the Assyrian conquest of this area, so it is impossible that the Middle Assyrian scribes could give the site the name Muṣru and then the Hittites bring the name into Hittite as Mazuwati.

83. Giusfredi (2010, 51) proposes a higher date "more or less contemporary to the dynasty of the *tarwanis*'s in Karkemiš, if not even a little earlier."

| **Family Side 1** | **Family Side 2** |
|---|---|
| Hapatila (Ruler 1) | |
| (Hapatila's son) | |
| Ariyahina (Ruler 2) | Hamiyata's father (Ruler 3) |
| | Hamiyata (Ruler 4) (late tenth/early ninth centuries) |
| Ariyahina's son (Ruler 6)[84] | Hamiyata's son (Ruler 5)[85] |

These six kings extend over four generations, and two, Ariyahina and Hamiyata's son, seem to have reigned only briefly.

Based on these inscriptions, the kingdom of Masuwari seems to have been rather extensive for at least a short time (Bunnens 1999, 613). According to Ariyahina's son's inscription (Hawkins 2000, 239–43), in the days of his great-grandfather, Hapatila, the borders of the kingdom extended "in the west and the east." In fact, his great-grandfather died "in the country of Ana" (*á-na*[REGIO]-*pa-wa/i-sa*) (Hawkins 2000, 240). This Ana is probably to be identified with 'Ana(t) on the middle Euphrates.[86] However, Fales (2014b, 36) has suggested that it might be better to understand this as the designation Ḫana, implying the more northernly area around the confluence of the Ḫābūr and the Euphrates. In any case, it seems that sometime in the late tenth century (925 BCE) a king of Masuwari died in 'Ana(t)/Ḫana perhaps in battle (Hawkins 2000, 240). Around 900 BCE, Hamiyata claims that he settled the "Anaitean things" (*á-na-i-tá*[REGIO]-*wa/i-na-'*), which may mean that he established the districts of 'Ana(t)/Ḫana.[87] According to Bunnens, the extent of Masuwari roughly corresponded to the area associated with the Aramean tribal state of Bīt-Adīni in Aššurnaṣirpal II's inscriptions (Bunnens 1999, 613). However, this is based solely on these two texts and the assumption that the two entities are one and the same.

Masuwari's status as a powerful state in the late tenth and early ninth centuries, however briefly, raises two questions. First, what was its relationship with Karkamiš, especially in light of the short distance between the two cities? Second, what was its relationship with the Aramean entity of Bīt-Adīni, since the Assyrians, in all known inscriptions, identify the polity as Bīt-Adīni and the city as Til-Barsib, not Masuwari?

84. One must also consider here the stela of ALEPPO 2 in which the author Arpas describes Hamiyata as "his lord and brother." Hawkins (2000, 226) comments: "that Arpas's openly expressed royal ambitions must have had their place in the tangled story outlined by Ariyahina's son on TELL AHMAR 1."

85. Hawkins 2000, 226.

86. Hawkins 2000, 242, note to §10. See Ismail, Roaf, and Black 1983.

87. Hawkins 2000, 227–30, esp. 228 (TELL AHMAR 2 §10). See also p. 229, note to §10.

The first question is very difficult to analyze, since there is no real evidence. But it seems likely that early on, from the time of the fall of the Hittite Empire and perhaps throughout the twelfth century, Masuwari was under the control of Karkamiš. Perhaps, like Malatya, there was some kind of connection between the ruling families. There might have been some sort of political agreement or integration between the two powers. But like the other Neo-Hittite states, Masuwari must have become independent of Karkamiš.

Tiglath-pileser I (ca. 1100 BCE) had campaigned in the region, exacting tribute from Karkamiš and "establishing"[88] the forts at Pitru (Tell Aušariye)[89] and Mutkīnu (across the river and right beside Til-Barsib, respectively).[90] This is mentioned in a text of Shalmaneser III (r. 858–824 BCE) dated to 856 BCE:[91]

> At that time, the city of (Ana)-Aššur-utēr-aṣbat, which the people of the land of Ḫatti call Pitru (and) which is on the River Sagu[ra by the opposite bank] of the Euphrates, and the city of Mutkīnu, which is on this bank of the Euphrates, which Tiglath-pileser (I), my ancestor, a prince who preceded me, had established (*ú-šá-ʳaṣ-bit-ú-niʾ*)—at the time of Aššur-rabi (II) (1012–972 BCE), king of Assyria, the land of Aram[92] had taken away by force—I restored these cites. I settled Assyrians in their midst.

The facts seem quite confusing. Perhaps Tiglath-pileser I's actions in the region precipitated Masuwari's break with Karkamiš. Since Middle Assyrian

88. The Kurkh Monolith's verb describes Tiglath-pileser I's establishing these cities, not necessarily capturing them (RIMA 3:19, A.0.102.2, ii.37: *ú-šá-ʳaṣ-bit-ú-niʾ*; and A.0.102.6, line 61: DAB-*šú-ni*).

89. Eidem and Pütt 2001. The Tell Aušariye excavation website states: "Aushariye is thus located precisely where ancient Pitru should be, and since there are no other similar sites nearby, it is a reasonable assumption that Aushariye hides the ruins of ancient Pitru. The excavations have not yet furnished any proof of this theory, but it is supported by the find of a stela with an Assyrian inscription, authored by exactly Shalmaneser III" (http://www.aushariye.hum.ku.dk/). Two fragments of this stela were discovered in 1999. The larger fragment (A) preserves portions of an inscription of Shalmaneser III, very similar the Assur Clay Tablets (RIMA 3:32–41, A.0.102.6). The smaller fragment (B) is a theoretical join to (A). Radner believes that this stela discovery makes the identification of the site almost certain. See Radner 2003–5b, 586; and Bagg 2007, 191.

90. This latter event is described in Shalmaneser III's Kurkh Monolith (RIMA 3:19, A.0.102.2, ii.35b–38) (see ch. 2 for the text). For a discussion of whether Aššur-dān II's inscriptions refer to this event, see below.

91. The Kurkh Monolith, RIMA 3:19; A.0.102.2, ii.35b–38.

92. Grayson (RIMA 3:19, A.0.102.2, ii.38) reads: MAN KUR *a-ru-mu* and translates, "the king of the Arameans." However, the sign MAN does not occur here, confirmed by separate collations by Yamada (2000a, 127) and Fuchs (1998b, col. 192). Personal collation: April 17, 2005.

pottery has been found at Tell Aḥmar, this indicates beyond doubt a period of Assyrian occupation. However, as discussed above, by the first half of the tenth century, it seems that Masuwari had become an independent and significant Neo-Hittite state. Yet, the Arameans captured the forts of Pitru and Mutkīnu during the reign of Aššur-rabi II (1012–972 BCE), which would appear to have occurred just before Masuwari's rise to power, if the round dates circa 975–875 BCE (given above) are roughly accurate. Certainly Masuwari was independent of Karkamiš by this point.

This leads to a discussion of the second question, namely, what was the relationship between Masuwari and the Aramean entity of Bīt-Adīni? The inscriptional evidence from Masuwari/Tell Aḥmar is Luwian, both in language and culture. In contrast, the names of the polity Bīt-Adīni and its ruler, Aḫuni, as well as the ethnicon *mār Adīni*, evidently point to an Aramean tribal confederation. The problem can be summed up thus: There is an apparent conflict in the data. Til-Barsib was conquered by Shalmaneser III from Aḫuni, the Aramean leader of Bīt-Adīni in 856 BCE; but most, if not all, of the excavated remains, which are assumed to be earlier than the Assyrian conquest, are Hittite in style. Nothing clearly Aramean has been discovered that can be assigned to this period. Different reconstructions have been proposed aiming at a reconciliation of the data.

(1) One view posits that Til-Barsib had been Hittite until its conquest by the Arameans at the beginning of the first millennium BCE (Thureau-Dangin 1936, 134).

(2) Another view has understood the data to indicate that the Luwian state of Masuwari was separate from the Aramean tribal entity Bīt-Adīni, and that only a short time before the Assyrian conquest, Til-Barsib/Masuwari came under the control of Aḫuni of Bīt-Adīni.[93]

(3) A third opinion is that Til-Barsib had been predominantly Aramean since the very beginning of the first millennium, but that, in the second half of the tenth or first half of the ninth century, a Hittite dynasty established its dominion over the city imposing its culture on the local Arameans to such an extent that Aḫuni had reliefs carved in the Hittite style.[94]

(4) It has been argued that Til-Barsib/Masuwari was a Neo-Hittite kingdom that was a vassal state of Aḫuni, the sheikh of the tribe of Adīni, who

93. Ikeda 1984, 34; Hawkins 1980, 156; 1982, 375; Yamada 2000a, 140–41; Fales 2011a.

94. Ussishkin 1971, 437. His argument was primarily based on the analysis of the artistic style of the Tell Aḥmar Luwian materials. See also Hawkins 1980; Orthmann 1971, 46–48; Genge 1979, 52–55 and 93–95.

controlled a vast area in northern Syria without being associated with a specific urban settlement.[95]

(5) Another opinion proposes that a lineage of Aramean tribal leaders (Hamiyata's father, Hamiyata,[96] and Hamiyata's son = Aḫuni[97]) were in the service of the Neo-Hittite dynasty as "mayors of the palace." These Arameans usurped "power in the city after the violent death of Hapatila" (Lipiński 2000a, 183–87).

(6) Bunnens has now proposed an alternative reconstruction. He identifies all three of the preserved personal names of the kings of Masuwari mentioned in the inscriptions from the city as being Semitic—possibly Aramaic—personal names written in hieroglyphic Luwian (Bunnens 2009, 75). He understands the name *Hamiyata* to be a Luwian rendering of a Semitic name such as *ʿammi-yadaʿ*, "my-(divine)-kinsman-knows-(me)" or *ʿammi-Ad(d)aʾ*, "(H)adad-is-my-(divine)-kinsman."[98] While *Hapatila* (the name of the earliest-known ruler) is usually understood as a Hurrian name, Bunnens posits a Semitic interpretation, *ʿAbd-Ila*, "servant-of-God/El." *Ariyahina* is interpreted as the combination of *ʾAri-* (like the first component in the Hebrew name *ʾAri-ʾEl*) with a verbal form of *ḥnn*. Such names, Bunnens (p. 80) suggests, could have been born by Arameans.

His reconstruction is highly dependent on these identifications. As a result, Bunnens envisions the two families of six kings as listed above as two Semitic speaking families, possibly Aramean, competing for the rule of the city. He puts it this way:

> If the interpretation of the personal names given above is correct, the conflict would have been between two Semitic speaking, possibly Aramaean, groups, although it cannot be ruled out that the two groups, or at least one of them, belonged to the traditional Semitic stock of the population as it is

95. Bunnens 1995, 19–20 and 25–26. See earlier, Bunnens 1989, 4; 1990, 3–4.

96. Lipiński (2000a, 185) sees this as "a Luwianized form of Aramaic *ʿAmmiya*, to which a suffix *-tta-s* was added."

97. Lipiński (2000a, 184) states: "The conflicting aspects of the evidence concerning Til-Barsib may be reconciled if Aḫūni, the ruler of Bēt-ʿAdīni according to the Assyrian sources, is none else but Hamiyatas' son who prevented the legitimate heir to the throne from exercising real power at Til-Barsib after the death of Hamiyatas. The Neo-Hittite prince recovered an apparent authority, at least for a short period, when Shalmaneser III forced Aḫūni to abandon Til-Barsib in 856 B.C. Aḫūni was captured in 855 on Mount Šittamrat and deported to Ashur with his gods, his troops, and his chariots. His final fate is not reported in the inscriptions of Shalmaneser III and this may imply indeed that he was then given up to Ariyahinas' son who had him decapitated at Til-Barsib, in 855 or in 854 B.C." There is no evidence to support this highly imaginative speculation. Fales (2014b, 37) calls it "far-fetched."

98. See the earlier suggestion of Dalley 2000, 80.

> known from Late Bronze Age epigraphic evidence. Anyhow, the usurpers, Hamiyata and his father, might have been Aramaeans and might thus illustrate an Aramaean takeover at Tell Ahmar (Bunnens 2009, 75–76).

However, because the Assyrian inscriptions of Aššurnaṣirpal II and Shalmaneser III only mention Aḫuni of Bīt-Adīni in connection with Til-Barsib, Bunnens suggests that the city was only Aḫuni's stronghold, and that his capital city was located elsewhere, possibly Šītamrat. He hypothesizes that Hamiyata ruled at Masuwari/Tell Aḥmar at the same time that Aḫuni was the leader of Bīt-Adīni; in fact, Hamiyata was probably a member of the same tribe. The coup perpetrated by Hamiyata's father might be understood either as resulting from a rivalry between branches of the tribe of Adīni or as an Aramean takeover of a city ruled by monarchs of another origin. Luwians as an ethnic element are totally absent in Bunnens's schema (p. 76). The problem of why these Arameans were using Syro-Hittite artistic style and the Luwian language is explained by Bunnens as simply a choice due to the close proximity to Karkamiš. In his words, "the new (Aramean) rulers of Tell Ahmar were naturally led to use the same language for their own inscriptions and the same style for their stelae and wall reliefs" (2009, 77).

As one can see from the foregoing, the problem is not solved. I will attempt to give a brief assessment of the reconstructions. Both views (1) and (3) face the problem of the extensive hieroglyphic Luwian inscriptions dating ca. 975–875 BCE. A further problem for (3) is the total absence of any evidence from the archaeology of the site that it was Aramean prior to the Neo-Hittite dynasty.

A difficulty for (2) is the lack of evidence that Aḫuni of Bīt-Adīni actually took control of Til-Barsib/Masuwari; the Assyrian texts speak only of his control of the city. On the other hand, nothing contradicts this position. Another potential difficulty for (2), however, is the possibility that an Aramean personal name(s) is found in the hieroglyphic Luwian texts. I will address this further below.

In the case of (4), there is, as Lipiński (2000a, 186–87) noted, no concrete evidence of such a vassal relationship between the Neo-Hittite city-state and Aramean Bīt-Adīni. Nonetheless in one sense this view could be completely compatible with (2).

Views (5) and (6) are very speculative. Would an Aramean leader of a powerful tribe like Bīt-Adīni be a "mayor of the palace" (i.e., a subordinate) of the king of a Luwian city-state? Was Aḫuni really the son of Hamiyata? This is not very likely,[99] but because the names of Hamiyata's father and son

99. Giusfredi (2010, 51 n. 74) states: "I am not entirely convinced such a solution

are unknown, it can be speculated. It is highly dependent on identifying the name Hamiyata as an Aramaic personal name.

Certainly, there is real doubt that *all* of these personal names in the hieroglyphic Luwian inscriptions are Semitic. Significantly, *Hapatila* (the earliest-known ruler) is very likely a Hurrian name. It is very doubtful that *Ariyahina* is a Semitic name. It is possible that *Hamiyata* is Semitic, though a far better etymology would be the actually attested Aramaic personal name עמיתע *ʿAmmī-yaṯaʿ* "the (divine paternal) uncle has saved."[100] But caution is still very much required; as it could also be analyzed as non-Semitic.[101]

Bunnens's speculation that there were two Semitic families competing for power, even more specifically two branches of the same Aramean tribe of Bīt-Adīni, is very questionable. A reconstruction like this that completely and purposely leaves out a Luwian component in the discussion is highly problematic. Aside from possibly the personal names, there is nothing in these inscriptions that hints that the rulers are Semitic or Aramean. The major deities invoked are typical of Luwian inscriptions (e.g., quite similar to those at Karkamiš). Their tone is Luwian. In fact, a reading of the Tell Aḥmar/Qubbah stela (Hawkins 2006) seems to paint a very different picture of Hamiyata. Nothing in this inscription indicates that this man or his father or son were subordinate to someone else (whether Aḫuni or another leader of Bīt-Adīni). Nothing hints at these individuals being part of an Aramean tribal group. Hamiyata claims to have defeated his enemies to the east and the west. This is typical rhetorical hyperbole, but the point is clear: he is a powerful "Ruler, Masuwarean king, the servant of Tarḫunza," who gives credit for his success to Tarḫunza of the army for whom he established a cult. There is absolutely no hint at subordination in this inscription.[102] In addition, there is no mention of any of these leaders at Til-Barsib/Masuwari being connected to the Adīni tribal confederation.[103] In the Assyrian inscriptions, Til-Barsib is never mentioned in connection with Aḫuni during the reign of Aššurnaṣirpal II. Only about twenty years later is Aḫuni credited with the possession of Til-Barsib.

---

would fit the new data coming from the new inscription TELL AHMAR 6 (Bunnens 2006) and prefer to preserve a higher date for these events."

100. Villard (1998, 104) understands the Assyrian-transcribed name $^{m}$*ha-mi-ia-ta-sa* "Hamiyata" to be Aramaic. There does not seem to be a good Anatolian explanation for the name, whereas the Aramaic explanation works. However, see next note.

101. In HAMA 7, §4, there is a land of Hamayara, which could be a rhotacized form of Hamiyata. See Hawkins 2000, 413.

102. Contrast the Azatiwada inscription from Karatepe; or Yariri of Karkamiš. In both, one sees a powerful man, but a subordinate to another ruler as clearly indicated.

103. Both Bunnens and Lipiński overly stress the use of the word "brothers," as though this indicates tribal affiliation. There is no mention of Adīni and it is far more likely that this has nothing to do with Adīni, but is an internal Masuwarean reference.

It would seem that there are no grounds for conflating the histories of Masuwari and Bīt-Adīni. All the evidence points to these being separate entities. What is clear is that the site of Tell Aḥmar was occupied in the Late Bronze/Iron I Age (Strata 6 and 7) with Middle Assyrian pottery (Bunnens 2009, 68) (see more below). Although the Arameans captured Pitru and Mutkīnu (ca. 1012–972), it is interesting that Shalmaneser III does not credit them with the capture and occupation of Til-Barsib. Instead, the evidence demonstrates that during the period of approximately 975–875 BCE[104] there was a Neo-Hittite polity centered at the city, whose name was called Masuwari. From this polity's inscriptions, it is clear that it had some successes in extending its borders and some internal strife, which, no doubt, weakened it. All the inscriptions in hieroglyphic Luwian and the Neo-Hittite art style demonstrate that there was a Luwian-speaking population group in the city (clearly the elite of the city). Obviously, there were Arameans in the area, some of whom may have lived in the city; but the material culture at the site does not help delineate the ethnic components in any way.

The last king of Masuwari would be placed in the first half of the ninth century, that is, roughly at the time that Aššurnaṣirpal II (r. 883–859 BCE) was already fully active in the northwestern sector of the Jezirah. The fact that a Neo-Hittite dynasty located in Til-Barsib/Masuwari is not mentioned in the early years of Aššurnaṣirpal II is simply a function of that king's campaigns being directed elsewhere. However, when, sometime between 875 and 867 BCE, Aššurnaṣirpal did campaign in the region,[105] it is clear that Karkamiš of the land of Ḫatti was the initial target (*ana āl Gargamiš ša māt Ḫatte aṣṣabat arḫu*, iii.57). The route of the campaign went through Bīt-Baḫiāni (tribute received), the land of Azallu (tribute received), Bīt-Adīni (tribute received from Aḫuni, the man of Bīt-Adīni), the land of Til-Abnâ (tribute received), and then across the Euphrates River to Karkamiš where Sangara, king of the land of Ḫatti (MAN KUR *ḫat-te*), submitted and paid tribute. In this context, the text states: "The kings of all the lands came down; they seized my feet" (*šarrāni ša mātāti kalîšunu ana elīya urdūni šēpēya iṣṣabtū*, iii.69). The king of Masuwari may have been included in this group (Fales 2011a, 217 n. 17). However, Til-Barsib may have been already absorbed by Bīt-Adīni.[106]

In any case, after around 875 (the date of the last hieroglyphic Luwian text), there is no further mention of an extant polity centered in Til-Barsib called Masuwari in any of sources. There is only Bīt-Adīni. The city of Til-Barsib is presented as a city of Bīt-Adīni.

104. Giusfredi (2010) would raise the date for these texts.

105. RIMA 2:216–17, A.0.101.1, iii.56b–77a.

106. For detailed discussion on the history of Bīt-Adīni, see §5.2.

### 3.1.5. Sam'al

Sam'al (modern Zincirli) was also known as Yā'diya.[107] It shows clear cultural continuity with the earlier Hittite period (Novák 2002, 2005). A study of its inscriptions reveals its mixed character. While its inscriptions are predominantly Aramaic (see Tropper 1993), Luwian played an important role. The kingdom's earliest inscription (ninth century) is in hieroglyphic Luwian, namely, a black basalt stela from Karaburçlu (5 km/3.125 mi north of Zincirli). Hieroglyphic Luwian was utilized up to the end of the kingdom of Sam'al, concurrent with Aramaic, as demonstrated by two seals of Barrākib (Lemaire 2001a). In fact, the recent discovery of a hieroglyphic Luwian inscription emphasizes this point.[108] Several of the Sam'alian kings had Anatolian names (also possibly a military officer, if Lemaire's analysis of an inscribed garnish of a shield is correct; Lemaire 2001a, 188; Younger 2007c, 143; Gubel 2012). Moreover, the architecture and reliefs reflect sure Neo-Hittite connections (Pucci 2008a, 2008b; Gilibert 2011). The Semitic monumental inscriptions (i.e., the non-Luwian texts) are not incised in the stone, but utilize a raised script that reflects a dependence on the hieroglyphic Luwian model (Hawkins 2006–8, 601; Greenfield 1998, 200). Yet, at Sam'al, the Sam'alian Aramaic dialect may reflect some type of Amurrite substrate. Sam'al exhibits significant acculturation (Novák 2005, 252–66).

### 3.1.6. Hamath

The ancient tell in the modern city of Ḥama was the location of the capital of the land of Hamath, known from ancient Near Eastern and biblical sources (Hawkins 1972–75b, 2000; Bryce 2012). In the eleventh century this area may have been part of the kingdom of Taita I. Certainly in the early tenth century it appears to have been ruled by Taita II (see above), whose kingdom appears to have continued down into the second half of ninth century. Excavations of the tell have uncovered evidence of Luwian material culture, manifested in the discovery of reliefs and monumental lions. Furthermore, the native hieroglyphic Luwian inscriptions from this region also attest to this cultural continuum. These inscriptions are primarily the work of Urhilina, the son of Parita, and Urhilina's son, Uratami. Urhilina, a contemporary of Shalmaneser III, reigned ca. 860–840 and his son Uratami reigned ca. 840–800 BCE. Parita perhaps reigned ca. 880–860 (a contemporary of Aššurnaṣirpal II).

107. See chapter 6 below for further discussion.
108. See now Herrmann, van den Hout, and Beyazlar 2016.

This cultural continuity can also be seen in the material culture at Tell Afis. A biconvex seal (TA.92.G.346) was discovered in a domestic context in area G in a level dating to the second half of the tenth century BCE (Cecchini 1998, 278). On both faces, the same name in hieroglyphic Luwian writing is engraved: *Sa-na-sà-li*, which corresponds to the Hurrian female name Šiniš-šal(l)i, well-attested in Nuzi documentation (Archi 1998, 367–68). On stylistic grounds, Archi (1998, 368) has dated this seal (TA.92.G.346) to the thirteenth century BCE. At Tell Ḥama, biconvex seals were found in the necropolis (Riis 1948, 159, fig. 201); bullae bearing Luwian and Aramaic names, impressed with this type of seal, are known from the citadel phase E (Archi 1998, 368). Thus, it appears that there was a tendency to treasure these kinds of objects. This is another indication of cultural continuity at both Tell Ḥama and Tell Afis.

Importantly, the recent discovery of a hieroglyphic Luwian text from Tall Šṭīb demonstrates the continuity of the Neo-Hittite dynasty of Urhilina. According to the inscription, Urhilina constructed the town at this site (ancient name still unknown), and erected his stela for the goddess Ba'alat (Gonnet 2010; Rousset 2010). It also shows that the power of the kingdom was not concentrated simply along the Orontes, but was, in fact, spread into the hinterland.

However, the architecture at Ḥama poses a difficult challenge for interpretation. This was, according to Matthiae (2008, 207–10), complicated by the attempts by the excavators to identify specific strata with the Luwian inscriptions and by an unwieldy complex of architectural analogy that ranged far and wide through the ancient Near East, both geographically and chronologically. He argues that a better method is to start with the Old Syrian architectural traditions before moving too quickly to neighboring traditions, with the result that the architecture at Luwian/Aramean Hamath (Ḥama) reflects an earlier south-central Syrian tradition that goes back to late third-millennium Ebla (Matthiae 2008, 210–12). While Hamath's tradition has links with some of these (e.g., Tell Ta'yinat), it is likely that the design of the citadel of Luwian-Aramean Hamath belongs to an architectural tradition of central and southern Syria, a tradition of which we know almost nothing so far.

The name of Hamath is not found in the historical sources of the Middle or Late Bronze Ages, suggesting that it was not one of the main urban centers, simply part of the territory of another state, perhaps Tunip.[109] A kingdom of Hamath is not firmly attested until the first millennium.

109. Hawkins 2000, 399. It may be attested in the third millennium texts of Ebla, but see chapter 7 below.

According to the Hebrew Bible, Hamath was a significant kingdom in the tenth century, an opponent of Hadad-ezer of Ṣobah. Around 980 BCE, its king To'i (*t'y*) seems to have entered into an alliance with Israel after David's defeat of Hadad-ezer (2 Sam 8:9–11, 1 Chr 18:9–11). Lipiński (2000a, 251) feels that To'î can hardly be regarded as a real historical figure. This position is understandable since there is no attestation outside of the Bible for such a monarch. Furthermore, the name of his son, Joram, looks very suspicious, having a Yahwistic thephoric element. However, the name To'î is very likely Hurrian.[110] This is in agreement with the known ninth-century king of Hamath, Urhilina, whose name is Hurrian.[111] Moreover, Uratami, the son of Urhilina, has a Luwian name, and the earlier king in the region, Taita (II), has a Hurrian name. Thus, the name To'î is consistent with what is known about the rulers of Hamath.

To'i's son, Joram (in the MT), is sent to greet and bless David after the victory over Hadad-ezer of Ṣobah. Importantly, the name "Joram" is preserved in a few manuscripts as Haddoram, which is clearly behind the Ιεδδουραν of the Septuagint. "Hadad-ram" is a common Aramaic personal name;[112] "Jo-ram" is a well-known Hebrew name. It appears that the theophoric element (the first component in each name) has been switched. This perhaps could be a result of the alliance in which a name change has taken place. Or, far more likely, it could be the result of redactional activity within the Hebrew text for theological reasons.

Thus other than this exception (if it is accepted as historically accurate), Hamath's rulers had non-Semitic, mostly Hurrian, names until the Aramean Zakkur—who was probably from the middle Euphrates city of 'Ana—seized power at the end of the ninth century, and his Aramaic inscription is followed by many others in the same language (Dion 1995a, 1283). Moreover, this dynastic change between Luwian and Aramaic elements, as Mazzoni (1994,

---

110. Hawkins (2000, 400 n. 30) identifies To'î with the Hurrian name *Tah'e*, "man," attested as a personal name at Meskene. As noted above, Steitler (2010) has attempted to identify Taita with To'î.

111. See Wilhelm 1998–2001, 127. See also Baker and Van Buylaere 2000. However, regarding this name, Yakubovich (2010, 396) has suggested that it should not be read Urhilina and interpreted as Hurrian, but should be read as Urahilina and analyzed as a Luwian name meaning "(having a) great gate." I have retained the spelling Urhilina for two reasons: (1) None of the cuneiform spellings of the name insert an /a/ vowel between *r* and *ḫ*. While it is possible that the Assyrians did not get it right, they very well may have; and importantly, (2) the spellings of the name Uratami (MAGNUS + *ra/i-tà-mi-sa*) and his father Urhilina (*u+ra/i-hi-li-na-sa*) seem to indicate a difference (the name is not spelled MAGNUS-*hi-li-na-sa*, which would unquestionably yield Ura-hilina.

112. E.g., *hdrm*, *'drm*, Ἀδωραμ, $^{m}$10-*ra-a-mu* $^{m}$10-*ra-me*, $^{m}$10-*ra-mi*. See Zadok 1977, 46, 84–85.

325) notes, is reflected in the foundation of Ḥaḏrak as a new capital (Soldi 2009; Venturi 2010). Hence, while suspicion may remain because of the generic issues surrounding 2 Sam 8, the personal names are not inconsistent with the known situation in Hamath.

## 3.2. The Assyrian Sphere

### 3.2.1. The Rise of the Middle Assyrian Empire

The Assyrian sphere corresponds to the Jezirah (see fig. 3.1). Geographically, this was "the natural hinterland of Assyria" and contributed to Assyria being "essentially 'a steppe-bound empire'" (Kühne 1995, 69). The need for dry-farming land seems to have been one of the primary motives for the constant Assyrian drive to the west, with "the other being the lack of natural resources, especially metal."[113] The result was that the Jezirah, especially the Ḫābūr area, became part of "Assyria proper" (Postgate 1992).

Prior to the ascent of Assyria, this region had undergone after the Middle Bronze Age a Hurrianization process (Zadok 1991, 108), which led to the establishment in the sixteenth century of the kingdom of Mittani[114] with its core in the Ḫābūr region, especially the Upper Ḫābūr.[115] While its origins are still ambiguous, by the early fifteenth century, this kingdom extended from Cilicia in the west to the foothills of the Zagros in the east. Its expansion eastward brought about the subjugation of Assyria (Wilhelm 2009–11), and this domination had a profound impact. While Assyria had certainly been under dominion in earlier times, notably going all the way back to the dynasty of Sargon the Great and Naram-Sin, the Mittanian rulers made a very strong impression, perhaps because, as one writer has put it, "the Mittani appear in the records more as plunderers than rulers" (Garfinkle 2007, 72–73). Thus the heavy tribute that these Hurrian overlords extracted from the Assyrians was a significant factor in their strong impulse to drive to the west, extending their power to the Euphrates, as an attempt to create a secure boundary for their state against the interference of outsiders. Garfinkle has concluded that

113. Kühne 1995, 72. Machinist (1982, 80 n. 31) notes that the Ḫanigalbat region, "was important to Assyria for at least two reasons: (1) it was a major breadbasket, especially in the Ḫābūr Valley; (2) it lay athwart the major east–west and north–south trade routes to which Assyria needed access." See also Postgate 1983–84a.

114. Kühne 1999, 210; de Martino 2004, 36; Wilhelm 1993–97; Cancik-Kirschbaum, Brisch, and Eidem 2014.

115. For example, note the evidence of Mittanian power at Tell Brak (ancient Nawar), including a palace and temple constructed on the highest point of the tell (Oates, Oates, and MacDonald 1997).

> we can view the militarism of the Middle Assyrian kings as a form of defensive imperialism that will be familiar to scholars of ancient Rome. This militarism though was also a direct outgrowth of the Assyrian king's relationship with divine authority. The king, first and foremost, was the priest of Ashur and the royal inscriptions of the Middle Assyrian kings placed a heavy emphasis on demonstrations of piety.[116]

Thus the humiliation of Mittanian hegemony was an important factor in the development of Assyrian militarism and its way of waging war.

The center of the Mittanian state was located in the Ḫābūr triangle, in particular at Waššukanni. The large site of Tell Fakhariya near the headwaters of the Ḫābūr has been proposed as a possible location of the Mittanian capital (Pruß and Bagdo 2002, 313). Although this identification is not absolutely certain, the recent petrochemical analyses of the clay of the letters of the Mittanian king, Tušratta, demonstrate an origination from the area of Tell Fakhariya, with a high degree of probability.[117] Thus, in addition to the clear vocal similarity and historical plausibility, there is good reason to posit the identification Tell Fakhariya = Sikānu = U/Aššukanni = Waššukanni.[118] Moreover, evidence of Mittanian power has been discovered at other sites, like Tell Brak (ancient Nawar) including a palace and temple constructed on the highest point of the tell,[119] as well as at Tell Ḫamīdiya (possibly ancient Ta'idu).[120]

During the fourteenth and thirteenth centuries, the kingdom of Mittani (also called Ḫanigalbat) was weakened by wars with Egypt, and eventually destroyed by the Assyro-Hittite conquest of its territory (Giorgieri 2011). A series of Middle Assyrian kings subjugated the Jezirah. The almost one hundred years of the combined reigns of Adad-nērārī I, Shalmaneser I, and Tukulti-Ninurta I (ca. 1298–1203) saw the establishment of the Middle Assyrian Empire over what traditionally was known as Ḫanigalbat (for dates, see

---

116. Garfinkle 2007, 73. See also Montero Fenollós and Caramelo 2012, 51.

117. See Goren et al. 2004, 38–44, esp. 44.

118. Cholidis and Martin 2010, 48 n. 88; Bonatz, Bartl, Gilibert, and Jauss 2008, 92; *pace* Szuchman 2007, 69; Lipiński 1994, 20–21.

119. Nuzi Ware, which was used throughout the Mittanian realm in the fifteenth to the fourteenth centuries, but rarely in great numbers, might serve as a Mittanian elite marker. First discovered at Yorgan Tepe (ancient Nuzi) in northern Iraq, it is characterized by light-colored painted motifs, either geometric or especially in the west, floral, applied to a field of dark paint. The typical shape is a tall thin-walled open vessel with a small pedestal or button base. In the Jezirah, the latest phases of Ḫābūr Ware overlap with the appearance of Nuzi Ware and consist of dark-painted motifs on "shoulder goblets" with button bases. Oates et al. 1997. However, see now Duistermaat 2008, 123–24.

120. Eichler et al. 1985, 53–70; Oates et al. 1997, 152; Röllig 1997, 282; Parpola and Porter 2001, 3; Tenu 2009, 103–4.

table 3.2 on p. 150).[121] This resulted in the region undergoing an Assyrianization process. I am using this term because in one sense this is an accurate description. However, Pongratz-Leisten (2011, 111) has demonstrated that even with the implementation of firm Assyrian control[122] supported by building activities, the settlement of Assyrians in particular areas, and the importing of Assyrian culture, the encounter with local traditions inevitably entailed the integration and adaptation of local cultural elements into the Assyrian discourse and vice versa, particularly in the forms of ideological expression and religious practice. In short, this was not a one-way street, though perhaps more traffic flowed in one direction than in the other.

This was also not an overnight process. Rather, it took the entire reigns of Adad-nērārī I, Shalmaneser I, and Tukulti-Ninurta I to complete through the utilization of both mass deportations and the implementation of a highly organized colonization. Yet, as the ceramic assemblages at various sites demonstrate, the Jezirah was relatively quickly and completely integrated into a new organism where the land underwent exploitation.[123] This was a "top-down process," for the very governmental reorganization with the creation of a *sukkallu rabiʾu* (grand vizier) and *šar Ḫanigalbat* ("king of Ḫanigalbat") was a move designed to give the appearance of a client-like status (retaining a "king" over the land) and yet provide at the same time a clear Assyrian governance by the highest Assyrian official possible (the "grand vizier"), who would guarantee this Assyrianization process.

An example of the technique of mass deportation can be seen in the 14,000 partially blinded Ḫanigalbatians who were uprooted.[124] To fill the vacuums created by the deportations, some other groups were brought in. For example, in the case of the Ḫābūr, there was a transfer of people from Katmuḫu (Röllig 1978, 428–29).

A general trend is encountered in the Late Bronze Age, namely, the decline in the number of occupied sites as over against the number for the Middle Bronze Age. The archaeological evidence indicates that there was a serious decline of settlements in the Jezirah during the Late Bronze Age.[125] This pattern of decline has sometimes been interpreted in terms of

---

121. For a recent narrative describing this process, see Fales 2011b.

122. Concerning the notion of Assyrian "control," see below.

123. See especially the comments of D'Agostino 2008 concerning Tell Barri/Kaḫat (and below). Also the comments of Tenu (2009, 246–47) and Postgate (2010, 26–29) on the Middle Assyrian ceramics.

124. Claimed by Shalmaneser I (RIMA 1:184, A.0.77.1, lines 74–75a).

125. Wilkinson and Tucker 1995, 58–62. It is possible that there is some blurring between Middle and Late Bronze pottery that may obscure some of the relevant data. See Yener et al. 2000.

Table 3.2. Chronology of the Middle Assyrian Empire

| | Brinkman 1977, 345 | Freydank 1991, 188–89 | | Jeffers 2013, 391* |
|---|---|---|---|---|
| Aššur-uballiṭ I | 1363–1328 | 1363–1328 | 1353–1318 | 1356.14–1322.10 |
| Enlil-nērārī | 1327–1318 | 1327–1318 | 1317–1308 | 1321.07–1313.80 |
| Arik-den-ili | 1317–1306 | 1317–1306 | 1307–1296 | 1312.77–1301.45 |
| Adad-nērārī I | 1305–1274 | 1305–1274 | 1295–1264 | 1300.42–1270.49 |
| Shalmaneser I | 1273–1244 | 1273–1244 | 1263–1234 | 1269.46–1241.60 |
| Tukulti-Ninurta I | 1243–1207 | 1243–1207 | 1233–1197 | 1240.57–1205.50 |
| Aššur-nādin-apli | 1206–1203 | 1206–1203 | 1196–1193 | 1204.47–1201.38 |
| Aššur-nērārī III | 1202–1197 | 1202–1197 | 1192–1187 | 1200.35–1195.20 |
| Enlil-kudurrī-uṣur | 1196–1192 | 1196–1192 | 1186–1182 | 1194.17–1190.05 |
| Ninurta-apil-Ekur** | 1191–1179 | 1191–1179 | 1181–1169 | 1189.02–1178.67 |
| Aššur-dān I | 1178–1133 | 1178–1133 | 1168–1133 | 1177.64–1133.30 |
| Ninurta-tukulti-Aššur (*ṭuppīšu*) | 1133 | 1133 | 1133 | 1132.27 |
| Mutakkil-Nusku (*ṭuppīšu*) | 1133 | 1133 | 1133 | 1131.24 |
| Aššur-rēša-iši I | 1132–1115 | 1132–1115 | | 1130.21–1114.70 |
| Tiglath-pileser I | 1114–1076 | 1114–1076 | | 1113.67–1076.54 |
| Ašared-apil-Ekur | 1075–1074 | 1075–1074 | | 1075.51–1074.48 |
| Aššur-bēl-kala | 1073–1056 | 1073–1056 | | 1073.45–1056.22 |

• Based on evidence that the Assyrians used solely a lunar calendar until they adopted the Babylonian luni-solar calendrical system in the eighth year of Aššur-bēl-kala. The decimal fractions reflect the calculation of the ever-changing position of the month of Ṣippu of the Assyrian calendar within the Julian calendrical system. See Jeffers 2013, 185–202; Jeffers, private communication.

•• There is uncertainty about the length of Ninurta-apil-Ekur's reign. In two copies of the Assyrian King List, the length is given as three years; in the Nassouhi version it is thirteen years (the difference of a single wedge). Freydank (1991, 195) assigns eleven *līmu* to his reign. Also Llop-Raduà (2008, 20) presents evidence from the eponyms to support the longer reign.

an increasingly exploitative urban elite whose oppressive demands forced the peasants to abandon their homes. The fleeing peasants either embraced a mobile pastoralist lifestyle (i.e., nomadization), or attached themselves to roving bands of refugees and outlaws like the rootless *ʿapiru* of the Amarna documents.[126] On the other hand, one might consider the denigrating effect of conflicts between external imperial powers (e.g., the devastation of Mittani) and of tributary obligations to such powers. The destructive effect of the Middle Assyrian aggression was the creation of a power vacuum. In this case, abandonment of the region could have been hastened by the policy of deportation, the destruction of villages, pestilence, and the general ravages of war. It is also possible that the Middle Assyrian aggression followed after a number of ecologically and socially induced disasters so that some of the population decrease may well have preceded the Assyrian occupation of the Jezirah (Lyon 2000, 104).

In contrast, the archaeological surveys have demonstrated a marked increase in Iron Age settlements. Again, however, it is difficult to know the causes for this strong intensification in settlement density. The increased Assyrian colonization and agricultural exploitation may be one reason; and/or a shift in living patterns of previously mobile Aḫlamû, Sutean, and Aramean peoples might be another.[127]

Be this as it may, there is, however, also the evidence of personal names that must be considered. The deportees from the Jezirah recorded at Kār-Tukulti-Ninurta bore mostly Hurrian names. None of them had a West Semitic name (Zadok 1991, 112). According to Zadok (2012, 572), this is an indication that no Suteans were integrated into the ruling class of Ḫanigalbat. Since the Assyrians generally did not rebuild the conquered and vacated Mittanian cities, the destruction of Mittani and its deportation meant that some portions of the Jezirah (particularly the western area) became prime targets for groups of West Semitic nomads.[128]

In addition to the deportations, as noted above, the Assyrians actively colonized the area, creating numerous self-contained Assyrian communities, a grid of nodes comprising a web of "administrative hubs and strongholds" (Fales 2011b, 9). The arrangement of these with a provincial center and surrounding cities were patterned after the imperial capital Assur (Machinist 1982, 84). A tight administrative system was exercised by the Assyrians as evidenced by the some six hundred administrative tablets discovered at the provincial capital Dūr-Katlimmu (modern Tell Šēḫ Ḥamad; Kühne 1983–84; Cancik-Kirschbaum 1996), in addition to numerous other sites in the Jezi-

126. Liverani 1987; On the *ʿapiru* in the Amarna materials, see now Fleming 2012.

127. Wilkinson et al. 2005, and the chart p. 39, which in particular demonstrates the vast increase in the Iron Age by giving the comparative quantities of sites from all surveyed areas dated to the LBA/Middle Assyrian and the IA/Late Assyrian periods.

128. Zadok notes that these were, with the exception of the Yaurians, ethno-linguistically undifferentiated.

rah[129] and the Assyrian homeland. Some of these "nodes" were located along the major routes going from Assur toward the west. Others—for example, Tell Ḥassaka (ancient Magarisu), Tell Taban (ancient Ṭābētu), Tell 'Ajaja (ancient Šadikanni), Fadghami (ancient Qatna), and Tell Šēḫ Ḥamad (ancient Dūr-Katlimmu)[130]—were set out along the Ḫābūr River Valley "at roughly regular intervals of 20–40 km, thus allowing a continuous administrative cover of the valley territory" (Morandi Bonacossi 1996, 19; 2000, 366). Recent archaeological research has demonstrated that the Assyrians built their administrative centers on top of former Mittanian settlements and local seats of government.[131]

The grid's nodes in each Assyrian "district" (*ḫalṣu*) were designated according to their settlement size and fortification. Hence, one encountered in decreasing order: *ālu* "city," *birtu* "fort," *dunnu* "fortified agricultural center" (Herles 2007a, 415). Thus the Middle Assyrian grid was invested systematically with various levels of fortifications. So for the Balīḫ area alone, Akkermans comments:

> Tell Ṣābi Abyad was evidently not the only Middle Assyrian fortress in the Balīḫ valley. Field surveys as well as the texts from Ṣābi Abyad and elsewhere point to a string of such fortified settlements less than one or two hectares in extent, distributed in a linear pattern from Harran in the north all the way down to Tuttul on the Euphrates in the south. (Akkermans 2006, 209)

A complex but functional system of main routes between the nodes produced a network that allowed political and administrative intercommunication and the forwarding of agricultural products to Assur. Yet, it would be very erroneous to think of a total occupation that "filled up" all of the Jezirah. In between this grid of fortified administrative nodes, Assyrian "control" was varied, both in the extent to which the Assyrians could gain it and in the level

129. E.g., Tell Fakhariya (Waššukanni; Güterbock 1958), more tablets discovered in 2009 and 2010; Tell Taban (ancient Ṭābētu) in 2009 in addition to those already published; Tell Šēḫ Ḥamad (Cancik-Kirschbaum 1996; Röllig 2008a); Tell 'Āmūdā (ancient Kulišḫinaš; see Machinist 1982); Tell Chuēra (ancient Ḫarbe, see Jakob and Janisch-Jakob 2009); Tell Ṣābi Abyad (mostly unpublished); Giricano (ancient Dunnu-ša-Uzibi; Radner 2004a); Tell al-Rimah (ancient Qaṭar or Karānā; Wiseman 1968); Tell Billa (ancient Šibaniba; J. J. Finkelstein 1953); Tell Ali (Ismail and Postgate 2008); and Tell Fray (unpublished; likely not Assyrian).

130. See §4.5.2 and table 4.3.

131. Postgate 2010, 27. For an up-to-date and thorough survey of the archaeological material from the Middle Assyrian period, see Tenu 2009, 57–147.

at which they could maintain it.[132] No doubt each decade experienced differences in this regard. Such a system was in a constant state of "a work in progress" (Fales 2011b, 23).

The *dunnu* ("fortified agricultural center") of the Grand Vizier (*sukkallu rabi'u*) and king of Ḫanigalbat (*šar māt Ḫanigalbat*[133]) at Tell Ṣābi Abyad has yielded over four hundred tablets.[134] The even smaller *dunnu* at Giricano (ancient Dunnu-ša-Uzibi) has yielded twenty-four tablets (Radner 2004a). These texts attest to the important agricultural orientation for the Jezirah and Upper Tigris during the Middle Assyrian period. This emphasis on agricultural intensification is highlighted by the implementation of a new canal system in the upper and lower Ḫābūr (Fales 2008a).[135]

Due to a perceived lack of Middle Assyrian texts saying much about pastoralism, Szuchman argued that this implied that this occupation was not a concern of the *dunnu*, but a purely local enterprise that employed local Suteans in this industry (Szuchman 2007, 26–28). However, a particular archive of a "flock-master" from Tell Ali (ancient Atmannu) demonstrates the Assyrian state's interest in animal husbandry as a source of meat for special occasions and of wool and goat hair to meet the state's requirements for everyday textile production.[136] To this can be added the Dūr-Katlimmu administrative documents regarding flocks and their products (mainly wool, but also sheep and goat skins, and hair) supplied to government officials, but especially to the palace workshops (Röllig 2008a; Postgate 2010, 24). It is interesting that the flocks attested in the Dūr-Katlimmu archives were of comparable sizes, varying between 265 and 840 animals (Ismail and Postgate 2008, 153).[137] Therefore, the Assyrians were not simply "subcontracting" pastoralism.

132. Brown 2013, 103–6. He cites the Ṭūr ʿAbdīn as an example of an area that was not as much under Assyrian control.

133. For a discussion of the (political, religious, ideological) significance of this title, see Fales 2011b, 53 n. 70.

134. Wiggermann 2000, 175; Akkermans and Rossmeisl 1990; Tenu 2009, 142. The texts will be published by Wiggermann. For the tentative identification with Amīmu, see Luciani 1999–2001, 97. Tell Ṣābi Abyad was not an administrative center, but the property of Ilī-padâ, *sukkallu rabi'u* "grand vizier" probably granted to him by the king, see Faist 2006, 151 n. 19.

135. Also a canal system may have been installed on the Balīḫ (Wiggermann 2000). See chapter 1.

136. Ismail and Postgate 2008; Postgate 2010, 29. Some of this was part of the *iškāru* system (Postgate 2010, 22–25). Both at Tell Ali (Atmannu) and at Tell Šēḫ Ḥamad (Dūr-Katlimmu), some of the wool is explicitly said to be issued for *iskāru*, but some also went just "for clothing (*lubulte*) of the serfs (*šiluḫli*)" (Tell Ali, Nos. 17–18; cf. Röllig 2008a, Nos. 48 and 51, just *ana lubulte*).

137. For the Dūr-Katlimmu data, see Röllig 2002, 592.

In general, archaeological research has documented the process of Assyrian territorial expansion and political and economic reorientation in the thirteenth through eleventh centuries in the Jezirah, documenting a process of succession from "Mittanian" to "Middle Assyrian" material-culture assemblages. Evidence of changes in material culture is drawn primarily from two sources: ceramic assemblages[138] and cylinder-seal styles.[139] The pottery produced during the Mittanian period is quite different from that of the later Middle Assyrian period, in morphology and technology. This means that in the archaeological record, the Assyrian integration of the Mittanian site is reflected in "a significant and identifiable way."[140]

In sum, this web of "administrative hubs and strongholds" evinced Assyria's "goals and objectives" for the Jezirah and yielded a "productive agricultural zone" that gave a level of prosperity to the empire.

### 3.2.2. Critical Issues in the Middle Assyrian Empire

There are two major issues in understanding the Middle Assyrian Empire. These are, in fact, interrelated: (1) the extent of the western borders and (2) when did the decline start and what was its nature.

---

138. The ceramic assemblages demonstrate a cessation of Hurrian Nuzi Ware and Ḫābūr Ware and the introduction of new popular types include carinated flat or ring-based bowls and various shapes with nipple bases. Assyrian imperial control is also evinced by the centralized production of a standard pottery repertoire throughout the Jezirah. See Pfälzner 1995, 1997.

139. The cylinder seal styles show a clear transition from Mitannian style cylinder seals to Assyrian style seals, characterized by balanced compositions with fantastic creatures. After the Mitannian period, seals of Middle Assyrian style predominate in the Jezirah. See Akkermans and Schwartz 2003, 355–57.

140. D'Agostino 2008, 525. Pfälzner (1995, 241) describes two contemporary traditions: a Middle Assyrian "official" ceramic, and the "domestic" ceramics. The pottery is "Assyrian" not merely in the chronological sense of pottery manufactured during the period of Assyrian domination, but also because it was made *for* Assyrians, in their own way, for their own purposes, and probably *by* Assyrians (Postgate 2010, 27). It should be noted that Duistermaat has challenged the ceramic assemblage argument (2008, 123–24). On the basis of comparisons between the ceramics from Tell Ṣābi Abyad and a number of other Middle Assyrian and non–Middle Assyrian or Late Bronze Age sites in northern Syria, Iraq, and southern Turkey, that "although the majority of the ceramics at Ṣābi Abyad was made in the well-known Middle Assyrian tradition, there are a number of more rarely occurring shapes that have closer connections to non–Middle Assyrian sites on the Euphrates. This shows that the inhabitants of Ṣābi Abyad had regular contacts with the west and with non-Assyrian sites" (Duistermaat 2008, 124). Perhaps, this gives an indication that there is a need for a more nuanced position. See the comments of B. A. Brown 2013, 107–8; Postgate 2010, 26–29.

### 3.2.2.1. The Location of the Western Boundary

Concerning the extent of the western boundaries (i.e., where was the western boundary located), there have been two contrasting scholarly views.[141] The traditional view understands the Assyrian conquest of Ḫanigalbat (the Jezirah) to have set the Assyrian border at the Euphrates River.[142] This view relies on the statements in the royal inscriptions and the archaeological evidence at some sites on the Euphrates. A second view claims that the Balīḫ River, not the Euphrates, was the border in the thirteenth century. In this view, the Assyrians did not settle beyond the Balīḫ. Thus the land between the Balīḫ and the Euphrates was more or less independent of the Assyrians, as well as the Hittites who controlled the right (west) bank of the Euphrates.[143] Scholars supporting this position point to the lack of Assyrian archives west of the Balīḫ River or of any official ceramics at the sites on the Euphrates. According to these scholars, the maximum expansion to the Balīḫ was only reached in the thirteenth century.[144]

However, Tenu has argued that the Assyrians settled on the left (east) bank of the Euphrates and that this was an occupation that continued uninterruptedly from the thirteenth to the eleventh centuries, until the reign of Aššur-rabi II (r. 1012–972 BCE) when these forts on the Euphrates were lost to the Arameans.[145] In addition to the royal inscriptions, she bases her arguments on the Middle Assyrian ceramic material found at sites on the banks of the Euphrates such as Būr-marina (Tell Shiukh Fawqani; Tenu, 2006b, 176) and Til-Barsib (Tell Aḥmar).

Tell Aḥmar is particularly of value in this instance. In its strata 6 and 7 (Late Bronze/Iron Age I phases), Middle Assyrian pottery occurs frequently, indicating a Middle Assyrian presence at the site (Bunnens 2009, 68). Progressively, however, shapes and wares characteristic of Iron II emerge, such as brown-burnished open bowls. Also a Middle Assyrian cylinder seal was found on a floor of Stratum 6. Radiocarbon dates seem to indicate a destruction around the end of the eleventh century (i.e., 1000 BCE). Bunnens interprets strata 6 and 7 to be from the period of Tiglath-pileser I and Aššur-

141. See the excellent summary in Llop-Raduà 2012a.

142. See for examples, Harrak 1987, 112–266; earlier Wilhelm 1982, 9–59, esp. 54.

143. See Cancik-Kirschbaum 1996, 34, fig. 4; Pfälzner 1997, 340; and Kühne 2000, 275, who states: "The Middle Assyrian sites of Tall Ṣābi Abyad and Hirbat as-Šanaaf probably marked the western periphery of the territorial extension of the Middle-Assyrian empire in the 13th century BC." For the village Khirbet esh-Shenef, see Bartl 1990.

144. Between these two positions is: Jakob 2003, 9–10; Jakob and Janisch-Jakob 2009, 11.

145. Tenu 2003; 2006b, 173; 2009, 247–49. See also Bunnens 2009, 68–71. However, see Luciani (1999–2001, 106) for a different interpretation.

bēl-kala and that the archaeology links the site with the occupation of Pitru and Mutkīnu and other sites. While Bunnens (2009, 68–71) does not directly connect the destruction to the Arameans, he certainly implies this by linking Tell Aḥmar's strata with those at Pitru and Mutkīnu, which were captured by the Arameans.

Additional evidence has recently been brought forth from Tell Qabr Abu al-ʿAtiq which confirms "the idea that the Euphrates, in accordance with textual sources, had actually functioned as a western border of the Middle Assyrian Empire" (Montero Fenollós and Caramelo 2012, 52; Montero 2010). Excavations at this site (located at the entrance to the Ḥalabiya Gorge), which may have been a *dunnu*, have yielded the typical repertory of "Middle Assyrian administrative pottery."[146] Typological comparisons with pottery from Tell Šēḫ Ḥamad on the Ḫābūr, and Tell Ṣābi Abyad on the Balīḫ, indicate a date for the Tell Qabr Abu al-ʿAtiq assemblage in the initial phase of the Middle Assyrian period (Montero Fenollós and Caramelo 2012, 56). In addition, the most important discoveries at the site were the cuneiform tablets, which were situated on the ground and partially covered by a bowl. The two texts were written in the Middle Assyrian dialect and describe administrative operations.[147]

In light of this recent evidence, the western border of the Middle Assyrian Empire appears to have been the eastern bank of the Euphrates—at least in the latter half of the thirteenth century.[148] It was a natural and possibly symbolic border. Llop-Raduà has recently shown that, on the basis of the royal inscriptions, the western border of the Assyrian kingdom certainly lay on the Euphrates at the time of Tukulti-Ninurta I (r. 1233–1197), possibly earlier in his father's reign (Llop-Raduà 2012a, 209–18; Fales 2012a). Moreover, the ceramic material from sites like Tell Shiukh Fawqani (*Marinâ*) seem to suggest some type of occupation (Capet 2005).

However, as Llop-Raduà points out, starting perhaps in the reign of Ninurta-apil-Ekur (r. 1182–1180), but definitively during the reign of Aššur-rēša-iši (r. 1132–1115), the western border of the Assyrian kingdom was located on the Ḫābūr River and not to the west of it.[149] No administrative

146. Montero Fenollós and Caramelo 2012, 56. For the Middle Assyrian pottery, see Pfälzner 1995, 250.

147. Ignacio Marquez Rowe is publishing the tablets.

148. There is reason to doubt that this occurred as early as Adad-nērārī I. See Llop-Raduà 2012a, 91–92; B. A. Brown 2013, 100.

149. Llop-Raduà 2012a, 215. On the extent of the Assyrian Empire in the mid-twelfth century, see Llop and George 2001–2, 12–16.

archives have presently been found west of the Balīḫ,[150] and this would seem to imply that there was no Assyrian administrative network as far as the banks of the Euphrates. In fact, no provinces west of the Ḫābūr are named in the documentation from the reign of Ninurta-apil-Ekur (r. 1182–1180) onwards.[151] Finally, the numerous razzias in the region by an unspecified enemy (possibly remnants of Hurrians and/or Aḫlamû or Suteans) indicate a certain lack of control that questions the extent of Assyrian occupation and whether such occupation was not interrupted. This eastward movement of the border leads to the second critical issue.

### 3.2.2.2. The Nature of the Decline

There is general agreement that Assyria's decline began following the death of Tukulti-Ninurta I. However, there are differences of opinion as to the nature of that decline. Liverani envisions that it began immediately upon the death of Tukulti-Ninurta I and did not abate until the tenth century (Liverani 1988b, 760; also Harrak 1987, 263–64). Liverani interprets the reign of the powerful and charismatic leader, Tiglath-pileser I, as only a temporary respite; a mere postponement of the certain, inevitable decline that would overtake Mesopotamia. Postgate also sees the decline as starting after the death of Tukulti-Ninurta I, but he divides it into two phases. The first was "a period of gentle recession, down to the reign of Tiglath-pileser I" followed by a second phase that was "a much more intense loss of power which saw Assyrian control wither to the minimal core of Assur itself and the cities to its north on the Tigris" (Postgate 1992a, 249). The cause of the second phase, while possibly climatic, was primarily the Arameans:

> The external political agents of this recession were not neighbouring states: Babylon was equally weak, the Hittite Empire had collapsed and fragmented, and the Mitannian state was only a memory. Rather, the damage was done by incursions of Aramaean tribes, who by 900 BC had established minor dynasties throughout most of North Mesopotamia and Syria. One contributory factor may well have been the climate, since poor rainfall both weakened Assyria's agricultural base and forced Aramaeans north in search of pasture. (Postgate 1992a, 249)

---

150. The eleven tablets from Tell Fray are still unpublished, although it seems likely that these are not Middle Assyrian.

151. If Freydank is correct in his redating of the *ginā'ū* tablet MARV 2.21 to the reign of Ninurta-apil-Ekur, this document would then be additional support for this position. See discussion below.

Recently, Fales (2011b) has also divided the decline into two phases. He sees the first phase of decline starting after the reign of Tukulti-Ninurta I (r. 1233–1197). The Middle Assyrian Empire reached its apex under his rule, extending from the Zagros to the Euphrates (at least its east bank),[152] and including the Upper Tigris area in the north and Kassite Babylonia in the south (at least temporarily). But the end of Tukulti-Ninurta's reign saw significant internal opposition to his building and religious policies, and culminated in his assassination. Fales observes that the Assyrian decline after the death of Tukulti-Ninurta I can be gauged from the absence of military feats attested in the royal inscriptions of his successors. It is thus commonly understood that under these kings the western limits of Assyrian occupation retreated back to the Balīḫ River Valley, though this retreat may have been partial with some isolated outposts being maintained, if the archaeological evidence is, in fact, present.[153]

The second phase of decline occurred during the last part of the reign of Tiglath-pileser I (r. 1114–1076), whose reign is marked by paradox. The royal inscriptions portray a monarch who again made the Euphrates the border of *māt Aššur* with a campaign on the left (east) bank of the Euphrates "from Sūḫu up to Karkamiš" that was waged against the Aramean-Aḫlamû[154] and who crossed the Euphrates to attack this particular group's settlements in the Jebel Bišri. In addition, the inscriptions record his reconquest of the territories lost to the *Mušku*; his campaigns in Katmuḫu and Nairi; his war in Babylonia; and his accomplishment of reaching the Mediterranean Sea.

Moreover, archaeological and textual evidence attests to his constructions of various fortifications on the Euphrates River during his reign (Herles 2007a): Pitru (Tell Aušariye) at the confluence of the Euphrates and the Sagura (modern Sajur) River, along with Mutkīnu (possibly Tall al-'Abr,[155] 2.5 km north of Tell Aḥmar) on the opposite (east bank) side of the Euphrates.[156]

In recent years, important synthetic studies of the excavations in the Middle Euphrates region have been published. These have demonstrated a significant Assyrian fort system in the region of Sūḫu that dates from the twelfth to eighth centuries (see table 3.3 and fig. 3.4). Some of these forts

152. There were probably no trans-Euphrates takeovers. See Galter 1988 and Fales 2011b, 49 n. 21.

153. Contrast Tenu 2009 and Luciano 1999–2001.

154. For this designation, see §2.5.1.

155. See Bunnens 2000a, 304; Yamazaki 1999; and Parpola and Porter 2001, 3, 18 (Tall al-'Abr). Another less likely candidate would be Tall Ḫamis, Lipiński 2000a, 168; Morandi Bonacossi 2000, 386, no. 28. For discussion, Bagg 2007, 180.

156. RIMA 3:19, A.0.102, ii.35b–40a.

were originally built in the Middle Assyrian period in order to control trade and nomadic movements in the region.[157] At Ḫaradu (modern Khirbet ed-Diniyeh),[158] two twelfth-century Middle Assyrian tablets have been discovered. Although their attribution to Tiglath-pileser I was initially announced, it seems that they come from earlier in the century.[159] In any case, the need to control the region was the clear motivation for the forts' construction. At some point later, the excavators believe that the fort at Ḫaradu came under Aramean control, which may well have been the case with a number of the other forts—or they were abandoned—until the Neo-Assyrian period (Aššurnaṣirpal II being a likely candidate for some of the reconstructions).

On the other hand, some administrative texts appear to attest to the onset of a second and graver phase of Assyrian decline and withdrawal from the previously conquered territories, both to the west and to the east. These are lists of regular offerings, called *ginā'ū*, and they may reflect the political situation in the provinces.[160] These are ruled, five-column lists that tabulate the quantities of commodities (barley, honey, sesame, and fruit) along with the toponyms from which these commodities were received at the Aššur temple in the city of Assur. There are as many as twenty-seven toponyms listed, which can be confidently identified as the provinces of the Assyrian state (Postgate 2013, 94 [table 4.1], 97), because they are occasionally explicitly identified as such ("offerings of the provinces received"[161]). Twenty-five of these tabular lists have been identified (Freydank 2006, 219). They were mostly compiled during a period spanning from the early twelfth century BCE (the earliest available documents can be dated to the reign of "obscure" kings: Aššur-nērārī III and Ellil-kudurrī-uṣur) to the reign of Tiglath-pileser I (r. 1114–1076 BCE).[162] In order to keep an annual record of deliveries, the scribes redacted these lists so that they noted the names of the different provinces (*pāḫatu*)[163] and the quantities delivered.

Rosa (2010, 337) addresses anew the issue of whether there is any geographic principle organizing these lists, concluding that:

157. Tenu 2006a, 217–45; 2008, 151–75; 2009, 222–23; Clancier 2006, 247–89. Likewise, the fort of Pitru was also founded by Tiglath-pileser I (Tell Aušariye). See Eidem and Pütt 2001.

158. Tenu 2006a, 2006b, 2008, 2009, 222–23; Kepinski 2006, 2009; and al-Shukri 1988, 1997.

159. They have not yet been published.

160. For a thorough discussion of the Offering House Archive and its system, see Postgate 2013, 89–146 (see 90 n. 8 for a treatment of the noun itself).

161. *gi-na-ù ša pa-ḫa-te maḫ-ru*, MARV 6.3:31.

162. This offerings-system survived into the Neo-Assyrian period (Sargonid period).

163. For the Middle Assyrian provincial system, see Llop-Raduá 2011b, 2012b.

Table 3.3. Summary of Assyrian Fort Systems

| Systems | Sites—Modern (Ancient) | Archaeological Evidence |
|---|---|---|
| First three-fort system | modern Sur Mur'eh | Middle and Neo-Assyrian pottery |
| | modern Glei'eh (Kār-Apladad) | Middle and Neo-Assyrian pottery |
| | modern Sur Jur'eh (Gabbāri-bānî) | Middle and Neo-Assyrian pottery |
| Second three-fort system | the Island of Bijan (Sapirutu?)[a] | Middle and Neo-Assyrian pottery |
| | 'Usiyeh | Middle and Neo-Assyrian pottery and Assyrian lamassu |
| | Yemniyeh | Neo-Assyrian pottery (ninth-century) pottery |
| Single forts/ cities | Sur Telbis (Sūru, capital of Sūḫu) | |
| | Island of Anat ('Anat) | |
| | Khirbet ed-Diniyeh (Ḫaradu) | Middle and Neo-Assyrian pottery; two texts dating to the first half of the twelfth century |

a. Sapirutu is mentioned by Tiglath-pileser I (RIMA 2, A.0.87.4, line 42; A.0.87.10, line 41) and Tukulti-Ninurta II (RIMA 2, A.0.100.5, line 66). See Gawlikowski 1983–84.

> Provinces laying on the borders of the kingdom are listed first, in the order: East; South (beyond the Euphrates); North; West ("Ḫābūr triangle"); South (between Tigris and Euphrates); West (course of the Ḫābūr); there follow provinces enclosed in these boundaries, with the Inner City of Aššur at the top of them, perhaps divided into two main groups ("western" and "eastern").

She notes that not all known Middle Assyrian provinces are included in the records of the regular offerings. Inner provinces, like Isāna and Nēmed-Ištar, do not appear where we would expect them. The ones lying beyond the far side of the Lower Zab, like Arrapḫa and Arzuḫina, were probably not yet under firm Assyrian control when the lists were redacted. In any case, the absence of certain places could simply mean that not all provinces forwarded regular offerings to the central temple of the capital town (exemptions for particular reasons are attested in the Neo-Assyrian period).

One particular tablet, published in MARV 2.21 (table 3.4) and one of the best-preserved of the *ginā'ū* lists, has been appealed to for establishing the status of the provinces at the time of Tiglath-pileser I. The dating to Tiglath-pileser I was based on the eponym Pa'uzu, which also occurs in the fragmentary section of the Middle Assyrian Eponym List (*KAV* 21.iii.10′)[164]

164. See Saporetti 1979, 164–65; Freydank 1991, 161; Bloch 2012a; Jeffers 2013, 151–58.

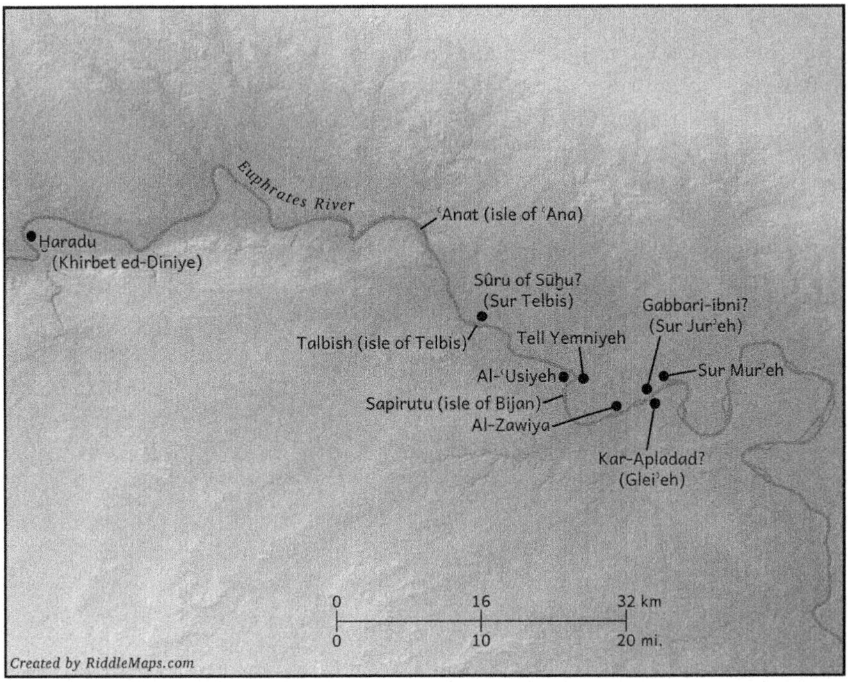


Fig. 3.4. Middle Euphrates forts

and which would seem to date the offering list to Tiglath-pileser I's next-to-last year, 1077 BCE (1077.54, Jeffers 2013). Hence, it has been used to reconstruct the provincial situation at this time (Postgate 1985, 96–99; Rosa 2010, 329 n. 20).

However, Freydank (2007, 70–77) has demonstrated through the publication of MARV 6.39 that there was another individual named Pa'uzu, who served as eponym at the beginning of the twelfth century. Thus, MARV 2.21 should be dated much earlier into the reign Ninurta-apil-Ekur (r. 1182–1170).[165] Consequently, this list has no bearing on the period of Tiglath-pileser I's reign. However, it is informative on Ninurta-apil-Ekur's reign (Freydank 2011). The hypothetical provincial boundaries for the twelfth century would seem to reflect a general loss of the Balīḫ area and a movement of the border to the Ḫābūr region (see fig. 3.5).

165. Freydank 2006, 219–21. Postgate (2013, 97 n. 22) states: "On the basis of MARV 6.39, Freydank 2007 has made it virtually certain that a Pa'uzu son of Erib-Aššur was eponym in the mid twelfth century, and MARV 2.21 should perhaps therefore be assigned to his term of office rather than to his much later namesake Pa'uzu, eponym for the thirty-eighth year of Tiglath-pileser (1077)."

That said, there may be another line of argument. Jeffers (2013, 331–36) has recently noted that the publication of numerous economic documents belonging to Tiglath-pileser I's reign permit a reconstruction of the approximate territory that was under Tiglath-pileser's direct provincial control. These texts, dated by eponym to the reign of Tiglath-pileser, document the *ginā'ū* transactions. He concludes that these texts can, at the very least, establish that the king was operating within the same territorial sphere as the one furnished by MARV 2.21,[167] and that the provincial system appears to be stable at the beginning of Tiglath-pileser's reign. While there is no evidence for the exact status of the kingdom in a single year (a snapshot as it were), all of the important administrative cities and regions attested in Tiglath-pileser's documents appear to be sending *ginā'ū*-offerings within the first seven years of his reign.

Postgate makes the important observation that several provinces listed in MARV 2.21 are virtually unknown outside of the *ginā'ū* lists, while some provinces that are well-attested in other contexts do not feature in the lists. He suggests that there may have been political reasons for this. Aminu, Saḫlala, Ḫarbu, Tuttul, and Naḫur are all in the northwestern region and are all mentioned in thirteenth-century texts. Thus, some of these may have fallen away from Assyrian control during the twelfth century.[168]

Finally, it should be noted that the Assyrian Chronicle 4 dates to the last years of Tiglath-pileser I's reign and is an important witness to the situation that occurred at this time and continued into the reign of Aššur-bēl-kala (see the discussion of this text below).

### 3.2.3. The Rise of the Aramean Polities in the Jezirah

During the twelfth–tenth centuries, perhaps starting earlier in the far-western areas, the Jezirah underwent an Aramaization process. Three stages for this process can be distinguished: (1) a stage of Aramean pastoralist expansion (ca. 1197–1114); (2) a stage of initial conflict (ca. 1114–1056); and (3) a stage of Assyrian weakness[169] and Aramean state formation (ca. 1055–935). Certainly by the end of the third stage, the overall Aramaization of the Jezirah was complete.

---

166. Rosa (2010, 330–35) suggests that the provinces named *pāḫutu elītu* (= Šadikannī) and *pāḫutu šaplītu* were located on the upper and lower Ḫābūr River. It would seem that Dūr-Katlimmu may have been connected with the *pāḫutu šaplītu*.

167. See Jeffers 2013, 332–33, table 5; and his maps on pp. 329 and 334.

168. Postgate 2013, 100–101; see Jakob 2003, 111–17.

169. This period is sometimes referred to as a "Dark Age," though such a designation is neither descriptive nor helpful.

Table 3.4. *Ginā'ū* Tabular List (MARV 2.21)

| | |
|---|---|
| 2 URU.*Ar-ba-il* | Arba'il |
| 3 URU.*Ki-li-zu* | Kilizu |
| 4 KUR.*Ḫa-láḫ-ḫu* | Ḫalaḫḫu |
| 5 URU.*Tal-muš-šu* | Talmuššu |
| 6 URU.*I-du* | Īdu |
| 7 KUR.*Kat-mu-ḫu* | Katmuḫu |
| 8 URU.*Šu-du* | Šūdu |
| 9 URU.*Ta-i-du* | Ta'idu |
| 10 URU.*A-ma-sa-ki* | Amasakku |
| 11 URU.*Ku-liš-ḫi-na-áš* | Kulišḫinaš |
| 12 URU.$^{d}$*A-šur* | Aššur |
| 13 *pa-ḫu-tu* AN.TA (*pāḫutu elītu*) | "Upper province" |
| 14 KIMIN KI.TA (*pāḫutu šaplītu*) | "Lower province"[165] |
| 15 URU.*Túr-šá-*[*an*] | Turšan |
| 16 URU.ŠÀ-*bi* URU | Libbi-āli |
| 17 URU.*Ni-nu-a* | Ninua |
| 18 URU.*Kur-da* | Kurda |
| 19 URU.*Ap-ku* | Apku |
| 20 URU.*Ad-da-rík* | Addarik |
| 21 URU.GEŠTIN-*na* | Karānā |
| 22 URU.*Ši-ba*$^{!}$*-ni-be* | Šib/manībe |
| 23 URU.*Ḫi-iš-šu-tu* | Ḫiššutu |
| 24 URU.*Ši-mi* | Šīmu |
| 25 URU.*Ḫu-sa-na-nu* | Ḫusananu |
| 26 URU.*Kal-ḫu* | Kalḫu |
| 27 URU.*Šá-ṣi-li* | Ša-ṣilli |
| 28 URU.*Šu-me-la* | Šumēla |
| final line [… *gi-n*]*a-ú maḫ-r*[*u ša l*]*i-me* $^{m}$*pa-'u-zi* | [Total(?), offer]ings received [of the] eponymate of Pa'uzu. |

3.2.3.1. Stage One: Aramean Pastoralist Expansion (ca. 1197–1114 BCE)

It appears from the most recent evidence that while Assyria extended its empire to the Euphrates, the region between the Euphrates and the Balīḫ Rivers was never fully part of the Assyrian grid of fortified agricultural production centers; it had no provincial system as the result of Assyrian

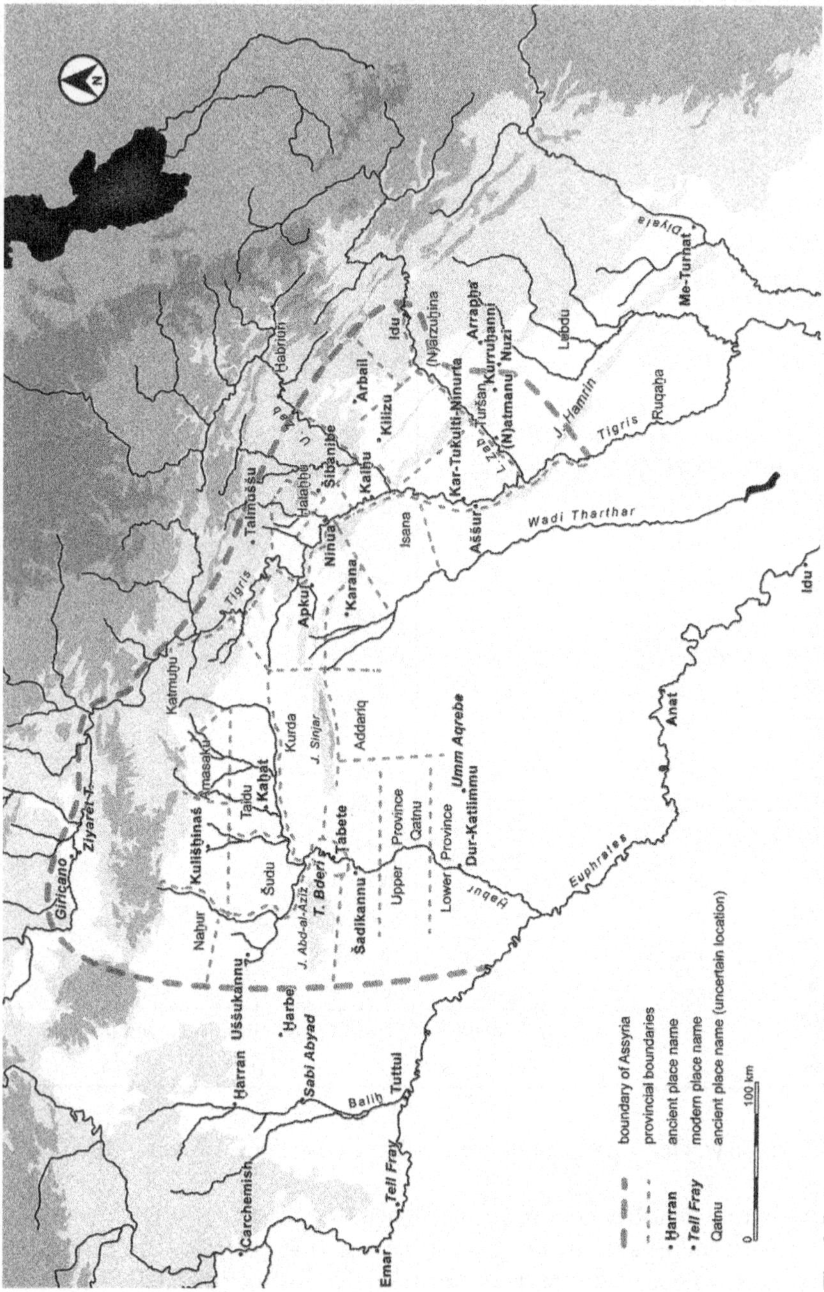


Fig. 3.5. Assyria in the twelfth century BCE showing hypothetical provincial boundaries (Postgate 2013, 31)

colonization. Hence, various tribal and clan groups that were located in this region and others may have migrated here before the demise of the Mittanian kingdom and throughout the early Middle Assyrian Empire.

However, the decline in Assyrian control in the Jezirah began in real terms with the death of Tukulti-Ninurta I. There is little documentation for the three weak kings that followed his death: Aššur-nādin-apli (r. 1196–1194), Aššur-nērārī III (r. 1193–1188) and Enlil-kudurrī-uṣur (r. 1187–1183). It appears that during the reign of Ninurta-apil-Ekur (r. 1182–1170), the western border was located on the Ḫābūr River. If Freydank's dating of MARV 2.21 to the time of Ninurta-apil-Ekur is correct, it would be further evidence in support of this.[170] The interruption of the administrative archives at Ḫarbe (Tell Chuēra)[171] and Dūr-Katlimmu (Tell Šēḫ Ḥamad)[172] during the last years of the reign of Tukulti-Ninurta I and the archive of Tell Ṣābi Abyad[173] at the beginning of the reign of Ninurta-apil-Ekur support a scenario of diminished territory. Although Tell Ṣābi Abyad was rebuilt with a much smaller facility, perhaps surviving into the reign of Aššur-rēša-iši, it seems surely abandoned during his reign. In short, it seems that for most of the twelfth century, the western Jezirah was not in Assyrian control. While it is possible that some enclaves remained (e.g., Tell Ṣābi Abyad), the Assyrian grid of hubs west of the Ḫābūr was severely diminished.[174]

However, Szuchman (2007, 98–99) argues that this supposed twelfth-century decline of Assyrian power might have been less severe than scholars traditionally propose. He posits that the period of instability was short, ending under Aššur-dān I (r. 1179–1134), who ruled for thirty-six or forty-six years, and Aššur-rēša-iši (1132–1115) who ruled for eighteen years before Tiglath-pileser I's own long reign. He argues that the power that Aššur-rēša-iši brought back to the throne of Assyria is also evident in the significant increase in the number of royal inscriptions documenting construction activities in Assur and Nimrud: twenty-two texts are attributed to Aššur-rēša-iši compared with only nine texts from the seven previous kings. Thus it was particularly the period after Tiglath-pileser I that saw a significant decline in Assyrian authority (Szuchman 2009c, 99).

---

170. This is also granting the assumption that these *ginā'ū* offering lists, in fact, reflect the provincial status of the text's dating.

171. The site was abandoned; see Jakob and Janisch-Jakob 2009, 6–7.

172. The tablets from Dūr-Katlimmu were discovered in a destruction layer. See Röllig 2008a.

173. The major fortification was destroyed around 1180. See Akkermans 2006.

174. Harrak (1987, 276) argued that Assyria must have lost its hegemony over Ḫanigalbat sometime after the reign of Aššur-nērārī III (r. 1193–1188).

Szuchman, however, is addressing the relative stability of the heartland and Ḫanigalbat. That Assyria had control of the Upper and Lower Ḫābūr[175] and that there was continuity in the settlement in that region is not at issue. Rather, the western Jezirah is the issue and the inability of these long-reigned kings to recover any of this area has implications concerning a continued recession in Middle Assyrian power.[176]

What appears to be driving this argument, however, seems to be Szuchman's conviction that nomads most often settle during periods of stability and strong urban authority (Szuchman 2007, 131; 2009c). Thus, the pastoral nomadic predecessors of the first-millennium Aramean kingdoms became sedentary farmers in the Jezirah at the end of the Late Bronze Age. In other words, the Arameans became sedentary before the collapse of the Middle Assyrian kingdom and hence simply filled the power vacuum after that collapse. However, Zadok (2012, 574) has recently countered:

> It is difficult to verify this claim from the ethno-linguistic identity of the individuals recorded in Middle Assyrian sources concerning the Jazira especially because the West Semitic (semi-)nomads are severely under-represented in the Middle Assyrian documentation. It stands to reason that the ensuing Aramean penetration into the Jazira was enhanced by the demise of the Late Bronze entities and urban centres there, notably Emar and Tuttul.

Moreover, as noted by van der Steen, there is never simply one explanation for why nomads settle, or why they take to nomadism and pastoralism again.[177] While it is entirely possible, in fact likely, that some groups of Arameans were sedentarizing during the period of the stable economic context of the Middle Assyrian Empire, it would be just as likely that many of these Arameans did not sedentarize until after the beginning of the demise of the empire after the death of Tukulti-Ninurta I, if not after Aššur-bēl-kala. There is no actual evidence for any of the Aramean sedentarizations.

Furthermore, if some of these Aramean socially constructed groups had sedentary components already, they may simply have moved to other sedentary contexts along with their mobile pastoralist components to other nearby pastures. If the Assyrians could no longer control large segments of

175. E.g., the Dūr-Katlimmu's continuity. See Kühne 2010.

176. When one comes to the inscriptions of Tiglath-pileser I, the purpose behind all this king's initial activities was to regain lost territory for Assyria, like for example Katmuḫu and to secure the kingdom by keeping outside threats at bay (see the comments of Jeffers 2013, 302–7 who states: "During the first years of his reign, Tiglath-pileser was in the process of reversing the political fortunes of the still relatively weak Assyrian kingdom so that he could assure his people that they were safe and secure in their land."

177. See discussion on pp. 70–71.

the western Jezirah, tribal and/or clan groups that had the ability and power to move and seize land did so. The perception of opportunity to seize land has been a major strong "pull" factor in migrations, just as much as a stable growing economy. Therefore, it is likely that Aramean chain migrations were taking place before the decline of the Middle Assyrian kingdom, but the empire's decline certainly added a further stimulus. A possible "push" factor may have been climate change (Lönnqvist 2008, 206–7).

Thus, an Aramaization process had been underway in the western Jezirah (Bunnens 1999, 611–12). It is also very probable that some of the western Ḫābūr provinces were experiencing Aramean migrations. A few of the toponyms in the region that are of Aramean derivation may originate from this time.

#### 3.2.3.2. Stage Two: Initial Conflict (ca. 1114–1056 BCE)

It is only with Tiglath-pileser I (1114–1076) that the gentilic form "Aramean" first enters the Assyrian usage: first associated with the Aḫlamû, then, from the time of Aššur-bēl-kala onward, as an autonomous designation.[178] Without the Assyrian inscriptions, a political history of the Arameans during the early Iron Age would be very difficult if not impossible to write (Klengel 2000). Therefore, it is prudent to provide the reader with the most important Assyrian texts relevant to the question of the Arameans. The following are the essential passages[179] from the texts of Tiglath-pileser I:

Text 1 (RIMA 2:23, A.0.87.1, v.44–63)[180]

> With the help of Aššur, my lord, I took my chariots and warriors (and) took off for the desert steppe (*mu-ud-ba-ra*). I marched against the Aramean-Aḫlamû (*aḫ-la-mì-i* KUR *ar-ma-ia*.MEŠ), the enemies of Aššur, my lord. I plundered from the edge of the land of Sūḫu to the city of Karkamiš of the land of Ḫatti in "a single day." I massacred them. I brought back their booty, possessions, and goods without number. The rest of their troops, who fled from the weapons of Aššur, my lord, crossed the Euphrates. I crossed the Euphrates after them on rafts (made of inflated) goatskins. I conquered six of their cities (6 URU.MEŠ-*šu-nu* : 6 *ālānīšunu*) at the foot of Mount Bišri

178. It should be stressed that this is the case as of our current knowledge. This should not be considered an absolute "firm" date, though it has often been treated as such.

179. Since the tenth-year annalistic text, RIMA 2:31–35, A.0.87.2 (lines 28–29) is the same as A.0.87.1, other than some condensing, I have not included a translation.

180. This "annalistic" text is dated by the eponymy of Ina-ilīya-allak: 1108.49 (Jeffers 2013).

(GÌR KUR *bé-eš-ri*), burned, razed (and) destroyed (them, and) brought their booty, possessions, and goods to my city Assur.

Text 2 (RIMA 2:37, A.0.87.3, lines 29–35)[181]

I crossed the Euphrates [...] times, twice in one year, in pursuit of the Aramean-Aḫlamû (*aḫ-la-mì-i* KUR *ar-ma-ia*.MEŠ), to the land of Ḫatti. I inflicted on them a decisive defeat from the foot of Mount Lebanon (GÌR KUR *lab-na-ni*), the city of Tadmor of the land of Amurru (URU *ta-ad-mar* [*š*]*a* KUR *a-mur-ri*), (and) Anat of the land of Sūḫu, as far as Rapiqu of Karduniaš (Babylonia). I brought their booty (and) possessions to my city Assur.

Text 3 (RIMA 2:43, A.0.87.4, lines 34–36)[182]

I crossed the Euphrates twenty-eight times, twice in one year, in pursuit of the Aramean-Aḫlamû (KUR *aḫ-la-me-e* KUR *ar-ma-a-ia*.MEŠ).[183] I inflicted on them a decisive defeat from the city of Tadmor of the land of Amurru (URU *ta-ad-mar šá* KUR *a-mur-ri*), (and) Anat of the land of Sūḫu, as far as Rapiqu of Karduniaš (Babylonia). I brought their booty (and) possessions to my city Assur.

Text 4 (RIMA 2:59, A.0.87.13, lines 4′–9′)[184]

By the command of Aššur and Ninurta, the [great] gods, [my lords], I conquered [from the *edge* of the land of Sūḫu] to the city of Karkamiš of the land of Ḫ[atti in a single day]. [I crossed] the Euphrates as though [it were a canal]. Seventeen of their cities (17 URU.MEŠ-*ni-šu-nu* : 17 *ālānīšunu*), from [the city of Tadmor of the land of Amurru, Anat of the land of Sūḫu, as far as Rapiqu of Karduniaš (Babylonia)], I burned, [razed, (and) destroyed. I brought their booty], their hostages, and [their goods to my city Assur].

Text 5 (Frame 2011, 127–34, No. 68 (MS 2004), lines 19–23, pls. XLIX–L)[185]

181. This first Summary Inscription is dated to the eponymy of Ninuʾāyu (twenty-third year): 1092.98 BCE.

182. This Summary Inscription is dated by eponymy to [Ta]klāk-ana-Aššur: 1091.95 BCE.

183. The KUR before *aḫ-la-me-e* is likely a scribal error, since it is almost everywhere absent. See discussion in 2.5.1.2 above.

184. Undated, fragmentary text. This text is "worn and pitted." However, it does seem, with due caution, to be narrating the events connected to the Aramean campaign of year 5. See Millard 1970, 168 and esp. pl. xxxiv.

185. This inscription was written on a completely preserved tablet and was dated to the second day of the month of Araḫsamnu (VIII) in the eponymy of Aššur-šaʾissunu,

> I crossed the Euphrates twenty-eight times, twice in one year, in pursuit of the Aramean-Aḫlamû. I defeated them from the foot/base of Mount Lebanon, the city of Tadmor of the land of Amurru to (as far as) Rapiqu of the land of Karduniaš. I brought their booty (and) their goods to my city Assur.

The inscriptions of Tiglath-pileser I and Aššur-bēl-kala remain far and away the earliest testimony to the Arameans that we possess. They give the impression of successful emperors who campaigned as far away as Lebanon and the Mediterranean Sea. But it is clear that both rulers struggled against the incursions of the Arameans into Assyrian territory, demanding a multitude of campaigns on their parts to halt these penetrations.

It seems that Tiglath-pileser I's actions were rooted in an attempt to recover former Assyrian territory. Fales has recently summed this up:

> ... perhaps it was exactly such a slow but unavoidable erosion of the Assyrian "hold" on the Jezirah—due to dynastic troubles at Assur, to the diversion of military energies toward Babylonia, to an increasing separatism in the diverse "lands" (Ḫanigalbat, Mari) that formed the western territories of the reign, and finally to an ever-growing menace posed by West Semitic gentilic groups on the Euphrates—that prompted Tiglath-pileser I to engage into a forceful attempt to *restore the borders of Assyria* established by his forebearers Shalmaneser I and Tukulti-Ninurta I. (Fales 2011b, 30–31, emphasis added)

The very wording of the initial account of Tiglath-pileser I's campaign against the Aramean-Aḫlamû[186] seems to support this understanding. Tiglath-pileser termed these Aramean-Aḫlamû as "the enemies of the god Aššur." This is because these Arameans are on "Assyrian soil," namely, on the left bank of the Euphrates, in the Jezirah. The "annalistic" text (Text 1) presents this military action as taking place in his fourth regnal year (1109.52 BCE), in which Tiglath-pileser fought an open-field battle in the steppe (*mudbaru*)[187] where he was able to utilize his chariots.[188] The geographic description for this battle

---

possibly ca. 1079 BCE (see Frame's discussion of the date at 2011, 134). Its account of Tiglath-pileser's encounters with Aramean-Aḫlamû closely follows RIMA 2:37–38, A.0.87.3, lines 29–35; and 2:43, A.0.87.4, lines 34–36.

186. The phrase *aḫlamî/aḫlamê armāyya*, with Aramean as a gentilic/ethnicon is only attested thus far in the genitive. See §2.5.1.2.

187. Schniedewind (2002, 278) rightly points out that *mudbaru* is better translated "steppeland" than "desert" (as Grayson RIMA 2:23): "In Ugaritic we find a helpful opposition between the *mdbr* 'steppeland' and the *nǵr mdrʿ* 'sown land'—that is, between the pastoral and the agrarian regions (cf. *Birth of the Twin Gods*, KTU 1.23:65–76; UT 52:65–76)."

188. RIMA 2:23, A.0.87.1, v.44–63.

makes it clear that this is not the Šamīya but the Jezirah. He claims to have then "plundered from the edge of the land of Sūḫu to the city of Karkamiš of the land of Ḫatti in a single day," that is, an area corresponding to the basin of the Middle Euphrates to the Upper Euphrates (a distance of some 200 km). While the claim is obviously hyperbolic, the toponyms (Sūḫu and Karkamiš) are important: this is the steppe of the Aramean pastoralists on the left (east) bank of the Euphrates (i.e., inside the Jezirah). Therefore, it is little wonder that Tiglath-pileser I designates these Aramean-Aḫlamû "enemies of Aššur," since to the Assyrian conception of their empire with the Euphrates being its border, these Arameans were "squatters." Furthermore, the construction of forts on the Euphrates by Tiglath-pileser at Pitru and Mutkīnu were very purposeful to his attempt to control these important crossing zones. It is also very possible that the Middle Assyrian fort system was established (or reestablished) at this time.

But there was a real need for a follow-up to this initial open-field battle and campaign in the Jezirah. In other words, as crushing of a loss as the Arameans may have suffered in the steppe of the Jezirah, they were by no means defeated. Hence, it was necessary that Tiglath-pileser I cross over the Euphrates and defeat them on the right (west) bank, i.e., in the Šamīya. He likely crossed the river at Ḥalabiya and Zalabiya, not far from Jebel Bišri (Pappi 2006, 251). He states: "I conquered six of their cities (6 URU.MEŠ-*šu-nu* : 6 *ālānīšunu*) at the foot of Mount Bišri (GÌR KUR *bé-eš-ri*)."[189] It is important to note that the text does not use a term like "fortified city" (*āl dannūti*), as this is done, for example, in connection with the campaign to Katmuḫu,[190] or "fortress" (*ḫalṣu*) as in the Babylonian campaign;[191] or "fort" (*birtu*). The term *ālānīšunu* "their cities" is important, likely referring here to town or village settlements similar to the use of the term *ālu* in the nomadic cycle as described by Streck[192] and in the ethnoarchaeological work

189. Jebel Bišri was naturally in earlier periods an area inhabited by various nomadic tribes who were perceived by the sedentary rulers in Mesopotamia as enemies. Šar-kali-šarrī reports a military campaign to the west against the nomadic Amurrites at Jebel Bišri. See Frayne 1993, 183, iv. The text reads: (1′) [*i*]*n* 1 MU *śar-kà-lí*-LUGAL-*rí* MAR.DÚ-*am in ba-śa-ar*.KUR [$iš_{11}$*-a-ru*] "The year Šar-kali-šarrī [was victorious over] the Amurrites at Mount Bašar."

190. RIMA 2:14–15, A.0.87.1, ii.6, 12.

191. RIMA 2:43, A.0.87.4, line 47.

192. Streck 2002, 159–70: "Dorf (*ālu*)," esp. the diagram on p. 167. Kreuzer (1996, 101) states: "bases and/or retreat areas in the mountains." Van Driel (2001, 109) noted that "for the Mesopotamians the congregated tents of the non-sedentaries also constituted an URU.'" See also the comments of Fadhil and Radner 1996, 423 n. 21. Also see the discussion in chapter 2 concerning the semantic range of *ālu* with *adurû*, "village, hamlet."

of Lönnqvist[193] (see §2.4.2 above). Archaeologically, sedentary remains in connection to Jebel Bišri are generally restricted to the Euphratic side and the western piedmont areas (Lönnqvist 2008, 202). Hence, they were more accessible to Tiglath-pileser's assaults.[194]

However, it is clear that the Arameans were quite resilient. In a later summary inscription, Tiglath-pileser I admitted that he had, in fact, "crossed the Euphrates 'twenty-eight times,' twice in one year, in pursuit of them, inflicting a decisive defeat on them from the city of Tadmor of the land of Amurru (URU *ta-ad-mar šá* KUR *a-mur-ri*), 'Anat of the land of Sūḫu, as far as Rapiqu of Karduniaš (Babylonia)."[195] In another summation of his campaigns, it is stated: "Seventeen of their cities (17 URU.MEŠ-*ni-šu-nu*), from [the city of Tadmor of the land of Amurru, 'Anat of the land of Sūḫu, as far as Rapiqu of Karduniaš (Babylonia)], I burned, [razed, (and) destroyed]."[196] Over the years, Tiglath-pileser's inscriptions widen the geographic scope of the campaigning against the Arameans with the clear "highlight" being his campaign to Lebanon: "I crossed the Euphrates [. . .] times, twice in one year, in pursuit of the Aramean-Aḫlamû (*aḫ-la-mì-i* KUR *ar-ma-ia*.MEŠ), to the land of Ḫatti. I inflicted on them a decisive defeat from the foot of Mount Lebanon (GÌR KUR *lab-na-ni*), the city of Tadmor of the land of Amurru (URU *ta-ad-mar* [*š*]*a* KUR *a-mur-ri*), 'Anat of the land of Sūḫu, as far as Rapiqu of Karduniaš (Babylonia)."[197]

These were numerous and extensive campaigns. The number "seventeen" underscores that it was more than "six" cities (again likely meaning "settlements") that were eventually destroyed. The emphasis on the lengthy zone of the Euphrates (especially the Middle Euphrates and Karkamiš), the oasis town of Tadmor, and climactically Mount Lebanon stresses the herculean effort being expended to defeat these Arameans.

The campaign to Mount Lebanon is narrated in a number of Tiglath-pileser I's inscriptions. The earliest account describes it as follows:

---

193. See the ethnographic and the ethnoarchaeological analogies, Lönnqvist 2008, 206–7. She observes concerning a seasonally abandoned village: "The plan of the village still corresponds to a nomadic camp, the houses are not yet agglutinated. The houses are rectangular in layouts and provide tent-like interiors. Open courtyards have household facilities with pens, kitchens, and silos. However, tents are still used on the courtyards as additional spaces of living and cooking" (p. 207).

194. The text (RIMA 2:31–35, A.0.87.2) is relatively close in date (five years) to the original annals of RIMA 2:7–31, A.0.87.1 (also speaking of the capture of "six cities").

195. RIMA 2:43, A.0.87.4, lines 34–36.

196. RIMA 2:59, A.0.87.13, lines 4′–9′. It appears to be conflating the Aramean campaigns; hence the total 17. The number is clear.

197. RIMA 2:37, A.0.87.3, lines 29–35. This is the earliest recording of this encounter in Tiglath-pileser's texts.

> I marched to Mount Lebanon. I cut down (and) carried off cedar beams for the temple of Anu and Adad, the great gods, my lords. I traversed to the land of Amurru; I conquered the land of Amurru in its entirety. I received tribute from the land of Byblos, the land of Sidon, (and) the land of Arvad. I rode in Arvadite ships; I achieved a successful journey, a distance of three double hours from the land of Arvad, which is in the midst of the sea (i.e., an island), to the city of Ṣamuru (Ṣimirra) which is in the land Amurru. In the midst of the sea, I killed a *nāḫiru*, which is called a sea-horse.
>
> Moreover, on my return, I [became lord] of the land of Ḫatti in its entirety [...]. [I imposed] upon Ini-Tešub, king of the land Ḫatti: hostages, tax, tribute, and cedar beams.[198]

This is an impressive campaign that demonstrates power and resources. Perhaps most interestingly, Karkamiš paid tribute. Hawkins observes: "It is hard to see where the centre of this country would have been if not in Karkamiš, and the king's name, recalling the famous Ini-Tešub of the Hittite Empire dynasty, reinforces the impression of dynastic continuity" (Hawkins 2000, 73–74).

Other than the open-field battle in the Jezirah (year 5), Tiglath-pileser's encounters with the Arameans are west of the Euphrates. Nothing in his inscriptions is said about any territory or cities located east of the Euphrates (Bunnens 1999, 606). Thus, it appears that the Arameans' activities on the eastern bank were primarily that of raiding Assyrian interests. But Tiglath-pileser I's inscriptions are only recording his engagements with particular groups of Arameans, and so it would be an error to assume that there were no Arameans in other parts of the Jezirah just because he does not mention them. It is also clear from a careful reading that Tiglath-pileser I's victories did not remove the Aramean threat.

The mention of "Sūḫu" and "Karkamiš" in Tiglath-pileser's initial campaign against the Aramean-Aḫlamû stresses the two important zones where trade and communication routes were located and where apparent tribal penetrations were occurring. The construction of forts on the Euphrates by Tiglath-pileser at Pitru and Mutkīnu was designed to control this crossing point of the Euphrates. At a much later time, it is not surprising that Til-Barsib was renamed Kār Shalmaneser and the *turtānu* Šamšī-ilu was stationed there. Tiglath-pileser's ability to found these two forts in this location is perhaps a result of the submission of Ini-Tešub. If the city of Til-Barsib was under Assyrian control, it was insufficient. Apparently, Til-Barsib (Luw. Masuwari) came under Luwian control some time later (see discussion above

198. RIMA 2:37, A.0.87.3, lines 16–28; see also the parallels in 2:42, A.0.87.4, lines 24–30; and 2:53, A.0.87.10, lines 33–35.

§3.1.4). In any case, it seems unlikely that Masuwari was an independent entity at this time who could oppose the constructions.[199]

On the Middle Euphrates a series of forts, many with Middle Assyrian pottery, have been surveyed and excavated (see table 3.3 above). While there can be little doubt that these forts served a role over against Kassite Babylonia,[200] it is very likely that their primary purpose was to control the river crossings. Historically, this is an area where tribal penetrations took place.[201]

With all the campaigning that Tiglath-pileser I did—to Lebanon, southeastern Anatolia, from Sūḫu to Karkamiš, Mount Bišri, the Upper Tigris, Babylonia—Assyrian resources were likely stretched to the limit, if not completely overextended. There were undoubtedly many enemies who were looking for a chance to rebel and/or get revenge.

It is important to remember that part of the reason that Tiglath-pileser I could conduct these campaigns was that, for his first two decades, there was relative peace between Assyria and Babylonia (Karduniaš), or at least he did not need to worry greatly about his southern frontier. This permitted the Assyrian king to devote his time and energy to all his other borders.

However, this changed drastically when Tiglath-pileser invaded Babylonia in two consecutive military campaigns. There are various speculations about Assyrian motives in these campaigns that are unnecessary for our discussion.[202] Two things are important in this: (1) It appears that Tiglath-pileser I's initial attack on Babylonia was a defeat; yet the Assyrian scribes found a way to gloss over this. This should caution us that the continuously successful campaigns against the Arameans that are narrated in his inscriptions may not be entirely accurate. Interestingly, one version of his texts from Nineveh, RIMA 2:50–56, A.0.87.10, [203] omits any account of the campaigns against the Arameans that appears in every other version of the king's inscriptions. While this could be explained as a telescoping of the king's campaigns, it appears to be rather blatant. It is more likely the result of the scribe of this

199. This is obviously only a deduction from the extremely limited knowledge of the situation at this time.

200. Cf. the letter (KBo I 10 + KUB ) from the Hittite king Ḫattušili III to the Kassite Kadašman-Enlil. The Middle Euphrates forts may have been the point where Assyrians intercepted messengers from either state (though Tuttul [Tell Bia] may have been another). For the letter, see Beckman 1999, 132–37; *COS* 3.31:52–53. For discussion, see Hoffner 2009.

201. See Clancier (2006, 269) who documents difficulties for later kingdoms to regulate this zone (Achaemenid, Seleucid, and Parthian).

202. For detailed discussions, see Bloch 2012a; Jeffers 2013; Younger forthcoming.

203. The name of the eponym is broken; so the date is unknown, although it was perhaps written around the same time as RIMA 2:38–45, A.0.87.4, or a little later.

version believing that these conflicts were not going so well for the Assyrian king, and so made no reference to them. Hence, the omission may be ideologically driven.

(2) As a result of the huge military efforts expended by Assyria under Tiglath-pileser I and Babylonia under Marduk-nādin-aḫḫē, which only ended with the treaty between Aššur-bēl-kala and Marduk-šāpik-zēri, both kingdoms were highly susceptible to Aramean penetrations. Ultimately these Aramean incursions brought both to their knees. In a sense, it was like two heavy-weight boxers punching each other silly—and then a feather-weight jumping into the ring and delivering knockout blows to each.

Not only did his "victories" not remove the Aramean threat, the very last years of Tiglath-pileser I's reign saw a significant reversal in Assyrian fortunes. This is found in Assyrian Chronicle 4, the so-called Tiglath-pileser I Chronicle:[204]

> (2) [In the eponymy of … great starvation(?) …]
> The peopl]e (the Assyrians) ate one another's flesh […]
> (3) […] the houses of the Arameans (É.MEŠ KUR.*Ar-ma-a-ia*.ME[Š]) (4) [increased(?)]
> they plundered[205] [the harvest of Assyria];
> they seized the roads;
> (5) They captured[206] (and) took [many districts of] Assyria.
> (6) [The people (the Assyrians) [(7)fled] (6)[t]o the mountains of Ḫabrūri[207] for (their) lives.
> (7) Their [gold], their silver, (and) their possessions they (the Arameans) took.
> (8) [Marduk-nādin-aḫḫē, king of] Karduniaš (Babylonia), passed away;
> Marduk-[šāpik]-zēri (9)ascended hi[s father's throne].
> Eighteen regnal years of Marduk-[nādin-a]ḫḫē.

---

204. Grayson 1975, 189; Glassner 2004, 188–91.

205. Tadmor (1958, 133) and Grayson (1975, 189) read: … *a*]*-lak tap-pu-tu ḫu-la-a-*[*ni*]meš *iṣ-bu-tu*, "… to] render aid they set out" understanding *alāku(m) tapputu* as an idiom "to go to someone's assistance." Glassner (2004, 188–89) reads: …] *iḫ-tab-ba-tu ḫu-la-a-ni*.MEŠ *iṣ-bu-tu*. See also Neumann and Parpola 1987, 178; and Na'aman 1994, 33–34.

206. While Grayson remarks that "it is difficult to say whether Aššur is the direct object in this sentence when the beginning is missing" (1975, 189, note to line 5), the subject must be plural and the most reasonable option is the *bītāt māt Aramāya* since these Aramean tribes are clearly the subject of numerous plural verb forms in the text.

207. While earlier read as Kirriuri (Tadmor 1958, 133; Grayson 1975, 189), Levine (1976–80) suggested reading Ḫabrūri based on a Sultantepe Eponym Chronicle text. He identified it with Dašt-e Ḥarīr located northeast of Arbail in the Zagros area closest to Assyria proper. See Parpola and Porter 2001, 9. For the reading, see now Millard (1994, 35, year 796).

> (10) [In the eponymy ...] the harvest of the land of Assyria, all of it, [was flood]ed.[208]
> (11) [The houses of the Arameans] increased;
> they proceeded along (lit. "took") the b[ank of the Tig]ris.[209]
> (12) [They plundered] [the land of $GN_1$, the land of $GN_2$, the land of] Īdu,[210]
> the district of Nineveh, (and) the land of Kili[zi].[211]
> (13) [In that year Tiglath-pil]eser (I), the king of Assyria, [marched] to Katmuḫu.

Assyrian Chronicle 4 is fragmentary and difficult to interpret. As a result, it has often been discounted as being able to offer much insight into the historical context. Thus Pitard (1996, 299) concluded that:

> the reconstruction is actually quite uncertain. What is actually preserved indicates that there was a famine that affected the Assyrians and the Arameans, but it remains entirely unclear whether the Arameans attacked Assyria.

But with closer scrutiny scholars have noted that in contrast to the Babylonian chronicles, the Assyrian chronicle fragments may be a bit more reliable when it comes to reconstructing history. Unlike the Babylonian chronicles, which are much later documents (from the seventh century or even later), the Assyrian probably date to the late Middle Assyrian period, making them almost contemporaneous with the Middle Assyrian narratives. Summing up the Assyrian chronicle materials, Postgate (2013, 60) states:

> These scraps of chronicle are tantalising out of proportion to their size, since they must be the remnants of at least two centuries of annual records main-

---

208. Tadmor (1958, 133) restored [*ra-ḫi*]-*iṣ* "was ravaged" speculating that the crop damage in this year was caused by excessive rains flooding the fields. Neumann and Parpola (1987, 178 n. 52) point out that "the verb can equally be read [*ma-ḫi*]-*iṣ*, which simply means 'was ruined' (by any agent, e.g., by locusts)." Recently Postgate (2013, 60) has pointed out that the restoration is likely [*ra-ḫi*]-*iṣ*, since there is the occurrence of the same verb in administrative texts from Dūr-Katlimmu (see Röllig 2008a, No. 67:12).

209. Na'aman (1994, 33–34) reads: *ši*[*d*]-*d*[*i* ÍD.]ID[IGNA]. Glassner (2004, 188) follows. Tadmor (1958, 133) reads: ⌜É.MEŠ⌝ [KUR *A*]*r-m*[*a-a-ia-e*] and Grayson (1975, 189) reads: *bītā*[*ti*]$^{\text{me}}$[$^{\text{š}}$ *māt A*]*r-m-a-a-ia*$^{\text{meš}}$].

210. While Grayson (1975, 189) and Glassner (2004, 188) understand this to be a reference to Īdu, Postgate (1985, 100) suggests a possible reading of either [Ta'i]du or Īdu. In my opinion, the mention of the Tigris in the immediate context would make Īdu more likely.

211. Although Grayson (1975, 189) reads KUR KI.TA "the land downstream," the reading KUR.*Kili*[*zi*, "the land of Kili[zi]" makes better sense in light of the mention of Īdu, Nineveh, and Katmuḫu (see Glassner 2004; Na'aman 1994; Postgate 1976–80b, 592). It was located in between Arbail and Kalḫu, at Qasr Šemamok (30 km south of Arbail).

> tained by Assyrian scribes in their vernacular dialect, to preserve factual information of a kind we do not find in the self-glorifying texts composed in Babylonian dialect to commemorate royal building projects.

The copy of the Tiglath-pileser Chronicle Fragment/Assyrian Chronicle Fragment 4 even comes from the so-called library of Tiglath-pileser from the southwest courtyard of the Aššur Temple (Pedersén 1986, 2:20, Archive N1:21; Jeffers 2013, 78–79).

This particular text reveals a number of important pieces of evidence. First of all, the events that it narrates can be accurately dated, since the text makes reference to the death of Marduk-nādin-aḫḫē and the accession of his son Marduk-šāpik-zēri. Thus, these events date to the latter part of Tiglath-pileser I's reign (1078/1077, Tiglath-pileser's I's thirty-seventh year; based on Bloch 2012a, 56; 2010d, 74 n. 48; see Jeffers 2013, 248–54).[212] This is important for contextualizing the data that is discernible in the text. Second, the vocabulary of war is clearly used in lines 3–7, and thus it is very likely that the conflict between the "houses of the Arameans" and the Assyrians is in view. More specifically, the grammar indicates the *bītāt māt Aramāya*, "houses of the Arameans" is the subject of a number of plural verb forms: "they plundered," "seized," "captured," "took" (2x), "increased," and "seized." The term *bītātu* is a powerful precursor of the later partition of the entire Jezirah into a number of polities—mostly Aramean—characterized by the *bītu*-formula. Third, it is manifest that there was famine bad enough that cannibalism took place. It may well be that the famine was the result of climate change during this period (Kirleis and Herles 2007; Neumann and Parpola 1987). Fourth, it is interesting that the Assyrian people escaped "[t]o the mountains of Ḫabrūri for (their) lives." This was an Assyrian province in the late Middle Assyrian period (ca. 1124–1120 BCE).[213] This is the very same place mentioned by Aššur-dān II, who "brought back the weary [people] of Assyria [who in the face of] famine, hunger, (and) shortage had abandoned [their cities (and) houses] (and) [had gone up] to oth[er] lands."[214] Fifth, a number of the same district names occur in this Chronicle that also occur in the *ginā'ū* lists: Kilizi, Īdu, Katmuḫu, and Nineveh. As mentioned above, in the past scholars have dated the *ginā'ū* list of MARV 2.21 to Tiglath-pileser I's reign (1077 BCE)

---

212. Brinkman (1987–90a, 1987–90b) gives the following dates: the death of Marduk-nādin-aḫḫē (r. 1099–1082 BCE) and the accession of his son, Marduk-šāpik-zēri (r. 1081–1069 BCE) = Tiglath-pileser's thirty-second year (1082/1081).

213. Ḫabrūri (modern Dašt-i Ḥarīr). See Zadok 2012, 578; Bloch 2012a, 69 n. 65. See MARV 6.86:16. It is mentioned after the province of the bank of the ḪUR-*ri* River (or $I_7$.*ḫar-ri* "the province of the bank of the ditch"?) in connection with Arbela.

214. RIMA 2:133–35, A.0.98.1, lines 54–67.

and have reconstructed the extent of the Assyrian loss (Postgate 1985, 100; 1992; 2013). However, in light of the redating of MARV 2.21 to Ninurta-apil-Ekur's reign, it appears that the Chronicle is the main witness to the end of Tiglath-pileser's reign. The Chronicle gives evidence of a significant struggle. The extent of the Assyrian loss is not entirely clear, but from the Arameans' actions on the Tigris, it is clear that the Aramean penetrations were east of the Tigris—this is now abundantly clear since Īdu must be equated with Sātu Qala[215]—and that at a minimum these districts mentioned in the last lines of the Chronicle were plundered, though not necessarily lost.[216]

The situation intensified during the reign of Aššur-bēl-kala (r. 1073–1056). The following are the relevant passages from this king's inscriptions.

Text 1 (RIMA 2:93, A.0.89.2, iii.27′–28′)
On [numerous] campaigns against the Ar[ameans (KUR *a-r*[*i-me*]), hostile to the god Aššur, who in the land …] I continually plundered […]

Text 2 (RIMA 2:94, A.0.89.3, line 6′)
On numerous [campaigns against the Ar]ameans ([KUR *a-r*]*i-me*), hostile to the god Aššur, who in the land [ … I continually plundered …]

Text 3 (The Broken Obelisk, RIMA 2:101–3, A.0.89.7, ii.13–iii.32)
(*1071 or 1070, third or fourth regnal year*)
In the month of Sivan (third month, May–June), the eponymy of Aššur[…], [he brought …] to the Inner City (Assur) to rebuild the temple of Anu and Adad.

In that year, in the same month, […]
he plundered [the land of Ḫim]me and the land […].

In that year, in the month of Kislev (ninth month, November–December), […]
From the Ḫābūr River, the land of Ḫarku (or Hirku, Hurku, Kinku, Murku) to the city of Karkamiš of the land of Ḫatti, he plundered.
[He crossed the Euphrates after them in] rafts (made of inflated) goatskins.
[…] *lacuna*
(Col. iii.1) In that year, in the same month,
on campaign against the Arameans (KUR *a-ri-me*),
he fought (with them) at the city of Šaṣiru, which is in the district of the city of […].

215. For the site's location east on the Lower Zab at Sātu Qala, see below.

216. The extent of the penetrations into the heart of Assyria may have caused Tiglath-pileser I to "beat a strategic retreat" westward to Katmuḫu (the eastern flank of the Kašiyāri Range [modern Ṭūr ʿAbdīn]; Brinkman 1968, 388; Fales forthcoming, 8).

In that year, in the month Tammuz,
on campaign against the Arameans (KUR *a-ri-me*),
he fought (with them) at the city [ ] of the land [ ].

(*1070 or 1069, fourth or fifth regnal year*)
In the month of Iyyar (second month, April–May), eponomy (*līmu*) of Aššur-rēm-nišēšu,
he conquered the city of Tur[x]tu of the land of Muṣri.

In that year, in the month of Shebat (eleventh month, January–February),
the chariots and [...] went from the Inner City (Assur) (and)
conquered the cities of [x-x]indišulu and [...]sandû, cities which are in the district of city of Dūr-Kurigalzu.
They captured Kadašman-Buriaš, the son of Itti-Marduk-balāṭu, governor of their land.

In that year, in the month of Iyyar (second month, April–May),
on the campaign against the Arameans (KUR *a-ri-me*),
he fought at the city of Pauza, which is at the foot of Mount Kašiyāri.

In that year, in the same month,
on campaign against the Arameans (KUR *a-ri-me*),
he fought at the head (front?) of the city of Nabula.

In that year, in the month of Sivan (third month, May–June),
he uprooted the troops of the land of Muṣri.

In that year, in the same month,
on campaign against the Arameans (KUR *a-ri-me*),
he fought at the city of [x]tibua, which is on the Tigris.

In that year, in the month of Ab (fifth month, July–August),
on campaign against the Arameans (KUR *a-ri-me*),
he fought at Dunnu-ša-Lišur-ṣala-Aššur[217]/Dunnu-ša-Libur-zānin-Aššur[218]
which is in the district of the city of Šinamu.[219]

---

217. Radner (2004a, 71 n. 122, 91 [collation by Cornelia Wunsch]) for the *dunnu*: *ina* URU.⌜*du*$^{!}$*-ni*⌝*-ša-*$^{m}$*li-šur-ṣa-la-*$^{d}$*a-šur*, instead of "cities" as Grayson RIMA 2:102, A.0.89.7, iii.14: *ina* URU.⌜MEŠ⌝*-ni ša* $^{m}$*li-šur-ṣa-la-*$^{d}$*a-šur*.

218. For the suggestion to read the personal name differently as: URU.⌜*du*$^{!}$*-ni*⌝*-ša-*$^{m}$*li-bur*$^{!}$*-za-nin*$^{!}$*-*$^{d}$*a-šur*, and linking this named *dunnu* to the Middle Assyrian *līmu* with this name, see Fales 2012a, 102–4.

219. This city is mentioned in the texts from Giricano (Text 10, line 12). See Radner 2004a, 90. Identified with Pornak by Kessler 1980, 117–21; Nashef 1982, 249. Lipiński (2002, 230–31) identifies Šinamu with Fafih, 30 km west of Midyat. It is also

In that year, in the same month,
he uprooted the city of Šūru[220] of the land of Ḫanigalbat.
He conquered the city of Ḫulzu, which is in the midst of Mount Kašiyāri,
and the city of Erēšu, which the people of the land of Ḫabḫu held.
He brought out 3,000 captives.

In that year, in the month of Elul (sixth month, August–September),
on campaign against the Arameans (KUR *a-ri-me*),
he fought at the city of Murarir(?) of the land of Šubru.

In that year, in the month of [Araḫ]samnu (eighth month, October–November),
he plundered the Arameans (KUR *a-ri-me*) from the land of Maḫirānu to the city of Šuppu (or Rupu) of the land of Harran.

*(1069 or 1068, 5th or 6th Regnal Year)*
In the month of Kislev (ninth month, November–December), in the eponymy of Ilī-iddina,
on campaign against the Arameans (KUR *a-ri-me*),
he fought at the city of Magrisu (Magarisu)[221] of the land of Māri.[222]

In that year, in the same month,
on campaign against the Arameans (KUR *a-ri-me*),
he fought at the city of Dūr-Katlimmu.
In that year, in the same month,

---

mentioned in a Middle Assyrian text *KAV* 119 as a place of civilian and military activities in the time of Shalmaneser I. See Jakob 2003, 9 n. 67.

220. Fales (2012a, 105) notes, "despite Grayson's edition, no sign should be actually missing, on the basis of the parallel with Š/Sūra of the later annals of Aššurnaṣirpal II" (see also Liverani 1992a, 59). Thus URU.*šu*-⸢*ú*⸣-[x]-*ra* should be read as URU.*šu*-⸢*ú*⸣-*ra*. See also Kessler 1980, 57–66, and n. 238 for the issues of correspondence of the sibilants between West Semitic and Assyrian for the possible connection of *šūru* with Aramaic *šr/ šwr* "wall, fortress."

221. Probably modern Tell Ḥassaka. See Kühne 1980, 54–58; 1995, 82; Morandi Bonacossi 2000, 366.

222. Grayson (RIMA 2:102, A.0.89.7, iii.21) read: KUR.[*i*]*a-ri*. Given the similarity of signs IA and MA, the partially preserved sign is likely MA. Thus, the land in view here is the land of "Māri" on the Middle Ḫābūr (capital at the city of Ṭābētu, modern Tell Taban; Fales 1992, 106–7). Maul (1992, 54 n. 218) states: "Die Nähe von Magrisu/ Tall Hasaka zu den Orten, die unter Tiglathpilesar I. zu dem 'Land Mari' gezählt wurden, spricht für dies neue Lesung. *Ein Land Iari hat es dann aber nie gegeben*" (emphasis added). See Jakob 2003, 13; Shibata 2012. Lipiński (2000a, 99 n. 133) argues against the reading [*ma*]-*a-ri* "because of the spelling and of the restricted use of the toponym Mari in kings' titles, where it is justified only by the legendary prestige attached to this ancient royal seat" and proposes the restoration [*Na*]-*a-ri*. However, in light of the abundant new evidence, this is unlikely.

[he fought] [Aram] opposite the city of Sangaritu [which is on] the Euphrat[es].
[In] that [year], in the same month,
[on campaign against the A]rame[ans] ([KUR *a*]-*ri*-*m*[*e*])
he fought [at the city of Ṭābe]te(?).[223]
[In] that [year, in the month of …],
[on campaign against the Arameans],
he fought in the land of Gulgulu.[224]
[In that year, in the month of …,]
[he fought(?) the Arameans at the city of …]ṣiku of Mount Ḫānu.
[In] that year, in the month of Araḫsamnu (eighth month, October–November),
[he plunder]ed [the Arameans] as far as the watering holes.
[In that year, in] the same [month],
[on campaign against the Arameans],
[he fought at …] […].

Text 4 (RIMA 2:98, A.0.89.6, lines 6′–15′)
[By the] command of Aššur, Anu, and A[dad, the great gods, my lords, …], [I crossed the Euphrates] twice in one year in pursuit of the Arameans (KUR *a-ra-me*). I inflicted on them [a decisive defeat] [from the city of An]at of the land of Sūḫu and the city of [Tadmor and as far as the city of Rapiqu of the land of Karduniaš(?)]. [I brought their] tribute and [tax to my city Assur]. The […]-adaiu ([ ]-*ʾa-da-ia*.MEŠ), the Suteans (*su-te*$_9$-*e*.ME[Š]), the […]miraiu ([ *m*]*i-ra-ia*.MEŠ), who [live] at the foot of Mount [Lebanon …]. [In] rafts (made of inflated) goatskins [I crossed the Euphrates]. [I conquered the city … which (is) on] the opposite bank of [the Euphrates, (on the Sagura River)]. [At that time, the region of the A]ḫlamû which […] the city of Mi[…].

Text 5 (RIMA 2:107, A.0.89.9, lines 3′–10′)
By the command of Aššur (and) Adad, [the great gods, my lords, …, I crossed the Euphrates twice] in one year [in pursuit of] the Arameans (KUR *a-ri-mi*.MEŠ). The Suteans (*su-te*$_9$-*e*.MEŠ), Naʾa[…] who [live] at the foot of Mount Lebanon […]. [I crossed the Euphrates in rafts] (made of inflated) goatskins. [I conquered the city … which (is) (on the opposite bank of the Euphrates)] on the Sagur[a] River.[225] At that time, the region of [the Aḫlamû which …] numerous […].

---

223. Compare Ḫābūr campaigns of Adad-nērārī II and Tukulti-Ninurta II.

224. Compare West Semitic *glgl* or Akk. *gulgullu* "skull." Lipiński (2000a, 99) suggests "the area of Tell Kawkab, east of Hassake, as suggested by the shape of this extinct volcan [*sic*: volcano] (alt. 533 m) and by the meaning of *gulgul(l)u*, 'skull.'"

225. Millard (1970, 168–69) and Kessler (1980, 191–92) observe that the event described here seems to be reflected in the later Kurkh Monolith of Shalmaneser III

From these passages, it can be seen that Aššur-bēl-kala fought the Arameans[226] not only on the Middle Euphrates, as far as Karkamiš, but also in the Ḫābūr region, an area considered by the Assyrians as their land. Some scholars have questioned the historicity of some of these events since the phraseology of Aššur-bēl-kala's texts is in some cases very similar to that of Tiglath-pileser I. But as Bunnens (1999, 606) has noted, it would be hyper-critical to doubt the very fact of an Aramean presence in the area and of the threat it represented to the Assyrians.[227]

In the Broken Obelisk, campaigns directed against the Arameans in various locations are mentioned at least sixteen times. This conspicuous role of the Arameans in the inscription implies, as Ornan has argued (2007, 63–64), that the two pairs of prisoners that are carved into the front squared niche of the Obelisk (facing King Aššur-bēl-kala who controls them with lead ropes) can be identified as Arameans, representing two different tribal leaders, perhaps followed by representatives of their peoples (see fig. 3.6). Ornan also argues that the earlier scenes of captives being led by ropes are led by deities, and that the Broken Obelisk manifests a shift in the pictorial relationship between the king and the gods regarding who actually controlled the subdued enemies. The deities, in fact, remain in charge of what happens within the scene, as they are represented by five symbols at the top of the scene; but in the Broken Obelisk the king takes over a function previously held by a god (Ornan 2007, 66–70). A god-like role appropriated by the king makes a powerful claim of control as the deities' representative. If she is correct in her analysis, then Aššur-bēl-kala is truly claiming complete and utter dominance over the Arameans both in text and relief.

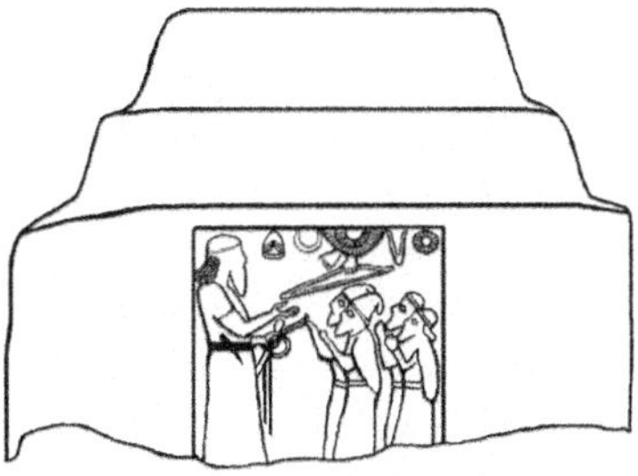
Fig. 3.6. Aramean tribal leaders "controlled" by Aššur-bēl-kala

(RIMA 3:23, A.0.102.2, ii.85–86). Thus the conquered city in the Aššur-bēl-kala texts is Pitru. Grayson (1991a, 98, note to 12′–13′) notes that there would not seem to be enough room in either of the two Aššur-bēl-kala texts for the full description given in Shalmaneser III's Monolith.

226. In Aššur-bēl-kala's inscriptions, the Arameans are a collective noun in the singular: **arumu*/**aramu*?, most commonly in the genitive for KUR *a-re-me*. They are a distinct group from the *aḫlamû*.

227. It is also important to remember that the Assyrian scribes used stereotyped phraseology so that accounts from different kings can appear quite similar (except, obviously, differences in the personal and place names, etc.).

Through his references to "the Arameans," Aššur-bēl-kala demonstrates that he has continued his father's policies. These Assyrian kings clearly believed that they had a right to rule over this region as their ancestors had in the thirteenth century. It is important to note that Aššur-bēl-kala's campaign against the Arameans in the Kašiyāri Mountains around the sources of the River Ḫābūr is the same area where his father had fought the Mušku.[228] Many of the towns mentioned in the account of year 1070/1069 are located in Mount Kašiyāri: Pauza, Nabula, Sūru, Ḫulzu, and Erisu.

Aššur-bēl-kala does not mention the conquest of any Aramean cities[229] or tribute paid to him by Aramean chieftains. The verb "fought" (*maḫaṣu*) is repeatedly used and "plundered" (*ḫabātu*) once or twice with reference to Arameans. All of the battles seem to be open-field engagements. This is important because it appears that these campaigns had ultimately little effect. The lack of concrete results suggests that the Aramean pressure was continuing unabated. It is clear from Aššur-bēl-kala's inscriptions that the Arameans were not highly organized; yet very resilient. Fales (2012a, 118) has aptly put it:

> the king's proud accounts of repeated victories against tribalist groups show an *overall geographical patterning* which points, instead, to tactics of difficult position-holding and to a movement of retreat eastwards on the part of the Assyrian forces. (emphasis added)

Thus, in spite of his claims of victory over these various Arameans, Aššur-bēl-kala was, in the end, unsuccessful. Most, if not all, of Aššur-bēl-kala's royal inscriptions date very early in his reign, which further suggests that the Arameans gradually gained the upper hand toward the end of his rule. This is supported by the dramatic decline in Assyrian power evident in subsequent reigns,[230] as well as new evidence.

Although the recently discovered texts from Giricano (ancient Dunnu-ša-Uzibi, "the fortified agricultural production center of Uzibu") are contracts (Radner 2004a), they bear testimony to the conflict between the Assyrians and Arameans in the Upper Tigris. All the texts (except one) are dated by eponym, mostly that of Ilī-iddina (either 1069 or 1068, the fifth or sixth year of Aššur-bēl-kala). During the eponym of Aššur-rēm-nišēšu (either 1070 or 1069, fourth or fifth regnal year), the year before that of Ilī-iddina, Aššur-bēl-kala's annals record fighting in Dunnu-ša-Lišur-ṣala-Aššur in the district

228. Tigath-pileser I (RIMA 2:14, A.0.87.1, i.62–88): LÚ.MEŠ KUR *muš-ka-a-ia*. MEŠ; Aššur-bēl-kala (RIMA 2:102, A.0.89.7, iii.8b–17a): KASKAL *šá* KUR *a-ri-me*.

229. He captured cities, but none are identified as Aramean.

230. RIMA 2:86; Lipiński 2000a, 99.

of Šinamu (see above). The city of Šinamu is located a mere 40 km west of Giricano on the southern bank of the Tigris (not far west of Üçtepe) and is mentioned in one of the Giricano texts (Radner 2004a, 90, line 12). More battles took place in the Kašiyāri Mountains (modern Ṭūr ʿAbdīn) south of the Tigris and in the region of Nabula (modern Girnavaz), located 90 km to the southeast of Giricano. In a text of Aššurnaṣirpal II (883–859 BCE) dating to 879 BCE,[231] that king related:

> I flayed Bur-Rammānu, the criminal, (and) draped his skin over the wall of the city of Sinabu. I appointed Ilānu, his brother, to the position of chief. I imposed upon him as annual tribute: 2 minas of gold, 13(?) minas of silver, 1,000 sheep, (and) 2,000 (measures) of barley. I repossessed the cities Sinabu (and) Tīdu—fortresses which Shalmaneser,[232] king of Assyria, a prince who preceded me, had garrisoned against the land of Nairi (and) which the Arameans had captured by force. I resettled the Assyrians—who in the land of Nairi had held fortresses of Assyria (and) whom the Arameans had trampled—in their (the Arameans) abandoned cities (and) houses. I placed them in a peaceful abode. I uprooted 1,500 troops of the Aramean-Aḫlamû of Amme-ba'al, a man of Bīt-Zamāni, (and) brought (them) to Assyria. I reaped the harvest of the land of Nairi (and) stored (it) for the sustenance of my land in the cities of Tušḫa(n), Damdammusa, Sinabu (and) Tīdu.[233]

The city of Šinamu (Aššur-bēl-kala) is the city of Sinabu (Aššurnaṣirpal II).

The Middle Assyrian occupation at Giricano included at least three strata and spanned about 120–160 years, perhaps indicating that the settlement existed from the reign of Shalmaneser I (1269–1241) to Aššur-bēl-kala (1073–1056).[234] The beginning of the Middle Assyrian remains at Giri-

231. Aššurnaṣirpal II's Kurkh Monolith, RIMA 2:261–62, A.0.101.19, lines 91–97.

232. The reference could be to Shalmaneser I (1263–1234) (Lipiński 2000a, 158) or to Shalmaneser II (1030–1019) (Grayson in RIMA 2:261). Shalmaneser I founding these fortresses seems perhaps more likely than Shalmaneser II who reigns during the time of Assyrian weakness and about whose military activities next to nothing is known (Radner and Schachner 2001).

233. Tušḫa(n) is Ziyaret Tepe; Tīdu is very likely Üçtepe (Kurkh); for Sinabu, see note above (Radner and Schachner 2001, 754–57; Liverani 1992a, 38–39 and Kessler 1980, 117–20).

234. Radner 2004a 72. Radner's calculations are based on the assumption that a mud-brick building lasts about 30–40 years; and obviously she is multiplying by four to obtain 120–160 years. However, if Shalmaneser I took control of the region around 1260 and the Assyrians lost the region during Aššur-bēl-kala's reign in 1069/68, this yields an occupation span of 191–192 years. Thus, either the length of each stratum should be extended to 48 years, or (if the length of each stratum remains 30–40 years) the beginning of the Middle Assyrian occupation must be dated later, i.e., 1230–1190 BCE (during the reign of Tukulti-Ninurta I [1233–1197]).

cano are directly above the remains of the Mittanian period; and the Middle Assyrian strata are separated from the early Iron Age remains by a layer of debris about 20–30 cm (8–12 inches) in thickness (Radner 2004a, 5). The early Iron Age remains contain the so-called grooved-type (Bartl 2001) or "groovy" pottery (Roaf and Schachner 2005, 119–22) known especially in eastern Anatolia.[235]

Although the Broken Obelisk of Aššur-bēl-kala does not provide us with an exact date for the collapse of Assyrian control over the Upper Tigris region, fortunately the tablets from Giricano offer a relatively secure clue as it is unlikely that the Assyrian control over the area lasted for long after the year 1069/1068 BCE. The information gained from the Broken Obelisk indicates that Arameans were responsible for the end of the Assyrian dominion in the entire region of the Upper Tigris. Roaf and Schachner conclude: "When the Assyrians returned to this region in the early ninth century, it was part of the lands of Nairi and was dominated by Arameans" (Roaf and Schachner 2005, 119).

Taking these Middle Assyrian sources together, the picture that emerges is that of "a 'multi-polar' movement of Arameans spreading out in the northern Syro-Mesopotamian region with possible mass movements upriver along the parallel axes of the Euphrates and Tigris."[236] When coupled with additional data from other sources, it becomes clear that there were many migrations of Aramean entities over the centuries headed in multiple directions, some more well-documented than others. When the plethora of entity reconfigurations are factored in, the picture becomes exponentially more complex. Figure 2.6 (p. 79 above) provides a glimpse at this by plotting some select known migrations from different periods. If one can envision many more of these added to the map, stretched out over roughly six centuries, then this complexity might begin to be realized.

### 3.2.3.3. Stage Three: Assyrian Weakness and Aramean Polity Formation (ca. 1055–935 BCE)

From roughly the end of the reign of Aššur-bēl-kala to Aššur-dān II, the Assyrian monarchy was characterized by political and military weakness. Eriba-Adad II (1055–1054) is the first in a series of obscure monarchs who ruled Assyria from 1055 to 935. Little direct information is available for any of these kings and their activities, but it is easy to deduce from events pre-

235. In the past, it has been assumed that this "groovy pottery" was a marker of the Mušku. It has been found at Tell Ḥalaf. For a full discussion, see §4.3 Gōzān/Bīt-Baḫiāni (Gūzāna).

236. Fales forthcoming, 9.

ceding and following these 120 years that the Arameans were the superior power and occupied much of what had once been regarded as Assyrian territory.

Although Assyrian domination over the Jezirah was dissipating throughout this period with the emergence of Aramean polities, Assyrian control of some strategic outposts seems to have persisted, indicating that the Assyrians did not lose the Lower, Middle, or eastern Ḫābūr areas. Evidence from Dūr-Katlimmu (Tell Šēḫ Ḥamad) demonstrates this for the Lower Ḫābūr.[237] Dūr-Katlimmu was the site of an Assyrian provincial center ruled by a district governor (*bēl pāḫete*). The significance of Dūr-Katlimmu to the Middle and Neo-Assyrian Empire is evident in the fact that the city's main god Salmānu (Radner 1998; 2002) was the theophoric element in five Assyrian kings' names between the thirteenth and the end of the eighth century BCE.[238]

In the Middle Ḫābūr, there is important textual evidence of two local polities that had a degree of independence, and yet were subordinate to Assyria. In addition, there is evidence of a similar situation on the Lower Zab. The first of these polities on the Ḫābūr came to light through excavations at Tell Bderi where inscriptions were discovered of a ruler named Aššur-ketta-lēšir (II)[239] who governed a city called Ṭābētu (modern Tell Taban) and who referred to himself as "the king of the land of Māri" (*šar māt Māri*),[240] even though he regarded the Assyrian king Tiglath-pileser I as his overlord.[241] His building inscriptions commemorated the reoccupation of the site of Tell Bderi (ancient Dūr-Aššur-kettī-lēšir) and building activities at Ṭābetu dated by Assyrian eponyms.[242] Thus the date for the beginning of Aššur-ketta-lēšir

237. Kühne 2009, 44; 1998, 282–84; 1995, 74–79; and Liverani 1988a.

238. Kühne (2009, 45–46) interprets this to imply a closeness in ties between Dūr-Katlimmu and the capital of Assur to be so intertwined as to constitute "a community of fate."

239. Regarding this king's name, see Shibata 2012, 489 n. 3. The thirteenth-century ruler with this name is consistently written syllabically $^{\text{m.d}}$*A-šur-ke-ta-le-šìr* in the archive from Tell Taban, while the second ruler with this name, the contemporary of Tiglath-pileser I, is written: $^{\text{m.d}}$*A-šur-ke-ti*-SI.SÁ. Shibata states: "as it is apparent that the name of this second local ruler was modelled after the former, Aššur-ketta-lēšir I, I would normalize his name as Aššur-ketta-lēšir II," even though it is grammatically incorrect.

240. Obviously, this land of Māri should not be confused with the earlier Middle Euphrates kingdom of Mari.

241. Maul 1992. A few of the texts' date formulae situate them "in the time (*ina tarṣe*) of Tiglath-pileser, king of Assyria, his lord," establishing Aššur-ketta-lēšir II as a contemporary of the Assyrian king.

242. These are dated by Assyrian eponyms from the reign of Tiglath-pileser I: construction of a wall at Dūr-Aššur-kettī-lēšir dated to the "eponymy of Bēlu-libūr" (Maul 1992, 28); and the construction of a city wall and gate at Ṭābetu dated to the eponymy of

II's reign appears to have been 1101, Tiglath-pileser's fourteenth regnal year (Jeffers 2013, 136 n. 339).

Excavations at Tell Taban (ancient Ṭābētu)[243] have recovered additional fragments of building inscriptions, but also an archive documenting the palace administration of the local rulers of this polity.[244] These texts mention an earlier ruler named Aššur-ketta-lēšir I (thirteenth century), his son Adad-bēl-gabbe II, and other rulers.[245] It appears that all the rulers were part of the same dynasty (Maul 1992, 47–57; 2006, 10–17), and that this dynasty was in power for almost two hundred years (from the late fourteenth to the mid-eleventh century) (Shibata 2011) as "the kings of the land of Māri" ruled from the city of Ṭābetu.

There is one thing that is especially interesting about this dynasty: it appears to have had Hurrian origins.[246] This can be seen in a brick inscription found in three exemplars written by Adad-bēl-gabbe I, whose grandfather bore a Hurrian name: "Adad-bēl-gabbe (I), son of Zumiya, king of the land of Mār[i], son of Akit-Teššub, [also] ki[ng of the Land of Māri]" (Shibata 2011). From Adad-bēl-gabbe I onward, all subsequent rulers had Assyrian names, displaying the effort exercised by this formerly Hurrian dynasty in adopting Assyrian names, and also to appropriate an Assyrian lifestyle (Pongratz-Leisten 2011, 117). Finally, these texts may also now record evidence for the presence of Arameans[247] in the Lower Ḫābūr a generation or two older than the Broken Obelisk of Aššur-bēl-kala (1073–1056 BCE).[248]

---

Mudammeq-Bēl (Maul 2006, 40: T I-23-1:2′ [text no. 5] and T II-25-1:13′ [text no. 6]). Another important inscription of Aššur-ketta-lēšir II is a large cylinder fragment written in honor of the building of a wall around the city Adališḫu (location unknown). Line 16 of this text mentions the eponym Aššur-apla-iqīša, an eponym of Tiglath-pileser I's reign (see Maul 1992, 35–41; earlier Lambert 1991, but without the benefit of the text discoveries).

243. Maul 2006. For the site, see Ohnuma, Numoto, and Okada 1999. Middle Assyrian texts have also been excavated at the site (Shibata 2007).

244. For these inscriptions, see Shibata 2007, 2010, 2011, 2012; Yamada 2008; and Maul 1992, 2006.

245. For a tentative list of the local rulers of Ṭābētu, see Shibata 2012, 492, table 1.

246. Pongratz-Leisten (2011, 118–19) points out other possible Hurrian cultural backgrounds.

247. S. Yamada personal communication to H. Kühne 2009, 46 n. 18.

248. The last known ruler of the land of Māri was Enlil-šar-ilāni, son of Aššur-ketta-lēšir II (attested by his inscriptions on bricks, Tab T06–44+46(+)Tab T07–37 // Tab T06–45 (see Shibata and Yamada forthcoming). Though the exact dating of his reign remains unclear, we can suspect it fell around the end of Tiglath-pileser I's reign and the beginning of Aššur-bēl-kala's, since his father was a known contemporary of Tiglath-pileser I, his overlord. Therefore, in 1069 or 1068, when early in his reign Aššur-bēl-kala fought the Arameans at the city of Magrisu of the land of Māri, the king of Māri would have been Enlil-šar-ilāni, not Tukultī-Mēr, as suggested by Brown (2013, 116), who he sees as making "some sort of alliance" with one or more local Aramean tribes. A Tukultī-

The second polity was located a little south of Tell Taban at the ancient site of Šadikanni (modern Tell 'Ajaja). Originally a Hurrian foundation, it became a local entity that initially was under Assyrian control.[249] At some point, direct Assyrian control was lost, but according to Aššur-bēl-kala's Broken Obelisk, Šadikanni acknowledged Assyrian overlordship in the context of Aramean incursions. A recently discovered inscribed clay cylinder of a local ruler, Bēl-ēreš, the *šangû* of Šadikanni records his deeds, particularly the building of a temple for the deities Samnuḫa and Kubaba, while mentioning the Assyrian kings Aššur-rabi II (r. 1012–972) and his son Aššur-rēša-iši II (r. 971–967).[250] It is a bit ironic that these two Assyrian kings's inscriptions are minimal, while Bēl-ēreš' text is twenty-nine lines in length. Excavations at Tell 'Ajaja (Šadikanni) have uncovered two halls of a palace. In hall B, two stelae have been discovered. They attest to the Assyrianizing of culture at the site, yet at the same time the integration of western artistic motifs.[251]

Newly discovered evidence demonstrates another example of a local independent polity that apparently was loyal to Assyria. A number of inscribed bricks have been discovered at Sātu Qala on the Lower Zab (southeast of modern Erbil). They were written in the Assyrian dialect and mention the names of seven kings who ruled over an entity called Īdu. For example, a three-line building inscription is preserved on three bricks:

---

mēr is mentioned in another fragmentary inscription of Aššur-bēl-kala. This Tukultī-Mēr (mGIŠ.*tukul-ti-dme-er*), king of the land of Mari (KUR.*m*[*á-ri*] in line 14′; spelled KUR.*má-r*[*i*] in line 15′), has been identified with Tukultī-Mēr, the king of the land of Ḫana, mentioned in a dedicatory inscription which reads: (2) [mGI]Š.*tukul-ti-me-er* MAN KUR.*ḫa-na* (3)[DUMU] mDINGIR-NÍG.BA MAN KUR.*ḫa-na* "Tukultī-Mēr, king of the land of Ḫana, [son] of Ilī-iqīša, king of the land of Ḫana." Podany (2002, 73–74) states: "This is probably the same king as Tukultī-Mēr, king of M[ari] who was a contemporary of Aššur-bēl-kala of Assyria (1073–1056)." Note that there is no Tukultī-Mēr in the list of local rulers of Ṭābetu composed by Shibata (2012, 492, table 1). Jeffers (2013, 345) also takes Tukultī-Mēr to be a king of Māri (Ṭābētu).

249. It is listed among the districts sending regular deliveries to the Assur temple in the thirteenth century BCE (Freydank 1997), and its status as a district in the Middle Assyrian provincial system is again attested during the twelfth century BCE with the reference to a district governor bearing the Assyrian name Kidin-Ninua (Millard 1970).

250. RIMA 2:126–28, A.0.96.2001. Note the Hurrian deities mentioned.

251. For Stela 1, see Rouault and Masetti-Rouault 1993, 378 (Catalogue no. 373). For Stela 2, see Mahmoud 2008. See also Kühne's comments (2009, 49). Pongratz-Leisten (2011, 119–20) points out Hurrian and Babylonian cultural influences.

> Palace of Abbi-zēri (m*ab-bi-ze-ri*), king of the land of the city of Īdu (MAN KUR URU.*i-di*), son of Šara[…]ni, also king of the land of the city of Īdu. The embankment wall of the palace of Abbi-zēri.[252]

At present, two groups of kings can be distinguished. One group is comprised of four kings: Šara[…]ni (reading uncertain), Abbi-zēri, Bā'ilānu, and KAM-*ti-e-ni*. The second group consists of Imzuyānu (reading uncertain), Edima and Ba'auri. Most of these names seem to defy easy interpretation and are unattested elsewhere (van Soldt et al. 2013, 214). The best paleographic comparison for these brick inscriptions is provided by the inscriptions from Tell Bderi and Tell Taban (van Soldt 2008, 73; van Soldt et al. 2013, 215). Consequently, it seems that the first group of kings would date to the time of Tiglath-pileser I or later; the second group appears to date to the early Neo-Assyrian period, prior to the reassumption of Assyrian direct control (van Soldt et al. 2013, 215). In light of these new data, this "land of the city of Īdu" should be distinguished from that of Īd(a) on the Euphrates River.[253]

During the Middle Assyrian period, the region in which Īdu was located came under direct Assyrian control, perhaps as early as the reign of Adad-nērārī I.[254] However, the first attestation of the city of Īdu is probably in connection with the payment of taxes during the reign of Tukulti-Ninurta I,[255] though it is not qualified as a province (*pāḫutu*). It appears as a province for the first time in the tabular lists of regular offerings of the twelfth century and other documents from the archive of the administrator of the offerings.[256] The last known governor of the province (*bēl pāḫete*) of

---

252. SQ 10-3, SM 1068, and Koya 3. See van Soldt 2008, 73; van Soldt et al. 2013, 210.

253. Some scholars have understood there to be only one Īdu, which is usually located at Ḥît (see e.g., Postgate 1985, 97–98). Other scholars have suggested another Īdu was located "in the north" (Nashef 1982; Na'aman 1994). Van Soldt's study (2008) demonstrates slightly different spellings of the names. Also he notes the river access to Assur from Sātu Qala (which may be an additional line of argument). With the discovery of the inscriptions of "the land of Īdu" and its kings, it seems best to posit two places with similar type names, one on the Euphrates, the other on the Lower Zab.

254. In general, see Tenu 2009, 170–72; Pappi 2012, 603; Llop-Raduà 2012b; van Soldt et al. 2013, 217–18.

255. MARV 4.127:12 and MARV 10.61:6; Īdueans are present in MARV 2.17:64. The question is whether the Īdu in the tablets of Tukulti-Ninurta I is the Euphratic Īdu (Ḥît) or Īdu (Sātu Qala) on the Lower Zab; campaigns against Sūḫu along the Euphrates by Tukulti-Ninurta are attested. Because of its position in the lists, the second option seems more probable (Llop-Raduà 2012b, 104).

256. MARV 7.27:6 (eponym Adad-rība, reign of Enlil-kudurrī-uṣur, 1192–1182); MARV 5.1:8 (eponym [Saggiu], reign of Ninurta-apil-Ekur, 1191–1179); MARV 5.2:9 (eponym Aššur-zēra-iddina, reign of Ninurta-apil-Ekur); MARV 1.21; MARV 2.21;

Īdu was Aššur-abuk-aḫḫe from early in the reign of Tiglath-pileser I.[257] Īdu is mentioned for the last time as a province in the regular offerings around the twentieth year of Tiglath-pileser I.[258] Finally and importantly, the Assyrian Chronicle 4 (lines 10–12, see above) documents Aramean incursions into the land of Assyria on the east side of the Tigris, where they plundered, beside unknown places, the land of "Īdu, the district of Nineveh, (and) the land of Kili[zi]." This action must have occurred after the thirty-second year of Tiglath-pileser I (see discussion above).

Based on the paleographic dating of the brick inscriptions, it would appear that the first group of local kings probably came to the throne at the very end of Tiglath-pileser I's reign or perhaps after Aššur-bēl-kala.[259] The political situation in Īdu was likely the same as with "the land of Māri" and with "the land of Šadikanni." While nothing is known about the history of this kingdom beyond the names of these kings, this "dynasty must have been stable enough to allow at least seven successive kings, most likely from the same dynasty, six of whom were able to undertake construction work on the site" (van Soldt et al. 2013, 219). Apparently, the kings of Īdu maintained political independence from Assyria over at least seven generations. However the palaeography, as well as the styles of the decorations discovered at Sātu Qala/Īdu, "reflect contemporary developments in Assyria, hinting at continued ties to the informal empire of Assyrian cultural dominance" (van Soldt et al. 2013, 219).

The title, "king of the land of the city of Īdu," indicates regional control beyond the immediate city environs. However, nothing is known of the extent of the kingdom's control. In this regard, it is important to note that at Hasanlu Tepe, south of the Urmia Lake, an inscription on a stone bowl that reads "Palace of Ba'auri, king of the land of Īdu," was discovered in the excavations of level IV.[260] This is none other than the last king attested at Sātu Qala "Ba'auri, king of the land of Īdu." The bowl is palaeographically similar to the glazed brick inscription of Ba'auri of Īdu (van Soldt et al. 2013, 213). How and why this inscribed object arrived at Hasanlu remains unknown. It may suggest some sort of relations between Īdu and the Zagros (hardly a

---

MARV 6.3–21, 22–70; MARV 7.22–58; MARV 7.13 (reign of Tiglath-pileser I, 1114–1076).

257. MARV 6.22:7′ (eponym Aššur-šallimšunu, around the accession year of Tiglath-pileser I). See van Soldt 2008.

258. MARV 1.25:16 (eponym Ninurta-aḫa-iddina). See Freydank 1991, 157.

259. Van Soldt et al. (2013, 219) prefer the end of the reign of Tiglath-pileser I.

260. See Salvini 1984, 55–56. The bowl is dated to the ninth century.

surprise). In any case, in the early Neo-Assyrian period, this polity lost its independence, being once again absorbed into the Assyrian domain.[261]

Switching back to the Ḫābūr region, the evidence from Kaḫat (Tell Barri) shows that the Assyrians maintained control there (D'Agostino 2009, 35). Thus, in the case of a number of enclaves on the Ḫābūr, political connections with the Assyrian state were never entirely severed.[262] In fact, Kühne (2009, 46) has suggested that these regional polities on the Lower and Middle Ḫābūr served as an Assyrian buffer zone against the Arameans, a type of Assyrian "limes" against the penetration of the Aramean tribes toward the nucleus of Assyria that deflected the "mainstream of the Aramean migration off to the north."

Interestingly, Aššur-bēl-kala's claim in the "Broken Obelisk" to have fought the Arameans throughout this region (most likely in open-field battles), not only appears to be accurate, but may be an indication of a partial success of the Assyrians against the Aramean penetrations, at least in this area. It may explain how some of these regional polities on the Lower and Middle Ḫābūr were able to survive and remain loyal to Assyria.

Yet, it was during the reign of Aššur-rabi II that "the land of Aram took away by force" the Assyrian forts on the Euphrates that Tiglath-pileser I had founded, namely Pitru and Mutkīnu.[263] Thus, between 1100 and 900 BCE a considerable change took place in the countryside so that by the ninth century much of the population of the Jezirah was now Aramean in areas formerly under the control of Assyria (Roaf 2001, 366). The impact of the various Aramean penetrations led to the abandonment of Assyrian farmland, with parts of the population taking refuge in other regions, for example, Šubria (B. J. Parker 2001, 169, 230–42) or Ḫabrūri.[264]

Many years later, the land of Ḫanigalbat, now fully "Aramaized," is cited frequently in the inscriptions of kings Adad-nērārī II, Aššurnaṣirpal II, and Shalmaneser III.[265] This is clearly a "fossilized" usage of the term. Grayson

261. For discussion, see van Soldt et al. 2013, 219–21. See also §4.6.2.

262. Fales (2011b, 59 n. 161) points out, no doubt correctly, that "Šadikanni and Ṭābētu prove to have played the role of non-hostile tributaries all through the Neo-Assyrian phase of reconquest of the Ḫābūr, possibly with the aim of warding off the main dangers of an Aramean invasion." The recent conclusion of Brown (2013, 118) that "renegade" Assyrians comprised "to a substantial degree" the Arameans must be rejected for lack of evidence.

263. RIMA 3:19, A.0.102.2, ii.35b–38.

264. It appears that at several sites there was a reduction of building activity in this period which was only resumed in the ninth century. For example, Tell al-Rimah was abandoned and the later Neo-Assyrian occupation was on a smaller scale than that of the Late Bronze Age (Roaf 2001, 366).

265. See Harrak 1987, 277; and now Fales 2012a.

observes that "the adoption of Middle Assyrian nomenclature is indicative of a feeling that they (the Neo-Assyrian kings) were recreating an old empire that was still rightfully theirs" (Grayson 1982, 280).

## 3.3. The Levantine Sphere

The Levantine sphere was under Egyptian domination during most of the Late Bronze Age, insofar as Egypt controlled the region through various local rulers and highly selective military interventions. Contemporaneous inscriptions confirm this, the stelae of Seti I from Qadesh and Ramesses II from Keswe near Damascus being the most recent examples (Taraqji 1999). The current consensus (insofar as there is one) pictures a gradual but uneven retreat of Egyptian imperial control during the two centuries following the battle of Qadesh accompanied in the decades around 1200 BCE by the coming of the so-called Sea Peoples, some of whom settled in the Levant (Philistines, Sherden, Tjekker, etc.).[266]

Circumstances facing the Arameans in the Levantine sphere were very different than those in the Hittite or Assyrian spheres. With the demise in the twelfth-century of the Egyptian Empire, Aramean peoples were competing not with large states like Assyria or significant Neo-Hittite polities, but with much smaller political entities (Dion 1995a, 1282). While the Aramean settlement in the Assyrian sphere was piecemeal and/or restricted initially to the periphery or isolated zones in the Jezirah, in the Levant, the small city-states were much more vulnerable, and it was precisely here that the Arameans appear to have been most successful in settling and seizing political control. Besides other West Semitic population groups, this sphere had Amurrite and Hurrian substrates (perhaps more so in central Syria, but to some extent in the southern part of the sphere too).

In the central and southern Syria, Arameans appear in control of new kingdoms that they have created (e.g., Ṣobah (Zobah), Bēt-Reḥob, Geshur, etc.). Unfortunately, the recent excavations at Qatna have not revealed much insight into this process (Al-Maqdissi et al. 2002). Damascus will be discussed in detail in a separate chapter below. The following presentation will be divided into larger and smaller polities (see fig. 3.7).

266. Singer 2012, 2000; Weinstein 1992, 1998; Mazar 1997, 218.

### 3.3.1. The Larger Polities: Ṣobah and Bēt-Reḥob

#### 3.3.1.1. Ṣobah (Zobah)[267] and Bēt-Reḥob

The earliest information so far preserved concerning the Aramean states of Ṣobah (*ṣwbh*) and Bēt-Reḥob (*byt-rḥb*) is found in the Hebrew Bible: time of Saul, 1 Sam 14:47;[268] time of David, 2 Sam 8:1–14 = 1 Chr 18:1–13; 10:6–19 = 1 Chr 19:6–19.[269] Fortunately, we have the biblical texts, for otherwise we would know virtually nothing about either entity. Unfortunately, the historical information in these texts is contained in passages that have many text critical, compositional, and various interpretive challenges. In other words, they cannot simply be summarized or paraphrased and assumed to be an accurate history. Such a simple approach is obviously problematic; but so too is the approach that simply declares that the biblical texts are religious, literary documents; and therefore they are utterly untrustworthy for any historical reconstruction.[270] All of the textual materials from the ancient Near East come out of a world that was utterly religious; and literary structuring is ubiquitous to narrative.[271] Therefore, a more *robust effort* is essential for historiographic purposes.

There is little doubt of the existence of a city of Ṣobah. It is attested in the second-millennium texts from Mari in the so-called Qatna dossier, designated there as Ṣîbat (Charpin 1998, 80–89). It is also attested in the Neo-Assyrian documents, spelled usually *Ṣubat* or *Ṣupite* (though with other variants).[272] It may be attested in the Aramaic graffiti from Hamath (eighth century) where the word *ṣbh* is identified by some scholars with *ṣwbh* of the Bible.[273] However, the frequency of this word and the words associated with it raise doubts about this identification (Dion 1997, 174 n. 15). In any

---

267. While English versions of the Bible transliterate the name as Zobah, Ṣobah will be used here.

268. MT: "kings of Ṣobah"; OG: "king of Ṣobah" (also mentions Bēt-Reḥob).

269. צוֹבָה, though צוֹבָא (2 Sam 10:6, 8; 23:36); OG: Σουβάς.

270. See Thompson 1992, 383–99; 1999, 179–225; and Lemche 1998, 86–132. However, this approach does not adequately deal with the textual material. For a more balanced assessment, see Na'aman 2002a, 200–203.

271. Importantly pointed out by Liverani (1973) decades ago. Note the literary and religious aspects in Sennacherib's Annals, see Younger 2003a, 247–60.

272. Bagg 2007, 233–34, s.v. Ṣubat. URU.*ṣu-ba-a* (SAA 11:21, 21.8′); URU.*ṣu-ba-te* (SAA 6:100, 109.r.9′); URU.*ṣu-bat* (SAA 11:5, 1.rs.i.12′); URU.*ṣu-bi-ti* (Asb A, vii.114); URU.*ṣu-pat* (SAA 1:141, 179.r.7); URU.*ṣu-pi-te* (Eponym 683 A9; SAA 11:80, 125.6′; SAA 1:141, 179.r.3, 13; 1:139, 177.r.11; SAA 6:78, 90.r.18; 6:97, 108.r.3; URU.*ṣu-pu-tú* (SAA 11:8, 6.7′; SAA 7:125, 116.10′, 11′.

273. Otzen 1990, 282 (HamG 8); 285 (HamG 11); 286 (HamG 12); 288 (HamG 14); 294 (HamG 20); 298 (HamG 26).

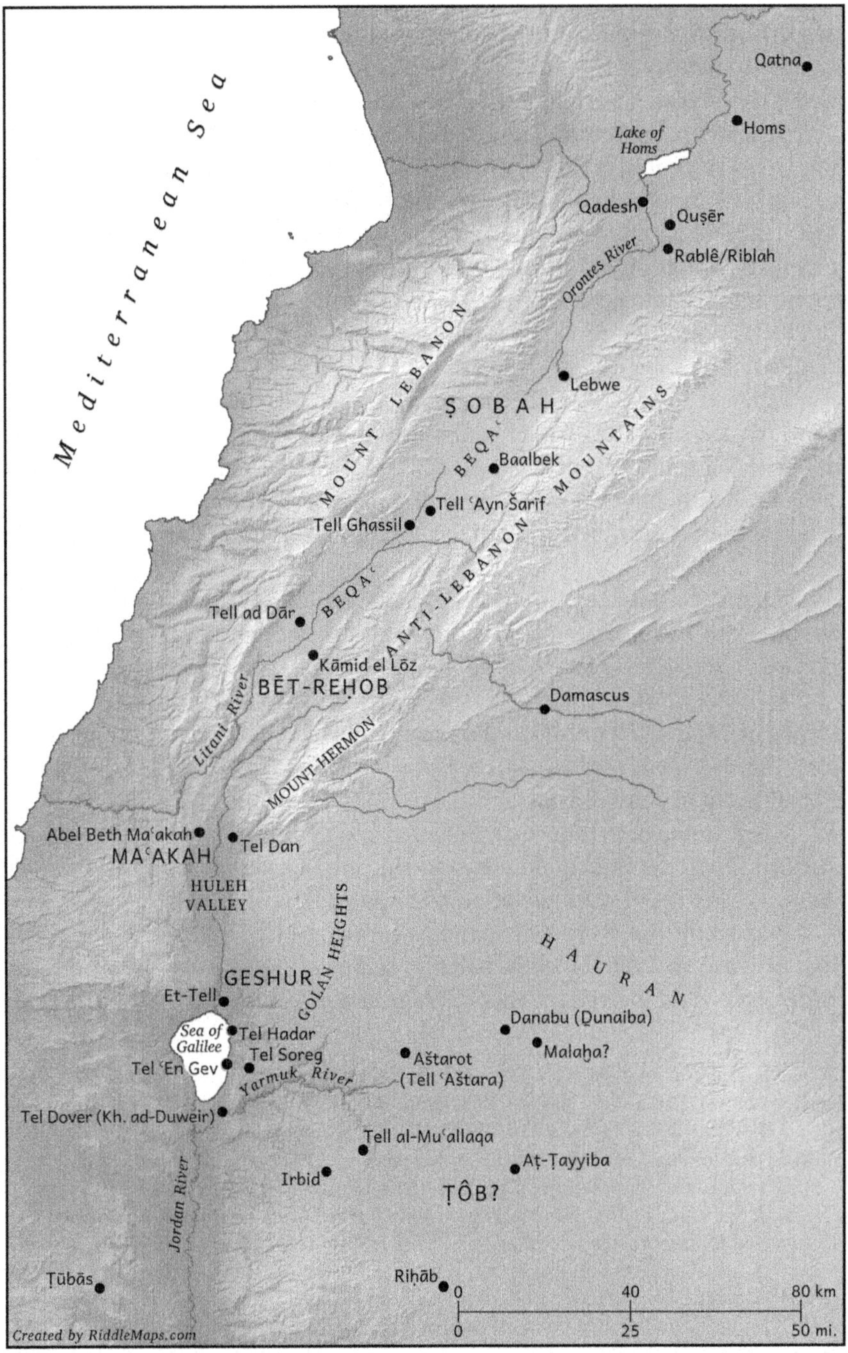


Fig. 3.7. The Levantine sphere

case, the cuneiform evidence documents an important city with this name[274] located somewhere in central Syria or the northern Beqaʿ Valley.[275] Unfortunately, the precise location of the city is not yet known.

Scholars have located Ṣobah/Ṣubat at a number of different sites, including Ḥoms in central Syria.[276] However, D. Charpin (1998), on the basis of a previously unpublished letter from Mari (M. 5423, part of the "Qatna dossier"), points out that this letter mentions a *têmtum*, in this context referring to a lake, which should be identified as the Lake of Ḥoms. Thus, according to his interpretation, the city of Ṣîbat (its earlier writing) was located south of this lake, most likely in the Beqaʿ at Baalbek. In his opinion, Ṣobah/Ṣubat should not be equated with Ḥoms.[277]

Lipiński (2000a, 326–27) has offered three possible sites for Ṣobah, all of which are south of Baalbek and north of Kāmid el-Lōz: (1) Tell Ghassil, about 16 km southwest of Baalbek; (2) Tell ʿAyn Šarīf, about 6 km southwest of Tell Ghassil, on the western bank of the Litani River; and (3) Tell ad-Dār, a large mound occupied in the Iron Age about 8 km northwest of Kāmid el-Lōz.

Finally, Na'aman (1999c, 424–25) has argued for a location just to the south of the Lake of Ḥoms, specifically near "present-day Quṣēr, halfway between Qidisi/Qidšu and Rablê/Riblah," with a territory extended "between Qidisi in the north and Labā'u in the south," while reaching "the northern slopes of Mount Lebanon" to the west, and bordering on the desert in the east. Similarly, both Fales (2002b, 134 n. 4) and Bagg (2007, 233–34) locate Ṣobah/Ṣubat in central Syria.

Later, in the area known as Ṣobah, a people known as the Ituraeans are attested. The relationship of Ṣobah to Hamath, as well as its position in the Assyrian provincial administration, is disputed.[278]

Regarding Bēt-Reḥob's location, Mittmann (1970, 225–28) suggested that because in 2 Sam 10:6 Bēt-Reḥob seems to be near to Ammonite territory, one could locate it at either Riḥāb, about 35 km southeast of Irbid, or

---

274. The toponym perhaps derives from the Semitic root *ṣbʾ*, "to flood a field" (suggestion of J.-M. Durand in Charpin 1998, 80 n. 11).

275. Pitard 1987, 89; Na'aman 1995b, 104; M. Weippert 1973–74, 62 and n. 84 ("im nördlichen Biqā) und dem nördlichen Antilibanus."

276. See, e.g., Parpola 1987, 238; Parpola and Porter 2001, maps 8, 24.

277. Charpin (1998, 90–92) argues that Forrer's earlier proposal is preferable. Because of its importance as a regional center in later times, Forrer (1920, 62) equated Ṣupat = Baalbek, suggesting that Ṣobah was the old name of Baalbek (classical Heliopolis). He was followed by Lewy 1944, 443–54, esp 449.

278. Was it the seat of an Assyrian governor, an independent province, a district of Hamath? See Lipiński 2000a, 319–30; Na'aman 1999c; Dion 1997, 172–76; Radner 2006–8a, 62–63.

at Tell al-Mu'allaqa, about 10 km east–northeast of Irbid. However, even if 2 Sam 10 is giving accurate information, it is not necessary to understand the text in this manner. Moreover, as Bagg (2007, 53) notes, that Bēt-Reḥob was a Transjordanian state is no longer maintained.[279] Two biblical references (Num 13:21; Judg 18:28) indicate that Bēt-Reḥob was the name of area north of Dan that stretched up to Lebo-Hamath (modern Lebwe).[280] The relationship of Bēt-Reḥob to Ṣobah will be discussed in detail below.

It seems that both states (Ṣobah and Bēt-Reḥob) lay to the west of the Anti-Lebanon mountain range with Bēt-Reḥob being located in the southern Beqa' and Ṣobah to the north.

Ṣobah appears to have been the dominant political power in central and southern Syria during the early part of the tenth century.[281] The biblical texts (2 Sam 8 and 10 ‖ 1 Chr 18 and 19) recount battles fought between the Arameans of Ṣobah and the Israelites under the leadership of David. Hadad-ezer, son of Reḥob,[282] king of Ṣobah, is designated as the leader of the Arameans. The name Hadad-ezer was a common Aramaic personal name.[283] Later, one of the ninth-century kings of Damascus bore this name (in Assyrian texts: Adad-idri, an enemy of Shalmaneser III). Hadad-ezer's intervention in the Transjordan appears to be an indication of a long-standing Aramean interest in that area (2 Sam 10).

While 2 Sam 8 and 10 provide the most important biblical material, there are two major problems within these texts. Both of these problems are exacerbated by the impoverished state of the archaeology in this part of Syria, in particular, the lack of excavations done in the area where Ṣobah was located, as well as the most important Aramean city in the region, Damascus.

The first major problem is the relationship between the chapters. Some scholars think that the description of Aramean conflicts in these chapters are really two different versions of the same war. Hence, 2 Sam 10 is simply a variant account. Among those who hold this view, there is disagreement over which chapter (2 Sam 8 or 10) is the more reliable witness. This is very evident in the two most recent full-length monographs devoted to the history of the Arameans. Thus, Dion (1997, 172–73) maintains that "certain concrete details of [2 Sam 8], such as the city names, the booty, the reaction of the king of Hamath after the victories of David" suggest a higher degree

279. Contra Dion 1997, 175 n. 22. See Mittmann and Schmitt 2001, B IV 16.

280. Yamada 2000a, 160; Na'aman 2002a, 204; Bagg 2007, 53.

281. Perhaps, it was earlier, but there is presently no evidence.

282. The phrase בן־רחב will be discussed below.

283. Hadad-ezer: Aramaic: Hadad-ʿiḏr, *hdd-ʿḏr*; Hebrew: Hadad-ezer, *hdd-ʿzr*, means "Hadad is (my) help" and is a well-attested Aramaic personal name. See Maraqten 1988, 155; Zadok 1977, 46, 97, 243, 246; Schwemer 1998a.

of authenticity here than in 2 Sam 10, which conformed "the facts to the context of the Ammonite wars and to the parameters established by Samuel 10:6–14."[284] On the other hand, Lipiński (2000a, 338) thinks that 2 Sam 8 is derived from 2 Sam 10 in addition to a second etiological source related to "'king David's quivers, which were in Yahweh's house' (2 Kgs 11:10; cf. v. 7), and to Solomon's 'sea of bronze, pillars, and bronze vessels' in the temple (1 Chr 18:8)."[285] Thus, for Lipiński chapter 10 is more reliable.[286]

But other scholars would see two separate conflicts, that is, two different events (McCarter 1984, 247–48). Many scholars would distinguish 2 Sam 8:3–8 as the description of a "separate battle, usually thought to have occurred after those described in 2 Samuel 10" (Pitard 1987, 216). In the first place, 2 Sam 8 appears possibly to be derived from a type of summary inscription.[287] Second, it is not an essential that 2 Sam 8 and 10 follow a strict chronological arrangement.

However, if these are two separate battles, the time lapse between them is not clear, and the circumstances attendant to the 2 Sam 8 battle depends to some extent on one's interpretation of the enigmatic expression, בְּלֶכְתּוֹ לְהָשִׁיב יָדוֹ בִּנְהַר (2 Sam 8:3). One problem lies in the understanding of the infinitive לְהָשִׁיב and its subject. If its subject is Hadad-ezer and it is from the root שׁוּב (*hiphil* "to restore"; cf. NRSV), then the Aramean king went to "restore his power" at the Euphrates (Lemaire 2001, 128). David, accordingly, was not slow in seizing this opportunity to attack Hadad-ezer from behind. However, McCarter (1984, 243) observes that the parallel verse in 1 Chronicles has the verb לְהַצִּיב (1 Chr 18:3) as a synonym, and the LXX of 2 Sam 8:3 has ἐπιστῆσαι. These readings suggest that the Hebrew verb in 2 Sam 8:3 is actually יָשֵׁב (*hiphil* "to cause to dwell/stay/remain") with David as its subject: David goes to set up his stela (יָדוֹ) at the Euphrates (McCarter 1984, 247–48). Another problem is the identification of the river: 1 Chr 18:3 reads בִּנְהַר־פְּרָת

284. Hertzberg (1964, 305) similarly argued for the priority of 2 Sam 8 on the basis of the numbers.

285. Concerning these textual additions, see the balanced assessment of Edenburg 2010, 167–68

286. S. B. Parker (1997, 68–74, esp. 74) feels that it is impossible to determine since the two chapters derive from variant oral stories. However, the parallel pointed out by Na'aman with the Mesha Inscription would argue that 2 Sam 8 was not based on oral tradition, but on a written summary text.

287. Good 2001. According to Halpern (2001, 134, 137–38), "2 Sam 8 employs the conventions of display inscriptions. Indeed 2 Sam 8 punctuates the reports of conquest by interlarding them with statements that David was saved by Yahweh or made temple donations or was just. This technique is reminiscent of Tiglath-pileser's annals with their intermittent titulary or characterization of the king in between reports of the campaigns." For a critique, see Holloway 2003.

"at the River Euphrates," which seems to be a later gloss. But is it accurate? Other scholars have suggested that it is not the Euphrates that is in view but another river, such as the Jordan, Jabbok, or Yarmuk.[288] Finally, the text of 1 Chr 18:3 adds after "the king of Ṣobah" the word חֲמָתָה,[289] the toponym חמת plus a directional ה. This seems to imply that David attacked Hadad-ezer from the south at a time when he was vulnerable being far to the north at the Euphrates River.[290]

What I have shown so far is illustrative of the various complexities in the biblical texts narrating the stories of the interactions between Israel and Ṣobah. Therefore, dogmatism about what these passages are attempting to communicate must be avoided.

It is also important to recognize that both narratives in 2 Sam 8:1–14 and 1 Chr 18:1–13 are part of a larger context and therefore were shaped in order to convey different views of the part that David's conquests play in Samuel and Chronicles respectively. A close reading of both accounts demonstrates that each has been purposely composed along different ideological lines. For example, both accounts are "loosely"[291] connected to the dynastic oracle given to David in the preceding chapter in their respective narratives (2 Sam 7:1–29; 1 Chr 17:1–27). Yet the narratives differ in chronological settings: 2 Sam 7:1 ("After the king was settled in his palace and Yahweh had given him rest from all his enemies around him"); 1 Chr 17:1 ("After David was settled in his palace"). It becomes clear that neither narrative (2 Sam 8 or 1 Chr 18) is truly arranged in a chronological fashion, but in accordance with its ideological purposes.[292]

However, it is important to recognize the fact that 2 Sam 8 and 1 Chr 18 anticipate the later Ammonite wars; and therefore the present form of 2 Sam 8 is integrally linked to 2 Sam 10. So, for example, Hadad-ezer is first mentioned in the 2 Sam 10 account in verse 16. Hadad-ezer's name appears eight times in chapter 8 (vv. 3, 5, 7, 8, 9, 10 [2x], 12); it appears only three times in chapter 10 (10:16 [2x], 19). The fact that he is not mentioned until 10:16 means that the writer of the 2 Sam 10 account is assuming prior knowledge of the 2 Sam 8 narrative, especially since Hadad-ezer is not iden-

---

288. Klein 2006, 405; Knoppers 2004, 722; Na'aman 2002a, 208; S. B. Parker 1997, 69; Halpern 1996, 65; Stoebe 1994, 243, 249–50; Japhet 1993, 346.

289. The NRSV translates "toward Hamath {meaning of the Hebrew uncertain}"; the NIV: "as far as Hamath."

290. 1 Chr 18:3 also omits בֶּן־רְחֹב as a designation for Hadad-ezer.

291. The very indeterminate phrase וַיְהִי אַחֲרֵי־כֵן is used in 2 Sam 8:1, 10:1 and in 1 Chr 18:1, 19:1, 20:4.

292. For the achronographic character of the summary in 1 Chronicles, see Knoppers 2004, 702–3.

tified in verse 16 as "the king of Ṣobah" (as he is in 2 Sam 8:3, 5). Even if this is the product of editing, the result is the same: there is an assumption of a knowledge of 2 Sam 8 on the part of readers.

Second Samuel 8 certainly reads like a type of summary inscription with David's victories arranged geographically (not chronologically). There is also a possible geographic arrangement, with the conquest developed along two axes: west (Philistia) to east (Moab) in 2 Sam 8:1–2; and north (Aram) to south (Edom) in 2 Sam 8:3–8, 13–14).[293] In this regard, Edenburg has correctly noted that narratives of both 2 Sam 8 and 1 Chr 18 are shaped according to geographic principles and that such use of fourpoint structures in boundary descriptions occur in a number of different types of documents, where they are best understood as a merism, in which the polar opposite extents of the border are used to represent the totality.[294] This, in turn, undergirds the text's ideological emphasis on the completeness of David's conquest.

Furthermore, the verb נָכָה is used with rhetorical value to begin each new section concerning a different foe: the Philistines (v. 1), Moab (v. 2), and Hadad-ezer (v. 3). The sections on Moab (8:2) and Hadad-ezer (8:3–6) begin and end with an almost identical expressions:

וַיַּךְ אֶת־מוֹאָב ...
וַתְּהִי מוֹאָב לְדָוִד לַעֲבָדִים נֹשְׂאֵי מִנְחָה

Now he struck down Moab, …
and Moab became servants to David, bearers of tribute. (8:2a, e)

וַיַּךְ דָּוִד אֶת־הֲדַדְעֶזֶר בֶּן־רְחֹב מֶלֶךְ צוֹבָה ...
וַתְּהִי אֲרָם לְדָוִד לַעֲבָדִים נוֹשְׂאֵי מִנְחָה

Now David struck down Hadad-ezer, son of Reḥob, king of Ṣobah, …
and Aram became servants to David, bearers of tribute. (8:3a, 6b)

If this passage in 2 Sam 8 originally belonged to an official document of David's victories, it is not surprising that the most decisive victory against the various enemies should be the one listed. Thus, 2 Sam 8 describes the

293. See the same pattern in 1 Chr 18: west to east: 1 Chr 18:1–2; north to south: 1 Chr 18:3–8, 12–13.

294. Edenburg (2010, 161–62) argues that this reflects the Mesopotamian notion of "king of the four quarters" and an emulation of Neo-Assyrian style. Since merism is a very common literary device and the compass points are frequently invoked in such a device, it is unnecessary to posit an emulation of Neo-Assyrian style. But her point about the literary power of the device is very much on target. It reinforces one of my points here: that a thorough understanding of the literary aspects of the text must precede historical reconstruction.

climactic battle of David against the Arameans, an event that would have occurred in real time after the battles mentioned 2 Sam 10. It is worth quoting Na'aman's comment (1996, 178) on this passage:

> It seems to me that the conclusion of every war with a reference to a distinct booty is an original trait of the early chronicle and was adopted by the Deuteronomistic historian. A good parallel is offered by the Mesha inscription in which the capture of important towns culminates with the taking of a distinct spoil and its dedication to the god as his preferential share in the booty.

Indeed, 2 Sam 8:11–12 seems to mark the end of this "summary inscription," a fact supported by its concluding mention of all three subjects dealt with previously: "Philistines," "Moab," and "Hadad-ezer, son of Reḥob, king of Ṣobah." Na'aman's observation of the parallel with the Mesha inscription is important because it suggests that the writer of 2 Sam 8 was perhaps following a rhetorical design. In this regard, certain Assyrian summary inscriptions would provide additional parallels. This only explains the way the narrative is working; one must be cautious not to take the rhetoric in every instance literally.[295]

Thus one might reconstruct the following. After the outbreak of war between Ammon and Israel, Hadad-ezer came to the support of Ammon, along with a number of vassals, and fought to a stalemate with the Israelites (2 Sam 10:6–14 || 1 Chr 19:6–15). Hadad-ezer returned to Ṣobah, where he gathered new troops and prepared to meet Israel again (2 Sam 10:15–19 || 1 Chr 19:16–19). But David marched his army northward and met Hadad-ezer in a battle at Helam, where the army of Ṣobah was decisively defeated. Several of Hadad-ezer's allies and vassals subsequently sued for peace and became David's vassals. A further confrontation between David and Hadad-ezer is described in 2 Sam 8:3–8 || 1 Chr 18:3–8. The third and final battle[296] occurred near Hamath in central Syria, and it is described as a decisive defeat for Hadad-ezer. It is during the course of this conflict that Aram-Damascus makes its first appearance in the Hebrew Bible. According to 2 Sam 8:5–6, troops from Damascus were sent to aid Hadad-ezer, but David defeated them as well and went on to place Israelite garrisons in Damascus, apparently making it an occupied territory (Pitard 1994a, 216). Since Hadad-ezer

---

295. A point that must be remembered as one interprets conquest accounts. See Younger 1990.

296. Three battles were fought by Aram-Ṣobah led by Hadad-ezer and Israel led by David (2 Sam 8 and 10); the three battles were fought by Aram-Damascus led by Ben-Hadad (Hadad-ezer?) and Israel led by Ahab (1 Kgs 20 and 22).

had made himself overlord of all Syria, David's final conquest of him and his forces gave Israel suzerainty over the whole of that territory at one blow.

(2) The second problem is the relationship of Ṣobah (2 Sam 8:3, 5, 12; 10:6, 8) and Bēt-Reḥob (2 Sam 10:6) to each other. This problem is complicated by four issues. First, Hadad-ezer, the king of Ṣobah (*ṣwbh*) is designated the "son of Reḥob (*bn rḥb*)" which could be a patronymic (B. Mazar 1962, 102) or gentilic affiliation.[297] Second, there is confusion in the description of the entities and their contingents. Bēt-Reḥob and Ṣobah are described as sending a single contingent of twenty thousand foot soldiers (2 Sam 10:6). However, in the same verse the contingents from Ma'acah and Ṭob are separately mentioned, even though their number of men (one thousand and twelve thousand respectively) is considerably smaller than that of Bēt-Reḥob and Ṣobah. Third, 1 Chr 19:6, which parallels 2 Sam 10:6, mentions only the involvement of Ṣobah and omits reference to Bēt-Reḥob. It also omits any reference to Ṭob, which is mentioned in 2 Sam 10:6. Fourth, there are textual difficulties: the Septuagint witness differs from the Masoretic reading. In 2 Sam 10:6, the Hebrew reading (אֶת־אֲרַם בֵּית־רְחוֹב וְאֶת־אֲרַם צוֹבָא) is shortened in the Greek τὴν Συρίαν Βαιρθοωβ. Therefore, it is not surprising that scholars are in disagreement concerning the relationship.

Some scholars have attempted to resolve the difficulties by suggesting that the two names refer to a single political entity. For example, B. Mazar (1962, 102) understood there to be simply "the important kingdom in southern Syria, Aram-Zobah, ruled by the dynasty of Beth-rehob." Recently, Lipiński endorses this approach: "Aram-Ṣoba must obviously be identified with Bēt-Reḥob."[298]

Most scholars, however, propose that Bēt-Reḥob and Ṣobah are two different political entities (perhaps intricately linked through Hadad-ezer) (cf. 2 Sam 10:6: "Aram-Ṣobah" and "Aram-Beth-Reḥob").[299] For example, Na'aman (2002a, 204) explicates:

> Scholars recognized that '*ben* Rehob' does not refer to Hadad-ezer's father, but is an abbreviated form of '*ben* (Beth)-Rehob,' and that his kingdom included two regions: Beth-rehob and Zobah. Two biblical references (Num 13:21; Judg 18:28) indicate that Beth-rehob covered most of the Beqa' of Lebanon, from the area north of Dan up to Lebo-hamath (modern Lebwe). Zobah was located in the northern Beqa', north of Lebwe, and in the area

---

297. Thus, for example, Pitard (1994a, 215) suggests that the phrase should better be translated "the Rehobite," since Hadad-ezer also appears to have been the ruler of another small Aramean state called Bēt-Reḥob.

298. Lipiński (2000a, 333–4) adds: "The right approach was already formulated in a few words of B. Mazar, namely: 'Aram-zobah, ruled by the dynasty of Bēt-Reḥob.' "

299. Note the syntax: אֶת־אֲרַם בֵּית־רְחוֹב וְאֶת־אֲרַם צוֹבָא.

north of Mt. Anti-Lebanon, bordering the north with the kingdom of Hamath.

Thus the two regions that were originally independent entities were united as one political entity under Hadad-ezer and thus have a joint army.[300] According to Malamat's scheme, Hadad-ezer was initially the king of Bēt-Reḥob, but later obtained the kingship of Ṣobah as well, "amalgamating the two kingdoms into a *Personalunion*, similar to David's *personalunion* of Judah and Israel."[301] Malamat adds: "While Aram-Beth-Rehob was apparently located in the southern Lebanon valley, Aram-Zobah lay in the north, extending north-east of the Anti-Lebanon into the Syrian desert, towards Tadmor."[302] Dion (1997, 173) notes that biblical tradition purports the existence of the state of Ṣobah in the tenth century, and that this state enjoyed a certain authority over the Arameans of Bēt-Reḥob, over the people of Ṭob and Ma'acah, and over the Arameans established beyond the Euphrates. Ṣobah may not have had the exact same authority over Damascus (2 Sam 8:5). McCarter (1984, 248) seems to cautiously concur with Malamat's position, especially with his analogy drawn from David's kingship over both Judah and Israel.

While Malamat's reconstruction is perhaps overly speculative (i.e., the issue of *Personalunion*), it seems clear from the evidence that there were two regions—Bēt-Reḥob and Ṣobah—and that during this time period Ṣobah was the dominant force in central and southern Syria under the leadership of Hadad-ezer.

It is important to note that in Shalmaneser III's Kurkh Monolith, in the listing of coalition participants, an enigmatic phrase occurs: $^{m}$*ba-ʾa-sa* DUMU *ru-ḫu-bi* KUR *a-ma-na-a-a*.[303] The debate concerning this participant has centered primarily on KUR.*A-ma-na-a-a*. Commonly scholars have

---

300. In 1 Sam 14:47, the plural וּבְמַלְכֵי צוֹבָה "and the kings of Ṣobah" is singular in the Greek εἰς βασιλέα Σουβα. Malamat thinks that in 1 Sam 14:47, "not only Zobah, but also Bēt-Reḥob is specifically listed among the enemies of Saul." See Malamat 1963, 2 n. 8; 1973, 141. However, it is not at all certain that the Greek βαιθεωρ in 1 Sam 14:47 refers to Bēt-Reḥob. Elsewhere the name "Bēt-Reḥob" is translated by οἴκου Ρααβ (Judg 18:28) and βαιθροωβ (2 Sam 10:6), while the name "Reḥob" is most frequently spelled Ρααβ (Num 13:21; Josh 19:28; 21:31; 2 Sam 8:2, 12) and Ροωβ (2 Sam 10:8; 1 Chr 6:60 [75]; Neh 10:12). See also the comments of Edelman 1984, 207.

301. Malamat 1963, 2; 1973, 141. While this is saying more than the evidence grants, obviously the two areas were under Hadad-ezer's authority.

302. Malamat 1973, 141–42. He adds: "In his heyday Hadad-ezer ruled over vast territories, founding an empire of complex political structure, comprising even Aram-Damascus and other vassals and satellites, such as the kingdom of (Aram-)Ma'akah, in the upper Gaulan, and the land of Tob, somewhere in northern Transjordan."

303. RIMA 3:23, A.0.102.2, ii.95. For a recent discussion, Younger 2007b, 260–61.

understood this to refer to Ammon, the small Transjordanian state.[304] Others have understood the word to refer to Amanah, the Anti-Lebanon mountain range (cf. 2 Kgs 5:12Q; Song 4:8).[305] Moreover, beside the similarity of place name, Forrer equated the patronym with Reḥob, father of Hadad-ezer of Ṣobah, named in 2 Sam 8:3, suggesting Reḥob was the dynastic name of the kings of Ṣobah (Forrer 1928).

The spelling of KUR.*A-ma-na-a-a* does not automatically point to Ammon or Mount Amanah, since KUR can be the determinative for land or mountain. The name Ba'asa (*bʿšʾ*) is West Semitic; it is the name of an Israelite king in 1 Kgs 15:16; is found on an Ammonite ostracon;[306] and also occurs in Punic (Benz 1972, 101). Consequently, it is impossible based on this name to identify the ruler's ethnicity. But Mount Amanah is never attested as a state in any other source, and here, in this context—compare the formulation of the preceding allies—the form is clearly a gentilic (Neo-Assyrian: *-āya*), which makes Mount Amana even less likely (Younger 2007b, 254). Therefore, it seems most probable that KUR.*A-ma-na-a-a* should be understood as "Ammonite" (Rendsburg 1991; Bagg 2007, 53).

However, no other individual in this list has a double attribution (whether one understands DUMU *ru-ḫu-bi* as a gentilic or a patronymic).[307] Thus quite a few scholars have followed Weidner's suggestion that these are really two entities: Bēt-Reḥob and Ammon. Galil (2002, 46) concludes: "the provincial author presumably was mistaken. The complement should be "[xxx troops of] the Ammonite," like the short and anonymous indications for rulers from Egypt, Usnu, and Que (or Byblos)." This assumes that the writer left out the signs X ME ÉRIN.MEŠ or X LIM ÉRIN.MEŠ between DUMU *ru-ḫu-bi* and KUR.*a-ma-na-a-a*. While possible, there is no way of proving this assumption.

Since the Kurkh Monolith contains numerous errors, the enigmatic phrase ${}^{m}$*ba-ʾa-sa* DUMU *ru-ḫu-bi* KUR.*a-ma-na-a-a* should not be used as the grounds for explaining the less-than-clear biblical text. Nor is it good methodology to do the opposite, that is, explain the Assyrian text based on the biblical material.

---

304. *COS* 2.113A:264; Luckenbill 1926–27, 1:§611; *ANET*, 279; Na'aman 1976, 98 n. 20; Millard 1992b, 35; and Yamada 2000a, 161; Bagg 2007, 53.

305. Cogan 1984; Dion 1997, 176, 186; Na'aman 1995a, 385–6; 2002a, 204–5.

306. Ḥesbân Ostracon A1. See *COS* 3.84:202 and *CAI*, 214–19. Lipiński (1999c) does not note this evidence in his discussion of the name.

307. Interestingly, an epigraph on a bronze band from Imgur-Enlil (Balawat) reads: "Adinu, (the man) of Bīt-Dakkūri, the Chaldean" (${}^{m}$*a-di-ni* A ${}^{m}$*da-ku-ri* KUR [*kal*]-*da-a-a*). See RIMA 3:145–46, A.0.102.79.

Some scholars have speculated on the extent of Ṣobah's empire at the time of its contact with David. Based on an earlier reading, the Kurkh Monolith of Shalmaneser III seemed to indicate that at the time of Aššur-rabi II, king of Assyria, "the king of the land of Aram" had captured two cities on the Euphrates (Pitru and Mutkīnu).[308] Since Aššur-rabi II (r. 1012–972 BCE) was a contemporary of David, Malamat, followed by a number of other scholars, identified "the king of Aram" with Hadad-ezer of Aram-Ṣobah, who campaigned up to the Euphrates and even "beyond the river" (2 Sam 8:3; 10:16–19; 1 Chr 19:16).[309] On the other hand, Ikeda (1999, 275 n. 12) has suggested taking the king of "the land of Aram" to be Hapatila, one of the rulers of the Neo-Hittite state of Masuwari (Til-Barsib), who is said to have "governed in the west and in the east (of the Euphrates)" by his great-great-grandson, author of a text from Tell Aḥmar. However, it seems somewhat odd that the king of the Neo-Hittite state of Masuwari be called "the king of Aram."[310] A third identification has been suggested by Bunnens (1999, 606–7), who has argued that "the king of Aram" might be identified with a king of Yaḫān (Bīt-Agūsi/Arpad) based on a restoration in an inscription of Aššur-dān II.[311]

Although Grayson read MAN KUR *a-ru-mu*, recent separate collations have demonstrated that the sign MAN (*šarru* "king") does not occur here; the text simply reads KUR *a-ru-mu* "the land of Aram."[312] Therefore, the reference is not to a specific monarch. It may refer to some unidentified Aramean tribal group's raid and capture of these two cities. There are simply no grounds for connecting the events of the Monolith with the biblical texts.

While it seems clear that there were two polities Ṣobah and Bēt-Reḥob, there naturally is disagreement about the location of the names of the towns of Hadad-ezer in 2 Sam 8:8 (Beṭaḥ [בֶּטַח] [see next note] and Berotay [בֵּרֹתַי]) and 1 Chr 18:8 (Ṭibḥat [טִבְחַת][313] and Kûn [כּוּן]; Dion 1997, 174; Lipiński 2000a, 323–24).

Since Bēt-Reḥob and Ṣobah were subdued by David (2 Sam 8), it is not surprising that Israelite influence should be reflected in names connected with Bēt-Reḥob or Ṣobah. Charpin has noted that some of David's elite military men were recruited from Ṣobah (Charpin 1998, 90). Thus in 2 Sam 23:36

---

308. RIMA 3:19, A.0.102.2, lines 35b–40a. See §3.1.4 above.

309. Malamat 1973, 142; 1983. See also Hawkins 1982, 381.

310. Moreover, Hapatila's dates may not fit with those of David.

311. See detailed discussion in §4.1.1.3 Yaḫānu below.

312. See Fuchs 1998b; Yamada 2000a, 127, 363. Also personally collated April 20, 2005. See section 3.1.4, and n. 92 above.

313. Thutmose III List, no. 6: *d-b-ḫ-w*; EA 179:15, etc.: URU.*ṭú-bi-ḫi*; Papyrus Anastasi I, 19:1: *d-b-ḫ*; Gen 24:24: טֶבַח; and metathesis in 2 Sam 8:8: בֶּטַח for טֶבַח?

there is a certain "Yigal, son of Nathan, from Ṣobah" (יִגְאָל בֶּן־נָתָן מִצֹּבָה). But the Old Greek for this verse is different: *Ιγααλ υἱὸς Ναθαν ἀπὸ δυνάμεως*." In 1 Chr 11:47, three men from Ṣobah are enumerated: "Eli'el, and 'Obed, and Yaasi'el, the Meṣobayah (Ṣobah?)" (אֱלִיאֵל וְעוֹבֵד וְיַעֲשִׂיאֵל הַמְּצֹבָיָה; OG: Αλιηλ καὶ Ωβηδ καὶ Ιεσιηλ ὁ Μισαβια). In any case, Charpin's suggestion seems very plausible.

As best as can be ascertained, at the time of David (ca. 980 BCE), Damascus was still rather insignificant politically. It is evident from 2 Sam 8:5 that Damascus had close relations with Ṣobah, but the type of relationship is not known; it may have been an ally, a vassal, or an occupied territory of the more powerful state, although the former seems most likely. Certainly Hadad-ezer, king of Ṣobah, did not rule in Damascus. There is no information on the internal political situation in Damascus before its defeat by David (Pitard 1987, 89).

### 3.3.2. The Smaller Polities: Geshur, Ma'akah, and Ṭob

#### 3.3.2.1. Geshur

Geshur seems to have been a small kingdom located in the Golan on one of the routes connecting the Bashan with the Phoenician coast (Ma'oz 1992). The name Geshur (גְּשׁוּר) is found primarily in the biblical sources (Hess 2004, 49). The etymology of the name has been linked to the spelling of Gether (MT: גֶּתֶר; LXX: Γαθερ), one of the sons of Aram in Gen 10:23 (cf. 1 Chr 1:17), understanding the name to be preserving the original pronunciation *Gtr* < **G*ṯ*r* "to be very strong," so that the name "Geshur" has been taken to mean "stronghold, fortress."[314]

314. Albright (1956a, 12) was the first scholar to suggest that "*g*ṯ*r* reflects the original Aramaic pronunciation of the name that appears as *Gešūr* in MT." Lipiński (1993, 202) pointed out that the Old Greek spelling of גשר is, in the majority of instances (seven times), Γεδσουρ (though Γεσιρ[ι] is also found four times), and that this seems to be related to the Semitic root *g*ṯ*r*, "be strong," which would give **Ga*ṯṯ*ūr* the meaning "fortress." He concludes: "C'est **Ga*ṯṯ*ūr*, puis **Gattūr* que l'endroit devait s'appeler en araméen, et *Gtr* serait alors la forme normale du toponyme dans l'orthographe purement consonantique." See also Lipiński 2000a, 336. Hendel (2005, 111) has recently concluded that "the etymology from **g*ṯ*r* indicates that *Gešūr* represents the orthography and phonology of the Old Aramaic period."

Although a root *gšr/gtr* < *g*ṯ*r* does not appear in Aramaic, the verb *gašāru* "to be or become very strong" occurs in Akkadian (see *AHw*, 283 s.v. *gašāru*, which also notes the Arabic *ǧšr*). Thus it is possible that the name comes from an earlier period in the second millennium, being possibly tied to a personal name of an important chieftain of Semitic origin in the region. In Ugaritic, the root *g*ṯ*r* occurs as an epithet of the dead and deified king (Olmo Lete and Sanmartín 2003, 314).

As far as ancient Near Eastern sources go, some scholars have attempted to identify the land of Gari in the Amarna Letters (EA 256:23) with Geshur, positing a scribal omission of a ŠU sign between GA and RI, emending the text to KUR.*ga-<šu>-ri*.[315] This proposal was first suggested by B. Mazar, who felt that

> it may be taken as certain that the land of Garu mentioned in the Amarna letter under discussion was a large tract of territory in the Golan, as suggested by Albright, stretching southward as far as the Yarmuk and identical with the biblical Geshur.[316]

However, recent study indicates that the fourteenth-century land of Gari of this Amarna letter should be sought in the area between the cities of Aštarot and Piḫilu, and "its extent is irrelevant for the study of the Aramean kingdom of Geshur in the early first millennium BCE."[317] Mazar's proposed emendation is unnecessary and only creates confusion.

Another possible ancient Near Eastern source is the Broken Statue of Shalmaneser III from Nimrud. This is an important source for Shalmaneser's 838 campaign and will be discussed in more detail in chapter 9 below. The text is fragmentary, though it preserves enough toponymy to demonstrate the general route of the campaign. The text lists four cities of Hazael that Shalmaneser claimed to capture, two of which are preserved (Danabu and Malaḫa) whose location is most likely in the Ḥauran, south of Damascus.[318] Next, the text relates the following:

> Ba'il (*ba-a'-il*), the G[i-x-r]a-*ite* (KUR.G[I-x-R]A-*a-a*), seized my feet. I received his tribute. I placed my royal image in the temple in Laruba (URU.*la-ru-ba*),[319] his fortified city. Moreover (*u*), I received the tribute of the Tyrians, the Sidonians and the Byblians. I went as far as the land of Muṣuruna (KUR.*mu-ṣu-ru-na*).

Can Ba'il's land be identified? Table 3.5 gives the proposed readings of the cuneiform.

315. Besides the problem of emending the text with the ŠU sign, there is the problem of reading GA, not GI in EA 256:23, a problem not addressed by Mazar.

316. B. Mazar 1961, 20. But see Moran 1992, 309. For other older proposed emendations that can safely be discarded, see Weidner 1957–71.

317. Na'aman 2012, 91–92 with supporting bibliography cited, esp. Na'aman 1988b, 181–82.

318. See §9.2.

319. Possibly to be read *Ma-ru-ba*, understanding a scribal error of the LA sign for the MA sign (Yamada 2000a, 209). But see Na'aman 2012, 93.

Table 3.5. Proposed Readings of RIMA 3:79

| Reference | Reading |
|---|---|
| Grayson 1996, 79 | ˹KUR˺ x-[x x-*r*]*a*?-*a*-*a*(*) |
| Lipiński 1999a, 242 | ˹KUR˺ [*Ṣi-mir-r*]*a-a-a* |
| Yamada 2000a, 206 | ˹KUR˺ Z[I](?)-[x]-[*r*]*a-a-a* (text: II) |
| Yamada 2000b, 80 | ˹KUR˺ *Ṣ*[*í-mir-r*]*a-a-a* (text: 2) |
| Na'aman 2002a, 205 | ˹KUR˺ *G*[*i-šu*(*r*)-*r*]*a-a-a* |
| Arav 1995b, 196–8; 2004, 13 | "Tzer … could also qualify for the identification." |
| Na'aman 2012, 93 | ˹KUR˺ *G*[*i-šu-*(*ú*)-*r*]*a-a-a* |

Grayson's initial reading did not have Peter Hulin's hand copies and thus was disadvantaged. Hulin's copies demonstrate that enough of the wedges are preserved to yield either the sign ZI (which can have the value ṢÍ) or the sign GI. The proposal of Lipiński and Yamada to read the sign as ṢÍ (hence yielding *ṣ*[*imir*]*ra*) was a reasonable possibility based on the value of the sign and an understanding that the episode of Ba'il was connected to the following lines of the inscription that speak of tribute on the Phoenician coast. Yamada (2000a, 208) argued that the passage concerning Ba'il:

> is connected by the conjunction *u* with the following sentence: "and I received the tribute of the people of Tyre, Sidon and Byblos" (ll. 161'b–162'a). This implies the closeness of the country of Ba'il to Tyre, Sidon and Byblos. On these grounds, it seems safe to regard Ba'il as a ruler on the south Phoenician coast.

However, there are three problems. First, Ṣimirra is always written with the city determinative (URU), never the land determinative (KUR). Second, the city is always spelled with the ṢI sign, never the ZI/ṢÍ sign—this is an important point.[320] Third, the conjunction *u* is actually introducing a new subject. In Neo-Assyrian, "*u* coordinates sentences which are not closely connected. Often it marks the boundary of two entirely unconnected sentences, the latter of which is the beginning of a new thought."[321] In my opinion, this is what is taking place in the context. Therefore, there is no

320. Bagg 2007, 231–32; Belmonte Marín 2001, 251–52. This point is missed by Pakkala (2010, 168–70) who opts for Ṣimirra.

321. Hämeen-Anttila 2000, 123 (§4.4.1.2). See, e.g., Sennacherib's Rassam Cylinder line 39.

compelling reason to posit the location of Ba'il's kingdom on the south Phoenician coast. In the context, it follows immediately after Shalmaneser's activities in the Ḥauran.[322]

Consequently, by a process of limitation, the likelihood is that the sign should be read as GI. In addition, a route[323] from the Ḥauran area (the likely location of Danabu and Malaḫa) to the Phoenician coast would likely pass north of the Sea of Galilee. On this logic, Na'aman (2002, 205; 2012, 93) proposed reading the name Geshur in the inscription, reading the first sign as *gi*, restoring the second as *šu* and the last as *ra*, yielding KUR *g*[*i-šu-(ú)-r*]*a-a-a* "the G[eshu]rite." Although the middle sign(s) is unfortunately not preserved, there is a high degree of probability that the first and third signs are GI and RA, followed by the Assyrian gentilic form. In my opinion, the restoration proposed by Na'aman has a very high probability of being correct, far better than other proposals.

The land of Geshur is first highlighted in the biblical texts in the so-called Deuteronomistic History (Deut 3:14; Josh 12:5; 13:11, 13).[324] According to Deut 3:14 and Josh 12:5, Geshur appears to be located "in the land that remains," that is, outside the borders of Israel "up to (עַד) the border of the Geshurites and Ma'akahites." On the other hand, it was included in Og's kingdom, the kingdom of Bashan, that which was given to Israel, although "the Geshurites and Ma'akahites still live among the Israelites to this day" (Josh 13:11, 13). Na'aman suggests that these passages are reflective of the scribes in far-away Jerusalem and their lack of knowledge of the region. This is a possible explanation, but I would prefer to see it as part of the numerous, and at times contrasting, land ideologies preserved in the book of Joshua (Younger 2003b, 174). In any event, they do not contradict the existence and general location of Geshur, just whether it was or was not in the kingdom of Bashan or later Israel.

In these verses, Geshur and Ma'akah occur together. Lipiński (2000a, 336) has argued that "Geshur and Bēt-Maaka were not distinct states, but one kingdom called either Geshur, according to its capital city, or Bēt-Maaka, according to the name of the ruling dynasty." He feels the frequent occur-

---

322. Arav's suggestion (2004, 13) to see the city of "Tzer" in Shalmaneser's inscription is out of the question. The proposal ignores the fact that there was most certainly a sign in between the GI sign and the RA sign (perhaps two?). The form is a gentilic with the KUR determinative; so there is no chance that this is the "Ṣērite" (totally unknown)! See further discussion of the ancient name of the city of et-Tell below.

323. See §9.3.5.4.

324. The Old Greek versions render גְּשׁוּר: Γεδσουρ (2 Sam 13:37; 14:23, 32; 15:8; 1 Chr 2:23; 3:2); Γεσουρι (Josh 12:5); Γεσιρ (2 Sam 3:3); Γεσιρι (Josh 13:11, 13), and Γαργασι (Deut 3:14).

rences of "the Geshurite and the Maakathite," as well as the fact that "the daughter of the king of Geshur was called Maaka" (2 Sam 3:3) indicate "that Geshur was the royal residence of Bēt-Maaka."

However, there is important evidence that both Ma'akah and Geshur were autonomous states. First, there is evidence that Ma'akah is mentioned in the Egyptian execration texts dating from the nineteenth and eighteenth centuries BCE. In E 37 it reads: *ḥkꜣ n mʿkyw šmš*[...] "the ruler of Ma'akayu," followed by the personal name "*Šamaš*-[...]." E 62 reads: *wrw nw mʿkyw* "the chiefs (clan leaders) of Ma'akayu."[325] Aḥituv (1984, 132) makes the important observation that the differentiation between "the ruler" (*ḥqꜣ*) in E37 and "the chiefs (clan leaders)" (*wrw*) in E 62 indicates that "the land of Maacha was inhabited by settled as well as by semi-nomadic elements." Moreover, the phrase "the chiefs (clan leaders)" of Ma'akayu melds nicely with the fact that the *bītu*-formula is used with Ma'akah in the biblical formulation and indicates its tribal entity status, with Abil being the name of the city (see further below).

Second, Geshur is absent in the accounts of 2 Sam 8 and 10, while the "king of Ma'akah" is an active participant.[326] Lipiński (2000a, 336) argues that Ma'akah is the name of the dynasty of Geshur; hence Geshur is, in fact, mentioned. Many scholars, however, reject this interpretation, asserting that Geshur had not opposed David in his Aramean battles.[327] The grounds for supposing an alliance between David and Geshur is the fact that David married "Ma'akah,[328] the daughter of Talmai, king of Geshur" early in his rule in Hebron (2 Sam 3:3 ≈ 1 Chr 3:2). Levenson and Halpern (1980) have demonstrated how David frequently employed the strategy of political marriages to secure his position within Israel, especially in the period of transition from Saul's dynasty. Malamat (1963, 8) argued that "the bond of marriage [with Ma'akah] gained for David an ally to the north of Ishbaal's [Ish-bosheth's] kingdom and placed the latter in a precarious strategic position between Geshur and Judah." That good relations were maintained between David and Geshur may be inferred from the fact that Absalom could seek asylum

325. Posener 1940, 83 (E 37), 93 (E 62). See Rainey and Notley 2006, 58. For discussion, see Mazar 1961, 22; and Dion 1997, 80. Lipiński (2000a, 335 n. 81) rejects this identification, but most scholars accept it (see Aḥituv 1984, 132). The common formulation throughout is *ḥkꜣ n* followed by *Place Name*. Therefore since this is the pattern in E 37, there seems to be every reason to see *mʿkyw* as a place name, not a personal name (especially since it is then followed by a personal name beginning with the component *šmš*.

326. It is not insignificant that Tyre is also absent, probably because it too, like Geshur, was an ally of David. See Na'aman 2002, 200.

327. E.g. Dion 1997, 81; Arav and Rousseau 1993, 422.

328. Na'aman (2012, 91 n. 4) feels that the oddity of the personal name might bring into question the princess's name.

at Geshur, under the protection of Talmai his grandfather (2 Sam 13:37).[329] These friendly relationships between Israel and Geshur suggest that Geshur was not part of the Aramean league in the time of David. It is unlikely that Geshur should have been allowed to remain neutral in the war, if it had been a vassal of Hadad-ezer.[330]

Third, evidence for Geshur's autonomy may also be gleaned from archaeological evidence. Evidence from Tel Hadar, a small site (2 ha) on the northeastern shore of the Sea of Galilee, may be helpful.[331] Dion (1997, 82) interprets the data at Stratum IV of Tel Hadar (eleventh century BCE) to indicate a culture that is "neither Aramean nor Israelite." Kochavi affirms that there are "many of the architectural features of Tel Hadar that have no parallels in ancient Israel, and several of the pottery styles and shapes are not found at Israelite sites."[332] However, it is uncertain whether enough is known about the material culture of the Arameans to claim that eleventh-century Tel Hadar is distinctively non-Aramean. Furthermore, excavations have uncovered "objects from Phoenicia, Greece, Syria and Jordan [which show] that Tel Hadar enjoyed cultural contacts of an international nature" (Kochavi et al. 1992, 38).

Fourth, Na'aman has suggested a preferable understanding:

> In this light, I suggest that Geshur was the name of the city located at et-Tell and that given the city's prominence, the kingdom was called by its name. The derivation of the kingdom's name from the root **gṯr* ("to be strong") and it meaning "stronghold, fortress" fit nicely the exceptional strength of the city walls (between six and eight meters width).[333]

The assumption that Maʿakah and Geshur were non-Aramean at the time of David is based on the onomastica, namely, that the personal names Maʿakah and Talmai are not Aramean.[334] However, a recent study of Geshurite onomastics provides a better assessment of the evidence. Analyzing the Bronze Age data, R. S. Hess (2004) concludes that "the Bronze Age in and around

329. The verses 2 Sam 14:23 and 32 where Geshur is mentioned are part of this same tradition.

330. Miglio 2014 investigates the international political context particularly looking at Absalom as a type of *kaltum*.

331. Kochavi 1993, 1994, 1996, 1999; Kochavi et al. 1992.

332. Kochavi et al. 1992, 41.

333. See discussion in note 345 below.

334. Lipiński (2000a, 336) states: "Neither Maaka nor Talmay—the name of the king of Geshur in the 10th century BC (2 Sam 3:3; 13:37; 1 Chr 3:2)—are Aramaic names and the kingdom of Bēt-Maaka was presumably not Aramean at that time. It was later considered as such, when its territory became part of the Aramean kingdom of Damascus."

Geshur is dominated by West Semitic onomastica. In the Middle Bronze period, there is a preponderance of Amurrite names with a possible Akkadian name. In the Late Bronze Age, the evidence suggests the appearance of Hurrian names among the largely West Semitic onomastica" (Hess 2004, 53). The Hurrian and other northern influences of the Bronze Age disappear in the Iron Age, with no clear attestations after the tenth century.[335] While Talmai (תַּלְמַי) is certainly Hurrian, Ma'akah (מַעֲכָה) is most likely West Semitic (Hess 2004, 57). The name of Talmai's father, Ammihud (עַמִּיהוּד), is West Semitic.[336] Thus the three biblical names of royalty from Geshur reflect three generations that may be ascribed to the eleventh and tenth centuries. The youngest and oldest generations possess West Semitic names while the middle generation, that of Talmai, possesses a Hurrian name. This generation, Hess (2004, 58) notes, is "the last period in which the Bible or any other source preserves such northern derived names. Their influence is on the wane and disappears altogether. It is replaced by entirely West Semitic names throughout Iron Age II."[337] In this connection, it is noteworthy that 2 Sam 15:8 describes Geshur as "in Aram." This situation is perhaps similar to that in Hamath, Masuwari, Sam'al, and other states where some mixed population that included West Semitics, specifically Arameans, lived (see the discussion above concerning the population substrates).

Recent excavations of et-Tell on the northern shore of the Sea of Galilee have uncovered the remains of an Iron Age city, which may have been the capital of the kingdom of Geshur (Arav 1995a, 1999a, 1999b, 2004, 2008, 2009, 2013). Particularly important was the discovery of a city-gate complex, one of the largest and best preserved in the region. Also excavated was a palace (*bīt ḫilāni* type) linked to the gate complex (Arav and Bernett 2000). Another important discovery was the Bull Stela (fig. 3.8), with its interesting iconography suggesting moon worship, but no inscription; Bernett and Keel 1998; Niehr 2010, 306 with bibliography).[338] An ostracon from et-Tell that may also point to moon-god worship does bear an inscription: *lšm* "belonging to the name." This is followed by a symbol that likely represented the

---

335. The Iron Age evidence includes from et-Tell, epigraphic: *'qb'*, *mky*, *zkryw*; and biblical: Ma'akah, Talmai, Ammihud, Absalom, and Tamar; from Tel En Gev, epigraphic: *lšqy'*, which is not a personal name but a title, "belonging to the cupbearer."

336. While the MT's *ketiv* is Ammiḥur (עַמִּיחוּר) is not attested elsewhere, the *qere*, Ammihud, is supported by all the versions.

337. A number of the Iron Age inscriptions from the Golan are Aramaic: from et-Tell: עקבא (Hess 2004, 54); from Ein Gev: לשקיא; and from Tel Hadar: לשדאל נזאא (Kochavi 1996, 192).

338. For the head of the bull, one should reference the shield fitting or garnish published by Krebernik and Seidl 1997. For a drawing and discussion of the shield fitting, see Younger 2007c, 143–44; Gubel 2012.

Moon God of Harran (Sîn/Śahr; Arav 1999b, 78–91; Savage 2009). The ostracon is a unique dedicatory inscription (Arav 2004, 34).

Fig. 3.8. Bull stela from Bethsaida (courtesy of Rami Arav)

It has been suggested that et-Tell is "Bethsaida" of the late Second Temple period and was probably a fortified city known as Zēr (צֵר) on the Sea of Galilee and mentioned in the Hebrew Bible (Josh 19:35).[339] Josh 19:35 reads: וְעָרֵי מִבְצָר הַצִּדִּים צֵר וְחַמַּת רַקַּת וְכִנָּרֶת. Arav (1995b, 196) argues: "The word הַצִּדִּים may be derived from the Aramaic *the fisherman* …," and the translation should be "and the fortified cities of the fishermen are Tzer (Tzed?), Hamat, Raqat, and Kinneret." This is not possible. In the first instance, Arav has confused two different roots, ציד "hunter" (*HALOT*, 1021, s.v. צַיָּד) and צד "side" (*HALOT*, 1000–1001, s.v. צֵד and צִדִּים).[340] Furthermore, there is a place name צדד (probably modern Ṣadad, 100 km north of Damascus (Num 34:8; Ezek 47:15).[341] Arav (1995b, 198) suggests an "interchange of *resh* and *dalet* so that the reading of *Tzer* could have been *Tzed*," which he identifies with Bethsaida.[342] It is true that Bethsaida means

339. Arav 1995b, 195–98; Greene 2004 (who follows Arav without assessment of the evidence and with the use of very dated sources).

340. I realize that there are forms צָדָה, צְדֶה, and צָדוּ that occur in Exod 21:13; 1 Sam 24:12 and Lam 4:18 respectively being derived from a root צדה (*HALOT*, 1000–1001, s.v. I צדה). However, this is not Arav's argument. See Olmo Lete and Sanmartín 2003, 778 s.v. /ṣ–d/; and McDaniel 1968, 49.

341. There is also a strong possibility that in 2 Sam 2:16b, הַצֻּרִים should be read הַצִּדִּים, based on context.

342. Arav (1995b, 198) argues: "Two facts support this suggestion: (1) The toponym Bethsaida in Aramaic means "the house of fishermen," and (2) there are several First Temple period place names to which the word בית (house) was added during the Second Temple period. These are Gilgal (Deut 11:30; Josh 4:19, 5:9–10; etc.) and Beth-Gilgal (Neh 12:29); Succoth (Gen 33:17; Josh 13:27; etc.) and Beth Socoth (Hieronymus, *Quaest. in Gen.* 53:8). In this manner Tzer/Tzed was transformed into Bethsaida during the Greco-Roman period."

"house of the fisherman." But it should be noted that the second component in the place name preserves the middle radical of the root (בֵּית צַיְדָא),[343] and it is very doubtful that the original name contained a *resh* that was then changed to a *dalet*, and that the original name meant "fisherman," even though it was spelled with a *resh*! Finally, the attempt to see the name צר preserved in Shalmaneser III's Broken Statue from Nimrud is based on an incorrect understanding of the cuneiform (see above).[344] Whether et-Tell is Bethsaida is not the concern here; only the linguistic analysis for the identification of the Iron Age city. Simply put, there is no evidence that the name of the site of et-Tell during this period was Zēr as preserved in Josh 19:35.

More likely, "Geshur" may have been the name of the city located at et-Tell and that given the city's prominence, the kingdom was called by its name (Na'aman 2012, 96).[345] This identification must remain tentative, but makes reasonable sense. The territory of Geshur appears to have extended along the Sea of Galilee to the Yarmuk River in the south. Perhaps Tel Dover (Kh. ad-Duweir), located southeast of the Sea of Galilee on the Jarmuk River and having an Iron I–IIa small settlement, was the kingdom's southern border.[346] Geshur's northern border must have been located somewhere south of Tel Dan in the north. Its territory included a narrow strip of plain on its western side and vast highland areas, including the Golan Plateau on its east.

Based on surveys conducted in the Golan Heights (Epstein and Gutman 1972; Kochavi et al. 1992), there do not appear to have been many other settlements in the land of Geshur. The sites like Tel Hadar (see above), Tel 'En Gev[347] (B. Mazar et al. 1964; Kochavi and Tsukimoto 2008) and Tel Soreg

---

343. BDAG, 140, s.v. βηθσαϊδά.

344. Such a reading ignores the fact that (1) there was clearly an additional sign in the middle (perhaps two) in the cuneiform text; (2) the Assyrian term is a gentilic; (3) Josh 19:35 is listing the fortified cities of Naphtali on the other side of the boundary (v. 34: the Jordan!); (4) the text in Joshua does not place Zēr on the Sea of Galilee; and (5) the determinative in the Assyrian text is KUR, not URU, so this is not referring to the name of a city, but the name of a land as a gentilic form.

345. Na'aman (2012, 96) feels that "The derivation of the kingdom's name from the root **g̱tr* ('to be strong') and its meaning 'stronghold, fortress' fits nicely the exceptional strength of the city walls (between six and eight meters width)." However, this is the inner city wall of the eighth-century city (Stratum V, see Arav 2009), so surely this structure itself did not give the city its name. This is the wall and gate that was destroyed by Tiglath-pileser III. For the period when et-Tell was the capital of an independent land of Geshur, one must examine the remains of Stratum VI, a less-impressive city than that of Stratum V (Arav 2009, 112–13). See the assessment of Wolff 2012.

346. See Wolff 1998, 775. Only the lower city has been excavated; so there may have been a much larger city at this site.

347. Na'aman 2012, 96. He also suggests that "LaRUba, Ba'il's stronghold," as mentioned in Shalmaneser III's Broken Statue from Nimrud (see above) was "possibly the

(Kochavi 1989, 6–9) were likely within the territory of Geshur. Certainly, agriculture and trade were the main components of Geshur's economy.

According to 2 Sam 13:37 and 14:23, Geshur appears to exercise a certain degree of independence. When Absalom fled to his grandfather, Talmai, David did not demand extradition of his son. If Geshur were a client polity bound by treaty, then there would have been grounds for such a demand (Na'aman 2002a, 205). Instead, three years later, Joab is sent to convince Absalom to return.[348] Unfortunately, it is not known how long Geshur had its own monarchy and at what point it completely lost its independence. But if Ba'il (*ba-aʾ-il*), the G[i-x-r]a-*ite* (KUR.G[I-x-R]A-*a-a*) in Shalmaneser III's Broken Statue inscription is a ruler of Geshur, the kingdom submitted itself to vassalage under Assyrian rule in the mid-ninth century. Perhaps it was Hazael that ended Geshurite independence, but we do not know for sure.

### 3.3.2.2. Ma'akah

As noted above, an entity called Ma'akah (מעכה) appears to be known in Egyptian sources. The name Ma'akah occurs as both a masculine and feminine personal name in the Hebrew Bible.[349] The feminine usage of the name naturally raises the possibility that the entity's name derives from an ancestress (like in the case of Bīt-Ḫalupē).[350] However, since the name is also used as a masculine personal name, Zadok (1988, 83) correctly notes "that *āh* is merely a suffix here seems clear from its absence in the homonym's transcription in the Egyptian Execration Texts and in the variant *Māʿôk* referring to a Philistine king (provided it is not due to a popular etymology)." Although Noth (1928, 250) suggested an etymology of the name from Arabic *maʿ(i)k* "stupid," this has been rightly rejected.[351] The name occurs in the Egyptian

ancient name of Kh. el-'Ashiq/Tel 'En Gev, the fortified settlement located about 13 kilometer south of et-Tell." See earlier, Na'aman 2002a, 206.

348. Alternatively, David may have simply chosen not to exercise the treaty demand.

349. See *HALOT*, 612, s.v. II מעכה. Zadok 1988, 434. Three masculine uses: the son of Nahor by his concubine, Reumah (Gen 22:24); the father of Achish, the king of Gath (1 Kgs 2:39 = מָעוֹךְ* 1 Sam 27:2); and a Simeonite leader (1 Chr 27:16). At least six feminine uses which include among others: the mother of Absalom, daughter of the king of Geshur (2 Sam 3:3; 1 Chr 3:2); the daughter of Absalom, the favorite wife of Rehoboam and mother of Abijah (1 Kgs 15:2; 2 Chr 11:20–22; contra 2 Chr 13:2 [מִיכָיָהוּ]); the mother of Asa (1 Kgs 15:10–13; 2 Chr 15:16); and wives of a number of Israelites.

350. On the Laqē confederation, see §4.5, especially p. 276.

351. Zadok 1988, 83. He posits: "Hebrew has *M-ʿ-K* 'rub, crush,' but this root does not produce names. Could it be a *maqtVl* formation deriving from a Canaanite equivalent of Arab. *ʿāka* (ʿ-W/Y-K) 'attack'? The name is in all likelihood Semitic." If correct, the name might mean something like "crusher," or "attacker."

literary masterpiece, Sinuhe (B 219), where a prince (*ḥḳꜣ*) of *Ḳdm* (קדם) is named *Mʿky*.

The city of Abel Beth-Maʿakah is commonly identified with Tell Abil al-Qamḥ, a large mound located about 7 km northwest of Tel Dan.[352] The first component of the name (אבל) is a fluvial term meaning "brook," or "meadow" that is often prefixed to another toponymic descriptor.[353] Thus Abel Beth-Maʿakah would mean "the brook/meadow of the tribal polity Maʿakah." The site of Abil al-Qamḥ is located on a high plateau overlooking the northern Huleh Valley near the Bareighit River (Naḥal ʿAyoun), a tributary of the Jordan River (Dever 1986, 210). The site is 10 ha in size (Panitz-Cohen, Mullins, and Bonfil, 2013, 27). Tell Abil al-Qamḥ is in the beginning stages of excavation.[354]

A city of "Abel" first appears in the Execration Texts (E 47) of the nineteenth–eighteenth century (Posener 1940, 87), where it is stated: *ḥḳꜣ n ʾibwꜣm* "the ruler of *ʾIbwꜣm*" (= *ʾIbwlm*).[355] Originally the text also contained the name of this ruler of this city. This particular occurrence of the Semitic term *ʾbl* in Egyptian hieroglyphic transcription has been understood to be a reference to the site of Tell Abil al-Qamḥ (Aḥituv 1984, 45). If this is correct, the fact that there was a ruler (*ḥḳꜣ*) of "Abil," and a ruler (*ḥḳꜣ*) in addition to chiefs or clan leaders (*wrw*) of "Maʿakayu (*mʿkyw*) may very well indicate that in this period there were separate political entities, Abil and Maʿakayu.[356] Later in the fifteenth century, the city of Abil is found in a list of conquered cities of Thutmose III (no. 92: *ʾi-b-r* = אָבֵל).[357]

It is important at this point to mention the occurrence of a place name in the Ugaritic texts: *ʾablm* (probably to be vocalized as ʾAbilūma[358]). The toponym occurs only in the ʾAqhatu Legend (*COS* 1.103:343–56), where it is described as "the city of prince Yariḫu" (*qrt zbl yrḫ*). It has thus been under-

352. Completely contrary to the commonly held opinion, Lipiński (2006, 256–65) identified ancient Laish/Dan at Abil al-Qamḥ and Abel Beth-Maʿakah at Tell el-Qādi (Tel Dan).

353. *HALOT*, 7, s.v. אָבֵל II.

354. For initial excavations, see Panitz-Cohen, Mullins, and Bonfil 2013. Of particular interest is the discovery of a silver hoard from a Late Bronze–early Iron Age I context. One hopes that excavations at the site will provide much needed insight. For recent information, http://www.abelbethmaacah.org.

355. The Egyptian *ꜣ* is one of the ways that Semitic *l* is transcribed (*r* being another; hence the spelling *ʾibr* is also encountered).

356. The land determinative is used for both *ʾibwꜣm* and *mʿkyw*.

357. *Urk. IV,* 781–786; Simons 1937, 27–38, 111–18; Rainey and Notley 2006, 72–73; and Aḥituv 1984, 46. Originally proposed by Albright 1924–25. See also Aharoni 1979, 162. For the various occurrences of *ʾbl* in the ancient toponymy, note the Greek Αβιλα.

358. Belmonte Marín 2001, 1; earlier Astour 1975, 254–55; Pardee 1989–90, 480.

stood as a mythical city,[359] although a few interpreters have suggested an actual city, some even connecting it with Abel Beth-Ma'akah (though this is unlikely).[360]

It seems that at some early stage the city of Abil became the capital of the tribal entity Beth-Ma'akah. However, there is some question about whether Beth-Ma'akah was originally Aramean. Dion (1997, 80–81) has suggested that Ma'akah's mention in the execration text (see above) would indicate that it was not Aramean, at least originally. Since the *Bēt*-X formulation can be used with any tribal entity (compare *Bēt* David or other *bītu*-formulations like Kassite groups, etc.), it is not necessary that Ma'akah was originally Aramean.[361] In this case, like others, the element "Aram" may have been added to an already extant toponym yielding Aram-Ma'akah (like Aram-Naharaim, Aram-Ṣobah, or Aram-Damascus). Thus "Ma'akah" may have been originally the personal name of an eponymous ancestor of an early West Semitic tribal group (hence, the usage of the *Bēt*-X formulation), which gave its name to the area that later came under the control of the Arameans. But at the time of the biblical writer or his historical source, it had become an Aramean polity.

---

359. Astour 1975, 254–55 (with discussion of earlier studies); Olmo Lete and Sanmartín 2003, 8; Watson 2001, 110.

360. Barton (1940, 33; 1941, 219) and MacLaurin (1978, 113–14) proposed that the city of *'ablm* in the Ugaritic epic of 'Aqhatu should be equated with Abel Beth-Ma'akah, i.e., Tell Abil al-Qamḥ. MacLaurin (1978, 113) explained the final *m* as a dual ending, which led him to suggest that there were twin towns, the main one being Beth-Ma'akah on one bank of the creek and the other being Abel ("the designation of the agricultural settlement on the other bank which supplied the city proper with most of its food" [114]). Far more likely, the *-m* in both the Egyptian and Ugaritic spellings is a witness to mimation in early West Semitic. Layton (1990, 157) notes that "the execration texts are an early witness to the existence of mimation in West Semitic." This is demonstrated in his examples (158–59). This mimation occurs in numerous other early West Semitic witnesses (159–97). Therefore, the *m* in the spelling of the toponym reflects either the nominative singular case ending (most likely) or the enclitic *m* (less likely). In either instance, the spellings without the *m* would simply reflect the loss of mimation. See also Pardee 1989–90, 480.

Margalit (1976, 178–81) discusses the etymology and proposes that *'ablm* should be equated with Beth-Yeraḥ/Sennabris (Khirbet el-Kerak, located on the southwestern shore of the Sea of Galilee and at the outlet of the Sea to the Jordan). See also Margalit 1981, 1989. However, this is based on a "Kinneret" interpretation of the 'Aqhatu text based on the single occurrence of a debated reading *knrt* (also read *knkt*) (Pardee *COS* 1.103:353 n. 114). Pitard (1994b, 36) correctly comments: "If the word {*knrt*} is a proper name, then the context requires that it be understood as the name of a town or region, not a lake (Margalit's interpretation of this passage—and indeed of most of 1.19—is far too problematic and speculative to be convincing)." Note Olmo Lete and Sanmartín 2003, 450, s.v. *knkt*. Simply, there is nothing compelling for understanding the location of the Ugaritic text's toponym.

361. See §2.3.1.

The passage in 2 Sam 10:6 where the king of Ma'akah is mentioned contains significant difficulties (see above). In its parallel in 1 Chr 19:6, Ma'akah is called Aram-Ma'akah which seems to indicate its independent status, though there are textual issues in the verse too.[362] Thus it is necessary to discuss these passages in some detail. According to 2 Sam 10:6, "When the Ammonites saw that they had become odious to David, the Ammonites sent and hired …

אֶת־אֲרַם בֵּית־רְחוֹב וְאֶת־אֲרַם צוֹבָא עֶשְׂרִים אֶלֶף רַגְלִי
וְאֶת־מֶלֶךְ מַעֲכָה אֶלֶף אִישׁ
וְאִישׁ טוֹב שְׁנֵים־עָשָׂר אֶלֶף אִישׁ׃

Aram-Beth-Reḥob and Aram-Ṣobah, 20,000 foot soldiers,
and the king of Ma'akah, 1,000 men,
and the men of Ṭôb, 12,000 men."

Although Bible translations have uniformly taken "the king of Ma'akah" and "the men of Ṭôb" in this manner, the connection between the two is ambiguous. The parallel in 1 Chr 19:6–7 reads: "When the Ammonites saw that they had made themselves odious to David …

וַיִּשְׁלַח חָנוּן וּבְנֵי עַמּוֹן אֶלֶף כִּכַּר־כֶּסֶף לִשְׂכֹּר לָהֶם מִן־אֲרַם נַהֲרַיִם וּמִן־אֲרַם מַעֲכָה וּמִצּוֹבָה רֶכֶב וּפָרָשִׁים׃

Hanun and the Ammonites sent a thousand talents of silver to hire, from Aram-Naharaim, from Aram-Ma'akah, and from Ṣobah, chariots and cavalry.…

וַיִּשְׂכְּרוּ לָהֶם שְׁנַיִם וּשְׁלֹשִׁים אֶלֶף רֶכֶב וְאֶת־מֶלֶךְ מַעֲכָה וְאֶת־עַמּוֹ

They hired 32,000 chariots and the king of Ma'akah with his army."

One thing quickly noticeable is the absence of all numbers in 1 Chr 19 as over against 2 Sam 10, except the figure 32,000. Also notable is the absence of any mention of Ṭôb in 1 Chr 19 (though there is a mention of Aram-Naharaim which is lacking in 2 Sam 10). In addition, the versions evince some different readings.

A possible way forward has been suggested. Wee (2005, 195–96) argues that אֶלֶף אִישׁ in 2 Sam 10:6 is not original for the following reasons:

---

362. B. Mazar (1961, 27) suggested that "the present text is corrupt, and that the true reading is not 'from Aram Maacah and from Zobah,' but 'from Aram Zobah and from Maacah.'" See most recently, Wee 2005, 195–96.

1. The expression אלף איש seems easily to have been influenced by the identical expression at the end of the verse (as noted by Driver 1913, 288). Importantly, in 4QSam[a], אלף איש appears to be lacking after מלך מעכה; and Josephus listed a "total of 12,000 for both Ma'akah and Ṭôb" (*Ant.* 7.121).
2. In the absence of אלף איש, the word immediately following מלך מעכה would have been (ו)איש. It is not difficult to see how the presence of איש could have mistakenly induced אלף איש.
3. The marker את, which precedes and coordinates the direct objects (ארם בית־רחוב, ארם צובא, and מלך מעכה), is absent before אלף איש. This may suggest that מלך מעכה and אלף איש were originally perceived as a single unit.

Wee (2005, 197) also asserts that איש טוב is not being used as a plural gentilic for "the men of Ṭôb." This is statistically borne out (see Wee 2005, 199, table 1). He concludes that there is no instance in the biblical usage whereby a foreign group of people is designated with X-איש.[363] Furthermore, the Old Greek rendering for איש טוב is Ιστωβ, taking this as a proper name. Hence Wee (2005, 197) argues:

> the Greek, Latin, and Syriac versions, as well as Qumran 4QSam[a] and Josephus, consider the expression to be a proper name. Kraeling (1918, 42 n. 1) also concurs with this interpretation. Alternatively, several scholars have considered the possibility that the איש element denotes a king (perhaps a lesser one), although Pitard's caution (1987, 94 n. 42) deserves to be reiterated here: "[איש for מלך] does not appear to have been an Israelite usage."

From this it appears that מלך מעכה and איש טוב refer to the same person, with the absence of אלף איש between them. Consequently, Wee (2005, 197–98) concludes:

1. That איש טוב was, from early times, understood to be an individual rather than a group ("men of Ṭôb") is clear from the fact that the different versions and non-Masoretic traditions have considered the term a personal name.[364]

363. Wee 2005, 197. However, it should be noted that the Mesha Stela (lines 10–11) reads: *w'š . gd . yšb . b'rṣ . 'ṭrt . m'lm . wybn . lh . mlk . y*[(11)]*śr'l . 't . 'ṭrt*, "Now the Gadites (lit., 'man of Gad') had settled in the land of 'Aṭarot from antiquity; and the king of Israel had fortified for him (the Gadite) 'Aṭarot."

364. See *HALOT*, 44. Note also the suggestion "governor of Tob" (*HALOT*, 43, s.v. אִישׁ 3b).

2. The absence of אלף איש accords well with the 32,000 figure in 1 Chr 19:7. Also, the awkward order of military numbers in 2 Sam 10:6 (the 1,000 men mentioned before the 12,000 men) is eliminated.
3. The apparent reversal of order in 2 Sam 10:8 (ואיש־טוב ומעכה) can be explained. Here איש־טוב refers to the king of Ma'akah, whereas in context the term מעכה refers to the troops. An analogous example of troops designated by the name of their state (after the mention of their commander) is found in 2 Chr 13:15: "God defeated Jeroboam and all Israel (יָרָבְעָם וְכָל־יִשְׂרָאֵל) before Abijah and Judah (אֲבִיָּה וִיהוּדָה)" (NRSV). Thus, in 2 Sam 10:8, איש טוב is portrayed as commander over the men of Ma'akah.
4. The absence of the expression איש טוב in 1 Chr 19:7 is accounted for. Here the same individual (i.e., the king of Ma'akah) *is* mentioned without being qualified as איש טוב.

Finally, איש טוב does not have to be understood as a substitute for the title מלך טוב, nor is it necessarily the personal name of the king of Ma'akah. There are a number of instances in the Hebrew Bible where איש-X is used as an ethnic qualifier mentioned after an individual's name/title: "Gideon son of Joash, an Israelite (lit. 'a man of Israel')" (Judg 7:14), "Tola son of Puah, son of Dodo, an Issacharite (lit. 'a man of Issachar')" (Judg 10:1). This can also be seen in the Zakkur inscription where איש-X appears as an ethnic qualifier: "I am Zakkur, king of Hamath and Lu'ash. I was a man of 'Anah [איש ענה] ..." (see Millard 1990). If Ṭôb in 2 Sam 10:6, 8 is to be identified with the place of Jephthah's refuge (Judg 11:3, 5; see below), its location fits well within or near the kingdom of Ma'akah (Wee 2005, 196–97). Hence, the final part of 2 Sam 10:6 might be understood to read: וְאֶת־מֶלֶךְ מַעֲכָה אִישׁ טוֹב שְׁנֵים־עָשָׂר אֶלֶף אִישׁ, "and the king of Ma'akah, the Ṭôbite (lit. 'the man of Ṭôb'), 12,000 men."

In the biblical texts, the city of Abel Beth-Ma'akah is referred to as an Israelite city (2 Sam 20:18; 1 Kgs 15:20; 2 Kgs 15:29, with a variant in 2 Chr 16:4: אבל מים). However, there is no information on this in terms of when and how it became Israelite. It may be inferred that this was one of the results of David's defeat of the Arameans; but it is not so stated.[365] The passages of 1 Kgs 15:20 and 2 Kgs 15:29 appear to list the city as part of an itinerary of conquest. Since the city controlled Israel's northern approaches, Bar-Hadad I of Aram-Damascus (1 Kgs 15:20) may have captured Abel Beth-Ma'akah sometime between 900 and 880. Was this an Israelite city or a entity allied with Baasha? The former seems to be implied. Geshur may have fallen too at

365. The phrase in 2 Sam 20:19, "mother in Israel," seems to imply an earlier context. Or is this mere rhetoric meant to accomplish its persuasive purpose?

this time, but the text is not clear. Certainly, by the time of Hazael's campaigns in the region, both kingdoms had been subsumed under Aram-Damascus's control.[366] It has been suggested that Abel is the restoration of ʾ⌜*b*⌝[ ] in the Tel Dan Inscription (Schneidewind 1996, 77; Na'aman 2012, 95 n. 10), but this is obviously far from certain.[367] Their histories definitely ended when the Assyrian army under Tiglath-pileser III (2 Kgs 15:29) conquered the entire region in 733.[368]

### 3.3.2.3. Ṭôb

That a polity named Ṭôb participated in the wars of Hadad-ezer against David is acknowledged by most interpreters (see above). But the location of the polity Ṭôb is greatly debated. The land of Ṭôb is apparently mentioned in Thutmose III's toponym list as *t-b-y* (Simons 1937, 111, 116: List 1, no. 22); and "a city of Ṭubu" is mentioned in the Amarna letters (EA 205:3: URU. *ṭú-bu*). A number of scholars have identified this tiny political entity with Aṭ-Ṭayyiba (located between Derʿā and Boṣrā aš-Šām; see fig. 3.7), and have taken it to be the "Ṭôb" of Judg 11:3–5 and 2 Sam 10; 1 Macc 5:13; and 2 Macc 12:17.[369]

Some scholars distinguish between the "Ṭôb" of Judges 11:3–5, and the "Ṭôb" of 2 Sam 10 (and 1 Macc 5:13). Thus de Vaux (1978, 820) argued that Aṭ-Ṭayyiba may be valid for the location of Ṭôb for the period of David, but not for Jephthah which he located in the "sparsely inhabited district to the north and north-west of the Jabbok."[370] However, Lipiński (2000a, 336–37) has rejected the identification of Ṭôb with Aṭ-Ṭayyiba, and instead suggested that the "men of Ṭob," either lived "west of the Jordan River, in the area of Ṭūbās, or settled later in the province of ʿAmmān." Finally, while rejecting the identification of Aṭ-Ṭayyiba with Ṭôb, Dion (1997, 80) underscores the paucity of external attestations to this biblical location: "we know nothing of Ṭôb, except that its name is West Semitic and that the activities [connected with it] take place in the Transjordan (as in Judg 11:3)."[371]

---

366. For this scenario, see Arie 2008, 34–38. However, while there is no problem with positing the conquest of the Aramean entities by Hazael, the reasons for this according to Arie are not all acceptable.

367. See §9.3.5.1.

368. See §9.3.6.3.

369. Maisler 1929, 83; Abel, 1933–38, 2:10; Aharoni 1979, 159, 443; Aḥituv 1984, 190–1; Rainey and Notley 2006, 140. However, the possible references in 1 Macc 5:13 and 2 Macc 12:17 to the land of Ṭôb are debated.

370. In this, de Vaux appears to have been following the view of Noth 1960, 156 n. 2.

371. "De Ṭôb on ne sait rien, sin on que son nom est ouestsemitique et que l'action se passe en Transjordanie (comme en Jug 11.3)."

While the location of Ṭôb remains debated (with the best option still perhaps Aṭ-Ṭayyiba), there can be no doubt of the entity's existence based on the Late Bronze Age attestations. Furthermore, the lack of first-millennium attestations is likely the result of the polity's absorption into the kingdom of Aram-Damascus.

# 4
# THE ARAMEAN POLITIES OF THE JEZIRAH

## 4.1. The Early Renewal of Conflict between Arameans and Assyrians (934–884 BCE)

The surviving Mesopotamian sources do not preserve much historical data for the roughly 120-year period between 1056 and 934 BCE. During this period, the Arameans gained control in a number of areas. The Assyrian monarchs were unable to cope with this "Aramean situation," and the same was true of Babylonia after Nebuchadnezzar I. Before any serious attempt could be made at expansion west of the Euphrates, the Assyrian kings of the tenth and early ninth centuries spent a long time reconquering and subduing the northern territories and the area of the Ḫābūr River that their predecessors had colonized in the thirteenth century and then lost to the Arameans. The Aramean penetrations had established new polities, but there were "pockets" or "islands" of Assyrians that managed to endure even in precarious circumstances (see discussion in previous chapter).

So it was that Aššur-dān II, Adad-nērārī II, and Tukulti-Ninurta II were the Assyrian kings that began the process of the resubjugation of the Jezirah. For these early Neo-Assyrian kings, there was a great ideological pressure to recreate the "Land of Aššur" (i.e., Assyria) as it had been in the second millennium, during the days of the Middle Assyrian Empire, particularly its zenith in the reign of Tukulti-Ninurta I. Grayson (1982, 280) observes that the Neo-Assyrian kings deliberately adopted the very nomenclature of the earlier Middle Assyrian kings and that this is "indicative of a feeling that they were re-creating an old empire that was still rightfully theirs." Postgate (1992, 257) puts it this way:

> The [early Neo-Assyrian] kings lovingly record the resettlement of erstwhile Assyrians on erstwhile Assyrian land, and tell us in whose reign

> recaptured cities had fallen to the Aramean intruders. The years when the Euphrates was the frontier to the west had not been forgotten.

Thus there is an important point of similarity between the Middle Assyrian and early Neo-Assyrian periods. Just as Mittanian domination stimulated the Middle Assyrian militaristic response, so one of the catalysts for the renewed militarism and expansion of Assyria in the first millennium was the result of the pressure created by the Aramean penetrations into the Jezirah (Joannès 2004, 25–29). However, unlike the Middle Assyrian kings, the early Neo-Assyrian kings were not motivated by "defensive imperialism." Instead, they developed into an aggressive military power, whose fundamental understanding of warfare was that it should be preemptive and reactive rather than defensive, and that it was their right to act accordingly. Melville (2009, 4–5) states:

> In other words, the Assyrians recognized that the best defense was a good offense. By the 9th century, the impulse to defend the "land of Assyria" had combined with the religious mandate for imperial expansion to reinforce its cultural expectation of war.

In the early Neo-Assyrian period, Assyria became an awesome offensive military machine. Accordingly, all the major battles of the Neo-Assyrian period (until the empire's collapse) took place outside of the heartland.[1]

The Aramean groups that penetrated the Jezirah created political entities (e.g., Bīt-Baḫiāni and Bīt-Zamāni, and possibly Azallu). Others appear as confederations of various sedentary groups with significant pastoral nomadic components (e.g., the Laqē confederation including Bīt-Ḫalupē; the Temanites). Still others are confederations of largely nonsedentary tribal affiliations (e.g., the Ḫaṭallu confederation, composed of the Sarūgu, Luḫūya/Luḫu'ātu, and Amatu clans; see ch. 10).

### 4.1.1. Tribal Entities Mentioned in the Inscriptions of Aššur-dān II

With Aššur-dān II, the Assyrians began the recovery of territory captured and held for more than a century by Arameans (particularly to the south and east of the city of Assur) and the resettlement of Assyrians in these lands. The main source for the reign of Aššur-dān II (934–912 BCE) is an annal-

1. Melville 2009, 8. Obviously, this excludes internal fighting that occurred with rebellions, civil wars, etc.

istic text that divides the episodes by rulings on a less than fully preserved tablet.[2] The relevant passages read:

> (lines 6–15)
> [In my accession year (and) in] my first regnal year, after [I nobly ascended] the royal throne, [...] the troops of the Yausu (KUR *ia-ú-sa-a-ia*) came up (*elû*) (the river), [...] they trusted in their own [stre]ngth, *they brought their* [...].[3] With the support of Aššur, my lord, [I] mustered [... my chariots (and) troops]. I plundered their settlements from the city of Ekal-pī-nāri[4] [(...) to ...]. I massacr[ed many of them]; the rest of them I brought to an end (i.e., destroyed). [I carried off] their [... herds] (and) flocks without number. [I] burned [...], their [cities] (and) their inhabitants (lit. "sons"). I brought up [heavy booty] from the midst of the land of Aram (KUR.*a-ri-mi*) [...]
>
> (lines 16–22)
> [... who] from the time of Shalmaneser, king of [Assyria, my forefather], had destroyed [the people of Assyria by ...] and by murder, had sold [all] their [sons (and) daughters] for silver; [by the command of Aššur], my lord, I took captives, I massacr[ed many of them]; I carried off their booty, possessions, [property, oxen, (and)] sheep; I br[ought up][5] to my city [Assur]. The land of Ruqāḫu (KUR.*ru-qa-ḫu*), the Zab River of the land (KUR) of [...]
>
> (lines 23–32)
> [the land of Uluzu?[6]... Y]aḫānu ([KUR.*i*]*a-ḫa-a-nu*), the land of Aram (KUR.*a-ru-mu*), which is behind the land of Pi/Ya(?)[ ], [which from the time of Aššur-ra]bi (II)(1012–972), king of Assyria, my forefather, the cities of the district of [my land, ...] they captured for their [own]; [I mustered] chariots (and) troops. [I plundered...] I massacred many of them. [I

2. RIMA 2:131–35, A.0.98.1. See also Weidner 1926, 154–55 (drawings).

3. Grayson (RIMA 2:132, note to line 9) suggests that this is an error: *ú-bi-ul* for *ūblū* (G pret 3mp [*(w)abālu*]). Schramm (*EAK* 2:1) suggested that this might be the end of a place name. He states: die Form *ú-bi-ul* ist grammatikalisch nicht möglich. Vielmehr dürften die Zeichen ]-*nu-ú-bi-ul* zu einem Länder- oder Ortsnamen gehören." My translation follows Grayson, though tentatively.

4. Ekal-pī-nāri "the palace of the mouth of the river/canal." Nashef (1982, 218) listed a place name Pī-nāri (written sometimes KA $I_7$-DA; hence perhaps to be read Ekal-ka-i-da? But here in Aššur-dān written: URU.É.GAL-pi-i-ÍD—clearly Ekal-Pī-nāri. It must be located down the Tigris from Assur, probably south of the confluence of the Lower Zab and Tigris.

5. I would suggest restoring at the beginning of line 22: [*ú-še*]-*li*, since the LI sign is clear and there is the parallel in line 15.

6. "Perhaps one should restore *māt Uluzu* ... from A.0.98.2 line 6 at the beginning of this line" (Grayson RIMA 2:133, note to line 23).

destroyed], ravaged, (and) burned their [cities]. [I pursued the rest of their troops which] had fled from my weapons [from …] to the city Ḫalḫalauš of the land Sa[…]zi. I massacred many of them. [I carried off their booty (and) possessions]. The rest of them I uprooted; [I settled them???] in […]; I counted them [within] the borders of Assyria.

(lines 60–67)
I brought back the weary [people] of Assyria [who in the face of] famine, hunger, (and) shortage had abandoned [their cities (and) houses] (and) [had gone up] to oth[er] lands.[7] [I settled] them in [proper] cities (and) houses. They dwelt in security. I constructed [palaces in the distri]cts of my land. [I hitched up] plows in the districts of my land; I [heaped up] more grain than ever before. I hitched up horses trained to the yoke [… for the armed forces of] Assyria.

4.1.1.1. Yausu

The first Aramean group encountered by Aššur-dān II was called the Yausu (KUR.*ia-ú-sa-a-ia*) (lines 6–15). The mention of KUR.*a-ri-mi* at the end of the episode obviously serves to label them. Furthermore, the fact that they came up (*elû*; the Tigris River is intended here) indicates that the Yausu (perhaps **Yaʾūš* > *ʾwš*) were located south of Assyria. Undoubtedly, their implied intent in coming up, according to the text, was to raid Assyria, perhaps as Aramean groups had done before.[8] Unfortunately, the city of Ekal-pī-nāri cannot at present be located, but Aššur-dān's plundering of their settlements ([TÚG(?).*m*]*aš-kan-na-te*.MEŠ-*šu-nu*) proceeded from this place to another (unfortunately) unidentified site. However, the use of the term *maškanu* "tent" is an important indication that this group likely had a significant mobile pastoralist component (also note the clause "[carrying off] their flocks without number"). Yet, since the best restoration in line 14 is [URU(?).M]EŠ-*šu-nu*, the Yausu also had a sedentary component. The text leaves little doubt that Aššur-dān II is avowing his massive extermination of the Yausu. That the tribe is not mentioned henceforth may corroborate his claim.

---

7. With the mention of the reconquest of Ḫabrūri, it is possible that this passage refers to descendants of Assyria who had abandoned their homes during the famine in the days of Tiglath-pileser I about 160 years earlier and seems to indicate that the conditions in Assyria had continued to be adverse so that an earlier return was not possible. See Neumann and Parpola 1987, 181.

8. Note here the Assyrian Chronicle 4 and particularly the activities on the Tigris River. See pp. 174–77 above.

### 4.1.1.2. Ruqāḫu

In the episode of lines 16–22, the text is unfortunately unclear as to what entity might be in view. On the one hand, this unidentified entity might be Aramean, since the Arameans are clearly in view in the preceding (lines 6–15) and subsequent sections (lines 23–32). On the other hand, since the text is broken, it is impossible to be sure. However, this entity appears to have been destroying Assyrians through murder and exploitation of their children from the time of Shalmaneser II (r. 1030–1019) until the days of Aššur-dān II and his intervention (probably in the early years of his reign[9]). The "land of Ruqāḫu" is mentioned at the end of the section, along with "the Zab River of the land of [...]." However, it is unclear how this relates to the preceding narrative.[10] The fact is the subject in the bulk of the episode prior to the mention of the Ruqāḫu might be another tribe. One cannot simply assume that the episode is about this tribe. Brinkman (1968, 176) commented on this reference to the "land of Ruqāḫu":

> there is a brief, but badly broken passage referring to Assyrian interest or activities in the land of Ruqāḫu, probably to be located somewhere near where the Lower Zab flows into the Tigris. Since this land otherwise is part of the central province of Assur itself, it is surprising to see it mentioned in a context which would suggest its having lapsed from Assyrian royal control. There is no direct evidence that would suggest that Ruqāḫu had fallen into the hands of either the Arameans or the Babylonians; but its defection from the jurisdiction of the Assyrian central government would point up the grave territorial limitations of Assyria at this time. These Assyrian troubles in the region east of the Tigris could be dated during the reigns of either Mār-bīti-aḫḫē-iddina or Šamaš-mudammiq in Babylon.

The general location of Ruqāḫu is based on a suggestion of Forrer who placed it on the east bank of the Tigris between the Lower Zab and the Jebel Hamrin.[11] From this passage, it is far from clear whether this tribe was Aramean or not.

The earliest occurrence of the Ruqāḫu tribe is in a Middle Assyrian text (BM 122635+), which is unfortunately not well-preserved.[12] It is an administrative text that records "audience gifts" (*nāmurtu*) from various governors

---

9. This is surmised based on where the episode comes within the rulings on the tablet.

10. Since the verb is missing in the sentence, it is impossible to know why Ruqāḫu was mentioned here. Most of the lands and cities referred to in this text of Aššur-dān II were objects of attack by the Assyrian army.

11. Forrer 1920, 12 and 47; Weidner 1926, 156 n. 9.

12. Millard 1970, 172–73 and pls. xxxiii and xxxiv.

and client rulers. Line obv. ii.22′ of the text reads: [ ] ⸢KUR⸣.*ru-qa-ḫa-iu*.[13] Postgate (1985, 99–100) has pointed out that the client rulers are regularly referred to as "the ...ian"; the governors are named and their cities specified. Thus Katmuḫu, Ṭābētu, the Ruqāḫu tribe, and another tribe appear as clients, while Īdu, Burallu, Ninua, Šadikanni, Qatnu, and Ḫalaḫḫu are within the Assyrian provincial system.

The dating of this text has been based on analogy with the well-dated text (Ass. 6096) from the Ninurta-tukulti-Aššur archive (1133 BCE).[14] However, the text importantly preserves in rev. i.7′ $^{\mathrm{md}}$IM-DUMU-UŠ URU.DÙG.GA-*a-iu* "Adad-apla-iddina, the Ṭābētean (*Ṭāb(e)tāyu*)," the gentilic form of the territory of the city of Ṭābētu. The same gentilic form (*Ṭābdāyu*) is also attested for another ruler of Ṭābētu named Mannu-lū-yā'u in a document *KAJ* 195, which records his audience gift to Ninurta-tukulti-Aššur (see Freydank 2011). Therefore, this text (BM 122635+) probably dates to a slightly later time, though exactitude is not possible according to Shibata (2012, 492).

Later, Ruqāḫu was certainly part of the administrative system of Assyria. It is mentioned on two stelae from Assur as within the jurisdiction of governors of that city who served as eponyms: Ilu-issīya (804 BCE) and Adad-bēlu-ka''in (748, 738).[15] There are a number of texts from the reign of Sargon II that mention Ruqāḫu. One letter, sent by Ṭāb-ṣill-Ešarra, the governor of Assur, attests to members of this tribe serving in the Assyrian army: "As to the reserves of the royal troops of the Ruqāḫu (and) the Ḫallatu...." ($^{[14]}$*ša ku-tal* ERIM–MAN $^{[\mathrm{r}.1]}$*ša* KUR.*ru-qa-ḫa-a-a* $^{[\mathrm{r}.2]}$*ša* KUR.*ḫal-lat-a-a*).[16] The Ḫallatu tribe is one of the tribal groups that is very likely Aramean, though never, as yet, explicitly stated as so. Two other fragmentary letters mention KUR.*ru-qa-*[*ḫa-a-a*][17] and ⸢LÚ$^{?}$.*ru*$^{?}$⸣-*qa*$^{?}$-*ḫa*$^{!}$-[*a-a*].[18] Another document that mentions members of the tribe will be discussed below.

---

13. One might assume that the name and title (perhaps *nasīku*, though this cannot be proven) occurred just before the gentilic ⸢KUR⸣.*ru-qa-ḫa-iu*. Even so, this in itself does not prove or disprove that the Ruqāḫu were Arameans. Contra Lipiński (2000a, 48), who states: "The mention of the Ruqāḫaean sheikh, whose name and title are lost, implies that *the Aramaean tribe* had a recognized territory on the Middle Tigris by the mid-12th century and that it maintained good relations with the Assyrians" (emphasis added).

14. Thus Zadok (1991, 117) states: "The independent(?) ruler of the West Semitic (possibly Aramean) tribe Ruqāḫu presented his *nāmurtu* to either Ninurta-tukulti-Aššur or one of his immediate successors."

15. Number 38, Ilu-issīya: *ṣa-lam* $^{\mathrm{m}}$*ili-it-ti-ya* | LÚ.*šá-kìn* URU.Aššur | URU.kār-tukúlti-ninúrta | URU.ēkallāte.MEŠ | URU.i-tu | URU.*ru-qa-ḫu*; Number 37, Adad-bēlu-ka''in: *ṣalam* $^{\mathrm{md}}$Adad-bēla-úkin | LÚ.*šá-kìn* URU.Aššur | URU.Kār-tukúl-ti-$^{\mathrm{d}}$Ninurta | URU.ēkallāte.MEŠ | URU.i-tú | KUR.*ru-qa-ḫa*. See Andrae 1913, 439.

16. SAA 1:79, 91.14–r.2 (= *ABL* 94.r.1). See Brinkman 1968, 176 n. 1085.

17. SAA 1:201, 262.7 (= Parpola 1979, 618).

18. SAA 1:79, 92.6 (= *ABL* 1086).

The major question concerning the Ruqāḫu is whether the tribe was Aramean or not. Lipiński (2000a, 47–49) has argued that the Ruqāḫu were an Aramean tribe attested in the region in the mid-twelfth century. His argument is primarily based on the etymology of the name. He derives the tribal name "from the root *rṣḥ*, well known in Arabic (*raḍaḫa*) and in Hebrew (*rāṣaḥ*)," and argues that "the Aramaic phoneme *ṣ́* (*ḍ*) is transcribed in Assyrian by signs with *q* or *ḫ*, like in the name *Raqiānu*/*Raḫiānu* of a king of Damascus" (Lipiński 2000a, 48). Zadok (2013, 313) has countered that this lacks credibility since one would expect Assyrian transcriptions reflecting a variant, such as <**Ru-ḫa-ḫu*>,[19] which they do not.

Yet Zadok's claim that the tribal name is "hardly explicable in Aramaic terms (*rqḥ* is recorded only in Canaanite-Hebrew)" (Zadok 2013, 313) may not be entirely on target. The word *mrqḥ* "ointment, perfume(?)"[20] occurs in Egyptian Aramaic (Porten and Yardeni 1986–99, C3.18 V15) and *mrqḥh*/*mrqḥt*ʾ "compounded spiced dish" occurs in Jewish Palestinian Aramaic.[21] Furthermore, there may be additional evidence. First, in the Deir ʿAlla plaster inscriptions, there is the phrase *rqḥt mr* "a compounder/perfumer of myrrh." Thus depending on how one classifies the language of these inscriptions whether Aramaic or not, this could be considered.[22] Second, if one counts the occurrence of the root *rqḥ*, "to compound" in Samaritan Aramaic (Tal 2000, 849), then there is another occurrence. Thus it seems that Zadok's wording is somewhat overstating matters on this point. There is certainly some basis for understanding a root *rqḥ* in Aramaic.[23]

A text from the first half of the eighth century from the Governor's Palace Archive[24] provides a list of eleven criminals who had undertaken a raid and had stolen seventy sheep. The first seven individuals named are grouped as a subtotal "seven Ruqāḫeans (LÚ.*ru-qa-ḫ-a-a*). The man who was in charge of these thieves is designated as Yada-'ilu, the sheikh of "the Naqari" (LÚ.*na-si-ku ša* LÚ.*na-qi-ra-a-a*)[25] and was actually caught red-handed with the

19. Lipiński's appeal to the transcription of the tribal name with *ḫ* or *q* occurs in KUR.*ra-ḫi-ḫa*, LÚ.*ra-ḫi-qu*, or LÚ.*re-ḫi-ḫu* does not pay attention to the vowels, which means that these cannot all be variants of the same name.

20. Whatever the meaning in this passage, the point is that the root *rqḥ* occurs in an Egyptian Aramaic text.

21. Sokoloff 2002b, 332.

22. *DNWSI*, 1083.

23. Zadok (2013, 313) notes the "quasi-homonymous tribal name" *Rqḥ*ⁿ in Sabean (Arbach 2002, 453).

24. Postgate 1973, 143–44, text 119.

25. For the Naqru tribe, see chapter 10 on southern Mesopotamia below.

stolen sheep, yet is not included in the total of "11 criminals." Yada-'ilu has a clear Aramaic name.[26]

Concerning the "seven Ruqāḫeans," Postgate asserted that "all (except perhaps the second) of the Ruqahaeans have uncomprisingly Aramaic names" (Postgate 1973, 144). However, this surely is overstating the case. The seven names are: ᵐ*sa-[a]b-ḫar-ru* "Sabḫarru"; ᵐ*id-na-a-ni* "Idnānu"; ᵐDINGIR-x-QI "Ilu[...]qi?"; ᵐ*nap-ʾa-d[u]-lu* "Nap'adulu"; ᵐ*mu-da-da* "Mudadi"; ᵐ*me-ʾi-i-⸢su⸣* "Me'isu"; and ᵐ*ḫa-ra-a-nu* "Ḫārānu." One name is unknown. Out of the six remaining names, two are definitely Aramaic: "Idnānu" and "Mudadi"; two are West Semitic (possibly Aramaic): "Me'isu" and "Ḫārānu"; one is uncertain ("Sabḫarru"[27]); and one is very difficult: "Nap'adulu."

In conclusion, there is still considerable uncertainty about the question of the Ruqāḫu being Aramean. While it is possible that the tribe was Aramean, there is no firm evidence and so it remains also possible that the tribe was not. At the present time, this question cannot be definitely answered.

#### 4.1.1.3. Yaḫānu

The major interpretive issue in the Aššur-dān text is how to understand lines 23–32. Bunnens has asserted:

> The first name can be restored Yahanu, which is the earlier name of the Aramaean state that will be called Bit Agusi (Arpad); Pi[ ]could be Pi[tru]; [Ashur-ra]bi is a very plausible restoration as there is only one name ending in *bi* among the "forefathers" of Ashur-dan II. We would thus have a description of the conquest of Pitru by the Aramaeans of Yahanu, also referred to by Shalmaneser III. This interpretation has been rejected, however, because the name Halhalaush sounds like toponyms from the Zagros region and because Ashur-dan does not mention his crossing of the Euphrates. The entire story should therefore be located to the east of Assyria, not on the Upper Euphrates. These objections are not as strong as they might look. The very plausible restorations [Y]ahanu, Pi[tru] and [Ashur-ra]bi, together with the sure mention of a king of Arumu (i.e., an Aramaean king), so well match the information we can get from Shalmaneser III's inscriptions that it is hard to believe that Ashur-dan II's text does not refer to the

26. Lipiński (2000a, 471) states Yada-'ilu "bears a perfectly Aramaic name, which is not common in North-Arabian."

27. See Baker, Perroudon and Zadok 2002. Perhaps the name is related to Safaitic *šbḥr* (see Lipiński 2000a, 48). But the name is perhaps found in Middle Babylonian Sambiḫari written ᵐ*sa-bi-ḫa-ri*. Besides this person, the name occurs as the sheikh of Ḫindaru (Fuchs 1994, Ann 279g). Thus there seems to be connection(s) to Aramean entities.

same events. The lacunae prevent us from putting too much weight on the absence of mention of the Euphrates. Similarly, there is a long lacuna before the mention of Halhalaush and it is not impossible that Ashur-rabi [sic: Aššur-dān] changed the orientation of his campaign. Shalmaneser III did exactly the same after his conquest of Til-Barsib: he went to Urartu and came back to Assyria via Arbela.[28]

There is certainly some appeal to Bunnens's interpretation.[29] However, there are four significant problems. First, Pitru is *never* determined by KUR "land," only URU "city."[30] Second, Aššur-dān's activities in the context of this passage indicate an area east of Assyria. Third, between the text that is preserved and what can be restored from the other Aššur-dān II text, there really is not that much of a lacuna to provide grounds for a switch in geographic location from the Upper Euphrates (if Bunnens's interpretation is accepted) and the area east of Assyria. In other words, it is highly unlikely that there is a geographic switch in the narrative, and thus the mention of Ḫalḫalauš is very significant to locating the place of the action against the Yaḫānu. Fourth, the city of Ḫalḫalauš is mentioned again in another text of Aššur-dān II[31] and the "White Obelisk" of Aššurnaṣirpal II;[32] its location is not in the Upper Euphrates. The mention of Ḫalḫalauš is the place that the "remainder" of the Yaḫānu fled (lines 27–29 above; Weissbach 1928, 291; Hawkins 1976–80b). The text states "[I pursued them] to the city Ḫalḫalauš of the land Sa[...]zi (URU.*Ḫal-ḫa-la-uš ša* KUR *sa*-[xx-(x)]-*zi*)." The land of *Sa*[...]*zi* does not resemble any known toponym in the west. The mention of Ḫalḫalauš in the White Obelisk is important. While there is debate about whether the White Obelisk belongs to Aššurnaṣirpal I or II, this inscription seems clearly to demand a location of Ḫalḫalauš (along with the city of Ḫarira) that is in rough proximity of the land of Gilzānu. Reade (1975, 136) gives this summary:

> The sense of column A would then be as follows: "In a particular year (*rabîš ūšibu*), I mustered my army, but did not capture any places worth naming. The most notable item of incoming tribute was horses from Gilzanu. Harira and Halhalauš failed to send their quota, so I marched against them. I, Aššurnaṣirpal, was eponym when I recaptured this area. I brought the loot home, &c."

---

28. Bunnens 1999, 606–7. Weidner argued also for a north Syrian location. See Weidner 1926, 156, and n. 10. Malamat (1973, 142 and 151 n. 21) equates with Bīt-Adīni.

29. See earlier Younger 2007a, 159 n. 55.

30. See Bagg 2007, 191. See Weidner, 1926, 156 n. 12.

31. RIMA 2:136, A.0.98.2, line 13′: URU.*Ḫal-ḫa*-[*la-úš*].

32. RIMA 2:255, A.0.101.18, line 6′: URU.*Ḫa-ri-ra* URU.*Ḫal-ḫa-la-uš*.

Fifth, the text is on a ruled tablet with self-contained episodes within the rulings; thus the idea of a sudden change in content within the rulings is questionable.

On the basis of these points, it seems clear that the episode transpired in an area near the Assyrian homeland. Thus, Lipiński has suggested that the Aramean tribe of Yaḫānu was located in the area east of the Tigris and that "the same Aramean tribe or some of its clans finished by emigrating from Assyria to northwestern Syria."[33] This seems very likely, given the parallels of tribal migrations already discussed (see fig. 2.6, p. 79). It should be emphasized that there was an obvious "push" factor in this particular migration.

The last episode (lines 60–67) given above emphasizes Aššur-dān II's role in restoring the Assyrian people to their rightful place, as well as the prosperity that resulted from his many deeds. This set the foundation for the following Assyrian monarchs' activities.

## 4.2. Temanites

In the region of Mount Kašiyāri and the Upper Ḫābūr, groups of Arameans known as the Temanites seized power and settled (see fig. 4.1). The name "Temanites" is derived from the Aramaic term *tymn* "south" (Lipiński 2000a, 109–10). This designation seems to indicate that these were Aramean groups that settled on the southern side of Mount Kašiyāri (Ṭūr ʿAbdīn). The Temanites were comprised of a significant sedentary component as is seen in their cities (some quite formidable militarily). But it is probable that they also had a significant mobile pastoralist component, given the terrain.

The Temanites are considered by scholars to be groups of at least three separate polities (Zadok 2012, 576; Fales 2011a, 214 n. 7). In his campaigns, Adad-nērārī II (911–891 BCE) encountered these entities. This Assyrian monarch initiated a series of annual campaigns to recover the land of Ḫanigalbat, the Assyrian designation for the area in which the Temanites were now resident.[34] On the one hand, this was certainly part of the effort of the early Neo-Assyrian kings to recreate the Middle Assyrian Empire; but on the other hand, it was also important as a crucial strategic move "to guarantee security along the piedmont route from the Assyrian heartland towards the Balīḫ" (Fales 2012a, 112).

Thus, in 901 BCE, Adad-nērārī II conducted his initial campaign against a certain Nūr-Adad, the Temanite:

33. Lipiński 2000a, 195. This is contrary to Hawkins 1976–80b.

34. Ḫanigalbat in this context seems to mean the Mount Kašiyāri Range (the modern Ṭūr ʿAbdīn). See Fales 2012a, 109–12.

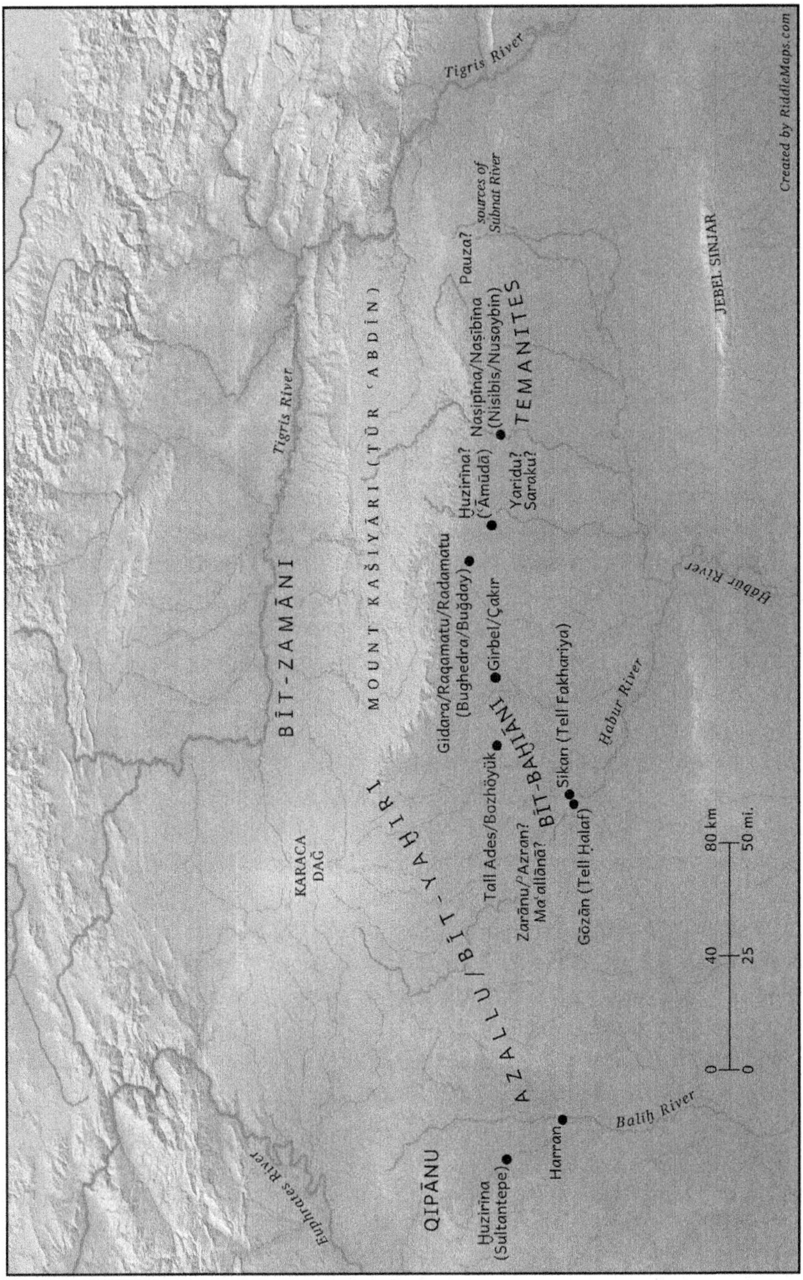


Fig. 4.1. Upper Ḫābūr

In the eponymy of Dūr-māt-Aššur,
I marched to the extensive land of Ḫanigalbat.
Nūr-Adad, the Temanite, mustered his troops.
We drew up in battle formation at the city Pauza at the foot of Mount Kašiyāri.
We fought with one another;
I inflicted a decisive defeat on him from the city of Pauza to the city of Naṣīpīna (and)
I destroyed his numerous chariots.[35]

This is the first explicit mention of the Temanites[36] (KUR.*te-ma-na-a-a*; Aramaic: *tymn* "southern," see above) who occupied the area south of Mount Kašiyāri (the Ṭūr-ʿAbdīn mountainous plateau) with their major fortified city being Naṣīpīna/Naṣībīna (Nisibis) (modern Turkish: Nusaybin).[37] This city was located along one of the northern sources of the Upper Ḫābūr River, and on the major route from Nineveh to Harran. Thus it was important to Assyrian recovery and expansion. However, while Adad-nērārī II claimed a victory in what appears to be an open-field battle involving chariots, the city of Naṣīpīna/Naṣībīna was not captured at this time. The name of the leader Nūr-Adad (ᵐ*nu-ur-*ᵈIŠKUR "Light of Adad") is an Akkadian personal name usually written by the Assyrian scribes as either ᵐZALAG-ᵈIM or ᵐZALAG-ᵈ10 (Brinkman 2001). In this case, the syllabic spelling of the name might point to the root *(nwr)* being West Semitic, even Aramaic.

Besides Naṣīpīna/Naṣībīna, the Temanites also have other cities (e.g., Pauza), chariots and developed agriculture in this Upper Ḫābūr region. They were likely the same group of Arameans that Aššur-bēl-kala encountered, since "the city of Pauza, which is at the foot of Mount Kašiyāri" was the focal point in both accounts.[38] In brief, they had seized this land in an earlier conflict; had sedentarized to a certain extent (it is likely that this group still had a significant mobile component); and during the roughly 150-year period since their battle with Aššur-bēl-kala, they had developed into a rather formidable foe (it took Adad-nērārī II a number of campaigns and some innovative efforts to subdue them, see below).

Yet, the Temanites were never described as a *bīt(u)* "house." They are not an organized singular entity, but as noted above, a number of groups with

35. RIMA 2:149, A.0.99.2, lines 39–41.

36. Concerning the mention of "Teman" in the inscription of Yariri of Karkamiš, there are different opinions. Some think this is a reference to this Teman; others think it is a reference to Teima in the Arabian desert. See now Younger 2014a.

37. Streck 1998–2001b. The spellings with a /ṣ/ probably speak for an Old Aramaic folk etymology *nṣībīn* "pillars."

38. RIMA 2:102, A.0.89.7, iii.8b–10a.

multiple leaders (as the following episodes demonstrate). Since Adad-nērārī II was apparently able to engage them in separate battles, it seems that they were not able (or willing) to join and coordinate as an effective fighting force. This indicates that they were not an effective political unity (Dion 1997, 33). They seem to be ruled by local dynasts or, in some instances, chiefs (*nasīku*). In the case of Nūr-Adad, he is explicitly called a king (line 71).

As the site of this initial battle involved chariotry and the pursuit led to the city of Naṣīpīna/Naṣībīna, Radner has rightly noted that "all this suggests a location in the plain just south of the eastern ranges of the Ṭūr-'Abdīn" for the city of Pauza.[39] Adad-nērārī II records his campaign of the next year (900 BCE) as follows:

> In the eponymy of Ilī-e<mū>qāya,
> I marched a second time to the land Ḫanigalbat.
> I fought with him (Nūr-Adad) at Naṣīpīna/Naṣībīna.
> I dyed the countryside red with the blood of his warriors.
> I entered the city Yaridu.
> I reaped the harvest of his land.
> I counted the city Saraku as mine;
> I heaped up in it barley and straw.[40]

In this second campaign against the Temanites, Adad-nērārī II seems to have fought another open-field battle at Naṣīpīna/Naṣībīna, though the city remains untouched. While the Temanites do not join their forces, the fact that they choose to engage the Assyrian army in open-field battles means that they felt confident in going against the Assyrians. Otherwise, they would certainly have avoided such engagements. The text mentions two other cities (unfortunately as yet of uncertain location) that were captured. What is clear from the latter clauses of the account is that Adad-nērārī executed this attack at harvest time in a clear attempt to deny the Arameans food and fodder, the latter likely hampering the Temanites' chariot force for a future engagement.

The third campaign (899 BCE) contains,[41] after the introduction (line 45a–b), three staccato vignettes (lines: 45c–46a; 46b–47; 48).

> (45) In the eponymy (*līmu*) of Ninuāya,
> I marched a third time to the land Ḫanigalbat.
> I captured the city of Ḫuzirīna.

39. Radner 2006, 285. Radner states: "No identification for 'the town of Pa'uzu at the foot of the Kāšiēri' has been suggested so far, but from the description it is clear that the site must be situated at the southern foothills of the Ṭūr 'Abdīn" (2006, 285).

40. RIMA 2:149, A.0.99.2, lines 42–44.

41. RIMA 2:149, A.0.99.2, lines 45–48.

(46) I completely surrounded the wall.
The cities at the foot of Mount Kašiyāri, which Mamli, the Temanite, had seized, (47) seized my feet.
I regarded his palaces as mine.
(48) At that time,
I received a large female monkey (and) a small female monkey, a shipment from Bīt-Adīni (lit. "the land of the man of Bīt-Adīni"), which lies on the bank of the Euphrates.

The introduction gives the date (*līmu*) and records a third campaign to the land of Ḫanigalbat. The first vignette recounts the capture of Ḫuzirīna. This city has been identified with Sultantepe (16 km southeast of Urfa) located on the western side of the Balīḫ River, north of Harran, in the Harran Plain.[42] This identification has been questioned since this location is 200 km to the west of Naṣībīna (Postgate 1972–75b; Radner 2006, 286 n. 29). It has been suggested that there may have been another city with the same name (i.e., homonym) closer to Naṣībīna (possibly at the site of 'Āmūdā, roughly 30 km west of Naṣībīna).[43] Moreover, if Sultantepe is the Ḫuzirīna of this narrative, it may not have been part of the Temanites' territory[44] or Ḫanigalbat. The vignette ends with a statement in line 46a "I completely surrounded the wall." This is obviously out of logical sequence (see discussion below). Furthermore, one might have expected a report on the journey to Ḫuzirīna; instead it is simply "I captured the city of Ḫuzirīna."

The second vignette (lines 46b–47) reports that the cities at the foot of Mount Kašiyāri (which had been seized by Mamli, the Temanite, ${}^{m}$*ma-am-li* KUR *te-man-na-a-a*)[45] submitted to Adad-nērārī II. The Assyrian king reckoned Mamli's palaces as his own. Mount Kašiyāri is not near Sultantepe (some 120 km west of Mount Kašiyāri's westernmost point). Thus it is hard to see the connection with this campaign, unless there is another Ḫuzirīna closer to Mount Kašiyāri. Furthermore, the Temanites are only found in the Mount Kašiyāri area. That Ḫuzirīna in the Annals of Adad-nērārī II is Sultantepe seems to run counter to all the other geographic data given in the text.[46]

42. Lipiński (2000a, 114) argues for Ḫuzirīna's location on the Balīḫ as the city intended in Adad-nērārī's text. See also Dion 1997, 33; Bunnens 1999, 607; 2009, 76; and Yamada 2000a, 70. See also Gordon 1967, 85–88.

43. Parpola and Porter 2001, map 3, D3. Radner 2006, 286 n. 29.

44. Dion (1997, 33) suggests that this passage where Adad-nērārī II describes the capture of Ḫuzirīna (Sultantepe) gives the impression that the Assyrian advance was perceived as a liberation of Assyrian territory wrongly seized. See also Mayer 1995a, 262.

45. Edzard 1987–90. *PNA* does not have an entry for this name.

46. Since Ḫuzirīna is captured on the campaign to Ḫanigalbat (RIMA 2:149–50, A.0.99.2, 45–48), one would need to suggest he left the region to travel to Sultantepe either without mentioning crossing the Ḫābūr, as he did when he went to Guzāna and Sikan (2:153,

Topping off the campaign is the third vignette (line 48), which narrates that Adad-nērārī II received a gift of a large female monkey and a small female monkey from Bīt-Adīni (KUR DUMU *a-di-ni*—a very unusual formulation), "which lies on the bank of the Euphrates" (*a-ḫi šá* ÍD *pu-rat-te* GAR-*nu*). The ruler of Bīt-Adīni was probably not the same as the ruler of Masuwari (ca. 900 BCE) because the Arameans had not gained control over Til-Barsib. At this time, it seems that Bīt-Adīni had control over the territory east of the Euphrates, including all of the great bend of that river, and the territory between the Euphrates and the Balīḫ, though it did not control Til-Barsib (Masuwari). Clearly, a location of Ḫuzirīna at modern Sultantepe would make better sense of the submission of this gift, then a location near Mount Kašiyāri.[47] Furthermore, the submission would be more compelling if Ḫuzirīna was located at Sultantepe. With an Assyrian foray into this location, Bīt-Adīni's control in the Balīḫ would have been threatened. Much less so, if a location in the western Mount Kašiyāri area were the location of Ḫuzirīna.

All three vignettes pose problems. The first with its dischronologized statement about surrounding the city completely after the city's capture (no need to surround it, if it had already been captured!).[48] The second vignette mentions Mamli, and promptly leaves blank what transpired with him. The third vignette utilizes a very unusual formulation, KUR DUMU *a-di-ni* in its identification of the one giving the display gift. In addition, the overall geographic flow is dischronologized: capture of Ḫuzirīna in the west (before) the submission of cities at Mount Kašiyāri in the northern Jezirah, (then) a display gift of monkeys given (in Ḫuzirīna, back in the west, if Ḫuzirīna is to be identified with Sultantepe).

It would seem that there are significant ancient scribal issues in this passage where errors have been introduced through recopying of an annalistic

---

A.0.99.2, 98–102), or that he took a northerly route without mentioning Mount Ḫasamu (modern Tektek Dağı) as Shalmaneser did (RIMA 3:15, A.0.102.2, i.29; 3:17, ii.14; 3:19, ii.31). There is also the problem of explaining Adad-nērārī II's strategy to take Ḫanigalbat from the Temanites. Adad-nērārī's tactics against the Temanites and their stronghold/capital of Naṣībīna is like that of Shalmaneser III concerning Til-Barsib: if the capital cannot be taken outright, and an extended siege is not feasible, then the state is reduced and weakened by attacking its fortified cities before readdressing the capital. The question is why would Adad-nērārī II travel to the Harran Plain when the Temanites seem to be restricted to the Ḫābūr triangle. See Postgate 1995, 10.

47. Lipiński (2000a, 112–14) does not eliminate the possibility of an eastern Ḫuzirīna, but he points out that a gift of two monkeys from the ruler of Bīt-Adīni, located in the Great Bend of the Euphrates would most likely take place in a western location like Sultantepe.

48. RIMA 2:149–50, A.0.99.2, lines 45b–46: URU *ḫu-zi-ri-na aṣ-ba-at* ⁽⁴⁶⁾ BÀD *a-na na-al-ban lu al-bi-šu* :: *dūra ana nalbân lu albīšu*, lit. "the wall completely I encircled it."

account for a single year.[49] In my opinion, the dischronologized statement is the first, but by no means the only hint.

Years ago, Grayson perceived this problem, commenting "Reiner's interpretation, which I have adopted, provides an awkward sequence of action (encirclement should come before capture) and the meaning of this passage remains uncertain."[50] The crux is the phrase *ana nalbân*.[51] Deriving *na-al-ban* from *nalbānu* "brick mold," earlier scholars translated "Die Mauer bekleidete ich(?) mit Ziegelwerk(?)"[52] or "aus geformten Ziegeln [verkleidete ich]."[53] Recently Lipiński has understood this to be a reference to the repair of the city's wall, stating "The annals recount the capture of the city (Ḫuzirīna) and the repair of its wall...."[54] However, if *nalbân* is derived from *lawû/lamû* (Assyrian: *labû*) as Reiner convincingly argued,[55] then this sentence is about the encirclement of the wall, not its repair.[56]

Fales (2012a, 108) proposes the following rearrangement: "I marched a third time to the land Ḫanigalbat" → "The (people of) the cities at the foot of Mount Kašiyāri ... submitted to me" → "I captured the city Ḫuzirīna" → "I received ... a shipment from the land of Bīt-Adīni." He suggests:

> With this light shuffling of the clauses, we would in point of fact obtain the coherent account of a campaign which started out against Ḫanigalbat," and specifically touched the southern Kašiyāri range, but thereupon continued along the E–W road which was to be further, and frequently, trodden by Aššurnaṣirpal II, and finally reached the Balīḫ at Ḫuzirīna/Sultantepe—an area and a city which quite surely had nothing to do with Ḫanigalbat itself, but were fully adjacent to Bīt-Adini. (Fales 2012a, 108)

To this, I would add that the *Vorlage* copied by the scribe of Adad-nērārī II's annals, mistakenly switched the encirclement of Ḫuzirīna and its capture; omitted some pieces of information about Mamli and what Adad-nērārī was

49. For the same suggestion, see now Fales 2012a, 108.

50. Grayson 1972–76, 2:88 n. 358; RIMA 2:149, note to line 46. See Reiner 1970.

51. See *CAD* 11.1:199, s.v. *nalbân*.

52. Seidmann (1935, 37) renders "I(?) dressed the wall with brick work(?)."

53. *AHw* 724a, s.v. *nalbanu(m)*; and 522b, s.v. *labānu*. "Out of molded bricks [I dressed up] (the wall)."

54. Lipiński 2000a, 114. See *CAD* 9:72, s.v. *lamû* 2.d which lists this text under the heading "to wall a city, a precinct."

55. Reiner 1970, 90. She rightly notes that line 55 of this same inscription demonstrates the idiom of *ana nalbân*: URU-*šu a-na na-al-ban hi-ri-ṣa lu ih-ru-«ṣu»-uṣ* "He had dug a moat all around his city."

56. Interestingly, *CDA* 179 s.v. *lawûm* does not list the meaning "to wall a city, a precinct." Also compare *ālšu ana nalbân ḫirāṣa lu iḫruṣ* "he dug a moat all around the city" (Adad-nērārī II, same inscription, line 55).

able to do with him (fought him, defeated him, etc.?), and mistakenly inserted a KUR in front of DUMU *a-di-ni*.

Finally, it seems manifest that, if Ḫuzirīna is Sultantepe (as argued here), it was most certainly not a Temanite city. The text does not identify it as Temanite, but nor does it give any indication of its affiliation. However, a very staccato passage in the Ninurta Temple Inscription of Aššurnaṣirpal II may be helpful:

> In the eponymy of Šamaš-nūri (866), ... I departed from Kalḫu. I crossed the Tigris; I went down to the land Qipānu. I received in the city of Ḫuzirīna the tribute from the city rulers of the land of Qipānu.[57]

A close reading of this passage seems to indicate that Aššurnaṣirpal entered into the land of Qipānu, and then received in the city of Ḫuzirīna the tribute of the various "city-lords" (LÚ.EN.URU.MEŠ-*te*) of the land of Qipānu. Thus from this passage it would seem that Ḫuzirīna was one of the many independent city-states that comprised the land of Qipānu.[58] In any case, the land of Qipānu was just to the north of Ḫuzirīna (see Radner 2006–8c).

The fourth campaign of Adad-nērārī II against Ḫanigalbat (898 BCE) was centered on the city of Gidara ("which the Arameans call Raqamatu"):

> In the eponymy of Likberu,
> I marched a fourth time to the land of Ḫanigalbat.
> At that time Muquru, the Temanite, broke the oath of the great gods; and he became hostile against me for war and battle. He trusted in his fortified city, his strong bow, his extensive troops, and the Arameans; and (so) he (Muquru) rebelled against me.
>
> I mustered my chariotry (and) troops; I marched to the city of Gidara, which the Arameans call Raqamatu (and) which the Arameans had taken away by force after the time of Tiglath-pileser, son of Aššur-rēša-iši, king of Assyria, a prince who preceded me.
>
> In my cunning, I placed siege forts[59] all around it (the city), (a tactic) which had never been utilized by (lit. "did not exist among") the kings my fathers. He (Muquru) had dug a moat all around his city; (but) they took fright in the

57. RIMA 2:219, A.0.101.1, iii.92b–93.

58. Perhaps not unlike the political situation in Media in the later Neo-Assyrian period. The rulers of the Medes, as well as others in that region, are designated "city lords." This term (singular: *bēl āli*) suggests the limited scope of their power. See Radner 2003, 52, who likens these to "robber-barons."

59. *ālāni battubattēšu*, translated "redoubts" (Grayson, RIMA 2:150, A.0.99.2, line 55); "posts" (*CAD* 2:169, s.v. *battubattu*); "bulwarks" (Melville).

face of my fierce weapons, my raging battle, (and) my strong forces, and I entered into the city of Raqamatu with force (and) violence.

That fellow I brought down from his palace. I personally inspected his property, precious stone of the mountain, chariots, horses, his wives, his sons, his daughters—(all) his heavy booty. That fellow together with his brothers I fastened in bronze clasps; (and) I brought (them) to my city Assur.

(Thus) have I constantly established the victory and strength of Aššur, my lord, over the land of Ḫanigalbat.[60]

On this campaign, Adad-nērārī II encountered a third Temanite leader called Muquru, who had allegedly broken "the oath of the great gods." Adad-nērārī besieged Muquru's capital of Gidara that the Arameans called by the name Raqamatu/Radamatu.[61] Gidara has been identified with modern Bughedra (Buğday), possibly deriving from *Abu Gidara—a location about half-way between Nusaybin (ancient Naṣībīna) on the southeast and Mardin on the northwest.[62]

As for the toponym Rad/qamatu, it occurs in the annals of Šamšī-Adad V,[63] being written as URU.*Raq-mat*, where it is named in a list of rebellious cities during the latter years of Shalmaneser III's reign, being mentioned after Urakka (near Naṣībīna) and before Ḫuzirīna (Sultantepe). It was a provincial capital according to the eponym list for 836, 812, 795, and 773 BCE (see Postgate 1995, 4; 2005, 247; Radner 2006–8a, 52).

This was an important city that had been conquered by the Arameans at the time of either Tiglath-pileser I (r. 1114–1076), son of Aššur-rēša-iši I (r. 1132–1115), or Tiglath-pileser II (r. 966–935), son of Aššur-rēša-iši II (r. 971–967), although the former is more likely given the troubles with Arameans in that king's reign. Fales (2012a, 109) observes that this historical note about the capture of Gidara by the Arameans in the days of Tiglath-pileser I is

60. RIMA 2:150, A.0.99.2, lines 49b–60a.

61. Written in line 52: URU.*ra-qa-ma-tu*; in line 57: URU.*ra-dam-ma-te*. The variant spelling in Neo-Assyrian indicates the Old Aramaic phoneme *ḍ*. See Weippert 1973, 46–47 n. 83; Millard 1980b, 369; Dion 1997, 32 n. 30.

62. Lipiński 2000a, 114. But Fales (2012a, 109 n. 59) comments: "However, it may be noticed that if—as maintained by Lipiński himself in a footnote (ibid.)—Gidara should be related to West Semitic *gdr*, 'wall,' 'enclosure,' the suggested toponym formation *Abu Gidara does not seem today convincing."

63. RIMA 3:183, A.0.103, lines 47–48, esp. line 48. Grayson reads URU.*sal-lat*, but see Postgate 1995, 10.

a first ideological clue to the overall aims of Adad-nērārī's thrusts vis-à-vis Ḫanigalbat—that of reclaiming territory which had formed part of māt Aššur in Middle Assyrian times. This "grand strategy" will be most forcefully continued under Aššurnaṣirpal II for the entire area up to the bank of the Euphrates, and even under Shalmaneser III for the areas on the riverbank itself.

Adad-nērārī captured the city using a new siege technique of building seven "siege forts"[64] around the city. The fact that there were "seven" of these means that there was an individual aspect to them, and yet they are clearly part of a siege technique, howbeit one that had not, according to Adad-nērārī II, been utilized before. If the Arameans in whom Muquru trusted were outside the city of Raqamatu, these facilities (whatever they exactly were) were designed to eliminate their help in breaking the siege.[65] Adad-nērārī personally inspected Muquru's property and family, and took him and his brothers as captives back to Assur. This Muquru may be mentioned on the very fragmentary remains of a black stone with traces of scenes in relief and inscriptions, perhaps the remains of "an obelisk of Adad-narari II similar in form to the Black or Rassam Obelisk of Ashurnasirpal II from Calah."[66]

In his fifth campaign to Ḫanigalbat (897), Adad-nērārī simply collects tribute. However, the next year, the sixth campaign to Ḫanigalbat, there was a revolt by Nūr-Adad in Naṣībīna. This is the same Nūr-Adad against whom the first two campaigns had been directed with open-field engagements at Pauza and Naṣībīna, though the city of Naṣībīna had not been captured. The narrative for this campaign is climactic, with flowing poetic praises lauding Adad-nērārī II at its end.[67]

64. See n. 59.

65. These *ālāni battubattēšu* were similar in their function to the siege walls and fortifications built by Julius Caesar in his siege of the town of Alesia where the confederation of Gallic tribes were hold up under the leadership of Vercingetorix.

66. Grayson, RIMA 2:277. Muquru is possibly mentioned also on a fragment of an obelisk from Nineveh (RIMA 2:161), see Brinkman, 2001a, 770. A tripod from Nimrud is inscribed *lmwqr* "belonging to Mwqr," see Barnett 1967, 6*. Brinkman (2001a, 770) states: "'Heavily burdened, hard of hearing, deaf'; West Semitic; masc. written: $^{m}$*mu-qu-ru*, $^{m}$*mu-qu-ri* (gen.), $^{m}$*mu-qur*." The meaning was suggested by Zadok 1977, 140, 312–13; 1996, 723–24. Lipiński (2000a, 115–16) disagrees and suggests "an Aramaic passive participle of the causative stem of *wqr*, thus *mawqar* < *məhawqar*, meaning "hardened" or "honoured," "venerable," like Arabic *muwaqqar* derived from Stem II (intensive)." See also Kessler 1993–97.

67. RIMA 2:150–51, A.0.99.2, lines 62–79.

(lines 62–79)
In the eponymy of Adad-dān, with the rage of my strong weapons, I marched a sixth time to the land Ḫanigalbat.

I confined Nūr-Adad, the Temanite in the city of Naṣībīna, (and) I established seven siege forts around it. I stationed therein Aššur-dīnī-amur, the *turtānu* (commander-in-chief). He (Nūr-Adad) had dug a moat, which had not previously existed, in bedrock all around it (the city). He had made (it) nine cubits wide; in a downward direction he made the foundation pit reach the (subsoil) waters. The wall was next to the moat.

I encircled his moat with my warriors like a flame; they (the enemy) screamed like children (lit. "the cry of children") about it. [I laid] traps as strong as the destructive flood for him; I deprived him of grain.

By the command of Aššur, the great lord, my lord, I carried off from the midst of his city: his [...], his gold, his property, precious stone of the mountain, his gods, chariots with teams of [horses], [...?], a staff, his battle-equipment, a gold throne, polished gold dishes, decorated [couches with] inlay, weapons, arrows, ?, a golden "tent" (*kultāru*) a symbol of his kingship, [...] the weight of which I did not determine, and the extensive property of his palace. [...]

He (Adad-nērārī) ascended his lordly throne. Within his shrine, he slaughtered holy sacrifices; he offered oxen; made a libation of best/ritual beer, (and) completed the offering with holy sweet wine of the mountain. (Thus) he made his offerings; and had himself exalted with elaborate praise:

"In all lands, kings are suffering constant anguish[68] (and)
mountains quake!

The king spoke [...-ly?][69] to his nobles:

"The young hero of Aššur,
praises of his warriorship are exalted;
his deeds are of the god Dagan;
the king who magnifies his praises!"

I brought back in my presence Nūr-Adad together with his extensive troops as hostages. I granted cities with people to Assyria; I counted them.

68. *CAD* 12:235, s.v. *pašāqu* III/3: "to undergo continually anguish, difficulty."
69. *CAD* 17.3:213 "mng. uncert." Grayson translates as "humbly."

Just as he had besieged and captured Gidara/Raqamatu, Adad-nērārī utilized the siege fort technique in the capture of Naṣībīna. Just like Muquru, Nūr-Adad had dug a moat, in this case a quite substantial one: 9 cubits wide (ca. 13.5 ft or 4.11 m) and down to a depth that reached water. By means of an archery attack and a tight siege that apparently starved the city into submission, Adad-nērārī was able to plunder Nūr-Adad's possessions thoroughly.

This is followed by sacrifice and celebration, with poetic exaltation praising the Assyrian king for his great victory. In the lines that relate this ceremony (73b–78b), there are numerous elements of the "Assyrian War Ritual."[70] Almost anticlimactically, the statements follow about Nūr-Adad being taken hostage, along with many of his troops. Assyrian complete control was established.

While these Aramean leaders did not combine their forces, apparently believing that they could defeat the Assyrians on their own, in two instances they built significant defensive works (moats) and in the case of Nūr-Adad were able to field a credible chariot force (at least it appears that he was confident that it was sufficient for victory). While Mount Kašiyāri may have served as a base of sorts for the Temanites, it is clear that they had a good hold on the plains of the Upper Ḫābūr just to the Ṭūr ʿAbdīn's south. Finally, there is a summary passage that ends this section.

> By the command of Aššur, the great lord, my lord, and Ištar, mistress of battle and strife, who goes at the head of my extensive troops, in the month Sivan, in this same eponymy (Šamaš-abūya, 894 BCE), I marched for a fifth time (sic[71]) to the land Ḫanigalbat. I received the tribute of the land Ḫanigalbat above and below (*eliš u šapliš*). (Thus) I became lord of the extensive land of Ḫanigalbat to its entire extent (and) I brought (it) into the boundaries of my land. I brought them under one authority.[72]

This was the end of Temanite independence from Assyria. From this point on, the area was firmly under Assyrian control. However, this also meant that a substantial area where the population was primarily speakers of Aramaic had become fully integrated into the Assyrian Empire.

The gentilic form is later used to designate four "Temanite" sheep (4 UDU KUR.⌜*te-man*⌝ *-a-a*) that belonged to Aššur-eṭer, the cohort commander (Fales and Postgate 1995, 55, no. 85:1). Perhaps this referred to a specific breed from the region?

70. Deller 1992. See also Parpola's partial translation in Annus 2002, 74–75; May 2012.

71. Possibly a scribal interpolation, perhaps from the fifth campaign, according to Fales (2012a, 109). See also Ponchia 2004, 260–61.

72. RIMA 2:152–53, A.0.99.2, lines 97–100a.

Finally, the *taimaniti tupalaliti* "the Taimani script" (*tymn* "southern" script) mentioned in the hieroglyphic Luwian inscription of Yariri[73] is not to be identified with the "Temanites" (Younger 2014a). It is most likely the North Arabian script, though the South Arabian script cannot be ruled out.

## 4.3. Gōzān/Bīt-Baḫiāni

The ancient city of Gōzān[74] (Gūzāna) was located at modern Tell Ḥalaf, on the south bank of the Nahr al-Jibjib, the westernmost tributary to the Ḫābūr River. It was the capital of the Aramean polity Bīt-Baḫiāni, a tribal state that had its jurisdiction over the far western area of the Ḫābūr triangle (see fig. 4.1). One of the main trade routes connecting Assyria with the Levant passed through Gōzān. This was known as the King's Road (*ḫarrān šarri*) in the Neo-Assyrian sources and ran through Harran, Gōzān, Naṣībīna to Nineveh.

The Assyrian spelling *Baḫiāni* reflects the Aramaic *Baǵyān*/*Ba'yān* "the desired one" from the verb *bǵy*/*b'y* "to desire" (Lipiński 1994, 23; 1999c). The name is attested in Aramaic *b'yn* (Fales 1977, 51, no. 77). Besides its sedentary component located in Gōzān and nearby Sikan (Tell Fakhariya), this tribal entity probably had a reasonably good-sized pastoralist component, given the areas surrounding Gōzān. The fact that there were few sedentary towns or villages south and west of the city during the period of Aramean domination may be indicative of this pastoralist component (Dion 1997, 39).

Although in northern Mesopotamia many of the urban centers of the Late Bronze Age still existed, the Aramean rulers typically founded new cities as residences (Novák 2004; Mazzoni 1994). This was exactly the case with Gōzān, which was founded as the capital in the late tenth century even though the site of Sikan (modern Tell Fakhariya "pottery sherd mound") was only about 2.5 km west.

The ancient settlement at Tell Fakhariya covers a total area of approximately 90 ha, twelve of which form the high mound or citadel. The remaining 78 ha constitute the lower town. Thus Tell Fakhariya is one of the largest sites in this region. The name of the modern town Rās al-'Ain has the meaning "head of the spring," which, in fact is one of the main sources of the Ḫābūr River, which made it a major cult center for the deity Hadad of Sikan, the Lord of the Ḫābūr.

---

73. KARKAMIŠ A15b (Hawkins 2000, 130–33, pls. 36–37).

74. The spelling in Aramaic and Hebrew is *gwzn*. "Gōzān" is the vocalization in the Bible (2 Kgs 17:6; 18:11; 19:12; Isa 37:12; 1 Chr 5:26).

The identification of Tell Fakhariya (first-millennium Sikan) as the Mittanian capital and Middle Assyrian administrative city Wa/Aššukanni has been debated. Opitz (1927) suggested the identification of Tell Fakhariya as Waššukanni, taking Sikan to be an Assyrianized version of the Hurrian original (Wa)Sikan(ni). On the other hand, Lipiński has argued that the toponym Sikan is the earlier West Semitic word designating a sacred stone or stela and that this was the name of the site as early as circa 2000 BCE, when an Ur III tablet mentions the goddess ${}^{d}$Ḫa-bu-u-rí-tum si-kà-an$^{ki}$ [75] (*sic*: ${}^{d}$ḫa-bu-rí-tum-si-ga-an$^{ki}$; Edzard and Farber 1974, 164). Lipiński (2000a, 120) states:

> The retention of the same West-semitic place name Sikkan through the Mittannian period, from the end of the third to the first millennium B.C., speaks strongly against the identification of Sikkan with Waššuganni, the name of which can by no means be considered as a Hurrianized form of Sikkan.

However, that the name was originally Sikan does not invalidate the phonetic similarity (Sikan = Aššukanni = Waššukanni)[76] nor the geohistorical plausibility that still make the identification of Tell Fakhariya with Waššukanni quite likely (Jakob 2003, 291–92). Furthermore, in the 2009 excavations in the Middle Assyrian building designated as *House I*, some cuneiform text fragments were discovered along with numerous seal impressions. One motif that is clearly represented on the impressions (e.g., TF 7746) consists of "a contest scene depicting an anthropomorphic winged-lion and a winged-bull, as well as a smaller winged-bull or calf crouched underneath both rearing protagonists" (Bartl 2011, 7, fig. 8). Bartl notes that this is an identical impression to one on a clay tablet found at Tell Šēḫ Ḥamad (Dūr-Katlimmu) making an identification of the seal owner possible. The Assyrian vizier, later grand-vizier, Aššur-iddin has been identified as the owner by Cancik-Kirschbaum (1996, 22–23 n. 76). Aššur-iddin had his administrative seats at Dūr-Katlimmu and Aššukanni (Tell Fakhariya) from where he governed the province of Ḫanigalbat during the reigns of Shalmaneser I (1264–1234 BCE) and Tukulti-Ninurta I (1233–1198 BCE). Another seal impression belongs to Sîn-mudammeq (TF 6293), a high official and vizier in the Assyrian administration, whose seal impression has been found on a sealed letter from Tell Khuera (Ḫarbe) (Jakob and Janisch-Jakob 2009, 185, seal motive 3). Since Sîn-mudammeq temporarily had his official residence in Aššukanni, this adds to the idea of both officials playing an important role in the administra-

75. Lipiński 2000a, 120; 1994. See also recently Szuchman 2007, 69.

76. Del Monte and Tischler 1978, 479–80, s.v. *Wašukana*; and Nashef 1982, 277–78, s.v. *Uššukani*.

tion of the western province at about the same time and that a part of these activities took place at Tell Fakhariya (Bartl 2011, 8). All this means that Middle Assyrian Aššukanni is Neo-Assyrian Sikan, located at Tell Fakhariya. Finally, recent petro-chemical analyses show that the clay of two letters of the Mittanian king Tušratta have a very high degree of probability of originating from the region of Tell Fakhariya.[77] The significance of Sikan as a central cultic place for the storm god and his wife Šala can also be traced back to the Ur III period at the end of the third millennium BCE (Kessler and Müller-Kessler 1995, 240–41).

Tell Fakhariya has occupation levels from prehistoric times to the Late Roman period. The excavations carried out at Tell Fakhariya are as follows:

(1) Excavations in 1940 by an American expedition (McEwan et al. 1958). In sounding VI of these excavations, a Middle Assyrian house was exposed where cuneiform tablets were found dating to the reign of Shalmaneser I and Tukulti-Ninurta I (Güterbock 1958).
(2) A series of soundings by a German team led by Moortgat in 1955 and 1956 (Moortgat 1956, 1957, 1959).
(3) The accidental discovery of the Tell Fakhariya Inscription in 1979 (Abou-Assaf, Bordreuil, and Millard 1982).
(4) Investigations by Pruß and Bagdo in 2001 (Pruß and Bagdo 2002).
(5) Ongoing excavations since 2006. Discoveries of Middle Assyrian cuneiform tablets and sealings (2009 and 2010 seasons; Bartl 2011).

Yet, for the site of their new capital city, the Arameans chose Tell Ḥalaf (Gōzān), with Sikan being primarily a cult center. This was a prehistoric ruin mound that had been apparently unoccupied during the entire Bronze Age since no settlement remains of the third or second millennia BCE have been observed (Novák 2009, 93). Numerous soundings dug into the mound confirmed that, in general, the Iron Age structures were built directly above the prehistoric Ḥalaf layer. Tell Ḥalaf consists of a high mound (where the Iron Age citadel was located) and an extended lower city, enclosing the citadel to the west, south, and east. This Iron Age city covered approximately 75 ha (Novák 2013, 294). The site of Tell Ḥalaf was excavated before and after the First World War by Max von Oppenheim (seasons: 1911–1913, 1927, and

77. Goren, Finkelstein, and Na'aman 2004, 38–44. They state: "When these petrographic results are combined with the textual and archaeological evidence, Tell Fakhariyeh seems to become the only possible site for the location of Waššukanni, the capital city of Mitanni" (p. 44).

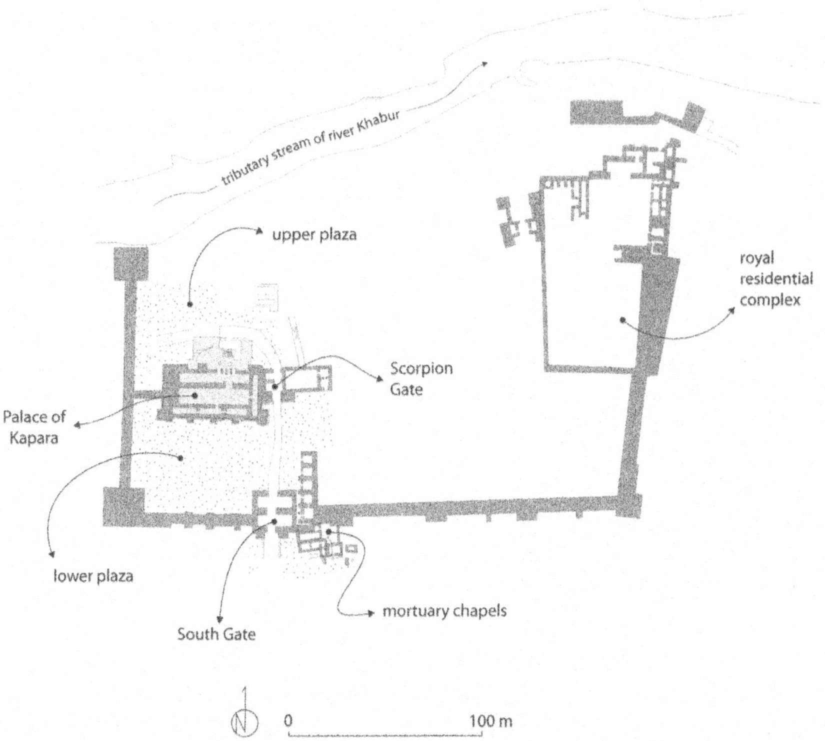


Fig. 4.2. Archaeological excavations of Tell Ḥalaf (Gilibert 2013, 62, fig. 3)

1929).[78] Further excavations have been resumed at the site, starting in 2006 (Baghdo et al. 2009; Cholidis and L. Martin 2011; see fig. 4.2).

However, there may have been a small settlement from the early Iron Age at Tell Ḥalaf (Novák 2013, 297). Some "groovy" pottery pieces from unsecured stratigraphic contexts have been identified from the earlier excavations.[79] Some has been found in recent excavation campaigns (Dornauer 2010, 48 n. 91). The so-called grooved-type (Bartl 2001) or groovy pottery (Roaf and Schachner 2005, 119–22) is especially known in eastern Anatolia.[80] Novák has recently suggested a connection of this "groovy pottery"

78. Von Oppenheim 1931, 1933; Schmidt 1943; Naumann 1950; Moortgat 1955; Hrouda 1962; 1972–75; Cholidis and Martin 2010.

79. Novák 2009, 93. The pottery is in Schmidt 1943, and identified by K. Bartl (Bartl 1989, 261).

80. Interestingly, some sherds of this "groovy pottery" have been found at Kaḫat (Tell Barri) in phase 2 dating to the period immediately after the reign of Aššur-bēl-kala (1073–1056). See d'Agostino 2009.

with the Mušku and Kaška as part of a migration of Anatolian groups into the area around Tell Ḥalaf (Novák 2013, 296–97; 2009, 93–94;Wittke 2004). He connects this with the report of Tiglath-pileser I (1114–1076 BCE)[81] that in his accession year he fought a battle with and defeated twenty thousand Mušku warriors and their five kings, who had conquered and occupied the countries of Alzu and Purulumzu for some fifty years earlier and had now conquered the land of Katmuḫu.

However, as Bartl (2001, 398) notes, "the broad distribution of that pottery which is found in an area of nearly 700 km (E–W) × 500 km (N–S) which exceeds the documented 'Mušku area' by far, makes this assumption impossible, apart from the fact that the identification of a cultural complex mainly defined by pottery with specific ethnic groups seems highly speculative." Thus, on historical and geographical grounds, a direct identification with the Mušku should probably be ruled out (Summers 1994, 245–47). While the distribution of the "groovy pottery" corresponds to some extent with the Nairi lands, it is apparent that this pottery should not be associated with any one ethnicity since it was used by a variety of peoples in the region. It is attested in Iron Age I contexts at Norşuntepe, Ziyaret Tepe, Üçtepe, Gre Dimse, and Giricano where it follows the Middle Assyrian ceramic forms. At none of these sites can it be assigned to the material culture of the Arameans.[82] In the Upper Tigris region, "groovy pottery" may be considered an indicator of the end of Middle Assyrian control (Roaf and Schachner 2005, 120).

Whether the "groovy pottery" should be connected to the Mušku or not, it is important to note that it was the Mušku with whom Tiglath-pileser I fought in this region, not the Arameans. Novák (2009, 94) rightly observes that this indicates that at this time the Aramean nomadic tribes were not the main threat to Assyrian dominance of this particular area, only later. Aššur-bēl-kala had to engage the Arameans throughout the Ḫābūr region, which certainly speaks to a different situation than his father's. The paucity of subsequent Assyrian documentation does not, of course, reflect the outcomes of all these conflicts; but the necessity of military operations by the early Neo-Assyrian kings to reconquer the region and the presence of established Aramean polities in it, can only mean that Assyria, without doubt, lost much territory in the Upper Ḫābūr (Cholidis and Martin 2010, ii).

Beside the prehistoric occupation and the limited early Iron Age "groovy" pottery, the early German excavations at Tell Ḥalaf uncovered significant Iron Age architectural remains, including carved orthostats, and

81. RIMA 2:14, A.0.87.1, i.62–88. For discussion, see pp. 122–23.

82. Dornauer 2010, 48 n. 92. For Giricano, see Radner 2004a, 115–17. See p. 183.

tombs with associated artifacts. These excavations were carried out on three areas of the acropolis: the northwestern, southern, and northeastern sides (see fig. 4.2). A number of surveys were also conducted in the area of the city apart from the enclosure wall enclosure of the acropolis. The excavators interpreted the evidence as reflecting three main phases, the first and second of which were followed directly one upon the other, and which intermingle at times: (1) the Old Building period (*Altbauphase*) with subphasing 1–5; (2) the Kapara period (*Kaparaperiode*; named for a ruler attested in cuneiform inscriptions, for which see below); and (3) the Assyrian period (Naumann 1950, 376–80). The exact date of the Kapara period is very much debated while the Neo-Assyrian period is represented on only part of the tell.

The first and second phases are not separated by either destruction or prolonged abandonment. Sader (1987, 31) rightly pointed to the *bīt-ḫilāni* (the so-called *Tempelpalast* in the reports, that is, the palace of Kapara) as an example of the coexistence of architectural units of the first phase with others of the second phase of construction. One is thus dealing with a long period of occupation without major interruption and characterized by the erection of imposing monuments. This continuity came to a clear and brutal stop. The layers of ashes that have been found indicate that a fire devastated the city (see further comments below). Indeed, structures of this period were not rebuilt or restored and the constructions from the Assyrian period were much simpler and only built on part of the ruins (Sader 1987, 31).

The early excavations discovered a number of cuneiform inscriptions, particularly of a ruler named Kapara; but also two archives: one that belonged to an Assyrian governor, Mannu-kī-māt-Aššur (minimum: 793–783 BCE)[83] and another that belonged to Il-manāni, son of Sagib from the town of Mehini, active in Gūzāna after the reign of Aššurbanipal and post-612 BCE.

The real crux for interpreting the archaeological data from Tell Ḥalaf and for reconstructing its history lies in the dating of the period of Kapara (and his two predecessors). The cuneiform inscriptions of "Kapara,[84] the son

83. Baker 2001a. The name is most often written with the KUR (*māt*) sign before Aššur.

84. For the much-discussed personal name Kapara, a number of different etymologies have been suggested (see Sader 1987, 42 n. 116): (1) the name is derived from the Hebrew root כְּפִיר "young lion" (Galling 1941, 121–22; Lemaire 1977a, 214; Röllig 1976–80b; Maraqten 1988); however, the suggested nominal *qatal* form of the Kapara inscriptions speaks against this derivation; (2) from the word כֹּפֶר "henna"; (3) Zakok (1977, 338, numbers 13 and 19) gives two possibilities: כִּפֵּר "to erase/clear, forgive/pardon" and the root כבר "to be great, strong," favored by Lipiński 2000a, 132. Recent evidence indicates that it is a *qatall* form: *Kaparra* (Dornauer 2010, 50 n. 99).

Fig. 4.3. The entrance portico of Kapara's Palace (Gilibert 2013, 64, fig. 6)

of Ḫadiānu,[85] the king of Palē" have fueled speculation since Kapara and his land, Palē (if this is the correct normalization of the Akkadian), are unknown.

Following the publication of the excavation reports, scholars have focused mainly on two different sets of data in attempting to determine historical sequence at Tell Ḥalaf: some have concentrated on the iconography and style of the reliefs and statuary; others have centered their attention on the inscriptions. Predictably, the results of these scholarly investigations have produced widely varying dates for the Kapara period. A further complicating factor is the apparent reuse and inscribing of reliefs by Kapara, and the question of whether these inscriptions indicate Neo-Assyrian influence or not (Moortgat 1955, 16). Similarly, there is disagreement about the extent of Neo-Assyrian influence in the reliefs. While Naumann (1950, 376–80) originally dated the Kapara period to the ninth century (ca. 850–830), there are six different dates on which scholars have tended to settle:[86]

85. The patronym Ḫadiānu is derived from West Semitic *ḥdw/y*, "to rejoice," + *-ān* suffix (Baker 2000a). See, however, Lipiński 2000a, 370 and the derivation of Arabic *ḥḏw/y*, "replica." This is also the name of a ruler of Damascus during the reign of Shalmaneser IV (773 BCE); see RIMA 3:240, A.0.105.1, line 6.

86. For an evaluation of some of these, see Schwemer 2001, 612–13 with comment in nn. 49–50.

(1) tenth century
(2) ninth century in general
(3) early ninth century
(4) late ninth century
(5) early eighth century
(6) late eighth century

Fig. 4.4. Kapara Inscription on Ištar statue

Table 4.1 provides the reader with an impression of the complexity of the debate, listing the scholar, the proposed date of the Kapara period and the basis used by this scholar for the dating. The table is selective and is arranged in chronological order.

A second difficulty associated with the Kapara period is the name of his land and its identification. The cuneiform inscriptions of "Kapara, the son of Ḫadiānu," are inscribed on a number of orthostats and statues of the *bīt ḫilāni* (*Tempelpalast*) excavated at Tell Ḥalaf (see fig. 4.4). A few of these state that he was "the king of the land of Palē" (MAN KUR.*pa*-LID(*le*$_8$)-*e*):[87]

> (1) É.GAL-*lì* m[*ka-pa-ra*] A m*ḫa-di-a-ni*] (2) MAN KUR.*pa*-LID(*le*$_8$)-*e*
> *ša* [AD-*ia* AD AD-*ia* NA$_4$.NU.MEŠ/NA$_4$.TI.ME] (3) *la e-pa-šú-ni*
> *a-na-*[*ku e-tap-šá*
> *ma-nu šá* MU *i-pa-ši-ṭu-ni*]
> (4) MU-*šú i-šá-ka-*[*nu-ni*]
> 7 DUMU.MEŠ-*šú* IGI IM] (5) *li-ši-ru-pu*
> m*ab-di-*[DINGIR-*mu um-man* IN.SAR]

Palace of [Kapara, son of Ḫadiānu], king of the land of Palē.

87. (1) full reading of the name on an inscription found on statue fragments. Meissner 1933, 74–76, Number III (fragments 60 + 61 + 59); Sader 1987, 12–13, I Ba$_{2-3}$; (2) partial reading of the name on an inscription found on fragments. Meissner 1933, 76, numbers 62 + 63; Sader 1987, 13–14, I Ba$_5$. Albright (1956b) proposed reading *Ḫat-tí-e*. The first sign, of course, could be read *ḫat*, but the second sign is most certainly not *tí*.

Table 4.1. The Dating of the Kapara Period (Scholars and Their Dates and Methods)

| Scholar | Date | Basis for Dating |
|---|---|---|
| Meissner 1933 | tenth century | Ductus of the inscriptions; Assyrians are not mentioned |
| Naumann 1950, 381 | 850–830 | Evolution of the Ḫilāni layout |
| Frankfort 1954 | ninth century | Style of the orthostats |
| Moortgat 1955 | second half of ninth century (850–800) | Style of the orthostats and statues of Temple-Palace |
| von Soden in Moortgat 1955 | second half of ninth century (850–800) | Palaeographic analysis of the inscriptions |
| Albright 1956 | tenth century | Absence of any Assyrian influence in the monuments and reliefs |
| Hrouda 1962 | ninth/eighth century (900–700) | Style of the small finds |
| Akurgal 1966, 1979 | end of eighth century (720–700) | Layout of the Temple-Palace shows a canonical form of the *Bīt-Ḫilāni*, the bases of the statues are a later development of the bases flanked by lions |
| Orthmann 1971, 127 | beginning of the ninth century (900–850) | Style of the small finds |
| Sader 1987, 37–42 | dated between the end of ninth and the end of the eighth century (ca. 800–700) | Sader maintains that the philological and archaeological information do not fit each other. |
| Winter 1989 | first half of ninth century (900–850) | The ivories are exact parallels of Syrian pieces found at Nimrud and dated to the ninth century |
| Dion 1997, 41–44 | early ninth century (882–870) | Absence of Assyrian influence in the style of the orthostats; Abi-salāmu could be Kapara's unnamed grandfather |

| | | |
|---|---|---|
| Lipiński 2000a, 130–32 | second half of ninth century (ca. 830) | Reliefs show no Neo-Assyrian influence and must predate period of Assyrian domination; ivories are like those from Nimrud of ninth century date (cf. Winter 1988) |
| Sass 2005, 93–95 | ±875 or ±860 | Paleography of the epigraphic evidence |
| Pucci 2008, 81–126 | early eighth century (800–775) | Architectural/Building sequence with dating the end of the first period on the basis of Mannu-kī-māt-Aššur archive (793–783) and assuming that the temple to the storm god was still in use since it is mentioned in Assyrian correspondence; the Kapara period is the second Building phase and must date after this. |
| Novák 2013; 2009; 2004, 324 | mid-tenth century (950) | Kapara claims in his inscriptions: "What my father and my grandfather did not do (in their) lifetime, I have done." This must refer to the act of building a palace in an urban capital (2013, 228). His principality is named Palē. Baḫiāni was a successor of Kapara. |
| Cholidis, Dubiel and Martin in Cholidis and Martin 2010, 360 | early ninth century: 890–870 (?) | Archaeological context |
| Dornauer 2010, 47–52 | late tenth century – early ninth century | Ductus of inscriptions, esp. in light of more recent discoveries; the red coating of the small orthostats suggests a relatively early dating of the inscriptions. |
| Fuchs 2011, 354 | mid-tenth century (950) | Art is somewhat crude; Kapara's claim to be the first to build such a palace should be believed because of the unskilled execution of the accompanying inscriptions; one of the inscriptions evinces an attempt, albeit half-hearted, to dishonor the memory of Kapara, and this may indicate a violent change of dynasty. |
| Schaudig 2011, 360 | second half of the ninth century during the reign of Šamšī-Adad V (823–811) | Destruction of *Tempelpalast* must date to 759–758 (reign of Aššur-dān III, 772–755) |

> What [my father and my grandfather did not make, namely, statues/columns[88]],
> I [have made].[89]
> [Whoever erases (my) name],
> (and) affix[es] (his) name,
> may he burn [his seven sons in front of Hadad (as a sacrifice)];
> ʿAbd-[ʾilīm,[90] the skilled man, has written].[91]

While the choice to inscribe in cuneiform rather than the linear alphabetic script (cf. the Tell Fakhariya Inscription) is somewhat surprising, the identification of *Pa-le/i$_8$-e* has eluded scholars since the name of such a kingdom is unknown. Moreover, Kapara is not mentioned in any other inscription from the ancient Near East.

Meissner (1933, 75) put forth the hypothesis to see in *Pa-li$_8$-e* the pre-Assyrian name of Gōzān. Another possibility would be to suggest that Kapara was not originally king of Gōzān, but the king of the land of Palē, and that he seized the city at some point. A third possibility would be to see in Palē the name of the area in which the city of Gōzān/Gūzāna was located. But this last option seems very unlikely since the Assyrians never use this designation, instead designating the area starting at the beginning of the ninth century the land of Bīt-Baḫiāni (Sader 1987, 11). Picking up on the second possibility, Lipiński (2000a, 132) has argued that the PA sign should be read BÁ both in the name and the land: hence, *Kabbārāʾ māt Bá-li$_8$-e*. Understanding the E sign as indicating the pharyngeal *ḥ*, he suggests that the land should be identified as "the land of Balīḫ." He speculates that

> Kapara, son of Ḫadyān, was most likely a later successor of Giammu, who was killed by his own subjects when Shalmaneser III was approaching in 853, and he obviously managed to extend Balīḫ's territory to the east in the latter part of Shalmaneser III's reign, probably around 830 B.C.

---

88. Restorations based on the readings of other inscriptions. The statue of a goddess (Meissner 1933, 72–73): Meissner read: DINGIR$^{lim}$ and translated: "die Vergöttlichten (d.h. gestorbenen)," i.e., the divinized dead. However, von Soden (in Moortgat 1955, 20) read: TI.ME = *balṭūte* "lifetime." Postgate (1983–84b) read TI.ME, and suggested understanding this as *timmū* (pl. of *timmu*) "columns." He also restored this in the Sphinx inscription. Sader (1985; 1987, 11) followed von Soden in reading *balṭūte* "lifetime." It is clear that the inscription on a sphinx reads: NA$_4$.NU *ṣalma* (Meissner 1933, 76–77, number IV; Sader 1987, 13, I Ba$_5$). None of these inscriptions claim to have built a palace or a temple.

89. See comments on this sentence below.

90. Phoenician: *ʿbdʾlm*, "servant of the gods." Fales 1998, though this individual is not cited there.

91. The restorations are based on the second text.

This implies that Assyria was not in control of Gōzān/Gūzāna from roughly 830 to 808 BCE, that is, during the reign of Šamšī-Adad V (823–811). This may have been true to some extent, however, there is no actual evidence for this speculation, and particularly that Kapara comes from the land of Balīḫ. The Kurkh Monolith of Shalmaneser III only mentions the cities of Giammu on the Balīḫ River; it does not speak of "a land of Balīḫu" (*a-na* URU.MEŠ-*ni* (79) *ša* m*gi-am-mu* ÍD KASKAL.KUR.A *aq-ṭí-rib*, "I approached the cities of Giammu on the Balīḫ River").[92] There was a Neo-Assyrian city of Balīḫu (URU.*Ba-li-ḫu*) as attested in the stela of Bēlu-lū-balaṭ,[93] the *turtānu*, *rab nāgiru*, and holder of other offices (the eponym for 814 BCE). The problem is he was governor of the city of Tabitu, the city of Harran, the city of Ḫuzīrīna, the city of Dūru of the land of Qipānu, the land of (A)zallu, (and) the city of Balīḫu.[94] This means that Kapara could not be ruling in the city of Balīḫu in 814 BCE and that Bēlu-lū-balaṭ controlled much of the very area that supposedly, according to Lipiński, was the base of Kapara's kingdom, if, in fact, Kapara was from this area.

Of the six suggested dates given above (p. 253), three can be eliminated: the ninth century (no. 2) is too general, and the early and late eighth century (nos. 5 and 6) are too late. What about the other proposed dates? The major sticking point has been how to fit the evidence together with the archaeological phases as envisioned by the original excavators. With the renewed excavations, this may be changing.

It now appears that Langenegger mistook the foundations for Kapara's palace, the *Tempelpalast*, for the remains of an almost identical, antecedent building, which he called the "Altbau" (Langenegger 1950, 30–33). The recent reexamination of the stratigraphy on the site has confirmed that the *Altbau* never existed.[95] This means that the *Tempelpalast* was the result of a

92. See also Zadok (1995, 332): "not Balīḫu."

93. Andrae 1913, no. 44; Millard 1994, 90, s.v. 814; RIMA 3:178, A.0.102.2002.1; Mattila 1999.

94. Lipiński (2000a, 124) locates the city of Balīḫu near the main source of the river, ʿAyn al-ʿArūs, possibly at Tell Abyāḍ (Akçakale). See also Parpola and Porter 2001, map 3.

95. Cholidis (Cholidis and Martin 2010, 69–70) states: "Der Palast, der sich auf einer Substruktion aus Lehmziegeln deutlich über das Stadtgebiet und die Zitadellenbebauung erhob, konnte nur noch in Teilen näher untersucht werden, da die westliche Hälfte bereits stark erodiert war. Entgegen der Annahme von Langenegger haben jüngste Nachuntersuchungen ergeben, dass das Gebäude nicht auf den Mauerstümpfen eines Vorgängerbaus—dem sog. Altbau—errichtet worden war. Gleichwohl belegen einzelne Mauerreste, die bei der Errichtung des Fundamentes durchschlagen worden waren, dass es in diesem Areal eine ältere früheisenzeitliche Bebauung gegeben hat. See also Martin and Fakhru 2009, 19–20, figs. 2–4. The existence of this *Altbau* was also already doubted by Pucci (2008, 95).

single planning and construction effort undertaken during the reign of King Kapara (Gilibert 2013, 42–43). In addition, a closer inspection of the ductus of the cuneiform of Kapara's inscriptions indicates that it is older than the Assyrian ductus of the Tell Fakhariya bilingual that dates to the mid-ninth century (Kaufman 1982, 140); and yet, in light of comparison to the texts from Dunnu-ša-Uzibi (modern Giricano) of the eleventh century, the inscriptions of Kapara appear somewhat later (Dornauer 2010, 51). Moreover, since Kapara's inscriptions on the limestone orthostats were coated with a layer of red coloring that was probably applied already in the original preparation of the orthostats, it is likely that at least these inscriptions of Kapara were produced prior to their use in the construction of the Bīt-Ḫilāni (*Tempelpalast*). This suggests a relatively early dating of the inscriptions (Dornauer 2010, 51).

In 894, Adad-nērārī II mentioned in his annals the receipt of tribute from Abi-salāmu, a man of Bīt-Baḫiāni at the city of Gūzāna (see discussion below). Since Kapara refers to Ḫadiānu as his father and at no point references Baḫiāni, he was not a ruler of an entity named Bīt-Baḫiāni, which was named after the eponymous ancestor of Abi-salāmu, as well as other rulers of this polity mentioned in the inscriptions of Aššurnaṣirpal II for the years 882, and ca. 870. This seems to make a date in the early ninth century (no. 3 above) unlikely.

There is a brief period between 840 and 808 for which there is no documentation for the rulership of Gūzāna. Although this is still a possible period for Kapara's reign (Schaudig 2011), and coincides with a late ninth century (840–810) date (no. 4), it leaves only about twenty to thirty years for the three-generation dynasty of Kapara's grandfather (name unknown), his father Ḫadiānu and Kapara to fit. This does not seem to be enough time to squeeze in these three rulers. It also seems odd that the kingdom is called Palē at this point, instead of Gōzān or Bīt-Baḫiāni.

All this means that a date in the tenth century (no. 1) is the most likely for Kapara's reign. Since Kapara's kingdom is named Palē, with no reference to Baḫiāni, it would seem that Baḫiāni must have been a successor of Kapara (Novák 2009; 2013, 228).

If there were no destruction or prolonged abandonment, and if the *Tempelpalast* was destroyed in 759–758 (as convincingly argued by Schaudig 2011), then this means there was a very extended use of the *Tempelpalast*," namely, over 176 years. However, Gilibert (2013) points out that the facility underwent a number of modifications and so this is not a problem. Table 4.2 presents my understanding of the chronology of Gōzān.

Table 4.2. The Chronology of Gōzān

| | Gōzān/Gūzāna Ruler | Attributed Title/Rank/Designation | Synchronism /Assyrian King |
|---|---|---|---|
| ca. 1125–1000 (?) | East Anatolian "groovy" pottery | | Tiglath-pileser I (1114–1076) |
| ca. 970 (?) | *name unknown*: Kapara's grandfather | | |
| ca. 950 (?) | Ḫadiānu (Ḥadyān) | | |
| ca. 935 (?) | Kapara, son of Ḫadiānu (Ḥaḏyān) | "son of Ḫadiānu, king of Palē(?)" | |
| | other ruler(s)? | | |
| ca. 915 (?) | Baḫiāni | | |
| | other ruler(s)? | | |
| 894 | Abi-salāmu | "son of Baḫiānī" (gentilic: *mār Baḫiāni*) | Adad-nērārī II (911–891) (paid tribute in 894) |
| 882 | *unnamed local ruler* | "son of Baḫiānī" (gentilic: *mār Baḫiāni*) | Aššurnaṣirpal II (883–859) |
| ca. 870 | *unnamed local ruler* | "son of Baḫiānī" (gentilic: *mār Baḫiāni*) | |
| 866 | Šamaš-nūri (eponym in 866, = father of Had(d)-yiṯʿī?) | governor (*šaknu*) of Gūzāna; king (*mlk*) of Gōzān | |
| ca. 850 | Had(d)-yiṯʿī (son of Šamaš-nūri = eponym of 866?) | governor (*šaknu*) of Gūzāna; king (*mlk*) of Gōzān | Shalmaneser III (859–824) |
| 841 | Adad-rēmanni | | |
| | | | Šamšī-Adad V (823–811) |
| 808 | Revolt | | Adad-nērārī III (810–783) |
| 793 | Mannu-kī-māt-Aššur (eponym in 793) | | |
| 763 | Būr-Sagalê (eponym in 763) | governor of Gūzāna | Aššur-dān III (772–755) |
| 759–758 | Revolt suppressed: destruction of "Tempelpalast" | | |
| ca. 750 (?) | Kammaki | scribe, possibly a prince (*rubû*) | |
| 727 | Bēl-Ḫarrān-bēl-uṣur (eponym in 727) | governor of Gūzāna (*šaknu*) | Tiglath-pileser III (744–727) |
| before 705 | Mannu-kī-Aššur-le'ī | governor of Gūzāna | Sargon II (722–705) |
| 706 | Mutakkil-Aššur (eponym in 706) | governor of Gūzāna | |
| 672–669 | Šamaš-amuranni | governor of Gūzāna (*bēl pīḫāti*) | Esarhaddon (680–669) |
| ca. 610 | Nabû-mār-šarri-uṣur | commander-in-chief (*turtānu*) | Aššur-uballiṭ II (?) |

### 4.3.1. Territory

The territory of Gōzān/Bīt-Baḫiāni may possibly be determined by the seated images discovered at Girbel (today Çakır), about 17 km southwest from Kızıltepe (province of Mardin) and at Bozhöyük (Tall Ades), about 50 km southwest from Kızıltepe (Schachner, Schachner, and Karabulut 2002). Four statues of seated figures in the Syro-Hittite style (one found at Bozhöyük and three at Girbel) served undoubtedly as funerary monuments (*Grabdenkmäler*). They evince very close stylistic and iconographic similarities to funerary monuments from Tell Ḥalaf, indicating a date in the tenth and early ninth century BCE.[96]

In the Tell Fakhariya bilingual inscription, the Assyrian version states "The statue of Adad-it'i, governor of Gūzāna, Sikānu, and Zarānu," while the Aramaic version states: "The statue of Had(d)-yiṯʿī, the king of Gōzān, and of Sikan, and of Azran" (*ṣlm . hdysʿy* (13) *mlk . gwzn . wzy . skn . wzy . ʾzrn*).[97] It is clear that the city of Zarānu/'Azran was an important city, perhaps on a par with Gōzān and Sikan. This city is also mentioned in a letter to Sargon II from Mannu-kī-Aššur-le'ī, governor of Gūzāna in the late 700s.[98] The location of this city, however, is still unknown (Lipiński 2000a, 123–24). Other towns are also mentioned in this letter and were likely located near Gōzān. Apparently, the city of Maʿallānā (*Mʿlnh, Ma'allanate*), the probable site where the seventh-century, bilingual Assyrian-Aramaic archive of the Gōzān-Harran area was located, is also still not known (Lipiński 2000a, 124–26).

### 4.3.2. History

The area around Tell Ḥalaf may have been lost to the Arameans at or just after the time of Aššur-bēl-kala. Prior to this, there may have been some type of Anatolian village at the site, based on the presence of the groovy pottery. In the early tenth century or slightly earlier, one should fit the three generation dynasty of Kapara, and his father Ḫadiānu (Ḥaḏyān), and grandfather (name unknown). It is not known whether Kapara's grandfather or father actually ruled at Tell Ḥalaf, though it is certainly a possibility. Some of the earlier structures at the site may have been their residences.

However, it was Kapara who conducted a massive building program that saw the construction of the *Tempelpalast*, Kapara's palace, to which the

96. Dornauer (2010, 50 n. 97) suggests that these give indication of the extent of the land of Palē.

97. Abou-Assaf, Bordreuil, and Millard 1982: Assyrian: lines 19–20; Aramaic: lines 12b–13a.

98. SAA 1:182, 233.16 URU.*za-ra-na* (also line 8 restored).

inscriptions mentioned above attest. This facility (*bīt-ḫilāni*) communicated power to his internal (i.e., his domestic) audience (Osborne 2012). It is an imposing structure, overshadowing its immediate surroundings. It functioned as a landmark, being visible from well beyond the surrounding city walls, even shaping the skyline of the city from faraway. The building had emotional impact on its observers (Gilibert 2013, 40).

In a stimulating article, Gilibert (2013, 36) has recently suggested that "the Palace of Kapara served as "theatre palace," an architectural device for spectacular practices in which place, performance and public were intimately bound together. Yet, it served as a royal mausoleum where performances of the cult of the royal ancestors took place.[99]

To the northwest of the temple-palace, the first excavators discovered two crypts. The southernmost (Tomb 1) was an arched vault tomb of a monarch.[100] The entrance faced east and was bricked up after the funeral with a threshold where ancestor cult rituals were held. Fortunately, the tomb had not been robbed in antiquity. The body of the deceased was positioned with the head facing east (Niehr 2006, 123). Thus, the construction and body positioning speak clearly to a solar component in the cult. Gilibert (2013, 52) suggests that, given the high status of this tomb in its apparent context, this may very well be the tomb of Kapara.[101]

In any case, the *Tempelpalast* of Kapara served as a statement of the power of this polity, and was, no doubt, because it could be seen from afar, a major attraction for the Neo-Assyrian kings who desired the tribute that could be extracted from this kingdom. It also explains why its destruction was perhaps so important in 759–758 when Assyrian building phase started.

It is not known when Baḫiāni took control of this kingdom, but this man was the eponymous ancestor to at least three, perhaps five, later rulers (e.g., Abi-salāmu, see below). The polity was known by the Assyrians as Bīt-Baḫiāni.

What may be one of the earliest Old Aramaic inscriptions was found on a small limestone object from Tell Ḥalaf. Paleographically, it appears to date

99. Gilibert 2013, 50–54. She rejects the usual interpretation of the triad of caryatids at the front of the *Tempelpalast* as a triad of deities, since the two male figures wear a horned crown and all three stand on the back of a lion or of a bull (Orthmann 2002, 68). Instead, she suggests that the Palace caryatids are images of deceased members of the royal dynasty, the center one being Kapara (Gilibert 2013, 50–51). Contrast Novák (2013, 298–99) who states: "The area became the building ground for a representative palace in the western Syrian '*Hilani* style,' decorated with huge caryatide statues of the main deities at its entrance and a large number of relief slabs along the south and north façades."

100. Oppenheim 1931, 192–94; Langenegger 1950, 100–103; Naumann 1950, 394; Orthmann 2002, 47–49.

101. However, contrast the assessment of Novák 2013, 298–99.

to the late tenth to early ninth century.[102] However, it is unclear as to what the piece's exact function was. It is commonly referred to as the Tell Ḥalaf Altar Inscription, but the object could be the base or pedestal of a statue or a stela.[103] The reading and interpretation of the inscription are also difficult.[104] Nevertheless, there is general agreement between scholars that the inscription speaks of "this image" (*zdmt*) which is followed by a personal name, a relative clause (*zy*) with perhaps another personal name.[105]

In 894 BCE, Adad-nērārī II (911–891 BCE) expanded his rule over territory in the western Upper Ḫābūr. His annals state:

> I crossed the Ḫābūr River; I marched to the city of Gūzāna which Abi-salāmu, a man of Bīt-Baḫiāni, held. I entered the city of Sikānu which lies at the source of the Ḫābūr River. By the exalted strength of Šamaš, lord of my diadem, who loves my priesthood, I received from him: his numerous chariots, teams of horses, silver, gold, the property of his palace. I imposed upon him tribute.[106]

Gōzān's ruler, Abi-salāmu,[107] is designated a man of Bīt-Baḫiāni (DUMU *ba-ḫi-a-ni*).[108] Adad-nērārī II chose to enter the city of Sikan (Tell Fakhariya), only a few kilometers away from Gōzān. This may have had to do with the fact, as noted in the text, that it was the "source" of the Ḫābūr River, always an important point to reach for Assyrian monarchs.[109] According to the Aramaic version of the Tell Fakhariya bilingual inscription, this was the home of the deity:

> Hadad of Sikan: the controller of water in heaven and earth (*gwgl . šmyn . wʾrq*), who brings down wealth, and gives pasture and watered ground to

---

102. This means that from this time on the linear alphabet was in use alongside the cuneiform scribal tradition at Tell Ḥalaf.

103. Schwiderski 2004, 197. Friedrich, Meyer, Ungnad and Weidner 1940, 69; Lipiński 1994, 15.

104. Works on the inscription prior to the new edition of Dankwarth and Müller (1988) can be disregarded because they were not based on the photos and squeeze that Dankwarth and Müller used.

105. Dankwarth and Müller: (1) *zdmt* (2) *bʿm*[x] (3) *zy* (4) *k* (*z*) [...]*ḥy* [ ... ] [(5) leer]. "Dieses (ist das) Bild des (st. c.) PN/GN?, welches (+Verbalform) PN?"; Lipiński (1994, 15): (1) *z dmt* (2) *pʿm*[*y*] (3) *zy* (4) *klḥy* [| *hw*?] "This is the figurine of Piġami, who is a man from Kalḫu"; and Cross (1) *zdmt* | *bʿm*[*r*] (2) | *zy* | *knn* [|] (3) *ḥy*[ ] (4) [ ] "This is the image of Bʿm[r?] which Ḥayya [ ... ]set up." See Cross 1995, 397.

106. RIMA 2:153, A.0.99.2, lines 100b–104.

107. "The father is peace" or "Shalom is [my] father." See Brinkman 1998. Cf. ʾ*byšlwm* and ʾ*bšlwm* in the Hebrew Bible.

108. For the formulation, see the discussion of the terminology in chapter 2.

109. For the importance of the Tigris source, see Schachner 2009.

> all lands, and gives prosperity and offering to all the gods, his brothers; the controller of all rivers (*gwgl . nhr . klm*), who makes all the lands luxuriant, compassionate god, to whom one's prayer is good, who dwells in Sikan (*ysb* (6) *skn*), ... the Lord of the Ḫābūr (*mr*ʾ . *ḥbwr*).[110]

Thus this was apparently an important cult center for a significant deity. Receiving the tribute in the cult center of Sikan would have also provided the occasion for a loyalty oath to be sworn in the presence of the local storm god. This is demonstrated in a text from the reign of the next Assyrian monarch, Tukulti-Ninurta II, who had Amme-ba'li, the ruler of Bīt-Zamāni—along with apparently his magnates—swear this oath by Aššur, the Assyrian deity, before the statue of, most likely, Adad, the storm god:

> "If you (plural: *attunu*) give horses to my enemies (or) my allies, may the god Adad [strike your] land with dangerous lightning."[111]

But there may have been a symbolic move as well in Adad-nērārī's choice to enter this city over against Gōzān. If, in fact, Sikānu had been the earlier Mittanian capital city and the Middle Assyrian provincial capital, Wa/Aššukanni,[112] then this may have also served as a statement of reaffirmation of Assyrian domination of the region—another way of "restoring" the former Middle Assyrian Empire.

Finally, a third reason was a matter of military practicality. The Assyrian army avoided frontal attacks on heavily fortified capital cities, if possible (Fuchs 2008b). When one of the Aramean capitals would submit without a long siege, this opportunity was quickly grasped.

Abi-salāmu gave Adad-nērārī II a rich tribute. While up to 894, this Aramean polity had been independent, it appears that the campaigns of Adad-nērārī II against the Temanites and the gift of Bīt-Adīni convinced Abi-salāmu that submission was the better decision rather than opposing the Assyrians. The conquest of Naṣībīna meant that Gōzān, no matter how strong, could not withstand an Assyrian siege. Furthermore, Abi-salāmu may have been intimidated by what had happened to Nūr-Adad.

This policy of submission appears to have been in force during the reign of Adad-nērārī II's son Tukulti-Ninurta II. In 885, after his tribute-collecting Ḫābūr River "campaign," Tukulti-Ninurta II left Naṣībīna and traveled to Ḫuzīrīna (Sultantepe)[113] bypassing Gōzān. The lack of mention of Gōzān or

110. Lines 2–6, 16.
111. RIMA 1:172, A.0.100.5, lines 24b–25.
112. See pp. 243–44 and chapter 3 for dicussion.
113. See discussion above, pp. 234–37.

Bīt-Baḫiāni seems to indicate that this Aramean polity was paying its regular tribute.

The same rationale that caused Bīt-Baḫiāni's submission in the days of Adad-nērārī II was likely operative in 882 BCE. Aššurnaṣirpal II, Tukulti-Ninurta II's son, had campaigned extensively in Nairi and had just finished a brutal subjugation of Bīt-Zamāni. Then Aššurnaṣirpal recorded:

> At that time, I received tribute from Aḫi-ramu, the man of Bīt-Yaḫiri, the Zallean (i.e., a chief of the Azallu); the man of Bīt-Baḫiāni, the Hittite; and the kings of Ḫanigalbat: silver, gold, tin, bronze casseroles, oxen, sheep, (and) horses.[114]

There are three problems in this short passage. First, the number of entities paying tribute. The text reads: *ina* $u_4$*-me-šú-ma ma-da-tu* ⁽²²⁾*šá* ᵐ*a-ḫi-ra-mu* DUMU *ia-ḫi-ri šá* KUR *zal-la-a-a* DUMU *ba-ḫi-a-ni* KUR *ḫat-ta-a-a ù* MAN.MEŠ-*ni šá* KUR *ḫa-ni-gal-bat ... ma-da-ta-šú-nu am-ḫur*. Grayson indicates by his translation[115] that there are five tributaries: "At that time, I received tribute from (1) Aḫi-ramu, a man of Bīt-Yaḫiri, from (2) the (A)zallean, (3) a man of Bīt-Baḫiāni, (4) men of Ḫatti, and (from) (5) the kings of the land of Ḫanigalbat ..." On the other hand, Liverani (1992a, 43–44) would see only three tributaries mentioned: "At that time, I received the tribute of (1) Aḫi-ramu, the man of Bīt-Yaḫiri, the Zallean, (2) the man of Bīt-Baḫiāni, the Hittite, and (3) the kings of Ḫanigalbat...." It would seem that (*ša*) DUMU X (*ša*) KUR *Hat-ta-a-a* is a parallel formulation to *šá* DUMU X *šá* KUR *Zal-la-a-a*, though in the former the *ša* was elided (Liverani 1992a, 44). If this is correct, then there are two double specifications here: Aḫi-ramu, who belonged to "Bīt-Yaḫiri" (Aramean tribal designation) and the "Zallean" (gentilic designation); paralleled by an *unnamed ruler*, who belonged to "Bīt-Baḫiāni" (Aramean tribal designation) and the Hittite (gentilic designation).[116] Regarding this last double specification "the man of Bīt-Baḫiāni, the Hittite," Fales (2011a, 220) has recently remarked that this may reflect the mixed culture at Gōzān:

114. RIMA 2:203, A.0.101.1, ii.21b–23a.

115. RIMA 2:203.

116. Liverani 1992a, 43; Dion 1997, 45. This should not be linked with the outdated and impossible reading of the king of Ḫatti in the Kapara inscription as Albright suggested. See Albright 1956b, 81–83. The reason that this view should be rejected lies in the reading itself, not in the use or lack of use of the *ša* (*pace* Sader 1987, 7). However, Aššurnaṣirpal II's use of *ša* does not correspond necessarily to Sader's objection. See e.g., RIMA 2:202, A.0.101.1, ii.12–14.

> So wird z.B. Gūzāna (das heutige Tell Halaf), das schon im 10. Jh. als befestigte Stadt mit gemischter Kultur (luwischer und aramäischer) gegründet worden war, zum urbanen Kern der politischen Gruppe von Bit-Bahjāni, obgleich die Erinnerung an die Vergangenheit mit dem Adjektiv "hethitisch" (*Ḫattajju*), das den Herrscher beschreibt, erhalten bleibt.

Certainly, the cremation practices at Tell Ḥalaf and the *Grabdenkmäler* found at and around Tell Ḥalaf may point to this mixed culture. Perhaps, the "groovy pottery" may also be an indicator.[117] Thus, it appears that at least in the ninth century, from the Assyrian perspective, the region of "Greater" *māt Ḫatti* began at borders of Bīt-Baḫiāni so that the subjugation of this land was a key bridgehead for Assyrian control of the western Jezirah (Dornauer 2010, 55).

The second problem is the meaning of the designation "Zallean." Do Azallu, Izalla, and Zalla refer to the same entity? Some scholars do not accept this equation.[118] On the other hand, other scholars equate these (Liverani 1992a, 34–35, 43–44; Postgate 1976–80c). Izalla—located in the Ṭūr ʿAbdīn or part of it—was apparently well-known for its wine as suggested by classical and Syriac sources (Dion 1997, 44–49).

The third problem is the identity of the unnamed Aramean ruler of Bīt-Baḫiāni (Gōzān). Perhaps on the basis of the Tell Fakhariya bilingual inscription (Aramaic-Akkadian),[119] one might surmise that it was Šamaš-nūri, the father of Had(d)-yiṯʿī (*hdysʿy*/$^{m}$10-*it*-*ʾi*). If the Tell Fakhariya Inscription dates to the mid-ninth century (ca. 850), then Šamaš-nūri would have ruled ca. 885–855(?), and would hence be a contemporary of Aššurnaṣirpal II. Philological arguments based on the cuneiform inscription speak for dating the bilingual to the middle of ninth century.[120] The fact that the eponym for Aššurnaṣirpal's eighteenth regnal year (866) was a Šamaš-nūri would strengthen this possibility. Furthermore, the fact that the governors of Gūzāna held the eponymate for the eighteenth regnal years of later Assyrian kings makes it very tempting to suppose that Šamaš-nūri, the governor of Gūzāna, mentioned in the Tell Fakhariya Inscription, was the

117. However, it should also be considered that the term "Hittite" is being used as a pejorative.

118. For example, see Parpola and Porter 2001, map 3: Izalla (D3), (the Ṭūr ʿAbdīn) and Azallu (C4) (between Bīt-Baḫiāni and Bīt-Adīni).

119. *COS* 2.34:153–54.

120. First, the use of the sign SAG with the value *šak* does not occur in Assyrian royal inscriptions before the time of Aššurnaṣirpal II; second, the writing RÉM-*ú* = *rēmēnu* is a feature of Aššurnaṣirpal's texts, and third, the phrase DINGIR RÉM-*li šá si-pu-šú* DÙG.GA is found in Aššurnaṣirpal's texts. See Abou-Assaf, Bordreuil, and Millard 1982, 22. See also Grayson, RIMA 2:390.

eponym for 866 BCE.[121] It is possible that this unnamed ruler of Bīt-Baḫiāni (Gōzān) who pays tribute in 882 BCE was a ruler just prior to Šamaš-nūri, even if the individual of the eponym for the eighteenth regnal year is the same person as the father of Had(d)-yiṯʿî of the Tel Fakhariya Inscription. However, it seems more likely that the unnamed ruler is Šamaš-nūri.[122]

In the Aramaic version of the inscription, both Had(d)-yiṯʿî and his father Šamaš-nūri are designated as "king of Gōzān (*mlk . gwzn*)," while in the Akkadian version they are both called "governor of the city of Gūzāna (GAR.KUR URU.*gu-za-ni*)." This implies that Bīt-Baḫiāni (Gōzān) became an Assyrian province under Aššurnaṣirpal II (sometime around 870 BCE).

Aššurnaṣirpal's eleventh campaign (see table 4.4)[123] is not dated in his annals but likely occurred between 875 and 867 BCE, often rounded by scholars to 870 BCE. The text relates:

> In the month of Ayyāru (Iyyar) on the eighth day, I departed from Kalḫu. I crossed the Tigris; I took the road for the city of Karkamiš of the land Ḫatti. I approached Bīt-Baḫiāni (É *ba-ḫi-a-ni*). I received tribute from the man of Bīt-Baḫiāni: harnessed chariots, horses, silver, gold, tin, bronze, (and) bronze casseroles. I took with me the chariots, cavalry, (and) infantry of Bīt-Baḫiāni. I departed from Bīt-Baḫiāni. I approached the land of Azallu. I received tribute from Adda-imme, the (A)zallean: harnessed chariots, horses, silver, gold, tin, bronze, bronze casseroles, oxen, sheep, (and) wine. I took with me the chariots, cavalry, (and) infantry. I departed from the land of Azallu.[124]

---

121. If one considers all the eponym lists in which a governor of Gūzāna appears, the governor of Gūzāna follows almost always the governor of Tušḫan (in the seventeenth position) in the sequence of eponym officials. See Dornauer 2010, 66–67, table I. It is therefore plausible that Šamaš-nūri of the eponym lists who was governor of Gūzāna in 866 should be identified with the Šamaš-nūri of the Tell Fakhariya Inscription. For the eponym lists, see Millard 1994, 10. See also Abou-Assaf, Bordreuil, and Millard 1982, 103–5. The Akkadian version of the inscription has $^{md}$UTU.ZÁLAG; the Aramaic has *ssnwry*.

122. Had(d)-yiṯʿî's name is Aramaic. His father's name, Šamaš-nūri "Šamaš is my light," is usually analyzed as Akkadian. But it is possible to analyze the name as Aramaic, since both components are found in Aramaic personal names. A possible analogy can be seen in the name from the Tell Ḥalaf-Harran region, Śahrnūri (*šhrnwry*). See Lipiński 2010, 278 (list of occurrences).

123. Or in Liverani's scheme (1992a), campaign IX. Some scholars believe that this campaign divides into two campaigns (Brinkman 1968, 393–94; Grayson 1976, 138–40; Yamada 2000a, 74–75; Na'aman 2002b, 293). Other scholars argue against dividing up the narrative, e.g., Schramm 1973, 27–29; Hawkins 1982, 388 with n. 135; Liverani 1992a, 73 n. 336 and 119 n. 475. In her discussion of the problem, de Filippi (1977, 27–30) chose to keep the question open.

124. The campaign is found in RIMA 2:216–19, A.0.101.1, iii.56b–92a.

Again, as in the previous passage, it seems likely that Šamaš-nūri is the unnamed "man of Bīt-Baḫiāni."

In some senses, this campaign is more like a "reconnaissance in force," and much of the expedition is on the whole peaceful (at least as the "annals" present it; Liverani 1988a, 85). It began with a march to the Euphrates with Karkamiš as its initial objective, following the main route that took the army through Gōzān. Aššurnaṣirpal II received the tribute from "the man of Bīt-Baḫiāni" (DUMU *ba-ḫi-a-ni*). He then marched west to the land of Azallu (KUR *a-zal-li*) and received the tribute of Adda-imme, the Zallean (i.e., a chief of Azallu).[125] Interestingly, both lands supply Aššurnaṣirpal with "chariots, cavalry, (and) infantry," no doubt as part of their client-oath obligations.

Fig. 4.5. The Tell Fakhariya Inscription

Since the anonymous "man of Bīt-Baḫiāni in the inscriptions of Aššurnaṣirpal II paid *maddattu* "tribute," a form of levy required of independent political organizations that are Assyrian clients, this may indicate the still independent character of Gōzān at this time. Furthermore, the fact that no conquest of Bīt-Baḫiāni is reported in the Assyrian royal inscriptions is probably due to the fact that there never was a conquest. The annexation of Gūzāna into the Assyrian provincial system appears to have been more or less bloodless.

Unfortunately, the king/governor of Gōzān/Gūzāna, Hadad-yis'ī/Had(d)-yiṯ'ī/Adad-it'i, is not mentioned in any other texts which would permit a clear identification and dating. In part due to this, Lipiński (2000a, 129) has speculated:

125. See discussion of Azallu in §4.4 below.

> One might surmise that the eponym of the eighteenth year of Shalmaneser III, i.e. 841 B.C., was Hadd-yiṯʻi whose name means "Haddu is my help." In fact, the Akkadian name of the eponym of 841 is dIM-ARḪUŠ-*ni*, i.e. *Adad-rēmanni*, what means "Adad, show pity on me!" This quite common type of Akkadian proper names may have been used as an Assyrian adaptation of Hadd-yiṯʻi's Aramaic name. Incidentally, no other eponym of that period bears a name with the theophorous element Hadd/Adad.

The argument is that Adad-rēmanni and Had(d)-yiṯʻî are the same person. This is argued as a possibility for three reasons: because Adad-rēmanni is a good translation of the Aramaic Had(d)-yiṯʻî[126]; both Šamaš-nūri and Adad-rēmanni were governors of Gūzāna and eponyms; and chronologically it seems to work. Dornauer (2010, 57) concludes:

> Hadd-yiṯ'i [*sic*] und Adad-rēmanni waren beide etwa gleichzeitig Statthalter von Gūzāna beziehungsweise Bēt-Baḫiāni. Entweder war Adad-rēmanni also ein Nachfolger des Hadd-yiṯ'i, oder es handelt sich bei Hadd-yiṯ'i und Adad-rēmanni um ein und dieselbe Person. Letzteres ist meines Erachtens wahrscheinlicher.[127]

Unfortunately, this is not as straightforward as it seems. First of all, it is true that Adad-rēmanni was very likely the governor of Gūzāna. Finkel and Reade (1998, 249) note that Adad-rēmanni was either governor of Tamnuna or governor of Gūzāna since the reading preserves the end of his province's name: [...]-*na*, which would suggest Gūzāna, particularly since the written evidence for a province of Tamnuna appears to begin only in 785 and thus making it unlikely that Tamnuna was a province in 841.[128] Furthermore, the normal order of the eponyms by province would suggest that Gūzāna is the province in view in 841.

The real crux is the personal name. If Adad-rēmanni is really a match for Had(d)-yiṯʻî, then the identification is possible, though not proven. The name *hdysʻy* (Had(d)-yiṯ'î) is clearly an Aramaic name of the pattern "DN is my Y" where the Y is the noun from the root *yṯʿ/yšʿ*, thus "Hadad is my deliverance/salvation." The name Had(d)-yiṯʻî is now found in an Old Aramaic contract in the Louvre (AO 29696), where it is written: *hdyšʿy* (Bordreuil 1993b, 265–66; Lemaire 2001c, 120–25). Thus the only difference is orthro-

126. Argued by Dornauer 2010, 57.

127. "Hadd-yiṯʻi and Adad-rēmanni were both approximately governor of Gūzāna or Bīt-Baḫiāni at the same time. Either Adad-rēmanni was a successor to the Hadd-yiṯʻi, or Hadd-yiṯʻi and Adad-rēmanni are one and the same person. The latter is more likely in my opinion."

128. Radner 2006–8a, 56, s.v. 38. Tamnunu.

graphic: *s* (Tell Fakhariya) and *š* (the Louvre AO.29696), with both letters standing for the phoneme *ṯ*. This name is the name of the father of a witness: *tkltšr br hdyšʿy* "Tukulti-šarru, son of Had(d)-yiṯʿî." The identification of this person with the king of the Tell Fakhariya statue is out of the question due to the date of the tablet.[129] The name *hdyšʿ* is also attested as the first in a list of witnesses in a sale of barley recorded on a clay tablet in the musée Champollion (Figeac).[130] The same components of this name occur in the cuneiform writing of the name Adda-iata' (mdIM-*ia-ta-a*', m10-*ia-t*[*a-a*']).[131]

On the other hand, Adad-rēmanni is an Akkadian name of a different pattern meaning, "O Adad, have mercy or compassion on me!"[132] The two names do not match. The Akkadian scribes were entirely capable of translating the Aramaic name into Akkadian: Adad-it'i (as in the Akkadian version of the bilingual; Schwemer 1998c). Therefore, it is likely that Adad-rēmanni is a different individual from Hadad-yisʿi/Adad-it'i. Moreover, there is more than enough time between the Tell Fakhariya Inscription and the 841 eponym date for another individual, namely, Adad-rēmanni, to fit into the chronology. There are twenty-five years between Šamaš-nūri (866) and Adad-rēmanni (841), which is more than adequate time for Hadad-yiṯʿî to be king/governor of Gōzān/Gūzāna before Adad-rēmanni served. Hence, it is more likely that they are not the same person and that Adad-rēmanni followed Had(d)-yiṯʿî.

It has also been recently argued that neither Šamaš-nūri nor Had(d)-yiṯʿî were native rulers of a local Aramaic dynasty; instead they were well-to-do Assyrian officials, father and son (Dornauer 2010, 58). This seems contradicted by the Aramaic personal name Had(d)-yiṯʿî (see above). If the man's name was Adad-rēmanni, why write it as Had(d)-yiṯʿî and Adad-it'i? In addition, the fact that he calls himself *mlk gwzn* would seem to be out of place if he is an Assyrian official appointed by the Assyrian king. It seems very likely that an Assyrian official would give a better indication of this situation in his inscription. It is far better to see Šamaš-nūri and Had(d)-yiṯʿî as native dynasts who were given status as provincial governors. The proper analogy from the Ḫābūr region would be the kingdom of Ṭābētu and Māri, or the kingdom of Šadikanni, where local rulers were incorporated into the provincial system, probably with little real choice, though it may have been to their individual advantage.

Another interesting proposal has been made by Dion (1997, 46). He has suggested that the individual named Itti' of (A)zallu, who paid tribute to

129. Lemaire 2001c, 123: late eighth century; see now Bordreuil 2012, 92: the third quarter of the seventh century.

130. Lemaire 2001c, 46–50; Lemaire 2010, 191–95, and fig. 1 (photos).

131. Schwemer 1998d. Zadok 1977, 201. Tell Fakhariya: m10-*it-'i*.

132. This name is attested in Aramaic as *'drmny*. See Maraqten 1988, 30.

Aššurnaṣirpal II in 866,[133] should be identified with (Adad)-it'i of Gūzāna and Sikan of the Tell Fakhariya Inscription. Hence, Had(d)-yiṯ'î ruled at the same time in Azallu, while his father Šamaš-nūri was ruler in Gōzān. But the name is written with a doubled /t/: <sup>m</sup>*it-ti-ʾi* which raises significant doubts about this suggestion.[134]

After the apparent governorship of Adad-rēmanni around 841 BCE, there is no mention of Gūzāna in the Assyrian texts until the Eponym Chronicle notes for the year 808 in its typical brief form: "to the city of Gūzāna" (*a-na* URU.*gu-za-na*; Millard 1994, 33). Such a brief notice after a long lacuna makes it very difficult to know what the exact circumstances were that caused the Assyrian action in 808. Some have taken this as an indication that Gōzān was out of Assyrian hands for a number of years preceding this reconquest (Lipiński 2000a, 133). Some scholars have placed the reign of Kapara in this time period, though this is probably not correct (see discussion above). It has also been suggested that the Assyrian action of 808 was simply putting down a revolt that occurred when Adad-nērārī III came to the throne in 810 BCE, and that Gūzāna had not been involved in the great civil war (826–820) at the time of Šamšī-Adad V (Dornauer 2010, 59). Without further data, it is impossible to know.

What is clear is that the territory of Gūzāna became once again a province, administered by Mannu-kī-māt-Aššur (Baker 2001a; minimum: 793–783), whose archive has been recovered. He was followed by Būr-Sagalê, who was eponym in 763 during the reign of Aššur-dān III. The name Būr-Sagalê is Aramaic meaning "son of Sagalê."[135] A few years later (759–758) a revolt in Gūzāna was suppressed.

In 1999, a seated statue with an inscription from this period was found during construction work in the area of Tell Ḥalaf (Röllig 2003). When the inscription was published, the upper part of the statue was missing. That a bust of a man with an Assyrian-style beard, discovered in the early excavations of Tell Ḥalaf, is a match for the lower part of the statue with inscription

133. For the passage, see the next section below, p. 273.

134. Dion (1997, 47) minimizes this stating: "mais cela n'a rien de plus grave que, par exemple, l'omission de la syllabe initiale *It-* dans la version akkadienne *Tu-ba-a-lu*$_4$ du nom d'Ittobaal, roi de Sidon." However, this is not a convincing argument since in the case of אתבעל, there was probably a simple apheresis of the *aleph* in the Phoenician name that preceded in the cuneiform form *Tu-ba-a-lu*$_4$, whereas in the case of Itti' there is an extra *t* added to the root, if the name Had(d)-iṯ'î is the name from which the second component (Aramaic *yšʿ*) is being shortened. Moreover, the first component of the Phoenician name * אִתּוֹבַּעַל "with him is Ba'al" is a different component than the second component in the name Had(d)-iṯ'i.

135. Brinkman 1999. During this year, there was a revolt in Assur and a near-total solar eclipse.

cannot be ruled out.[136] On the basis of its inscription, it represents the figure of Kammaki,[137] a scribe (LÚ.A.BA), who may have been a prince of the royal family of Gūzāna (although this is not absolutely certain).[138] The statue can be dated to the middle of the eighth century (ca. 750 BCE). Since Kammaki holds a cup in his right hand for libations, the statue, like earlier types from Tell Ḥalaf, was connected to the ancestor cult. The inscription (DeZ 7970) reads:

> (1) NU $^{m}$*Kam-ma-ki* A $^{m}$DINGIR-ZU LÚ.A.BA
> (2) *man-nu* NUN-*u* EGIR-*u* LÚ.ZA.DÍM! (3) *la ta-da-ki*
> *ik-kib* $^{d}$EN.ME.ŠARA

> (1) The image of Kammaki, son of Ilu-lē'i, the scribe.
> (2) Whoever is a later prince, (3) may you not muster (2) a stone mason,
> (3) interdict of the god Enmešarra!

What is particularly interesting here is that the deity invoked is not Hadad, the storm god, as one might expect from the Tell Fakhariya and Kapara Inscriptions, but Enmešarra, whose name means "Lord of all the rites," and who was a chthonic deity, the ancestor of Enlil and lord of the underworld. A *pitiqtu*-ritual (Borger 1971) that includes a incantation invoking Enmešarra is, I believe, very informative (only the incantation relating to Enmešarra is included here):

> MAŠ-MAŠ ŠU NUN DIB-*ma*
> *ki-a-am* DUG$_4$-GA
> (42) ÉN $^{d}$*En-me-šár-ra*

> EN KI-*tim* NUN *šá A-ra-*⸢*al*⸣ ⸢*li*⸣ (43) EN *áš-ri u Kur-nu-gi*$_4$ *šá-du-ú šá* $^{d}$*A-nun-na-ki* (44) *pa-ri-is* EŠ-BAR KI-*tim mar-kás* GAL-*ú šá An-durun-na* (45) EN GAL-*ú šá ina ba-li-šú* $^{d}$*Nin-gír-su* AŠ-GÁN(Borger: IKU) *u pal-gi* (46) *la uš-te-eš-še-ru la i-ban-nu-ú ab-še-na*

> (47) EN *ú-ma-ši šá ina dan-nu-ti-šú* KI-*tim i-bé-lu* (48) RAB *šá-*⸢*piṭ*⸣ *dan-ni-nu ṣa-bit kip-pat ki-gal-li* (49) *na-din* GIŠ.GIDRI *u* BALA *ana* $^{d}$*A-nu u* $^{d}$*En-lil* (50) *áš-ri šá-a-šú ina qí-bi-ti-ka te-me-en-šú* (51) *ina mah-ri-ka li-bur*

> IM-DÙ-A BI (52) GIM *šu-bat be-lu-ti-ka ina* KI-*tim lu* DI(read *ki*)*-na-át*

> The *mašmašu* (incantation priest) takes the hand of the prince

---

136. See photo in Cholidis 2010, 251, fig. IX.23.

137. There are some difficulties with this name, see Röllig 2003, 422.

138. The clause in line 2, *mannu rubû* "Whoever is a later prince," may be simply formulaic, not strictly literal.

and speaks as follows:
Incantation: Enmešarra,

lord of the Earth (Underworld), prince of Aralli (the Netherworld), lord of the Place (heaven/sky?)[139] and the Kurnugû (Netherworld), mountain of the Anunnaki, the decider of decisions for the Earth (Underworld), great link of Andurunna, great lord, without whom Ningirsu could not keep the dykes and channels in good condition, (and) grass seed is not created.

Strong lord, who in his strength rules the Earth (Underworld), neck stock who judges the Netherworld, holder of the circle of the (foundation of the) Underworld, granter of scepter and rule to Anu and Enlil, may the foundation of this place according to your order stay in good repair in your presence.

May this mud-brick wall be as firmly grounded in the Earth as the seat of your lordship.

Horowitz (1998, 361) comments on this text: "The only known evidence for the shape of the underworld is found in the epithet of Enmešarra *ṣābit kippat kigalli* 'Holder of the Circle of the Underworld.' If 'circle' in this context can be taken literally, then this epithet reveals that the underworld, like the heavens and earth's surface, was circular in shape." Finally, it is important to note that the Sebettu (Pleiades) are Enmešarra's seven sons and that Enmešarra was associated with the constellation Auriga. Thus it is really not so surprising that Enmešarra is invoked in the curse formula of Kammaki.[140]

In 727, Bēl-Ḫarrān-bēl-uṣur, governor of Gūzāna, was eponym during the reign of Tiglath-pileser III. Mannu-kī-Aššur-le'ī (Jursa 2001), who was eponym in 709 (being governor of Tillē), was governor of Gūzāna before 705 (during the reign of Sargon II, 722–705 BCE). In 706, Mutakkil-Aššur was governor of Gūzāna and eponym.

In a long and difficult letter from the reign of Esarhaddon,[141] there is fascinating insight into the dynamics of governance, in particular the role of the elders of Gūzāna. The letter contains a warning to the king about a number of crimes being committed in Gūzāna by six men and a woman, servants of the local governor, as well as the corruption of the governor himself. Among their crimes, they have falsified a legal document, abused the royal stamp-seal, taken a bribe, violated a religious item, and acted rebelliously. Šamaš-amuranni, the governor of Gūzāna, ordered the elders of the

139. Horowitz (1998, 225) states: "Akkadian *ašru* is a poetic name for heaven … In the incantation to Enmešarra, *ašru* is paired with the underworld name, *kurnugû*."

140. Van der Toorn 1996, 159; Black and Green 1992, 76–77; Livingstone 1986, 153.

141. SAA 16:58–62, text 63. The text seems to date from 672–669 (see introductory comments in SAA 16:xxx–xxxi). See also the comments of Barjamovic 2004, 87.

city to assemble in front of the palace of the crown prince, asking them: "To whom are you [devoted]." Adda-sakâ, a chariot-driver (and apparently one of the elders), answered the governor: "Tell us, why do you ask us? Ask our sons!" But the governor replied: "It is you I have asked, so tell me!" They said in unison: "(Although) we have eaten a slice of our sons and daughters ... we keep the t[reaty of the king]; we are devoted to Esarhaddon." At this, the governor threw the scepter from his hands in apparent disgust that they refuse to support him and yells some kind of rebuke at them (the text is fragmentary and difficult at this point). While the letter is clearly biased against the current leadership in Gūzāna, it is an important example of the political power of the elders.

Finally, Nabû-mār-šarri-uṣur, the commander-in-chief (*turtānu*) who is a postcanonical eponym of the year 611/610 (reign of Aššur-uballiṭ II?), is attested in the date formulae of documents from Gūzāna (only one instance with his title).[142]

## 4.4. Azallu, Bīt-Yaḫiri

Early in his campaign of 882 BCE (see table 4.4), Aššurnaṣirpal II claimed, "At that time, I received tribute from the land Izalla (KUR *i-za-la*), oxen, sheep, (and) wine."[143] Later, at the end of this campaign, he stated: "At that time, I received tribute from Aḫi-ramu, the man of Bīt-Yaḫiri, the (A)zallean (m*a-ḫi-ra-mu* DUMU *ia-ḫi-ri šá* KUR *zal-la-a-a*)," in connection with the receipt of tribute from Bīt-Baḫiāni and the kings of Ḫanigalbat.[144]

This raises a number of questions. Is Izalla the same place as Azallu? What is the connection between Bīt-Yaḫiri and Azallu, if any? Some scholars do not accept the equation: Azallu = Izalla = Zalla.[145] But other scholars do.[146] Liverani (1992a, 34) sums up this view: "the writings Izalla, Azalla for the toponym, and Zallayu for the adjective, refer to the same entity."[147]

142. Millard 1994, 105; Mattila 2001, 846, no. 7.

143. RIMA 2:201, A.0.101.1, i.106.

144. RIMA 2:203, A.0.101.1, ii.21b–23a. See p. 260 above for discussion of the problems.

145. For example, see Parpola and Porter 2001, map 3: Izalla (D3), (the Ṭūr ʿAbdīn) and Azallu (C4) (between Bīt-Baḫiāni and Bīt-Adīni).

146. Liverani 1992a, 34–35, 43–44; Postgate 1976–80c.

147. See also Dion 1997, 45 n. 95 with others cited there. On the contrary, Parpola and Porter (2001, map 3) place "Azallu" directly between Harran and Gōzān, with the designation being placed south of the main road, and place an entity "Izalla" in the western Kašiyāri Range. However, a better placement would be, in my opinion, having the designation "Azallu" just north of this main road and stretching into the western Kašiyāri.

The country seems to have been fiscally centered around Ḫuzirīna,[148] and eventually was centered in Harran (Liverani 1992a, 34). This is apprehended by a look at the territorial list of the governor, Bēlu-lū-balaṭ (814 BCE): the city of Tabitu, the city of Harran, the city of Ḫuzīrīna, the city of Dūru of the land of Qipānu, the land of (A)zallu (KUR.*za-al-lu*), (and) the city of Balīḫu.[149] The land seems to be located in the western part of Mount Kašiyāri, on the plateau between the city of Urfa and the shield volcano Karaca Dağ, an area that is in agreement with the itineraries of Aššurnaṣirpal, and with the location of classical Izala.[150]

Therefore, it seems that the Azallu was a geographic designation for an area with Harran and Qipānu on the west and Gōzān and the central Mount Kašiyāri on the east (see fig. 4.1). Part of western Kašiyāri would be part of Azallu. The fact that later in 870 Adda-'imme, the (A)zallean (KUR *zal-la-a-ia*) will give to Aššurnaṣirpal II (among other things as tribute) "oxen, sheep, (and) wine"—the same items as the land Izalla (KUR *i-za-la*) gave in 882 ("oxen, sheep, (and) wine") argues in favor of Liverani's analysis of the data.

While there may appear to be a difficulty with this 882 campaign's connection of Izalla's tribute with the Subnat sources, the problem is only apparent, since the text obviously omits as irrelevant everything that transpired between the Subnat sources to the receipt of the Izalla tribute, which must have taken place in a much more western area, just before Aššurnaṣirpal's penetration of the western Mount Kašiyāri area to approach the city of Damdammusa (Liverani 1992a, 35). In other words, the receipt of the tribute did not have to take place at the sources of the Subnat.

While Azallu was the geopolitical designation—and "(A)zallean" its gentilic form, the man of Bīt-Yaḫiri (DUMU *ia-ḫi-ri*) was the Aramean tribal designation. Dion cites the parallel of "Sam'alian" (geopolitical designation) and Bīt-Gabbāri (the Aramean tribal designation; Dion 1997, 45).

There is additional evidence for Aḫi-ramu of Bīt-Yaḫiri. A. H. Layard discovered fragments of embossed bronze sheathing that are parts of long bronze bands for decorating gates, apparently in the North West Palace at Nimrud. According to Curtis (Curtis and Tallis 2008, 75), the pieces appear to belong to three or more bands (NIM 1–3) and show mostly chariot scenes and the king receiving officials and tributaries. All three bands have epigraphs recording tribute from different places or individuals; but in only one case (NIM 2) is detailed information still preserved, recording that the tribute was from Aḫi-ramu of Bīt-Yaḫiri (fig. 4.6). The epigraph reads:

148. As seen in RIMA 2:219, A.0.0101.1, iii.94. See below.

149. RIMA 3:178, A.0.102.2002.1; Andrae 1913, no. 44.

150. Liverani 1992a, 34.

Fig. 4.6. The tribute of Aḫi-ramu, a man of Bīt-Yaḫiri (NIM 2)

> *ma-d[a]-tú šá* ${}^{m}$*a-[ḫ]i-[r]a-mu* DUMU ${}^{m}$*ia-ḫi-ri am-[ḫur]*
> I recei[ved] the tribute of Aḫi-ramu, a man of Bīt-Yaḫiri.[151]

Curtis's description of the relief on the band states:

> the king stands, facing left, staff in right hand and left hand resting on the pommel of his sword. Facing the king is a group of four men in Assyrian dress. The first, who may be the crown prince, is bearded, clad in a long fringed garment and armed with sword in "voluted" scabbard. He is followed by two men clad in long, fringed garments who walk together; one is bearded, one beardless. The beardless figure wears a sword. The fringe at the hem of his garment possibly consists of large tassels. The fourth Assyrian introduces tributaries, only the first of whom survives. *He is clad in a long garment and wears boots with upturned toes.* Behind the king are three armed attendants. The first is bearded and wears a tunic of medium length; he is armed with quiver, spiked shield with lion's head, and sword in "voluted" scabbard and carries a mace. The second and third men are beardless and wear long tunics; they are armed with quiver, bow, sword in "voluted" scabbard, and carry maces. To the right is the king's pavilion with a tasselled covering resting on posts with pomegranate finials. On the far right is the royal chariot with driver; at the horses' heads is a soldier clad in a tunic of medium length and armed with a sword in a voluted scabbard. (Curtis and Tallis 2008, 77, emphasis added)

Interestingly, this scene may record the incident of Aḫi-ramu's tribute to Aššurnaṣirpal in 882.[152]

In addition, another bronze band records a military campaign against Bīt-Yaḫiri with an attack on a town whose name is not preserved as shown on

151. Curtis and Tallis 2008, 77, and photo and drawing on p. 197, fig. 96.

152. It is also very interesting that the one surviving tributary wears a long garment and boots with upturned toes (Curtis and Tallis 2008, 77).

the Balawat gates of Aššurnaṣirpal II (fig. 4.7).[153] This band has an epigraph which reads:

> URU [x-x]-x-*su šá* É-$^{m}$*ia-ḫi-ri* KUR-*ud*
> "the city of [ ]su of Bīt-Yaḫiri, I captured."[154]

Fig. 4.7. Attack on a town of Bīt-Yaḫiri

The relief shows an Assyrian chariot attack from both the left and the right against a fortified city on a mound. The battle seems to be an open-field engagement. The defenders of the town in Bīt-Yaḫiri are wearing knee-length kilts and are barefoot. The enemy is taking casualties and is generally in confused flight. Aššurnaṣirpal's chariot is leading the attack on the left side, trampling a naked fallen enemy. On both sides of the city, however, a single enemy archer stands tall taking aim at the Assyrian charge. In the city are women who watch from the battlements holding one hand to the ear and raising the other, palm upward, in a gesture of supplication or submission.

This battle against a city of Bīt-Yaḫiri is not recorded in Aššurnaṣirpal's Annals. While this could point to other later campaigns of Aššurnaṣirpal not

153. Curtis and Tallis 2008, 40, 128–29, fig. 27 and 28 (BM 124688). King 1915, pls. LXXVIII–LXXX; Barnett 1973; 1972; Grayson, RIMA 2:321–22, A.0.101.51 (introduction) and 2:345–51, A.0.101.80–97 (all the captions of the reliefs). See also Russell 1999, 56–57.

154. RIMA 2:346, A.0.101.83. The restoration of the city name as [*ma*(?)-*ga*(?)-*r*]*i*(?)-*su* was a suggestion of F. M. Fales in Grayson RIMA 2:346. However, this city is located in the Ḫābūr region and is not close to the Azallu region.

recorded in Annals, it is important to note that it is not uncommon for the reliefs with their epigraphs to record events not mentioned in the "annals" and vice versa (e.g., Tiglath-pileser III [Gezer] and Sennacherib [Lachish]).

Later, in his eleventh campaign (Liverani's IX; see table 4.4),[155] often rounded by scholars to 870 BCE, Aššurnaṣirpal first went to Bīt-Baḫiāni (see above). He then marched west to the land of Azallu (KUR *a-zal-li*) and received the tribute of Adda-'imme (Hadad-'imme, written: mdIŠKUR-*ʾi-me* KUR *zal-la-a-ia*),[156] the (A)zallean, which included harnessed chariots, horses, silver, gold, tin, bronze, bronze casseroles, oxen, sheep, (and) wine. Afterwards, he took chariots, cavalry, (and) infantry from the Hadad-'imme and departed from the land of Azallu (KUR.*a-zal-li*),[157] marching to Bīt-Adīni where he received the tribute of Aḫunu of Bīt-Adīni and Ḫabīnu of Til-Abnâ.

Aššurnaṣirpal's final campaign (his twelfth) took place in 866 BCE (his eighteenth regnal year).[158] The march followed the usual main road in upper Mesopotamia with a stop in Ḫuzirīna (Sultantepe) where he received tribute from the nearby land of Qipānu. Then the text states:

> While I was in the city of Ḫuzirīna, I received tribute of Itti', the (A)zallu (m*it-ti-'i* KUR.*zal-la-a-ia*), (and of) Giri-Dadi,[159] the Aššu (KUR.*áš-šá-a-ia*): silver, gold, oxen, (and) sheep.[160]

The name Itti' may be Aramaic (Fuchs 2000). Aššurnaṣirpal received the tribute of two previous chiefs of Azallu: in the previous campaign (ca. 875–867), that of Adda-'imme (Aramaic), the Zallean (iii.59), and in the 882 campaign, the tribute of "Ahi-ramu (West Semitic), the man of Bīt-Yaḫiri, the Zallean" (ii.22).

155. The full campaign is found in RIMA 2:216–19, A.0.101.1, iii.56b–92a.

156. The name is Aramaic and means "Adda (Hadad) is with him." See Schwemer 1998b.

157. RIMA 3:216, A.0.101.1, iii.58b–60a.

158. For the campaign, see RIMA 2:219–21, A.0.101.1, iii.92b–113a. The eponym for the eighteenth regnal year, Šamaš-nūri, may be the same person who is the father of Had(d)-Yiṯʿī of the Tell Fakhariya Inscription. See discussion above, pp. 261–62.

159. For this name, see Schwemer 2000b.

160. RIMA 2:219, A.0.101.1, iii.94b–95a.

## 4.5. The Laqē Confederation

Laqē[161] was an important land on the Middle Euphrates around the confluence of the Ḫābūr with the Euphrates, first attested in the reign of Adad-nērārī II (r. 911–891; see fig. 4.8). It was created during the Aramean occupation of the area sometime between 1100 and 950 BCE. It was a tribal confederation, "a sort of mosaic of polities" (Liverani 1992a, 108; Dion 1997, 56). Laqē seems to have emerged in the general area where the kingdom of Ḫana had existed (Buccellati 1990b). In fact, both Ḫana and Laqē seem to have had ruling classes with West Semitic and nomadic backgrounds.[162]

It had a significant sedentary component with a heterogenous conglomerate of cities, each ruled by a king.[163] Some of the more significant cities included: Sūru, the capital city of the Bīt-Ḫalupē tribe,[164] Sirqu, Ṣupru, and Naqarabanu. It is also clear that there were many smaller settlements, simple farming villages/hamlets (*adurû*).[165] The local rulers of these cities paid separate tributes to the Assyrians, demonstrating the loose nature of the ties between them. The land of Laqē was never under the unifying control of one ruler (Postgate 1980–83, 494). Thus, it seems that the relationship of these various politically divided kingdoms is explainable through a common league. Lipiński (2000a, 77) has suggested that the very name Laqē may "designate a tribal confederacy."

However, the area's geography meant that Laqē would have certainly had a significant mobile pastoralist component, no doubt comprising an important part of the tribal confederation. This mobile component was located throughout the land of Laqē on both sides of the rivers, and had many unfortified towns. The leaders of these mobile tribal entities were chiefs or sheikhs (*nasīku*).

Interestingly, one of the more important tribes of the confederation, Bīt-Ḫalupē, is written with a feminine determinative: Bar-atara, a man of

161. For the tribal name, see Zadok 1976, 114 n. 9, who takes the form as a causative precative from the root *yqy* "to guard." Lipiński (2000a, 77) understands the derivation to be from Arabic *laqiya* "to encounter," and hence designates a confederation. *La-qí-e* is also recorded as a personal name (*ABL* 520:15).

162. In addition, there seems to have been connections in both kingdoms with Jebel Bišri. See Lönnqvist 2011, 204–5.

163. RIMA 2:200, A.0.101.1, i.94: MAN.MEŠ-*ni šá* KUR *la-qe-e a-na si-hír-ti-šú-nu.*

164. Bīt-Ḫalupē has a king in its capital city of Sūru with a palace, treasury, harem, officials and eunuchs.

165. See chapter 2 discussion of the *adurû* of Laqē mentioned in Ninurta-kudurrī-uṣur. See RIMB 2:296, S.0.1002.2, i.28 (É.DURU$_5$.MEŠ).

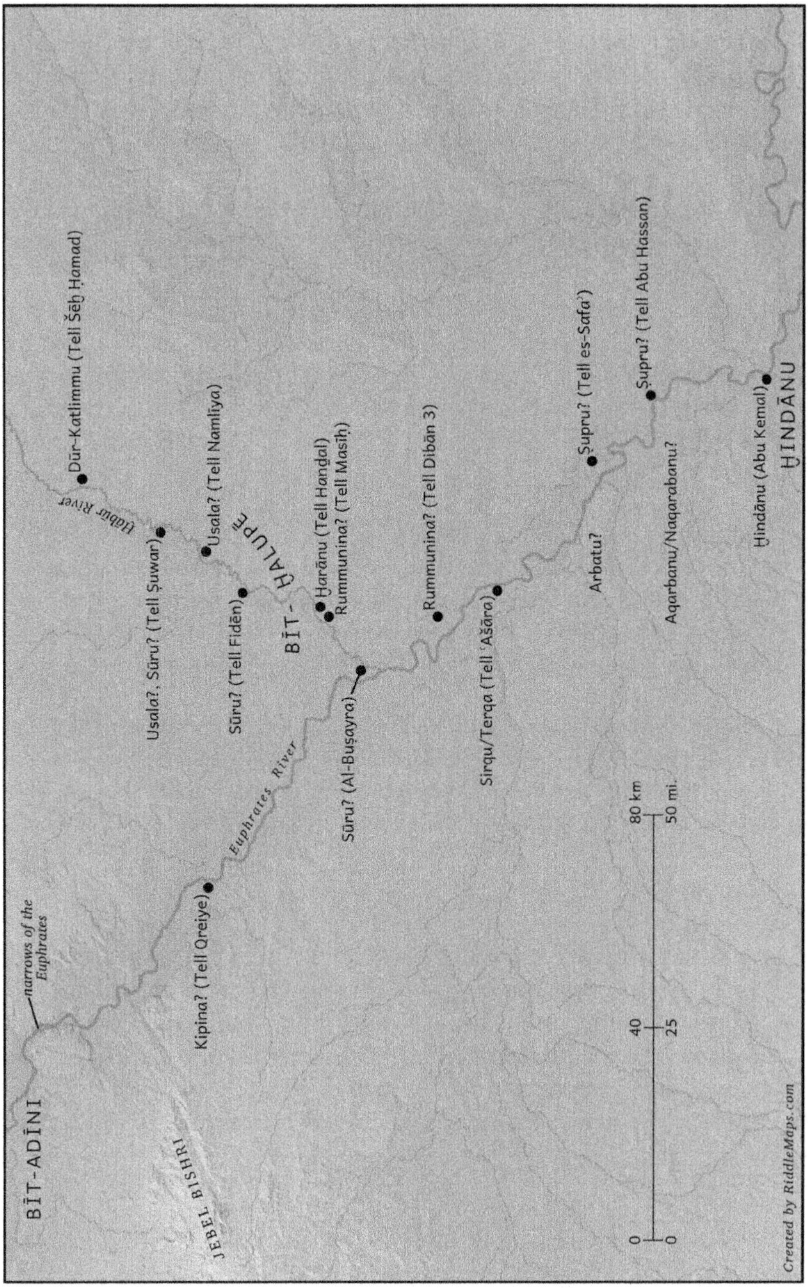


Fig. 4.8. Lower Ḫābūr and Middle Euphrates

Bīt-Ḫalupē (mba-ar-a-ta-ra DUMU fha-lu-pé-e).[166] This seems to imply that the name Ḫalupē derives from a female tribal leader. It has been speculated that this may indicate its origins in a priestly clan headed by a priestess, whose function could be comparable to the North Arabian queens-priestesses who were active in the eighth and seventh centuries (Lipiński 2000a, 78–80). But other than this one occurrence, there is no other evidence for the feminine link.[167]

There is later possible evidence for this tribe from Nippur in the mid-eighth century. In two letters from the so-called Governor's archive, the tribe of Ḫalupē appears to be mentioned. In the first letter, the *šandabakku* of Nippur had entered into a treaty with the sheikhs of the Chaldean tribe of Bīt-Awkāni and the Aramean tribe of Rupū' (Cole 1996a, 49–50, text 6). However, in violation of this treaty, a man identified as "son of Šaknu, son of Ḫalapē" (DUMU m*Šak-nu* DUMU m*Ḫa-*⌜*la*⌝*-pi*) seems to have carried off a slave belonging to a member of Mukīn-zēri's tribe, that is Bīt-Awkāni. Cole (1996a, 49) comments:

> "The offender's patronym identifies him as a member of the Šaknu clan of the Bīt-Ḫalupē, an Aramean tribe whose territory included the banks of the lower Ḫābūr. His clan must have been living in Nippur or among the Rupū' tribe at this time, or he would not have been covered by the provision(s) of the agreement in question. He is identified solely by his lineage."

In the second letter,[168] the Ḫalupē tribe (LÚ.*Ḫa-la-pi*) is mentioned along with several other Aramean tribes. These attestations demonstrate that by the mid-eighth century, some of the members or clans of Bīt-Ḫalupē had migrated to northern Babylonia in the Nippur area.

### 4.5.1. Territory

The land of Laqē was centered on the confluence of the Ḫābūr and Euphrates. It stretched down the Euphrates to the border with Ḫindānu (Abu Kemal). Up the Euphrates, its border was with Bīt-Adīni; and on the Ḫābūr, it comprised the land south of Dūr-Katlimmu (Tell Šēḫ Ḥamad). Laqē had settlements and cities on both sides of both rivers. Thus in one sense, it was riverine in character. But on the other hand, the steppe, never far from the rivers, was its

---

166. Annals of Adad-nērārī II (RIMA 2:153, A.0.99.2, line 114). This is the only instance of the feminine determinative being used with the name.

167. See the discussion of the name Ma'akah in chapter 3.

168. Cole 1996a, 62–63, text 13:10. See chapter 10.

pastoralist hinterland and gave it a special quality. The following presentation outlines what is known of the cities of the land of Laqē by their regions.

#### 4.5.1.1. Cities South of Dūr-Katlimmu and North of the Confluence

The reading of the name of the first city south of Dūr-Katlimmu in the land of Laqē that Adad-nērārī II encountered poses a difficulty. Grayson read the name (URU.*zu-ú-ri-iḫ*) "the city of Zurīḫ."[169] Lipiński has suggested reading the name as URU.*ṣu-ú-ri-iḫ* and normalizes as *Ṣūriḫ or possibly *Ṣuwwariḫ. He identifies it with Tell Ṣuwār, west bank of the Ḫābūr, 18 km south of Dūr-Katlimmu (Lipiński 2000a, 83). Between this city and the city of Sūru (*Su-ú-ru*) of Bīt-Ḫalupē was the city of Usala (URU.*ú-sa-la-a*). Kühne (1980, 61–62) identifies Usala with Tell Ṣuwār; Lipiński (2000a, 83) suggests Tell Namlīya. The city of Sūru (*Su-ú-ru*) has been equated in the past with Tell Ṣuwār (Scheil 1909, 49; Lewy 1952, 267). However, this was based almost entirely on the assonance of names, and is unsatisfactory. Kühne (1980, 61–62) locates Sūru at Tell Fidēn. Liverani (1992a, 32–33) also places it there. Lipiński (2000a, 83–89) locates the city of Sūru at Al-Buṣayra, which is on the west bank of the Ḫābūr at the confluence of the Ḫābūr with the Euphrates. Finally, the site of Rummunina has been located by Kühne at Tell Masīḥ, 18 km south of Tell Fidēn (Kühne 1980, 64); Lipiński (2000a, 84–85) locates it at Tell Dibān 3, 17 km south of Al-Buṣayra, on the Dawwarīn canal near a meander of the Euphrates.

#### 4.5.1.2. Cities South of the Confluence of the Ḫābūr and Euphrates to the Border with Ḫindānu

There is agreement that the city of Sirqu (ancient Terqa) was located at Tell ʿAšāra (Luciani 1999; Chavalas 1996; Masetti-Rouault 2001). In the annals of Adad-nērārī II, there is a city between Ṣ/Zurīḫ and Sirqu, recorded as URU.*šá* ᵐ*ḫa-ra-a-ni*, which could be understood as "the city that belongs to Ḫarānu" or "Āl-ša-Ḫarānu." In any case, it is not to be confused with another city in the annals of Tukulti-Ninurta II, "the city of Arbatu" where "Ḫarānu, the Laqēan" (ᵐ*ḫa-ra-a-ni* KUR *la-a-qa-a-ia*) paid his tribute. Lipiński rightly points out that there were two different Ḫarānu connected with two different places. In this case, Tell Hanḏal, 3 km below Tell Abū Ḥā'iṭ, has been identified with URU.*šá*-ᵐ*Ḫa-ra-a-ni*, the Laqēan settlement that the annals of Adad-nērārī II locate between URU.*Zu*/*Ṣú-ú-iḫ* and URU.*Si-ir-qi* (Kühne 1980, 67–68; Lipiński 2000a, 93). The exact location of Arbatu (in

169. RIMA 2:153, A.0.99.2, 114.

Tukulti-Ninurta II's Annals) is not known. The city of Ṣupru has been identified with Tell eṣ-Ṣafa' (in the area in front of Dura Europos; Musil 1927, 174 n. 87, 204, 206); more probably it should be identified with Tell Abu Hassan.[170] The city of Aqarbanu is to be equated with the city of Naqarabanu, but its modern location is still unknown (Liverani 1992a, 65).

#### 4.5.1.3. Cities North of the Confluence of the Ḫābūr and Euphrates on the Euphrates

The city of Kipina is only attested in the Annals of Aššurnaṣirpal II,[171] as being located on the right bank of the Euphrates, at a two-day march (presumably a fast march) downstream from the Jebel Bišri and the border with Bīt-Adīni. Liverani felt that this placed the site roughly at the confluence of the Ḫābūr and Euphrates (Liverani 1992a, 70; Musil 1927, 209). On the other hand, Lipiński suggests the area near Deir ez-Zor; in fact, a location 14 km upstream at Tell Qreiye, the location of a later important Roman fort.[172] Herles (2007a, 429–30) has recently followed Lipiński's suggestion noting that Tell Qreiye is near the modern village of Ayyash. Lipiński (2000a, 97) also pointed out that the name of the city of Kipina probably reflects the Aramaic root *kp* "rock."

In an area just south of the border cities of Bīt-Adīni (Dummetu and Azmu), a Laqēan enclave of a certain Ilâ, a Laqēan chief, was conquered by Aššurnaṣirpal II.[173] Unfortunately, the Assyrian text does not name any sites connected to this individual and his tribal group, even though the text does credit him with having chariots (which seems to imply that the group had some sedentary element).

### 4.5.2. History

During his campaign of 894 BCE, Adad-nērārī II (911–891 BCE) marched down the Ḫābūr receiving tribute along the way. This was basically a "show of strength" expedition. The "itinerary" structure used to describe this collection and imposition of tribute is used by the next two Assyrian monarchs, Tukulti-Ninurta II and Aššurnaṣirpal II, in their narratives concerned with this same region (see table 4.3). Thus Adad-nērārī II initiated a pattern of

---

170. Herles 2007a, 428–29; Geyer, Monchambert, Besançon, and Coqueugniot 2003, 143; Liverani 1992a, 65.

171. RIMA 2:215, A.0.101.1, iii.37b–39.

172. Lipiński 2000a, 97–98; so too earlier, Horn 1922, 146–7. Liverani asserts that this seems too much upstream (Liverani 1992a, 65).

173. RIMA 2:215, A.0.101.1, lines 43–44; cf. line 42. See Lipiński 2000a, 98.

repossession of the Ḫābūr region for Assyria (Liverani 1988a, 81–98; Postgate 1992, 255–56), just as he had done in the case of the land of Ḫanigalbat. In this instance, Adad-nērārī II started his expedition in Gōzān where he received the tribute of Abi-salāmu (see 4.3.2 above). He proceeded down the Ḫābūr: to the city Arnabānu, to the city of Ṭābētu, to the city Šadikanni (tribute received), to the city of Kisiru, to the city of Qatnu (Amēl-Adad gave his tribute), to the mountains of Būṣu (which) are by the Ḫābūr River, and to the city of Dūr-Katlimmu.

After departing Dūr-Katlimmu, Adad-nērārī II marched into the land of Laqē.[174] While Aššur-bēl-kala only spoke of Arameans in the descriptions of his campaigns in this region, Adad-nērārī II and his successors speak only of the Laqēans in this same region. This change in terminology by the Assyrian scribes does not simply attest to a better knowledge of the Aramean tribes in the Middle Euphrates area. It also reflects a change in the situation in the region. The Arameans had become the overlords of this territory.

Adad-nērārī II received tribute from three of this confederation's rulers. The first of these was a ruler named Bar-atara, a man of Bīt-Ḫalupē (ᵐ*ba-ar-a-ta-ra* DUMU ᶠ*ḫa-lu-pé-e*), ruler of the city of Zurīḫ (URU *zu-ú-ri-iḫ*). The name Bar-atara is Aramaic: Bar-ʿAttār, "son of Attār."[175] For the discussion of the possibility of feminine ancestress, see above. The second, whose name was Ḫārānu (URU *šá* ᵐ*ḫa-ra-a-ni*), was a ruler of an unnamed city. Ḫārānu is Aramaic name from the root *ḥwr* "white" with the ending *an*.[176] The third ruler was a man identified as Mudadda,[177] the Laqēan, the ruler of the city of Sirqu on the Euphrates. Sirqu should be identified with Tell ʿAšāra, known as Terqa in the earlier sources.

During his 885 campaign, Tukulti-Ninurta II, like his father, led a "show of strength" expedition along the Ḫābūr, although his march went up the Ḫābūr rather than down the river. Once again, an itinerary structure is used to describe this collection and imposition of tribute, though there is more detail in Tukulti-Ninurta's annals. Among those of the Laqē confederation who submitted and paid tribute were two rulers who had yielded to Adad-nērārī II: Mudadda of Sirqu (ᵐ*mu-d*[*a*]*-da* URU.⌜*sir*⌝*-aq-a-ia*) and Ḫārānu, the Laqēan (ᵐ*ḫa-ra-a-ni* KUR.*la-q*[*a*]*-a-*[*i*]*a*).

A new tributary was Ḫamatāya ("the Hamathite"), the Laqēan (KUR. *ḫa-ma-ta-a-ia* KUR.*la-qa-a-ia*), the ruler of the city of Ṣupru and the city

174. RIMA 2:153–54, A.0.99.2, 113b–119.

175. Note the form *bar*-DN, like *Bar*-Hadad. See below.

176. Baker 2000. This person is, however, not listed in this entry. See Zadok 1977, 160, 180, 183. *ḥwr* "white."

177. The name is written ᵐ*mu-da-ad-da* KUR *la-qa-a-*⌜*ia*⌝. The name is Aramaic: *mwdd*, "friend of Dadi?" See Baker 2000d.

Table 4.3. Ḫābūr and Middle Euphrates Segments of the "Show of Strength" Campaigns

| Aššur-bēl-kala (1073–1056) (Broken Obelisk) | Adad-nērārī II (911–891) (894 BCE) | Tukulti-Ninurta II (890–884) (885 BCE) | Aššurnaṣirpal II (883–859) (878 BCE) | Modern Site |
|---|---|---|---|---|
| | | Kaḫat | | Tell Barri |
| | Arnabānu | Tabite | Tabite | |
| Magrisu of the land of Māri | | Gurete<br>Magarisu | Magarisu | Tell Ḥassaka |
| [Ṭābe]te(?) | Ṭābētu<br>Šadikanni | Ṭābētu<br>Šadikanni | Šadikanni | Tell Taban<br>Tell 'Ajaja |
| | Kisiri/Sikiri<br>Qatna | Latiḫi<br>Qatna | Qatna | Tell Šaddāda/Tell Baḫza<br>Tell Fadhgami*/Tell Ašamšani** |
| Dūr-Katlimmu | Mount Būṣu<br>Dūr-Katlimmu | xxx<br>Dūr-Katlimmu | Dūr-Katlimmu | Tell Šēḫ Ḥamad |
| | Zurīḫ / Ṣurīḫ<br>City of Ḫarānu | Usala<br>Sūru | Bīt-Ḫalupē | Tell Ṣuwār<br>Tell Ṣuwār<br>Tell Fidēn/Tell Ṣuwār |
| Sangaritu | Sirqu | Rummunina<br>Sirqu | Sirqu | Tell Masīḥ<br>Tell Abū Ḥā'iṭ (Kühne 1980, 253); Tell al-Jubn (Lipiński 2000a, 92)<br>Tell 'Ašāra (Terqa) |
| land/mountain of Gulgulu | | | | |
| city of . . . ]ṣiku of land of Ḫānu*** | | | | |

*Kühne 1980, 48; Morandi Bonacossi 1996, 19; 2000, 366. **Parpola and Porter 2001, 14; Nashef 1982, 221. ***Tenu 2006a, 229 n. 37: equals the Ḫana of the Old Babylonian period.

Sūru[178] on the Ḫābūr in the land of Bīt-Ḫalupē. In Tukulti-Ninurta II's text, the name is written: KUR.*ḫa-ma-ta-a-ia* and [KUR.*ḫa-ma-t*]*a-a-ia*.[179] This led Lipiński (2000a, 101 and 251) to argue that "Ḫamatāya" is not a personal name, but "an ethnic qualification," and is a reference to the "Hamathite" governor of Laqē. In his opinion, this is evidence that "the Ḥamathite king ruled, at least nominally, also in a part of the territory of the Laqē tribes, near the confluence of the Euphrates with the Ḫābūr ... and characterizes 'the land of Laqē' as Ḥamathite." Moreover, Lipiński argues that:

> This interpretation of *Ḫamatāya*, which implies an extension of the Ḥamathite territory until the land of Laqē beyond the Euphrates, is confirmed by the mention of the "valley" or "river-land of Laga" in one of the hieroglyphic Luwian inscriptions of king Uratami and by the letter sent to him by his neighbour Marduk-apla-uṣur, the semi-independent ruler of Sūḫu, a region southeast of the land of Laqē, on the Middle Euphrates. The relations of Uratami with this area are confirmed by the reference to "Naharima" in the same hieroglyphic Luwian inscription.[180]

However, this interpretation is problematic on a number of counts. First, this is a personal name formed from the gentilic. This is proven by the writing of the name in Aššurnaṣirpal II's inscriptions where it appears with the masculine determinative (i.e., the *Winkelhaken*): ᵐ*Ḫa-ma-ta-a-ia*,[181] in a context that is obviously referring to the same person. The fact that there is a variant of this passage that spells the name with the KUR determinative demonstrates that this is the same personal name as in Tukulti-Ninurta II's text.[182] Importantly, Ḫamatāya is found in other later contexts proving that it was a personal name (Baker 2000e). Therefore, it is not evidence of Hamathite territorial extension.

Second, the text of Uratami (HAMA 2, Hawkins 2000, 413) does not support Lipiński's interpretation. His interpretation of the term "Naharima" is based on a discarded reading. HAMA 2 is one of a group of building inscrip-

178. Sūru is probably Tell Fidēn. See Kühne 1980, 61. Lipiński (2000a, 86–89) disagrees and places Suru at Al-Buṣayra. But see Parpola and Porter 2001, 16 (Sūru is Tel Fidēn); Dion 1997, 58 n. 155.

179. RIMA 2:176, A.0.100.5, lines 87 and 101.

180. Lipiński 2000a, 251–52. The identification of Laka with the Middle Euphrates land of Laqē was made earlier by Meriggi (1962, 78, s.v. Lakawanas). Hawkins (1995c, 97) alluded to the possibility.

181. RIMA 2:198, A.0.101.1, i.75. Correctly noted by Russell 1985, 73 n. 111, and Hawkins 1972–75b, 67.

182. RIMA 2:198, apparatus i.75 attested in RIMA 2:234, A.0.101.9; King 1902, 254 (BM 90830). Rightly pointed out by Bagg 2007, 88.

tions of Uratami in which Uratami claimed to have built fortresses which certain river-lands made. Hawkins (2000, 414) comments:

> From the view point of Hama, one would expect the "riverlands" to be districts of the Orontes river under Hamathite sway, such territories as those controlled from the two unnamed cities whose building by Uratamis's father is recorded on the stelae RESTAN and QAL'AT EL MUDIQ. It is perhaps not surprising that the names are largely unfamiliar to us.

Hence, there is no reason to connect the river land of Laka in HAMA 2 with the land of Laqē. It is extremely unlikely that Uratami (ca. 840–820) during this time period would have had any "control" in the Lower Ḫābūr, following Shalmaneser III's reduction of Hamath to vassalage.[183] There is no indication that Shalmaneser lost control of the region of Laqē or granted Uratami any power there.

Third, the letter of Marduk-apla-uṣur attests to a relationship between Hamath and Ana(t) on the Middle Euphrates. It is not attesting to the region of Laqē, and it does not imply any type of control or extension of Hamathite territory. While there can be no doubt of relationships between Hamath and the Middle Euphrates, caution is preferred here.

Ḫamatāya, in addition to his other tribute gifts, gave his two sisters[184] to Tukulti-Ninurta II with bountiful dowries. This probably concluded an alliance, sealed by a double political marriage. It will also explain Aššurnaṣirpal II's actions, when the people of Sūru assassinated Ḫamatāya and replaced him with a man of Bīt-Adīni (see below).

In Sirqu (Tell 'Ašāra), Tukulti-Ninurta II erected a basalt stela (height: 90 cm / 35.5 in) with a cuneiform inscription that commemorated both his father, Adad-nērārī II, and himself and their victorious campaigns in the land of Laqē. This four-sided stela was discovered prior to controlled excavation, and hence its original location and possible function in that location is lost, although Kühne (2009, 49) labels it as a *kudurru* (which it very well may have been). While the iconography evinces a mixture of Assyrian and local artistic elements, the latter are clearly the more dominant. Thus it is clear that the monument is not an Assyrian work, but a local one with some Assyrian influences. Hence, the inscription testifies to a later secondary use by Tukulti-Ninurta II, an appropriation and adaptation of the much earlier work.

183. See discussion in §7.2.2.3.

184. Gen 29:15–30 (Jacob marries Leah and Rachel); Lev 18:18 (injunction against marrying two sisters while one is living).

Unfortunately, the inscription is badly worn.[185] Masetti-Rouault has published an edition that provides a more readable text than past attempts.[186] Lines 1–5 praise Adad-nērārī II with such epithets as "trampler of the city of Laqē," "flattener of the evil horns of the snake," etc. Lines 6–8 praise Tukulti-Ninurta II: "wise king," "the one that his father made," etc., concluding with mention of "the most eminent of deities, Ištar of Arbela." Lines 9–12 are more difficult, but seem to continue epithets for Tukulti-Ninurta. How the inscription may have functioned with the artwork will be discussed below.

As for the reliefs themselves (see fig. 4.9), sides 1–2 present a male deity (clearly marked by the double-horns—although uniquely protruding from the forehead rather than the helmet) standing in the position of a smiting god. In his left hand, he is grasping a large snake; and in his right hand, he is holding a battle-axe. Behind this deity, a stream flows from the top of the helmet, and perhaps represents "an aquatic element often part of the representations of the stormgod, as in the stele from Ras Shamra" (Bellino 2008, 274). On sides 3–4, behind the snake, facing the smiting scene are two other male figures. Side 3 has a fish-cloaked man, represented in a smaller scale, holding two sticks; and side 4 depicts a male without headgear wearing a long short-sleeved vest leaning on a rod and holding three ears of wheat. For each character, one may indicate pertinent comparisons within the Syrian milieu (Bellino 2008, 274). On the other hand, the southern Anatolian style is obvious (Pongratz-Leisten 2011, 123).

Masetti-Rouault has suggested that the iconography represents the Syro-Hittite storm god, choking and killing a big snake in the presence of another god, possibly Dagan, the overlord of the Euphrates Valley, who had a famous temple in Terqa (unless it is an image of the local king), with an *apkallu* priest in between.[187]

There can be no doubt about sides 1–2. They depict the storm god in a smiting pose in the myth of the defeat of the snake-monster (Bunnens 2006). The Anatolian dress and battle-axe are evinced in other works.[188] The *apkallu* of side 3 and the figure in side 4 face the action of the storm god; the

185. So much so that Grayson did not offer an edition in RIMA 2:188, A.0.100.1003.

186. Masetti-Rouault 2001, 103–14; see also Tournay 1997; Güterbock 1957; and Tournay and Saouaf 1952.

187. Masetti-Rouault 2009, 144. She labels only three sides with sides 1–2 being side 1, etc.

188. However, Pongratz-Leisten (2011, 123) has argued that although southern Anatolian in style, the origin of the iconography in the stela can be traced back to early Hurrian tradition.

Fig. 4.9. The stela of 'Ašāra (Gundlach 2000, 239), © Aleppo Museum

*apkallu* is performing a ritual, probably apotropaic,[189] and the figure is holding a bundle of wheat in his left hand, while his right hand is placed on the top of a staff, cane or club.

The identity of the figure on side 4 is difficult. Does it represent a deity—possibly Dagan (as suggested by Masetti-Rouault 2009, 144)—or a human, perhaps the local king? What seems clear is that the primary (i.e., original) function of the stela was to convey an important scene known from texts: the Storm God (of Aleppo) in the act of killing the mythical serpent (Bordreuil and Pardee 1993). Since only after defeating the snake does the storm god offer royalty and its attributes to the king, the scene could be understood to

189. The fish-cloaked priest (*apkallu*) occurs in Assyrian art of the slightly later reign of Aššurnaṣirpal II (883–859), son of Tukulti-Ninurta II, in the Temple of Ninurta in Nimrud (Kühne 2009, 49). The Middle Assyrian evidence remains confined to the glyptic (Pongratz-Leisten 2011, 123). Interestingly, the *apkallu* is also represented on a slab from the newly excavated Temple of Aleppo with clear Anatolian artistic traditions; thus the imagery does not have to be attributed to Assyrian influence (Bellino 2008, 274). In fact, it is possible that the Assyrians have borrowed the imagery from their contact with the west or perhaps earlier Hurrian tradition.

render the precise moment in which the king is about to receive the royal insignias; he is without emblems because the battle is still in progress (Bellino 2008, 276). But the victory over the snake also signifies the control over the chaotic forces and consequently the regularization of natural cycles. The ears of wheat would be an offering from the king paying tribute to the storm god as governor of this sphere.

However, side 4 has been interpreted to represent Adad-nērārī II. Gundlach (2000) has suggested that Tukulti-Ninurta II had this image made of his father Adad-nērārī II. On the other hand, Kühne (2009, 49) has suggested that it may represent Tukulti-Ninurta II. Masetti-Rouault (2009, 144) has suggested that with the cuneiform inscription added, the observer of the stela is invoked

> to read the images as the portraits of Tukulti-Ninurta II, his father Adad-nērārī II (now deceased), and the local Aramean tribes of the Laqē people, depicted here as the snake of the steppe, destroyed by the Assyrian intervention in the area. In her view, the stela is the product of the palace at Sirqu (i.e., the local urban elite) who have "readjusted" the object "to welcome the Assyrian masters, trying not only to avoid immediate destruction, but also, and even better, to exploit their military strength in their ongoing conflict with the semi-nomads, probably menacing trade through the steppe routes, as usual.

She admits that from the Assyrian point of view this would be very unorthodox, representing a king as the storm god. It is also problematic in that the "urban elite" are part and parcel of the Aramean Laqē confederation[190] that includes its own mobile steppe groups. Unfortunately, without a better preservation of the inscription, it is very difficult to posit with any confidence what the secondary appropriation exactly was. Finally, these interpretations assume a connection between the inscription and the iconography, an assumption that is not necessary and perhaps misleading (Bellino 2008, 276).

During his first full regnal year (883 BCE), Aššurnaṣirpal II conducted two campaigns (table 4.4). The first (in the spring) was directed against the mountainous hinterland of Assyria. The political entities here were non-Aramean: Tummu, Kirruru, Ḫabḫu, Gilzānu, and Ḫubuškia. His second campaign (in the autumn) started with the conquest of Katmuḫu. As he completed this, Aššurnaṣirpal received a report that the city of Sūru of Bīt-Ḫalupē (URU *su-ru šá* É-*ḫa-lu-pe-e*) had rebelled. Its inhabitants had killed

190. While he is called: [m]*mu-d*[*a*]-*da* URU ⸢*sir*⸣-*aq-a-ia* by Tukulti-Ninurta II, in Adad-nērārī II's annals he is called: [m]*mu-da-ad-da* KUR *la-qa-a-*⸢*ia*⸣. Thus Mudadda is an Aramean sheikh of the Laqē confederation. It would make little sense for him to present Tukulti-Ninurta II with a stela depicting the Assyrian king smiting his own people!

Ḫamatāya, their governor (LÚ.GAR/*šaknu*), a Laqēan chief, who had given his two sisters with bountiful dowries to Tukulti-Ninurta II, Aššurnaṣirpal's father (see above). Moreover, the people of Sūru had installed a usurper, "Aḫi-yababa,[191] the son of a nobody,[192] whom they brought from the land of Bīt-Adīni, as their king (*a-na* MAN-*ti*)."[193] There can be little doubt that Bīt-Adīni was very concerned with the rise of Assyrian power in the lower Ḫābūr and Middle Euphrates. It therefore used its influence (which must have been substantial) to aid in the instigation of the overthrow in Laqē, hoping that the Assyrians would not be able to handle the crisis.

But the punitive expedition to Bīt-Ḫalupē was quite swift. On the way down the Ḫābūr River to Sūru, Aššurnaṣirpal received the tribute of Samnuḫa-šar-ilāni, the vice-regent (*iššakku*) of the city of Šadikanni,[194] and Amēl-Adad[195] of the city of Qatna/Qatnu (he had paid tribute to Adad-nērārī II in 894, 11 years earlier). The action in Laqē was concentrated solely on Sūru. The nobles and elders of the city came out to Aššurnaṣirpal and pled for mercy. Nevertheless, the city was besieged and captured; Aḫi-yababa was also captured, along with his soldiers. After extracting great booty—after its lengthy enumeration, it is summed up as "his valuable tribute which, like the stars of heaven, had no number"—, Aššurnaṣirpal installed a new governor over the city, a man named Azi-ili.[196] Based on this West Semitic name, this man was probably a non-Assyrian, local elite, likely an Aramean. Some of the rebellious leaders and soldiers were executed and their bodies heaped in a pile in front of the city gate. Others were flayed or impaled. As for Aḫi-

191. Brinkman 1998a (West Semitic: "The brother has cried"); also Ebeling 1928.

192. The phrase *mār lā mammāna* refers to an upstart or usurper. The expression, common in historical documents from Assyria and Babylonia, indicates someone whose father was not a legal member of the major branch of the contemporary royal family, and expresses a value judgment with negative connotations, i.e., "usurper" or "an upstart?" Seux 1980–83, 150–52; Younger 2005, 247.

193. RIMA 2:198–99, A.0.101.1, i.74b–99a. See Bunnens 1999, 613.

194. The case of Šadikanni is interesting: at the time of Aššur-rabi II and Aššur-rēša-iši II, Bēl-ēreš seems to have been the local ruler (see chapter 3). He is followed by a line of tribute-payers at the time of Adad-nērārī II, Tukulti-Ninurta II and Aššurnaṣirpal II. The last of these, Samnuḫa-šar-ilāni, is the father and grandfather of the fully Assyrianized "vice-regents" / "governors" (LÚ.ŠID) Ninurta-ēreš and Mušēzib-Ninurta respectively as seen on a cylinder seal (RIMA 2:392, A.0.101.2005, line 3). See Liverani 1988a, 89; and Baker 2002c: "The inscription on a cylinder seal identifies it as the seal of Mušēzib-Inurta, vice regent (LÚ.ŠID), son of Inurta-ēreš, the same (i.e., vice-regent), son of $^{md}$DI-*ma-nu-ḫa*–MAN–DINGIR.MEŠ-*ni*, also the same (i.e., vice-regent) *RIMA* 2 A.0.101.2005:3."

195. Brinkman 1998c. Amēl-Bēl: Akk. "man of Adad" (formerly read Ilu-Adad).

196. Brinkman 1998d. Azi-il (West Semitic: "the god [or (El] is strong"). The name is attested in Old Aramaic, Ammonite and Hebrew (עזיאל). Note עזכר at Tell Šēḫ Ḥamad (Röllig 2001, 46–52).

yababa, he was brought back to Nineveh, flayed and his skin draped over the wall of the city. As a final act, the Assyrian king imposed an exceptionally large tribute, tax and duty upon all the kings of the Laqē confederation, no doubt to discourage any further rebellion.

Although the Aramean state of Bīt-Adīni was apparently involved in this revolt, Aššurnaṣirpal took no action against it at this time.[197] Nonetheless, the Assyrian intervention was effective since the rest of the Aramean confederation of Laqē sent its tribute to Aššurnaṣirpal at Sūru. Furthermore, the effectiveness of the intervention can be seen in the tributes sent by Ḫindānu and by Sūḫu (other states on the Middle Euphrates). Hence, Ḫayānu, the ruler of Ḫindānu, and Ili-ibni, the governor of Sūḫu, presented their tribute to Aššurnaṣirpal II. This is the same Ili-ibni who gave tribute to Tukulti-Ninurta II a few years earlier (i.e., 885).[198] But in this instance, Ili-ibni brought the tribute to Nineveh after Aššurnaṣirpal had returned there at the end of the campaign, "in order to save his life together with (that of) his brothers (and) his sons."

This tribute is perhaps depicted on the bands of the Palace Gates of Aššurnaṣirpal II at Balawat, where a epigraph reads:

> Palace of Aššurnaṣirpal, king of the universe, king of Assyria, son of Tukulti-Ninurta, king of Assyria, son of Adad-nērārī, (who was) also king of Assyria: tribute from the land of Sūḫu (*ma-da-tu šá* KUR *su-ḫi*).[199]

However, this could be a depiction of a later tribute, that of Kudurru, (clearly shown in other bands of the temple of Mamu, see below).

Aššurnaṣirpal's 878 campaign (his sixth regnal year) was a "show of strength" in the Ḫābūr and Middle Euphrates regions.[200] Like the "show of strength" campaigns of his predecessors, Adad-nērārī II and Tukulti-Ninurta II, Aššurnaṣirpal's campaign narrative utilizes the "itinerary" structure with its daily listing of station to station movement to describe the collection and imposition of tribute (see table 4.3).

The itinerary form is used to express the procedure of "a regular contact of established links between known centers" (Liverani 1988a, 87; see also Roskop 2011, 102–15). For the Ḫābūr area, the form goes back to the thirteenth century (Röllig 1983). As pointed out in chapter 3 above, while

197. The reason is not specified. Time of year, military and/or political concerns could be possible reasons.

198. RIMA 2:174–75, A.0.100.5, lines 67–73a.

199. Band BM ASH II R7 (BM 124693 / Rm 1073). See Curtis and Tallis 2008, 44 and figs. 35 and 36.

200. RIMA 2:212–14, A.101.1, iii.1–26a.

the Aramean penetrations had significant impact, the Ḫābūr was retained both through "pockets" or "islands" of Assyrians (like Dūr-Katlimmu) or through local dynasties that remained loyal to Assyria. Thus before these "show of strength" campaigns, there were already a number of places that were Assyrian and/or alternated with places that were loyal in nature, creating a piecemeal pattern of different forms of territorial control in the Ḫābūr region. This patchwork formed the basis for, as Liverani (1988a, 87–92) has termed it, a "network of communications" by which the Assyrian control was spread by means of the thickening of the mesh of the network. The other form of expansion that worked in conjunction with this was the basic component of Assyrian territory (constantly existing from the time of Middle Assyrian period onwards): the provinces. These were the basis for a spreading of control over the land.[201]

While this campaign of 878 BCE resembles those of Adad-nērārī II and Tukulti-Ninurta II, the major difference is that Aššurnaṣirpal, unlike his predecessors, received a very strong military challenge from the city of Sūru in the land of Sūḫu (located on the left side, i.e., north side, of the Euphrates River) where Babylonia had supplied a contingent of troops to confront him. This is a different Sūru than the Sūru of Bīt-Ḫalupē located on the Ḫābūr River—the focus of a previous campaign (campaign 2 in 883 BCE); and different from Sūra in the Mount Kašiyāri region.[202] This Sūru of the land of Sūḫu is probably to be identified with modern Sur Telbis (Tenu 2008, 163; Kepenski, Lecomte and Tenu 2006, 13).

Sūru was the fortified city of Kudurru,[203] the governor of the land of Sūḫu. This is a new ruler. Ili-ibni of Sūḫu had paid tribute to Tukulti-Ninurta II (885) and to Aššurnaṣirpal II (883). Kudurru—perhaps a usurper since Aššurnaṣirpal did indicate that he was Ili-ibni's son—wanted to escape tribute obligations.

If Bīt-Adīni was worried about the arrival of Assyrian power in the lower Ḫābūr and Middle Euphrates (thus instigating unrest and revolt in Laqē), on this occasion it was the Babylonian king Nabû-apla-iddina who was not willing to accept Assyrian influence in a zone that, for a long time, had had Babylonian connections (Clancier 2006, 253). Undoubtedly, this was even more crucial as far as the Babylonians were concerned because the outlet for the trade caravans from Tadmor and the Levant was in this zone (Dion 1997,

201. See the comments of Postgate 1992 255–56; and Yamada 2000a, 299–305.

202. Ninurta Temple Annals, RIMA 2:209, A.0.101.1, ii.93.

203. See Baker 2000f. In the inscriptions of Šamaš-rēša-uṣur, an early eighth-century governor of Sūḫu, Šamaš-rēša-uṣur traces his ancestry back through several generations, including "Adad-nadin-zeri, son of Kudurru" (RIMB 2:283, S.0.1001.2, line 2; also 2:284, S.0.1001.3, lines 2 and 4).

359–60 and n. 173). Thus the Babylonian intervention added to the general upheaval in the Middle Euphrates. With the significant support given to the land of Sūḫu, Aššurnaṣirpal II had no choice but to react.

With Aššurnaṣirpal's attack the resistance crumpled. Kudurru escaped via the Euphrates along with seventy of his soldiers. But the Assyrian king captured a sizeable haul of Babylonians, including fifty cavalrymen and other troops of Nabû-apla-iddina,[204] the king of Babylonia (886–851 BCE), Zabdānu (the brother of the Babylonian king), along with his three thousand troops, and Bēl-apla-iddina, the diviner (*bārû*), their commanding officer. Aššurnaṣirpal II took a great deal of plunder from the city and erected a stela commemorating his victory.

Kudurru's flight during this battle across the Euphrates may be pictured in a relief from Room B of the North West Palace at Nimrud (BM 124538) (Curtis and Reade 1995, 48–49). In the relief, three high-status enemies are depicted in the river attempting to escape Assyrian archers. One is swimming, but appears to be wounded with an arrow in his back; the other two (one is a beardless eunuch) are using inflated animal skins to support themselves in the water, blowing into them as they struggle toward a fort on the other side of the river (or perhaps an island in the middle). Later, the tribute of Kudurru of Sūḫu is depicted on a number of bronze bands (see below).

However, some time later (perhaps even the next year 877, but certainly between 877–866), Aššurnaṣirpal II received a report in Kalḫu that "all the lands of Laqē, Ḫindānu, and Sūḫu" were in revolt. The revolt was this time without Babylonian support (as opposed to the revolt in 878). Nevertheless, it appears to have had at least the passive support of the Aramean state of Bīt-Adīni who supplied a safe haven for the escapees. Aššurnaṣirpal immediately conducted a campaign (his ninth)[205] to deal with this new threat. The Assyrian king probably used the desert route to get to the Lower Ḫābūr quickly. The swiftness of his appearance in Laqē must have caused Azi-ili to flee the city. Aššurnaṣirpal then used Sūru of the land of Bīt-Ḫalupē as a staging area to prepare his next move against the rebels. He built boats to transport his troops down the river. Instead of marching, this conserved his army's energy and perhaps added an element of surprise since the rebel forces may not have expected attacks from the river.

Ironically, Azi-ili had been appointed governor in Sūru by Aššurnaṣirpal II after the 883 campaign that avenged the murder of Ḫamatāya by executing the usurper Aḫi-yababa (see above). Yet now it is this same Azi-ili (referred

204. For the king, see Brinkman 2001c.

205. RIMA 2:214–16, A.0.101.1, iii.26b–50a. Liverani designates this campaign VII (counting the double campaigns of 883 and 881, this would be his ninth campaign). See table 4.4.

to as Azi-ili, the Laqēan, $^{m}$*a-zi*-DINGIR KUR *la-qa-a-a*[206]) who has rebelled. He was not just a late addition to the rebel cause, but apparently had been one of the main conspirators all along.

In the initial phase of his campaign, Aššurnaṣirpal captured and destroyed the towns of Azi-ili and those of Hemti-ili[207] (another Laqēan/Aramean ruler). This phase took Aššurnaṣirpal down the Ḫābūr and then down the Euphrates, "from the mouth of the Ḫābūr River as far as the city of Ṣibatu of the land Sūḫu."

However, the revolt was still in full swing and Aššurnaṣirpal needed to deal with it by crossing to the other side of the Euphrates. This was accomplished by the boats that he had made in Sūru earlier and by rafts made of inflated goatskins. After crossing the river at Ḫaridu/Ḫaradu (modern Khirbet ed-Diniyeh),[208] all the combined troops of Sūḫu, Laqē, and Ḫindānu were encountered in the most significant engagement of the campaign.

It is apparent that the strategy of the rebels was to combine their forces in order to defeat the Assyrians in an open-field battle at a place of their choosing. Aššurnaṣirpal put it this way: "The Sūḫeans, Laqēans, (and) Ḫindāneans trusted in the massiveness of their chariotry, troops, (and) might; they mustered six thousand of their troops; they arose against me to wage war and battle."

Ḫaridu/Ḫāradu was about midway between Ḫindānu and Anat and Sūru of Sūḫu. It was across the river from Bīt-Šabāya and perhaps "the city of Ṣibatu of the land Sūḫu." Excavations of Khirbet el-Diniyeh have revealed that there was an Aramean phase in the tenth–ninth century BCE. But Aššurnaṣirpal II apparently recaptured the fort at this time (and later did construction work on it; Kepinski 2009, 152). It had been originally a fort built in the Middle Assyrian period.[209] In fact, the fort shows the marks of numerous sieges that it suffered, though apparently at this point Assyrian power prevailed in the region after Aššurnaṣirpal's campaign.

The crossing of the river itself is significant: since "the river is considered the border of the empire, its left bank being 'Assyrian,' and its right bank being 'outer' (on which Aššurnaṣirpal did not yet venture in campaign I B or in campaign VI)" (table 4.4; Liverani 1992a, 94; Lönnqvist 2011, 205). The result of the battle was 6,500 causalities for the combined forces

206. RIMA 2:214, A.0.101.1, iii.30, 38.

207. The name is West Semitic: Ḥamdi-'Il "My praise of God," or "My ardor is my god." See Fuchs 2000a. The name is spelled $^{m}$*ḫe-en-ti*-DINGIR and $^{m}$*ḫe-em-ti*-DINGIR.

208. For the original town on this site from the Old Babylonian period, see Joannès 1993; 2006. For the Iron Age fort on the site, see Kepinski 2009.

209. Tenu 2006a, 222–23. Built as part of the Middle Assyrian fort system. See chapter 3 above.

of Laqē, Sūḫu, and Ḫindānu.[210] Following this engagement, Azi-ili blocked the Assyrians at another river crossing at the city of Kipina. In the ensuing battle, one thousand more troops of the Laqēan ruler were killed, and his chariotry was destroyed. Azi-ili fled to Mount Bišri (KUR *Bi-su-ru*).[211] The mountain may have marked the border between Laqē and Bīt-Adini (Liverani 1992a, 70). A day later, Aššurnaṣirpal pursued after him, felling the remainder of his troops. But Azi-ili fled into the territory of Bīt-Adīni. Aššurnaṣirpal pursued, attacking and destroying two of Bīt-Adīni's cities (Dummetu and Azmu), and once again destroying the "rest of his troops" and carrying away "his valuable booty, oxen (and) sheep that, like the stars of heaven, had no number."[212] But somehow Azi-ili escaped, vanishing deeper into Bīt-Adīni's territory.

The last statement in this episode relates that after the destructions of Dummetu and Azmu, Aššurnaṣirpal "emerged from the narrows of the Euphrates" (*ina hi-in-qi šá* ÍD *pu-rat-te*). This is most likely a reference to the narrows of Hanuqa, halfway between Der ez-Zor and Raqqa.[213] It is very significant that Bīt-Adīni's territorial possessions were this far down the Euphrates from the confluence with the Balīḫ.

Although Azi-ili escaped, as a consolation, Aššurnaṣirpal II captured another Laqēan sheikh (*nasīku*) named Ilâ, and deported him, along with his troops, to the city of Assur. Finally, with Azi-ili and Ilâ neutralized, a third Laqēan (tribal) ruler, Hemti-ili, was confined to his city (*ina* URU-*šú e-sir-šu*). Aššurnaṣirpal records that he became afraid, submitted to him, and paid his (back) tribute. Nonetheless, Aššurnaṣirpal imposed a greater tribute upon him as a result of the revolt. However, the phrase "I confined him in his own city" may be an indication that Hemti-ili successfully resisted the siege of his city, remaining on the throne.[214]

After this campaign, the area of Laqē was satisfactorily under control. The exact status of Ḫindānu and Sūḫu is not clear. It is likely that although defeated, they kept some degree of independence. But it appears that Kudurru also paid tribute. This is clear from the three bronze bands on the Gate of the

---

210. Note this figure is five hundred more than the number given for the troops of the coalition (six thousand).

211. In the inscriptions of Tiglath-pileser I, Mount Bišri (KUR *bé-eš-ri*) was a homeland of some of the Arameans that he battled (RIMA 2:23, A.0.87.1, v.59).

212. RIMA 2:215, A.0.101.1, iii.42b–43a.

213. Liverani 1992a, 70 and fig. 8; Lipiński 2000a, 182; Bagg 2007, 38, s.v. Azmu; 62–63, s.v. Dummutu; Herles 2007a, 430–31 suggests Azmu (Zalabiya) and Dummetu (Ḥalabiya).

214. Liverani 1992a, 94–95. Note the parallel situations with Shalmaneser III and Hazael; Sennacherib and Hezekiah.

temple of Mamu that depict formal tribute being sent from Sūḫu to Assyria, two of which have epigraphs declaring the tribute as belonging to Kudurru.

> Band MM ASH II L6[215]
> *ma-da-tu šá* $^{\text{m}}$*ku-dúr-ri* KUR *su-ḫa-a-a*
> "Tribute of Kudurru.[216] the Sūḫean"
>
> Band MM ASH II R1[217]
> URU *im-gur-*$^{\text{d}}$*Enlíl ma-da!-tú šá* $^{\text{m}}$*ku-dúr-ri šá* KUR [*su-ḫi*]
> "The city Imgur-Enlil. Tribute from Kudurru of the land [Sūḫu]"
>
> Band MM ASH II R3[218]
> [ . . . . . KUR] *su-ḫi*
> "[ . . . . . the land] of Sūḫu"

There is a clear emphasis made on the reduction of Sūḫu to tributary status in the famous Banquet Stela of Aššurnaṣirpal II.[219] Moreover, to insure this status Aššurnaṣirpal rebuilt the fort at Ḫaradu and founded two others to protect Assyrian interest in Laqē and Sūḫu:

> I founded two cities on the Euphrates. I called the name of one on this bank of the Euphrates: Kār-Aššurnaṣirpal; I called the name of one on the other bank of the Euphrates: Nēbarti-Aššur.

Excavations at Tall Masaikh seem to confirm that this is Kār-Aššurnaṣirpal because of the discovery of an Assyrian stela on the site. The findspot enabled the recognition of four phases of the Neo-Assyrian occupation, including a perimeter wall and the so-called palace and associated outbuildings (Masetti-Rouault 2004; 2007; and Herles 2007a, 429). In the case of Nēbarti-Aššur, its equation with al-Graiye 3 is not yet confirmed, but Neo-Assyrian pottery has been found on the site (See Geyer et al. 2003, 84).

---

215. See Curtis and Tallis 2008, 59 and figs. 67 and 68.

216. Curtis and Tallis (2008, 59) note: "The phonetic writing of the name $^{\text{I}}$*ku-dúr-ri* here and on Band MM ASH II Rl confirms the reading proposed by Streck 1905–6, 252, and Brinkman 1968, 185 n. 1129."

217. See Curtis and Tallis 2008, 62 and figs. 73 and 74. See RIMA 2:351, A.0.101.97. See also Barnett 1973, esp. the unnumbered plate following p. 22; Oates 1983.

218. Curtis and Tallis 2008, 64 and figs. 77 and 78.

219. RIMA 2:289, A.0.101.30, line 12. See also Curtis and Tallis 2008, 44 (Band BM ASH II R7).

## 4.6. Bīt-Zamāni

The Aramean polity of Bīt-Zamāni is first assuredly encountered in the inscriptions of Tukulti-Ninurta II (890–884 BCE; see fig. 4.10).[220] Lipiński (2000a, 135) suggests that the name upon which the tribal eponym is based occurs as an Amurrite personal name in southern Babylonia in the eighteenth century: *Za-am-ma-a-nu-um, Za-am-ma-nu-um*. The personal name is also found in a seventh-century Neo-Assyrian document written: $^{m}$*Za-am-ma-a-ni*.[221] It also occurs in North Arabian inscriptions.[222] The original meaning of the name is uncertain. One possibility is to see the name as coming from the root *zmm* "to tie up," hence "fastener."[223] Another possibility is to derive the name from $zmn_1$ "to invite" or $zmn_2$ "appointed," "prepared," "set."[224]

In a text from Tell Billa (the ancient Assyrian city of Šibaniba) dating from the thirteenth century BCE, J. J. Finkelstein (1953, 124: Billa 6:8) read and translated: $^{md}$*A-šur*-KUR-*id* $^{(6)}$ DUMU EN-*qarrād* $^{(7)}$ LÚ.*ḫa-síḫ-li* $^{(8)}$ *ša ḫal-ṣí* É-*za-ma-ni* "Aššur-kāšid, son of Bēl-qarrād, *ḫassiḫlu* of the district of the city of Bīt-Zamāni." Finkelstein (1953, 119) understood this to be a possible reference to the Aramean tribal entity stating: "Bīt-Zamāni (if the reading should be borne out) is the westernmost place mentioned (Bi 6 8)."[225] Lipiński has assumed this reading is correct and has constructed a Middle Assyrian province of Bīt-Zamāni.[226]

The difficulty with this is not the occurrence of an Aramean entity this early (though it would be considerably earlier than Tiglath-pileser I's inscriptions).[227] The Aramean groups surely predate the Tiglath-pileser reference, at least by a couple of centuries or so. The problem with the Tell Billa text is threefold. First, in spite of Finkelstein's assurance (1953, 124), "repeated collation of the tablet, however, has convinced the writer that the given reading is correct," his drawing is not so convincing.[228] Frankly, I doubt that this is in any way a reference to the Aramean tribal group. Second, it is very odd that a Middle Assyrian provincial name is based on an Aramean tribal entity in the thirteenth century in the Upper Tigris region in an area that was likely under the jurisdiction of the province of Tušḫan.

---

220. For a recent discussion of Bīt-Zamāni, see Szuchman 2009a.
221. Ahmad 1996, especially Text 4, line 2. See also Lipiński 2011.
222. Harding 1971, 301, s.v. *zm*, but note also *zmn*.
223. Lipiński 2000a, 135; 2011. The another root $zmm_2$ could also mean "to buzz."
224. *DNWSI*, 332, s.v. *zmn*. See Syriac.
225. See also Nashef 1982, 74, s.v. Bīt-Zamāni.
226. Lipiński 2000a, 135. Followed by Szuchman 2009, 56 n. 1, and 58.
227. If the Egyptian reference to "Aram" is considered (see chapter 2), this being a reference to an Aramean entity is not impossible.
228. Finkelstein 1953, 150, number 6, line 8. I have real doubts about the É sign.

Third, and importantly, there is not a single scrap of other evidence for Bīt-Zamāni being a province in the Middle Assyrian period. No mention of Bīt-Zamāni as a province is found in any of the *ginā'ū* texts (Rosa 2010; Freydank 2012). After the Neo-Assyrian conquest of the Aramean entity, Bīt-Zamāni became a province (Radner 2006–8a, 49–51; see discussion at the end of section 4.6.2 below). Therefore, there is significant doubt as to the validity of Lipiński's interpretation.

### 4.6.1. Territory

It is clear from the historical data preserved in the inscriptions of Tukulti-Ninurta II and Aššurnaṣirpal II that at the beginning of the Assyrian recovery of the Upper Tigris, the chiefs (*nasīku*) of Bīt-Zamāni (with its capital at Amedi) controlled the cities of Damdammusa, Sinabu, and Tīdu (and perhaps at some point earlier, the city of Tušḫan; see history below).

Many of these cities can now be identified. Amedi, the ancient city of Bīt-Zamāni, was located at modern Diyarbakır.[229] Sinabu (earlier Šinamu of Aššur-bēl-kala's Broken Obelisk) was Tell Pornak, roughly 30 km west of the modern city of Bismil.[230] This city (in the form Šinamu) is mentioned in the newly published texts (Text 10, line 12) from modern Giricano (ancient Dunnu-ša-Uzibi).[231] Tīdu is very likely Üçtepe (Kurkh),[232] roughly 13 km west of Bismil, and Tušḫa(n) is modern Ziyaret Tepe,[233] roughly 12 km east of Bismil. However, Damdammusa is more difficult to locate, perhaps to be identified with Aktepe.[234]

229. The name Amedu is West Semitic and is not attested in the texts of the second millennium before Aramean autonomous rule in the region. The site was likely occupied, but had a different name. See Lipiński 2000a, 153.

230. Radner and Schachner 2001, 754–57; Liverani 1992a, 38–39; and Kessler 1980, 117–20; Nashef 1982, 249.

231. See Radner 2004a, 90. Lipiński (2002, 230–31) identifies Šinamu with Fafih, 30 km west of Midyat. But see Kessler 1980, 117–20; Liverani 1992a, 38–39.

232. Köroğlu 1998, Resim (Image) 3, 4. See Szuchman 2009a, 59–60; Kessler 1980, 117–21; Liverani 1992a, 38–39; Radner and Schachner 2001, 754–57; Contra Lipiński 2002, 233–34. See Younger 2007a, 247 n. 11.

233. The confirmation that Ziyaret Tepe is Tušḫan is now very likely through the implications of the Neo-Assyrian texts discovered at the site. See Parpola 2008, 25–27. Contra Lipiński (2000a, 142) who argued that Tušḫan was Kurkh.

234. Kessler 1980, 119; Liverani 1992a, 36. Lipiński (2000a, 148) suggested placing Damdammusa at Pornak.

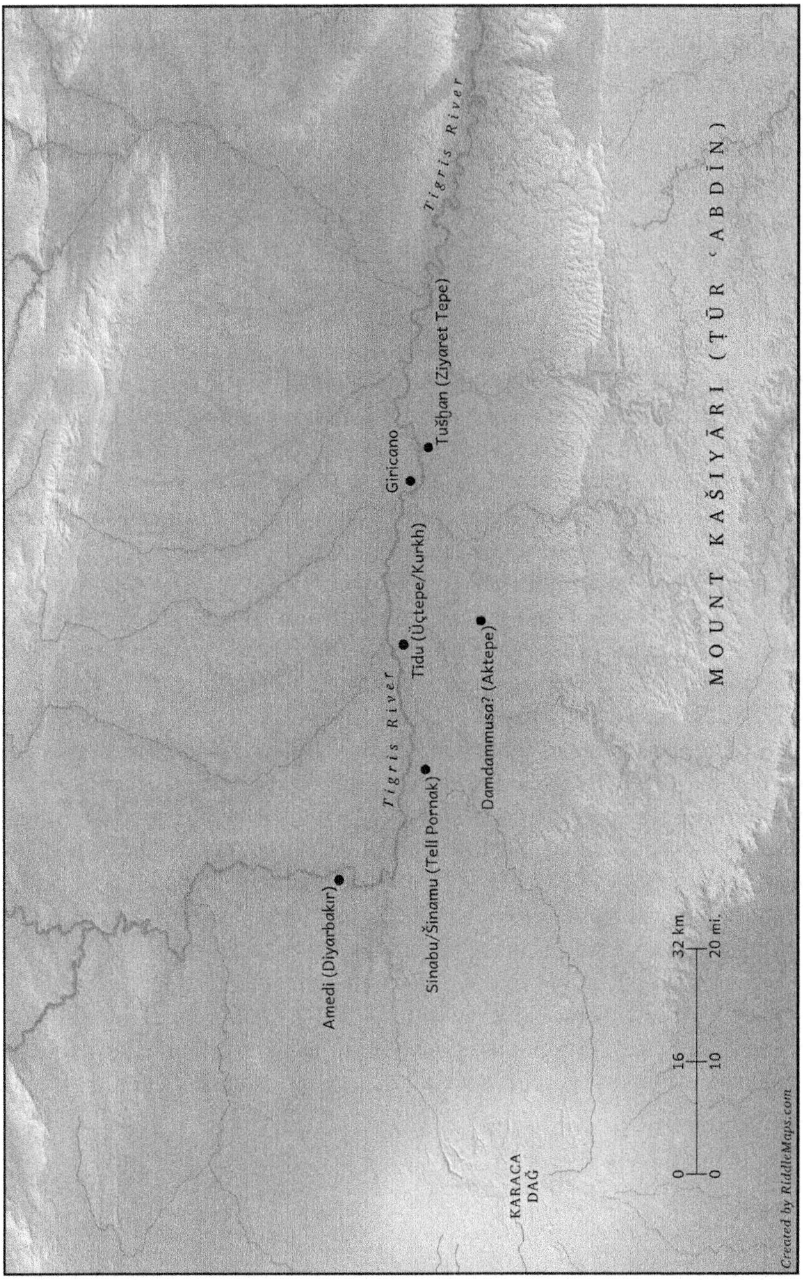


Fig. 4.10. Upper Tigris

4.6.2. History

The Middle Assyrian Empire controlled the region from roughly the time of Adad-nērārī I, establishing an important provincial center at Tušḫan (Ziyaret Tepe). The 2009–2010 excavations of this site have uncovered an underlying Bronze Age, that is, Middle Assyrian building (Matney et al. 2011), in addition to many Neo-Assyrian discoveries at the site.

However, in spite of Aššur-bēl-kala's claims of victory over the various Arameans that he fought in the region, it is clear that this was, at best, a holding action (see ch. 3 above). The evidence points to an Aramean seizure, for when the Assyrians again come back into the region the Arameans are in possession, although there is evidence that there was a significant substrate of Šubrians, as well as perhaps others who cannot yet be fully identified.[235] Moreover, some of the toponyms and personal names (e.g., Damdammusa) may be Hurrian or Urartian (Zadok 1995, 270). The very nature of the Nairi lands (see below), of which Bīt-Zamāni was a part (as the Assyrian inscriptions demonstrate) means that the region was a porous frontier zone, where many cultures came into contact (Szuchman 2009a, 59; Parker 2001).

It was Tukulti-Ninurta II (890–884 BCE) who was the first Assyrian king to penetrate the Upper Tigris in an effort to restore Assyrian control. While he campaigned in the years 889–885 (his second to sixth regnal years), it was only during his 886 and 885 campaigns that he had contact with the Arameans.

In 886 BCE, Tukulti-Ninurta II campaigned north of Mount Kašiyāri, encountering the Aramean tribal state of Bīt-Zamāni, which was part of the larger region of Nairi (Roaf and Schachner 2005, 119). The Nairi lands were a very loosely organized group of allied entities, under the direction of "kings" (the Middle Assyrian texts give the totals of 23, 60, or 30 *šarrānu*), who were really tribal chiefs (Salvini 1998–2001). There was no real central governance or organization. So far as we know, Bīt-Zamāni was the only Aramean entity counted by the Assyrians as being part of the Nairi lands.

At the time of Tukulti-Ninurta II's campaign, Bīt-Zamāni was under the rule of an individual named Amme-Ba'al.[236] Bīt-Zamāni's capital was Amedu (modern Diyarbakır). This city is at the head of the navigation of the Tigris, at the junction of important roads and near rich copper mines. Tukulti-Ninurta II relates:

235. As perhaps seen in a cuneiform tablet from Ziyaret Tepe. See MacGinnis 2011; 2012.

236. For this name, see chapter 10 (the name Balammu of the Amatu tribe).

> With the support [of Aššur, my lord], in the month Simānu (Sivan), the first day, the eponymy of Ilī-milku, I departed from Nineveh. [I marched] to the lands of [Nairi ...] [At] the Subnat River, I crossed to Mount Kašiyāri.
>
> I approached the city P[a]tiškun [belonging to Amme-Ba'al], a man of Bīt-Zamāni. I established ... against ... [...] I destroyed two cities in its environs. The grain (and) straw of his land [...]; [...]; I carried off the people of his land as prisoners. I decisively defeated them. His sons [...] I felled many with the sword.
>
> I had mercy on him. His son ... [...]. In order to save his life he seized my feet; I pardoned him. [...] my officers inside [...]. Bronze, tin, iron, pots, ... [...]. Horses, mules before my officers [...] I took away for myself. I was merciful toward Amme-Ba'al, a man of Bīt-Zamāni (m*am-me-ba-a'-li* DUMU m*za-ma-a-ni*).
>
> I established (them) in abandoned cities (and) settled them in peaceful dwellings. I had him take an oath by Aššur, my lord, before the statue of [*the storm god Adad*]:
>
> "If you (plural: *attunu*) give horses to my enemies (or) my allies,[237] may the god Adad/Hadad [strike your] land with dangerous lightning."[238]

Tukulti-Ninurta's destruction of some of Amme-Ba'al's cities and plundering his people and grain apparently caused Amme-Ba'al (m*am-me-ba-a'-li*)[239] to beg for mercy, which was shown to him.[240] Tukulti-Ninurta

---

237. The term *salmēya* in the phrase *a-na* KÚR.MEŠ-*ia sa-al-me-ia* has been understood as referring to "my foes." See Schramm 1970, 156: "meinen Feinden, meinen Gegnern"; and Grayson RIMA 2:172, A.0.100.5: "to my enemies (and) foes." However, see *CAD* 15:104–5. An important parallel is seen in the Esarhaddon loyalty oath: *lu-u ina pi-i* LÚ.KÚR-*šú lu-u ina pi-i sal-me-šú* "(If you hear any evil ... against Aššurbanipal ... either from the mouth of his enemy or from the mouth of his ally (or his brothers, sons, or daughters ...)" (SAA 2:33, 6.111b–112). Clearly, the juxtaposition of *nakru* and *salmu* formulates the connotation "anyone." In the case of the Tukulti-Ninurta II passage, the word pair is probably forming a merism. Hence, no trade of horses except with Tukulti-Ninurta II of Assyria is acceptable.

238. RIMA 1:172, A.0.100.5, 12b–25.

239. Lipiński (2000a, 153) suggests that the name means "My ancestor is lord" since Ba'al is not a "theophorous element here but a predicate, while the subject of the sentence forming the name is the suffixed word *'amm*, 'ancestor.'" Since Ba'al is not commonly a theophoric element among Aramean personal names, Lipiński's point has merit. However, see Åkerman and Radner 1998: "Ba'al is [my] paternal uncle."

240. It is very unclear whether there is a relationship between this passage and an earlier passage that mentions a certain m*bi-x*[...]-*šú šá* m*am-me-b*[*a-a'-li*] (if the restoration is correct) (line 4). Since in the passage of lines 12b–25, the personal name seems to

Table 4.4. Aššurnaṣirpal II's Campaigns (parts 1 and 2)

Column 1 designates the two major sections of the "Ninurta Temple Annals" that narrate the campaigns: 1 = i.43–ii.124 (first to fifth regnal yrs.; 2 = iii.1–112 (sixth to eighteenth regnal years) * Liverani's datings. **According "The Ninurta Temple Annals" from Kalḫu; *RIMA* 2, A.0.101.1). ***Standard Inscription (A.0.101.23:9); Bulls (A.0.101.2:13); Banquet Stela (A.0.101.30:14). ****Note that all campaigns are introduced by some date formula. This is the only exception. Thus it may not be a separate campaign.

| | Year | Regnal Year | Liverani's Numbering | Campaign | Dating | Places Campaigned |
|---|---|---|---|---|---|---|
| 1 | | acc. | | none | | |
| | 883 | first | IA (spring) | campaign 1 (i.43b–69a)** | "In my accession year (and) my first regnal year" | Tummu, Kirruru, Ḫabḫu, Gilzānu, Ḫubuškia |
| | | | IB (fall) | campaign 2 (i.69b–99a) | "In this same eponymy on the 24th day of Ab" | Katmuḫu, Sūru of Bīt-Ḫalupē; Ḫindānu and Sūḫu |
| | 882 | second | II | campaign 3 (i.99b/101b–ii.23a) | "In the eponym year of my name" | Nairi (Urumu/Nirbu, Bīt-Zamāni, Shubru, Nirdun); esp. Urumu/ Nirbu |
| | 881 | third | IIIA (spring) | campaign 4 (ii.23b–33a) | "In the eponym of Aššur-iddin" | Zamua |
| | | | IIIB (fall) | campaign 5 (ii.33b–49a) | "On the 15th day of Tishri" | Zamua |
| | 880 | fourth | IV | campaign 6 (ii.49b–86a) | "In the eponymy of Miqti-adur" | Zamua |
| | 879 | fifth | V | campaign 7 (ii.86b–125a) | "On the 1st day of Sivan, in the eponymy of Ša-ilima-damqa" | Nairi: focus on Nirdun, Bīt-Zamāni, and Shubru |

| | | | | | | |
|---|---|---|---|---|---|---|
| | 878 | sixth | VI | campaign 8 (iii.1–26a) | "On the 22nd day of Sivan, in the eponymy Dagan-bēla-uṣur" | "Show of strength" in Ḫābūr and Middle Euphrates; Sūru of Sūḫu |
| | 877 | | VII | campaign 9 (iii.26b–50a) | "On the 18th day of Sivan" | Revolt of Laqē, Ḫindānu and Sūḫu |
| | 876–868* | | VIII | campaign 10 (iii.50b–56a) | "On the 20th day of Sivan" | Attacked the city of Kaprabi, Yalligu/Alligu, Rug(g)ulitu, and Marinâ; tribute of Bīt-Adīni and Til-Abnâ |
| 2 | 875–867* | | IX | campaign 11 (iii.56b–92a) | "On the 8th day of Iyyar" | Patina; Karkamiš; Yaḫānu; plundering Luḫuti |
| | | | | campaign 12? (iii.77b–92a)? | "At that time"**** | *to the Mediterranean*. Brinkman; Grayson; Na'aman; but see Schramm; Hawkins; Liverani |
| | 866 | eighteenth | X | campaign 12/13 (iii.92b–113a) | "In the eponymy of Šamaš-nūri" | tribute of Qipānu, (A)zallu, Kummuḫ; Aššа; dealt with Bīt-Zamāni's seizure of Damdammusa |
| | ? | ? | | campaign 13/14 *** | — | Urartu |

had Amme-Ba'al (and apparently his magnates since the second-person plural *attunu* is used) swear a loyalty oath in the name of Aššur in the cult center in front of the statue of the local storm god. The text continues and notes that two-thirds of the silver taken from Amme-Ba'al of Bīt-Zāmani was given to the god Aššur, and one third was kept for the palace treasury.[241] It appears that Amme-Ba'al kept his oath and fulfilled his obligations as an Assyrian vassal throughout the remainder of Tukulti-Ninurta's reign and the beginning of Aššurnaṣirpal II's reign, until his murder.

In 882 BCE, Aššurnaṣirpal, like his father, focused his third (Liverani's II) campaign (table 4.4)[242] on the geopolitical entity of Nairi (corresponding in this instance to roughly the upper Tigris basin; Liverani 1992a, 41, 89). At this time, Nairi seems to have been comprised of a group of four autonomous polities that included: Bīt-Zamāni, Šubru, Nirdun, and Urumu/Nirbu, that is, all the countries around the upper Tigris, on the north and south sides of the river. In the Tigris Valley, the Assyrians had two fortified towns, Damdammusa and Tušḫan. It was an attack on the former that provided Aššurnaṣirpal II with the excuse for invading Nairi.

> In the same eponymy, while I was in Nineveh, a report was brought back to me: "men of Assyria (and) Ḫulāya, their city-lord—whom Shalmaneser ('Salmānu is foremost'), king of Assyria, a prince who preceded me, had settled in the city of Ḫalziluḫa—had rebelled; they had come to capture the city of Damdammusa, my royal city."[243]

The city of Ḫalziluḫa[244] (located in Urumu/Nirbu) had been settled by Shalmaneser.[245] Some Assyrian colonists and their "city-lord," Ḫulāya,[246] had rebelled and brought about the seizure of Damdammusa. Aššurnaṣirpal

be qualified by DUMU ᵐ*za-ma-a-ni*, which is missing in lines 4–5, this may not be the same person. Moreover, there is uncertainty as to who is speaking in the passage. On the other hand, if it is the same person, then lines 12b–25 are recording a rebellion. But this raises the question as to when Bīt-Zamāni became a vassal. In my opinion, due to the fragmentary and otherwise difficult to interpret passage from the initial lines of the inscription, it is safer to assume that these two stories are not connected and that Amme-Ba'al became vassal with the loyalty oath administered in line 25. Rebellious vassals are not usually spared. Lipiński (2000a, 138–41) offers a full interpretation of lines 4–8.

241. RIMA 2:171–72, A.0.100.5, lines 11–29.

242. RIMA 2:200–203, i.99b/101b–ii.23a.

243. RIMA 2:200, A.0.101.1, i.102–103.

244. Ḫalziluḫa (URU *ḫal-zi/ṣi-lu-ḫa*); compare *ḫassiḫlu ḫalṣi* (Tell Billa 6:8).

245. RIMA 2:200, i.101b–103. The reference could be to Shalmaneser I (r. 1263–1234) or to Shalmaneser II (r. 1030–1019). See discussion below.

246. The name Ḫulāya is Akkadian and he may have been an Assyrian himself. See Baker and Fuchs 2000.

captured Kinabu, a fortified city of Ḫulāya, and then captured him. Ḫulāya was flayed and his skin draped over the wall of Damdammusa. Aššurnaṣirpal used this attack on Damdammusa as a pretext to target all of Urumu/Nirbu. In order to help secure the gains in the region, he renovated Tušḫan (modern: Ziyaret Tepe). While the other states of Nairi (Bīt-Zamāni, Šubru, and Nirdun) remained outside the military operations against Urumu/Nirbu, they paid their tribute. Thus Amme-Baʿal, a man of Bīt-Zamāni, Ilī-ḫite[247] of Šubru, and Labṭuri, the son of Ṭubusu/Ṭupusu of the land of Nirdun brought their tribute to Aššurnaṣirpal II at Tušḫan. Bīt-Zamāni appears to be the only Aramean tribal polity among the four.[248]

A parallel to this political situation may be seen in Aššurnaṣirpal's campaigns of 881 and 880 (campaigns 4, 5, and 6), which were directed against Zamua in the east. The initial part of these campaigns was against a certain Nūr-Adad, the sheikh of the land of Dagara (ᵐZÁLAG-ᵈIŠKUR LÚ.*na-si-ku šá* KUR.*da-ga-ra*) who was able to get the entire land of Zamua (KUR.*za-mu-a*) to band together against the Assyrians. The Assyrian king defeated Nūr-Adad at the Babitu Pass where the enemy had attempted to build a wall to block the pass.[249] Some scholars understand the name Nūr-Adad as Akkadian.[250] Others have suggested that this sheikh (*nasīku*) was an Aramean.[251] Zadok (2013, 312) suggests that the Neo-Assyrian writings of KUR/URU.*da-ga-ra* may derive from the root *dgr* "to heap, gather together,"[252] just as similarly Neo-Assyrian URU.*di-gi-ri-na* in a letter from the reign of Sargon[253] would be the root plus the Aramaic plural -*īn*. The fact that Arameans penetrated Īdu (modern Sātu Qala),[254] upstream on the Lower Zab, not all

247. Ilu-ḫiti (written: DINGIR–*ḫi-ti*) "May the god smite" (*ḫiti* being G imperative of *ḫatû* "smite"). Note the Šubrian has a Semitic name, unless this has been improperly analyzed.

248. Liverani (1992a, 40) suggests the possibility that the designation given to Labṭuri, "the son of Ṭupusi/Ṭubusi," may indicate a member of a tribe called Bīt-Ṭubusi; hence possibly another Aramean tribal entity. However, the name Labṭuri is probably Urartian/Biainilian. See Fuchs 2001b; Salvini 1987–90. Thus it seems more likely that "son of Ṭupusi" is Labṭuri's patronym or an Urartian tribal designation. See Grayson's translation in RIMA 2:202; and Lipiński 2000a, 154.

249. RIMA 2:203–4, A.0.101.1, ii.23b–31a.

250. Brinkman 2001b; Lipiński 2000a, 495: "he is probably no Semite and bears the Assyro-Babylonian name."

251. Dion 1997, 35 n. 46; Zadok 2013, 312. Note the name of a Temanite sheikh: Nūr-Adad (see above, pp. 232–33, 240–41).

252. Jastrow 1950, 280; *HALOT*, 214.

253. SAA 19:124, 123.11; see earlier Saggs 2001, 95–96, and pl. 20 (ND 2786), line 11.

254. See discussion on pp. 188–90.

that far from the Babitu Pass,[255] means that some Arameans may have come into the region of Zamua, at least in its westernmost areas. Three additional facts are noteworthy: (1) Tukulti-Ninurta II (r. 890–884), Aššurnaṣirpal II's father, appears to have engaged Arameans in the region. His inscription reads: "I approached the cities of the land of Ladānu which the A[rameans and] (KUR.⸢*a*⸣-[*ru-mu u*]) the Lullu held."[256] In light of the Assyrian Chronicle 4 and the location of Īdu, Grayson's restoration is more probably correct. (2) Aramaic was used in the Bukān inscription (Tapeh Qâlaychi) in Mannea (see fig. 1.6).[257] (3) An Aramean sheikh gave testimony in Mannea[258] (presumably in Aramaic). This means that Arameans and the Aramean language may have penetrated this zone much earlier than might have been expected. The political status of Zamua is likely analogous to that of Nairi: a series of local kingdoms, not yet tributary to Assyria (Liverani 1992a, 90). Thus it may be, that like Nairi with different entities with at least one being Aramean, Zamua had multiple polities with perhaps one being Aramean.

In 879, his fifth regnal year, Aššurnaṣirpal II conducted his seventh campaign, vying again for control of Nairi (completing what he had started in 882).[259] There was no need to attack Urumu/Nirbu which had been conquered in 882; the focus was now on the other three polities that comprised Nairi: Nirdun, Bīt-Zamāni and Šubru. Nirdun was subdued; its ruler, however, Labṭuri escaped. In the case of Bīt-Zamāni, Amme-Ba'al had apparently kept his oath and had fulfilled his obligations as an Assyrian vassal. But his loyalty to Assyria was not approved of by some of his nobles and people. They rebelled against him and murdered him. It is likely that these magnates had sworn the oath earlier (see above). Aššurnaṣirpal marched to Bīt-Zamāni in order to avenge his death. The nobles submitted quickly, and Aššurnaṣirpal received the palace treasure (chariots, horses, metals, bronze vessels, textiles, and furniture) as well as livestock, Amme-Ba'al's sister, and the daughters of the nobles, all with their dowries.[260]

It is worth noting that at this stage in the reassertion of the Assyrian Empire the place played by political marriage, particularly in the case of Aššurnaṣirpal II. It is also noteworthy that neither Amme-Ba'al in 882 nor

255. Identified with the Bazian Pass. See Liverani 1992a, 46.

256. RIMA 2:172, A.0.100.5, lines 34b–35a. See now Pappi 2012, 606.

257. Fales 2003; Lemaire 1998b, 1998c, 1999.

258. SAA 10:94, 113.r.7b–r.10a (= *ABL* 1109+). See chapter 10, under the discussion of the Yaqīmānu tribe.

259. This campaign is recorded in his annals (RIMA 2:208–11, A.0.101.1, ii.86b–125a) but also in a more detailed account in Aššurnaṣirpal II's Kurkh Monolith Inscription (RIMA 2:256–57, A.0.101.19, lines 25b–103).

260. Aššurnaṣirpal's Annals, RIMA 2:211, A.0.101.1, ii.118b–125a.

the nobles in 879 were executed. Both remained in power. Consequently, it may be surmised that Assyrian power in the region, while obviously the superior force on the battlefield, was not able to secure the region alone. Political allies were still important, since the very composition of the Nairi lands worked against Assyrian domination.

However, not every noble escaped execution. Only Aššurnaṣirpal's Kurkh Monolith adds the following details about this 879 campaign in Bīt-Zamāni.

> I flayed Bur-Rammānu, the criminal (*bēl ḫiṭṭi*), (and) draped his skin over the wall of the city of Sinabu. I appointed Ilānu, his brother, to the position of sheikh/chief (*nasīkūte*). I imposed upon him as annual tribute: 2 minas of gold, 13(?) minas of silver, 1,000 sheep, (and) 2,000 (measures) of barley. I repossessed the cities of Sinabu (and) Tīdu—fortresses which Shalmaneser (I),[261] king of Assyria, a prince who preceded me, had garrisoned against the land of Nairi (and) which the Arameans (KUR *a-ru-mu*) had captured by force (*ina dannāni*). I resettled the Assyrians—who in the land of Nairi had held fortresses of Assyria (and) whom the Arameans had trampled—in their (the Arameans') abandoned cities (and) houses. I placed them in a peaceful abode. I uprooted 1,500 Aramean-*Aḫlamû* (*aḫ-la-me-e* KUR *ar-ma-a-ia*) troops of Amme-Ba'al, a man of Bīt-Zamāni (DUMU *za-ma-a-ni*), (and) brought (them) to Assyria. I reaped the harvest of the land of Nairi (and) stored (it) for the sustenance of my land in the cities of Tušḫa(n), Damdammusa, Sinabu (and) Tīdu.[262]

Thus Aššurnaṣirpal II had Amme-Ba'al's murderer, a certain Bur-Rammānu ("son of Rammān [lit. thunderer]"),[263] flayed alive and his skin placed on display on the wall of the city of Sinabu. The choice of the wall of the city of Sinabu (Šinamu) for the "drapping" of the skin of the flayed Bur-Rammānu (clearly an Aramean) is not fortuitous! This city, founded early in the establishment of the Middle Assyrian Empire by Shalmaneser I, was the site of a battle in the days of Aššur-bēl-kala, and was, at some point, seized by force by the Arameans. So drapping the skin on the wall of this city had special significance to the Assyrians. It is also not fortuitous that Aššurnaṣirpal

261. The reference could be to Shalmaneser I (r. 1263–1234) (Lipiński 2000a, 158) or to Shalmaneser II (r. 1030–1019) (Grayson RIMA 2:261). Shalmaneser I's founding of these fortresses seems perhaps more likely than Shalmaneser II who reigned during the time of Assyrian weakness and about whose military activities next to nothing is known. See Radner and Schachner 2001.

262. Aššurnaṣirpal's Kurkh Monolith, RIMA 2:261–62, A.0.101.19, lines 91–97.

263. Baker 1999. The importance of the cult of the storm god in Bīt-Zamāni appears already in the imprecation that sealed the oath imposed on Amme-Ba'al by Tukulti-Ninurta II (see above pp. 296–97).

chose to use the phrase Aramean-*Aḫlamû*[264] to harken back to the days of Tiglath-pileser I. Thus, while these Arameans had inflicted damage on the Assyrian kingdom, ironically Aššurnaṣirpal II was now making things right, "uprooting" (*nasāḫu*) 1,500 men of Bīt-Zamāni, "Aramean-*Aḫlamû*" from the land that had been Assyrian! Finally, Ilānu, his (probably Bur-Rammānu's) brother,[265] was appointed as the new chief (*nasīku*)[266] and vassal of Assyria. Such an appointment is somewhat surprising, but perhaps Ilānu was the rightful heir(?). In any case, this man will not prove to be loyal.

It also becomes clear from this passage that Aššurnaṣirpal used the murder of Amme-Ba'al as an excuse to repossess (*ana ramēnīya utterra*, lit., "turned back to my own") the two cities, Sinabu and Tīdu,[267] which had been Assyrian fortresses in the region since the days of Shalmaneser I, but had been seized at some point in the past by the Arameans "by force" (*ina dannāni*).

Aššurnaṣirpal's last involvements in Bīt-Zamāni were during his final campaign (his twelfth) which took place in 866 BCE (his eighteenth regnal year).[268] After marching to the west to Ḫuzirīna where he received the tribute of Qipānu, Azallu, Kummuḫ (classical Commagene), and the land of Ašša, he invaded the land of Ḫabḫu.[269] This apparently was the first major military objective of the campaign.[270] This also put the Assyrian army more or less directly west of Bīt-Zamāni and in a position to fulfill the second objective of the campaign, namely, the reconquest of Damdammusa, the Assyrian fortress that had once again been captured and occupied by the Arameans of Bīt-Zamāni under the leadership of Ilānu, "a man of Bīt-Zamāni."[271] Ironically, this is the brother of the rebel Bur-Rammānu that Aššurnaṣirpal II had installed in 879 after the murder of Amme-Ba'al.

---

264. While his grandfather, Adad-nērārī II, used the phrase KUR *aḫ-la-me-e* KUR *ar-ma-a-ia*.MEŠ, one must go back to Tiglath-pileser I to find its use. So while it is an archaic usage, it is intended to produce irony.

265. The nearest antecedent for -*šu* on *aḫīšu* would be Bur-Rammānu.

266. The term obviously reflects the tribal structure of Bīt-Zamāni. See discussion in chapter 2 and Szuchman 2009a, 57.

267. For the identifications, see above.

268. For the campaign, see RIMA 2:219–21, A.0.101.1, iii.92b–113a. The eponym for the eighteenth regnal year, Šamaš-nūri, may be the same person who is the father of Hadad-Yith'i of the Tell Fakhariya Inscription. See discussion above.

269. For its location, see Liverani 1992a, 82–83.

270. Ḫabḫu seems to have been a loose term encompassing the more precise toponyms: Adanu, Dirria, Mallanu, and Zamba. None of these appear to be Aramean, and the political situation seems to be one of fragmentation. The entire area is plundered and laid waste; no local kings are mentioned.

271. Of course, a similar situation had already occurred in the 882 campaign. See above.

Although Damdammusa was besieged, stormed, and captured, Aššurnaṣirpal was not able to complete the punishment of Bīt-Zamāni. Its capital city, Amedu, was attacked, but it appears to have successfully resisted the siege. So Aššurnaṣirpal eventually vented his anger by impaling some prisoners-of-war, beheading others, and chopping down the city's orchards. Szuchman (2009a, 57) notes that "this campaign marked the beginning of the end for Amedi as the capital of a dependent, but autonomous polity of Bīt-Zamāni."

However, the reign of Shalmaneser III marked the real end for Bīt-Zamāni's independence. Shalmaneser III mentions Bīt-Zamāni in the account of his campaign in 856 BCE against Urartu. The Kurkh Monolith records:

> I departed from Kār-Shalmaneser (Til-Barsib); I traversed Mount [Ḫa?]sumu; I went down to the land of Bīt-Zamāni (KUR.É-*za-ma-a-ni*); I departed from the city of Bīt-Zamāni (URU.É-*za-ma-a-ni*).[272]

Thus while his father may not have been able to capture Amedu in 866, Shalmaneser "departed from the city of Bīt-Zamāni" which likely refers to the city of Amedu. A few years later (853/852 BCE), Shalmaneser III erected his Kurkh Monolith in Tīdu (Üçtepe). Thus the area had importance in these early campaigns. Some years later in 830 BCE, Bīt-Zamāni is mentioned in connection with the route taken by Dayyān-Aššur, the *turtānu* ("commander-in-chief") in a campaign against Urartu in which Dayyān-Aššur "filled the wide plain with the corpses of his (Sēduru, the Urartian's) warriors."[273] This was Sarduri I, son of Lutipri, king of Urartu.[274]

It is clear from these texts that the Assyrians were using a route to attack Urartu that led through Bīt-Zamāni. The significant increase in the size of the army of Shalmaneser III as over against his father[275] meant that a very powerful force was moving through Bīt-Zamāni's land—no doubt, compelling Bīt-Zamāni by sheer weight of numbers to comply with total submission. This certainly set the stage for the formal annexation of Bīt-Zamāni as an Assyrian province.

Radner (2006c, 49) has suggested that this may have occurred as early as 849, since the eponym for that year is described in Shalmaneser III's clay

272. RIMA 3:19, A.0.102.2, ii.40b–41a.

273. RIMA 3:69, A.0.102.14, 141b–146a (Black Obelisk); fuller account in RIMA 3:81, A.0.102.16, 228′–244′ (Broken Statue from Nimrud).

274. Kroll et al. 2012a, 10.

275. Liverani (2004b, 215–16) concludes that "we can reasonably maintain that Shalmaneser had to venture into Syria with armies of the size of 60,000 soldiers or more" (about three times the size of Aššurnaṣirpal's army).

cone inscription[276] as the governor of Nairi (Millard 1994, 94, s.v. Ḫadi-lipūšu; Ambos 2000b). Nairi was the archaic, literary name for the province (Radner 2006–8a, 49). It could also be known as the province of Sinabu (Millard 1994, 109, s.v. Nasḫurbēl; this city had been a major administrative center in the region during the Middle Assyrian period). The eponym for 838, Ninurta-kibsī-uṣur, was the chief cupbearer (*rab šaqê*) for Shalmaneser III, as well as governor of Nairi, Amedi, Sinabu, Suḫna, Mallani, and Alzi.[277]

Other governors include: Marduk-išmānni (799), "governor of Nairi, Amida, Sinabu, Mallani, [...], Suḫna" (Millard 1994, 100); Aplāya (768), "governor of Zamua, Amida, and Assur" (Millard 1994, 81); Ṭāb-bēlu (762), "governor of Amida" (Millard 1994, 41); Marduk-bēlu-uṣur (726), "governor of [URU.*A-mi*]-*di*"(Millard 1994, 45); and Bēl-iqbi (postcanonical), apparently governor of "the land of Zamāni," though also written as "of Tušḫan" and Bīt-*z*[*a-ma-ni*] (Millard 1994, 90).

Thus Bīt-Zamāni was fully integrated into the Neo-Assyrian Empire at the end of the ninth century BCE. In a seventh-century inscription, the longest and best preserved Aramaic inscription from Tell Shiukh Fawqani (TSF Number 47 = TSF 95 F 204 I/3), a contract mentions *bny zmn* "men of Bīt-Zamāni.[278] The opening lines read:

> [seal of Ša]'il and Maya' and Palṭî, (2) men of the contingent of the king (i.e., the home army) (3) from Bīt-Zamāni, have pledged[279] a man, (4) Nasuḥa' (is) his name, to Še'-'ušnî, (5) for eight shekels of silver.

## 4.7. Aramean Tribal Entities of the Jezirah

A number of sources attest to the various Aramean groups in the Jezirah, whether clans, tribal entities, and/or confederations (the interrelationships are not always clear). Because much of the evidence concerning these entities is contained in source materials that are intertwined with the Aramean tribal units in southern Mesopotamia, for the sake of a coherent analysis, the discussion will be presented in chapter 10.

276. RIMA 3:88–89, A.0.102.18, lines 19′–22′.

277. Millard 1994, 111, s.v. Ninurta-kibsī-uṣur. In the Eponym Chronicle this man is called the governor of Raṣappa (p. 29). Finkel and Reade (1998, 248–49) attribute the difference in titles to a mistake in the Eponym Chronicle and suggest that the correct province would have been Nairi to agree with the Assur Stela. See also Mattila 2000b.

278. Fales 1996b; 2005, 655–60; Lemaire 2001c, 123–26; Younger 2007c, 140–41.

279. Fales read *rhnn* (*qal* ptc.). However, the last letter in the word appears to be *waw* (cf. with the *waw* at the beginning of line 6). A reading *rhnw* corresponds precisely to Fales 1986, no. 13:2.

# 5
# BĪT-ADĪNI

THE ENTITY CALLED BĪT-ADĪNI IS FIRST ENCOUNTERED IN THE NEO-ASSYRIAN texts written É $^{(m)}$*A-di-ni* (Bagg 2007, 44–45). This renders adequately a putative Aramaic *Bēt-'Eden* (Millard 1993, 173; Lemaire 1981). However, no Aramaic writing of the name has yet been found. While the Aramaic Assur Ostracon[1] mentions an entity *byt 'dn* in lines 14 and 15, this is a homonymic group in Babylonia—a Chaldean, not an Aramean, entity that seems to have been a clan or subtribe of the Bīt-Dakkūri tribe/confederation that according to this ostracon was deported by Shalmaneser V.[2] It should not be confused with the Upper Euphrates polity conquered by Shalmaneser III. The same Chaldean entity, Bīt-Adīni, is one of the groups fighting against the Assyrians in the battle of Ḫalulê (691 BCE).[3]

The root *'dn* is used in the mid-ninth-century Tell Fakhariya bilingual as a factitive (*m'dn*) "enrich," "make abundant or luxurious" (Abou-Assaf, Bordreuil, and Millard 1982, 30). The term is also found in personal names: Adānu (the ruler of the Aramean tribe Yaḫān)[4] and Adīni (name used by Chaldeans in southern Mesopotamia, see above),[5] both of which have *'dn* as their root. Thus the tribal entity was likely founded on an eponymous ancestor having this root in his name.

The Upper Euphrates polity of Bīt-Adīni is only mentioned a few times in the biblical texts. It appears in the gentilic form בְנֵי־עֶדֶן (2 Kgs 19:12 = Isa 37:12). In Ezek 27:23, עֶדֶן occurs alone. Many scholars assume that this is

1. *KAI* 233. See now Fales 2010a, 193–99.

2. Brinkman 1968, 244 n. 1567; Fales 2010a, 197 n. 39.

3. RINAP 3.1:182, 22, v.47; 3.1:199, 23, v.38, both read: KUR.É.-$^{m}$*a-di-ni*; see Lipiński 2000a, 163.

4. Frahm and Zadok 1998. This individual is a contemporary and ally of Aḫuni of Bīt-Adīni.

5. Frahm 1998. The occurrences are later and in the south, but they attest to the root's use.

a reference to Bīt-Adīni[6]; however, there are problems with this identification.[7] The occurrence of בֵּית עֶדֶן in Amos 1:5 has generated much discussion and will be discussed in detail in §5.3.3 below.

The early history of the tribal entity Bīt-Adīni must not be conflated with the history of the city of Til-Barsib/Masuwari (modern Tell Aḥmar). There is no convincing evidence that the two polities were, in fact, the same. The conflation of the two only leads to highly speculative reconstructions with an uncritical mixture of the evidence. The reconstruction of the history of the city of Masuwari and the polity based there is given in §3.1.4 and will not be repeated here.

## 5.1. Territory

In the earliest occurrence of the entity Bīt-Adīni (in the annals of Adad-nērārī II dated 899 BCE), it is clear that Bīt-Adīni's primary place of settlement was on the bank of the Euphrates River (*aḫi ša Puratte šaknu*)[8]—no doubt referring to the Great Bend of the river, and that since it paid tribute to the Assyrian king in the city of Ḫuzirīna,[9] Bīt-Adīni had spread its control up the Balīḫ for some distance (Fales 2011a, 219). The campaigns of Aššurnaṣirpal II between 875–866 confirm that the upper Balīḫ was in Bīt-Adīni's control. They also confirm that while Bīt-Adīni's territory had expanded down the Euphrates impacting the Laqē confederation, the territory west of the Euphrates was not yet in its domain. As discussed in chapter 3, the tribal polity expanded its territory west of the Euphrates, most likely in the last years of Aššurnaṣirpal's reign, for when Shalmaneser III campaigns in the west, Bīt-Adīni has significant holdings west of the river. The city of Til-Barsib became the tribal state's possession in connection with this expansion (Fales 2011a, 219; for further details, see below).

---

6. Liverani 1991, 69 (assumes the equation). However, Diakonoff (1992, 191) states: "*ʿdn* is certainly not Assyrian Bīt-Adīni, an accepted, but false, interpretation." He suggests ʿAden in south Arabia. He is followed by Corral (2002, 12).

7. In the first place, it is lacking in the Old Greek and there is evidence of textual corruption (see, e.g., Kanne in the same verse). Moreover, Bīt-Adīni had not been an entity for 250 years or more, and there is no evidence that the name continued in use during this span (see discussion below, §5.3.3). Finally, it is never referred to as simply Adīni/Eden. If עֶדֶן in Ezek 27:23 is a reference to Bīt-Adīni, the text of Ezekiel is drawing from much earlier sources that had the actual writing בֵּית עֶדֶן that was subsequently corrupted to just עֶדֶן.

8. RIMA 2:150, A.0.99.2, line 48.

9. See §4.2: "the Temanites."

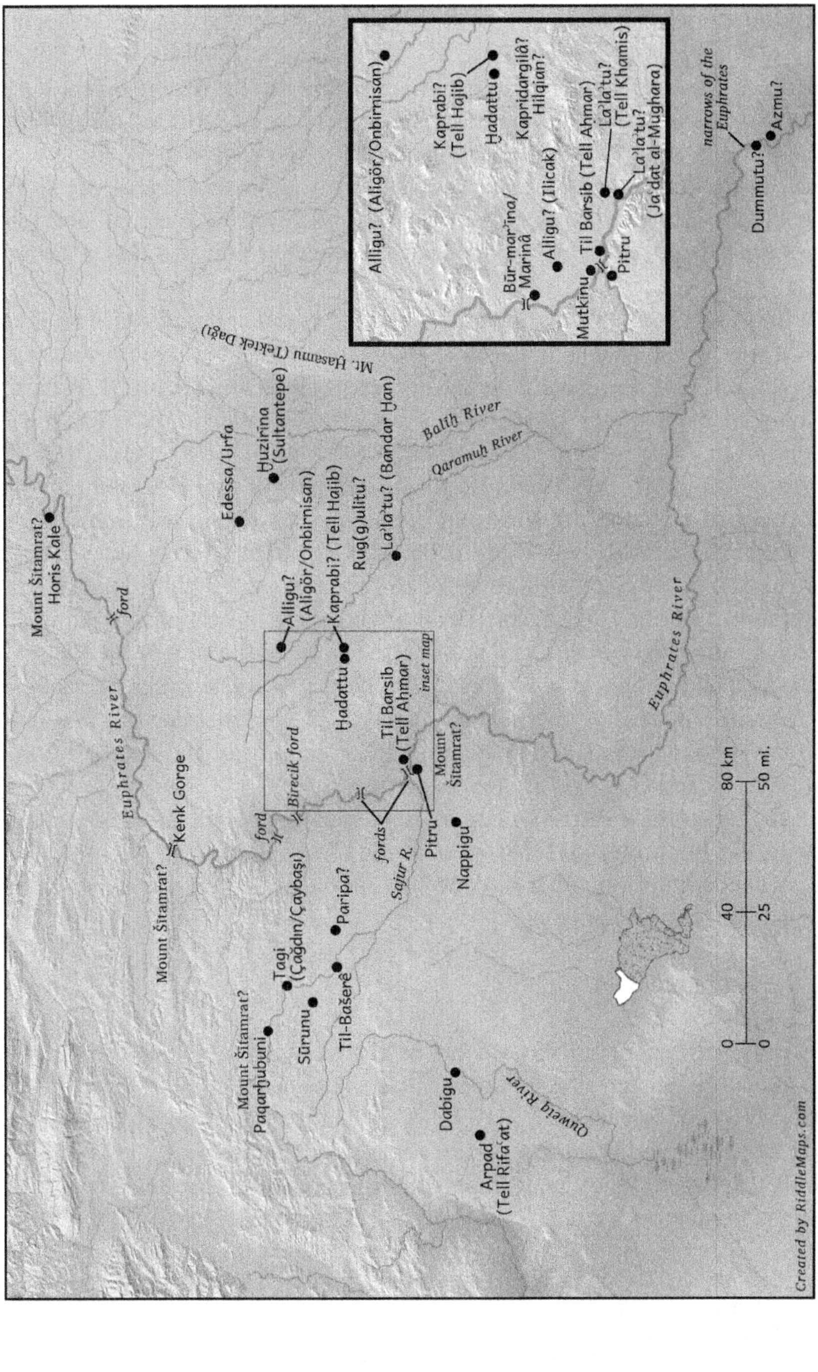


Fig. 5.1. Territory of Bīt-Adīni

On account of the Assyrian sources, it is possible to envision the extent of the territories that made up this Aramean polity (see fig. 5.1). At the beginning of the reign of Shalmaneser III, the area controlled by Bīt-Adīni is perhaps larger than that of any other Aramean state in the region. Its holdings extended from La'la'tu in the east to the borders of Tell Rifa'at in the west, from the area around Gaziantepe in the north to the narrows in the Euphrates in the south. It was, however, an area that was occupied at specific points or in a specific direction, often in river basins or valleys where agricultural villages were found, or on high ground with a defensive potential (Fales 2011a, 227).

Bīt-Adīni had both mobile and sedentary tribal components. The idea that it was largely nomadic because Shalmaneser III does not use the term "king" (*šarru*) to designate Aḫuni is incorrect (Bunnens 1995, 25). A close reading of Shalmaneser's texts reveals that virtually none of the rulers mentioned in his inscriptions are referred to as "king" (*šarru*); they are only referred to by one of two gentilic forms: GN-*a-a* or *mār* PN. Thus this is not proof of nomadic organization, but simply a stylistic feature of Shalmaneser's texts. Moreover, as Yamada (2000a, 142) correctly notes, while Bīt-Adīni may be founded like all *bīt*-Xs on a tribal structure, it seems to have had a clear and significant sedentary component who possessed many fortified cities on *both sides* of the Euphrates. In addition, it fielded a very well-equipped army that was able to take on the Assyrian military machine on numerous occasions in open-field battles. The very mention of "chariots" within the booty from Bīt-Adīni has significant ramifications, since these are not typically found as part of nomadic armies!

The territory of Bīt-Adīni can be conveniently divided into the territory east of the Euphrates and that west of the river (Bagg 2007, 44–45). The following will discuss what is known of its major settlements as revealed through the Assyrian sources.

### 5.1.1. East of Euphrates

Presently, the easternmost known city of Bīt-Adīni appears to be La'la'tu.[10] It was probably on the eastern border of Bīt-Adīni, since it was the first town attacked by Shalmaneser III.[11] While the location is unknown, because of the route taken by Shalmaneser and because of the use of the verb *elû* "to climb," "go up" (which may imply that the people of the town "fled up" into the mountains), scholars have suggested a location for the town in the

10. Bagg 2007, 153–54, s.v. La'la'tu. La'la'tu may be *qalqal* formation of *l'y* "be strong." See Zadok 1995, 278.

11. RIMA 3:15, A.0.102.2, i.30.

western Tektek Dağı (Lipiński 2000a, 174; Yamada 2000a, 88). This verb is frequently used to describe people fleeing to the mountains; however, when it means this, *elû* is usually followed by *ana* KUR-(*i*), "to the mountain(s)." For example, *Arramu ana šūzub napšātīšu ana šadē marṣi ēli*, "Arramu, in order to save his life, went up to a steep mountain."[12] In this Shalmaneser III passage, *ana* KUR-(*i*) is lacking. Thus, it is possible that the meaning is that the residents "fled upstream."[13] This would indicate that La'la'tu was located on a river. Interestingly, Morandi Bonacossi (2000, 377 n. 140) has suggested identifying La'la'tu with Tell Khamis (Matilla Séiquir 1999) or Ja'dat al-Mughara (Coqueugniot 1999), only about 9 km and 5 km respectively south of Til-Barsib. If he is correct, then the city was not in the eastern border area. The Assyrian narrative does not exclude such a location. It is not clear how far the Assyrian army marched beyond Mount Ḫasamu[14] before approaching the city of La'la'tu, and the very next city mentioned in the account is Til-Barsib. On the other hand, one might have expected a location nearer to the eastern border of the polity. Thus a location on the Balīḫ or Qaramuḫ might be a possibility.[15] In any case, the town must not have been much of a fortified site for no resistance was put up by its inhabitants, and it was destroyed by the Assyrian army.

Also on the eastern border of Bīt-Adīni was the city of Kaprabi.[16] Its exact location is not known.[17] Lipiński (2000a, 172) has suggested two places in the region of Tektek Dağı: Kapaklı and Mohammed Hanı, 45 km and 60 km east of Urfa/Şanlıurfa, respectively. Bagg assesses Lipiński's localizations as purely hypothetical. Furthermore, such localizations place Kaprabi to the northeast of Harran, which seems very unlikely. Parpola and Porter have very

---

12. RIMA 3:20, A.0.102.2, ii.51–52.

13. Note Grayson's translation, RIMA 3:15.

14. Mount Ḫasamu can be reasonably identified with Ḥasmī Ṭūrā (Tektek Dağı). See Parpola and Porter 2001, map 3.

15. An interesting site on the Qaramuḫ River, about 25 km from Aslan Taş and 25 km to the Balīḫ, is Bandar Ḫan. See Einwag 2000, 313.

16. Bagg 2007, 133–34, s.v. Kaprabi. For the etymological discussion, see p. lxxxix.

17. See Liverani 1992a, 72 n. 332; and Sader 1987, 94 n. 140; 2000, 74. The supposed later reference to Kaprabi in the inscriptions of Tiglath-pileser III (Luckenbill 1926–27, 1:§821) was based on an incorrect restoration: URU.*kap*-[*ra-bi*] URU.MEŠ *ša* KUR.É-*a*-⌜*di*⌝ -*ni* (Rost 1893, 85, line 32). However, this must be rejected since Bīt-Adīni had been incorporated into Assyria long before the reign of Tiglath-pileser III and the list is only enumerating newly conquered territories. Thus the text should be read: URU.*kap*-[*ra-bi*] URU.MEŠ *ša* KUR.É- *a* -[*gu-si*] "Kap[rabi] – cities of Bīt-A[gūsi]." See Tadmor 1994, 146–47, Summary 5, ii.6–7; and RINAP 1:109, 43, ii.6–7. It is also the case that a supposed reference in SAA 6:100, 109.r.6′, cannot be proven to be the same city (see Bagg 2007, 134).

tentatively suggested Urfa/Şanlıurfa, a proposal that goes back to Olmstead,[18] but such a location has been deemed by Liverani (1992a, 72 n. 332) to be "too northerly."

In Aššurnaṣirpal II's inscription,[19] Kaprabi is mentioned along with the city of Til-Abnâ. This city should be located north of the Suruç-Birecik road (Fales 2011a, 219; 2014). As a result, Kaprabi may be located "some 80 to 100 km north of the circum-Euphratic zone" (Fales 2011a, 219), on the eastern edge of Bīt-Adīni, perhaps not too far from the Balīḫ (Liverani 1992a, fig. 9). The Ninurta Temple text of Aššurnaṣirpal (see n. 19 above) states:

> In the month of Simānu (Sivan), on the twentieth day, I departed from Kalḫu. I crossed the Tigris; I marched to the land Bīt-Adīni; I approached the city of Kaprabi, their fortified city. The city was well fortified; it hovered like a cloud in the sky. The soldiers trusted in their numerous troops; they did not come down; they did not seize my feet. By the order of Aššur, the great lord, my lord, and Nergal (the divine standard) which goes before me, I besieged the city; I conquered the city by means of breaches, battering-rams, (and) siege-towers. I massacred many of them; I slew 800 of their fighters; I carried off captives (and) property from them. I uprooted 2,500 of their troops; I settled them in Kalḫu. I razed, destroyed, burned, (and) consumed the city. I imposed the awe of the radiance of Aššur, my lord, upon Bīt-Adīni.

A few comments are in order. First, the description "it hovered like a cloud in the sky" is obviously figurative, and one should be cautious about assuming that the city was located in mountainous terrain.[20] Second, as pointed out by Liverani (1992a, 147), the siege may have been a long one. Third, the number killed and the number deported (800 + 2,500) indicates that this was a fairly substantial city of Bīt-Adīni.

One of the largest Iron Age settlements between Harran and Til-Barsib was located at the site of Tell Hajib, a few kilometers east of Arslan Taş (Einwag 2000, 312). Tell Hajib may well have been the center of the Saruj Plain during the Iron Age. Arslan Taş, on the other hand, was probably only

18. Parpola and Porter 2001, 3, 25. They do rate this identification as uncertain (p. 10). See Olmstead 1918, 245.

19. RIMA 2:216, A.0.101.1, iii.51; full account of the city's capture on lines 50b–54.

20. Compare the description of Azekah in the so-called Azekah Inscription of Sennacherib: "Azaqâ … is situated upon a mountain peak. Like the blade(s) of daggers, without number, they rise up high into the heavens […]" (RINAP 3.2:352, 1015, lines 5′–7′). The hill of Azekah is only 319 m high; and while imposing from the north, it is not so much from the south. This description is surely a case of overstatement. In Shalmaneser III's Kurkh Monolith, the place of Auni's final stand, Šītamrat, is also described as "a mountain peak on the bank of the Euphrates which hovers like a cloud from heaven" (RIMA 3:21, A.0.102.2, ii.69b–70a).

a short-lived Neo-Assyrian establishment that came to an end with the fall of that Empire. Tell Hajib is over 30 ha with a citadel more than 20 m high situated in the center overlooking a vast lower city (Einwag 2000, 312–13, 323–24) and must have been a major city in the territory of Bīt-Adīni. Hence, if Kaprabi was located "some 80 to 100 km north of the circum-Euphratic zone" (Fales 2011a, 219), perhaps Kaprabi was located at Tell Hajib.

The city of Ḫadattu[21] was clearly within the territory of the tribal polity. This can be firmly equated with modern Arslan Taş. Alligu was another city of Bīt-Adīni.[22] Shalmaneser III renamed it Aṣbat-lakūn and made it a royal city in 856. An earlier attack and capture of the city is pictured on one of the bronze bands from Aššurnaṣirpal II's palace Gates at Balawat.[23] The band contains an epigraph that reads: URU *i*[*a*(?)-*l*]*i-gu* [*šá* É]-*a-di-ni* KUR-*ud* "The city Y[all]igu of [Bīt]-Adīni I conquered."[24] Alligu has been identified with Aligör/Onbirnisan, about 40 km east of Birecik (Forrer 1920, 25). Lipiński (2000a, 168–69) has suggested that Alligu should be identified with Ilicak, about 5 km north of Tell Aḥmar.[25] Both suggestions are based purely on phonological similarity.

Two cities of Bīt-Adīni are known from their destruction by Aššurnaṣirpal II: Azmu and Dummutu. The last statement in the episode in Aššurnaṣirpal's annals relates that, after the destructions of these two cities, Aššurnaṣirpal "emerged from the narrows of the Euphrates," which is most likely to be identified with the narrows of Hanuqa, halfway between Der ez-Zor and Raqqa.[26] Obviously, Bīt-Adīni's territorial possessions were at least this far down the Euphrates from its confluence with the Balīḫ.

The city of Rug(g)ulitu is first mentioned on one of the bronze door bands of Aššurnaṣirpal II from the palace gate of Balawat/Imgur-Ellil.[27] The city is depicted being attacked and captured by Assyrian troops and the epigraph reads:

---

21. Bagg 2007, 82–83, s.v. Ḫadattu. Not to be confused with Ḫadattâ.

22. Bagg 2007, 6–7, s.v. Alligu. Its derivation is unknown. See Zadok 1995, 278.

23. Band BM ASH II L7, BM 124692. Curtis and Tallis 2008, 36, figs. 19 and 20. For earlier publications and studies, see King 1915, pls. LXXVIII–LXXX; Barnett 1973; 1972; Grayson, RIMA 2:321–22, A.0.101.51 (introduction); and 3:345–51, A.0.101.80–97 (all the captions of the reliefs).

24. Curtis and Tallis 2008, 36; RIMA 2:348, A.0.101.87.

25. See also Dussaud 1927, 462 n. 4 and map XIII; Morandi Bonacossi 2000, 386, no. 22–23.

26. RIMA 2:215, A.0.101.1, iii.42–44a. See Liverani 1992a, 70 and fig. 8; Lipiński 2000a, 182. For Azmu, see Bagg 2007, 38, s.v. Azmu; for Dummutu, see Bagg 2007, 62–63, s.v. Dummutu. Herles 2007a, 430–1 suggests Azmu (Zalabiya) and Dummutu (Ḥalabiya).

27. Band BM ASH II R2, BM 124691/Rm 1077. Curtis and Tallis 2008, 39, figs. 25 and 26.

> É.GAL [$^{m}$AŠ-PAB]-A *šar*$_4$ Š[Ú *šar*$_4$ KUR AŠ A TUKUL.MAŠ *šar*$_4$ KUR AŠ] A U-ERÍN.TAḪ *šar*$_4$ KUR AŠ-*ma* URU [*r*]*u*?-*gu-lu-tú* šá É-$^{m}$*a-di-ni* KUR-*ud*
>
> "Palace of Aššurnaṣirpal, king of the world, king of Assyria, son of Tukulti-Ninurta, king of Assyria, son of Adad-nērārī, (who was) also king of Assyria: the town of Rugulutu of Bīt-Adīni I conquered."[28]

In 856, Shalmaneser declared that he took the cities of Til-Barsib, Alligu, Nappigu and Rugulitu to be his royal cities, building palaces in them, and renaming them. Rugulitu was renamed Qibīt-[Aššur?]. The city is not mentioned again until 611 BCE when it was besieged and captured by the Babylonians under Nabopolassar (r. 625–605), who executed all the inhabitants.[29] Lipiński (2000a, 169) equates the city with Urfa, classical Edessa, but Bagg (2007, 204) argues that it would seem more likely in the southern area of Bīt-Adīni. It was certainly located somewhere between Til-Barsib and Harran (Radner 2006–8d).

The city of Būr-mar'īna (Marinâ) was located at modern Tell Shiukh Fawqani.[30] The city was on the Euphrates, just 18 km north of Til-Barsib (Tell Aḥmar) and only about 8 km south of Karkamiš, although it was on the opposite side of the river from Karkamiš. A seventh-century Aramaic text from Tell Shiukh Fawqani gives the reading *brmrn*.[31] Fales states:

> This line contains the indication of the toponym which should represent the ancient name of Tell Shiukh Fawqani. In its sole attestation in cuneiform, URU.*bur-mar-ʾi-na*, the second element of the toponym seems to point to the Aramaic noun **mrʾ*, "lord", with pronominal suffix of the 1st person plural. As for the first element, it may well be asked whether a divine name **Būr* should not be taken into account here, taking up a suggestion offered as long ago as 1895 by A. H. Sayce, and again by R. Zadok in 1977, thus yielding a nominal sentence name "*Būr* is our lord." The recently published evidence from Tell Šēḫ Ḥamad concerning many personal names built with the divine element *Būr* at Dur-Katlimmu, and which points to a cult of this deity spread in the region between Harran and Hindanu on the middle Euphrates lends additional probability to this interpretation. At the same time, however, one should not rule out the possibility that such a formation represented a case of secondary etymologization on the part of Aramaic-

---

28. Curtis and Tallis 2008, 39 and RIMA 2:347, A.0101.86.

29. Grayson 1975, 95, Chronicle 3, lines 56–57; Glassner 2004, 222–23, Text 22, lines 56–57.

30. Excavations have confirmed the site's identification with Būr-mar'īna. See Bachelot and Fales 2005. See also Bagg 2007, 55.

31. No. 46: TSF 95 F 204 I/2, obv.2.

> speaking peoples. This is suggested by two place names attested for the same general region: *Marina ša šadê* near Karkemiš, which appears in the Middle Assyrian texts from Tell Šēḫ Ḥamad, and *Marinâ*, said to be "in Bīt-Adīni" in an epigraph on the Balawat gates from Assurnaṣirpal's reign. In other words, it is possible that the original toponym was pre-Aramaic in time, and non-Aramaic in its meaning—perhaps Hurrian.[32]

A number of other etymologies have been proposed: (1) *br mrʾn*, "Son of our Lord;"[33] (2) *br mrʾn*, "Well of our Lord;"[34] and *brmrʾn*, "Well of the Pasture Grounds."[35]

The city of Marinâ is depicted on the Balawat Palace Gates of Aššurnaṣirpal II (Band BM ASH II L2, BM 124686).[36] The bronze band contains the epigraph: *ti-du-ku šá* URU *ma-ri-na-a šá* É-[m]*a-di-ni* "Battle against the city Marinâ of Bīt-Adīni."[37] It is also featured on a bronze band of the gate of the temple of the dream god, Mamu (MM ASH II R2), where it is shown being attacked and having the epigraph: URU *ma-ri-n*[*a*]*-a* šá É-*a-di-ni* "City of Marinâ of Bīt-Adīni."[38] Shalmaneser III attacked and captured the city of Būr-mar'īna early in his reign (see below).

The cities of Mutkīnu (probably Tell ʿAbr) and Til-Barsib (Tell Aḥmar) have been previously discussed.[39] But the city of Ḫilqian has not been identified. It is only found on one of the bronze bands from the Mamu Temple Gates (MM ASH II R7) where it is shown under attack and has the epigraph: [U]RU *ḫi-il-qi-an šá* É-*a-di-ni* "City of Ḫilqian of Bīt-Adīni."[40] It must be located, however, on the east side of the Euphrates. This is also true of the singularly attested city of Kapridargilâ (Bagg 2007, 134), which appears to have been a village in the vicinity of Til-Barsib (Parpola and Porter 2001, 3, 25).

---

32. Fales 2005, 654; Zadok 1977, 65; 1995, 278.

33. Dion 1997, 92 n. 43; Olmstead 1921, 350; Bunnens 1999, 611. However, Bagg and Lipiński see this option as the least likely. See Bagg, 2007, lxxxvii; and Lipiński 2000a, 176 n. 75.

34. Bunnens 1999, 611; Yamada 2000a, 89 n. 38; and Lipiński (2000a, 176 n. 75) as an alternative proposal from his main suggestion.

35. Lipiński 2000a, 176. He argues that "Marina is a derivative of the root *rʿy* with a preformative *ma-*. The absorption of *ʿain* by the contiguous *r* is not surprising if the latter was pronounced as a guttural or uvular [R]. If the termination *-īna*, comparable to the one of Classical Arabic, is Proto-Aramaic, this would imply the Aramaean presence in this area as early as the 14th–13th centuries B.C., possibly under the name of 'Sutaeans.'" This is certainly the least likely etymology for the place name.

36. Curtis and Tallis 2008, 31, figs. 9 and 10.

37. Curtis and Tallis 2008, 31. RIMA 2:345–46, A.0.101.81.

38. Curtis and Tallis 2008, 63, figs. 75 and 76.

39. For Mutkīnu, see pp. 138, 156, 158 n. 154; for Til-Barsib, see §3.1.4.

40. Curtis and Tallis 2008, 68, figs. 85 and 86.

### 5.1.2. West of the Euphrates

On the west side of the Euphrates, the following cities are attributed to Bīt-Adīni:

Just across the river from Mutkīnu was the city of Pitru. Tiglath-pileser I had made it a fortified Assyrian outpost; it was captured by the Arameans in the days of Aššur-rabi II. In the Neo-Assyrian period, Shalmaneser III restored it to the Assyrian Empire renaming it Ana-Aššur-utēr-aṣbat.[41]

Dabigu was a walled city in Bīt-Adīni. It has been identified with Tall Dābiq on the upper part of the Quweiq River, 13 km east of 'Azāz and 11 km east-northeast of Tell Rifa'at, and about 30 km northwest of Aleppo.[42] A bronze band of Shalmaneser III from Balawat shows the attack on the town of Dabigu.[43]

Nappigu was a city in northern Syria which belonged to Bīt-Adīni at the time of Shalmaneser III's conquest (Bagg 2007, 181–82). He renamed it Līt-Aššur,[44] although the name change does not seem to have stuck since the city's name was later cited as Nappigu. It has been identified on phonological grounds with Mambīj (Mem/nbij*), classical Bambyke and Syriac Mambog or Mabbog, an important center of communication in classical, Christian and medieval Islamic times.[45]

Bagg, however, raises concern about the issue that Nappigu lay on the Euphrates, if the restoration of Tadmor (1994, 102, line 6′) ÍD.A.[RAD] is correct, because Mambīj is approximately 20 km away from the river.[46] The answer may lie in the Assyrian phrase *ša kišād*, "on the bank," and how rhetorical it may be.[47] In other words, does the phrase's semantic range allow for "in the general vicinity of the bank?"

Paqarḫubuni[48] was one of the cities belonging to Aḫuni, (the man) of Bīt-Adīni. In fact, it was the site of an open-field battle in 858 between Shalmaneser III and Aḫuni. The city is mentioned in a number of historical sources, though with different spellings. It was located near the border with

41. See pp. 138–39, 156, 158.

42. Bagg 2007, 57, s.v. Dabigu. See Schiffer 1911, 70–71; Kraeling 1918, 60; Dussaud 1927, 468; Noth 1961b, 137 n. 54; Sader 1987, 96 n. 157; Yamada 2000a, 115–17; Lipinski 2000a, 179; Parpola and Porter 2001, 18.

43. Band SHAL III R4.

44. RIMA 3:19, A.0.102.2, ii.30–34.

45. Dussaud 1927, 450; Postgate 1998–2001, 164; and Lipiński 2000a, 180.

46. Bagg (2007, 182) states: "but it seems clear that Nappigu was on a watercourse." See Zadok 1996a, 12.

47. See Yamada 2000a, 137 n. 207, who cites Šītamrat as a possible analogy.

48. Bagg 2007, 186, s.v. Paqarḫubuni. Hawkins 1995c, 94; Yamada 2000a, 93 n. 59; Parpola and Porter 2001, 2, 18.

Kummuḫ and Gurgum and should probably be identified with Gaziantepe (Yamada 2000a, 93).

Paripa was another walled city in Bīt-Adīni (Bagg 2007, 187–88). Its location is not certain. Dussaud cautiously suggested Tall ʿIfar, about 14 km northwest of Manbij on the basis of similarity of the name through a metathesis.[49] However, this location does not seem to fit with the itinerary of Shalmaneser III (Bagg 2007, 188). Lipiński argues for a location at Ekinveren (former Tilsevet), about 9 km east of Tall Bāšir.[50] He notes that about 1,500 m south of the village a tomb was discovered that contained a funerary stela written in hieroglyphic Luwian.[51] Bagg expresses doubts because, based on Lipiński's equations of Tagi and Sūrunu with Çağdın/Çaybaşı and Sazgın respectively, a localization of Paripa at Ekinveren would mean that Shalmaneser III would have to double back in his conquest route (Bagg 2007, 188). But this is not an insurmountable objection since armies must sometimes cut off communication and supply before attacking a position; this may be an instance of such here.

Sūrunu may be identified with Saruna, attested in Tiglath-pileser III's list of the cities of Bīt-Agūsi, with *šrn* of the Aramaic Sefire treaty, and perhaps with *Šurun* of the Suppiluliuma-Sattiwaza treaty.[52] Three possibilities for the location of Sūrunu have been given. It has been identified with (1) Ṣawrān (Ṣauran in Dussaud), 5 km northwest of Tell Dābiq;[53] (2) Tell Ṣūrān, 22 km northwest of Aleppo;[54] and (3) Sārīn (Sazgın) on the Kızılhizar Çay, a tributary of the Sajur River, some 15 km southeast of Gaziantepe and 11.5 km northwest of Tell Bāšir (Tilbeşar).[55] The problem with the first option is that the modern site has no tell.[56] The second site seems to be located too

49. Dussaud 1927, 470 n. 6, map XIII, B2.

50. Lipiński 2000a, 179. Hawkins 2000, 178 states that Tilsevet/Ekinveren is 35 km southeast of Gaziantepe.

51. Hawkins 2000, 43, 178, pl. 62. The stela dates, however, to the eighth century. Thus it is from a later time than Shalmaneser's campaign of 857 BCE. The stela would date to the last century of the history of Karkamiš.

52. See Yamada 2000a, 115; Noth 1961b, 136 n. 54. For Tiglath-pileser III's list, see Tadmor 1994, 146–47, ii.5. For the Sefire treaty, see *KAI* 222:A34. For the Suppiluliuma-Šattiwaza treaty, see Weidner 1923, 22–25 [= KBo I, no. I], r. 17′; Hawkins 1983, 135–36. See also Zadok 1995, 277.

53. Honigmann 1932, col. 1592; Dussaud 1927, map XII, 2C; Parpola and Porter (2001, 16) identify Sūrunu with Tell Ṣūrān, Šewirin. Olmstead (1921, 254 n. 22) suggested this as possibility.

54. See Astour 1963, 234, no. 116.

55. The identification was proposed by Noth (1961b, 136 n. 54); see also Sader 1987, 96 n. 154; Tadmor 1994, 147; Olmstead 1921, 254 n. 22; Lipiński 2000a, 178; Yamada 2000a, 115; and Bagg 2007, 223–24.

56. According to Lipiński 2000a, 178.

far south. Tell Ṣūrān might be the *šrn* of the Sefire treaty, but it seems to be in Bīt-Agūsi's territory. The third option seems preferable, especially since it is near Tell Bāšir (Tilbeşar).[57] Zadok (1995, 277) has suggested that Sūrunu might be connected with the earlier Eblaite city of Zurum. Bagg (2007, 224) argues that this is too far south.

It seems best to identify the city of Tagi with the modern village of Çağdın/Çaybaşı, about 9 km southeast of Gaziantepe and 1.5 km north of the ruin mound Bayramlı.[58] Lipiński notes that a stela picturing the storm god was found at the site.[59]

The city of Til-Bašerê has been identified with Tell Bāšir (Tilbeşar), on the western bank of the Sajur River, 26.5 km southeast of Gaziantepe.[60] The site has been recently excavated,[61] but without confirmation of its identification.

Finally, there is the location of Aḫuni's final stand: Šītamrat. Was it located in Bīt-Adīni or Kummuḫ? This will be discussed in more detail below.

## 5.2. History

It is very important to observe that what is known about the history of Bīt-Adīni is derived primarily from the inscriptions of Aššurnaṣirpal II and his son, Shalmaneser III. This is supplemented by some of their reliefs. There are no native written sources that contribute.

As pointed out above, the history of Bīt-Adīni should not be confused with the history of Masuwari/Til-Barsib. From the passage in the annals of Adad-nērārī II at the very beginning of the ninth century (899), it is clear that Bīt-Adīni was an entity located to the east of the Euphrates River, primarily in the Great Bend, but with some expansion up the Balīḫ. This is confirmed by the inscriptions of Aššurnaṣirpal II. When this king campaigned (between

57. Archi, Pecorella, and Salvini 1971, 53, no. 18 and pl. XII, fig. 39; and p. 91, no. 166, pl. L, fig. 189.

58. Bagg 2007, 246–47; Lipiński 2000a, 178; Archi, Pecorella, and Salvini 1971, 53, No. 18.

59. Lipiński 2000a, 178. For the stela, see Bossert 1951–53, 106–12 and pl. V. The stela is kept in the Museum of Adana. It does not appear in the catalogue of Bunnens 2006 that I can verify.

60. Fales 2014–16c; Bagg 2007, 255–56, s.v. Tilbašerê. Schiffer 1911, 69; Kraeling 1918, 60; Dussaud, 1927, 468; Sader 1987, 96 n. 156; Yamada, 2000a, 115; Lipiński, 2000a, 179; Parpola and Porter 2001, 17.

61. Kepinski-Lecomte et al. 1996; Kepinski-Lecomte and Ergeç 1997; Rousset and Ergeç 1997; Kepinski 2005 (summary of 1994–2000 seasons); and Kepinski, Lecomte, and Tenu 2006a.

875 and 867 BCE),[62] he received the tribute of Aḫuni, the man of Bīt-Adīni, before he crossed the Euphrates where "the kings of all the lands came down; they seized my feet." Undoubtedly, the king of Masuwari was included in this group (Fales 2011a, 217 n. 17). Thus, even at this point, Masuwari and Bīt-Adīni appear to have been separate political units.

In 883, Aššurnaṣirpal II received a report of a rebellion in the city of Sūru of Bīt-Ḫalupē where the people killed Ḫamatāya, the governor, and installed "Aḫi-yababa, son of a nobody, whom they brought from the land of Bīt-Adīni, as their king."[63] Since Bīt-Ḫalupē was a confederation located near the confluence of the Ḫābūr and Euphrates Rivers, there was a natural geographical connection with Bīt-Adīni via the Euphrates. Although the coup ended in a bloodbath, with the punishment of Aḫi-yababa and the upper class of Bīt-Ḫalupē who had brought him to the throne, Aššurnaṣirpal II undertook no immediate retaliation against Bīt-Adīni for its apparent involvements.[64] Obviously, Bīt-Adīni's power and influence was significant.

However, in 877, in pursuit of another rebel, Azi-ili of Laqē, Aššurnaṣirpal claimed to have conquered and destroyed two frontier fortresses Dummutu and Azmu, "cities of Bīt-Adīni," that apparently were harboring the fugitive Azi-ili. These fortresses were apparently located halfway between Der ez-Zor and Raqqa (see above).[65] Clearly Bīt-Adīni had control quite a significant distance down the Euphrates from the confluence with the Balīḫ and in both the Jezirah and the Šamīya.

Aššurnaṣirpal's next campaign (his tenth)[66] is not dated in his annals, but likely took place sometime between 876–868 BCE.[67] While the main objective of the campaign was Karkamiš, Aššurnaṣirpal also targeted Bīt-Adīni, probably because of Bīt-Adīni's involvements in the previous campaign. He attacked the city of Kaprabi (see above), a fortified city of Aḫuni. After he besieged and captured the city, Aššurnaṣirpal II received the tribute of Aḫuni, the ruler of Bīt-Adīni and Ḫabīnu, the ruler of Til-Abnâ.

However, this is not the whole story. This seems to be an instance where the royal inscriptions have chosen to narrate certain events, leaving out others. It seems that on this occasion, the Assyrians must have also besieged and captured other cities of Aḫuni, based on the reliefs from Balawat/Imgur-

62. RIMA 2:216–17, A.0.101.1, iii.56b–77a.

63. RIMA 2:198, A.0.101.1, i.75b–76a. See §4.5.2 (pp. 285–86).

64. The reason is not specified. Time of year, military and/or political concerns could be possible reasons. Or it may be that Bīt-Adīni's role in the affair was rather minor.

65. RIMA 2:215, A.0.101.1, iii.42–44a. See chapter 4, pp. 290–91.

66. The tenth campaign is Liverani's campaign VIII (1992a). See table 4.4 (pp. 298–99).

67. RIMA 2:216, A.0.101.1, iii.50b–56a.

Ellil. Three cities are shown being attacked, one on two different bronze bands: Yalligu/Alligu,[68] Rug(g)ulitu,[69] and Marinâ (palace gate and Mamu temple gate).[70] While these depictions could refer to some later campaign of Aššurnaṣirpal II, it is more likely that they portray events connected to this campaign that the scribes of the annals chose not to narrate (though fortunately they have been preserved in gate reliefs).[71]

For the history of Bīt-Adīni, these reliefs are important. If one reconstructed the history of the polity during the period of Aššurnaṣirpal II based on the Assyrian texts alone, the impression would certainly be one of some conflict with the Assyrians, but not too much. With the testimony of the reliefs, it is clear that Bīt-Adīni suffered much more at the hands of the Assyrians. It means that Aḫuni had to sustain some significant defeats throughout his land. Yet, he was able "to bounce back." This evidence demonstrates the significant capacity of his tribal state and the determination that he and his people must have had.[72]

Aššurnaṣirpal's next campaign (his eleventh),[73] like the previous one, is not dated in his annals, but likely occurred between 875–867 BCE, often rounded by scholars to 870 BCE.[74] In some senses, this campaign is more like a "reconnaissance in force," and much of the expedition is on the whole peaceful (at least as the "annals" present it; Liverani 1992b, 85). It began with a march to the Euphrates following the main route, which took the army through Gōzān/Gūzāna, then through the land of Azallu (see §4.4), and then Bīt-Adīni. Each of these three paid tribute and supplied Aššurnaṣirpal with "chariots, cavalry, (and) infantry."

After crossing the Euphrates, Aššurnaṣirpal received the impressive tribute of Sangara,[75] the king of the rich and powerful Neo-Hittite city-state of

68. Band BM ASH II L7, BM 124692. Curtis and Tallis 2008, 36, and 120–21, figs. 19 and 20.

69. Band BM ASH II R2, BM 124691/Rm 1077. Curtis and Tallis 2008, 39, and 126–27, figs. 25 and 26.

70. Band BM ASH II L2, BM 124686. Curtis and Tallis, 2008, 31, and 110–11, figs. 9 and 10; MM ASH II R2, Ibid., p. 63, and 176–77, figs. 75 and 76.

71. This situation is not unique. It can be observed in other instances where there are reliefs but no narrative in the "annals" and vice versa (e.g. Tiglath-pileser III [Gezer], Sargon II [Gath], and Sennacherib [Lachish]).

72. Some parallels with Hazael of Aram-Damascus immediately come to mind.

73. Or in Liverani's scheme (1992a), campaign IX. See table 4.4. Some scholars believe that this campaign divides into two campaigns: Brinkman 1968, 393–94; Grayson 1976, 138–40; Yamada 2000a, 74–75; Na'aman 2002a, 293. Other scholars argue against dividing up the narrative: Schramm 1973, 27–29; Hawkins 1982, 388 with n. 135; Liverani 1992a, 73 n. 336 and 119 n. 475. This is not the place to discuss the arguments.

74. The campaign is found in RIMA 2:216–19, A.0.101.1, iii.56b–92a.

75. The meaning of the name is unknown. See Baker 2002.

Karkamiš (Sangara is called here "the king of the land of Ḫatti"). Sangara ruled approximately 870–848 BCE (Hawkins 2000, 75). His massive tribute included gold, silver, bronze and iron, as well as many luxury items. This payment of tribute apparently occurred early in Sangara's reign; later he was active in coalitions opposing the Assyrians at the time of Shalmaneser III (see below).

Like the previous campaign against Bīt-Adīni, the textual evidence apparently does not tell the entire story when compared with the reliefs. There is no account of any actual fighting between Aššurnaṣirpal II and Sangara in the Assyrian texts. However, in four bronze bands from the Balawat palace gates, the evidence for military action against Karkamiš is clear. The first band (Band BM ASH II L3, BM 124695) depicts an attack on a city and has an epigraph that reads: URU *ú-[l]u-ba šá* ^m^*sa-ga-ra* [ŠAR$_4$ K] UR *Ḫa-te* KUR-*ud*, "The city Ulluba of Sa(n)gara, [king of] the land of Ḫatti, I conquered."[76] The city of Ulluba does not occur in other texts and has not yet been identified. Yamada has suggested reading the toponym as: *sa-*[*z*]*a-ba* (Yamada 2000a, 74 n. 188). Since a city of Sazabê was conquered by Shalmaneser in his second regnal year, Yamada suggests equating the two. However, having collated the bronze band, he notes that the first sign resembles *ú* rather than *sa* (Yamada 2000a, 74 n. 188). Moreover, according to Curtis and Tallis, the drawing makes the reading and equation with Sazabê very unlikely (Curtis and Tallis 2008, 32). In a second band from the palace gate,[77] the epigraph reads: *šal-lu-tu šá* ^m^*sa-an-ga-ra* KUR *ḫat-ta-a-a*, "The plunder from Sangara, the Hittite"[78] and naked prisoners are shown as part of the plunder. On a third band,[79] the plunder of the city of Ellipu of the land of Ḫatti is depicted.[80] This city (Ellipu in northern Syria) is also not otherwise known in Assyrian historical texts. Finally, a fourth band[81] shows "the plunder from the city Mari[ru] of the land Ḫatti," another city of unknown location.

These bands, through their depictions and epigraphs, indicate clearly that there was some kind of military action against Sangara of Karkamiš with subsequent plunder. On the other hand, at least two bands, one from the

76. Curtis and Tallis 2008, 32, figs. 11 and 12. RIMA 2:349, A.0.101.90.

77. Band BM ASH II L6, BM 124685. Curtis and Tallis 2008, 37, figs. 21 and 22.

78. RIMA 2:345, A.0.101.80.

79. Band BM ASH II R1, BM 124687/Rm 1067. Curtis and Tallis 2008, 38, figs. 23 and 24.

80. For the epigraph, see RIMA 2:346, A.0.101.82.

81. Band BM ASH II R8, BM 124696/Rm 1076. Curtis and Tallis 2008, 45, figs. 37 and 38.

palace gates at Balawat[82] and the other from the Mamu Temple[83] appear to portray the earlier tribute of Sangara that was probably connected to the mention of the envoys from the land of Ḫatti who were invited to Aššurnaṣirpal's banquet at Nimrud held in his Year 5, 879 BCE, as recorded in the Banquet Stela.[84]

As in the other instances of tribute paid, Aššurnaṣirpal II recorded that he took with him "the chariots, cavalry, (and) infantry of the city of Karkamiš." In addition, "All the kings of the lands came down; they seized my feet. I took from them hostages; they marched to Mount Lebanon in front of me and behind(?)."[85]

In his march from Karkamiš, Aššurnaṣirpal appears to have bypassed the land of Yaḫānu (Bīt-Agūsi). He entered the territory of Lubarna,[86] the Patinean, at the city of Ḫazāzu (modern 'Azāz). The Neo-Hittite state of Patina appears to have been a substantial political target of this campaign.[87] Patina does not appear to have resisted at this time—perhaps the massive army of Assyrians and their vassals was a major factor in the decision not to fight! Earlier Aššurnaṣirpal received Patinean envoys at the inauguration of Kalḫu,[88] and settled Patineans in the newly built city of Kalḫu.[89]

Patina allowed passage through its territory, and this gained Aššurnaṣirpal an opening to campaign still further south. After crossing the Apre River (modern 'Afrin), he descended on the Patinean capital, Kunulua (modern Tell Ta'yinat), where he received a massive tribute, hostages, and cavalry and infantry to accompany him.

While he had bypassed the land of Yaḫānu, Aššurnaṣirpal's success in the region stimulated its ruler, Gūšu,[90] to pay tribute at this time. From Kunulua, Aššurnaṣirpal crossed the Orontes River. That he was still in Patinaean territory after crossing the Orontes is evidenced by the ninth–eighth century hieroglyphic Luwian inscriptions found at Jisr el Hadid and Tuteil.[91] Aššurnaṣirpal marched to Aribua, a fortress of Lubarna, the Patinean, and

82. Band BM ASH II L8, BM 124690. Curtis and Tallis 2008, 37, figs. 21 and 22.

83. Band MM ASH II L1. Curtis and Tallis 2008, 54, figs. 57 and 58.

84. RIMA 2:293, A.0.101.30, line 144.

85. RIMA 2:217, A.0.101.1, iii.69–70.

86. Lubarna may be the illustrious Hittite title: Labarna. See Fuchs 2001. On the other hand, the title may have become a personal name. For further discussion, see below.

87. Patina territorially would correspond to the area of second millennium Mukish.

88. Banquet Stela (RIMA 2:293, A.0.101.30, iv.144).

89. Banquet Stela (RIMA 2:290, A.0.101.30, i.35–36); Annals (RIMA 2:222, A.0.101.1, iii.134)

90. For a discussion of the name, see ch. 8.

91. Hawkins 2000, 378–83.

established an Assyrian base there. Aribua was apparently located on the southern border of Patina.[92]

In 2002, a Late Bronze–Early Iron I basalt relief was discoverd in the area of Jisr esh-Shughur, which may come from a temple (Al-Maqdissi 2011). It has seven standing figures with the one on the far left in profile, standing on a platform. The other six figures are identical, being females with the typical Hathor hairstyle and holding their breasts. Thus, the scene may be that of a great god or goddess standing on a platform addressing a message to an audience that is characterized by female figures symbolizing fertility.

From Aribua, Aššurnaṣirpal II launched an attack on Luḫuti with the obvious objective of plunder, especially of grain. According to his "Annals," this was the only military action taken on the campaign. Luḫuti is usually identified with Lu'aš (*l'š*, occuring in the Old Aramaic inscription of Zakkur) and with Nuḫašše of second-millennium texts (see chapter 7). Thus Luḫuti was located in the hills east of the Orontes in the neighborhood of modern Idlib.[93] Aššurnaṣirpal II does not mention Hamath specifically on this western campaign, but, according to Hawkins, it seems that at this time Luḫuti would have probably formed part of Hamathite territory and indeed was likely already a province.[94] If this were the case, there was no military response on the part of Hamath to the invasion of one of its provinces.[95]

Aššurnaṣirpal concluded his campaign by marching to Lebanon (the term is used in its general, not specific, sense). He probably crossed the Jebel Ansariyah through the Bdama Pass, and reached the Mediterranean near Latakia.[96] The result was the influx of tributes from many of the Phoenician city-states (from as near as Arvad to as far away as Tyre). The text states:

92. Generally located by scholars at Jisr esh-Shughur (et-Tell; west bank of the Orontes, north of modern Jisr esh-Shughur). See Liverani 1992a, 76–77; Yamada 2000a, 73, 174; Dion 2000, 134, 138. For a different opinion, see Na'aman 2002b. See p. 431 n. 26 below.

93. Earlier scholarship located Luḫuti west of the Orontes. See Elliger 1947, 73–76. Cifola (1997–98) has attempted to locate Luḫuti in the central Orontes River Valley south of Jisr esh-Shughur. For a refutation of this view, see Dion 2000, 136–37.

94. Hawkins 2000, 362 and 400. See also Hawkins 1987–90a. Luḫuti should be equated with Lu'aš (*l'š* of the Zakkur Inscription) and the kingdom of Nuḫašše of the Hittite Empire period.

95. Perhaps without forming a coalition to fight the Assyrians, the Hamatheans felt that they could only protect their territory on the Orontes. See discussion below.

96. Liverani 1992a, 77. Three different reconstructions of the route of Aššurnaṣirpal II's campaign to the Mediterranean have been offered: (1) *A southern route*. The Assyrian army proceeded from the Middle Orontes southward along Jebel Ansariyah. It then passed through the "Ḥoms Gap," and reached the Mediterranean coast at the 'Akkar Plain near Tripoli (Cifola 1997–98). Beside the fact that the route south of Jisr esh-Shughur is on the other side of the Orontes River, this puts the Assyrian army deep into the territory

> I received tribute from the kings of the seacoast, from the lands of the people of Tyre, Sidon, Byblos, Maḫallatu, Maizu, Kaizu, Amurru, and the city of Arvad which is (on an island) in the sea ...[97]

What did this extensive campaign mean to Bīt-Adīni? One thing that is clear from the description of the campaign is this: there is no mention of territory belonging to Bīt-Adīni west of the Euphrates, nor is there any indication that Til-Barsib or the area around it was in the control of Bīt-Adīni. Aḫuni's territory appears to be extensive, but all east of the Euphrates. Again, there is no mention of Til-Barsib being in his possession.

At some point in the last years of Aššurnaṣirpal II, however, Aḫuni took advantage of the less powerful Assyrian pressure in the region. It would seem that this is the point at which Aḫuni drove out the Neo-Hittite kings of Til-Barsib/Masuwari. Whether he had possession of Pitru and Mutkīnu before this is unknown (it appears that he already had possession of Būr-mar'īna).

Therefore, it seems very likely that it was Aššurnaṣirpal's extensive campaign west of the Euphrates that may have actually helped Aḫuni. By weakening the area west of the Euphrates (or at least undermining the status quo of the region), the area was in a position to be seized by Aḫuni. The Assyrian documents from the reign of Shalmaneser III detail Aḫuni's holdings on both sides of the Euphrates, which required multiple campaigns to subjugate. In fact, due to the annals of Aššurnaṣirpal II and Shalmaneser III,

---

of the strong potential adversary, Hamath where it could be caught by surprise or have its way blocked from return (for a detailed criticism, see Dion 2000, 133–38). On the other hand, since Hamath did not respond to the attack on Luḫuti, perhaps it would not have reacted to a further penetration of its territory. But this is too speculative. Thus, this route does not seem to fit the historical situation. (2) *A northern route*. Aššurnaṣirpal proceeded from Aribua westward along the lower Orontes River, and reached the Mediterranean sea near the Gulf of Alexandretta (Kestemont 1972, 1983). (3) *A central route*. Aššurnaṣirpal crossed Jebel Ansariyah through the pass of Bdama, and reached the Mediterranean near Latakia, where he received the tribute (Schramm 1973, 28 n. 1; Liverani 1992a, 77 and fig. 10). This route, which connects the middle Orontes Valley with the Mediterranean coast, was often used in the past. For example, during the Old Babylonian period, Zimri-Lim, king of Mari, took it on his visit to the king of Ugarit. It was possibly called "the road(s) of Pitḫana" in the Ugaritic texts, and was frequently used in the Late Bronze Age (van Soldt 1997, 689–90). See Courtois 1973, 60.

Na'aman (2002b) suggests that some Assyrian contingents departed from the Assyrian main force when it camped near Jisr esh-Shughur, and proceeded westward via the pass of Bdama. Arriving at the Mediterranean coast near Latakia, these troops marched southward along the coast and collected tribute from the Phoenician cities. In this way they "took the way along Mount Lebanon." On their way back they must have arrived in the area of Latakia, and either crossed Jebel Ansariyah on their way back to Patina, or forced the Phoenician cities to assemble boats and sailed by sea to the Gulf of Alexandretta.

97. RIMA 2:218–19, A.0.101.1, iii.85b–88a.

it is possible to understand the expansion of the territories that made up the Aramean polity of Bīt-Adīni.

This expansion that took place in the last years of Aššurnaṣirpal II's reign made Bīt-Adīni the largest Aramean polity in the region. However, as pointed out above (p. 310), it is best to envision Bīt-Adīni's control as specific to certain essential points rather than a solid fill of territorial occupation.

In the case of Til-Barsib, it is described by Shalmaneser III most frequently as a simple fortress of Aḫuni (*āl dannūti*),[98] although in the inscriptions of Kenk (855) and in the summary versions that were written after 842, it appears as his *āl šarrūti*, that is, his capital.[99] Consequently, there is some doubt and disagreement about whether Til-Barsib was Aḫuni's capital city. If it did serve as a type of capital city, this seems to have been a very recent development. It may well be the reason that no evidence from his reign has been uncovered in excavations at Tell Aḥmar.

Although Bīt-Adīni had a very large number of fortified towns in different parts of its territory, it had no real "center of power" from which the polity was truly organized. Without a doubt, the most important place, both from a strategic point of view as well as in terms of expansion, was Til-Barsib. Yet, when the city is seized by the Assyrians, there is no report of rich treasuries coming forth. Instead, it is Mount Šītamrat, which Aḫuni made his fortress (*dannūtīšu*), that Shalmaneser III claimed: "I brought into my presence Aḫuni, with his armies, (his) chariots, his cavalry, and much property of his palace, the weight of which is immeasurable" (*makkūr ēkallīšina māʾdu ša šuqultîšu lā ṣabtat*). Hence, it seems that Aḫuni simply kept moving; and whatever royal possessions he had kept, these kept moving too, until he was cornered and captured.

In addition, Aḫuni is never designated a "king" (*šarru*) in the Assyrian texts, but only the simple gentilic *mār Adīni*, "man of Bīt-Adīni." Even though this may be the result of a type of indirect *damnatio memoriae* (Fales 2011a, 222), Aḫuni was a very significant, challenging opponent who apparently wielded real power over both sides of the Euphrates. His charismatic leadership apparently was a significant factor. Probably, he was considered by the people of his tribe as their "chief/king."[100] He is really only second to Hazael as a persistent resistor of the Assyrians among Aramean leaders.

Due to the manner of territorial control and Aḫuni's leadership, Fales (2011a, 227) has dubbed Bīt-Adīni a "shifting tribal state." He sees this as connected to the deeprooted and persistent migration of civilians and armed

98. Kurkh Monolith (dated 853): RIMA 3:15, A.0.102.2, i.31 (URU *dan-nu-ti-šú*).

99. Kenk Gorge (dated 855): RIMA 3:91, A.0.102.20, line 10 (URU MAN-*ti-šú*); Clay Tablets from Assur (dated 842): RIMA 3:35, A.0.102.6, i.58 (URU MAN-*ti-šú*).

100. See the discussion in ch. 2 regarding the flexibility in the terminology.

men in Upper Mesopotamia and the Transeuphratic basin (Fales 2011a, 227–28). His analysis is in complete accordance with the *bītu*-formula as discussed in chapter 2 above.

5.2.1. Shalmaneser III's 858 Campaign

In 858 (his first full regnal year), Shalmaneser III undertook his first campaign to the west with the ultimate target of reaching the Mediterranean Sea (see fig. 5.2).[101] To a certain extent, this campaign was an emulation of his father's Mediterranean campaign, which took place over a decade earlier (875–867 BCE). But Aššurnaṣirpal's last appearance in the region was in 866, and it is clear that with the accession of Shalmaneser to the throne, the lands in the west from whom Aššurnaṣirpal had extracted tribute were withholding it from the new monarch. The Kenk Gorge Inscription[102] states:

> m*a-ḫu-ni* DUMU *a-di-ni ša* TA MAN.MEŠ-*ni* AD.MEŠ-*ia* (8)*šip-ṣu u da-na-a-nu il-ta-ka-nu* GUN *u ma-da-tú* (9) *ša aš-šur* EN-*ia ik-lu-ú*
>
> Aḫuni,[103] the man of Bīt-Adīni, who had conducted obstinate resistance[104] against the kings, my fathers, (and) who withheld the tribute and tax of Aššur, my lord …

Manifestly, one of the campaign's major goals was the reestablishment of the lines of tribute. In order to accomplish this, the major political barrier on the western Euphrates would need to be removed, namely Bīt-Adīni.

Thus Shalmaneser began the dual strategy of maintaining pressure upon the major fortified city of Til-Barsib, while at the same time enacting the political/military isolation of Bīt-Adīni through the conquest of its important towns on both sides of the Euphrates. With this strategy, Shalmaneser intimidated the northern Syrian states into submission, and put Til-Barsib, the center of the still resisting state of Bīt-Adīni, under siege.

---

101. Specified in the Two-Year Annals (RIMA 3:9, A.0.102.1, lines 41–42): "In that year, I went to the western sea, even the sea of the land of Amurru."

102. RIMA 3:91, A.0.102.20 (Kenk Gorge Inscription), lines 7–9a. See also Taşyürek 1979.

103. Aḫuni's name means either "our brother" (see Yamada 2000a, 139 n. 214); or perhaps better, "Little brother" (a diminuative of *'aḥ*), a typical West Semitic name written *'ḥwn*. See Radner 1998.

104. The phrase *šipṣu u danānu* + the verb *šakānu* expresses the idiom of "conducting obstinate resistance," an idiom occurring primarily in the early Neo-Assyrian royal inscriptions. See *CAD* 17.3:85 s.v. *šipṣu* A.

The first objective of this campaign[105] was to begin the isolation of Bīt-Adīni by seizing control of the Euphrates's crossings in the area of the western bend of the river (Lipiński 2000a, 190). Since Bīt-Adīni controlled territory on both sides of the Euphrates, this would prove a challenging objective. Moreover, from the resistance put forth by Bīt-Adīni as recorded in Shalmaneser's texts, it is clear that militarily this was not an easy objective (three more years of campaigning will be required to finally achieve it). The apparent further expansion of Aḫuni during the time between Aššurnaṣirpal II's last campaign (866) and this campaign (858) had strengthened the tribal entity against the Assyrian onslaught. In many ways, this was a war of attrition.

The campaign began in the month of Ayyar (April/May) with Shalmaneser departing from Nineveh, crossing the Tigris and passing by Mount Ḫasamu (see p. 311 n. 14) and Mount Diḫnunu. Taking such a route indicates that the Assyrians had control over the northern Ḫābūr region and that Shalmaneser was able to approach Bīt-Adīni without any opposition. The first town in Bīt-Adīni attacked by Shalmaneser was La'la'tu. The location of this city is unknown (see pp. 310–11 above). After destroying this town, Shalmaneser approached the city of Til-Barsib (Tell Aḥmar) on the Euphrates. Aḫuni decided to oppose Shalmaneser by massing his troops and fighting an open-field battle near the city. Obviously, Aḫuni felt confident in his chances to win this battle, perhaps based on battles fought in the process of expanding his territory on the west side of the Euphrates. Shalmaneser's inscriptions claim that he inflicted a decisive defeat on Aḫuni and confined him to his city. While it must be true that Shalmaneser won this battle (at least in some fashion), Aḫuni's confinement was brief since he regrouped and fought again in the two coalitions that formed to oppose Shalmaneser on the west side of the Euphrates.

Shalmaneser moved northward up the river 18 km to attack the city of Būr-mar'īna (Tell Shiukh Fawqani).[106] After besieging the city, Shalmaneser captured it, slaughtering 300 of its fighting men and making a tower (*dimtu*) of heads in front of the city.[107] Sometime after the conquest of Būr-mar'īna and before crossing the Euphrates, Shalmaneser received "the tribute of

105. The primary sources for this campaign are: Ann. 2 = RIMA 3:9–10, A.0.102.1, 41–82'a; Ann. 3 = RIMA 3:15–17, A.0.102.2, i.29b–ii.13a; and Ann. 1 = RIMA 3:25, A.0.102.3, obv. 42b–r.46. See also *COS* 2.113A:261–62, i.29b–ii.10a.

106. See pp. 314–15 above.

107. An earlier battle may have been fought here by Aššurnaṣirpal II. See band 9 of Aššurnaṣirpal II's Balawat Gates above. It is unclear why Aššurnaṣirpal II seems to play down his military activities against Bīt-Adīni.

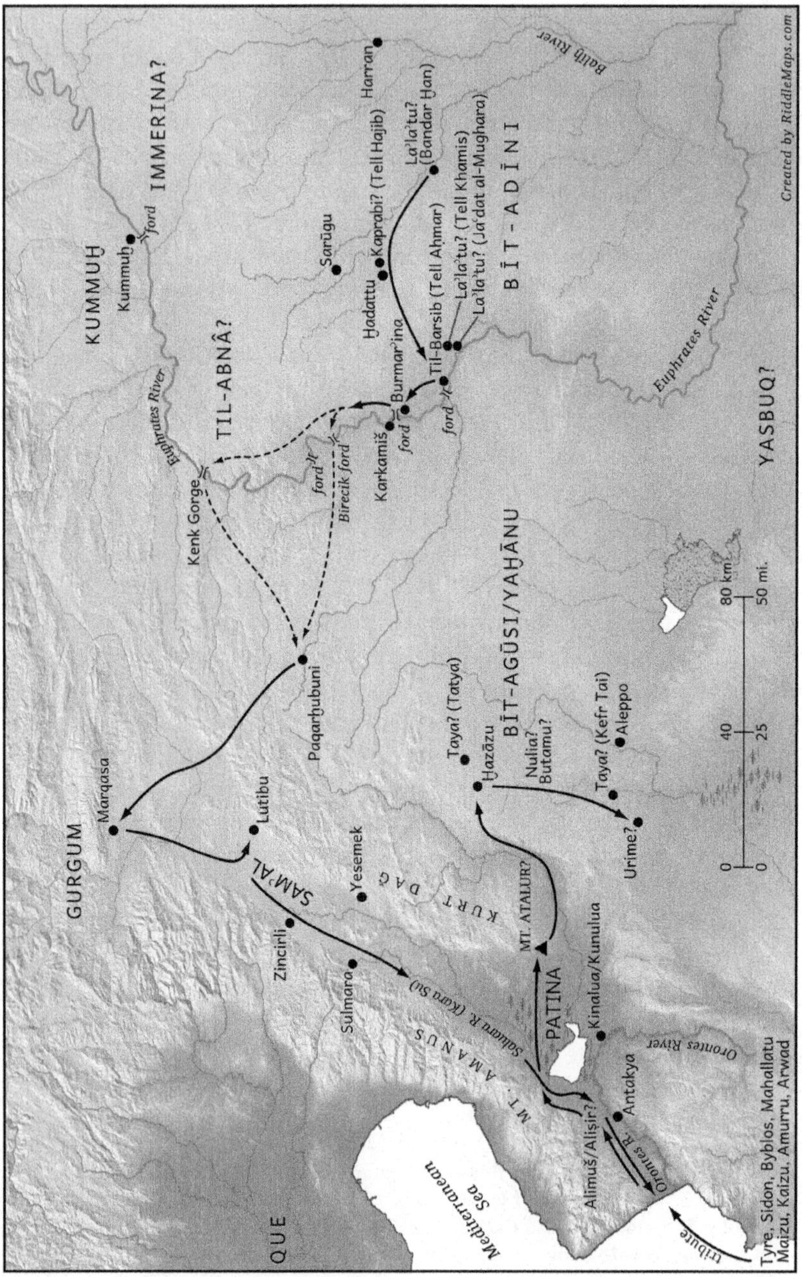


Fig. 5.2. Shalmaneser III's 858 campaign

Ḫabīnu, the Til-Abnâean, Ga'ūnu, the Sarūgaean, and Giri-Adad, the Immerinaean: silver, gold, tin, bronze, oxen, sheep, (and) wine."[108]

Ḫabīnu[109] was the city lord of Til-Abnâ (located east of the Euphrates, opposite Kummuḫ, and north of Bīt-Adīni).[110] Aššurnaṣirpal had extracted tribute from Ḫabīnu during his tenth campaign (between 876–868, that is, ca. 870, see above). During his eleventh campaign (between 875–867), Aššurnaṣirpal had received tribute from Ḫabīnu again—four minas of silver and 400 sheep; but at this time, he imposed on him an annual tribute of ten minas of silver.[111] The fact that Ḫabīnu paid his tribute after Shalmaneser's successful attacks on Aḫuni likely indicates that Ḫabīnu had not been as forthcoming with his annual tribute as he should have been.

Ga'ūnu (m*ga-ʾu-ú-ni*) was a ruler of a city polity, identified by the gentilic form (URU.*sa-ru-ga-a-a*) "the man of Sarūgu, the Sarūgaean."[112] The name Ga'ūnu is West Semitic derived from the root *gʾy* "to be proud, exalted."[113] The city of Sarūgu[114] was located northeast of Til-Barsib (Parpola and Porter 2001, map 3; Bagg 2007, 214–15). Like Til-Abnâ, Sarūgu perhaps waited until the outcome of the initial battles with Bīt-Adīni before paying its tribute to Shalmaneser III.

Giri-Adad (Gīr-Adda)[115] was the ruler of the city of Immerina, which may be identified with Emerion in much later Syriac sources.[116] Yamada (2000a, 91) equates this person with Giri-Dadi of the land of Aššа who paid tribute to Aššurnaṣirpal II when he was in the city of Ḫuzirīna near Urfa on

108. RIMA 3:15, A.0.102.3, lines 35b–36. The passage is somewhat ambiguous as to the exact location where the tribute was received. While it is possible that these rulers (or their envoys) brought their tribute to Shalmaneser at Būr-mar'īna, it is also possible on the basis of the phrase "in the course of my advance" (*ina mētaqtīya*) to understand the text to refer to specific corps branching out from the main Assyrian army on the Euphrates, with the task of reaching these outlying cities and exacting tribute from them under the menace of armed attack (Fales 2005, 619 n. 155).

109. The origin and meaning of the name are presently unknown. See Ambos 2000.

110. For the location of the city, see Liverani 1992a, 72.

111. RIMA 2:217, A.0.101.1, iii.63–64.

112. Sarūgu should be identified with modern Suruç in Turkey. See the earlier mention of the city in Aššurnaṣirpal's Balawat Gates (Band BM ASH II L1 [BM 124689]): Curtis and Tallis 2008, 30, fig. 7 and 8. Epigraph (RIMA 2:347, A.0.101.84): *ma-da-tú šá* URU *sa-ru-ga-a-a* "Tribute of the people of the city of Sarūgu."

113. Reynolds 1999; Zadok 1977, 88, 208, 291 n. 3; 1988, 142. Note *gʾn*, attested in Phoenician and Hebrew, and in Aramaic the second component in the name: *br-gʾyh* (*KAI* 222:A1, etc.).

114. See §4.7 for a discussion of the city name.

115. The name is analyzed as Canaanite (Phoenician?) meaning "Client of Adda"; see Schwemer 2000a. However, the noun *gr* "guest, client" occurs in Palmyrene, Nabatean, Jewish Aramaic (see *DNWSI*, 232). See also n. 118 below.

116. For the location, see Fales 1973, 128.

the Balīḫ River during his final (twelfth) campaign (866 BCE, eighteenth regnal year).[117] He concludes that Immerina was included in the land of Aššša.[118]

Where exactly Shalmaneser was when he received the tribute of these kings (see n. 108 above) and where he crossed the Euphrates are difficult to determine. There are three possible crossing points: (1) south of the Sajur River near Til-Barsib (Na'aman 1976, 96); (2) between Til-Barsib and Karkamiš (Sader 1987, 95–96) (3) at a northern point opposite the territory of Kummuḫ (Winter 1983, 190–91 n. 73; Lipiński 2000a, 190). The first of these, as Yamada (2000a, 92) notes, appears to be incompatible with Shalmaneser's movements, since he marched from Til-Barsib northwards along the east bank of the Euphrates to Būr-mar'īna. A crossing south of the Sajur River near Til-Barsib would require a doubling back by Shalmaneser's army. The second option means that Shalmaneser would have had to establish a bridgehead into the heart of the kingdom of Karkamiš. This seems unlikely since the crossing surely would have been met with stiff resistance. Yamada (2000a, 92) concludes that

> It is most probable, therefore, that Shalmaneser avoided crossing the river into the hostile land of Carchemish and chose a more northerly crossing-point, opposite the territory of friendly Kummuh, which extended along the Euphrates and lay to the north of Carchemish.

There are two possibilities that fit this conclusion: a crossing-point a little north of modern Birecik, or a crossing-point at Kenk Gorge (Kenk

117. RIMA 2:219, A.0.101.1, iii.94–96.

118. For the possibility that the city of Immerina was located in a territory known as Ašša, see Fales 2005, 619 n. 156; Lemaire and Durand, 1984, 66 n. 24. Fales gives four points: (1) *Gi-ri-da-di* (king of Ašša) might be homonymous with *Gi-ri-*$^{d}$IM (king of Immerina), in view of the "improper encoding" *Bir-da(-ad)-da* = *Bir-*$^{d}$IM of the name of an Arab ruler in royal inscriptions of Aššurbanipal. However, in *The Prosopography of the Neo-Assyrian Empire*, the name Giri-Dadi (Gīr-Dādi) is treated as being a separate name meaning "Client of Dadi" from the name Gīr-Adda based on the theophorics (Schwemer 2000a, 2000b). (2) Ašša has been located on the left bank of the Euphrates slightly to the northwest of Ḫuzirīna (20 km north of Harran), where *Gi-ri-da-di* came to bring tribute to Aššurnaṣirpal together with Qipānu and (A)zalla, and adjoining Til-Abnâ (Liverani 1992a, 83). (3) many local kings (Aḫuni, Ḫabīnu of Til-Abnâ, Sangara of Karkamiš, Qatazilu of Kummuḫ, etc.) are attested in both Aššurnaṣirpal's annals and the accounts of Shalmaneser's early campaigns. (4) the three toponyms mentioned by Shalmaneser, Til-Abnâ, Sarūgu and Immerina, as well as Qipānu, are attested more than once in the "Harran census" of the age of Sargon II (cf. most recently Fales and Postgate 1995, 180–82)—i.e., they all seem to pertain to a geographical area encircling the great cultic center of the moon god on the northern Balīḫ, and all refer to a territory or administrative district centering on an urban site and comprising minor villages in its midst.

Boğazı).[119] Yamada has recently argued in favor of the former. But the later cannot be ruled out, since after the crossing, it would place Shalmaneser within Kummuḫ, and clearly the Kenk Gorge was used by Shalmaneser for some of his crossings as evinced from his inscriptions at the site.

After the crossing, Shalmaneser received the tribute of Kummuḫ. Kummuḫ had paid tribute to Shalmaneser's father Aššurnaṣirpal II. It maintained loyalty to Assyria for many years against various western coalitions until its submission to Sarduri II of Urartu and subsequent participation in the anti-Assyrian league led by Urartu and Arpad (middle of the eighth century).

Having secured Kummuḫ's tribute, the Assyrian army approached the city of Paqarḫubuni (modern Gaziantepe), one of the cities belonging to Aḫuni, (the man) of Bīt-Adīni (see §5.1.2). It was apparently an important part of the northern section of Bīt-Adīni's territories west of the Euphrates. For a second time, Shalmaneser defeated Aḫuni's troops in an open-field battle, killing 1,300 men.

This victory opened the door for Shalmaneser's march into Gurgum (Bagg 2007, 80–81) where he received "the tribute of Mutalli, the Gurgumite: silver, gold, oxen, sheep, wine, (and) his daughter with her rich dowry." Gurgum's capital city was located at Maraş (ancient Marqasa). The presenting of the king's daughter with her dowry indicated Gurgum's peaceful acceptance of Assyrian overlordship.

With the submission of these polities on both sides of the Euphrates, north of Bīt-Adīni's territory, Shalmaneser III was now in a position to begin the isolation of Bīt-Adīni by defeating its western allies. This began with the invasion of Sam'al. Marching south from Maraş, Shalmaneser approached Lutibu (modern Sakçagözü), the fortified city of Ḫayānu, the Sam'alite, located 21 km northeast of Zincirli on the western slopes of Kurt Dağ.[120] At Lutibu, Shalmaneser III faced his first coalition of western forces: "Ḫayānu, the Sam'alite, Sapalulme II,[121] the Patinean, Aḫuni, the man of Bīt-Adīni, (and) Sangara, the Karkamišean" (see table 5.1).

---

119. According to Taşyürek, "still today it is possible to cross the Euphrates easily at this point by simple rafts buoyed up by goat-skins, especially in summer when the water level in the river is low" (1979, 47; 1975).

120. See discussion in §6.2: Sam'al "territory."

121. In light of the newly discovered inscribed statue of Sapalulme II. See table 3.1. For the name, see Baker 2002b.

Table 5.1. The Two Battles against Coalitions in 858 BCE

| Ruler | Polity | Formulation | Battle of Lutibu | Battle of Alimuš |
|---|---|---|---|---|
| Aḫuni | Bīt-Adīni | $^{m}$*a-ḫu-ni* DUMU *a-di-ni* | ✓ | ✓ |
| Sangara | Karkamiš | $^{m}$*sa-an-ga-ra* KUR/URU *gar-ga-miš-a-a* | ✓ | ✓ |
| Sapalulme II | Patina | $^{m}$*sa-pa-lu-ul-me* KUR *pa-ta-na-a-a* | ✓ | ✓ |
| Ḫayānu (Ḥayyā') | Sam'al (Bīt-Gabbāri) | $^{m}$*ḫa-a-ni/ḫa-a-a-nu* KUR *sa-am-ʾa-la-a-a* | ✓ | ✓ |
| Katiya | Que (Adana; Danunians) | $^{m}$*ka-te-a* KUR *qu-ú-a-a* | | ✓ |
| Piḫirim | Ḫilukku (Cilicia) | $^{m}$*pi-ḫi-ri-im* KUR *ḫi-lu-ka-a-a* | | ✓ |
| Bur-Anate | Yasbuq (north Ṣubat region) | $^{m}$*bur-a-na-te* KUR *ia-as-bu-qa-a-a* | | ✓ |
| Adānu | Yaḫānu | $^{m}$*a-da-a-nu* KUR *ia-ḫa-na-a-a** | | ✓ |
| | | | | |
| Lubarna | Patina | $^{m}$*lu-bar-na* KUR *pa-ti-na-a-a* | — | — |
| Arame | Bīt-(A)gūsi | $^{m}$*a-ra-me* DUMU $^{m}$*gu-ú-si* | — | — |

* The Kurkh Monolith text is not well preserved here; this reading is confirmed from the Ann. 1 (RIMA 3:25, A.0.102.3; Mahmud and Black 1985–86, lines 28–29).

The coalition was apparently defeated in this open-field battle, though not thoroughly, since the members regrouped for another battle later during this very campaign. Lutibu was not besieged and captured, nor was the royal capital city of Sam'al/Yādiya (Zincirli). Both were bypassed. This demonstrates that the Assyrian intentions in this campaign were not to conquer and destroy every single point of resistance, but to accomplish two things: (1) to reduce the main military capacity of these western states in order to cut off support for Aḫuni; and (2) to secure their tribute, thus establishing future obligations from these entities.

After the battle, Shalmaneser set up his royal image "at the source of the Saluara River at the foot of Mount Amanus." The river may be identified with the modern Kara Su. This means that the source of the river was probably located not too far southwest of Zincirli, near the village of Sulmara/Sulumağara (west of Yesemek; Elliger 1947, 77 and n. 24). During this campaign, according to the One Year Annals, Shalmaneser III set up four monuments: three images (*ṣalmu*) and one stela (*asumettu*).[122] This is the first of the narratives concerned with the erection of monuments by Shalmaneser. It is also the longest and most developed of these narratives, giving credit to the deities (specifically Aššur and Šamaš). Noteworthy is the importance of the sources of rivers for the locations of these stelae.

After this, Shalmaneser III marched south into Patina. He crossed the Orontes River and approached the city of Alimuš or Aliṣir, "the fortified city of Sapalulme, the Patinean." The last cuneiform sign in the spelling of the city name can be read either MUŠ or ṢIR.[123] One suggested location for Alimuš/Aliṣir is in the neighborhood of Antioch, modern Antakya, which means that Shalmaneser bypassed, by some distance to the west, the Patinaean capital Kinalua/Kunulua (Tell Ta'yinat).[124] Recently, Casana (2009, 22) has accepted Astour's equation of *A-li-muš* with *A-li-me* of the Alalaḫ tablets (Astour located Alime south of the Orontes, see n. 123). Thus Casana argues against locating Alimuš/Aliṣir in the area of Antioch, and instead, suggests that the site of Bozhöyük/Tell Uzunarab is "the only site that has been recorded in this area that was clearly a fortified town during the Iron Age." However, Zeeb (1998, 861) has suggested that the town of Alime of the Alalaḫ texts be associated with the town of *A-rí-me*.KI of the Ebla tablets (see Bonechi 1993, 51) which was probably located on the Euphrates River between Karkamiš and Emar. Therefore, a location for Alimuš in the area of Antioch cannot be ruled out.

At Alimuš/Aliṣir, Shalmaneser faced the second coalition force of this campaign (see table 5.1). This force was comprised of the four coalition members that fought Shalmaneser at Lutibu, plus four additional members

122. The passages are: r.21: *ṣa-lam* MAN-ti-ia *šur-ba-a* (*ṣalam šarrūtīya šurbâ*) "a very great image of my kingship"; r.35: *ṣa-lam* EN-*ti-a šur-ba-a* (*ṣalam bēlūtīya šurbâ*) "a very great image of my lordship"; r.40: *ṣal-mì* (*ṣalmī*) "my image"; r.44: $NA_4$ *a-su-me-ta* ($NA_4$.*asumetta*) "a stela." The baseline semantic field of *ṣalmu* is image, representation; context alone determines whether a statue in the round, relief image, or stela is meant. See Winter 1992, 15 n. 5.

123. See Bagg 2007, 6, s.v. Alimuš. Porter and Parpola (2001, 5 and map 2) read Aliṣir; Grayson (RIMA 3:16, A.0.102.2, i.51) reads: *a-li*-ṢIR; Olmstead (1921, 351) reads: *a-li-ṣir*; Yamada (2000a, 96 n. 73) follows Astour (1963, 236, no. 132) in identifying the city with *A-li-me* attested in the Alalaḫ tablets, arguing that the reading *A-li-muš* is preferred to the alternative reading *A-li-ṣir*. Hawkins (1995c, 94) seems to favor Alimuš (though he lists the alternative Aliṣir).

124. Hawkins 1995c, 94; Harrison 2001a, 117; reading Aliṣir, Parpola and Porter 2001, 5 and map 2.

(doubling the opposition): Katiya,[125] the Quean; Piḫirim,[126] the Ḫilukaean; Bur-Anate,[127] the Yasbuqean; (and) Adānu, the Yaḫānean. Que was located on the Adana Plain; and Ḫilukku was Cilicia (Toros Dağları).

The term "Yasbuqean" is difficult to identify. Scholars since Delitzsch (1885, 92) have seen a connection between the Monolith's KUR *ia-as-bu-qa-a-a* and the personal name יִשְׁבָּק (OG: Ιεσβοκ) in Gen 25:2 and 1 Chr 1:32. Furthermore, a land of Yasbuq (KUR.*ia-su-bu-qi*) is also attested in a Neo-Assyrian letter from the time of Sargon II.[128] This letter was sent to Sargon II by Bēl-(l)iqbi,[129] the governor of Ṣubat/Ṣupat (Fales 2002b, 148). He reports that he has driven out of his towns in the Ṣupat area the people ("the farmers and gardeners") of the Arabian sheikh, Ammi-li'ti of the tribe of Amiri (DUMU [m]*a-me-ri*), and has torn down his large sheepfold that he had constructed (SAA 1:140, 17.8b–12a). Yet, Bēl-(l)iqbi granted fields and orchards "in the land of Yasbuq" to Ammi-li'ti. The letter also reveals that the governor of Ṣupat had some influence on the city of Ḫuzāza (URU.*Ḫu-za-za*) at that time. If Ḫuzāza is identified with the well-known Ḫazāzu (modern 'Azāz) (Yamada 2000a, 97),[130] Bēl-(l)iqbi's sphere of influence would have extended from his seat, Ṣupat/Ṣubat, to northern Syria around Ḫazāzu. Thus Yasbuq may be located close to Patin, which, at that time, extended as far as Ḫazāzu (Yamada 2000a, 97–98). However, this seems to be too great a distance from Ṣupat. And in addition, a number of scholars have dissociated the city with Ḫazāzu ('Azāz), and instead have given a localization of Ḫuzāza directly south of Ṣupat (Lipiński 2000a, 327 [= Tell Ǵazza]; Parpola and Porter 2001, 24; Bagg 2007, 112–13).

Hence, there are two issues that have not been fully resolved: (1) the ethnic connections of Yasbuq and (2) the tribe's geographic location. A number of scholars have assumed a north Arabian ethnicity of Yasbuq (e.g., Eph'al 1982, 231–33; Lipiński 2000a, 192). This is clearly based on an assumption that the biblical passage in Gen 25:1–6 is assigning an Arabian

125. Shalmaneser III's inscriptions confirm that the real stem of the name Katî was /Katiya-/. It is likely derived from this root **ke/ot-* "enmity, spite" and would be an **iyo-* adjective from the /kata-/ of hieroglyphic Luwian: thus "hostile, inimical." See Younger 2009, 159–66. For earlier discussion, see Baker 2000b.

126. The meaning of Piḫirim's name is also unknown, though likely Anatolian. See Weszeli 2002.

127. Bur-Anate's name is Aramaic meaning "son of Anat." See Fuchs 1999.

128. SAA 1:140, 179.18. For a discussion of the Ṣupat dossier, see Fales 2002b.

129. The name is written [m]EN–*liq-bi*; but this might be a Sandhi writing for Bēl-iqbi (Gesche 1999).

130. However, Parpola and Porter (2001, 24) give a location of Ḫuzāza directly south of Ṣupat. For discussion, see p. 511 below.

derivation for all the "sons" of Abraham and his wife Qeturah.[131] However, as with other texts of this sort (e.g., Gen 10), this is hardly a straightforward lineage.[132] Shuah (שׁוּחַ) in Gen 25:2, if this is a reference to Sūḫu in the Middle Euphrates as is typically understood,[133] cannot be taken as having Arabian derivation.[134] On the other hand, Yamada (2000a, 97–98) feels that on the basis of the Aramaic name of its ruler mentioned in the Monolith, Bur-Anate ("son of the goddess Anat"), Yasbuq was probably an Aramean tribal entity. Furthermore, the letter from Bēl-(l)iqbi to Sargon II seems to differentiate the Arabian sheikh, Ammi-li'ti, from fields and orchards in the land of Yasbuq (KUR.*ia-su-bu-qi*) that were not his until granted by Bēl-(l)iqbi. Since the root *šbq* is found in Aramaic, Yašbuq/Yasbuq is more likely an Aramean tribal entity than a North Arabian group. Later, in the time of Esarhaddon, Yasbuqeans were part of the Assyrian army.[135]

Geographically, on the basis of this letter of Bēl-(l)iqbi, Na'aman (1999, 424) places the land of Yasbuq in the northeastern area of the Ṣupat region. Zadok (2008, 326) suggests that perhaps the North Arabian tribe penetrated the area through the Ḥoms/Akkar gap. However, Eph'al (1982, 240) suggested locating the land of Yasbuq in the Upper Euphrates region. The fact is that a location in the region of Ṣupat at the time of the battle of Alimuš/Aliṣir means that the "Yasbuqean" had quite some distance to come to the battle site through the territories of Hamath and Lu'aš/Luḫuti. A possible resolution is proposed by Zadok (2008, 327):

> It seems that the polity ruled by Bur-Anate almost 150 years before the occurrence of Yasbuqu in the Emesenian gap, is to be sought not in Ṣubat, but—as can be expected of semi-nomads who are notoriously mobile—further north, presumably somewhere on the fringe of the desert east of Bīt-Agūsi and not far from Bīt-Adīni.

---

131. While some of the "sons" are clearly ancestors to Arabian tribal groups (e.g., "Midian," the sons of Yaqšan ("Sheba and Dedan"), the text is a complex combination of "socially constructed identities." Westermann (1985, 395) states: "Gen 25:1–6 belongs neither to P's or J's overall plan and must be a secondary addition."

132. Others living in Sheba and Dedan did not come from Abraham, but from Cush, at least according to the tradition in Gen 10:7.

133. Based on the occurrence of הַשּׁוּחִי in Job 2:11, etc. "Bildad the Shuhite." However, Hamilton (1995, 166) argues "Gen 25's connection of Shuah with names like Sheba and Dedan argues for a Shuah farther to the south."

134. This is proven beyond any doubt by the inscriptions from Sūḫu, see RIMB 2:275–331.

135. Based on the extispicy texts (SAA 4:154–56, texts 144 and 145) with the readings of Fales. See Fales 2001, 59–61, 77–78.

In my estimation, this makes eminent sense. Some similarity will be seen in a number of the southern Mesopotamian tribes (see chapter 10).

The last coalition member is Adānu the Yaḫānean. The name has been analyzed as being Aramaic, a *qatal* formation of *ʿdn* "to give abundance" (Frahm and Zadok 1998), in which case it is from the same root as the eponymous ancestor of (Bīt-)Adīni. The land of Yaḫānu was mentioned in the Annals of Aššurnaṣirpal II during his eleventh campaign (875–867 BCE) when he received the tribute of Gūšu the Yaḫānean (see also chapter 8 below).

Some scholars have raised the question as to how the coalition forces, which had already fought a difficult battle at Lutibu, were able to appear again at Alimuš/Aliṣir to encounter the Assyrian force. Years ago, Kraeling (1918, 69–70) suggested that either Shalmaneser after the battle of Lutibu, was engaged in other unrecorded operations, so that "he gave the allies from Asia Minor and Syria time" to assemble at Alimuš/Aliṣir, or the scribe of the Annals was inaccurate in recording that Ḫayānu was present at Alimuš/Aliṣir and that the others participated in the battle of Lutibu.

Neither of these options is necessary. First, the Assyrian account of the battle of Lutibu employs the usual stereotypical language of Assyrian conquest accounts and should not be pressed too literally. The description of massive defeat is no doubt hyperbolic. Based on the casualty numbers given ("300" felled at Būr-mar'īna; "1,300" at Paqarḫubuni; and "700" at Alimuš/Aliṣir),[136] it is apparent that Shalmaneser was not facing the full combined forces that he faced in later engagements (e.g., at Qarqar). The coalition was defeated, or perhaps better, failed in its attempt to block Shalmaneser's advance. But it was intact and militarily still a viable force ready to fight another day. On the other hand, the coalition could not prevent Shalmaneser from attacking some of Sam'al's more vulnerable cities/towns (line 51a: "I razed, destroyed (and) burned his cities," though with the obvious exceptions of the cities of Lutibu and Sam'al/Yādiya). Second, significant time was spent in setting up the image at the source of the Saluara River at the foot of Mount Amanus and its accompanying rituals (no doubt included was time for the Assyrian troops' recovery from the engagement at Lutibu). Third, Lutibu and Alimuš/Aliṣir are approximately 120 km apart (Yamada 2000a, 97) and so time was necessary for the army to cover this distance.

Not only did Shalmaneser defeat the coalition for the second time in an open-field battle, he also successfully besieged and captured the city of Alimuš/Aliṣir. It seems that the crowning achievement in the battle was the

136. These numbers are not only round figures, but 300 and 700 look like "ideal" type numbers and 1,300 is 300 + 1,000 in the text. How accurate are these numbers? Nevertheless, they give some indication of the size of the forces opposing Shalmaneser.

capture of Bur-Anate of Yasbuq.[137] His fate is not described. In the case of the other rulers in the coalition, most fought Shalmaneser III again in subsequent years.

It is clear from the One Year Annals[138] that after the battle at Alimuš/Aliṣir, Shalmaneser III marched southwest to the Mediterranean Sea, presumably following the Orontes River to its mouth. This text records the ritual cleansing of weapons in the sea in conjunction with offerings to the gods, and the setting up of a royal image with dedicatory praises to Aššur and Shalmaneser's battle achievements written on it.

However, the Kurkh Monolith (and possibly the Two Year Annals) records the conquest of cities on the shore of the Mediterranean as well as the tribute of the kings of the seashore. The Mediterranean Sea receives the double attribution: [*tâmti*] ⁽⁶⁾ *e-li-ni-te šá* KUR *a-mur-ri u tam-di* <SILIM>-*um* ᵈ*šam-ši* "the upper [sea] of land of Amurru, even the western sea." Yamada comments:

> The name *tâmti* (*elēnīte*) *ša māt Amurri* was applied to the Mediterranean by the scribes of Tiglath-pileser I, whereas *tâmdi ša šulme/u* ᵈ*Šamši* is the term introduced first in the inscriptions of Shalmaneser III. Therefore, the juxtaposition of the two names in Shalmaneser's texts can be understood as an effort of Shalmaneser's historiographer(s) to show the correspondence between the traditional name and the new name of the Mediterranean Sea by paraphrasing both of them.[139]

It is noteworthy that this double attribution is found in a "provincial document" that has a number of errors (Tadmor 1961).

Due to the vague description, the exact location on the seashore reached by Shalmaneser cannot be determined, but the most probable location would simply be the mouth of the Orontes River. The receipt of tribute of the kings of the seashore is absent in the One Year Annals, but is recorded in the Kurkh Monolith,[140] as well as in the Balawat Gate and Calah Throne Base inscriptions.[141] Exactly who were the kings of the seashore who paid tribute

---

137. Yamada (2000a, 98 n. 82) notes that from this point on, Yasbuq is never mentioned in the inscriptions of Shalmaneser, and that this may imply that the land was incorporated by a neighboring country, probably Yaḫān/Bīt-Agūsi. But see the discussion above.

138. RIMA 3:25, A.0.102.3, lines 85b–89a.

139. Yamada 2000a, 101. He concludes: "It is unlikely that the two names should be seen as the appellatives of two different parts of the Mediterranean Sea, as suggested by J. Elayi, since there is no indication that Shalmaneser reached the sea twice at two different points." See Elayi 1984, 83.

140. RIMA 3:17, A.0.102.2, ii.7.

141. RIMA 3:29, A.0.102.5, ii.4; 3:103, A.0.102.28, line 20.

to Shalmaneser is not stated in *any* text. On analogy with Aššurnaṣirpal II, one could suggest Tyre, Sidon, Byblos, Maḫallatu, Maizu, Kaizu, Amurru, and Arwad. Interestingly, two bronze bands of the gates from Balawat[142] are usually associated with this tribute, both of them depicting Phoenician boats crossing the sea from an island, apparently Tyre, to the mainland, as well as people unloading cargoes from a boat and carrying tribute to Shalmaneser. Both bands have epigraphs: Band III, upper register: "I received the tribute of the ships of the Tyrians and Sidonians";[143] Band N, lower register: "I received the tribute of the Tyrians and Sidonians: silver, gold, tin, bronze, wool, lapis lazuli (and) carnelian."[144] On Band III, an aged king of Tyre, probably Ittobaal I, is pictured standing on an island. That the Tyrian king did not lead the delegation himself may imply that the actual site where the tribute was received was far from the island.[145]

On his return from the sea, Shalmaneser III climbed Mount Amanus and cut down timbers of cedar and juniper. The scene is likely depicted on Balawat Bronze Band N, upper register (Schachner 2007, 306, pl. 14). This probably occurred somewhere on the southern Amanus Range, not particularly far from the Orontes River.

Next, Shalmaneser climbed another mountain, Mount Atalur, where he erected a royal image (the third of the campaign) beside the image of a previous king, Anum-ḫirbe—an eastern Anatolian king of the Old Assyrian period (first part of the eighteenth century BCE).[146] Anum-ḫirbe was the king of Mama, a country that was perhaps located in the vicinity of modern Elbistan, or the region of Comana Cappadocia and Göksün, that is, the modern Turkish district of Maraş.[147] A number of scholars have suggested that Mount Atalur should be identified with one of the (southern?) peaks of the Kurt Dağ.[148] In the later texts of Shalmaneser III, the mountain is not called Atalur but

142. Schachner 2007, 38. In contrast to Schachner's proposed order of the bands, see Curtis and Tallis 2008, 72. They conclude that the pictorial schemes of these gates were not haphazard at all, but instead designed according to "a carefully formulated plan, with a strong, but not overriding, emphasis on visual and thematic symmetry in design and content." See also Hertel 2012. However, this issue is not an essential part of the argument made in this work.

143. RIMA 3:141, A.0.102.66: *ma-da-tú šá* GIŠ.MÁ.MEŠ *šá* URU *ṣu-ra-a-a* URU *ṣi-du-na-a-a am-ḫu-ur*.

144. Or alternatively for the last items: "wool, blue and red." RIMA 3:147, A.0.102.84: [*ma-da*]-*tú šá* URU *ṣu-ra-a-a* URU *ṣi-du-na-a-a* KÙ.BABBAR.MEŠ KÙ.GI. MEŠ AN.NA.MEŠ ZABAR.MEŠ SÍK.MEŠ $NA_4$.ZA.GÌN $NA_4$.GUG *am-ḫur*.

145. Yamada 2000a, 103 and n. 97.

146. This is quite remarkable when one considers the time distance between the two (ca. 1775–858 = 917 yrs.—over nine centuries!).

147. Balkan 1957, 31–34; Nashef 1991, 82–83.

148. Yamada 2000a, 105 and n. 106; Hawkins 2000, 363 n. 23; Röllig 1980–83.

Lallar. Since the name Atalur is attested in the earliest texts of Shalmaneser, as well as in the Hittite sources, it is difficult to reject its authenticity. Yamada (2000a, 105–6) argues:

> If the form Lallar, attested only in the later texts, is not an error, we may explain, with E. Weidner, that the original non-Akkadian name of the place, **Tlallor* was normalized differently into "Atalur" and "Lallar"; perhaps the latter reflects the contemporary Assyrian transcription of the toponym, as against the former, traditional version.

Na'aman (1976, 95) argued that Mount Atalur and Mount Lallar were different peaks. He identifies Mount Atalur with Kurt Dağ, the actual place visited by Shalmaneser III and assumed that the scribe of the later version, being misled by the confusing text of his *Vorlage*, the Kurkh Monolith, "modified" Atalur into Lallar (the southern spur of the Amanus Range). However, the One Year Annals text—which very clearly indicates the course of the campaign—was very likely the *Vorlage* for the later version rather than the Kurkh Monolith.[149] This makes Na'aman's explanation less tenable.[150]

After this erection of a royal image on Mount Atalur, the One Year Annals record the conquest of Taya and Ḫazāzu, "the great cities belonging to the Patinean."[151] The Kurkh Monolith enumerates four cities, Taya, Ḫazāzu, Nulia, and Butāmu. Only Ḫazāzu can be securely identified, namely, with modern ʿAzāz (Hawkins 1972–75c). The Balawat Gates of Shalmaneser III (Band III, lower register) picture the capture and destruction of Ḫazāzu, with the epigraph reading: "the battle of the city of Ḫazāzu" (*ti-du-ku šá* URU.*ḫa-za-zi*).[152] The relief shows the city of Ḫazāzu under the attack of the Assyrians and in flames, with captive Patineans (men and women—the men are naked and bound) being brought out before the Assyrian king. Taya (URU.*ta-ia-a*) is probably the same place as Tae (URU.*ta-e*) mentioned in the Annals of Tiglath-pileser III as a city of Patina/Unqi (Tadmor 1994, 66, Ann 13, line 4). It has been identified with modern Kefr Tai,[153] 12 km west of Aleppo or with the site of Tatya (between Kilizi and ʿAzāz).[154] Part of the

149. As pointed out by Yamada 2000a, 106 n. 109. Would the errors of the Kurkh Monolith be preserved on a wax writing tablet?

150. The One Year Annals had not been published (1985–86) when Na'aman wrote his article (1976).

151. RIMA 3:25, A.0.102.3, lines 92b–94a.

152. RIMA 3:141, A.0.102.67; Schachner 2007, 40.

153. Elliger 1947, 78–79 n. 27; Astour 1963, 237, no. 153.

154. Dussaud 1927, 469 n. 2; and Yamada 2000a, 106 n. 111.

difficulty is establishing the route of Shalmaneser's march. The locations of Nulia and Butāmu are uncertain.[155]

The results of the attacks on Taya and Ḫazāzu according to the One Year Annals were: "I killed them" (GAZ.MEŠ-*šú-nu* ḪI.A *a-duk*) and "I carried off 4,600 captives" ((r.42) 4 LIM 6 ME *ša-la-su-nu aš-lu-la*). The Kurkh Monolith states: "I killed 2,800 (of them)" (2 LIM 8 ME GAZ.[MEŠ-*šunu*] (12) *a-duk*) and "I carried off 14,600 captives" (14 LIM 6 ME *šal-la-su-nu áš-lu-la*). However, the Monolith backtracks the campaign by stating "I de[parted] from the sea" and adds the other two cities (Nulia and Butāmu) to the list. Thus while the Monolith's 14,600 may be a manipulation of the One Year Annals' 4,600, it may be that some kind of total is being given for the entire campaign (?) or the seashore and Patinean portion (?).[156]

In the One Year Annals, one final itinerary statement is given: "I departed from the city of Ḫazāzu." This introduces an episode[157] concerning the conquest and destruction of another Patinean city, Urime.[158] This city is described as the fortified city of Lubarna, the Patinean. The Patinean ruler mentioned previously in the text was Sapalulme II.[159] There are three possible ways to deal with this problem.

First, some have suggested that there were two Patinean rulers at this time: one was Sapalulme who participated in the anti-Assyrian coalition in the two battles of Lutibu and Alimuš/Alişir (described as his fortified city); and the other was Lubarna whose fortified city was Urime. In the Annals of Aššurnaṣirpal II, a Lubarna of Patina paid tribute. He controlled the cities of Kunulua, Aribua, and Ḫazāzu, and permitted Aššurnaṣirpal II to make Aribua an Assyrian outpost (ca. 870 BCE). Thus, according to this view, it is most

155. Nulia has been identified with modern Niyara, east of ʿAzāz (Kraeling 1918, 70 n. 1), though Astour (1963, 223–24, no. 15) identified it with either Jebel Lailun, modern Jebel Seman or Jebel Barakat located between Antakya and Aleppo. Butāmu has been identified with Beitan (Kraeling 1918, 70 n. 1) and with Badama of Yaqut (Olmstead 1923, 353 n. 20). Both of these locations are near ʿAzāz. Astour proposed Bdama located in the pass in the Ansariyah Mountains. Note also the possible identity of Butāmu with Bumame found in Tiglath-pileser III's inscriptions (Tadmor 1994, Ann. 19, line 9). See Weippert 1973, 42 n. 61; Yamada 2000a, 106 n. 112.

156. The number of slain previously given are: 300 + 1,300 + 700 equaling 2,300 (× 2 = 4,600!).

157. RIMA 3:25, A.0.102.3, lines 94b–99.

158. The location of Urime is likely south of Ḫazāzu, since apparently after its conquest, Shalmaneser received the tribute of Arame, the Gūšite, whose territory was probably located around Aleppo and Arpad (Tell Rifaʿat). Urime has been identified with Urima of the Idrimi Inscription and Urume of the Alalaḫ texts. See Astour 1963, 234 n. 118. See also Bagg 2007, 268., s.v. Urime.

159. Both rulers bore illustrious Hittite names, Labarna and Suppiluliuma, respectively.

probable that the Lubarna of Aššurnaṣirpal II's campaign and the Lubarna of Shalmaneser III's campaign are the same person.[160] Lubarna would be the king of Patina and Sapalulme, who is mentioned only in this campaign, was "merely a viceroy of the aged king Lubarna, whose reign ended in this year; he was succeeded by Qalparunda in the next year, Year 2."[161] Hawkins (2000, 363) understands the Lubarna of the Aššurnaṣirpal II and Shalmaneser III texts to be the same person, but supposes that "at this time the land was divided between him and Shalmaneser's opponent Sapalulme."[162]

Second, some scholars have understood the Lubarna of the Annals of Aššurnaṣirpal II (i.e., Lubarna I) as a different ruler than the Lubarna of this campaign of Shalmaneser's (i.e., Lubarna II). Thus there was a sequence of rulers: Lubarna I, succeeded by Sapalulme II, then Lubarna II, and then Qalparunda. Yamada criticizes this view stating: "This is theoretically possible but less likely, since it implies too many changes of ruler during a short period, including the reign for Lubarna II that lasted less than one year" (Yamada 2000a, 107–8 n. 116). But there are many examples of very short reigns and changes of rule within short periods, particularly when there are strong outside military pressures on a small or internally weak state.[163] Sometimes, internal political conflict can be a nation's greatest enemy.

Third, since *Lubarna* means "king," it may not be a personal name, but a title.[164] In this case, both in Aššurnaṣirpal II's and in Shalmaneser III's inscriptions the word simply refers to the ruler of the Patineans, without giving the personal name. However, the tendency in the Assyrian royal inscriptions is to use the personal name rather than a dynastic title. It is possible that the title had become a personal name.

Now adding to this is the 2012 discovery at Tell Taʿyinat of a large statue with a fragmentary hieroglyphic Luwian inscription of a king Suppiluliuma which appears to date to the ninth century and may be in fact Sapalulme (II).[165]

---

160. Mahmud and Black 1985–86, 137; Yamada 2000a, 107.

161. Yamada 2000a, 107. This is also an Anatolian name = Halparuntiya (note the name of the Gurgum ruler).

162. For a similar view, see Fuchs 2001; Weeden 2013, 15.

163. For example, one can cite the changes of government within Mexico in 1846 in the midst of the Mexican-American War. In 1846 alone, the presidency changed hands four times, the war minister changed six times, the finance minister changed sixteen times. Again, all of this change in the midst of a war! See Stevens 1991, 11. Note also the year 883–882 in Israelite history: Elah, Zimri, Omri, Tibni.

164. Weeden 2013, 15 suggests that the Assyrian confused the title for a personal name. For the meaning of the name and this suggestion, though he does not follow it, see Fuchs 2001.

165. See §3.1.3 and table 3.1 above.

In 829 BCE, Shalmaneser received a report that the Patineans had killed their ruler Lubarna and that they had replaced him with a usurper Surri. This Lubarna (II, III) could be another ruler of that name, but possibly is the ruler known from the records of 870 and 858.[166]

According to the One Year Annals, Shalmaneser erected a fourth and final victory stela in the ruins of the city of Urime. After Urime's conquest, Shalmaneser received the tribute of Arame, the Gūšite. At the battle of Alimuš/Alişir, one of the coalition members was Adānu the Yaḫānean. This poses a similar problem to that of "Sapalulme, the Patinean," and "Lubarna, the Patinean," implying that both Adānu of Yaḫān and Arame of Bīt-Agūsi held power in the same area. This problem will be discussed in §8.2.1.

As stated at the beginning of the discussion of this campaign, Shalmaneser seems to be attempting to emulate his father's Mediterranean campaign(s) (875–867 BCE). In both cases, the Neo-Hittite state of Patina was a substantial political target. In the days of Aššurnaṣirpal II, Patina does not appear to have resisted, but allowed passage through its territory in combination with its tribute. But in Shalmaneser III's time, it chose to resist.

Not one single capital city of the western states was captured and destroyed by Shalmaneser in 858. But the focus of the campaign seems to have been twofold: (1) the beginning of the process of the isolation of Bīt-Adīni, and (2) the collection and reestablishment of the lines of tribute. In these matters, the campaign appears to have been successful.

### 5.2.2. Shalmaneser III's 857 Campaign

In his second year (857), Shalmaneser III renewed his attack on Aḫuni of Bīt-Adīni (fig. 5.3).[167] The encounter is narrated in terms very similar to those of the previous year: Aḫuni trusted again in the might of his own army and fought Shalmaneser in an open-field battle; Shalmaneser defeated him and confined him in his city of Til-Barsib, and then departed and crossed the Euphrates. It appears that "I confined him in his city (*ina* [*ālīšu*] *ēsiršu*)" is a stereotyped syntagm (Yamada 2000, 114). Thus the confinement was hardly

166. Hawkins (2000, 363 n. 28) states: "It has always been assumed that this Lubarni was a different individual from the opponent of Aššurnaṣirpal ca. 870 B.C., but the new evidence {the One Year Annals} that Lubarna was still alive in 858 B.C. when he was earlier thought to have been succeeded by Sapalulme, raises the possibility here that the same Lubarna had survived also the reign of Qalparunda to be assassinated at this date." This would give this Lubarna a minimum 41 year rule. But is this really the best understanding of the data? This is a long reign. See Table 3.1

167. The details of this campaign are set out primarily in two of Shalmaneser's texts: the Two-Year Annals (RIMA 3:10–11, A.0.102.1: 82′–95′) and the Kurkh Monolith (RIMA 3:17–19, A.0.102.2: ii.13b–30a).

substantial. Shalmaneser had no more success in capturing Til-Barsib than in the previous campaign, but he had renewed success on the other side of the Euphrates. Hence, the dual strategy was working.

As in the case of the previous year, the point of Shalmaneser's crossing of the Euphrates is not specified.[168] According to the Kurkh Monolith (ii.16b–17a), Shalmaneser conquered six fortified cities of Aḫuni (the man) of Bīt-Adīni: [...]gâ, Tagi[...], Sūrunu, Paripa, Til-Bašerê, Dabigu (⌜URU⌝ *x-ga-a* URU *ta-gi-*[...] URU *su-ú-ru-nu* URU *pa-ri-pa* URU.DU$_6$-*ba-še-re-e* URU *da-bi-gu*), in addition to destroying two hundred towns in their environs, with great massacre and plundering. These six fortified cities and their towns and villages were located in the area between Gaziantepe and Tell Rifaʿat (ancient Arpad), on the west bank of the Sajur River and on the upper Quweiq River.

The first city's name is not fully preserved. Lipiński (2000a, 178) suggests restoring URU [*Du-lí*]-*qá-a* here in the Kurkh Monolith (ii.16), as well as restoring *ma-da-tu šá* URU [*Du-li*]-*qá-*[*a*] "the tribute of Doliche" on one of the bronze bands of Aššurnaṣirpal II's gate at Balawat.[169] This is a possible reading of the preserved signs (hence [...]*qâ*).[170] But it appears that Lipiński is assuming a name based on a possible preservation in the name of a modern site.[171] The other cities have been discussed in detail above.

The battle of Dabigu is depicted on Balawat Bronze Band IV.[172] The upper register of the band bears the epigraph "the battle of Dabigu of Aḫuni, a man of Bīt-Adīni."[173] It shows a walled city being attacked from both sides by sappers, archers, and chariots. In the lower register, which has no epigraph, the scene depicts in its left half the final assault on a walled city by sappers

168. Since the cities of Pitru and Mutkīnu which control the crossing nearest to Til-Barsib were not captured until the next year (856 BCE), it is perhaps more likely that Shalmaneser III crossed the Euphrates near Būr-mar'īna, or at the crossing a little north of modern Birecik. Perhaps the latter is most likely. Lipiński (2000a, 177) argues: "The order in which the cities are enumerated [referring to the six cities of Bīt-Adīni west of the Euphrates listed in the Kurkh Monolith] does not suggest that the crossing had taken place at Pitru. It points rather to a crossing at Balkis {same crossing spot referred to in Yamada as Birecik; Balkis is on the west bank, Birecik is on the east bank}, where also Ashurnasirpal II may have crossed the Euphrates before receiving the tribute of Carchemish."

169. See RIMA 2:348, A.0.101.89.

170. Reading GA as *qá*. See von Soden and Röllig (1991, no. 170): possible for this period.

171. He suggests that the ancient city should perhaps be identified with Karhöyük, a large ruin mound in the valley of Güreniz Dere, 3 km northeast of Dülük. See Lipiński 2000a, 178 n. 91.

172. Schachner 2007, 41–43; 296, pl. 4; photos: pls. 28a–30b; King 1915, 24, pls. XIX–XXIV.

173. For the epigraph, see RIMA 3:142, A.0.102.68.

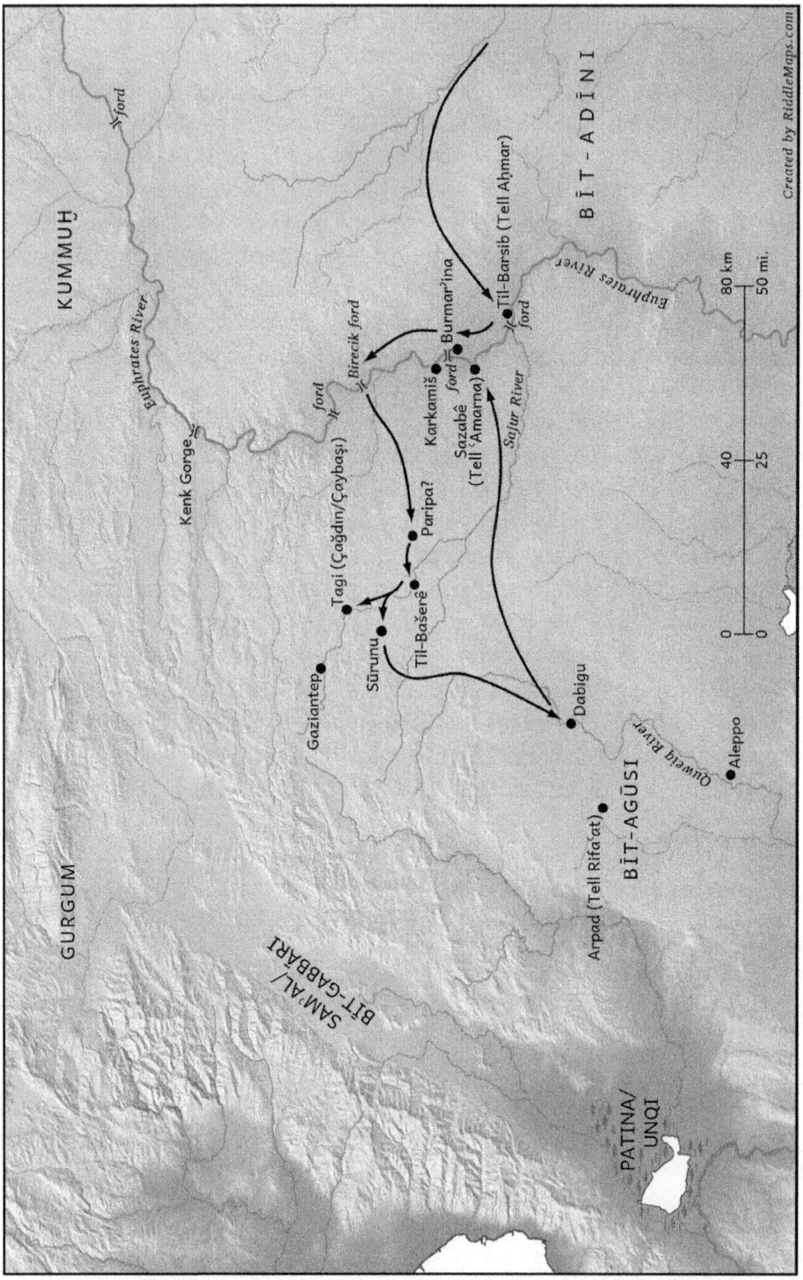


Fig. 5.3. Shalmaneser III's 857 campaign

and a siege engine, with enemy corpses being impaled near the city;[174] on the right half is engraved another scene, with captives led by Assyrians to a walled city which already seems to be under Assyrian occupation.[175] The two walled cities engraved on the lower register are similar to each other and resemble the city in the upper register as well. Thus, it appears that all three are intended to represent Dabigu, and that each of them represents a different stage of the same battle, that is, its beginning, the assault on the city, and the taking of captives after the fall of the city.[176]

The Two Year Annals[177] record a separate narrative concerning the battle at Dabigu as opposed to the Kurkh Monolith, which relates the fight against the six cities. The episode concerning Dabigu in the Two Year Annals and that in the Kurkh Monolith concerning the city of Sazabê[178] are narrated in virtually the same way. Thus at the end of each episode, the tribute of the western kings is given. The Two Year Annals, however, demonstrate that it was after the battle at Dabigu, while Shalmaneser was still there, that he received the tribute (*maddattu*) of four of these kings (see table 5.2).

Table 5.2. First Tribute List of 857 BCE (according to the Two Year Annals, Kurkh Monolith, RIMA 3:11, A.0.102.1, lines 93′–95′)

| Ruler | Nation | Formulation |
|---|---|---|
| Qalparu(n)da (II) | Unqi (Patina) | $^{m}$*qàl-pu-ru-un-da* URU *un-qa-a-a* |
| Mutalli | Gurgum | $^{m}$*mu-tal-li* URU *gúr-gu-ma-a-a* |
| Ḫayānu (Ḥayyā’) | Sam’al (Bīt-Gabbāri) | [$^{m}$*ḫa*]*-ia-a-ni* KUR *sa-am-ʾa-la-a-a* |
| Arame | Bīt-Agūsi | $^{m}$*a-ra-me* DUMU [$^{m}$]⌜*a-gu-si*⌝ |

Yamada interprets this to imply that these countries, having failed to organize an anti-Assyrian coalition, adopted a wait-and-see policy when Shalmaneser attacked Aḫuni's cities. Thus with the capture of the six cities culminating in Dabigu's seizure, the kings brought their tribute to him there. The absence of Karkamiš among the tributaries in the list indicates that country's still-determined resistance that necessitated Shalmaneser's invasion of its territory.

174. King 1915, pls. XX–XXI.

175. King 1915, pls. XXII–XXIV.

176. Schachner 2007, 222; Yamada 2000a, 116; Billerbeck and Delitzsch 1908, 25. King (1915, 24) and Olmstead (1921, 354) were of the opinion that the scenes in the lower register depict the sack of a neighboring town, which Olmstead identified it as Til-Bašerê.

177. RIMA 3:11, A.0.102.1, lines 90′–95′.

178. RIMA 3:18, A.0.102.2, ii.18b–20a.

Departing from Dabigu, this is exactly what Shalmaneser III did. He approached Sazabê, the fortified city of Sangara of Karkamiš. The city is identified with Tell Amarna, located 8 km south of Karkamiš (Jerablus) on the west bank of the Euphrates River.[179] As noted above, the Kurkh Monolith which gives a detailed episode concerning its capture, lists the tribute of all the western kings immediately after this (see table 5.3).

Table 5.3. Second Tribute List of 857 BCE (according to the Kurkh Monolith, ii.20b–30a

| Ruler | Nation | Formulation |
|---|---|---|
| Qalparu(n)da (II) | Patina (Unqi) | $^{m}$⸢*qal*⸣-[*pa-ru*]-*un-da* KUR *pa-ti-na-a-a* |
| Ḫayānu (Ḥayyā') | Bīt-Gabbāri (Sam'al) | $^{m}$*ḫa-ia-a-nu* DUMU *gab-ba-ri* |
| Arame | Bīt-Agūsi | $^{m}$*a-ra-mu* DUMU *a-gu-ú-si* |
| Sangara | Karkamiš | $^{m}$*sa-an-ga-ra* URU *gar-ga-miš-a-a* |
| Qatazilu | Kummuḫ | $^{m}$*qa-ta-ẓi-lu* KUR *ku-mu-ḫa-a-a* |

Obviously, the tribute of Sangara of Karkamiš is now listed, along with that of Qatazilu of Kummuḫ. But the Monolith omits Mutalli of Gurgum from its list, perhaps due to scribal error (Yamada 2000a, 118–19).

The scenes of tribute brought by Patina and Karkamiš are depicted in the reliefs from Balawat. Bronze Bands V and VI are generally associated with the tribute of the 857 campaign.[180]

In conclusion, the 857 campaign of Shalmaneser III was another step in the political and economic subjugation of the north Syrian states, in particular Bīt-Adīni. Its primary goal was the continued attrition of Bīt-Adīni's resistance capacities. By targeting Bīt-Adīni's territory west of the Euphrates, Shalmaneser not only accomplished this, he was able to intimidate the north Syrian states into submitting to him; and therefore, to complete the isolation of Til-Barsib so that its eventual fall was assured. The attack on the single city of Sazabê of Karkamiš forced that state's quick submission through tribute payment.

179. Bagg 2007, 216, s.v. Sazabê. Parpola and Porter 2001, 16 (listed with high certainty). However, there is no trace of Iron Age remains at the site of Tell 'Amarna according to the field surveys. See Sanlaville 1985, 171; and Bunnens 1989.

180. Schachner 2007, 43–48, 221–22, 297–98 (pls. 5–6), 323–29 (pls. 31a–37b).

### 5.2.3. Shalmaneser III's 856 Campaign

The campaign of 856, Shalmaneser III's third regnal year, was made up of two phases: (1) the western phase: the attack on Bīt-Adīni (with the capture of Til-Barsib and a number of other cities; fig. 5.4), and (2) the northern phase: the attack on Urartu (with Shalmaneser traversing the northern lands from west to east, especially targeting Urartu with the climax coming in the battle at Arṣašku(n)/ Arzashku(n), the capital of Arramu,[181] king of Urartu).

While the concern of this study is with the Arameans, a few comments must be given on the northern phase as the two are integrally tied together, at least literarily.[182] Furthermore, the 856 campaign as it regards Aḫuni of Bīt-Adīni is integrally tied in a number of Shalmaneser's texts with the 855 campaign. The Kenk Gorge inscription is the earliest account of this campaign, but it is a very brief part of a summary inscription (i.e., a nonannalistic text), so its usefulness is limited. The Kurkh Monolith is by far and away the most detailed text and serves as the primary source for the campaign;[183] the other annalistic accounts abridge it.[184] The Monolith is unique among the annalistic texts because it uses resumptively a narrative that is a type of résumé of the accounts found in the Kenk Gorge Inscription and the Balawat Gates Inscription. Neither of these two texts uses this résumé in a resumptive fashion, since they do not include the initial narrative concerning Shalmane-

---

181. Radner (1998c) notes the suggestion by Salvini (1995a, 26–27) to interpret *A-ra-mu*, not as a personal name, but a designation "the Aramean." This would imply that the Urartian kingdom was initially founded by a Aramean and later acquired by the actual Urartians themselves, requiring a change in dynasty with Sarduri I. This seems unlikely, since, as pointed out by Radner (1998c) and Fuchs (2012, 159), it is contradicted by the form of the name *Arrame/u*, which the Assyrian scribes never use to designate an Aramean entity (the personal name is written the following ways: $^{m}$*ar-ra-mu*, $^{m}$*a-ra-mu*, $^{m}$*ar-ra-me*, $^{m}$*a-ra-me*, *a-ra-me*). Compare the Greek Ἄραμος. Fuchs (2012, 159) also speculates whether Ar(r)ame might represent a mutilated form of the toponym that is inconsistently written Aramalē, Armarilī, Armarijalī and Armiraliu, i.e., Aram(al)ē; that the Assyrian scribes used it mockingly; and whether Lutibri, the father of Sarduri I, might be this person, yielding: (Lutibri, the lord of) Aram(al)ē. Alternatively, perhaps Ar(r)ame is reflective of Erimena? (Fuchs 2012, 158, tab. 09.05).

182. The composition *STT* 43 appears to belong to Shalmaneser III and connects the two phases of the 856 campaign. See Livingstone 1989, 44–47; Foster 2005, 779–82. Cf. Grayson 1982, 259–69; Yamada 2000a, 129.

183. RIMA 3:13–24, A.0.102.2.

184. These include: the Assur Clay Tablets or 16 Year Annals (RIMA 3:35–36, A.0.102.6–7, i.57–61a, Urartu i.61a–ii.2); the Marble Slab or 20 Year Annals (RIMA 3:51–52, A.0.102.10, i.36b–44a; Urartu i.44b–48a); the Assur Stone Fragment Inscription (RIMA 3:71–72, A.0.102.15); the Black Obelisk (RIMA 3:64–65, A.0.102.14, lines 35b–41a; Urartu 41b–44); and the Broken Statue from Nimrud (RIMA 3:74, A.0.102.16, 14b–17; Urartu 18–20a). For a discussion of these sources, see Yamada 2000a, 120–23.

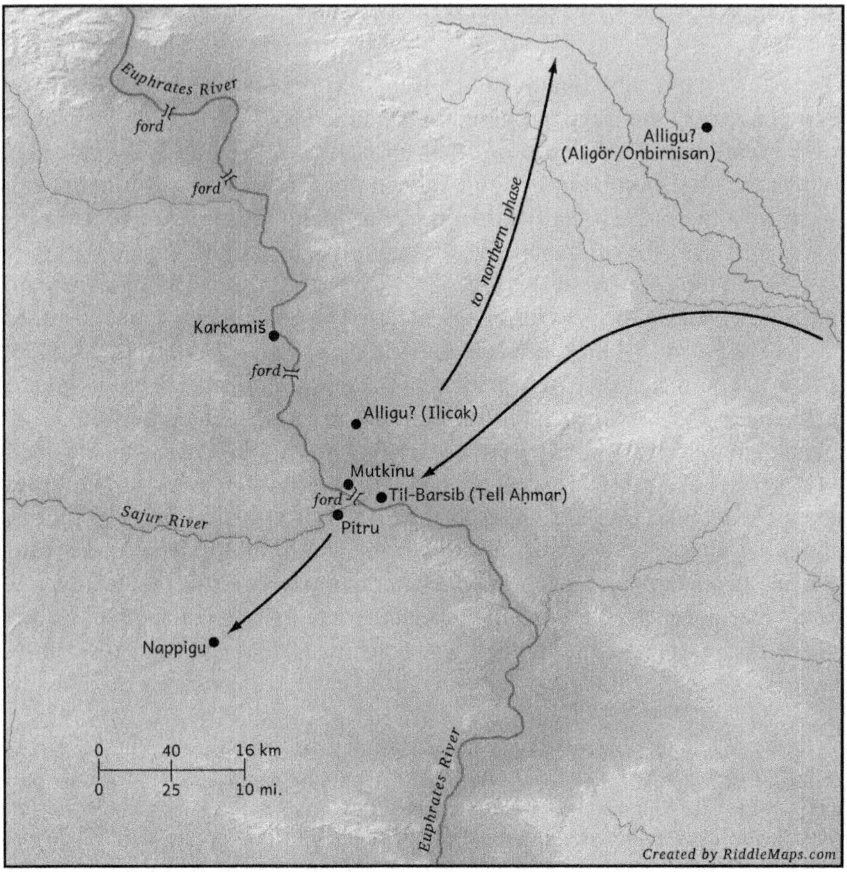


Fig. 5.4. Shalmaneser III's 856 campaign

ser's conflict with Aḫuni of Bīt-Adīni before their summaries of the Urartian phase of the campaign. For the Monolith's narration of the 856 campaign, the use of this résumé creates an inclusio that frames the Urartian episode with Bīt-Adīni.[185]

185. Yamada (2000a, 131–32) argues that the résumé functioned as an introduction to the fourth year account, drawing the reader's attention away from the Urartian war, which ends the account of the previous year (the 856 campaign), back to the events in the west. It also effectively commemorates the entire process of the reduction of Bīt-Adīni in a single literary framework, giving it a special emphasis. The editor may have been unable to find any appropriate place for relating the fall of Til-Barsib within the usual framework of the Annals; hence the special résumé, an element alien to the Annals.

There are problems with the length and route of the Urartian campaign. Salvini (1995b, 47; 1995a, 30) summarizes:

> Russell (1984) follows substantially the traditional interpretation of the campaign. He calculated an itinerary of roughly 2,380 km. It is 600 kms from Nineveh to Til-Barsib, which can be covered in daily stages of 20–25 km. The long march through the mountains of roughly 1,780 km, however, could not be covered at a rate of more than 12 km a day. This means approximately 170–180 days of marching without taking into consideration stops, battles, raids or the erection of 4 victory stelae. With a campaign of such dimensions, that could last for more than six months, the army which left Nineveh in the second half of April (13th of Ayyaru) risked finding itself in the late autumn (the second half of October) in the difficult region of the Zagros, still beyond the mountain passes which separated it from the Assyrian plain.

Salvini proposes that these are two separate campaigns that have been presented as one.[186] His hypothesis is that the report for the third year (856) brings together reports of two separate campaigns, carried out simultaneously, one to the west and the other toward the east by two armies led, respectively, by the king and the *turtānu* ("the commander-in-chief"). In his opinion, the scribes combined two distinct itineraries for the third year. The first, the western expedition (ii.30b–47), was a campaign in the Euphrates region in which the narrative culminates with the statement "I departed from the land of Dayeni." This expedition returned via the Enzite Pass with Til-Barsib serving as "an excellent base both for departure and the return" (Salvini 1995b, 46; 1995a, 31). The other expedition (ii.48–66a) would have taken much longer and faced greater difficulties. The narration of its itinerary begins with the statement "I approached the city of Arṣašku(n)" and culminates with the statement "I emerged by the mountain pass of Kirruru in front of the city of Arbela." This campaign returned via the Kirruru Pass.

While it is entirely possible that the scribes could combine two separate itineraries into one, Salvini's reading of the text of the Kurkh Monolith is not convincing. Liverani notes a fundamental problem stating: "the reconstruction by Salvini … is based on a misunderstanding of the text. 'I entered (into Nairi or into the mountains) from the Enzite pass, and I went out from the Kirruru pass' [ii.65b–66a] refers to the entire itinerary, where Enzite is the western end and Kirruru the eastern end, and explicitly confirms the unity of the campaign (that Salvini would divide into two)."[187] Recently Kroll (2012)

186. Salvini 1982; 1995a, 30–35; 1995b, 47. See also Kessler 1986, 66–71.

187. Liverani 1992a, 24 n. 56. If the composition *STT* 43 belongs to Shalmaneser III, it connects the two phases of the 856 campaign. For bibliography, see n. 200 below.

has endorsed Russell's reconstruction and this seems to be the preferred understanding.

Both the initial narrative and resumptive narrative (or résumé) give details concerning the capture in 856 of Til-Barsib with Aḫuni's flight to Mount Šītamrat that is not found in the other narrative. Til-Barsib was undoubtedly Bīt-Adīni's most important fortress because of its dominance of a major crossing point over the Euphrates River.[188] Thus its conquest was a major political and military feat. It was not an easy achievement. It took several years to accomplish. The resumptive narrative seems to imply a more protracted siege of the city. Yamada (2000a, 125) suggests that Aḫuni had fled the city before Shalmaneser had even left Nineveh with the city falling in such a manner that Shalmaneser's trip was "only for the sake of inspection, reserving plenty of time to traverse the entire land of Urartu." He bases this on the fact that the statement "I departed from Nineveh" follows Aḫuni's abandonment of the city in the Assur Clay Tablets account. However, this statement may be out of place due to scribal error.[189] The statement normally occurs after the date formula at the beginning of the narrative as in the Kurkh Monolith. It does not occur in the other annalistic accounts at all. Therefore, I would be somewhat cautious of this.

But it is clear that the campaign to Bīt-Adīni with its capture of the cities of Til-Barsib, Alligu, Nappigu, Rugulitu, Pitru, and Mutkīnu was a speedy military action that, no doubt, was enhanced by the earlier campaigns that diminished Bīt-Adīni's resistance capacities and softened up its defenses.[190]

### 5.2.4. Shalmaneser III's 855 Campaign

In 855,[191] the fourth year of Shalmaneser's reign, the Assyrians launched a full-scale attack against Mount Šītamrat where Aḫuni had centered his final

188. On the modern site of Tell 'Abr (meaning "crossing," "ford") nearby, see Bunnens 1989, 2.

189. In this same text, the wording is problematic for the taking of Til-Barsib and Pitru. Something looks conflated here.

190. For the locations of these cities, see above.

191. The eponym for 855 was Aššur-būnāya-uṣur ("Oh Aššur, protect my features!"). He was the chief cupbearer (*rab šaqê*) and eponym of the years 855, 825, and 816 (reigns of Shalmaneser III and Šamšī-Adad V). As an eponym, Aššur-būnāya-uṣur served for the first time in 855, and he may well have assumed office during the reign of Aššurnaṣirpal II. In contrast to Aššur-bēlu-ka"in, the commander-in-chief, and Abu-ina-ekalli-lilbur, the palace herald, he was not removed from office in Shalmaneser III's fifth regnal year (cf. Olmstead 1915, 346–47). Aššur-būnāya-uṣur served as eponym for the second time in 825, yet again in 816, Šamšī-Adad V's eighth regnal year. His exceptionally long career lasted therefore at least thirty-nine years (cf. Grayson 1993, 33).

resistance (see fig. 5.5). After three days of fierce battle, Aḫuni, perhaps the most defiant of Aramean leaders aside from the later Hazael (see §9.3.5), came down before the king with his troops, chariots, and cavalry, the lavish "immeasurable" wealth of his palace. All of this, along with his sons, daughters, and gods, were brought to the city of Assur. No punishment seems to have been served upon this rebellious Aramean leader. In the text of the Balawat Gate, Shalmaneser III states "I reckoned them among the people of my land."[192] Apparently, Shalmaneser promised Aḫuni and his family leniency in exchange for his surrender (Ikeda 1999, 276).

A number of suggestions have been given for the location of Mount Šītamrat.[193] It has been located by some scholars on a mountain ridge to the west of the Kenk Gorge.[194] Dion (1997, 91) suggests that Šītamrat and Paqarḫubuni were in the same region. Ideka locates it "probably deep in the land of Kummuḫ," in the area northeast of Samsat, perhaps at Horis Kale.[195] However, Parpola and Porter locate Mount Šītamrat on the west side of the Euphrates south of Tell Aḥmar (Til-Barsib).[196]

Since Kummuḫ was a firm Assyrian ally, it seems unlikely that the ruler of Bīt-Adīni would have his final stronghold located there. It is assumed that Mount Šītamrat was located in the region of Kummuḫ on account of the discovery of Shalmaneser III's relief and inscription in the Kenk Gorge which gives a narrative about the 855 campaign. But the question is whether either bank of the Euphrates in the area of the Kenk Gorge belonged to the territory of Bīt-Adīni (Lipiński 2000a, 175). Shalmaneser could have conducted

---

The Bible Lands Museum Jerusalem houses a stela commissioned by "Aššur-[būnāya-uṣu]r, the eunuch, chief cupbear[er]," ${}^{m}$*aššur*-[DÙ-*a*-PA]B LÚ.SAG GAL LÚ.KAŠ.LU[L] Bible Lands Stela: 20. The text names the location in which the stela has been erected as "City of Aššur-būnāya-uṣur," URU ša ${}^{m}$*aš-šur*-DÙ-*a*-PAB (Bible Lands Stela: 6)—possibly the renamed administrative center of his province. The name of the male deity to whom the stela has been dedicated is not preserved in the extant text. Judging by his warlike epithets, however, he may be identified as a local hypostasis of either Adad or Ninurta, "residing in the City of Aššur-būnāya-uṣur" (Bible Lands Stela: 20). See Weissert 1998.

192. RIMA 3:22, A.0.102.2, ii.75a.

193. Bagg 2007, 241–42, s.v. Šītamrat.

194. Taşyürek 1979, 52; Hawkins 1982, 392; Sader 1987, 97.

195. Ikeda (1999, 275–76 and n. 14) states: "it also seems possible to find Mount Shitamrat further north among the sites in today's Kahta district northeast of Samsat, among them Horis Kale (Horis Fort), situated on a steep rocky ridge overlooking the flood-plain and the Euphrates. To our great regret most of these areas including Samsat, the important site of the capital of Kummuḫ, have been submerged under the water of the dam."

196. They give this a certainty rating of 2 (1–4, 1 being certain). See Parpola and Porter 2001, 15. Based on an unpublished manuscript of M. Astour 1995.

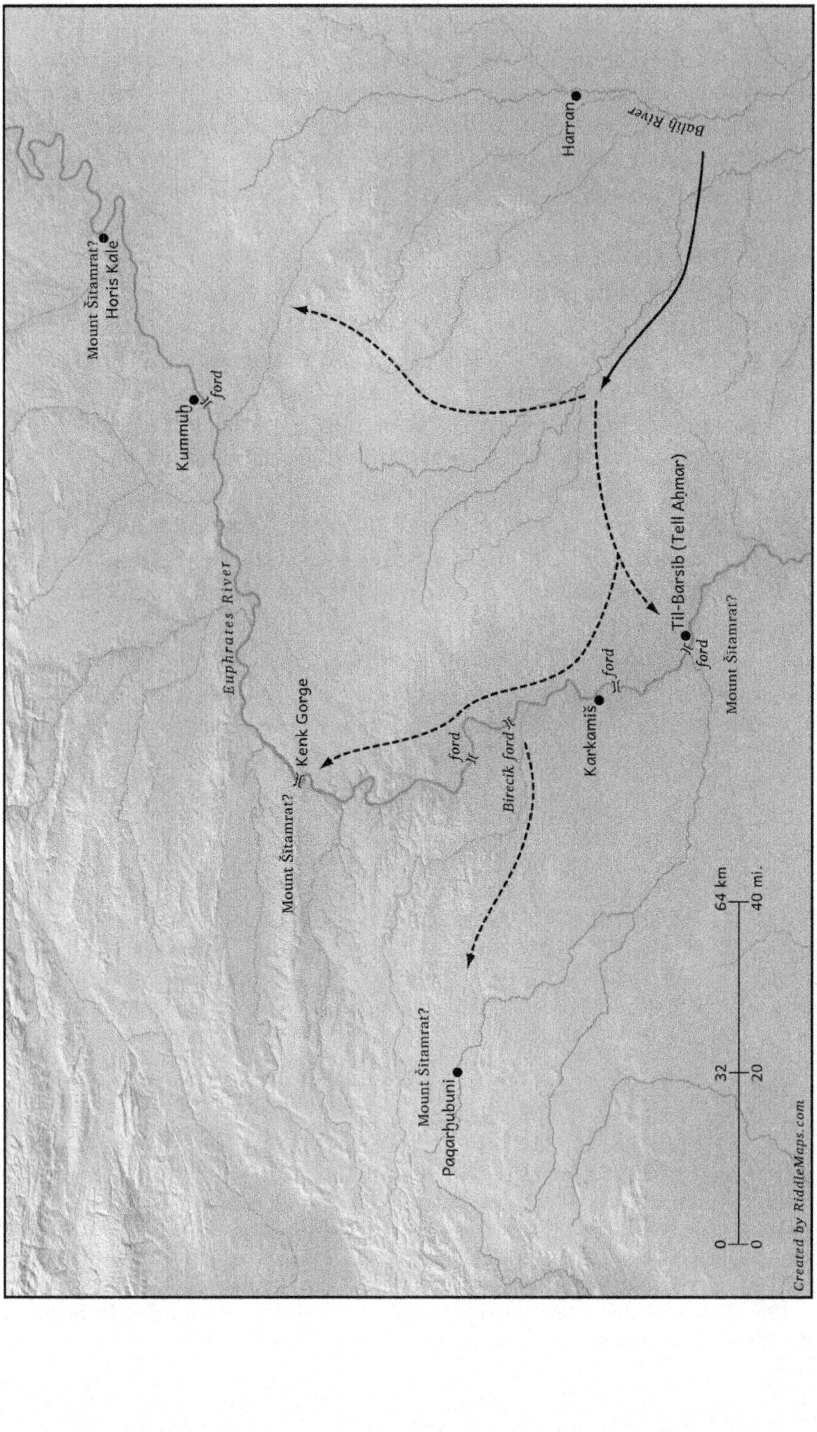


Fig. 5.5. Shalmaneser III's 855 campaign

a campaign on the west side of the Euphrates, south of Til-Barsib, and then returned across the Euphrates at the Kenk Gorge.[197]

Furthermore, some scholars have doubted that Til-Barsib was the capital of Bīt-Adīni. For example, Sader (1987, 92–93) suggested that Til-Barsib was only a strategic fortress, while proposing that Šītamrat was the actual capital of Aḫuni. This is based on two arguments. First, it is claimed that the mention of the palace property and the divine images taken from Šītamrat by the Assyrians is evidence for the existence of palaces and temples at Šītamrat—hence a capital city. However, these items had probably been carried by Aḫuni to Šītamrat at the time of the abandonment of Til-Barsib.[198] Another passage from Shalmaneser's Annals serves as a strong analogy. Shalmaneser took the royal treasure (*niṣirti šarrūti*) after pursuing Arrame, the king of Urartu, who had abandoned his royal city Arṣašku(n) and fled to Mount Adduri. Thus it is questionable whether the fortress of Šītamrat contained palaces and temples, though it cannot be ruled out. Although Šītamrat is occasionally called "his city," it is never called the "royal city (*āl šarrūti*)" or even "the fortified city (*āl dannūti*)" of Aḫuni. It is most often preceded by the determinative KUR (*šadû*) with only a few exceptions, and it is specifically described as a "mountain peak (*ubān(at) šadê*)." Thus Šītamrat was likely a mountain with perhaps a small fortified town. Second, it is asserted that Til-Barsib could not have been the capital of Bīt-Adīni because in the Kurkh Monolith, as well as in the One Year Annals, it is designated "the fortified city (*āl dannūti*)," and not "the royal city (*āl šarrūti*)," as it is designated in the later versions of Shalmaneser's Annals. While the Neo-Assyrian inscriptions usually refer to the capital city of a kingdom as *āl šarrūti*, not as *āl dannūti* (Ikeda 1979, 78–80), there is fluidity in the uses of the two designations.[199] If Fales (2011a, 227) is correct in his dubbing Bīt-Adīni a "shifting tribal state," then in a sense, Bīt-Adīni's capital was wherever Aḫuni was.

Four years of campaigning had snuffed out the largest Aramean polity in north Syria. Shalmaneser III renamed Til-Barsib, Kār-Shalmaneser (Kār-$^{d}$Salmānu-ašarēd; see Pongratz-Leisten 1997, 328–29). It would serve as an Assyrian provincial administrative center for years to come. The Assyrian victory over Bīt-Adīni secured the Euphrates's crossing, with former Bīt-Adīni lands providing the base for the further reduction of the states west

---

197. This question is linked to the issue of the Kenk Gorge inscription's date. The mention of Muṣaṣir is an issue that causes some scholars to believe that a later date is in order, but Grayson (RIMA 3) and Yamada (2000a, 29) give a reasonable explanation that allows for an early date.

198. As pointed out by Yamada 2000a, 141 n. 222.

199. Yamada (2000a, 142) points out two clear exceptions to the general usage of the designations.

of the river. An important testimony concerning the city of Til-Barsib is found in the poetic text about the conquest of Bīt-Adīni,[200] Shalmaneser III declares:

> (7) the arrogant/obstinate sl[ave],[201] (man) of Bīt-Adīni, (and) his allies,
> [**they*(the gods)/he/I *defeated**][202]
> (8) The strong cult city[203] of Til-Barsib I have [ignited] with fire.[204]
> The kings of the land of Ḫatti their dwellings I have laid waste,
> he spoke sharply (to) Aššur-bēlu-ka"in, the commander-in-chief (*turtānu*),
> thus:
> (11) Let the fortresses be entrusted to you;
> let your vigilance be steady,
> (12) your organization strong!
> Receive their tribute!
> (13) The king of the land of Ḫatti I have made bow down at my feet;
> (14) now let me go (and)
> see how the Urartians fight!

This passage demonstrates that Shalmaneser entrusted the *turtānu*, Aššur-bēlu-ka"in with the task of guarding the conquered region around Til-Barsib and ordered him to receive the tribute, while the king himself hastened off to the Urartian campaign (see §5.2.3, campaign of 856). It has been suggested that it was Aššur-bēlu-ka"in "who actually took the city *manu militari* from Aḫuni and proceeded to the reorganization of the conquered cities" (Fales 2014–16b, 37; Yamada 2000a, 121–22). This was the beginning of the tradition that the city of Til-Barsib was the seat of the *turtānu* (Yamada 2000a, 129), as it was later in the days of Šamšī-ilu, who described Kār-Shalmaneser (Til-Barsib) in his own inscription: "my lordly city (*āl bēlūtīya*)."

At some later time, a palace was erected on the model of the Assyrian royal palaces (Thureau-Dangin and Dunand 1936, 8–52). It was decorated with wall paintings that still form the largest collection of Near Eastern wall paintings ever discovered (Bunnens 2014–16). Among the discoveries of this period are a collection of carved ivories (Bunnens 1997a), 22 cuneiform texts (Dalley 1996–97; Radner 2004b) and 2 Aramaic texts (Lemaire 2001, 126–29; Younger 2007c, 141).

---

200. *STT* 43. RIMA 3:86, A.0.102.17, lines 7–8; Livingstone 1989, 44–47; Foster 2005, 779–82.

201. [*ur*]*du ekṣu*, i.e., Aḫuni. For *ekṣu*/*akṣu* see *CAD* 1.2:281–82.

202. Grayson RIMA 3:86: "They (the gods) defeated."

203. *CAD* 10.1:87.

204. There is no indication in the Kurkh Monolith that Til-Barsib was burned. In fact, it is turned into the Assyrian city Kār-Shalmaneser! Thus this is likely poetic hyperbole.

## 5.3. ŠAMŠĪ-ILU

Šamšī-ilu[205] was the commander-in-chief (*turtānu*) during the reigns of Adad-nērārī III, Shalmaneser IV, Aššur-dān III, and Aššur-nērārī V (Mattila 2000a, 110–11). Thus he was truly the most active of all *turtānu*s, having an exceptionally long period of administration. He was eponym for the years 780, 770, and 752 (Millard 1994, 38, 40, 42). His own contemporary inscriptions attribute to him accomplishments which would normally belong to the king alone, thereby indicating the relative weakness of Assyrian royal power at this time.[206]

For example, in 1908, two colossal, dark gray basalt lions were discovered at Tell Aḥmar (Til-Barsib/Kār-Shalmaneser) which contained an inscription.[207] While the text is in the form of a royal dedicatory inscription, its author is not an Assyrian monarch, as would be expected, but Šamšī-ilu. It highlights among his victorious campaigns his expedition against the Urartian king Argišti I and the erection of the two lions with their fierce names.[208] There is no mention of the Assyrian king.[209] Yet, Šamšī-ilu is mentioned in the royal inscriptions of several Assyrian monarchs. In the Antakya

205. His name is written mdUTU-DINGIR / mdŠam-ši-DINGIR / mdŠá-mas-DINGIR. See Baker 2006–8; Mattila 2002b.

206. He is known from a number of sources besides the Assyrian Eponym Chronicle: (1) Antakya Stela (RIMA 3:203–4, A.0.104.2; *COS* 2.114A:272); (2) Pazarcık Stela (RIMA 3:204–5, A.0.104.3; *COS* 2.114B:273); (3) the Šamšī-ilu Inscription / Stone Lions Inscription from Tell Aḥmar (Til-Barsib) (RIMA 3:231–33, A.0.104.2010; *COS* 2.115A:278); (4) the Dohuk Stela (RIMA 3:233–34, A.0.104.2011); (5) a Stone Bead from the Aššur temple in Assur (RIMA 3:236, A.0.104.2013); (6) a golden bowl found in the grave of Mullissu-mukannišat-Ninua (RIMA 3:236, A.0.104.2014); (7) perhaps a broken text on a stone tablet from Assur (RIMA 3:235, A.0.104.2012), though the name Šamšī-ilu does not appear in the fragmentary text; (8) the inscription of Ninurta-bēlu-uṣur (Tadmor and Yamada 2011, 161–63; Röllig 2009); and (9) a fragmentary, carefully engraved inscription on the rim of an ivory pyxis found at Nimrud. This inscription reads: "[... at the re]quest of the gods as a gift from al[l of ...... to RN] king of Assyria, his lord, Šamšī-ilu f[or his life has given]" (Herrmann, Laidlaw, and Coffey 2009, 178–79, pl. 33). Unfortunately, the name of the Assyrian monarch to whom Šamšī-ilu dedicated the ivory pyxis is not preserved and so dating is impossible.

207. RIMA 3:231–33, A.0.104.2010; Thureau-Dangin 1930. A study of one of the lions in 1988 revealed that it was 258 cm in height; with a length of 250 cm; and a width of 120 cm (Roobaert 1990, 127).

208. For the importance of this text in discerning Šamšī-ilu's year of appointment, see below.

209. While some of the evidence gathered in Dalley's essay (2000) on Šamšī-ilu demonstrates the wide semantic range of *šarru/mlk*, which is undoubtedly correct, her proposal to see Šamšī-ilu simply as the SUKKAL.MAḪ (*sukkallu rabû*) "vizier/viceroy," "the king of Ḫanigalbat" does not really address this important issue of the absence of acknowledg-

Stela, Adad-nērārī III and Šamšī-ilu establish the border between Zakkur of Hamath and Attār-sumkī I of Arpad, son of Abi-rāmu.[210] In the Pazarcık Stela (Reverse), which Shalmaneser IV set up in 773 for Ušpilulume, king of Kummuḫ, the text proclaims that Šamšī-ilu marched to Damascus forcing the Damascene king, Ḫadiānu (Ḥadyān) to pay tribute to the Assyrian king.[211]

Scholars have generally understood Šamšī-ilu to have been *turtānu* until at least 752, and perhaps as late as 745, if he was removed from office when Tiglath-pileser III ascended to the throne following the revolt against Aššur-nērārī V (Zawadzki 1997, 384–85). However, exactly when he was appointed to the office has been the source of much debate.

### 5.3.1. The Year of the Appointment of Šamšī-ilu as Turtān and the Date of His Gate Lions Inscriptions

Since Šamšī-ilu served as *turtānu* under the monarchs listed above and was eponym for the years 780, 770, and 752, the minimum period of his office would be from 783, the last year of Adad-nērārī III, until his last Eponymate in 752. The maximum extends from the Eponymate year of his predecessor Nergal-ilāya to the eponymate of his successor Nabû-da''inanni (i.e., 808 to 742). Thus Šamšī-ilu was head of the Assyrian army at least for thirty-one years and not more than sixty-six years.[212]

A number of scholars have advocated that Šamšī-ilu began his role as *turtānu* around the year 800 BCE, or shortly thereafter, usually basing this on the Antakya Stela.[213] Ikeda (1999, 282) and Hawkins (2000, 400) have attributed this demarcation as a consequence of the campaign against Manṣuāte in 796. On the other hand, Grayson states that the border was set "presumably just after Arpad had been reconquered (c. 800)."[214] Lipiński (2000a, 284)[215]

---

ment of the Assyrian king. The example of Šamšī-ilu's eunuch, Ninurta-bēlu-uṣur, shows such acknowledgment of his lord (see below).

210. RIMA 3:203–4, A.0.104.2. For discussion, see pp. 484–85.

211. RIMA 3:239–40, A.0.105.1. See discussion at §9.3.6.2.

212. Fuchs 2008a, 131. While nothing is known about the minimum age for a person to be appointed to *turtānu*, it seems that it surely required some age and experience. Even if Šamšī-ilu was roughly thirty years old when he assumed this high office, he would have led the army until his sixty-first birthday (minimum and reasonable) or until his ninety-sixth birthday (maximum and very doubtful).

213. RIMA 3:203–4, A.0.104.2, esp. line 5.

214. Grayson 1993, 27. Followed by Mattila 2000a, 110; and Baker 2006–8, 639.

215. Following Kuan 1995, 77–78. Kuan (2001, 137) states: "In the Antakya Stela, dating from the last decade of the ninth century BCE (807/806), Šamšī-ilu is mentioned as the *turtānu*. His tenure, however, must have begun after 808/807 BCE, since Nergal-ilāya was identified as the *turtānu* for that year. It is therefore likely that he had a career that lasted more than half a century."

places Šamšī-ilu's appointment even earlier before Attār-sumkī I's "high treason, around 807–806."

However, as Fuchs (2008a, 132) has pointed out, none of these approaches is mandatory because the Antakya Stela actually does not offer the slightest hint of any such dating. While the Pazarcık Stela (observe) must be dated with some certainty to 805 (because its inscription reports about the battle against Attār-sumkī, son of Abi-rāmu, which can be linked to an Assyrian campaign mentioned in the Eponym Chronicle), the Antakya Stela offers no such clue. The fact that war is not mentioned in the Antakya Stela means that the border demarcation was, in fact, probably not connected to any of the Assyrian campaigns in north Syria. Thus, Fuchs (2008a, 133) concludes that there is no need to put Šamšī-ilu's work at the beginning or in the middle of the reign of Adad-nērārī III.

An additional problem that does not seem to have been adequately addressed is this: if Šamšī-ilu became *turtānu* in 808/807 or even in 800, he would have served an extraordinarily long time before ever holding the eponymate (28/27 years and 20 years respectively, since he is only for the first time eponym in 780). Being over two decades in office without holding the eponymate is simply impossible. No *turtānu* served this long without being an eponym.

Fuchs's study (2008a) has greatly clarified the discussion of the year of Šamšī-ilu's appointment. He starts with a fresh look at Šamšī-ilu's inscriptions, not only on the two lions, but in a partially preserved inscription on a black stone statue.[216] From these, it is clear that Šamšī-ilu claims to have won two victories over the Urartian king Argišti I: one victory in Guti (KUR. *Gu-te*$_9$*-e*), that is, in northwestern Iran, and the other in a place that, according to the text, was located near a river, most likely in northern Syria or the Murad Su.[217]

The Gate Lions text gives a detailed description of the victory that Šamšī-ilu achieved against the Urartian king Argišti I in the area of Guti. The inscription itself was probably written in the same year as this victory, that is, 774. This was almost certainly the same campaign that Argišti, son of Minua, claimed in his Annals as a victory over the Assyrians.[218] Moreover,

216. RIMA 3:233–34, A.0.104.2011. It is evident that the inscription on the Gate Lions of Til-Barsib (RIMA 3:231–33, A.0.104.2010) and this statue (RIMA 3:233–34, A.0.104.2011) have been erroneously assigned by Grayson to the period of Adad-nērārī III, when they must belong to early in the reign of Shalmaneser IV. Schramm (1973, 120–21, sub c) assigned these to the period of Shalmaneser IV.

217. RIMA 3:234, A.0.104.2011, lines 1′ (⸢ÍD⸣ *x*), 2′ (*a-ge-e pal-ḫu-*[*ti*?]), 4′ (ÍD *x*), and 14′ (⸢ÍD?⸣ *x-bi*), which make reference to water or a river. See Fuchs 2012, 150.

218. Fuchs 2012, 150; Kroll et al. 2012a, 15. For the text of Argišti I, see Salvini

this inscription gives a reliable indication of the start of his career when one looks closely at the military successes that are mentioned,[219] and coordinates these with the Eponym Chronicle.

> (lines 8b–11a)
> $^{md}$[*šam-ši*]-⸢DINGIR LÚ.*tar*⸣-*ta-nu* ⸢NIMGIR GAL-*ú*⸣ [*šatam* É.KUR.M]EŠ GAL ÉRIN.ḪI.A DA[GAL] $^{(9)}$ *šá-pi-ir* KUR.*ḫat-ti* KUR.*gu-te*$_9$*-e u gi-mì-ir* KUR.ZA[LAG *ka*]-*šid úḫ*(*u*)-*ma-tú šá* SILIM $^{d}$UTU-*ši mu*-[*š*]*aḫ-r*[*i*]-*bu* x [...] $^{(10)}$ *mu-šam-qit* KUR.*mu-us-ki u* KUR.*ú-ra-ar-ṭu šá-li-lu* UN.MEŠ-*šú sa-pin* KUR.*ú-tu-'u* KUR.[*ru*]-*bu-'u* $^{(11)}$ KUR.*ḫa*-⸢*ṭa*⸣-*lu* KUR.*lab-du-du šá-ki-nu ka-mar-šú-nu*
>
> [Šamšī]-ilu, the commander-in-chief (*turtānu*), the great herald, [the administrator of] temples, chief of the extensive army, governor of the land of Ḫatti (and) of the land of the Guti, and all the land of Namri, conqueror of the mountains in the West (Lebanon?), who lays waste [...[189]], who overthrows the lands of Mušku and Urartu, who plunders its people, who devastates the lands of Utû, Rubû, Ḫaṭallu,[220] (and) Labdūdu, who brings about their annihilation.

Since Šamšī-ilu was as vain as the kings that he imitated, what he considered important to transmit to posterity was included in the accounts of his successes. Thus, when the toponyms listed by Šamšī-ilu are collated with the Eponym Chronicle, the density of occurrences demonstrates the time period to which these campaigns belong.

The table 5.4 demonstrates that the campaigns by Šamšī-ilu that are mentioned in his Gate Lions inscription could only have taken place in the very last years of Adad-nērārī III and the very beginning of the reign of Shalmaneser IV. After the 774 campaign, there are no campaigns against Urartu until Assyria's revival under Tiglath-pileser III, because of military weakness and internal dissensions within Assyria.[221]

---

2008, 336–39: Salvini 2008, A 8–3 III. Three of the toponyms in Argišti's Annals (Baruata, Babilū, and Parsua) are located in the area designated Guti in the Assyrian texts (for the documentation, see Fuchs 2012, 150 and notes).

219. RIMA 3:231–33, A.0.104.2010; *COS* 2.115A:278.

220. KUR.*ḫa*-⸢*ṭa*⸣-*lu*. Grayson reads KUR.*ḫa*-⸢*da*(?)⸣-*lu*, *RIMA* 3:232, A.0.104.2010, 11a. Liverani (1992b, 37) reads this as a reference to the Ḫaṭallu tribe (or better, confederation of tribes). This is the correct reading. See chapter 10.

221. Kroll et al. 2012a, 15. And perhaps also because of Urartu's strength during the period.

Table 5.4. Šamšī-ilu's Successes Coodinated with the Eponym Chronicle (adapted from Fuchs 2008a, 134)

| Year | Campaign Goal of the Eponym Chronicle | Successes of Šamšī-ilu in his Til-Barsib Inscription | King | *Turtānu* |
|---|---|---|---|---|
| 810 | in the land | | Adad-nērārī III | Nergal-ilāya |
| 809 | Media | | (810–783 BCE) | (810–787 BCE) |
| 808 | Guzāna | (*eponym: Nergal-ilāya*) | | |
| 807 | Mannea | | | |
| 806 | Mannea | | | |
| 805 | Arpad | | | |
| 804 | Ḫazāzu | | | |
| 803 | Ba'alu | | | |
| 802 | the Sea (= Arwad) | | | |
| 801 | Ḫubuškia | | | |
| 800 | Media | | | |
| 799 | Media | | | |
| 798 | Lušia | | | |
| 797 | Namri | | | |
| 796 | Manṣuāte | | | |
| 795 | Dēr | | | |
| 794 | Dēr | | | |
| 793 | Media | | | |
| 792 | Media | | | |
| 791 | Ḫubuškia | | | |
| 790 | Itū'a | | | |
| 789 | Media | | | |
| 788 | Media | | | |
| 787 | Media | | | |
| 786 | Kisku | = Mušku | | Šamšī-ilu |
| 785 | Ḫubuškia | | | (786–746) |

| | | | | |
|---|---|---|---|---|
| 784 | Ḫubuškia | | | |
| 783 | Itū'a | = Utū'a | | |
| 782 | Itū'a | = Utū'a | | |
| 781 | Urartu | = Urartu | Shalmaneser IV (782–773) | |
| 780 | Urartu | = Urartu (eponym: Šamšī-ilu) | | |
| 779 | Urartu | = Urartu | | |
| 778 | Urartu | = Urartu | | |
| 777 | Itū'a | = Utū'a | | |
| 776 | Urartu | = Urartu | | |
| 775 | "Cedar Mountain" | = the western mountains | | |
| 774 | Urartu, Namri | = Victory over Argišti I in Guti | | |
| 773 | Damascus[a] | | | |
| 772 | Ḫatarikka | | | |
| 771 | Gannānāte | | Aššur-dān III (772–755) | |
| 770 | Marad | (eponym: Šamšī-ilu) | | |
| 769 | Itū'a | | | |
| 768 | in the land | | | |
| 767 | Gannānāte | | | |

[a] not mentioned in Šamšī-ilu's inscription

Fuchs points out that the mention of Namri is of particular importance because this country (located in western Iran) had resisted the attempted conquests of Shalmaneser III and was not defeated by Šamšī-Adad V. It must have been conquered under Adad-nērārī III, probably recorded in the Eponym Chronicle for the year 797, which was expressly directed against Namri. In his inscription, Šamšī-ilu describes himself as "the governor of all the land of Namri," but does not claim to have been the one who conquered it (i.e., he does not claim to be "the conqueror of Namri").

Furthermore, even more telling is the fact that Šamšī-ilu does not claim any victories for himself in Media. Although the Assyrian army campaigned for three years in a row (789–787) in the land of the Medes, Šamšī-ilu does not claim to have directed a single one of these campaigns. This omission is in contrast to the *turtānu* Nergal-ilāya who was apparently so closely associated with these campaigns to Media that he immortalized himself on a stone, which expressly originated "from the mountains of the Medes." This is an inscription on a duck weight found in the antecella of Tašmetum in the palace of Adad-nērārī III in Kalḫu (Nimrud).[222] Under his military leadership, Assyria pursued its expansionist interests in western Iran. From 809–787, a total of thirteen campaigns were aimed at Media (8x), Namri, Mannea (2x) and Ḫubuškia (2x).[223] By far, this is substantively more in this direction than any other. So there is every indication that Nergal-ilāya remained as *turtānu* of the Assyrian army until 787 (Fuchs 2008a, 135).

No campaign to Damascus is mentioned by Šamšī-ilu. This is a highly significant omission. The campaign in the reign of Adad-nērārī III (796) is not mentioned. Certainly one would have expected it to have been mentioned for at least three reasons: (1) since this was a defeat of the most important central Levantine power; (2) since there was such a sizeable tribute given; and (3) since the campaign brought about the submission of a number of other Levantine states! Furthermore, the campaign against Damascus during the reign of Shalmaneser IV is also not mentioned, even though it is mentioned in that king's inscription that notes Šamšī-ilu's role in the campaign (Pazarcık Stela, reverse). This is a further indication that Šamšī-ilu's lion gate inscription must date after the Damascus campaign of Adad-nērārī III (796) and before that of Shalmaneser IV (773).

Šamšī-ilu's victory over the land of Mušku does not connect at first sight with the details of the Eponym Chronicle. It appears, however, that Mušku refers to the Anatolian entity that Šamšī-ilu may have fought against in the far northwestern regions of the Assyrian Empire, and that the only link in the Eponym Chronicle would be to 786 against Kisku (Bagg 2007, 137–38). Thus, Fuchs concludes that 786 was the first year that Šamšī-ilu led the Assyrian army after being appointed as *turtānu* either in this year or in the previous year 787. If Šamšī-ilu remained in office until the rebellion of 746, this means that his tenure as *turtānu* was 40–41 years, a considerable period indeed, since not one Assyrian king ruled for so long!

---

222. Mattila 2000a, 109 (ND 5544). It reads: (1) 5 MA.NA $NA_4$.KUR-*nu* GI.NA *šá* dMAŠ.MAŠ–DINGIR-*a-a* LÚ*.*tur-ta-ni* (2) GAL–ERIM.ḪI.A ⌜x x⌝ *ul-tú* KUR-*i* KUR.*ma-da-a-a* "Five minas, of real *šadānu*-stone, belonging to Nergal-ilāya, *turtānu*, commander of the army [. . .] from the mountains of the Medes."

223. These campaigns seem to attest to the fact that western Iran had become the major source for "horses, a commodity of unappeasable demand to Assyria" (Radner 2003, 42–43).

Nonetheless, the two victories against the king of Urartu, Argišti I, were the highlight of Šamšī-ilu's military career, at least at the point of the incising of the inscription at Til-Barsib. These are what he chose to immortalize in a thoroughly Assyrian royal style in the form of two inscriptions on the monumental lions that "I (Šamšī-ilu) set up on the right and left in the city gate of Kār-Shalmaneser, my lordly city."[224] The traditional royal motifs of conquering hero and builder are credited to Šamšī-ilu without any word about the king.

Thus there is relative clarity as to when Šamšī-ilu held his position as *turtānu* and the extent of the power that he wielded.[225]

### 5.3.2. The Inscription of Ninurta-bēlu-uṣur/Inurta-bēl-uṣur

Another important piece of evidence is found in a trilingual inscription, written in Neo-Assyrian cuneiform, Aramaic, and hieroglyphic Luwian, that has been discovered on monumental gate lions at ancient Ḫadattu (modern Arslan Taş) about 30 km east of the Euphrates near the Turkish border (Younger 2007c). The inscription belonged to Ninurta-bēlu-uṣur, the provincial governor of Kār-Shalmaneser (Kār-šulmānu-ašarēd/Til-Barsib). This man was also a eunuch of the Assyrian *turtānu* Šamšī-ilu. The inscription seems to date to around 780 BCE.

A pair of basalt lions were at the east gate of the city and a pair were at the west gate. The east gate lions both bear an incised nine-line Assyrian, a nine-line Aramaic, and a four-line hieroglyphic Luwian inscription (Galter 2004a, 449, and fig. 6; 2004b). The west gate lions have only the bilingual Akkadian-Aramaic inscriptions (i.e., they lack the hieroglyphic Luwian text). All the texts were inscribed on the surfaces of the lions that abutted the wall next to which they were placed. The Akkadian and Aramaic inscriptions record that Ninurta-bēlu-uṣur/Inurta-bēl-uṣur (^mdMAŠ.EN.PAB; Aramaic: *ʾnrtblṣr*) constructed Ḫadattu's wall and gates, in which the lion colossi were stationed.[226] The Luwian text has been published (Hawkins 2000, 246–48), and appears to be somewhat independent of the Assyrian and Aramaic texts (the personal name at the beginning of the inscription is not preserved), although it reports on the building activity of the "country lord" of the city of Masuwari (Luwian name for Til-Barsib) in the city of Hatata (= Ḫadattu). While the Aramaic text is poorly preserved, it follows that of the Assyrian

224. Again, these inscriptions date to the reign of Shalmaneser IV, not Adad-nērārī III. See note 216 above; Schramm 1973.

225. For a discussion of his role in the history of Aram-Damascus, see chapter 9.

226. For a complete discussion of all the Akkadian inscriptions, see Tadmor and Yamada 2011, 161–62; Galter 2004a, 2004b, 2007.

(Röllig 2009). In order to facilitate the discussion the three inscriptions are presented here.

The Akkadian Text:[227]

> [I, Ninurta-bēlu]-uṣur, provincial governor (EN.NAM = *bēl pīḫāti*) of the city of Kār-Shalma[neser], erected solid basalt [lions ...] ... (which are) in the gate[s of] the city of Ḫadattu.
>
> Ninurta-bēlu-uṣur ($^{md}$MAŠ-EN-PAP) of the city of Ṣirani, which is (in the area of) the city of Ḫalaḫḫi, which is in front of the city of Lipapan in the mountains, the city of the house of my father (i.e., "my *bēt ʾab*");
>
> At that time, I created, built, (and) completed the city of Ḫadattu.
>
> (As for) a future ruler who repairs its dilapidated section(s but) erases my inscribed name and inscribes his (own) name (in its place), may (the god) Aššur, the great lord, in the assembly of the gods verily order his destruction ... and his name ...Lacuna

The Aramaic Text[228]

> and I built fortifications (?) [in (?)] Ḥadattu (*ḥdš* = *ḥdt*)[229] to set (my?) name:
>
> Inurta-bēl-uṣur (*ʾnrtblṣ?r?*), the one who (is) of/from the town of Ṣiran(i) (*Ṣrn*) which (is) (in) the area of Ḥalaḫḫu (*ḥlḥ*) that (is) before Lilaban (*llbn*), the town of the house of my father (*qryt . byt . ʾby*).
>
> In my days, I made Ḥadattu (*ḥdš* = *ḥdt*) and I built it and I brought it order(?) Its ... and the gates of his ... I made good (?). Four (?) lions (?), I had erected in its gates.

The Luwian Text[230]

> ... x ... -tas Masuwarean Country-Lord (*ma-su-wa/i+ra/i-za-sa*(URBS) REGIO-*ni*(-) DOMINUS-*ia-sá*).

227. RINAP 1:161–63, 2001.

228. Röllig 2009 (Aramaic Text A). I have not included the curse formulation since it is very fragmentary and adds little to the discussion.

229. For discusion, see Röllig 2009, 275.

230. Hawkins 2000, 246–48.

I founded[231] the city of Hatata (= Ḫadattu) in one year;
*and for me the gods ... (?) he/they will buy.*
*But he ...*
*... I [...]ed.*
*... who with ox(en) Y*[232]

A few comments on the Luwian text are necessary. Line 1 is longer than lines 2–4, and there are approximately a half-dozen signs at the beginning of line 1 that are very difficult to make out. Hawkins's drawing (2000, pl. 104) does not accurately represent this (compare with pl. 105). While one would have expected the inscription to begin with EGO (*amu*) "I (am)," this cannot be read, nor can the name of the author of the inscription. Hawkins (2000, 247) suggests that the word ending in *-tas* may be the ending of a title. Clearly in the Luwian, "*Masuwarizas*(URBS) REGIO-*ni*(-)DOMINUS-*ias* ('Masuwarean Country-Lord') seems to correspond to the EN.NAM URU. *Šulmān-ašarēd* on the adjoining Assyrian cuneiform text, although it is still not clear that the two inscriptions are by the same author" (Hawkins 2000, 247). However, the placement of the hieroglyphic Luwian inscription is such that it appears to be integral with the Akkadian and the Aramaic—all three are contained in the same prepared surface area on the lion (see Hawkins 2000, pl. 105; Galter 2004a, 449, fig. 6).

Bunnens has emphasized this trilingual, making a number of assertions based on it:

> Besides the use of Luwian, another surprising fact was the name used by Ninurta-bêl-uṣur to refer to Tell Ahmar in the Luwian version of his inscription. It was Masuwari, the very same name as the one used in earlier, pre-Assyrian, Luwian inscriptions. This is the more surprising as, in the Aramaic inscription, Ninurta-bêl-uṣur used the name Kâr-Shalmaneser as he did in Akkadian. Luwian tradition, at Tell Ahmar/Kâr-Shalmaneser, did not come to a halt with the Assyrian conquest (Bunnens 2009, 78).

And:

> Another conclusion that can be drawn from Ninurta-bêl-uṣur's inscriptions is that Šamši-ilu was not governor of Kâr-Shalmaneser/Til-Barsib. The city was under Ninurta-bêl-uṣur's immediate authority and only secondarily under Šamši-ilu's power. This weakens the possibility that Šamši-ilu had his residence at Tell Ahmar as is often assumed by scholars. The idea stemmed

231. ("AEDIFICIUM") *upaha*—perhaps lit. "I brought about the construction of."

232. The latter part of line 2 through line 4 are very difficult. The translation follows Hawkins's discussion (2000, 247–48).

> from the words "my lordly city" referring to Tell Ahmar in the inscription of Šamši-ilu carved on the two lions that adorned the east gate of Tell Ahmar. As the inscription was written in the style of a royal inscription, it was admitted that Šamši-ilu behaved as a local ruler with his capital city at Tell Ahmar. Although it can be admitted that Šamši-ilu behaved as a local ruler, his capital city must have been located elsewhere (Bunnens 2009, 79).

Neither of these is accurate. In the first instance, the Aramaic does not preserve mention of the city of Til-Barsib, either by that name or by the name Kār-Shalmaneser. Furthermore, the use of the name Masuwari for the city is naturally the name that would be used in a Luwian inscription.[233] All this demonstrates is that Luwian was apparently still spoken in the region (hardly surprising).

In the second case, just because Ninurta-bēlu-uṣur was the *bēl pīḫāti* of the city of Kār-Shalmaneser (Fales 2014–16b, 37) does not mean that Šamšī-ilu did not have his residence there. The wording of Šamšī-ilu's inscription "Then I set up two great lions to right and left at the gate of Kār-Shalmaneser, the city of my dominion" makes it clear that Til-Barsib was the place from which he ruled.

There can be no doubt as to who was the underling, this "eunuch of Šamšī-ilu."[234] Röllig (2009, 277) rightly points out that the long and complicated emphasis on the origin of the (N)inurta-bēlu-uṣur stands out, which seems to underline the legitimacy of this process; yet, at the same time because there is the absence of any filiation, it is reasonable to assume that this governor is a parvenu,[235] who was moreover of Aramean origin (note the reference to the *bīt abīya* / *byt ʾby*), although he does not bear an Aramaic name. His name (N)inurta-bēlu-uṣur, "O Ninurta, protect the lord!"[236] seems to have been characteristic of the second-level provincial officials, particularly in this period (Galter 2004a, 450). Consequently, one might suggest that it was an assumed name when he took the office. In any case, this trilingual does not support Bunnens's contentions.

---

233. There is absolutely no proof of the existence of a continued political entity called "Masuwari," as Makinson (2005–7) speculates; only that the city continued to exist and that that name was used by Luwian speakers, where Aramean and Assyrian speakers used Til-Barsib or Kār-Shalmaneser. Not only is there no evidence that the political entity Masuwari survived the Assyrian conquest of the region, there is no clear evidence that the designation was used to describe a political entity that existed at the time of the Assyrian conquest!

234. Galter 2004b, 175–76; Röllig 2009, 276; Tadmor and Yamada 2011, 162.

235. In other words, a person of obscure origin who has gained wealth, influence, or celebrity.

236. For this name, see Baker 2000g. A few examples: Aššur-bēlu-uṣur, Nabû-bēlu-uṣur, etc.

### 5.3.3. Amos 1:5

With the discovery in the nineteenth century of the Assyrian royal inscriptions that mention Bīt-Adīni, biblical scholars began to connect the occurrence of בֵּית עֶדֶן in Amos 1:5 with the polity of Bīt-Adīni.[237] Today, a large percentage of biblical scholars assume this identification. For example, Kuan (2001, 147) states: "That Beth-Eden in Amos 1:5 is to be identified with Bīt-Adīni is quite certain."[238] This verse is the last verse in "the oracle against Damascus" (Amos 1:3–5). After the refrain that introduces "the transgressions of Damascus," including its particular crime (v. 3), verses 4–5 declare the coming judgment:

(4)וְשִׁלַּחְתִּי אֵשׁ בְּבֵית חֲזָאֵל
וְאָכְלָה אַרְמְנוֹת בֶּן־הֲדָד׃
(5)וְשָׁבַרְתִּי בְּרִיחַ דַּמֶּשֶׂק
וְהִכְרַתִּי יוֹשֵׁב מִבִּקְעַת־אָוֶן
וְתוֹמֵךְ שֵׁבֶט מִבֵּית עֶדֶן
וְגָלוּ עַם־אֲרָם קִירָה
אָמַר יְהוָה׃

(4)I shall send fire on Bēt-Hazael (the kingdom of Damascus),
and it will consume the fortresses of Ben-Hadad (the kingdom of Damascus).[239]

---

237. For some discussion and earlier references, see Lemaire 1981. Hallo (1960, 38–39) understood the reference in 1:5c to be Aḫuni, the Aramean ruler of Beth-Eden during the time of Shalmaneser III, an entire century before the time of Amos. He states: "The fate of Beth-Eden still served Assyria as an intimidating example another fifty years later (2 Kgs 19:12 = Isa 37:12)." While the last statement is undoubtedly true, the identification of 1:5c with Aḫuni of Bīt-Adīni is eliminated by the *weqatal* verbal form that demands a future nuance here.

238. Andersen and Freedman (1989, 256) assert that "'the house of Eden' is almost certainly the Aramaean state of Bît-Adini, located between the Upper Euphrates and the River Balīḫ. It was conquered by Shalmaneser III as early as 855 B.C.E., and Assyrian penetration into the region is now attested by the Tell Fekherye bilingual inscription in the ninth century." This last clause is entirely off the mark: Bīt-Adīni is not mentioned in the Tell Fakhariya Inscription, and Tell Ḥalaf/Gōzān is in the Ḫābūr region not the area of Bīt-Adīni.

239. Paul (1991, 50) comments "Even though both royal names are amply documented, it is nevertheless suggested here that Amos is not referring to two respective Aramean kings but rather to two dynastic titles for the kingdom of Aram per se … the recurrent throne name, Ben-Hadad, is also used as a title for the Aramean kingdom, as is evidenced by the almost exact passage in Jer 49:27, where 'the wall of Damascus' is paralleled by the phrase 'the fortresses of Ben-hadad,' the latter obviously representing an epithet for Aram." Jer 49:27 reads:

(5)And I will break the (gate) bars of Damascus;
and I will cut off the one who reigns[240] from the Valley of "Awen";
and the one who grasps a scepter from "Bēt-eden";
and the people of Aram will be deported to Qir,
says Yahweh.[241]

In addition to בֵּית עֶדֶן in Amos 1:5c being a reference to Bīt-Adīni, Malamat (1953, 25–26) identified Šamšī-ilu, the Assyrian *turtānu*, as the ruler "who grasps the scepter." He argued that Amos, who preached in the middle of the eighth century, knew only the Assyrian province, which had replaced the ancient Aramean principality of Beth-Eden. At the time of Amos, "Beth-Eden was administered by an Assyrian governor to whom the title, 'who holdeth a sceptre,' may aptly be applied, as the Hebrew idiom does not exclude a subroyal status" (Malamat 1953, 25). A number of scholars have followed Malamat.[242]

In fact, Hayes (1988, 74) proposes that Amos 1:5 reveals the existence of a three-ruler alliance made up of: (1) Rezin of Aram-Damascus, the primary target of the oracle (although Rezin is not specifically named); (2) Pekah, a rival king of Israel (identified in the text with יושב מבקעת־און); and (3) Šamšī-ilu. These rulers formed "an anti-Assyrian front in the west."

Kuan (2001, 146) rightly points out the problem with the identification of "the one who grasps a scepter from Beth-Eden" with Šamšī-ilu: there is no reason why an Assyrian governor of Šamšī-ilu's stature and power—and who was virtually the Assyrian king of the west—would enter into an alli-

---

וְהִצַּתִּי אֵשׁ בְּחוֹמַת דַּמֶּשֶׂק
וְאָכְלָה אַרְמְנוֹת בֶּן־הֲדָד

240. The term יוֹשֵׁב does not refer to the inhabitants as clearly seen in its usage in 1:8 and 2:3 (see Paul 1991, 51–2). Compare also 1 Kgs 15:18: מלך ארם הישב בדמשק, "the king of Aram who was enthroned in Damascus." The phrase וְתוֹמֵךְ שֵׁבֶט refers to the "ruler"; compare the Hadad inscription 24b–25a: *y'ḥz. ḥṭr* "seizes the scepter" … *wyšb. 'l. mšby* "sits on my throne."

241. The Old Greek of Amos 1:5 reads: καὶ συντρίψω μοχλοὺς Δαμασκοῦ καὶ ἐξολεθρεύσω κατοικοῦντας ἐκ πεδίου Ων καὶ κατακόψω φυλὴν ἐξ ἀνδρῶν Χαρραν καὶ αἰχμαλωτευθήσεται λαὸς Συρίας ἐπίκλητος λέγει κύριος, "And I will shatter the bars of Damascus; and will put to death the inhabitants out of the plain of On; and I will cut a tribe out of the men of Harran; and the specially summoned people of Syria shall be led captive, says the Lord." Bordreuil (1998, 56) comments: "Le remplacement de Bet Eden par Χαρραν dans la LXX d'Amos 1:5 ne peut pourtant tenir lieu d'argument car il s'agit vraisemblablement ici d'une harmonisation avec la notice de II Rois 19:12 (= Isa 37:12) qui cite Eden avec Gozan, Harran et Rezeph, trois villes situées audelà de l'Euphrate : Gozan-Tell Khalaf aux sources du Khabour, Harran sur le Balih et Rezeph, cette dernière correspondant à la région appelée Rasappa qui serait située à l'est du Khabour."

242. E.g., Wazana 2008, 713; Paul 1991, 53; Hayes 1988, 74–79; Hawkins 1982, 404; Wolff 1977, 156.

ance with Aram-Damascus, a state frequently opposed to Assyrian power in Syria-Palestine, particularly because coalitions in the west were often formed in order to oppose Assyria's domination in the region. Thus, Šamšī-ilu's participation in the coalition would have meant rebellion against the Assyrian central administration, which seems unlikely. He proposes that Amos 1:5c is a reference to a native ruler of Bīt-Adīni, and suggests that with the death of Šamšī-ilu, a rebellion broke out, leading to the defacement of his monuments at Til-Barsib and Arslan Taş. A native of Bīt-Adīni, who was able to take over the throne, then joined the anti-Assyrian coalition headed by Rezin. While ingenious, there is no evidence to support this proposal: no mention of a rebellion, no naming of a native ruler, and no hint of the necessity of an Assyrian reconquest or any Assyrian military action in the region.

Kuan (2001, 147), following Hayes's suggestion that the ruler of the Valley of Awen may be identified with Pekah, states: "The Valley of Aven was thus probably the Suweinit Valley and its continuation as the Wadi Qelt to the Jordan River. Pekah, with the backing of Rezin, appears to have begun encroaching on territories west of the Jordan after securing his hold in Transjordan." This identification seems highly unlikely.

However, a number of scholars do not see an alliance, but rather a description of a ruler of Aram-Damascus. Paul (1991, 54), not accepting the equation with Šamšī-ilu, argues that the passage reflects an earlier period of the kingdom of Aram-Damascus. He states:

> A more probable solution is to understand the reference here as reflecting an earlier period when בִּקְעַת־אָוֶן and בֵּית עֶדֶן represented the two polar extremes of Aram, thus comprising a geographical merism: from Lebanon to Beth-eden on the Euphrates, that is, the entire kingdom of Aram from west to east, is destined for destruction.

Along similar lines Wazana (2008, 725) has argued that בִּקְעַת־אָוֶן and בֵּית עֶדֶן reflect a geographic merism, in spite of the fact of the absence of the מן ... עד formula. She states:

> Though the two places mentioned, the Valley of Aven and Beth-eden, are preceded by the preposition "from," this is due to their syntactical position (as the places from which the rulers will be cut off) and not because of an incomplete extremities formula ("from ... to ..."). The merismatic role of this verse derives from the context and not from the syntactical function of the places mentioned or their form of conjunction.

However, Amos 1:8 flatly contradicts this, for it has the same syntax and is most certainly not a merism.

Moreover, if 1:5c is a reference to an earlier period when Aram-Damascus conquered and ruled over the former territory of Bīt-Adīni (which is in itself problematic!)[243] and which is no longer the case (i.e., Damascus certainly has no hegemony over the area at the time of Amos's oracle—no matter when one dates it[244]), it is very hard to make sense of the use of the "tense" of the *weqatal* verbal form וְהִכְרַתִּי in 1:5b (especially when it immediately follows וְשָׁבַרְתִּי in 1:5a).

If, as proposed by Malamat, Amos only knew the province, not the kingdom, Amos would have in no case used בֵּית עֶדֶן. This is because the province is never referred to as Bīt-Adīni, only as Til-Barsib (Radner 2006–8a, 56). The evidence is clear: (1) Til-Barsib is found in a fragmentary list of provinces (SAA 11:7, 3.ii.1′). (2) The governor of Til-Barsib is referred to in two letters (SAA 1:8, 4.10′; 1:32–33, 32,r.13′). (3) A small tablet lists a number of workmen or soldiers that are "at the disposal of the governor of Til-Barsib" (*ina* IGI EN.NAM *ša* URU.*tur-bu-si-bi*) (Parker 1961, 43, ND 2684, r.5′–6′). (4) Also Til-Barsib is mentioned in Tell Shiukh Fawqani texts and Tell Aḥmar texts, never Bīt-Adīni (see Lemaire 2001). Bīt-Adīni is never used in cuneiform sources after the fall of the city of Til-Barsib to Shalmaneser III to refer to this area! Neither is Aramaic בית עדן.

The bottom line is this: after 855, there is not a single usage of either the West Semitic *byt ʿdn* or the Akkadian *Bīt-Adīni* to identify the Assyrian province or an independent polity in Upper Mesopotamia![245] And there is no evidence of a rebellion and reestablishment of the entity Bīt-Adīni. Hence, it is highly doubtful that בֵּית עֶדֶן in Amos 1:5c is to be identified with Bīt-Adīni.

Consequently, with the discovery and publication of the Tell Fakhariya Inscription, which states *mʿdn* (5) *mt . kln* "who makes all the lands luxuriant,"[246] Millard (1993, 176*) argues that the older understanding of בֵּית עֶדֶן as a pleasure house is reinforced, the unacceptable aspects of it emphasized by the parallel Biqʿat 'Awen, "Valley of Sin." Thus whether Biqʿat 'Awen

> was the present Beqʿa of Lebanon, more specifically Baalbek, or another place, and where Beth Eden lay, cannot be known; Beth Eden may have

243. There is no clear evidence that the kingdom of Aram-Damascus ever conquered and ruled over the former territory of Bīt-Adīni. See full discussion in ch. 9.

244. With the dates for Šamšī-ilu's administration established above, i.e., 786–752 (possibly to 745), Jeroboam II would have been a rough contemporary.

245. The use in 2 Kgs 19:12 (= Isa 37:12) is a historical reference by use of the Gentilic from to the polity by this name that existed *before* 855.

246. Abou-Assaf, Bordreuil, and Millard 1982, 30. The Akkadian has *muṭaḫḫidu kibrāti*, "who makes prosperous the regions."

> been a location within Biq'ath Awen. The expression Beth Eden has analogies in the "summer house" and "winter house" of 3:15 and the Aramaic inscription of Bar Rakkab of Sam'al later in the eighth century BCE.

Wolff (1977, 129) translated 1:5b–c as "and cut off the one who reigns from Sin Valley and the one who holds the scepter from House of Pleasure," and commented (p. 156): "Both of these are … meant to characterize the natures of the districts: 'Sin Valley' and 'House of Pleasure.'" Paul (1991, 54) labeled the use of אָוֶן in the phrase בִּקְעַת־אָוֶן "a cacophemism," that is, a word or expression that is generally perceived as harsh, impolite, or offensive.[247] It is interesting that the use of בֵּית עֶדֶן in the very next colon with the meaning of "house of pleasure"[248] could be understood as a euphemism (the exact opposite of a cacophemism); and hence, the passage is delivering a scathing condemnation of Aram-Damascus whose people will go into exile.

Most interpreters understand בִּקְעַת to refer to the Beqaʿ Valley. Some make a specific identification with Baalbek through an interpretation of the Old Greek πεδίου Ων, "the plain of On" being equated with the later Heliopolis in the Beqaʿ.[249] However, it is difficult to know whether Ων was the reading (און/אן?) that was polemically modified to אָוֶן or whether the Greek translators have merely transliterated the Hebrew letters און with Ων as they have in Hos 4:15; 5:8; and 10:5, 8 (where Heliopolis absolutely cannot be in view).

Bordreuil (1998, 58–59) has argued that it is less likely that בֵּית עֶדֶן designates a territory than a city or a palace located in the north of the Beqaʿ. He suggests the root *ʿdn* allows an identification with the place name known as Triparadeisus of Diodorus and Paradeisos of Strabo, which was located in the upper Beqaʿ.[250] Thus, according to Bordreuil, בֵּית עֶדֶן should be situated in the area of El Qaʿ. In this interpretation, בֵּית עֶדֶן is a place in the territory of Aram-Damascus at the time of Amos (see Hasegawa 2012, 130–31).

---

247. Note the use of בֵּית־אָוֶן (Hos 4:15; 5:8; 10:5) for בֵּית־אֵל (Amos 4:4; 5:5). Amos 5:5 states: "Do not seek Bethel, Do not go to Gilgal, Do not traverse to Beer-sheba; because Gilgal shall go into exile, and Bethel shall belong to/shall become "evil" (וּבֵית־אֵל יִהְיֶה לְאָוֶן). Cf. Hos 10:8: וְנִשְׁמְדוּ בָּמוֹת אָוֶן חַטַּאת יִשְׂרָאֵל, "The high places of evil, the sin of Israel, shall be destroyed."

248. Note that בֵּית עֶדֶן is translated in the Vulgate: *domus voluptatis*, "house of pleasure."

249. For the best detailed explication of this, see Bordreuil 1998, 57–58. Lipiński (2000a, 390) has a different view. See the discussion in ch. 9.

250. Keil and Delitzsch (1900, 244) state: "Bēth-Eden, i.e., house of delight, is … the *Παράδεισος* of the Greeks, which Ptolemy places ten degrees south and five degrees east of Laodicea."

Whether this identification is correct or not, the main point is that בֵּית עֶדֶן in Amos 1:5 is not to be connected with the long-extinct polity of Bīt-Adīni. In my opinion, the likelihood of a cacophemism (בִּקְעַת־אָוֶן) in 1:5b followed by a euphenism (בֵּית עֶדֶן) in 1:5c yields the best explanation of the meaning of the passage.

# 6
# SAM'AL/YĀDIYA/BĪT-GABBĀRI

## 6.1. Introduction

The small kingdom of Sam'al was located in the rift valley between the Amanus Range (Nur Dağları) and Kurt Dağ (about 50 km/31 mi. north–south by 35 km/22 mi. east–west; fig. 6.1). The capital of Sam'al, bearing the same name as the kingdom, was located at the site of modern Zincirli, Turkey, between modern Maraş[1] and Antakya, some 6 km northeast of the exit of the Nur Dağı Pass at Fevzipaşa. Sam'al was thus located at a strategically important point along the east–west piedmont highway, the so-called saddle route,[2] that connected northern Mesopotamia with southeastern Anatolia.[3]

Since the Amanus Range receives an average of over 1,000 mm of rainfall each year, in antiquity, its slopes supported dense forests consisting mainly of coniferous species such as fir, spruce, cedar, pine, and juniper.[4] As a result, the region was a major source of high-quality timber and other tree products such as resin. These were exported from very early times to the great cities of Mesopotamia. The kingdom had a Mediterranean coastal climate,[5] and consequently was agriculturally very prosperous.

### 6.1.1. Excavations

Excavations of the site were initially carried out by the German Orient-Comité during five campaigns between 1888 and 1902.[6] These excavations

1. 110 km north of Antakya; 55 km southwest of Maraş. Latitude 37 6′ north, longitude 36 40′ east.

2. For more on the piedmont "saddle route," see Comfort, Abadie-Reynal, and Ergeç 2000; Comfort and Ergeç 2001.

3. For a excellent discussion of the geographical setting, climate and resources of Sam'al, see Schloen 2014, 27–31.

4. Modern deforestation has changed all this.

5. See §1.1.2.1.2.

6. Carl Humann, Felix von Luschan, Robert Koldewey, and Gustav Jacoby directed

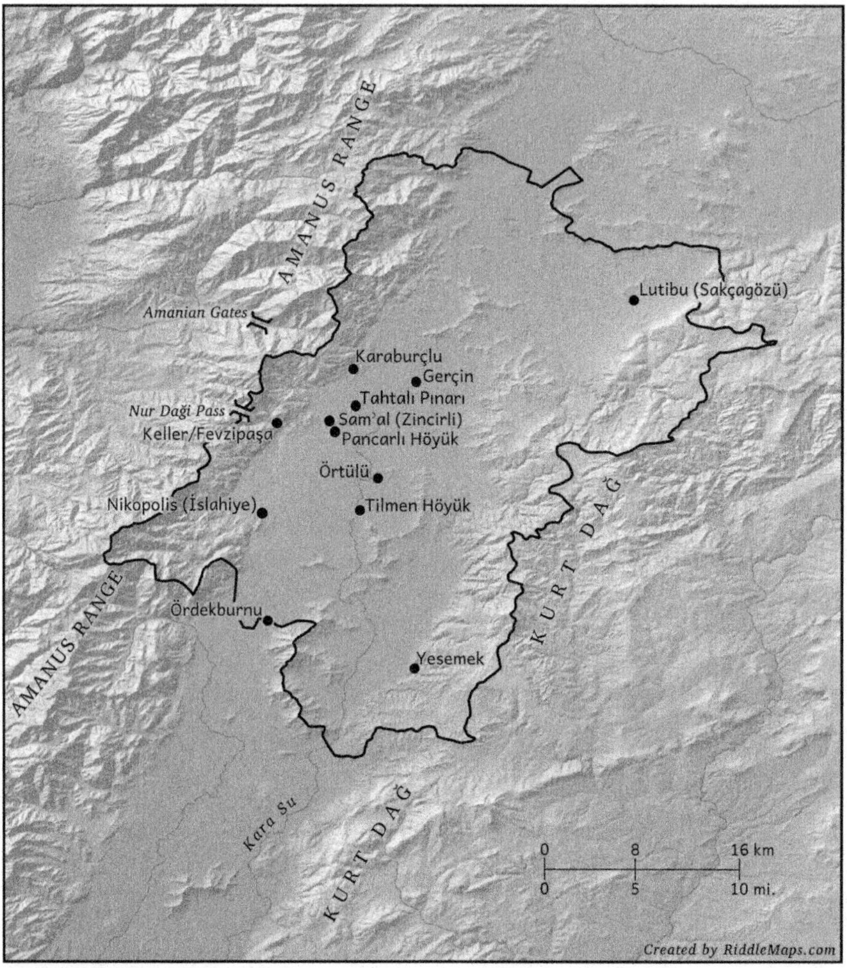


Fig. 6.1. Territory of Sam'al

concentrated on the acropolis and yielded rich inscriptional and archaeological evidence of a small kingdom. Perhaps the biggest deficit to these early excavations, due to the methods of the day, was the lack of the development of a clear ceramic stratigraphy. Nevertheless, the volume of artifacts and information have enabled scholars for over a century to delve into the study of the richness of this ancient tiny kingdom.

---

five expeditions to Zincirli between 1888 and 1902. For a excellent summary, see Wartke 2005, 7–56. Also see von Luschan 1893; 1902; 1911; *AiS* 5; Lehmann 1996, 272–81.

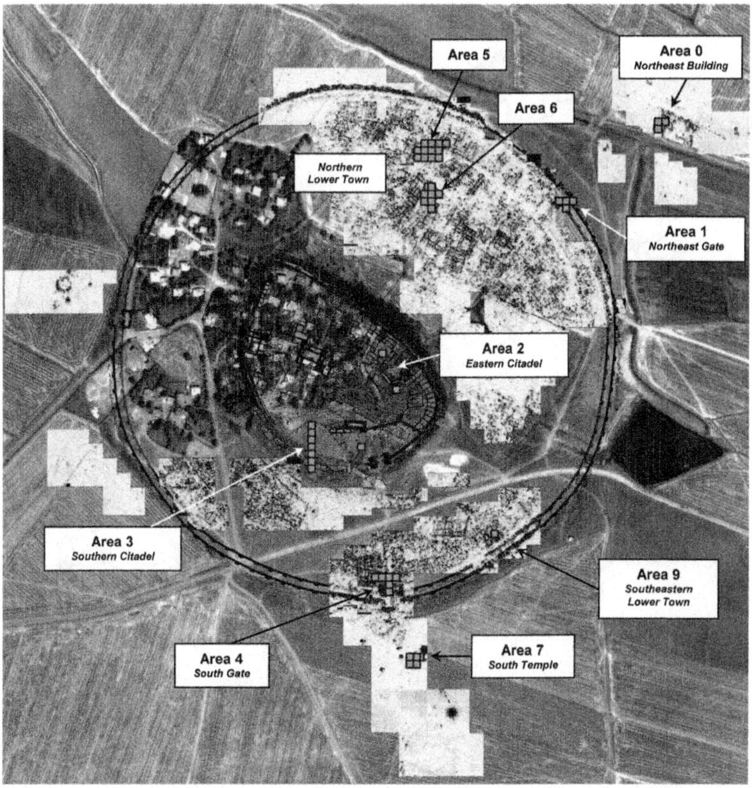


Fig. 6.2. Sam'al excavation areas (Herrmann and Schloen 2014, fig. 2.4, courtesy of J. David Schloen and the Neubauer Expedition to Zincirli)

In 2006, excavations at the site were renewed by the University of Chicago under the direction of J. David Schloen (Schloen and Fink 2009a; 2009b; Herrmann and Schloen 2014). These ongoing excavations have exposed sections of the northern lower city (Areas 5–6), two of the outer wall gates (Area 1 and 4), the southern acropolis (Area 3), two buildings outside the outer city walls (Area 9: a northeast building, and Area 7: a South Temple structure), a small section of the eastern citadel (Area 2), and a section of the southeastern lower city (Area 9; fig. 6.2).

The oval, 8 ha upper citadel mound is approximately 15–18 m higher than the valley floor and is surrounded by a lower residential town that is only about 2 m higher than the valley (fig. 6.3). This citadel had a massive gate, fortification walls, and stone-faced rampart. It also had palatial structures built during the different phases of the kingdom (see discussion below).

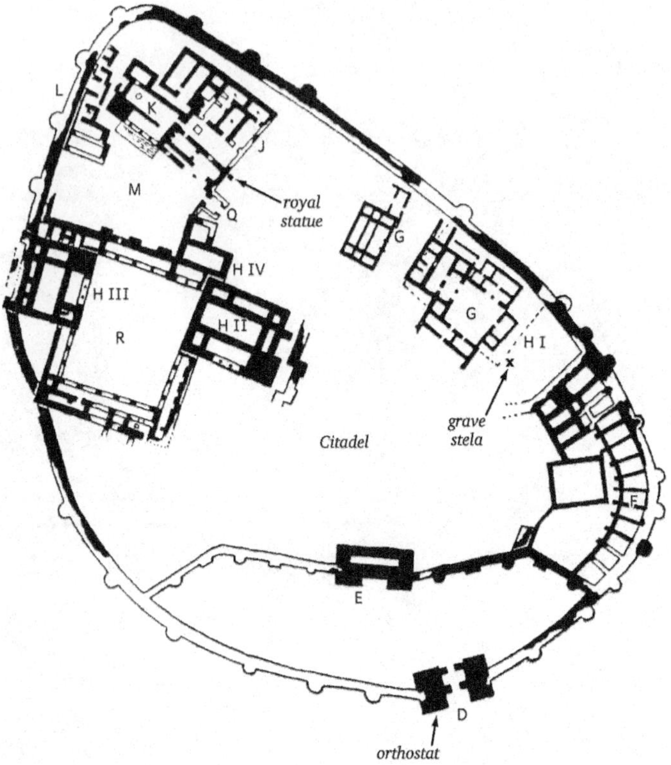


Fig. 6.3. The Zincirli citadel

The mound evinces occupation during the mid-second millennium BCE, and perhaps earlier. However, at the present according to the ceramic data, there seems to have been a gap in occupation of around three to four centuries (Lehmann 1994).

The lower city was enclosed by a perfectly circular double wall[7] that was approximately 2,200 m long, with one hundred projecting towers. The double wall was built on stone foundations upon which mud-brick superstructures (now eroded away) rose to a height of at least 10 m. There was a distance of 7 m between the walls. Apparently the two walls were not built at different times (contra the conclusion of the early excavators). The two were integral to one another, the inner wall's foundation served to support a mud-brick superstructure on which the inner ring of defenders could stand (Schloen and

7. Gilibert (2011, 56) points out that at Karkamiš, fortification walls are often double.

Fink 2009b, 209). Both walls have one hundred evenly spaced towers protruding from them, creating positions for archers to assail attacking forces (Casana and Herrmann 2010, 63). In addition, recent excavations have found evidence of a water-filled moat outside the walls (Schloen and Fink 2009b, 209). Thus, this fortification system would have been a formidable obstacle to any attacker, who, having crossed the moat and captured the outermost wall, would have been trapped in the corridor between the two walls and subjected to a withering fire from the defenders who had fallen back to man the inner wall (Pucci 2008, 8). The entire Iron Age city was about 40 ha in size.[8]

This outer wall had three double gates (northeast, south and west). The inner portion of the South City Gate was the only gate to be decorated with monumental art and it led directly to the Southern Citadel Gate ("Äußeres Burgtor"). This was the only entrance into the walled acropolis. Both the South City Gate and the Southern Citadel Gate were decorated with relief orthostats. Gilibert has suggested that the choice to employ orthostats decorated with images of ritual spectacles at the South City Gate suggests that the gate was conceived as a ceremonial public space from the beginning and that the orthostats commemorated ritual events that first took place in connection with the foundation of the city (Gilibert 2011, 61). This is also true for the Outer Citadel Gate (Gilibert 2011, 67). The "iconography of the reliefs (war, hunt, procession of gods, and ancestral cults)"[9] clearly connects with "the celebration of rituals" (Gilibert 2011, 67). Gradiometry survey seems to indicate that there was only one road that connected the South City Gate and the Southern Citadel Gate, and excavations in this area demonstrate that it was at least partially paved, signaling its monumental character (Casana and Herrmann 2010, 65). Thus this was likely a ceremonial, processional road, perhaps lined with relief orthostats.[10] All of this must have provided an impressive entrance to the city for any visitor or foreign envoy (figs. 6.2 and 6.3).

The survey extended more than 100 m south of the gateway and revealed evidence for what may be a continuation of this road in the form of an unpaved trail leading out of the city toward a square building that may be a small temple, indicated by the discovery of an orthostat in its vicinity (Casana and Herrmann 2010, 65).

8. Wartke 2006–8, 605; Schloen and Fink 2009a, 1–2; 2009b, 205; Schloen 2014, 27.

9. On representations of the royal ancestral cult at the gates of the city, as opposed to representations of mortuary rituals *stricto sensu* on funerary stelae (i.e., *Ahnenkult* versus *Totenkult*), see Bonatz 2000a, 158. Gilibert (2011, 67 n. 125.) notes also a child burial that indicates a use of the area for ceremonial and burial purposes, perhaps related to ancestor worship.

10. Schloen and Fink 2007, 2009.

In the magnetic gradiometry data, two circular tracks are visible. These appear to be planned roads inside the lower city, since they follow the course of the outer fortification walls. This survey data also reveals a number of residential housing blocks around these roads, though these do not appear to be designed in an authoritative fashion. Several of these housing compounds in the lower town are considerably larger than the Upper Palace on the citadel. Interestingly, in the present survey data there appears to be an absence of "poor" districts within the lower city. It may be that these residential areas belonged to prominent patrimonial households, since this would explain the apparent absence of spatially manifested class distinctions (Casana and Herrmann 2010, 66, 71). From this evidence, Casana and Herrmann (2010, 75) conclude that "Zincirli strongly suggests a pattern of distributed authority in creating the built environment of the city, whereby the king and his administrators planned and constructed the circular walls, streets, and citadel, but according to which individual elite households were probably left to plan and build their own residential compounds."

In Area 5, two important buildings on the outer ring road have been excavated. Part of Building A/II was a small, urban mortuary chapel, in which the Katumuwa stela was discovered (Herrmann 2014, 51, fig. 5.2). The room contained no evidence of a burial or cremation. Consequently, Katumuwa's body or cremation urn must have been located elsewhere, perhaps in the necropolis at Gerçin. Yet, this chapel was the place for the perpetuation of Katumuwa's name and "soul." The room contained proper features necessary for the depositing of food and drink offerings. This room, which was secured by door and lock-system, was entered from the east and, importantly, the stela itself faced east, its back to the wall. On the other side of this wall was another larger and important building (A/III). It shows no features of the typical monumental temples of the region, but has been understood by the excavators as a smaller neighborhood temple, likely popular since it could be entered from the ring road. Perhaps this was the temple of the deity who received the most significant of the sacrifices at the dedication of Katumuwa's stela, Hadad *qrpdl*. It seems that by establishing his mortuary chapel literally right next to this temple, Katumuwa intended to ensure that his "soul" would eat and drink with the gods through simultaneous offerings.

### 6.1.2. The Names

#### 6.1.2.1. The Name Šmʾl

The Iron Age city-state located at Zincirli was known by three names: *Šmʾl*, *Yʾdy* and *Bīt-Gabbār*. There is evidence that this city-state had a mixed population made up of Luwians and Arameans. This has led scholars to look to these languages for possible etymologies for the names *Šmʾl* and *Yʾdy*. For example, Landsberger[11] argued that both names were Anatolian (Hittite/Luwian) in origin. Lipiński (2000a, 235–36) has argued that both names have Semitic etymologies. Tropper opines that *Šmʾl* has a Semitic etymology and *Yʾdy* has a non-Semitic etymology.[12]

*Šmʾl* (vocalized Sam'al) was the name by which the city-state was called by its neighbors in almost every instance. The lone exception is the Aramaic Sefire inscription (*KAI* 222:B9) where the city-state is designated *Yʾd*[*y*]. In Akkadian sources (Bagg 2007, 206–8), the place name is abundantly attested as *Sa-am-al-la* (with variants *Sa-ma-al-la* and *Sa-am-al*), written with the determinative KUR or URU, as well as the gentilic form *Sa-am-a-la-a-a*. The gentilic form with the KUR determinative[13] is used earlier than the plain toponymic form, which is used almost exclusively after Sam'al became a province.[14] In Aramaic, the city-state is called *Šmʾl* in the Zakkur Inscription from Tell Afis (ca. 796 BCE),[15] as well as in local Aramaic texts of king Barrākib from Zincirli (B1:2–3,17; B2:1). Significantly, these are the latest native inscriptions from the site and very likely reflect the influence of Assyrian overlordship.

There is a scholarly consensus that *Šmʾl* should be vocalized as /*Śamʾal*/ and has a West Semitic etymology, meaning literally "left side," indicating the "north" (hence: "North City" or "Northland").[16] Whether this is tied to an early immigrate group of the second millennium like the *mārū Simʾal* "northerner (tribes)," or to later Aramean settlers of the Iron I period, or some other explanation is not known. This depends, in part, on whether there are second-millennium attestations connected to the site of Zincirli. Citing two texts, Schloen and Fink believe that Sam'al occurs in second-millennium

11. Landsberger 1948, 22 n. 42, 36 n. 76, and 40 n. 93.

12. Tropper (1993, 9–10) states: "Bei einem Nebeneinander zweier antiker Namen für ein und denselben Ort ist grundsätzlich davon auszugehen, daß diese auf unterschiedliche ethnische Gruppen zurückgehen."

13. The URU determinative is used almost exclusively in the inscriptions of Tiglath-pileser III with reference to "Panamuwa, the Sam'alian" (mPa-na-am-mu-u/ú URU *Sa-am-'a-la-a-a*). The only exception is in a contract dated by the postcanonical eponym Sîn-šarru-uṣur, governor of Ḫindānu (636 BCE): "Seal of Zabdî and Adad-zēru-ibni, sons of Kēnî, the Sam'alian (URU.*S*[*a-a*]*m-*⌜*'a*⌝*-*<*la*>*-a-a*), the owner of the man to be sold." Deller and Millard 1985, 38, Vs. 2.

14. The one exception is found in an administrative text (a fragmentary list of contributions (Dalley and Postgate 1984, 86:13; SAA 11 8, 6.2′: mEN-KASKAL-KI-*ia* IGI URU.*Sa-*⌜*am-al-la*⌝ URU.*kàl-zi* "Bēl-Ḫarrān-issīya (serving) over Sa⌜m'al⌝ (and) Kilizi" (reign of Tiglath-pileser III according to Dalley and Postgate 1984, 144).

15. *KAI* 202:A7.

16. Tropper 1993, 7; Dion 1997, 100; Lipiński 2000a, 235.

sources: an Old Assyrian text from Kültepe and the Egyptian toponym list of Thutmose III:

> That the name Sam'al was known already in the Amorite period (the Middle Bronze Age) is shown by an Old Assyrian text of the 19th century B.C. (Kültepe c/k 441; published by Nashef 1987:18–20, text no. 7). This text records payments made by an Assyrian merchant for various expenses related to an expedition to what must be the Amanus Mountains to procure timber and wine, including a payment to "the employee from Sam'al" (*a-na ṣú-ḫa-ri-im ša sá-am-a-al*), who was presumably hired at Zincirli, at the foot of the mountains, to assist with the expedition.
>
> The place-name Sam'al (written *ś-m-i-r-w*) appears also in an Egyptian list of North Syrian toponyms carved on the wall of the temple of Amun at Karnak to celebrate the exploits of the pharaoh Thutmose III, who campaigned repeatedly in the region, conquering the Orontes River and its tributaries and marching as far as the Euphrates in his eighth campaign around 1450 B.C.[17]

However, in both texts it is far from certain that these are references to a toponym centered at Zincirli. In the Old Assyrian text (Nashef 1987, 18–20, text no. 7), the determinatives are lacking throughout and since the other place names are in a different region, there is little way of assuring that this is a reference.[18] The Egyptian list likewise lacks sufficient context to say with any degree of certainty that this is a second-millennium reference to an entity located at Zincirli. While the Egyptian hieroglyphics could be spelling Sam'al, it is also possible that they are spelling a different place name.

My point is simply to emphasize the very tentative nature of these data. Whether the name existed in the second millennium or not has really no bearing on the question of the Arameans. Since the Arameans are clearly identified by the Gabbāri tribal entity (Bīt-Gabbāri), the name Sam'al is not relevant to this group's identity. In other words, it does not appear that Sam'al

---

17. Schloen and Fink 2009a, 6. They cite Astour 1963, 233: "314. *ś-m-i-r-w* (Albright III:A:22 *Sa-m(a)-'a-ra-wa*) Sam'al (*Šm'l*), the well-known city-state of the Assyrian age. Recognized by Müller, 291 n. 6 (who could not explain, by that time, the ending *-wa*). It is so far the earliest evidence of the existence of that city, already under its West Semitic name. Geographically, Sam'al's location in the upper valley of the Kara-su links it with the region of Alalah." However, all of the toponyms in this group that can be located are found in the Alalaḫ, Aleppo, and Karkamiš areas. Nothing near Zincirli can be safely identified. See Simons 1937, 121.

18. Nashef himself did not take the mention of Sam'al to be a station in the itinerary sequence, but only a vague connection (1987, 19 n. 32). The cuneiform spelling (*sá-am-a-al*) also does not match the Neo-Assyrian writing of Sam'al.

was the name of the Aramean tribe in this locale. The same point applies to the name Yādiya (see below).

Finally, an earlier scholarly attempt at the identification of this name with the city name Simala occurring in the Old Assyrian texts from Cappadocia is to be rejected (Tropper 1993, 7).

6.1.2.2. The Name Yādiya (*Y'dy*)

In the earliest domestic inscriptions, the polity was called *Y'dy*. This was also its designation in the Old Aramaic inscription from Sefire.[19] Since *Y'dy* was replaced in the Standard Old Aramaic inscriptions of the king Barrākib by *Šm'l* and only occurs once outside of the city-state's own indigenous texts, *Y'dy* may be the older, non-Semitic name of the city that enjoyed primarily local use.[20]

The vocalization of *Y'dy* has been debated. It has been traditionally vocalized as Ya'udī. This vocalization was based on a misinterpretation of a Neo-Assyrian cuneiform fragment that was wrongly attributed to Tiglath-pileser III with the result that the place name KUR/URU *Ia-u/ú-du/da/di(-a-a)* in this text was equated with the *Y'dy* found in the local inscriptions from Zincirli.[21] However, Na'aman demonstrated that the fragment was a join to the so-called Azekah inscription (Na'aman 1974), which has now been attributed to Sargon II or, more likely, Sennacherib (Younger 2002b, 292–93). In any event, the place name in the cuneiform actually refers to the kingdom of "Judah"; and therefore the equation of *Y'dy* with the *Yaudi* of this inscription is wrong.[22] This false identification led some scholars to designate the local dialect of this city-state as "Jaudisch," "yaoudien," and "yaudico."[23] How-

19. Sefire I: *KAI* 222:B9: *Y'd*[*y*].

20. As already noted above, ŠM'L, not Y'DY, is not used in the Old Aramaic Zakkur Inscription from Afis as well as in the Akkadian sources.

21. Initially put forward by Winckler 1893, with a first study entitled "Das Syrische Land Jaudi und der angebliche Azarja von Juda." Thereafter followed by many.

22. Often overlooked is the fact that there is a significant philological difficulty in equating יאדי with Neo-Assyrian KUR *Ia-u-di* (well pointed out by Luckenbill). KUR *Ia-u-di* is clearly the Neo-Assyrian rendering of יְהוּדָה where the *u* renders the ה, for which there are good examples. An א would have been rendered by the cuneiform sign ('). "If the Assyrian scribe had had before him the Aramaic form יאדי, he would have rendered it *Ia-'-di-(i)*, not *Ia-u-di*. In a word, יאדי is not a good Aramaic writing of יְהוּדָה and *Ia-u-di* is not a probable rendering of יאדי. But יְהוּדָה is regularly rendered in the cuneiform by *Ia-u-di*." See Luckenbill 1924–25, 222–23.

23. Jaudisch: Friedrich 1951, 153–61; Donner and Röllig 1968, 216–17; yaoudien: Dion 1974; yaudico: Garbini 1976; 1988, 69–80.

ever, for roughly the last three decades, the local dialect of Zincirli has been designated "Sam'alian" and/or simplifying "Samalian."

The difficulty in vocalization is complicated by disagreement over whether the term is Semitic or Anatolian. Scholars have suggested various vocalizations for *Y'dy*, including:

(1) Ya'di (Cooke 1903, 163–64;[24] Luckenbill 1924–25);[25]
(2) Ya'diya (Landsberger 1948, 22 n. 42; 36 n. 76);[26]
(3) Yu'addiya (Rosenthal, *ANET*, 654);[27]
(4) Ya'ady (Lemaire and Durand 1984, 81–82);[28]
(5) Yu'addī (Lipiński 1983, 18; 2000a, 235).

Lipiński (2000a, 235–6) has been a strong advocate for a Semitic derivation. He argues that *Y'dy* cannot be explained by a known Anatolian language, and therefore must be a Semitic tribal name (either "Aramean or North Arabian"), derived from a personal name:[29]

> It belongs to the same root as the Arabic verb *'dy*, stem II of which (*'addā*) means "to lead." The personal name **Yu'addī* is probably attested in the Neo-Assyrian census of the district around Harrān, datable in the late 8th century B.C. We find there a patronymic ᵐ*Ú-a-di-i*, which was rightly related to Old Arabian personal names. Although this name may be inter-

24. Cooke gives no explanation for his vocalization. One can assume that he understood the *a* and *y* as *matres lectionis* for *ā* and *ī* respectively. He commends Winckler's hypothesis, but does not follow it.

25. Luckenbill simply utilizes this vocalization without explanation, apparently following Cooke 1903, 163–4.

26. Landsberger's arguments are primarily targeted against the Semitic origins of the name and its possible homonymous link with Judah. He, more or less, simply postulates the vocalization of Ya'diya as being based on Luwian/Hittite, but without analogies or reasons for these vowels.

27. Rosenthal (*ANET*, 654) stated: "*Y'dy*, whose vocalization is uncertain, might be the capital city of the realm, to be vocalized Yu'addiya or the like (cf. Azitawadda-Azitawaddiya), which later on came to be known as Sam'al. The latter, however, might have been the name of the larger region or country." Clearly Rosenthal is using the analogy of Azatiwada/Azatiwadiya in his understanding of *Y'dy*, although it is not clear why the initial vowel is *u*. While there is coincidental similarity, Lipiński's vocalization (Yu'addī) is independent and original, being carefully explained as being an Arabic derivation (Lipiński 1983, 18; 2000a, 235).

28. They only state: "Ya'ady est le nom indigène (louvite?) du royaume de Sam'al situé à l'est de l'Amanus." No comment on the reasons for this vocalization.

29. Lipińksi (2000a, 236) suggests that this Aramean or North Arabian tribe called *Y'dy* should be related to the inhabitants of Sam'al designated as the *b'rrm* "the nomadic or semi-nomadic group" distinct from another group the *mškbm* "the sedentists" in the Kulamuwa Inscription (Tropper 1993, 39–45, lines 10, 13–15). See discussion below.

> preted as *Waddī*, it is more likely that Ú stands there for initial *yu-* like in the next following name ${}^{m}$*Ú-a-si-i* of the Ḫarran Census, which is identical with Thamūdic *Y's¹y /Yu'aššī/*, and like the name ${}^{m}$*Ú-a-a-te-'* designating the same person as ${}^{m}$*Ia-u/ú-te/ta-'* and standing for **Yuwaiṯiʿ*. The spelling in Ú- occurs in other names as well, like in ${}^{m}$*ú-a-bu* corresponding to *Wahb* rather than to *Y'b* or *Y'b*. The root *'dy* is attested also in the Old Arabian personal names *'dy* (*'Udaiy*) and *'dyn*, both Ṣafaitic. We suggest therefore that *Y'dy* should be vocalized **Yu'addī*, "he leads," a shortened name in which only the first element is preserved.

Landsberger (1948, 36 n. 76) pointed out a difficulty in positing a third weak consonantal root for *Y'dy*: it is doubtful in the Phoenician inscription of Kulamuwa that the prefixed form of a III-*y* verb would have a *y* written at the end of the word. However, since Sam'alian Aramaic does have the *y* at the end of III-*y* verbs (e.g., *yrqy* - Hadad 22), Landsberger's argument is not determinative. However, the root 'DY does not occur in any Northwest Semitic language (including Ugaritic). Thus, while Lipiński's proposal might be a possible explanation, it is far from certain. Based on cognate propinquity, it is certainly questionable.

On the other hand, from the inscriptional evidence, *Y'dy* is clearly an *indigenous* name. It might, therefore, be based on Luwian.[30] Starke has argued for an Anatolian derivation based on analogies with other place names in which the *-iya* ending is utilized, for example, Wilus(s)*a* → Wilu*siya*; Arzaw*a* → Arzaw*iya*; Adan*a* → Adan*iya*; hence: Yad*a* → Yad*iya*. Perhaps Azatiwad*a* → Azatiwad*iya* should be added to this list, particularly given the Semitic renderings: *'ztwd* / *'ztwdy* in the Karatepe bilingual. In the Cebel Ires Dağı Inscription,[31] a place name occurs written alphabetically: WRYKLY. This may be a place name linked to the name *wryk* in line 8.

Another kingdom in the region seems to have had both Anatolian and Semitic names: Patina and 'Umq, respectively. This example may serve as an analogy. In light of the present data available, an Anatolian etymology is more likely. While the name of the city unfortunately is not yet attested in hieroglyphic Luwian script,[32] it seems likely that *Y'dy* was the Luwian-derived name for the city-state. If *Y'dy* has a Semitic derivation, then this city-state would be utterly unique among all ancient Near Eastern political

30. Starke (2003, col. 122 = 1999, col. 122) states: "based on a Luwian ethnicon pl.N.A.n. **Yādiya* (to the country name of **Yāda-*) – 'the Yādaean (country).'" See also Starke 1997a, 458 n. 121.

31. *KAI* 287:3b.

32. The suggestion that *Y'dy* (in contrast to the city name *Šm'l*) was the designation of the land around Zincirli, but not the city itself (see Donner and Röllig 1968, 216), is not likely to be correct (Tropper 1993, 8).

entities in having three Semitic derived names: Sam'al, *Y'dy* and Bīt-Gabbār. It seems best to understand *Y'dy* as the indigenous name Yādiya.

6.1.2.3. The Name Bīt-Gabbār[33]

One king of this city-state was designated in the Kurkh Monolith inscription of Shalmaneser III as ${}^{m}$*ḫa-ia-a-nu* DUMU *gab-ba-ri šá* GÌR KUR *ḫa-ma-ni* "*Ḫayānu mār Gabbāri*, which is at the foot of Mount Amanus"[34] and ${}^{m}$*ḫa-ia-ni* DUMU *ga-ba-ri*.[35] The phrase *mār Gabbāri* is a gentilic or ethnicon and indicates that Gabbār[36] was the eponymous founder of an Aramean tribal entity based at this city-state known as Bīt-Gabbār (contra Sader 1987, 272). He is the only definitely known ruler of this dynasty, although the Kulamuwa inscription may imply a dynastic succession (see discussion of history below).

It has been suggested that Sam'al may have been known as Uša in the Hittite period (Schramm 1983; Lipiński 2000a, 234). This is based on a small steatite tablet allegedly from Zincirli which Schramm (1983, 458) interpreted to read: (1') [PN] (2') King (3') of the land of Uša. However, uncertainty over provenance, authenticity (Bossert 1958) and reading of the cuneiform render such a conclusion speculative, and hence doubtful (Hawkins 2006–8, 601; Jasink 1995, 111 n. 48).

6.1.3. Native Written Sources

Inscriptions in the area of the ancient kingdom of Sam'al/Yādiya were written in hieroglyphic Luwian, Phoenician, and Aramaic.[37] The Luwian inscriptions include the Karaburçlu Inscription,[38] a hieroglyphic Luwian seal of Barrākib,[39] and a hieroglyphic Luwian fragment that was discovered in 2008.[40]

Only the Kulamuwa Inscription was written in Phoenician (ca. 830–820), clearly a prestige language at the time of its composition. Phoenician was

33. Bagg 2007, 48, s.v. Bīt-Gabbāri.

34. RIMA 3:18, A.0.102.2, ii.24, dated to 857 BCE.

35. RIMA 3:23, A.0.102.2, ii.83, dated to 853 BCE.

36. The name Gabbār, "warrior, hero" is a *qattāl* formation of the root *gbr* "to be strong."

37. Tropper 1993, 47; Lemaire 2001, 188; 2013; Young 2002; Río Sánchez 2006, 178.

38. See 3. Karaburçlu below.

39. Hawkins 2000a, 576 and pl. 329.

40. Schloen and Fink 2009a, 9. See now Herrmann, van den Hout, and Beyazlar 2016.

very important for trade in the region (attested on both sides of the Amanus mountain range). Even Yariri, a regent of Karkamiš (ca. 800) a few years later, boasted of his knowledge and ability in the Tyrian language and script (Younger 2014a).

The Aramaic inscriptions attest to two sure dialects: Sam'alian Aramaic[41] and Standard Old Aramaic.[42] The bulk of the lengthy inscriptions are written in Sam'alian Aramaic. These include: the Kulamuwa Golden Case Inscription (ca. 830–820), the Ördekburnu Inscription (ca. 820–760), the Hadad Inscription (ca. 755–750), the Katumuwa Inscription (ca. 735), and the Panamuwa Inscription (ca. 732). Pardee (2009) has suggested that the Katumuwa inscription is another additional dialect. However, Lemaire (2013) argues that it is Sam'alian, and not a distinct dialect. If correct, it is intriguing that all of the major Sam'alian Aramaic inscriptions are connected with the ancestor cult (see table 6.2 below). The only exception is the Kulamuwa Golden Case Inscription. The Standard Old Aramaic texts are on six basalt orthostats, a seal impression, as well as three small inscribed silver ingots, all belonging to Barrākib (ca. 732–727), the last known king of Sam'al.[43] Interestingly, all of the Semitic monumental inscriptions are not incised in the stone, but utilize a raised script that seems to reflect a dependence on the hieroglyphic Luwian model (Hawkins 2006–8, 601; Greenfield 1998, 200). The nonmonumental Semitic texts are incised.

Finally, there are, of course, Neo-Assyrian cuneiform inscriptions discovered at the site that come from the period of the Assyrian province.[44]

41. Although Friedrich (1951, 152–53) attempted to attribute Panamuwa and the Hadad inscription to the "Canaanite" branch of Northwest Semitic, there can be no doubt that these belong within the Aramaic dialects. Greenfield (1968; 1978, 94) has shown that these texts belong to Aramaic; see also Tropper 1993, 283–311; Noorlander 2012. Therefore, there is no reason to doubt that Sam'alian is Aramaic, as Schloen and Fink (2009a, 9) do, stating: "Thus, Samalian could instead be an otherwise unattested branch of Northwest Semitic that developed in this topographically isolated region on the east side of the Amanus Range, being derived from the Amorite dialect brought there during the Middle Bronze Age." However, in the same *BASOR* issue as Schloen and Fink's article, Pardee asserts concerning the Katumuwa Inscription: "One may legitimately claim that *the more clearly Aramaic character of the language of the new inscription*, in conjunction with its strong isoglosses with Samalian (in particular {'ank} and {wt-}), provides a new argument in favor of the identification of Samalian as a dialect of Aramaic characterized by the even more archaic retention of case endings in the plural and the absence of nunation" (Pardee 2009, 68, emphasis added).

42. Or using Fales's designation (2011c, 560): "Syrian Old Aramaic."

43. For all these inscriptions, except the Ördekburnu Inscription and the Katumuwa Inscription, see Tropper 1993. For the Ördekburnu and Katumuwa Inscriptions, see below.

44. Most notably the stela of Esarhaddon; see RINAP 4:181–86, 98.

## 6.2. Territory

Aside from the city of Sam'al itself, only one other city in the kingdom is mentioned in the sources: Lutibu (Bagg 2007, 160). On his 858 campaign, Shalmaneser III reports:

> I departed from the city of Gurgum. I approached the city of Lutibu (URU. *lu-ti-bu*), the fortified city of Ḫayānu, the Sam'alite.[45]

The issue surrounding this toponym has been its location. Two possible locations have been proposed: (1) Sakçagözü,[46] 21 km northeast of Zincirli, on the western slopes of Kurt Dağ; and (2) Yesemek,[47] about 20 km southeast of Zincirli (see fig. 6.1).

Sakçagözü lies on the route from Gurgum (Maraş) to Sam'al (Zincirli), and hence automatically made a good candidate. The excavations of Sakçagözü[48] uncovered the entrance to the vestibule of the palace, which was decorated with orthostats with reliefs that were found nearly completely in situ. Stylistically these belong to the later phase of the Neo-Hittite "späthethitische" art from Zincirli and Karkamiš and hence can be dated to the second half of the eighth century (Orthmann 2006–8, 558). However, the lion-hunt scene that is found on other orthostats (now in Berlin; see fig. 6.6) appears to be connected with the outside entrance to the palace complex and can be assigned to a somewhat older phase of Neo-Hittite "späthethitische" art (first half of the eighth century).[49] In many ways, the best analogies are still found at Zincirli.[50]

Nevertheless, Hawkins (1982, 423; 1995, 95) argued against Sakçagözü, in spite of its proximity to Zincirli, feeling that the site might have belonged to the territory of Gurgum or Kummuḫ. Thus his proposal to equate Lutibu with Yesemek was mainly based on the rejection of Sakçagözü. However, the site of Yesemek seems too far south to be a reasonable candidate for

45. RIMA 3:16, A.0.102.2, i.42; also RIMA 3:9, A.0.102.1, line 53′.

46. Kraeling 1918, 69 n. 1; Sader 1987, 173 n. 57; Ponchia 1991, 94 n. 11; Lipiński 2000a, 237.

47. Hawkins 1982, 377; 1995, 95. Following Hawkins's arguments, see Dion 1997, 102–3; less committedly, Yamada 2000a, 95.

48. For a recent summary, see Orthmann 2006–8. The site was excavated (see Garstang 1908; 1913; 1929, 262–78; du Plat Taylor, Seton Williams and Waechter 1950).

49. According to Ussishkin (1966), the gate reliefs, and therefore the wall and the gate, belong to the first half of the eighth century. However, the main wall and the gate may be earlier in date than the gate reliefs. See also Orthmann 1971, 79–82.

50. But see Hawkins 1982, 423; Güterbock 1961. The palace was still in use as late as 650–625 BCE according to Hanfmann 1960.

Lutibu. Hence, Hawkins himself has reassessed the evidence and states: "In 858 Shalmaneser marching from Gurgum to Sam'al passed the city of Lutibu, 'strong city of Ḫayānu,' plausibly identified with Sakçagözü."[51]

In sum, Sakçagözü is the best candidate for Lutibu. However, there is no inscription confirming this, and there is, of course, no knowledge of exactly where the border between Gurgum and Sam'al was located.

While Lutibu is the only city known by ancient name from the polity of Sam'al, some modern sites have yielded evidence connected to it (fig. 6.1).

(1) Gerçin is located about 7 km northeast of Zincirli. The site was apparently the royal necropolis for some period of the history of the kingdom. The Hadad statue with its inscription,[52] dating from the last years of the reign of Panamuwa I (r. 790–750 BCE), was discovered here.
(2) İslahiye (Nikopolis; 10 km south of Zincirli), a *Grabdenkmal* dates to ca. 800–700 BCE.[53] It has the same structural design as the stela of the royal lady from the Ḫilāni I grave on the acropolis of Zincirli, as well as the Katumuwa Stela, though without an inscription.
(3) At Karaburçlu (5 km north of Zincirli), a basalt mortuary stela with a banquet scene was discovered.[54] It contains an inscription in hieroglyphic Luwian, although only a few words are readable; thus the content is unclear. The relief and inscription can be dated on stylistic and paleographic grounds to ca. 925–850 BCE (Bonatz 2000a, 19).
(4) Keller (modern Fevzipaşa; 3 km west of Zincirli).
(5) Ördekburnu (20 km south–southwest of Zincirli), a *Grabdenkmal,* dates to 820–760 BCE (Lemaire and Sass 2012, 2013).
(6) Karapınar Mezarlık (2 km from Ördekburnu) may be the site of an early royal necropolis and the place from which the Ördekburnu Stela originated (Lemaire and Sass 2013, 129–30).
(7) Pancarlı-Höyük (2–3 km southeast of Zincirli).
(8) Tahtalı Pınarı (2 km northeast of Zincirli). Here a statue was discovered at a spring. It is a statue set up by king Barrākib for his deceased father Panamuwa II and bears the Panamuwa Inscription (*KAI* 215). The statue was in a secondary location,

51. Hawkins 2006–8, 601. See also the arguments of Lipiński 2000a, 237–38.

52. *KAI* 214. Vorderasiatisches Museum, Inv. Nr. VA 2882: height: 2.85 m.

53. Bonatz 2000a, 19 [C 30], pl. XIII; Kalaç 1975, 189, pl. XLIII, fig. 10.

54. Altorientalische Museum Istanbul, Inv.-Nr. 7729. Bonatz 2000a, 19, C 32; pl. XIV; Hawkins 2000a, 276, pl. 127; Orthmann 1971, 487 (Karaburçlu 1), pl. 14d; Darga 1992, fig. 299.

having been moved apparently from the necropolis at Gerçin (Wartke 2005, 69, fig. 62).

(9) Yesemek quarry (northeast of Ördekburnu; Lipiński 2000a, 238; Duru 2004). A sphinx dating to the ninth century was discovered at the site (Genge 1979, 1:185–86).

(10) Tilmen Höyük (7 km southeast of Zincirli). Significant MB/LB with Iron remains, a regional center.[55]

(11) Örtülü (7 km southeast of Zincirli), a *Grabdenkmal* (stela or orthostat?) was discovered that dates to around 900–800 BCE (Bonatz 2000a, 19: C 26, pl. XIII).[56]

## 6.3. History

The two challenges in reconstructing the history of Sam'al are the chronology and the interpretation of the archaeological evidence from Zincirli. First, there is only a relative chronology for the history of Sam'al, which is provided mainly by the native inscriptional evidence. The inscriptions only provided a general outline. This relative chronology of the Sam'alian kings is supplemented by four absolute dates: (1) in 858, Shalmaneser III records marching from Gurgum into Sam'al and approaching the city of Lutibu, "the fortified city of Ḫayānu, the Sam'alian"; (2) In 857, Shalmaneser III records the tribute paid by Ḫayānu, "man of Bīt-Gabbāri"; (3) in 853, Shalmaneser III records again the tribute paid by Ḫayānu, "man of Bīt-Gabbāri"; and (4) in 738, Tiglath-pileser III records the tribute given by "Panamuwa, the Sam'alian."

One of the major difficulties in establishing the relative chronology of Sam'al is knowing the dynastic connections or lack thereof between the attested monarchs. This is also complicated by possible gaps. For example, in his inscription, Kulamuwa lists four of his predecessors: Gabbār, BMH/BNH, his father Ḥayyā', and his brother Ša'il. The relationships between the first three are not specified, whether familial or not. Scholars have advocated possible dynastic connections or no possible dynastic connections. Just because the Assyrian sources describe Ḫayānu as *mār Gabbāri* does not mean that there was an actual biological connection between Ḫayānu (Ḥayyā') and Gabbār, since the construction *mār* X can be an ethnicon (i.e., a gentilic form; see the discussion in ch. 2).

55. Marchetti 2006, 2007. See also Dion 1997, 102; and Mazzoni 1994, 324.

56. Gaziantepe Museum, Inv.-Nr. 5600; basalt: height 0.56 m; width: 0.90 m; depth 0.50 m.

On the other hand, the evidence for dynastic changes between the two is weak, being completely dependent on the interpretation of the differences in "personal protective deities" of Gabbār, BMH/BNH and Kulamuwa (dynasty of Ḫayānu).[57] Thus Kulamuwa pronounced a curse against anyone who might damage his inscription (Tropper 1993, K1: lines 15–16):

*yšḥt. rʾš. bʿl. ṣmd. ʾš. lgbr*
*wyšḥt. rʾš. bʿlḥmn. ʾš. lbmh. wrkbʾl. bʿl. bt*

may Baʿal Ṣemed,[58] (the god) of Gabbār, strike his head;
and may Baʿal Ḥammon, (the god) of Bamah, and Rākib-El, the lord of the house, strike his head.

While this may signal a difference in dynasty, it does not have to. Thus the precise line of succession is difficult to establish (Sader 1987, 175), and any reconstruction of the history of Sam'al is, to a certain extent, tentative (table 6.1).

The second challenge has recently been highlighted by Gilibert (2011, 58). She points out that the exposed architectural features from the excavations of the citadel could not have been in use all at the same time. Consequently, Koldewey attempted to sequence them (*AiS* 1:172–78). But there has been debate concerning the construction date and life histories of the single buildings (see Gilibert 2011, 58 n. 117), and as yet no general agreement has been reached. The general lack of documentation on the archaeological deposits in connection with the architectural features makes it impossible to reconstruct the stratigraphy of the excavated areas (Lehmann 1994, 106). Thus, the building phases have been reconstructed according to architectural relationships along with some dateable artifacts (Pucci 2008a, 15). However, there is significant disagreement, and it is not easy to resolve the differences as Gilibert's work demonstrates.[59] Where there is a datable artifact, however, it is possible to posit certain structures to certain periods. For example, the Kulamuwa orthostat with its structural connection with Building J allows attribution of this building's construction to this king. The styles of the reliefs can also contribute to determining the dates of construction for certain structures, but their value is also limited (Gilibert 2011,

57. E.g., Landsberger 1948, 47–51; Lipiński 2000a, 239.

58. Schmitz (2009, esp. pl. 1) has recently suggested that Baʿal Ṣemed "the mace" is to be connected with the relief from the temple of the Storm God of Aleppo that has the hieroglyphic Luwian symbol of a mace (Orthostat 7).

59. See especially her illustration of the different views. Gilibert 2011, 138 pl. 3.

Table 6.1. Kings of Sam'al/Yādiya

| Period | Kings of Sam'al/Yādiya | Kings of Assyria |
|---|---|---|
| Early History (920–870) | Gabbār (ca. 920/900–880) | Aššur-dān II (934–912)<br>Adad-nērārī II (911–891) |
| | *Dynastic Change?*<br>BMH/BNH (ca. 880–870) | Tukulti-Ninurta II (890–884) |
| The Dynasty of Ḥayyā' (870–815/810) | *Dynastic Change?*<br>Ḥayyā'/Ḥayyān (ca. 870/860–850) | Aššurnaṣirpal II (883–859)<br>Shalmaneser III (858–824) |
| | Ša'īl, son of Ḥayyā' (ca. 850–840) | |
| | Kulamuwa, brother of Ša'īl (ca. 840–815/810) | Šamšī-Adad V (823–811)<br>Adad-nērārī III (810–783) |
| | *Dynastic Change?*<br>King X? (ca. 815/810–810/805)? | |
| The Period of Local Autonomy (815/810–743) | Qarali (ca. 810/805–790) | Shalmaneser IV (782–773)<br>Aššur-dān III (772–755) |
| | Panamuwa I, son of Qarali (ca. 790–750) | |
| | Barṣūr (ca. 750–745?) | Aššur-nērārī V (754–745) |
| | Usurper (ca. 745–743) | Tiglath-pileser III (744–727) |
| Period of Assyrian Vassalage (743–711) | Panamuwa II, son of Barṣūr (743?–733/732) | |
| | Barrākib, son of Panamuwa II (733/732–713/711) | Sargon II (722–705) |

58–59). One must keep these challenges in mind as the polity's history is reconstructed.

### 6.3.1. Before the Establishment of the Aramean Polity

Ceramic finds and other small finds show that the site of Zincirli was originally settled during the Early Bronze Age.[60] It was also occupied during the Middle Bronze Age, in the period of the Amurrite Empire of Yamḫad based in Aleppo, though it is at the nearby site of Tilmen Höyük that a palace and temple have been excavated that have close parallels to Amurrite sites farther south (Marchetti 2006).

60. See Lehmann 1994. See earlier, Landsberger 1948, 12.

For a period in the middle of the seventeenth century, it came under the influence of the Hittites during the period of their first Syrian expansion (about 1650–1590 BCE, middle chronology) until the murder of Muršili I, when the Hittites were pushed back into Anatolia. In the middle of the second millennium, the Hurrian Empire of Mittani dominated this region and this probably remained the situation until Suppiluliuma I (ca. 1370). The Hittites, along with the Middle Assyrian kings destroyed the Mittanian Empire in northern Syria. Thus began the period of Hittite dominance that continued until the collapse of the empire ca. 1180, after which the Hittite successor states, particularly Karkamiš, flourished. For the early Iron Age, it would seem that the area that would become Sam'al would have initially been under "the Great King" of Karkamiš, and then perhaps under the dominance of Taita I (see ch. 3). Unfortunately, there is not really any information directly from the area.

The origins of the first-millennium kingdom of Sam'al are not known. Being surrounded by Hittite successor states, the Neo-Hittite/Late-Hittite artistic tradition is well-evident at the site of Zincirli. While the first-known monarch, Gabbār, bore a Semitic name, at least four of its other dynasts had Luwian names: Kulamuwa, Qarali, Panamuwa I, and Panamuwa II. In addition the high official Katumuwa also had a Luwian name. Even though there are more Aramaic inscriptions than Luwian inscriptions from within its territory, it is significant that perhaps the earliest is Luwian (Karaburçlu, ca. 925–850 BCE)[61] and one of the last is a hieroglyphic Luwian seal[62] of Barrākib, the last king of Sam'al (this is in addition to an Aramaic seal impression of this same king: Tropper 1993, 150: B7). In 2006 a hieroglyphic Luwian royal inscription fragment was discovered at Pancarlı Höyük (1 km from Zincirli; see note 40 above). It dates to the tenth or early ninth century and is perhaps from a Luwian dynasty that preceded the Arameans.

Since evidence is lacking for the Iron I period (1200–900 BCE), it is not known when exactly and how the Arameans came to power. Some scholars have concluded that, since the first significant architectural structures date from the later Iron Age II, the Yādiya/Sam'al was probably an insignificant

61. See above under Karaburçlu.

62. A gold signet ring set with black and white onyx bearing a four-sign inscription in hieroglyphic Luwian of Barrākib was excavated in small room J9 of Kulamuwa-building in 1902. See von Luschan, *AiS* 4:248 and pl. L; see Hawkins 2000a, 576 and pl. 329. The inscription reads: *pa* + *ra/i-ki-pa-sa* "(of) Parakipas," and can be dated to 732–720 BCE. Hawkins (2000a, 576) argues that the seal is important for establishing the correct vocalization of the final syllable in the name Barrākib since *-ki-* is the spelling. It is also important in demonstrating that the first syllable is *bar*, not *bir* or *bur*. See also Fales 1999: "son of the chariot rider, perhaps as an epithet for Ba'al."

place, certainly not yet a political center (Sader 1987, 174; Tropper 1993, 10). But since excavations have not really reached the Iron I levels, this is not based on actual data. Landsberger argued that it is archaeologically evident that a number of walls in the city citadel were established before Kulamuwa.[63] Again, this may be simply the result of the archaeological excavations which have not yet clarified the earlier historical situation.[64]

Two groups mentioned in the Kulamuwa Inscription (see fig. 6.4) have been understood as possible indicators of the two different population groups in the Sam'alian kingdom: *bʿrrm* and the *mškbm* (Tropper 1993, 39–45, K1: lines 10, 13–15). In the inscription, it is clear that these are polar opposites.

In the case of *bʿrrm*, there are two possible derivations: (1) *bʿr* "cattle" (as in Hebrew), and hence meaning of "ranchers," or perhaps "roamers"; or (2) *baʿrīrā* "cruel, savage, barbaric" (as in Syriac), and hence meaning "wild barbarians."[65] Thus, particularly if one follows the first possible derivation, it may be that this group referred to the dominant, mobile, immigrant Aramaic group in the land (as opposed to the *mškbm*).[66]

In the case of *mškbm*, there is agreement that this term is derived from *škb*, "to lie down," "settle." Thus this group is understood as the sedentary population.[67] While the two groups might represent the mobile pastoralist and sedentary components with the tribal entity of Bīt-Gabbāri itself, it is perhaps more likely that the two terms refer to the Aramean and Luwian (i.e., non-Aramean) population groups; and in this case, using obviously Semitic

63. Landsberger 1948, 40–41 and n. 95. Dion (1997, 106) argued that one cannot exclude that the city received its first fortifications and its first monuments before the arrival of the Arameans.

64. Casana and Herrmann (2010, 67) state: "It is notable that the best parallels for the Zincirli buildings seem to come from eastern areas, as this may lend support to the arguments of numerous scholars that Zincirli was settled by Aramaean peoples who moved west from their traditional homeland in the Euphrates Valley (e.g., Dion 1997; Lipiński 2000a). On tbe other hand, Schloen and Fink (2009, 9–11) argue that there is little reason to assume that Zincirli was occupied by Aramaean conquerors and that inscriptional evidence points instead to the development of a local West Semitic culture."

65. See the discussion in Swiggers 1983, 145–46. Lipiński (2000a, 236) prefers the first option *bʿr* (a *paʿlel* form) "to roam"; Tropper (1993, 45) prefers the second stating: "*bʿrrm* : Bezeichnung der zugewanderten aramäischen Bevölkerung von Y'DY/Sam'al; wahrscheinliche Vokalisation */baʿrīrīm/*, d.h. "die Wilden" (vgl. syr. *baʿrīrā*)"; see *DNWSI*, 185, s.v. *bʿrr*. Schmitz (2013, 76) suggests understanding *b* + *ʿrrm* "among the destitutes."

66. *COS* 2.30:148 n. 18. See Dion 1997, 253–54; 285–86.

67. See Swiggers 1983, 142–43; Lipiński 2000a, 236; Tropper 1993, 41, stating: Bezeichnung der einheimischen, nichtaramäischen Bevölkerung von Y'DY. Die Form ist wahrscheinlich als */muškabīm/* (G-Part. pass.) zu vokalisiern: "die Gelegten," d.h. "die Eingesessenen." See *DNWSI*, 701, s.v. *mškb*$_2$. Schmitz (2013, 74) offers the meaning "suzerains."

Fig. 6.4. The Kulamuwa Inscription (S 6579 © Staatliche Museen zu Berlin - Vorderasiatisches Museum, photo: Olaf M. Teßmer)

terms to designate them. The terms may not have had an inherent ethnic nuance, but in the context of Kulamuwa's time, in reality did. Clearly, there was significant disparity between the two groups with consequent tensions.

It is clear from his inscription that Kulamuwa made a special effort to gain the support of the *mškbm* that, apparently, worked:

> Before the former kings, the *Muškabīm* (the sedentary non-Aramean population) were living like dogs. But I was to some a father; and to some I was a mother; and to some I was a brother. Now whoever had never possessed a sheep, I made lord of a flock. And whoever had never possessed an ox, I made owner of a herd and owner of silver and lord of gold. And whoever from his childhood had never seen linen, now in my days wore byssos. And I took the *Muškabīm* by the hand, and they showed (me) affection like the affection of a fatherless child toward (its) mother (Tropper 1993, K1: lines 9b–13a).

Since no such effort was made to ingratiate himself to the *bʿrrm*, this probably indicates that Kulamuwa came from within their ranks (the mobile pastoralist Arameans, if the term *bʿrrm* is rightly understood). Moreover, Kulamuwa's curse formula demonstrates the ever-present potential for conflict between the two groups within his kingdom:

> Now whoever of my sons who will sit (reign) in my place and damages this inscription, may the *Muškabīm* not honor the *Baʿrīrīm*, and may the *Baʿrīrīm* not honor the *Muškabīm* (Tropper 1993, K1: lines 13b–15a).

Thus this portion of the inscription is a particularly informative window into the social composition of this small political entity.[68] This disparity that Kulamuwa claims to have resolved had clearly been a long-term problem that "the former kings" had not been able to deal with, and which had the potential to develop very quickly again.

Yet it is very evident that with the Aramean takeover the native Luwian culture did not become extinct by any means. There is evidence for the use of the Luwian language within Sam'al for almost two hundred more years (920–730) and the art and pantheon of Sam'al exhibit numerous Luwian links, not to mention the use of Luwian-derived personal names. The recently discovered Katumuwa *Grabdenkmal* confirms these Luwian cultural interconnections.

### 6.3.2. Early History of the Aramean Entity (920–870)

This is the period of the history of Sam'al before Assyrian campaigns. In his orthostat inscription,[69] Kulamuwa listed four of his predecessors: Gabbār, BMH (or BNH), his father Ḥayyā' and brother Ša'īl. The text puts it this way in a rather staccato form:

68. For discussion of the ethnicity issues, see Brown 2008.

69. Tropper 1993, 27–46 (K1); *KAI* 24; Donner and Röllig 1968, 30–34, 338; *SSI* 3:30–39; *editio princeps*: *AiS* 4:374–77.

Gabbār ruled over Yādiya,
but he achieved nothing.
BNH/BMH also (ruled over Yādiya),
but he achieved nothing.
And then my father Ḥayyā',
but he achieved nothing.
And then my brother Ša'īl,
but he achieved nothing.
But I am Kulamuwa, son of *TML* —
what I achieved (my) predecessors had not achieved.

All of his predecessors "did or achieved nothing (*bl . p'l*)." This is a common ancient Near Eastern literary topos/motif serving hyperbolically to heighten the presently ruling king over his predecessors.[70] The fact that the Assyrians call the kingdom Bīt-Gabbāri indicates that in their opinion Gabbār was very significant as the eponymous ancestor of the tribal entity (see pp. 46–48 and table 2.1).

Some scholars have taken Gabbār to have been Kulamuwa's great grandfather, but this assumes a straightforward genealogical linkage. As noted above, it is unclear, in fact, whether there was any familial relationship between Kulamuwa and the first two rulers. Beside the fact that no father-son relationship is spelled out for the first kings mentioned, a number of interpreters have taken the difference in protective deities mentioned at the end of the Kulamuwa inscription to be an indication of different dynasties (see p. 389 above).

The name Gabbār is a *qattāl* formation of the root *gbr* "to be strong," hence "hero." This is, of course, a West Semitic root, which could imply that this individual was Aramean, but not necessarily.[71] Gabbār is commonly dated to approximately 920/900–880 BCE. He would have been roughly a contemporary of Aššur-dān II (r. 934–912) and Adad-nērārī II (r. 911–891) of Assyria.[72]

70. Interestingly, see Ninurta-kudurrī-uṣur inscriptions for the topos (RIMB 2:297, S.0.1002.2, ii.27–29a). In fact, the accomplishments of the first building period would mitigate the claims (see pp. 396–97).

71. Lipiński's comment (2000a, 239) that "the name of Gabbār suggests that he was an Aramaean or North-Arabian chieftain" is misleading. There is no reason whatsoever to posit a North Arabian connection here.

72. Interestingly, and long overlooked, are the remains of a very fragmentary black, stone obelisk that Thompson discovered at Nineveh that shows traces of scenes in relief and inscriptions and that may be the remains of an obelisk of Adad-nērārī II similar in form to the Black or Rassam Obelisk of Aššurnaṣirpal II from Calah (RIMA 2:277–78, A.0.101.24); see Thompson 1937, 45 no. 12. One of the names that appears among the fragments is Gabbār; on another fragment appears the name Muquru, a Temanite leader.

In a study of the building phases at the site of Zincirli, Pucci (2008a, 15–80; 2008b) has assessed the structural relationships between the buildings. She has done this through a study of the local sequence of style of the orthostats (integral parts of these buildings) in order to establish the building phases on the acropolis of Zincirli. She has also utilized the inscriptions to aid in this study of sequencing of the architecture. She is able to identify three building periods.

Pucci dates the beginning of the first building period to the second half of the tenth century and its end to the last decades of the ninth (ca. 950–800 BCE)[73] based on the fact that:

> Kilamuwa in his inscription lists four kings before him. Therefore, if Kilamuwa was the one who constructed building K, the other structures, also attributed to this period, were possibly built by his ancestors. Considering that the style of the reliefs belonging to the structures of this period, according to Orthmann and Mazzoni, dates to the 10th century, we could consider the second half of the 10th century as the starting point of this building period.[74]

During this period, the citadel wall and outer double city wall were constructed.[75] She argues that the concentration on the defensive system suggests that there was an insecure political situation (Pucci 2008b, 546). While this may be the case, it is not a necessary conclusion.[76] What it certainly indicates is sufficient power and resources within the realm to accomplish the construction.

The citadel was divided between northeastern and northwestern complexes. The citadel had two gates (D and Q) that were decorated with orthostats and controlled access. Gate D served as the entrance onto the citadel, while the northwestern complex of the acropolis was accessed through Gate Q (comprised of a stone socle and flanking lion jambs).

Gate Q served as a demarcation point, marking the entrance to a separate large courtyard in the northwestern complex (designated by M + R). Stone stairs led up northwards to the columned porch of Building K and the

---

Based on the rough chronology, this Gabbār might well be the Gabbār of the Kulamuwa inscription, though obviously without more information, it is impossible to be certain. See Börker-Klähn 1982, no. 156–60 (photo, study); Kessler 1993–97; and Hunger 1999, 411.

73. Pucci 2008b, 547–48; see map on p. 554, fig. 2.

74. Pucci 2008b, 547–48; Orthmann 1971, Stilgruppe: Z I–II; and Mazzoni 1997b, 314.

75. See pp. 375–77 and fig. 6.2.

76. It is not uncommon for strong fortifications to be built in periods of peace and stability.

entrance to Building J. Both buildings had reception areas, dwelling and work areas, and bathrooms. The Building J can be identified as the palace of Kulamuwa since his Phoenician memorial inscription was found therein, as well as his inscribed Sam'alian Aramaic golden case. Kulamuwa reigned from around 840 to 810 BCE. Buildings L and Ab3 served as storage areas.

The northeastern complex (designated Ḫilāni I [HI]) was a large building located in the northeastern area (Pucci 2008a, 25–26). Since a grave was built near this structure, it is possible that the building had a religious significance, but this is far from certain, particularly since the grave was a later addition.

Schloen and Fink (2009a, 8) have commented on some of the difficulties in assigning dates to the constructions at Zincirli:

> It is not yet known precisely when the expansion and fortification of Sam'al took place, although the relatively shallow accumulation in the lower town (only 1.5–2 m) and the presence of only two or three main architectural phases argue against a date earlier than the mid-ninth century. As we have noted, the Neo-Hittite orthostats and sculptures could be much older, having been brought from another site, so we cannot rely on stylistic dating of this material based on comparisons to similar sculptures found at Carchemish and other Luwian sites, but must wait for the analysis of radiocarbon and ceramic evidence (currently in progress) in order to establish the chronology.

Thus they feel that while the "reconstruction of Sam'al is often attributed to Gabbār himself, in the late tenth or early ninth century," it could have been accomplished as late as "the reign of Kulamuwa in the latter part of the ninth century, in response to the Assyrian invasion under Shalmaneser III in 858 BCE, which occurred during the reign of Kulamuwa's father, Ḥayyā'—especially since the original royal palace of Sam'al is attributed to Kulamuwa in the Aramaic inscription of Barrākib commemorating Barrākib's construction of a new palace in the late eighth century."

However, in 858, Shalmaneser III chose not to attack the cities of Lutibu and Sam'al (see below). If these cities were easy targets without good defenses, it is highly doubtful that the Assyrians would pass on an opportunity to plunder them. During Kulamuwa's reign, he faces the significant challenge of the Danunians (Que)—a significant enough challenge that it required his "hiring" of the king of Assyria to remove the threat. Schloen's point is that the double wall was not built by Gabbār; it dates to a later time. If Kulamuwa was the one who constructed it, the likelihood is that this was part of this defense against the king of the Danunians. Kulamuwa likely built his palace after the Assyrian intervention; but it is difficult to imagine that the Assyrians would have permitted him, under these circumstances, to build really serious fortifications like the double outer wall.

It seems very likely that a 2.5 m tall basalt statue of a king should be identified with Gabbār (fig. 6.5),[77] yielding perhaps the earliest evidence for an ancestor cult at Sam'al. This statue was erected in front of the southeast wall of Building J, approximately 10 m northeast of Gate Q (fig. 6.3).[78] Building J has been identified as the palace of Kulamuwa because the orthostat that contains his Phoenician inscription[79] was discovered on the left side of the entrance to the vestibule of that building. The statue is older than Building J and comes from Stratum V.

Niehr and others[80] have suggested that the statue should be identified with Gabbār. While this cannot be absolutely proven, it seems likely based on two facts: (1) the kingdom was referred to by the name *Bīt-Gabbāri* by the Assyrians, indicating that kingdom's patronymic founder of the tribal entity was Gabbār;[81] and (2) the placement of the statue in connection with Building J where the Kulamuwa Inscription was found that mentions Gabbār indicates a continuity of a state-sponsored royal ancestor cult headed by Gabbār (Tropper 1993, K1: 2, 15).

The statue stood on a base on which a "kneeling hero" restraining two lions was portrayed. Due to the use of animal bases as pedestals for deity-statues, one can easily infer the "divine" status of this king. Moreover, there are three cup holes drilled into the top of the heads of the lions and the hero that served for the reception of libations.[82] Thus it appears that a state-sponsored ancestor cult was established for Gabbār. Finally, during this building period at Zincirli, the area in front of the statue (i.e., to the east of the palace

77. Wartke 2005, 29 fig. 28. This statue was originally interpreted as a weather god (Koldewey in *AiS* 2; von Luschan *AiS* 3), however, see now Bonatz 2000a, 157. While Felix von Luschan saw correspondences between this statue and the Hadad statue from Gerçin, it is particularly noteworthy that the headdress is different: Hadad wears a horned crown; Gabbār wears a tight-fitting, decorated cap, a *lupanni* (a small, tight-fitting cap worn on the head by kings in the Hittite tradition; see van den Hout 1994, 41 and n. 21).

78. The statue was discovered in the fifth excavation season (1902) and is today in the Altorientalische Museum Istanbul, Inv.-Nr. 7768. Concerning the precise foundation and erection site of the statue, see Jacoby in *AiS* 4:288–89 with fig. 194 and pl. LI; concerning the statue, see von Luschan *AiS* 4:362–69; Orthmann 1971, 69, 545 (Zincirli E/1) and pl. 62c–e (E/1); Niehr 1994, 58; Bonatz 2000a, 25–26, 76–78, 105–6, 150–51; Wartke 2005, 29 figs. 28 and 29a–b. Concerning Building J, see Naumann 1971, 413–17 with fig. 549.

79. Discovered in 1902: Vorderasiatisches Museum, Inv.-Nr. S 6579. Orthmann 1971, 545 (Zincirli E/2).

80. Niehr 2006, 114; Bonatz 2000b, 207 n. 52; Lipiński 2000a, 239.

81. Kurkh Monolith of Shalmaneser III: Grayson, RIMA 3:18, 23, A.0.102.2 ii.24, 83.

82. The cup holes in the two lion heads are 7 cm in diameter with a depth of 3 cm; the cup hole in the head of the hero is 5.5 cm in diameter with a depth of 2 cm. See Ussishkin 1975, 94–95 and fig. 14; Bonatz 2000a, 154; Niehr 2006, 114.

complex) was an open area that appears to have had a religious function connected to this ancestor cult (Pucci 2008a, 77; 2008b, 546). At the end of this Building period, the statue was ritually "buried" next to its base.[83]

Gate Q was not defensive in nature;[84] its main function was not to block but to regulate passage. The only figurative decoration at the gate were portal lions. Since the gate was in use for at least two centuries, the exposed basalt surfaces acquired a shiny patina, which the excavators found to be located particularly on the lion's socles, suggesting that people sat there on a regular basis and that Gate Q functioned as a place for assembly over a long time (Gilibert 2011, 75). Thus, the gate functioned as a liminal demarcation point, a meeting point, a powerful visual frame for the impressive stairs and the colonnade of Building K (Gilibert 2011, 75).

However, it would be a mistake to see this colossal statue as only an artifact of the royal ancestor cult at Sam'al. This had a powerful political message. Towering over the beholder at a highly visible, relatively accessible location on the exterior of the palace complex, it struck the viewer with a simple, yet powerful iconography that stimu-

Fig. 6.5. The statue of Gabbār? (photo courtesy of Dominik Bonatz)

83. This burial is proven by the fact that the overturned statue was surrounded by stones as though by the walls of a grave (Niehr 2006, 115; Jacoby in *AiS* 4:289 and pl. IL).

84. Jacoby in *AiS* 4:271.

lated deep reflections of political connectedness to the eponymous ancestor of the political entity of Bīt-Gabbāri. This colossal statue enjoyed a very special status, catalyzing beliefs and ritual behavior for generations of rulers. Its position outside the palatial complex, in an open space of relatively easy access—on the one hand, past the citadel gates, but on the other hand, still clearly outside the palace quarters—meant that the rituals connected with the statue had a public or semipublic nature and that they were performed in front of a crowd of spectators. Thus its location, its rhetoric and its age—by the end of the ninth century BCE, the statue had been "in use" already for four generations[85]—suggest that "the rituals it involved addressed a large, non-elite public familiar with the local monumental tradition and its ritual embedment" (Gilibert 2011, 83).

Gabbār's successor, who may or may not have been his son, poses an immediate difficulty. While the name is written *bnh* in line 3 of the Kulamuwa Inscription, the reading in line 16 is *bmh*.[86] Since *bnh* and *bmh* can hardly be explained as phonetic variants, either one or the other in line 3 or line 16 must be seen as a mistake of the stonemason (Tropper 1993, 32 and esp. pls. 6 and 7). Lipiński (2000a, 240) opts for the error in line 16, "because of its faulty engraving in line 16, where the two strokes of *nun*'s head parallel the upper part of the shaft instead of forming a triangle at its top." Consequently, he posits that "the name is likely to correspond to cuneiform ᵐ*Ba-ni-ú*, namely *Bānihu*, 'the builder,' with an archaic suffixed pronominal element *-hu* functioning as a demonstrative-determinative.

On the other hand, Tropper (1993, 32) feels that from the epigraphic viewpoint it is more likely that the error is in line 3 where the letter that is read as *n* can be considered an unfinished *m*. He also points out that the orthography speaks against reading *bnh*, since if the name is derived from the root *bny*, the Sam'alian orthography would expect a writing *bn*ʾ.[87] Finally, Tropper (1993, 32) argues that since the etymology of BM/NH is uncertain, it must remain open whether the *h* in the name has consonantal value or represents a *mater lectionis* for a long vowel /ā/. In any case, this ruler, BMH/BNH, who followed the eponymous founder of Bīt-Gabbāri must have ruled sometime between 880–870 BCE.

85. Gabbār, BMH/BNH, Ḥayyā', and Ša'īl/Kulamuwa (more or less the same generation).

86. Contra Lipiński 1974, 49; and Swiggers 1983, 136–37.

87. Tropper 1993, 32. He lists a number evidences for this, including this very root *lbn*ʾ "to build" in the Hadad Inscription (H: 13, 14).

Fig. 6.6. Sakçagözü chariot scene (VA 00971 © Staatliche Museen zu Berlin - Vorderasiatisches Museum, photo: Olaf M. Teßmer)

6.3.3. The Dynasty of Ḥayyā' (870–815/810)

The third king listed in Kulamuwa's Inscription is Ḥayyā'. This name is attested in Neo-Assryian cuneiform sources (Ambos and Fuchs 2000), which demonstrate that the full form of the name read: *Ḫayyān(u)* and is derived from the Aramaic root *ḥyy*. It is therefore a hypocoristic name consisting of the elements /*ḥayy*/, "He (the god) is alive," and a nominal suffix /*-ān*/.[88] Throughout this chapter, I will primarily use Ḥayyā'.

On account of the Assyrian inscriptions, it is known that Ḥayyā' was a contemporary of the Assyrian king Shalmaneser III (r. 858–824) and that he must have been on the throne of Sam'al a minimum of 858 to 853 BCE. The accession of Ḥayyā' was probably sometime between 870 and 860 BCE.[89]

The year 858 BCE was a watershed in Sam'al's history, for it was in this year that the kingdom first encountered the expanding Assyrian Empire. Shalmaneser III was in the midst of this initial campaign to bring down Bīt-Adīni. Part of his strategy[90] was to isolate Bīt-Adīni by defeating its western allies. Having forced the submissions of Kummuḫ and Gurgum, Shalmaneser III advanced into Sam'alian territory from the north and approached Lutibu (modern Sakçagözü), "the fortified city of Ḫayānu, the Sam'alite," just 21

88. Tropper 1993, 31. See also Zadok 1977, 158. Ḥayyā' is mentioned in K1: 1 *Ḥy* (defective spelling); in Kl: 3 and 9: *Ḥy'*; and K2: 3: *Ḥy* (defective spelling). The ' in *ḥy'* (line 3, 9) very likely represents a *mater lectionis* for the long vowel /ā/.

89. Landsberger 1948, 37 n. 82 (870 BCE); Lipiński 2000a, 247 (870 BCE); Sader 1987, 287 (860 BCE).

90. See discussion at §5.2.1, pp. 331–33, 342.

km northeast of Zincirli.[91] Here at Lutibu, Shalmaneser III faced his first coalition of western forces: "Ḫayānu, the Sam'alite, Sapalulme, the Patinean, Aḫuni, the man of Bīt-Adīni,[92] (and) Sangara, the Karkamišean."

While the coalition was defeated in this battle, its members regrouped for another battle. Lutibu was not besieged and captured, nor was the royal capital city of Sam'al (Zincirli); both were bypassed. Evidently, the Assyrians' aim was to reduce the military capacity of these western states in order to cut off support for Aḫuni, as well as to secure their tribute. However, it is also manifest that the fortifications of Sam'al must have been sufficient at this time to serve as a deterrent to the Assyrians; otherwise, it is hard to believe that they would not have taken advantage to gain easy plunder. Sometime later in this year, the coalition did, in fact, regroup, this time with double the number of allies to fight Shalmaneser at the battle of Alimuš/Aliṣir (see table 5.1). Once again, the Assyrians won this open-field battle; then they besieged and captured the city of Alimuš/Aliṣir, "the fortified city of Sapalulme, the Patinean."[93] For Ḥayyā', he had twice in one year fought the Assyrian military machine and lost.

The very next year (857) saw the Assyrian army back on the west side of the Euphrates in an attempt to further isolate Bīt-Adīni. After the battle of Dabigu, Shalmaneser III recorded the receipt of the tribute (*maddattu*) of four western kings including "Ḫayānu, the Sam'alian" ([m*ḫa*]-*ia-a-ni* KUR *sa-am-ʾa-la-a-a*). It seems that these western kings had failed to organize an anti-Assyrian coalition. This may have been partly due to the results of the engagements the previous year, but it is also evident that at this point they have adopted a wait-and-see policy. Aḫuni was the main target, and if his cities could resist successfully the Assyrian onslaught, there would be no need in expending any more of their own resources. However, with the capture of six of Aḫuni's cities culminating in Dabigu's seizure, the kings quickly brought their tribute in order to forestall any action against them by Shalmaneser III.

Yet, at this point (857), Sam'al's cities were intact. Undoubtedly, Ḥayyā' must have calculated his position, and paying tribute was a much better option. He may not have had a real choice, if the Sam'alian casualties were substantial in the previous year's battles. Nonetheless, while in Kulamuwa's Inscription he is credited with "achieving nothing," the reign of Ḥayyā' seems to have at least saved Sam'al's territory from complete ravaging.

---

91. See discussion above, pp. 386–87.

92. Aḫuni had already fought two open-field battles with the Assyrians earlier in the year: in the area of Til-Barsib and in the area of Paqarḫubuni.

93. RIMA 3:10, A.0.102.1, lines 64–80; 3:16–17, A.0.102.2, i.51b–ii.10a.

This policy of submission rather than resistance, was applied a few years later in 853, when Shalmaneser III records again the tribute paid by "Ḫayānu, man of Bīt-Gabbāri."[94] At this point, Shalmaneser has destroyed Bīt-Adīni, with the highly resistant Aḫuni being taken away captive; and Shalmaneser is aiming at another target: Hamath with all its allies. But the north Syrian states line up to pay their tribute, which included Ḥayyā'.[95]

Around 850 BCE, Šaʾīl, son of Ḥayyā', the brother of Kulamuwa, came to the throne. It appears that he had a smooth succession to the throne. The name Šaʾīl is West Semitic.[96] This being the case, Lipiński notes correctly that the Anatolian name of his brother Kulamuwa[97] does not prove a Luwian descent of the ruling dynasty, but either reflects the ethnically and linguistically composite nature of the population of Sam'al or simply implies that Kulamuwa's mother was of Luwian stock. She is perhaps mentioned in line 4 in order to distinguish Kulamuwa from Šaʾīl, who may have had a different mother.[98] Šaʾīl ruled roughly 850–840 BCE.[99]

Next, Kulamuwa "sat on the throne of his father" (ca. 840–815/810 BCE). As noted above, through his use of the topos of achieving what the ancestors had not, Kulamuwa presents himself in a quite positive light. Not even Gabbār, the eponymous ancestor of the polity (Bīt-Gabbāri), measured up to Kulamuwa. The alternating contrasts in the inscription between the past and the present allows Kulamuwa to portray himself in the most positive fashion.

94. RIMA 3:23, A.0.102.2, ii.82b–86a.

95. See §7.2.2.2.1.

96. For example, attested in Hebrew: *Šāʾûl*. See: Swiggers 1983, 137; Noth 1966, 257, no. 1294.

97. The name *Klmw* is undoubtedly Anatolian, comprising two elements, *kl* and *mw*. Starke (1990, 236 n. 806) understands the two elements as the Luwian components *Kl(n)mw* as Kulana-muwa, thus Kulamuwa, and defines the name as "die Wehrhaftigkeit des Heeres besitzend," that is, "possessing the fighting ability of the army"). Lidzbarski (1915, 223–24) suggested the vocalization of the *kl* element as *kila*; see also Lipiński 2000a, 234 n. 11 and Tropper 1993, 30; hence Kilamuwa. However, in the Cebel Ires Dağı inscription (*KAI* 287), the name *klš* occurs (*š* obviously is the nominative ending). See *COS* 3.55:137–38. The name is comparable to Kula/Κουλας. See Mosca and Russell 1987, 12.

98. Since Kulamuwa's father has already been given (Ḥayyā'), it does seem likely that whatever the reading of the name, it would be Kulamuwa's mother. However, that the name is Luwian is not proven. Lipiński (2000a, 242), reads it as *tmn*. The name has also been read as *tml*. See Young 1993; and Tropper 1993, 33. For a reading *tmʾ*, see Swiggers 1981, 2 n. 6; 1983, 138.

99. Šaʾīl was probably replaced, after a short reign, by Kulamuwa, before Shalmaneser's first campaign to Que in Year 20, i.e., 839, or less probably, at some time in the period between the first Que campaign and the fourth and last one (839–831). See Yamada 2000a, 199 n. 422; Lipiński 2000a, 242.

One of the obvious challenges to his success in outperforming his ancestors was his conflict with various surrounding kingdoms, especially "the Danunians" (i.e., Que). Either just before Kulamuwa's reign or at its beginning, the kingdom of Que exerted power over Sam'al. Kulamuwa's inscription puts it this way:

> The house of my father was in the midst of mighty kings; and each one stretched forth his hand to fight.
>
> But I was in the hand of the kings like a fire consuming the beard and like a fire consuming the hand.
>
> Now the king of the Danunians (*mlk . dn*[*n*]*ym*) was more powerful than I (or: too powerful for me),
>
> But I engaged (lit. "hired") against him the king of Assyria.
>
> A young woman was given for a sheep and a young man for a garment.

Thus, the dynasty of Ḥayyā'[100] was fighting for its very survival. While there were numerous "mighty kings" attacking Sam'al, it was "the king of the Danunians" who was the particular power that the Sam'alian dynasty could not overcome. At this time, the king of Que seems likely to have been Katiya (Katî of the Assyrian inscriptions).[101] Because the site of Sam'al (Zincirli) was located at the eastern exit of the main Amanus Pass (modern Fevzipaşa), it is not surprising that Que would desire to dominate this area, particularly as a means of preparation for an anticipated Assyrian attack. The Assyrian Annals of Shalmaneser III do not give the reason for the 839 campaign against Que. But in light of Kulamuwa's text, it would seem probable that Shalmaneser used the excuse of the "obligatory" protection of an Assyrian vassal as a pretext to march against Que.[102] As for the results for Kulamuwa of his "hiring" of the king of Assyria,[103] there were immediate economic

---

100. Since *bt . 'by* in this context refers to the dynasty of Ḥayyā', there is a hint that this is a different dynasty than that of Gabbār.

101. Commonly normalized as Katî. See Baker 2000b. However, the earliest writings of the name, along with comparative analysis, shows that the real stem of the name is Katiya-. See Younger 2009, 161–66. I favor the vocalization of the name of the *ktmw* inscription as Katumuwa, in part, because of the proximity of Karkamiš, but also because it seems that there was enmity between Que and Sam'al on more than one occasion.

102. Yamada 2000a, 199. For the protection of a protégée as a reason for war in the Assyrian royal inscriptions in general, see Oded 1992, 61–68.

103. See Liverani 1991; Lipiński 1974, 50. Cf. 2 Sam 10:6; 1 Kgs 15:18; 2 Kgs 7:6; and 2 Kgs 16:7.

benefits. While he credited his own work for this, the prosperity[104] that Kulamuwa brought to the disadvantaged *mškbm* was likely very much the result of the Assyrian king's intervention.

This prosperity made it possible for Kulamuwa to have an active building program in which he built Palace J.[105] Certainly Kulamuwa's proud boast that "what I achieved (my) predecessors had not achieved" is, in part, based on his construction projects.

The placement of Kulamuwa's orthostat was on the left side of the entrance into his palace (J). The slab, the inscription, and Building J date to the last part of Kulamuwa's reign or, if the orthostat was a posthumous work, immediately thereafter.[106] This orthostat (fig. 6.4, p. 397) utilized text, image, form and architectural setting in order to generate a single visual message (Brown 2008) to the elite of his kingdom. Rather than placing his orthostat in a very public place (like the location of the Gabbār statue), Kulamuwa's orthostat addressed only visitors who were entering the large reception room of his palace and thus was created for the courtly elite, the special few who would enter his court. While the nameless colossal statue outside the palace promoted the royal ancestor cult to create "national identity" through the widely known eponymous ancestor, "inside the royal compound, for the eyes of the few, the royal figure was given a name and became a multi-layered political locus, a testimony to a newly developed elite identity that developed further in the century to follow" (Gilibert 2011, 79).

Furthermore, the choice of language (Phoenician, not Luwian or Aramaic) and the emulation of an Assyrian style in the relief (especially evident in Kulamuwa's clothing),[107] which broke in a sense with the Karkamiš style, were part of an attempt to create a new discourse for both the Aramean elite

---

104. An object that should be mentioned is a small golden case that was incised with a seven-line dedication inscription of Kulamuwa to the deity Rākib-El (Tropper 1992, 50–53, K2; *KAI* 25). During the excavations of the palace of Kulamuwa, it was discovered in the debris from the building's destruction. The case is 6.7 cm long and 2.2 cm in the diameter. According to the traditional interpretation, it served as a case or "sheath" for the handle of a staff or a scepter. This was the interpretation of the excavator, F. von Luschan; see Andrae in *AiS* 5, pl. 47f–g. Galling (1950, 16) notes Andrae's doubt concerning this interpretation. However, Lemaire (1990) argues that it may have served as an amulet case.

105. This is the palace referenced by Barrākib. See Tropper 1993, B1: 17–18.

106. Gilibert (2011, 79 n. 135) observes: "Facing the Kulamuwa slab, at the right side of the main entrance, was an aniconic basalt orthostat of similar dimensions. Both orthostats were placed upon squared foundation socles, and both had two mortises on their top to receive a tenon and joint into the mud-brick wall. These features indicate that the orthostats were planned and erected together with the entrance walls. and not added at a later time."

107. Including the Assyrian *yā'uru* (i.e., *ayyaru*) bracelets on both wrists. See Hamilton 1998, 222; and Brown 2008, 345.

and the Luwian social substratum through "ethnically neutral" elements (Brown 2008, 346). Thus, through this work Kulamuwa attempted to meld the two disparate elements of his kingdom into a unity built on a policy of connectedness.

### 6.3.4. The Period of Local Autonomy (815/810–743)

Starting with the revolt in Assyria during the last part of Shalmaneser III's reign (826–824), there was a period of decline in Assyrian power that was the result of both internal and external factors. Within Assyria, there was an "inner crisis" (Liverani 2004b, 220), which was—to a certain extent—the result of the rapid expansion of the empire and particularly the internal structure installed by Shalmaneser for its administration. As the empire expanded, Shalmaneser III developed an administration that delegated power to various members of the Assyrian cabinet (e.g., the *turtānu*, "commander-in-chief") and the provincial governors. With this investment of power, some of these officials pursued their own independent political ambitions and personal advantages. Thus this period has been coined the "period of local autonomy."[108] However, there is no indication that during this period, especially in the time of Adad-nērārī III, that there was any disloyalty to the throne. If anything, there seems to be a clear indication of loyalty and gratefulness for the empowering on the part of those to whom it was given (Fales 2012b, 136–37). In any case, the period seems to have lasted for a little over eighty years (until the advent of Tiglath-pileser III in 745 BCE).

The initial decline that occurred with the revolt in Shalmaneser's last years continued under Šamšī-Adad V (r. 823–811). It was followed by a partial recovery under Adad-nērārī III (r. 810–783).[109] However, during his reign there were indications that the monarchy was not as powerful (e.g., the roles and power of his mother, Sammu-ramat [Semiramis] (see Bernbeck 2008) and the *turtānu*, Šamšī-ilu[110]). But then, under Adad-nērārī's three sons, there was again a general weakness in Assyrian power. From a sys-

108. Brinkman uses this designation for the period in both Assyria as well as Babylonia. See Brinkman 1968, 218–19; 1984. For Sam'al, see Dion 1997, 108.

109. Oded (1998, 32) puts it well in these terms: "Adad-nērārī III ascended the throne when the kingdom of Assyria was politically unstable. Control of the lands west of the Euphrates had slipped out of Assyrian hands in the final days of Shalmaneser III. Adad-nērārī III embarked on a rigorous policy of restoring the Assyrian kingdom. He regained control over the territories which had been under Assyrian suzerainty under his ancestors, broadening the imperial borders and exacting tribute from countries located near and far. And indeed, his reign marks the recovery of the realm, expressed in military endeavours and building enterprises."

110. See §5.3.

temic standpoint, these monarchs were either content to, or not able to, do more than hold formal suzerainty over the states of northern Syria, not interfering unless they acted against Assyrian interests. Thus the strong, cohesive political entity represented in the reigns of Aššurnaṣirpal II and Shalmaneser III became geographically fragmented with various districts being ruled by a select few "powerful men" who received their powers from the king. Millard (1983, 106) has suggested that these empowered men of the Assyrian provinces might have been members of local princely houses who had accepted Assyrian suzerainty and remained loyal to their conditions of vassalage. Hence they could be referred to as *šaknu* "governor" in Akkadian as well as *mlk* "king" in Aramaic.[111] On the other hand, a number of these men were eunuchs that bore Assyrian names and show clear ties to the elite of the kingdom. Nonetheless, the apparent weakness of Assyria, particularly between 800 and 745, is partially belied by some limited campaigns against Aramean states on several separate occasions, and by Assyria's role in determining the boundary between two of these polities.[112]

Externally, on Assyria's northern border, there was a corresponding "period of the ascendency of the kingdom of Urartu/Biainili" (ca. 830–708 BCE)[113]—certainly a contributing factor to the demise of Assyrian power. Thus, for example, the Urartian king Argišti I conducted a military campaign against the land of Parsua in the Zagros region around 784–783 BCE (approximately forty years before the accession of Tiglath-pileser III).[114] After this Urartian campaign, certainly Parsua entered into the Urartian sphere of influence, very likely as a tributary state. It is entirely understandable that Tiglath-pileser III's action against Parsua in his second *palû* was a first successful step in denying military support to Urartu and to stabilize in pro-Assyrian terms the political landscape of the central Zagros region (Lanfranchi 2003, 100).

At this same time in the Levant, there was a renewed independence among the Aramean political entities of the region. In a number of respects, this was a period in which the polities of the Levant, including many of Aramean states, flourished, as manifest especially in Aram-Damascus and Arpad/Bīt-Agūsi.

---

111. Something illustrated in the early Tell Fakhariya Stela (see above discussion under Gōzān, §4.3.2, esp. pp. 261–66).

112. See chs. 7 and 8. For further discussion, see Blocher 2001; also Millard 1992a; Dion 1995b; 1995c; Grayson 1993, 1994, 1995, 1999.

113. "The earliest inscriptions in this kingdom appeared around 830 BC." See Zimansky 2006, 257 and n. 1 which delimits the usage of "Biainili."

114. The expedition of Argišti I to B/Parsua is celebrated in his "Horhor" inscription from Van (König 1955, 91, no. 80 §5, Kol. iii.12–13).

All of this had significance for the small kingdom of Sam'al, as well as the other kingdoms of north Syria. After the reign of Kulamuwa, there is uncertainty about who the next king was and whether there was a dynastic change or not (Tropper 1993, 13). One of Kulamuwa's sons should have ascended the throne of Sam'al, but there is no information.

According to the Hadad inscription, Panamuwa I was the son of a king whose name is written QRL. This name appears to be non-Semitic[115] (Panamuwa's name is Anatolian, see below). The hieroglyphic Luwian name ${}^{I}$*ha+ra/i-li-sa* "Harali" occurs in Cekke, Inscription 2 §17b (Hawkins 2000, 145), and is likely derived from *harali-* "shield." This would yield "Qarali" in Aramaic transcription.[116]

Thus, if there were a king before Qarali, possibly a son of Kulamuwa, his likely reign would have been roughly 815/810–810/805. Qarali might have reigned ca. 810/805–790. On the other hand, Qarali may have reigned 815/810–790. We simply do not know for sure. However, it would seem that, based on the relative chronology, Qarali would have been the unnamed "king of Sam'al with his army" (*wmlk . šm'l . wm[ḥnt]h*) who joined the other kings allied against Zakkur, king of Hamath and Lu'aš, in besieging Ḥaḏrak mentioned in the Zakkur Inscription (796 BCE).[117]

Pucci (2008b, 548) argues that the first building period came to an end with "a partial destruction" and that a different political situation seems to have caused the break with the consequent change to the second building phase. The evidence for this partial destruction is attested, in Pucci's opinion, by the ritual burial of five statues of lions, along with some female figurines and bone knives, in a pit between Gates D and E, and the apparent ritual burial of the Gabbār statue.[118] According to Orthmann's analysis (1971, 64–68), three of the lions are of an older style than the other two. Pucci understands the older lions to date to the late tenth century; the two younger lions date to the end of the ninth century, giving the date for the "partial destruction" (Pucci 2008a, 21; 2008b, 548). Thus she links this "partial destruction" to the Assyrian campaigns against the rebellious north Syrian

115. On the right track, Lipiński (1994, 204 n. 5) vocalized the name as Qarli, based on Laroche 1966, 61 (no. 305; *Há+r-li-s*). Other suggestions are apparently based on Anatolian names of the Hellenistic and Roman periods: Tropper (1993, 60): "Qurala"; and Wartke (2005, 59, 90): "Qurila."

116. The *h/q* interchange is well documented. See Yakubovich 2010.

117. *KAI* 202:7. Numerous interpreters have posited this. Landsberger 1948, 60 n. 152; Sader 1987, 175; Dion 1997, 137; Lipiński 2000a, 242–43.

118. She states: "Five statues of lions were found lying on their side in a 1.5m thick layer of ash. Next to each statue a stone bowl was found.... The ash around them and the bowls near their heads witness that a ritual took place in this area.... This tradition of burying was also employed with the Hadad (*sic*: Gabbār) statue" (Pucci 2008b, 548).

kings (described as the "eight kings of Ḫatti") under the leadership of Attār-sumkī, son of Abi-rāmu, of Arpad in the days of Adad-nērārī III (805–804 BCE, or perhaps 803–802 BCE).

This campaign in which the Assyrians fought Attār-sumkī and the "eight kings" at the battle of Paqarḫubuni is usually dated to 805 BCE.[119] Paqarḫubuni is located approximately 60 km east of Sam'al, and some scholars have suggested that Sam'al might have been one of the "eight" allies of Attār-sumkī.[120]

However, there are two problems for this reconstruction. First, it is not known if, in fact, Sam'al was in the alliance in 805 against Assyria. Kummuḫ certainly was not, and perhaps Sam'al, which had been and would be a vassal, did not rebel. If KARKAMIŠ A24a §§6–10[121] relates to Adad-nērārī III's campaign against Attār-sumkī, then perhaps Karkamiš may have been part of the eight-king alliance. A more likely context for some kind of military action against Sam'al might be found in the Zakkur Inscription, where Sam'al is definitely listed as a participant in the war against Hamath and Luǵath, with the besieging of the city of Ḥadrak (Ḫatarikka) in 796 BCE, which brought about the intervention of Adad-nērārī III.[122]

Second, while the three older lions are in the "Zincirli I" style and may date to the late tenth century, in her recent study, Gilibert (2011, 70) dates the two later lions to the "Zincirli IV" style (711–670 BCE).[123] If Gilibert is correct, this means that the "partial destruction" does not date to the end of the ninth century, but to the end of the eighth or the beginning of the seventh century, in other words, to the destruction of Zincirli that took place between

119. See discussion in §8.2.3.

120. For example, Grayson states: "The composition of this alliance may be surmised from later similar groupings, and probably included (besides Arpad), Que, Unqi, Gurgum, Sam'al, and Melid, and excluded Kummukh and Carchemish" (Grayson *CAH* 1982:400).

121. Hawkins 2000, 133–39. The inscription of Yariri/Kamani (ca. 800 BCE) refers to the Assyrian king carrying off Halabean Tarḫunza (the Storm God of Aleppo).

122. See §7.2.3. A shield garnish may come from this period at Zincirli (Younger 2007c, 143; Gubel 2012).

123. Gilibert (2011, 72) gives this history of the lions in the pit: (1) At the end of the tenth century BCE, five basalt portal lions were set up in a passageway. Since the portal lions always go by twos, we must assume the existence of a *sixth lion* (emphasis mine) that has not been found or that has been destroyed. (2) At the end of the eighth–beginning of the seventh century BCE, {700 BCE} the above-mentioned passageway (or what remained of it) was dismantled and the portal lions removed and reused in a new passageway. The layout of the new gate must have been similar to the older one in order to accommodate the lions. In the course of this building phase, two of the five (six) portal lions, presumably designed to occupy a prominent position, were recarved in the style of the age. (3) Following the destruction or dismantlement of the second passageway, the five lions were ritually buried in the pit in front of Gate E.

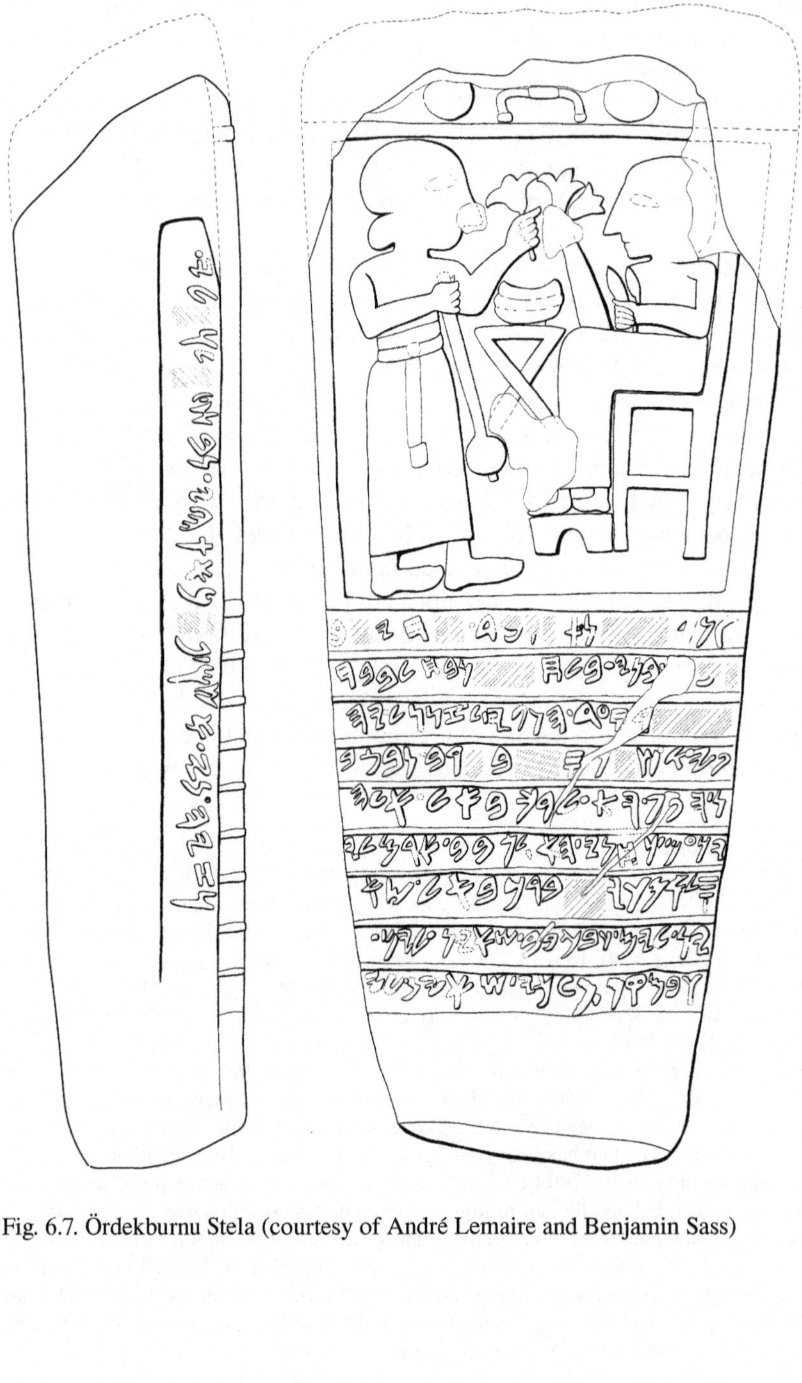

Fig. 6.7. Ördekburnu Stela (courtesy of André Lemaire and Benjamin Sass)

676 and 671/70, which must have taken place before the erection of a stela by Esarhaddon in 671.

More definitely from this period of local autonomy is a *Grabdenkmal*, which may have belonged to a female of the royal family. This long-known and neglected mortuary stela with a banquet scene comes from Ördekburnu (20 km [12 mi.] south–southwest of Zincirli), and has recently been studied afresh by Lemaire and Sass (see fig. 6.7).[124] Although it is in a poor state of preservation, the relief and inscription appear to date to 820–760 BCE and yield some important data (Lemaire and Sass 2013, 131). The fragmentary text reveals that this was a *Grabdenkmal* of someone in the royal family of Sam'al. Four things point to this conclusion: (1) the use of the term *ḥlbbh* "domain, succession"[125] found especially in the Hadad Inscription where Panumuwa I credits the deities with giving him "the scepter of dominion" (*ḥṭr . ḥlbbh*);[126] (2) the use of the symbol of the yoke at the very middle of the top of the stela which is the symbol for the dynastic protective deity Rākib-El; (3) this dynastic deity, Rākib-El, is explicitly mentioned twice in the Ördekburnu Stela (lines 5 and 7); and (4) the animal sacrifice for the deceased is to be made in the "royal necropolis" (*mqm . mlky*, line 9).[127]

Above the banquet scene, there are three symbols standing in a row (there may have been others, but none are preserved). These three are badly worn. Lipiński (2000a, 233–34) interprets these as hieroglyphic Luwian signs (see also Laroche 1960, xxviii; Tropper 1993, 6). However, no reading of these signs as hieroglyphic Luwian is offered. According to Lemaire and Sass (2013, 74), they do not appear to be hieroglyphic Luwian. Lidzbarski (1915, 3:195) interpreted the symbol on the left as the lunar crescent and disk; the symbol on the right as the solar disk. The center symbol he identified with the yoke of Rākib-El as in the Barrākib inscription 1, although he guessed that it represented Rašap. Lemaire and Sass (2013, 74) interpret the center symbol as the yoke of Rākib-El, which is undoubtedly correct (it is the best preserved of the three). The symbols on the left and the right appear to be disk-shaped. In the iconography from ancient Sam'al, the sun god, Šamaš, appears always to be represented by a winged solar disk, never a simple disk with radiant lines drawn inside it. Lemaire and Sass admit that they cannot see a crescent and disk in the left symbol and the right symbol may have had

---

124. Lemaire and Sass 2012, 2013. *Editio princeps*: Lidzbarski 1915, 3:192–206.

125. *DNWSI*, 373. The CAL suggests *ḥlp* + *bh* *ḥᵉlēbbāh*?

126. Hadad Inscription: lines 3, 9, 10, 12, 13, 19.

127. Lemaire and Sass (2012) give two additional indications of the owner of the stela being royal; however, these are not compelling (as they admit), and I am not convinced.

something inside it, though now worn away.[128] The two most likely symbols, based on analogy with other Sam'alian materials, are a lunar crescent and disk (the moon god Śahr/Sîn of Harran), and a circle with five-pointed star (like Barrākib inscription 1), possibly symbolizing Rašap.[129]

The relief, which is contained within a carved out rectangular field, shows a two-figure banquet scene with a crossed-legged table in between. The left figure stands; the right figure is seated with feet on a footstool. The seated figure on the right is holding two spindles in the left hand,[130] a typical motif of females in *Grabdenkmäler*, as seen in the Karaburçlu Stela[131] and the Örtülü Stela.[132] In fact, the women in all three of these monuments are pictured on the right side of the relief facing left. Beside the deity Rākib-El, one other deity is mentioned twice in the inscription: the Karkamišean goddess Kubaba. Hence, the combination of spindles and the mention of Kubaba signals important things in Syro-Hittite art. Recently, Rova has rightly observed:

> On some Syro-Hittite reliefs, the general appearance of Kubaba and of human women can be considerably similar (they are shown in the same position, wear similar garments, and hold the same mirror in one hand). We probably have here an intentional ambiguity, whose aim is to visually suggest some form of connection with the divine (if not of proper divinization) of the deceased woman, and at the same time, her quality of being, like Kubaba, a "lady." The ambiguity is, however, not pushed to the point of making these figures identical to each other: this message is conveyed, among other (e.g., by the lion on which Kubaba's chair is resting), by the spindle and distaff which, in the human lady's hand, appear in the place of Kubaba's pomegranate (or poppy capsule). On the other hand, through their chthonic associations, spindle and distaff underscore the funerary meaning of these scenes.[133]

---

128. My students, Scott Booth and A. D. Riddle, have personally inspected the stela in Istanbul (May, 2010) and feel that two disks on either side of the the yoke are indeed present. I thank them for their photos that aided me in my study.

129. Note that the Tell Sifr Inscription mentions both Rašap and Kubaba. See Michelini Tocci 1962.

130. Lemaire and Sass 2012; 2013, 68. Also Bonatz (2000a, 79) interprets the figure in the Ördekburnu Stela to be a woman holding a spindle.

131. Altorientalische Museum Istanbul, Inv.-Nr. 7729. See Orthmann 1971, 487 (Karaburçlu 1), pl. 14d; Darga 1992, fig. 299; Bonatz 2000a, 19, C 32, pl. XIV; Hawkins 2000, 276, pl. 127. It contains an inscription in hieroglyphic Luwian, although only a few words are readable; thus the content is unclear. The relief and inscription can be dated on stylistic and paleographic grounds to ca. 925–850 BCE (Bonatz 2000a, 19).

132. Gaziantepe Museum, Inv.-Nr. 5600; basalt: height 0.56 m; width: 0.90 m; depth 0.50 m. See Bonatz 2000a, 19, C 26, pl. XIII; Kalaç 1975, 188–89, pl. XLIII, fig. 10.

133. Rova 2008, 563. See also Bonatz 2000a, 83–84.

Lemaire and Sass feel that the evidence converges to indicate that the deceased, whose name is partially preserved in line 10, beginning with the element "Piya-" (*py-*),[134] was a woman in the royal family: a queen or wife or mother of the king. The person standing on the left in front of her, holding a mace,[135] is perhaps her son. Of course, it could also be her husband.

Finally, they note that the inscription suggests that the stela was originally erected in the royal necropolis of the kings of Sam'al. During the reign of Panamuwa I, a royal necropolis was located Gerçin, 7 km northeast of Zincirli.[136] However, this necropolis is more than 20 km from Ördekburnu. Therefore, Lemaire and Sass speculate that there was another, perhaps earlier royal necropolis that the Ördekburnu stela is referring to that is closer to Ördekburnu.[137]

Panamuwa I, son of Qarali, ruled Sam'al ca. 790–750 BCE. He was the contemporary of three Assyrian kings: Adad-nērārī III (r. 810–783); Shalmaneser IV (782–773) and Aššur-dān III (772–755). None of these, however, mention Panamuwa, and it is very likely that Sam'al enjoyed a degree of independence from Assyria that it had not been available prior. Thus Panamuwa I reigned in the very heart of the period of local autonomy.

His name is Anatolian. In his analysis of the hieroglyphic Luwian feminine name, [(f)]Panamuwati, Zehnder has recently demonstrated the meaning of Panamuwa.[138] The initial component *pana-* is probably just a late allomorph of No.21 Luwian *puna* "every, all."[139] The second component *-muwa* seems to be something like "reproductive power, fertility, abundance," a more general "might, power" is likely in compound names (Younger 2009, 160 n. 5). Thus the two components, Pana-muwa, would yield a meaning of "(having) all the might."

---

134. It is very possible that the name is simply Piya. See, e.g., [f]*Piya* BOR 9 "gift," (which is probably a reduction of a double root name like [(f)]Kupapiya as in the SHEIZAR inscription, or Boğ./hier. [f]Ḫepapiya ([f]Ḫepa-SUM) NH 365. See Zehnder 2010, 89–90. While masculine names with the Piya- component are attested, the spindles seem to make it likely that this is a woman.

135. Is this a *ḥṭr* "mace-scepter"? Such a mace-scepter is mentioned at Zincirli.

136. Others have suggested that the royal necropolis was based here because this is where Panamuwa I erected the statue of Hadad (according to Hadad, line 14).

137. One could think of the tell of Karapınar Höyük or that of Karapınar Mezarlık. The latter, located about 2 km from Ördekburnu, may have been the origin of the stela.

138. Zehnder 2010, 240–41. [I]*pa-na-mu-wa/i-ti-(i-)sa* Boybeypınarı 1 und 2 passim (Hawkins 2000a, 336–37). For the occurrences of the name in cuneiform sources, see Fuchs 2002.

139. Zehnder 2010, 240–41. He notes importantly: "Ein analoges Verhältnis besteht zwischen *[m]*Punamuwa* ([m]*Puna*-A.A) NH 1050 einerseits und dem Namen zweier Könige von Samal im 8. Jahrhundert v.Chr., Enkel und Grossvater, [(m)]*Panamuwa* NH 927 (Reallex. 10, 293b) andererseits."

Panamuwa I seems to have had a smooth succession to the throne as indicated in the text of the colossal statue of Hadad[140] erected Gerçin. The statue was intended to mark Panamuwa I's grave (along with a statue of Panamuwa himself which has not been recovered).[141] The inscription identifies the statue as the god Hadad (Tropper 1993, H1; *KAI* 214). This is the only statue of a deity found in the land of Sam'al thus far. Panamuwa I credits the deities with his accession:

> The gods Hadad and El and Rašap and Rākib-El and Šamaš supported me. And Hadad—and El and Rākib-El and Šamaš and Rašap—gave the scepter of dominion (*ḥṭr . ḥlbbh*) into my hands ... And I, Panamuwa, reigned also on the throne of my father. And Hadad gave into my hands a scepter of dominion (*ḥṭr . ḥl*[*bbh*]) (H1: lines 2–3a, 8–9a).

Furthermore, the inscription depicts his reign as long, happy, and prosperous, and does not allude to any external troubles: "And in my days also Yādiya ate and drank," and "whatever I asked from the gods of the land they gave me" (H1: line 9b, 12b). While there was an Assyrian campaign to the Amanus Range ("Cedar Mountain") in 775 BCE (Millard 1994, 39, 58), there is every indication that this was a peaceful expedition to cut down cedar trees. Thus it would appear that Panamuwa I reigned over Sam'al at perhaps the time of its greatest peace and prosperity.

However, while Panamuwa's reign was peaceful and prosperous, it seems that Panamuwa anticipated problems in his succession. In a passage that is reminiscent of the Hittite composition "The Proclamation of Telipinu" (*COS* 1.76), with its interest in the shedding of royal blood and procedures given to deal with such, Panamuwa declares:

> Whoever of my house seizes the scepter in Yādiya and sits on my throne and reig[ns in my place], [may he not] stretch his hand with the sword against [ ] of my [hou]se [either out of] anger or out of violence; may he not do murder, either out of wrath or out of [ ]; and may no one be [put to death], either by his bow or by his word [or by his command] (Tropper 1993, 86–87; H: 24b–27a).

140. The Hadad statue (VA 2882) was discovered at Gerçin (7 km northeast of Zincirli) in 1890. Today it is in the Vorderasiatisches Museum in Berlin. The present height of the statue is 2.85 m (originally about 4 m); in the center, the circumference is 2.36 m; and on the lower part, it is 2.94 m.

141. The inscription's contents are a very important witness to the royal ancestor cult at Zincirli.

Unfortunately, his edict went unheeded. According to the inscription written on the lower part of the statue of Panamuwa II[142] erected by his son Barrākib, there was trouble in the reign of Barṣūr, the father of Panamuwa II. Barṣūr,[143] who probably reigned ca. 750?–745?, was murdered in a coup d'état that also eliminated "seventy" of Panamuwa's brothers. Panamuwa himself barely escaped.[144]

There is a supposed Sam'alian Aramaic seal of an official of Barṣūr.[145] The text reads: *lʿzbʿl ʿbd brṣr* "Belonging to 'Ozba'al, the servant of Barṣūr." However, the authenticity is doubted (Hawkins 2006–8, 604). Clearly the personal name 'Ozba'al is Phoenician, which seems very odd for a high functionary at Sam'al at this time.[146]

A contemporary of Barṣūr was the Assyrian king, Aššur-nērārī V (754–745 BCE), who is perhaps best known for his treaty with Mati'-'El (ᵐ*ma-ti-i'*-DINGIR), son of Attār-sumkī II, king of Arpad.[147] The treaty date is lost, but should probably be dated to 754.

With the power that Arpad/Bīt-Agūsi had in the region at this time, it is natural to wonder if this usurpation was purely internal, or whether the

---

142. The statue was discovered in 1888 (the first excavation season of the German expedition) at the spring of Tahtalı Pınarı (2 km northeast of Zincirli). Only the torso of a king dressed in a tasseled garment and laced shoes was preserved. It may have had an original height of approximately 3.50 m, but today only 1.54 m remains. The statue contains an inscription in raised script. See Tropper 1993, 98–139 (P); *KAI* 215). Apparently, it was originally erected at the royal necropolis at Gerçin not long after the death of Panamuwa II by his son Barrākib, though at some point not long before its discovery in 1888, it was transported to Tahtalı Pınarı to mark a recently dug grave there. Today it is in the Vorderasiatisches Museum.

143. Tropper 1993, 102. The second component *ṣr* may be a theophoric; hence, *brṣr* "Son of *ṣūr* (the Rock)." Note the Hebrew personal name פְּדָהצוּר "Ṣūr ('the Rock') has ransomed" (Num 1:10).

144. Tropper 1993, 106–9, P: 2b–5a. There is no basis for the proposal by Margalit to merge the two different Panamuwa's into one (i.e., Panamuwa I and Panamuwa II were the same person) and to have this Panamuwa murder his father Barṣūr and brothers. His interpretation is based on a highly doubtful restoration in P5, a misinterpretation of the events relating the murder of Barṣūr, and an ignoring the clear differences between the Hadad and Panamuwa Inscriptions. Margalit 1994a, 1994b, 1994c. See also Weszeli (2003–5, 293), although he appeals to the seal of the servant of Barṣūr (whose authenticity is very doubtful, see above) as an argument against Margalit's proposal.

145. Deutsch and Heltzer 1995, 74–76, fig. 74. See also Lemaire 2001, 187 and fig. 1; and Lipiński 2000a, 243.

146. While the choice of the Phoenician language by Kulamuwa for his inscription is understandable for the reasons detailed above, evidence for Phoenician personal names in this region seems to be lacking, and so caution is best exercised on this matter.

147. SAA 2:8–13, 2.i.7′, etc.

usurper was backed by Arpad. The revolt in Kalḫu in 745 BCE may have stimulated various regional actions. Unfortunately, at present, we cannot know.

### 6.3.5. Period of Assyrian Vassalage (743–711)

The usurper probably reigned only a short time (ca. 745–743), since Panamuwa II was able to get Assyrian support to regain his throne. This was likely coordinated with the Assyrian action against Arpad by Tiglath-pileser III. Mati'-'El, king of Arpad, had instigated a revolt against Assyria in 743. He was joined by Sarduri of Urartu (Biainili), Sulumal of Melid (Malatya), Tarḫu-laru of Gurgum and the land of Kummuḫ. Although Mati'-'El appears as the subordinate partner in both the treaty with Aššur-nērārī V and the Sefire treaty (see §8.2.6), it is clear that Arpad/Bīt-Agūsi was the leading power of northern Syria—"the Aram." Allied with Urartu, it appears as the moving force behind the opposition to Assyria. The alliance was severely defeated by Tiglath-pileser III.[148]

As a result of the Assyrian intervention, Panamuwa II,[149] the son of Barṣūr, came to the throne in 743, or possibly a year or two later. The usurper's reign was characterized by terror and destruction in Sam'al in which many suffered—"filling prisons," "ruining numerous cities," and destroying the economy—at least this is Panamuwa's version (P: lines 4–5). The turning point is interestingly described:

> Then my father, Pana[muwa, son of Ba]rṣūr, brought a gift to the king of Assyria. And he made him king over the house of his father. And he killed the stone of destruction (*'bn . šḥt*) from the house of his father (P: lines 6b–7a).

With his restoration to power, Panamuwa reversed the usurper's work and brought peace and prosperity once again to the land: releasing the captives, bringing cheap prices and abundance to Yādiya.

> And it abounded with wheat and barley and ewe and cow in his days. And then [the land] ate [and drank[150] … ] The price was cheap (*zlt. mwkrw*).[151]

148. Yamada and Tadmor, RINAP 1:84–85, 35, i.21′–27′a; Tadmor 1994 Iran Stela B 21′–27′a.

149. For the meaning of the name, see above.

150. Compare H: 9b: *wbymy gm 'bl wšt' y'dy* "And in my days also Yādiya ate and drank" (Panamuwa I).

151. Concerning the motif of "ideal prices" in Panamuwa's day as compared to the previous depressionary conditions in *Y'dy*, see Hawkins 1986, 93–102; and Younger 1986, 96–98.

His loyalty is seen in that he is listed as a payer of tribute in the annals of his overlord in 738 BCE.[152] According to the Panamuwa inscription, Panamuwa was esteemed by his fellow kings and he was an ardent military supporter of Tiglath-pileser III, running at the wheel of his lord's chariot. Hence, "[to] his territory his lord Tiglath-pileser, the king of Assyria, [added] cities from the territory of Gurgum" (P: lines 14b–15a). Just before this statement, there are a few sentences that have caused some uncertainties. The text reads:

> [*wrṣ* .] ⁽¹³⁾*bglgl* . *mrʾh* . *tgltplsr* . *mlk* . *ʾšwr* . *mḥnt(?)* . *ʾw* . *mn* . *mwqʾ* .
> *šmš* . *wʿd* . *mʿrb* . *ʾ*[*w* .] *mn* … [ca. 19 signs] … ⁽¹⁴⁾ *rbʿt ʾrq* .
> *wbnt* . *mwqʾ* . *šmš* . *ybl* . *mʿrb* .
> *wbnt* . *mʿrb* . *ybl* . *mw*[*qʾ* . *š*]*mš* .
> *wʾb*[*y* . *ʿml* . *mn* . *kl* . *mlky* . *kbry* (?)]

> [And he ran] at the wheel of his lord,[153] Tiglath-pileser, king of Assyria, (in) campaigns from the east to the west [and from the north to the south, over] the four quarters of the earth.
> And the population (*bnt*) of the east he brought to the west;
> and the population (*bnt*) of the west he brought to the east.
> And [my] father [profited more than all other mighty kings[154]].

The term *bnt* translated "the population" is literally "the daughters." Although the majority of commentators understand it in this way, it is not without its problems. In the first place, *bnt* designating "daughters" would refer exclusively to the female population of a country or a city (which can hardly be the meaning here). However, it seems that *bnt*, "daughters" should simply be understood as a synecdoche for the whole population.

But a second problem is more difficult. Tropper (1993, 122) notes that it is historically not demonstrable that the Assyrian client kings were ever authorized to perform deportations. One way of explaining this would be to see this applying only when the client king functioned as an Assyrian army commander under the Assyrian king's orders. Donner and Röllig (1968, 229) suggest that perhaps the Assyrian client kings imitated the Assyrian monarch by doing smaller-scale deportations within their own lands. However, Tropper (1993, 122) feels that this is not at all likely.[155] The land of Sam'al was small.

152. Tadmor 1994, 87:4 n. 3 and elsewhere, see Lipiński 2000a, 244, n 79.

153. Cf. Bar-Rakib 1:8–7. Cf. 1 Sam 8:11; 2 Sam 15:1; 1 Kgs 1:5.

154. Tropper's suggested restoration based on Bar-Rakib 7–8 (1993, 122).

155. Yet, a vizier of Que, Azatiwada states: "And I humbled strong lands in the west, which no king who was before me ever humbled. But I, Azatiwada, have humbled them. I brought them down. I settled them in the far regions of my borders in the east. And I settled the Danunians there (i.e. in the west)." See Röllig 1999, lines i.18b–ii.1a. But Que is a much larger polity than Sam'al, so one can make sense of it.

Fig. 6.8. Katumuwa Stela (drawing by Karen Reczuch, courtesy of J. David Schloen and the Neubauer Expedition to Zincirli)

What would deportations from the eastern side of the country to the western part have involved? And why would a Sam'alian king carry out such a short distanced bidirectional deportation within his own land?

It is certainly the case that Assyrian officers were given specific duties and responsibilities for carrying out deportations.[156] However, there does

156. E.g., Aššur-šallimanni, see Saggs 2001, 49 (ND 2634); SAA 19:85–86, text 81;

not seem to be evidence that client kings did this. Perhaps the subject of the verb *ybl* should be understood as Tiglath-pileser III. He is the one who led the campaigns to the east and the west (and the north and south), in which Panamuwa participated, and so it may be Tiglath-pileser who should be understood as the one carrying out the deportations from east to west, etc.

In any case, Panamuwa profited from these. Loyalty had its dividends. But it also came at a price. While he was on campaign with Tiglath-pileser III against Damascus in 733–732, he was killed (thus his reign was relatively short: 743–733/32). A funerary rite took place in the Assyrian camp, in which Tiglath-pileser III, other vassal kings, and the whole army lamented his death. A funerary image was erected for him by the Assyrian king and he was buried in Assyria (P: lines 16–19a).[157]

During the 2008 excavation season, a well-preserved, basalt stela was discovered in the north lower city in Area 5 (see above for archaeological context).[158] It was the mortuary stela of a high official named Katumuwa,[159] the servant of Panamuwa II, with an inscription in a dialect of Aramaic (see fig. 6.8).[160] Since Panamuwa II died in 733/732 and Katumuwa declares himself the servant of Panamuwa and not Barrākib, it seems likely that Katumuwa's death occurred prior to Panamuwa's death. Thus the stela should be dated 743–733 BCE (perhaps more likely toward the last years). In the inscription, Katumuwa establishes an ancestor cult ritual. Hence the stela's text and relief provide important insights for understanding this cult at late eighth-century Sam'al.[161]

With Panamuwa's death, the natural heir to the Sam'alian throne was Barrākib.[162] However, it is clear from the Barrākib Inscription (Tropper

---

Aššur-remanni and Nabû-bēl-aḫḫēšu, see Saggs 2001, 304–5 (ND 2735), lines r.7′–14′; SAA 19:8–9, text 6.

157. There is a difficulty in line 18. Tropper (1993, 126) states: "Ich nehme eine unvollständige Schreibung (Schreibfehler) des ortsnamens Assur an, der sonst stets plene als *ʾšwr* geschrieben ist." On the other hand, Sader (1987, 168) reads *ʾšr* and translates: "et il fit transporter mon père de Damas à (cet) endroit." Epigraphically, the third letter cannot be *r*, because the head is open at the top, which means that *w* is most likely. It would seem to me that the text should read *mn. dmšq. lyʾdy* "from Damascus to Yādiya," if Sam'al were the intended place where Tiglath-pileser brought the body of Panamuwa.

158. Schloen and Fink 2009a, 1–2; Struble and Herrmann 2009; Herrmann and Schloen 2014.

159. For the vocalization of the name, see Younger 2009.

160. Pardee (2009, 66–69) suggests the inscription is perhaps written in a distinct dialect. Recently, Lemaire (2013) argues that it is Sam'alian, and not a distinct dialect.

161. For a discussion of the iconography, Struble and Herrmann 2009; Bonatz 2014. For the most recent discussion of the ancestor cult and bibliography, see Herrmann and Schloen 2014; Sanders 2013; Niehr 2013, 2014a, 2014b.

162. For his inscriptions, see §6.1.3.

1993, 132–39: B1) that he reigned at the pleasure of the deity Rākib-El and his lord, Tiglath-pileser III:

> I am Barrākib, son of Panamuwa, king of Sam'al, the servant of Tiglath-pileser (III), lord of the four quarters of the earth. On account of the loyalty of my father and on account of my loyalty, my lord, Rākib-El, and my lord, Tiglath-pileser, caused me to reign upon the throne of my father.

Thus Barrākib, son of Panamuwa II, reigned 733/732–713/711 BCE and followed the policy of his father so that his kingdom prospered under Assyrian protection. Like his father, he "ran at the wheel of my lord, the king of Assyria." Hence, he claims "I made it (the dynasty) better than the house of any powerful king, and my brother kings were desirous for all that is the good of my house." A letter from Kalḫu (Nimrud), that perhaps dates from the reign of Shalmaneser V, reports the arrival of LÚ.MAḪ.MEŠ-*ni* (*ṣīrāni*) "emissaries" from several western states, including Sam'alians.[163] Barrākib would have been the one who sent his representatives to this Assyrian king.

However, Barrākib's biggest accomplishment (according to his inscription) was the construction of a new palace.

> But there was not a good house (palace) for my fathers, the kings of Sam'al. They had the house of Kulamuwa; and it was a winter house for them; and it was a summer house (too). But I built this house!

There can be little doubt that "this house" refers to the building identified by the excavators as Ḫilāni IV. The façade of the entrance to Ḫilāni IV had basalt orthostats on both sides. On the eastern side, there was an orthostat that depicted Barrākib sitting on a throne with a scribe standing before him (see fig. 6.9). At the top of the orthostat, a short epigraph in Standard Aramaic reads:

> "My lord is Ba'al-Ḥarran" {centered image} "I am Barrākib, son of Panamuwa."[164]

The centered image is a crescent and full moon erected on a pole with tassels and is thus identified as Ba'al Ḥarran (the lunar deity: Sîn of Harran, Aramaic: Śahr).

163. SAA 19:10, 8.9–15; Saggs 2001, 182–84, pl. 34; Radner 2003–4, 100–101.
164. The so-called *Schreiberorthostat*. See Tropper 1993, 145–46: B3; *KAI* 218. VA 2817: height: 1.13 m; width: 1.15 m.

Fig. 6.9. The Barrākib orthostat (VA 2817 © Staatliche Museen zu Berlin, Vorderasiatisches Museum, photo: Olaf M. Teßmer)

On the opposite side of the entrance a very fragmentary orthostat (convincingly reconstructed by Voos[165]) depicts Barrākib sitting on a throne banqueting. Gilibert (2011, 86–87) notes that the scene mirrors the eastern side orthostat so that in both, Barrākib sits on a throne, holding a blossoming stem in his left hand; in both, he faces a standing courtier, and is backed by another one, who swings a feather-fan; the eastern side shows Barrākib engaged in administrative matters, while the western side depicts him banqueting. These scenes were painted with strong colors (Gilibert 2011, 87 n. 139). While Barrākib wears the same attire in both scenes, the implements

165. Voos 1985, 71–86. See already tentatively Orthmann 1971, 369, 373, 462.

involved differ, especially the thrones. On the eastern side administrative scene, Barrākib is seated on an Assyrian-style throne; on the western side banqueting scene, he is seated on a western Syrian type throne (Gilibert 2011, 86–87).

In addition, two other inscribed orthostats were found out of context, but connected to the northern portico. One is the famous Barrākib Inscription (Tropper 1993, 132–39: B1) which was found in front of Ḫilāni IV.[166] The other is an orthostat that appears to preserve a banquet scene that has numerous deity symbols at the top and nine lines of broken inscription.[167] Barrākib was the last king of Sam'al, so far as we know.

### 6.3.6. Assyrian Province

Landsberger (1948, 77) suggested that it was likely that Sam'al became an Assyrian province after the death of Barrākib; and while Shalmaneser V may have accomplished this, the exact date and circumstances are uncertain because of the absence of inscriptions from this king's reign.[168] At least by 713 BCE, it was a province, since Sargon II mentions it in the fragmentary Nineveh Prism (the so-called 711 Annals; Fuchs 1998a, 43, 72: VIe, 4). This text gives a list of governors of the western provinces involved in the campaign against Am(ba)ris of Tabal/Bīt-Purutaš (713 BCE). Obviously, Sam'al must have become the province known as Sam'alla sometime before this event (Radner 2006–8a, 62 and map on 59). Since there are no traces of a violent destruction of Zincirli that can be dated from this period, it seems that the annexation of Sam'al was a peaceful process (Lipiński 2000a, 246). Additional evidences for Sam'alla as a province are found in administrative texts from Sargon II's reign.[169] Later in the year 681, Nabû-aḫḫē-ēreš, the governor of Sam'alla, held the eponymate (Millard 1994, 51, 102–3). This province, as Radner understands it, was roughly equivalent to the present-day Turkish province of Hatay, with the governor's residence located at Zincirli (Millard 1994, 51, 102–3).

A destruction of Zincirli took place between 676 and 671/70 in which the northwest palace was burnt. A cuneiform tablet (S3566) dated to 676

166. *AiS* 4:377. Tropper 1993, B1.

167. Tropper 1993, 140–44: B2; *KAI* 217. VA 6581: height: 44.5 cm remaining; width 45.5 cm remaining.

168. See the discussion of Radner 2006–8a, 62. Also see Radner 2003–4.

169. SAA 7:143, 136.r.i.10′: [LÚ.EN.NA]M URU.*sa-am-al*; SAA 7:125, 116.11′: URU.[*s*]*a-am-al-la*; SAA 11:5, 1.r.14′: URU.*sa-am-al-la*; SAA 11:8, 6.2: URU.*sa-*[*am-*ʾ*a-al*]; SAA 11:53, 80.r.5′: URU.*sa-ma-al*; SAA 11:20, 19.r.4′: [URU.*sa-m*]*a-al-la*; Dalley and Postgate 1984, 86.13: ᵐEN-KASKAL-KI-*ia* IGI URU.*sa-*⸢*am-al-la*⸣ URU.*kàl-zi*.

indicates that this unit still existed into 676, but the destruction occurred before the erection of a stela by Esarhaddon in 671, at which time the Assyrians rebuilt the acropolis according to an extremely different plan to serve as headquarters for the Assyrian administration. A comparative study of the pottery from the destruction level of the northwest palace confirms this dating (Lehmann 1994, 1996).

This third and final Building Phase[170] saw the construction of a new administrative center on the highest part of the citadel mound and the erection of Esarhaddon's massive stela (3.5 m in height), which commemorated his conquest of Egypt in 671[171] in the gatehouse of the Outer Citadel Gate (see fig. 6.3), where it was excavated in fragments. Its positioning at this spot was clearly intentional. It dominated the entrance into the renovated citadel complex so that its visual message was easily perceived and reinforced (Porter 2004, 2005).

In a document from Esarhaddon's reign, a *maqaltānu*(-priest?) of [the god] *Bi-ʾi-li ra-kab-bi ša* URU.*Sa-ma-al-la* is mentioned. The divine name has been identified as the Sam'alian protective deity RKBʾL.[172] The province is mentioned in an administrative list from the time of Aššurbanipal.[173]

At some point as the Assyrian Empire began to fall—perhaps as late as the last Assyrian king, Aššur-uballiṭ II (r. 611–605), who reorganized the Assyrians at Harran after the fall of Nineveh in 612—the city of Sam'al was abandoned. It was not destroyed but was apparently evacuated in an orderly manner, leaving no people or goods behind. Thus, in the entire lower town and in most places on the citadel mound remains of the seventh century BCE form the final stratum and are easily accessible for excavation.[174]

---

170. See Pucci 2008a, 39, 42–43; 2008b, 551–52.

171. RINAP 4:181–86, 98; Borger 1967, 96–100, §65 (Mnm. A).

172. SAA 16:61, 63.r.11. See Fales 1980, 144, line 11.

173. SAA 7:143, 136.9; SAA 11:5, 1 iii.14.

174. Schloen 2014, 38. He also points out that there was a small area of subsequent occupation on the upper mound, probably a fortress built under the aegis of the Achaemenid Persian Empire to control the nearby pass over the Amanus Mountains. But Zincirli was abandoned again soon after Alexander's conquest of the Persian Empire. A new Greek city called Nikopolis (modern İslahiye) was built in the Amanus foothills 10 km to the south (p. 38).

Table 6.2. Major Sam'alian Aramaic Inscriptions Connected with the Ancestor Cult

| Statues | Mortuary Stelae |
|---|---|
| | **Ördekburnu Stela** (820–760 BCE) (relief of a royal woman with inscription) |
| **Hadad** (755–750 BCE) (statue of the god with the royal inscription of Panamuwa I) | |
| **Panamuwa** (733–732 BC) (statue of the king with the royal inscription of Panamuwa II) | **Katumuwa Stela** (735 BC) (relief of high official with inscription) |

# 7
# HAMATH AND LUǴATH

HAMATH WAS THE NAME OF THE ANCIENT CITY AND STATE LOCATED AT THE TELL in the modern city of Ḥama on the middle Orontes River (fig. 7.1).[1] The acropolis of Tell Ḥama was excavated in 1932–1938 by a Danish archaeological team who uncovered twelve levels (labeled M to A) that indicate a near continuous occupation from the fifth millennium BCE.[2] The best architecturally represented strata are the Iron Age levels (F and E), the so-called Aramean citadel with its gatehouse, courtyard, and monumental buildings (Fugmann 1958). Hawkins (2000, 399) suggested that this might be better termed the "Hittite" rather than "Aramean" citadel. Matthiae has recently emphasized that the design of the citadel of Luwian/Aramean Hamath belongs to an architectural tradition of central and southern Syria.[3]

One of the more important structures in the city was a temple to the goddess Ba'alat. This temple is attested in several Luwian hieroglyphic inscriptions.[4] Lion sculptures of Neo-Hittite type flanked the entrances and staircases of several buildings. However, the overall sculptural remains of this period are minimal.

While the occupation of the tell was quite lengthy, the name Hamath (*ḥmt*) is not firmly attested before the Iron Age. Although the name seems to be attested possibly in the Eblaite texts (*ʾà-ma-tù*^ki^ or *ʾà-ma-at*^ki^), this toponym appears to be located north of Ebla.[5] Lipiński (2000a, 249–50) has suggested that the city's name may appear in Egyptian texts: first in the Execration Texts of the early second millennium as *ʿḫwmwt*,[6] then in the geographical list of Thutmose III as *ḥ-m-t*.[7] The former is unlikely, but the latter

1. *ḥmt* < *ḥmh*, "wall"? see *DNWSI*, 381; Hawkins 2000, 399 n. 15.
2. Ingholt 1934; 1940; Fugmann 1958; Riis 1948; Riis and Buhl 1990.
3. See Matthiae 2008, 207–10. See also §3.1.6.
4. See especially HAMA 4 (Hawkins 2000, 405).
5. Bonechi 1993, 36, s.v. *ʾà-ma-tim*^ki^.
6. Sethe 1926, *e* 29; Posener 1940, E 26.
7. List I a–c, see Sethe 1907, 781, no. 16.

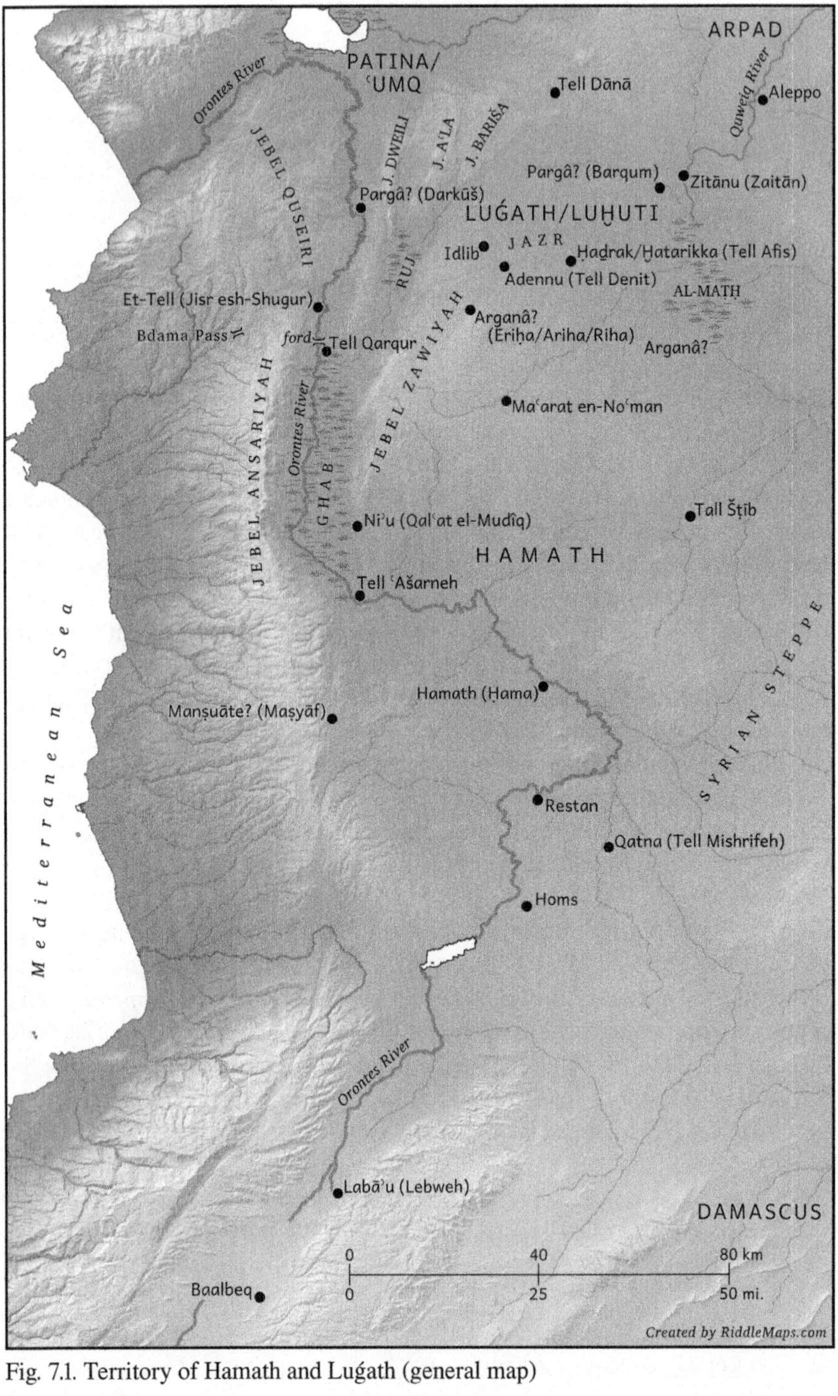


Fig. 7.1. Territory of Hamath and Luǵath (general map)

is possible, particularly since it occurs in a sequence of other toponyms and a land determinative is used, although there are different opinions.[8] If this is correct, then the site was called by this name in the fifteenth century BCE. However, it was certainly not one of the main urban centers and was likely part of the territory of another state, probably Tunip (Hawkins 2000, 399).

The first "allusion" to Hamath in the Assyrian texts is from the time of Tukulti-Ninurta II (890–884 BCE), where in 885 a Laqēan chief, the ruler of the city of Sūru on the Ḫābūr in the land of Bīt-Ḫalupē, bore the personal name Ḫamatāya, "the Hamathite."[9] The personal name is built off the ethnicon of Hamath[10] and indicates that the city and state of Hamath existed for some time before this attestation. Most frequently in the Assyrian sources, the determinative KUR "land" is used with Hamath, although URU "city" is used four times in the extant Assyrian texts.[11] In the letter of Marduk-apla-uṣur to Uratami (ca. 840), the city determinative is used (URU.*Ḫa-ma-ti*; Parpola 1990, 259, r. 13′). The hieroglyphic Luwian references, always found in the kings' titularies, refer to the "land of Imatu."[12] *Ḥmt* is also attested in Aramaic and Hebrew texts.

The land of Luǵath (*lʿš*) is the Aramaic form of the name[13] for the area north of Hamath and east of Jebel Zawiyah (figs. 7.1 and 7.2). It was known in Assyrian texts as Luḫuti, which is derived from the second-millennium name for the region, Nuḫašše.[14] While the exact borders of Luǵath/Luḫuti cannot

8. Simons 1937, 160–61; Rainey and Notley 2006, 72, no. 16; Aharoni 1979, 147, no. 16. Aḥituv (1984, 112) identifies this reference with Hamath-gader (el-Ḥammāh) on the Yarmuk River. But would such a small site as this be given a land determinative, as *ḥ-m-t* in list c is?

9. RIMA 2:176, A.0.100.5, lines 87, 101.

10. See discussion at §4.5.2, Laqē.

11. See Bagg 2007, 87–91, s.v. Ḫamat. Hawkins (2000, 399 n. 12) observes: "The toponym is most frequently mentioned by Shalmaneser III, Tiglath-pileser III and Sargon II. The first and the last use forms with initial *a-* and *ḫa-* indiscriminately; Tiglath-pileser only forms in *ḫa-*. The alternation shows typical Akkadian doubt on the rendering of West Semitic *ḥ*." To this, it can be added that in the spellings the consonant *m* can be doubled, as too the *t*. Ikeda (1979, 82) suggests that Hamath may be the royal city depicted along with Aštammaku on Band XIII of the Bronze Gates of Balawat in connection with the campaign of 848 BC.

12. Hawkins 2000, 399. Written mostly, *i-ma-tu-wa/i-ni*(REGIO) REX "Hamathite king": see Urhilina: HAMA 4 §1; QAL'AT EL MUDIQ §1; RESTAN §1; HINES §1; Uratami: HAMA 2 §1; HAMA 3 §1; and HAMA 6 §1; and HAMA 7 §1. Urhilina: HAMA 8 §1: *i-ma-tu-wa/i-ni-i-sa*(REGIO) REX. See also Starke 2003, col. 123.

13. Found in the Zakkur Inscription (*KAI* 202).

14. The change *n* > *l* explains the Assyrian and Aramaic forms; *ṯ* is represented by *š* in the Aramaic. The vocalization of *lʿš* as Luǵath is based on the forms Nuḫašše and Luḫuti. The *ḫ* in the cuneiform writings and the letter ʿ in the Aramaic writing are, in fact,

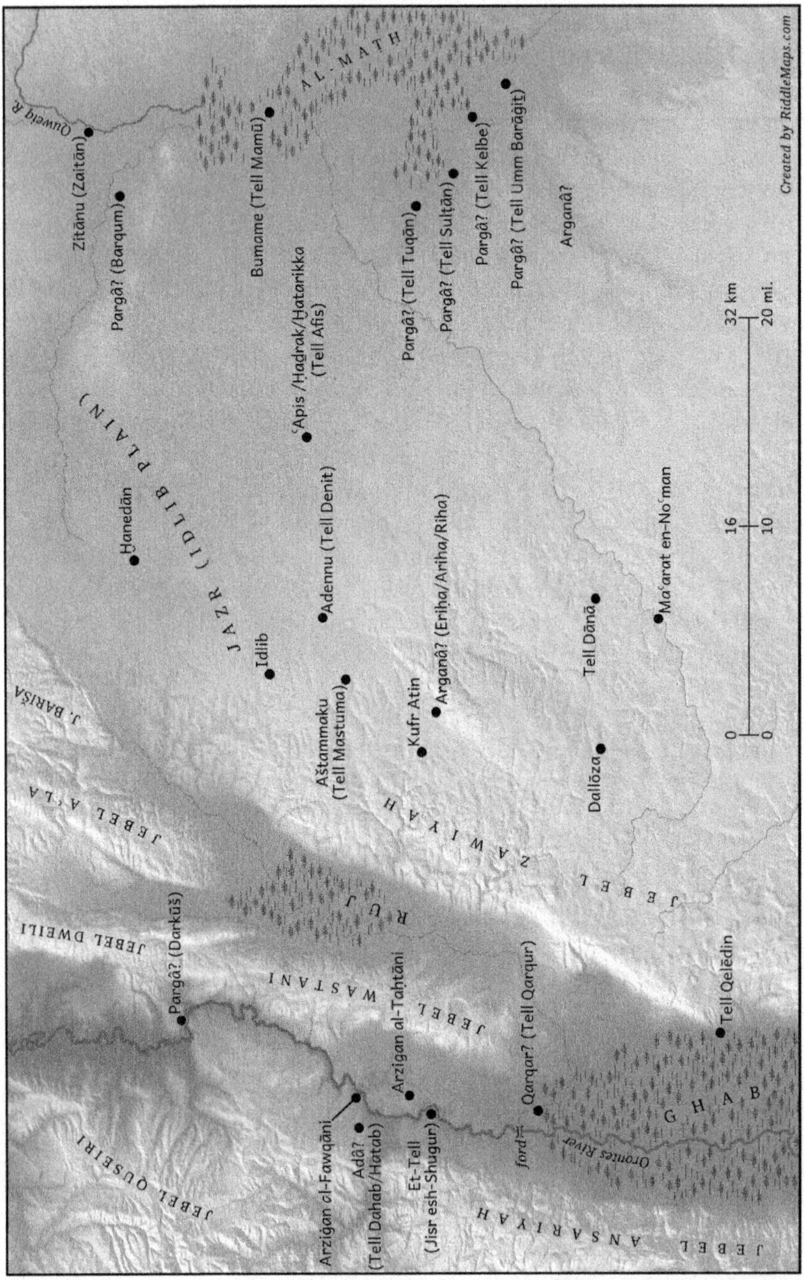


Fig. 7.2. Territory of Luġath

be specified,[15] its territory stretched probably between Aleppo and Ma'arat en-No'man and was centered on the city of Ḥadrak/Ḫatarikka. Mazzoni (2001a, 110) has summed up the geographic demarcations for Luǵath/Luḫuti as consisting of four parts: the left and eastern bank of the Lower Orontes above Darkūš, the Ruj, the Jazr, and al-Maṭḥ. These areas are adjacent to each other and permeable by means of a series of internal routes. The Jazr was particularly important as a communications route but was also important to the regional agricultural economy, especially the production of cereal crops, horticulture, and the growing of olives (Mazzoni 2001a, 110).

When the Assyrian king Shalmaneser III invaded the area (853 BCE), Luḫuti was apparently under Hamathite control, since a number of the cities are attributed to Urhilina, king of Hamath (ca. 860–835 BCE; see below). Prior to this, however, it is unclear as to its status when Aššurnaṣirpal II plundered it. Later, under King Zakkur (sometime after the death of Hazael and before 796 BCE), Luǵath was merged together with Hamath—at least Zakkur ascribed to himself the title "king of Hamath and Luǵath" (*mlk ḥmt wlʿš*).[16]

## 7.1. Territory

Based on the historical sources, Hamath's northern border was with Arpad and Patina/'Umq; its southern border was with Damascus.[17] While the western border was the range of the Jebel Ansariyah, its eastern border was the Syrian steppe.

One of the major cities of Hamath whose identification is intertwined with a number of other Hamathite cities is the city Qarqar.[18] In the scholarly study of the region, the identification of Qarqar[19] has posed problems. Early

both writing systems' way of representing the phoneme *ǵ*. Hence the vocalization Luǵath. See Lipiński 2000a, 257; Bagg 2007, 159; Hawkins 1987–90a.

15. For the southern border of Luḫuti, see Dion 2000.

16. *KAI* 202:A1, 2; see also *mlk mt wl*[*ʿš*], *KAI* 202:B17–18. Beside the Zakkur Inscription, *lʿš* is also inscribed on an ivory piece from Nimrud (ND 10359). See Millard 1962, 41–42.

17. In the Hebrew Bible, Lebo-Hamath was considered the idealized northern border of Israel.

18. See Bagg 2007, 194–95, s.v. Qarqaru; and Lehmann 2002, 364. The execration texts (E 56), which mentions the ruler of *Qrqrm* (written: *ḳ3ḳ3m*) may refer to the Qarqar on the Orontes River (Aḥituv 1984, 157).

19. A place name Qarqar (קַרְקֹר) occurs as a hapax in the Hebrew Bible (Judg 8:10), though this must be Karkor of the Wadi Sirḥan. *HALOT*, 1148: "probably an epithet meaning 'water-holes, springs, wells.' cf. Ugaritic *qr* 'spring, fountain, pool, pond.'" For the Ugaritic root, see Olmo Lete and Sanmartín 2003, 707, *qr* (I).

on, scholars did not try to identify the site. Those that did assumed that Qarqar must have been located south of the swampy lands of the Ghab (Ǧab). Thus, in 1900, Maspero (1900, 70 n. 4) identified Qarqar with Apamea (modern Qal'at el-Mudîq) asserting that "it is agreed that Qarqar must be sought not far from Hamath, whatever the exact site may be." Winckler, as well as Kraeling, argued along similar lines.[20] But Dussaud (1927, 242) proposed the site of Tell Qarqur (7 km south of Jisr esh-Shughur) because of the similarity in name. This has become the general view of many scholars.[21]

In the 1980s, Sader (1987, 223–25) argued that there was no *city* of Hamath;[22] rather Qarqar was the capital of the *country* of Hamath; therefore Qarqar should be identified with present-day Ḥama. She based her arguments mainly on the fact that Qarqar is designated a "royal city" (*āl šarrūti*), and hence the capital,[23] and that Hamath is attested mainly with the determinative KUR "land" (Sader 1986; 1987, 223–25). However, the epigraphic evidence argues against Sader's identification (Lipiński 2000a, 265). First, there are the inscribed weights from both Qarqar and Hamath: *šql qrqr*, "šeqel of Qarqar" (Bordreuil 1993c, 266–67, no. 231) and the *šql ḥmt*, šeqel of Hamath," (Heltzer 1995). In addition are the *šqly ḥmt* (Bordreuil 1983, 219–20, no. 251) and *šṭ šql ḥmt* (Bron and Lemaire 1991, pl. CXLV). Furthermore, an inscribed ostracon from the seventh century BCE found in the excavations of Ḥama reads *qrqr*, while another reads *ḥmt*.[24] And, most convincing, the letter of Marduk-apla-uṣur of 'Anat to Rudamu (Uratami), king of Hamath, discovered in the excavations of Ḥama, ends with the invocation: "May the city of 'Anat and the city of Hamath be strong" (Parpola 1990, 257–65). Thus Tell Ḥama cannot be Qarqar; it is indeed Hamath (Hawkins 1972–75b; 2000, 398–403).[25]

Pitard (1987, 126 n. 79) expressed doubts concerning the identification with Tell Qarqur, arguing that the tell appears to be some distance from the

---

20. Winckler 1903, 43; Kraeling 1918, 73.

21. Tell Qarqur (name correspondence, but no archaeological evidence as yet to confirm) Noth 1955, 39–41, 72 [with reservations]; Astour 1969, 412; Klengel 1982, 77–78; Ikeda 1979; 2003; Mittmann and Schmitt 2001, B IV 14; Streck 2003–5, 131.

22. But Amos 6:2 states: "Cross over to Kalneh (כַּלְנֵה) and see; go from there to Great Hamath (חֲמַת רַבָּה); and go down to Gath of the Philistines (גַּת־פְּלִשְׁתִּים); are [you] better than those kingdoms, or is their territory larger than yours?" Bordreuil (2012, 285) argues that since the first Kalneh (= Kunulua/Kullania, modern Tell Ta'yinat) and the third (Gath, modern Tell eṣ-Ṣafi) are cities, logically Hamath should also designate a city. In addition, the designation "Great Hamath" refers to the city's regional importance.

23. However, as pointed out by Yamada (2000a, 175 n. 344), several cities in Hamath can be considered as *āl šarrūti*.

24. Otzen 1990, 292–93, *AramGraf* 18 and 19.

25. For the archaeology of Ḥama, see above.

most important part of the trade route. Thus, in his estimation, the most likely candidate for the site of Qarqar is a mound known as et-Tell, located at the modern town of Jisr esh-Shughur and one of the largest tells in the northern Ghab. This site, however, has been identified by a number of scholars with the ancient city of Aribua mentioned in Aššurnaṣirpal II's annals, though this is not proven.[26]

In a critical note, Na'aman has proposed that Qarqar should be identified with Tell 'Ašarneh:[27]

> From the early days of research, Qarqar was identified with Tell Qarqur, located 3 kms (sic) south of Jisr esh-Shughur. The identification is mainly based on the similarity of names and the location of the site on the Orontes river, near the northern edge of the marshes of el-Ghab. However, the city of Qarqar is not included in the list of places conquered by Tiglath-pileser III and annexed to the province of Hatarikka, whereas Tell Qarqur is located within the confines of the newly-established province. Qarqar remained in the territory of Eni-ilu, the king of Hamath, outside the area annexed by Assyria in 738 … In this light I would suggest that Tell 'Asharneh was the site of the city of Qarqar.

Finally, in their recent atlas, Parpola and Porter (2001, 14) list Tell Qarqur as Qarqar and Tell 'Ašarneh as an alternative location, rating the level of certainty for both possibilities as 3 (their next-to-lowest rating). Recent excavations at both sites have yielded significant Iron II pottery remains.[28] However, neither tell has yielded anything firm for its identification in the Iron II period.[29] All this highlights the ongoing difficulties. Is Qarqar to be located north or south of the Ghab?

---

26. There have been six proposals for the identification of Aribua (the first is most likely in my opinion): (1) et-Tell, west bank of the Orontes, north of modern Jisr esh-Shughur (Liverani 1992a, 76–77; Cifola 1997–98, 156; Yamada 2000a, 73, 174; Dion 2000, 134, 138; Mittmann and Schmitt 2001, B IV 14; Bagg 2007, 22); (2) Rubeda (ca. 7 km west of Ma'arat en-No'man, about 17 km south of Riha; Lewy 1952, 401–2, 418–19); see also Na'aman 1978, 232; Ikeda 1979, 76–77 and nn. 11, 86; (3) The city of Aribua was probably located near Patina's southeastern corner (Na'aman 2002b, 295). This area was later captured by Arpad so that Patina lost control over this territory and city; (4) Rab'o (east of Maṣyāf; Dussaud 1927, 241; Honigmann 1928, 144); (5) Qal'at Arba'in (southwest of Shughur; Wäfler, *NND*, 222); and (6) The possibility of its location further north should not be excluded (Ikeda 2003, 92*; 1977, 76–77 and nn. 11, 86).

27. Na'aman 1999d. A view voiced by F. Thureau-Dangin (as quoted by Dussaud 1927, 242 n. 5) on the basis of the discovery of the stela of Sargon II there.

28. For Tel Qarqur, see Dornemann 1997a, 1997b, 2000, 2003, 2012; for Tell 'Asharneh, Cooper, and Fortin 2004; Fortin 2006; Fortin and Cooper 2013.

29. The first-millennium name for Tell 'Ašarneh is still unknown (Fortin and Cooper 2013, 148). The site was Tunip in the third and second millennia (Klengel 1995; Goren,

In the Kurkh Monolith's description of the campaign,[30] Shalmaneser attacks the city of Qarqar after his capture of three "royal" cities[31] of Irḫulēni/Urhilina, the king of Hamath (ca. 860–835 BCE): "Adennu, Pargâ, (and) Arganâ, his royal cities" (URU *a-de-en-nu* URU *pár-ga-a* URU *ar-ga-na-a* URU MAN-*ti-šú* KUR-*ud*).[32]

Beside this sentence in the Monolith, Shalmaneser's attacks on different cities of Hamath are depicted on the upper and lower registers of Band IX of the Bronze Gates from Balawat/Imgur-Enlil (fig. 7.3).[33] The upper register of the Band IXa depicts an Assyrian attack on two walled cities. One is being attacked with a siege engine and bears the epigraph "I conquered the city of Pargâ" (URU *Pa-ar-ga-a* KUR-*ud*).[34] The other is being scaled with ladders and bears the epigraph "I captured the city of Adâ of Urhilina (= Irḫulēni) the Hamathite" (URU *A-da-a šá* [m]*Ur-ḫi-le-ni* KUR *ḫa-ma-ta-a-a* KUR-*ud*).[35] Arganâ is not depicted. This pictorial evidence introduces two further complications. First, many scholars believe that Adâ should be identified with the Monolith's Adennu, although this is an assumption made without explanation.[36] It would seem that this is based on two factors: that Pargâ is mentioned or paired with Adennu and Adâ; and that the *nn* in Adennu have

Finkelstein and Na'aman 2003, 9; Goren, Finkelstein, Na'aman, and Artzy 2004). A Late Bronze city wall was found in the 2010 excavations (Fortin and Cooper 2013, 156–58).

30. RIMA 3:23, A.0.102.2, ii.87b-97b.

31. Elliger (1947, 82 n. 42) assumed that Shalmaneser approached and subjugated two cities, Adennu and Pargâ, without giving battle, and then attacked Arganâ, the royal city. His interpretation was based on the incorrect copy of G. Smith in III R, 7–8 that read a numeral "II" before "*ālāni ša* [m]*Irḫulēni māt Amatāya*" (ii 87f.). This incorrect reading was also followed by Oppenheim (*ANET*, 278) and Astour (1969, 412–13). The numeral does not exist on the Monolith (see the collations of J. A. Craig (Hebraica 3 [1886–87] 218, 232; Grayson, RIMA 3:23, A.O.102.2, ii.87; and Yamada 2000a, 367). Furthermore, such an interpretation contradicts the evidence from Balawat Bronze Band IX, upper register, which depicts the attack on Pargâ; and if Adâ is Adennu, then the attack on this city too.

32. The phrase *āl šarrūtīšu* "his royal city" may relate to Arganâ alone (Elliger 1947, 82 n. 42; Ikeda 1979, 79 n. 33). On the other hand, it could refer to each of the three cities, Adennu, Pargâ, and Arganâ (Luckenbill 1926–27, 1.610; Noth 1955, 40; Sader 1987, 187 n. 7; Grayson, RIMA 3:23, A.0.102.2). While the phrase *ālāni šarrūtīšu* might be expected if all three cities were intended (Ikeda 1979, 79), the singular could still be used to attribute each of the three cities as Yamada points out (2000a, 153 n. 261; see also von Soden, *GAG*, §134c). In any case, the fact that the attacks on the walled cities of Pargâ and Adâ, as well as Qarqar, were depicted on Balawat Bronze Band IX may suggest that these two cities were no less significant than Arganâ.

33. Schachner 2007, 53, pl. 9 (IXa, left: Pargâ; IXa, right: Adâ); King 1915, pls. XLXIII–LIII.

34. RIMA 3:144, A.0.102.74; Schachner 2007, pl. 9 (IXa, left: Pargâ).

35. RIMA 3:144, A.0.102.75; Schachner 2007, pl. 9 (IXa, right: Adâ).

36. For example, Kraeling 1918, 73; Astour 1969, 412; Grayson 1996, 144; Yamada 2000a, 155: "Ada should apparently be identified with Adennu"; Schachner 2007, 223.

Fig. 7.3. Shalmaneser III's attacks on Pargâ (top) and Adâ (bottom) (Schachner 2007, pl. 9, IXa)

dropped or back assimilated in Adâ. Other scholars understand these to be different cities.[37]

Second, both Pargâ and Adâ are depicted on the Band as standing on low mounds alongside water. This indicates that they were located near a river or swamp (Astour 1969, 410–13). This fact yields two different possible routes (Yamada 2000a, 155) that the Assyrian army of Shalmaneser III may have taken: (1) from Aleppo west to the Lower Orontes, and then south along the Orontes; or (2) from Aleppo south along the Quweiq River to the marsh al-Maṭḥ, and then west to the Ruj Valley and the Orontes. In the Monolith, Adennu is mentioned first; in the bronzes, Pargâ is first.[38] It is, however, difficult to determine which of these possibilities is the correct one.[39]

37. Lipiński (2000a, 259 and 262) proposes two other possibilities: Tell Dahab or Hatab (5 km northwest of Ariĝan) or ʿAyn at Tall (just north of Jisr esh-Shughur). These suggestions are based on his understanding of the Assyrian army's route to Qarqar. Bagg treats with separate entries (2007, 2 [Adâ]; 35 [Atinnu/Adennu]).

38. Since the Monolith uses the itinerary pattern for narrating the campaign and since geographic grouping is at work in the art rather than chronologic concern, Adennu/Adâ was likely the first city encountered by Shalmaneser III.

39. Astour (1969, 411–14) favored the second route option. Ikeda (2003, 93*) asserts that these cities must have been located in the land of Luḫuti; and Dion (2000, 135–36) feels that they were likely north of the Ghab.

Fig. 7.4. Qarqar, Band IXb (Schachner 2007, pl. 9, IXb)

Five different sites have been proposed for the location of Adennu.[40] However, recent studies have pointed to Tell Denit (5 km southeast of the modern city of Idlib; only 4 km northeast of Tell Mastuma).[41] Pargâ has been equated with Barqum, about 25 km southwest of Aleppo.[42] But Astour and Lipiński have argued that Barqum cannot be Bargâ/Pargâ for onomastic reasons.[43] Astour placed Pargâ/Bargâ at "one of the numerous tells on the southern coast of al-Maṭḥ: Tell Tuqān, Tell Sulṭān, Tell Kelbe, Tell Umm Barāġiṯ, and others."[44] Lipiński (2000a, 260–61) located it at Darkūš (20 km north of Jisr esh-Shughur).

The lower register of Band IXb[45] contains an epigraph: "I captured the city of Qarqar, which belonged to Urhilina, the Hamathite" (URU *qa-ar-qa-ra šá* ^m^*ur-ḫi-le-e-ni* KUR *ḫa-ma-ta-a-a* KUR-*ud*). It pictures the Assyrian army advancing on the left through fruit trees alongside a river to attack the city of Qarqar, which is shown burning, with captives and spoils from the city being led away to be presented to Shalmaneser (fig. 7.4).

Thus if these cities were located on a river or marshland, the first route option, which would place them along the Orontes River, might seem to be a better option than the second. However, if the location of Aribua (mentioned

40. These are: (1) Tell Denit/Dānīt/Tall Dann (see next note); (2) Tell Dānā (= ad-Dānā 1, Bagg 2007, 35; 38 km west of Aleppo, 4 km southwest of Turmanin; Forrer, 1920, 58; Dussaud 1927, 243; Elliger 1947, 82; Lipiński 2000a, 259 n. 46); (3) Tell Dānā (= ad-Dānā 2, Bagg 2007, 35; 6 km north of Ma'arat en-No'man; 14 km south and west of Eriha; Dussaud 1927, 243; Elliger 1947, 82; Astour 1969, 412 n. 3, 414). But see Arganâ (below); (4) Ḫanedân, 12 km northwest of Idlib (Elliger 1947, 82 n. 42); and (5) Kufr Atin, 2 km west of Riha (Abu Taleb 1973, 159).

41. Ikeda 2003, 93* n. 22; Wakita, Wada, and Nishiyama 2000, 555; Kraeling 1918, 73; Shaath 1981–82, 216; Sader 1987, 222; Mittmann and Schmitt 2001, B IV 14.

42. Barqum near Zeitan and Zirbe southwest of Aleppo (Dussaud 1927, 243 and 513; cf. Elliger 1947, 82; Belmonte Marín 2001, 52; Radner 2003–5a; Schachner 2007, 223).

43. Egyptian spelling and lack of mimation in Syrian personal and geographical names of the Old Babylonian period; thus perhaps Old Aramaic *b*(*t*)-*rqm*. See Astour 1969, 412 n. 5.

44. Astour 1969, 410–13, quote from p. 413. Hittite texts (particularly *KBo* III 3) locate the KUR URU *Bar-ga* ("the land of the city of Barga") "somewhere in the region of Nuḫašše" (Astour 1969, 411).

45. RIMA 3:144, A.0.102.76; Schachner 2007, pl. 9 (IXb, Qarqar).

in the Aššurnaṣirpal II Annals) is to be located at Jisr esh-Shughur (et-Tell) as argued by a number of scholars, this presents a situation in which Hamath has control of cities north of this site on the Lower Orontes that would seem to have been (at least according to Aššurnaṣirpal's text) part of Patina/'Umq. If one adopts the first route option, then there must be an assumption that the area north of Jisr esh-Shughur was seized by Hamath in the years in between Aššurnaṣirpal II's campaign (ca. 870) and Shalmaneser III's foray (853).[46] Although this is, of course, possible, there is no direct evidence. On the other hand, perhaps the fact that Luḫuti appears to be under Hamathite control in 853, perhaps this section of the Lower Orontes had also come under Hamath's domain. Another problem with the first route option is that there is a significant narrowing of the Orontes Valley from Jisr esh-Shughur to Darkūš forming a gorge between Jebel Wastani and Jebel Quseiri.[47] Militarily, it is a more difficult route; however, armies have been known to negotiate such narrow valley roads.

On the Kurkh Monolith, Shalmaneser continues his narration stating: "I departed from the city of Arganâ. I approached the city of Qarqar. I razed, destroyed and burned the city of Qarqar, his royal city." This is followed by an open-field battle with the "twelve-king" coalition of which Shalmaneser claims: "I decisively defeated them from the city of Qarqar to the city of Gilzau" (TA URU *qar-qa-ra a-di* URU *gíl-za-ú* $BAD_5$.$BAD_5$-*šú-nu lu áš-kun*). Obviously, if one could identify Arganâ and/or Gilzau, then the general location of Qarqar (either north or south of the Ghab) would be fixed.

Unfortunately, this is not an easy task. At least six possible identifications have been proposed for Arganâ.[48] The first and the second listed seem

46. Dion (2006, 44) assumes this stating: "Aribua probably did not last long; other ancient records, beginning with those of Shalmaneser III, Aššurnaṣirpal's own son, when he marched through the region, do not preserve any further mention of it. It must have fallen under the control of Neo-Hittite Ḥamath some time before 858."

47. Mazzoni (2001, 107–8) notes that "north of Qarqur and Jisr esh-Shughur, the settlements appear to decrease in number as the valley narrows. The only one of note is the tell below Qnayé, consisting of deposits from EB III–IV to the west and Iron II–III toward the river to the east. Further downstream, after the gorges, a few settlements on the right eastern bank are found at the foot of the hills sloping gently down from Jebel Dweili. Amongst these, the largest is Tell Bek, occupied from the Late Chalcolithic to the Byzantine era."

48. These are: (1) Eriḥa/Ariha/Riha (15 km south of Idlib; Kraeling 1918, 73; Sader 1987, 222); "perhaps identical with the modern Rīḥā on the north side of the mountain of the same name" (Kraeling 1918, 73); (2) ad-Dānā (Parpola and Porter 2001 maps 2, 24, but their coordinates do not match a place named ad-Dānā); (3) the name of the swamp er-Ruj, northwest of Qarqar (Dussaud 1927, 243: cf. Elliger 1947, 82); (4) in the area of Apamea (Qal'at el-Mudîq; Honigman 1929, 143); and (5) Arziǵan al-Fawqāni (about 10 km north of Tell Qarqur) or Arziǵan al-Taḥtāni (about 6 km north of Tell Qarqur; Lipiński 2000a, 262).

to present the best possibilities: Eriḥa/Ariha/Riha (15 km south of Idlib) and (ed-)Dana.

In the case of Gilzau, Yamada (2000a, 162) notes, "we cannot be entirely sure whether the Assyrians actually advanced or retreated, since the location of Gilzau is unknown." Thus, on the one hand, Kraeling argued that the Assyrian army advanced until Gilzau and then was halted there by the coalition.[49] On the other hand, Ideka (1977, 173) postulates that Gilzau is located north of Qarqar and that the retreating Assyrians passed Gilzau and went further westwards in the direction of the Mediterranean Sea.

Furthermore, what has complicated the identification is the fact that there is a variant spelling of the toponym. In the Kurkh Monolith, it is spelled: URU *gíl-za-ú*.[50] But in two of Shalmaneser's Summary Inscriptions it is spelled: URU *di-il-zi-a-ú* "the city of Dilziau."[51] Neither spelling of the toponym has been identified, so the full ramifications for Shalmaneser's claim of pursuing the coalition forces to this toponym cannot presently be assessed. Lipiński (2000a, 265) has suggested that the reading URU *gíl-za-ú* is a scribal error:

> The location of Qarqar and of the area reached in 853 B.C. by Shalmaneser III's army is confirmed besides by the king's claim to have defeated the allies "between the towns of Qarqar and of *Di-il-zi-a-ú*," with a variant *Gíl-za-ú* in the Monolith Inscription II, 97. The first reading, provided by the inscription on Shalmaneser III's throne-base, is certainly correct since the village of Dallōza, built in the middle of ancient ruins, is situated 19 km east-southeast of Qarqūr. The uniqueness of this toponym excludes the possibility of a casual similarity, while *Gíl-za-ú* can be explained easily as a scribal error occasioned by the Urarṭian place name *Gíl-za-a-ni* which is mentioned higher in the Monolith Inscription II.60–61 and 63.

This is certainly a possible explanation of the variant spellings of the toponym. However, while it is well documented that there are scribal errors

---

Abu Taleb (1973, 160) suggested that Tell Arguni is near Ma'aret en-No'man. However, there does not seem to be any evidence of a Tell Arguni near Ma'aret en-No'man at all.

49. Kraeling 1918, 73. He even suggested that Gilzau be located at Qal'at Seğar (Seleucid Larissa): "Here the retreat from Qarqar would most logically reach the Orontes" (Kraeling 1918, 75 n. 1). But Kraeling's identification is tied to his identification of Qarqar at Apamea (Qal'at el-Mudîq). Dussaud (1927, 242) suggested that Gilzau might be identified with 'Ašarneh.

50. Kurkh Monolith: RIMA 3:24, A.0.102.2, ii.97; *COS* 2.113A:261–64; Yamada: Annals 3.

51. Fort Shalmaneser Stone Throne Base (RIMA 3:103, A.0.102.28, line 32; Yamada: Summary Inscription 6); the Engraved Door Sill from Fort Shalmaneser (RIMA 3:107–8, A.0.102.30, line 27; Yamada: Summary Inscription 9).

in the Monolith (Tadmor 1961), I have reservations concerning Lipiński's suggestion. First, there are hundreds of cuneiform signs between the occurrence of Gilzānu and Gilzau. This can hardly be a case of the scribe's eye seeing a sign in the previous line or two and mistakenly copying it here, a type of *homoeoarkton*, which coincidentally, just so happens also to preserve the second consonant in the place name: *l*. Second, Gilzānu is determined by KUR, while here the determinative is URU.[52] Third, it is methodologically problematic to decide on an ancient variant reading based on a highly speculative identification with a modern site. In fact, the village of Dallōza (Delloze) is located on the other side of the Jebel Zawiyah from Tell Qarqur, which causes doubts militarily with this site as the place to which the coalition forces were pursued. Fourth, it may be unnecessary to posit a scribal error in the Monolith at this juncture. From around 1900 on, scholars have read the first sign of the toponym in the Monolith with the value GÍL (before this it was read KÌR or the text was emended to read *Gilzan(u)*).

It may be suggested that a better reading would be with the value QIL,[53] resulting in the name "Qilzau." Reading the name with this value would yield another instance in Neo-Assyrian transcription of the proto-Semitic interdental phoneme *ḏ*, still preserved in Aramaic at this time.[54] An example of this was noted by a number of scholars[55] in the case of the toponym Raqammatu / Radammatu (= the city of Gidara[56]) found in the Annals of Adad-nērārī II[57] where the name is spelled: URU *ra-qa-ma-tu* (line 52) and URU *ra-dam-ma-te* (line 57). The name Gidara is apparently a dialect of Aramaic; but the Assyrian sources state that it is also called Raqammatu or Radammatu by the Arameans,[58] perhaps in another Old Aramaic dialect (Dion 1997, 32). Thus

---

52. Only twice out of 33 occurrences is Gilzānu determined by URU rather than KUR. See Parpola 1970, 132.

53. See Borger 1979, no. 483; also von Soden and Röllig 1991, no. 280.

54. A. R. Millard suggested this possibility to me while discussing other issues surrounding Shalmaneser III's inscriptions (personal communication, Feb., 2004). I assume full responsibility for any errors in pursuing it.

55. Weippert 1973, 46–47 n. 83; Millard 1980, 369. See also Parpola 1970, 290, 292; Dion 1997, 32 n. 30.

56. On the dialectal situation of the root *gdr*, see Meshen and Knauf 1988, 129; Timm 1989, 328.

57. RIMA 2:150, A.0.99.2, lines 52 and 57. See §4.2, pp. 237–39.

58. It should be noted that Lipiński (2000a, 114–15) argues that the variants *Ra-qa-ma-tu* and *Ra-dam-ma-te* cannot go back to a name *Raḍamat*, as it has been suggested, because a root *rḍm* is so far unknown in Semitic (see Zadok 1977, 434). Lipiński states: "*Raqamat*, related to the Semitic name *Rqm* of Petra and of some other sites, should be considered as the correct form, while the sign DAM must result from a confusion." But Dion (1997, 32 n. 30) concludes: "*Ra-qa-ma-tu* (A.0.99.2, ligne 52) fait penser à RQM, le nom araméen de Pétra en Jordanie (see Stacky 1965; Weippert 1966). La forme **ra-dam-*

the interchange of *q*/*d* may be seen in the Monolith's "Qilzau" (URU *qil-za-ú*) and the Throne Base's and Door Sill's "Dilziau" (URU *di-il-zi-a-ú*).

Another example of the *ḏ* phoneme is seen in the Neo-Assyrian transcription of the name of the last king of Aram-Damascus, known in the Hebrew Bible as Rezin. Hebrew רְצִין reflects the Aramaic Raḏyān,[59] and this is seen in the Neo-Assyrian spellings of *ra-qi-a-nu*, *ra-ḫi-a-nu*, *ra-ḫi-a-ni*, attesting to the later shift in Aramaic *ḏ* > ʿ.[60]

While the location of this toponym in Shalmaneser's inscriptions remains uncertain, it is hoped that by noting the possible reading of Qilzau, instead of the traditional Gilzau, this will perhaps aid in its eventual identification. With *all* due caution, could Tell Qelēdin be Qilzau (assuming *qld* < *qlz*)? The tell[61] is roughly 150 × 100 m at the base and lies on the route[62] from Tell Qarqur to Tell Qalʿat el-Mudîq (apparently Ni'u in Neo-Assyrian times),[63] and is only 14.5 km / 9.1 mi from Tell Qarqur, representing a very reasonable distance from that tell. It is also located near the swampy Ghab (as opposed to Dallōza) and would thus seem to fit the context of the battle description in the Monolith. Whether this is the correct identification or not, the reading of

---

*ma-tu* apparaît cependant à la ligne 57 de la même source, ce dont on peut déduire que la véritable racine du nom araméen avait un \ḏ\ au lieu d'un \q\ (ainsi Weippert 1973, 47, n. 83)."

59. For a discussion of this name, see Pitard 1987, 182. The name Raḏyān is from the Old Aramaic verb *rqy*$_1$ / *rʿy* [cf. Heb. *rṣy*] + *ān* ending. See also Fuchs and Hunger 2002, 1028; *DNWSI*, 1083, s.v. *rqy*$_1$.

60. The interdentals are represented as follows: ṯ = š / ḏ = z / ẕ = ṣ / ḏ̣ = q. It is generally agreed that the shifts that characterize later Aramaic (ṯ > t / ḏ > d / ẕ > ṭ / ḏ̣ > ʿ) had not yet taken place, i.e., that the earlier proto-Semitic phonemes were still preserved and that the closest approximation to their sounds were selected from the graphemes available in the Phoenician alphabet.

61. The survey speaks of a clear Bronze Age stratigraphy (Courtois 1973, 84), but says nothing about Iron Age remains. Obviously, if there are no Iron Age remains, the site cannot be identified with the Shalmaneser account.

62. A longitudinal road began near the site of Alalaḫ (Tell Açana)—of course, not far from Kunulua (Tell Taʿyinat)—and went south along the east side of the Orontes River to Tell Qarqur, then on to Qalʿat el-Mudîq (Neo-Assyrian Ni'u) and crossed the Orontes at its bend near the huge mound of ʿAšarneh (and then further south). For this road, see Astour 1995, 1415; Balty, Balty, and Dewez 1970, 27; Mouterde and Poidebard 1945, map 1).

63. Importantly a hieroglyphic Luwian stela—a monument of king Urhilina—was discovered at Qalʿat el-Mudîq (classical Apamea), a major site that dominated the Ghab on the east side. The stela was "excavated in autumn 1937 in a sondage in a classical building at Apamea (Qalʿat el-Mudîq), apparently *in situ*" (Hawkins 2000, 408). It is a building inscription of Urhilina, king of Hamath that records "the construction of 'this city'" (the ninth-century predecessor of Apamea, i.e., Ni(u) and erection of the stela to Baʿalat (Hawkins 2000, 408). Hawkins translation (p. 409): "I (am) Urhilina, Paritas's son, Hamathite king. This city I built, and this stele I set up to the deity Baʿalatis." See also Parpola and Porter 2001, 14, 29; Balty, Balty and Dewez 1970, 27.

the name as Qilzau seems, at a minimum, to solve the problem of the variant reading.

The efforts to locate Qarqar south of the Ghab[64] have not been based on any positive evidence, but on objections to locating Qarqar at Tell Qarqur. Two main objections have been leveled: topographic and textual. In the first instance, it has been argued that the topography around the site of Tell Qarqur is not strategically suitable for the battle as described in the Monolith. This was discussed at length by Noth (1955, 39–41) who depicts Tell Qarqur as more or less enclosed on three sides (south: the Ghab; west: the Ansariyah Mountains; north: a river gorge).[65] Noth (1955, 39) questioned why Shalmaneser went straight to Qarqar and why the coalition forces waited for his attack at Qarqar.

While Noth's assessment of the topography is correct in the basics, it does not fully represent the situation. To the west, not far from Tell Qarqur, is the Bdama Pass, which was the main central route throught the mountains to the Mediterranean near Latakia, a route that Aššurnaṣirpal II probably utilitzed, as well as during the Old Babylonian period, Zimri-Lim, king of Mari, who took it on his visit to the king of Ugarit (see Courtois 1973, 60). Just north of Tell Qarqur was the important crossing of the Middle Orontes that facilitated east–west traffic through the region (Klengel 1982, 66–67). Directly to the north, a secondary longitudinal road went to Kunulua (Tell Ta'yinat; in earlier times, to Aleppo), as Astour (1995) has pointed out. Another route went northwest to the area around Antioch. And to the south there was an important longitudinal road that ran east of the Ghab southward to Qal'at el-Mudîq (Neo-Assyrian Ni'u) and then onward to Tell 'Ašarneh. It was probably on this road that the coalition forces marched to engage Shalmaneser at Qarqar. Shalmaneser most likely approached Qarqar from the east traveling from the Tell Denit–Ariḫa area to Qarqar (a natural route that is still used today). His interest in Qarqar may have been linked to the Assyrian outpost of Aribua, if et-Tell (Jisr esh-Shughur) was the location of that city as Liverani and others have argued.[66] In any case, the city of Qarqar fell before the coalition forces could arrive on the scene; otherwise, the open-field battle would have occurred before the capture of the city by Shalmaneser. The coalition forces may have withdrawn to Tell Qelēdin just south of Qarqar on this same longitudinal road. But the coalition succeeded in halting the Assyrian advance, and Shalmaneser III had to campaign in north Syria in 849, 848, and 845 before the coalition could be broken.

---

64. Sader 1986; 1987; Na'aman 1999.

65. The impression given by Noth is that militarily Tell Qarqur is practically located in a "box canyon."

66. See n. 26 above.

In the case of the textual objection, it is argued that since the city of Qarqar is not mentioned in the lists of places conquered by Tiglath-pileser III and annexed to the province of Ḫatarikka, and since Tell Qarqur is located within the confines of the newly-established province, Qarqar must have remained in the territory of Eni-ilu, the king of Hamath, outside the area annexed by Assyria in 738 BCE.[67] There are two summary inscriptions of Tiglath-pileser that record town lists for Ḫatarikka: Summary Inscription 4[68] and Summary Inscription 5.[69] However, this is not that strong of an argument.[70] While it is true that Qarqar is not included in either list, both texts are very fragmentary and therefore cannot be used as definitive proof that Qarqar was not included in either list.[71] In fact, in the case of Summary Inscription 4, what text is preserved is on a second slab and was probably not the first line of that slab. Moreover, there is no statement that Eni-ilu retained the possession of Qarqar;[72] this is a deduction from its absence in the lists. Na'aman has also argued that the northern boundary of Hamath after 738 may tentatively be established on the basis of the letter ND 2644.[73] He asserts that the mention of Ni'u (Qalʿat el-Mudîq) in the letter (line 6 or 22 in Saggs edition) was the northern border of the kingdom of Hamath. But again, this letter is fragmentary, and the section in question appears to read:

(r. 3) KASKAL *ša* URU.*ta-ab-*⸢URU-*a-a*⸣
(4) *ú-šaḫ-ka-mu-k*[*a* x?]
(5) *ki-i ša bir-te* URU.x[x x x]
(6) [*bir-t*]*e* URU.*ni-u*
[space of about 2 lines?]
(7) *bir-te* ⸢URU.*qi*⸣*-di-ši*
(8) ⸢*bir*⸣-te [x x x x]x

(r. 3) (As to) the campaign against the Tabalean(s),
(4) they will explain to you [...].
(5) When (those) between the city of [...]
(6) [betwe]en the city of Ni'u,

67. Na'aman 1999, 89; Sader 1986, 133.
68. RINAP 1:104–7, 42, lines 1′–5′; Tadmor 1994, 136–43, Summary 4: lines 1′–5′a.
69. RINAP 1:107–10, 43, ii.16–24; Tadmor 1994, 144–49, Summary 5: lines ii.16–24.
70. See the discussion of Liverani 1992a, 76–77; and Grayson 2001, 185–87.
71. A perusal of the plates demonstrates this, see RINAP 1:40–44, 13, lines 6b–11; Tadmor 1994, pls. LI and LII.
72. The texts simply record that Eni-ilu paid tribute (Ann. 13*:11; Ann. 27:4; and Summ. 7 r.8′). See Tadmor 1994.
73. Most recent edition: SAA 19:5–6, text 3; earlier editions: Saggs 2001, 175–77; 1955, 142–43. See the transcription of the tablet, Saggs 2001, pl. 35.

(7) between ⸢the city of Qa᾽desh,
(8) between the [city of ...]

As can be seen, there are only two cities (fortresses as Saggs interpreted *bir-te*) whose names are preserved. From this context, as much as can be discerned, it is hardly self-evident that the city of Ni'u represents the northern border! Therefore, there is no evidence that proves that Tell Qarqur cannot be the location of Qarqar. While there is presently no absolute proof that Tell Qarqur is Qarqar, there is also no evidence that disproves it.[74]

In 848 BCE, Shalmaneser captured the city of Aštammaku (URU *áš-ta-ma-ku*).[75] This event is also depicted on a bronze band from Balawat with epigraph,[76] that notes Shalmaneser's capture of another eighty-six cities (var. eighty-nine and ninety-nine). Tell Mastuma is very likely ancient Aštammaku.[77] Excavations carried out at the tell have revealed that it was part of a series of garrisons established in this area in order to meet the continuing Assyrian pressure.[78] A grand-type house found in level 1–2b appears to have been the residence of a governor from the time period of the battle of Qarqar. Perhaps these other cities, Adennu, Pargâ, and Arganâ had similar functions.

As discussed above, the center of Luǵath was Ḥad̮rak/Ḫatarikka (Bagg 2007, 93–5). It is mentioned a number of times in the Aramaic inscription of Zakkur (*ḥzrk*)[79]and occurs in biblical Hebrew (*ḥadrāk*).[80] The spellings with *z*/*d* interchange indicate an original *d̮*. While the Zakkur inscription was found at Tell Afis, both Ḥad̮rak and a toponym 'Apis are mentioned in the inscription. Thus, some scholars have suggested that since Tell Afis should be identified with the Apis (*ʾpš*) in the inscription, Ḥad̮rak should be located

74. See the comments of Makinson 2009, 29.

75. See the Assur Annals (RIMA 3:38, A.0.102.6, iii.1–2); the Calah Bulls (RIMA 3:47, A.0.102.8, 36′–37′); and the Marble Slab (RIMA 3:53, A.0.102.10, ii.55–57).

76. RIMA 3:146–47, A.0.102.82; Schachner 2007, 64–65, pl. 13.

77. Tell Mastuma (modern Stoumak/Stumak; halfway between Idlib and Riha). See Ikeda 1979, 79; 2003, 93* n. 23; Sader 1987, 222; Watika, Wada and Nishiyama 1995; 2000, 555–56; and Iwasaki 2009. The Iron Age settlement was about 10,000 m$^2$ in size (2000, 538 n. 4). Astour (1963, 236) suggested identifying Neo-Assyrian Aštạmmaku with the city of Aštakamu mentioned in some Alalaḫ VII texts. See Zeeb 1998, 863; Mittmann and Schmitt 2001, B IV 14; Parpola and Porter 2001, 6 (level 1 of certainty).

78. Wakita, Wada and Nishiyama 2000, 555–56.

79. Zakkur Inscription (*KAI* 202:A4, 9, 10, B1, 4).

80. See Zech 9:1, where it is mentioned in connection with Damascus and Hamath.

elsewhere.[81] One suggestion has been that Ḥaḏrak/Ḫatarikka was the ancient name of Ḥoms.[82]

However, a number of scholars have argued that the 'Apis in the inscription refers to a particular part of the city of Ḥaḏrak (possibly the acropolis), so that both names can be identified with Tell Afis.[83] Lipiński (2000a, 257) argues that both Ḫatarikka and 'Apiš are non-Semitic place names, with *ʾpš* being the non-Semitic, second-millennium name for "the sacred precinct," and Ḫatarikka being the city's name in the first millennium. Alternatively, others have suggested that *ʾps* was the Semitic name of the city, while Ḫatarikka was the Hittite name.[84]

Located approximately 45 km southwest of Aleppo, Tell Afis[85] is the largest tell (25 ha) between Aleppo and Ḥama with very significant Iron Age remains. It consists of a large lower town of circular shape and an acropolis located in the northern half of the tell. Its significance as a town in the Late Bronze Age Hittite Empire has recently been affirmed by the discovery of Hittite administrative tablets.[86] There is evidence for the identification of *ʾps*/Tell Afis in texts from Ugarit, Alalaḫ, and Ebla.[87]

That the acropolis contained an ancient sacred precinct is proven by two recent discoveries. First, an ostracon reading [ ]*lwr*[88] was found on the eastern part of the acropolis (Area G, square EaV6).[89] The building (L.1344)

81. Hawkins (1990, 161) states: "For the location of the city of Ḫatarikka itself, the site of Afis where the Zakkur Stele was found has been proposed, but is apparently ruled out by the probable identification of *ʾpš* on the stele as the ancient name of this site. The probability remains that Ḫatarikka should be sought in the neighbourhood of Afis." A location near Qinneṣrîn has been suggested. See Lewy 1944, 449 n. 108; 1952, 419. Millard (1962, 43) states: "The site of Ḥaḏrak (Assyrian *Ḫatarikka*; Hebrew *Ḥazrak*) has been located near Qinneṣrîn, 15 miles south-west of Aleppo. The Zakir stele itself was found at Afis, 14 miles south-west of Qinneṣrîn." See also Sader 1987, 226 n. 104; Margalit 1994, 13; Noth 1929, 137. Dion (1997, 142 n. 19) points out that the mention of URU.*qi-na-as-ri-na* by Tiglath-pileser III (see Tadmor 1994, 102, St. IIB, line 8′) shows that Qinneṣrîn was already the name of a city at the time when Ḥaḏrak was still called Ḫatarikka in the Neo-Assyrian inscriptions.

82. Rainey in Rainey and Notley 2006, 221; Dussaud 1927, 237–39.

83. Dion 1997, 139–43; Lipiński 2000a, 255–57; Mazzoni 1994, 323; 2001, 99–100; Mazzoni 2005, 12–13; 2008a, 7–11.

84. See for discussion, Bagg 2007, 95.

85. For discussion of the archaeological finds from the early periods, see §3.1.6.

86. Note the connection between Kizzuwatna and Tell Afis in the newly discovered correspondence at Tell Afis. See Archi and Venturi 2012, 32–55.

87. Belmonte Marín 2001, 27–28; Bonechi 1993, 12–13.

88. Paleographically, the text seems to date to the early eighth century (Cecchini 2000b, 204).

89. An ostracon (found in the same square EaV6) is engraved on the two sides and may be an eighth-century letter (Cecchini 2000a; 2000b, 203).

where the sherd was discovered was a large open-air court, apparently dating to the Iron II and having a religious, ceremonial function (Cecchini 2000b 201–3). The preserved letters are three of the four letters of the name of the god Elwer (*ʾlwr*), and based on similar inscriptions on pottery, the inscription likely read [*lʾ*]*lwr* "belonging to/for Elwer" (Younger 2007, 139–40; Amadasi Guzzo 2014, 56). This was the deity for whom Zakkur erected his stela and who was probably pictured in the now-missing upper relief portion of that monument. Elwer was a weather god known in east and north Syria (Millard 1990: 51).

J. F. Ross (1970, 20–22) has identified the god Mer worshiped at Mari with El-wer, the deity to whom Zakkur dedicated his stela. This deity, whose name is also written in cuneiform as Wer and Ber, is attested in the Mari region throughout the second millennium and into the first. The Middle Assyrian god-list, *An* = *Anum*, equates Ber with the storm god Adad (Litke 1998). His name stands beside Aššur's and Adad's in a Neo-Assyrian deed, and the Old Babylonian Pennsylvania tablet of Gilgamesh names Wer while the Neo-Assyrian account of the same episode has the name Enlil instead (Lambert 1985, 534–35). The god was evidently not central to the Babylonian pantheon, but it is not clear that his worship was centered in the Mari region. Importantly, he is mentioned in Adad-nērārī III's Antakya Stela: MU *aš-šur* ᵈIŠKUR *u* ᵈ*be-er* ᵈBAD *aš-šur-ú* [ᵈNIN.LÍ]L *aš-šur-tú* MU ᵈ30 *a-šib* URU.KASKAL-*ni*, "By the name of the deities Aššur, Adad, and Ber, the Assyrian Enlil, the Assyrian [Ninli]l, and the name of Sîn, dwelling in Harran." Line 17 reads: [*aš-šur*] ᵈIŠKUR *u* ᵈ*be-er* ᵈ30 *a-šib* URU.KASKAL, "[Aššur] Adad and Ber, Sîn dwelling in Harran."[90] It may be that Zakkur honored this deity because he recognized a god he knew from his days in ʿĀna, if he came from there, and according to the end of the Zakkur inscription he built a temple to the deity.[91] Thus the discovery of this ostracon is an important witness to this deity and to the fact that Apis (*ʾpš*) was "the ancient sacred district, i.e., the acropolis" (Soldi 2009, 104).

Second, the discovery on the western side of the acropolis of a typical *in antis* temple (designated Temple AI) with a tripartite plan on a north–south axis is additional evidence (Mazzoni 2001a, 2008, 2010, 2012, 2014). This is an impressive structure, being 38/32 × 28 m with large stone foundations and hard plastered floor. The striking and unparalleled dimensions of the building have led the excavators to identify this as the main temple of the city, the one representing the major cult on the acropolis of the Aramaean town, namely, that of the Storm God. More importantly, this temple is built on the

90. RIMA 3:204, A.0.104.2, lines 11b–12; *COS* 2.114A:272.

91. See also Lipiński 2000a, 616; Niehr 2003, 91–95.

remains of two earlier temples (Temple AII and Temple AIII). Temple AIII has a plastered shrine and appears to date to the eleventh–tenth century BCE. Soldi notes the discovery of a seal in the fill of this temple that depicts the Storm God on a bull, as well as the recovery of a *kernos* vessel with a bull's head found on the floor during the last excavation campaign, both of which support an identification with a storm-god temple complex (Soldi 2009, 108).

Thus these two discoveries, from different sides of the acropolis, in conjunction with the longevity of the location of the storm-god temple, strengthen the identification of the acropolis of Tell Afis with the part of the town called Apis (*ʾpš*) in the Zakkur Inscription. Perhaps, the dynastic change with Zakkur is reflected in the foundation of Ḥaḏrak as a new capital (Venturi 2010). Later, Ḫatarikka is attested in Neo-Assyrian inscriptions as the seat of a Neo-Assyrian governor.[92]

Zitānu was another city of Hamath, mentioned in Tiglath-pileser III's list, which is identified with Zaitān on the western bank of the Quweiq River, about 20 km southwest of Aleppo.[93] The city of Bumame was also a city that belonged to a district of Hamath named in Tiglath-pileser's list. Lipiński suggests identifying it with Tell Mamū, ca. 22 km south of Aleppo in the al-Maṭḥ marshes.[94]

An important city on the southern end of the kingdom was Labāʾu[95] (URU.*La-ab-ʾu-ú*) mentioned immediately after the summation of the cities of Hamath by Tiglath-pileser III.[96] In this list, it heads the unpreserved list of cities of Bīt-Ḫazaʾili (Aram-Damascus). Hence, Labāʾu appears to have been a border town; though in the middle of the eighth century, it must have belonged to Damascus, not Hamath.[97] It was a city near Ṣubat, most likely modern Lebwe,[98] 25 km northeast of Baalbek in the northern Beqaʿ Valley of Lebanon.[99]

---

92. Radner 2006–8a, 58, no. 50. However, she excludes Tell Afis from being identified with Ḫatarikka.

93. Dussaud 1927, 239; Sader 1987, 290; Lipiński 2000a, 296; Bagg 2007, 276.

94. Lipiński 2000a, 296. According to Bagg (2007, 55) Weippert's suggested emendation (1973, 42 n. 61) to read URU.*bu-ta*!-*me* has no basis.

95. Lebwe appears to be attested in Thutmose III List (no. 10: *l-b-n*); the Amarna texts: EA 53:35, 57; EA 54:27, 32 (URU.*la-bá-na*); and the Hebrew Bible: לבוא-(חֲמָת).

96. RINAP 1:107–10, 43, ii.25; Tadmor 1994, 148–49, Summary Inscription 5, ii.25.

97. Naʾaman 1978, 232–33; 1999c, 421–25.

98. For possible archaeological evidence, see Lehmann 2002, 316; Kuschke 1954, 128; 1958, 96.

99. Bagg 2007, 151, s.v. Labāʾu; and the extended discussion of Rainey in Rainey and Notley 2006, 35; Aḥituv 1984, 131; Lipiński 2000a, 320–22: Naʾaman 1999c, 425; Sader 1987, 291; Tadmor 1994, 149; Weippert 1992, 59 n. 100; Parpola and Porter 2001, 8, 22.

The city of Manṣuāte (most often KUR.*Man-ṣu-a-te*[100]) appears also to have been a border town that at times was considered Hamath's territory and at other times Damascus's (Bagg 2007, 166–68). The Aramaic spelling was possibly **Maṣṣuat*, **Maṣṣuah*.[101] It has been suggested that the region is reflected in the Egyptian transcription *Mnḏ'wt* in an inscription of Amenhotep II (ca. 1427–1401), but this is far from certain.[102] Sure occurrences of the toponym occur only in the Neo-Assyrian period (from 796 BCE onwards). A restoration of the toponym in the Sefire inscriptions (Sefire I B 10) is doubtful (Bagg 2007, 167).

Generally, the proposed locations for Manṣuāte have fallen into two main areas: (1) the Beqa' of Lebanon, around Baalbek, north–northwest of Damascus (thus in the territory of Aram-Damascus);[103] or (2) in the southern territory of the kingdom of Hamath at the modern site of Maṣyāf (45 km southwest of Ḥama).[104] Makinson (2009, 30–31) proposes a northern location, arguing that, although the central Beqa' appears as a logical step in the expedition of Adad-nērārī III against Damascus, the proposed identifications in this area are speculative. Regarding the equation of Manṣuāte with Maṣyāf, he argues that there are two problems: (1) the absence of Iron Age remains at the site; and (2) the location of the place within the kingdom of Hamath makes little sense, because Hamath was a polity ruled at the time of the battle of Manṣuāte by Zakkur, an ally of the Assyrians. He asserts that the Aramaic spelling of the name would have been MNSH or MNS' and that with the assimilation of the N, the Aramaic form would be MSSH or MSS', which resembles the Hellenistic and Roman period name Ἔμεσα (modern Ḥoms). However, Makinson's proposed Aramaic form is most cer-

---

100. Written only once with the land determinative (KUR).

101. Zadok 1978, 56; Millard and Tadmor 1973, 65 n. 21: "The Aramaic form was apparently *mṣwh* like *ḥdwh*, *Ḫanduati* in Akkadian." Zadok suggests that the toponym may possibly be the same word as Syriac *maṣṣūtā* (> **maṣṣuatā*) "strife"; that the proposed Egyptian attestation of the toponym in the second millennium poses no linguistic difficulty since the root *nṣy*, "to quarrel, strive" is also found in Canaanite; that this meaning may suit a border district; and that the *n* of *Manṣuāte* may be either original (i.e., the first consonant of the root) or dissimilatory. There is one anaptyctic spelling (URU.*man-nu-ṣu-a-te*, SAA 7:125, 116, 7′) out of the eleven occurrences (which might indicate that the /n/ is part of the root).

102. Bagg (2007, 167) asserts that it is impossible.

103. Honigmann 1924, 16 (no. 302), s.v. Μασσυας; Mazar 1962, 97–98; Donner 1970, 56; Elliger 1947, 104–5; Millard and Tadmor 1973, 63; Na'aman 1995b, 104, with map, p. 105; Weippert 1992, 50–52.

104. Honigmann 1924, 15 (no. 298); Lipiński 1971; 2000a, 306–9; Na'aman 1999c, 427–28; Radner 2006–8a, 61; Hasegawa 2012, 116; Siddall 2013, 17. Hawkins (1987–90b, 67) understands Manṣuāte to be a province within Hamath.

tainly wrong, since he has not paid close attention to the *ṣ* in the spelling.[105] In light of the current data, the location of the city of Manṣuāte and the limits of the Assyrian province cannot be accurately determined. This is unfortunate since this was the site of a crucial battle in 796 (see §7.2.3.1).

Tell Mishrifeh/Qatna is located about 170 km north of Damascus. Excavations have revealed a tenth–eighth-century occupation of the site following its destruction and abandonment at the end of the second millennium (Bonacossi 2007, 80–86). The precise name of the site during this period is uncertain. It is likely that it was connected with the kingdom of Hamath, with it serving as a center for one of the districts in the southern part of the kingdom (Sader 2014, 34). Yet, for part of this period it was under the control of Aram-Damascus (most certainly at the time of Hazael). The city declined at the end of the eighth century in connection with the Assyrian conquest.

## 7.2. History

### 7.2.1. Early Period

It is not known for certain when the kingdom of Hamath came into existence (for a list of the kings, see table 7.3). In the eleventh century, this area may have been part of the kingdom of Taita I; in the late eleventh–early tenth century, it appears to have been ruled by Taita II, whose kingdom may have continued down into the second half of ninth century. The storm-god temple at Tell Afis, Temple AIII (see §3.1.6 above) might possibly date to the eleventh–tenth century and belong to the reign of one of these monarchs. As for Luǵath/Luḫuti in this period, there is no evidence to indicate the political circumstances, whether it was part of these rulers' domains or was independent.

The fact that in the ninth century the dynasty in control of Hamath utilized hieroglyphic Luwian for its inscriptions may be taken as evidence for some kind of continuity with the eleventh–tenth-century monarchs. But the exact relationship is very unclear.

The Hebrew Bible refers to Hamath as a significant kingdom in the early tenth century, with its king To'î (*t'y*) entering into an alliance with David (2 Sam 8:9–11; 1 Chr 18:9–11). The assessment of this evidence was presented in §3.1.6 and will not be repeated here.

105. This does not mean that Ḥoms could not have been ancient Manṣuāte. It just means that Makinson's philological discussion is flawed.

### 7.2.2. The Ninth-Century Luwian Dynasty

In ninth-century Hamath, the native hieroglyphic Luwian inscriptions from this region attest to a cultural continuum with the earlier period of Taita I and Taita II. These inscriptions are primarily the work of Urhilina, the son of Parita, and his son, Uratami. Urhilina was a contemporary of Shalmaneser III, and reigned ca. 860–840.[106] Uratami reigned approximately 840–820. Thus Parita probably reigned ca. 880–860 (making him a contemporary of Aššurnaṣirpal II). In the HAMA 4 inscription,[107] Urhilina contrasts the situation regarding the temple of the goddess Ba'alat "in my age" (*á-mi-za ara/i-za*)(§12) with that "in my father's and also great-grandfathers' age" (*á-mi-za tá-ti-za* AVUS-*ha*||-*tà-za-ha-wa/i ara/i-za*) (§10).[108] This seems to imply that at least two generations are unnamed: his grandfather "Y" (who may have reigned ca. 900–880 BCE) and his great-grandfather "X" (ca. 920–900 BCE). Thus, this dynasty appears to have been at least five generations, possibly more.

#### 7.2.2.1. The Reign of Parita

Urhilina's father, Parita, ruled Hamath in 880–860 BCE. Parita is known only from three inscriptions of his son Urhilina. While he is never given a royal title in any of these occurrences, the HAMA 4 inscription contrasts his time of rule with that of Urhilina.

Interestingly, Aššurnaṣirpal II does not mention Hamath on his western campaign of 870 BCE, even though he raided and plundered the land of Luḫuti (Luǵath) from his base at Aribua:[109]

> I entered the city of Aribua, the fortified city of Lubarna, the Patinean; I took the city for my own. I reaped the barley and straw of the land Luḫuti; I stored (it) inside. I staged a banquet in his palace. I settled people of Assyria in (the city).
>
> While I was in the city of Aribua, I conquered the cities of the land Luḫuti. I massacred many of their (inhabitants); I razed, destroyed, (and) burned. I captured soldiers alive; I impaled (them) on stakes before their cities.[110]

---

106. In the Assyrian sources, Irḫulēni (Urhilina) is attested with a minimum reign of 853–845 BCE.

107. Hawkins 2000, 405, HAMA 4 §10.

108. Kloekhorst (2008, 353) analyzes the term as a dat.-loc.pl. of *huhant(i)-*.

109. For the location, see n. 26 above.

110. RIMA 2:218, A.0.101.1, iii.81b–84a.

This raises a question about the status of Luḫuti/Luǵath vis-à-vis Hamath. One possibility is that Hamath did not control Luḫuti/Luǵath at this time. From Aššurnaṣirpal's text, it appears that Luḫuti/Luǵath is not unified; it has no king (at least mentioned), and it seems to consist of a "plurality of cities" (Liverani 1992a, 110).

Another possibility is that Luḫuti/Luǵath was part of Hamathite territory already at this date, but since there is no effort on the part of Parita (perhaps the ruler at the time) to engage the Assyrian army (and all of its allies that Aššurnaṣirpal II had accumulated on his campaign westward), there must have been a deliberate choice not to fight. Perhaps without forming a coalition to fight the Assyrians, the Hamathites felt that they could only protect their territory on the Orontes, and that Luḫuti would need to fend for itself. Another possibility is that Urhilina ascended the throne around this time (ca. 870 BCE) and perhaps was not in a good position to oppose Aššurnaṣirpal's invasion.

The episode raises many questions, even if Hamath was not in control of Luḫuti/Luǵath at the time of Aššurnaṣirpal's action. Was Hamath caught off guard? Was Assyrian strength too much for a response without forming a coalition, although Aššurnaṣirpal's army would not be the size of Shalmaneser III's?[111] Why did Aššurnaṣirpal II attack Luḫuti, if he could have simply forced a tribute payment? Was the grain simply a means of supplying Aribua or feeding all the army? While these and other questions remain unknown, it is clear that Aššurnaṣirpal II established an Assyrian outpost at Aribua, which appears to have been on the border of Patina and Hamath. When the Assyrian king Shalmaneser III invaded the area in 853, Luḫuti was apparently under Hamathite control, since a number of the cities are attributed to Urhilina, king of Hamath (both in the inscriptions and the Balawat Gates).

### 7.2.2.2. The Reign of Urhilina

By 860 BCE, it is likely that Urhilina was ruler over Hamath.[112] It seems that he was one of the more significant monarchs in Hamath's history, perhaps its most outstanding. From his inscriptions, it is clear that his building activities were more substantial than his predecessors. From his ability to put together, and keep together, a major and, overall, very effective coalition, it is evident that he must have been a person of diplomatic skills. From his involvements

---

111. Liverani (2004b, 215–16) concludes that "we can reasonably maintain that Shalmaneser had to venture into Syria with armies of the size of 60,000 soldiers or more" (about three times the size of Aššurnaṣirpal's army).

112. For a discussion of the name, see §3.1.6 n. 111.

in battles with the Assyrians, it seems that he was, at least, an above average military leader.

A recently discovered hieroglyphic Luwian stela from Tall Šṭīb, 41 km north–northwest of Ḥama, demonstrates this monarch's building activities. According to its inscription, Urhilina constructed the city at this site (ancient name still unknown), and erected his stela for the goddess Ba'alat:[113] "I am Urhilina, son of Parita, king of Hamath. This city, I constructed; and I erected this stela for Ba'alat." This stela is very similar in its wording to the RESTAN, QAL'AT EL-MUDÎQ, and HINES stelae of Urhilina (Hawkins 2000, 409). Together they indicate that Urhilina was not only an important member of the anti-Assyrian coalition, but was a successful builder. The Tall Šṭīb stela shows that the power of the kingdom was not concentrated simply along the Orontes, but was, in fact, spread into the hinterland.

Early in his reign, there seems to have been a period of peace and expansion. Luǵath was recovered and built up. Many of the cities that the Assyrians must later vanquish were located in Luǵath and it is likely that they were reinforced in preparation for what was coming. Hamath had not been drawn into the Bīt-Adīni campaigns at the very beginning of Shalmaneser's western expansion. Urhilina, however, certainly observed what was transpiring north of his land. In the years running up to 853 (Shalmaneser III's first campaign in his land), Urhilina took the initiative to construct a powerful coalition of very different polities. In fact, Hamath and Damascus had been, and later would be, enemies; the same was true of Aram-Damascus and Israel. That Urhilina was the organizer of the coalition seems to be the inference from Shalmaneser's statement "these 12 kings he (Urhilina) took as his allies" (Kurkh Monolith ii.95b, see below).

However, after this first segment, the bulk of his reign saw a constant attrition of his territory. Hamath and Luǵath bore the brunt of the resistance to Assyria: most of the major battles were fought on his country's soil (other than the 849 campaign), and it was his land's cities that were mauled one by one as the Assyrian military pressure persisted against Hamath for almost a decade.

#### 7.2.2.2.1. Shalmaneser III's 853 Campaign

Shalmaneser III's campaign of 853[114] is reported in nine of his inscriptions,[115] the most detailed of which is found on the Kurkh Monolith. This is an annal-

113. Gonnet 2010, 97–99; see also Rousset 2010, 101–3.

114. For a detailed analysis of this campaign, see Younger 2007b, 237–71.

115. Six of the nine texts are "Annals": the Kurkh Monolith (RIMA 3:22–24, A.0.102.2, ii.78b–102; Yamada: Annals 3; *COS* 2.113A:261–64); the Aššur Clay Tablets:

istic text that dates the campaign by eponym.[116] On account of its abrupt ending with the narration of the battle of Qarqar, scholars date it from 853–852 BCE. It was apparently carved in great haste resulting in numerous scribal errors (Tadmor 1961, 143–44). This is quite unfortunate since the stela contains the most detailed extant account of the battle of Qarqar (see figs. 7.5, 7.6). The portion concerning the 853 campaign reads:

> *Episode 1* (ii.78b–81a)
> In the eponymy of Dayyān-Aššur (853),[117] in the month of Iyyar (the second month = April-May), the fourteenth day, I departed from Nineveh. I crossed the Tigris. I approached the cities of Giammu on the River Balīḫ. They were afraid of my lordly fearfulness (and) the splendor of my fierce weapons; and with their own weapons they killed Giammu, their master. I entered the cities of Saḫlala[118] and Tīl-ša-turaḫi. I took my gods into his palaces; (and) celebrated the *tašīltu*-festival in his palaces. I opened his treasury (and) saw his stored-away wealth. I carried off his possessions (and) property. I brought (them) to my city, Aššur.

> *Episode 2* (ii.81b–86a)
> I departed from the city of Saḫlala. I approached the city of Kār-Shalmaneser. I crossed the Euphrates in its flood,[119] for a second time[120] in rafts (made of inflated) goatskins. <In> the city of Ana-Aššur-utēr-aṣbat, which is by the opposite bank of the Euphrates on the River Sagura (and)

(RIMA 3:36–37, A.0.102.6, ii.19b–33; Yamada: Annals 5; *COS* 2.113B:264–66); the Calah Bulls (RIMA 3:45–46, A.0.102.8, lines 12′b–19′; Yamada Annals 6; *COS* 2.113C:266–67); the Marble Slab (RIMA 3:52, A.0.102.10, ii.13–25; Yamada: Annals 7; *COS* 2.113D:267–68); the Black Obelisk (RIMA 3:65, A.0.102.14, lines 54b–66; Yamada: Annals 13; *COS* 2.113F:269–70); the Broken Statue from Calah (RIMA 3:75, A.0.102.16, lines 28–38a; Yamada: Annals 14). The three other texts are "summary inscriptions": the Fort Shalmaneser Stone Throne Base (RIMA 3:103, A.0.102.28, lines 29–34a; Yamada: Summary Inscription 6); the Engraved Door Sill from Fort Shalmaneser (RIMA 3:107, A.0.102.30, lines 22–28a; Yamada: Summary Inscription 9); and the Assur Basalt Statue (RIMA 3:118, A.0.102.40, i.14–24; Yamada: Summary Inscription 19; *COS* 2.113G:270).

116. This version is identified by Schramm as Recension A (see *EAK* 2:70–72, 87–90), while Yamada labels it Annals 3. See Yamada 2000a, 14; and Fuchs 1998, cols. 191–192.

117. See Millard 1994, 27, 93.

118. Hallo (1964, 78) proposed that the city of Saḫlala be identified with Tell Sahlan (about 20 km south of Ain al-Arūs). Also see Yamada 2000a, 151; and Lipiński 2000a, 128 n. 57.

119. This would likely have been around April–May when the Euphrates is in flood in this part of the river as reflected in modern gauge reading at Jerablus (obviously prior to dam constructions). See Ionides 1937, 38, table 18.

120. Yamada (1998, 92–94) argues that the phrase *ša šanûtēšu* means "another time, again," not "for a second time."

which the people of the land of Ḫatti call the city of Pitru, in (this city) I received the tribute of the kings on the opposite bank of the Euphrates—Sangara, the Karkamišean, Kundašpu, the Kummuḫite, Arame, (the man) of Bīt-Agūsi, Lalla, the Melidite, Ḫayānu, (the man) of Bīt-Gabbāri, Qalparuda, the Patinean, (and) Qalparuda, the Gurgumite: silver, gold, tin, bronze, (and) bronze bowls.

*Episode 3* (ii.86b–87a)
I departed from the Euphrates. I approached the city of Aleppo (Ḫalman). They were afraid to fight. They seized my feet. I received their tribute of silver (and) gold. I made sacrifices before Hadad of Aleppo (Ḫalman).

*Episode 4* (ii.87b–89a)
I departed from the city of Aleppo (Ḫalman). I approached the cities of Irḫulēni, the Hamathite. I captured Adennu, Pargâ, (and) Arganâ, his royal cities. I carried off captives, his valuables, (and) his palace possessions. I set fire to his palaces.

*Episode 5* (ii.89b–90a)
I departed from the city of Arganâ. I approached the city of Qarqar.[121] I razed, destroyed and burned the city of Qarqar, his royal city.

(ii.90b–95a)
1,200 chariots, 1,200 cavalry, (and) 20,000 troops of Hadad-ezer (*Adad-idri*) of Damascus; 700 chariots, 700 cavalry, (and) 10,000 troops of Irḫulēni, the Hamathite; 2,000 chariots, (and) 10,000 troops of Ahab, the Israelite (*Sir'alāia*); 500 troops of Byblos; 1,000 troops of Egypt; 10 chariots (and) 10,000 troops of the land of Irqanatu (Irqata); 200 troops of Matinu-Ba'al of the city of Arvad; 200 troops of the land of Usanatu (Usnu); 30 chariots (and) [ ],000 troops of Adon-Ba'al of the land of Šianu (Siyannu); 1,000 camels of Gindibu' of Arabia;[122] [ ] hundred[123] troops of Ba'asa, (the man) of Bīt-Ruḫubi, the Ammonite—these 12 kings he took as his allies.

121. See discussion above concerning the location of Qarqar.

122. It is hard to understand the basis for Ahlström's statement (1993, 577 n. 2): "Gindibu' participated in the battle with 1,000 camels, which may have contributed to the coalition's victory *in scaring the horses of the Assyrians. They do not like the smell of a camel*" (emphasis added)! If this is true, why didn't the camels scare the coalition's horses? They were much closer than the Assyrian horses!

123. Or [ ],000, if it is [L]IM instead of ME. See Yamada 2000a, 368.

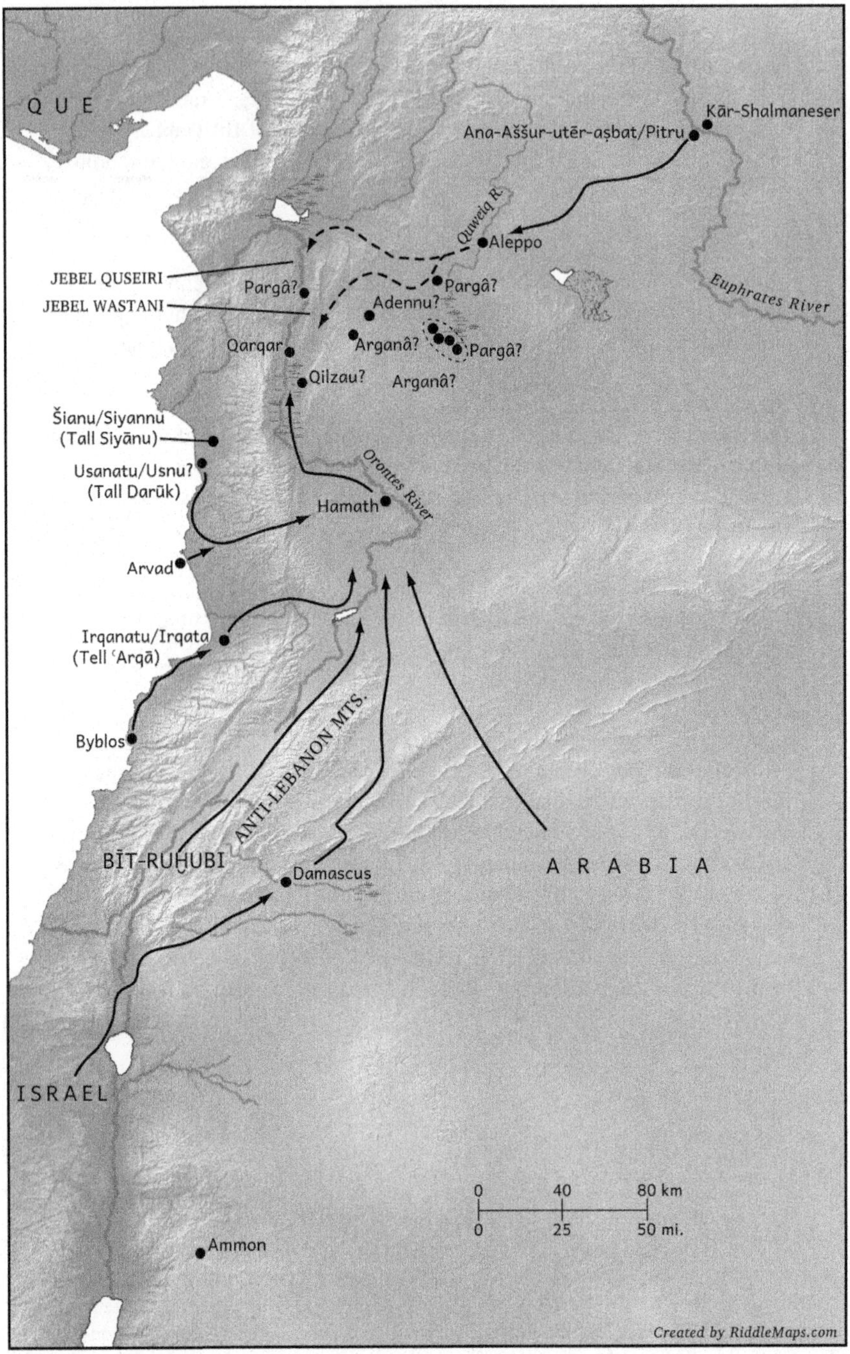


Fig. 7.5. Map of Shalmaneser III's 853 BCE campaign

(ii.95b–102)
They marched against me [to do] war and battle.[124] With the supreme forces which Aššur, my lord, had given me (and) with the mighty weapons which the divine standard,[125] which goes before me, had granted me, I fought with them. I decisively defeated them from the city of Qarqar to the city of Qilzau.[126] I felled with the sword 14,000 troops, their fighting men. Like Adad, I rained down upon them a devastating flood. I spread out their corpses (and) I filled the plain. <I felled> with the sword their extensive troops. I made their blood flow in the *wadis*(?) [ ]. The field was too small for laying flat their bodies (lit. "their lives"); the broad countryside had been consumed in burying them. I blocked the Orontes River with their corpses as with a causeway. In the midst of this battle I took away from them chariots, cavalry, (and) teams of horses.

The structure of the account of the 853 campaign on the Kurkh Monolith (fig. 7.6) contains five episodes built on the itinerary phrase: TA URU X *at-tu-muš*, "I departed from X" (ii.78b; ii.81b; ii.86b; ii.87b; and ii.89b).[127] The first three episodes (1–3) narrate Phase One of the campaign, the subjugation of northern Syria, and the last two episodes (4–5) relate Phase Two, that is, the subjugation of central and southern Syria. Phase One sets the stage for Phase Two. The campaign is related in terms of the easiest (no fighting of the Assyrian army is necessary to subdue northern Syria) to the most difficult (the Assyrian army must capture and destroy cities and fight a twelve king alliance in central and southern Syria). This order creates a literary effect, slowly increasing the tension by progressing from the easy to the difficult and is similar to the narration of the third campaign in Sennacherib's Annals.[128] This is important to keep in mind as one comes to the longer, climactic account of the battle of Qarqar at the end of the narrative.

Throughout the account, religious aspects are stressed: Shalmaneser's gods are taken into Giammu's palaces for a celebration; through sacrifices, the support of Hadad of Aleppo (a major Syrian deity, also known to have been worshiped in the city of Assur[129]) is obtained; and in the battle of Qarqar, Aššur, Nergal, and Adad insure Assyrian victory. This is in complete agree-

124. Based on the internal data of the inscription, it seems likely that the battle of Qarqar was fought during July or early August. See n. 119 above.

125. Yamada notes that RIMA 3 reads ÙRI.GAL, but the text reads $^{d}$ÙRI.GAL (2000a, 368, 383). As protective divine standard, Nergal accompanies the Assyrian army on campaigns. See Pongratz-Leisten, Deller and Bleibtreu 1992, 291–98, 330–39, 341–46.

126. For this reading of the toponym, see the discussion on pp. 436–39.

127. This clause as an excerpt from the Neo-Assyrian itineraries is found in the texts starting with Adad-nērārī II on. See Liverani 1988a.

128. See Tadmor 1985, 71, 73. See also Younger 2003a, 235–63.

129. Menzel 1981, 128, T 154 116 (VAT 8918, Ass Ph 4681).

| |
|---|
| Phase One: Subjugation of Northern Syria: Nonfighting Phase (ii.78b–87a) |
| Episode 1 – The Killing of Giammu, Submission and Plunder of Balīḫ (ii.78b–81a) |
| Episode 2 – The Tribute of the Seven Kings of Ḫatti (ii.81b–86a) |
| Episode 3 – The Tribute of Aleppo (Ḫalman) (ii.86b–87a) |
| Phase Two: Subjugation of Central and Southern Syria: Fighting Phase (ii.87b–102) |
| Episode 4 – The Capture, Plunder, and Destruction of the Cities of Irḫulēni of Hamath (ii.87b–89a) |
| Episode 5 – The Battle of Qarqar (ii.89b–102) |
| Part 1: Capture and Destruction of Qarqar (ii.89b–90a) |
| Part 2: Enumeration of Alliance (ii.90b–95a) |
| Part 3: Description of Battle and Results (ii.95b–102) |

Fig. 7.6. Kurkh Monolith's Structure of Shalmaneser III's 853 Campaign

ment with the fact that, as Reade (1979a, 342) points out, the royal stela was "the Assyrian equivalent of a political poster." Since the stela's iconography includes a depiction of the Great King and various divine symbols, either independent of the figure of the king or engraved as components of his necklace, the Neo-Assyrian royal stela portrayed "visible religion" to its onlooker (Hollaway 2002, 68–69). Since the Monolith was discovered at Kurkh, the stela falls into Morandi's class 1 ("stele di intervento militare," Morandi 1988, 113–17) ,which were placed along the routes taken by the Assyrian army on campaigns. Thus it is not surprising that the account of year 853 BCE in the Monolith is the most detailed and propagandistic of all of Shalmaneser's inscriptions that narrate the events of his sixth regnal year.

In episode 1, in the initial action of this campaign, by simply marching to the Balīḫ River, Shalmaneser removed a pocket of insubordination in northern Syria—specifically a group of cities that were under the rule of an individual named Giammu. In order to ward off a hopeless conflict, a pro-Assyrian opposition group in the country killed Giammu[130] and submitted to Shalmaneser without a fight.

130. For a discussion of the variants concerning the death of Giammu, see Younger 2005, 255–57.

Table 7.1. The Seven Tributary Kings of Ḫatti (853 BCE) (Kurkh Monolith ii.82b–86a)

| Ruler | Nation | Formulation |
|---|---|---|
| Sangara | Karkamiš | $^{m}$*sa-an-ga-ra* URU *gar-ga-miš-a-a* |
| Kundašpu | Kummuḫ | $^{m}$*ku-un-da-áš-pi* URU *ku-mu-ḫa-a-a* |
| Arame | Bīt-Agūsi (Yaḫānu; Arpad) | $^{m}$*a-ra-me* DUMU *gu-si* |
| Lalla | Melid | $^{m}$*lal-li* URU *me-li-da-a-a* |
| Ḫayānu (Ḥayyā') | Bīt-Gabbāri (Sam'al) | $^{m}$*ḫa-ia-ni* DUMU *ga-ba-ri* |
| Qalparunda | Patina (Unqi) | $^{m}$*qàl-pa-ru-da* KUR *pa-ti-na-a-a* |
| Qalparunda | Gurgum | $^{m}$*qàl-pa-ru-da* KUR *gúr-gu-ma-a-a* |

After a celebration, in episode 2, Shalmaneser departed and marched to Til-Barsib (Kār-Shalmaneser). Crossing the Euphrates, he marched to the city of Pitru (biblical Pethor), another city that he had renamed, Ana-Aššur-utēr-aṣbat. Here he received the tribute of seven kings of "the land of Hatti" (table 7.1).

In episode 3, advancing through the territory of Bīt-Agūsi, Shalmaneser arrived at the city of Aleppo (Ḫalman). There he received that city's tribute and sacrificed to the important Syrian deity, Hadad of Aleppo. At this point, the narrative has demonstrated the utter suzerainty of Shalmaneser III over north Syria, especially with the ease at which he accomplished this.

In Phase Two, in episode 4, the Assyrian army fights for the first time during the campaign, though it appears to easily capture, plunder and destroy three of Irḫulēni's cities. The capture of the Hamathite cites of Pargâ, Adâ (= Adennu) and Qarqar (along with the city of Aštammaku captured in the 848 campaign) are represented in the reliefs on Shalmaneser's bronze gate bands from Balawat (Imgur-Enlil; see above figs. 7.3 and 7.4).[131]

Episode 5 describes the greatest challenge to Assyrian suzerainty over central and southern Syria—the twelve king alliance, headed surprisingly not by Irḫulēni/Urhilina, the king of Hamath, whose land is being invaded, but by Hadad-ezer (Adad-idri) of Aram-Damascus.[132] The challenge is heightened by the enumeration of the extent of participation, size, and military hardware exhibited by the coalition forces (table 7.2). The severity of the alliance's defeat, as it is graphically described in full detail, reinforces the climactic

131. See the discussions of Marcus 1987; Reade 1979b, 66–68; Bär 1996, 113–30.

132. For a possible reason for the organization of this coalition at this time, see Grayson 2004, 5.

Table 7.2. Coalition Members at the Battle of Qarqar 853 BCE (Kurkh Monolith ii.86b–102)

| | Ruler | Nation | Formulation | Chariots | Cavalry | Soldiers | Camels |
|---|---|---|---|---|---|---|---|
| 1 | Hadad-ezer (Adad-idri) | Damascus | $^{md}$IŠKUR-*'I-id-ri* [*ša* KUR] ANŠE-*šú* | 1,200 | 1,200 | 20,000 | |
| 2 | Irḫulēni (Urhilina) | Hamath | $^{m}$*ir-ḫu-le-e-ni* KUR *a-mat-a-a* | 700 | 700 | 10,000 | |
| 3 | Ahab | Israel | $^{m}$*a-ḫa-ab-bu* KUR *sir-'a-la-a-a* | 2,000 | | 10,000 | |
| 4 | | Byblos | KUR *gu-<bal>-a-a* | | | 500 | |
| | | Egypt | KUR *mu-uṣ-ra-a-a* | | | 1,000 | |
| 6 | | Irqanatu/Irqata/ Arqā | KUR *ir-qa-<na>-ta-a-a* | 10 | | 10,000 | |
| 7 | Matinu-Ba'al | Arvad | $^{m}$*ma-ti-nu-ba-'a-li* URU *ar-ma-da-a-a* | | | 200 | |
| 8 | | Usanatu/Usnu | KUR *ú-sa-na-ta-a-a* | | | 200 | |
| 9 | Adon-Ba'al | Šianu | $^{m}$*a-du-nu-ba-'a-li* KUR *ši-a-na-a-a* | 30 | | [ ],000 | |
| 10 | Gindibu' | Arabia | $^{m}$*gi-in-di-bu-'u* KUR *ar-ba-a-a* | | | | 1,000 |
| 11 + 12? | Ba'asa | Bīt Reḥob? (+?) Ammon | $^{m}$*ba-'a-sa* DUMU *ru-ḫu-bi* KUR *a-ma-na-a-a* | | | [ ]00<br>[ ],000 | |
| | Totals | | | 3,940 | 1,900 | 53,000*<br>69,900* | 1,000 |

*minimum: 51,900 + [1],000 + [1]00 = 53,000
*maximum: 51,900 + [9],000 + [9],000 = 69,900
De Odorico (1995, 103–4) estimates 62,900 infantry (+ 3,940 chariots + 1,900 cavalry) ≈ 75,000 fighting men. If the 14,000 casualties figure is correct, then slightly less than 20% (actually 18.7%) of the coalition troops would have been killed during the battle.

message that the Monolith communicates in this 853 campaign: Since Shalmaneser III, on account of his armed forces and powerful deities, exercises complete sovereignty over those who might oppose him, humble submission (as in the case of the Phase One) is preferable to the utter destruction suffered when he is opposed (as in Phase Two).

At this point, some observations on the other texts of Shalmaneser III that narrate the 853 campaign are worth pointing out. Two of the five other annalistic texts (the Assur Clay Tablets [842 BCE] and the Calah Bulls [841 BCE]) contain all five episodes of the Kurkh Monolith, although episodes 2, 4, and 5 are significantly truncated. In episode 5 (the battle of Qarqar), these two "Annals" change the number of dead for the alliance forces from 14,000 to 25,000. They also add three sentences at the end of the episode:

> In order to save their lives they ran away.
> I boarded ships (and)
> I went out upon the sea.

None of the other texts (including the three "Summary Inscriptions") have any of these sentences at the end of episode 5, except the Assur Basalt Statue (a Summary Inscription), which contains only the sentence: "In order to save their lives they ran away."

The remaining three "Annals" (the Marble Slab Inscription [839 BCE], the Black Obelisk [828–827 BCE], and the Broken Statue from Calah [828–827 BCE]) narrate only episodes 1, 2, and 5, though these are shortened in similar ways to these episodes in the Assur Clay Tablets and the Calah Bulls. The number of allied dead are 25,000 (Marble Slab), 20,500 (Black Obelisk), and 29,000 (Broken Statue from Calah).

The Summary Inscriptions (the Fort Shalmaneser Throne Base [846 BCE], the Fort Shalmaneser Door Sill [844 BCE], and the Assur Basalt Statue [833 BCE]) narrate only episode 5 in truncated form. Since the first two summary inscriptions predate all of the annalistic texts, except, of course, the Kurkh Monolith, the truncated form of episode 5 in them probably served as the base text for the truncated forms in the Annals. Line ii.97b of the Monolith has been read "I decisively defeated them from the city of Qarqar to the city of Qilzau (URU *gíl-za-ú*)."[133] Finally, the Assur Basalt Statue credits Shalmaneser with slaying 29,000 allied troops, a reading that is followed in the Broken Statue from Calah.

Also important as a historical source are the bronze bands with multiple registers devoted to depicting the battle scenes from this campaign (853), as well as others that portray the conflict with Hamath in 848, etc. In chrono-

133. For the reading, see above discussion in §7.1, pp. 436–39.

logical order these are: Adâ (IXa, left, pl. 9; fig. 7.3) and Pargâ (IXa, right, pl. 9; fig. 7.3), Qarqar (IXb, pl. 9; fig. 7.4), Aštammaku (XIIIa, pl. 13), and other unnamed settlements of Hamath (XIIIb, pl. 13).[134] Schachner observes that this intense portrayal of the struggles with Hamath reflects the importance of this region in the early years of the reign of Shalmaneser III and that since the images also show the troops of Hamath as the best-equipped opponents, the significance of the opponent is graphically emphasized (Schachner 2007, 223).

#### 7.2.2.2.1.1. Shalmaneser III's Claim to Victory

From the detailed, gory narration of the Kurkh Monolith, it would certainly seem that Shalmaneser III won a great victory at the battle of Qarqar in 853 BCE. However, while Shalmaneser appears to have captured the city of Qarqar along with the other three cities listed in the Monolith and Balawat Bronzes, most scholars believe that his claim to victory over the coalition in the ensuing battle of Qarqar was in reality an Assyrian defeat, since he returned in 849 (his tenth year), 848 (his eleventh year) and 845 (his fourteenth year) to fight against the coalition with little greater success.[135] Of course, there may have been some limited successes during these campaigns (e.g., in 848 he was apparently able to capture the royal city of Aštammaku[136] from the Hamathites and the city of Aparāzu from Arpad),[137] but the Assyrians never once claim to have conquered Hamath, Damascus, or Israel while this coalition remained intact. Aside from Aštammaku, neither looting, nor the destruction of enemy territory, nor tribute is mentioned by Shalmaneser III, let alone an annexation (Bagg 2011, 197). Since the coalition's goal was to halt the Assyrians' southward advance and prevent their domination over the west, it seems that as long as the coalition remained united, this goal was achieved.

Another indication of Assyrian overall failure is the fact that opposition to Assyria increased after the 853 campaign among some of the northern states that had paid tribute previously. In both 849 and 848, even Karkamiš and Arpad fought against Assyria, and consequently the Assyrian army was forced to reconquer cities and territories that on the eve of the battle of Qarqar were submissive to Assyria.[138] It is important to note that Sangara,

134. Schachner 2007, pls. 9 and 13. For Adâ, Pargâ, and Qarqar, see §7.1.

135. See Hawkins 1972–75b, 67. For the resistance to Shalmaneser, see Dion 1995d.

136. For the identification of Aštammaku, see §7.1.

137. See the Assur Clay Tablets (*COS* 2.113B:264–66, ii.68–iii.15).

138. Assur Clay Tablets, ii.55–iii.15; Calah Bulls, 29′–41′; Marble Slab ii.51–iii.5.

the Karkamišean, and Arame of Arpad (Bīt-Agūsi) were kings who paid tribute in 853, but are still on the throne and fighting Assyria in 849 and 848.

Finally, the Balawat Gates of Shalmaneser III hint at a defeat (or at least the halting of Shalmaneser's advance). In Band IX (see fig. 7.4), the capture and destruction of Qarqar is depicted. However, the actual open-field battle with the coalition, led by Hadad-ezer and Irḫulēni, is not shown—a subtle, but significant omission that may reveal a conscious concealment of the Assyrian defeat.[139]

According to two annalistic texts (the Assur Clay Tablets [842 BCE] and the Calah Bulls [841 BCE]), after the battle of Qarqar, Shalmaneser boarded a ship and took a boat ride in the Mediterranean. While some scholars (e.g., Yamada 2000a, 163) accept Shalmaneser's claim of maritime entertainment, this event is missing in the earliest Assyrian record of the battle and its addition to the narrative is only found in these two annalistic texts. And these are the texts that begin the pattern of inflation of the number of allied dead from 14,000 in the Monolith to 25,000, finally culminating in the figure of 29,000 found in the Broken Statue from Calah and the Assur Basalt Statue. Of course, even the 14,000 figure may be exaggerated. Thus some scholars (Galil 2002, 46) see Shalmaneser's cruise as a rhetorical device used to disguise the Assyrian army's failure to gain its objectives in this battle.[140]

Another indication of Shalmaneser's failure, as Hallo has pointed out, may be the total silence of the Bible. He states: "Had Ahab and his allies really suffered the massive defeat which the Assyrian annalists inflicted on them, an account of the battle would certainly have served the didactic purposes of the canonical Book of Kings."[141]

Therefore, the strategy of a combined opposition to the Assyrians worked and spared the region from Assyrian ambitions for roughly twelve years (853–841 BCE). This proved that it was possible to stand up to the Assyrian Empire. However, only the common opponent held this coalition together. By 841 BCE, the coalition had disintegrated—partly the result of the repeated Assyrian campaigns, and partly the result of changes in rulership in two of the most powerful states involved, Damascus (the usurpation of Hazael) and Israel (the usurpation of Jehu).[142] Thus time worked in Assyria's favor. Shalmaneser was on the throne long enough to outlast the coalition. With the changes in Damascus and Israel, Hamath came to terms with Assyria.

---

139. See Schachner 2007, 224 in combination with pp. 191–92.

140. If the battle were a defeat for the Assyrians as the vast majority of scholars believe, it seems doubtful that one would go on a boat ride after such a defeat.

141. Hallo 1960, 40; Hallo and Simpson 1998, 127–30.

142. Kuhrt 1995, 2:488.

The fact is, Shalmaneser's inscriptions do not relate an encounter with Hamathite troops during the 841 campaign, nor later in the campaign of 838–837 BCE. Obviously between 844 and 841, the relationship between Hamath and Assyria had changed. More than a century later, Sargon II claimed that his predecessors had imposed tribute on Irḫulēni (see the Borowski Stela, Lambert 1981, 125; *COS* 2.118B; Hawkins 2004). But since Shalmaneser himself never claimed this, some scholars feel that it is more likely that Shalmaneser brought Hamath over to an Assyrian alliance by diplomatic means, perhaps even some type of bilateral agreement with Assyria that allowed Shalmaneser to pass through its territory (Astour 1971, 384; Green 1979, 36 n. 10; Yamada 2000a, 190 n. 387). One thing is sure: items from Hamath are found at Kalḫu (modern Nimrud), the capital city of Shalmaneser III. For example, there is an ivory with the name of Hamath incised on it.[143] In addition, sixteen burnt-shell ornaments (that were perhaps clappers or castanets) have been discovered at Fort Shalmaneser (room T 10; Barnett 1963, 82–84; Oates and Oates 2001, 181; Hawkins 2000, 410–11). Seven of these are inscribed in hieroglyphic Luwian "Urhilina, the king" (Hawkins 2000, 411). Excavations at Ḥama (ancient Hamath) have produced a similar shell inscribed with the same name (with the same orthrography; Riis and Buhl 1990, 213, 215, no. 800). Also found in the same room (T 10) were some ivories, one of which belonged to Hazael (see §9.3.5.3).[144]

Interestingly, an inscription of Irḫulēni/Urhilina was discovered in the Iraqi village of Hines (1 km from Bavian) about 70 km north of Kalḫu (Nimrud). The inscription, reported in 1935 by Jacobsen (Frankfort and Jacobsen 1935, 101–3, fig. 107 [photo]), is a duplicate of two other Irḫulēni/Urhilina building inscriptions found in Syria (Restan and Qalʿat el-Mudîq) (Hawkins 2000, 408–9). But the stone and incised style of the inscription differ markedly from the basalt and relief script of its duplicates and the other Hamath inscriptions (Hawkins 2000, 409). Because of these differences, Hawkins speculates that it is a copy made in antiquity of an original inscription taken to Assyria by Shalmaneser III, Irḫulēni's/Urhilina's contemporary, or Sargon II, the conqueror of Hamath.[145] On the other hand, Dion

143. Possibly dating to the ninth century on paleographic grounds (note esp. the *mem*). See Millard 1962, 42.

144. Barnett (1963, 81, 85) argued that all of the ivories and other objects from Hamath found in the excavations at Fort Shalmaneser were part of booty that Sargon II carried off after his 720 BCE campaign. A recent study on the Neo-Assyrian attitude toward the use of ivory may explain the storage of ivories of this sort. See Herrmann and Millard 2003.

145. Hawkins 2000, 409. Landsberger (1948, 33 n. 66) went so far as to speculate that Irḫulēni had somehow penetrated deep into Assyria and had written this inscription commemorating this event.

speculates that the reference in the Borowski Stela to Irḫulēni's final submission to Sargon's forefathers favors the reign of Shalmaneser for the time when the Hines inscription was made (Dion 1995b, 487–88).

7.2.2.2.1.2. The Total "Twelve Kings"

Another problem is the number of coalition forces. In the Monolith (ii.95), it states: "these twelve kings he took as his allies" (12 MAN.MEŠ-*ni an-nu-ti a-na* ÉRIN.TAḪ-*ti-šú il-qa-a*), implying that Irḫulēni was the one who organized a coalition of twelve kings to assist him. Oddly, there are only eleven members listed, not twelve; and Irḫulēni is included in the eleven (though not listed first, but second); and only the names of seven kings are entered!

This has brought about a number of different proposals. Grayson suggests that this is an erroneous addition since only eleven kings are listed.[146] Tadmor (1961, 144–45) concludes that this is one of many scribal errors in the Monolith: in this case, the name and country of the twelfth participant were erroneously omitted. A number of scholars think that the last entry "Ba'asa, (the man) of Bīt-Ruḫubi, the Ammonite" is really a reference to two entities: Bēt-Reḥob and Ammon, and that the name of the ruler of the Ammonites has been lost.[147] Among those that hold this view, there is disagree on the identification of the last entity (is it Ammon or Amanah? see the discussion below). Finally, it is also possible that the Assyrian scribes are simply rounding off the number to an even dozen, a conventional number with symbolic significance.[148] The last option seems preferable.

Interestingly, one text of Shalmaneser III, carved along with a second inscription into a rock face at the Tigris's source, gives the number of the allied enemies as "fifteen cities of the seashore."[149] Moreover, the formulation found in three of the Annalistic texts and one Summary Inscription is: "Hadad-ezer (Adad-idri), the Damascene, (and) Irḫulēni, the Hamathite, *together with twelve kings*[150] of the shore of the sea, trusted in their combined

146. See RIMA 3:23 n. ii.90–95.

147. Weidner suggested this (apud Michel 1947, 70 n. 13). Na'aman (1976, 98 n. 19) states: "It should be noted that this combination of names does not appear elswehere in the Assyrian inscriptions, so Weidner's proposal to complete the number of allies to 12 makes very good sense." See also Kuan 1995, 32–34; Ikeda 1999, 278; Yamada 2000a, 160–61; Galil 2002, 42.

148. De Odorico 1995, 133–36; Na'aman (1976, 98 n. 19) recognized this possibility.

149. Tigris Rock Face Inscription 2: RIMA 3:94–95, A.0.102.23, line 21. Grayson (RIMA 3:95 n. 21) notes: "The numeral 15 is clear, according to Lehmann-Haupt, although one expects 12."

150. In the Annals (Assur Clay Tablets, Calah Bulls, Marble Slab): *a-di* 12 MAN. MEŠ-*ni*; in a Summary Inscription (Assur Basalt Statue): *a-di* 12 *mal-ki*.MEŠ.

forces" (emphasis added), while the formulation in two Summary Inscriptions is: "Hadad-ezer (Adad-idri), the Damascene, (and) Irḫulēni, the Hamathite, *and twelve kings*[151] along the seashore trusted in their combined forces" (emphasis mine). All these texts imply two major named kings plus twelve others, giving a total of "fourteen" participants. In light of this, it would seem that the number "twelve" is used in a figurative, conventional way. It is noteworthy and, perhaps not fortuitous, that there are "seven" named kings in this list of "twelve" (Hadad-ezer, Irḫulēni, Ahab, Matinu-Ba'al, Adon-Ba'al, Gindibu', and Ba'asa), a figure that corresponds in number to the tributary kings listed earlier in the account of the 853 campaign (episode 2). The number "seven" is also a conventional figure.

7.2.2.2.1.3. Identification of the Coalition Partners

Interrelated to the question of the "twelve kings" is the issue of the identification of the coalition partners (see table 7.2). These identifications give rise to the question of whether there is a discernible arrangement in the presentation of the participants.

While the first participant seems straightforward, Hadad-ezer (Adad-idri) of Damascus (Schwemer 1998a), there is, in fact, a problem. Since Ahab, the Israelite, is mentioned in the Monolith (third participant listed in the coalition), it is evident that the two kings were contemporaries. However, the only king of Damascus during the reign of Ahab that the Hebrew Bible mentions is Ben-Hadad. In reconstructing the history of the period, two different possibilities have been proposed and these will be discussed at §9.3.4.

The second participant is identified in the Monolith as Irḫulēni of Hamath, who is none other than Urhilina of some of the hieroglyphic Luwian inscriptions from Ḥama, an important king of the Neo-Hittite dynasty that ruled over Hamath during the ninth century (ca. 860–840 BCE).[152] All nine of Shalmaneser's inscriptions that narrate the battle of Qarqar mention him and he, along with Hadad-ezer, forms the leadership for the united front against the Assyrian king, not only in 853, but in 849, 848, and 845. After 845, the coalition disappears and Hamath does not participate in resistance to Shalmaneser in 841 or 838–837 BCE.[153]

151. Fort Shalmaneser Throne Base and Fort Shalmaneser Door Sill read: *ù* 12 MAN. MEŠ-*ni*.

152. Hawkins 2000, 400.

153. Irḫulēni may be pictured lying on his couch within a city of Hamath on the Balawat gates. See King 1915, pl. LXXVII; Barnett 1963, 83.

The third participant is Ahab, the Israelite. This is the only occurrence of the term "Israelite" in the Assyrian inscriptions.[154] The first three participants supply the largest number of troops, chariots, and cavalry to the alliance.

The fourth participant poses a difficulty. The text of the Monolith reads: KUR *gu-a-a* and many early translations understood this to be a variant spelling of Que/Quwe, that is, Cilicia.[155] However, in 1961, Tadmor argued that it is improbable that *gu-a-a* is a variant spelling of the gentilic form on phonetic grounds. He suggested the emendation: KUR *Gu-<bal>-a-a*—the gentilic form for "Byblos." It has also been argued that Que's participation in the military organization of the central Syrian states was unlikely since neither Patina/Unqi or Sam'al/Bīt-Gabbāri were involved, making it difficult to supply troops from Que to Qarqar (Yamada 2000a, 158).

Recently, some scholars have opted once again for understanding the Monolith's KUR *gu-a-a* as Que/Quwe.[156] In fact, Galil (2002, 42) has argued that since only five hundred troops were sent to the battle, it is possible that they sailed from Que to the land of Hamath.

But none of these scholars have addressed the cuneiform spelling issue raised by Tadmor. While it is possible to read the sign GU as QÙ, Que/Quwe is not once spelled with this sign in any of Shalmaneser's inscriptions.[157] It is always spelled with the signs: QU, or QA. In fact, the gentilic form for Que/Quwe occurs in the Monolith (i.54): QU-Ú-A-A. There is not one spelling of Que/Quwe throughout the Neo-Assyrian inscriptions with the first sign being QÙ (Parpola 1970, 288–89). Therefore it is highly unlikely that Que/Quwe is the entity involved in the battle of Qarqar. Tadmor's emendation makes the best sense.[158]

The fifth participant was Egypt (KUR *mu-uṣ-ra-a-a* "Egyptian"). Egypt is referred to in some other contexts in Shalmaneser's inscriptions and it makes good sense here.[159] It is interesting to remember that Osorkon II demonstrated "a lifetime preoccupation with affairs in Asia" (Redford 1992, 339),

154. The spelling of *sir-ʾa-la-a-a* may be the result of metathesis of the first two letters in the name of Israel (*ysrʾl* → *syrʾl*) by the Assyrian scribe. See Lipiński 1979, 74 n. 77. Alternatively, it could be simply an apheresis of the *y*.

155. For example, see Oppenheim in *ANET*, 279; Wiseman in *DOTT*, 47.

156. Lipiński (2000a, 303–4) suggests reading: KUR *qù-a-a* :: "Que." See also Miller and Hayes 1986, 269.

157. See Yamada 2000a, 157 n. 279. But Byblos is spelled with the GU sign (see e.g., Black Obelisk, 104 and Broken Statue from Calah, 162′).

158. Kuan 1995, 33. Fuchs (1998b, col. 192) reads: KUR *x-gu-a-a* and he suggests possibly reading the first sign as MA or ÁŠ. But Yamada's collation seems better.

159. See Tadmor 1961, 144–45; Borger *TUAT* 1/4:361 n. 92a; Kitchen 1986, 325; Redford 1992, 339–40.

which the gifts of alabaster (presumably sent to Ahab) discovered in excavations at Samaria illustrate.[160]

In a recent article, Lemaire (1993, 152*) suggests that there was a metathesis of the first two signs so that the proper reading is: KUR *ṣu-mu-ra-a-a* "Ṣumuraean." Some other scholars have followed in this interpretation.[161] While this is appealing since it yields another Phoenician coastal ally, it seems completely unnecessary.[162] Good sense of the text can be made without it. Therefore, reading the text as is (KUR *mu-uṣ-ra-a-a* "Egyptian") seems best.

The next four, participants 6–9, are all northern Phoenician coastal city-states: Irqanatu/Irqata/Arqā,[163] Arvad,[164] Usanatu/Usnu (Dion 1997, 185 n. 66), and Šianu/Siannu (Bounni and Al-Maqdissi 1992). The names of two kings are given: Matinu-Baʿal of Arvad and Adon-Baʿal of Šianu/Siannu. The sequence of entities follows a south to north order. The identity of participant 10 is clear: Gindibu' of Arabia. Damascus's dominant position on the King's Highway may have been a factor in the participation of the Phoenician city-states and the Arabs. Dion (1997, 188) notes the ninth-century cylinder seal that is inscribed in Aramaic, carries astral symbols, and honors ʿAttār-šamayn, a deity that was particularly popular among the Arabs.[165]

The last participant listed reads: ${}^{m}$*ba-ʾa-sa* DUMU *ru-ḫu-bi* KUR *a-ma-na-a-a*. The debate concerning this participant has centered primarily on the word KUR *A-ma-na-a-a*. Commonly scholars have understood this to refer to Ammon, the small Transjordanian state.[166] Some scholars have understood the word to refer to Amanah, the Anti-Lebanon mountain range (see 2 Kgs 5:12Q, Song 4:8).[167] Moreover, beside the similarity of place name, Forrer equated the patronym with Reḥob, father of Hadad-ezer of Ṣobah, named in 2 Sam 8:3, suggesting Reḥob was the dynastic name of the kings of Ṣobah (Forrer 1928).

The spelling of KUR *A-ma-na-a-a* does not automatically point to Ammon or Mount Amanah, since KUR can be the determinative for land or mountain. The name Ba'asa is West Semitic (*bʿšʾ*) and is known from the

160. Reisner et al. 1924, 1:247, fig. 205; 2:pl. 56g.

161. See Dion, 1997, 164–65; Lipiński 2000a, 303.

162. See the objections of Na'aman 2002c, 207 n. 29.

163. Tell ʿArqā northeast of Tripoli, Lebanon (Borger *TUAT* 1:361 n. 92b). See also Thalmann 1991. Cf. Gen 10:17.

164. See Badre 1997; Bonatz 1993; Dion 1997, 113–36.

165. For the seal, see Bordreuil 1993, 78 and fig. 5. For the goddess *ʿtršmn*, see Weippert 1973–74, 44–45.

166. Luckenbill 1926–27, 1.611; Oppenheim *ANET*, 279; Na'aman 1976, 98 n. 20; Millard 1992b, 35.

167. Cogan 1984; Dion 1997, 176, 186; Na'aman 1995a, 385–86; 2002c, 204–5.

name of an Israelite king (1 Kgs 15:16), found on an Ammonite ostracon,[168] as well as in Punic (Benz 1972, 101). Consequently, it is impossible from this name to identify the ruler's ethnicity. But Mount Amanah is never attested as a state in any other source; and here, in this context—compare the formulation of the preceding allies (table 7.2), it is clearly a gentilic form, which points to a political/ethnic entity. Therefore, it seems most probable that KUR *A-ma-na-a-a* should be understood as "Ammonite."[169]

However, no other individual in this list has a double attribution (whether one understands DUMU *ru-ḫu-bi* as a gentilic or a patronymic).[170] Thus quite a few scholars have followed Weidner's suggestion that these are really two entities: Bēt-Reḥob and Ammon. Galil (2002, 46) most recently concludes: "the provincial author presumably was mistaken. The complement should be "[xxx troops of] the Ammonite," like the short and anonymous indications for rulers from Egypt, Usnu, and Que (or Byblos)."

7.2.2.2.1.4. The Number of Chariots, Cavalry, and Troops Ascribed to the Different Coalition Kings

There is debate over the accuracy of the numbers in this passage and especially the number of chariots attributed to Ahab. Some scholars argue that this is an accurate number.[171] Some suggest that Ahab's force may have included auxiliaries from Jehoshaphat of Judah and from vassals such as Moab and Edom.[172] But other scholars argue that the number of chariots is a scribal error.[173]

A well-known, and oft-quoted, passage from Shalmaneser's Assur Clay Tablets (RIMA 3:41, A.0.102.6, iv.47–48), dated to 842 BCE, records his claim to have "hitched up teams of horses to 2,002 chariots and 5,542 cavalry for the forces of my land."[174] In another text (the Marble Slab, RIMA 3:55,

---

168. Ḥesbân Ostracon A1. See *COS* 3.84 and *CAI* 214–219. Lipiński (1999a) does not note this evidence in his discussion of the name.

169. For a fuller discussion, see Rendsburg 1991.

170. Interestingly, an epigraph on a bronze band from Imgur-Enlil (Balawat) reads: "Adinu, (the man) of Bīt-Dakkūri, the Chaldean" ([m]*a-di-ni* A [m]*da-ku-ri* KUR [*kal*]*-da-a-a*). See RIMA 3:145–46, A.0.102.79.

171. For example, Elat 1975, 29; Briquel-Chatonnet 1992, 80–81; Kuan 1995, 34–36.

172. Malamat 1973, 144; Miller and Hayes 1986, 270.

173. For example, Na'aman 1976; Mitchell 1982, 479.

174. A Stone Slab from Assur (ca. 839 BCE) reads: "I mustered 2,001 chariots (and) 5,242 [cavalry] for the forces of my land" (RIMA 3:58, A.0.102.11, left edge ii.1–2a). Figures from Egyptian royal inscriptions serve as useful comparisons. During the eighteenth dynasty, Thutmose III captured 924 Canaanite chariots on his first campaign (ca. 1458 BCE; cf. *COS* 2.2A:5–13), and Amenhotep II captured 730 and 1,092 (60 + 1,032) chari-

A.0.102.10, iv.34b–40a) Shalmaneser gives grand totals for his campaigns through his twentieth year:

> 110,610 prisoners, 82,600 killed, 9,920 horses (and) mules, 35,565 oxen, 19,690 donkeys, (and) 184,755 sheep – booty from the beginning of my reign up to my twentieth regnal year.

A "Horse List" from Fort Shalmaneser from the reign of Sargon II is very informative regarding the muster of the Assyrian army's chariot and cavalry contingents. The tablet (TFS 103) seems to date from 709–708 BCE and to constitute a BE-*qu* muster, "a record of all the horses and mules in the chariotry and some, if not all, of those in the cavalry, of the army gathered by Sargon for one of the years of his Babylonian campaign" (Dalley and Postgate 1984, 200). The tablet gives totals for different musters (like that for Borsippa, lines iii.7–8) as well as a grand total: "3,477 (horse and mules)."

In the case of the number of infantry mustered by the coalition, M. de Odorico has discussed the problem and concludes that the scribe decided on what had to be the approximate size of the Syro-Palestinian army (≈ 70,000) and tenfolded some numbers until he got this value. It was the first three contingents (i.e., Damascus, Hamath, and Israel), as well as those referring to the camels of the Arabs and to the troops of Arqā, that were all intentionally multiplied by a factor of ten (de Odorico 1995, 103–7).

Finally, a thorough quantitative study of the Assyrian musters for war by F. M. Fales (2000c, 52–53) has demonstrated that the size of the Assyrian army at the battle of Qarqar was approximately 86,000 men (excluding all civilian and auxiliary personnel). Based on the size of the Assyrian army, Fales concludes that the numbers given for the coalition forces at Qarqar may, in fact, reflect roughly the true numbers.

In the case of the number of casualties, as A. R. Millard has observed,[175] the Monolith's 14,000 becomes 25,000 in the Assur Clay Tablets, the Kalḫu Bulls, and the Marble Slab, and then 29,000 in the Broken Statue from Kalḫu and the Assur Basalt Statue.[176] Since the figure 14,000 may already be an exaggeration, the other figures most certainly are. As noted above, this infla-

---

ots respectively on his official first and second campaigns (ca. 1421, 1419 BCE; cf. *COS* 2.3:21, 22). During the nineteenth dynasty, the Hittites reputedly fielded 2,500 chariots against Ramesses II at the battle of Qadesh (1275 BCE; cf. Kitchen 1996–99, 1:5, 7, 20; *COS* 2.5A:34, 35) and Ramesses II himself probably fielded 2,000 chariots (Kitchen, 1996–99, 2:40).

175. Millard 1991, 219. See also the discussions of de Odorico 1995, 107 and Mayer 1995, 46–47.

176. The Black Obelisk reads 20 LIM 5 ME "20,500," instead of the 20 LIM 5 LIM "25,000" of the other annalistic texts. Thus it can be treated as an error for 25,000.

tion of the casualties' number is one of the items that point to the Assyrian failure at Qarqar.

7.2.2.2.2. Shalmaneser III's 849 Campaign

For two years (851–850 BCE), Shalmaneser was heavily involved in giving assistance to the Babylonian king Marduk-zakir-šumi to suppress the rebellion in his country.[177] Having successfully accomplished this, Shalmaneser again turned attention to the west (849).[178] Although the primary targets of this campaign were Karkamiš and Bīt-Agūsi, the "twelve-member" coalition was again engaged by Shalmaneser,[179] probably because his clear intentions were to invade Hamath. And so they sought to once again block him.

In stereotypical phraseology, Shalmaneser III claimed to raze, destroy, and burn the cities of Sangara, the Karkamišean. Karkamiš, however, was not attacked, and the action probably was designed on the one hand to force the submission of Sangara, and on the other, to open the way for a clear attack on Bīt-Agūsi. However, the fact that Shalmaneser had to attack Karkamiš again the next year (848) meant that he had not effectively reduced its fighting capacity.

In any case, Shalmaneser captured and destroyed the city of Arnê, the royal city of Aramu of Bīt-Agūsi, as well as another one hundred towns.[180] But at some point in his attack on Bīt-Agūsi, Shalmaneser encountered the "twelve-king" coalition led by Aram-Damascus and Hamath, just like in 853. The account states:

> At that time, Hadad-ezer (Adad-idri) of Damascus (and) Irḫulēni, the Hamathite, together with 12 kings of the seashore, trusted in each other's strength; they marched against me to do war and battle; I fought with them; I decisively defeated them; (and) I took from them their chariots, cavalry and their military equipment. In order to save their lives they fled.[181]

177. This was in fulfillment of the bilateral peace treaty made between the Assyrian and Babylonian royal houses (see Grayson 1975, 167, lines 22–36 [Synchronistic History]).

178. The earliest and full version of the Annals which includes an account of the 849 campaign is Annals 5 = the 16 Year Annals (ii 55–67); its account was reproduced in Annals 6 = the Bull Inscription (lines 84b–89). Other texts abridge the account. See Yamada 2000a, 166–67.

179. For discussion of the historicity of the battle, see Yamada 2000a, 167 and Pitard 1987, 129 n. 84.

180. See §8.2.2.

181. RIMA 3:37–38, A.0.102.6, ii.60b–67 (Annals 5); and RIMA 3:46, A.0.102.8, 32′b–34′ (Annals 6).

However, just like the battle of Qarqar, there are three reasons why this "supposed" Assyrian victory cannot "be taken at face value" (Yamada, 2000a, 169). First and most importantly, Shalmaneser III did not conquer a single city of Hamath before or after the engagement. It would appear that he did not, in fact, penetrate Hamathite territory on this campaign. This indicates that the coalition effectively halted his campaign within the territory of Bīt-Agūsi. Second, the use of many of the same stereotyped syntagms to describe this battle as were used in the 853 narrative gives indication of a less than favorable outcome. Third, Shalmaneser needed to fight the same coalition in the following years 848 and 845. Yamada (2000a, 169) has rightly observed that the coalition must have remained largely the same since it would need to field similar numbers as at Qarqar in order to turn back Shalmaneser a second time. Hence, it is probable that Urhilina contributed a similar number of men and equipment to this engagement as in 853.

#### 7.2.2.2.3. Shalmaneser III's 848 Campaign

In his eleventh regnal year (848), Shalmaneser III—having reorganized and refitted—marched against Hamath and encountered for the third time the "twelve-king" coalition.[182] As in the previous year's campaign, the Assyrian king first attacked Karkamiš and Bīt-Agūsi, claiming to have captured ninety-seven cities of Sangara the Karkamišean, as well as having captured and destroyed one hundred cities of Aramu of Bīt-Agūsi. These engagements with Karkamiš and Bīt-Agūsi were, no doubt, due to the fact that these two countries were encouraged by the military action of the coalition in the previous year. However, having apparently been successful against these two, the Assyrians brought the war onto Hamathite territory for the first time since 853.

> I took (the way along) the slopes of the Amanus Range (*ši-di* KUR *ḫa-ma-a-ni*); I traversed Mount Yaraqu; I descended to the cities of the Hamathite (i.e., Irḫulēni). I captured the city of Aštammaku, together with eighty-nine towns. I massacred them; I plundered them.
>
> At that time, Hadad-ezer (Adad-idri) of Damascus (and) Irḫulēni, the Hamathite, together with twelve kings of the seashore, trusted in their combined forces; they attacked me to wage war and battle. I fought with them;

182. The account of the present campaign is included in five versions of the Annals: RIMA 3:38, A.0.102.6, ii.68–iii.15 (Annals 5); 3:47, A.0.102.8, lines 35′–41′a (Annals 6); 3:53, A.0.102.10, ii.51–iii.5 (Annals 7); 3:66, A.0.102.14, lines 87–89a (Annals 13); and 3:76, A.0.102.16, lines 71′b–81′ (Annals 14); as well as in some summary texts. There is an abridgement process of the account in these texts. See Yamada 2000a, 170–71.

> I defeated them. I felled 10,000 of their fighting men with the sword. I took from them their chariotry, cavalry, (and) military equipment.
>
> On my return, I captured the city of Apparāzu, the fortified city of Aramu.
>
> At that time, I received tribute of Qalparunda: silver, gold, tin, horses, donkeys, oxen, sheep, blue-purple wool, (and) linen garments. I climbed Mount Amanus (and) cut beams of cedar.

The wording (*ši-di* KUR *ḫa-ma-a-ni*) places Shalmaneser on the eastern slopes of the Amanus Range marching south toward Tell Ta'yinat when he then traversed along the eastern side of Mount Yaraqu (Jebel Quseiri).[183] It makes little sense to march along the Amanus and then go to the eastern side of Jebel Bariša. Coming down the Orontes, Shalmaneser would have marched through the Ruj Valley to attack Aštammaku (Tell Masṭūma/Stūma).

Yamada has rightly observed that by taking the long way around, Shalmaneser outflanked the coalition whose combined forces must have been massed on Hamath's northern border (based on the previous year's engagement).[184] Marching through his client Patina's land permitted Shalmaneser to attack the important Hamathite city of Aštammaku before the coalition was able to respond. The logistic support of the Assyrian outpost at Aribua (Jisr esh-Shughur) was likely important to the success of this manoeuver (provided that it was still garrisoned). At some point after the capture of Aštammaku, and perhaps in the general area of that city, the coalition engaged the Assyrian army in an open-field battle. On this occasion, Shalmaneser claimed to have felled 10,000 of the coalition. This round and probably exaggerated number does not prove that the Assyrians decisively defeated the enemy since the coalition remained intact and viable as a fighting force and Shalmaneser was not able to follow up this "victory." Importantly, it is three years later (845) before he campaigned again in the region.

This campaign is depicted on Shalmaneser III's Balawat Bronze Band XIII (fig. 7.7).[185] It includes an epigraph engraved on its upper register (the gray blocks in the upper register of the drawing) that reads: "I captured the

183. This also fits the route of Aššurnaṣirpal II who departed "Kunulua, the royal city of Lubarna, the Patinean. I crossed the Orontes River. I pitched camp (and) spent the night by the Orontes; I departed from the Orontes; I took the way between Mounts Yaraqu (and) Yahturu." See RIMA 2:218, A.0.101.1, iii.78b–80a; and Liverani 1992a, 75; Yamada 2000a, 174. Two proposed locations for Mount Yaraqu are: (1) Jebel Bariša (Dussaud 1927, 238; Röllig 1976–80a, 267; Sader 1987, 225 n. 99; Schiffer 1911, 188; Astour 1969, 401); (2) Jebel Quseiri (Kraeling 1918, 67; Elliger 1947, 72–73, 83 n. 44; Lewy 1952, 399 n. 2; Ikeda 1979, 79, n. 36; Liverani 1992a, 75; Yamada 2000a, 173).

184. Yamada 2000a, 174; also Schachner 2007, 224.

185. Schachner 2007, 305, pl. 13; Pinches, Birch 1882–1902, pls. L1–L7; King 1915, pls. LXXII–LXXVII.

city of Aštammaku, the royal city of Irḫulēni, the Hamathite, together with 86 cities" (URU.*áš-ta-ma-ku* URU MAN-*ti-šú šá* [m]*ir-ḫu-le-e-ni* KUR <*ḫa*>-*ma-ta-a-a a-di* 86 URU.MEŠ KUR-*ud*).[186] In that this epigraph is located on the left, above the chariot scene to the left of the first city that is being attacked on both sides, with dead hanging from the city's wall, with the epigraph continuing across the register, this first city must be Aštammaku.[187] However, the interpretation of the rest of the Band is not as clear and has raised problems for historical reconstruction. First, what is being conveyed in the remainder of the Upper Register? Second, what is the relationship of the Upper and Lower Registers?

In the Upper Register, there are three scenes in which a city is depicted. As already noted, the first scene on the left portrays the attack and capture of Aštammaku. To the right of this first city, there is an Assyrian camp with another city being attacked from both directions. Then to the far right is a third scene with a city being attacked from only the left side. On the wall of this city, a despairing Hamathite noble lies on a couch, attended by his servants, and making a gesture of supplication (Yamada 2000a, 175). In the Lower Register (no epigraph), on the left is a procession from the Assyrian camp; on the right, another procession, of captives being led off from a city on the far right. The processions meet with Shalmaneser III being depicted with bow turned and a man bowing down to the ground in front of Shalmaneser, accompanied by two standing Assyrian officials.

Some scholars have identified the man lying on the couch in the Upper Register and the one bowing before Shalmaneser in the Lower Register as Irhuleni/Urhilina.[188] These scholars have understood that after the fall of Aštammaku, many other cities of Hamath were destroyed (as pictured in the Upper Register of Band XIII), and as a result Urhilina decided to surrender as depicted in the Lower Register.[189] Thus in 848, Hamath was subjugated by Shalmaneser.

This is problematic firstly because the coalition was not broken in 848. Shalmaneser III had to engage it again in 845. Furthermore, it is doubtful that such an event, the submission of Urhilina, would have not received an

186. RIMA 3:146–47, A.0.102.82.

187. So Yamada 2000a, 175; Schachner 2007, 225.

188. Billerbeck and Delitzsch 1908, 75–77 and 119–20; Olmstead 1921, 370; and Ikeda 1977, 190–2. Ikeda identifies the old noble lying on the couch with Irhuleni but the man in the lower register with the Hamathite crown prince Uratami.

189. Arguing against this, Yamada (2000a, 175) suggests that all representations of the Band XIII are the same city, Aštammaku, drawn from different angles, for the artist's purposes. However, there is too much difference in the detail and since some of the eighty-six or eighty-nine cities that Shalmaneser conquered in the area of Aštammaku must have been walled, there is no reason to posit that all these four cities are depicting one.

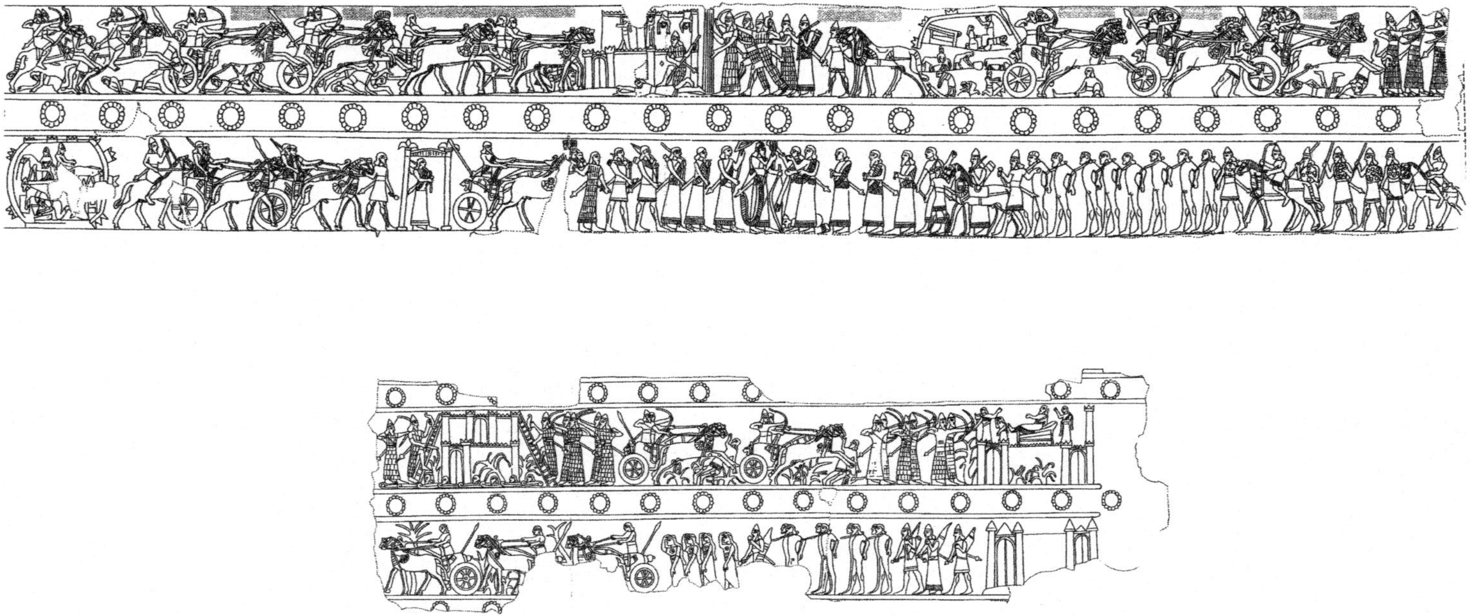

Fig. 7.7. Shalmaneser III's Balawat Bronze Band XIII: Aštammaku's capture (Schachner 2007, pl. 13)

epigraph, clearly attributing the event. Yamada (2000a, 176) suggests that the man lying on the couch and the man bowing could be a Hamathite governor or governors, and need not be identified with Urhilina, who fought as a leader of the coalition in 845. Schachner (2007, 225 n. 152) suggests that the man prostrating himself was an Assyrian dignitary, which in my opinion, is likely since his horse is depicted being retained by a squire just to the right. Finally, Schachner argues that the production of the bronze bands must have been completed at the latest in fourteenth regnal year, that is, 845 BCE.[190] While Balawat Gate Band P contains a battle fragmentary scene with an epigraph that reads: *ti-du-ku šá* KUR(?) *ḫa-m*[*a-t*]*a-a-a*, "Battle against the Hamathite,"[191] it is uncertain whether this band refers to 853, 849, 848, or 845 (although if Schachner is correct, the last date is unlikely).

Thus, at the end of the campaign, Shalmaneser had once again failed to break the coalition. It survived to fight another day—actually three years later. This was, no doubt, due to the persistence of Urhilina and Hadad-ezer of Damascus who were able to coax the other "twelve" members to stay the course.

On his return march Shalmaneser conquered Apparāzu, the fortified city of Arame of Bīt-Agūsi, received the tribute of Qalparunda of Patina, and climbed Mount Amanus to cut cedar timber. The recording of such events seems anticlimactic in light of the greater surprise of destroying the coalition.

#### 7.2.2.2.4. Shalmaneser III's 845 Campaign

In his fourteenth regnal year (845), Shalmaneser III mustered all of his resources for another attempt (his fourth try) at breaking the "twelve-king" coalition by smashing Hamath.[192] While the account is more vague in many respects than the previous, and utilizes almost entirely stereotypical phraseology, there is one significant difference: the number of troops mustered. Conscripting 120,000 troops, Shalmaneser crossed the Euphrates at flood in order to overpower this persistent coalition. The appearance of such a large number has engendered much discussion.[193] The discussion about this problem in the 853 campaign will not be repeated here. Whatever the

---

190. Schachner 2007, 253–54; and see his analysis on pp. 105–6. Hertel dates them to the fifteenth regnal year, 844. See Hertel 2004, 312.

191. RIMA 3:148, A.0.102.86.

192. The account of the present campaign is included in five versions of the Annals: RIMA 3:29, A.0.102.6, iii.24–33 (Annals 5); 3:47, A.0.102.8, lines 44′b–47′a (Annals 6); 3:53–54, A.0.102.10, iii.14–25 (Annals 7); 3:66–67, A.0.102.14, lines 91b–92a (Annals 13); and 3:77, A.0.102.16, lines 87′b–95′ (Annals 14). See Yamada 2000a, 179–83.

193. See Yamada 2000a, 181 and de Odorico 1995, 107–12.

case (whether accurate or hyperbole), the impression from this number is that Shalmaneser is holding nothing back. Neither is the coalition who is said to have mustered troops too numerous to be counted. Yet, the stereotypical syntagms that have been used repeatedly in the earlier narrations of the other campaigns creates doubts about Shalmaneser's success in this campaign as in the past. The fact that he must bring such a large force to the west in 845 leads to the conclusion that his claims of success in 853, 849 and 848 have not been quite accurate.

Schachner observes that the relatively precise dating for the Balawat Gates that he advocates is very likely reinforced by the fact that Shalmaneser III does not have a victory over this coalition to insert on one of the bronze bands when the gates were erected.[194] In fact, there is no concrete evidence of an Assyrian conquest of any of the cities in central Syria or of the subjugation of the coalition partners; only the empty phrases of "I destroyed their chariotry, cavalry (and) I took away their military equipment"—stated for all the campaigns against the coalition.

There are, nevertheless, two pieces of information that aid in historical reconstruction. First, four years later in 841, when Shalmaneser marched against Hazael of Damascus, he no longer encountered the blocking action of the anti-Assyrian coalition which had always included the Hamathite army. This unquestionably alludes to a changed political situation in the central Levant. Second, an inscription of Sargon II provides data about this situation. It states:

> I gathered from them 200 chariots, 600 cavalry, shield and lance (bearers); and I added them to my royal contingent. I pardoned 6,300 guilty Assyrians; and showed mercy on them; and I settled them in Hamath. I imposed on them tribute, gifts, and corvée work, as my royal fathers had imposed on Irḫulēni of Hamath.[195]

Thus it seems manifest that Urhilina had submitted to Assyria at some point after the 845 campaign and before the 841 campaign in order for the Assyrian troops to move unencumbered through Hamathite territory on their way to attack Hamath's former ally (at least for these years 853–845). Moreover, Urhilina was responsible to supply troops to Assyria, a clear duty of a vassal or client king. This also means that until the coalition collapsed, the allied front against Assyria was, in general, effective. But with the usurpation of Hazael in Damascus, the old alliance could not stay intact and this led to the eventual demise of the entire Levant.

194. Schachner 2007, 254.
195. *COS* 2.118B:294; Lambert 1981; Hawkins 2004.

7.2.2.3. The Reign of Uratami

It seems that Uratami (ca. 840–820 BCE) probably came to the throne not long after the 841 campaign. Five of his inscriptions have been recovered (all from Ḥama). All of these appear to be part of the masonry of a rebated portal or gate. In HAMA 1–3 and 6–7 (Hawkins 2000, 411–14), he recorded the construction of "this fortress/wall" (*harnisanza*)—in other words, the walls of Hamath. In each of these, it appears that a particular section of the wall (towers or gate structure?) was built by different "riverlands" (areas of the Orontes or districts under Hamathite control). These include the riverlands of Ḫurpata, Musanipa, Laka, Mount Labarna, as well as the Kusunites and the land of Tuhayata. Thus these inscriptions were placed at various points, probably in gateways of the fortifications of the ancient city, to commemorate the construction of the respective sectors. Moreover, an additional statement in three of the five inscriptions is that various peoples "(are) in (it)," which suggests that perhaps these towers or gatehouses were linked by curtain walls and garrisoned by those named: the Halabeans, the land Nikima, and the land of Hamayara.

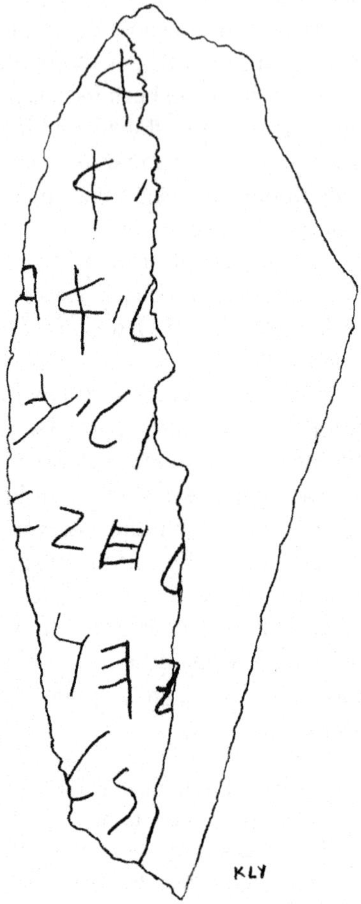


Fig. 7.8. The Tell Afis Stela fragment (Drawing by K. Lawson Younger Jr.)

Certainly part of his reign saw a level of independence from Assyria and a trade relationship with the Middle Euphrates. This is attested by the letter of Marduk-apla-uṣur of Sūḫu (Anat in the letter) to Uratami (written: Rudamu; Parpola 1990, 258–59). Marduk-apla-uṣur had paid tribute to Shalmaneser III between 842 and 832 BCE. So, this may imply that the correspondence between the two rulers took place after 832.[196] In any case, the letter provides witness to Hamath's relative strength and independence during a part of Uratami's reign.

During the last part of the reign of Uratami or shortly after his reign, Hamath faced another different threat, this time from the south, from a former ally, Damascus. Hazael had usurped the throne of Damascus sometime around 844–843, 842 at the very latest. He reigned until ca. 803. It is now clear that he extended Aram-Damascus's power northward, likely controlling Hamath and Luǵath. It would seem that Hazael's control over Hamath and Luǵath did not occur before the 820s, perhaps not until the revolt in Assyria began in the last part of Shalmaneser III's reign (826–824 BCE). Whether Uratami or his successor became vassal to Hazael is presently not known, but the Hazael Booty Inscriptions mention Hazael's campaign northward that crossed the Orontes River in his campaign against ʿUmq/Patina,[197] when he obtained the horse frontlet and blinker on which the inscriptions were incised.

A fragment of a basalt stela with an Aramaic inscription was discovered in excavations of the ruins of a temple (A1) at Tell Afis in 2003 (fig. 7.8).[198] M. G. Amadasi Guzzo has published a study of the inscription of which only bits of seven lines are preserved.[199] She has suggested reading line 5′ as [...]*lḥz*⸢ʾ⸣[*l*], thus yielding the name of Hazael (*ḥzʾl*), probably a reference to the king of Damascus. Moreover, she also has suggested that line 6′ (which reads: [...]*yhw*[ ]) might have contained a Yahwistic type name, possibly Jehu, although Jehoram (*yhwrm*) and Ahaziah (*ʾḥzyhw*) would be other possibilities. If the name Jehu occurred in line 6′ of this stela, then there would have been an ʾ after the *w* (what is now in the break), since Jehu's name is consistently spelled *yhwʾ*.[200]

In any case, Amadasi Guzzo correctly notes that paleographically the fragment's letters resemble those on the Zakkur Inscription. She points out that this is especially seen in the *zayin*, though the shape of this letter also

---

196. Parpola 1990, 257 (he dates the letter to ca. 840).

197. Though not across the Euphrates. See Younger 2005 for a discussion of the identification of *nhr* in these two inscriptions. See the discussion 9.3.5.5.2.

198. For the archaeological context, see Mazzoni, et al. 2005, 17–19 and fig. 12–14; 2014, 44–47.

199. See Amadasi Guzzo 2009, 336–41; 2005, 21–23, fig 18; 2014, 54–55; see also Younger 2007c, 139.

200. Younger 2005, 253–54. Amadasi Guzzo (2014, 55) has recently suggested that "since it is not possible to link Hazrak with any known event involving Damascus and either Israel or Judah, it is preferable to derive the letters YHW from the root HYH, 'to be' (imperfect, third person plural?)." Unfortunately, without additional pieces of the stela, it is impossible to reconstruct.

resembles the *zayin* in the duplicate Hazael booty inscriptions from Eretria and Samos. One can also note the similarity of the *kaph* in both this fragment and the Zakkur inscription. Therefore, this text likely dates to the last third of the ninth century BCE. Numerous other broken fragments of carved basalt were also recovered in the excavation and show that all around this area iconographic and epigraphic documents were displayed.[201] If the reading of Hazael's name is correct, it would seem that Hazael had authority over Luǵath (and certainly over Hamath) for some time during this period (ca. 825?–803?), and that this stela was set up by Hazael at this time. Whether Uratami's reign extended down into this time or whether one of his sons ascended the throne is unknown. But sometime in the last decade of the ninth century, it seems very probable that the Luwian dynasty that had ruled in Hamath for over a century came to an end.

### 7.2.3. The Reign of Zakkur (ca. 803–780)

Around the time of Hazael's death (a typical time for rebellions, usurpations, etc.), or possibly a few years earlier, a new king, Zakkur, usurped the throne of Hamath and Luǵath. The attempt by Bar-Hadad (Hazael's son) to besiege Ḥaḏrak was likely an attempt to restore the power of Damascus over the region. Very simply, the king of Damascus could not remain indifferent to this reformulation or resurrection of Hamath and Luǵath, which threatened to undo all the work of his father. The Zakkur inscription[202] is the main source for our knowledge of this event (fig. 7.9). It reads:

> The [st]ela which Zakkur,[203] king of [Ha]math and Luǵath, set up for Elwer, [his lord / in Apis].[204]
> I am Zakkur, King of Hamath and Luǵath.
> A man of ʿAnah (or "an ʿAnaean") am I;[205]

---

201. Unfortunately, once this area began to serve as an open quarry, most all of these were lost. See Soldi 2009, 108.

202. AO. 8186 in the Louvre Museum. See *KAI* 202; Schwiderski 2004, 422. *Editio princeps*, Pognon 1907, 156–78 pls. IX–X, XXXV–XXXVI.

203. The vocalization of the name is Zakkur, not Zakir. This is assured from the Antakya Stela (RIMA 3:203, A.0.104.2; *COS* 2.114A:272), as well as other cuneiform evidence (Dion 1997, 137 n. 2). Also note the fragment of black limestone sculpture from Nineveh, which bears the name ᵐ*za-ku-r*[*i*] which could refer to the same individual (Millard 1990, 47 n. 1). See Reade 1981, 151; fig. 7.10 here and discussion below.

204. *KAI* (202:A1) restores *mrʾh*. Millard 2000a restores [*bʾpš*] and states in n. 5: "The name is restored on the basis of its later occurrence in the text and the likely provenance of the stele." This restoration makes excellent sense.

205. Regarding the translation of *ʾš ʿnh ʾnh*, following Millard's article (1990), most recent scholars have translated "I was a man of Anah" (*COS* 2.35:155), not "I was a humble

and Ba'alšamayn[206] [delivered m]e,
and stood with me;
and Ba'alšama[yn] made me king [over[207] Ḥ]aḏrak.
and Bar-Hadad, son of Hazael, king of Aram, united against me 1[6] kings:[208]
Bar-Hadad and his army,
and Bar-Gush and his army,
and the king of Que and his army,
and the king of 'Umq and his army,

man" (see Dion 1997, 147–50; Lipiński 2000a, 299–301). 'Anah = (Ḫ)ana(t) on the middle Euphrates. Connections between the lands of Hamath and 'Ana(h) are enhanced by the cuneiform letter of Marduk-apla-uṣur of 'Anat to Rudamu (Urtamis), king of Hamath, discovered in the excavations of Ḥama, which ends with the invocation: "May the city of Anat and the city of Hamath be strong" (Parpola 1990). I realize that this may appear to undercut a part of Greenfield's argument about the use of the Danklied in the Zakkur inscription. However, Greenfield's argument rested on more than this, and I believe still holds. The phrase *'š 'nh* could be understood as a gentilic (nisbe) form: "the Anaean."

206. See Niehr 2003.

207. *KAI* 202 reads at the end of line 3 beginning of line 4: *b'lšm[yn . 'l]* (4)*[ḥ]z⌜r⌝k*. However, in my opinion, there does not seem to be enough room at the end of line 3 for four letters plus a word divider. Thus restoring *b* instead of *'l* would fit better.

208. Some scholars have restored "seventeen kings." Friedrich (1966, 83) gave the rationale for the restoration "seventeen" in line 4. He argued that both line 4 and line 8 should have the same restoration *šb't 'šr* and thus the restoration of [*mlkn*] at the end of line 8 (in *KAI* 202) is wrong. But this ends up with a restoration in the break of line 8 of "[und zehn andere Könige, insgesamt] sie[bzehn (sind) s]ie." Donner and Röllig's restoration has "seventeen kings" in both lines 4 and 8 (which while they do not offer the restoration "ten other kings," this must be assumed in the break of line 8: (8)*['šr . mlkn . 'ḥrn] ⌜w⌝šb'⌜t⌝ . ['šr . mlkn]*. There is most certainly not enough room for the two words *'šr . mlkn* at the end of line 8 after the *wšb't*: so either one or the other, but not both. On the other hand, the break from the end of line 7 to the word *wšb't* is too long to just contain the words *'šr . mlkn . 'ḥrn*. It would seem virtually certain that the kings of two other political entities were listed in the break.

Thus, many recent commentators (and I too) understand the last part of line 7 and most of line 8 to contain in the break the names of two kings; thus: [*wmlk*] (8)[ X ] [*wmḥnth*] [*wmlk* Y *wmḥnth*] *wšb't* [*mlkn*]. If this is correct, then there would be nine kings listed (the seven for which the political entity's name is preserved + these two missing names in the break) + "the seven [kings]" (line 8). Thus, this equals sixteen (which is one of the proposed restorations for the end of line 4 and beginning of line 5: *š*(5)*[št] 'šr mlkn*). Restorations have been proposed for the two kings X and Y. Gibson (*SSI* 2, 1975, 14) proposed to restore the entities Kummuḫ and Karkamiš. However, Kummuḫ is most certainly not correct, since it was a client of the Assyrians. In particular, see the discussion of Na'aman 1991, 84. Lemaire opts also for a restoration of Karkamiš. See Lemaire 1993, 151*. Lipiński (2000a, 254, 302–3) has argued against Karkamiš and has posited the following in the break: "the king of Melid [and his a]r[my, the ki(8)ng of Tābal? and his army, the king of Kittik? and his] a[rm]y, a[nd] seven k[ings of (9)A]murru and their armies"). I have preferred not to restore the names of the entities.

and the king of Gurgu[m] and his a[rmy],
and the king of Sam'al and his [army],
and the king of Melid and h[is army],
[and the king of [ X ] and his army],
[and the king of [ Y ] and his army],
and seven [kings], them and their armies.
And all these kings laid siege on Ḥaḏrak.
and they raised a rampart higher than the rampart[209] of Ḥaḏrak.
and they dug a moat deeper than its moa[t].
But I lifted up my hands to Baʿalša[may]n,
and Baʿalšamayn answered me.
[And] Baʿalšamayn [spoke] to me [through] the hand of seers and the hand of envoys,
[and] Baʿalšamayn [said to me]:
"do not be afraid
because I have made [you ki]ng,
[and I will st]and with you,
and I will deliver you from all [these kings]
[who] have raised a siege against you."
Then [Baʿalšamayn] said to [me]:
[ ] all these kings
who have raised [a siege against you].
[....] and this rampart which [they have raised(?) ...]
[....] Ḥaḏrak [..........]
[....] for chariot [and for] calvary
[....] its king in its midst.

I [built (repaired)] Ḥaḏrak;
and I added [to it] the whole circle/district [of "strongholds"];
and I established it as [my king]dom;
and I [established it] as [my la]nd;
[and I repaired] all these strongholds throughout [my] entire territo[ry].
[And] I bui[lt] the temples of the gods throughout my en[tire terri]tory.
and I built ........;
[and I built] Apis;
[and I installed] [the gods] in the temple of [.......];
[.........]
[and] I have set up before [Elwer] this stela;

---

209. At present, excavations have not uncovered the wall/rampart (*šr*) to which Zakkur refers. Soldi (2009, 105) states: "There is currently no archaeological data answering this question, because it seems that the excavated layers in Area B rest directly on Middle Bronze Age ruins. We can assume that the MB rampart was still functional for the Iron Age town, and probably part of the Iron Age II wall has been lost with heavy erosion of the tell on this side of the settlement."

Fig. 7.9. Zakkur Stela (Musée du Louvre AO 8155) © Baker Publishing Group and Dr. James C. Martin. Courtesy of the Musée du Louvre.

and [I] have wr[itten on] it the record of my achievements.
[Who]ever erases the record of the achieve[ments of] Zakkur king of Hama[th and Lu]ʿaš from this stela;
whoever removes this stela from [befo]re Elwer,
and drags it away from its place;
or whoever stretches forth
[ …? …]
[Then Baʿa]lšamayn and El[wer]
and [______] and Šamaš and Śahar
and [ ] and the gods of heaven
and the gods of earth and Baʿal
[______] the man and [______]
[ ] his root(?)
[ ]
[But may] the name of Zakkur and the name [of his house be forever]!

Zakkur seems to have reigned ca. 803–780 BCE. Some scholars have suggested that since he ascribed to himself the title "king of Hamath and Luǵath" (*mlk ḥmt wlʿš*) that under Zakkur, Luǵath was merged together with Hamath, thus implying a united double kingdom (Dion 1997, 140). However, Hamath appears to have controlled the area of Luḫuti/Luǵath for a good part of the ninth century (see the discussion above about Urhilina's efforts in the region). Nevertheless, it is noteworthy that Zakkur chose to use Ḥaḏrak as his center of resistance, rather than Hamath. Apparently, Ḥaḏrak was more the base of Zakkur's power than Hamath. In the first lines of the inscription, it is revealed that Zakkur was a usurper. The lack of patronym, the citation of his place of origin ('Ana) as a patronymic replacement, and the immediate religious legitimation of his reign ("and Baʿalšamayn [delivered m]e, and stood with me; and Baʿalšama[yn] made me king [over Ḥ]aḏrak") combine as indicators of Zakkur's illegitimacy.[210]

Obviously at the point of the organization of the alliance against Zakkur, Bar-Hadad, the son of Hazael (here designated "king of Aram"), still had substantial influence in the region. The fact that Arpad/Bīt-Agūsi (here "Bar Gūš"[211]) is listed next evinces the ascendence of this kingdom as a regional

210. Interestingly, the Tel Dan inscription likewise provides legitimation for the monarch through a religious explanation for the positive turn of events, crediting the storm god (Hadad in the place of Ba)alšamayn of Zakkur). For the Tel Dan inscription, see Knapp 2012.

211. See p. 46 for discussion of the form.

power,[212] even if its king's name is omitted (ostensibly Attār-sumkī I).[213] The inclusion of many of the other polities attests to the fact that Zakkur's coming to power in Hamath and Luǵath was a cause of great superregional concern.

The circumstances of his coming to power are unfortunately obscure. It is generally assumed that he usurped the throne in Hamath and Luǵath around the time of Hazael's death or perhaps slightly before. Dion (1997, 149–50) has speculated that being from ʿAna and his calling for Assyrian help against the coalition allied against him might indicate that Zakkur came to power by means of Assyrian support or at least with Assyrian consent. Of course, this is possible; but there is no real evidence. It is interesting that Amadasi Guzzo (2009, 341) emphasizes the nearness in time between the Tell Afis stela fragment that appears to belong to Hazael and the Zakkur inscription based on paleographic analysis and the fact that we do not know the context in which Hazael was mentioned, especially if he was an ally or an opponent of Zakkur. This raises the possibility that Zakkur came to power as a result of the action of Hazael, or perhaps with his consent.[214] In such a scenario, Zakkur was then rebelling after the death of his overlord. But again there is no real evidence. We simply do not know the time and circumstances of Zakkur coming to power, though it must have been around 803.

#### 7.2.3.1. The Date of the Siege and Deliverance of Ḥaḏrak

When the siege and deliverance of Ḥaḏrak took place is also debated. Four different dates have been proposed in the scholarly literature: just before 805, just after 805 (i.e., 804), 796, and 772. There are a number of pieces of sundry data that must be considered along with the various interconnections with the Assyrian campaigns against Arpad and Damascus. The discussion here will center directly on the dating of the siege of and deliverance of Ḥaḏrak as reflected in the Zakkur Inscription. Further discussion of Adad-nērārī III's campaigns can be found in chapters 8 and 9.

---

212. Na'aman (1991, 84) puts it this way: "Since Arpad (*brgš*) appears first in this list, it may safely be regarded as the leader, second only to Damascus who had assembled the anti-Hamathean coalition."

213. Since there will be a border adjustment between Hamath (Zakkur) and Bīt-Agūsi (Arpad) (Attār-sumkī) that will be made by the Assyrians—in favor of Attār-sumkī, it is not surprising that his name is omitted by Zakkur in this inscription that was undoubtedly erected some years after the events that it describes. See the Antakya Stela (RIMA 3:203, A.0.104.2; *COS* 2.114A:272) and discussion below. Dion notes that the Zakkur inscription is datable paleographically to the first decades of the eighth century (Dion 1997, 139–40).

214. Perhaps not entirely unlike the situation in Israel as hinted at in the Tell Dan Inscription.

Early in the study of the Zakkur Inscription and Aramean history, a number of scholars proposed that the siege and deliverance of Ḥaḏrak should be dated to the campaign of Aššur-dān III in 772 based on the Eponym Chronicle which lists "to Ḫatarikka" as a target for the Assyrian army.[215] This date is no longer seriously considered because of more recent additional data that has ruled it out, particularly inscriptions belonging to Adad-nērārī III.

A date just before 805, just prior to Adad-nērārī III's campaigns, has also been proposed (Dupont-Sommer 1949, 47). In this scenario, the coalition was formed in opposition to Assyria; Zakkur refused to join it; he was besieged; and the Assyrian army's action in 805 rescued him. However, Adad-nērārī's campaign of 805 was directed against a Syro-Hittite "eight-king" coalition headed by Attār-sumkī of Arpad (not Bar-Hadad as in the Zakkur Inscription). The Assyrian army's action was instigated at the request of Ušpilulume, the king of Kummuḫ,[216] not Zakkur. The decisive battle was fought at Paqarḫubuni (with no mention of Ḥaḏrak). This intervention may have been a "miraculous deliverance" for Ušpilulume, but there is nothing to indicate that there was any military action as far south as Ḥaḏrak. Thus it is doubtful that this was in any way connected to Zakkur's "miraculous" deliverance.

A date just after 805 (i.e., 804) was proposed by Na'aman (1991, 86). Having surveyed the other options, he suggested that "the episode described in the Zakkur Stela reflects the efforts of Damascus to unite an all-inclusive Syro-Hittite coalition against Assyria immediately after the defeat of the northern alliance in 805." He feels that this may explain Damascus's leading role in the Zakkur Inscription vis-à-vis Bēt-Gūš (Bīt-Agūsi). Thus following the battle of Paqarḫubuni, it was evident that only a large, fully participating coalition could hold back the Assyrian war machine, and Bar-Hadad was the driving force behind this. Zakkur's refusal brought on the coalition's attack with the Assyrian intervention occurring in 804 with its attack on Ḫazāzu causing the coalition "to hurry northwards in order to defend their homeland and thus Hamath was saved" (Na'aman 1991, 86).

This scenario is certainly right on a number of points. However, it is not problem free. Dion (1997, 151–52, and n. 61) points out that such a scenario involves a series of reactions that are a little too rapid, especially as the Pazarcık Inscription seems to indicate that Adad-nērārī III had time to exploit his victory by fixing the border between Kummuḫ and Gurgum. Moreover, it is difficult to imagine that Bar-Hadad of Damascus would want to count on the northern allies so immediately after their defeat. Finally, and importantly,

215. This was first formulated by Lidzbarski 1915, 3:8–9; Kraeling 1918, 101–2; Noth 1929, 128–30; Albright 1942, 23–25; Unger 1957, 85–89.

216. Pazarcık/Maraş Stela (RIMA 3:204–5, A.0.104.3, lines 7b–18).

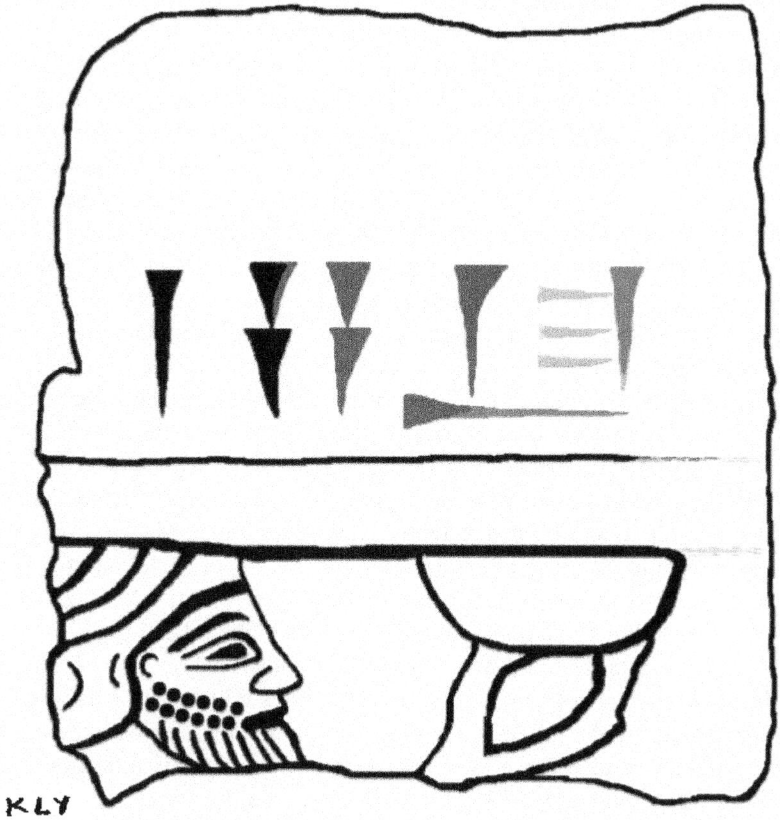


Fig. 7.10. Zakkur's tribute? (BM 120429; drawing by K. Lawson Younger Jr.)

Bar-Hadad, who was a contemporary of Joash of Israel, could hardly be on the throne of Damascus at this time (i.e., before 803).

The fourth date for the siege of Ḥadrak, proposed by a number of scholars, is 796 BCE.[217] In the case of Lipiński, the argument is based on the Eponym Chronicle's "to Manṣuāte" and his location for this toponym.[218] For other scholars who hold this date, it is considered the most likely option, especially because: (1) the issue of the chronology of Bar-Hadad's accession

217. Jepsen 1941–44, 164–70; Lipiński 1971; 1979, 86–93; 2000a, 309–10; Hawkins 1982, 400, 403–4; Lemaire 1993, 151*; Millard and Tadmor 1973, 62–64; Pitard 1987, 162–65; Dion 1997, 152–54; and Weippert 1992, 57.

218. Lipiński 1971; 1979, 86–93; 2000a, 305–10. See below.

to the throne in Damascus, and (2) the possibility of a connection with the Assyrian campaign of Adad-nērārī III against Damascus.

Having defeated sufficiently Arpad and its northern allies (805–803), and having dealt with other issues between 802 and 797 (on his northern and eastern borders), Adad-nērārī III was able to return to Syria in 796. Damascus—for which there is no actual mention of its involvements in the northern coalition wars of 805–803, organized by Attār-sumkī of Arpad in 805, with subsequent targeting of Arpad's territory by Adad-nērārī in 804–803[219]—had a new king on the throne, Bar-Hadad, son of Hazael, who now organized a new and more comprehensive anti-Assyrian coalition. As Na'aman (1991, 86) has noted, it was clear that only a large, fully participating coalition could hold back the Assyrian war machine, and Bar-Hadad was the driving force behind this particular coalition. The Eponym Chronicle indicates that Adad-nērārī III headed to Manṣuāte—whose location is still not certain.[220] Despite this yet-rather-obscure destination, the campaign of 796 seems to be the only one which can be identified with the expedition of Adad-nērārī III to Damascus in which the invention on behalf of Zakkur likely took place (Dion 1997, 153; Millard and Tadmor 1973, 62–4). That Adad-nērārī III campaigned against Damascus in 796 is firmly established by the chronologies of Adad-nērārī III inscriptions integrated with those of his official, Pālil-ēreš.[221]

Zakkur's vassalage to Assyria may well be illustrated by a tiny fragment of a black stone obelisk found at Nineveh that has a little bit of its inscription preserved (see fig. 7.10).[222] There is a scene in a register with the traces of two lines of inscription above the register. The piece is a corner fragment and its register presents, on its left-hand side, a tributary in a turban or cap which flops backward on the top; he moves right, raising a bowl in one hand. It appears that he is a westerner, not an Assyrian. The inscription only preserves the name Zakkur: ᵐ*za-ku-r*[*i*]. It is very probable that this is none other than Zakkur, king of Hamath and Luġath, paying tribute to Adad-nērārī III,[223] especially since this spelling is precisely the same as that in the Antakya Stela: ᵐ*za-ku-ri*.[224]

Even so, while Zakkur may be depicted in this manner, probably reflecting a tribute payment either in connection with the 796 campaign or another

219. See §8.2.3.

220. See discussion above.

221. See §§8.2.3 and 9.3.6.1.

222. BM 120429. See Reade 1981, 151–52 and pl. XXc. For the inscription, see RIMA 3:225, A.0.104.1003. G. Smith brought it back from Nineveh in 1874. See Smith 1875, 141 and 430 (provenance).

223. Lipiński 2000a, 302; Grayson, RIMA 3:225, A.0.1003; and Reade 1981, 151.

224. RIMA 3:203–4, A.0.104.2, line 4.

annual *maddattu*, the Assyrian interests and agenda in the region meant that Zakkur would be handled in a rather ruthless fashion. This is seen in the Antakya Stela[225] which records the reassignment of the border between Arpad and Hamath at Zakkur's expense:

> (lines 4–8a)
> The boundary which Adad-nērārī (III), king of Assyria, (and) Šamšī-ilu, the commander-in-chief (*turtānu*), established between Zakkur (*ᵐza-ku-ri*), the Hamathite, [and] Attār-sumkī, son of Abi-rāmu: the city of Naḫlasi[226] together with all its fields, its orchards [and] its settlements is Attār-sumkī's property. They divided the Orontes River between them. *This is* the border.[227]
>
> (lines 8b–11a)
> Adad-nērārī (III), king of Assyria (and) Šamšī-ilu, the commander-in-chief (*turtānu*), have released it (from obligations) free and clear to Attār-sumkī, son of Abirāmu, to his sons, and his subsequent grandsons. He has established his city (and) its territories [...] to the border of his land.

Hawkins (1995c, 96) argues that it is very difficult determine where this border reassignment took place based on the findspot of the stela which would have been in ancient times in the middle of Patina/'Umq. Thus it has been suggested that the stela was conveyed down the Orontes from an original emplacement in the neighborhood of Jisr esh-Shughur, where the location of an Arpad-Hamath frontier seems much more probable (Hawkins 1995c, 96). However, other scholars believe that the findspot indicates that the city of Naḫlasi probably originally belonged to Patina/'Umq, even though it is being transferred into the possession of Attār-sumkī of Arpad by Adad-nērārī III from Zakkur of Hamath. Hence they seek to locate the city in the area between Antakya and Samandağ where the stela was found.[228]

In any case, this event is surely some years after 805, and for that matter after 796, because, unlike the arbitration between Kummuḫ and Gurgum where Adad-nērārī III and Sammuramat were involved, in this border or frontier reassignment it was Šamšī-ilu, the *turtānu* "commander-in-chief"

225. RIMA 3:203–4, A.0.104.2, lines 4–11a; Donbaz 1990; *COS* 2.114A:272; Weippert 1992.

226. Naḫlasi is an obscure toponym. This is its only mention (Bagg 2007, 181).

227. NAM.A is unclear. Probably refers to the territory of the city in question, i.e., Naḫlasi (Fuchs 2008, 132 n. 179).

228. As does Weippert 1992, 58–59, and n. 97; Wazana 1996, 62–63; Dion 1997, 155; Lipiński 2000a, 282–83 n. 188 ("it is unlikely that the stela was conveyed down the Orontes, over 100 km, from an assumed original emplacement near Ğisr aš-Šuġur to the neighbourhood of Antakya"). See also now Bagg 2007, 181.

who was involved. In fact, notably, it is Adad-nērārī III and Šamšī-ilu who may be portrayed at the top of the stela with the perpendicular pole of the moon god Sîn of Harran standing between them. Fuchs (2008, 131–35) has demonstrated that the year of Šamšī-ilu's appointment as *turtānu* must date to 787/786.[229] This means that this border adjustment occurred some time in the latter years of Zakkur's reign, at a time that suited the Assyrians. There were perhaps two reasons for the Assyrian decision:

(1) to drive a wedge between enemies (Bīt-Agūsi had been one of the armies besieging Zakkur, and Damascus was already an adversary of Hamath during this period) (Galil 1992, 59; Ikeda 1999, 283; 2003, 91*; and
(2) in order to maintain a level of desired cooperation with Bīt-Agūsi/Arpad due to that kingdom's strategic position at the node of the routes of northern Syria and Anatolia (Dion 1997, 154–55).

Zakkur does not mention the Assyrian deliverance in his inscription, instead crediting the god Baʿalšamayn. This may be due to his disappointment with the policy of the Assyrians as a result of this border reassignment.[230]

7.2.4. The Period after Zakkur (780–740 BCE)

After this border settlement, the history of Hamath and Luǵath is somewhat obscure. It is reasonable to assume that tensions between Arpad and Zakkur and his successors (none of whom are known by name) continued. The relationship with Assyria was also no doubt strained, though there is no record of rebellion for over two decades (perhaps throughout Zakkur's reign). But the resistance of Hamath and Luǵath to Assyria becomes evident in the Eponym Chronicle's notations "to Ḫatarikka" for the years 772, 765, and 755 BCE. It is possible that only Luǵath was the problem (see below).

Interestingly, the archaeological evidence from Tell Afis portrays the general picture of a flourishing Aramean city during the eighth century, reaching its maximum width on the northern and southern limits of the Lower Town (Soldi 2009, 104). While Zakkur lays claim in his inscription to certain building projects in Ḥaḏrak, it seems that the recovered archaeological evidence does not link to the period of Zakkur's reign (i.e., the very end of the ninth century and the first quarter of the eighth century), but to a few decades later (Soldi 2009, 104). Soldi attributes this to a period "when

229. See the discussion in §5.3.1.
230. This may be an indication that Zakkur's stela dates toward the end of his reign or it may be simply a function of the glorification of Zakkur's deity.

the Lu'ash kingdom was still independent between the time of the *Turtānu* Šamšī-ilu and the campaigns of Tiglath-pileser III in northern Syria."[231]

Perhaps the action of Šamšī-ilu's march through Hamath's territory in order to attack Damascus in 773,[232] in combination with the past Assyrian abuses, caused protests of resentment, such that "the bitter discontent of the people naturally erupted" (Ikeda 1999, 283), particularly in Luǵath. This necessitated an Assyrian response in 772, though nothing is known about it. Seven years later (765), and again seventeen years later (755), Assyrian military action was required. It can be assumed that Šamšī-ilu was involved in leading these expeditions, but nothing is known about them and no destruction layer has been identified with any of them in the excavations at Tell Afis.

These three actions, especially the last two, against Ḫatarikka within less than twenty years is in contrast to the silence of the sources about any Assyrian campaigns to Hamath or to central or southern Syria. It may be that Ḥaḏrak was more susceptible to the influence of Arpad than Hamath and that these were isolated, local rebellions, not part of the kingdom's overall policy. However, this perceived difference between Ḥaḏrak and Hamath has also been taken as possible evidence of the double monarchy and the lack of centralization within the region.[233] The fact is, any interpretation of the situation is not based on any actual evidence only the lack of data. Therefore, it is better to refrain from too much speculation.

There is some evidence that indirectly indicates that the kingdom of Hamath, in fact, may have expanded during the eighth century. This evidence is primarily from texts of the later Assyrian king Tiglath-pileser III, who gives an extensive list of territory that he annexed in 738 BCE, which was "nineteen districts (*nagû*) of [the city of Hamath]" (fig. 7.11).[234] Unfortunately, it is impossible to determine exactly when or how Hamath expanded and came into possession of the territory that is located on the Mediterranean coast.

The texts of Tiglath-pileser III can be compared with the list of Shalmaneser III found in the Kurkh Monolith. Most of the differences between the two which were written over a hundred years apart is that Shalmaneser listed kingdoms, while Tiglath-pileser listed cities and districts. The only

231. Soldi 2009, 104. It is unclear in the context whether Soldi means that Luǵath was independent both of Assyria and Hamath or was still joined to Hamath and that this entity as found in the Zakkur inscription was independent of Assyria.

232. Pazarcık Inscription of Shalmaneser IV, RIMA 3:240, A.0.105.1, lines 4–10; and the Eponym Chronicle for 773, Millard 1994, 39.

233. Alt 1934, 241 (= 1959, 222).

234. RINAP 1:42–43, 13, lines 1–12 (Tadmor 1994, 58–65 [Ann. 19*], esp. p. 63, line 9.); RINAP 1:75–76, 31, lines 1–8 (duplicate of text 13:7–11 and text 14:10).

| RINAP 1:42–43, No. 13, lines 2–12<br>(Ann. 19*:1–12; Tadmor 58–63)<br>eighth *palû* (738) | RINAP 1:75–76, No. 31, lines 1–8<br>Duplicate of text no. 13:7–11 and text no. 14:10 |
|---|---|
| (2)[…;] Azriyau […] I seized and (3)[…] [I imposed upon them] tribute like that [of the Assyrians] (4)[…] the city of *kur*… […] his helper(s). | (1) [...] ... |
| The city of El[…], (5) the cities of [Usnu], Siannu, ⸢Ma⸣[…], Kašpūna, which are on the seashore, together with the towns […] [up to Mount Saue], (6) [which] nudges [the Lebanon]—Mount Ba[(ali]-ṣapūna, up to Mount Amma[nā]na (Anti-Lebanon)*—the boxwood mountain—all Mount Saue, [the province of the city of Kār-Adad], (7) [the city of Ḫatarikka], [the province] of Nuqudina, Mount [Ha]su[atti, to]gether with the towns of [its environs, the city of Arâ …, both of them, (8)the towns of their en]virons, [all] of Mount Sa[r]būa, [the city of Ašḫani, (and) the city of Yaṭabi, all of Mount Yaraqu], [the city of x-x-ri], (9)[… the city of El]litar[bi], (and) [the city of Zi] tānu, up [to] the city of Atin[ni] […], [the city of Bumame—19 districts] (10) [of Hamath] together wit[h the t]owns of their [en]virons, which are [on the] western [sea]shore, (and) which [in sin and criminal outrage were seized for Azriyau], (11)I anne[xed to Assyria].<br>I placed two of my [eun]uchs over them as governors.<br>[…] 83,000 (people) (12)[…] in/from those cities in the province of Tuš[ḫan] I settled. I settled 1,223 people in the province of Ulluba. | […...] […...] both of them, the towns in their environs, all of Mount Sarbūa, the city of Ašḫani (and) the city of Yaṭabi, all of Mount Yaraqu, x-x-ri, the city of Ellitarbi, (and) the city of Zitānu, up to the city Atinnu, … […], (5) the city Bumame—19 districts of Hamath together with the towns (6)of their environs, which are on the western seashore, (and) (7)which in sin <and> criminal outrage were seized for Azriyau, (8)I annexed to Assyria.<br>I placed two of my eunuchs over them as governors. |

*Tadmor and Yamada (RINAP 1, 42, note line 6) state: "⸢KUR.*am-ma*⸣-[*na*]*na*, 'Mount Amma[nā]na': The full name appears in text no. 46 line 23 and text no. 47 rev. 26′. It has been discussed if this mountain is to be identified with the Anti-Lebanon (Tadmor, *Tigl. III* p. 61), Jabal an-Nusairiya (*Helsinki Atlas*), or the Amanus (Zadok 1996a, 11–13); see also Bagg, *Rep. Geogr.* 7/1 pp. 8–9 s.v. Ammanāna. A. Bagg (*SAAB* 15 [2006] pp. 184–92) has persuasively argued that Ammanāna is to be identified with the northern part of the Anti-Lebanon." See also Cogan 1984, 255–59.

Fig. 7.11. Duplicate texts of Tiglath-pileser III

really significant difference is the presence of Arwad in the Shalmaneser text while it is absent from Tiglath-pileser's lists. This may be simply due to the fact that Arwad (alternatively Armada) was probably still able to maintain its independence at the time of Tiglath-pileser due to the insular position of its capital (Dion 1997, 165).

Another source for this obscure period of Hamath's history is found in 2 Kgs 14:23–29, the account of Jeroboam II's reign. Unfortunately, this source is fraught with difficulties. Two of its verses (25 and 28) give the following information:

> (25) He restored the border of Israel from Lebo-Hamath as far as the Sea of the Arabah, according to the word of Yahweh, the God of Israel, which he spoke by his servant Jonah, son of Amittai, the prophet, who was from Gath-hepher.
>
> (28 )Now the rest of the acts of Jeroboam, and all that he did, and his might, how he fought, and how he recovered for Israel Damascus and Hamath, which had belonged to Judah, are they not written in the Book of the Annals of the Kings of Israel? (NRSV)

The first clause of verse 25 states rather straightforwardly that Jeroboam II restored (הֵשִׁיב) the border of Israel from one point to another: *from* (מִן) Lebo-Hamath (לְבוֹא חֲמָת, very likely is a reference to ancient Labā'u, modern Lebwe, 25 km northwest of Baalbek in the northern Beqa' Valley of Lebanon[235]) *to* (עַד) the Sea of the Arabah (i.e., the Dead Sea).[236] In the inscription of Tiglath-pileser III, it is clear that the city of Labā'u was on the border and was, at that time, a possession of Damascus. The association in the biblical tradition of Labā'u with Hamath may derive from an earlier time when this was reflective of that kingdom's territorial extent.[237] Although the second part of the verse attributes this to a prophecy of Jonah, the son of Amittai, the initial statement is understood by many scholars to refer to an

235. See Territory of Hamath discussion above, §7.1.

236. Cf. the description in Amos 6:14: "and they shall oppress you *from* (מִן) Lebo-hamath *to* (עַד) the Wadi Arabah." See §5.3.3 for discussion of this verse.

237. Weippert (1992, 59 n. 100) argued that it is not well understood how this city could be called "Lebwe of Hamath." Dion (1997, 167) expresses it in a slightly different way: "Son association artificielle avec le Hamath dans les textes bibliques, qui réinterprètent son nom comme l''Entrée de Hamath,' vient peut-être de ce que l'abaissement de Damas sous Jéroboam II ouvrit cette région à Israël, faisant ainsi de Lebweh le dernier bastion israélite avant d'entrer au Hamath." Thus Jeroboam's reduction of Damascus made Lebweh the Israelite border town that was then artificially associated with the "entrance to Hamath."

expansion of Israelite territory in the days of Jeroboam II (though with various views about the extent and timing).

However, the NRSV translation of verse 28b is interpretive and obscures the significant problems in the verse. The MT reads: וַאֲשֶׁר הֵשִׁיב אֶת־דַּמֶּשֶׂק וְאֶת־חֲמָת לִיהוּדָה בְּיִשְׂרָאֵל, lit. "and how he restored Damascus and Hamath to Judah in Israel." While some scholars have attempted to explain this clause as it reads, most scholars agree that this is senseless. That this verse is to be connected with verse 25 is clear from the repetition of the verb הֵשִׁיב "restored," but the last two words are a hub of confusion. There are four ways in which scholars have attempted to deal with the problem.

(1) Some scholars have attempted to make sense of the passage by emendation, a complete rewriting in some cases. Burney rewrote it as:

אשר נלחם את דמשׂק ואשר השׁיב את חמת יהוה מישׂראל

"how he fought with Damascus and how he turned away the wrath of YHWH from Israel."[238]

Lipiński (1970, 48–49) offered another rewriting, which he himself has now abandoned in favor of an understanding of the passage that is utterly unique: "How he warred, and how he pushed back Damascus and Hamath to his glory in Israel, isn't this recorded in the annals of the kings of Israel?"[239] Such creativity does not yield a solution.

(2) This view can be seen in the original NIV translation "how he recovered for Israel both Damascus and Hamath, which had belonged to Yaudi,"[240] or the NEB translation "in Jaudi for Israel," which take the consonants יהודה to be a reference to Yaudi/Sam'al, the modern site of Zincirli. This is based on Winckler's suggestion (1893, 1–23) that identified Y'DY (ancient Sam'al) with Yaudi in the Assyrian inscriptions. But this has been thoroughly discredited, since all the references in the Neo-Assyrian sources to Yaudi are to the kingdom of Judah and the north Syrian kingdom of Y'DY is always referred to in these same sources as Sam'al or Bīt-Gabbāri.[241]

(3) Translating the clause in question as "how he recovered Damascus and Hamath for Judah in Israel," Sweeney (2007, 368) has suggested

238. Burney 1903, 320–21. He is followed by Gray 1970, 616.
239. Lipiński 2000a, 311, with explanation on p. 312.
240. However, with the text note: "or *Judah*." Revised in 2011 to read "Judah."
241. See §6.1.2.2.

that "this brief account indicates that Jeroboam's reign holds utmost significance for the kingdoms of Israel and Judah since he was the first and only monarch ever to restore control over the entire extent of the empire once controlled by David and Solomon." With Lebo Hamath "identified with the region of Hamath in upper Syria," and the Sea of Arabah "with the Red Sea to the south," he argues that "Jeroboam's control of Hamath and Damascus restores Aram to Israel's control for the first time since the Arameans revolted against Solomon (1 Kgs 11:23–25). Because Joash subdued Amaziah, who in turn had defeated Edom, Jeroboam controlled Edom." Thus, "Jeroboam's reign sees an end to the greatest challenge faced by Israel through the ninth and early eighth centuries: the Arameans."

However, Sweeney's understanding of the geographic descriptions is questionable and the reference "to Judah" (לִיהוּדָה) remains problematic.[242]

(4) Finally, a number of scholars have suggested that יהודה ב is a scribal insertion. Cogan and Tadmor (1988, 161–62) argue: "The easiest solution is to omit 'for Judah' and read 'for Israel.'" Thus the verse originally read "for Israel," and a later Judahite scribe added the word "for Judah" as a gloss so that "the claim to these territories in the far north might be connected to the achievements of David and Solomon (Judahite kings)."

Furthermore, the boundary description "from Lebo-Hamath to the Sea of the Arabah" can be understood as presenting Jeroboam's reign as an ideological reflection of the achieving of the glories of David and Solomon, perhaps as a feature of the earlier northern kingdom composition upon which the later Kings's version is based. Thus the scribal gloss, if it is accepted as such, was in some sense in line with the *Vorlage* that he was working with. While there is no textual variant upon which to posit such a gloss, this, nevertheless, may be the best solution.

Regarding when this expansion may have occurred, Haran (1967, 279) argued that the most likely time for the Israelite expansion under Jeroboam was during the last six years of his reign (754–748 BCE in his understanding). On the other hand, Tadmor has argued that the expansion would have taken place in the early to middle years of Jeroboam II's reign because the

242. I would certainly agree, however, with his emphasis on the small pericope and its importance as the culmination of the Jehu history (Sweeney 2007, 369).

latter part of his reign was already experiencing the disintegration of his "empire."[243]

That the biblical text presents this as the work of Yahweh and as an ideological link to the Davidic story is also, no doubt, the result of the northern source being redacted into the present history through a Judahite lens. Nevertheless, in spite of the lack of certainty and disagreements on a number of the issues as outlined here, most scholars do see some type of expansion of Israelite political influence northward to Labā'u of Hamath in the days of Jeroboam II.[244] However, the preposition מִן attached to Lebo-Hamath (לְבוֹא חֲמָת) makes clear that this expansion did not include Hamath itself.[245]

### 7.2.5. The Demise of Hamath (740–720)

Less than a century after Zakkur, Hamath was eliminated as a polity. Its end came in two stages initiated by Tiglath-pileser III and finalized by Sargon II. Both stages are largely enveloped in obscurity. The first stage began in 738 with the northern half of the kingdom being conquered and made into Assyrian provinces; the second stage transpired in 732 with the rest of the kingdom being annexed (Radner 2006–8a, 66). A rebellion led by Yau-bi'di could not reverse this.

#### 7.2.5.1. Azriyau

After Tiglath-pileser III had defeated Sarduri, the king of Urartu and his Anatolian allies, and after he had eliminated Mati-ilu of Bīt-Agūsi/Arpad (743–740), he was forced to suppress a revolt in 738 led by Tutamuwa[246] of Patina/ʿUmq/Unqi. In his account concerning this revolt, Tiglath-pileser mentions a leader whose name is Azriyau (written in cuneiform: ${}^{m}$*az-ri-ia-a-ú* and ${}^{m}$*az-ri-a-ú*; Cole 1998). However, the land of this Azriyau is not clearly identified. In one of his inscriptions, Tiglath-pileser III states:

> I annexed to Assyria 19 districts of Hamath together with the towns of their environs, which are on the western seashore, (and) which in sin <and> criminal outrage were seized for Azriyau.[247]

---

243. Tadmor 1961b, 240. See also Hallo 1960, 166–69; Kuan 1995, 127–28.

244. Lipiński 2000a, 312–15; Dion 1997, 166–67; Cogan and Tadmor 1988, 161–62; Sweeney 2007, 368.

245. See further discussion at §9.3.6.1.

246. Novotny and Zadok 2011.

247. RINAP 1:75–76, 31, lines 5–7. For more detail, see above.

The identification of this individual is uncertain. The second component of the personal name contains the Yahwistic theophoric (Younger 2002), while the first element (*ʿzr* "help") is Hebrew or Phoenician, not Aramaic (*ʿḏr*) typically written in cuneiform: *id-ri-(i)*. The name could imply that this person was an Israelite. On the other hand, he could be a native of Hamath that had an Israelite background or a strong Israelite influence (perhaps due to Jeroboam II's power having reached Labāʾu [Lebo] of Hamath).[248] A future king of Hamath had the name Yau-biʾdi, perhaps another individual that bore a Yahwistic name.[249]

Concerning this Azriyau's identification, three proposals have been made. Two of these were based on a supposed join of Ann of 19* of Tiglath-pileser III with K 6205—a fragmentary tablet that contains an account of a war against the land of *Yaudi* and a certain individual called [... *i*]*a-a-u* KUR *Ia-u-da-a-a*. Thus the first proposal was that Azriyau was the king of *Yʾdy*/Samʾal, the southeastern Anatolian state (Winckler 1893). This view, however, is out of the question since the land of *Yʾdy*/Samʾal was always rendered KUR/URU.*Samʾal(la)* in Assyrian records, whereas *Yaudu*/*i* exclusively refers to Judah. A second proposal was that Azriyau was none other than Azariah, the powerful king of Judah.[250] The third proposal was put forth by Naʾaman (1974, 25–39). He argued convincingly that the cuneiform fragment K 6205 should be joined to another fragment and that both of these derive from the reign of Sennacherib.[251] This meant that the Azriyau of Tiglath-pileser's annals not longer was attributed to a particular land. Thus Naʾaman (1995d, 276–77) argued that this Azriyau was an otherwise unattested king of Ḫatarikka (Ḥaḏrak), part of Hamath or possibly the land of Luġath. He postulated an alternative reconstruction of the events of 739 and especially 738, the year in which Tiglath-pileser III annexed Patina/ʿUmq/Unqi, Ḫatarikka and the "19 districts of Hamath."[252] While accepting this, Tadmor (1994, 273–74) argued that since the attribution of Azriyau's land is still unknown, it cannot be ruled out that this is still a reference to Azariah of Judah. Unfortunately, until new evidence is discovered, the identification of Azriyau must remain conjectural.[253]

248. Lipiński 2000a, 315; Dalley 1990; Zevit 1991; and Becking 1992, 35 n. 59. Yahweh's worshipers could be descendants of the Israelites who were living in the ninth century under Aramean rule.

249. Yau-biʾdi might be analyzed as "Yahweh is behind me" (Fuchs and Parpola 2000). See below.

250. Tadmor 1961b; Roberts 1985, 158–64.

251. Now commonly referred to as the Azekah inscription, see *COS* 2.119D:304–5.

252. See text in fig. 7.11. See also Weippert 1976–80; Hawkins 1976–80a, 273.

253. For further discussion, see Tadmor 1994, 273–76.

Archaeological evidence from Tell Afis demonstrates that in the latter half of the eighth century "it became necessary to provide Afis with a big defensive wall, probably built in a very short time on leveled debris sealing IA II materials still in situ: the well-stratified pottery leaves us in no doubt that we are not dealing with the wall Zakkur claims to have built around Ḥaḏrak as defence against the army of the king of Aram-Damascus and his seventeen allies, but with a wall that had to defend the town at least half a century later" (Soldi 2009, 104). The Tell Afis excavators feel that this wall was built to defend the city from either the army of Tiglath-pileser III or Sargon II (Soldi 2009, 104). In the former instance, the wall was constructed in connection with the 738 rebellion; in the latter case, it was hurriedly built as part of the anti-Assyrian revolt in the western province led by Yau-biʾdi in 720 (see below). In my opinion, the former is more likely, given the Assyrian campaigns against Arpad, the necessity for the wall's construction would be greatly underscored.

One of the further complications of the ʿAzriyau "episode" lays in the interpretation of the text quoted above about "the nineteen districts of Hamath." If one assumes that only nineteen districts, including Ḥaḏrak, followed ʿAzriyau in his revolt, then it might imply a split kingdom (i.e., Luǵath in the north and Hamath in the south). On the other hand, as Lipiński notes, this passage may be simply enumerating the districts of Hamath that were annexed to Assyria by Tiglath-pileser III and hence are alluding to the reduction of the kingdom to a rump state centered at Hamath with Eni-ilu as the Assyrian nominee.[254] Again, obscurity makes it difficult to know which scenario is right.

The fate of ʿAzriyau after his defeat is also unknown. If one accepts the heavily restored passage of Tiglath-pileser III's annals proposed by Na'aman (1995d, 276–77), it may indicate that he fell into Assyrian hands, was deported to Assyria, and was doubtless dealt with as a treaty-breaker. But the actual fate is not clear. There is indication, however, that large-scale deportations took place, a rather common feature of Tiglath-pileser III's policy. Because of the fragmentary nature of the text, it is not clear, but a figure of 83,000 people (Hamathites?) is given, with a settling process stated in the following clauses (see the text in fig. 7.11). Kunulua (capital of Patina/ʿUmq/Unqi) was made into an Assyrian provincial administrative center,[255] as too Ḫatarikka (Ḥaḏrak). Thus in 738, the northern half of Hamath and Luǵath

254. Lipiński 2000a, 314. An analogy would be Tiglath-pileser's action against Israel, where it was reduced to only the rump state of Samaria under Hoshea (with Pekah's elimination).

255. Radner 2006–8a, 61, no. 52: Kullani(a) (also Kinalua), modern Tell Taʿyinat.

was divided into the Assyrian provinces of Ḫatarikka and Ṣimirra (Radner 2006–8a, 66).

### 7.2.5.2. Eni-il

In the year 738,[256] a certain Eni-il (ᵐ*E-ni-ìl* URU.*Ḫa-am-ma-ta-a-a*; Brown 1999) is listed as the ruler of Hamath paying tribute to Tiglath-pileser III.[257] Once again, there is uncertainty. Why is he absent from the narrative until this point? Did Eni-il, the king of Hamath, simply remain on the sidelines during this struggle (an indication that Luǵath was independent from Hamath?) and hence was not punished by Tiglath-pileser III, not being held liable?[258] Or is Eni-il's absence an indication that at the point of his mention, he is now a newly appointed king of the rump state of Hamath (analogous to Hoshea of Israel)? Whatever the case, he is listed as a tributary along with numerous other western monarchs. It is interesting to note that in all three of the texts that mention him he is listed just before Panamuwa of Sam'al, a known loyalist of Tiglath-pileser III.[259]

Eni-il reigned at least until 732 BCE, since he is included in the list of Tiglath-pileser III's tributaries following the capture of Damascus.[260] He may be mentioned in a letter[261] from Šamaš-aḫu-iddina (see Ambos 2011), the chief eunuch (LÚ*.GAL–SAG), who was active in the west during the reign of Tiglath-pileser III. In this letter addressed to the king, Šamaš-aḫu-iddina mentions an Eni-il (ᵐ*a-i-ni*-DINGIR)[262] along with others from the cities of Riblah (URU.*ra-ab-le-e*) and Qadesh (URU.*qi-di-si*). When he first published this letter, Saggs suggested that this Eni-il was perhaps the ruler of the tributary kingdom of Hamath. This understanding has been accepted by a number of scholars.[263] While this may, in fact, be a reference to the

256. For the date, see Tadmor 1994, 267–68. Dion (1997, 168) notes that the absence of this king of Hamath in the Iran Stela, the earliest version of this list, must be an accident.

257. Tadmor 1994, 68–69, Ann. 13, line 11; 89, Ann. 27, line 4; 170–71, Summary 7, r. 8′.

258. Dion 1997, 168.

259. See §6.3.5.

260. RINAP 1:122, 47, line r.8′; Tadmor 1994, 170–71, Summary 7, line r.8′.

261. ND 2766. SAA 19:42–44, text 37; Saggs 2001, 161–63; 1963, 79–80 (no. LXX) and pl. XIV.

262. The spelling of the first component (*'yn*) is perhaps more accurately reflective of the diphthong, as is normal in Old Aramaic. Interestingly, the spelling of the name as *'yn'l*, a king of Byblos in the fourth century, is curious in light of Phoenician phonetics. See Elayi 1993.

263. Dion 1997, 168; Lipiński 2000a, 316; Ambos 2011.

same Eni-il, king of Hamath, as in Tiglath-pileser's inscriptions, the association is based on the mentioning of Riblah and Qadesh. Perhaps a caution should be signaled since the letter does not identify this person as the king of Hamath (or for that matter with Hamath at all—apparently a verb follows the name and so there is no actual identification associated with the name in the letter). So then, it is certainly possible that this is another person with this name, and not a reference to the ruler mentioned in Tiglath-pileser's texts. It seems that at this point in 732, the second stage of Hamath's demise came to pass with the annexation of the rump state. It was divided into the provinces of Ṣubutu[264] and Manṣuāte.[265] There does appear to be any evidence that a province named Ḫamattu existed.[266]

### 7.2.5.3. Yau-biʾdi

Around two decades later in 722, the crippled land of Hamath was led in a final revolt against Assyria by Yau-biʾdi. With the death of Shalmaneser V and the seizure of the throne by Sargon II, Hamath revolted. In spite of the addition of a number of other entities in the rebellion, there probably was little real prospect of success. Assyria was simply too strong and the coalition too weak.

Frahm (2013) has recently published a slab that appears to have an early version of Sargon II's annals.[267] It has added to our knowledge of the events of this year. It appears that with the demise of Hamath as brought about through Tiglath-pileser III's action, there was significant resentment throughout the region (Bagg 2011, 215–16). The new slab reveals that Yau-biʾdi and his rebels went on a killing spree, murdering every Assyrian they could find.[268] This demonstrates the incredible hatred that many people in the west

264. Radner 2006–8a, 62–63, no. 61: Ṣubutu. See the discussion on the location of Ṣobah at §3.3.1.1.

265. See discussion above regarding the date of the siege and deliverance of Ḥaḏrak/Ḫatarikka (§7.2.3)

266. Radner 2006–8a, 66; see also Hawkins 1995, 97; Lipiński 2000a, 317; Dion 1997, 170; pace Na'aman 1995b, 104.

267. In addition to this text, the following texts mention this campaign: Aššur Charter (Saggs 1975, 14–15, line 20); the Borowski Stela (Hawkins 2004; Lambert 1981, lines 5–12); Annals (Fuchs 1994, 87–8); Room 5 (Albenda 1986); the Iran Stela (Levine 1972, 25–86); ʿAšarneh Stela (Frame 2006), and the "Cyprus Stela" (VAS 1, no. 71, Malbran-Labat 2004); Sargon's "Cylinder Inscription" (Fuchs 1994, 29–44), his "Display Inscription" (Fuchs 1994, 189–248), a cylinder inscription from Nimrud (Gadd 1954, 198–201); and the so-called "Juniper Palace Inscription" from Nimrud (Winckler 1889, 168–73). See also Fuchs 2009–11, 52.

268. Frahm 2013, 46, 50; lines 14b–16a: "He killed the citizens of Assyria who were present in [...] altogether [and left no one alive (...)]."

Table 7.3. The Kings of Hamath (and Luǵath)

| |
|---|
| Taita II (ca. 1000–985) |
| To'î (ca. 985–950)<br>*Hdrm*? and/or others? (ca. 950?–935?) |
| Urhilina's great-grandfather "X" (ca. 935–910)<br>Urhilina's grandfather "Y" (ca. 910–885)<br>Parita (ca. 880–860)<br>Urhilina (ca. 860–840) – 870–840 (Liverani 2005, 106)<br>Uratami (ca. 840–820) – 840–807 (Liverani 2005, 106)<br>? (ca. 820?–803?) |
| Zakkur (ca. 803–780) – 807–780 (Liverani 2005, 106) |
| ? (ca. 780–750) :: Jeroboam II of Israel's expansion ‖ Šamšī-ilu |
| Azriyau? (ca. 750–738?) – 730–738 (sic: 738–730) (Liverani 2005, 106) |
| Eni-il (ca. 738–732?) – 738–730 (Liverani 2005, 106) |
| ? (732?–722?) |
| Yau/Ilu-bi'di (ca. 722–720) – 730–720 (Liverani 2005, 106) |

felt toward Assyria and its imperial agents. With Sargon's seizure of power and the unrest within Assyria at the beginning of his reign, the opportunity to regain independence was more than enough stimulation for rebellion.

So it was that Yau-bi'di (also called Ilu-bi'di)[269] organized a coalition against Sargon II including the cities of Arpad, Ṣimirra, Damascus, Ḫatarikka, and Samaria (Samaria is listed last in all the sources; Younger 1999, 471–72). No doubt the very recent outcome of Sargon's battle with Ḫumbannikaš I of Elam at Dēr greatly encouraged the rebels.[270] Sargon II expresses his contempt: "Yau-bi'di [(5)] [of Hamath, (who was) not the rightful throne-holder, (who was) unfit for (living in) a palace, and as whose] fate it had not been decreed [that he would (ever) shepherd] the people."[271] The new slab pre-

269. This king's name is spelled: Ilu-bi'di or Yau-bi'di. Concerning the Yahwistic theophoric, see §7.2.5.1 and note 249.

270. Brinkman 1984, 48–9. Sargon seems to admit to a severe defeat at Dēr according to the Borowski Stela (Lambert 1981, 125, lines 5–12).

271. Frahm 2013, 46. Yau-bi'di's rulership is only indirectly described in Palace Door 4 lines 22–23: "subjugator of the kings (*malkī*) of Hamath, Karkamiš (and) Kummuḫ"). See Fuchs 1994, 261.

serves some information not found elsewhere in Sargon's texts: namely, the Assyrian monarch's immediate reaction to the revolt:

> [*I lifted my hands*] to Sîn, the king of the gods and lord of the lands [..., who *vanquishes*] the foes and destroys the enemies, my lord; and I appealed to him (to help me) to [*reconquer*] the land of Hamath, overthrow [... and ...] the wide land of Amurru.[272]

In his prayer to the moon god, Sîn, in which he implores for his help in reconquering Hamath and the rest of the Levant, Sargon is appealing to a deity very special in the northern Levantine context (Staubli 2003). This is no doubt purposeful, for having this deity's support meant victory.

The new slab does not preserve the outcome. However, from other texts, it is known that Sargon II defeated the coalition decisively at the battle of Qarqar (the same site where Shalmaneser III had fought a western alliance in 853, see above). It may be that Qarqar on the Orontes was the major stronghold of Yau-bi'di, rather than Hamath (Frahm 2013, 49). Major deportations followed, including one from Samaria of 27,000 people (cf. 2 Kgs 17:6) (Younger 1998, 1999). Sargon II also pardoned and settled 6,300 "guilty Assyrians," apparently his political opponents, in Hamath, and imposed on them the same tax and corvée duties that "the kings, my royal fathers, had imposed on Irḫulēni the Hamathite."[273] Sargon, it seems, was well informed about the events that had taken place in the west during the reign of Shalmaneser III.

As for Yau-bi'di, he and his family were carried off to Assyria. Later, his public flaying while still alive was depicted in realistic detail on one of Sargon's reliefs,[274] with an epigraph: "Yau-bi'di the Hamathite, I flayed his skin ([*ma*]*šakšu akūṣ*)."[275] Sargon's Cylinder inscription adds an important detail: "(I am the one), who stained red the skin of the rebel Ilu-bi'di as *nabāsu*-wool" (*ša mašak* ᵐ*Ilu-bi'di hammā'i iṣrupu nabāsiš*).[276] Rollinger and Wiesehöfer (2012, 504–13) have demonstrated that this sentence refers to the tanning of the peeled skin, giving it a reddish color. Thus the skin was removed and preserved by tanning, giving it this particular color and preserving it for display as a trophy of Sargon's victory over the coalition in 720.

272. Frahm 2013, 46, lines 16b–19.

273. The "Borowski Stela." See Hawkins 2004, 160, B 5–9.

274. Botta and Flandin 1849–50, 2 pl. 120; 4 pl. 181, no. 2. Albenda 1986, pl. 78, room 8, slabs 24–25.

275. Saal VIII:25, lines 1–2; Fuchs 1994, 278, 364; see also the Great Summary Inscription (Groß Prunkinschrift) line 35: *šâšu mašakšu akūṣ* (Fuchs 1994, 201, 345).

276. Fuchs 1994, 35, line 25; Reiner 2006, 327.

There can be little doubt that Yau-biʾdi received this "special treatment" because this was a particularly serious rebellion. Three of the participants—Arpad, Ṣimirra, and Damascus—were Assyrian provinces and not just vassal states,[277] and Samaria had just been conquered less than two years earlier in 722 by Shalmaneser V (Younger 1999). Thus the threat to the Assyrian Empire was dire, and the leader of such a major treasonous act deserved a particularly horrendous punishment.

The citadel of Hamath (modern Ḥama) was destroyed and plundered as is seen in the level of its stratigraphy that corresponds to this event (Fugmann 1958), and as Sargon commemorated his victory by erecting a stela at ʿAšarneh,[278] among other sites (e.g., Samaria). The destruction was such that the citadel of Hamath did not seem to be rebuilt until Hellenistic times,[279] although the town continued to exist as attested by Sargonid period letters and administrative texts.[280] As mentioned above, there were significant deportations both from and to the entire region such that Sargon claimed the epithet, "uprooter of Hamath" (*na-si-iḫ šur-uš* KUR/URU.*a-ma-at-te*) (Fuchs 1994, 35 and 291). He incorporated three hundred charioteers and six hundred cavalry of Hamath into the Assyrian army.[281] Thus Hamath and Luǵath were thoroughly integrated into the Assyrian Empire and remained so until its demise.

---

277. See the comments of Bagg 2011, 229, 233–36.

278. Frame 2006. See earlier, Thureau-Dangin 1933.

279. The Hellenistic city was called Epiphaneia.

280. SAA 1:135, 172.16; 1:135, 173.6; 1:136, 174.7; 1:179, 230.r.5; 1:197, 252.5; SAA 11:5, 1.r.1, 8′, and 12′.

281. Fuchs 1994, 201 and 345, Display 35–36; Lambert 1981; Hawkins 2004; Dalley 1985.

# 8
# BĒT-GŪŠ/ARPAD

THE *BĪTU*-FORMULATION WAS USED BY THE ASSYRIANS TO DESIGNATE THE TRIBAL state of Bēt-Gūš, which was, of course, based on the eponymous ancestor Gūš. This leader was mentioned by Aššurnaṣirpal II as "Gūš, the Yaḫānean" ($^{m}$*gu-u-si* KUR.*ia-ḫa-na-a-a*) who paid tribute to Aššurnaṣirpal II during his campaign to the Mediterranean Sea around 870 BCE.[1] This text implies that an Aramean entity called Yaḫān was firmly established in northern Syria. Nevertheless, the entity would be referred to from this point on in the Assyrian sources as Bīt-(A)gūsi and in Aramaic texts as Bēt-Gūš (fig. 8.1).

The ninth-century tribe of Yaḫān in this north Syrian location is the same Aramean tribe that is mentioned in the tenth century in the annals of Aššur-dān II (934–912 BCE)[2] where it is located in the Tigris area, more specifically Jebel Ḥamrīn (see fig. 2.6). Lipiński rightly notes that this is evidence that the tribe had immigrated to northern Syria.[3] Hawkins disagrees (1977, 238), feeling that "the name {Yaḫanu} is not to be identified in the annals of Aššur-dān II (third campaign, in connection with the land of Aram [KUR *i*]*a-ḫa-a-nu*)."[4] The rationale for this statement is not given, but it would appear to be the improbability of having the same tribe in two different locations (one in central Mesopotamia and the other northern Syria). However, the evidence for migration by the Aramean tribal entities, as discussed in the earlier chapters of this volume as well as in chapter 10, negates this objection. There are simply too many examples of the same Aramean tribal

1. RIMA 2:218, A.0.101.1, iii.78.

2. RIMA 2:133, A.0.98.1, line 23. In the 1926 *editio princeps* of Aššur-dān II's Annals, Weidner (1926, 156 n. 10) connected this mention of the Aramean tribe of Yaḫānu with the north Syrian Aramean tribe of Bīt-Agūsi, though he felt that this was an indication that Aššur-dān II campaigned in the Karkamiš area.

3. See the discussion §4.1.1.3.

4. See also apparently Bagg, 2007, 122, s.v. Jaḫānu 1. He does not list the Aššur-dān II text and seems to be separating it from the other entry, presumably his Jaḫānu 2, which he states: "Nicht mit Jaḫānu 2 zu verwechseln."

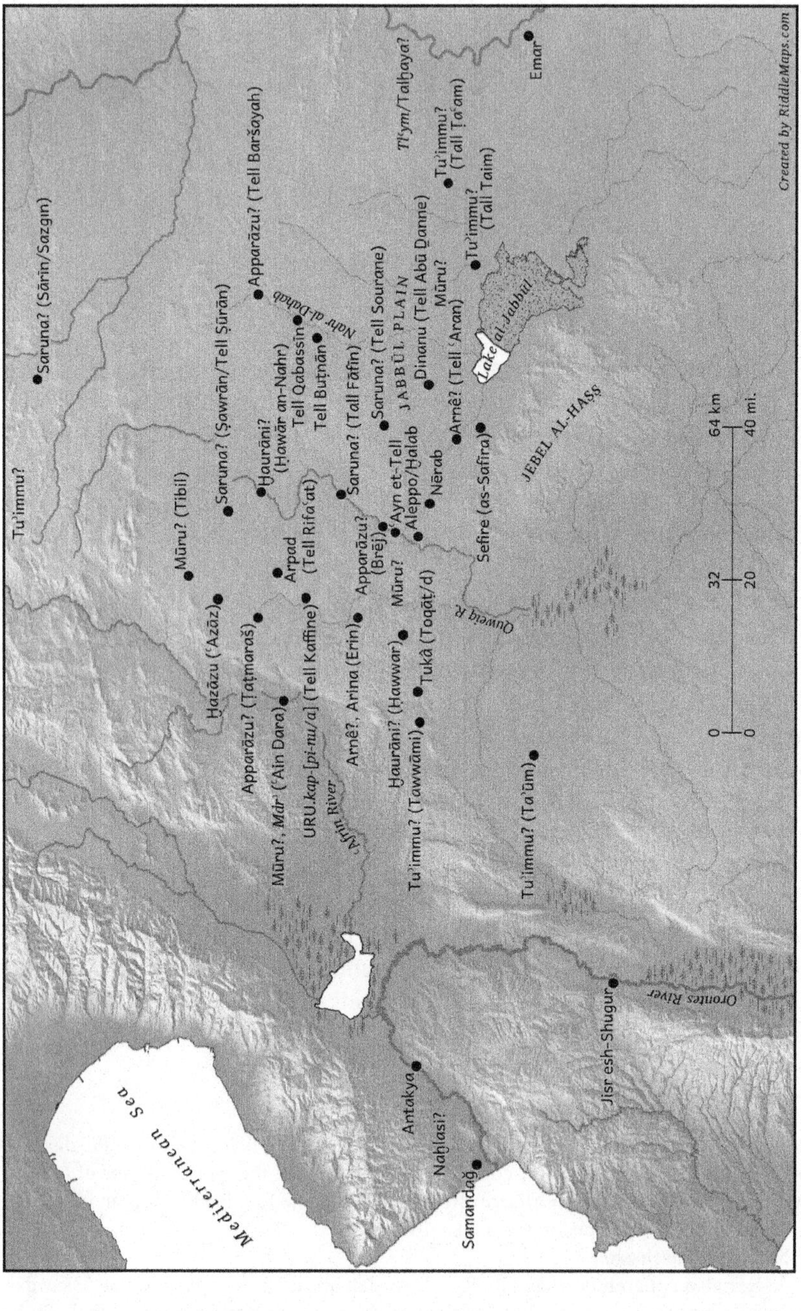


Fig. 8.1. Territory of Bēt-Gūš/Arpad

name popping up in different locations for this to be a case of two different Aramean tribes with the same name!

Lipiński (2000a, 196) suggests that Yaḫān (*Yaḥan*) is a West Semitic shortened personal name, paralleled by Amurrite *Ia-ḫu-un-*[5] and Phoenician *Yḥn-/-yḥn.*[6] It must therefore be considered as an Aramaic tribal name and not as an original toponym. Such an understanding is completely in line with what is known about the names of the Aramean tribal entities, who take their names in most instances from ancestors, not from toponyms (in fact, the toponyms may often be taken from the ancestral name or the tribal name). This is an important point that impacts the understanding of the narrative of Aššurnaṣirpal II referred to above.

Around 870 BCE, as Aššurnaṣirpal II marched from Karkamiš to the city of Ḫazāzu (modern ʿAzāz), which was at that time in the kingdom of Patina/ʿUmq:

> I departed from the land Karkamiš; I took the way between Mount Munziganu (and) Mount Ḫamurga. I left (alone) KUR *a-ḫa-a-nu* on my left side (i.e., to the south); I approached the city of Ḫazāzu of Lubarna, the Patinean.[7]

Dion and Grayson have understood the determinative KUR to refer to a mountain (i.e., Jebel Simʿān).[8] Dion (1997, 114) even suggests that the gentilic tribal name of Yaḫānāya associated with Gūš (m*gu-u-si* KUR *ia-ḫa-na-a-a*) is derived from the geographical name of "Mount Aḫanu." However, most scholars understand the determinative in the writing KUR *a-ḫa-a-nu*/*a-ḫa-nu* as a determinative for "land," and thus see this as a reference to "the land of (Y)aḫānu."[9] Thus Yamada (2000a, 98 n. 80) states: "Ahan and Yahan in this context undoubtedly refer to the same place." The gentilic form of the tribal polity will only be used through the reign of Shalmaneser III, at which point the polity will be referred to by its other names: Bēt-Gūš and Arpad.

The name Gūš appears to be a hypocoristic form, though its etymology is not entirely clear (Dion 1997, 113 n. 5). Its spellings in Neo-Assyrian (Luukko 1998) are: m*a-gu-su*, m*a-gu-si*, m*a-gu-ú-si*, m*gu-si* and m*gu-ú-si*.

5. See Gelb 1980, 6, and 83.

6. He suggests that "the vowel *a* probably results from the influence of the pharyngeal *ḥ* and it is lengthened as a consequence of the shortening of final *n*: *yaḥunn* > *yaḥann* > *yaḥān*" (Lipiński 2000a, 196 n. 2).

7. RIMA 2:217, A.0.101.1, iii.70–71. See also RIMA 2:227, A.0.101.2, line 46, where it is written: KUR *a-ḫa-nu*.

8. Dion 1997, 114–15; and RIMA 2:217 and 227.

9. Bagg 2007, 122, s.v. *Jaḫānu 1; Lipiński 2000a, 196–99; Yamada 2000a, 98 n. 80; Liverani 1992a, 73–74; Zadok 1977–78, 45; Kessler 1980, 217 and n. 785; and Hawkins 1976–80b.

Only the first is a spelling used for individuals other than the eponymous ancestor of the polity Bīt-Agūsi (Bagg 2007, 45–46).

Zadok (1978, 50–51) suggested that *gūš* might be a theophoric element in personal names. He collected examples of the Neo-Babylonian personal name *A-a-ga-a-šú*, *A-a-i-ga-a-šú*, and *A-a-i-ga-a-ši* that clearly reflect the interrogative pronoun *ʾAyya* seemingly attached to a second component that is a theophoric: "Where is *Gaš?"[10] However, Lipiński (2000a, 211, and n. 100) argues against Gūš being a theonym. While the personal name at Ugarit ᵐDUMU-DINGIR-*gu-ši*[11] might suggest that *gūš* is a theonym,[12] Lipiński rightly notes that this name can be read as "*Bin-Il-gūši* with *gūšu* qualifying Il." In my opinion, the meaning of this name might be "the son of ʾIlu is solid, substantial."[13] Thus there does not seem to be any strong evidence that *Gūš* was a deity, and in any case, there is a very reasonable alternative.

In Aramaic, the polity's name *gš* occurs on the Sefire stelae.[14] It also likely occurs on an ivory pyxis from Nimrud.[15] It is also found in the form *brgš* in the Zakkur Inscription (*KAI* 202:A5; see §2.3.1).

The tribal state was also called Arpad. The city of Arpad was the polity's capital city after 849 BCE when the city of Arnê was destroyed by Shalmaneser III. This name of the city/country occurs in Aramaic,[16] in Hebrew,[17] as well as in Akkadian (Bagg 2007, 23–25). It has been suggested that the hieroglyphic Luwian inscription of Uratami (ca. 840–820) from Ḥama,[18] that mentions "the river-land of Ḫurpata," whom Uratami credited with building one of the gate structures at Hamath, is a reference to Arpad (modern Tell Rifaʿat), particularly because the text adds "and therein (are) Halabeans" (i.e.,

---

10. Zadok (1978, 51 n. 109) states: "Possibly a *qal* nominal formation which is related to *Gus*. The two vocalized names in Ugarit which include *Gš*, namely *Girgišu* and *Giše* (see Gröndahl, PNU 130f. s.v. *Gs/š*) point to a *qil* formation. Late Baby. has also *Gu-sa-a-a*, i.e., from *Gus/š*; see Fales, ACF 13/3, 181 No. 5 (NA *Ba-gu-su* which is discussed there, may be interpreted differently: 'son of *Guš*,' cf. Zadok 1976b, 28 n. 93."

11. *PRU* 3, 199 and pl. LXXXI (RS 16.257+, A I, 5″).

12. The reading of the cuneiform alphabetic script name in *CTU*/*KTU*, 328, text 4.309, 16 is *bn gšl*(?), not *bn gš*.

13. The Neo-Babylonian names may also be understood along similar lines.

14. Sefire I: *KAI* 222: B11: [*b*]*yt gš*; Sefire II: *KAI* 223:B10: *byt gš*; possibly Sefire I: *KAI* 222:A16 ([*bny* or *byt*] *gš*) and B3: (*bny gš*).

15. Reading: *l*[xxxx]*bytgš* "Belonging to [ ] of Bēt-Gūš." See Puech 1978, 165. Mitchell (1996) states: "Since there is nothing to determine its position precisely, the space available for the personal name allows for at least four characters and possibly more."

16. Aramaic: *ʾrpd*: Sefire I: *KAI* 222:A1, 3, 4 (2x), 12, 14, 26, 29, 30, 32, 35, B1, 4, 5, 6, 22, 30, 41; Sefire II: *KAI* 223:B2, 3, C1, 5; Sefire III: *KAI* 224:1, 3, 16, 27.

17. Hebrew: *ʾarpād*. See *HALOT*, 90.

18. HAMA 1 §§2–4. See Hawkins 2000, 413.

the inhabitants of Aleppo).[19] However, while obviously the reference to the Halabeans is clear, it is not certain that Ḫurpata is, in fact, the Luwian rendition of *ʾrpd*, since there is some question as to whether the Quweiq riverland would be named in Luwian after Arpad, which had only recently become the capital city, and is not even located on the Quweiq River. Later after the Assyrian conquest, Arpadda was a province (see below).

Finally, in the Sefire stelae, there are two phrases that have received much attention: *ʾrm klh*, "all Aram" and *kl ʿly ʾrm wtḥth*, "all of Upper-Aram and Lower-(Aram) (lit. 'its lower')."[20] Part of the debate has centered around the fragmentary border description in I B 9–10. Scholars have made various proposals on the understanding of these two phrases. Mazar (1962, 112, 116–20) proposed that "all Aram" referred to "all Syria," a unified Aramean state that Bar-Hadad II (Adad-idri) established whose hegemony had been moved from Aram-Damascus to Arpad.[21] Fitzmyer (1995, 65; 1967, 29, 62–5, 134–5) argued that "all Aram" expressed the extent of the coalition or union which Bar-Ga'yah had set up.[22] Na'aman (1978, 221–24) proposed that the border description in I B 9–10 describes the borders of Aram-Damascus, not Arpad or all of Syria, because in his assessment the name "Aram" always refers to the kingdom of Damascus.[23] Pitard (1987, 152–58, 178–79) believed that "all Aram" refers to the Aramean states in northern Syria that were dominated by Arpad, without delineating its exact borders. Grosby (2002a, 2002b) proposed that the phrase "all Aram" has a sociological significance, implying a certain kind of collective unity like "all Israel" in the Hebrew Bible. He sees its use as anticipatory of a territorial entity, which in reality is a military ad hoc confederation of all independent cities/kingdoms in an alliance with Arpad as its head. Somewhat similar to Grosby, Wazana (2008, 728–29) states:

> The existence of the term "all Aram" probably indicates, as Grosby noted, the emergence of a "nation" (practically in the modern sense) in process that was united by more than just a military alliance of city-kingdoms bound by a common enemy—the expanding Neo-Assyrian force—but was not yet a crystallized political entity. However, the term does not necessarily indicate that this entity had restrictive, compulsory borders. In the current state of scholarship, we have no indication whatsoever that the geographical-religious-sociological (though not political) entity "all Aram" had linear,

19. Savaş 1998, 189; Lipiński 2000a, 207; Jasink 1995, 101–2.

20. Most recently see Talshir 2003; Kahn 2007; Wazana 2008.

21. This highly speculative proposal has been sufficiently criticized, see in particular, Na'aman 1978, 220–22 and Pitard 1987, 178.

22. See criticisms of Na'aman 1978, 220; Pitard 1987, 178; Kahn 2007, 77.

23. Pitard (1987, 178–79) points out the evidence of the use of "Aram" (Melqart Stela) and the biblical material (e.g., Aram-Ṣobah) that invalidates Na'aman's position.

> recognizable borders in reality. In my study of border descriptions in the ancient Near East, I found that boundary-lines were marked in the field and put into writing only when deemed necessary to solve an acute military or fiscal problem. It is unlikely that the still vague, emerging concept of "all Aram" required delineation. The claim that the description indicates borders, without further proof, stems from the misconception that all territories were demarcated, reflecting modern ideas about borders, and cannot be maintained.

However, Kahn (2007, 79) has rightly noted that the term "all Aram" appears in a vassal treaty (a legal contract between two parties) and that in a contract an abstract between not yet existing parties is never what is being delineated. "All Aram" had linear, recognizable borders in reality. It was not a vague, emerging concept, but an existing entity with clear borders under the sovereignty of Mati''El, king of Arpad.

There are two points that can be added to Kahn's observation. First, when one looks closely at the structure of the treaty as dictated by the repetitive usage of *ʿdy* and *ʿm*, the referent of *ʾrm klh* becomes clear. The text (Stela I A 1–6a) reads:

(1) ʿdy brgʾyh mlk ktk ʿm mtʿʾl br ʿtrsmk mlk [ʾrpd]
[wʿ](2)dy bny brgʾyh ʿm bny mtʿʾl
wʿdy bny bny brgʾ[yh wʿqr](3)h ʿm ʿqr mtʿʾl br ʿtrsmk mlk ʾrpd
wʿdy ktk ʿm [ʿdy] (4) ʾrpd
wʿdy bʿly ktk ʿm ʿdy bʿly ʾrpd
wʿdy ḥb[wr](5)w ʿm ʾrm klh
  wʿm mṣr wʿm bnwh zy ysqn bʾšr[h]
  w[ʿm mlky/bʿly(?)] (6) kl ʿly ʾrm wtḥth
  wʿm kl ʿll byt mlk

(1)The treaty of Bar-ga'yah, king of KTK **{A}**, with Mati'-'El, son of 'Attār-sumkī, the king of [Arpad] **{B}**;
[and the trea(2)]ty of the sons of Bar-ga'yah **{A}** with the sons of Mati'-'El **{B}**;
and the treaty of the grandsons of Bar-ga'[yah and] (3)his [offspring] **{A}** with the offspring of Mati'-'El, son of 'Attār-sumkī, king of Arpad **{B}**;
and the treaty of KTK **{A}** with [the treaty] of (4)Arpad **{B}**;
and the treaty of the lords of KTK **{A}** with the treaty of the lords of Arpad **{B}**;
and the treaty of *ḥb*[*wr*](5)*u* "the union" **{A}** with all Aram (lit. "Aram, all of it") **{B}**,
  and with *Muṣr* and with his sons who come up in [his] place (i.e. "come after [him]"),

> and [with the kings/lords] of (6)all of Upper-Aram and Lower-(Aram) (lit. "its lower"),
> and with all who enter the royal palace (lit. "house of the king").

There can be no doubt that the treaty was between the lands of KTK **{A}** and Arpad **{B}**: between Bar-ga'yah and Mati'-'El; between their sons; between their grandsons; between their polities; between their lords; between [the union?] of *ḥb*[..]*w* with "all Aram." With the last *wʿdy* in line 4, the **{A}**–**{B}** sequence ends; and with the use of *wʿm*, a further delineation of **{B}** is given (prior to this, it is only *ʿm*). The same structure recurs throughout the stelae. In my opinion, scholars have been so engaged with the identification of the entities mentioned that the structure has not been closely observed. So, while the identification of KTK is still uncertain,[24] the repetition throughout the stelae demonstrates that these are the "two entities" in view. This is even observable in the more fragmentary section I B 2–4, where "all Aram" occurs again in a restored passage, parallel with *bny gš* "the Gūšites" (the people of Arpad), the otherwise unknown Bēt-ṢLL, and "the offspring of whatever king who (3)[comes up and reigns] in his place."

The second point is that the understanding of *kl ʿly ʾrm wtḥth*, "all of Upper-Aram and Lower-(Aram)" is elucidated by Akkadian materials. In the *ginā*ʾ*ū*-lists from the Middle Assyrian period, one encounters two provinces: *pa-ḫu-tu* AN.TA (*pāḫutu elītu*) "the Upper province" and KIMIN KI.TA (*pāḫutu šaplītu*) "Lower province."[25] Rosa (2010, 334) rightly notes that adjectives like "upper" and "lower" are almost meaningless if we do not know the cultural horizon, or merely the point of view, of people using them. Therefore, the context is paramount for understanding the referents. Based on various data, Rosa (2010, 330–35) suggests that the provinces named *pāḫutu elītu* (= Šadikanni)[26] and *pāḫutu šaplītu* were located on the upper and lower Ḫābūr River. A particular text of Adad-nērārī II is informative:

> GUN *ma-da-tu* NÍG.GA É.GAL-*šú* $GU_4$.MEŠ (118) ANŠE *a-ga-li*.MEŠ GUN *ù ma-da-tu šá* KUR *la-qe-e a-na paṭ gim-ri-šá e-liš* (119) *ù šap-liš lu am-ḫur*

24. See detailed discussion below.

25. MARV 2.21:13–14. See discussion of this text in chapter 3.

26. The Tell Šēḫ Ḥamad archives have revealed that the Upper Province and Lower Province are on the Syrian Ḫābūr (Postgate 2013, 99 and n. 27). See also Jakob 2003, 316; Röllig 2008a, text 22.

> I received tribute, tax, the property of his palace, oxen, *agālu*-donkeys, tribute and tax of the land of Laqē to its entire extent (i.e. "all of it") above and below (i.e. the Upper and the Lower).[27]

Here, one can see an almost perfect parallel to the Sefire phrases: "the land of Laqē to its entire extent" (*māt Laqē ana pāṭ gimrīša*) = "all Aram" (*ʾrm klh*), and "above and below, i.e. the Upper and the Lower" (*eliš u šapliš*) = "all of Upper-Aram and Lower-(Aram)" (*kl ʿly ʾrm wtḥth*).[28] In this instance, "Upper" and "Lower" are likely referencing "north" and "south," as Talshir 2003 and Kahn 2007 have suggested (just as *eliš* and *šapliš* are referencing "north" and "south" in the case of Laqē).[29]

Therefore, it is apparent from the structure and the parallel wordings that *ʾrm klh* and *kl ʿly ʾrm wtḥth* are references to the entity of Arpad in its political condition at the time of the Sefire treaty inscriptions. The border description given in I B 9–10, unfortunately, is fragmentary. But the general delineations given in the *mn–ʿd* formulation describe the boundaries of the polity. Thus, within these parameters (to the best that they can be determined) are the subordinates of the king of Arpad (= "all Aram"; Kahn 2007, 80; Bunnens 2015).

## 8.1. Territory

During its history as a north Syrian kingdom, Bēt-Gūš/Bīt-Agūsi saw significant changes in its territory. In its earliest phases, one encounters three issues: (1) there is some uncertainty concerning its unity;[30] (2) the location of its first capital city Arnê has been debated (Bagg 2007, 23); and (3) the borders of the land moved over its history. Complicating this, few of its cities can be firmly identified. Therefore, the knowledge about this polity is still tentative (see fig. 8.1).

---

27. RIMA 2:154, A.0.99.2, lines 117b–119a.

28. One can see another parallel in this same inscription of Adad-nērārī II (RIMA 2:153, A.0.99.2, lines 98b–99a): *ma-da-tu šá* KUR *ḫa-ni-gal-bat* (99) *e-liš ù šap-liš lu am-ḫur* KUR *ḫa-ni-gal-bat* DAGAL-*tu a-na paṭ gim-ri-šá lu a-pél a-na mi-ṣir* KUR-*ia* (100) *lu-te-er* 1-*en pa-a ú-še-eš*$_{15}$-*ki-šu-nu-ti*, "I received the tribute of the land Ḫanigalbat above and below (upper and lower). (Thus) I became lord of the extensive land of Ḫanigalbat to its entire extent (and) I brought (it) into the boundaries of my land. I brought them under one authority.

29. So, too, in the case of Ḫanigalbat. See previous note.

30. See discussion below.

8.1.1. Capitals

The first capital city of this polity was Arnê. Two different sites have been proposed for its location. Some scholars have equated Arnê with Erin, about 20 kilometers southwest of Tell Rifaʿat (Arpad).[31] Lipiński and others have argued for an identification with Tell ʿAran,[32] about 15 km northeast of Lake al-Jabbūl, some 6 km northwest of Sefire and about 18 km southeast of Aleppo. He identifies Erin with ancient Arina. Matthers et al.[33] argued that "Arne is more likely to be identified with Tell Aarane than with Erine" (*their spellings of the modern place names*) because of several factors. Erin is a much smaller site than Tell ʿAran, being located on the eastern edge of the hills that divide the ʿAfrin and Quweiq valleys and is, therefore, more vulnerable to attack than ʿAran. Tell ʿAran is a large, imposing tell rising from the Jabbūl Plain and has a mud-brick wall over 20 m in width. Yet the tell is covered by a thick destruction layer.[34]

The problem with Tell ʿAran being identified with Arnê is that such an identification would mean that places like Aleppo, Nērab and Tell Abū Ḏanne were all part of Bēt-Gūš/Bīt-Agūsi during the ninth century before the 849 destruction of the site by Shalmaneser III. But when Shalmaneser III came to Aleppo on his 853 campaign, there is no indication that this city was part of Bēt-Gūš/Bīt-Agūsi. In fact, it seems to be independent.[35] It would seem that Aleppo only became a city of Bēt-Gūš sometime later.

In any case, sometime after the destruction of Arnê in 849, the city of Arpad became the capital of Bēt-Gūš (Bagg 2007, 23–5). Because Attār-sumkī, son of Abi-rāmu, is described in the Pazarcık Stela as the Arpadite (URU.*ár-pa-da-a-a*), a stela that is recording events that occurred in 805, it can be assumed that at a minimum around 805, with all probability much earlier, the city of Arpad had become the capital. It remained so until 740 BCE when Tiglath-pileser III captured the city.

The identification of Arpad with Tell Rifaʿat, about 25 km north of Aleppo, has long been proposed on etymological and geographical grounds. While this identification is not absolutely certain, it has been generally accepted.[36] This site has an imposing tell that rises 30 m high. It was 89

31. Dion 1997, 116–17; Dussaud 1927, 468; Elliger 1947, 79; Sader 1987, 147.

32. Located at N 36°07′; E 37°20′. See Lipiński 2000a, 198, 203, 210, with map on 201. See also Parpola and Porter 2001, 2, 6 (Tall ʿAran); Fales and Mazzoni 2009–11, 343.

33. Matthers, et al. 1978, 144. See also their map on p. 121, no. 3.

34. Matthers, et al. 1978, 144.

35. See the translation of the passage in §7.2.2.2.1.

36. Schiffer 1911, 137 n. 9 (Tell Arfad); Kraeling 1918, 65 (Tell Erfad); Forrer 1920, 56 (Tell Rfad); Seton-Williams 1961, 70; Matthers et al. 1978, 144–45; Kessler 1980, 187;

ha/220 acres in size and had a double fortification wall (the inner wall was 18 m wide).[37] The excavation of the tell yielded a large quantity of the eighth-century Red-Slipped Burnished Ware that matches well that found at Ḥama level E in the destruction level (Matthers, et al 1978, 144). On the western side of the tell, excavations discovered a large palace 923 m wide and 30 m long with a large porch with two columns and a great paved courtyard. The palace was flanked by two rooms, in front of which there had been a large hall. The palace belongs to the first millennium BCE.

### 8.1.2. Major Cities and Borders

A very important site in Bēt-Gūš is Sefire (Arabic as-Safīra), which is located between the Jebel al-Ḥaṣṣ and Lake al-Jabbūl on the southern route linking Aleppo to the Euphrates, in the vicinity of Emar (Fales and Mazzoni 2009–11). Although the identification of Sefire with the URU.*Ši-ip-ri* in Aštata by Dussaud (1928, 171) and Dossin (1930) was accepted by many,[38] there is, in fact, no first-millennium attestation of this toponym (Fales and Mazzoni 2009–11, 342). Lipiński (2000a, 204–6) has suggested that its ancient name was *mrbh* based on the Sefire stelae (Sefire I: *KAI* 222:A34). However, from the context of Stela I, this is hardly self-evident, being based on Lipiński's interpretation of a very difficult fragmentary line (Stela I: *KAI* 222:B12). Thus, as Fales and Mazzoni (2009–11, 342) conclude, the Iron Age name of the site remains uncertain.

In addition to the three Sefire stelae,[39] a fragmentary basalt statue[40] has also been recovered from Sefire (Warmenbol 1985, fig. 2–5). It is a male figure holding a cup in the right hand and wearing a pleated garment with wide belt. On the front hangs a short sword with the sheath decorated with complex geometric patterns. The head is missing and the legs are only partially preserved. On the back, there is a cuneiform inscription of Adūni-abīya, son of Enna-Aya who dedicates a sacred place and a statue to the god of *Nir-rú-bi*[ki] (probably the city of Nērab). It had been dated by scholars to the fifteenth or fourteenth century but is now dated, on the basis of the

---

Sader 1987, 289; Weippert 1992, 49; Mazzoni 1995, 181; Lipiński 2000a, 208; Radner 2006–8a, 58, no. 46; Parpola and Porter 2001, 2, 24. The suggestion that Arpad be identified with Tell as-Safīra (Sefire; Warmenbol 1985) and the suggestion to identify Arpad with ʿAin Dara (Abou-Assaf 1990, 24) are both highly unlikely.

37. Seton Williams 1961; 1967; Matthers and Collon 1981.

38. KBo I 1 rs.17′. See del Monte and Tischler 1978, 359–60.

39. *KAI* 222, 223, 224. See Lemaire and Durand 1984; Fitzmyer 1995.

40. Aleppo National Museum, no. M. 6525. Current height: is 42 cm. For photos, see Lipiński 2000a, 209, 213.

inscription, to a period after Assyrian annexation of Arpad (740; Warmenbol 1985, 168–69; Lipiński 2000a, 206–7). The Egyptianizing style of the pleated garment suggests a Phoenician cultural context, and can be compared with the kilt of the royal iconography of the Twentieth Dynasty worn in statues from Tyre, Zarephath, ʿAmrīt, the stela of Melqart from Brēj (but more probably from the nearby ʿAyn et-Tell, see discussion below), and the stela from Qadbun (al-Qadmūs).

The city of Ḫazāzu is important for the delineation of the territory of Bēt-Gūš/Bīt-Agūsi (Bagg 2007, 102–3). The identification of Ḫazāzu with ʿAzāz, about 15 km northwest of Tell Rifaʿat (Arpad) is generally accepted.[41] In the middle of ninth century, the city was in the territory of Patina/ʿUmq according to the texts of Aššurnaṣirpal II and Shalmaneser III,[42] though these texts make it clear that the border with Bēt-Gūš was to the south of this city. Sometime in the late ninth century, the city became part of the territory of Bēt-Gūš, and in the inscriptions of Tiglath-pileser III it is listed as being in Bīt-Agūsi (mid-eighth century). Thus, the firm identification with ʿAzāz provides a significant insight into the history of the polity of Bēt-Gūš.

Another city of Bēt-Gūš was Apparāzu (Bagg 2007, 17–18). Three possible identifications have been proposed. First, Forrer identified Apparāzu with modern Brēj (classical Abarara), on the eastern bank of the Quweiq River, about 30 km southwest of Tell Rifaʿat (Arpadda).[43] Yamada (2000a, 177 with n. 74) also considers this proposal possible. Second, Yamada prefers a location at Ṭaṭmaraš, about 9 km northwest of Tell Rifaʿat.[44] Third, Lipiński (2000a, 207 with n. 74) proposes a localization at modern Tell Baršayah or al-Barša;[45] thus placing it beyond the Nahr al-Dahab in the northeastern boundary region of Bēt-Gūš/Bīt-Agūsi. Other tells in this area with Iron Age II ceramics are Tell Qabassīn and Tell Buṭnān.[46] One issue with this location is whether these localities belonged to Bīt-Agūsi or not; and this is far from evident.[47] Furthermore, from the other subsequent events in Shalmaneser III's annals subsequent to the destruction of Apparāzu—namely, the tribute of Qalparunda of Patina and Shalmaneser's cedar cutting expedition on Mount

41. Dussaud 1927, 469; Olmstead 1918, 247 n. 67; Forrer 1920, 56; Astour 1963, 236; Hawkins 1972–75c, 240; Matthers et al, 124, no. 6; Sader 1987, 146, n 114; Liverani 1992a, 74; Weippert 1992, 49; Lipiński 2000a, 196, 199; Yamada 2000a, 106–8; Parpola and Porter 2001, 2, 24.

42. Aššurnaṣirpal II: RIMA 2:217, A.0.101.1, iii.71; Shalmaneser III: RIMA 3:17, A.0.102.2 ii.1; RIMA 3:25, A.0.102.3, i.92–94.

43. Forrer 1920, 26, 56; Mittmann and Schmitt 2001, B IV 10.

44. See already Kraeling 1918, 78.

45. Location: N 36°29′; E 37°35′, ca. 14 km northeast of Al-Bab.

46. Matthers et al. 1978, 121, no. 26 and 9.

47. Matthers et al. 1978, 147. See also Sader 1987, 137–38.

Amanus—it seems that a location in the western part of Bēt-Gūš would be preferable (see further discussion below for the year 848).

The city of Dinanu (Bagg 2007, 62) is listed in the inscriptions of Tiglath-pileser III.[48] While some have understood it to be listed in the Sefire treaty, reading the toponym as *dynn*,[49] the reading seems to be *bynn*,[50] which of course, would not be an attestation of this toponym. A possible candidate for Dinanu is the Tell Abū Ḏanne,[51] some 15 km northeast of Sefire, where an Iron Age II–III settlement is archaeologically attested.[52]

The city of Ḫaurāni (URU.*ḫa-ú-ra-a-ni*)[53] also occurs in this same list of Tiglath-pileser III. It may be connected to [ʿ]*rnh* in the Sefire text (Stela I, A, 34–35). Lipiński (2000a, 203) identifies it with Ḥawwār, 15 km west of Aleppo. However, it has also been identified with Ḥawār an-Nahr, 14 km east northeast of Arpad.[54] Lemaire and Durand (1984, 114, 122) and Fitzmyer (1995, 46–47) both restored the reading as [ʾ]*rnh* and translate [ʼA]rneh, and understood this to be a reference to the city of Arnê. However, this city was destroyed by Shalmaneser III, and there is no evidence for it in the sources after this. Therefore, a restoration [ʿ]*rnh* and link with Ḫaurāni is preferable.

The modern city of Aleppo was known in Neo-Assyrian sources as Ḫalman/Ḫalab,[55] in Aramaic as *ḥlb*,[56] and in Luwian as Ḫalpa. While the city's political preeminence was lost with the collapse of the Hittite Empire, Ḫalab retained its importance as the cult center for the worship of the Storm God of Aleppo (Hawkins 2000, 388–89). The invoking of this deity in the treaty between Aššur-nērārī V of Assyria and Matiʿ-ʾEl of Arpad,[57] as well as in the treaty of Bar-gaʼyah and Matiʿ-ʾEl,[58] emphasizes the importance of

48. URU.*di-na-nu*. Tadmor, 1994, 146, Summary 5: ii.6; RINAP 1:109, no. 43, ii.6.

49. Sefire I: *KAI* 222:A34; Lemaire and Durand (1984, 76) note that the reading *dynn* is as possible as *bynn*.

50. *KAI* 222:A34; Fitzmyer 1995, 46 and 91.

51. Lipiński 2000a, 203 and n. 47; Sader 1987, 122 n. 31, 148; Lemaire and Durand 1984, 114.

52. Tefnin 1980; Tefnin, Doyen, and Warmenbol 1980; Lebeau 1983.

53. RINAP 1:109, 43, ii.1; Tadmor, 1994, 146, Summary 5: ii.1. Noth (1961b, 137) proposed this.

54. Parpola and Porter 2001, 2; earlier Elliger 1947, 93.

55. Bagg 2007, 84, s.v. Ḫalman 1. The spelling "Halman" is found only in the inscriptions of Shalmaneser III. This writing of the name must be carefully distinguished from the URU.Ḫalman, also called URU.Arman, modern Ḥolwān See Hawkins 1972–75a. This form of the name as applied to Ḫalab has not been adequately explained. See Landsberger 1948, 23 n. 45. For earlier attestations in other various languages see Bagg 2007, 84 and Hawkins 2000, 388.

56. Sefire I: *KAI* 222:A11; Sefire III: *KAI* 224:5.

57. SAA 2:13, 2.r.vi.18.

58. *KAI* 222 and 224 (see n. 61).

the deity, even if the city had diminished in political significance. There is uncertainty about when Bēt-Gūš/Bīt-Agūsi came to control Aleppo (see the discussion below).

In 833/832, Shalmaneser III annexed Mūru (Bagg 2007, 177), the fortified city of Aramu, the man of Bīt-Agūsi, rebuilding the gates and building a palace in it.[59] Since no attack on Mūru is mentioned, this may imply that the Assyrians annexed the city with the consent of the ruler of Bēt-Gūš/Bīt-Agūsi, their loyal vassal (Yamada 2000a, 219), although how much a choice this was undoubtedly is suspect. The city became an Assyrian outpost in the west[60] and must have had strategic value (Sader 1987, 148). The exact location of Mūru is unknown. Many proposals have been given. Forrer (1920, 26) proposed a site north of Lake al-Jabbūl, but this seems unlikely being too far to the south (Sader 1987, 147; Bagg 2007, 177). Sader (1987, 147–48) proposed to seek a location for Mūru northwest of Aleppo. Parpola and Porter (2001, 2, 13) suggest modern Tibil. Lipiński (2000a, 202) argues that since

> the local dialect articulated the cluster *dr* almost like *r*, as shown by the usual Assyrian spelling *A-ra-me* of the name *Hadrām*, URU.*Mu-ú-ru* is most likely the same city as *Mdrʾ* in the Sefire treaties and URU.*Mu-ud-r*[*u*-?] in Tiglath-pileser III's inscriptions,[61] where the city is considered as belonging to ʿUmq.

He proposes identification with ʿAin Dara,[62] on the right bank of the ʿAfrin, about 22 km southwest of Tell Rifaʿat. However, Yamada (2000a, 219 n. 490) equates Mūru with Murūa (URU.*mu-ru-u-a*), mentioned in the next line in the same inscription of Tiglath-pileser III as the occurrence of URU.*mu-ud-*⌜*ru*⌝-[..].[63] This equation seems more likely, which permits the equation of URU.*mu-ud-* ⌜*ru*⌝-[..] with *Mdrʾ* of the Sefire treaty to work separately.

The ancient name of ʿAin Dara remains obscure.[64] As noted, Lipiński (2000a, 202) identifies it with the city of *Mdrʾ* mentioned in the Sefire treaty.[65] The site is about 40 km northwest of Aleppo and 25 km west of Tell

59. URU.*mu-ú-ru*. RIMA 3:68, A.0.102.14, lines 130–131.

60. Yamada 2000a, 219 and 223 n. 508, not necessarily a provincial center, as Zadok 1989, 169.

61. Tadmor 1994, 148–49, Summary 5, ii.13: URU.*mu-ud-*⌜*ru*⌝-[..]; RINAP 1:109, no. 43, ii.13.

62. He argues that the name Dārā is "a Semiticized form of the probably Hurrian place name *Mudrā/u*. See Lipiński 2000a, 202.

63. Tadmor 1994, 148–49, Summary 5, ii.14; RINAP 1:109, no. 43, ii.14.

64. In spite of the fact that a hieroglyphic Luwian inscription was discovered there, see Hawkins 2000, 386–87, s.v. VII.11 ʿAFRIN.

65. Obviously, a preferable suggestion to the identification of ʿAin Dara with Arpad (Abou-Assaf 1990, 24).

Rifa'at (Arpad) on the east bank of the 'Afrin River. The citadel mound is about 125 m (north–south) by 60 m (east–west), with the southwestern edge near the 'Afrin (Novák 2012, 43). The lower city is 270 m to 170 m (Stone and Zimansky 1999). Excavations demonstrate a more or less continuous occupation of the site from Neolithic to medieval times, with a dense settlement in the Late Bronze Age as well as Iron I–II. However, 'Ain Dara is best known for its temple located on the northern quarter of the citadel mound, the dating of which has been debated.[66]

The city of Naḫlasi (URU.*na-aḫ-la-si*) became part of the territory of Bēt-Gūš/Bīt-Agūsi after the border settlement by Adad-nērārī III and Šamšī-ilu between Attār-sumkī and Zakkur.[67] The city may have originally belonged to Patina/'Umq.

The modern name Nērab preserves the ancient name of the site.[68] Two grave markers with inscriptions of priests of Śahr that were discovered at the site contain the toponyn *nrb*: Sîn-zēr-ibni and Si'gabbār.[69] Today, Nērab is a suburb of modern Aleppo, and is home to the Aleppo International Airport. But in the nineteenth century CE, Nērab was approximately 67 km southeast of Aleppo. According to Clermont-Ganneau (1897), the tell rose 19 m in height and was approximately 130 m in length.

---

66. See Abou-Assaf, 1990; Orthmann 1993; Kohlmeyer 2008; Weippert 2003; Novák 2012. The excavations of the Aleppo citadel temple complexes has aided in clarifying this issue. Novák (2012, 50) has recently proposed "in a time between 1250 and 1100 B.C.E."

67. Antakya Stela. RIMA 3:203–4, A.0.104.2, line 6. See Bagg 2007, 181 and in previous chapter.

68. The first attestation of the place name is on a statue fragment from the time of Man-ištūšu: [É]NSI-*nir-ra-ab*.KI (RIME 2:314, E2.0.0.1007, lines 2–3). It also appears in the topographical list of Thutmose III as *nyrb* (Simons 1937:113, no. 189 [100]). Nīrabu is mentioned in texts from Alalaḫ and Ugarit, as well as in Middle Babylonian (Belmonte Marín 2001, 210). From the Neo-Assyrian period (see Bagg 2007, 182, s.v. Nīrabu), Nērab (URU.*ni-ra-bu*) appears in a list of Arpadite cities in Tiglath-pileser III's Summary Inscription 5 (RINAP 1:109, text 43: ii.3). A legal text discovered at Nineveh records the purchase of a town by Remanni-Adad (a charioteer during the reign of Aššurbanipal), namely, the town Musina-aplu-iddina, which adjoined the city of Nērab (URU.*né-ri-bi*; SAA 6:264, 326.6′). Nērab also appears in a letter from the reign of Sargon II (URU.*né-ri-bi*, SAA 1:149, 189.8). In Neo-Babylonian texts, the name is written URU.*né-re-eb* or URU.*né-re-bi* (RGTC 8, 238). Of particular interest is one reference to $^{d}$XXX [Sîn] *šá* URU.*né-re-bi* (Zadok 1985a, 238). I thank my student, A. D. Riddle, for helping compile this note.

69. In 1865, Clermont-Ganneau acquired the two stelae, presently in the Louvre: Nērab 1 (AO 3026; *KAI* 225), appropriately named since it contains the representation of a single figure, and Nērab 2 (AO 3027; *KAI* 226), which has two figures portrayed in relief. See most recently Yun 2006.

The city of Saruna (URU.*sa-ru-na*) occurs in the list of Arpadite cities in Tiglath-pileser III's inscriptions,[70] and seems to be the city *šrn* in the Sefire treaty.[71] A number of different proposals for its location have been made; the main ones are:

(1) modern Sārīn (Sazgın), 15 km southeast of Gaziantepe;[72]
(2) Ṣawrān, modern Tell Ṣūrān, 15 km northeast of Tell Rifa'at;[73]
(3) Tall Fāfīn, 17 km north of Aleppo on the Quweiq River;[74]
(4) Tell Sourane northeast of Aleppo (Matthers no. 29, midway between Bab and Aleppo).[75]

Another city mentioned in Tiglath-pileser III's list as being in the territory of Arpad is Tukâ (URU.*tu-ka-a*).[76] Lipiński (2000a, 203) proposes Toqā(ṭ/d), 24 km west of Aleppo as a possible candidate.

The city of Tu'immu (Bagg 2007, 259–60) which is mentioned in Tiglath-pileser III's annals[77] and the Iran Stela,[78] as well as in other Neo-Assyrian texts,[79] is the *t'wm* of the Sefire treaty.[80] This city may be equated with Tawwāma, about 25 km southwest of Aleppo (Lipiński 2000a, 203; Zadok 1985, 314). The location proposed by Forrer, namely Ta'ūm,[81] about 10 km northeast of Idlib is rightly questioned by Zadok (1985, 314), because this

70. Bagg 2007, 215; Tadmor 1994, 146, Summary 5, ii, 5.

71. Sefire I: *KAI* 222:A34.

72. Forrer 1920, 56; Elliger, 1947, 93; Noth 1961, 136–37 n. 54; and Tadmor 1994, 147. Yamada (2000a, 115) states: "Surunu may probably be identified with Saruna, attested in Tiglath-pileser III's list of the cities of Bit-Agusi, with *šrn* of the Aramaic Sefire treaty, and perhaps with *Šurun* of the Suppiluliuma-Šattiwaza treaty. The name of the place may be preserved in the modern Sarin located 15 km south-east of Gaziantep." Fales states: "Thus, *Šrn* (Sefire I A: 34) = Tiglath-pileser (Tigl.) III's *Sa-ru-na* and already *Su-ru-nu* (Sūrunu), a city to the west of the Euphrates, previously part of Bīt-Adini, mentioned by Shalmaneser III (RIMA 3, 18: 17)" (Fales in Fales and Mazzoni 2009–11, 343). However, some scholars see this as a confusion of Surunu, a city of Bīt-Adīni with Saruna, a city of Bīt Gūš/Bīt-Agūsi (Sader 1987, 148).

73. Lemaire and Durand 1984, 74–75; Parpola and Porter 2001, 2, 16.

74. Lipiński 2000a, 210f with map on page 201.

75. Sader (1987, 148) states: "Tell Sourane au nord-est d'Alep."

76. Bagg 2007, 261, s.v. Tukâ. See RINAP 1:109, text 43, ii.4; Tadmor 1994, 147, Summary 5, ii.4.

77. RINAP 1:46, text 14, line 8: *i-na* NAM(*pīḫat*) URU.*Tu-'i-im-me*; Tadmor 1994, 66, Ann. 13, line 8.

78. RINAP 1:86, text 35, ii.14′: URU.*Tu-'a-am-mu*; Tadmor 1994, 104, Iran Stela II B, 14′.

79. Dalley and Postgate 1984, 86:14 (part of a provincial list): URU.*tú-im-m*[*e*].

80. Sefire I: *KAI* 222:A34. See also Lemaire and Durand 1984, 75.

81. Forrer 1920, 59. See also Sader 1987, 148–49; Parpola and Porter 2001, 2, 17.

would have been in Hamath's territory.[82] The proposal of Astour (1977a, 141 with map), of Tall Taim, about 25 km east of al-Safira, is disputed by Lemaire and Durand (1984, 75), since only a Hellenistic settlement is attested there. They suggest another location: Tall Ṭa'am, about 15 km northeast of Tall Taim. According to Na'aman (1998a, 16), Tu'immu should be sought on the northern border of Arpad/Bīt-Agūsi near Til-Karme. On account of the wording in Tiglath-pileser III's Annals 13 text: *i-na* NAM(*pīḫat*) URU.*Tu-ʾi-im-me*,[83] Tu'immu was either a district within the newly established province of Arpadda by Tiglath-pileser III,[84] or one of (at least) two provinces (the other would be Arpadda), in which the territory of Bēt-Gūš/Bīt-Agūsi was divided.[85]

In Tiglath-pileser III's list an URU.*kap*-[x-x] occurs, which has been restored as URU.*kap*-[*ra-bi*].[86] This restoration goes back to Schiffer (1911, 71) and Luckenbill (1926–27, 1.820), and has been the basis for a historical reconstruction of an eastward expansion of Bēt-Gūš/Bīt-Agūsi (Ikeda 1979, 76). Sader (1987, 120, 148) proposed to restore URU.*kap*-[*pi-nu/a*] and to see this as a reference to Tell Kaffine west of Tell Rifa'at. None of the other cities in this list is located east of the Euphrates, which certainly should cause doubt about the restoration of Kaprabi. Furthermore, to posit such an expansion on a restored text is highly problematic.

Finally, the city *Tlʾym*, mentioned in the Sefire stelae[87] as having belonged to *Br-gʾyh*, then having fallen to Arpad, but reverting by treaty to its previous master "forever," has been identified with Talḫaya/Talḫayum known from the Mari texts, and localized not far from Emar.[88]

## 8.2. History

As discussed above and in §4.1.1.3, the Aramean tribe of Yaḫān moved from the middle Tigris region where it was located at the time of Aššur-dān II[89] to the north Syrian location where it was encountered by Aššurnaṣirpal II during his eleventh campaign (ca. 870 BCE) when he received the tribute of "Gūš the Yaḫānean."

82. See also Kessler 1975–76, 62; Na'aman 1977–78, 233.

83. RINAP 1:46, text 14, line 8; Tadmor 1994, 66, Ann. 13, line 8.

84. Na'aman 1998a, 16; Zadok 1985, 314.

85. Radner 2006–8a, 63; Weippert 1982, 404 n. 11.

86. RINAP 1:109, text 43, ii.6; Tadmor 1994:147, Summary 5, ii.6.

87. Sefire III: *KAI* 224:23b–27.

88. Fales and Mazzoni 2009–11, 343; Lemaire and Durand 1984, 66–67; contra Lipiński 2000a, 223–24.

89. RIMA 2:133, A.0.98.1, line 23.

### 8.2.1. Early Foundations of the Kingdom

In this campaign Aššurnaṣirpal II stated that he bypassed the land of (Y)aḫān (KUR *a-ḫa-a-nu*), which lay to the south of his march to the Patinean city of Ḫazāzu.[90] When he reached the capital city of Patina, Kunulua, he received the tribute of Gūš, the Yaḫānean (^m^*gu-u-si* KUR *ia-ḫa-na-a-a*).[91] Three things can be gleaned from this passage of Aššurnaṣirpal's Annals. First, the Aramean polity of Yaḫān was firmly established in this region by this time. Second, this entity's territory was south of the line of march from Karkamiš to Ḫazāzu. Third, the later name Bēt-Gūš/Bīt-Agūsi was clearly based on this person Gūš who was considered its eponymous founder and who must have begun his reign sometime around 890–880.

In Shalmaneser III's 858 campaign, the last member listed in the coalition that opposed him at the Battle of Alimuš was "Adānu the Yaḫānean" (^m^*a-da-a-nu* KUR *ia-ḫa-na-a-a*).[92] The name has been analyzed as being Aramaic, a *qatal* formation of *ʿdn* "to give abundance" (Frahm and Zadok 1998), in which case it is from the same root as the eponymous ancestor of (Bīt)-Adīni (*ʿdn*). Later in this same campaign (858), Shalmaneser III attacked a city of Patina called Urime.[93] After the conquest of this city, Shalmaneser received the tribute of "Arame, the man of Bīt-Gūsi" (^m^*a-ra-me* DUMU ^m^*gu-ú-si*).[94] While the spelling of the name of the ruler "Arame" is an issue (to be discussed below),[95] the real difficulty seems to be: Were there two rulers in the same territory or had the polity divided? The lack of titles for these rulers makes it difficult to assess the relations between them. There are three possibilities:

(1) One of these rulers might be a subordinate of the other. Thus Yamada (2000a, 98) has attempted to argue this, stating: "The presence of the two rulers might be taken as testimony to the fragmentation of the area of Yaḫan/Bīt-Agūsi into two smaller Aramaean polities. It is, however, more likely that Adānu was a commander or viceroy of king Arame, since the former is mentioned only in this context, in contrast with the latter, who is attested consistently in Years 1, 2, 6, 10, 11 and 26/27 as the leader of Bīt-Agūsi." However, while it is true that Adānu is only mentioned in connection with the battle of

90. RIMA 2:217, A.0.101.1, iii.70–71. See discussion above.
91. RIMA 2:218, A.0.101.1, iii.77–78.
92. RIMA 3:10, A.0.102.1, line 69′; 3:17, A.0.102.2, ii.1. See table 5.1 above (p. 332).
93. See pp. 340–42 above.
94. RIMA 3:25, A.0.102.3, lines 96b–97a; 3:17, A.0.102.2, ii.12b–13a.
95. See in §8.2.3, especially pp. 530–31 below.

Alimuš, he is listed alongside other kings and rulers leading their military contingents in the battle. There is nothing in the context to indicate that he is the only one of the eight listed who is not a king/ruler.

(2) Some scholars have interpreted the two designations "the Yaḫānean" and "man of Bīt-Gūsi" to be an indication that the tribal entity was divided. In other words, the "Yaḫān" group was a separate group with its leader and the Bēt-Gūš entity was another group with its own ruler. Eventually the latter group seized control. "Gūš and his people were probably not yet in possession of all of Yaḫān.... As the Yaḫānean (i.e., Adānu) seems to bear a Semitic name ('Lord'), one could imagine that the legacy of Gūš was divided after his death, but it is simpler to assume that Gūš did not command all of the Yaḫāneans."[96] This is certainly a possibility given the flexibility in the tribal structures (see ch. 2). However, it seems odd that Gūš "the eponymous ancestor" was not, in his day, in control of the entire tribe.

(3) It is also possible that "Adānu the Yaḫānean" was replaced by "Arame, the man of Bīt-Gūsi," either by death due to wounds suffered in the battle of Alimuš, or a natural death, or an usurpation of the leadership of the tribe by Arame; and that the terminology "Yaḫānean" and "man of Bīt Gūsi" is synonymous and interchangeable, i.e. no different than referring to Ḫayānu, the Sam'alian (*ᵐḫa-a-ni* KUR *sa-am-ʾa-la-a-a*) or Ḫayānu, the man of Bīt-Gabbāri (*ᵐḫa-ia-a-nu* DUMU *gab-ba-ri*).[97] This is also a possibility; but without additional data, it is impossible to decide between options 2 and 3.

Clearly the city of Arnê was the capital in 849 when Shalmaneser III attacked it. However, it is not known how long it had been the capital. Moreover, if the Yaḫāneans were not united, we also do not know what may have served as the capital of this other part of the entity.

### 8.2.2. The Reign of Arame

In any case, Arame is the only ruler henceforth mentioned and it can be assumed that the tribe was now fully united under his rule. However, Bēt-Gūš was not in any shape to take on Assyria. Thus, the next year (857), Arame,

96. Dion 1997, 114; Lipiński 2000a, 212; Hawkins 2000, 363 n. 22.
97. See table §2.3.1 and table 2.1.

"the man of Bīt-Agūsi" (ᵐ*a-ra-me* DUMU [m] ⌜*a-gu-si*⌝) paid tribute to Shalmaneser III;[98] and so too in 853, he paid his tribute.[99] This was the year of the battle of Qarqar in which the coalition led by Hadad-ezer of Damascus and Urhilina/Irḫulēni of Hamath halted the Assyrian advance. For the next three years (852–850 inclusive) there were no Assyrian expeditions to the west and the annual tribute from these entities ceased, including states like Bīt-Agūsi. In 849, Shalmaneser III began the process of reasserting Assyrian dominance over the region.[100]

Having attacked some of the cities of Karkamiš, Shalmaneser zeroed in on Bīt-Agūsi. His annals record:

> I approached the cities of Aramu; I captured the city of Arnê, his royal city. I razed, destroyed (and) burned (it) together with one hundred cities in its environs. I slaughtered them (and) I plundered them.[101]

Balawat Bronze Band XII[102] depicts the Assyrian attack and gives two epigraphs. The epigraph on XIIa[103] reads: "I captured the city of Arnê, belonging to Arame" (URU.*ar-né-e šá* ᵐ*a-ra-me* KUR-*ud*), while the epigraph on XIIb[104] reads: "I captured the city of [...]agdâ, belonging to Arame, the man of Gūsi" (URU.[...]-*ag-da-a šá* ᵐ*a-ra-me* DUMU ᵐ*gu-si* KUR-*ud*).

In the upper register (XIIa), the walled city of Arne is depicted being attacked from both sides by Assyrian archers and chariots (figs. 8.2 and 8.3). The lower register is composed of two scenes: On the far left side, the captives and booty from an unidentified conquered city (perhaps Arnê?) are seen being led to an Assyrian camp.[105] On the right side of the lower register (XIIb), the city of [...]agdâ (the epigraph is on the city itself) is portrayed under attack from both directions with the participation of the king himself (fig. 8.3). Unfortunately, the fragmentary name [...]agdâ cannot be identified with certainty.

98. RIMA 3:11, A.0.102.1, lines 93′–95′.

99. RIMA 3:23, A.0.102.2 ii.83: ᵐ*a-ra-me* DUMU *gu-si*.

100. For further discussion of this campaign, see §7.2.2.2.2.

101. RIMA 3:37, A.0.102.6, ii.58–60a.

102. Schachner 2007, 221 and pl. XII.

103. RIMA 3:146, A.0.102.80.

104. RIMA 3:146, A.0.102.81. Yamada (2000a, 169) has suggested that the name might be read: URU [*Pa-á*]*r*!-*ra*!-*za*!, instead of generally accepted URU.[x]-*ag-da-a*. Thus it could be equated with the city of Apparāzu that was conquered in 849.

105. It is possible to consider the captives in the lower register to be associated with the victory shown in the upper register; in which case the city should be identified with Arnê at an advanced stage of the conquest. See Reade 1979b, 65.

Fig. 8.2. Attacks on the city of Arnê belonging to Arame of Bēt-Gūš (Schachner 2007, pl. 12, Band XIIa). The upper and lower registers are continued in fig. 8.3.

Dion (1997, 116) argues that despite the current trend to prefer the large site of Tell ʿAran, about 20 km east-southeast of Aleppo, the identification of Arnê with Tell Erin, 20 km southwest of Arpad is historically plausible. He feels that the western part of Bēt-Gūš had to be the victim of the attacks of Shalmaneser and that it is difficult to assign territories east of Aleppo to Bēt-Gūš during this time period since Aleppo appears still to be independent.

But Schachner (2007, 221) has countered such an argument. He asserts that the Assyrian army's attack was on the southern side of Bēt-Gūš because this offered the most direct route for engaging the coalition forces. The Assyrian army wanted to take the direct line from the Euphrates to Aleppo and this gave it a line of march through the plain of Jabbūl. Therefore the city of Arnê and the city of [...]agdâ should probably be sought between the Euphrates and the region of Aleppo in the catchment area of the River Quweiq. He argues that the Assyrians were not attempting to reduce Bēt-Gūš, but only control the southern routes.

The issue certainly swings largely on the status of Aleppo in 853. Schachner's interpretation is not entirely accurate here. The Kurkh Monolith states in very staccato fashion:

> I approached the city of Aleppo. They were afraid to fight. They seized my feet. I received their tribute of silver (and) gold.[106]

Thus Shalmaneser III's visit to Aleppo during his sixth campaign was peaceful and for the purpose of worshiping the Storm God. There is no mention of plundering. The fact that the people of Aleppo pay tribute seems to imply that they are independent of Arame who paid his tribute in the episode just

106. RIMA 3:23, A.0.102.2, ii.86b–87a.

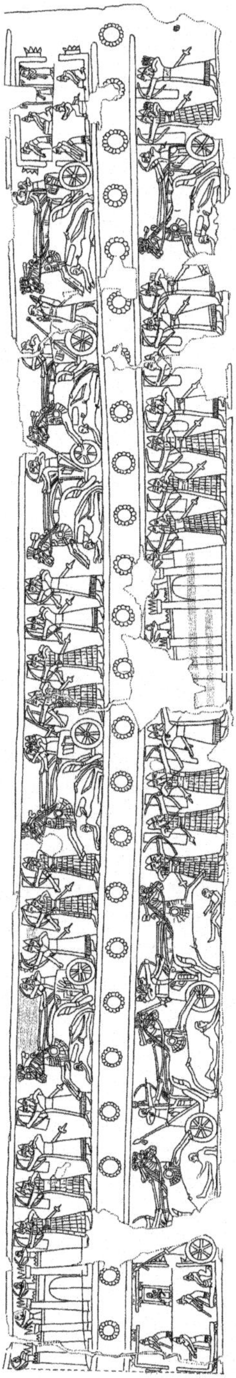

Fig. 8.3. Attack on the city of […]agdâ belonging to Arame of Bēt-Gūš (Schachner 2007, pl. 12, Band XIIb)

before this one in the Monolith's narrative. On the other hand, the other points in Schachner's argument are substantive. A direct line to engage the coalition does make sense, particularly if the intent of the campaign is to secure a route for future campaigns. Since the campaign in 848 will take a route on Bēt-Gūš's northern and western territories in order to outflank the coalition, it seems more likely that this campaign in 849 took the direct line.

Another issue is what was the ancient name of Tell 'Aran, if it was not Arnê. It is a large site and certainly the Assyrians would have had to reduce it at some point, especially if they needed to secure a line of passage into the heart of Hamath and Luǵath. When Arame paid tribute in 853 there was no need to attack it, only in 849 when tribute had been withheld. Aleppo may simply have been a small independent city-state in the midst of Bēt-Gūš with its eventual absorption into Bēt-Gūš taking place in the period of 852–850 BCE.

In his 848 campaign,[107] Shalmaneser III struck Bēt-Gūš/Bīt-Agūsi at the beginning and end of the campaign. As in his 849 campaign, he attacked Karkamiš first, claiming to have captured 97 cities of Sangara. He then struck Bēt-Gūš. The apparent halting of Shalmaneser III's advance by the coalition of Hadad-ezer and Urhilina/Irḫulēni in 849 caused Karkamiš and Bīt-Agūsi to continue in their resistance, clearly in the hope of a successful outcome.

However, Shalmaneser claimed that he captured and destroyed one hundred cities of Arame.[108] In fact, for each year (849 and 848) Shalmaneser III claimed the destruction of "one hundred cities" in Bēt-Gūš/Bīt-Agūsi. While this is at the least a round number and

107. For the narrative of the entire campaign, see RIMA 3:38, A.0.102.6, ii.68–iii.15.

108. RIMA 3:38, A.0.102.6, ii.68–71a.

is probably somewhat inflated, it is evident that Bēt-Gūš, as compared to the other allied anti-Assyrian states, was suffering greater loss.

Furthermore, because the text continues by describing the route of the Assyrian campaign as passing south alongside the slopes of the Amanus,[109] there can be no doubt in this instance that the campaign of Shalmaneser in 848 struck the northern part of Bēt-Gūš. This means, if the understanding of the 849 campaign as striking the southern part of the country is correct, that Bēt-Gūš was being pounded on both its southern and northern flanks. On top of this, after his battle with the coalition, Shalmaneser claims that on his return march he captured the city of Apparāzu,[110] the fortified city of Arame. Since the tribute of Qalparunda of Patina is listed next in his annals, followed by Shalmaneser's going up to Mount Amanus in order to cut cedar, it seems best to see him retracing the route of his campaign so that the location of the city of Apparāzu must in all likelihood be sought in the western part of Bēt-Gūš. It seems evident that Shalmaneser received the tribute of Qalparunda of Patina at Apparāzu.[111]

What is known about the events of the next few years testifies to the results of the 849 and 848 campaigns on the kingdom of Bēt-Gūš/Bīt-Agūsi. In 847, the kingdom was not directly attacked. However, Shalmaneser III's campaign targeted the land of Paqarḫubuni.[112]

In 858, Shalmaneser had destroyed this city with other towns in its environs, which were under the control of Bīt-Adīni.[113] In 847 the campaign was directed against the land (KUR *pa-qa-ra-ḫu-bu-ni*), which was probably located in the mountainous terrain stretching to the north of Gaziantepe (Yamada 2000a, 179). It seems that, although Bīt-Adīni was eliminated in 855, the area around Paqarḫubuni may have remained under a local Aramean government. Yamada has suggested that it was politically loosely organized and while maintaining some type of independence, was nonallied, making it an easy target for the Assyrians. Shalmaneser ruthlessly slaughtered the land's inhabitants who had sought refuge on a mountain.

The message contained in this act of raw terrorism was not lost on Arame and Bēt-Gūš. When combined with the significant destruction that

---

109. It was from this point that Shalmaneser launched his attack on Hamath, capturing the city of Aštammaku before engaging the coalition. See §7.2.2.2.3.

110. See n. 93 above.

111. Consequently, the location of Apparāzu in the northeastern area of Bīt-Agūsi (Lipiński 2000a, 207 n. 74) would seem the least likely of the options for the city's location (see the discussion in §8.2.2). Del Fabbro (2012, 214) follows Lipiński without considering the alternatives.

112. RIMA 3:38–39, A.0.102.6, iii.16–20. See Yamada 2000a, 178–79.

113. See §5.2.1.

it had suffered, it is entirely understandable why Bēt-Gūš/Bīt-Agūsi chose not to be part of the resistance in 845. There is no statement in Shalmaneser's text that records a tribute payment, but there is no indication that Bēt-Gūš was involved any longer in the northern Syrian resistance during the reign of Shalmaneser III.

A number of years later (recorded in his twenty-fifth *palû* in Shalmaneser's Annals),[114] on his return from a campaign against Katî (Katiya) of Que, Shalmaneser reports that he annexed Mūru, the fortified city of Arame, the man of Bīt-Agūsi (URU *mu-ú-ru* URU *dan-nu-ti-šú šá* ᵐ*a-ra-me* A ᵐ*a-gu-si*), rebuilding its gates and constructing for himself a palace in it.[115] Since no attack on Mūru is mentioned, this may imply that the Assyrians annexed the city with the consent of the ruler of Bēt-Gūš/Bīt-Agūsi, Arame, implying that he was a vassal (Yamada 2000a, 219). The city became an Assyrian outpost in the west[116] and must have had strategic value (Sader 1987, 148). The exact location of Mūru is unknown (see the discussion in §8.1.2, p. 513).

Therefore, Arame was still the leader of Bēt-Gūš/Bīt-Agūsi in the late 830s, having survived numerous Assyrian attacks, the destruction of his capital at Arnê, and the humiliation of the annexation of one of his cities outright. However, it seems that Arame was able to move his capital from Arnê to Arpad. Perhaps, he was even the one responsible for the city's initial strong defense works. Certainly, he put his kingdom in a position to take advantage of the weakness that Assyria suffered from the revolt at the end of Shalmaneser III's reign.

Moreover, there is no indication that Hazael's expansion during the last decades of the 800s was able to bring Arpad under his control.[117] Instead, the picture that emerges is that of a resurgence of Bēt-Gūš that produced a

114. On the date of this campaign, see Yamada (2000a, 64–65, 218). He understands the Annals to register only two successive Que campaigns (the twenty-fifth and twenty-sixth *palûs*) as against the Eponym Chronicle's three (Years 26-28) and thus, in the annals, either one of the campaigns of Years 26 and 27 has been omitted, or these two campaigns have been somehow conflated into the single account of the twenty-fifth *palû*. See the discussion of Lanfranchi 2002.

115. URU.*mu-ú-ru*. RIMA 3:68, A.0.102.14, lines 130–131.

116. Yamada 2000a, 219 and 223 n. 508, not necessarily a provincial center, as Zadok 1989, 169.

117. Lipiński suggests that the Hazael fragmentary ivory plaque discovered from Arslan Taş (*KAI* 232) might possibly speak of the capture of the city of Ḫazāzu of Bēt-Gūš/Bīt-Agūsi by Hazael. However, as Lipiński also rightly notes, only the first letter of the place name is preserved, *ḥ*[...], which could be restored as *ḥ*[*ṣr*] "Ḥ[azor]," *ḥ*[*mt*] "Ḥ[amath]," *ḥ*[*zrk*] "Ḥ[azrak]," or *ḥ*[*zz*] "Ḥ[azazu]." Without the discovery of another fragment the restoration must remain uncertain. Thus, due to its fragmentary nature and highly uncertain readings, this booty inscription of Hazael offers very little for historical reconstruction. On the other hand, perhaps *ḥ*[*zrk*] "Ḥ[azrak]" would be a better choice now

significant challenge to Assyrian power in the region, a power that will be labeled simply "Aram" as an indicator of the kingdom's potency.

### 8.2.3. The Reign of Attār-sumkī I

In 810 BCE, Adad-nērārī III (810–783) ascended the throne in Assyria.[118] The reign of Attār-sumkī I of Arpad/Bēt-Gūš seems to have more or less coincided with that of Adad-nērārī III's.[119] In 805, Adad-nērārī campaigned in the west in an attempt to reinstate Assyrian dominion and was opposed by a coalition led by Attār-sumkī.[120] This was the first in a series of annual campaigns over a three year period (805–803) aimed especially at Arpad.

Unfortunately, there is a major challenge to the historical reconstruction of events in these years because Adad-nērārī III's royal inscriptions do not date any of these events.[121] Hence, one of the main sources for his campaigns is the Eponym Chronicle. Adad-nērārī III campaigned in the west early in his reign, only a handful of times: 805–803, 796 (802 was perhaps not so much a campaign as an expedition). The Eponym Chronicle for his reign yields (Millard 1994, 32–7, 57–58):

Table 8.1. Eponym Chronicle (810–782)

| | YEAR | REGNAL YEAR | EPONYM | OFFICE | TARGET |
|---|---|---|---|---|---|
| | 810 | accession | Bēl-qātē-ṣabat | [*šakin* of M]azāmua | in the land |
| ‡ | 809 | Year 1 | Adad-nērāri (III) | king of Assyria | to Media |

that the Tell Afis Stela fragment has been found, though as Amadasi Guzzo points out the ḥ could be the letter in the name Hazael. See Amadasi Guzzo 2009, 342 n. 14.

118. His rule is somewhat enigmatic. On the one hand, he seemed to have accomplished the military/political restoration of the empire as well as a number of building projects. On the other hand, much of what is accomplished in his reign is through the power and preeminence of others—including his mother Sammu-ramat and many officials who increased their power, composing their own inscriptions. See Oded 1998; Siddall 2013.

119. Siddall 2013, 36. This syncretisim is further evidenced by the treaty that their sons signed (SAA 2:8–13, text 1).

120. The name Attār-sumkī means "(the god) Attār is my support." See Fales and Radner 1998.

121. At present, no annalistic texts of Adad-nērārī III have been discovered. The probability that there were annals devoted to his reign is reasonably high.

| | YEAR | REGNAL YEAR | EPONYM | OFFICE | TARGET |
|---|---|---|---|---|---|
| | 808 | Year 2 | Nergal-ilāya | [*turt*]*ānu* [commander-in]-chief | to the city (URU) of Guzāna |
| * | 807 | Year 3 | Bēl-dān | [*nāgir*] *ekalli* palace [herald] | to the land (KUR) of Mannea |
| * | 806 | Year 4 | Ṣil-bēli | [*rab*] *šāqê* [chief] cupbearer | to the land (KUR) of Mannea |
| ♦ | 805 | Year 5 | Aššur-taklāk | *masennu* treasurer | to the land (KUR) of Arpad |
| ♦ | 804 | Year 6 | Ilu-issīya | *šakin māti* governor of the land | to the city (URU) of Ḫazāzu |
| ♦ | 803 | Year 7 | Pālil-ēreš | [*šakin*] of Raṣappa | to the city (URU) of Ba'alu |
| | 802 | Year 8 | Aššur-balṭi-ekurri | [*šakin*] of Arrapḫa | to the sea (= Arwad); plague |
| | 801 | Year 9 | Ninurta-ilāya | of Aḫi-zuḫina | to the city (URU) of Ḫubuškia |
| * | 800 | Year 10 | Šēp-Ištar | of Naṣībīna | to the land (KUR) of Mannea |
| * | 799 | Year 11 | Marduk-išmānni | of Amedi | to the land (KUR) of Mannea |
| | 798 | Year 12 | Mutakkil-Marduk | *rab ša-rēši* chief eunuch | to the city (URU) of Lušia |
| | 797 | Year 13 | Bēl-tarṣi-ilumma | of Kalḫu | to the land (KUR) of Namri |
| ♦ | 796 | Year 14 | Aššur-bēlu-uṣur | of Ḫabrūri | to Manṣuāte |
| | 795 | Year 15 | Marduk-šadûni | of Raqmat | to the city (URU) of Dēr |
| | 794 | Year 16 | Mukīn-abūa | of Tušḫan | to the city (URU) of Der |
| ✗ | 793 | Year 17 | Mannu-kī-māt-Aššur | of Guzāna | to Media |
| ✗ | 792 | Year 18 | Mušallim-Ninurta | of Tillē | to Media |
| | 791 | Year 19 | Bēl-iqīšanni | of Šibḫiniš | to the land (KUR) of Ḫubuškia |
| ★ | 790 | Year 20 | Šēp-Šamaš | of Isāna | to the land (KUR) of Itū'a |

| | YEAR | REGNAL YEAR | EPONYM | OFFICE | TARGET |
|---|---|---|---|---|---|
| ✗ | 789 | Year 21 | Ninurta-mukīn-aḫi | of Nineveh | to Media |
| ✗ | 788 | Year 22 | Adad-mušammer | of Kilizi | to Media; foundations of Nabu temple in Nine[veh la]id |
| ✗ | 787 | Year 23 | Ṣil-Ištar | of Arbela | to Media; Nabû entered the new temple |
| | 786 | Year 24 | Nabû-šarru-uṣur | of Talmusa | to the land (KUR) of Kiski |
| | 785 | Year 25 | Adad-uballiṭ | of Tamnuna | to the land (KUR) of Ḫubuškia; the Great God went to Dēr |
| | 784 | Year 26 | Marduk-šarru-uṣur | of [Arb]ela | to the land (KUR) of Ḫubuškia |
| ★ | 783 | Year 27 | Ninurta-nāṣir | of [Z]amua | to the land (KUR) of Itū'a |
| ★ | 782 | Year 28 | Iluma-lē'i | of [Naṣ]ībīna | to the land (KUR) of Itū'a |

♦ campaign west of the Euphrates * campaign against Mannea ✗ campaign against Media ★ campaign against Itū'a

Of the royal inscriptions of Adad-nērārī III, there are several that bear on these events.[122]

Pazarcık/Maraş Stela[123]

> (lines 1–7a) Boundary stone of Adad-nērārī, king of Assyria, son of Šamšī-Adad, king of Assyria, (and) Sammuramat (Semiramis),[124] the palace-woman of Šamšī-Adad, king of Assyria, mother of Adad-nērārī, mighty king, king of Assyria, daughter-in-law of Shalmaneser, king of the four quarters.

122. For the Antakya Stela, see §7.2.3.1, p. 484. For a chronology of Adad-nērārī III's inscriptions, see Siddall 2013, 45, table 7, 50–56.

123. RIMA 3:204–5, A.0.104.3; *COS* 2.114B:273; Donbaz 1990; Timm 1993; Hasegawa 2010, 1–5. This must be one of his earliest inscriptions (Fales 2012b, 120).

124. For Semiramis, see most recently Rollinger 2009–11. For a critical evaluation of the shifting interpretations of Sammu-ramat's political role vis-à-vis her son, see Bernbeck 2008, 356–59.

(lines 7b–15a) When Ušpilulume, king of the Kummuḫites, caused Adad-nērārī, king of Assyria, (and) Sammuramat (Semiramis), the palace woman, to cross the Euphrates,[125] I fought a pitched battle with them—with Attār-sumkī, the son of Abi-rāmu, the Arpadite, together with eight kings who were with him at the city of Paqiraḫubuna. I took away from them their camp. In order to save their lives they ran away.

(lines 15b–18) In this year, they erected this boundary stone between Ušpilulume, king of the Kummuḫites, and Qalparuda, son of Palalam, the king of the Gurgumites.

## Orthostat Slab[126]

... [...] They drew the yoke of [my lordship. The kings of the extensive land of Ḫatti] who, in the time of Šamšī-[Adad, my father, had become strong and caused] the lords of the River Or[ontes?][127] to rebel ...] he heard [of my approach] and Attār-š[umkī ...] trusted [in his own strength, attacked to wage war and battle. I decisively defeated him. I took away his camp. [...] the treasure of [his pal]ace [I carried off.] [... Attār-sumkī], the son of Abi-rāmu, [...] I received without number [...]

## Tell Sheikh Hammad Stela[128]

(lines 3–9a) [At the command of Aššur], I mustered my [chariotry, troops] (and) camp. [I ordered (them) to march] to the land of Ḫatti. I crossed the Euphrates in its flood. I descended [to the city of Paqarḫu]buni. Attār-sumkī [son of Abi-rāmu, together with 8 kings] of the land of Ḫatti who had rebelled and [trusted in their own strength,] the fearful splendor of Aššur, my lord, [overwhelmed them]. [In a sin]gle year, [I con]quered the land of Ḫatti [in its entirety].

125. Hasegawa (2010, 3–5) has argued that the verb *ušēbirūni* should be understood as the third-person plural Š-stem of *ebēru* plus the ventive, yielding a translation of "they caused Adad-nērārī (III) king of the land Assyria, (and) Sammuramat (Semiramis), the palace woman, to cross the River Euphrates," and that the anonymous "they" can be identified with Attār-sumkī and the eight kings" depicted in lines 11–13. However, understanding the initial clause as subordinate (as Donbaz 1990, 9 and Grayson RIMA 3:205, A.0.104.3; Younger, *COS* 2.114B:273) is not only still grammatically possible but is more natural and hence preferred.

126. RIMA 3:205–6, A.0.104.4; *COS* 2.114C:273–74; Millard and Tadmor 1973, 60–61; Scheil 1917; Schramm, *EAK* 2:118.

127. See *COS* 2.114C:273 n. 1.

128. RIMA 3:206–7, A.0.104.5; *COS* 2.114D:274; Radner 2012a; Siddall 2013, 193–204.

(lines 9b–13a) [I went] to the s[ea] in the west (lit. the setting of the sun).[129] I erected [an image of my lordship] in the city of Arwad,[130] which is in the midst of the sea. I ascended Mount Lebanon. I cut sturdy strong logs of cedar.

(lines 13b–18) At that time, I brought back those cedars from Mount Lebanon. I placed in the gate of the temple of the god Salmānu, my lord. The old Temple, which Salmānu-ašarēd (Shalmaneser I), my ancestor, had built, had become dilapidated; and I, with intuitive understanding,[131] rebuilt that temple from its foundation to its parapet. I placed the beams of cedar from Mount Lebanon on top *as a roof.*

(lines 19–20) When that temple becomes old and dilapidated, may a future prince renovate its dilapidated parts (and) return the inscription (lit. written name) to its place.

## Saba'a Stela[132]

(lines 11b–20) In the fifth year, <after> I had ascended nobly the royal throne, I mustered the land; (and) I ordered the extensive troops of the land of Assyria to march to the land of Ḫatti. I crossed the Euphrates in its flood. The kings of the extensive [land of Ḫatti] who, in the time of Šamšī-Adad (V), my father, had become strong and had withheld(?)[133] their [tribute], by the command of Aššur, Marduk, Adad, Ištar, the gods who support me, (my) fearful splendor overwhelmed them; and they submitted to me (lit. "they seized my feet"). Tribute (and) tax [...] they brought to Assyria (and) I received.

I ordered [my troops to march to the land of Damascus]. I [confined] Mari' in the city of Damascus. [He brought to me] [x] hundred (100?) talents of gold (and) 1,000 talents of silver, (and) [60?][134] talents of [...] as tribute.

129. New, and specifically relevant for Dūr-Katlimmu, is that a visit to Mount Lebanon at that time resulted in cedar logs being brought back in order to renovate the temple of Salmānu, the god of Dūr-Katlimmu. This shrine is said to be a foundation of "my father Salmānu-ašarēd." It would appear that this is a reference to the first king of that name (ca. 1263–1234 BCE), who indeed has already been suggested as the temple's founder on independent grounds (Radner 1998a: 49–51).

130. Arwad, off the shore of the modern city of Tartus in Syria.

131. *CAD* 6:201–2, s.v. *ḫissatu*, 1, c (*ḫissat libbi*).

132. RIMA 3:207–9, A.0.104.6; *COS* 2.114E:174–75; Tadmor 1973, 144–8; Unger 1916, 8–12; Hasegawa 2008.

133. ⸢*ik*(?)-*lu*(?)⸣-*ú*(?). Reading is uncertain. See *CAD* 8:95–104, s.v. *kalû*.

134. Grayson (RIMA 3:209, A.0.104.6, line 20) does not indicate the presence of a numeral. But a quantity of 60 has been read by scholars (Oppenheim, *ANET*, 282; Page 1968, 144; de Odorico 1995, 51). Tadmor (1973, 145) read [x].

Tell al-Rimah Stela[135]

(lines 4–9a) I mustered (my) chariots, troops and camps; I ordered (them) to march to the land of Ḫatti. In a single year: I subdued the entire lands of Amurru and Ḫatti. I imposed upon them tax and tribute forever.

I (text: "he") received 2,000 talents of silver, 1,000 talents of copper, 2,000 talents of iron, 3,000 linen garments with multi-colored trim—the tribute of Mari' of the land of Damascus. I (text: "he") received the tribute of Joash (*Iu'asu*) the Samarian, of the Tyrian (ruler), and of the Sidonian (ruler).

Calah Orthostat (Nimrud Slab)[136]

(lines 11–14) I subdued from the bank of the Euphrates, the land of Ḫatti, the land of Amurru in its entirety, the land of Tyre, the land of Sidon, the land of Israel (Ḫumrî), the land of Edom, the land of Philistia, as far as the great sea in the west. I imposed tax (and) tribute upon them.

(lines 15–21) I marched to the land of Damascus. I confined Mari', the king of Damascus in the city of Damascus, his royal city. The fearful splendor of Aššur, my ("his") lord, overwhelmed him; and he submitted to me. He became my vassal. 2,300 talents of silver, 20 talents of gold, 3,000 talents of bronze, 5,000 talents of iron, linen garments with multi-colored trim, an ivory bed, a couch with inlaid ivory, his property (and) his possessions without number—I received inside his palace in Damascus, his royal city.

The Orthostat Slab inscription bears witness to the fact that, during the reign of Šamšī-Adad V, the lands west of the Euphrates had grown strong and independent of Assyria, apparently withholding their tribute. This is the *casus belli* and justification for Adad-nērārī III's action (Hasegawa 2008). The Pazarcık Stela, however, presents the reason for the war as Adad-nērārī III and Sammuramat fulfilling a treaty obligation to Ušpilulume, king of Kummuḫ (Siddall 2013, 40).

When Adad-nērārī III began his program of restoration of Assyrian sovereignty in 805, he faced significant opposition, and it was Attār-sumkī I, the son of Abi-rāmu, the Arpadite (m*a-tar-šúm-ki* A mAD-*ra-a-me* URU *ár-pa-da-a-a*) who organized and led a coalition of "eight kings" (in addition to himself) to oppose the Assyrians. This coalition fought Adad-nērārī III at the battle of Paqarḫubuni. This battle is dated on the basis of the Eponym Chronicle's "to Arpad (805)," since all of Adad-nērārī III's inscriptions are nonannalistic texts and hence do not preserve the date. Paqarḫubuni (modern

135. RIMA 3:209–12, A.0.104.7; *COS* 2.114F:175–76.

136. RIMA 3:212–13, A.0.104.8; *COS* 2.114G:276; Tadmor 1973, 148–50.

Gaziantepe), which had been the site of an open-field battle in the days of Aḫuni of Bīt-Adīni and Shalmaneser III (858 BCE; see p. 331) and had been the target area for Shalmaneser III's 847 campaign (see p. 522) became the site of yet another engagement.

Grayson (1982, 400) has suggested that "the composition of this alliance may be surmised from later similar groupings, and probably included (besides Arpad) Que, Unqi, Gurgum, Sam'al, and Melid, and excluded Kummukh and Carchemish." However, there is really no evidence as to who exactly the "allies" of Attār-sumkī were, though these are certainly possibilities. In the case of Kummuḫ, it was an Assyrian client state. Thus, as mentioned above, the Assyrian action was in part a fulfillment of a treaty obligation.[137]

According to the textual evidence, the Assyrians were led by Adad-nērārī III and his mother Sammu-ramat. They defeated the coalition and afterwards reestablished the border between Gurgum and Kummuḫ. Notably, Šamšī-ilu is not mentioned in connection with the 805 campaign; he had not yet become the *turtānu*.[138]

The patronym of Attār-sumkī is written ${}^{m}$AD-*ra-a-me*, which yields the same name as the king in the days of Shalmaneser III: Arame, if one understands *a-ra-me* to be a shortened form of Abi-rāmu or A(b)-rāmu meaning "the father is exalted" (cf. Aramaic *ʾbrm*; Mattila and Radner 1998). In Shalmaneser III's inscriptions, the name is written ${}^{m}$*a-ra-me*,[139] except in one instance where it is written ${}^{m}$*a-ra-mu*.[140] In Shalmaneser's inscriptions the name is never spelled with the sign AD. But in the Pazarcık and Antakya stelae, one encounters the spelling ${}^{m}$AD-*ra-a-me* and ${}^{m}$AD-*ra-a-mu* respectively.[141] Lipiński (2000a, 212) has attempted to understand the AD element as the theophoric element "Hadad." He posits the meaning "Hadad is exalted." But this is unlikely since the name Adda-rāmu in cuneiform is always written with the sign "10" for the theophoric element: ${}^{m}$10–*ra-a-mu*, ${}^{m}$10–*ra-me*, ${}^{m}$10–*ra-mi*.[142] Importantly, there is a stone frag-

137. Pazarcık/Maraş Stela (RIMA 3:204–5, A.0.104.3, lines 7b–18). See §7.2.3.

138. See §5.3.1.

139. RIMA 3:25, A.0.102.3, lines 96b–97a; 3:17, A.0.102.2, ii.12, ii.83; etc.

140. RIMA 3:18, A.0.102.2, ii.27. Kroll et al. (2012a, 10 n. 18) criticize Mattila and Radner (1998) for their analysis of ${}^{m}$*a-ra-me* and ${}^{m}$*a-ra-mu*. However, the later Grand Vizier, who was eponym in 677 (reign of Esarhaddon) demonstrates the interchange of the component *ra-me*/*ra-mu* where his name is spelled AD-*ra-mu* and AD-*ra*-[*m*]*e* (Millard 1994, 52); hence clearly "Abi-rāmu" is intended.

141. RIMA 3:205, A.0.104.3, line 11; 3:203, A.0.104.2, lines 5 and 9.

142. The theophoric for Hadad is never written simply with the sign AD. When written syllabically, it always has more than one syllable (NA: *a-da* or *a-di*). Otherwise, it is written with the signs "10" or IM.

ment[143] that must belong to Adad-nērārī III, which helps, in my opinion, to clarify this issue. In line 9′ it reads: DUMU $^{m}$*a-ra-me* and this is undoubtedly a reference to $^{m}$AD-*ra-a-me* (Pazarcık Stela). Therefore the name $^{m}$AD-*ra-me* can be written $^{m}$*a-ra-me*. There is a slight possibility that this is a different person with the same name.[144] However, as outlined above, Arame was still on the throne as late as around 830–825 BCE, and it seems most likely that Attār-sumkī was the son of this A(bi)-rāmu, king of Bēt-Gūš. Interestingly, Attār-sumkī is called an "Arpadite," which is a testimony to the fact that the city of Arpad was the new capital of the tribal entity and had become significant in its own right.

The Eponym Chronicle's "to Ḫazāzu" for 804 and "to Ba'alu" for 803 indicate that the Assyrians needed to continue their campaigning in north Syria particularly against Bīt-Agūsi/Arpad. Clearly, the open-field battle of Paqarḫubuni was not decisive. The identification of Ḫazāzu with Tall 'Azāz,[145] about 15 km northwest of Tell Rifa'at (Arpad) is taken as clear evidence of this, even though the identification of Ba'alu is not known for certain, but is likely located in northern Syria.[146] Therefore, in the two years following the defeat of the coalition at the battle of Paqarḫubuni in 805, Adad-nērārī III had to fight further battles to bring Bīt-Agūsi/Arpad into submission. Yet, Bīt-Agūsi/Arpad was by no means done as a political and military force any more than Damascus was after Shalmaneser III's numerous attacks in the days of Haza'el.[147]

The Eponym Chronicle's entry for 802 reads: *a-na* UGU *tam-tim mu-ta-nu*, "to the sea; plague."[148] Brinkman, who recognized the uncertainty of the phrase *ana muḫḫi tâmtim*, argued that since the mention of a body of water as the destination of a campaign would be unique in the Eponym Chronicle, it

143. RIMA 3:205–6, A.0.104.4. Grayson argues that "the fragment can with some certainty be ascribed to Adad-nērārī III." The predecessor's name in line 3′ must be Šamšī-Adad V and the same phrase is used in another text of Adad-nērārī III (A.0.104.6, line 14): *šá ina tar-ṣi* $^{m}$*Šam-ši*-10, as in this text (line 3′): *šá ina tar-ṣi* $^{m}$*Šam-ši*-[Adad]. The name Attār-sumkī almost definitely appears in line 5′ who is undoubtedly the same man as mentioned in Adad-nērārī III's texts (A.0.104.2 and A.0.104.5).

144. Mattila and Radner (1998, 13, no. 2) list this father of Attār-sumkī as a separate person from the early ruler of Bēt-Gūš/Bīt-Agūsi, although they note the text RIMA 3:205–6, A.0.104.4 line 9′.

145. Ḫazāzu had been captured by Shalmaneser III in his 858 campaign. See p. 339 above.

146. Some scholars have argued that the Eponym Chronicle's 803 "to Ba'alu or 802 "to the Sea," link to Adad-nērārī's campaign against Damascus. Ba'alu is understood as a reference to Ba'al-re'si. But this seems too far to the south. See Millard and Tadmor 1973, 59–60; Millard 1973, 161–62.

147. See §9.3.5.

148. Millard 1994, 34, 57, B1:16′; Glassner 2004, 168–69.

is more probable that *tâmtu* should be understood as "Sealand."[149] However, the use of UGU (*muḫḫi*) may signal that the reference is to the seacoast, not the Sealand.[150] In light of Adad-nērārī III's expedition to the island of Arwad "in the midst of the sea" (*ša qabal tâmtim*) and Mount Lebanon where he "cut sturdy logs of cedar," it would seem that the Eponym Chronicle's reference is to this campaign. Most of the lumber from this expedition went to Dūr-Katlimmu for the refurbishment of the temple of Salmānu (see n. 129).

There is no direct evidence that Karkamiš was involved in any of these events in northern Syria. However, an interesting inscription from that city may allude to some kind of Assyrian action against it, or at the very least, to a significant tribute extraction. A fragmentary inscription of Yariri[151] that dates to around 800 BCE states:

> [Whe]n(? ) the Assyrian king carried off Halabean Tarḫunza, and he smote Assyria with the firebrand, and it […] […] Kubaba (nom. or acc.? ) brought forth, and Assyr]ia(? ) she (the goddess) ?ed[152] away; and up to Halabean Tarḫunza … […]he/they [. . .]-ed. It/them the Talupatean king … […]

It would appear that this is a reference to the "god-napping" of the image of the Storm God of Aleppo from his temple in Karkamiš to Assyria and that this resulted in the Storm God "smiting" Assyria. According to Hawkins, "The context suggests that the clause describes the Storm-God's punishment of Assyria with *marusana-* (abl.), perhaps some fiery or celestial phenomenon (but not thunder [= TONITRUS] or lightning [= (FLUGUR)*pihas-*]). The Hittite *kalmisana-* 'firebrand,' also a celestial phenomenon wielded by the Storm-God, might be compared."[153]

It is interesting, and perhaps not coincidental, that the Eponym Chronicle for the year 802 BCE reports, in addition to the expedition to the sea, that there was "plague" (*mūtānu*; see above). Could this be the Storm God's "smiting" of Assyria, at least in the eyes of the Karkamišeans? The time frame for this may be around 800 BCE. Whether there is any connection of this inscription to the Eponym Chronicle's entry for 802 or not, the fact that there was a plague in Assyria recorded for that year is not insignificant. This may

149. Brinkman 1964, 12 n. 36; 1968, 217 with n. 1359, 262 n. 1676. He notes that the Sealand can be referred to by *tâmtu* without a preceding determinative KUR, as seen in the title LUGAL *tam-tim* "king of the Sealand" as a designation of Marduk-apla-iddina II. A number of scholars have scholars have followed Brinkman's interpretation (e.g., Lipiński 1971, 393–9; 2000a, 392; Pitard 1987, 163).

150. See now the comments of Siddall 2013, 22, 66.

151. KARKAMIŠ A24a2+3, §6–10. See Hawkins 2000, 133–39 pls. 38–39.

152. The meaning of the verb KARI- is not presently known.

153. Hawkins 2000, 136, §7.

well be part of the reason for the bold move on the part of the western polities in 796 BCE.

In addition, the Eponym Chronicle shows that Adad-nērārī III was occupied north and east from 801 to 797 (see table 8.1). This granted Attār-sumkī and his allies respite to regain their strength after their defeats at Paqarḫubuni, Ḫazāzu, and Ba'alu in order to be ready to oppose Adad-nērārī in 796. While the Zakkur inscription mentions the king of Bēt-Gūš without giving his name, there can be no doubt that this was Attār-sumkī I who joined the grand coalition that Bar-Hadad mounted against Zakkur. Very likely, Attār-sumkī was the one who brought Que, 'Umq (Patina), Gurgum, Sam'al, and Melid into this sixteen kingdom coalition that besieged the city of Ḥaḏrak.[154]

A few years later, in spite of the fact that Zakkur was by all appearances a loyal vassal of the Assyrians, Adad-nērārī III in coordination with Šamšī-ilu, now his *turtānu*, reassigned the border or frontier between Arpad and Hamath at Zakkur's expense.[155] This indicates the importance of Bēt-Gūš/Bīt-Agūsi to Assyrian policy in the region and drove a wedge between potential coalition partners in an attempt to limit Hamath.[156]

### 8.2.4. The Reign of Bar-Hadad

A short Old Aramaic inscription on a stela of around sixteen or so words, commonly known as the Melqart Stela,[157] has been the subject of a huge number of studies. The stela was discovered in 1939 at Brēj, just north of Aleppo, in a Roman period wall,[158] although it may have been brought there from a nearby site, the nearest being 'Ayn at-Tell, 3 km to the south of Brēj.[159]

The dedicatory inscription was incised on the lower part of a basalt stela just over a meter in height, with a relief of the Phoenician god Melqart on the upper part where he is depicted striding to the left carrying a fenestrated axe over one shoulder and an Egyptian *'ankh* in his right hand. The relief is without question stylistically Phoenician (see Cecchini 2013); but the inscription is clearly Aramaic. There is agreement that the inscription dates on the basis of its paleography to last part of the ninth or the beginning of the eighth century BCE.

---

154. See §7.2.3 on Hamath. For the date of the campaign, see §9.3.6.1.
155. The Antakya Stela. RIMA 3:203–4, A.0.104.2, lines 4–11a.
156. See pp. 484–85; and Dion 1997, 154–55.
157. *KAI* 201; *COS* 2.33:152–53.
158. See Matthers et al 1978, 416.
159. Suggested by Warmenbol 1985, 169 n. 19; Lipiński 2000a, 211.

The crux of the text is the identity of the donor, "Bar-Hadad, the king of Aram," which is centered on attempts to read the damaged name of his father in line 2, in addition to anything that might follow in that line (otherwise, all the other words in the inscription are read the same by scholars). As representative of the major readings, the following table is offered:

Table 8.2. Representative Readings of the Melqart Stela[160]

| | |
|---|---|
| Albright 1942 | br . ⌜h⌝(2)dd . br . ṭ⌜br⌝[m]n . [b]⌜r⌝ . ⌜ḥzy⌝[n] |
| *KAI* 201 | br . ⌜h⌝(2)dd . br . ⌜ḥzyn br⌝ . [ ] |
| Cross 1972 and 2003 | br . h(2)dd . br . ʿzr [.] ⌜d⌝mš⌜qyʾ⌝ b[r] |
| Pitard 1988 | br . ⌜h⌝(2)dd . br . ⌜ʿtrhmk⌝ [vacat] |
| Puech 1992 | br . ⌜h⌝(2)dd . br . ⌜ʿtršmk⌝ br . ⌜hdrm⌝[?] |

The first three readings of the damaged name of Bar-Hadad's father in line 2 have led scholars to identify Bar-Hadad with one of the kings of Aram-Damascus who had that name (cf. 1 Kgs 15:18; 2 Kgs 8:7–15; 13:24–25, where Ben-Hadad is the Hebrew rendering of the name). Pitard's and Puech's readings broke this connection to Damascus (leading instead to a possible connection with Arpad). Cross (2003) reiterated his 1972 view that Bar-Hadad's father's name (*ʿzr*) was a hypocoristicon of Hadad-ezer (*hddʿzr*) and had Damascene connections (reading ⌜*d*⌝*mš*⌜*qy(*⌝), a view that has had some recent supporters.[161]

Over the last four decades (since Cross 1972), there has been a consensus that the first letter of the name of Bar-Hadad's father is an *ayin*, that the third letter is a *reš*, and that a fifth letter is a *mem*. The disagreement over the second letter is whether it is a *taw* or a *zayin*. If it is a *taw*, the possibility of a connection with Damascus is very remote because it would require a whole new explanation, which has not, and perhaps cannot be offered. If it is a *zayin*, this does not automatically mean a connection with Damascus, since it is entirely possible that there was a Bar-Hadad, son of *ʿzr*(…), who was not a king of Damascus. The mention of *mlk ʾrm* at the beginning of line 3 means that the monarch in question was either a king of Damascus or Arpad, since these are the only two polities that are designated alone as "Aram" in all known texts. Even if the reading *ʿzr* is taken to be correct, there is no

160. For more complete tables, see Hafþórsson 2006, 39; Ghantous 2013, 77.
161. Reinhold 2003; Mykytiuk 2009, 69–85.

evidence that the king of Damascus known as Hadad-ezer (Adad-idri in Neo-Assyrian) was ever written as simply *ʿzr* in a royal inscription.

In light of the photos available on Inscriptifact,[162] the second letter appears to be a *taw* and the letter following the *mem* appears to be a *kaph*. I am not confident that much else can be read in the rest of the line with any degree of certainty, because what letters were in the remainder of the line have been so worn that they are nondiscernible. Therefore, I am completely doubtful about the reading ⌜*d*⌝*mš*⌜*qy*ʾ⌝; but I am just as doubtful about the reading of Puech: reading ⌜*hdrm* ⌝.[163] My reading of line 2 is: *br* ⌜*h*⌝ ⁽²⁾*dd* . *br* . ⌜*ʿtr*⌝[*š*]⌜*mk*⌝ [uncertain letters] "Bar-Hadad, son of ⌜ʿAttār⌝[šu]⌜mkī⌝ [ ].

There are two items of circumstantial evidence that must be factored into the assessment of this stela. First, while the stela's findspot was secondary, it was not moved a great distance from its original setting. This means that the stela derived from the Aleppo area. This has always posed a significant problem for understanding the stela as having been set up by a king of Damascus. While Hadad-ezer of Damascus might have been in this area briefly in 849–848 (though this is not in any way certain), nothing indicates that his son[164] would have been in the region in order to erect the stela. It makes far better sense to see this stela as having been erected by a king of Arpad.

Second, the dedication to the deity Melqart seems to fit better with the evidence for a king of Arpad than a king of Damascus. In the treaty between Aššur-nērārī V and Mati'-'El of Bīt-Agūsi, Melqart appears to be invoked: $^{d}$*m*[*i-il-qar-tu* $^{d}$*ia-s*]*u*$^{!}$*-mu-na* KI.MIN "M[ilqartu (and) E]šmun, ditto."[165] Lipiński (2000a, 215) notes the Phoenician influence in the region during this period. This would include the presence of the Phoenician scribe 'Abd-'ilīm at Gōzān in Kapara's reign, the use of Phoenician in Kulamuwa's inscription at Zincirli, and the claim of Yariri of Karkamiš that he knows "the Tyrian script" (see Younger 2014a).

In light of this understanding of the stela, it would appear that Bar-Hadad was the son of Attār-sumkī I and was a king of "Aram," in other words, Arpad/Bīt-Agūsi. If the adjustment of the border between Attār-sumkī I and Zakkur occurred some time after 796, then this Bar-Hadad may not have

162. See www.inscriptifact.com.

163. I believe that both readings are influenced by other texts (biblical or Neo-Assyrian). *Hdrm* is clearly based, not on actual readable letters, but on the Assyrian inscriptional evidence, in this case wrongly understood (see the discussion of the name $^{d}$AD-*ra-a-me* on pp. 530–31 above). Moreover, I disagree with Ghantous (2013, 79) who claims that "Puech's identification … is preferable because it does not read the epigraphist's preconceptions into the text (Hafþórsson 2006, 38)."

164. There is no text that actually documents a "son of Hadad-ezer (Adad-idri)" of Damascus.

165. SAA 2:13, 2.vi.22; collations, 2:122.

come to the throne until sometime around 790.[166] His length of reign is unknown, perhaps fifteen years.

8.2.5. The Reign of Attār-sumkī II

Very little is known about this king. Three inscriptions give evidence of his reign, none of them belonging to him. The clearest testimony is found in the Sefire Stelae where he is mentioned as the father of Mati'-'El (*mtʿʾl br ʿtrsmk mlk ʾrpd*).[167] Since Mati'-'El is known from other documents from the mid-eighth century (see below), this Attār-sumkī cannot be identified with Attār-sumkī I, but must be Attār-sumkī II. Because his son Mati'-'El likely ascended the throne around 760, Attār-sumkī probably reigned roughly 775–760. He is also mentioned in the Iran Stela of Tiglath-pileser III: "Mati'-'El, [son of A]ttār-sumkī (ᵐ*ma-ti-ìl* [DUMU ᵐ*a*]-*tar-šúm-qa*).[168] Finally, he is mentioned on a seal inscription of one of his officials *lnšʾ ʿbd ʿtrsmk* "belonging to Nūr-Šiʾ, servant of Attār-sumkī.[169] The seal dates from the first half of the eighth century.

8.2.6. The Reign of Mati'-'El

The last king of Bēt-Gūš/Bīt-Agūsi, Mati'-'El,[170] the son of Attār-sumkī II, seems to have come to the throne around 760 BCE. According to the Eponym Chronicle, there was a campaign to Ḫatarikka in 755 and one to Arpad in 754 (Millard 1994, 42). Such information seems to indicate the possible formation of an anti-Assyrian coalition, although these two campaigns, about which there is no other information, may have countered this to some degree. It would appear that Aššur-dān III led the campaign in 754 against

166. Lipiński (2000a, 215) offers a different understanding. He understands "the border adjustment between Attār-šumkī (Arpad) and Zakkur (Hamath and Luǵath) to have occurred much earlier around 806, since Shamshi-ilu was not appointed *turtānu* before 807/6 B.C., while Attār-sumki I had become a declared foe of Assyria in 805 B.C. Besides, Bar-Hadad, Attār-šumkī I's son reigned already over Upper-Aram around 800 B.C." The last statement is a fact not entered in evidence. Lipiński (2000a, 216) speculates that "Bar-Hadad's vow and Melqart's hearing of his prayers, alludes to a victory won by Bar-Hadad, north of Aleppo, on Zakkur's army and was followed by the siege of Ḫadarik, Zakkur's residence."

167. Sefire I: *KAI* 222:A1, 3.

168. RINAP 1:84, 35, line 21′; Tadmor 1994, 100, line 21′.

169. Bordreuil 1986, no. 86; 1993a, 75 and fig. 2.

170. Mati'-'El "Saved by (the god) El." The Aramaic name is written *mtʿʾl* (see Maraqten 1988, 182–83); and ᵐ*ma-ti-iʾ*-DINGIR, ᵐ*ma-ti*-DINGIR (see Jursa 2001b). See the earlier discussion of the form (*qatīl* of *mtʿ* + *ʾl*) in Donner and Röllig 1962–64, 2:234.

Arpad, which had at this point been an Assyrian vassal for approximately one hundred years.

Probably shortly after this campaign in 754, Aššur-nērārī V, king of Assyria (754–745), concluded a treaty with Mati'-'El, king of Arpad.[171] That Mati'-'El had been beaten militarily is unlikely—later Tiglath-pileser III had to expend three campaigns (742, 741, 740) to conquer Arpad (Bagg 2011, 212). Mati'-'El may have entered into the treaty out of expediency in order to avoid conflict for the time being. Matters seem to have been quelled in north Syria for the remainder of Aššur-nērārī V's reign since no other campaigns are known to the region.[172] However in the end, it simply meant that the Assyrian actions of 755–754 had temporarily delayed the inevitable. They certainly had not crushed Arpadite independence. Mati'-'El took advantage of the time to formulate a powerful alliance.

Unfortunately, since the treaty is poorly preserved, only the curses for Mati'-'El's breach of the treaty are known. There is no mention of the obligation of paying tribute, though Mati'-'El's obligations to not harbor enemies of Assyria and his duties for providing armed forces to the Assyrians on campaign are preserved.[173] The deities invoked are first and foremost Assyrian, but a handful of deities that can be attributed to Arpad are listed at the end.[174] Obviously, the curse formulas had little impact on Mati'-'El's plans, since he revolted against Assyria a little over a decade later.

However, the great conundrum of Mati'-'El's reign is contained in the Sefire inscriptions.[175] According to these texts,[176] at some point in his reign, Mati'-'El, king of Arpad, entered into a treaty with a certain BR-G'YH of KTK. If the border description in I B 9–10 is outlining the borders of the polity (see pp. 505–8), Arpad was certainly a significant polity in the region.

---

171. SAA 2:13, text 2.

172. This is based on the Eponym Chronicle entries.

173. SAA 2:11, 2.iii.19′–28′ and iv.1–3.

174. SAA 2:13, 2.vi.6–26 (esp. lines 18ff.).

175. Editions: Dupont-Sommer and Starcky 1958; *KAI* 222–244; Fitzmyer 1967; 1995; Lemaire and Durand 1984.

176. On account of their design and lapidary style these were intended for display in a local temple. The emphasis on the role of the gods in all three in conjunction with the warning against removing them from "the dwellings of the gods" (Sefire II C 2–3, 9–10) proves this. Moreover, the first two stelae were probably inscribed on all four sides, suggesting that they were originally intended to be displayed in an open area, providing access to all the inscribed faces. Finally, the addition of Mati'-'El explicitly marks the first stela as a "memorial" (*zkrn*) specifically aimed at his progeny (Sefire I C 2–8), inscribed for the purpose of maintaining the "good" and avoiding the "evil" in the treaty relationship which is enforced by a series of invocations to the gods (I C 15–25).

It is the name of Bar-Ga'yah[177] and of his polity, who are not otherwise attested in ancient Near Eastern texts, that have made these inscriptions such a source of great debate from the moment of their discovery. The number of proposals and their variants is quite large.[178]

There are some basic limitations. Table 8.3 presents the proposals, noting the nature of each proposal in light of the following. (A) Bar-Ga'yah is the unknown name of a known ruler or (B) an unknown ruler. The toponym KTK could be (a) a well-known toponym; (b) the unknown name of a known toponym; or (c) an unknown toponym. Hawkins notes that each proposed identification must also consider the following factors: (1) KTK has a dominant position in the treaty, so it must be an important state; (2) KTK probably bordered Bīt-Agūsi/Arpad; (3) among the gods of KTK and Arpad, which are called as witnesses (Sefire I A, 7–14), a significant number are from the Assyrian-Babylonian pantheon; (4) a place *tl'ym* (Sefire III, 23–27), whose identification is still unknown, belongs to KTK; and (5) if one assumes the proposal of an unknown name of a known ruler and an unknown name of a known place, the explanation must be truly convincing, including an explication of why other names were used in this treaty in place of the known names.[179] While the identifications of both Bar-Ga'yah and KTK are interdependent, they both unfortunately remain unidentifiable (no explanation as yet has proven truly convincing).[180] Yet, these stelae evince a clear interchange, both on the lexical and motif levels, indicating a confluence of Aramean and Assyrian thought at the political level, what Fales (1990, 150) calls "an ideological hybridization" ("un'ibridazione ideologica") between the two cultures.

The seventeen proposals themselves are as follows:

(1) The earliest real proposal was made by J. Cantineau (1931, 177–78) who suggested that BR-G'YH to be a second name of Aššur-nērārī V and

---

177. The Aramaic name Bar-Ga'yah means "Son of Majesty" (Fitzmyer 1995, 59). Being Aramaic does not necessarily identify nationality or ethnicity, but must be considered a piece of evidence. The name may be symbolic, possibly suggesting a throne name (though there is no genealogical list given), or possibly that Bar-Ga'yah was a usurper (similar to Zakkur of Hamath). However, there is a reference in Sefire III 23–25 to "my father's house" which may rule out usurpation. If Bar-Ga'yah is a throne name, it may parallel another possible throne name Bar-Hadad (see discussion in §9.3.4).

178. For the most recent summary and critical engagement of the seventeen different proposals, see Bagg 2011, 41–52. Earlier summaries included: Hawkins (1981, 255): nine proposals; Fitzmyer (1995, 167–74): eleven proposals; Fales (1990, 151–54; Fales and Mazzoni 2009–11, 343–44): eight proposals. See also Kitchen and Lawrence 2012, 218–20.

179. Following Hawkins 1981, 255 and Bagg 2011, 41.

180. Some of the proposals can be eliminated because of the discovery of new data. These are noted in the presentation.

KTK to be a deliberate misspelling of Kalḫu, the capital of the Assyrian Empire. He understood the Sefire treaty to be the Aramaic version of the Akkadian version of treaty between Mati'-'El and Aššur-nērārī V. Along similar lines, Dossin (1944) proposed that KTK was a cryptogram for KUR. AŠ.KI, equalling *māt Aššur* (see also Contenau 1957). Cantineau's basic proposal has been argued by Parpola (SAA 2:xxvii–xxviii) who sees the Sefire inscriptions as the Aramaic counterpart—though not an exact translation—of the Assyrian treaty between Aššur-nērārī V and Mati'-'El of Arpad. He points out that "all the essential features in these treaties (the treaty gods, the structure and formulation of the texts, and the actual treaty terms) imply that the other contracting party was the king of Assyria." For Parpola all this leads to the inevitable conclusion "that Barga'yah ('son of majesty') is a pseudonym for this king. Liverani (2000) also holds this view, though he understands KTK as an Aramaic cryptogram for *k*(*br*) *t*(*mm*) *k*(*bd*), which is the Aramaic translation of the titles of the Assyrian king: *šarru rabû/šar kiššati/šarru dannu*. Thus Mati'-'El was able to enter into a treaty with Assyria and yet was protected from the anti-Assyrian opposition within Arpad by this cryptogram. However, as Fales and Mazzoni (2009–11, 342) point out "numerous differences make it clear that the Aramaic stelae do not represent in any way a rendering of the Assyrian treaty, nor vice versa." Bagg (2011, 42) rejects this proposal. He believes that the treaty document itself would have to be hidden. Futhermore, since the god Aššur is mentioned in the treaty, there does not seem to be a reason for a cryptogram.

(2) A. Alt vocalized KTK as Katikka and understood it to be the non-Semitic name of a Syrian state, which should be sought in the Lake al-Jabbūl area, allegedly Sūdjīn (1.3 km northeast of Sefire and 25 km east–southeast of Aleppo). BR-G'YH would be the Aramaic name of an unknown ruler of that country. However, the mention of Assyrian-Babylonian gods poses one of many problems for this view (Fitzmyer 1995, 168; Bagg 2011, 42).

(3) Since KTK appears in the treaty as more powerful than Arpad, B. Landsberger (1948, 59 n. 147) proposed that BR-G'YH was an unknown ruler of Hamath/Luḫuti and that KTK was a variant pronunciation of the city of Ḫatarikka, the center of Luḫuti. However, the linguistic connection between KTK and Ḫatarikka is difficult (not to mention the fact that the city appears in the Aramaic inscription of Zakkur as Ḥzrk). The view also does explain adequately the problem of the mention of the Assyrian-Babylonian gods.

(4) A. Dupont-Sommer (1949, 58–60 with n. 24) identified BRG'YH with Dadīlu (or his father) and KTK with Kasku,[181] found in the inscriptions

181. Although a phonetic objection to the equation Kasku = KTK has been raised (Degen 1967–68; Fitzmyer 1995, 170), in light of the Tell Fakhariya Inscription, where /ṯ/

of Tiglath-pileser III ($^{m}$*da-di-i-lu* URU.*kas-ka-a-a*).[182] He was followed in this proposal by von Schuler (1965, 88).[183] However, the toponym Kasku in the Neo-Assyrian sources can be localized in northeast Anatolia, approximately between Urartu and Mušku (Bagg 2011, 43). Thus that country does not directly border Arpad.

(5) A. Dupont-Sommer changed his earlier opinion and proposed to identify BRG'YH of KTK with Sarduri III of Urartu.[184] BRG'YH would be the Aramaic name of Sarduri and KTK could be a new foundation of that king, perhaps even during his regnal period it was the capital of the Urartu. Besides the lack of direct evidence, there are the problems of the mention of the Assyrian-Babylonian deities, and the lack of mention of Urartian deities.

(6) M. Noth (1961b, 165–67) held that BRG'YH was an unknown Aramean ruler and KTK the southern Babylonian city of Kissik. This theory is no longer tenable. Noth's theory was based on an alleged reading Kissik ([*ki*]-*sik*$^{ki}$) in the annals of Tiglath-pileser, but the reading is LÚ.⌜*na*⌝-*sik-ki*, the name of an Aramean tribe.[185]

(7) J. A. Fitzmyer (1967, 132–35) cited a proposal by Y. S. Kassouny that identified KTK as a toponym Katuk (Syriac *gʾdwg*/Gâdûg; via very late Armenian sources) as a Katuk in the Maraş (Gurgum region). Because of the almost two thousand years that separate these sources from the Sefire Inscriptions, this identification was rejected later by Fitzmyer (1995, 172–73).

(8) In 1976, A. Malamat suggested that KTK was a royal city of Bīt-Adīni, based on a reading of URU.*Ki*-[*it*]-*qa*, or URU.*Ki*-[*ta*]-*qa* in Shalmaneser III's Kurkh Monolith (col. i.33). In addition, he identified BR-G'YH with Šamšī-ilu. However, this reading is incorrect; the correct reading is URU.$DU_6$-*bar*-[*si-i*]*p*.[186] Therefore, the alleged presence of KTK is completely eliminated.

(9) N. Na'aman (1978) interpreted *ʾrm klh*, "all Aram" in Sefire I A, 5 as Aram-Damascus and the passage in Sefire I B, 9–10 as a description of the boundaries of this state which would lie south of KTK. Rejecting Landberger's dubious phonetic connection between KTK and Ḫatarikka, Na'aman (1978, 227) nevertheless followed Landsberger (1948, 59 n. 147) sug-

can be represented by /t/ or /s/, this objection cannot be considered decisive (von Soden 1985, 136–37).

182. RINAP 1:48 text 15, line 1; RINAP 1:77, text 32, line 6; RINAP 1:87, text 35 (Iran Stela), iii.15.

183. Albright (1953, 370–71) also adopted this view, locating KTK at Sakçegözü, east of Zincirli.

184. Dupont-Sommer and Starcky 1956, 38–41; 1958, 22.

185. For a discussion, see chapter 10.

186. RIMA 3:15, A.0.102.2, i.33 and the text note there.

gesting "that KTK was the name of the united state of Hamath + Hadrach (distinguishing it from the two component states),[187] or that KTK was the local name for the kingdom of Hadrach." BRG'YH would be the successor of Zakkur to the throne of this state in the second half of the eighth century BCE. *Tl'ym* as well as the findspot of the inscriptions were cities in the border between Arpad and Hamath/Ḫatarikka. Hawkins (2000, 390) believes the thesis of Na'aman to be likely. However, Fales and Mazzoni (2009–11, 343) correctly note that "this, historically seductive, theory does not justify the presence of an Assyrian pantheon in the stelae."

(10) In an unpublished doctoral thesis, H. Farzat (1972, 71–94, 101–13) equated BR-G'YH with the Chaldean prince (Nabû)-mukīn-zēri (or his father), who revolted against Tiglath-pileser III and for a short time was the ruler of Babylon at the end of the eighth century BCE. A relationship between this ruler and Arpad is otherwise not attested. Furthermore, because of the distance between Babylon and the place of the display of the Sefire inscriptions, the theory is very unlikely.

(11) J. C. L. Gibson (1975, 21–3) looked at KTK as a vassal state of Urartu. He proposed that BR-G'YH was an Aramean ruler over a population that was Kaškaean in origin. The inhabitants of KTK are descended from the Kaškaeans that Tiglath-pileser I (1114–1076 BCE) defeated and were located in the area of the Ṭūr 'Abdīn. The name KTK would make reference to this origin. Accordingly, Gibson localized KTK in northern Mesopotamia, near the Ṭūr 'Abdīn, on the border between Assyria and Urartu. This proposal is unlikely due to the distance between Arpad and the postulated Urartian vassal state in northern Mesopotamia. It also provides no explanation for the mention of Mesopotamian gods in the treaty.

(12) A. Lemaire and J.-M. Durand adopted the thesis of Malamat (no. 8 above) and tried to back it up with additional arguments. They suggested that the alleged city of Kitqa in the Kurkh Monolith of Shalmaneser III was the Luwian name of Til-Barsib and that BR-G'YH was the *turtānu* Šamšī-ilu.[188] Again, there is no city named "Kitqa." Moreover, it is now known that the Luwian name of Til-Barsib was Masuwari (Hawkins 1983; 2000). Thus this proposal is impossible.

(13) R. Zadok (1984, 534) localized KTK east of the Euphrates and held that BR-G'YH was an Assyrian governor. He based his proposal for this

187. However, if this were the case, then one would have expected the Zakkur inscription (line 2) to read: [']*nh* . *zkr* . *mlk* . *ktk*, "I am Zakkur, king of KTK"; but instead it reads: [']*nh* . *zkr* . *mlk* . *ḥmt* . *wl'š*, "I am Zakkur, king of Hamath and Lu'aš."

188. Recently, Kitchen and Lawrence (2012, 219) have suggested: "The likeliest answer is that this is Bar-Ga'yah's local title and status, while serving also as Governor in some district not too far from North-Syrian Arpad."

location on the assumption that the etymology of KTK was Hurrian. Bagg (2011, 46) rightly notes the improbability that the Aramean ruler of Arpad would have concluded a treaty with an Assyrian governor of a still unattested province in the Jezirah.

(14) W. von Soden (1985) combined KTK with the country of Kiski where Adad-nērārī III had campaigned according to the entry in the Eponym Chronicle for the year 786. Nothing is known about this campaign. He argued that there are no phonetic objections to the equation, since /s/ can be used for etymological /ṯ/ as shown in the Tell Fakhariya Inscription. He located the land Kiski/KTK in northern Syrian territory. But it is not clear whether Kiski is inseparable from Kasku in the inscriptions of Tiglath-pileser III and Sargon II, which would give reason for adopting a more southerly location of Kasku (Bagg 2011, 46). Von Soden, following Lemaire and Durand, identified BR-G'YH with Šamšī-ilu. For him, Šamšī-ilu was a son of Adad-nērārī III, the second oldest, or even a twin brother of Shalmaneser IV, which would explain the title BR-G'YH "son of majesty."

(15) F. M. Fales (1990, 154–57, 172–73) identified BR-G'YH as a hitherto unknown Aramean, pro-Assyrian ruler, of an unknown polity KTK (perhaps located around Maskana/Emar), that is, near the Great Bend of the Euphrates.[189] KTK was able to make a treaty with Arpad because it had the support of Assyria. Thus the mention of the Mesopotamian gods, especially the Assyrian ones, would indicate this support. He equated *tl'ym* with the Old Babylonian toponym *Talḫayum* that appears in the Mari texts. Talḫayum was located in the vicinity of Emar. Sefire could have been its center or a city on the northwestern border with Arpad. Bagg (2011, 47) endorses Fales's study, stating: "Fales Argumentation ist stichhaltig und lässt keinen Aspekt unberücksichtigt."

(16) Y. Ikeda (1993; 1999, 288–89) argues that Šamšī-ilu is the most plausible candidate for the enigmatic BR-G'YH. Since the identification of KTK with Til-Barsib (Lemaire and Durand) or with any other city of Bīt-Adīni (Malamat) have been invalidated, Ikeda thinks that KTK is the abbreviation of a federation consisting also of Kummuḫ, Til-Barsib and Karkamiš, whose initials form the acronym. He dates the treaty to around 754 BCE (i.e., around the same time as the treaty between Aššur-nērārī V and Mati''El of Arpad), or perhaps a little earlier. Due to his age Šamšī-ilu wanted to secure Arpad, preventing an anti-Assyrian move against any member of this federation. Beside the obvious criticism that the concept of an acronym seems anachronistic, the fact that Til-Barsib was conquered in 856 by Shalmaneser III and probably made an Assyrian province (Yamada

189. See also Fales and Mazzoni 2009–11, 344.

2000a, 128) means that it was no longer an independent entity, like Kummuḫ or Karkamiš.[190]

(17) E. Lipiński (2000a, 221–31) identified KTK with an Aramean polity Kasku/Kittik, whose dynastic name was *bt ṣll*. He identified BR-G'YH with the predecessor of Dadīlu. Lipiński (2000a, 222) identifies KTK, the capital of the polity, with a site Tel Baba, 15 km northwest of Tell Rifa'at on the basis of a dubious equation with a late Roman place name Kittika (variant: Kitta), which is mentioned by Theodoret of Cyrus (fifth century CE). He also identified *tl'ym* of the Sefire treaty with a town Tillima mentioned by Theodoret (Lipiński 2000a, 223). However, such a location places KTK north of Arpad and thus fails to explain why the stelae of the treaty would have been erected at Sefire itself (Fales and Mazzoni 2009–11, 344). I agree with Bagg's assessment (2011, 49) that because of the methodological weaknesses of his argument, Lipiński's proposal should be considered as hypothetical. It really cannot be given serious consideration.

Having surveyed these proposals, one can sum up this way. The identity of the mysterious BR-G'YH and the location of his polity KTK must remain open. Most theories do not provide a satisfactory answer to all the questions, and/or are based on phonetic acrobatics, cryptograms, acronyms or aliases. Since both the individual and the entity are unknown, it is methodologically sound to wait for more definitive textual evidence before identifying Bar-Ga'yah with a known ruler or KTK with a known region/city.

Whoever Bar-Ga'yah might have been, and wherever KTK may have been located, both appear to be primarily Aramean while casting an Assyrian shadow. Equating Bar-Ga'yah with an Assyrian ruler, attractive as it might be, does not explain very well the prevailing Aramean flavor of the inscriptions. In a similar vein, the existence of a treaty between Assyria and Mati'-'El, king of Arpad, makes another treaty between them superfluous, especially one using pseudonyms.

At present, it would seem that KTK must be an Aramean entity in northern Syria that bordered Arpad (though its exact location cannot be accurately determined); it was supported and culturally influenced by Assyria;[191] and it was ruled by a yet-unknown "philo-Assyrian" Aramean monarch/governor, who bore the title Bar-ga'yah (Fales and Mazzoni 2009–11, 344; Bagg 2011, 50).

190. For further discussion, see Bagg 2011, 47–48.

191. Regarding the cultural issues, see the discussion of Morrow 2001.

Table 8.3. Proposals for the Identifications of Bar-ga'yah and KTK (proposals numbered in the first column; order follows Bagg 2011, 51–52)

| | BAR-GA'YAH | KTK | NATURE OF PROPOSAL* | PROPONENT(S) |
|---|---|---|---|---|
| 1 | Aššur-nērārī V | Assyria | A + b | Cantineau 1931; Dossin 1944; Contenau 1957; Parpola 1988; Liverani 2000 |
| 2 | Unknown ruler | non-Semitic name of Aramean entity in the area of Sefire | B + c | Alt 1968 |
| 3 | Unknown ruler | Ḫatarikka | B + a | Landsberger 1948 |
| 4 | Dadīlu/unknown ruler | Kasku | A/B + a | Dupont-Sommer 1949; von Schuler 1965 |
| 5 | Sarduri III | Urartu/Kasku | A + a/b | Dupont-Sommer and Starcky 1958b |
| 6 | Unknown ruler | Kissik (in S. Mesopotamia) | B + a | Noth 1961 |
| 7 | Unknown ruler | Katuk/Gâdûk | B + a/b | Fitzmyer 1967 |
| 8 | Šamšī-ilu | Kittiqa, a city of Bīt-Adīni | A + a | Malamat 1976 |
| 9 | Unknown ruler following Zakkur | Hamath/Ḫatarikka | B + b | Na'aman 1978; Hawkins 2000 |
| 10 | (Nabû)-Mukīn-zēri of Bīt-Amukāni or his father | Babylonia | A + b | Farzat 1972 |
| 11 | Unknown Aramean ruler | Vassal state of Urartu in northern Mesopotamia | B + a/c | Gibson 1975 |
| 12 | Šamšī-ilu | Kittika = the Luwian name of Til-Barsib | A + b | Lemaire and Durand 1984 |
| 13 | Assyrian governor | East of the Euphrates KTK < Hurrian? | A/B + c | Zadok 1984 |
| 14 | Šamšī-ilu | Neo-Assyrian: Kiski = Kaška in NE Anatolia | A + a | von Soden 1985 |

| | | | | |
|---|---|---|---|---|
| 15 | Aramean ruler | Polity in northern Syria, perhaps in the area of Maskana | B + c | Fales 1990 |
| 16 | Šamšī-ilu | Federation of Kummuḫ, Til-Barsib and Karkamiš | A + b | Ikeda 1993 |
| 17 | Predecessor of Dadīlu | Polity 15 km NW of Arpad (= Neo-Assyrian: Kasku) | B + a | Lipiński 2000a |
| * For the nature of the proposal, see the representation of the letters on page 538. | | | | |

Although Aššur-nērārī V led an Assyrian campaign against Arpad in 754, which seems to have been the context for the treaty discussed above, recent study has demonstrated that early in the reign of Aššur-nērārī V, there was a battle in which Sarduri II, king of Biainili/Urartu, claims in a royal inscription to have defeated the Assyrian king in battle.[192] Fuchs suggests that this took place early in Sarduri II's reign, as well as early in Aššur-nērārī V's reign (between 755 and 753).[193] A date in 753 seems to make better sense in light of the Assyrian campaigns to the west in 755 and 754 mentioned in the Eponym Chronicle.

In any case, this defeat, coupled with the later revolt in Kalḫu in 746 (according to the Eponym Chronicle) were most certainly catalysts that stimulated Mati'-'El to revolt against Assyrian sovereignty, although it is entirely possible that he revolted more or less immediately after the Assyrian defeat by Urartu and did wait until the revolt in Kalḫu.

Whether the instigator of the broad rebellion that eventually included a number of north Syrian and Anatolian lands was Mati'-'El or Sarduri (II) is unclear.[194] Perhaps they should simply be considered co-conspirators. It is certain that Mati'-'El broke his loyalty oath and sent messengers fomenting rebellion. Fales (2003, 147) has suggested a possible anti-Assyrian coalition between Mati'-'El and an unknown Mannean ruler based on the Bukān Inscription. It is interesting to note that when Tiglath-pileser III ascended the throne in 745 BCE, having seized power in the revolt of 746, he faced signifi-

192. Salvini 2008, A 9-1: right side 8–9. "Aššurnirarini Adadinirariehi" = Aššur-nērārī V, son of Adad-nērārī III.

193. Fuchs 2012, 140, 153–54.

194. Mati'-'El, according to the Iran Stela, Tadmor 1994:100, i B, 21′–22′; RINAP 1:84, no. 35, i.21′–22′. Sarduri, according to Summary Inscription 1 (Tadmor 1994:124–5, lines 20–22); Summary Inscription 3 (Tadmor 1994:132–3, lines 15′b–23′.

cant challenges, and in one of his first campaigns, he forced a submission of an unnamed Mannean ruler (744).[195]

However, it was only in his third regnal year (743) that Tiglath-pileser marched to the Levant to engage the anti-Assyrian coalition.[196] The inclusion in the coalition of the only true rival power to Assyria, namely Urartu, must have stimulated the other polities to participate in the opposition. The coalition included: Sarduri (II) of Urartu, Mati'-'El of Arpad, Sulumal of Melid, Tarḫulara of Gurgum and probably Kuštašpi of Kummuḫ, on whose territory the decisive battle took place ("between the lands of Kištan and Ḫalpi, districts of the land of Kummuḫ").[197]

Tiglath-pileser III used a forced, day and night march to arrive suddenly and surprise the coalition forces. He was able to rout them easily. Sarduri (II) fled on a mare at night in order to escape! According to the Assyrian sources, Tiglath-pileser followed up this victory with further action against Tarḫulara of Gurgum.[198] While the capital of Gurgum apparently was spared and the land was not annexed, "one hundred" cities of Gurgum were overwhelmed.

However, the settling of accounts with Mati'-'El took place over the next three years. Three campaigns against the city of Arpad are attested, the first two (742 and 741) are only mentioned in the Eponym Chronicle. In his third attempt in 740, Tiglath-pileser III succeeded in conquering the city. In the newly captured Arpad, the victorious Tiglath-pileser received the tribute from Raḫi[ā]nu (Rezin) of the land of Damascus, Kuštašpi of Kummuḫ, [...] of the land of Tyre, Uriakki (Urikki) of the land of Que, Pisīri of Karkamiš and Tarḫulara [of the land of Gurgum].[199]

Nothing is known about the fate of Mati'-'El, except that in 2 Kgs 19:13 (|| Isa 37:13) the *rab šaqē* before the wall of Jerusalem rhetorically queries "where is the king of Arpad?" (perhaps implying that it was a fate similar to that of the king of Hamath in 720).[200] After a great deal of booty was taken away to Assyria—including a bronze four-headed lion scepter-head with the inscription *lmtʿʾl* "belonging to Mati'-'El,"[201] Bīt-Agūsi was annexed,

195. RINAP 1:84, (Iran Stela), text 35, i.15′–20′.

196. RINAP 1:34, text 9, lines 2′–16′; RINAP 1:84–85, text 35, i.21′–43′.

197. RINAP 1:84, text 35, i.25′–26′.

198. RINAP 1:85, text 35, i.38′–42′.

199. RINAP 1:38, text 11, lines 1′–10′ and no. 12, lines 1′–2′; Tadmor 1994, 54–56, Annals 21, lines 1′–10 and Annals 25, lines 1′–2′.

200. The rhetorical question in 2 Kgs 18:34 and Isa 36:19 "where are the gods of Arpad?" should also be noted.

201. Barnett 1967, 5*, no. 258 and pl. VIII 2.

becoming an Assyrian province.[202] It was named after its capital, Arpadda, and the polity name Bīt-Agūsi is no longer used in the Assyrian texts.[203]

### 8.2.7. The Assyrian Provinces of Arpadda and Tu'immu

While there was no administrative reorganization of the empire along the lines postulated by Forrer,[204] the policy of Tiglath-pileser III was innovative, not because the king introduced a new administrative system, but because he consistently applied an existing process, namely "annexation" (Bagg 2011, 213). During a twelve-year span of his reign (743–732) in which eight campaigns were undertaken, a significant number of countries lost their independence and were annexed into the Assyrian Empire.

Consequently, whether or not it was because of the rebellion of Mati'-'El and the difficulty incurred in the conquest of Arpad that caused the annexation or whether it had been Tiglath-pileser's plan all along is unknown. What is certain is that Tiglath-pileser decided to initiate the direct control and eliminate the polity of Arpad all together. With such a move, one might think that the other entities in the region would have been intimidated, but, in fact, Hamath, Patina/Unqi, and the states to the south chose a course of opposition and experienced the same fate as Bēt-Gūš/Bīt-Agūsi.

However, when Tiglath-pileser III incorporated Bēt-Gūš/Bīt-Agūsi into the provincial system, he did not keep the former territory intact. Rather, the polity was divided into two provinces with the Quweiq River serving as perhaps a rough demarcation: Arpadda and Tu'immu (Tawwāma).[205] Radner understands the river to be a hard border, but it is possible that there was some variance with perhaps the city of Arpad being the capital of the area east of the river, even though it was located a bit to the west of it. Examples

202. RINAP 1:114, text 46, lines 20–21; RINAP 1:131, text 49, lines 24′–25′; Tadmor 1994, 152, Summary 6, lines 20–21; 1994, 186, Summary 9, lines 24′–25′.

203. Bagg 2011, 214. He observes in n. 120 that the only exception is the Borowski Stela (Rs 18), where Bīt-Agūsi is mentioned together with Unqi (line 19), Ḫatti and Arumu (line 17). Since Unqi was annexed two years after Bīt-Agūsi (738), it is clear in this stela of Sargon II (ca. 708) that the names of states are used that have not existed for thirty years. Unfortunately, the text of line 19 is no longer preserved, so that the context of the reference is not known. Since the stela treats mainly the conquest of the remaining independent part of Hamath, it is possible that the scribe wanted to make a parallelism with the first annexations of Tiglath-pileser III (Hawkins 2004, 162), in the sense that Hamath, like the others, ceased to exist as an independent state.

204. Forrer 1920, 5–6, 49–50. Forrer's theory was definitively refuted by Postgate 1995, 2–5.

205. Radner 2006–8a, nos. 58 (Arpadda) and 63 (Tu'ammu).

of the division of a conquered land into two provinces can be seen in the cases of Katmuḫu (Šaḫuppa and Tillē) and Šubria (Kullimeri and Uppumu).

During the reign of Sargon II, the province of Arpadda is mentioned in a letter[206] and in administrative texts.[207] Under Sennacherib, the governor of Arpadda, a man named Zāzāya, was eponym for the year 692.[208] In addition, the province is mentioned in letters to Esarhaddon[209] and Aššurbanipal,[210] and a charioteer of Aššurbanipal acquired a village in the province of Arpadda.[211]

The province of Tu'immu is first mentioned in the reign of Tiglath-pileser III (Radner 2006–8a 63). Tiglath-pileser created the province of Tu'immu after his campaign of 740.[212] It is likely to be identified with the toponym *tw'm* in the Sefire treaty (Stela I A 34).[213]

Table 8.4. Rulers of Yaḫān/Bēt-Gūš/Arpad

| | |
|---|---|
| Gūš | ca. 890–870/860 |
| Adānu the Yaḫānean | ?–858 |
| Arame (Abi-rāmu)<br>‖<br>Attār-sumkī I<br>‖<br>Bar-Hadad | ca. 860–825<br><br>ca. 825–790<br><br>ca. 790–775 |
| ? | |
| Attār-sumkī II<br>‖<br>Mati'-'El | ca. 775–760<br><br>ca. 760–740 |

206. SAA 1:149, 189.12.

207. SAA 11:16, 15.iii.9; 11:17, 16.r.i.2; and 11:52, 80.6′; Dalley and Postgate 1984, 86:14 (mentioned with the province of Tu'immu).

208. For documentation, see Baker 2011, 1439, no. 3.

209. SAA 13:75, 86.r.13; 13:87, 110.9; 13:90, 116.14.

210. SAA 10:73, 96.16.

211. SAA 6:264, 326.13′–14′.

212. Tadmor 1994:104, Iran Stela II B 14′–15′.

213. For further discussion on the location of Tu'immu, see §8.1.2.

# 9
# ARAM-DAMASCUS

## 9.1. Introduction

Aram-Damascus is a compound name used only in some biblical texts as a designation for the most important Aramean city-state in southern Syria from roughly 1050 to 732 BCE. In the Hebrew Bible, it can also be referred to as simply Aram or Damascus. This city-state flourished especially in the ninth to eighth centuries and was a major Levantine opponent to the Assyrians during this period.

In the Hebrew Bible, this polity was sometimes known simply by the term "Aram" (*ʾrm*). This is also the case in the Aramaic inscription of Zakkur (line A 4). Thus during the ninth and early eighth centuries the kingdom ruled by Damascus could be simply called "Aram" by the other Levantine states.[1] Both Aram-Ṣobah in the tenth century (before Damascus became a dominant state), and Arpad (Bīt-Agūsi) in the mid-eighth century (after Damascus had declined in power) were referred to during their periods of strength simply as "Aram." This fact suggests that the dominant Aramean power in Syria could be called "Aram" without any qualifying modifiers. This was true only while it was recognized as the strongest of the Aramean kingdoms, and lesser states were referred to with more specific designations (Aram-Bēt-Reḥob, etc.).[2]

In the Assyrian sources, "Aram" is never used to designate Damascus. Instead, the kingdom is designated by two toponyms and a *bītu*-fomulation. First, it is frequently referred to simply as "Damascus" (Bagg 2007, 60–62). Second, it is often called in Assyrian texts from 853–732: *imērīšu*, "his

1. The exception being the Panamuwa Inscription which mentions *dmšq* in connection with Panamuwa's involvement in Tiglath-pileser's campaign against Damascus (734–732 BCE).

2. Pitard 1987, 13. See chapter 2 for the discussion of the biblical usage of the term Aram.

donkey(s)" or *māt Ša-imērīšu,* "land of his donkeys."[3] Both of these toponyms will be discussed below. A third way that the kingdom was designated was the use of a *bītu*-formulation: Bīt-Ḫaza'ili, "the house of Hazael," after that king's important reign (Bagg 2007, 49).

It has been suggested that the Assyrians refused to give the kingdom of Damascus the name "Aram," preferring to stress the city's reputation as the center of caravan traffic utilizing donkeys,[4] and to reserve the term Aram for one of their designations for the kingdom of Arpad. Yet, perhaps the refusal was motived by an ideological reason, namely, to deny Damascus this status. Unfortunately, neither suggestion can presently be verified. What is perhaps important to note is that the name Bīt-Ḫaza'ili, according to Assyrian usage, likely implies that this Aramean entity was a "political and geographical entity founded on a tribal system."[5]

### 9.1.1. Etymology and Use of the Toponym: Damascus

In Egyptian hieroglyphics, Damascus occurs with the spellings *ti-ms-s-ḳ-w* and *ti-ms-ḳ-w*. The first appearance of the city's name is in the geographical list of Thutmose III (1479–1425): *T-m-ś-q* (*ti-ms-ḳ-w*).[6] It also occurs in the List of Amenhotep III ($B_N$3r: *tí-mas-qa*). In cuneiform, it occurs in the Tell el-Amarna texts: URU *di-mas-qa* (EA 197:21); URU *di-ma-às-qì* (EA 197:21; EA 53:63); and URU *di-ma-às-qa* (EA 107:28). It also occurs in a letter discovered at Kāmid el-Lōz (Kl 69: 277, line 1): URU.*dá-ma-àš-qá* (Edzard 1970, 55–56 [= Hachmann 2012, 20–21]; Cochavi-Rainey 2011, 38).

In first-millennium texts, Damascus only occurs once in Old Aramaic in the Panamuwa Inscription from Zincirli: דמשק (*dmšq*).[7] No native Aramaic inscription from the kingdom preserves what it called itself. In the Hebrew Bible it occurs frequently. The forms דַּמֶּשֶׂק and דַּמָּשֶׂק (*Dammeśeq* and *Dammāśeq*) occur forty times (Samuel, Kings, and the Latter Prophets, two times in Gen 14–15 and once in the Song of Songs).[8] Once the form is

3. For the occurrences, see Bagg 2007, 238–39. In a Neo-Assyrian legal text (Donbaz and Parpola 2001, no. 53), the form LU*.*si-me-ri-šu-a-a* might be understood as "a Damascene." However, Ponchia (2003, 275) has argued that this should be read as LU*. *si-me-ri-na*!-*a-a*, "a Samarian," which fits the context of the document better.

4. Sader 1987, 260–65; Dion 1997, 171 n. 3.

5. See chapter 2 for full discussion.

6. See Rainey in Rainey and Notley 2006, 72, no. 13ac; Simons 1937, 111, List I, no. 13a–c; Aḥituv 1984, 87. For a recent discussion, see Elitzur 2004, 193–200.

7. *KAI* 215:18.

8. Gen 14:15; 15:2; 2 Sam 8:5, 6; 1 Kgs 11:24 (2x); 15:18; 19:15; 20:34; 2 Kgs 5:12; 8:7, 9; 14:28; 16:9, 10, 11, 12; Song 7:5; Isa 7:8 (2x); 8:4; 10:9; 17:1(2x), 3; Jer 49:23, 24, 27; Ezek 27:18; 47:16, 17, 18; 48:1; Amos 1:3; 1:5; 5:27; Zech 9:1.

דּוּמֶּשֶׂק (*Dummeśeq*; 2 Kgs 16:10). In the book of Chronicles, a late dissimilated spelling[9] can be seen: דַּרְמֶשֶׂק and דַּרְמָשֶׂק (*Darmeśeq* and *Darmāśeq*) occur six times.[10]

In Neo-Assyrian texts (Bagg 2007, 60–62; Parpola 1970, 103–4), the following forms are found: KUR *di-maš-qa* (twice); URU *di-ma-áš-qi* (twice); URU *di-maš-qa* (twelve times, two are restorations) URU *di-maš-qi* (five times, one restoration); URU *di-maš-qu*; URU *di-maš-qa-a-a-a* (gentilic); URU *dim-maš-qa* (legal text of Sennacherib's reign); and *dim-maš-[qi]* (in eponymous list of Sennacherib's reign).

In Arabic, the city is called *Dimašq al-šām*, although this is often shortened to either *Dimašq* or *al-šām* by the citizens of Damascus, of Syria and other Arab neighbors. Al-Shām is an Arabic term for "north" and for "Syria"; the latter, and particularly historical Greater Syria, is called Bilād al-šām ("land of the north").

Earlier scholarship attempted to posit a Semitic origin for the name, but all of these were plagued with serious unresolved problems (Pitard 1987, 7–10). Consequently, the general consensus today is that the word may have a non-Semitic origin.[11]

### 9.1.2. Meaning and Use of the Toponym: Imērīšu / Ša-imērīšu

Another toponym that occurs only in Assyrian text from the period 853–732 BCE (in fact, only in the royal inscriptions of Shalmaneser III, Adad-nērārī III, and Tiglath-pileser III[12]) is *Imērīšu / Ša-imērīšu*.[13] In cuneiform, the toponym was usually written by a mixture of logographic and syllabic signs in several variant forms. Whether the original basic form, *imērīšu*, should be

---

9. For another example, see Tell Fakhariya line 13: *krs'h* "his throne" = *krs'* + third masculine singular suffix – *rs* dissimilated from *ss* (i.e., *kss* > *krs*). The dissimilation is Akk. *kussiu* (*kussû*). Compare OT: *drmsq* (*Darmeseq*) < *dmsq* (*Dammeseq*). Later Aramaic spellings of the name often include an intrusive *resh*, perhaps influenced by the root *dr*, meaning "dwelling." Thus, the Qumranic Darmeśeq (דרמשק), and *Darmsûq* in Syriac. The English and Latin name of the city is "Damascus," which was imported from Greek Δαμασκος," which originated in Aramaic: דרמשק "a well-watered place."

10. 1 Chr 18:5, 6; 2 Chr 16:2; 24:23; 28:5, 23.

11. Sauvaget 1934, 435; Pitard 1987, 7–10; Lipiński 2000a, 347; Elitzur 2004, 193–200, esp. 195.

12. The only exception is that the toponym is mentioned in the colophon of an astrological text dated to the eleventh regnal year of Sennacherib (694 BCE), which, however, is a learned usage and should not be considered in the discussion. See Lanfranchi 2012, 414 and n. 44.

13. For the occurrences, see Bagg 2007, 238–39. Ponchia (2003, 275–76) points out that KUR.*Ša-imērīšu* is not used in epistolary or legal documents.

understood as the singular or the plural form of the word "donkey" has been debated (see below).

In the past, scholars have suggested various interpretations of the meaning of *Ša-imērīšu*. However, Pitard (1987, 7–10) demonstrated the weaknesses in these. He also argued that since the toponym is mentioned together with the city of Damascus, it must refer to the land/territory not the city itself, and the designation likely refers to the oasis-city's reputation as an important commercial center on the early caravan routes where this animal was particularly utilized in caravans before the domestication of the camel (Pitard 1987, 14–17).

Lipiński (2000a, 347) argues that the pronominal suffix -*šu* is to be understood as an old device expressing determination. It either implies that a particular breed of donkeys is meant (see Lewy 1961, 73–74) or, more likely (in Lipiński's view), it simply marks species determination.

Lanfranchi (2012, 410–29) has provided an important recent study that advances the study of this toponym. Surveying all the uses in the royal inscriptions of Shalmaneser III, Adad-nērārī III, and Tiglath-pileser III,[14] he concludes that the original formulation in Shalmaneser III's texts was KUR. ANŠE-*šu* (= "land *Imērīšu*"); and that *ša* was not part of the toponym; and that this was an innovation introduced during his reign.[15] Thus, in Lanfranchi's opinion, the meaning of this invented toponym in the context of Shalmaneser III's reign is determinative. Rather than the word "donkey" being an accurate rendering of a factual reality, the linkage of this artificial exonym with the name of the king of Damascus should be attributed to "the will of making humour and of producing an ironical laughter in the reader." The Assyrian scribes reserved to Damascus and particularly to its king/kings the unique position of having their names being deformed and associated to an animal like the donkey, so as to solicit laughter. Since at present there is no evidence that this exonym was used by any of the neighboring polities, Lanfranchi concludes, "it can be safely deduced that this was neither the Aramaean, nor the local, Damascene name of Damascus. Thus, the compound toponym cannot have been the Assyrian transcription of a regional or local endonym." Finally, he sees this coined derogatory exonym with humorous connotations that also has links to the notion of the donkey as a sacrificial animal used in a treaty ritual (particularly the treaty alliance [*kitru*] established by Hadad-ezer/Adad-idri in the Levant to confront the Assyrian westward expansion). In the days of Tiglath-pileser III, the scribes attempted

14. See especially his table on pp. 415–16.

15. Lanfranchi 2012, 415–16. It is highly significant that this toponym does not occur before 853 BCE. There is no evidence that it is a late second-millennium toponym that is being preserved.

to clarify the ambiguity of the exonym through the writing of the gentilic form: KUR *šá*-ANŠE.NÍTA.MEŠ-*šú-a-a*, "the man of the land of his donkeys" (p. 418). Their interpretation indicates that the plural form is likely intended.

A few comments are necessary. The Akkadian term *imēru* is cognate with West Semitic *ḥmr* "donkey" (*AHw* 375). This means that ANŠE-*šu* or *imērīšu* could be the Assyrian translation of Aramaic *ḥmrh*. Since there are no native inscriptions found in Damascus, we cannot say with absolute certainty that this was a purely Assyrian exonym. While the probability is high that this is a coined, derogatory toponym (stimulated by ideological concerns), caution is important here. In my opinion, it is easier to see the possible humor connections than to see the treaty-ritual connections, especially since the examples marshaled by Lanfranchi are from the second millennium. Nonetheless, the fact that the use of this toponym is limited in time to only three Assyrian monarchs' royal inscriptions, where it occurs 93 percent of the time immediately after the name of a king of Damascus, seems to point to a wordplay.

### 9.1.3. Archaeology of the City-State of Aram-Damascus

The following brief overview of the archaeology of Aram-Damascus in the period under investigation looks at the city of Damascus and then the region. It will also survey items that come from Damascus, but have been found in secondary contexts.

#### 9.1.3.1. The City of Damascus

Since the city has been continually occupied from antiquity, very little excavation has been possible in Damascus. While there have been a few limited excavations (Will 1994), none have found the Iron Age remains of the city. What has been discovered is mostly from late antiquity (mainly from the Roman period or later).

According to Late Bronze sources, southern Syria was in the Egyptian orbit. This has been corroborated by stelae of Seti I and Ramesses II (1279–1213 BCE) that have been recently discovered at Keswe and the eastern outskirts of the city (Taraqji 1999). Excavations at Tell Sakka have exposed Late Bronze Age pillared houses.

At present, the exact location and extent of the original city are still uncertain. Scholars have proposed that the Grand Umayyad Mosque, located on a plateau in the northwest part of the city, was probably built on the site of the Iron Age temple of Hadad-Rammān, "Hadad-the-Thunderer" (cf. 2 Kgs 5:18; Martinez Borobio 2008, 387–91). Remains of a third-century CE temple of Jupiter are found on the west side and the southern part of the current mosque, and it has been assumed that this temple was located where the Hadad-Rammān temple first stood (Freyberger 1989). A recognized historical phenomenon, according to which sanctuaries of different religions follow one another in the same place, lends support to this assumption.

But as for the rest of the Iron Age city, some scholars suggest a location to the west and south of the temple, while others propose that a group of hills to the east and southeast of the mosque area covers this city's remains. One mound, located some 300 m to the south of the mosque, is generally thought to be the prime candidate for the location of the Iron Age citadel. Only excavation will clarify this problem.

9.1.3.2. The Region

As with Damascus, very little excavation has been carried out in southern Syria. A lion of Neo-Hittite stylistic tradition was discovered at aš-Šēḫ Sa'd (Qarnīnu of the Assyrians, see Sader 1987, 267, 270; and below). An Assyrian inscription also attests to the existence of a temple of the god Śahr, the Aramean moon god in Malaḫa, "the royal city of Hazael"[16] (for the location of Malaḫa see the discussion below). At Tell Aštara in the western Ḥauran (ancient biblical Ashtaroth), a metallurgical workshop was excavated (Abou-Assaf 1968, 1969). Finally, a fortification wall was detected at Salihiyeh near Damascus (von der Osten 1956).

9.1.3.3 Items Found in Secondary Contexts

A few items dating to the Iron Age have been discovered in secondary contexts.

(1) A carved basalt orthostat (80 × 70 cm; fig. 9.1) was found incorporated into the eastern corner of the north side foundation of the Damascene Jupiter temple, which is now part of the outside enclosure wall of the Umayyad mosque. It belonged very likely to the temple of Hadad-Rammān. It has a carved relief of a crowned, winged androsphinx (human head on lion body), which evidences a Phoenician-Egyptianizing style, datable to the ninth century BCE (Trokay 1986; Abd el-Kader 1949). The winged androsphinx is a theme characteristic of a number of carved ivories from the Levant.[17]

16. RIMA 3:151, A.0.102.92; *COS* 2.113H:271.

17. The recently excavated temple of the Storm-God of Aleppo has uncovered an orthostat that is similar to the Damascene orthostat having the same motif (Gonnella, Khayyata, and Kohlmeyer 2005, 96, fig. 133, Orthostat 4). The only difference is that the

Fig. 9.1. Damascus orthostat with sphinx. Copyright © Erich Lessing, Art Resource, New York

(2) Two carved ivories, each containing a short inscription of Hazael, have been found: one in Ḫadattu (modern Arslan Taş) in northern Syria and the other at the Assyrian capital Kalḫu (modern Nimrud). They belonged to the Damascene king of that name and were taken away from Damascus as booty by the Assyrians. These will be discussed below.

(3) Two bronze horse ornaments, each one containing the same inscription of Hazael, have been discovered: a trapezoidal horse frontlet with figures in relief that was excavated in the Hera temple at Samos in 1984 (fig. 9.2; Kyreleis 1988); and a horse blinker with relief that was uncovered in excavations of the temple of Apollo Daphnephoros

Damascene orthostat manifests Egyptian influence, while the Aleppo orthstat shows Anatolian influence.

Fig. 9.2. Bronze horse frontlet with an inscription of Hazael from the Heraion on Samos, Greece, ninth century BCE. Samos Archaeological Museum. Photography: Gösta Hellner, DAI Neg. no. D-DAI-Ath-1984/371. Copyright © Deutsches Archäologisches Institut. All rights reserved.

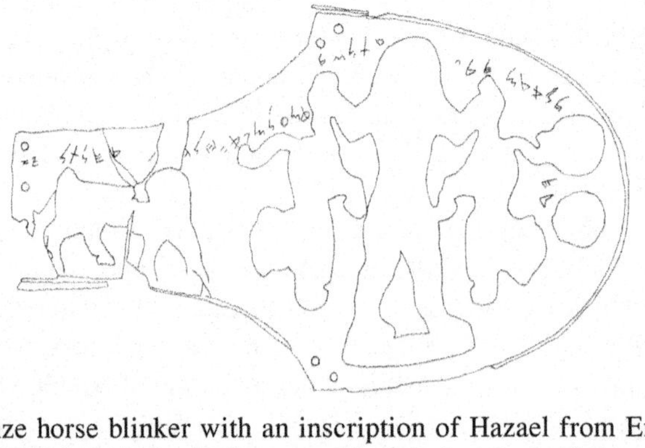

Fig. 9.3. Bronze horse blinker with an inscription of Hazael from Eretria, Greece, ninth century BCE (inscription is shown upside down). Athens, National Museum, inv. no. 15070. After Amadasi Guzzo 1996, fig. 1; courtesy of Dr. Amadasi Guzzo).

in Eretria in Greece (fig. 9.3; Charbonnet 1986). Both are from tertiary contexts. They were probably looted from somewhere in Syria, perhaps the temple of Hadad in Damascus and passed through several hands to Greece (see below). Their placement in the temple of Hadad in Damascus was their secondary context. They originated in a northern Syrian workshop. Since both identify ʻUmq/Unqi/Patina in their inscription, it is not unlikely that they came from a workshop in Kunulua (Tell Taʻyinat).

(4) A fragmentary stela from Tell Dan contains part of an Aramaic inscription that most scholars attribute to Hazael (see below).

## 9.2. Territory

In the earliest periods, the territory of Aram-Damascus was in all probability the area of the al-Ghutah Oasis, simply the city and the towns of its environment with their respective fields and pastures.[18] As the Aramean kingdom of Damascus grew and developed, its initial expansion was northeastward and southward, dictated by the Anti-Lebanon Range (fig. 9.4). Some of the northeastward expansion may have occurred much earlier as a result of the need to secure the important trade routes (both to north Syria and to Tadmor and the Middle Euphrates). The southward expansion brought the kingdom into the regions of the Ḥawran (Ḥauran) Plateau, the Golan and Transjordanian Gilead. Some westward expansion seems eventually to have taken Damascene interest into the Beqaʻ Valley. In the areas to the south and west, Damascus came into contact with some of the smaller Aramean entities of the southern Levant and with the kingdoms of Israel, Judah, and Philistia. In the north, the kingdom of Hamath limited Damascus's expansion until the last third of the ninth century.

The cities of Yabrūdu and Ḫāurīna were important towns in the northern part of the kingdom of Damascus due to their locations on the major trade routes. Yabrūdu can be identified with the modern town of Yabrūd on the eastern slopes of the Anti-Lebanon mountain range, about 42 km east of Baalbek.[19] Ḫāurīna was a town northeast of Yabrūd on the edge of the desert, 110 km west of Tadmor (Palmyra).[20]

---

18. See the geographic discussion in chapter 1.

19. Bagg 2007, 121, s.v. Jabrūdu; Parpola and Porter 2001, 10, map 8; Eph'al 1982, 149 n. 514; Lehmann 2002, 620–21; Weippert 1973–74, 61–62. Ḫāurīna (modern Ḥawārīn) Parpola and Porter 2001, 10, maps 8, 22; Weippert 1976, 62.

20. Bagg 2007, 102, s.v. Ḫāurīna 1. Eph'al 1982, 149–50 n. 514; Schiffer 1911,

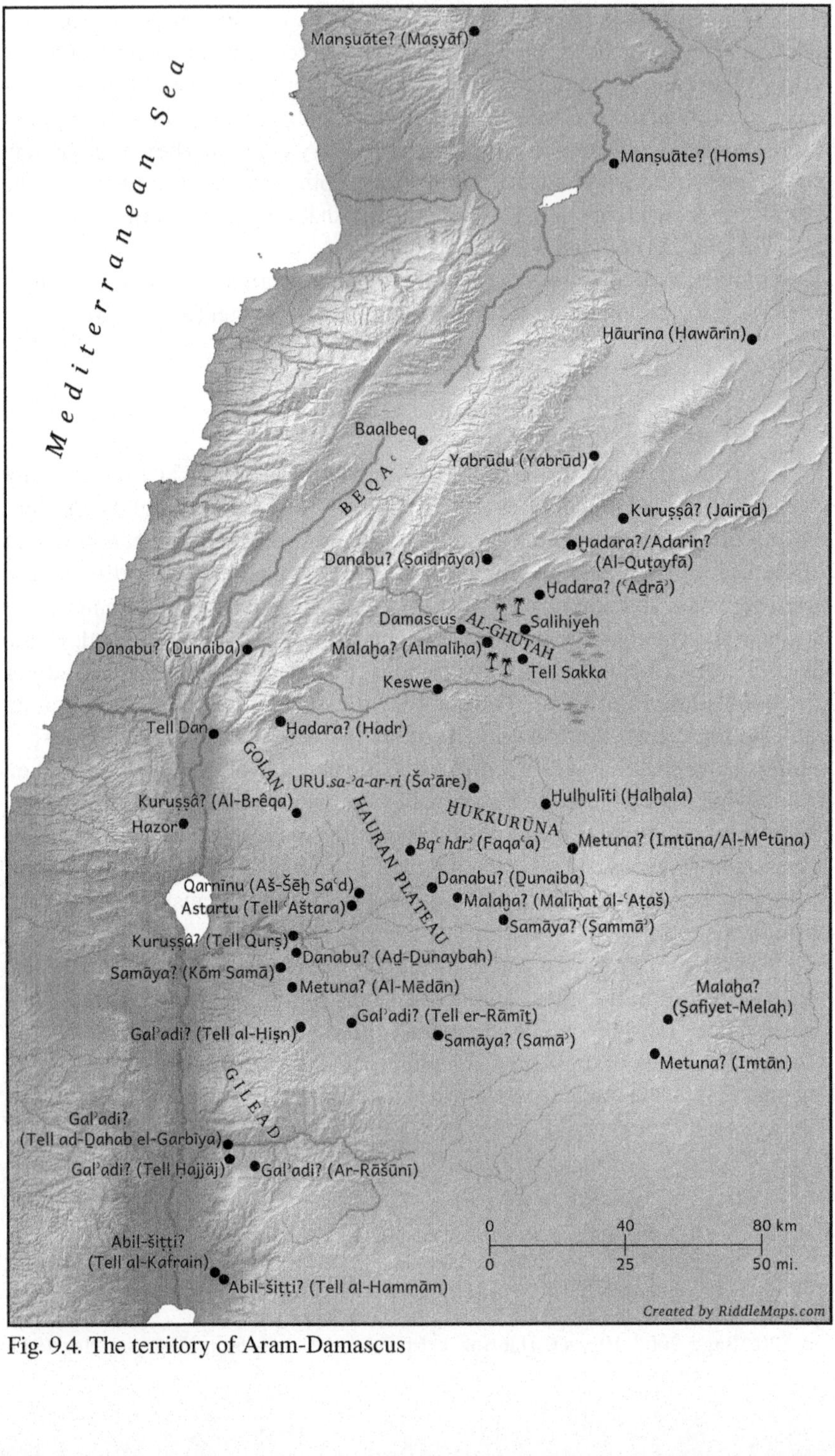
Mediterranean Sea
Manṣuāte? (Maṣyāf)
Manṣuāte? (Homs)
Ḫaurīna (Ḥawārīn)
Baalbeq
Yabrūdu (Yabrūd)
BEQAʿ
Kuruṣṣâ? (Jairūd)
Ḫadara?/Adarin? (Al-Quṭayfā)
Danabu? (Ṣaidnāya)
Ḫadara? (ʿAḏrāʾ)
Damascus
AL-GHUTAH
Salihiyeh
Danabu? (Ḏunaiba)
Malaḫa? (Almalīḥa)
Tell Sakka
Keswe
Tell Dan
Ḫadara? (Ḥadr)
GOLAN
URU.sa-ʾa-ar-ri (Šaʾāre)
Ḫulḫulīti (Ḫalḫala)
Kuruṣṣâ? (Al-Brêqa)
ḪUKKURŪNA
Hazor
HAURAN PLATEAU
Bqʿ hdrʾ (Faqaʿa)
Metuna? (Imtūna/Al-Metūna)
Danabu? (Ḏunaiba)
Qarnīnu (Aš-Šēḫ Saʿd)
Malaḫa? (Malīḥat al-ʿAṭaš)
Astartu (Tell ʿAštara)
Samāya? (Ṣammāʾ)
Kuruṣṣâ? (Tell Qurṣ)
Danabu? (Aḏ-Ḏunaybah)
Samāya? (Kōm Samā)
Metuna? (Al-Mēdān)
Malaḫa? (Ṣafiyet-Melaḥ)
Galʾadi? (Tell er-Rāmīṯ)
Galʾadi? (Tell al-Ḥiṣn)
Samāya? (Samāʾ)
Metuna? (Imtān)
GILEAD
Galʾadi? (Tell ad-Ḏahab el-Garbīya)
Galʾadi? (Tell Ḥajjāj)
Galʾadi? (Ar-Rāšūnī)
0 40 80 km
0 25 50 mi.
Abil-šiṭṭi? (Tell al-Kafrain)
Abil-šiṭṭi? (Tell al-Hammām)
Created by RiddleMaps.com

Fig. 9.4. The territory of Aram-Damascus

About 45 km south of Damascus was the region designated in the Assyrian inscriptions as Ḫukkurūna. This seems to be the mountainous area known today as al-Lajā (classical Trachōnitis).[21] One town located in this region was Ḫulḫulītu, which is likely to be identified with the modern town of Ḫalḫala (Ḥululē), on the eastern edge of the al-Lajā, about 56 km southeast of Damascus.[22] This distance is roughly equivalent with the distance specified in a Neo-Assyrian text, namely 6 *bēru* (ca. 65 km).[23]

A significant fortified city of Damascus in the days of Hazael mentioned in Shalmaneser III's 838 campaign was Danabu (Bagg 2007, 59–60; Hasegawa 2012, 86). Its exact location is unknown. Four different proposals have been made for its identification, either around Damascus or in the Ḥauran (i.e., Jebel Druze area).

First, it has been equated with classical Danaba, which a number of scholars have placed at modern Ṣaidnāya (20 km north of Damascus).[24] However, no Iron Age settlement at this place is so far attested (Lehmann 2002, 515).

Second, Dussaud identified classical Danaba with Ḏunaiba, about 70 km south of Damascus, between aš-Šēḫ Miskīn and Izra', about 18 km east of Nawā (Naveh; Dussaud 1927, 332; Lemaire 1991a, 101). A number of scholars have located the city at this site.[25] Aḥituv identified it with Dunubu of the list of Amenhotep III (Aḥituv 1984, 89). However, this site is yet to be confirmed archaeologically (Lehmann 2002, 177–78).

Third, Lipiński (2000a, 352–53) suggests that Danabu should be identified with Aḏ-Ḏunaybah (Tell Ābil/Quwailibī), about 15 km north of Irbid in Gilead.[26] At this tell, Iron Age remains have been found (Mare 1993, 214; Zwickel 1990, 331–32 and map 6). Lipiński argues that Tell Ābil, classi-

---

139–40 n. 7; Weippert 1973–74, 62–63. Mentioned in Asb A, vii, 111: *ina nagie ša Ḫāurīna*, Assyrian Province? see Radner 2006–8a, 58–61, no. 51.

21. Bagg 2007, 109–10, Ḫukkuruna. Abel 1933–38, 10; Eph'al 1982, 163–64; and Weippert 1973–74, 65–66.

22. Bagg 2007, 110, s.v. Ḫulḫulītu. Eph'al 1982, 163; Weippert 1973–74, 65–66; Parpola and Porter 2001, 10, maps 8, 23.

23. Another possible town might be the URU.*sa-'a-ar-ri* of Aššurbanipal's inscription (Asb A, vii, 112) that could be equated with the modern town of Ša'āre, about 44 km south of Damascus, although it is more likely that this is a reference to Edomite territory. See Bagg 2007, 205, s.v. Sa'arri; and Weippert 1973–74, 62. For identification with the modern town, see Parpola and Porter 2001, 15 and map 8.

24. Kraeling 1918, 80; Honigmann 1938, 116; and Pitard 1987, 150.

25. Dussaud 1927, 332; Dion 1997, 198 n. 120; Sader 1987, 265–66; Lemaire 1991a, 100–101; Röllig 1988, 73; Yamada 2000, 207–8 and n. 446; Na'aman 2002, 205.

26. Bagg erroneously attributes Lipiński's proposal: "Lipiński (2000a) 352f. schlägt vor, Danabu mit dem Tall Ābil/Quwailibī, ca. 15 km nordwestlich von Irbid, zu identifizieren."

cal Abila would be identical with biblical דִּנְהָבָה (Gen 36:32: "Bela son of Beor reigned in Edom, the name of his city being Dinhabah"; cf. 1 Chr 1:43 דִּנְהָבָה). Lipiński must assume a correction from "Edom" to "Aram."[27]

Fourth, Parpola and Porter (2001, 8, map 8) have given a very different location: modern Ḏunaiba, 52 km west of Damascus.

In my opinion, the second option is the most likely, even though it has not yet been confirmed archaeologically.

Another important city of Damascus attributed to Hazael during this campaign of Shalmaneser III was the city of Malaḫa (Bagg 2007, 165–66, s.v. Malaḫu 1). Like Danabu, its precise location remains uncertain,[28] although a number of different proposals have been made. First, Almalīḥa, several kilometers east of Damascus has been suggested (Sader 1987, 266). Second, Lipiński has argued that Malaḫa was "the early Aramaic name of Hazor." Yet this is very doubtful. Lipiński's arguments are less than persuasive.[29] Many scholars have located Malaḫa in the Ḥauran region.[30] Sader (1987, 266) proposed Ṣafiyet-Melaḥ, 17 km east of modern Ṣalḫad. Lemaire (1991a, 100–101) believed that this site is too far to the east, and suggested that Malaḫa should be identified with one of a number of sites south of Buṣr al-Ḥarīr that contain the root *mlḥ* in their names and where the rabbinic site of Malaḥ ez-Ezraʿ was located.[31] Thus, the site of Malīḥat al-ʿAṭaš has been suggested (Mittmann and Schmitt 2001, B IV 14), but other sites such as Malīḥat aš-Šarqīyah, Malīḥat ʿIyun, and Malīḥat al-Garbīya (?) cannot be ruled out.

In his inscriptions, Tiglath-pileser III listed a number of cities that he captured from the Arameans of Damascus. Some of these were located in Gilead, having been captured earlier from Israel (Amos 1:3), although there may have been swings in control over this Transjordanian territory through-

27. See also Lemaire 1990b.

28. Malaḫa is identified as a royal city of Hazael (URU MAN-*ti-šú*) (RIMA 3:151, A.0.102.92, line 3), one of the fortified cities (URU.MEŠ-*ni dan-nu-te*) (3:79, A.0.102.16, line 157′), and one of his important cities (with a cult center) (*ma-ḫa-zi-šú*) (3:67, A.0.102.14, line 103). In the Eponym Chronicle, it is preceded by the determinative KUR.

29. Lipiński 2000a, 350–51. He states: "The identification of Hazor with *Mal(l)aḫa* apparently receives a confirmation from the cult of the Moon-god which is attested for *Mal(l)aḫa* by the inscription found in Ashur and for Hazor by a sanctuary and some artefacts from the 13th and early 9th centuries, discovered at the site" (351). As common as moon-god worship was in the ancient Near East, it is truly astounding that this is put forth as an argument. A change in the name from Hazor (attested in the eighteenth century BCE onwards) to Malaḫa is highly unlikely (Hasegawa 2012, 56 n. 25).

30. Sader 1987, 266; Lemaire 1991a, 100–101; Dion 1997, 198; Yamada 2000a, 207–8; Parpola and Porter 2001, 13, map 8; Na'aman 2002a, 205; Hasegawa 2012, 56.

31. Unfortunately at present, the precise location of this toponym cannot firmly be established.

out the eighth century. One of these is only partially preserved: Abil[...].[32] Tadmor suggests a possible reading for *a-bi-il-⌜šit-ti⌝*, with reference to biblical *Ābēl haššiṭṭîm*.[33] This means that the southern boundary of Bīt-Hazā'ili/Dimašqa ran about 40 km south of the Nahr al-Zarqā'. The place should be sought east of Jericho, with Tell al-Hammām (Neef 1984, 100–101) and Tell al-Kafrain (Parpola and Porter 2001, 7, 23) being possible candidates.

Another city mentioned by Tiglath-pileser III, in this case in an epigraph on a relief, is Astartu (URU.*as-tar(a)-tu*).[34] This is no doubt biblical Aštarot, present day Tell 'Aštara, approximately 40 km east of the Sea of Galilee.[35]

Tiglath-pileser also mentions the city of Gal'adi (URU.*ga-al-ʾa-a-di*).[36] According to 2 Kgs 10:32–33, Hazael of Damascus seized "all the land of Gilead" from Israel. However, it is impossible to give a precise localization of this toponym because it is not clear to which biblical city the Assyrian text's "Gal'adi" refers (i.e., *yābēš gilʿād, miṣpeh gilʿād, rāmôt gilʿād*). Furthermore, there is some disagreement about the locations of these biblical place names that contain the term *gilʿād*. For example, Gal'adi could be equated with biblical Rāmôt Gil'ad, but there is no consensus on that site's modern identity. Some scholars have identified Rāmôt Gil'ād with Tell ar-Rāmīṯ (7 km south of Ramtha, near the modern border of Jordan and Syria),[37] but others have identified it with Tell al-Ḥiṣn (16 km southwest of Ramtha).[38] But Lipiński (2000a, 354–55 with map on page 357) sees in Tell al-Ḥiṣn a plausible candidate for Gal'adi; however, he identifies the place not with Rāmôt Gil'ad (which for him should be equated with Tell ar-Rāmīṯ), but with Gil'ad. In contrast, Na'aman equates Gal'adi with biblical Miṣpeh Gil'ad,[39] a

32. Bagg 2007, 1, s.v. Abil[...]. Summary Inscription 4, line 6′; Summary Inscription 9, Rs. 3. According to Tadmor (1994, 139) [URU].*a-bi-il-x-x* is clearly read (see also Weippert 1972, 152), so that the old reading URU.*a-bi-il-ak-k*[*a*] (Rost 1893, 78, line 6) and an identification with biblical Abel Beth-Ma'akah (Tell Ābil al-Qamḥ; *HALOT*, 7) appears to be ruled out. It is agreed that only two signs follow after URU.*a-bi-il*. The restoration of Rost URU.*a-bi-il-ak-k*[*a*] and the interpretation of this toponym as Abel Beth Ma'akah requires a corruption of *-maʿakah* > *-akka*, which is highly doubtful in any case.

33. Tadmor 1994, 139; Weippert 1972, 152 and 1997, 31 n. 59; Na'aman 1995c, 105, 110 and map on p. 111.

34. Tadmor 1994, 210, misc. II, 2.

35. Tadmor 1994, 210; Bagg 2007, 32; Lipiński 2000a, 365; Galil 1998; Oded 1970, 179. On the excavations: Lehmann 2002, 52–53. Parpola and Porter 2001, 7, 23.

36. Tadmor 1994, 138, Summary 4, line 6′; Tadmor 1994, 186, Summary 9, line Rs. 3; Tadmor 1994, 192, Summary 10, Rs. 3. Bagg 2007, 68–69, s.v. *Gal'adi/Gal'ad(d)a.

37. Pitard 1987, 188. Galil (2000, 41) states: "Tell Rāmīṯ has the advantage of etymological ties with Rāmôt, a strategic location as a 'height,' and Iron Age pottery that dates from the time of Solomon to that of Tiglath-pileser III." See also Younker 2000.

38. Weippert 1997, 32–33; Zwickel 1990, 313; Ghantous 2013, 21.

39. Na'aman 1995c; 1995a, 104.

city that he locates on the Nahr al-Zarqā' (the biblical Yabbōq) near biblical *maḥᵃnayim* (Tell Ḥajjāj or Tell ad-ḏahab al-Garbīya). However, other localizations for Miṣpeh Gil'ad have been proposed, including a more southerly site at ar-Rāšūnī, about 2.5 km northwest of Khirbet Jal'ad.[40]

Whether Gal'ad was the seat of a governor and a province is not clear. In a list of provinces, recent collation demonstrates that Gal'ad is not attested.[41] Another source, namely, the inscriptions of Tiglath-pileser III, does not clarify the situation.[42]

A fourth city mentioned by Tiglath-pileser is Metuna (URU.*metuna*).[43] Its exact location is unknown. One proposal is to locate it at al-Mēdān, about 5 km north of Irbid where Iron Age pottery is attested (Zwickel 1990, 324). Two other localizations (Lipiński 2000a, 364–65) have been proposed: Imtūna or Al-Mᵉtūna, east of Al Lejā, on the road of the Wadi al-Liwā (Abel, 1933–38, 103); and Imtān, the Roman period site of the town of Mothana, about 15 km southeast of Ṣalḫad (Forrer 1920, 63).

A fifth town is Kuruṣṣâ (URU.*ku-ru-uṣ-ṣa-a*).[44] Again, the exact location is unknown. Kraeling equated Kuruṣṣâ with classical Geroda, modern Jairūd, about 50 km northeast of Damascus.[45] According to Forrer, the old name is preserved in the mountain Ḥāmi-Qurṣu and thus he identifies Kuruṣṣâ with the place at the foot of this mountain located at al-Brêqa (Forrer 1920, 62). Lipiński (2000a, 364), who normalizes the name as Quruṣṣā, sees a possible candidate in Tell Qurṣ (Jordan), about 5 km north of Quwailibī. Iron Age remains are attested there (Zwickel 1990, 332).

A sixth town is Qarnīnu (URU.*qarnina*/*qarnini*).[46] This city became a seat of a governor and the center of a province south of Damascus after Tiglath-pileser III's annexation of the kingdom of Damascus (Radner 2006–8a, 61–62, no. 56). This town in the Assyrian list can be equated with the biblical Qarnaim and classical Carneas (Amos 6:13; also 1 Macc 5:43; 2 Macc 12:21), and identified with aš-Šēḫ Sa'd, about 4 to 5 km northeast of Aštara (Aštartu).[47] Although the site was excavated briefly in 1924 by B. Hrozný, no publication of the findings followed, only short newspaper articles. Apparently, however, Bronze and Iron Age strata were uncov-

40. Na'aman 1995c, 105–6, with n. 5.

41. SAA 11:6, 2.ii.7; contra Forrer 1920, 54.

42. For further discussion, see Bienkowski 2000, 46–47; and Na'aman 1995c, 110 n. 12. For the territory of biblical Gil'ād: MacDonald 2000, 195–208.

43. Tadmor 1994, 80, Ann, 23, line 16′. See Bagg 2007, 175, s.v. Metuna.

44. Tadmor 1994, 80, Ann, 23, line 15. See Bagg 2007, 149, s.v. Kuruṣṣâ.

45. Kraeling 1918; Honigmann 1923, 190, Nr. 194.

46. SAA 7:236, 136.ii.4′; SAA 11:4–6, 1.r.i.7′. See Bagg 2007, 193–94, s.v. *Qarnīnu.

47. Forrer 1920, 62; Lipiński 2000a, 353, 365–66; Sader 1987, 267 and 270; Porter and Parpola 2001, 8, 23.

ered, as well as a portal lion in Neo-Hittite style (now in the Damascus Museum).[48] It has become clear with the recent publication of the Esarhaddon Loyalty Oath tablet from Tell Ta'yinat that the city of Qarnīnu's god "Aramiš" became important in the northern Levant in the Late Neo-Assyrian period being included in one of the curse formulae of the tablet. The curse reads (T vi 44)

> ᵈ*a-ra-miš* EN URU KUR SI EN URU KUR ⸢*az-a-i?*⸣ A.MEŠ SIG$_7$.MEŠ *li-mal-li-*⸢*ku-nu*⸣
>
> "May Aramiš, lord of the city and land of Qarnê (and) lord of the city and land of Aza'i, fill you with yellowish-green water."

Lauinger (2012, 119) notes that the god Aramiš (or Aramis), is known primarily from a few personal names, and that these indicate that Aramiš was probably the head of a local pantheon. The persons bearing these names appear to come from north Syria. The fact that Aramiš is designated as "lord of the city and land of Qarnê (and) lord of the city and land of Aza'i" means that he was especially associated with Qarnê/Qarnīna.

A seventh town mentioned by Tiglath-pileser III is Samāya (Samā) (URU.*sa-ma-a-a*).[49] Its exact location is unknown. Kraeling (1918, 118) located Samāya east of Damascus. Lipiński (2000a, 364) suggests Samā', about 15 km north of al-Mafraq, or Ṣammā', between Izra' and as-Suwēdā' as potential candidates. Bagg observes that if one equates Kuruṣṣâ with Tell Qurṣ, then Kōm Samā, about 6 km south from Quwailibī, might be identified with Samā. At both places Iron Age sherds have been found (Bagg 2007, 206; see also Zwickel 1990, 323).

The hometown of Rezin (Raḍyān; רְצִין), the last king of Aram-Damascus, is mentioned in Tiglath-pileser III's inscriptions. Unfortunately, it is a fragmentary reading: [URU x-(x)-]-*ḫa-a-da-ra*.[50] Some scholars have understood the name to be Ḫadara and have identified it with modern 'Aḏrā', 22 km northeast of Damascus (Dupont-Sommer 1949, 72 n. 34; Dussaud 1927, 264; Sader 1987, 267), or with Adarin (Kraeling 1918, 118), perhaps modern Al-Quṭayfā, 18 km further to the northeast (south of Yabrūd), or even with Ḥadr, 53 km southwest of Damascus (Forrer 1920, 62).

However, Tadmor (1994, 80, note to line 13′) notes that from Layard's copy it is clear that at least two signs are missing before *ḫa*, and he conjec-

---

48. Zwickel 1990, 335; Lehmann 2002, 519–20.

49. Tadmor 1994, 80, Ann, 23, line 16′. See Bagg 2007, 206, s.v. Samāja.

50. Tadmor 1994, 80, Ann. 23, line 13′. See Bagg 2007, 280–81, s.v. [...]ḫādara.

tures a restoration of [URU *Bīt*]-*ḫa-da-a-ra*. Lipiński takes this a step further and offers a suggestion based on Amos 1:3–5:

> where "the ruler from the Valley of Wickedness" (*yōšēb mib-Biqʿat-ʾĀwen*), mentioned after Hazael and Bar-Hadad II, must be Raṣyān. This is an obvious cacophemy which indicates that the original place name meant something like "Beautiful Valley." We may therefore restore the name of Raṣyān's home town as [uru*Bi-qa*]-*ḫa-da-a-ra*, reproducing Aramaic **Bqʿ hdr*(ʾ), "Valley of Beauty."[51]

Although one may agree with certain aspects[52] of the interpretation of Amos 1:3–5, a restoration based on numerous interpretive assumptions cannot be uncritically accepted.

Mention should be made of the city of Manṣuāte, since this city was certainly for some period under the authority of Aram-Damascus (at the very least during the time of Hazael, Mariʾ/Bar-Hadad). This is dependent on the location of the city.[53]

## 9.3. History

### 9.3.1. Early History

The earliest mention of the city of Damascus occurs in the Toponym List of Thutmose III and in the Amarna letters[54] (where it is one of the cities and kingdoms that fought against Thutmose III at the battle of Megiddo in 1479 BCE, see *COS* 2.2A:7–13). In the Late Bronze Age texts, the region around Damascus was known as Āpum/Upi.[55]

From the time of Thutmose III's conquest until shortly after the battle of Qadesh, the region remained under Egyptian sovereignty. During the Egyptian domination of the region, very little is known about the local population. Damascus is mentioned in three Amarna letters. One ruler of Damascus

---

51. Lipiński 2000a, 363. Furthermore, he suggests "Since the other cities mentioned in this passage seem to belong rather to the area south of Damascus, we might suggest tentatively that the village of Faqaʿa, situated on the Wādī al-Ḥarīr, south of Aṣ-Ṣanamayn, preserves the first element of the ancient toponym."

52. See §5.3.3.

53. See §7.2.

54. For details, see above §9.1.1.

55. KUR *a-pí* (EA 197:34, 42) and KUR *ú-pí*/*ú-pí* (EA 53:57, 59, 62, 63; 189:rev. 12). Egyptian texts refer to *ʾiwpʾ* (Gardiner 1947, 152). Hittite texts have: *a-pí-na* or *a-pa* (KUB XXI 17 I 18–20). Other variant spellings include: Aba/Apa/Apina/Apum/Upi/Upu. For the history of Āpum/Upi, see Pitard 1987, 27–80.

during this period, known from these letters, was a certain Biryawaza (*Bir*$_5$-*ia-wa-za*) who was the representative of the Egyptian administration in the land of Upi.[56] The name is generally analyzed as Indo-Aryan (Hess 1993, 60–61, no. 54). At this time, Upi was subject to pharaoh Akhenaten. With due caution, Na'aman (1988b, 190) has concluded that Zalaya may be considered as Biryawaza's successor to the throne of Damascus.

Around 1340, Damascus was captured by the Hittites during Suppiluliuma I's one-year Syrian campaign against Mittani and its Syro-Palestinian vassals. However, not long after the campaign, Suppiluliuma relinquished control of the town in an attempt to achieve peace with the pharaoh.

In 1274, following the Egyptian retreat from Qadesh, the Hittite army marched as far as the Damascus area and devastated the land. Thus Ḫattušili III related in his Apology:

> Because my brother Muwatalli campaigned against the king of Egypt and the king of Amurru, when he defeated the kings of Egypt and Amurru, he went back to Aba. When Muwatalli, my brother defeated Aba/Apa, he … went back to Ḫatti, but he left me in Aba/Apa.[57]

Thus, Ḫattušili was in charge of Damascus for a time. However, once again the Hittites did not stay in Apa. After the Hittite withdrawal, Damascus and its surrounding region marked part of Egypt's northern frontier with the Hittites (Bryce 2012, 175). With the collapse of the Egyptian Empire in the Levant, Damascus seems to have been seized by a group of Arameans (Sader 2000, 71).

With the paucity of archaeological evidence (including any inscriptions found in Damascus itself), the main sources for the history of Aram-Damascus are Assyrian and biblical texts.[58] Since these textual

56. Na'aman (1988b, 179–87) investigated the issues surrounding Biryawaza. He concluded: "Biryawaza was a king, who ascended his throne according to dynastic principle and operated in the land of Canaan side by side with the Egyptian authorities. It is also evident that Damascus is the logical candidate for his residency. All the documentary evidence perfectly fits this location whereas no other place in the land of Upi can fill these requirements" (p. 187).

57. KUB XXI 17 (CTH 86) I 14–21, with duplicate KUB XXXI 27:2–7, 51. See Beal 1992, 307. For discussion, see Collins 2007, 55; Bryce 2005, 240. KUB XXI 171:14–21; KUB XXXI, 27:208. At the time that [Muw]atalli took to the field against the king of the land of Egypt and the country of Amurru, and when he then had defeated the king of the land of Egypt and the country of Amurru, he went to the country of Apa. When Muwatalli, my brother, had conquered Apa, he [returned to] the land of Ḫatti, but [left] me in the country of Apa.

58. The exception to this is those texts that are directly attributable to Hazael (Booty Inscriptions) or likely belong to Hazael (Tel Dan) and the Zakkur Inscription.

sources are quite naturally concerned with their own national interests, they provide only a partial record. Furthermore, there is complexity and scholarly debate concerning the historicity of the biblical texts (particularly the narratives about David and Solomon, but not limited to these). Even the types of sources utilized in the composition of the biblical texts pose difficulties. Nonetheless, some of the basic information given about (Aram)-Ṣobah and Hadad-ezer, and Damascus and Rezon is accepted by historians of the Aramean states.

According to the record of 2 Sam 8:3–6 (‖ 1 Chr 18:3–6), in the early tenth century, Aram-Damascus joined with Hadad-ezer (Aramaic: Hadad-ʿid̲r), king of Aram-Ṣobah,[59] in the fight against David, the king of Israel. David won this war and garrisoned troops in Damascus. There is no information on the internal political situation in Damascus before its defeat by David, and it seems likely that for some time previous it was vassal to Hadad-ezer.

### 9.3.2. Rezon

The biblical sources also mention Solomon's control over southern and central Syria with his fortification of Tadmor, a key town on the trade route from southern Syria to Mesopotamia (Pitard 1987, 89), and his building of some store cities in Hamath (2 Chr 8:3–4), and his trade of horses and chariots with the "kings of the Hittites and the kings of Aram."[60]

According to the biblical tradition, the birth of the Aramean kingdom of Damascus (as it comes to be known) began sometime in Solomon's reign. The establishment of this kingdom in Damascus was in opposition to the Israelites. That Arameans were present in Damascus prior to this can be assumed; and that there may have been an earlier dynasty subject to Hadad-ezer of Ṣobah is also possible. The fact that there was kingship in Damascus during the Amarna period means that there had been some tradition of independent governance in the city before this Aramean dynasty was established in the days of Solomon. But the biblical writer was not interested in recording the history of Damascus *per se*, but in emphasizing that this Aramean kingdom was set up in opposition to Israel, having impact on the two Hebrew kingdoms' history, as well as emphasizing that this was due to God's opposition to Solomon (hence the emphasis on שָׂטָן, "adversary" throughout 1 Kgs 11:14–40). Thus 1 Kgs 11:23–25—at least as the MT presents the story—puts it this way:

59. See §3.3.1.1 on Ṣobah.

60. This reference to the Luwian and Aramean "kings" reflects the realities of the political diversity of the Levant during the Iron Age. However, this does not speak to the historical accuracy of Solomon's trade per se.

(23) God raised up (another) adversary (שָׂטָן) against him (Solomon), Rezon (רְזוֹן), the son of 'Elyada (אֶלְיָדָע),[61] who had fled from Hadad-ezer, the king of Ṣobah, his lord. (24) He gathered men to himself, and became leader of a band of raiders,[62] while David was slaughtering them (the Arameans of Ṣobah). They (Rezon and his band) went to Damascus; and they settled in it; and they made (him) king in Damascus. (25) He was an adversary of Israel all the days of Solomon, and he was trouble (הָרָעָה) as Hadad was; and he abhorred Israel; and he reigned over Aram.

The precise date when Rezon seized power in Damascus cannot be determined. A number of scholars believe that it occurred early in Solomon's reign;[63] others think that it occurred well along in Solomon's reign as the empire began to weaken.[64] The statement "They went to Damascus" does not indicate when this occurred, only that it was sometime after David's slaughter. The phrase "all the days of Solomon" is rhetorical. In any case, Rezon must have come to power at some point during the third quarter of the tenth century, and Damascus began its rise to domination as the "Aram" in the region.[65] It would seem that Solomon must have had some kind of control over Damascus at the beginning of this reign. If he did not, then the presence of this statement in 1 Kgs 11:23–25 makes little sense.[66] Of course, controlling Damascus at this point in the late tenth century is not the same as later—this is not yet the Damascus of the ninth and eighth centuries!

There are, however, many problems of textual criticism (the Greek text is quite different from the MT), as well as literary criticism and historical criticism.[67] The MT's text of 11:23–25a appears at a different place in the Old Greek (3 Kgdms 11:14).[68] These difficulties have led some scholars

61. 1 Kgs 11:23 MT reads: רְזוֹן בֶּן־אֶלְיָדָע, "Rezon the son of Eliada"; OG in 3 Kgdms 11:14b reads: Εσρωμ υἱὸν Ελιαδαε (some manuscripts Εσρων): "Esrom/n son of Eliadae." For a discussion of the old theory that Hezion and Rezon were the same person, see Pitard 1987, 101–3; and Lipiński 2000a, 369.

62. Such Aramean bands of raiders are well attested in ancient Near Eastern (Sūḫu Annals) and biblical sources (2 Kgs 5:2; 6:23; 24:2).

63. Noth 1960, 206; Mazar 1962, 104; Unger 1957, 54; Na'aman 1992, 74 ("The revolts of Hadad the Edomite and Rezon the Aramean are dated to Solomon's early years, whereas Jeroboam's revolt took place during the second half of his reign").

64. Pitard 1987, 97; Lemaire 2001, 130.

65. See discussion on "Aram" at the beginning of the chapter.

66. Solomon is presented in a very negative way, hardly the stuff of royal propaganda.

67. Winckler (1892, 1–2; 1900, 269) understood 1 Kgs 11:14–22 to be two accounts interwoven that he can isolate. See also Burney 1903, 157–60.

68. The text reads (translation mine; different font = OG variant): "(14) And the Lord raised up a *satan* against Salomon, (H)ader the Idumean (11:23) and (H)esrom son of Eliadae who was in Raemmath, (H)adrazar, king of Souba, (was) his master, (11:24) and men were

to the proposal to read "Aram" instead of "Edom" in this story, resulting in Hadad being an Aramean rather than an Edomite, a prince from the royal family of Hadad-ezer of Aram-Ṣobah.[69] For Lemaire (2001, 131–33), there is only one main character in the narrative of 1 Kgs 11:14–25, Hadad, who fled from the extermination of the royal family after the defeat of Hadad-ezer to Egypt, and then after living there for some time under the protection and blessing of the Pharaoh, returned to his country where he became the "king of Aram." Lemaire (2001, 134–35) also argues that the words "Rezon (*rzwn*), son of Elyada" should be understood as giving Hadad's title (*rzwn* = "prince") and his patronym, yielding the reading: "Hadad, the Aramean, the prince, son of 'Elyada."[70] This Hadad was the "first" Aramean king of Damascus.

This "Aramean" interpretation is based primarily on three assumptions: (1) that there was a confusion of *d*/*r* in the writing of the names of the polities (*'dm* being confused with an original *'rm*); (2) that Hadad could not have ruled in Edom, since the monarchy was only established there in the second half of the ninth century BCE; and (3) that the name Hadad was typically Aramean and is unknown in the Edomite onomastica.

There is, of course, no problem with a proposal of the confusion of *d* for *r*.[71] However, why was there a change from ארם to אדם? This must have been a systematic, intentional change, not just a one-time confusion of *d* for *r*, because it would have required six changes in the text (toponymic and gentilic forms). Someone would deliberately have had to change the reading to Edom. This seems very doubtful.

In a recent thorough investigation of the Old Greek of 3 Kgdms 11, Turkanik (2008, 32–34) concludes: "a reconstruction of the original text based on G is very difficult. It appears that either the *Vorlage* of G was very corrupted or, and this seems more probable, G tried to conflate two accounts which it considered would be better interwoven. In spite of the difficulties, therefore I take MT's version to be better" (p. 34).[72]

---

gathered around him, and he was leader of a band, {omitted: when David slew them} and he first captured Damasek, (11:25) and they were a *satan* to Israel all the days of Salomon. And (H)ader the Idumean was of the seed of the kingdom of Idumea. [15] And it happened, when Dauid utterly destroyed Edom while Ioab, commander of the army went to bury the casualties, that they cut off every male in Idumea."

69. Lemaire 1988; 1997, 85; 2001, 130–32; Knauf 1988; 1990: col. 469; and Lipiński 2000a, 368–69 (though with a different understanding of "Rezon, the son of Elyada" than Lemaire's).

70. "Dès lors, le v. 23 ne ferait que donner le titre et le patronyme du futur roi de Damas: le 'prince fils d'Elyada' " (Lemaire 2001, 134).

71. For a discussion, see Fernández Marcos 2001.

72. For a different assessment that sees the OG's version as original, see Schenker 2000, 112–14. However, the string of names in verse 14 following one another in the OG

The particular issue of whether monarchy existed in Edom at the time of David has been specifically addressed by Na'aman.[73] He argues that

> all Semitic kingdoms in the ancient Near East were hereditary, the dynastic principle was deeply rooted in the structure of the Semitic patriarchal family. Whatever the sources, date and function of the Edomite king-list in Gen 36:31–39, it certainly cannot support a theory of an early non-hereditary monarchy in Edom.

In addition, he asserts that "Hadad's origin from the royal family of Edom is explicitly mentioned in the story, a fact that explains the readiness of the Pharaoh to give him an Egyptian princess (1 Kgs 11:19–20). Whether his father was actually king of Edom is unknown. It is clear that according to the story of 1 Kgs 11:14–22 there was an hereditary monarchy in Edom in the time of David. How old was this "monarchy" cannot be established, and how long it was to last remains to be seen.

To this can be added the fact that the semantic range of the term *mlk* includes "tribal chiefs."[74] Therefore, the statement in 11:14b is simply saying that Hadad came from the ruling family among the Edomites.

Na'aman (1992, 75) rightly points out that Hadad appears as a theophoric element in the names of rulers situated in the Shephelah of Judah, north of the Negev area, in the Amarna period (EA 288:45; 329; 333:6, 9; 335:10). I would add that this is even the case at an earlier period as seen in the numerous personal names of rulers in the Execration Texts with the Hadad theophoric.[75] Na'aman (1992, 75) asserts that

> Hadad was also the name of two rulers mentioned in the Edomite king-list of Gen 36:31–39 and 1 Chr 1:43–51, who were apparently connected with the area of Moab. The list of "Edomite kings" is a mixed registration of central and south Transjordanian personae and has nothing to do with Aram (*pace* Lemaire 1988, 14–15; 1990). It is therefore clear that we have to follow the text of 1 Kgs 11:14–22 and regard Hadad as an Edomite.

Finally, it should be pointed out that Lemaire's proposal obtains a textual order that is highly unlikely: "Hadad, the Aramean, the prince, son of 'Elyada."

---

version is difficult to figure out. This alone seems to argue for a corrupted state of the OG in comparison with the MT's account.

73. Na'aman 1992, 75–76. While Na'aman's criticism of Lemaire's proposal has many good points, he is mistaken in his criticism of Lemaire arguing that Hadad was "the son of Hadad-ezer of Aram Zobah." Lemaire's argument (2001, 134–35) is that Hadad was from the royal family, his father being 'Elyada.

74. See discussion on tribal structure in chapter 2 above.

75. See Posener 1940, 62–96: E 4, E 6, E 7, E 19, E 46.

Surely the patronymic would have followed immediately after the personal name yielding something like: "Hadad, son of 'Elyada, the Aramean prince."

Hadad and Rezon were each described as an "adversary" to Solomon (vss. 14a, 25a). The use in the narrative of 11:14–25 of the terms "adversary" (שָׂטָן) and "trouble" (רָעָה) is a deliberate contrast to the beginning of Solomon's reign which was characterized by "there was no adversary and no trouble" (אֵין שָׂטָן וְאֵין פֶּגַע רָע; 1 Kgs 5:18). The multiple adversaries is an important narrative structural and thematic strategy.

Intriguingly, in this vignette of 11:23–25, Rezon is portrayed as a leader of a band of raiders whose career is similar to that of David. He had been a commander of Hadad-ezer who rebelled against his lord and fled, then assembled a band (*gdwd*) and after David's death conquered and ruled Damascus (1 Kgs 11:23–25a). In fact, there are certain similarities between the passages describing the nominations of David and Rezon as leaders of bands (1 Sam 22:2; 1 Kgs 11:23–24a). Both passages use the noun *śr*, the verb *qbṣ*, and the concept of "band" (*gdwd*; see Na'aman 1992, 76 n. 2).

Lastly, a few words must be said about the personal name "Rezon" (רְזוֹן).[76] Old Greek has variants galore: LXX$^{A}$ in 11:23 (22): Ραζων; LXX$^{B}$ in 11:14b: Εσρωμ; LXX$^{L}$ in 11:14b: Εσρων; with Αζρων or *ναζρων*.[77] Lipiński (2000a, 368–69) has argued that:

> the name is Ezron, son of Elyada, whose name was changed in the Hebrew Bible into *rᵊzōn*, "prince," apparently by metathesis (1 Kgs 11:23). The Greek transcriptions Εσρωμ/ν and Αζρων in III Kings 11:14 fortunately preserve the original form of the name. It goes back to a well attested Aramaic anthroponym *ʿEḏrān/ʿEḏrōn* or *ʿIḏrān/ʿIḏrōn*, that occurs in ancient Aramaic and in several Neo-Assyrian cuneiform texts *Ed-ru-nu*, *Ed-*[*ra*]*-a-nu*, *Ed-ra-ni*, *Ed-ra-nu*.

However, the Neo-Assyrian name *Idrūnu* is from the Aramaic *ʿḏr* "help" with the *ōn/ān* suffix (Baker and Streck 2000). If Lipiński is correct, this means that the Hebrew *Vorlage* of these Greek manuscripts containing Εσρωμ/ν must have had an original עזרן. It is hard to conceive of how this could have become רזן. The fact is that other than this passage in 3 Kgdms 11:14 in these Greek manuscripts, Εσρωμ/ν and Εζρων are the Old Greek's rendering of the personal name חֶצְרוֹן.[78] It is far more probable that a Greek translator has

76. There are personal names in Old South Arabian (Sabean) with the root *rzn*: *rzn*, *rznm*, *ʾrzn* as well as a toponym *trznn* (Harding 1971, 36, 131, 277).

77. Josephus: Ράζος; Vulgate follows the versification of MT and reads in 11:23: Razon filium Heliada.

78. Εσρωμ/ν is used, along with Εζρων, for the translation of חֶצְרוֹן in Josh 15:3; Ruth 4:18–19; 1 Chr 2:5, 9, 18, 21, 24, 25; 4:1; 5:3 (though here Luc has Ασρων).

confused the names and has mistakenly transposed Εσρωμ/Εσρων into the text in conjunction with the transposition of verse 11:23–25 into 3 Kgdms 11:14, creating untold confusion thereafter.[79]

### 9.3.3. The Early Kings of Aram-Damascus after Rezon

Around the beginning of the ninth century, Asa of Judah (ca. 911–870) made an alliance with "Ben-Hadad (Bar-Hadad), son of Tab-Rimmon, the son of Hezion, king of Aram, who was ruling in Damascus" against Baasha of Israel (ca. 909–886), who had fortified Ramah on the border between Israel and Judah (1 Kgs 15:16–22 ‖ 2 Chr 16:1–6).[80] The 1 Kgs 15 passage describes these events as follows (my translation):

> There was war between Asa (אָסָא) and Baasha (בַּעְשָׁא) king of Israel all their days. Baasha king of Israel marched against Judah, and fortified Ramah, to prevent anyone from going out or coming in[81] to Asa king of Judah. Then Asa took all the silver and the gold that were left in the treasuries of the house of Yahweh and the treasuries of the house of the king,[82] and gave them into the hands of his servants. King Asa sent them to Ben-Hadad (בֶּן־הֲדַד), son of Tab-Rimmon (טַבְרִמֹּן), son of Hezion (חֶזְיוֹן), king of Aram, who ruled in Damascus, saying, "(Let us make) a treaty (בְּרִית) between me and you, (a treaty) between (the house of) my father and (the house of) your father."[83] To this end, I have sent to you a "present" (שֹׁחַד) of silver and gold; go, break your treaty (הָפֵרָה אֶת־בְּרִיתְךָ) with King Baasha of Israel, so that he may withdraw from me." Ben-Hadad listened to King Asa, and he sent the commanders of his armies against the cities of Israel. He attacked Iyyon,[84] Dan, Abel Beth-Ma'akah,[85] and all of Kinneroth, with all the land of Naphtali. When Baasha heard (about this), he ceased fortifying Ramah and stayed in Tirzah. Then King Asa made a proclamation to all Judah; no

---

79. Perhaps this is similar to the transposition in the Old Greek of Αδωνιβέζεκ into Josh 10:1 from Judg 1:5 in the place of אדניצדק. This was a move that was made by a Greek translator who did not know that Hebrew בזק is a toponym and is not productive of personal names; thus Αδωνιβέζεκ is not a personal name and should be understood as "lord of Bezek." Nevertheless, a Greek translator treated it as a personal name and then placed it in the Josh 10:1 narrative creating untold confusion. See Layton 1990, 117.

80. For discussion, see Adam 2010, 49–68. The account in 2 Chr 16 is not an exact parallel. The chronological statement in 16:1 is clearly mistaken and cannot be used in historical reconstruction and the passage in 16:7–10 appears to reflect antithesis (Kalimi 2005, 342).

81. Cf. Josh 6:1. See Cogan 2001, 399.

82. Following the *qere* and the parallel in 2 Kgs 16:8: וּבְאֹצְרוֹת בֵּית הַמֶּלֶךְ.

83. See discussion below.

84. Located at Tell ed-Dibin.

85. Located south of Iyyon at Abil el-Qamḥ.

> one was exempt: they carried away the stones of Ramah and its timber, with which Baasha had been building; with them King Asa fortified Geba of Benjamin and Mizpah.

The basic historicity of the account is generally accepted by historians[86] (but see the discussion of Finkelstein's analysis below). This account follows on the heels of the introduction to the reign of Asa with its emphasis on his religious activities, which culminate in his dedication of "sacred" objects into the house of Yahweh, items that belonged to his father and himself (15:15). The use of these same items, now belonging to Yahweh, in order to secure a political/military objective is undoubtedly the reason for the inclusion of this account, that is, to criticize Asa's abuse of these.

It seems evident that a Judahite, nomistic perspective permeates this account. Not only is this perceived in the issue of the use of items belonging to Yahweh in order to "acquire" help (something that Asa should look to Yahweh for), but in the use of the term שֹׁחַד, "present." Parker has argued that in 1 Kgs 15:19 the word is used in an international relations context, not a legal context (where it would connote "bribe") and

> Further, it is used by the person sending the present in an address to the person receiving it, not by someone—whether outside observer or threatened third party—who might view the act negatively. There are, therefore, no grounds for claiming that the use of *šoḥad* by Asa is an expression of the narrator's condemnation of the act. Certainly this *šoḥad* was understood by both parties to require something in return, as in modern political life. But in Asa's message, it remains distinguished, as a present, from the opprobrium of a "bribe," as also from an enforced gift or "tribute" (Parker 1997, 92).

However, while שֹׁחַד means simply "present," it can mean and most frequently means "bribe." As Parker (1997, 91–92) rightly notes, it is used in the direct speech of Asa to his servants as instruction of what they are to say to the king of Damascus. In the parallel action of Ahaz in his sending a שֹׁחַד given to Tiglath-pileser III in 2 Kgs 16:8, it is the narrator's choice of words. Thus in 1 Kgs 15:19, the term is used as an ironic wordplay: on the one hand, it may simply be a present, but on the other hand, in light of the use of Yahweh's treasuries, and the lack of trust on the part Asa, it is nothing short of a

86. Fritz (2003, 167) states: "The historicity of the conflict must not be doubted, since all its details can be verified." I am unsure what "details" Fritz had in mind since not a single detail is actually verified. See also Dion 1997, 182–83; Lipiński 2000a, 372.

"bribe."[87] It is, therefore, used by the narrator to taint Asa's action, to express his disapproval of Asa. Na'aman (2008, 58) has perceptively observed that

> Even more remarkable is Asa's request that Ben-Hadad break his covenant with Baasha (v. 19). Asa is portrayed as instigating a violation of a covenant, an act of serious implications in biblical literature (compare, e.g., Deut 31:16, 20; Jer 11:10, 31:31, 33:20; Ezek 17:11–21). Finally, Asa is shown as indirectly responsible for bringing heavy destruction upon the Northern Kingdom (v. 20). The passage includes a harsh criticism of Asa and is based upon an early source that the author of Kings reworked extensively according to his own historical outlook.

The opening statement of this account ("there was war between Asa and Baasha, king of Israel, all their days") is clearly formulaic,[88] and should not be taken literally for the final clause of verse 21 indicates that from the point of Ben-Hadad's military action in the north, Baasha could not engage Asa in the south. The fortification of Ramah (modern er-Ram), only 8 km from Jerusalem and on the north–south road through the Jerusalem hills, is portrayed by the biblical narrator as a significant threat, that is, a shut down of the border with all the concomitant ramifications.[89] Asa's response was to take what was in the treasuries of the temple and the palace, and open a second front by inducing Ben-Hadad (Bar-Hadad) to attack Israel's northern border region.

Upon arriving in Damascus, Asa's emissaries present the first part of his message in 1 Kgs 15:19a: בְּרִית בֵּינִי וּבֵינֶךָ בֵּין אָבִי וּבֵין אָבִיךָ.[90] Exactly how best to understand these words has been debated. Many scholars and

---

87. Cogan (2001, 400) suggests that it was not the word used in the actual speech of the emissaries of Asa to Ben-Hadad. Based on the word's occurrences in West Semitic inscriptions, this seems correct. Parker (1997, 163 n. 50) acknowledged the term's clear negative connotations in the Sefire treaty. While fragmentary, the immediate context demands a negative nuance "bribe" (Sefire III, 27–28). His argument that the use of Yahweh's treasuries to secure the foreign alliances are not condemned is contradicted in the explicit condemnation of Hanani in 2 Chr 16:7–10 (which makes explicit what is implicit in the 2 Kgs 15 passage), as well as the overwhelming condemnation of the prophets for foreign alliances. Adam (2010, 61–62) considers the Chronicler's condemnation of the alliance of Asa to be in contradiction to the "synchronistic chronicle of Kings."

88. In the immediate context, note 1 Kgs 14:30 (Rehoboam) and 15:6 (Abijah in context). See Adam 2010, 67.

89. For a discussion of the intentions and objectives in Baasha's action, see Elgavish (2000). However, while the historical circumstances are outlined well, there seems to be a bit of a confusion about the grammatical status of the *lamed* attached to Asa (לְאָסָא) and the negative purpose clause introduced by לְבִלְתִּי in 1 Kgs 15:17.

90. Parallel 2 Chr 16:3.

versions understand this as a nominal sentence that is indicative,[91] and therefore it speaks to the present relationship between Judah and Damascus as allied kingdoms, under a treaty dating from the reigns of their fathers (a fact not mentioned elsewhere): "There is a pact between you and me, and between your father and my father" (e.g., NJPS 2nd edition). J. Gray (1970, 351) writes:

> This passage indicates that Abijah the father of Asa had an agreement with Damascus which Kings does not mention. It was probably this that enabled Abijah to attack and defeat Jeroboam, the Aramaeans possibly intervening at a critical moment when Jeroboam held the advantage (2 Chr 13:13–15).

This understanding seems based on the assumption of a comparison between the two parts of 15:19a: between בְּרִית בֵּינִי וּבֵינֶךָ and בֵּין אָבִי וּבֵין אָבִיךָ, yielding, "There is an alliance between us, *as* there was between our fathers." Rudolph (1951, 206) went so far as to propose an emendation, restoring a כ before בֵּין that he felt had fallen out by haplography. However, there is no trace of this in the Hebrew manuscript tradition, or in the versions. Nevertheless, quite a few scholars, while not endorsing the emendation, seem to see an implicit comparison between the two parts.

On the other hand, other scholars understand this to be a nominal sentence expressing a wish (e.g., Noth 1968, 339; see NRSV, NIV, etc.). This interpretation, however, is rejected by DeVries (2003, 191) who states that "there is no solid basis for Noth's proposal." He also observes that the "G$^{L}$ Διαθήκη ἔστω 'let there be a treaty' might be a legitimate paraphrase except for the fact that a subjunctive is not suitable when referring to something that occurred in the past—the forefathers' treaty" (2003, 189).[92]

It seems that how one understands the phrase בֵּין אָבִי וּבֵין אָבִיךָ is a factor. While the emendation of כ as suggested by Rudoph should be rejected, this part of the sentence might be an implicit comparison, except for rather strong contextual reasons. The context of 1 Kgs 15 argues that this is a request for a treaty to be established between the Judah and Damascus. If there were an already existing treaty between Judah and Damascus, then there are significant problems (see Lemaire 2007a, *49). First, it is not clear why the king of Aram would not have intervened earlier to rescue the king of Jerusalem (he would have been obligated by an extant treaty to do so). Second, Asa would

91. E.g., the Vulgate renders: *foedus est inter me et te*, "a treaty is between me and you."

92. Note nevertheless Cogan (2001, 400) who comments: "However, it cannot be ruled out that this declaration represents the initial contact between Asa and Ben-hadad, with Asa proposing a renewal of his father's treaty."

not have needed to send a שֹׁחַד of silver and gold: he could have simply asked for *an implementation of the extant treaty terms.*[93] Furthermore, since the text explicitly mentions an existing treaty between Aram-Damascus and Israel, it seems highly unlikely that Asa is making an indicative statement about a previously existing treaty that Abijah of Judah had made with Ṭāb-Rammān of Damascus, because it is very improbable that Damascus had extant treaties with both Israel and Judah at the same time! In fact, 1 Kgs 11:23–25 suggest that at an earlier time Aram-Damascus was on hostile terms with the Davidic dynasty, and nothing seems to demonstrate that this situation had changed in the days of Asa's and Ben-Hadad's fathers.[94]

In an insightful article, Lemaire (2007a, *50–*51) has suggested that there is an ellipsis of בית before אָבִי and אָבִיךָ. This would yield a translation: "(a treaty) between (the house of) my father and (the house of) your father."[95] In support, he notes the meaning of the phrase בית אב is attested a number of times in the Bible with ellipsis of the first term (בית).[96] Thus it does not seem impossible that in 1 Kgs 15:19 there is an ellipsis of (בית), which would give a meaning that would be perfectly appropriate in a historiographical context. Even if there is no ellipsis, the text is expressing an appeal to a wider commitment of the families, not just the two individuals.[97]

Lemaire (2007a, *50) also argues that the nominal sentence is nonindicative as clearly signaled from the Old Greek. Whether one reads διάθου Διαθήκην (with the aorist imperative, second singular) "conclude a treaty," or the G^L variant Διαθήκη ἔστω (with the present imperative third singular) "let there be a treaty," the Old Greek translators were evidently perceiving that this sentence reflects a nonindicative (in this case, optative) nuance. According to Joüon (1965, 501, s.v. §163b), nominal sentences can be used to express an optative nuance.[98] A very clear example of an optative nominal sentence can be seen in Ruth 2:9: עֵינַיִךְ בַּשָּׂדֶה אֲשֶׁר־יִקְצֹרוּן, "Let your eyes be on the field which they are harvesting."

Typically, the verb כרת occurs in contexts of the request to make a

93. If the wording was יֵשׁ (לָנוּ) בְּרִית בֵּינִי וּבֵינֶךָ בֵּין אָבִי וּבֵין אָבִיךָ, then this would reflect an existing treaty.

94. What meager evidence there is seems to point to Judah not having enough political or financial clout to be a desirable ally.

95. See also Barr 1978.

96. See also *HALOT*, 2, s.v. number 5; *DCH* 1:91. See Exod 6:25; Num 31:26; 32:28; 36:1; Jos 14:1; 19:51; 21:1; 1 Kgs 8:l; Ezra 1:5; 8:29; 1 Chr 29:6; 2 Chr 5:2.

97. An analogy certainly can be seen in the Sefire treaty (*KAI* 222, 223, 224).

98. "Une proposition nominale peut avoir le sens optatif; ainsi dans les formules de salutation: שָׁלוֹם לְךָ *salut à toi!* Jug 6,23 etc. עִמָּכֶם יהוה *Jéhovah soit avec vous!* Ruth 2,4 (Opp. Jug 6,12 Jéhovah est avec toi)…." In Ruth 2:4, the context makes clear that this nominal clause is optative.

treaty. For example, in Gen 31:44, Laban urges Jacob: נִכְרְתָה בְרִית אֲנִי וָאָתָּה וְהָיָה לְעֵד בֵּינִי וּבֵינֶךָ, "Let us make a treaty, me and you, and let it be a witness between me and you."[99] Perhaps in certain situations it was unnecessary to express the verb, though as attested here, the nominal clause could be optative by context.

In any case, Asa is clearly invoking Ben-Hadad to break his extant treaty with Israel and establish a new treaty with him. Apparently, in this instance, the sending of such a large monetary sum was necessary to induce Ben-Hadad to break an existing treaty and turn against a treaty-brother (i.e., Baasha). Therefore, the sentence should be translated: "(Let us make) a treaty between me and you, (a treaty) between (the house of) my father and (the house of) your father."[100]

The text does not record the Aramean king's thinking on this, but surely he saw this as a win, win. Thus, while the two Hebrew kingdoms warred, he would, on the one hand, accept a "pretty present" from Judah; yet, on the other hand, because the king of Israel was occupied on his southern border with Judah, he could not protect his northern border, affording Damascus with a perfect opportunity to raid a significant part of valuable Israelite territory with impunity. Bar-Hadad attacked a number of Israelite cities north of the Sea of Galilee:

> Iyyon, Dan, Abel Beth-Ma'akah, and all of Kinneroth, with all the land of Naphtali
>
> אֶת־עִיּוֹן וְאֶת־דָּן וְאֵת אָבֵל בֵּית־מַעֲכָה וְאֵת כָּל־כִּנְרוֹת עַל כָּל־אֶרֶץ נַפְתָּלִי

The verb נכה used in this instance (as opposed to לכד) may indicate that the military action of Bar-Hadad was that of a razzia, not a complete conquest and annexation. However, it is surely not impossible that some territory was seized. It was a sufficient plundering that forced Baasha to withdraw from Ramah.[101] However, it is possible—though there is no direct evidence—that at this time Bar-Hadad I annexed the Aramean kingdoms of Geshur and Ma'akah to Damascus (Dion 1997, 180).

Recently, Finkelstein (2013, 74–76) has questioned the historicity of 1 Kgs 15:16–22. This is based on his analyses of the archaeological evidence from two sites—Tel Dan and Hazor—and his assessment of the text of

99. Compare especially Gen 26:28; Josh 9:6, 7, 11; 1 Sam 11:1; 2 Sam 3:12; and Ezra 10:3. In every occurrence listed here, an optative form of the phrase διατίθημι Διαθήκην is used to render כרת ברית, as it is in 1 Kgs 15:19.

100. Understanding "(house of) my father" referring to Judah or the Judahite dynasty, and "(house of) your father" referring to Damascus or the Damascene dynasty.

101. The date for this conflict is debated due to internal biblical difficulties, which are too complex to enter into here, but see Pitard 1987, 109–14; Galil 1996, 17–20.

1 Kgs 15. Concerning Tel Dan, Finkelstein relies on the work of Arie (2008) who argued, among other things, that there was a gap in occupation in Iron IIa at the site. In the case of Hazor, although Yadin (1972, 143) attributed the destruction of Stratum IX at the site to this campaign of Bar-Hadad I described in 1 Kgs 15,[102] Finkelstein (2013, 75–76; 1999, 59) argues that radiocarbon results put the destruction of this stratum in the late ninth century and leave no destruction layer at Hazor for this campaign (he attributes the stratum's destruction to the work of Hazael). Since there was no occupation of Dan during this period, and because there is no destruction layer at Hazor, the campaign of Kgs 15 must not have happened. Instead, because there is some similarity between the itinerary of 1 Kgs 15:20 and the one in 2 Kgs 15:29, the campaign must be a later fabrication and "there is good reason to doubt its (1 Kgs 15) historicity."

However, there are problems with Finkelstein's historical analysis. First, excavations in Area T at Tel Dan have uncovered material that contradicts Arie's conclusion about an occupational gap at the site.[103] At present, there is uncertainty on the length of Aramean presence at Tel Dan, but the Tel Dan Inscription (see below) and the discovery of a bowl with an Aramaic inscription[104] are sure evidence that the site was under Aramean control for some period of time. In any case, the archaeological evidence does not support Arie's conclusion (or Finkelstein's). Second, Hazor is not actually listed by name in the itinerary of 1 Kgs 15:20 (it is in 2 Kgs 15:29).[105] So whether there is a destruction layer at Hazor from the early ninth century or not is, in one sense, really irrelevant. The absence of archaeological evidence from a site that is not even specifically listed is a nonstarter.[106] But moreover, in the publication of the 1990–2009 excavations at Hazor, the archaeologists concluded that "the transition between the major urban settlements (i.e., Strata X–Vb) at the site was quite gradual, and in the relatively large areas excavated by the new expedition there was no clear-cut evidence of a wholesale

102. See also Ben-Tor 2000, 12 and Lemaire 2010b, 62–3.

103. See Greer 2013, 46 n. 11, 56 n. 46, 74 n. 76, 97–123; and Ilan forthcoming.

104. Avigad 1968. The inscription reads: *lṭb[ḥ]y*' "belonging to the butchers (sacrificers)." For possible cultic connections, see Greer 2013, 78 n. 86.

105. The phrase כָּל־אֶרֶץ נַפְתָּלִי should not be pressed too literally. The fact is Hazor is unnamed in the passage.

106. There are two other cities mentioned in 1 Kgs 15:20 (Iyyon and Abel Beth-Ma'akah), which have not really been excavated. Ultimately, it is only the archaeological evidence from Tel Dan that may speak to the issue of the historicty of 1 Kgs 15:20. One must remember that cities could and did capitulate without a fight, leaving no destruction layer! Just because there is no destruction layer found at a site does not allow one to conclude that there was no campaign.

destruction—neither in Stratum IX nor in Stratum VII."[107] If they are correct, there is no evidence at Hazor for a destruction by either Ben-Hadad I or Hazael. Third, most scholars have seen the use of the itineraries in these accounts as grounds to accept the historicity of the campaigns (not necessarily everything in the accounts per se).[108] Fourth, Finkelstein has ignored the three generation kinglist in 1 Kgs 15:18, which actually argues in favor of the historicity of Bar-Hadad and this campaign. If the whole account is a fabrication of "later historical realities" (Finkelstein 2013, 76), then these kings of Aram-Damascus disappear, and nothing is known about the history of Aram-Damascus at the end of the tenth and the beginning of the ninth centuries. The only Bar-Hadad of Damascus mentioned outside of the Bible is Bar-Hadad, the son of Hazael, in the Zakkur Inscription. However, although the existence of this first Bar-Hadad (Ben-Hadad) of 1 Kgs 15:18 cannot be presently proven by extrabiblical texts, many scholars hold to the existence of at least two Bar-Hadads (Lemaire 1984, 343–6; Grabbe 2007, 165). That there was a Bar-Hadad I who campaigned in the region is very likely.

In fact, ultimately what is most important for the history of Aram-Damascus that can be gleaned from this account is found in the three-generation king list: Ḥadyān I (Hebrew: חֶזְיוֹן) who apparently ruled in the fourth quarter of the tenth century,[109] Ṭāb-Rammān (Hebrew: טַבְרִמֹּן) at the end of the tenth century, and Bar-Hadad I (Hebrew: בֶּן־הֲדַד) during the early decades of the ninth century.

Since the father and grandfather of Bar-Hadad I, Ṭāb-Rammān and Ḥadyān I, are not mentioned in any other text, some past scholars have attempted to argue that Rezon (רְזוֹן) of 1 Kgs 11:23–25 and Hezion (חֶזְיוֹן), the grandfather of Bar-Hadad, are the same person (e.g., Kraeling 1918, 48 n. 2). This theory was based originally on a supposed corruption of an original *Ḥezron (חזרון) somehow reflected in the Greek versions Εσρων or Εσρωμ (Burney 1903, 198). While this line of argument was discarded, some scholars continued to equate the two names with the same person: for example, Malamat (1973, 151–52 n. 23)[110] followed an etymological sug-

107. Ben-Tor, Ben-Ami, and Sandhaus 2012, 3. Contra Yadin (1972, 143, 200) who posited a Stratum IX destruction to Ben-Hadad I and a Stratum VII destruction to Hazael.

108. Lemaire's statement (2007a, *46) seems to be to the point: "La démarche du roi Asa envoyant une ambassade demander l'intervention du roi araméen de Damas Ben-Hadad fils de Tabrimmon a peu de chance d'avoir été inventée par un historien, deutéronomiste ou autre, et reflète la pratique des alliances/vassalités politiques au Levant à cette époque, comme un peu plus tard, vers 735/4, le roi Akhaz de Jérusalem demandant l'intervention du roi néo-assyrien Tiglat-phalazar III contre Péqah, roi d'Israël, et Rezin, roi de Damas (2 Rois 16:7–9)."

109. There was a later Ḥadyān II, attested in Assyrian inscriptions (see below).

110. See also Unger 1957, 56–57; Mazar 1962, 104; Gray 1970, 353.

gestion of Landsberger (1964, 60) that the two forms were merely phonetic variants of the same name, based on a proposed phonetic shift of *ḥ* to *r*, which would result in Hebrew *rzn* yielding Akkadian *ḫazan(n)u*, "mayor, potentate." However, a phonetic shift of *ḥ* to *r* is quite dubious (Pitard 1987, 104–7). The publication of the Pazarcık Stela provided knowledge that another king of Aram-Damascus, in fact, bore the name Ḥadyān II (spelled m*Ḫa-di-a-ni*).[111] This is also the same name that is attested at Tell Ḥalaf, namely, the father of Kapara, the king of Palē(?) (written: m*Ka-pa-ra* A m*Ḫa-di-a-ni*).[112] Therefore, Hezion (חֶזְיוֹן) is the Hebrew rendering of the name of Ḥadyān I of Damascus, who is absolutely a separate person from Rezon (רְזוֹן).

Ṭāb-Rammān is also otherwise unknown. He has an Aramean name, meaning "Good is (the god) Rammān" where Rammān was a characteristic epithet "Thunderer" of Hadad (2 Kgs 5:18).[113] Bar-Hadad, meaning "son of Hadad," is "probably a dynastic epithet" (Liverani 2005, 107; see discussion below). Clearly, this is the first person known to bear it; hence, Bar-Hadad I.[114] Opinions differ as to whether this is the same Bar-Hadad/Ben-Hadad of 1 Kgs 20 (see discussion below).

A suggestion of Eshel (1984, 1990) should be mentioned. He proposed that Isa 8:23 [Eng. 9:1] makes an allusion to the incursions of two kings (the "former" and the "latter") that he proposed to identify with Ben-Hadad I as "the former" and Tiglath-pileser III as "the latter."[115] Obviously, Eshel assumed that in this text הָרִאשׁוֹן and הָאַחֲרוֹן were substantives: "the former (king)" and "the latter (king)." There is no question that this verse is one of the most difficult to interpret in the Hebrew Bible. However, a number of scholars have demonstrated that these two words are more likely adjectives modifying עֵת, based primarily on their usage elsewhere in the book of

111. See below for discussion.

112. Also an individual from Dūr-Katlimmu (m*ḫa-di-ia-nu*). See Baker 2000 and ch. 4 above.

113. Note the name Bur-Rammānu "son of Rammān" (Baker 1999). One of the leaders in Bīt-Zamāni had this name (see ch. 4 above).

114. Albright (1942, 25–26) read the king's name and his ancestry as given in the present text (1 Kgs 15:18) in the very ill-preserved second line of the Melqart Stela: *Br-h*(2) *dd . br . Ṭ⌜br⌝[m]n [b⌜r⌝ . ⌜Ḥzy⌝[n]* "Bir-Hadad, son of Ṭâb-Rammân, son of Ḫadyân." See also his translation in *ANET*, 655: "Barhadad, the son of T[abrimmon, the son of Hezion]." However, this reading cannot stand. See §8.2.4 (discussion of the Melqart Stela's reading, pp. 534–36).

115. For earlier discussion, see Emerton 1969.

Isaiah. Hence, it is not likely that Bar-Hadad I/Ben-Hadad I is in view in this verse, whatever the best interpretation of it might be.[116]

Finally, it is important to note that this account in 1 Kgs 15:16–22 attests to the local conflicts that were to be so dominant in the politics of the region during this period. These conflicts might be interspersed with temporary unions of old enemies against a common enemy (Assyria); but when that common enemy was no longer an immediate threat, there was a quick resumption of the old local conflicts (Liverani 2014, 438–39). Ben-Ami and Wazana (2013) have explicated the local emphasis that is seen in the biblical texts as well as in the bulk of the native inscriptions from the region. Only Hazael will truly achieve a hegemonic position in the region among Levantine rulers.

### 9.3.4. Hadad-ezer (Adad-idri) // Bar-Hadad (II)?

The Assyrian texts of the mid-ninth century mention the kingdom of Aram-Damascus for the first time. It is clear from these references that Aram-Damascus had become one of the most important Levantine powers. In 853, Shalmaneser III invaded the kingdom of Hamath and a coalition was formed to oppose him. Shalmaneser's Kurkh Monolith describes this coalition, listing as the first of the conventional "twelve" participants, Adad-idri/ Hadad-ezer of Damascus.[117] Listed third is Ahab, the Israelite. Although Shalmaneser III claimed victory against the coalition in the battle of Qarqar, most scholars believe that this battle resulted in an Assyrian defeat, since he returned in 849, 848, and 845 to fight this same coalition without any real success.[118] Adad-idri of Damascus is always listed as the head of this coalition in Shalmaneser's inscriptions, indicating Damascus's leading role in the coalition.

One of the major historical cruxes concerning the history of Aram-Damascus arises in the Assyrian and biblical sources.[119] While the Monolith

116. See especially Williamson 1993; and Gosse 1996. For a discussion of the grammar, see Wegner 1991. Moreover, it is difficult to see how in this context Tiglath-pileser III could be "the latter."

117. *COS* 2.113A:263–64; Younger 2007b, 256–57; see chapter 7 and table 7.2.

118. For additional reasons, see chapter 7 on Hamath. Younger 2007b, 253.

119. The Bible seems to refer to three Ben-Hadads of Aram-Damascus: (1) the Ben-Hadad, the contemporary of Baasha and Asa (1 Kgs 15:16–21); (2) Ben-Hadad, the predecessor of Hazael, the contemporary of Ahab and his sons (1 Kgs 20–2 Kgs 8); and (3) Ben-Hadad, the son of Hazael, contemporary of the Joash of Israel (2 Kgs 13). Only (3) is attested outside of the Bible. A few scholars see (1) and (2) as the same person. Albright (1942, 26), for example, identified the Ben-Hadad of 1 Kgs 20 and 22 with the Ben-Hadad of 1 Kgs 16:18, based on his reading of the Melqart Stela, stating: "biblical historians have

lists Adad-idri/Hadad-ezer[120] and Ahab as contemporaries and allies, the Hebrew Bible only mentions a king by the name of Ben-Hadad (Bar-Hadad "son of Hadad") as king of Damascus during Ahab's reign. In reconstructing the history of the period, scholars have proposed two different possibilities.[121]

One option is to equate Hadad-ezer with Ben-Hadad of 1 Kgs 20 and 22. Since an earlier Ben-Hadad is mentioned in 1 Kgs 15:18–20 in the days of Asa and Baasha, the Ben-Hadad of 1 Kgs 20 and 22 is usually designated Ben-Hadad II by those following this option (Hallo 1960, 39–40; Wiseman 1972–75; 1993, 185; Elat 1975, 30–31; Mitchell 1982, 479; Ikeda 1999, 277; Rainey 2001, 140–49; Cogan 2001, 471–4; Galil 2002, 46–48; Liverani 2005, 106–10[122]; 2014, 407; Lamb 2007, 200–204). The Assyrian materials make it quite clear that Adad-idri (who is not equated with "Bar-Hadad" in the Assyrian texts) was Hazael's predecessor (Stith 2008, 45). Thus, a fundamental problem with this option is that the name in the Monolith, Adad-idri, does not equate with Ben-Hadad (other than the theophoric element). A possible explanation[123] of this has been to argue that the name Bar-Hadad (Ben-

been mistaken in distinguishing between Benhadad son of Tab-rimmon son of Hezion, the contemporary of Asa and Baasha (I Kings 15:18), and Ben-hadad the contemporary of Elijah and Elisha. The first two kings of this name are one and the same, and must both be called Ben-hadad I, while Ben-hadad son of Hazael (the Bir-Hadad son of Hazael of the Zakir Stele) becomes Ben-hadad II instead of III." See also Unger 1957; Lambert 1994; 2004, 369; Mazzoni 2013.

120. Hadad-ezer (Aramaic: *hdd-ʿḏr*, Hadad-ʻiḏr; Hebrew: Hadad-ezer, *hdd-ʿzr*) means "Hadad is (my) help" and is a well-attested Aramaic personal name. See Maraqten 1988, 155; Zadok 1977, 46, 97, 243, 246; Schwemer 1998a. In the Hebrew Bible, this is one of the Aramaic personal names that is partially altered. Layton (1990, 19) states: "The Aramaic PN *br hdd* occurs in the Bible under the Canaanite form *ben-hădad*, and the Aramaic PN *Hadad-ʻidrī appears in Hebrew guise as *hădadʿezer*." Zadok (1982, 120) notes that the name pattern: divine name + abstract noun + possessive pronoun first-person singular is found both in Aramaic and Akkadian names, but not in Hebrew. He opines: "The lack of the above-mentioned onomastic type in Hebrew may be—in my opinion—the reason why Biblical Hebrew has *Hadad-ʿezer* and not **Hadad-ʿezrī.* Hadadʻezer refers to an Aramean king and may be the same name (not the same individual) as Neo-Assyrian ᵈIM-(ʿ-)*id-ri*, U-*id-ri*, the same person as biblical Ben-Hadad. It seems to me that Aramaic **Hadad-ʿiḏrī* (> **Hadad-ʿedrī)* was interpreted by the Hebrew-speaking scribes as Hadad-ʻezer, which is of the same pattern as the common Hebrew names 'Elîʻezer, 'Abîʻezer, etc." It is interesting that tradition has the servant of Abram from Damascus named אליעזר (Gen 15:2).

121. While there are a few variants, these are the two major reconstructions.

122. Liverani 2005, 106: table with three Ben-Hadads, p. 107: "Ben-Hadad II (Hadad-ʻezer)"; pp. 109–10: "Ben-Hadad (Bar-Hadad in Aramaic, and probably a dynastic epithet)"; 1 Kgs 20 and 22 record Ahab's victory over Ben-Hadad and his death at Ramoth-Gilead.

123. Another explanation has been given by Provan, Long, and Longman (2003, 369 n. 30) who have suggested that the same individual was carrying more than one personal

Hadad) was a dynastic title or throne name (e.g., Mazar 1962, 101; Liverani 2005, 107). The evidence for this will be evaluated below.

The second option, which has gained wide endorsement over the last four decades and is today the consensus view, understands 1 Kgs 20, 22 and 2 Kgs 8:7–15 as reflecting a later political situation in the days of Jehoram, Jehoahaz, or Jehoash; and thus the passages are not a source of the history of the Omride dynasty, but the Jehuite dynasty.[124] Scholars who follow this option believe that Hadad-ezer (Adad-idri) should not be equated with Ben-Hadad of 1 Kgs 20 and 22. They point out that the only Ben-Hadad (Aramaic: Bar-Hadad) known from extrabiblical sources is Ben-Hadad/Bar-Hadad, the son of Hazael, who ruled over Damascus in the early eighth century and who is clearly identified in 2 Kgs 13:3, 24–25, and the Zakkur Inscription. Thus, this view understands the names "Ahab" (1 Kgs 20) and "Ahab" and "Jehoshaphat" (1 Kgs 22) to be erroneous insertions by a later redactor. These narratives really belong to Jehoahaz (2 Kgs 13:10–25). The major problem with this view is the lack of any actual evidence.[125] It stands solely on hypothetical arguments[126] concerning the compositional history of the biblical texts.

There is another piece of evidence that has further complicated past discussions: the Melqart Stela. This inscription mentions a Bar-Hadad

---

name in the ancient sources (thus, in this case: Hadad-ezer and Bar-Hadad). For an example, they cite 2 Chr 21:17; 22:1 where the same person is called Jehoahaz and Ahaziah. But here, the names contain the same two elements simply reversed: אחז + יהו = יהו + אחז. This is no different than the various spellings for Jehoiakim's son (e.g., יְהוֹיָכִין [2 Kgs 24:6] and יְכָנְיָהוּ [Jer 24:1], etc.) Therefore, this is not the same case as with Hadad-ezer and Ben/Bar-Hadad, where only the theophoric element matches.

124. Jepsen 1941–44; Whitley 1952; Miller 1966; 1967a; 1967b; 1982; Timm 1982, 214; Pitard 1987, 114–25; 1992; 1994, 207–30; H. Weippert 1988; Halpern and Vanderhooft 1991, 230–35; Kuan 1995, 36–38; Dion 1997; Yamada 2000 with modification; Lipiński 2000a; Stith 2008, 62; Knapp 2012, 219–20; Ghantous 2013, 78–79.

125. The hypothetical nature of the option has resulted in varying mutational views. Thus while Yamada (2000a, 311 n. 13, 315) in general principle follows Miller (1966, 1967a, 1967b, 1982), he admits to the historicity of 1 Kgs 20:1–34, i.e., the first and second battles between Ahab and Ben-Hadad, though he believes that 1 Kgs 22 is displaced. On the other hand, Na'aman (2002, 2007) admits the historicity of 1 Kgs 22, though he believes 1 Kgs 20 is displaced! On 1 Kgs 22, see Block 2005.

126. Another development has been to see 1 Kgs 20 as a literary unity that is a fictional (theological), late composition of the Persian period that contains no historical information for the time of the Jehuite Dynasty (and obviously not for the Omride Dynasty either). See Sroka 2006, 5–35; Hasegawa 2012, 112–13. Similiarly, Ahlström (1993, 575–77), while equating Ben-Hadad and Adad-'idri, believes that 1 Kgs 20, 22 contain no historical data for this period since they must be dated to a later time; contra Sweeney 2007, 240 and Cogan 2001, 472–74.

(*br.⌜h⌝dd*) who is designated "king of Aram" (*mlk ʾrm*).[127] The reading of this Bar-Hadad's father's name is very difficult. From the time of its discovery, many scholars understood this to be a reference to Bar-Hadad, the king of Aram-Damascus,[128] though the reading of the patronym has varied. One particularly popular understanding of line 2 has been the patronym "(Hadad)-Ezer" and the other part to contain the gentilic *dmšqy*, "the Damascene" (Cross 1972; 2003; Reinhold 1986; 2003; and Mykytiuk 2009).[129] However, in more recent years, most scholars have understood this Bar-Hadad to be a king of Arpad, reading the patronym as Attār-sumkī (Puech 1992; Lipiński 2000a; Pitard 1988 [reading the name as Attar-hamek]). The evidence seems to point to a king of Arpad.[130] Therefore, this inscription has no bearing on the question discussed here.

During the past three decades, the scholarly interpretation of 1 Kgs 20, 22 and 2 Kgs 8:7–15 as being displaced narrations has controlled the reconstructions of the history of Aram-Damascus. On the one hand, because of the hypothetical nature of the arguments used to endorse this interpretation, there is a need to scrutinize their strength. An objective assessment of these arguments shows that this interpretation is far from certain.[131] On the other hand, due to the textual and literary complexity of 1 Kgs 20, 22, uncertainties remain. Table 9.1 presents some of the reconstructions of the king list of Damascus based on different understandings of the Melqart Stela and 1 Kgs 20, 22.

Methodologically, there seems to be a better way forward in the discussion. Rather than allowing the debate to be centered on the biblical texts to determine the history of Aram-Damascus,[132] the key is to focus the analysis on the ancient Near Eastern sources, primarily the Neo-Assyrian materials. Therefore, a thorough investigation of the Neo-Assyrian data is the place to start.

It may appear to be a rather obvious observation, but it is nevertheless important: the Assyrians always designated the Aramean kings, including the kings of Damascus, by their actual personal names, not their titles. The kings of Damascus mentioned in the Assyrian texts are Hadad-ezer, Hazael,

---

127. *KAI* 201. For full discussion, see §8.2.4.

128. See the table in Hafþórsson 2006, 39, table 1.

129. For the resultant reconstructed king-list, see table 9.1 and Mykytiuk 2009, 79. However, note that this Bar-Hadad, son of Hadad-ezer, who only reigns a year or two, is the author of the Melqart Stela found in the north around Aleppo! This is very unlikely.

130. See the discussion in §8.2.4.

131. Glatt (1993, 110 n. 135) notes that it "creates more problems than it solves." See Lamb 2007, 200–204.

132. The internal biblicist debate about 1 Kgs 20, 22 and 2 Kgs 8:7–15 will undoubtedly continue.

Mari',[133] Ḫaḏyān, and Rezin. They do not, on any occasion, use the name Bar-Hadad. The use of Bar-Hadad/Ben-Hadad is only found in West Semitic inscriptions and the biblical texts.

The formation of *br* (Bar/Bir/Bur) plus divine name is replicated in the Assyrian transcriptions of a number of Aramaic personal names: Bir-ammâ ("Son of the paternal uncle"); Bir-Attār ("Son of Attār"); Bir-Bariaš ("Son of Bariaš"); Bir-Dāda ("Son of Dada"); Bar-il/Bir-il ("Son of god"); Bir-Šamaš ("Son of Šamaš"); Bur-Anate ("Son of Anat"); Bur-Attār ("Son of Attār"); and Bur-Rammānu ("Son of Rammān"). However, at present, *brhdd* ("Son of Hadad") does not actually occur in the Neo-Assyrian texts of any genre. Nor does it occur in Aramaic sources, other than in two royal inscriptions (Zakkur and Melqart). In other words, it does not appear to function as a common everyday personal name. Although this may appear to be odd given the high occurrence of the form *br*-DN listed above this is what the present data reveal. So while theoretically it is entirely possible that Bar-Hadad was a personal name, there is actually very little evidence for it. Consequently, it seems very possible that Bar-Hadad was a dynastic name, perhaps based on a personal name, similarly to Hittite "Labarna," Latin "Caesar," or a dynastic title like Egyptian "Pharaoh" ("Great House"), etc. Hence, in this instance, Bar-Hadad appears to have been used as a title or honorific. It is also possible that Bar-Hadad, "son of Hadad," functioned as an honorific, expressing adoption language, not unlike Ps 2:7: "You are my son; today I have begotten you."[134] Possibly there were some similarities between the ideology of kingship in the Hebrew kingdoms and their Levantine Aramean counterparts.

Of all the names of the kings of Damascus mentioned in the Assyrian inscriptions, the only name that has been taken other than a personal name is Mari'. Three times in the texts[135] the name is written: $^{m}$*Ma-ri-i'* rendering Aramaic *mārē'*, "lord" or *mārī'*, "my lord." This has been understood as a title, especially since in Hazael's Booty Inscriptions the term occurs with this usage in the phrase *lmr'n ḥz'l*, "Belonging to our lord, Hazael."[136] There is no doubt that *mr'* could be and was used as a title. However, scholars have too quickly and simply assumed that this is the usage in the Adad-nērārī III texts.[137] For example, Lipiński (2000a, 390) states:

133. The issue surrounding the use of Mari' will be discussed at length below.

134. Note the very likely symbolic name Bar-ga'yah in the Sefire texts (perhaps also a dynastic title?). Even if the Psalm is dated exilic or postexilic, it records a conception of adoption that is attested in other ancient Near Eastern cultures.

135. RIMA 3:209, A.0.104.6, line 19; 3:211, A.0.104.7, line 7; 3:213, A.0.104.8, line 15.

136. The term appears in all four inscriptions of his Booty Inscriptions, see below.

137. Page 1968, 149; Vattioni 1969, 368–69; and Heltzer 1983.

Table 9.1. Scholarly Reconstructions of the King List of Damascus
(see also the list of kings of Aram-Damascus at the end of this chapter)

| Lipiński 2000a, 407 | Albright 1942 | Cross 2003, 177 | Pitard 1987, 144, 166 | Liverani 2005, 106 |
|---|---|---|---|---|
| Hadad (?) (mid-tenth century) | | | | Hadad-‘ezer (960) |
| Ezron (third quarter of the tenth century) | | | Rezon (mid-tenth century) | Rezon (940) |
| Ḥadyān I (fourth quarter of the tenth century) | | | Ḥazyān (Hezion) (late tenth century) | (Hezyon) |
| Ṭāb-Rammān (end of the tenth century) | | | Ṭab-Rammān (late tenth–early ninth century) | (Tab-Rimmon) |
| Bar-Hadad I (ca. 900–ca. 880) | Ben-Hadad I (Adad-idri) (ca. 883–843) | Ben-Hadad I (son of Ṭābramān) (ca. 885–ca. 870) | Bir-Hadad I (early ninth) | Bar-Hadad I (900–875) |
| Hadad-ezer (ca. 880–ca. 843) | | Ben-Hadad II (= Hadad-‘iδr) (ca. 870–844) | Hadad-‘iḏr (mid-ninth–ca. 844) | Bar-Hadad II (Hadad-‘ezer) (875–845) |
| | | Ben-Hadad III (son of ‘Iδr) coregent (?) (ca. 845?–844?) | (Bir-Hadad II?) (ca. 844/842 | |
| Hazael (ca. 843–ca. 803) | Hazael (founder of a new dynasty) (ca. 843–796?) | Ḥaza’el (“son of nobody”) (ca. 844?–ca. 796) | Hazael (ca. 844/842–?) | Haza’el (845–800) |
| Bar-Hadad II (ca. 803–ca. 775) | Ben-Hadad II (Mari’) (ca. 796?–?) | Ben-Hadad IV (Mari’) (“son of Hazael”) (ca. 796–?) | Bir-Hadad III (Mari’) | Bar-Hadad III (800–780) |
| Ḥadyān II (ca. 775–ca. 750) | | | Ḫadiānu | Khadyanu (780–750) |
| Raṣyān (ca. 750–732) | | | Raḏyān | Rezin (750–732) |

> Since the proper name *māri*', "lord," is not attested in ancient Aramaic, the Assyrian $^{m}$*ma-ri-*' must go back to the Damascene royal title used in Hazael's inscriptions and on the jar handle stamped *lmr*', which parallels Hebrew *lmlk*, and certainly in the royal correspondence, in which Hazael, as suzerain, may have been called even *mr*ʾ *mlkn*, "lord of kings."

Also working with this assumption, Miller and Hayes (2006, 332) conclude: "*Mari*' is an Aramaic title, 'lord,' not the name of the king of Damascus. It was probably Bar(= Ben)-Hadad II, son of Hazael, who had recently succeeded Hazael his father." While this assumption is based on a natural first impression, there is significant evidence that points to a different conclusion. No one questions that *mr*ʾ was used as a title, or better an appellative. The question is whether this is the usage of $^{m}$*Ma-ri-i*' in the inscriptions of Adad-nērārī III.

When one peruses the Neo-Assyrian evidence, it becomes very clear that the root *mr/mr*' is a highly productive component in Aramaic personal names:

> (1) Mār-barakka ("The Lord has blessed"); (2) Mār-bi'di ("The Lord is behind me"); (3) Mār-gubbi ("[The] Lord is my cistern"?); (4) Mār-iababa ("[The] Lord has wept"); (5) Mār-iate' or Mār-Iate' ("[The] Lord has saved" or "Yate' is the lord"); (6) Mār-ia[ ... ] ("[The] Lord [ ... ]"); (7) Māri-barakka ("[The] Lord has blessed"); (8) Māriddi ("My lord is Adda," with crasis[138]); (9) Māri-li'ti ("[The] Lord is my strength"); (10) Mār-ilūti or Mār-ilūti ("[The] Lord is my divinity/god" or "Son of god"); (11) Māri-[...] ("The] Lord ..."); (12) Mār-larim ("May the Lord be exalted"); (13) Mār-liḫia ("O Lord, may he live"); (14) Mār-nūrī ("[The] Lord is my light"); (15) Mār-samsī ("[The] Lord is my sun"); and (16) Mār-sūrī ("[The] Lord is my bulwark").[139]

In addition, Mari' ($^{m}$*ma-ri-i*ʾ) itself occurs as the name of the father of a witness to the sale of a house in Maganuba by Šamaš-abu'a, son of Kakia, probably during the period of Sennacherib:[140]

| | | |
|---|---|---|
| 8′ | [IGI $^{m}$x x x x DUMU $^{m}$x]-*x-u-ni* | [witness XX, son of] X-uni, |
| 9′ | [IGI $^{m}$x x x x DUMU $^{m}$]*ma-ri-i*ʾ | [witness XX, son of] Mari', |
| 10′ | [IGI $^{m}$x x x x] DUMU $^{m}$PAB-*u-a*-SU | [witness XX], son of Aḫu'a-eriba, |

138. Crasis is a type of contraction in which two vowels or diphthongs merge into one new vowel or diphthong.

139. See *PNA* 2.2, 702, 737–38, 740–41.

140. SAA 6:158–59, 200.r.9′. See Baker 2001b, 737.

11′ [IGI ^m^x x x x] *šá* URU.*ḫa-ta-ia-te* [witness XX] of the city of Ḫatayate.

The name Mari' is written at the end of the line with the next line beginning a new witness. Hence, there is no other component to the name. This demonstrates that Mari' can be a hypocoristic form.[141] Moreover, an additional attestation of the name is found in a contract for the sale of an estate from a certain ^m^*ma-*⌜*ri*!⌝-[x].[142]

Of course, linear alphabetic transcriptions of Aramaic personal names[143] with this component are also attested: (1) *mr'hd* – seal (*CIS* 2.1, no. 79; Lidzbarski 1898, 317; Galling 1941; Vattioni 1971; Herr 1978, 14, no. 8; Maraqten 1988, 88; Avigad and Sass 1997, 303, no. 809);[144] (2) *mrbrk* – seal (*CIS* 2.1, no. 85; Lidzbarski 1898, 317; Maraqten 1988, 89); (3) *mr'yš'* – (Ammonite) seal (Giron 1922; Herr 1978, 31 n. 53; Maraqten 1988, 88; Avigad and Sass 1997, 304, no. 811); (4) *mrsmk* – seal (Herr 1978, 35, no. 65; Maraqten 1988, 89); (5) *mr'l* (Hammond 1960); (6) *'bdmr'n* – ostracon (Naveh 1973, 270–71; Maraqten 1988, 95); and (7) *mr'ybb* – seal (Avigad and Sass 1997, 303, no. 810).

The continuation of the use of the personal name *mr'* can be seen in the Neo-Babylonian Murašû documents (written: *ma-ri-e*).[145] It also occurs in the Palmyrene Inscriptions (e.g., *nbwmr*, "Nabû is lord");[146] and in the Hatran Inscriptions (written: *mry'*; Abbadi 1983, 126).

This evidence shows that Lipiński's assertion that the proper name *māri'* is not attested in ancient Aramaic is very misleading. Not only is the root highly productive in personal names, the form Mari' itself occurs as a hypocoristicon (see further below).

A number of scholars have used a stamp seal impression from a jar handle that reads *lmr'* to argue that *mr'* must be understood as a title.[147] For

141. Contra Lipiński's statement (2000a, 390) that Mari' is not attested as a personal name.

142. SAA 14:175, 223.14.

143. See Maraqten 1988, 181.

144. This carnelian scarab has a single line border with a camel centered, and the inscription around the edge. It must be genuine having been known since 1828.

145. BE 9, IX:1. See Coogan 1976, 29, 77; Zadok 1977, 64. Lipiński (2000a, 390 n. 232) discounts the NB name *ma-ri-e* arguing that it means "fat," "well-fed." But this is clearly nothing but special pleading. The evidence leads manifestly to another conclusion.

146. Stark 1971, 98. Stark also notes the name *Nbwm'* which he suggests is a hypocoristic of *Nbwmr*. See Caquot 1962, 251 and n. 4. The name *mr'* also occurs, although Stark (1971, 96) attributes this to a different root (although without explanation).

147. Published initially by Heltzer (1983, 9). See also Avigad and Sass (1997, 303, no. 808); Dion 1997, 153 n. 66; and Lipiński 2000a, 390. Schwiderski 2004, 2: 285, s.v. JarH:1; and 1: 544 where he lists *mr'* as a proper name.

example, like Lipiński (2000a, 390) in the above quote, Dion (1997, 153 n. 66) has argued:

> Mari (MR', "Lord" in Aramaic), was more a title of the kings of Damascus at the height of their influence, than a personal name somehow worn by Hazael or Bar-Hadad. In the abstract, one might conceive MR' as the hypocoristic of a proper name, like Baal of Tyre or Ahaz of Israel. But, there is no solid example of a duality of names among the Aramaic kings, and we know a jar-handle of Damascene provenance, stamped LMR' as many Judahite jars are embossed LMLK ... (citing Heltzer) ... It is therefore quite likely to understand Mari'/MR' as a title of the kings of Damascus, at least about 800, at the zenith of their power.[148]

However, there are significant problems. First, the stamp seal impression is unprovenanced, allegedly from the Damascus region, although its present location is unknown and only a modern cast exists.[149] There are significant doubts that it is genuine,[150] and therefore it cannot be used as evidence. Second, even if it were genuine—which it is not, there is no border and no iconography; thus it is a poor comparison to the *lmlk* stamps; and since there are no other examples, there is significant doubt whether there was any kind of royal stamp like the *lmlk* stamps from Judahite sites in Damascus. Third, again even if it were genuine, on the basis of the evidence discussed above, it would appear to be additional evidence of the hypocoristic personal name *mr'*, not evidence of some type of hypothetical jar stamps by the Damascene monarchy. Again, there is no doubt about the use of *mr'* as a title or appellative. The question is whether it can be a personal name and the evidence is most affirmative.[151]

Interestingly, Oppenheim (1939; see also de Vaux 1934) suggested that the Assyrian scribes misunderstood ${}^{m}$*Ma-ri-i'* (Mari') as a proper name.

148. Translation mine. It should be noted that Heltzer (1983, 10) was the first to argue that *lmr'* should be likened to *lmlk* and hence *mr'* was "the royal title of the King of Damascus."

149. My attempts to locate this cast have proved fruitless. I am inclined to doubt its existence.

150. The first paragraph of Heltzer's article (1983, 9) should set off loud sirens especially the first sentence: "This paper will deal with *a gypsum-cast of a jar-handle in the possession of the author, the original of which is now lost* (emphasis mine). The original jar handle came from the Damascus region or at least from the region where in ancient times the Kingdom of Damascus flourished." How does Heltzer know this and how can it be verified? This is not evidence! Wisely, Lemaire (2007b, 283) does not mention it among the Aramaic inscriptions from Damascus.

151. Sader (1987, 260) argued that Mari' was the proper name of a brother of Bar-Hadad, who had preceded him on the throne for a short time.

However, after nearly a century of contact with Arameans in the process of the recovery of their empire, the Assyrian scribes of Adad-nērārī III's day surely knew full well the difference between a title and a personal name in Aramaic. The fact that *mr'* is a component in numerous Aramaic personal names, as well as a stand-alone form, means that they *knew* that they were using a personal name, not a title.

It appears that Pitard's observation (1987, 166) is right on target: "The conclusion that מרא qualifies as a title of the kings of Aram seems a bit strained. The parallel biblical Hebrew term, אדני 'My lord' is a term of address to the king in Israel, not what could be called a title." Just as the root אדן is highly productive of personal names in Hebrew, so it is that מרא is highly productive of personal names in Aramaic, and can be a short form.

The evidence as presented here for Mari' being a personal name has not really been fully part of the analysis of those advocating that Mari' be understood as a title. But on the basis of the evidence for the use of this root in Aramaic personal names, it is abundantly clear that מרא/מר was a highly productive component of personal names in Aramaic just as אדן or בעל were productive components in other West Semitic personal names, and just as also *bēlu* was in Akkadian. Therefore, it is much more likely that Mari' is a shortened form of the king's own name[152] similar to that of Ba'al of Tyre[153] and to 'Adon in an early Aramaic letter.[154] It is apparent that the Assyrians only used the personal names of the kings of Damascus. Millard and Tadmor (1973, 63 n. 22) noted this stating:

> ... it is very unlikely that they (the Assyrians) would refer to a foreign king as "the lord" or "my lord" even if that was the accepted appellative of the Aramaean ruler among his subjects ... The Assyrian scribes usually used the personal names of the foreign kings, including those of Aram: Adad-idri (and not the dynastic name Ben-Hadad), Haza'ilu, Rahianu. In the same fashion, Mari' appears to be the abbreviated form of a personal name, perhaps *Mari-Hadad.

In the Assyrian inscriptions, not one single Aramean ruler is designated by his title or appellative alone.[155] In fact, the vast majority of the time no title or appellative is given. In every instance for the Aramean rulers of the Levant, the personal name is used. The Assyrians appear to designate the

152. Millard 1987–90, 419.

153. RINAP 4:17 and 23, 1, iii.17 and v.55; 4:46, 5, vi.7′; 4:87, 34, 12′; 4:135, 60, 7′.

154. *KAI* 266.

155. It is true that *pir'û* "pharaoh" (loanword from Egyptian *pr'ȝ*) is used as a title by Sargon II (3x). But this is clearly an exception, derived from the "great king" mentality. Aramean rulers do not so rate in Assyrian scribal eyes.

kings of Damascus only by their personal names: Hadad-ezer, Hazael, Mari', Ḥad̠yān, and Rezin.[156] Bar-Hadad is not used by the Assyrians whether in reference to a king of Damascus, or a king of Bēt-Gūš/Bīt-Agūsi/Arpad, or any other Aramean entity. The absence of its usage appears to be intentional.

Therefore, in view of the repeated occurrences of the root *mrʾ* in Neo-Assyrian and other sources in the composition of personal names (including the hypocoristic form), it is overwhelmingly more likely that *Mari' must be a hypocoristic form of the actual personal name of the king of Damascus* (emphasis mine). There is no evidence to the contrary, only an assumption that Mari' is a title—an assumption that the above data and analysis show cannot stand.

The king of Damascus whose personal name was Mari' is also called Bar-Hadad, the son of Hazael,[157] but not by the Assyrians (Liverani 2014, 407). Consequently, in this instance, "Bar-Hadad" was likely used as a title or honorific (see above discussion). If this is correct for Mari'/Bar-Hadad, then it is entirely possible that "Bar-Hadad" (Ben-Hadad) was also used as a dynastic title or honorific for Hadad-ezer (Adad-idri), as well as others.[158] At least two, possibly three kings of Damascus, as well as a king of Arpad, were so designated "Bar-Hadad/Ben-Hadad."

Therefore, in one sense, it does not matter whether 1 Kgs 20, 22 and 2 Kgs 8 are actual sources for the history of Aram-Damascus. The late ninth–early eighth-century kings of Damascus are known from other sources and there is no reason to complicate that kingdom's history with hypothetical rulers. For example, there is no reason to posit a "Ben-Hadad III (son of ʿ'ðr) / Bir-Hadad son of Hadad-ezer" (Cross 2003). Rather, what I have proposed seems to be the simplest and best solution.

However, if Hadad-ezer was referred to by the dynastic name or honorific title Bar-Hadad, just as the Damascene king Mari' was referred to by this dynastic title or honorific, then it permits the possibility to posit anyone of the passages (1 Kgs 20, 22 and 2 Kgs 8) as containing possible historical

---

156. The use of the *Winkelhaken* determinative is not happenstance. These are all personal names.

157. Mari' absolutely cannot be Hazael. The Assyrian scribes knew and used the name "Hazael" earlier in the numerous inscriptions of Shalmaneser III, and it is simply inconceivable that they would not have used his name here—especially since naming him here paying tribute to Adad-nērārī III would have humiliated their long-time nemesis. See discussion below.

158. Hasegawa (2012, 119) has recently and correctly stated: "more plausible is to regard Mari' as a hypocoristicon of the king's real name, and Ben-Hadad as a throne name. Mari', meaning "my Lord" in West Semitic, probably formed a part of the real name of Ben-Hadad, son of Hazael."

information (provided that additional arguments can be mounted and without having to accept all of the prophetic stories' details).

Hadad-ezer (Adad-idri) was highly successful in his involvements in the coalition that resisted the Assyrians in 853, 849, 848, and 845 in the land of Hamath.[159] During Hadad-ezer's reign the Arameans of Damascus became a very significant power, perhaps the most significant in the Levant. It seems reasonable, based on the Damascene historical interests, that Hadad-ezer had some military involvements in the Transjordan and in the land north of the Sea of Galilee. Ben-Ami and Wazana (2013) have investigated the potential enemy threats that may have stimulated the building of Israelite fortifications. Regarding this period, they (2013, 378) make the important observation:

> Although most commentators agree that the stories about the three battles between Ahab and Ben Hadad (1 Kgs 20:1–22, 26–36; 22:29–36) reflect events more relevant to the days of the dynasty of Jehu, it is more than likely that there were confrontations and hostilities between Israel and Aram during Ahab's 22 years of rule as well. The two kingdoms competed for supremacy in the area and for control of the lucrative trade passing through trans-Jordan and Gilead, while cooperating as allies against Assyria … the Arameans were a continuous threat during the Omride dynasty, but succeeded in realizing their potential in the full during the days of Hazael and his son Bar-Hadad, in the second half of the ninth century.

It is very likely that the early Omrides restored certain territory and power lost to Bar-Hadad I in the days of Baasha. It would be highly unusual for there to be no conflict between the two rising powers. While peaceful cooperation surely existed, there were a number of "hot spots" that flared up from time to time.

### 9.3.5. Hazael

Hazael of Aram-Damascus was undoubtedly the most defiant[160] and resilient of Aramean leaders against Assyrian aggression. Furthermore, he was, far and away, the most successful in the creation of an Aramean mini-empire (the powerful kings of Arpad really do not come close to matching Hazael's accomplishment). Not surprising then is his later deification (see below).

The discoveries of the last few decades have greatly enriched our understanding of this true Aramean "hero." The discovery and publication of the fragments of the Tel Dan inscription in 1993 and 1995 (Biran and Naveh

159. For these, see chapter 7.

160. Second place in this regard might go to Aḫuni of Bīt-Adīni.

1993, 1995) provided scholars with a new source for the reign of Hazael of Aram-Damascus.[161] The inscription is generally dated, on paleographic grounds, to the last quarter of the ninth century BCE (Schniedewind 1996, 78; Lemaire 1998, 11). Although it does not preserve the name of its author, a general consensus has emerged that the inscription belongs to Hazael, the king of Aram-Damascus (ca. 844/843–803/802 BCE).[162] This seems to be the best fit historically, since the restoration of "[Jo]ram, son of [Ahab] king of Israel" in lines 7b–8a seems virtually certain (see below). Other additions to our knowledge have come from the publication of the short "booty inscriptions" of Hazael (Röllig 1988; Bron and Lemaire 1989; Eph'al and Naveh 1989), as well as the publication of a stela fragment from Tell Afis that appears to contain the name of Hazael (Amadasi Guzzo 2005; 2009, 336–41; Younger 2007c, 139). Finally, recent excavations at Tell eṣ-Ṣāfī (Gath) seem to supply evidence of Hazael's activity there (Maeir and Ehrlich 2001; Ehrlich 2002),[163] to which now can be added other evidence from additional sites.

All of these discoveries and publications have reenergized the study of this Aramean king of Damascus.[164] But they have also introduced a number of interpretive problems (see Stith 2008). In particular, due to its fragmentary nature, the Tel Dan Inscription has presented a number of challenges to epigraphists and historians. But Hazael's booty inscriptions also present some difficulties that interpreters have not always addressed.

#### 9.3.5.1 Hazael's Usurpation and the Initial Events of his Reign

The discovery of the Tel Dan inscription has resulted in a plethora of new proposed reconstructions for Hazael's rise to the throne in Damascus.[165] In order to facilitate this discussion, the text and translation of the Tel Dan

---

161. Most scholars accept the placement of the fragments by the *editio princeps* (Biran and Naveh 1995) with perhaps the slight modification proposed by Schniedewind 1996. For a very different reconstruction of the fragments, see Athas 2003. See now Hasegawa 2012, 35–38.

162. For a summary of the discussion, see Hagelia 2009, 32–43.

163. Also important are the full-length monograph devoted to the study of Shalmaneser's inscriptions, as well as Peter Hulin's hand copies of some of Shalmaneser's texts including that of a broken statue from Nimrud that contains a passage preserving information about Shalmaneser's 838 BCE campaign against Hazael (see Yamada 2000a, 2000b).

164. For a more comprehensive study of all the issues concerning Hazael, see the still very useful article by Lemaire (1991a), although the Tel Dan material was, of course, unknown to him at the time.

165. The following discussion is based in part on Younger 2005, 245–57.

inscription is presented here.[166] On account of its fragmentary nature,[167] a number of important textual and interpretive matters have been included in the notes.

Tel Dan Inscription (see fig. 9.5)

[ ]
(1)[ *ʾ*]*mr* . *ʿ*[ ]
*wgz*⸢*r*⸣ [ ]
(2)[ *ʾ*]⸢*l*⸣ . *ʾby* .
*ys*⸢*q*⸣ [. *ʿlwh* . *bh*]⸢*t*⸣*lḥmh* . *bʾ*⸢*b*⸣[ ]
(3)*wyškb* . *ʾby* .
*yhk* . *ʾl* [. *ʾbhw*]*h* .

[*Some lines are missing at the beginning*]
(1)[ s]aid [ ]
and cut [ [168] ]
(2)[ [169] ]⸢*ʾl*⸣ my father;

166. It should be noted that there are other proposed arrangements of the inscription's fragments (Galil 2001; Athas 2003, 178–89), though these have not been accepted. For further discussion, see Hafþórsson 2006, 49–65; Ghantous 2013, 43.

167. The fragmentary nature of the inscription means that the need for caution is essential. Irvine (2001) and Na'aman (1999b, 10–11) argue for the historical reliability of the inscription's report over against the pro-Jehu account in 2 Kgs 9. Hasegawa (2012, 43–46) argues similarly. Thus a fragmentary and very difficult text to interpret can be declared historically more reliable than the biblical text. Both texts (Tel Dan and the 2 Kgs 9) are ideological and require close critical reading. One text should not a priori be deemed historically more reliable than the other.

168. While the word *wgz*⸢*r*⸣ is clear and a restoration based on the combination *gzr ʿdy*, "to make a treaty" (Biran and Naveh 1995, 13) is possible (see also Kottsieper 1998, 478–79; Na'aman 2000, 97), it is unwise to speculate too much on this.

169. Speculative restorations have been suggested for the beginning of the line. Puech (1994, 221) restores [*wb*]*r*[.]*hdd* . *ʾby* "mais Ba]r Hadad, mon père." Kottsieper (1998, 477–80) restores [*lb*⸢*r*⸣*hd*⸢*d*⸣ ] "[mit] meinem Vater [Bar-hadad]." *KAI* (310:2) also similarly reads: [*b*]⸢*r*⸣[*h*]⸢*dd*⸣. Schniedewind and Zuckerman (2001, 88–91) have suggested reading line 2 of the Tel Dan inscription: [*b*]⸢*rqʾl*⸣ . *ʾby* "[Ba]⸢raq'el⸣, my father." If their restoration is correct, then this Baraq-El would have been Hazael's father who was king of Damascus before him and whose land the king of Israel invaded (see lines 3–4: *wyʿl* . *mlky*[*ś*](4)*rʾl* . *qdm* . *bʾrq* . *ʾby* "And the king of I[s]rael formerly invaded the land of my father"). But the *resh* and the *qoph* are very doubtful, as also the *beth*. In fact, there is no compelling reason that there must be a proper name preceding *ʾby*. Their speculation, based on this entirely restored name Baraq-El, that there was some kind of religious rivalry and tension within Aram-Damascus between the adherents of El versus the adherents of Hadad makes little sense in that the son of Hazael (an adherent to the "El-clan") is desig-

he went up[170] [against him[171] when] he fought at A⸢b⸣[el?].[172]
(3)And my father lay down;
he went to his [fathe]rs.

*wyʿl . mlky*[*ś*](4)*rʾl . qdm . bʾrq . ʾby* [.]
[*w*]*yhmlk . hdd . ʾ*[*yty*] (5)*ʾnh .*
*wyhk . hdd . qdmy* [.]
[*w*]*ʾpq . mn . šb*⸢*ʿ*⸣[ ](6)*y . mlky .*
*wʾqtl .* ⸢*ml*⸣[*kn . šb*]⸢*ʿn*⸣ *. ʾsry . ʾ*[*lpy .r*](7)*kb . wʾlpy . prš .*

---

nated by a Hadad theophoric in the appellation "Bar-Hadad." In the Zakkur Inscription line 4, he is called Bar-Hadad, son of Hazael, king of Aram."

All of these, however, are, in my opinion, highly doubtful. Working back from the *ʾby*, it is difficult, but it seems possible to make out a *lamed*. I do not see a *dalet* (so Kottsieper 1998 and *KAI* 310 are ruled out). Next, I cannot really make out the *aleph*, though it could be there. Again a *dalet* does not appear to be the reading. Next, *qoph* is not impossible; but I do not think *resh* is out of the question (or even a *he*). The last two possible letters are not preserved. *There is simply not enough here to speculate a reading with any confidence*. While it is possible that a proper name was found before *ʾby*, it does not have to be a proper name. In fact, the preposition *ʾl* is a possibility—the construction *ʾl* + *ʾb* occurs twenty-five times in the Hebrew Bible.

170. Is *ʾby* the subject of the verb *ysq* or does *ysq* begin a new sentence? Not one *yqtl* verbal form in the inscription has the subject preceding it. When the subject is expressed, it follows the *yqtl* form. The other two times that *ʾby* occurs in the inscription, it is the last word in the sentence. Thus it seems likely that *ysq* begins a new sentence, though the antecedent of the third masculine singular verb could be [*xxxxx*] *ʾby*, "[PN], my father."

171. Scholars have generally assumed that the enemy in line 2 is a king of Israel (who fought with Hazael's "father"). Irvine (2005, 344–46) proposes that the enemy of Hadad-ezer is Shalmaneser III and that the line refers to a battle at Abel (specifically, "Abila of Lysanius") located "on the ancient road leading from the southern end of the Beqaʿ Valley through the Anti-Lebanon range to Damascus. It was probably here or nearby that Hazael stationed his forces in 841 BCE to check the advance of the Assyrian army. The location would make equally good strategic sense for the last battle of Hadad-ezer against Shalmaneser four years earlier" (346). Thus the fragmentary Tell Dan Inscription in line 2 refers to an attack by Shalmaneser III against Hadad-ezer during the former's 845 campaign, and that this was the last battle fought by Hadad-ezer.

This interpretation is not possible. In the 845 campaign, as in the earlier 853, 849, and 848 campaigns, Shalmaneser faced the western coalition headed by Hadad-ezer and Irḫulēni. In all of these instances, the coalition was able to prevent Shalmaneser from accomplishing his strategic goals. Hamath, in fact, was the center of the struggle. Most scholars believe after the death of Hadad-ezer the usurpation of Hazael brought about the disintegration of the coalition. And it wasn't until the coalition dissolved that Hamath permitted Assyrian troops through its territory during Shalmaneser III's attack on Hazael of Damascus in 841.

172. See Schniedewind 1996, 79. There are two possibilities: (1) reading a *bet* would perhaps yield: *ʾbl* "Abel (Beth-Maakah)" or *bʾ*⸢*b*⸣[*y*] (Kottsieper 1998, 477); or (2) a *pe*

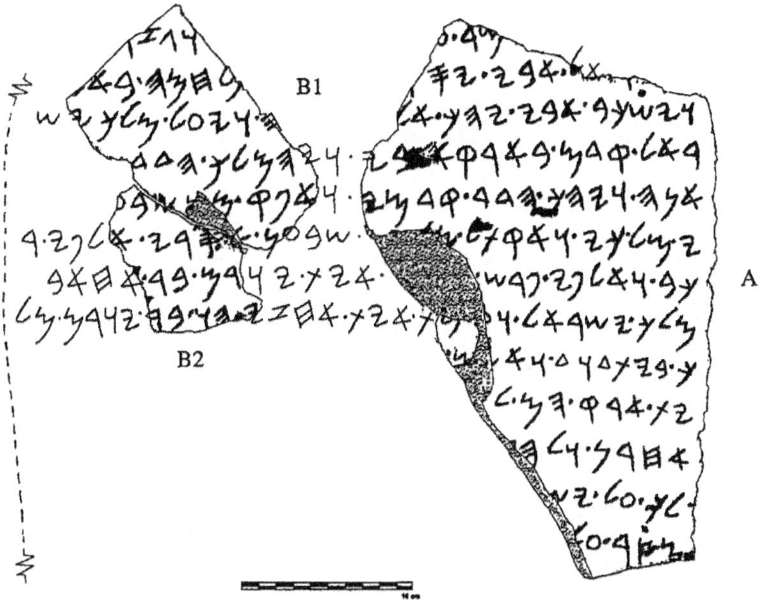


Fig. 9.5. The Tel Dan Stela (courtesy of William Schniedewind)

*[qtlt*[173] *. ʾyt . yw]rm . br . [ʾḥʾb]* (8)*mlk . yśrʾl .*
w⌜*qtl*⌝[*t . ʾḥz*]*yhw . br* [*ywrm*]
[*wʾhp*](9)*k . bytdwd .*

---

yielding: *ʾpq* "Aphek." The *aleph* is clear. The next letter only has the curved tail at the bottom which could be a *bet* or a *pe*. However, the *pe* in line 5 has a long tail and this does not. All the *pe*s in the inscription go significantly lower on the lines than the *bet*s. Thus probably a *bet*. Stith (2008, 43 n. 31) states: "Presumably Abel-Beth-Maacah (see Dever 1986 for background on this site). Yamada (2000a, 315 n. 21) suggests reading *ʾpk* (Aphek) in place of *ʾbl* (Abel), but this reading is explicitly an effort to preserve the essential historicity and attribution to Ahab of the battle account in 1 Kings 20."

173. Schniedewind 1996, 77 restores: [*wqtlt*]; Biran and Naveh 1995 restore: [*qtlt ʾyt yhw*]*rm*; but there doesn't appear to be enough room. Dion (1999, 148) restores: [*wʾky*]. Since the next verbal form in line 8 is a *waw* plus suffix conjugation (*wqtl*), it is most likely that the form in line 7 is a simple suffix conjugation form (*qtl*). In the Hebrew Bible, in a narrative context, a *waw* plus prefix conjugation (*wyqtl*) followed by a *waw* plus suffix conjugation (*wqtl*) only occurs in 1 Sam 1:4 where the first verbal form is in a subordinate clause to the second verbal form. Thus a suffix conjugation (*qtl*) followed by a *waw* plus suffix conjugation (*wqtl*) used to coordinate the actions is most likely.

Now the king of I[s]⁽⁴⁾rael earlier[174] invaded the land of my "father";
[but] Hadad made me, ⁽⁵⁾myself, ⁽⁴⁾king.
⁽⁵⁾And Hadad went before me;
[and] I departed from seven [ [175] ] ⁽⁶⁾of my kingdom/kings.
And I killed {"two" *based on context*} [power]ful ki[ng]s,[176] who harnessed thou[sands of ch]ari⁽⁷⁾ots and thousands of horsemen;

---

174. CAL takes *qdm* as "an adj. possibly adv." Lemaire argues that the word *qdm* is not a temporal adverb "formerly, previously," but is a local adverb specifying the verb *wyʿl* (Lemaire 1994, 88; 1998, 5; see also Na'aman 1995b, 389). Hence, the text is referring to the attack (penetration) of the kingdom of Damascus at the precise time of the king's death (Lemaire 1998, 5). I really do not see any clear usage of *qdm* in *DNWSI* that corresponds to this. Na'aman (2000, 97) argues similarly and suggests that the sentence should be translated something like: "and the king of Israel invaded, advancing in my father's land." The report supposedly explains that Israel's aggression began during Hadad-ezer's reign (line 2) and subsequently resumed between the king's death and Hazael's enthronement (lines 3b–4a). Irvine (2005, 343–44) argues against this understanding.

Naveh (1999, 119–20) notes that the idiom *ʿll b-* occurs in the Aramaic Elephantine papyri with the meaning of "to enter by force. It also occurs in Jewish Aramaic, Syriac, and Mandaic with the meaning "to penetrate, invade." (See also *DNWSI*, 857 s.v. *ʿll*, number 3 "indicating forced entry"). *ʿll b-* occurs in a Neo-Babylonian decree and in the Tel Dan inscription with this meaning. Naveh translates lines 3–4: *wyʿl . mlky*[*ś*]⁽⁴⁾*rʾl . qdm . bʾrq . ʾby*, "And formerly the king of Israel invaded the land of my father."

The Tell Fakhariya stela (line 15) reads: *dmwtʾ . zʾt . ʿbd . ʾl . zy . qdm . hwtr*, "He made this likeness; he made it better than the earlier (one)." Kaufman (1982, 168) noted that this is "a direct calque of the usual Assyrian formula *eli ša maḫri ušātir*. (But note that our Akkadian text omits the *ša*!)." Thus *qdm* = *maḫrû*, an adjective, "first, former, earlier, previous, older." There is no way that *qdm* here is spatial; it is clearly temporal. I believe that this is the usage in the Tel Dan Inscription.

Knapp (2012, 232, 399 n. 795; 2014) and Kottsieper (2007, 113–14) interpret *qdm* as a geographic entity (Qedem) located in northern Transjordan, in the Ḥauran region. This is intriguing and deserves consideration. It seems, however, that there are difficulties with this suggestion. First, given the idiom *ʿll* + *b*, one would have expected the *b* to be attached to *qdm*; and that *ʾrq* would not have the *b* so that *ʾrq ʾby* might be in apposition to *bqdm*. Kottsieper (2007, 113 n. 36) argues that *ʿll* can occur with the nuance of "invade" without the preposition *b*. But the *b* is here attached to *ʾrq*. Second, and importantly, there is no clear evidence that the land of Qedem existed in the first millennium (all the evidence outside of the Bible comes from the second millennium). Third, the name for the region is Ḫaurānu (Bagg 2007, 101), not Qedem; and the name of the Assyrian province was Qarnīna. Fourth, assuming that it did exist, if Israel's possession of northern Gilead is contested (Ramoth-Gilead?), how can the king of Israel invade Qedem? Or is Qedem located further to the east of the Ḥauran? If so, why would the king of Israel invade this area (Qedem)? This makes little military sense.

175. There is room for three or four letters + *y* at the end of a word before *mlky* in line 6. Restoring Yamada 1995, 612 n. 8.

176. Biran and Naveh (1995, 16) propose reading *ml*[*kn . šb*]*ʿn*; Dion (1999, 148) proposes *ml*[*kn . rbrb*]*n*; Lemaire 1998, 8 suggests the reading: *wʾqtl . ml*[*k*]*n* [*. tq*]*pn*, "and I

and [I killed Jo]ram, son of [Ahab], (8)king of Israel.
And [I] killed [Ahaz]yahu, son of [Joram];[177]
[and I overthr](9)ew[178] Bēt-David (Judah).

*w'*[*ś*]⌜*m*⌝ . [ ]
[']⁽¹⁰⁾*yt* . *'rq* . *hm* . *l*[ ]
(11)*'ḥrn* . *wlh* [ ]
[*wyhw'* . *br* . *nmšy* . *m*](12)*lk* . *'l* . *yś*[*r'l* ] [ ]
[*w'śm* .](13)*m*⌜*ṣ*⌝*r* . *'l* . [ ]

And I set [ ]
(10)their land [ ]
(11)another and [ ]
[*and Jehu, son of Nimshi*] (12)ruled over Is[rael ]
[And I] (13)besieged [ ]

The Assyrian and biblical texts declare that Hazael was a usurper. But if Hazael was a usurper on the throne of Damascus, and if he was the author of the Tel Dan stela, why does he talk about his "father" at the beginning of the inscription (*'by* is used three times in lines 2, 3, 4)? Dion (1999, 153–54) argues:

> It is important to realize, in this matter, that our previous sources about the accession of Hazael were not all that clear. In most of the Assyrian documents that usher him onto the historical scene, including the most detailed of those [Calah Bulls; RIMA 3:42–48, A.0.102.8, lines 1′–27′], his power in Damascus is simply taken for granted, without any hint at his being a usurper. Only one text [Assur Basalt Statue; RIMA 3:118, A.0.102.40, i.25–ii.6], always quoted, calls Hazael a "son of a nobody," and even this text falls short of saying explicitly that he killed or overthrew his predecessor, the soul of the Qarqar alliance.
>
> On the biblical side, most scholars believe that 2 Kgs 8:7–15 tells how Hazael murdered his predecessor by smothering him with a pillow, during a visit of the prophet Elisha; but serious doubt has been cast on this interpretation (Lemaire 1991a, 95–96). Even if one does not follow Lemaire, it remains that the evidence branding Hazael as a usurper is not very convinc-

killed two [power]ful kin[gs]," restoring [*tq*]*pn* and understanding it as a dual. The left top of an *ayin* or a *pe* appears to be discernible on Fragment B1. See below.

177. Dion (1999, 148) reads: *wqtl* [*qtlh* . *'bdh* .] *yhw* . *br* [*nmšy* .]; Schniedewind (1996, 77) reads: *wqtl*[*t* . *'yt* . *'ḥz*]*yhw* . *br* [. *ywrm* . *ml*](9)*k* . *bytdwd*.

178. See discussion below.

> ing, all the more so since it originated in the enemy camp. It may well have developed somewhat belatedly, and for propaganda purposes.

Methodologically, this approach is problematic since it takes the fragmentary and difficult passage in the Tel Dan Stela, which well may be more propagandistic than the other sources, and uses that passage to evaluate passages from two different sources that are much clearer. In the case of the Assyrian source, the Assur Basalt Statue states:

> Hadad-ezer (Adad-idri) passed away. Hazael, son of a nobody (DUMU *la ma-ma-na*), took the throne. He mustered his numerous troops; (and) he moved against me to do war and battle. I fought with him. I decisively defeated him. I took away from him his walled camp. In order to save his life he ran away. I pursued (him) as far as Damascus, his royal city. I cut down his orchards.[179]

"Son of a nobody" (*mār lā mammāna*) is a term referring to a usurper or upstart.[180] This strongly suggests that Hazael was not the first in line of succession and had seized the throne in an unusual manner (Yamada 2000a, 189; Stith 2008, 51–53). The expression, common in historical documents from Assyria and Babylonia, indicates someone whose father was not a legal member of the major branch of the contemporary royal family, and expresses a value judgment with negative connotations, that is, "usurper" or "an upstart."[181]

The phrase is used in the Assyrian King List with this nuance. For example, the section devoted to describing the reign of Aššur-dugul states (Grayson 1980–83, 106, §14):

> m*Aš-šur-du-gul* DUMU(*mār*) *la ma-ma-na la* EN(*bēl*) GIŠ. GU.ZA(*kussê*) 6 MU.MEŠ LUGAL(*šarru*)-*ta* DÙ-*uš*(*īpuš*)

> Aššur-dugul, the son of a nobody, not suitable to the throne,[182] ruled for six years.

179. RIMA 3:118, A.0.102.40, i.25–ii.6.

180. Niehr (2011, 340) points out that the fact that Hazael, in his own inscriptions, does not claim a clear affiliation is significant. Combined with the Assyrian designation (*mār lā mammāna*), this helps demonstrate that Hazael was a usurper on the throne of Damascus and did not belong to the ruling house.

181. For an earlier list of the attestations of the term, see Seux 1980–83, 150–52.

182. Following Yamada 1994, 26 n. 47. He states: "This phrase clearly expresses a value judgement with negative connotations, as seen in a sentence well attested in omen texts: *lā bēl kussî kussâ iṣabbat* 'one who is not suitable to the throne will seize the throne.'"

A propagandistic motive in the Assur Basalt Statue is possible. However, the fact that the passage is found in the context of a very concise summary of Shalmaneser III's western campaigns (lines i.10b–ii.6) and is otherwise a parallel to the other Hazael passages in Shalmaneser's inscriptions seems to argue against a specific propagandistic motive here. In line 25, the text, in a matter-of-fact fashion, records the death of Hadad-ezer (Adad-idri) ($^{md}$IŠKUR-*id-ri* KUR-*šú e-mi-id*[183]) who had been the subject of lines 14–24. It then notes that Hazael seized the throne and that Shalmaneser attacked him. There is no apparent reason to doubt the general veracity of the Assyrian statement that Hazael was the "son of a nobody," that is, a usurper.[184] Clearly, Shalmaneser did not refer to Jehu with this designation "son of a nobody," even though Jehu too was a usurper (Na'aman 1998, 237; Stith 2008, 53). But Jehu was Shalmaneser III's southernmost loyal vassal (according to the Black Obelisk, register 2).

There are actually two biblical texts that are relevant to Hazael's accession: 1 Kgs 19:15–17 and 2 Kgs 8:7–15. 1 Kgs 19:15–17 records Yahweh's command to Elijah to anoint Hazael and Jehu. Although some scholars have argued for 1 Kgs 19 being a pre-Deuteronomistic passage (Schniedewind 1996, 84) and others that it is post-Deuteronomistic (McKenzie 1991, 81–87), the text appears to reflect a tradition that considered the Hazael and Jehu usurpations as parts of one overarching whole (Knapp 2012, 218). In the case of 2 Kgs 8:7–15, even though it is part of a prophetic tradition concerning the work of Elisha, many critics and commentators have accepted that this passage also preserves a tradition that Hazael usurped the throne of Damascus (Noth 1960, 248). It is not necessary to accept all the detail of the story about the murder in order to recognize a base tradition in this regard.[185]

Thus, it is hermeneutically and historiographically sounder to reconstruct the historical events on the clear claims preserved in multiple different sources from different parts of the ancient Near East than to reconstruct the historical events on the basis of an interpretation of a fragmentary inscription

183. KUR-*šú e-mi-id* / *šadāšu ēmid* "he disappeared forever," lit. "he reached his mountain." The phrase is simply a euphemism for "to die" and, in and of itself, does not specific whether the death was due to natural or unnatural causes. See *CAD* 4:138–47, esp. 140, 1.d.3′.

184. The Assyrian ideology sought to portray enemy kings in a negative light. When reality could be used in service of this ideology, all the better.

185. Knapp (2012, 229) argues: "But even if one assumes that the Elisha cycle is a late critique and remains skeptical of the historical claims within these stories (cf. Van Seters 1983, 303–6), the mention of an assassination here deserves to be taken seriously. The correspondence of Hazael's usurpation in the Hebrew Bible with the contemporary Assyrian account suggests that the writer of the prophetic account did not fabricate the story out of whole cloth, but at worst molded the story according to a known tradition."

(an interpretation that may or may not be correct), and then make the multiple sources fit that reconstruction.

At the heart of the matter is the issue of how the Tel Dan Inscription is using *ʾby*.[186] The term *ʾby* may be used figuratively (1) or literally (2). If it is used literally, there are three possibilities: (2a) it could refer to Hadad-ezer himself; or (2b1) it could refer to a different father who was part of the royal family; or (2b2) it could refer to a different father who was not part of the royal family, but leader of another tribe. Each of these will be discussed in more detail.

**(1)** If the term *ʾby* is not literal but figurative, then Hazael is not referring to his literal "father," but to the previous ruler (most likely Hadad-ezer) as "father" in order to establish his legitimacy. Lemaire, who accepts that Hazael was a usurper, "the son of a nobody," suggests that in calling Hadad-ezer/Adad-idri his father Hazael was following an ancient Near Eastern historiographic tradition: kings of a new dynasty might refer to the previous king as "father." He cites for examples Tiglath-pileser III and David, who once calls Saul *ʾābî* "my father" (1 Sam 24:11 [Eng 12]). Thus Lemaire (1998, 6) concludes:

> one should not be surprised that Hazael, whose father is not known, could call Hadad-ezer: 'my father.' It was a traditional way to present oneself as a legitimate successor.

But there are some difficulties with Lemaire's examples. In the case of David, Saul is not dead and David is attempting to convince Saul that he is not a usurper and is, in fact, a member of Saul's family (Saul is his actual father-in-law). In the case of Tiglath-pileser III, matters are complicated by the Assyrian King List, which attributes Tiglath-pileser's filiation to his immediate predecessor Aššur-nērārī V,[187] while on two inscribed enameled bricks, Tiglath-pileser III declares that he is the son of Adad-nērārī III.[188] The filiation in the Assyrian King List is most likely wrong. As Yamada (1994, 34 n. 78) has rightly observed this incorrect filiation is not the result of a lack of information (since it is highly unlikely that the editor would not have accu-

---

186. See also Stith's (2008, 54–61) discussion.

187. Grayson's edition reads: [$^{m\ g}$]$^{iš}$*Tukul-ti-apil-É-šár-ra mār* $^{m}$*Aš-šúr-nērārī* 18 MU.MEŠ *šarru*$_2$*-ta īpuš*$^{uš}$ "Tiglath-pileser (III) son of Aššur-nērārī (V) ruled for 18 years." See Grayson 1980–83, 115; Millard 1997, 465.

188. Tadmor 1994, 212–13; L. Messerschmidt, KAH I 21: Assur 918 and 1559. Tadmor's transliteration reads: $^{(1)}$ *ekal* $^{m}$*Tukul-ti-apil-*É*-šár-ra* $^{(2)}$ *šar*$_4$ *māt Aš-šur apil* $^{m}$*Adad*(x)*-nērārī* (ÉRIN.TÁḪ) *šar*$_4$ *māt Aššur* $^{(3)}$ *ša ki-gal-li ša bīt Aš-šur*, "Palace of Tiglath-pileser (III), king of Assyria, son of Adad-nērārī (III), king of Assyria, from the platform of the temple of Aššur."

rate information for the next to last entry in the king list, who reigned not all that long before this edition [the SDAS list] was written); but rather is probably due to a miscopying of the original on account of the graphic similarity between the two royal names, Adad-nērārī and Aššur-nērārī. Yamada notes: "When the right half of the IM sign is ignored, $^{d}$IM = *Adad* is similar to *Aš-šur* and identical to AN.ŠÁR, the common Sargonid spelling of *Aššur* (the SDAS list is a product of the Sargonid period)" (Yamada 1994, 34 n. 78) Therefore it is very likely that the scribe miscopied the original $^{d}$IM-*nērārī* as *Aš-šur-nērārī*.

Tiglath-pileser III's claim on the enameled bricks to being the son of Adad-nērārī III, could, of course, be taken literally. As Tadmor (1994, 212–13) points out, Adad-nērārī III was young when he ascended the throne in 811, and he died in 783 after a twenty-eight year reign. If Tiglath-pileser was about fifty when he ascended the throne in 745, then he could have been born around the turn of the century. On the other hand, it is quite possible that he was Adad-nērārī III's grandson.

However, Tiglath-pileser III's filiation is curiously not indicated in his other inscriptions. Moreover, he substituted the typical royal parentage formula (i.e., "king X, son of king Y, grandson of king Z") with the phrase *pirʾi Bal-til*(BALA.TIL)$^{ki}$ "precious scion of Baltil," an apparent reference to the oldest part of the city of Assur. Tadmor (1994, 41) argues that "by tracing his descent to the seat of the ancient dynasty, Tiglath-pileser, who obviously was not in the direct line of succession, emphasizes his claim to the throne." Consequently, many scholars believe that Tiglath-pileser III deposed his predecessor Aššur-nērārī V in the rebellion of 746 BCE and set himself on the throne (745 BCE).[189]

Hence, while complicated, the case of Tiglath-pileser III supports Lemaire's contention regarding the use of the term *ʾby* "my father" in the Tel Dan stela.

**(2a)** This interpretation sees *ʾby* as literal: Hazael was a son of the previous king (Hadad-ezer), but he was not the first in line for succession, perhaps a younger brother or illegitmate half-brother. Possibly the legitimate heir was sickly and this provided the basis for the 2 Kgs 8 tradition. Pitard (1987, 133) suggested that the Ben-Hadad (Bar-Hadad) of 2 Kgs 8 may have been a son of Hadad-ezer whom Hazael murdered.[190] However, this remains as

189. For example, Tadmor 1981, 25–30. See the Eponym Chronicle for years 746–745 (Millard 1994, 43, 59).

190. Following the earlier suggestion of Jepsen 1941–44, 158–59. While some scholars have argued that the name "Ben-Hadad" has been added to the story in 2 Kgs 8:7–15 (e.g., Lipiński 2000a, 373; 1969, 172–73; Noth 1960, 245 n. 1), Pitard (1987, 134) emphasizes that this is not necessarily correct, since the name "Ben-Hadad" may have originally

speculative as when it was first proposed even with the Tel Dan Inscription's discovery.[191] Nevertheless, it is possible to understand Hazael as a minor son of Hadad-ezer who assassinated his father and eliminated his rival siblings.[192]

**(2b1)** This view sees *'by* as literal, being a reference to Hazael's father who was not Hadad-ezer, but belonged to a subsidiary royal branch (Yamada 2000a, 312; Na'aman 2002, 207). In this view, Hazael was the assassin of the legitimate heir, but he could refer to himself as a true son in "a broad sense" (Yamada 2000a, 312).

**(2b2)** The term *'by* is used literally as a reference to Hazael's actual father who was not a member of the dynasty of Hadad-ezer of Aram-Damascus, but was the leader of an Aramean tribe during the time of Hadad-ezer (Suriano 2007, 165); Hazael was the son of an important Aramean sheikh (Niehr 2011, 341; Sasson 1996). Ghantous (2013, 51, 60, 111, 136) has suggested that Hazael was the son of the king of the Aramean kingdom of Bēt-Reḥob who succeeded his father on the throne of that kingdom and then was successful in becoming king of Aram-Damascus by uniting the two kingdoms to create a greater Aramean kingdom of Damascus.[193]

To a certain extent, each of these options is possible. At this point, pivotal to the understanding of the use of *'by* in the Tel Dan Stela is a recognition of the inscription's use of the genre of apology (cogently argued by Suriano 2007 and Knapp 2012). It is manifest that Hazael was in all respects not the expected successor. Therefore, the repeated references to "my father," whether literal or not, clearly result from a need to convince the audience that his kingship is legitimate.

Of course, the Tel Dan inscription may be using the term *'by* figuratively as suggested by Lemaire; and at the same time, the actual literal father of Hazael may have been an Aramean tribal leader. The only thing that is actu-

---

appeared in the story and that it was partially responsible for the confusion that led to the insertion of the later Ben-Hadad stores in their present context. In my opinion, both options manifest methodological weakness having to rely on the historian's *intuition* in order to discern "additions" to various texts and to speculate about them, when there is no actual text-critical evidence in any of these passages that relates to this question.

191. It also appears to be contradicted by Shalmaneser III's text that has a succession of Hadad-ezer (Adad-idri) to Hazael, without a Bar-Hadad.

192. In other words, similar to what Esarhaddon's brothers apparent intentions were in the murder of Sennacherib, though thwarted by Esarhaddon.

193. This is too speculative, in my opinion. Ghantous bases this on Na'aman's (1995a, 386) understanding of Shalmaneser III's Kurkh Monolith in ii.95: ᵐ*ba-'a-sa* DUMU *ru-ḫu-bi* KUR *a-ma-na-a-a* "Ba'asa of Beth-Rehob and of Mount Amana (the Ammanite)." This is a doubtful interpretation. But Ghantous then couples it with his assumption that Hazael is the son of this Ba'asa, for which there is no actual evidence.

ally known—and this is from 2 Kgs 8—is that Hazael was in the service of the previous king (named Ben-Hadad according to the biblical narrative). On the other hand, the fact that Aram-Damascus will be designated in the Assyrian inscriptions after the death of Hazael as Bīt-Ḫaza'ili may well indicate that they considered Damascus to be a entity based on a tribal system (see discussion above and chapter 2). If correct, Suriano's remarks (2007, 174) are very germane:

> The fluidity of seminomadic tribal elements within a patrimonial society fits well with the aggressive and mobile character of Hazael, who may have conquered various tribal groups before he eventually seized control of Aram-Damascus.

So Hazael was in the service of the previous king, but being from another tribal entity within the Damascene tribal network, he seized upon his opportunity.

Some scholars believe that there is further evidence of the illegitimacy of Hazael's accession within the Tel Dan inscription itself. In 1995, Biran and Naveh (1995, 15) noted that the end of line 4 and the first word of line 5, [*w*] *yhmlk . hdd .* ʾ[*yty*] ⁽⁵⁾ʾ*nh* "[but] Hadad made me, myself, king," may hint that the succession between Hazael and his predecessor was not natural. Lemaire (1998, 6) reinforces this view arguing:

> Zakkur I, line 3, Panamuwa lines 6–7 and several biblical texts (1 Sam 8:22; 15:11–35; 1 Kgs 1:43; 12:1–20) show clearly that in ancient North-West Semitic historiography, the factitive of *mlk* was generally introduced when the succession was unusual and, somehow, problematic.

Naveh himself has published two articles (1999, 119–20; 2002, 240–41) asserting that in the Hebrew Bible, the *hiphil* is used "in those instances in which the king ascending the throne is not the legitimate heir or in which there is dissension concerning the throne" (2002, 241). He claims: "It is reasonable to assume that making somebody king (and anointing which was part of the ceremony) was not practiced when the king was the undisputed legitimate heir" (1999, 232*). "Whenever the legitimate heir ascends the throne, neither *mšḥ* nor *hmlk* is used in the biblical or epigraphic texts" (2002, 241).

While the Zakkur inscription certainly supports this assertion (using the *hapḥʿel* just like in the Tel Dan stela), the Panamuwa Inscription does not. Panamuwa is the legitimate heir being restored by the king of Assyria. While the *hapḥʿel* of *mlk* in the Tel Dan stela might indicate some irregularity in the accession, it does not prove that Hazael was illegitimate.[194] His status as a usurper comes from the Assyrian and biblical sources discussed above.[195]

If the Tel Dan Inscription manifests the rhetoric of an apology (Suriano 2007), then the use of the term *ʾby* must be an important element in a planned rhetorical strategy (Knapp 2012, 223–33). Therefore, it should be treated accordingly. It explains the rather odd way that Hazael narrated his succession in the Stela:

> (3)And my father lay down; he went to his [fathe]rs.
>
> Now the king of I[s](4)rael earlier invaded the land of my father; [but] Hadad made me, (5)myself, (4)king.

If Hazael had been the legitimate successor, one would have expected immediately following the statement about his father's death, a statement of his enthronement, just like one sees, for example, in the Mesha Stela and the Panamuwa Inscription. In other words, there is no natural succession here.[196] Instead, there are statements about the Israelite invasion and the emphatic attribution of the work of the god Hadad in making Hazael king. The parallel way in which the usurper, Zakkur, credited the god Baʿlšamayn with having made him king (*whmlkny . bʿlšm*[*yn . ʿl / b*](4)[*ḥ*]*z*⌜*r*⌝*k*)[197] demonstrates that Hazael's words are functioning apologetically. In this case, an assertion that there was a military crisis, and that in such a crisis, the chief deity of the nation himself raised Hazael to the throne, makes perfect sense.[198] Hazael forcefully claims that the god Hadad utilized a special divine election of him as king. Thus who can debate such a selection by divinity? Furthermore, Hazael asserts that the divine support is validated through his ensuing achievements in battle. Hazael relates that "Hadad went before me" (line 5)

---

194. The argument based on the usage of the *hiphil* in the Hebrew Bible would be more convincing if the *hiphil* were used in every instance where an usurpation takes place; but it isn't (e.g., Baasha, Athaliah, Shallum, Menahem, Pekah, etc.).

195. Perhaps better wording it, one might say that the *hiphil* of this verbal root occurs when there are extenuating circumstances. In the case of the Tel Dan Stela (*KAI* 310:4), it is the context that indicates the coup d'état. See Schniedewind 1996, 87 n. 89; Suriano 2007, 166–67; 2010, 88 n. 73.

196. Some might object based on the clauses in line 3, "And my father lay down; he went to his [fathe]rs," assuming that such wording automatically implies a natural death. However, this is not the case. See further discussion below.

197. *KAI* 202:3b–4a.

198. Dion 1999, 154. If this is sequential (the father dies, the invasion happens), the question should be asked: if one wanted to say "my predecessor died, and the king of Israel invaded the land of my predecessor …" how would you say it?

into war, and the justice of his cause is further highlighted by the contrast of his rise with the demises of Joram and Ahaziah.

The Tel Dan statements in line 3 (*wyškb . ʾby . yhk . ʾl* [. *ʾbhw*]*h*, "And my father lay down; he went to his [fathe]rs") closely resembles the so-called Deuteronomistic phrase "and he lay with his fathers" (וישכב עם־אבתיו). The biblical syntagm is commonly, but erroneously, understood to imply in all cases a peaceful death. Both V. Sasson (1995, 16–17) and Suriano (2010, 40–41; 2007, 165) have argued against the widely held, but poorly founded, idea.[199] The fact is 2 Kgs 14:20–22 notes that Amaziah "lay with his fathers" after being assassinated which refutes the theory.[200]

In the Hebrew Bible "the phrase relates to inheritance, specifically succession rights" (Suriano 2010, 42) and "signified dynastic integrity" (Suriano 2007, 165). The expression appears only in contexts where sons succeeded their fathers to the throne and therefore implies the integrity of the dynasty. It is used to bolster the successor's legitimacy; that a king lies with his fathers asserts that the king was not deposed and that he joined his forebears in the ancestral tomb. In royal genealogies and king lists, "various eponymous figures are collected into an aggregate whole that was used to buttress the lineage of a ruling house" (Suriano 2010, 49–50). Thus, Hazael's utilization of this phrase must be a deliberate rhetorical strategy (Knapp 2012, 230). Suriano (2007, 165) explicates:

> … how does this formulaic expression relate to Hazael? According to the Hebrew Bible and Assyrian sources, Hazael was a usurper, so it may seem odd that he would use terminology implying dynastic succession. The frequent references to his father in the inscription, however, show that Hazael's political legitimacy was a matter of perspective.

Hazael implies that the people need not concern themselves with any assassination that may or may not have happened; Aram has a king and the leadership is secure. The nature of this accusation lends itself perfectly to Hazael's response. Knapp (2012, 230) puts it succinctly:

> Barring a skillfully performed autopsy by an Aramean forensic team, an assassination like that described in 2 Kgs 8 would be undetectable. Nothing but rumor could link Hazael to such a murder by smothering, so whatever ambitious machinations one attributed to Hazael, there would be room for doubt—especially if Hadad-ezer were known to be ailing. By not even

199. See also Halpern and Vanderhooft 1991, 183–85, 230–32; Sasson 1995: 16–17; Galil 1996, 35 n. 4; Bin-Nun 1968.

200. For a full analysis of the biblical materials, see Suriano 2010, 32–50. With reference to Hazael, see Suriano 2007, 164–66; 2010, 71–72.

acknowledging the accusation and instead pointing to the positive aspects of his rule, Hazael would encourage the audience to ignore their suspicions and focus on the state's stability. This is a savvy rhetorical ploy and apparently an effective one. If the subjects feel secure and content with their lot, they are unlikely to go out of their way to stir up unrest.

### 9.3.5.2 The Events of 842–841 BCE Leading to Shalmaneser's Invasion

Since Hadad-ezer was still a participant in the coalition against Assyria that resisted Shalmaneser in 845, scholars have dated the usurpation of Hazael sometime between 844 and 842, usually tending toward 844/843.[201] It is reasonable to assume that a short period of consolidation of power took up Hazael's attention in 843–842.

Thus, it seems that it was in 842 that war broke out between Aram and Israel at Ramoth-Gilead (2 Kgs 8:28–29; 9:14–15a). Joram, king of Israel, was wounded and retired to Jezreel. It was in this context that Jehu assassinated Joram and Ahaziah, the king of Judah, on the same day (2 Kgs 9). With regard to the interconnections with these events, lines 7–9a of the Tell Dan Stela present a number of challenges to interpreters: first in terms of the reading and translation, and second in terms of its integration with 2 Kgs 9. The following table (table 9.2) lists some of the more important suggested restorations and translations.

Biran and Naveh (1995, 9) correctly observe: "The only king, either of Israel or Judah, whose name ends with *resh* and *mem* is Jehoram." In this light, the restoration *br* . [*'ḥ'b*], "son of [Ahab]" seems very likely. Schniedewind (1996, 80) points out that the Arameans would most likely spell the name as Joram (*ywrm*), according to the northern Hebrew orthography, without the *he* found in the Judahite dialect (*yhwrm*).[202]

The beginning of the sentence, however, is more difficult. As can be seen in the table, most scholars restore some form of the verb *qtl*, although there may be a problem with there being enough room for a form of this verb. As a reasonable alternative, Dion (1999, 148) has proposed restoring [*w'ky*]. Thus the restoration and translation of this sentence would be either: [*qtlt* . *'yt* . *yw*]*rm* . *br* . [*'ḥ'b*] [(8)]*mlk* . *yśr'l* "[I killed Jo]ram, son of [Ahab], king of Israel,"

201. E.g., Stith (2008, 41) states: "It seems most likely that Hazael took the Aramean throne in 844 (though 843 cannot be ruled out), and that the conflict at Ramoth-Gilead and Jehu's coup should be dated to 842." Ikeda (1999, 291) suggests 844. Lipiński (1979, 76) and Lemaire (1991, 97) suggest 843.

202. This is further supported by the analogy of spelling of the name of Joash/Jehoash (*yw'š*/*yhw'š*) in Neo-Assyrian without the *h* being represented: [m]*Iu-'a-su* in Adad-nērārī III's Tell al-Rimah Stela (RIMA 3:211, A.0.104.7, line 8).

Table 9.2. Proposed Restorations of the Tel Dan Inscription

| Scholar | Restoration and Translation |
|---|---|
| Biran and Naveh 1995, 12–13 | *[qtlt . ’yt . yhw]rm . br . [’ḥ’b] mlk . yśr’l .*<br>*wqtl[t . ’yt . ’ḥz]yhw . br [. yhwrm . ml]k . bytdwd*[a]<br><br>[I killed Jeho]ram son of [Ahab] king of Israel,<br>and [I] killed [Ahaz]iahu son of [Jehoram kin]g of the House of David |
| Schniedewind 1996, 77 | *[wqtlt . ’yt . yw]rm . br . ’[ḥ’b] mlk . yśr’l .*<br>*wqtl[t . ’yt . ’ḥz]yhw . br [. ywrm . ml]k . bytdwd*<br><br>[And I killed Jo]ram, son of A[hab,] king of Israel,<br>and [I] killed [Ahazi]yahu, son of [Joram, kin]g of the House of David |
| Lemaire 1998, 4 | *[qtlt . ’yt . yw]rm . br . [’ḥ’b] mlk . yśr’l .*<br>*wqtl[t . ’yt . ’ḥz]yhw . br [. ywrm . ml]k . bytdwd*<br><br>[I killed Jo]ram son of A[hab] king of Israel,<br>and I killed [Achaz]yahu son of [Joram, kin]g of the House of David |
| Kottsieper 1998, 478; see also 2007, 109 | *[w’qtl . ’yt . yw]rm . br . [’ḥ’b] mlk . yśr’l .*<br>*wqtl[t . ’yt . ’ḥz]yhw . br [. ywrm . ml]k . bytdwd*<br><br>[Dann I tötete ich Jo]ram, den Sohn [Ahabs], den König von Israel.<br>Und ich töte[te Ahas]jahu, den Sohn [Jorams, den Kön]ig vom Haus Davids. |
| Dion 1999, 148–49 | *[w’ky . ’yt . yw]rm . br . [’ḥ’b] mlk . yśr’l .*<br>*wqt?l[qtlh .‘bdh] . yhw . br [. nmšy .]*<br>*[wyh]k . bytdwd*<br><br>and [I struck Jo]ram, son of [Ahab,] king of Israel;<br>and [his servant] Jehu, son of [Nimshi], killed [him];<br>[and walk]ed away the House of David. |
| Millard 2000b, 162 and n. 10 | *[ ]rm . br .[ ] mlk . yśr’l .*<br>*wqtl[ ]yhw . br [. ]*<br>*[w’hp]k . bytdwd*<br><br>[ ]rm son of [ ] king of Israel<br>and kill[ed ]yahu son of [ ]<br>[I overthr]ew the house of David. |
| Rainey 2003 | *[wqtyl .yhw]rm . br . [’ḥ’b] mlk . yśr’l .*<br>*wqty[l .’ḥz]yhw . br [. yhwrm . ml]k . bytdwd*<br><br>[so that then was killed Jo]ram son of [Ahab] king of Israel,<br>and [was] killed [Ahazi]yahu son of [Joram kin]g of the House of David |

a. An elementary application of Ockham’s razor deduces that *bytdwd* is a simple metonymy put for the kingdom of Judah. See Couturier 2001; Dion 1997, 225–32; and chapter 2 above.

or [*w'ky . 'yt . yw*]*rm . br .* [*'ḥ'b*] ⁽⁸⁾*mlk . yśr'l* "[And I struck Jo]ram, son of [Ahab], king of Israel." The former seems preferable.[203]

Lines 8–9a present perhaps some of the greatest difficulties in the inscription. The first word appears to be *w*⌈*qtl*⌉[ ]. A common restoration has been: *w*⌈*qtl*⌉[*t . 'yt . 'ḥz*]*yhw . br* [*. yw'h'rm . ml*]⁽⁹⁾*k . bytdwd*, "and I killed Ahaziah, son of Je(ho)ram, king of Beth-David" (Biran and Naveh 1995, 12–13; Schniedewind 1996, 77; Lemaire 1998, 4; Kottsieper 1998, 478). While the restoration of the verbal form as a first person common singular makes logical sense in light of the clear reading of *w'qtl* in line 6, it is not, of course, certain. Rainey (2003) has suggested that the indeterminate third person plural *wqtl*[*w*] "[they] killed" may be the correct restoration.[204] This restoration is, of course, possible since the suffix to *wqtl* is unfortunately not preserved. However, the flow of the narrative in this part of the inscription would seem to necessitate a first person verbal form.

But there are two other problems with the common restoration as pointed out by Dion: (1) the spelling of Ahaziah: one would expect a northern spelling *'ḥzyw* without the *he*, as with Joram (*ywrm*) above; (2) there is a grammatical problem with *mlk bytdwd.* Only Millard and Dion have noted the grammatical problem with the restoration of [*ml*]*k bytdwd.* Millard (2000b, 166 n. 9) states:

> A restoration "[Jeho]ram son of [Ahab] king of Israel and killed [Ahaz]iah son of [Jehoram kin]g of Beth-David" is attractive historically (Kitchen 1997, 32–34), although 2 Kgs 9:14–28 names Jehu as the killer and the expression "king of the House of PN" has grammatical problems. Possibly Hadad was the subject here, for the first person ending of the verb is not preserved. The number of missing letters is impossible to calculate with certainty, for, even if only one is to be restored at the end of the third line (n. 2), there is no proof that the stele was symmetrical, or that the lines were of equal length.

Instead of reading [*ml*]*k bytdwd,* Millard (2000, 166 n. 10) suggests a restoration: [*w'hp*]*k*, "and I overthrew." He notes the usage in Sefire IC 19, 21 (*'hpk*) (see Fitzmyer 1995, 54) and 2 Sam 10:3 (*wlhpkh* "and to overthrow it

203. Since the next verbal form in line 8 is a *waw* plus suffix conjugation (*wqtl*), it is most likely that the form in line 7 is a suffix conjugation form (*qtl*). In the Hebrew Bible, in a narrative context, a *waw* plus prefix conjugation (*wyqtl*) followed by a *waw* plus suffix conjugation (*wqtl*) only occurs in 1 Sam 1:4 where the first verbal form is in a subordinate clause to the second verbal form. Thus a suffix conjugation (*qtl*) followed by a *waw* plus suffix conjugation (*wqtl*) used to coordinate the actions is most likely.

204. A second suggestion made by Rainey to read *wqtyl*, while syntactically possible, seems unlikely since there does not appear to be a *yod* after the *taw* and before the *lamed.*

[the city of Rabbath-Ammon]"). Dion (1999, 152) is more specific about the problem:

> In Old Aramaic as in Hebrew and other Northwest Semitic languages, *mlk* never is followed by "the house of So-and-so," and the rule is the same in the Assyrian inscriptions when they refer to smaller neighbours and vassals, in contrast, say to Ambaris, King of Tabal (Luckenbill 1927 §§24–25). In biblical Hebrew and in Ammonite inscriptions, *mlk bny ʿmn*, for instance, is very well documented; but one never encounters *mlk byt ʿmn*. In Aramaic, the normal pattern is represented by phrases like *mlk yśrʾl* in the Dan Stele, or *mlk ʾrpd* in the Sefîre inscriptions. The kingdom of Arpad could be called *byt gš* as the kingdom of Judah is called *bytdwd*; but one never finds *mlk byt gš*.

Dion (1999, 148) proposes the reading: *wqtl* [*qtlh* . *ʿbdh* .] *yhw* . *br* [*nmšy* .] [*wyh*]*k bytdwd*, "and [his servant] Jehu, son of [Nimshi], killed him; [and walked away] the House of David."

As seen in this restoration, Dion's solution to the spelling of Ahaziah is to suggest reading the name, not as Ahaziah, but as Jehu. But there are two problems with this. First, the name Jehu is consistently spelled *yhwʾ* in the Hebrew Bible. There is always an *aleph* at the end of the name; it is never spelled: *yhw*. Second, in the Neo-Assyrian spelling, it is important to note that the name of Jehu is consistently spelled ᵐ*Ia-ú-a* (Calah Bulls, Kurbaʾil Statue, and Black Obelisk).[205] Thus the final *aleph* is preserved in the Assyrian writing of the name. We could rightly expect this to be the case in the Aramaic spelling of the name too.

It is not impossible that the scribe of the Tel Dan Stela simply chose to use the southern spelling of *ʾḥzyhw*, if the reference is to the king of Judah. Also there is no attestation of spelling the name as *ʾḥzyw* in biblical or extra-biblical texts (whether in reference to the northern or southern kings who bore this name or anyone else). The attestations of the name in Neo-Assyrian evince the spelling *ʾḥzyhw*: ᵐ*aḫ-zi-iá-a-u* and ᵐ*aḫ-zi-i*[*a-a-u*].[206]

Concerning the grammatical problem with the restoration [*ml*]*k bytdwd*, there is one example of *mlk* before *byt* in the Hebrew Bible. Interestingly, it is found in a statement made by the counselors of Ben-Hadad of Aram-Damascus in 1 Kgs 20:31a:

205. RIMA 3:60, A.0.102.12, line 29; 3:149, A.0.102.88; and 3:48, A.0.102.8, 26″, respectively. See Brinkman and Schwemer 1999. The only exception is the Marble Slab, where it is spelled ᵐ*Ia-a-ú* due to scribal error (RIMA 3:54, A.0.102.10, iv.11).

206. See Selz 1998. In the Hebrew Bible, the name is most often spelled אֲחַזְיָהוּ and occasionally אֲחַזְיָה.

שָׁמַעְנוּ כִּי מַלְכֵי בֵּית יִשְׂרָאֵל כִּי־מַלְכֵי חֶסֶד הֵם

"we have heard that the kings of the house of Israel are merciful kings."

Although in this context *mlk* is a plural construct, there is no reason it could not be a singular. Thus there is a possibility that the inscription originally read *mlk bytdwd*, and that further evidence in support of this reading may come forth in the future. Such a restoration has great appeal because of the resultant parallel structure:

I killed A, son of B, king of Israel;
and I killed X, son of Y, king of Bēt-David (Judah).

Nevertheless, two facts are important to remember: (1) *mlk* is not the preserved reading (only a *kaph* is preserved), and (2) the evidence argues strongly that one does not normally find the construction *mlk byt X*. Hence one should be cautious in positing the restoration: [*ml*]*k bytdwd*. In light of these points, Millard's suggestion may be preferable: [*w'hp*]*k bytdwd*, "[and I overthr]ew Beth-David (Judah)." Such a restoration certainly fits the historical context since the death of Ahaziah of Judah threw that country into chaos with Athaliah seizing power.[207] Consequently, it seems best to read the two sentences: *w*⸢*qtl*⸣[*t* .*'yt* . *'ḥz*]*yhw* . *br* [*ywrm*] [*w'hp*][(9)]*k* . *bytdwd*, "And [I] ⸢killed⸣ [Ahaziah], the son of [Joram, and overthr]ew Bēt-David (Judah).

Since the author of the stela (Hazael) appears to claim "[and I killed Jo]ram, son of [Ahab], king of Israel …," there seems to be a contradiction to 2 Kings 9, which narrates Jehu's murder of both Joram of Israel and Ahaziah of Judah. A number of scholars have attempted to explain this by appealing to such claims by kings of the ancient Near East, in particular a passage in Shalmaneser III's inscriptions that describes the killing of a certain Giammu. Thus Lemaire (1998, 10–11) notes:

> One should note here, after B. Halpern and W. H. Schniedewind, that we have a very interesting parallel double claim in contemporary Assyrian royal inscriptions. In the Kurkh Monolith again, it is said that nobles, "with their own weapons," killed Giammu, their lord (on the Baliḫ), but in the Marmorplatte, about fifteen years later, Shalmaneser III claims to have killed Giammu himself. This parallel gives us another hint that Hazael is boasting here and that the Dan stela was probably not engraved immediately after 841 but several years later, at least late enough in Hazael's reign, when he controlled Israel, Judah and most of the Transeuphrates.

207. See also Ghantous 2013, 48.

But Scholars have not paid close enough attention to the cuneiform texts.[208] The following table (9.3) shows all the texts of Shalmaneser III that contain the Giammu episode and their precise wording concerning his death.

Table 9.3. Variants in the Account of Giammu's Death

| | **RIMA 3** | **Text** | **Translation** |
|---|---|---|---|
| Kurkh Monolith (853–852 BCE) | A.0.102.2, ii.79b–80a | *ina* GIŠ.TUKUL *ra-ma-ni-šú-nu* ᵐ*gi-am-mu* EN-*šú-nu i-du-ku* | "With their own weapons they killed Giammu, their lord." |
| Annals: Assur Clay Tablets (842 BCE) | A.0.102.6, ii.21b | ᵐ*gi-am-mu* EN URU-*šú-nu i-du-ku* | "They killed Giammu, the lord of their city." |
| Bulls from Kalḫu (841 BCE) | A.0.102.8, line 13b | ᵐ*gi-am-mu* E[N *ālīšunu idūkū*] | "[They killed] Giam-mu, [the lo]rd [of their city]." |
| Marble Slab (839 BCE) | A.0.102.10, ii.14b–15a | ᵐ*gi-am-mu* EN URU-*šú-nu* GAZ | "They killed Giammu, the lord of their city." |
| Black Obelisk (828–827 BCE) | A.0.102.14, line 55 | ᵐ*gi-am-mu* EN URU-*šú-nu* GAZ-*ku* | "They killed Giammu, the lord of their city." |
| Broken Kalḫu Stone Statue (828–827 BCE) | A.0.102.16, line 29a | ᵐ*gi-am-mu* EN URU-*šú-nu* GAZ-*ku* | "They killed Giammu, the lord of their city." |

Michel's edition of Shalmaneser's Marble Slab inscription reads:

> ᴵ*gi-am-mu* ⁽¹⁵⁾*bēl āli-šú-nu adūk*
> "Giammu ⁽¹⁵⁾ihren Stadtherrn tötete ich."[209]

However, Grayson's edition of this text reads:

> ᵐ*gi-am-mu* ⁽¹⁵⁾EN URU-*šú-nu* GAZ
> "They killed Giammu, their city ruler."[210]

208. At this point Na'aman's explanation (2000, 104) is unnecessary. He argues that the Giammu episode was an insignificant, marginal episode in Shalmaneser's inscriptions, while this dual killing in the Tel Dan inscription is central. Therefore, since the Tel Dan inscription is closer in time to the events, it is more reliable than the "prophetic narrative." "Hazael's contemporary inscription should be accorded primacy over the biblical prophetic narrative."

209. Michel 1954, 32–33, ii.14b–15a.

210. RIMA 3:52; A.0.102.10, ii.14b–15a.

Michel normalized the logogram GAZ as *adūk*, believing that the context demanded a first common singular verb form. Michel's edition is the one that Lemaire, Halpern and Schniedewind have used. But W. Schramm (1973, 77) noted in his study that GAZ in line ii.15 should be understood as *idūkū* on the basis of comparison with the Black Obelisk (line 55). To this, one can now add the text of the Broken Kalḫu Stone Statue (828–827 BCE).[211] The reading is clear in P. Hulin's copy published by Yamada (2000b, 77, line 29 of transcription):

> $^{(29)m}$*gi-am-mu* EN URU-*šú-nu* GAZ-*ku*
> "They killed Giammu, their city ruler."

Thus the Marble Slab's reading is not *adūk* "I killed" but *idūkū* "they killed." Therefore, this text from Shalmaneser III does not support the contention that Shalmaneser claims to have killed Giammu as well as stating that the citizens killed him.

This does not mean, however, that double claims are not found in ancient Near Eastern texts. Perhaps a better example can be seen in the claims of 2 Kgs 15:30 and the inscriptions of Tiglath-pileser III concerning the death of Pekah and the accession of Hoshea. Second Kings 15:30 states:

וַיִּקְשָׁר־קֶשֶׁר הוֹשֵׁעַ בֶּן־אֵלָה עַל־פֶּקַח בֶּן־רְמַלְיָהוּ וַיַּכֵּהוּ וַיְמִיתֵהוּ וַיִּמְלֹךְ תַּחְתָּיו

> Then Hoshea son of Elah made a conspiracy against Pekah son of Remaliah, attacked him, and killed him; he reigned in place of him.

Tiglath-pileser III states (Summary Inscription 4, lines 17′b–18′a) (Tadmor 1994, 141)[212]:

> $^{m}$*Pa-qa-ḫa* LUGAL(*šarru*)-*šú-nu* [...]-*du*-$x_1$-$x_2$-*ma*
> $^{m}$*A-ú-si-ʾi* $^{(18')}$ [*a-na* LUGAL(*šarru*)-*ti i*]-*na* UGU(*muḫḫi*)-*šú-nu áš-kun*
> [I/they killed] Pekah, their king, and
> I installed Hoshea [as king] over them.

The verb describing Pekah's fate is not fully preserved. The possible restorations include: [*i*]-*du*-[*ku-ma*], "they killed" or [*a*]-*du*-[*uk-ma*], "I killed" (Tadmor 1994, 141 n. 17′). But the first person singular verb *aškun* clearly indicates Tiglath-pileser's claim of involvement in the events that brought

211. See RIMA 3:75, A.0.102.16, line 29a.

212. See also Summary Inscription 9:r.10–11 and Summary Inscription 13:18′ (Tadmor 1994, 188–89 and 202–3).

Hoshea to the throne in Israel. Similarly, Hazael appears to be claiming a role in the removal of the Israelite king Joram that brought Jehu to the throne.

In conclusion, it is important to remember that like the Zakkur Inscription, the Tel Dan Inscription provides legitimation and propaganda for the monarch through a religious explanation for the positive turn of events, crediting the storm god (in the case of Zakkur: Baʿalšamayn and in Hazael's case: Hadad). In short, the Tel Dan Inscription is an apology (Suriano 2007; Knapp 2012). Interestingly then, in many ways, the answer to the question "who killed the two kings?"—as it appears that the ancients would have perceived it—is not Hazael versus Jehu, but Hadad versus Yahweh. Hazael is unquestionably claiming divine empowerment from Hadad himself in his slaying of the two kings.[213] This is in total concert with the theology and royal ideology found in his booty inscriptions (see below).

9.3.5.3. Hazael's Resistance during Shalmaneser III's 841 Campaign

Shalmaneser III faced a coalition in 853, 849, 848, and 845 that was led by Hamath and Damascus (Hadad-ezer/Adad-idri).[214] With these usurpations in Damascus and Israel, the coalition collapsed. As Yamada points out (2000a, 189–90), it is plausible that the allies had been bound to each other by an oath of loyalty, since this was common practice in the ancient Near East. If so, it is plausible that they would have been required to maintain loyalty to the royal family of Hadad-ezer (Adad-idri) and to oppose any usurper. Thus, with the change in dynasty in Damascus, the new political situation would have caused the disintegration of the coalition.

Consequently, Shalmaneser faced no opposition from Hamath;[215] and so in 841, he attacked Aram-Damascus. He claimed to have defeated Hazael's army at Mount Senir (the Anti-Lebanon Range) and subsequently to have confined Hazael within Damascus. He plundered the Ḥauran area (modern Jebel ed-Druz) and extracted tribute from Jehu. Shalmaneser III also campaigned

213. Yet, the biblical text credits Yahweh with the anointing of Hazael, trumping any Hadad claim of Hazael known to the biblical authors. In addition, the text of 2 Chr 22:1–9 contains a variant Yahwistic tradition of the death of Ahaziah crediting God specifically in his death (see esp. v. 7a: וּמֵֽאֱלֹהִים הָיְתָה תְּבוּסַת אֲחַזְיָהוּ). So just as Yahweh was credited directly in bringing about the death of Joram of Israel through the anointing of Jehu (with the coincidental killing of Ahaziah), so he is credited by the Chronicler directly with "the downfall" of Ahaziah (yielding a corresponding narrative to 2 Kgs 9). (Jehu's treatment of Ahaziah in 2 Chr 22:9a is in contrast to Ahab's treatment of Ben-Hadad in 1 Kgs 20:30b–34). The term תְּבוּסָה is a *hapax legomenon*. Intriguingly, the Peshitta has *həpīktā*, "the destruction/ruin/overthrow of (Ahaziah)" (from the root *hpk*).

214. See §§7.2.2.1–7.2.2.4.

215. See pp. 472–73 above.

against Aram-Damascus again in 838 and 837, though his Annals conflate the two years into one account. This campaign will be discussed below.

Shalmaneser III's 841 campaign is preserved in five annalistic texts and two summary inscriptions.[216] The Marble Slab, even though it dates two years later than the Calah Bulls, preserves the fullest account. It reads:

> *Episode 1* (iii.45b–iv.4a)
> In my eighteenth regnal year, I crossed the Euphrates for the sixteenth time. Hazael of Damascus trusted in the massed might of his troops; and he mustered his army in great number. He made Mount Saniru/Senir, a mountain peak, which (lies) opposite Mount Lebanon, his fortress. I felled with the sword 16,020 troops, his fighting men. I took away from him 1,121 of his chariots, 470 of his cavalry, together with his camp. In order to save his life he ran away. I pursued after him. I confined him in Damascus, his royal city. I cut down his orchards. I burned his shocks.
>
> *Episode 2* (iv.4b–7a)
> I marched to the mountains of Ḫaurānu. I razed, destroyed and burned cities without number. I carried away their booty.
>
> *Episode 3* (iv.7b–10a)
> I marched to the mountains of Ba'li-ra'si at the side of the sea and opposite Tyre. I erected a statue of my royalty there.
>
> *Episode 4* (iv.10b–12a)
> I received the tribute of Baʿal-manzēr, the Tyrian, and of Jehu (*Ia-a-ú*), (the man) of Bīt-Ḫumrî (Omri).
>
> *Episode 5* (iv.12b–15a)
> On my return, I went up on Mount Lebanon. I set up a stela of my royalty with the stela of Tiglath-pileser (I), the great king who went before me.

The narrative structure of the campaign divides into two phases (see fig. 9.6). The first phase is a fighting phase in which the primary enemy, Hazael, and his land are subjugated. This phase is narrated in two parts: the defeat of

---

216. The "Annals" are: the Calah Bulls (RIMA 3:48, A.0.102.8, lines 1″–27″; Yamada Annals 6; *COS* 2.113C:266–67); the Marble Slab (RIMA 3:54–55, A.0.102.10, iii.45b–iv.15a; Yamada: Annals 7; *COS* 2.113D:267–68); the Kurbail Statue (RIMA 3:60, A.0.102.12, lines 21–30a; Yamada: Annals 9; *COS* 2.113E:268); the Black Obelisk (RIMA 3:67, A.0.102.14, lines 97–99; Yamada: Annals 13; *COS* 2.113F:269–70); the Broken Statue from Nimrud (RIMA 3:77–78, A.0.102.16, lines 122′–137′; Yamada: Annals 14). The two Summary Inscriptions are: Walters Art Gallery Stela (RIMA 3:49–50, A.0.102.9, lines 1′–15′; Yamada: Summary Inscription 16); and the Assur Basalt Statue (RIMA 3:118, A.0.102.40, i.14–35; Yamada: Summary Inscription 19; *COS* 2.113G:270).

Hazael (Episode 1) and the continuation and conclusion of the campaign in the mountains of Ḥauran (Episode 2). The second phase is a nonfighting phase in which there are two instances in which a statue is set up on a mountain and the extraction of tribute from two noncombatant kings: Baʿal-manzēr of Tyre and Jehu of Bīt Ḫumrî. The receipt of the tribute from the two kings (Episode 4) is framed on either side by the erection of a statue at a specific location on a mountain (Episodes 3, 5). Most of the narration of the 841 campaign in the Slab is devoted to the description of the defeat of Hazael. This gives the feeling that episodes 2–5 are somewhat anticlimactic. Nevertheless, by framing the tribute of the two kings with the erections of the two statues, Shalmaneser is able to depict effectively his sovereignty over the entire region.

The Marble Slab and Broken Statue from Nimrud seem to follow the same version (with five episodes); the Calah Bulls and the Kurbail Statue give a slightly different version (with only four episodes). The Black Obelisk gives a significantly truncated version, but it also includes the relief and epigraph detailing the precise tribute of Jehu of Bīt Ḫumrî.

Regarding the "Summary Inscriptions," the Walters Art Gallery Stela is a fragmentary description of the 841 campaign, much of which can only be restored from parallels. The Assur Basalt Statue (*COS* 2.113G:270) contains a brief passage describing the death of Hadad-ezer (Adad-idri), the usurpation of Hazael, and a telescoped version of the campaign.[217]

From these inscriptions, it appears that Shalmaneser apparently took the route through the Beqaʿ Valley between the Lebanon and Anti-Lebanon mountains. In episode 1, he claims to have fought Hazael at "Mount Sanir, a mountain peak, which (lies) opposite Mount Lebanon, his fortress." Mount Sanir is the biblical Mount Senir which has been identified with the Anti-Lebanon Range. He claims to have killed 16,000/16,020 of Hazael's troops and to have confined him in Damascus.

In episode 2 of the Marble Slab, Shalmaneser continued the campaign, moving southward to plunder the towns in the Ḥauran, the modern Jebel ed-Druz which rises to the east of biblical Bashan. He states: "I razed, destroyed and burned cities without number. I carried away their booty." This concludes the fighting phase of Shalmaneser's campaign.

A piece of booty from this campaign (or possibly from a later one against Hazael in 838–837) has been discovered. It is an ivory found in the excavations of room T 10 at Fort Shalmaneser incised with a fragmentary inscription (Millard 1966; *COS* 2.40:163):

---

217. For Hazael's accession, see discussion above.

[ *mr*]*'n ḥz'l*
[ our lor]d Hazael.

In the next episode, Shalmaneser marched to the mountains of Ba'li-ra'si at the side of the sea and opposite Tyre and erected a statue of himself there. The identification of Ba'li-ra'si is debated. Three locations have been proposed: (1) in the vicinity of the Nahr el-Kelb (Honigmann 1928; Wiseman 1958, 49); (2) Mount Carmel (Astour 1971, 384–385; Green 1979, 36), and (3) Ras en-Naqura, the mountain demarcating the modern Lebanese-Israeli border (Borger, *TUAT* 1, 366 n. 21a; Dion 1997, 196–197; Yamada 2000a, 192). The last option seems best in light of the fact that the texts of the Marble Slab and the Broken Statue from Nimrud read "opposite the land of Tyre" (*ša pūt māt ṣurri*).

In his march from Ḥauran to Ba'li-ra'si, it is possible that Shalmaneser crossed Israelite territory. Some scholars have attempted to understand the enigmatic verse in the book of Hosea (Hos 10.14), "The ravaging of Beth-Arbel by Shalman on the day of battle," as a reference to an attack on the Israelite town by Shalmaneser III in connection with this campaign.[218] It is possible that this is a reminiscence of the town's destruction, but it might date from the 838 campaign.

In episode 4, Shalmaneser receives the tribute of Ba'al-manzēr of Tyre and of Jehu of Bīt Ḫumrî (Marble Slab and Broken Statue from Nimrud). The Calah Bulls and Kurbail Statue state this somewhat differently:

> At that time, I received the tribute of the Tyrians and the Sidonians, and of Jehu (man of) Bīt-Ḫumrî (Omri) (*ma-da-tu šá* KUR *ṣur-ra-a-a* KUR *ṣi-du-na-a-a šá* ᵐ*ia-ú-a* DUMU ᵐ*ḫu-um-ri-i*).

Some scholars (e.g., Yamada 2000a, 194) have concluded from the difference in wording between the Marble Slab and these two other inscriptions that Tyre and Sidon were unified under one ruler: Ba'al-manzēr of Tyre.[219]

There can be no doubt that the Assyrian cuneiform spelling *ia-ú-a* (the Marble Slab mistakenly writes *ia-a-ú*) is an accurate reflection of the Hebrew name of the Israelite king Jehu (יֵהוּא) (Zadok 1997; Na'aman 1997; Brinkman and Schwemer 2000; and Younger 2002, 207–18). The following cuneiform sign DUMU (*mār*) is used in this construction with ᵐ*ḫu-um-ri-i* to form a type of gentilic as part of the *bītu*-formulation (see ch. 2) "house."[220]

218. Beth-Arbel is identified with Irbid. See Aharoni 1979, 341; Astour 1971, 385.

219. However, see the formulation in the Black Obelisk 103b–104a (*šá* KUR *ṣur-ra-a-a* KUR *ṣi-du-na-a-a* KUR *gu-bal-a-a*). Cf. also lines 180b–183a.

220. Schneider (1995, 1996) has suggested that the phrase DUMU(*mār*) ᵐ*ḫu-um-ri-i* means "son (descendant) of Omri" and that Jehu was a descendant of the Omride dynasty,

| |
|---|
| The Fighting Phase: Subjugation of Aram-Damascus (iii.45b–iv.7a) |
| Episode1 – The Defeat of Hazael of Damascus (iii.45b–iv.4a) |
| Episode 2 – Continuation and Conclusion of the campaign in the Mountains of Ḥauran (iv.4b–7a) |
| The Nonfighting Phase: Setting Up of Stelae and Extraction of Tribute (iv.7b–15a) |
| Episode 3 – Erection of a Statue on the Mountain of Ba'ali-ra'si (opposite Tyre) (iv.7b–10a) |
| Episode 4 – Receipt of Tribute from Ba'al-manzēr of Tyre and Jehu of Bīt Ḫumrî (iv.10b–12a) |
| Episode 5 – Erection of a Statue on Mount Lebanon beside that of Tiglath-pileser (I) (iv.12b–15a) |

Fig. 9.6. The Marble Slab's structure of Shalmaneser III's 841 campaign

It seems very likely that the battle of Ramoth-Gilead where Jehoram of Israel was wounded and Jehu's *coup d'état* occurred between Tishri 842 and Nisan 841 BCE. Shalmaneser's attack on Damascus and Jehu's submission took place later in 841 BCE.

The Black Obelisk, the latest of all known obelisks, provides a visual of Jehu's tribute with an epigraph identifying the particulars.[221] Sculpted from black alabaster, it is 1.98 meters in height and contains the longest account of Shalmaneser's reign, stretching down to the king's thirty-first year. Discovered by A. H. Layard at Kalḫu (Nimrud) in 1846, the text dates to 828–827 BCE. The top of the Obelisk is formed in the shape of a ziggurat, having four sides with five registers or tiers on each side containing reliefs of the tribute being brought to the king (*ANEP*, 120–21).[222] This form may reflect the

perhaps by a different branch than the ruling descendants of Ahab. Lamb (2007, 29–40) persists in understanding *mār ḫumrî* as indicating that Jehu was an actual descendant. If anyone should have been designated *mār ḫumrî* "(literal) son of Omri," it should have been Ahab. But Shalmaneser III's scribes identify him as "the Israelite." But *mār*-X is an idiom connected to the tribal structure, as Assyriologists and Aramaists have consistently pointed out. See ch. 2.

221. See Uehlinger 2007. The known examples of obelisks date to the period from Aššur-bēl-kala to Shalmaneser III (Russell 2003–5, 4).

222. Register 4 contains an epigraph that identifies the tribute in the relief as that of Marduk-apla-uṣur of Sūḫu. Interestingly, a letter from this ruler to the Hamathite king Rudamu/Uratamis, the son of Irḫulēni/Urhilina, was discovered in excavations at Ḥama. See Parpola 1990 and chapter on Hamath above.

special appeal which these temple towers appear to have had for the Assyrians (Porada 1983, 16). While each register has an epigraph, the main text is found above and below the five registers on all four sides.

All Assyrian obelisks have apparently been found in the vicinity of temples, suggesting that their function was to display to the gods the economic success of the king—in pictures depicting the flow of wealth into the empire and in text describing how this wealth was obtained (Russell 2003–5, 6). On the other hand, their four-sided portrayals imply mobile viewers and a freestanding setting, suggesting that they were also intended for a human audience.

On the front side, the second register contains the famous relief of Jehu of Israel (or his envoy) paying his tribute to Shalmaneser. The first register holds a scene of Sūa, the ruler of Gilzānu, a land near Lake Urmia, paying his tribute. Through parallelism of the portrayals of the tribute from these two countries—the first being in the northeasternmost area of the empire and the second being in the southwesternmost area—the obelisk creates a pictorial merism stressing the gigantic extent of Shalmaneser's empire (see Keel and Uehlinger 1994; Green 1979, 385; Porada 1983, 13–18; and Lieberman 1985, 88). The epigraph (RIMA 3:149, A.0.102.88) reads:

> I received the tribute of Jehu (*Ia-ú-a*) (the man) of Bīt-Ḫumrî: silver, gold, a golden bowl, a golden goblet, golden cups, golden buckets, tin, a staff (*ḫuṭārtu*) of the king's hand, (and) javelins(?).[223]

M. Elat (1975, 33–34) notes that Sūa, king of Gilzānu, is pictured on the Obelisk giving Shalmaneser *ḫuṭārāte/ḫutārte*, "staffs." He argues for a distinction between *ḫuṭāru/ḫuṭārtu* and *ḫaṭṭu*, with the former being a symbol of protection or ownership of property, and the latter a symbol of royal authority (i.e. a scepter). Thus Jehu and Sūa, in handing over the *ḫuṭārtu* to Shalmaneser III, "wished to symbolize that their kingdoms had been handed over to the protection of the king of Assyria."[224] This *ḫuṭārtu*-staff may be pictured on the recently discovered alabaster vase from the Jezirah attributed to Shalmaneser III (Abou-Assaf 1992; Fortin 1999, 111; Heintz 2001, 473). The vase pictures Shalmaneser and an unidentified king "shaking hands," a motif seen on Shalmaneser's throne base from Fort Shalmaneser.[225]

223. In terms of the number of items delineated, Jehu's tribute contains the most: nine items.

224. See *CAD* 6:265 s.v. *ḫuṭāru* A.

225. For the theme of two kings "shaking hands," see Reade 1979a, 69–70.

### 9.3.5.4. Shalmaneser III's 838–837 Campaign

Shalmaneser III's 838 campaign against Hazael of Aram-Damascus is recorded only on the Black Obelisk (RIMA 3:67, A.0.102.14, lines 102b–104a) and the Broken Statue from Nimrud (RIMA 3:78–79, A.0.102.16, lines 152′–162a′).[226] The Broken Statue from Nimrud in particular is an important source for the campaign, and although the text is fragmentary, it preserves enough of the toponymy to demonstrate the general route of the campaign. It reads:

> [In] my [twenty-first regnal ye]ar, [I crossed] the Euphrates [for the twenty-first time]. I received the [trib]ute of all the kings of the [land of Ḫat]ti. I departed from [the land of Ḫatti?]. I took the route (along) the [Leba]non, trave[rsed] Mount Saniru (and) I descended to the cities [of] Hazael of Damascus. The cities [...] feared (and) they took to the difficult mountains. I conquered the fortified cities of Ya[...], [...], Danabu, Malaḫa, by means of [mines, battering]-rams and towers. I defeated and plun[dered] them. The [cit]ies I razed, I destroyed, I burned with fire.[227]

Unfortunately, the names of the first and second cities are not preserved, but it does supply the names of the last two, Danabu and Malaḫa (both are also mentioned in the Eponym Chronicle[228]). The locations of these two preserved city names are uncertain, though the best possibilities are in the Ḥauran region.[229] Yamada points out that this was probably a single campaign 838–837 even though the Eponym Chronicle lists two years.

Following the destruction of these cities of Hazael, Shalmaneser received the tribute of a certain Ba'il, whose name is probably a hypocoristic form of

226. In his critical edition of 1996, A. K. Grayson published two texts that added information concerning Shalmaneser III's campaign against Hazael in 838 BC. In the case of the first text, the Assur Stone Slab (RIMA 3:61–62, A.0.102.13) had not been published before, although E. Weidner may have mistakenly used part of it as a variant of a text of Shalmaneser I. In the case of the second, the Broken Statue from Nimrud (RIMA 3:72–84, A.0.102.16) had been published before by Laessøe (1959), but Grayson's edition of the inscription was based on Peter Hulin's unpublished copy and transliteration that deciphered much more than Laessøe's work. In 2000, S. Yamada published Hulin's hand copies (Yamada 2000b), as well as a monograph that discusses all these texts concerning Shalmaneser's 838 campaign. Before these publications, the only text which gave any information about this campaign was Shalmaneser's Black Obelisk (RIMA 3:62–71, A.0.102.14, lines 102b–104a).

227. The inscription continues with an episode involving Ba'il, probably of Geshur. See §3.3.2.1.

228. Millard 1994, 29: Malaḫa (838), Danabu (837).

229. A discussion is given above at §9.2.

a personal name that has the divine name Ba'al as its first element. Because of the most likely restoration of the gentilic, this may be a ruler of Geshur.[230] With the use of the conjunction "moreover" (*u*), an accessorial part is conjoined that elucidates the Assyrian army's return route on the Phoenician coast.

Thus Shalmaneser III conquered numerous cities belonging to Hazael during his campaigns, but failed to capture Damascus.[231] Not conquering Damascus was of crucial importance for it left Hazael's royal residence, the center of his further military and political power totally intact (Fuchs 2008b, 46–47). It would take another 124 years until the Assyrians, under Tiglath-pileser III, were able to gain complete control of the city (in 732).

#### 9.3.5.5. Hazael's Empire

After the 841 and 838–837 campaigns, Shalmaneser III was occupied with other concerns. While these campaigns were "successes" as far as Shalmaneser III was concerned, they were less than resounding defeats for Hazael. Soon he had a wide-open window for military expansion without Assyrian interference. The Assyrian Empire had enormous political weakness in the last years of Shalmaneser III's reign, especially with the revolt in 826–824. This was followed by the reign of Šamšī-Adad V (823–811) when the Assyrians appear to have withdrawn from the political arena of the Levant almost completely.[232] This empowered the emerging Damascene king who was more than eager to implement his own expansionistic plans (see fig. 9.7). Thus through a series of conquests, Hazael created a significant Levantine empire (the different regions that were brought under the hegemony of Hazael will be outlined below). The power that Hazael amassed must have been quite impressive as recognized by the Assyrians. After his death, they often refer to the kingdom of Aram-Damascus as Bīt-Ḫaza'ili (Suriano 2007, 175 n. 85). Moreover, it seems that Hazael was deified in some fashion after his death (see below).

A brief word should be said about the way that Hazael's empire has been treated in earlier scholarship. In B. Mazar's study (1962, 108–16), he proposed that the rule of Damascus under Hazael and his son Bar-Hadad reached far into the south as well as into north Syria and even east of the Euphrates. For Mazar (1962, 112–14), the evidence for Hazael's northern expansion was found in his analysis of 1 Kgs 20, as well as his appeal to the Melqart Stela and the Hazael Booty Inscription from Arslan Taş. Pitard (1987, 152–58) cor-

230. See §3.3.2.1.
231. Lemaire 1991a, 100–101; Dion 1997, 198–99; Yamada 2000a, 205–9.
232. For more details, see §6.3.4 above.

rectly pointed out the weaknesses in this evidence. The Melqart Stela does not belong to a king of Damascus, but rather to a king of Arpad;[233] the find spot in Arslan Taş is not an indication of Hazael's penetration into the region as Mazar argued, but rather that the piece of ivory was brought to Arslan Taş as booty by either Adad-nērārī III or Šamšī-ilu after one of the campaigns to Damascus (796 or 773);[234] and the text of 1 Kgs 20 does not really yield any evidence that relates to Hazael's kingdom, regardless of which king of Israel that may be in view in that passage.

Pitard (1987, 158) concluded that "there is no evidence that he (Hazael) was able to extend his influence farther north than his border with the kingdom of Hamath," though he argued for Hazael's southern expansion. However, this negative assessment of the northern expansion cannot be sustained today. There is evidence that points to Hazael extending his power into northern Syria, though most certainly not as far as Mazar envisioned[235] (see §9.3.5.5.2).

#### 9.3.5.5.1. The Southern Expansion

To the south of Damascus, the natural geographic link is the Transjordan. As witnessed in the Tel Dan stela, Hazael had success against Joram (Jehoram) of Israel, though the exact extent of his involvement in Jehu's revolt is not entirely clear. It appears that the Transjordan was a particular territory that Israel was forced to concede.

The region of the Ḥauran had likely already been a Damascene territory for quite some time (if the understanding of the location of the toponyms of Malaḫa and Danabu is correct, see above). However, this cannot be based on Hazael's booty inscription from Arslan Taş.[236] Puech (1981) proposed a restoration *ḥ*[*wrn*?] "Ḫa[wran?]" for this fragmentary inscription.

233. See §8.2.4 on Bīt-Agūsi/Arpad.

234. This is a fragmentary ivory plaque discovered in 1928 at Arslan Taş, ancient Ḫadattu, that some scholars believe to be from the edge of a bed. Winter (1981, 123) suggests that it may have been carried to Arslan Taş as booty by Šamšī-ilu after the capture of Damascus in 773. For other possibilities and the way that this ivory found its way to Arslan Taş, see Feldman 2014, 151–53. For the Arslan Taş ivories, see Cecchini 2009.

235. As a number of scholars early on have pointed out, based especially on Hazael's Booty Inscriptions. See Bron and Lemaire 1989; Eph'al and Naveh 1989; Millard 1993, 175 and discussion below.

236. See §9.1.3.3 (2) above; Younger 2005, 260–61 (Inscriptions 3 and 4); Amadasi Guzzo 1996; 2009; Ghantous 2013, 67–69; Feldman 2014, 150–53. The very fragmentary booty inscription from Kalḫu (modern Nimrud) simply reads: [ *mr*]'*n* *ḥz'l*, "[ our lor]d Hazael." It is too short to contribute anything historical.

The inscription reads: [ ]?? *ʿm*ʾ . *l//mrʾn* . *ḥzʾl* . *bšnt* //[. ]*zt* . *ḥ*[...?].[237] How to understand the beginning of the text is debated.[238] The middle of the inscription clearly reads: *l//mrʾn* . *ḥzʾl* . *bšnt* "to our lord Hazael in the year." Generally accepted is the restoration of [ʾ*ḥ*]*zt*. The majority of scholars (Bron and Lemaire 1989, 37; Ephʿal and Naveh 1989, 197 n. 24; Niehr 2011, 345) reject Puech's idea of an annexation of Ḥauran, arguing that [ʾ*ḥ*]*zt* speaks of the capture of a city (cf. Mesha 11, 14, 15–16, 20) and that one could restore *ḥ*[*ṣr*] "Ḥ[azor]," *ḥ*[*mt*] "Ḥ[amath]," *ḥ*[*zrk*] "Ḥ[azrak]," or *ḥ*[*zz*] "Ḥ[azazu]." Without the discovery of another fragment the restoration must remain uncertain, but it seems that Ḥauran is the least likely, and Ḥ[azrak] the most likely (in light of the Tel Afis Stela fragment, see below).[239]

In any case, the land of Gilead appears to have been one of the initial areas to fall under the political domination of Damascus.[240] This mastery over the Transjordan probably picked up steam in the context of the attempt of the kings of Israel and Judah, Jehoram, and Ahaziah, to make territorial gains at the expense of Damascus at a time of perceived weakness as the result of Hazael's coming to power (2 Kgs 8:28–29; 9:14b; Tel Dan stela, line 3b–4a[241]). However, it was not until the Assyrian pressure upon Hazael was abated that he was able to defeat them "throughout the territory of Israel: from the Jordan eastward, all the land of Gilead, the Gadites, the Reubenites, and the Manassites, from Aroer, which is by the Wadi Arnon, that is, Gilead and Bashan" (2 Kgs 10:32–33).[242] Not all of this area was necessarily cap-

237. The // represent the division points between the fragments.

238. The two partially preserved letters before the term ʿ*m*ʾ have been read as *br* ("son"), [*q*]*rb* ("offered") or [*h*]*dd* ("Hadad") (*KAI* 232; *SSI* 2:4–5; Puech 1981; Bron and Lemaire 1989, 37; Naʾaman 1995a, 382–83; Lipiński 2000a, 388). Perhaps the two words *br* and ʿ*m*ʾ should be read as one: *br*ʿ*m*ʾ, a proper name Bir-ammâ. The term ʿ*m*ʾ has been often understood as a personal name, ʿAmma, although some scholars have seen it as the noun "people" (e.g., Millard 2000c, 163). Lipiński (2000a, 388) is unique in understanding it as a toponym: ʿImma.

239. Unfortunately, this booty inscription of Hazael offers very little for historical reconstruction.

240. Perhaps some of the northern areas fell under Damascene control during the reign of Hadad-ezer (Adad-idri).

241. I am understanding the sentence "And the king of I[s](4)rael earlier invaded the land of my father" to be claiming, as part of Hazael's apology, that the king of Israel made the initial aggression; Hazael was simply empowered by Hadad to defend against a clear aggressor of the land that belonged to his predecessor ("his father")!

242. See Lemaire 1991a; Lipiński 2000a, 353–67; and Hafþórsson 2006, 201–5. Dion (1997, 199 n. 121) considers 2 Kgs 10:33 to be subject to caution since it attributes to Hazael the territories north of the Wadi Arnon which Mesha claims in his inscription to have conquered. However, Mesha's claim to have seized territory north of the Arnon is undoubtedly the situation in the days after the death of Ahab (i.e., more or less imme-

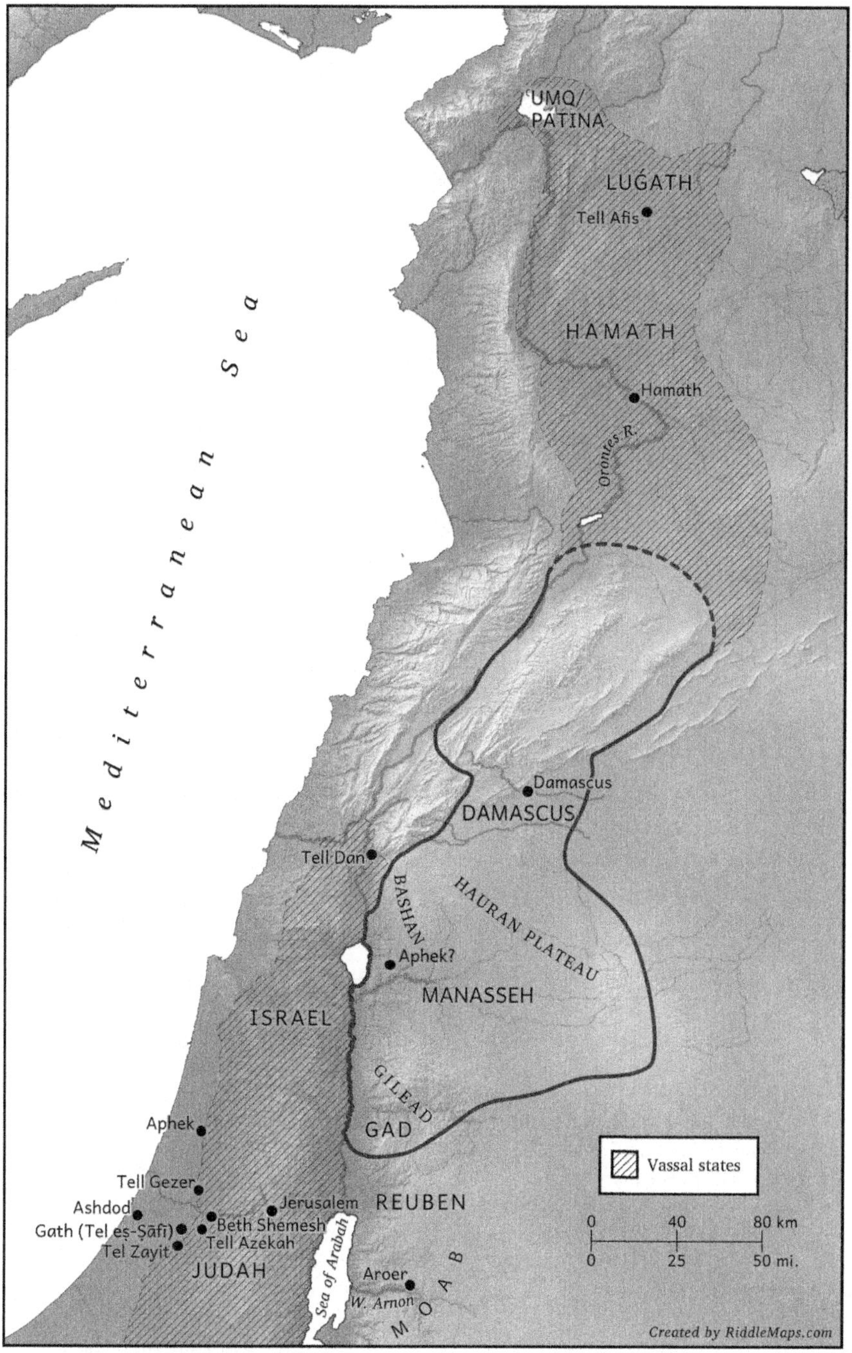


Fig. 9.7. The empire of Hazael

tured during the reign of Jehu; some of it likely was seized during the reign of Jehoahaz (2 Kgs 13:25). The final conquest of Gilead by Hazael was probably the result of several campaigns.[243] Although it has been speculated that there may have been alliances with the Ammonites and the Moabites (Lemaire 1991a, 102; 1991b, 158–60; Lipiński 2000a, 386), there is no actual evidence of such alliances (Niehr 2011, 345; Gaß 2009, 60 n. 286; Hübner 1992, 184).

As for Israel west of the Jordan, the magnitude of Hazael's military successes is especially attested by the Tel Dan stela. The conquest and the destruction of different sites have been attributed to Hazael's campaigns. For example, Finkelstein (1999; 2009; 2013, 120–21)[244] has attributed the destruction of level IX at Hazor to Hazael and proposed that Hazor VIII–VII was an Aramean city.[245] However, as pointed out above (p. 578 and note 107), there is no clear-cut evidence at Hazor for any proposed breaks in the occupational sequence, with no evidence of a wholesale destruction in either Stratum IX or Stratum VII (Ben-Tor, Ben-Ami, and Sandhaus 2012, 3). If this is correct, there is no evidence at Hazor for a destruction by Hazael. That some of the destructions at various sites may be attributed to Hazael is entirely possible, although some may be attributable to other Damascene monarchs. Without textual support, it cannot definitively be known. The fact is that "the destruction of any site in Israel during the time in question can be assigned to any Aramean king, depending on the chronology being advocated" (Ben-Tor 2000, 12; Ben-Ami and Wazana 2013). In any case, one has the impression that the kingdom of Israel was significantly reduced in the second half of the ninth century BCE.

By 810 BCE, Hazael had oriented his attention toward Judah and the royal cities of the Philistines. The reasons are not clear, though Niehr (2011,

---

diately post 853); the statement in verse 33 is reflecting much later developments in the region ca. 835–814.

243. See Lipiński 2000a, 386. This is probably the period reflected in the notice embedded in 1 Chr 2:23a: "But Geshur and Aram took Ḥavvoth-Jair from them, along with Qenath and its villages, sixty towns" (my translation follows Knoppers 2003, 295, 299). Being found in the midst of the genealogical material of Ḥezron, it is impossible to determine the date (see Pitard 1987, 151 n. 12).

244. He proposes the destructions of Dan IVA, Hazor IX, Megiddo VA–IVB, Yoqneam XIV, and Tanaach IIB are attributable to Hazael. However, see Ben-Tor 2000. Finkelstein (2013, 120–21) understands the destructions at Tel el-Ḥammāh (early), Hazor IX, Megiddo VA–IVB, and Tel eṣ-Ṣāfī to be the work of Hazael (830–800). For the low chronology, see Ghantous 2013, 21–35. For a survey following the high chronology, see Hafþórsson 2006, 185–246.

245. For a full presentation and discussion of Hazor, see Ben-Ami 2012. Earlier discussion Hafþórsson 2006, 229–34, 236–38.

348) has suggested that Hazael was interest in the Via Maris and the Mediterranean, since Damascus had no harbor itself. This is apparently based on an acceptance of Lipiński's evaluation of the archaeological evidence from Ashdod (see below). However, this is by no means an assured conclusion.[246]

According to 2 Kgs 12:18, Hazael captured the Philistine city of Gath (Tel eṣ-Ṣāfī). There is no date for this event indicated in the verse; it is simply attributed to the period of Joash, king of Judah. The archaeological exploration of the Tel eṣ-Ṣāfī has led to the discovery of a siege trench that the excavators have attributed to Hazael (Maeir and Ehrlich 2001; Ehrlich 2002; Maeir and Uziel 2007; Maeir 2009b). The trench was 6 m deep and 8 m wide and surrounded the city with a length of about 2 km on three sides. According to their interpretation, the ditch had been created to prevent the besieged from escaping. No doubt it also deterred any relief effort for the besieged city. The trench is dated based on the ceramics and because there is an analogy in the siege trench of Bar-Hadad, the son of Hazael, mentioned in the inscription of Zakkur (see *KAI* 202:10). However, this interpretation has also been disputed. Ussishkin has argued that the so-called siege trench is a natural phenomenon, since it is impossible artificially to create such an elaborate siege works (Ussishkin 2009). His arguments have been answered by Maeir and Gur-Arieh (2011). It is also important to underscore that the excavations of Tel eṣ-Ṣāfī/Gath have revealed Hazael's destruction of the site (both in the lower and upper city),[247] a destruction that had possible reverberations in Amos 6:2.[248] Other sites may have evidence of Hazael's campaign(s),[249] but caution should be applied since some of this "evidence" is based on different chronologies.[250]

Lipiński (2000a, 387–88) has attempted to attribute the destruction in Stratum IX at Ashdod (Lower Town) to Hazael, as too Beth-Shemesh (Stra-

246. Niehr's proposal, of course, is not invalidated; simply the basis for the suggestion may not necessarily stand.

247. This destruction's date is supported by radiocardon dating. See Maeir, Ackermann, and Bruins 2006. The remains of what might have been a victory stela (?) were found in earlier excavations at Tel eṣ-Ṣāfī/Gath. See Maeir 2009a; Berlejung 2014.

248. While Uzziah's action against Gath in 2 Chr 26:6 could be the reference in Amos, that text simply states that Uzziah "broke down the wall of Gath." The siege and destruction of Hazael seems a more probable candidate.

249. Additional evidence may have been discovered in destruction levels at Tel Zayit, Tell Gezer, and Tell Azekah as reported at the Sixteenth World Congress of Jewish Studies, Jerusalem, 2013.

250. Compare Hasegawa's survey (2012, 68–74) with the presentation of Ben-Ami and Wazana 2013, 371–3. For further discussion of the different chronologies, see Finkelstein and Mazar 2007; Frese and Levy 2010.

tum IIb).[251] It is clear that Lipiński has based his reconstruction on his understanding of the Lucianic Recension of 2 Kgs 13:22 and on his assessment of the archaeological evidence at Ashdod which is different than the excavator's interpretation. He argues that the partial destruction of Stratum IX at Ashdod is to be dated to the end of the ninth century, not the mid-eighth century, as M. Dothan (1993, 99) dated it, attributing it to Uzziah.[252]

In the case of 2 Kgs 13:22, the MT has "King Hazael of Aram oppressed Israel all the days of Jehoahaz." While many of the manuscripts of the Old Greek concur with the MT, the Lucianic Recenion has an additional sentence at the end of the verse:

> καὶ ἔλαβεν Ἀζαὴλ τὸν ἀλλόφυλον ἐκ χειρὸς αὐτοῦ ἀπὸ τῆς καθ' ἑσπέραν ἕως Ἀφέκ

Commentators who accept the recension's reading generally understand that Hazael conquered a Philistine territory between the Mediterranean Sea and Aphek in the coastal plain (Pitard 1987, 151–52; Lipiński 2000a, 386–87; Niehr 2011, 348). Nevertheless, caution should most certainly be exercised as pointed out by Cogan and Tadmor (1988, 149).

Richelle (2010) has done an outstanding study of the internal usages within the Lucianic Recension of two crucial items: the term ἀλλόφυλον and the phrase καθ' ἑσπέραν. Regarding the phrase καθ' ἑσπέραν, he demonstrates that while it has the possible meaning "in the west," the translators of the recension have, in fact, confused an original toponym ערבה "Arabah" as being from the root ערב "evening," a type of confusion that is also found in the Old Greek of Deut 1:1 and 11:30 (Dogniez and Harl 1992, 95). Thus Richelle (2010, 21–22) argues that the *Vorlage* must have read: ים הערבה.[253] Based on his analysis of the translators of the Lucianic recension, Richelle concludes that this additional sentence in 2 Kgs 13:22 refers to the region of the Transjordan between the Dead Sea and a site called Aphek in the Golan. Thus this verse may be compared to the description of Hazael's invasion in 2 Kgs 10:32–33.

While the term ἀλλόφυλον is generally used by the translators of the Septuagint to describe the Philistines (Lemaire 1991a, 103 n. 85), Richelle shows through his analysis of 2 Kgs 8:28 that the Septuagint translator

251. Niehr (2011, 348) has also followed Lipiński.

252. Herzog and Singer-Avitz (2011, 170) have recently observed that "Stratum IX should not be defined as a separate stratum. It was artificially created and some pottery has been attributed to it." See Finkelstein and Singer-Avitz 2001, 242–44.

253. Note also his remark: "Au passage, remarquons que cette difficulté de traduction constitue un indice très fort de l'existence d'une *Vorlage* hébraïque pour ce verset, qui n'est donc sans doute pas une invention d'un glossateur hellénisant" (Richelle 2010, 22).

decided to translate אֲרָם by ἀλλοφύλων.[254] Therefore, it is possible that in 2 Kgs 13:22 (only five chapters later) the translator has still used ἀλλοφύλων where he read אֲרָם. In light of this analysis, it would seem that the sentence should be rendered: "Hazael took from his (Jehoahaz's) hand "the Aram" from the Arabah (Dead Sea) to Aphek."[255] If Richelle is correct in his analysis, this means that there is no textual evidence of Hazael having a more extensive Philistine campaign, and so there is no reason to attribute the destruction of Stratum IX at Ashdod to Hazael (if, in fact, Stratum IX can be isolated, see n. 252 above).

After his destruction of Gath, Hazael threatened Jerusalem. This could only be averted by significant gifts to Hazael from king Joash taken from the treasuries of the Temple of the Lord (2 Kgs 12:18–19). Thus, Joash became vassal to Hazael at this time.

#### 9.3.5.5.2. The Northern Expansion

Due to the weakness of the Assyrian Empire, Hazael was able to expand his kingdom north of Damascus's traditional borders. One of the evidences of this is seen in his inscribed bronze horse frontlet and blinker, one of the so-called Hazael Booty Inscriptions (the inscription on each item is the same).[256] The established reading of the text of these inscriptions reads:[257] *zy ntn hdd lmr'n ḥz'l mn ʿmq bšnt ʿdh mr'n nhr*, "That which Hadad gave to our lord Hazael from ʿAmq in the year when our lord crossed the river" (see figs. 9.1 and 9.5).

The translation of the text, however, presents three difficulties. First, Bron and Lemaire (1989, 39, 43) have argued that *hdd* is not the deity Hadad, but is the personal name of the king of ʻUmq in the last part of the ninth century BCE who dedicated the object to Hazael. Similarly, Na'aman (1995a, 383) argues that Hadad is the personal name of one of the "officers or dignitaries in the court of Hazael, who offered gifts to their lord on the occasion of his victorious campaigns." On the other hand, Ephʻal and Naveh (1989, 193–94) have argued that while Hadad could be a personal name, it is more

254. MT: חֲזָהאֵל מֶלֶךְ־אֲרָם but Αζαηλ βασιλέως ἀλλοφύλων in LXX$^{B}$.

255. "Aram" is the direct object of the verb ἔλαβεν "he took"; hence the use of "Aram" for this territory would indicate that these areas have been annexed to the kingdom of Hazael. Hasegawa (2012, 81) suggests that the employment of the two toponyms in 2 Kgs 13:17 (Aphek) and 14:25 (the Sea of Arabah) are ideological and not historical.

256. See fig. 9.1 above; §9.1.3.3 (3); Younger 2005, 257–60 (Inscriptions 1 and 2); Amadasi Guzzo 1996, 2009.

257. Röllig (1988, 62) read the inscription: *zy ntn hdr lmr'n ḥz'l mn ʿmq bšn tʿrh mr'n nhr* "(Das ist es) was HDR gab unserem Herrn Haza'el von der Ebene von Basan. 'Stirnbedeckung' unseres erhabenen Herrn." Röllig understood HDR as the name of the one dedicating the object to Hazael.

probable that it is the divine name of the storm deity: "As the national deity played an important role in wars fought by the kings in antiquity (both in the Bible and in ancient Near Eastern sources), it appears that booty taken by Hazael from Umqi was considered as a gift of Hadad" (p. 194).[258]

Na'aman, however, argues against understanding Hadad as a divine name on the basis of genre. He sees this text involving the dedication of an object to a deity (Na'aman 1995a, 383). Thus he feels that "Eph'al and Naveh failed to appreciate properly the type of the inscription and their interpretation must therefore be abandoned." While Na'aman is correct in his assessment of the text as votive, it has been pointed out (e.g., Millard 2000c, 162) that such booty objects were often selected and then inscribed as votive offerings in accordance with the common practice of giving the deity part of the spoils of war (Gen 14:20; Num 31:25–54; 1 Chr 18:11). Millard (1993, 176*) states:

> it is preferable at present to treat them (the bronze duplicates) as celebratory notices, marking booty as the gift of the god Hadad to Hazael following an incursion across the Orontes into Umq.

Thus on this type of booty object, the inscription would function as a registration of its origin similar, for example, to the Black Stone Cylinder inscription of Shalmaneser III (*COS* 2.113H:271).

Moreover, Amadasi Guzzo (1996, 331–36) has thoroughly investigated the Old Aramaic dedicatory inscriptions and has concluded: (1) that if *hdd* were a personal name, it would have had a title or a patronym; (2) that the verb *ntn* is not used in Old Aramaic for a person dedicating an object whether to another human or to a deity, but rather for deities granting things to humans; and (3) the appellation "our lord" (*mr'n*) is wrong if a vassal king is donating the horse frontlet to Hazael; it should be "my lord" or "his lord" (i.e., a singular suffix, not a plural suffix). She argues that Hadad must refer to the deity and that the inscription is a type of label, tag or registration.

Bron and Lemaire's proposal that Hadad was the name of a ruler of ʿUmq during the latter part of the ninth century BCE is very unlikely, since the known rulers of Patina during the ninth and eighth centuries bore non-Semitic personal names (Hawkins 2000, 361–65). Moreover, the probability that there was an Aramean dynasty between Sasi (829 BCE) and Tutamuwa (738 BCE) that had a king with an Aramaic personal name "Hadad" reduced

258. Two biblical passages illustrate that booty from war was considered a gift from the deity: Deut 20:14 and 1 Sam 30:22–23.

to the sole theophoric element is very low,[259] especially since the archaeological evidence points to Neo-Hittite cultural continuity until the campaign of Tiglath-pileser III in 738 BCE (Harrison 2001, 2009). Therefore, it is most likely that *hdd* refers to the deity Hadad, whom Hazael credited with making him king and going before him in battle in the lines 4b–5a of the Tel Dan Inscription.

The second difficulty for interpreters has been the geographic identification of *ʿmq*. While most scholars have understood this to be a reference to the state of ʻUmq/Unqi/Patina, Na'aman (1995a, 381–94) understands *ʿmq* as Amqi, a geographic name for Bīt-Reḥob. However, Lipiński (2000a, 389 n. 227) disagrees stating: "There is not the slightest evidence that 'Amqi was a geographical name for Bēt-Reḥob, and the construction *ntn* – subject - *l* + complement - *mn* + complement perfectly corresponds to the use of *mn* in connection with verbal forms indicating acquisition and related concepts." It is most probable that ʻUmq/Patina is the referent.

The third difficulty has been the interpretation of the referent of *nhr*, "the river."[260] Dion (1997, 201–2) and other scholars[261] understand the reference to be to the Euphrates and reconstruct a historical context in which Hazael crosses the Euphrates to take advantage of Assyrian weakness in the last days of Shalmaneser III or in the reign of Šamšī-Adad V. "The river"[262] is understood to be the Euphrates in many biblical and cuneiform texts.

Nevertheless, in conjunction with the usage of *ʿmq*, there is a high probability that *nhr* here denotes the Orontes River (see Millard 1993b, 175*–76*; Amadasi Guzzo 1996, 334; Niehr 2011, 349). Lipiński (2000a, 389) puts it this way:

> This river might be the Euphrates, but the mention of ʻUmq rather suggests a crossing of the Orontes. The word *nāru*, "river," often occurs in Assyrian correspondence without any qualification and may designate any river, according to various contexts. Also in Hebrew "the river" must be identified

259. Lipiński 2000a, 388 n. 222; Hafþórsson (2006, 48–49) suggested that Hazael originally came from Patina/ʻUmq and later usurped the throne in Damascus. This suggestion can obviously be discarded.

260. A related question is whether the clause *bšnt ʿdh mr'n nhr* constitutes a "year name." See the discussion of Harrak 1992; and esp. Amadasi Guzzo (1996, 334–36) who concludes: "l'expression *bšnt* + complément de spécification était un formulaire de type historiographique plus répandu qu'on ne le supposait et qu'il n'était pas employé seulement à Damas" (contra Bron and Lemaire 1989, 41).

261. E.g., Harrak 1992, 67–73; Bron and Lemaire 1989, 40; Hasegawa 2012, 62.

262. The earliest Old Aramaic texts do not evince the postpositive (i.e., suffixed) definite article.

sometimes with the Jordan, as in Numb. 22, 5. Therefore, there is no stringent reason why *nhr* should be the Euphrates in Hazael's inscriptions.

Ikeda (1999, 291) dates this campaign of Hazael against Unqi (Patina) some time after the Assyrian intervention led by Dayyān-Aššur in 829 BCE. Like elsewhere, it is probable that Hazael forced 'Umq/Unqi/Patina into vassalage, but the details of such are, of course, lacking due to the sources.

How did Hazael campaign against 'Umq with the powerful kingdom of Hamath lying in between? Sometime late in the reign of Uratami or possibly his successor, Hamath and Luǵath must have become vassal to Hazael. Certainly the horse frontlet and blinker inscription would point to this.[263] However, the fragmentary basalt stela discovered at Tell Afis (TA.03.A.300) seems to be an additional witness to Hazael's power in the region. This was discussed in chapter 7 (Hamath and Luǵath). The inscription appears to contain the name of Hazael (line 5′: [...]*lḥz*⌜ʾ⌝[*l*]).[264]

The carved ivory containing a fragmentary booty inscription of Hazael from Arslan Taş (ancient Ḫadattu; fig. 9.8) may have originally made reference to Hazael's northern campaigns, since possible restorations suggest a northern city.[265] However, due to its fragmentary nature and highly uncertain readings, this booty inscription of Hazael cannot offer any sure information for historical reconstruction.

#### 9.3.5.5.3. Conclusion

While Hazael's reign began with a fight for survival, it became the period of Aram-Damascus's greatest power, a time when Damascus dominated a very large portion of the Levant. His empire reached far to the south with the destruction of Gath and vassalage of Judah being indicators of its extent. Although his empire did not have a border on the other side of the Euphrates as Mazar thought, its extent was certainly as far north as 'Umq/Patina. The impact of this empire of Aram-Damascus must have been significant economically, though nothing is really known about it. Certainly a promotion of the Aramaic language was a byproduct.

Resilience, perseverance, drive, military prowess, ruthlessness—these are some of the traits no doubt possessed by Hazael that led to Damascene hegemony. However, it must be remembered that Assyrian weakness was most certainly a major contributing factor.

---

263. See chapter 7 above.

264. See Amadasi Guzzo 2009, 336–41; 2005: 21–23, photo: fig 18. See fig. 7.8 and Younger 2007, 139.

265. For the inscription, see p. 523 above and n. 117.

### 9.3.5.6. Deification of Hazael

It was not just the Assyrians who recognized Hazael's power. He left an indelible mark on the memory of the region to the extent that there is evidence for the deification of Hazael after his death with a significant cult (Niehr 2011, 352). Flavius Josephus reports that in Damascus there was a cult of Ἀζάηλος "Hazael," together with one for Ἄδαδος (while this name is the name of the deity Hadad, it is very clear in the context of Josephus that this is a reference to the biblical person Ben-Hadad/Bar-Hadad whom Hazael murdered). Josephus's text states:

> Then Azaēlos, coming to Adados (Ben-Hadad), declared to him a good report concerning his illness; but the next day, he spread over him a soaked mesh-cloth, and by suffocation killed him. Then he (Azaēlos) himself took over the rulership, being a man of action and having much favor with the Syrians and the common people of Damascus, by whom Adados and Azaēlos (who ruled after him) are until now honored as gods because of their outstanding deeds and the building of temples by which they adorned the city of the Damascenes. And they (the Damascenes) lead processions every day in honor of these kings and with great pomp glory in (i.e. worship) their ancientness, not knowing that they are rather recent and these kings lived less than eleven hundred years ago.[266]

A number of scholars have misunderstood Josephus's references to Ἄδαδος as referring to the deity Hadad-Rammān (Niehr 2011, 352; Schwemer 2001, 623–24) or to Hazael's son Bar-Hadad (Dion 1997, 203). But clearly Josephus refers to the Ben-Hadad of the biblical text (Hadad-ezer/Adad-idri of the Assyrian sources?) as simply Ἄδαδος, and it is the deification of these two kings that Josephus is attesting to (note the wording "every day in honor of these kings … and these kings lived less than eleven hundred years ago").

It is generally thought that Josephus's source is Nicholas of Damascus, a historian of the first century BCE who certainly knew his own city's cultic practices. Thus it is probable that the deified Hazael and the deified Hadad(-ezer) (who proceeded him on the throne of Damascus) were wor-

266. My translation. The text reads: Ἀζάηλος μὲν οὖν παραγενόμενος πρὸς τὸν Ἄδαδον τῷ μὲν τὰ βελτίω περὶ τῆς νόσου κατήγγελλε, τῇ δ᾽ ἐπιούσῃ δίκτυον ἐπιβαλὼν αὐτῷ διάβροχον τὸν μὲν στραγγάλῃ διέφθειρε, τὴν δ᾽ ἀρχὴν αὐτὸς παρέλαβε δραστήριός τε ὢν ἀνὴρ καὶ πολλὴν ἔχων παρὰ τῶν Σύρων εὔνοιαν καὶ τοῦ δήμου τῶν Δαμασκηνῶν, ὑφ᾽ οὗ μέχρι νῦν αὐτός τε ὁ Ἄδαδος καὶ Ἀζάηλος ὁ μετ᾽ αὐτὸν ἄρξας ὡς θεοὶ τιμῶνται διὰ τὰς εὐεργεσίας καὶ τῶν ναῶν οἰκοδομίας, οἷς ἐκόσμησαν τὴν τῶν Δαμασκηνῶν πόλιν. πομπεύουσι δ᾽ αὐτοὶ καθ᾽ ἑκάστην ἡμέραν ἐπὶ τῇ τιμῇ τῶν βασιλέων καὶ σεμνύνονται τὴν τούτων ἀρχαιότητα οὐκ εἰδότες, ὅτι νεώτεροί εἰσι καὶ οὐκ ἔχοντες οὗτοι οἱ βασιλεῖς ἔτη χίλια καὶ ἑκατόν. See Marcus 1937, 6:48–50 (*Ant*. 9.4.3 §§92–94).

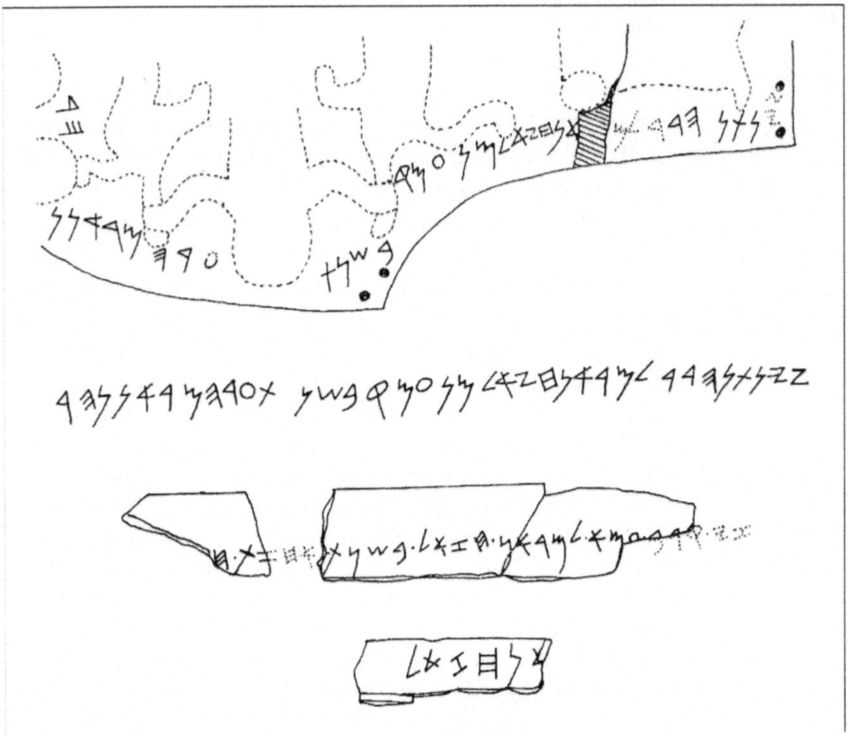

Fig. 9.8. Composite of the Hazael Booty inscriptions

shiped in Damascus in the first century BCE, and perhaps even beyond the time of the Christianization of the city (see Niehr 2011, 352).

### 9.3.6. Decline: The Loss of Aram-Damascus Hegemony

#### 9.3.6.1. Mari'/Bar-Hadad (II–III)

Hazael's son, Mari'/Bar-Hadad, became king after the death of his father sometime around 803. His personal name was undoubtedly Mari' (see discussion above). His rule over Aram-Damascus was roughly 803–775.[267] He is specifically mentioned in 2 Kgs 13:3, 24–25 and in the Zakkur Inscription (in all these instances, he is given the designation "Ben/Bar-Hadad, son of Hazael").[268] It would appear that this was how this ruler of Damascus

267. Jehoash/Joash appears to have ascended the throne in Israel in 798.

268. Zakkur adds "king of Aram."

was designated in the West Semitic sources but not in the Assyrian sources. Depending on how one understands the Adad-idri/Hadad-ezer identification and the Ben-Hadad references in connection with Ahab, he is either Bar-Hadad II or III. The Assyrian inscriptions of Adad-nērārī III record his attack on Damascus and his confinement of Mari' within the city in 796 BCE. Since the campaign must date to 796, Mari' cannot refer to Hazael, who was dead some years by this point.[269]

The certainty of this date is derived from the integration of the inscriptions of Adad-nērārī III and Pālil-ēreš (Nergal-ēreš).[270] Pālil-ēreš was a eunuch (*ša rēši*) and the Assyrian governor of Raṣappa. He was eponym in 803 and in 775 BCE (during the reigns of Adad-nērārī III [810–783] and Shalmaneser IV [782–773] respectively). Pālil-ēreš placed his own inscriptions on three stelae of Adad-nērārī III, on a mace-head discovered in Assur, and on a Black Stone Cylinder, all of which enumerated his various territorial holdings (see table 9.4).[271]

Pālil-ēreš did not control Ḫindānu until it was added to his holdings by a royal edict that is preserved on a tablet from the Ištar temple in Nineveh dated by eponym to 797 BCE (Bēl-tarṣi-ilumma).[272] Therefore, the Saba'a and Tell al-Rimah stelae must date after the issuance of this edict and after Adad-nērārī III's campaign to Damascus in 796 because they include Ḫindānu among his administrative territories. While Adad-nērārī III's Calah Orthostat (Nimrud Slab)[273] does not mention Pālil-ēreš, the fact that it describes the campaign to Damascus means that it must also date after 796.[274] Since the war against Aram-Damascus occurred before the submission of Israel, Phoenicia and Edom, the Tell al-Rimah stela must date slightly later than the Saba'a stela (Siddall 2013, 49).

---

269. For a discussion of the date, see §7.2.3. For a discussion of past proposals, see Pitard 1987, 165–67.

270. The reading of $^{d}$IGI.DU remains uncertain. It is unlikely to be Nergal (usually written in Neo-Assyrian: mostly $^{d}$U.GUR, but also $^{d}$MAŠ.MAŠ). Although in Neo-Babylonian names $^{d}$IGI.DU (= Pālil) stands for Nergal, there is no evidence of this for Neo-Assyrian. Thus there is still uncertainty whether Pālil is the correct reading of $^{d}$IGI. DU or not. See Radner in Kühne and Radner 2008, 31–32; Younger 2015b.

271. The Saba'a Stela (RIMA 3:209, A.0.104.6, lines 22b–25); the Tell al-Rimah Stela (RIMA 3:211–12, A.0.104.7, lines 13–21); the unpublished inscription on a mace head (Assur 10274) dedicated to Nergal by Pālil-ēreš (RIMA 3:230, A.0.104.2007; Weidner 1939–40, 318); the Tell Šēḫ Ḥamad Stela (Radner 2012a, 271–74; RIMA 3:207, A.0.104.5); and the Black Stone Cylinder (RIMA 3:229, A.0.104.2006).

272. RIMA 3:213–16, A.0.104.9; SAA 12:98–100, text 85.

273. See ch. 8.

274. Schramm 1973, 113; Tadmor 1973, 147–8; Kühne and Radner 2008, 32–33; Siddall 2013, 30, 32.

Table 9.4. The Inscriptions of Pālil-ēreš

| Black Stone Cylinder (ca. 805–800) | Tell Šēḫ Ḥamad Stela (ca. 801–797) | Mace-head (before 797) | Saba'a Stela (ca. 796 or later) | Tell al-Rimah Stela (ca. 795 or later) |
|---|---|---|---|---|
| city of Nēmed-Ištar | city of Nēmed-Ištar | | city of Nēmed-Ištar | |
| | city of Apqu | | city of Apqu | |
| | | | city of Marê | |
| land of Raṣappa | land of Raṣappa | land of Raṣappa | land of Raṣappa | land of Raṣappa |
| | | | land of Qatnu | |
| | | | city of Dūr-Katlimmu | |
| | | | city of Kār-Aššurnaṣirpal | |
| | | | city of Sirqu | |
| | | land of Laqē | land of Laqē | land of Laqē |
| | | | land of Ḫindānu | land of Ḫindānu |
| | | | city of Anat | city of Anat |
| | | land of Sūḫu | land of Sūḫu | land of Sūḫu |
| | | | city of Aššur-iṣbat | city of Aššur-iṣbat |

During Mari'/Bar-Hadad's reign, Aram-Damascus's power began to wane. When he came to throne after the death of his father, Hazael, Aram-Damascus's influence was still at its zenith (Lemaire 1993, 149*). It seems that Hazael had prudently stayed out of the north Syrian coalition that Attār-sumkī I of Arpad organized against Assyria (805–803). This kept Aram-Damascus in its powerful position. Mari'/Bar-Hadad inherited this dominant status until Zakkur's seizure of the control of both Hamath and Luġath (perhaps at the time of Hazael's death?), creating a serious problem in north central Syria.[275]

275. See §7.2.3.

Mari'/Bar-Hadad decided to organize his own coalition to deal with this problem. The prestige that Aram still possessed enabled him to gather quite an impressive alliance of entities (sixteen in number) to besiege Zakkur in Ḥaḏrak (Tell Afis). Not only did the Assyrians relieve Zakkur, they inflicted a significant defeat on Aram (perhaps in the Beqa' if this is the location of Manṣuāte[276] and the site of the battle). In any case, it was such a disastrous outcome that Mari'/Bar-Hadad was compelled to open up the gates of the city of Damascus to the Assyrian conqueror and render up a very great tribute from the treasures of the capital itself at the end of this 796 campaign. This was truly an unprecedented humiliation.[277] So, from roughly 803 to 796, Damascus had gone from the most powerful kingdom in the Levant to a much-weakened kingdom, one that now faced potential losses in its southern territories, namely to a renewed Israel under Joash/Jehoash. Even though Israel had also paid tribute to Adad-nērārī III at this time, it had not suffered the heavy losses in men and material in battle against the Assyrians that Damascus had.

In a highly telescoping and rhetorical passage in 2 Kgs 13:22–25, the biblical text summarizes the hegemony of Hazael in the days of Jehoahaz and the destruction of that hegemony in the days of Joash/Jehoash, when sometime after 796, Aram-Damascus lost territory on its southern border as well. It states:

> (22)Hazael king of Aram oppressed Israel all the days of Jehoahaz.[278]
>
> (23) But Yahweh was gracious to them; and he had compassion on them; and turned to them; on account of his treaty/covenant with Abraham, Isaac and Jacob.
>
> He was not willing to destroy them, nor did he banish them from his presence until now (עַד־עָתָּה). (24)Hazael, king of Aram, died; and Ben-Hadad his son reigned in his place.
>
> (25)Then Jehoash, son of Jehoahaz, recovered/restored and retook the cities from Ben-Hadad, son of Hazael, that he (Hazael) had taken from his father

276. See §7.2.3.1.

277. From the Saba'a and Tell Rimah stelae, and the Calah Orthostat (Nimrud Slab), it is clear that Adad-nērārī III considered the victory over Aram-Damascus as the high point of his military activities. The absence of the mention of Aram-Damascus in the Eponym Chronicle for the period of Adad-nērārī III is "nothing short of mystifying" (Siddall 2013, 25). Perhaps the victory at Manṣuate was so impressive, it was then cited in the Eponym Chronicle. It is also significant that Šamšī-ilu is not mentioned in these inscriptions.

278. For the Lucianic Recension's addition, see pp. 626–27 above.

> Jehoahaz in war. Three times Joash defeated him; and he recovered/restored the towns of Israel.

The narrative presentation of the contrast between the period of the oppression of Hazael in the days of Jehoahaz and the period of Joash/Jehoash's restoration at the expense of Ben-Hadad, the son of Hazael is very similar to the narrative presentation in the Mesha Inscription, where the period of the Israelite oppression in the days of Omri and Mesha's father are contrasted with the restoration in Mesha's day at the expense of the "son" (i.e., descendent) of Omri, including the divine activity referenced in each narrative account. The Mesha Inscription's narrative reads:

> Omri was king of Israel, and he oppressed (*yʿnw*) Moab for many days, because Kamoš was angry with his land. And his son followed him, and he also said: "I will oppress Moab!"
>
> In my day he said "[...]"
>
> But I saw (my desire) over him and his house, and Israel has utterly perished forever.
>
> Now Omri had possessed [all the la]nd of Madaba, and had dwelt in it his day (time) and half the days of his son (descendent's), forty years.
>
> But Kamoš restored it (*yšbh*) in my day.

It would be a mistake to read either account not discerning the rhetoric and figurative language. Thus, for example, one should not attempt to identify each of the "three" victories of Joash/Jehoash over Bar-Hadad.[279]

First Kings 20 is often seen as relating to this context, rather than the period of Ahab (Dion 1997, 204–5; etc.). Whether this is correct or not, the Calah Orthostat (Nimrud Slab)[280] is especially important, since it makes clear that Mari' suffered a devastating military and economic loss to the Assyrians in 796 BCE (table 9.5), paying this tribute inside his own palace (*ina qé-reb* É.GAL-*šú*) in Damascus.

In Adad-nērārī III's inscriptions, there are variations in the inventories and their quantities (table 9.5). Scholars have given different explanations for these variants. For example, Lipiński (2000a, 393) attributes the differences in the numbers to a lack of concern for accuracy among the Assyrian scribes. It has also been suggested that the scribes may have intentionally exagger-

279. See the comments of Lipiński 1969b, 97 and Dion 1997, 205. But see Yamada 2000a, 311 n. 13.

280. For translations of this inscription and the Saba'a and Tell al-Rimah stelae, see §8.2.3, pp. 526–29.

ated the quantities of those items so as to enhance the achievements of the king (Hasegawa 2012, 120). Yet, it seems inconceivable that the Assyrians defeated the Arameans of Damascus in battle, confined (besieged) the city, and that the city surrendered (giving access into the royal palace in Damascus without a fight—note Shalmaneser III was unable to take the city), but they only received the tribute found listed in the Saba'a Stela (100? talents of gold; 1,000 talents of silver; and some talents of another metal). Another suggestion is that the differences may reflect "totals" (i.e. the accumulative amount of tribute received; de Odorico 1995, 51 n. 31, 71; Siddall 2013, 42). In this case, the amount in the Tell al-Rimah stela is greater than that in the Saba'a stela because it is the total amount received from Aram-Damascus since its defeat.

It is important to emphasize that this payment of tribute[281] took place inside the royal palace in Damascus. This was something that Shalmaneser III did not accomplish! Even if one considers the Calah Orthostat (Nimrud Slab) to reflect a total of the tribute over a period of years, this huge extraction of wealth, combined with the military defeat inflicted on the Aramean forces of Mari' (Bar-Hadad), must have had a very significant impact on the ability of Mari' and Damascus to reload for war with Israel for some time (Dion 1997, 205).

Another biblical passage often attributed to Mari'/Bar-Hadad is 2 Kgs 6:24–7:20 (the siege of Samaria). Ikeda (1999, 292) dates the beginning of this siege of Samaria to the year 804 BCE, with its deliverance occurring in 802 BCE. Obviously, this is based on the assumption that the "Ben-Hadad" mentioned in 2 Kgs 6:24 is Ben-Hadad, the son of Hazael (i.e., Mari'). This is by no means problem free. 2 Kgs 8:7–15 narrates the usurpation of Hazael. 2 Kgs 9–10 narrates the usurpation of Jehu with Hazael being mentioned in 2 Kgs 10:32–33; while the text of 2 Kgs 12:17–18 describes Hazael's conquests. This means that a narrative about Ben-Hadad, the son of Hazael (Mari'), precedes the story of Hazael's ascension to the throne and Bar-Hadad's birth. However, since Elisha is the prophet involved in the story, the narrative may be placed here to connect it with the other Elisha stories.[282]

---

281. Hasegawa (2012, 118) has suggested that this campaign was led by Pālil-ēreš (Nergal-ēreš) and that "Mari' of Damascus paid tribute to Nergal-ēreš as representative of Adad-nērārī III." But there is no evidence, at present, to support this.

282. For discussion of the hiring of more powerful kings, see Parker 1997, 120–24; Liverani 1991. Makinson (2009, 27) takes 2 Kgs 7:6 to be a reference to Šamšī-ilu, "the king of the Muṣrites" who breaks the siege of Samaria: "De la même façon, l'expansionnisme d'Aram vers le sud a été mis en échec par l'arrivée du * roi des Murites +, un épisode mentionné en 2R 7 : 6. Ce dernier n'est pas le pharaon égyptien, mais Šamši-ilu, *turtânu* (général en chef et second personnage de l'Empire) gouvernant la province de Harran et l'Euphrate syrien depuis Kar-Šalmanezer/Mauwari (sic: Masuwari)." Such

Table 9.5. Mari's Tribute to Adad-nērārī III

| Saba'a Stela (RIMA 3:209, A.0.104.6, 19–20) | Tell al-Rimah Stela (RIMA 3:211, A.0.104.7, 6–7) | Calah Orthostat (Nimrud Slab) (RIMA 3:213, A.0.104.8, 15–21) |
|---|---|---|
| [x] hundred (100?) talents of gold ([x](?) ME GUN KÙ.GI) | | 20 talents of gold (20 GUN KÙ.GI) |
| 1,000 talents of silver (1 LIM GUN KÙ.BABBAR) | 2,000 talents of silver (2 LIM GUN KÙ.BABBAR) | 2,300 talents of silver (2 LIM 3 ME GUN KÙ.BABBAR) |
| [60?] talents of [...] ([x] GUN [...]) | 1,000 talents of copper (1 LIM GUN URUDU) | |
| | | 3,000 talents of bronze (3 LIM GUN ZABAR) |
| | 2,000 talents of iron (2 LIM GUN AN.BAR) | 5,000 talents of iron (5 LIM GUN AN.BAR) |
| | 3,000 linen garments with multi-colored trim (3 LIM *lu-bùl-ti bir-me u* TÚG. GADA.MEŠ) | linen garments with multi-colored trim (*lu-bùl-ti bir-me* GADA) |
| | | an ivory bed (GIŠ. NÁ.ZÚ) |
| | | a couch with inlaid ivory (GIŠ.*né-mat-ti* ZÚ *iḫ-zi tam-le-e*) |
| | | his property (and) his possessions without number (NÍG.GA-*šú* NÍG. ŠU-*šú a-na la ma-ni*) |

Šanda (1911–12, 2:49–51) attempted to pinpoint the exact date for this siege, namely 797 BCE shortly after the accession of Ben-Hadad, son of

an interpretation is nullified, among other reasons, by the fact that the text of 2 Kgs 7:6 reads: "the kings of Muṣri (Egypt) and the kings of Ḫatti (Luwian kings)." Collins (2007, 199) rightly comments: "2 Kgs 7:6 describes how the Arameans, while besieging Samaria, heard the approach of chariots and horses, the sound of a great army. They thus fled their camp, believing that the king of Israel had hired the kings of the Hittites and of Egypt to fight against them. The Hittites and Egyptians in this passage are not the two superpowers who fought the battle of Qadesh (1275 B.C.E.) and later brought a long-standing peace to

Table 9.6. Proposed Identifications of the "Savior" in 2 Kgs 13:5

| Identification | Representative Proponents |
|---|---|
| Adad-nērārī III | Winckler 1903, 260; Hallo 1960, 42; Lipiński 2000a, 395 (dating to 803 BCE) |
| Jehoash (Joash) | Cody 1970, 336–37 |
| Jeroboam II | Šanda 1911–12 2:153; Montgomery and Gehman 1951, 433 and 443 |
| Elisha | Noth 1943, 84; Gray 1970, 595; Hobbs 1985, 167–68 |
| Zakkur | Cooke CAH[1] (1925) 3:367 / 376 |
| The lifting of the siege (2 Kgs 6:24–7:20) | Cogan and Tadmor 1988, 144 |

Hazael. This was accepted by Gray (1970, 517–18). However such attempts at exact dating should be avoided. The evidence is too limited.[283]

Moreover, a number of scholars have connected the passage in 2 Kgs 6:24–7:20 with the mention of a savior in 2 Kgs 13:5. The passage (2 Kgs 13:3–5) reads:

> (3)Yahweh was angry with Israel and he repeatedly gave them into the hand of Hazael, king of Aram and into the hand of Ben-Hadad, the son of Hazael.
>
> (4)But Jehoahaz entreated Yahweh; and Yahweh heeded him; for he saw the oppression of Israel, how the king of Aram oppressed them.
>
> (5)So Yahweh gave Israel a savior/deliverer (מוֹשִׁיעַ), and they came out from under the hand of Aram; and the Israelites dwelt in their tents (homes) as before.

Various suggestions on the identity of the "savior" have been given. Table 9.6 shows the different proposed identities and a representative proponent of that identification. Obviously, the matter is not settled.[284] Siddall (2013, 6) rightly

---

the region, but their Iron Age descendents, who were nevertheless still powerful enough to intimidate the army of their Syrian enemy."

283. Cogan and Tadmor 1988, 85 n. 6, although they suggest the period of Jehoahaz as the time when a siege of Israel's capital city was most likely.

284. Hasegawa (2012, 87) suggests that verses 4–6 are "a secondary interpolation and thus should be excluded from the historical discussion." See also his discussion on pp. 76–79. Nevertheless, a number of the commentators listed in Table 9.6, while taking the

remarks: "unless we discover more illuminating sources, the saviour's identity shall continue to elude us."

9.3.6.2. Ḥadyān II (Ḫadiānu)

In 773 BCE, according to the Pazarcık inscription of Shalmaneser IV and the Eponym Chronicle,[285] Šamšī-ilu, the Assyrian commander-in-chief (*turtānu*), campaigned against Ḥadyān II (Ḫadiānu) of Damascus. This ruler is not mentioned in any biblical text, but his name is the same as the earlier monarch of Damascus, the biblical Hezion (חֶזְיוֹן), the grandfather of Ben-Hadad I (1 Kgs 15:18). The reign of Ḥadyān II (Ḫadiānu) would seem to be ca. 775–750 BCE.

> When Šamšī-ilu, the commander-in-chief (*turtānu*), marched[286] to the land of Damascus (KUR.ANŠE-*šú*), the tribute of Ḥadyān (ᵐ*ḫa-di-a-ni*), the Damascene (KUR.ANŠE-*šú-a-a*)—silver, gold, copper, his royal bed, his royal couch, his daughter with her extensive dowry, the property of his palace without number—I received from him.

Noteworthy is the mention of Ḥadyān's daughter and dowry.

Fuchs (2008a, 82) has argued that the few available sources from the time of Shalmaneser IV indicate clearly that this king never participated in a campaign. The two victories won against Argišti I of Urartu were recorded only by Šamšī-ilu in his Til-Barsib Lion Inscriptions dating to 774 as his own personal success, and the 773 campaign against Damascus was undertaken and is solely attributed to him. However, in line 10 of the Pazarcık inscription, the first person singular verb form is used (*amḫuršu*), and in lines 11–13a, Shalmaneser IV stated: "On my return (*ina tayyartīya*), I gave (*addin*) this boundary stone (*taḫūmu*) to Ušpilulume, king of the Kummuḫites," which clearly implies that Shalmaneser IV had some kind of participation in the Damascus campaign (however minimal that role might have been)—unless all this is purely rhetorical (for which I see no clear indication).[287]

---

verses as secondary, attempt an identification tied to the secondary context as they envision it.

285. RIMA 3:239–40, A.0.105.1, lines 4–10; *COS* 2.116:283–84; Millard 1994, 39.

286. Hasegawa (2010, 7–8) argues that *illikūni* is a 3mp plus the ventive (apparently having Shalmaneser IV and Šamšī-ilu as the subject). It seems much preferable to understand line 4 as beginning the narrative section of the royal inscription with a temporal clause that has Šamšī-ilu as the subject, taking *illikūni* as a 3cs plus the subordinate marker -*ūni*. For such a temporal clause, see *CAD* 8:316–17. The main clause *madattu* ... *amḫuršu* is typical of royal inscriptions. Thus Hasegawa's resorting to positing separate sources for the composition is, in my opinion, not necessary.

287. Hasegawa's conclusion (2010, 8) seems on target: "Šamšī-ilu might have indeed

Perhaps connected with or the result of the action of Šamšī-ilu, Israel experienced some political expansion at the cost of Damascus during the reign of Jeroboam II (first half of the eighth century BCE). Whether there was an agreement between Jeroboam II and Šamšī-ilu is not clear, though some have speculated that there may have been (Lipiński 1991, 175; 2000a, 312–13). In any case, the Assyrian incursions weakened Damascus, making the Israelite move northward easier (Kuan 2001).

One scholar has suggested that Ḥadyān is the referent of the term הָרִאשׁוֹן in Isa 8:23 [Eng. 9:1].[288] However, as noted above (p. 579), this is one of the most difficult passages in the Hebrew Bible and the likelihood is that the terms הָרִאשׁוֹן and הָאַחֲרוֹן may better reference, not kings, but עֵת "time" (see NRSV, NIV etc.). In any case, since the passage is not remotely clear, it cannot serve as real evidence.

The biblical narrative in 2 Kgs 13–14 presents a picture of the Israelite kingdom's reduction during the end of Jehoahaz, followed by Jehoash's reversal that retakes and restores Israelite cities from Aram, and culminates with Jeroboam II re-establishing the ideal borders for his mini-empire (2 Kgs 14:25, 28),[289] approaching in equivalence to the borders of the Solomonic kingdom (1 Kgs 5:1 [4:21]; 8:65). The particular linkage is seen in the reference to Lebo-Hamath (Labā'u)[290] as a border in 2 Kgs 14:25 and 1 Kgs 8:65.[291] Accordingly, Jeroboam II appears, at some point, to have dominated Aram-Damascus for a limited time.[292] However, the real crux is found in verse 28,[293] which reads:

conducted the campaign against Damascus, as other Assyrian royal officials led military expeditions on behalf of their sovereign, but he did give the credit of this accomplishment to his king."

288. See Kuan 2001, 142 and appendix on p. 151. He takes the terms הָרִאשׁוֹן "the former" and הָאַחֲרוֹן "the latter" as referring to kings, and identifies them as Ḫadiānu and Rezin, respectively.

289. For an outline of the scholarly views concerning the sources, see Hasegawa 2012, 124–26.

290. For this toponym, see §7.1.

291. However, it is technically inaccurate to see this as a full "restoration" of the Davidic-Solomonic empire (Sweeney 2007, 368), since the southern border is quite different: Solomon ("the Wadi of Egypt"); Jeroboam II ("the Sea of the Arabah"). Thus the Jeroboam border description avoids "suggesting that Jeroboam added Judah to his greater Israel" (Ghantous 2013, 157).

292. Many scholars see this as occurring in the earlier part of Jeroboam II's reign. See Cogan and Tadmor 1988, 163–64; Na'aman 1993b; Kuan 1995, 127–28; Miller and Hayes 2006, 352–54. Haran (1967, 280–81) argues that it was only during the last years of Jeroboam II's reign that the expansion occurred. This seems less likely.

293. See the discussion in §7.2.4.

אֲשֶׁר־נִלְחָם וַאֲשֶׁר הֵשִׁיב אֶת־דַּמֶּשֶׂק וְאֶת־חֲמָת לִיהוּדָה בְּיִשְׂרָאֵל

… how he fought and restored Damascus and Hamath to Judah in Israel.

Various proposals have been given on how to understand this enigmatic clause. Lipiński (2000a, 311–12) asserts that the "word *lyhwdh* must be understood as *l*ᵉ*hōdō* 'to his glory.'" This seems to be the least likely suggestion. Na'aman (1993b, 231) emends וְאֶת־חֲמָת לִיהוּדָה בְּיִשְׂרָאֵל "and Hamath to Judah" to ומלחמות ליהודה בישראל "the war(s) of Judah in Israel." Hasegawa (2012, 125) suggests that the phrase "for Judah" is an insertion of a later editor. Ghantous (2013, 158) sees this clause as a theological presentation giving precedence to Judah over Israel (i.e., Jeroboam's success is claimed "for Judah by Israel"). Hence, it reflects the convictions of the redactors of the book of Kings rather than any historical reality. Finally, a rather simple solution is to read the text as ואת־חמת לישראל, dropping out יהודה ב, and yielding "and restored Damascus and Hamath to Israel."[294]

The expansion during the reign of Jeroboam II is supported by the book of Amos, which describes the recapturing of Qarnaim and Lo-Debar[295] and the extension of Israelite territory from Lebo-Hamath to the Wadi Arabah (Amos 6:13–14).[296] See detailed discussion in §3.3.3.

#### 9.3.6.3. Rezin/Raḍyān

The last king of Damascus, Rezin (Hebrew: רְצִין; Aramaic: Raḍyān),[297] came to power sometime before 738,[298] though it is unknown exactly when his reign began. Moreover, the precise origins of this monarch are also uncertain. A passage in the inscriptions of Tiglath-pileser III states: "I surrounded

294. Montgomery and Gehman 1951, 446; Hobbs 1985, 175–76; Cogan and Tadmor 1988, 161. This is seen in the Syriac version, which omits יהודה ב. This is clearly an ancient and perhaps best solution.

295. For Qarnaim see discussion in §9.2 above. Lo-Debar may be identified with Tel Dover on the north bank of the Yarmuk River. While excavations at the site have yielded Iron I materials and little Iron II remains (Wolff 1998; Rapuano 2001), the upper tell has not been excavated. So, the site remains a good possibility for the location of ancient Lo-Debar.

296. See the comments of Hasegawa 2012, 128–29; Paul 1991, 219; Cogan and Tadmor 1988, 161.

297. The name was probably written *rqyn* in eighth-century Aramaic, being composed of the root *rqy* "desired" + *n* (hypocoristic suffix). Zadok 1977, 180, 262; Pitard 1987, 181–82; Lipiński 2000a, 404; Fuchs and Hunger 2002.

298. Since his name is included among vassals who brought tribute to Tiglath-pileser III of Assyria in that year, the year 738 is a terminus. See the Iran Stela (RINAP 1:80–87, 35, iii.1–23; Tadmor 1994, 91–110 and 260–64).

(and) captured [the city of ...]ḫādara, the home of the dynasty/the ancestral home (*bīt abīšu*, lit. "the house of his father") of Raḫiānu (Rezin) of the land of Damascus, [the pl]ace where he was born."[299] Unfortunately, as pointed out in §9.2 above, the actual name of the toponym remains unknown and any attempt at locating it must remain highly speculative. Since his father's name is not mentioned, only his hometown, it is very possible that Rezin was a usurper.[300]

Yet the year 738 marked a watershed in the history of the ancient Near East (as rightly noted by Na'aman 2008, 62). Following his western campaigns of 743–740 and 738, Tiglath-pileser III (745–727) annexed vast territories in north and central Syria and established new provinces in the region: Arpadda, Tu'ammu, Kullania, Ḫatarikka, and Ṣimirra (see chs. 7 and 8 on Hamath and Arpad). He performed numerous bidirectional deportations, displacing thousands all over the empire.

During the next three years (737–735), the Assyrian king conducted campaigns against Urartu and Media, and in his absence from the west, an anti-Assyrian coalition took shape (Irvine 1990; Ehrlich 1991; Tomes 1993; Na'aman 2008). The leader of this new coalition of Levantine polities was Rezin/Raḍyān, king of Damascus, who is mentioned in several biblical texts (2 Kgs 15:37; 16:5, 7; Isa 7:1, 5, 8–9; 8:6).

A pivotal moment in the formation of this coalition seems to have been the murder of Pekahiah of Israel. When Menahem, king of Israel, "rested with his fathers," he was succeeded by his son Pekahiah, who apparently continued his father's cautious policy toward Assyria. In around 736 BCE, an opportunistic individual[301] named Pekah assassinated Pekahiah, son of Menahem, and ruled as king in Samaria (2 Kgs 15:25). Pekah's political base of support came particularly from Gilead (note the "fifty men of Gilead" mentioned in 2 Kgs 15:25),[302] and it is entirely possible that he was an underling of Rezin/Raḍyān, the king of Damascus (Irvine 1990, 298; Na'aman 1995c). His accession marked the decisive step in the formation of

---

299. RINAP 1:57–59, 20, lines 13′–14′a; Tadmor 1994, 80–81, Ann 23, 13′–14′a.

300. Did Rezin/Raḍyān usurp from Ḥaḏyān II (Ḫadiānu) or his son?

301. The term *šlyšw* could be in apposition to either Pekah or Remaliah. Remaliah could have remained loyal to the royal house even though his son, Pekah, had taken a different course of action. If the term is in apposition to Remaliah, then there is no necessity to speculate when Pekah would have served as a *šlyš* in the royal army of the Menahem dynasty. On the difficult term *šlyš*, see the recent works by Na'aman 1988; Schley 1990; and Margalith 1992.

302. Whether Pekah had a rival kingdom in Gilead, see Kuan 1995, 126–27. Dion (1997, 213 n. 180) notes that Shallum might have been of Transjordanian origin, if בֶּן־יָבֵישׁ is taken as a gentilic and if the Yabesh where he seems to be born was Jabesh-Gilead (2 Kgs 15:10, 13).

the anti-Assyrian coalition, for a number of other kingdoms joined the rebels, as indicated by the Assyrian accusations against some rulers that they either joined Damascus (e.g., Ḫi-rumu, "Hiram," of Tyre)[303] or broke their loyalty oath (e.g., Mitinti of Ashkelon and Samsi, queen of the Arabs; Na'aman 2008, 63). Thus Damascus, Tyre, Israel, Gaza, Ashkelon, and the Arabs are listed together in Tiglath-pileser's summary inscriptions as participants in the rebellion.[304] It is possible that Egypt was also involved in the negotiations and that Rezin and Pekah had hoped for Egyptian military aid. This may very well explain why Tiglath-pileser III reacted to the formation of the coalition by conducting an immediate campaign to the Egyptian border (734), thereby blocking a possible advance of Egyptian troops to the coast of Philistia. Clearly, the main objective of this campaign in 734 was Philistia—Gaza and the Egyptian border to be precise as the Eponym Chronicle implies in its statement: *ana māt Pilišta* "to Philistia" (Millard 1994, 44).

Tiglath-pileser III's annals are not preserved for the events of this year,[305] and unfortunately only a few passages from the "Summary Inscriptions"[306] report on individual episodes of this campaign, in particular the expedition against Ḫanūnu of Gaza. This Philistine king fled in fear to Egypt, but Tiglath-pileser reinstated him and made the city an Assyrian *bīt kāri*. The Assyrian king also erected a stela in Ḫanūnu's palace and imposed a heavy tribute. Tiglath-pileser also moved further southwest to Naḫal-Muṣur, where he had another stela erected. At this same time, it appears that the Arab tribe of Mu'na (i.e., the Me'unites) submitted to Tiglath-pileser,[307] and Idibi'ilu was established as the "gatekeeper" in the area of Naḫal Muṣur.

Also in 734, perhaps very early in that year, Rezin and Pekah attempted to force Judah into the coalition, threatening a siege of Jerusalem (2 Kgs 15:37; 16:5–9; Isa 7:1–2). There may have existed a state of war for a few

303. Tadmor 1994, Summ. 9:r.5.

304. On the basis of this, Dubovský (2006, 158 n. 15) is correct in preferring to take all three campaigns (734, 733, 732) as part of one military operation aimed at reestablishing Assyrian control over the Levant.

305. The Hebrew Bible is also silent about this year's campaign.

306. Tadmor 1994: Summary Inscriptions 4:8′–15′; 7:r.12′–13′; 8:14′–19′; and 9:r.13–16 = RINAP 1:105–6, 42, lines 8′–15′a; 1:123, 47, lines r.12′–13′; 1:127, 48, lines 14′b–19′a; and 1:132, 49, lines 13–16.

307. Tadmor 1994, Summary 8:22′–23′; see Na'aman (1998) with hypothetical restoration for Summary 13, lines 15–16: (15) … *šul-ma-ni-šú-nu* [*qe-re*]*b*$^{!}$ É.GAL *ú*ʾ-[… $^{m}$*Si-ru*]-*at-t*[*i*] (16) [KUR *Mu-*ʾ*u-na-a-a ù*] $^{m}$*I-di-bi-*ʾ*i-i-lu a-na* LÚ.*q*[*e-pu*]-*ti* <*ina*> *muḫḫi* [x x KUR *Mu-uṣ*]-*ri ap-qid*, "Their gifts I [stored/exhibited] within the palace. [Siru]att[i the Me'unite and] Idibi'ilu I appointed as 'su[pervis]ors' over [the entrance? of Egy]pt." See also Bagg 2011, 217. However, Tadmor and Yamada (RINAP 1:111) read 44, line 15′b: *šùl-*⸢*ma-ni*⸣*-šú-nu* [x (x)] A ⸢É?⸣.GAL x […] AD x.

years prior to this (depending on how one understands 2 Chr 28:5–21).[308] This conflict has been dubbed by scholars as the Syro-Ephraimite war, despite the confusion such a designation causes. There is, of course, debate over the exact reason(s) for the war against Judah. Some believe that it was:

(1) To replace Ahaz with a ruler that would support the Damascus-Israel anti-Assyrian coalition (the traditional view) (e.g., Weippert 1982, 396–98, Na'aman 1991, 91–4; Dion 1997, 211; etc.);

(2) to expand territory starting earlier in Jotham's reign (Jotham had defeated the Ammonites, making them vassals [2 Chr 27:5]; thus in the initial conflict [2 Chr 28:5], Ahaz lost the Transjordanian gains of his father. The issue was the control of the Transjordan (Oded 1972);

(3) to solve inward struggles (odd that Damascus and Israel would want to weaken themselves in battle against Judah if they were susceptible to Assyrian attack; Tomes 1993, 55–71);

(4) to secure the profits from the lucrative Arabian caravan trade, preventing Assyrian seizure (Dion 1997, 213–14). In this view, the war was the result of an important economic factor.[309] The coalition could not tolerate the noncommittal attitude of Judah, who enjoyed a key position between Arabia and Philistia.[310]

(5) These are not necessarily mutually exclusive. But the need for Rezin and Pekah to secure their southern flank became acute with the Assyrian threat. Even a minor enemy can distract.[311] Hence, it was not so much that Judah would be a powerful addition to the coalition, as that it would siphon off Aramean and/or Israelite troops to deal with it. In addition, with the economic issue of the Arabian trade, Judah, due to its geographic location, was an important factor for the coalition's success. Having a "stooge" on the throne of Judah would greatly enhance Rezin's cause.[312]

308. For a recent discussion of the issues, see Siddall 2009. See also Kalimi 2005, 332–34; Knoppers 1999, 200–201; Dubovský 2006, 156–57.

309. This may explain the enigmatic 2 Kgs 16:6: "At that time King Rezin of Aram recovered Elath for Aram; he drove out the Judahites from Elath, and Edomites came to Elath and settled there, as is still the case."

310. This interpretation underscores the importance of the Transjordanian routes as well as the routes to the coastal ports.

311. E.g., the Nazi invasion of Yugoslavia before the invasion of the Soviet Union was intended to eliminate such a situation.

312. Interestingly, the writer of 2 Kgs 15:37 introduces an additional (obviously unverifiable) divine reason: "In those days, the LORD began to incite (לְהַשְׁלִיחַ) King Rezin of Aram and Pekah son of Remaliah against Judah" (NJPS). This expresses an ancient Judahite ideological perspective.

Certainly, according to Isa 7, it seems that Rezin and Pekah planned to replace Ahaz of Judah with an anti-Assyrian puppet ruler, Tabeel (Isa 7:6), clearly a man who was willing to join the coalition in exchange for a chance at the throne.[313] Ahaz apparently refused to join the coalition and instead paid tribute to Tiglath-pileser III.[314] So far as is known, this is the first tribute paid by a Judahite king to Assyria. It appears that the same narrator who composed 1 Kgs 15 (story of war between Baasha and Asa with Asa's sending a שֹׁחַד to Ben-Hadad/Bar-Hadad of Damascus) composed this narrative. In 2 Kgs 16:8, the use of the term שֹׁחַד is clearly the narrator's choice of words. Thus just as in 1 Kgs 15:19, the term is used as an ironic wordplay: on the one hand, it may simply be "a present," but on the other hand, in light of the use of Yahweh's treasuries (a major issue for the writer of these two stories), it is nothing short of "a bribe."

From one modern political angle, Ahaz's action might be evaluated as positive: his "adherence to the cautious policy of his ancestors and his avoidance of participation in the anti-Assyrian coalition proved correct and kept his kingdom safe and sound in a period of widespread annexations, destruction, and plunder" (Na'aman 2008, 63). However, from the perspective of the biblical writers Ahaz is censored. For the writer of Isa 7:1–17,[315] the use of Yahweh's treasuries and the lack of trust on the part Ahaz (note the rebuke in Isa 7:13 and the allusions to Deut 20:1–4) are interpreted negatively: he is one who fears "on account of the ragings (בָּחֳרִי־אַף) of Rezin and his Arameans, and the son of Remaliah (i.e., Pekah)" (Isa 7:4). In the case of the writer of 2 Kgs 16, Ahaz is a Judahite king who "did not do what was right (הַיָּשָׁר) in the eyes of Yahweh, as his ancestor David had done, but followed in the ways of the kings of Israel" (2 Kgs 16:2b–3). Importantly, none of these perspectives on the events is necessarily "wrong," just different.

The same is true for the reasons for Assyrian involvement in the region. From the Assyrian perspective, the aspirations of the Levantine states for economic independence and their attempt to expand their territories and/or control trade routes were perceived as an anti-Assyrian activity (Dubovský

313. Possibly a scion of the house of David (Na'aman 2008, 63).

314. Probably in the year 734. See Tadmor 1994, 170–71, Summary 7:r.11': ᵐ*Ia-ú-ḫa-zi* KUR.*Ia-ú-da-a-a* "Jehoahaz [i.e., Ahaz] the Judahite." See *COS* 2.117D:289. For the dating of this list, see Tadmor 1994, 268.

315. On the one hand, the writer of 2 Kgs 16 is more explicit than Isaiah calling the "tribute" to Tiglath-pileser III a "bribe," and thus evaluating the appeal for help from Tiglath-pileser as a horrendous act for the nation's well-being. Yet, on the other hand, Isa 7 is more explicit in rebuking Ahaz for a lack of trust and failure to implement the law of Deut 20:1–4, and does not explicitly criticize Ahaz's appeal to the Assyrian king, though the concluding statement in the prophecy (7:17) implies the ultimate disaster for Judah of the coming of the Assyrian king.

2006, 155). Certainly, a major reason for the Assyrian campaign against Damascus and Samaria in 733–732 was the increasing power of Aram and Israel (Galil 1992, 60). But the Assyrians were definitely also interested in the Arabian trade network. And while it would be naive to suppose that the Assyrians were solely motivated by the desperate call of Ahaz, king of Judah, or by his bribe, the Assyrians do show a significant tendency to support their vassals when possible. This was part of a combined "carrot and stick policy" carried out by the Assyrians.[316]

Tiglath-pileser's campaigns of 733 and 732 were directed primarily against Damascus since Rezin was unquestionably the ringleader of the coalition.[317] Tiglath-pileser's annals record the campaigns of these years against Damascus (Tadmor 1994, 78–81, Ann. 23:1′–17′; RINAP 1:58–9, 20, lines 1′–17′; *COS* 2.117A:286).

> [... of] Rezin (*ʳRaʾḫiānu*) [the Damascene ...]. [I captured] heavy [booty] [...] his advisor [...] [(With) the blood of his] war[riors] I dyed a reddish hue the river of [...], a raging [torrent]; [...], his tribal chief[tains] ([*ālik*] *pānīšu*), charioteers and [...], their weapons I smashed; and [...] their horses, [their mule]s, his warriors, archers, shield- and lance-bearers I captured; and I dispersed their battle array.
>
> That one (i.e. Rezin), in order to save his life, fled alone; and he entered the gate of his city [like] a mongoose. I impaled alive his chief ministers; and I made his country behold (them). I set up my camp around the city for 45 days; and I confined him like a bird in a cage. I cut down his gardens, [...] orchards without number; I did not leave a single one.
>
> [The town of ...]ḫādara, the home of the dynasty (*bīt abīšu*) of Rezin (Raḫiānu), the Damascene, [the pl]ace where he was born, I surrounded (and) captured. 800 people with their possessions, their cattle (and) their sheep I took as spoil. I took as spoil 750 captives from the city of Kuruṣṣâ (and) the city of Samāya, 550 captives from the city of Metuna. I destroyed 591 cities of 16 districts of the land of Damascus like mounds of ruins after the Deluge.

In 733, Tiglath-pileser routed the army of Rezin/Raḍyān near a river (unfortunately the name has not been preserved). Rezin's army was thoroughly shattered and dispersed. Then Tiglath-pileser besieged Damascus where Rezin had fled. The impaling alive of numerous high officials did not bring about the capitulation of the city. Realizing that they could not succeed in

316. See Younger 2015b; Fales 2010b.
317. For the following, see Younger 1998, 206–14; and more recently Dubovský 2006, 157–61.

taking the city in that year, the Assyrians wasted the surrounding 591 settlements, devoting particular attention to the birthplace of Rezin (Ann. 23:13′). They especially singled out gardens and orchards for destruction. Rezin's defeat demoralized the coalition, which apparently had not been able to join its forces in time to engage the Assyrian king. Thus the rebels were split up to be dealt with piecemeal. It appears that Tiglath-pileser had moved so rapidly into the land of Damascus that only Rezin/Raḍyān was in a position to fight the Assyrians.[318] The demoralization of the coalition resulted in a *coup d'état* in Ashkelon (Tadmor 1994, Ann. 18:9; Ann. 24:13′).

So, while Damascus underwent this siege, a two-pronged attack was launched by Assyrian troops on Israel in the Gilead and Galilee regions. The conquest of Gilead was connected with Tiglath-pileser's attack on Damascus. It was a logical continuation of this campaign from a military, geographic viewpoint. Also it would have greatly weakened Pekah since Gilead appears to have been the heartland of his political power. If Pekah were, as one interpreter remarks, "the stooge" of Damascus (Irvine 1990, 298), then his power was, for all practical purposes, eliminated with Damascus undergoing a withering siege and Gilead fallen into Assyrian hands. Tiglath-pileser III's annals do not preserve the section that described the campaign into Gilead. However, Summary Inscription 4 gives a fragmentary account (Tadmor 1994, 138–39, 140–41, Summary 4, lines 6′–7′, 15′a–19′a; RINAP 1:105–6, 42, lines 6′–7′, 15′a–19′a):[319]

> [… the cities of …]nite,[320] Gi[lead?, and] Abel-…,[321] which are the border of Bīt Ḫumri[a] (Israel)—I annexed to Assyria the en[tire] wide land of [Bīt-Ḫaza'i]li (Aram).
>
> I carried off [to] Assyria the land of Bīt-Ḫumria (Israel), [… its] "auxiliary [army,"] […] all of its people, […]

318. None of the other coalition members are mentioned as being present at this riverside battle.

319. An indirect reference in Summary Inscription 13 may also reflect the campaign.

320. Tadmor (1994, 139, note to 6′) states: "One might restore here [*adi libbi* $^{uru}$*Qa*]-⸢*ni*⸣-*te*: Biblical Kenath (Num 32:42; 1 Chr 2:23) modern Qanawat in the Ḫauran (Abel 1933–38, 2:418). However, other restorations are not excluded." Na'aman (1995c, 105) restores [*a-di* URU.*mi*]-⸢*ni*⸣-*te* "[as far as the city Mi]nite."

321. RINAP 1:105, 42, note to line 6′: "[URU].*a-bi-il-šiṭ-*⸢*ṭi*⸣ ['the city] Abil-šiṭṭi': So according to G. Smith's draft." Tadmor (1994, 139) notes that the earlier restoration of Abel Beth-Ma'akah (cf. 2 Kgs 15:29) "cannot be sustained any longer." Abil-šiṭṭi perhaps can be identified with *'bl hšṭym* of Num 33:48–49, which would indicate that Aram on the eve of its fall controlled a much larger territory east of Jordan (Tadmor 1994, 281 n. 10).

> [I/they killed][322] Pekah, their king, and
>
> I installed Hoshea[323] [as king] over them.
>
> I received from them 10 talents of gold, x talents of silver, [with] their [property] and
>
> [I car]ried them [to Assyria].

Two biblical passages seems to report the campaign to Gilead: 2 Kgs 15:29 and 1 Chr 5:26. The first passage states:

> In the days of Pekah king of Israel, Tiglath-pileser king of Assyria came and took Iyyon, Abel Beth-Ma'akah, Yanoaḥ, Kedesh and Hazor—Gilead and Galilee—all the land of Naphtali; and he deported the people to Assyria.

The second adds:

> So the God of Israel stirred up the spirit of Pul king of Assyria (that is Tiglath-pileser king of Assyria), who took the Reubenites, the Gadites and the half-tribe of Manasseh into exile. He took them to Halah, Habor, Hara[324] and the river of Gōzān, where they are to this day.[325]

In the case of the biblical accounts, the mention of Gilead in 2 Kgs 15:29 is problematic—probably a later gloss (as too the mention of Galilee). First Chronicles 5:26 is late and very difficult with at least one probable corruption: Hara.[326]

Unfortunately, the names of the cities in line 6′ are not fully preserved. Tadmor's suggested readings of URU.*Ga-al-*[*'a-a-di*], "the city of Gil[ead]" and [URU].*a-bi-il-šiṭ-*⌜*ṭi*⌝, "Abel-Shit[tim]" seem to be the best options. Thus, Tadmor (1994, 281), Irvine (1994) and Na'aman (1995c, 107) are probably right that the Transjordan on the eve of the Assyrian invasion was in the

322. For a discussion of this word's restoration, see Tadmor 1994, 141 n. to line 17′; RINAP 1:106, note to line 17′. But also see the discussion above in the section on Hazael and the Tel Dan Inscription.

323. The king of Assyria contented himself by mutilating the kingdom of Israel. The removal of Pekah was undoubtedly connected to a pro-Assyrian (anti-Damascus?) group within Israel, which since the time of Jehu had often been willing to serve Assyria. See Na'aman 1991, 94.

324. Hara is an unknown place and is probably a textual corruption. See Williamson 1982, 67. Hara (*hārā'*) is perhaps the result of confusion with *'ārê* "cities."

325. Also cf. 2 Chr 5:6: "and Beerah his son, whom Tiglath-pileser king of Assyria took into exile. Beerah was a leader of the Reubenites;" and also Judg 18:30.

326. The mention of the exile locations may be anachronistic or a confusion in transmission (Cogan and Tadmor 1988, 197).

possession of Aram-Damascus.[327] This is a very tentative conclusion and does not negate the ancient Israelite tradition that this was Israelite territory (1 Chr 5:26), of which there was a long history. In real terms, the population still consisted of a significant Israelite component (perhaps the majority), even if Aram-Damascus were in political control. That there was a deportation in the Transjordan seems assured since Tiglath-pileser's reliefs picture a deportation of men from a city that is clearly identified by the epigraph URU. *As-tar(a)-tu*, which is biblical Ashtaroth (Aštarot).[328]

Neither Ashtaroth nor Gezer (discussed below) is mentioned in any of the preserved portions of Tiglath-pileser's inscriptions.[329] These are—along with a third epigraph (*U-pa*?)—the first known appearance of epigraphs on the wall reliefs of an Assyrian palace,[330] and consist of a single city name written above the walls of the city that it labels (Russell 1999, 96). Given the very fragmentary nature of Tiglath-pileser III's inscriptions, it would not be prudent to make too much of the fact that none of the three cities mentioned by epigraph are mentioned in his inscriptions. However, it is worth noting that more than half of the toponyms in the epigraphs on the Khorsabad reliefs of Sargon II do not appear in his historical records.[331] This reinforces the fact that both the Assyrian inscriptions and reliefs are highly selective and partial. They supplement one another.

The campaign(s) to Galilee and the conquest of the "entire region of Naphtali" are recorded in the biblical text (cf. 2 Kgs 15:29 above), as well as in Tiglath-pileser's Annals (Ann. 18: 3′–7′; 24:3′–11′) and Summary Inscriptions (Summ. 4:15′–17′; and Summ. 9:r.9). While 2 Kgs 15:29 contains a gloss (the mention of Galilee and Gilead), it is clear that it is a selective listing of a campaign route or part of a campaign route. The former may be preferred since there is the parallel campaign route of Ben-Hadad/Bar-Hadad I given in 1 Kgs 15:20 (Becking 1992, 15–19; Na'aman 1993, 106). Second Kings 15:29 and the fragmentary list of Tiglath-pileser III contain different sites from one another with no overlap. Since Tiglath-pileser III campaigned

327. Irvine (1994) argues also that Galilee was annexed by Rezin before the invasion. However, the evidence can be read in a different (and perhaps more convincing) way. Until much more firm evidence is discovered this view must be held in reserve. See the objections of Dion 1997, 212 n. 177.

328. See Tadmor 1994, 210; Younger 2003, 36–37.

329. Furthermore, the accompanying texts on the two slabs showing these labeled cities, Aštartu and Gezer, do not refer to any western campaigns of Tiglath-pileser III, but to his campaigns against Urartu in his eleventh year and against Babylonia in his fifteenth year.

330. Earlier epigraphs like these are found on bronze gate bands or on obelisks.

331. On the function of descriptive epigraphs (one sentence or more) on palace reliefs, especially of the Sargonid kings, see Gerardi 1988; Russell 1991.

for two years (733–732) in the area of northern Israel, one cannot even be sure that the biblical and Assyrian lists refer to the same campaign, although commentators have typically taken them to refer to one and the same campaign (see Younger 1998, 208–10).

Based on Tadmor's analysis (1994, 210) of the order of Tiglath-pileser's slabs, the one containing the relief of the besieged city with the epigraph URU.*Ga-az-ru* should be dated to the campaigns against Israel and Damascus (733–732). If this is correct, then the capture of Gezer may have occurred in connection with the demise of Mitinti of Ashkelon some time after the initial defeat of Rezin in 733.[332]

No Assyrian sources for the year 732 are preserved.[333] However, it is clear that the siege was resumed (if, in fact, it was ever lifted), and Damascus was captured, its inhabitants were deported, and Rezin was executed (the capture and execution of Rezin is found in 2 Kgs 16:9).[334]

One particular causality on the Assyrian side is known. The Panamuwa inscription from Zincirli records the participation of Panamuwa II, the king of Sam'al, alongside Tiglath-pileser III in his campaign against Damascus. Panamuwa was killed in the attack on Damascus and mourned by the Assyrian king.[335]

The entire "wide land of Bīt-Ḫaza'ili" (Aram-Damascus) was annexed into the Assyrian imperial system. Designating the kingdom of Aram-Damascus as Bīt-Ḫaza'ili plays an important ideological role. It is not simply that the Assyrians recognize Hazael as a great military leader in the region. Giving the kingdom this name is a particular way that Tiglath-pileser III is glorified: he conquered the land that Shalmaneser III could not and that Adad-nērārī III could only extract tribute. He outdid his predecessors! Although this was the end of the independent political entity of Aram-Damascus, the city became an Assyrian provincial capital. A fragmentary

332. See Tadmor 1994, 82–83 (Ann. 18.8′–10′ and 24.12′–16′). See also the discussion of Ehrlich 1991, 56–58; Dubovský 2006, 157. For the most recent discussion of the Assyrian materials from Gezer, see Ornan, Ortiz, and Wolff 2013.

333. However, the fall of Damascus must be dated to 732, since in the next year (731) Tiglath-pileser III was already fighting in Babylonia. The Assyrian king would not have left the region without ending the siege of Damascus and dealing with its ringleader.

334. The mention of the deportation of the inhabitants of Damascus to Qir remains problematic for two reasons. First, there is a textual problem. Pitard (1987, 188 n. 113) notes that the word does not appear in most manuscripts of the Old Greek. In the Lucianic recension the reading appears to be *απωκισεν την πολιν*, which suggests a reading העיר in the *Vorlage*. The reference to Qir may be a gloss under the influence of the prophecy in Amos 1:5, "and the people of Aram shall go into exile to Qir." The second issue is due to the uncertainty of the location of the toponym "Qir." For this, see the discussion in ch. 2.

335. See §6.3.5, p. 419.

letter may mention construction works in Damascus (SAA 19:50–51, text 45; Saggs 2001, 181).

9.3.7. Postscript

About twelve years later, in the time of Sargon II, Damascus participated in a Levantine revolt[336] led by Yau-biʾdi of Hamath in 720 BCE. There are no further details given concerning Assyrian reprisals in Damascus as the result of the revolt's failure, but perhaps, based on analogy with Samaria's fate, there was some type of action against the city's leadership. There is an interesting letter[337] that records the Assyrian interception of a raid by the Arab tribe of Amiri (probably under the leadership of a man named Ammiliʾti, though he is not named in the text). This raid was intended to capture the booty (⸢LÚ⸣.*ḫu-ub-t*[*e*]) that was being transferred from Damascus to Assyria (*ša* T[A*] U[RU.*di*]-*maš-qa*). This could be interpreted as booty from Damascus itself or booty "which was from Damascus" meaning it was being shipped from Damascus but may have originated elsewhere (possibly from a later war of Sargon in the southern Levant?). In any case, two Assyrian governors, Adda-ḫāti (governor of Hamath) and Bēl-(l)iqbi (governor or vice-governor of Ṣupat) joined forces to preempt the Arab raid. However, apparently the Arab leader saw them approaching and laid an ambush for them. It seems that the battle turned in favor of the Assyrians who then pursued the Arabs. But due to the rugged terrain, the governors had to stop their pursuit and the Arabs escaped.

At the time of Aššurbanipal, the geographical position of Damascus played a pivotal role in the imperial operations in the Arab world.[338] Thus this city's advantages to the trade routes were so great that it never lost its place in the heart of the economic, political and cultural life of the ancient Near East, unlike many other "royal cities" of the Levant in the Iron Age.

---

336. Fuchs 1994, 200–201. Samaria is also listed among the rebels. See Younger 1999.

337. SAA 1:136–37, text 175; Saggs 2001, 167–68 (ND 2381). Dion (1997, 215 n. 190) mistakenly connects this letter with the time of Tiglath-pileser III, but it appears to belong to the period of Sargon II.

338. Prism A IX.8, 12. See Borger 1996, 65; see Weippert 1973–74, 65–66.

Table 9.7. List of Known Kings of Aram-Damascus

| | |
|---|---|
| ♦Hadad-ezer of Ṣobah (הֲדַדְעֶזֶר) (Aram: *hd-ʿdr*) | first quarter of the tenth century<br>(970 - Liverani) |
| - - - - - - - - - - | - - - - - - - - - - |
| ♦Rezon/Ezron (רְזוֹן / אֶזְרוֹן?) | third quarter of the tenth century<br>(950 - Liverani) |
| ♦Ḥadyān I (Aram: *ḥz/dyn*) (חֶזְיוֹן)<br>\| | fourth quarter of the tenth century |
| ♦Ṭāb-Rammān (טַבְרִמֹּן)<br>\| | end of the tenth century |
| ♦Bar-Hadad I (בֶּן־הֲדַד) | ca. 900–880<br>(900–873 - Liverani) |
| ——————— | ——————— |
| *Hadad-ezer (Akk: *Adad-idri*) // ♦Bar-Hadad (II) (בֶּן־הֲדַד) | ca. 880–844/843<br>(855–845 - Liverani) |
| *○♦Hazael (Aram: חזאל) (Akk: *Ḫazā-il*) (חֲזָהאֵל; חֲזָאֵל)<br>\| | ca. 844/843–803<br>(845–800 - Liverani) |
| *Mari' (Akk: *Māri'*) // ♦○Bar-Hadad II/III (Aram: בר הדד) (בֶּן־הֲדַד) | ca. 803–775<br>(800–780 - Liverani) |
| *Ḥadyān II (Aram: *ḥz/dyn*) (Akk: *Ḫadiānu*) | ca. 775–750<br>(780–750 - Liverani) |
| *♦Raḍyān (רְצִין) (Aram: *rqyn*) (Akk: *Raḫiānu/Raqiānu*) | ca. 750–732<br>(750–730 - Liverani) |

♦ Biblical source
* Assyrian source
○ Aramaic source
| genealogical relationship
- - - - above this line represents the earlier domination of Damascus
—— represents the division between kings known solely from the biblical sources and those known from Assyrian, Old Aramaic, and biblical sources
Liverani = Liverani 2014, 407

# 10
# ARAMEANS IN SOUTHERN MESOPOTAMIA

VARIOUS SOURCES ATTEST TO THE PRESENCE OF ARAMEAN TRIBAL ENTITIES IN southern Mesopotamia. While our knowledge of these groups has increased in substantial ways, there is still a lack of clarity about their origins in the lower Tigris and Euphrates alluvium. Fortunately, in a number of instances, it is possible to trace the movements of some of these Aramean groups from the Jezirah into the region.

For the sake of coherence, I have postponed the discussion of the Aramean tribes of the Jezirah that are also encountered in the southern Mesopotamian region. Thus, this chapter will first present the material that concerns these tribes. It will then deal with the complex diversity of the population in southern Mesopotamia, with special interest, of course, on its many Aramean tribal entities.[1]

## 10.1. ARAMEAN TRIBAL ENTITIES OF THE JEZIRAH

A number of sources attest to the various Aramean socially constructed groups in the Jezirah, whether clans, tribal entities, and/or confederations (the interrelationships are not always clear). Particularly important are the lists of these units in the inscriptions of Tiglath-pileser III who gives the names of thirty-six entities, though many of these are not located in the Jezirah proper.[2] An earlier list is given by Šamšī-ilu.[3] Although not in list form,

1. The spelling of the Aramean tribal names generally follows that used by Zadok (2013, esp. tables 1 and 2). For a list of the Aramean tribes and some information on their general location, see also Frahm 2003, 151–53; Streck 2014.

2. These can be seen in RINAP 1 and Tadmor 1994.

3. RIMA 3:232, A.0.104.2010, lines 10–11.

Ninurta-kudurrī-uṣur mentions a number of these groups in his inscriptions.[4] Sargon II and Sennacherib also provide lists of Aramean tribal units. Finally, administrative documents provide additional data, for example, the governor's archive from Nippur (Cole 1996a, 1996b).

The Neo-Assyrian lists provide evidence of these Aramean tribes that is explicit: that is, the groups are precisely and clearly expressed and identified as Aramean, leaving nothing to uncertainty. These data are presented in table 10.1 below. These lists evince certain sequences and patterns. Zadok (2008, 316–17; 2013, 274–75) has pointed out that some of the lists exhibit the use of conventional numbers. Two of the lists in Tiglath-pileser III's summary inscriptions utilize the number "seven" in this manner: the number of tribes is thirty-five (7 × 5) and fourteen (7 × 2; columns three and five respectively in the table below). It is also very likely that the fragmentary inscription, where eighteen tribes are preserved (column 4), had originally more tribes with a multiple of seven (Zadok 2013, 274). The shorter list (column 6) has ten tribes, which is also a number used conventionally.[5] Furthermore, the list in Sennacherib's inscriptions (basically identical in each inscription as a result of copying) has seventeen tribes, which is a combination of two typological numbers (10 + 7; Zadok 2013, 274).

Interestingly, the first tribes listed (except in the case of Sennacherib's list) were the initial tribes that the Assyrians encountered in Upper Mesopotamia. The pattern of the lists conforms with the pattern in the inscriptions of Šamšī-ilu. There are two exceptions: (1) the Ḫamarānu tribe is not listed in Šamšī-ilu's register, but this tribe is associated with the Sippar region, which bordered on the middle Euphrates; and (2) the Luḫu'ātu tribe is also not mentioned by Šamšī-ilu, but this tribe is very closely connected with the Ḫaṭallu confederation, again in a middle Euphrates context according to the inscriptions of Ninurta-kudurrī-uṣur.[6] Notably, Sargon II's first four tribes are precisely the same as the four tribes listed in Šamšī-ilu's list!

In all of the lists in the table, the tribal unit of the Utū'/Itū'[7] is listed first, followed by the Rupū' (except in one list of Tiglath-pileser III and in Sennacherib's list).[8] Apparently this sequence was established by Šamšī-ilu's list. There may have been an element of hierarchy in the pattern (Zadok 2013,

4. Cavigneaux and Ismail 1990, 343–57, 412–17; Frame 1995 (RIMB 2:294–300).

5. Compare the significant usage of ten in the genealogies in the book of Genesis and in Ruth 4.

6. See p. 57 in ch. 2.

7. For the spelling of the tribal name, see below. For simplicity, the later spelling Itū' will be used.

8. This includes Tiglath-pileser III's basalt bull inscription from Arslan Taş (see RINAP 1:139–42, 51, line 3).

274). The listing of Itū' first is very likely merited by the fact that Itū' was the most important of the Aramean tribes, at least from the Assyrian point of view, being located very close to Assyria proper (Zadok 2013, 274).

The case of the Labdūdu tribe is particularly interesting. While it is listed fourth in Šamšī-ilu's register, it is absent from Tiglath-pileser's lists. However, this tribe is mentioned as being deported by Tiglath-pileser III from the area near the Elamite border and settled within Assyria proper.[9] Šamšī-ilu most certainly did not campaign in the region of the Elamite border. Therefore, this is evidence that this tribe migrated from Upper Mesopotamia to the Elamite border region, or that some part of the tribe did.[10]

Although there was, of course, always a seasonal movement of the pastoralist components of a given tribe, it is doubtful that these seasonal orbits "extended from northern or eastern Syria across northern Babylonia to the banks of the lower Tigris" (Cole 1994, 224). The Ḫaṭallu did not move seasonally from near Til-Barsib to southeastern Babylonia each year.[11]

Although Tiglath-pileser III's long list (column 3) seems exhaustive, this is not the case. After the list, the inscription contains a digression about the Babylonian temple cities. This is followed by a section detailing Tiglath-pileser's defeat and annexation of the Puqūdu tribe and the deportation of Lab(a)dūdu tribe (neither entity is identified as Aramean).[12] However, Tiglath-pileser's shortest list records LÚ.*pu-qu-du* as an Aramean tribe,[13] perhaps in recognition of the prominence of this tribe in Babylonia (Zadok 2013, 275).

Tiglath-pileser III's shorter lists maintain the same sequence pattern. Even if there are gaps, there is no change in the order. The only exception occurs in the fragmentary list (Column 4) where number (32) Lītawu is listed eleventh in the list between number (12) Nabātu and (13) Raḫīqu (see column 4). The list of fourteen tribes (Column 5) retains the first seven (Itū' to Rāpiqu), although it omits most of the remaining ones. Tiglath-pileser III's shortest list (Column 6) retains only the first four tribes, yet is the only list that includes the Puqūdu as its last member, perhaps because of its prominence. All of Tiglath-pileser's lists have the Lītawu. Clearly, such inclusions as the Puqūdu and the Lītawu are the result of his Babylonian campaigns.

---

9. RINAP 1:118–19, 47, lines 13a–15a, esp. 14b–15a.

10. Perhaps, like the tribe of Dan in Judg 18.

11. Moreover, the movement of these tribes certainly was restricted at times by the imperial powers.

12. RINAP 1:118–19, 47, lines 13b–15a; Tadmor 1994, 160, summary 7.

13. RINAP 1:100, 40, line 6; Tadmor 1994, 130, summary 2.

A number of these tribal entities appear to have moved from Syria down the Euphrates into Babylonia over the course of the eighth century BCE (Cole 1996b, 25). Šamšī-ilu (787–746) described himself as "the devastator or flattener (*sāpin*) of the Utū', Rupū', Ḫaṭallu (and) Labdūdu."[14] The Eponym Chronicle has "to the land of Itū'a (*a-na* KUR *i-tu-(a)* for the years 783, 782, 777, and 769 (Millard 1994, 37–40). Since Šamšī-ilu's Lion inscriptions must date before the 773 campaign to Damascus,[15] the battles with these four tribes most likely occurred in the years 783, 782, and 777. Whether the four tribes formed a coalition or not is unknown, but it may be that the Eponym Chronicle's entry "Itū'a" stands for the four tribes by naming the most significant one.

That these tribes were located in Upper Mesopotamia is undoubted, for Šamšī-ilu did not campaign in Babylonia. Whether the tribes were located near Til-Barsib[16] or somewhere in the Jezirah is not entirely clear. Cole (1996b, 25) writes:

> Sometime in the decade or two before 750, two thousand Ḫaṭallu and Luḫu'aya tribesmen moved from Sarūgu, near Carchemish, in the Aramean domain of Bīt-Adīni and attacked the territory of Laqē on the lower Ḫābūr.

However, since the inscriptions of Ninurta-kudurrī-uṣur clearly state that the Ḫaṭallu had to pass by Sūḫu in order to attack Laqē (thus an east to west movement is implied), the Ḫaṭallu confederation was, as Liverani notes, "clearly occupying the area between (the city of) Assur and (the land of) Sūḫu, i.e., the area of the Wadi Tharthar, perfectly fitting as the abode of a nomadic tribe."[17] This was the Ḫaṭallu confederation's location at this time. However, this fact does not mean that the Ḫaṭallu confederation was located in this area at the time of Šamšī-ilu's engagements. The tribe may have been located nearer to Til-Barsib, perhaps in the Great Bend of the Euphrates.

As indicated by the quote of Cole above, some scholars have understood the references in the inscription of Ninurta-kudurrī-uṣur to the Sarūgu clan or tribe to be connected with the city of Sarūgu, mentioned in the inscriptions of Aššurnaṣirpal II and Shalmaneser III, identified with modern Suruç.[18] However, Lipiński (2000a, 174 n. 66, 427) points out that this city should be distinguished from the Aramean clan, asserting:

14. RIMA 3:232, A.0.104.2010, line 10.

15. See §5.3.1 and table 5.4 above.

16. Streck (2006–8a, 463) comments: "Šamšī-ilu nennt sich im frühen 8. Jahrhundert den Zerstörer des Landes der Rupū'u; offenbar lebte ein Stamm dieses Namens damals in der Umgebung von Til-Barsip."

17. Liverani 1992b, 37. See also Lipiński 2000a, 426.

18. For a discussion of these, see pp. 329–30.

> The first group {LÚ.*Sa-ru-gu*} cannot be identified with the city URU.*Sa-ru-gi* in Upper Mesopotamia, but its name may correspond to the Safaitic personal name *Śrg*. It is one of the numerous clans or tribes that cannot be identified as yet (p. 427).

Although the name of the city is written URU.*sa-ru-gi* in the Harran Census,[19] the gentilic form used in the royal inscriptions of Aššurnaṣirpal II and Shalmaneser III is URU.*sa-ru-ga-a-a* (for the occurrences, see Bagg 2007, 215). There is no compelling reason to distinguish the city from the tribe, especially when one considers the fact that a number of the tribal names appear as city names.[20] The fact that it is possible for the same clan or tribe to have sedentary and mobile elements means that parts of the mobile element of the Sarūgu may have migrated from Upper Mesopotamia to the Middle Euphrates.[21]

If Šamšī-ilu engaged the Ḫaṭallu and its clans in 783–782 and 777, he was either successful in driving a tribe east into the Wadi Tharthar from the Great Bend region or unsuccessful in subduing the confederation, if it was already located in the area of the wadi, because by the time of Ninurta-kudurrī-uṣur, the confederation was located in the wadi and was not subjugated.

Finally, there is significant evidence for the migration of a number of the tribes (or parts of them) found in the Assyrian list to eastern Babylonia, as they are encountered later in the so-called governor's archive from Nippur and other texts. Some of them were later collaborators with Mukīn-zēri (see Cole 1996a, 49–50) and Merodach-Baladan.

### 10.1.1. Specific Tribes of the Jezirah

The numbering of the presentation of the Aramean tribal entities follows that of Zadok (2013, 281–99).[22] However, I have added additional tribes in the section "Highly Likely Aramean Tribes" (§10.2.3 below). The first five

19. SAA 11:121–45, texts 201–220. The phrase where it occurs is consistently written: *ina* URU.*sa-ru-gi*. See Bagg 2007, 214–15.

20. See the discussion in Zadok 2013, 278–80.

21. Durand (2004, 194–95) suggests that Sarūgu is possibly a survival of *Ašarugāyum* of Old Babylonian Mari. Also compare the name of a Sabean clan *S²rgy* (Arbach 2002, 454).

22. In general, the numbering follows Tiglath-pileser III's longest list (column 3) with a few modifications: the tribes of the Jezirah, Lab(a)dūdu, Tu'mūna and Ḫaṭallu (mentioned in earlier texts), follow the Rupū'. The important tribe of Puqūdu, plus its close confederate Ubūlu, follow. Riḫiḫu is juxtaposed with Raḫīqu. At the end, one finds the Sargonid mentioned tribes of Gambūlu, Yādaqqu, and Malaḫu.

Table 10.1. Lists of Explicitly Aramean Groups in the Assyrian Royal Inscriptions

| Column 1 | Column 2 | Column 3 | Column 4 |
|---|---|---|---|
| Tribe | Šamšī-ilu (RIMA 3:232, A.0.104.2010, lines10–11) | Tiglath-pileser III (RINAP 1:118, text 47, lines 5–8 = Tadmor 1994, Summary 7) [a] | Tiglath-pileser III (RINAP 1:25, text 4, lines 3–7) [c] |
| Itū' | 1 KUR.*ú-tu-'u* | 1 LÚ.*i-tu-'u* | |
| Rupū' | 2 KUR.[*ru*]-*pu-'u* | 2 LÚ.*ru-pu-'u* | |
| Ḫamarānu | | 3 LÚ.*ḫa-mar-a-ni* | 1 LÚ.*ḫa-mar-a-ni* |
| Luḫu'ātu | | 4 LÚ.*lu-ḫu-ú-a-tu* | 2 LÚ.*lu-ḫu-ú-a-tu* |
| Ḫaṭallu | 3 KUR.*ḫa-*⌜*ṭa*⌝*-lu* | 5 LÚ.*ḫa-ṭal-lu* | 3 LÚ.*ḫa-ṭal-li* |
| Rubbū | | 6 LÚ.*ru-ub-bu-ú* | 4 LÚ.*ru-ub-bi* |
| Rāpiqu | | 7 *ra-pi-qu* | 5 LÚ.*ra-pi-qi* |
| Ḫīrānu | | 8 LÚ.*ḫi-ra-a-nu* | 6 LÚ.*ḫi-ra-a-ni* |
| Rabb-ilu | | 9 LÚ.*rab-bi*-DINGIR | 7 LÚ.*rab-bi-i-lu* |
| Naṣīru | | 10 LÚ.*na-ṣi-ru* | 8 LÚ.*na-ṣi-ri* |
| Gulūsu | | 11 LÚ.*gu-lu-su* | 9 LÚ.*gu-lu-si* |
| Nabātu | | 12 LÚ.*na-ba-tu* | 10 LÚ.*na-ba-a-tu* |
| Raḫīqu | | 13 LÚ.*ra-ḫi-qu* | 12 LÚ.*ra-ḫi-qi* |
| Kapīru | | 14 LÚ.⌜*ka*⌝-[*pi-ri*] | 13 LÚ.*ka-pi-ri* |
| Rummulūtu | | 15 ⌜LÚ⌝.*ru-mu-lu-tu* | 14 LÚ.*ru-mu-li-tu* |
| Adelê | | 16 LÚ.*a-di-le-e* | 15 LÚ.*a-di-le-e* |
| Kib/prē | | 17 LÚ.*kib/p-re-e* | 16 LÚ.*kib/p-re-e* |
| Ubūdu | | 18 LÚ.*ú-bu-du* | 17 LÚ.*ú-bu-di* |
| Gurūmu | | 19 LÚ.*gu-ru-mu* | 18 LÚ.*gu-ru-mi* |
| Ḫudādu | | 20 LÚ.*ḫu-da-du* | |
| Ḫinda/eru | | 21 LÚ.*ḫi-in-di-ru* | |
| Damūnu | | 22 LÚ.*da-mu-nu* | |
| Dunānu | | 23 LÚ.*du-na-nu* | |
| Nilqu | | 24 LÚ.*ni-il-qu* | |
| Radê | | 25 LÚ.*ra-de-e* | |
| Da⌜i⌝[x]⌜nu⌝ | | 26 LÚ.*da-*⌜*i*⌝-[x]-⌜*nu*⌝ | |
| Ubūlu | | 27 LÚ.*ú-bu-lu* | |
| Karmâ | | 28 LÚ.*kar-ma-'u* | |
| Amlātu | | 29 LÚ.*am-la-tu* | |

| Column 5 | Column 6 | Column 7 | Column 8 |
|---|---|---|---|
| Tiglath-pileser III RINAP 1:136, text 51, lines 5–6 = Tadmor 1994, Summary 11) [d] | Tiglath-pileser III (RINAP 1:99–101, text 40, lines 3b–11a = Tadmor 1994, Summary 2) | Sargon II (Fuchs 1994, 195 – Great Display Inscription 18b–19) [e] | Sennacherib (RINAP 3/1:36, lines 55–56) [f] |
| 1 LÚ.*i-tu-ʾu* | 1 ⸢LÚ⸣.*i-tu-ʾu* | 1 LÚ.*i-tu-ʾu* | |
| 2 LÚ.*ru-pu-ʾu* | 2 LÚ.*ru-pu-ʾu* | 2 LÚ.*ru-pu-ʾu* | |
| 3 LÚ.*ḫa-mar-a-nu* | 3 LÚ.*ḫa-mar-a-ni* | 5 LÚ.*ḫa-am-ra-nu* | 14 LÚ.*ḫa-am-ra-nu* |
| 4 LÚ.*lu-ḫu-ú-a-tu* | 4 LÚ.*lu-ḫu-ú-a-tu* | | |
| 5 LÚ.*ḫa-ṭal-lu* | | 3 LÚ.*ḫa-ṭal-lum* | |
| 6 LÚ.*ru-ub-bu* | | | |
| 7 [LÚ.*ra-pi*]-⸢*qu*⸣ | | | |
| | | | |
| | | | |
| | | | |
| | | | |
| 8 LÚ.*na-ba-tu* | 5 [LÚ].*na-ba-tu* | | 16 LÚ.*na-ba-tu* |
| | | | |
| | | | |
| | | | |
| | | | |
| | | | 5 LÚ.*kib/p-re-e* |
| | | | 4 LÚ.*ú-bu-du* |
| 9 LÚ.*gu-ru-mu* | | | 7 LÚ.*gu-ru-mu* |
| | | | |
| | 6 LÚ.*ḫi-in-di-ru* | 10 LÚ.*ḫi-in-da-ru* | 11 LÚ.*ḫi-in-da-ru* |
| | | | 9 LÚ.*da-mu-nu* |
| 10 LÚ.*du-na-nu* | | | |
| | | | |
| | | | |
| | | | |
| 11 LÚ.*ú-bu-lu* | | 6 LÚ.*ú-bu-lum* | 8 LÚ.*ú-bu-lum* |
| | | | |
| | | | |

| Column 1 | Column 2 | Column 3 | Column 4 |
|---|---|---|---|
| Ru'a | | 30 LÚ.*ru-'u-a* | |
| Qabi' | | 31 LÚ.*qa-bi-'u* | |
| Lītawu | | 32 LÚ.*li-i'-ta-a-ú* | 11 LÚ.*li-i'-ta-ú* |
| Marūsu | | 33 LÚ.*ma-ru-su* | |
| Amātu | | 34 LÚ.*a-ma-tu* | |
| Ḫagarānu | | 35 LÚ.*ha-ga-ra-a-nu* | |
| Puqūdu | | [b] | |
| Lab(a)dūdu | 4 KUR.*lab-du-du* | [b] | |
| Tu'mūna | | | |
| Raḫīḫu | | | |
| Yādaqqu | | | |
| Malaḫu | | | |
| Gambūlu | | | |
| Total | 5 | 35 | 18 |

Not included in this table is another inscription of Tiglath-pileser III on a basalt bull from Arslan Taş. Due to its fragmentary state, it only preserves the names of the first two tribes: ⸢*ka*⸣-[*šid* LÚ.*i*]-⸢*tu*⸣-*ú* LÚ.*ru-pu-'u* [...]. See RINAP 1:139–42, text 53, line 3; Tadmor 1994, 207, Misc. 1: 3.

[a] Tadmor 1994, 272 n. 10 stated: "Except for the Li'tau {line 6 of RINAP 1, text 4}, this sequence is identical to that appearing in Summ. 7:5–6, which is introduced there by the formula 'From the beginning of my reign until my 17th *palû*.' It would seem then that the scribe of that summary inscription copied the detailed list of the Aramaean tribes from the annalistic account of the first palû (745), as it appears on {excavation number}NA 9/76 {i.e., RINAP 1, text 4}." The 36 tribes (35[+1] = 12 x 3) could be a symbolic number (multiple of 12) (Zadok 2008, 317). Maybe the list reflects a geographically correct sequence of tribes from north to south. See Zadok, 1985a, 64–65; Stockhusen 2013, 225 n. 10.

[b] In this inscription, Puqūdu and Labdūdu are not recorded in the list of Aramean tribes, but are mentioned in the main narrative in lines 13b–15a.

[c] This slab was discovered during the Polish excavations at Nimrud in 1976 (excavation number NA 9/76). Not published in Tadmor 1994 (only commented on p. 272 n. 10; see next note. Published in RINAP 1, text 4; see also Frahm, *AfO* 44–45 (1997–98) 400–401.

| **Column 5** | **Column 6** | **Column 7** | **Column 8** |
|---|---|---|---|
| 12 LÚ.*ru-’u-a* | 7 LÚ.*ru-’u-ú-a* | 7 LÚ.*ru-’u-*$u_8$*-a* | 12 LÚ.*ru-’u-u-a* |
| | | | |
| 13 LÚ.*li-i’-ta-a-ú* | 8 [LÚ].⌜*li*⌝*-i’-ta-a-ú* | 8 LÚ.*li-i’-ta-a-a* | 17 LÚ.*li-i’-ta-a-ú* |
| 14 LÚ.*ma-ru-su* | 9 LÚ.*ma-ru-su* | | |
| | | | |
| | | | 15 LÚ.*ḫa-ga-ra-nu* |
| | 10 LÚ.*pu-qu-du* | 11 LÚ.*pu-qu-du* | 13 LÚ.*pu-qu-du* |
| | | 4 LÚ.*lab-du-bu* | |
| | | | 1 LÚ.*tu-’u-mu-na* |
| | | | 2 LÚ.*ri-ḫi-ḫu* |
| | | | 3 LÚ.*ia-daq-qu* |
| | | | 6 LÚ.*ma-la-ḫu* |
| | | 9 LÚ.*gam-bu-lu* | 10 LÚ.*gam-bu-lum* |
| 14 | 10 | 11 | 17 |

[d] Summary 11 and perhaps Summary 12 (RINAP 1:136, text 52, lines 5–7, fragmentary) artificially make the tribal list 14 (2 × 7) (Zadok 2008, 316).

[e] Paralleled by the Tangi Var, lines 31–32. See Frame 1999, 37.

[f] Same list is repeated with only the first occurrence in text 1 (multiple exemplars) giving waterway locations. RINAP 3/1:32–33, text 1, lines 12–14, 55–56; 3/1:42–43, text 2, lines 14–16; 3/1:51, text 3, lines 14–16; 3/1:61, text 4, lines 12–14; 3/1:76, text 8, lines 12–4; 3/1:80, text 9, lines 12–13; 3/1:93, text 15, i.21′–30′; 3/1:112, text 16, i.59–69; 3/1:129, text 17, i.50–60; 3/1:173, text 22: i.43–53; 3/1:190, text 23, i.38–44.

are tribes encountered first by the Assyrians in the Jezirah and are discussed here; the remainder are in southern Mesopotamia.

1. Utū'/Itū'

The etymology of the tribal name is uncertain. Lipiński (2000a, 437–38) argues for a derivation from *ʾty* "to come." However, Zadok (2013, 282) asserts that "any precise nominal formation, let alone a 'broken' plural, is doubtful due to its feeble base."[23] Since the spelling Itū' is recorded later than the spelling Utū', this can be attributed to the attenuation *u* > *i*.[24] Although the personal name occurring at Elephantine *ʾtw* (Porten and Yardeni 1986–99, B.2.2, 16) appears to be homonymous with the tribal name, its derivation is still uncertain, and therefore of little help to understand the tribal name (Zadok 2013, 282).

Utū'/Itū' is one of the earliest attested Aramean tribes. From his 885 BCE campaign, Tukulti-Ninurta II reported:

> I approached the Tigris; and I captured the encampments (*maškanāte*) of the land of the Utū'/Itū' (KUR *ú-tu-u'*) together with their villages (*kaprānīšunu*), which were situated on the Tigris. I massacred them (and) I carried off much booty from them.[25]

Clearly, the Utū'/Itū' had both mobile and sedentary elements at the point of this engagement with the Assyrians.[26] Based on this inscription, they occupied the west bank of the middle Tigris around present-day Tikrīt and Samarra, near the modern confluence of the River Aḍaim (Postgate 1976–80, 221). In the days of Šamšī-ilu, this tribe was still not yet subjugated, in spite of the *turtānu*'s claim. The mention of the tribe in his inscriptions seems to indicate their mobility and their political clout among the other Aramean groups within the Jezirah in the early eighth century. For at least a century, the Utū'/Itū' were a predominant force in the region that required Assyrian military actions.

However, about a generation later, Tiglath-pileser III brought them under Assyrian rule early in his reign. Their territory, together with that of the Ruqāḫu, was put under the jurisdiction of the governor of the province of Assur. A segment of the tribe apparently migrated further north into Assyria proper during the early Sargonid period. This is seen in a Neo-Assyrian

---

23. See also Zadok 1981, 197 with n. 3. Could the root be *wtʾ*, Akkadian (*w*)*atû*?

24. Zadok 2013, 282. This is an attenuation that is observable in other instances. See below.

25. RIMA 2:173, A.0.100.5, lines 49–50a.

26. See pp. 72–73.

letter (SAA 19:175–76, text 176) in which the provincial governor, Bēl-lešir, complained to the king about the Itū'eans abusing the grazing rights in the province of Kurbail, stating:

> After my departure, the Itū'eans (KUR.*i-tú-'a-a-a*) who hold (land) in the province committed a theft in the district. Instead of the fine (imposed on them), they plundered the sheep which were being grazed in the district and are holding [them] ... [The king] my lord kn[ows that] the Itū'eans hold [a who]le [di]strict in the province of Kurb[ai]l (lines 4–12 and r.4′–7′).

This letter (lines r.8′–9′) also demonstrates that the Itū' kept their tribal organization there, since they were represented by their sheikhs (LÚ.*na-si-ka-ni*) before the king. Later, in Sargon II's reign, the Itū' tribe was found on the Tigris in the Elamite border zone, indicating that perhaps another segment of the tribe had migrated from the middle Tigris region (Lipiński 2000a, 437–38).

From the reign of Tiglath-pileser III until the end of the Assyrian Empire, the Itū'eans served within the Assyrian army as permanent auxiliary units of infantry and cavalry being assigned to provincial governors to act as military police and put down small disturbances.[27] For example, in a letter to Tiglath-pileser III,[28] Qurdi-Aššur-lāmur states that when the Sidonians rebelled against the collection of Assyrian taxes, he sent in the Itū'eans as a police force who caused "panic" among the Sidonians. The result was their submission. Itū'ean auxiliaries in Assyrian service are frequently recorded in the Sargonid period and were requested by officials.[29]

The Itū' were the most important and longest-established of the Aramean units serving in this capacity, although others are found, often acting in conjunction with them (especially the Gurru[30] but also the Ḫamarānu). These Aramean units are depicted in the reliefs of Tiglath-pileser III (and in later Sargonid kings) as primarily archers.[31] The terms of their service with the army are not known, but there is slight evidence for the tenure of land in connection with it. Finally, Itū'eans were found in temple service in Assur.[32]

However, the segment of this tribe dwelling in Babylonia, like a number of other Aramean tribes in the region, collaborated with Merodach-Baladan (Marduk-apla-iddina). A letter reports that together with the Rupū' and the [Lī]tawu ([KUR.*li*]-*ta-a-a*), they crossed a river (presumably the Tigris) at

27. Postgate 1976–80, 221; Frame 1992, 45, 242.
28. SAA 19:28–29, 22.19.
29. SAA 19:79, 77.r.3′–14′ (= Saggs 2001, 124–25, ND 2488).
30. For this tribe's connections with Itū', see Parpola 1970, 137.
31. See the discussions in Postgate 1976–80a, 222; 2000, 223; and Zadok 2013, 278.
32. SAA 7:8, 5.i.30, ii.11. See Zadok's comments (2013, 281–82).

the town of *Ab/p-al-la-a*, although another tribe, the Raḫīḫu, spent the night at the town of Nunak.[33] According to a damaged letter from the Sargonid period, some people of the city of Sarrabānu (near Larak, east of the Tigris) "were in possession of" (*kullu*) houses(?) in several Babylonian cities and in the midst of the Itū'.[34]

2. Rupū'

The second sign in the name written *Ru-pu-*ʾ or *Ru-pu-ú* has been read *bu*, but based on the personal name *rpw*ʾ in Num 13:9,[35] the preferred reading of the second sign is *pu*. Hence, the name of the tribe is certainly derived from the root *rp*ʾ, "to heal."[36] However, while Lipiński posits that the name is a "broken plural," Zadok (2013, 283) suggests that "since this name is not recorded outside of Neo-Assyrian and does not have an attenuated form, one may suspect here a *qatūl* formation with Neo-Assyrian vowel harmony." Due to the fact that Rupū' and Rubbū are both mentioned in Tiglath-pileser III's lists (see above), they cannot be the same group (contra Parpola 1970, 295–96).

Rupū' was also one of the earliest attested Aramean tribes. Šamšī-ilu registers the tribe as part of the tribal confederation that he defeated.[37] Thus the tribe may have resided in Upper Mesopotamia. It must have been of some significant size in order to be mentioned as an achievement of Šamšī-ilu's military prowess. Later Tiglath-pileser III encountered them in the vicinity of Rapiqu in the middle Euphrates.[38] In the final decades of the eighth century, Sargon II encountered the tribe along the Uqnû and Surappu Rivers near the Elamite border (Fuchs 1994, 195, lines 18–19). Clearly the tribe or part of it had migrated to eastern Babylonia (Lipiński 2000a, 439–40). The Governor of Nippur concluded a treaty (*adê*) with the Rupū' and Mukīn-zēri (Cole 1996a, 48, no. 6:4–7a, esp. line 4). In another text from Nippur, the tribe/clan of the Gāmu had gone over to the Rupū' (Cole 1996a, 177–78, no. 83:6–7; Streck 2006–8a, 464).[39] Sargon II characterizes all the Aramean groups in his list as LÚ.*Su-te-e ṣa-ab* EDIN (*ṣēri*) "Suteans, steppe people," drawing particular attention to their nomadic way of life (Fuchs 1994, 195, 19). In a

33. SAA 15:124–25, 186.10–r.6 (= *ABL* 830).

34. SAA 16:132, 154.7′–11′a (= *ABL* 572).

35. Note that רְפוּא in Num 13:9 is rendered in the Old Greek as: Ραφου "healed" (Zadok 1988, 110).

36. Lipiński 2000a, 439; Streck 2006–8a, 463; Zadok 2013, 283.

37. RIMA 3:232, A.0.104.2010, line 10.

38. RINAP 1:118, 47, line 5.

39. For the passage, see below.

Neo-Assyrian letter, the Rupū' are listed with the Itū' and Lītawu as having crossed a river (probably the Tigris).[40]

3. Lab(a)dūdu

The name of this tribe is likely a *qat(a)lūl* formation of the Aramaic root *lbd* "thicken, make dense, heavy, opaque, compact."[41] This is also one of the earliest attested Aramean tribes, found in Šamšī-ilu's list, and located in the Jezirah. Although it is absent from Tiglath-pileser's lists, the tribe is mentioned in the narrative that follows the list as being deported by Tiglath-pileser III from the area near the Elamite border and settled within Assyria proper.[42] Šamšī-ilu certainly did not campaign in this region. Therefore, this is evidence that the tribe or part of it had migrated from Upper Mesopotamia to the Elamite border region, or that some part of the tribe did. It is also mentioned in a broken passage in another inscription of Tiglath-pileser III,[43] which was clearly a list of Aramean tribes living on the Tigris and Euphrates Rivers. Only two names are preserved: [LÚ.*ḫa*]-⸢*ṭal*⸣-*lu* KUR.*lab-du-di* "the Ḫaṭallu, the land of Labdūdu."

There is evidence that Labdūdean archers (LÚ.*Lab-du-da-a-a*) were incorporated as auxiliaries into the Assyrian army in the time of Aššurbanipal (*ABL* 1009). In a letter from Marduk-šarrāni to Sargon II, bulls of this tribe (if the restoration [LÚ/URU.*Lab*(?)]-*du*!-*du*!-*a-a* is correct) are conscripted for ploughing fallow fields (presumably those belonging to the tribe).[44] Two other documents mention issues concerning the Labdūdu.[45]

4. Tū'mānu/Tu'mūna

The name is certainly derived from the root *t'm* "twin" (Zadok 2013, 283; Lipiński 2000a, 425). A shift *-ān* > *-ōn* is observable in the cuneiform writings, a shift that must have occurred sometime in the middle to late eighth century, though the shift *ā* > *ō* in this name is first recorded in the inscriptions of Sennacherib.

Around 770–760 BCE, Šamaš-rēša-uṣur, the ruler of Sūḫu, recorded an engagement with this tribe. He proclaims:

40. SAA 15:124, 186.11. See Itū' above.

41. For the formation, see Zadok 1977, 137. For the derivation, see Zadok 1977, 432; 1985c, 77; Lipiński (2000a, 441) derives the name from the root *lbd*, but explains the form as a broken plural meaning "feltmakers."

42. RINAP 1:118–19, 47, lines 13a–15a, esp. 14b–15a.

43. RINAP 1:113–15, 46, line 5; Tadmor 1994, 151, summary 6:5.

44. SAA 15:125, 187.6.

45. SAA 15:84–85, 121.5 (= *ABL* 537:5); and 15:85, 122.6 (= *ABL* 798).

> 400 of the Tū'mānu (LÚ.*Tu-ʾ-ma-a-nu*) came and arose (to fight) against the city of Ribaniš.[46] I had gone to the New City for a festival and when in the town of Baqa I heard, I crossed over (the river) with the palace troops who were with me to the land side, and I pursued them. When I crossed over (the river), I defeated them in the territory of Aradātu;[47] and I killed 350 of the troops among them (and) the remainder I released (to go spread the news of my) glory.[48]

The tribe is not mentioned in any of Tiglath-pileser III's inscriptions; however it is mentioned by Sargon II, not in his list (see column 7 in table 10.1), but in an inscribed prism where the LÚ.*tu-ʾu-mu-na* is mentioned together with another confederate tribe the LÚ.*te-šá-a-a*.[49] They had delivered their pro-Assyrian chief to Marduk-apla-iddina of Babylon, no small crime. A newly published slab of Sargon mentions that the Teša and the Tū'mānu were deported from northern Babylonia to north Syria (the land of Ḫatti; Frahm 2013, 46, lines 2a–4a).

Also in a letter from the time of Sargon II,[50] perhaps from Il-yada', there is some segment of the Tū'mānu tribe (LÚ*.*tu-u*ʾ-⌜*ma-na*⌝-[*a-a*]) living among the Ḫaṭallu confederation (LÚ*!*ḫa*!-[*ta*]*l*!-*la*). Moreover, both the city of Anat (URU.*Ana-te*) and the Diyala River (ÍD.*tur-nu*) are mentioned here in a broken context. Later, in Sennacherib's inscriptions, the tribe is located on the Tigris.

5. Ḫaṭallu

Lipiński (2000a, 426–27) argues that the name "Ḫaṭallū should in fact be related to the Assyro-Babylonian noun *eṭlu,* 'male,' 'virile,' and to the Aramaic name *Ḥaṭṭīl* built on the adjectival pattern *qattīl* ... the Ḫaṭallū or Ḥaṭallū were simply 'valiant men' or the like." Zadok (1977, 186, 312 n. 2) argued that Ḫaṭallu was a *qatal* form from *ḥṭl* "to be loose, base" and might denote that the tribe belonged to a lowly class; the tribe might have been so named by other people.[51]

The tribe is first mentioned by Šamšī-ilu (sometime before 774; see column 2 in table 10.1).[52] At this time, the location of the tribe may have been in the area near Til-Barsib. According to Ninurta-kudurrī-uṣur's inscriptions,

46. Interestingly, four hundred is given as the number of David's men (1 Sam 22:2).

47. *CAD* 13:117, s.v. *qaqqaru* A, 3c. Or, Qaqqaru-Aradātu, if *qaqqaru* is understood as part of the toponym.

48. RIMB 2:280, S.0.1001.1, ii.17b′–26′.

49. Gadd 1954, 199 (line 16) and pl. 51.

50. SAA 15:107–8, 157.r.1′–12′, esp. r.6′ (= *ABL* 1041).

51. Note the clan בְּנֵי־חֲטִיל in Ezra 2:57 and Neh 7:59. See also *DNWSI*, 364, s.v. *ḥṭl*.

52. RIMA 3:232, A.0.104.2010, line 11.

the Ḫaṭallu attacked the land of Laqē ca. 770–760. From this narrative, it is clear that the Ḫaṭallu was a tribal confederation. The text's wording "from (*ultu*) the Sarūgu clan to (*adi*) the Luḫūya clan"[53] indicates only the basic parameters of the confederation. In parallel texts, one reads "to (*adi*) the Minū' clan" (LÚ.*mi-nu-ʾ-i*).[54] Thus, the Ḫaṭallu confederation was comprised of, at least, four clans or sub-tribes: the Sarūgu,[55] the Luḫūya (Li/uḫuātu), Minū', and the Amatu, and perhaps others.[56] It is clear from the mention of some of these in later Assyrian texts that they could act independently of the confederation. The leader of the Ḫaṭallu confederation was the herald (*nāgiru*) of the Sarūgu clan.[57] The Amatu tribe was also part of the confederation. At this time, when the raid on Laqē occurred, the Ḫaṭallu were located in the Wadi Tharthar region.[58] A letter from Fort Shalmaneser collaborates this location:

> (Obv)(1–2) Tablet of the governor of (the province of Assur) to Šarru-dūrī: (3) May there be well-being to my brother. (4–6) Your servants cast fire into the desert-steppe. (7–10) It devoured the entire desert-steppe up to the land of Sūḫu (and) up to the land of the Ḫaṭallu (KUR.*ḫa-ṭ*[*a*]*l-li*). (11) Make inquiries! (Rev)(1)[the city of the Ḫ]aṭallu which the fire burned (???) (2) they have not listened/obeyed. (3) I have written you.[59]

In addition, in recently published contracts from Dūr-Katlimmu (dating from the time of Aššurbanipal), a "city of the Ḫaṭallu" is mentioned; and "the land of the Ḫaṭallu" has its own governor (*šaknu*), Adad-bēl-šīmāti, who served as a witness.[60] Therefore, there seems to be little doubt that the "the land of the Ḫaṭallu" was located southwest of Assur and northeast of Sūḫu in the central Wadi Tharthar area.

Tiglath-pileser III's inscriptions (see columns 3–6 in table 10.1) listed the Ḫaṭallu as one of the Aramean tribes that he had defeated, but they do not supply any other data on the entity. Sargon II included the Ḫaṭallu in his lists. A fragmentary document from his reign mentions that there are five Ḫaṭallu (LÚ*.*ḫa-ṭal-*[*la-a-a*]) who are staying in the town of Minū' (URU.

53. RIMB 2:295, S.0.1002.2, i.9–10.

54. RIMB 2:292, S.0.1002.1, line 20. See also the comments of Zadok 1985a, 63–70.

55. Cf. discussion above.

56. For these clans/tribes, see below. The Luḫūya, see under 9. Li/uḫuātu (p. 694).

57. See Lipiński 2000a, 427. For the name, cf. the Sabean clan name *S²rgy*, Arbach 2002, 454. Durand (2004, 194) suggests that Sarūgu is possibly a survival of *Ašarugāyum* of OB Mari. Later in 615 BCE, a herald of the settlement of *Mì-ḫi-ni-ni-i* is recorded in a deed from 615 (see Friedrich et al. 1940, 106).

58. Liverani 1992b, 37. See also Lipiński 2000a, 426.

59. Postgate 1973, 187–88, Plate 67; Fales and Lanfranchi 1992, 60–61, no. 8.

60. See Radner 2002, 134 (no. 93), and 129 (no. 89).

*Mi-nu-*[ʾ]) in northern Babylonia.[61] Zadok (2013, 284) suggests that perhaps these Ḫaṭallu were attached to the Assyrian garrison as that town was fortified according to a report of Il-yada'.[62] In a letter dating to ca. 710 BCE, Marduk-šuma-iddina, an Assyrian official, who was based in Sippar, handed over ten[63] Ḫaṭallu men (LÚ.*ḫa-ṭal-la-a-a*) to the bodyguard of the king (LÚ. *šá–qur-ru-bu-ti šá* LUGAL).[64] In a fragmentary letter (date missing),[65] an official writes the king that he has used up the grain rations that were given to him by the king and then mentions the Ḫindaru (see no. 26 below) and the Ḫaṭallu, unfortunately without further context preserved. A very fragmentary letter mentions the Ḫaṭallu along with the Luḫu'ātu and Awkaneans.[66] There were apparently homonymous settlements in western Babylonia: NB/LB *Ḫaṭalluʾa* near Nippur and *Ḫa?-ṭal-la-ʾ* (possibly not far from Sippar).[67]

## 10.2. Aramean Tribes of Southern Mesopotamia

### 10.2.1. The Population Complexity

In the first half of the first millennium, the population of southern Mesopotamia was comprised of five different groups. The Arameans were only one part of a cultural heterogeneity unmatched in the ancient world. Scholars have generally understood this diverse population to be stratified into only two social groups: the older nontribal, urban inhabitants and the relative newcomers, that is, the tribal, rural, pastoralist groups (Frame 1992, 32; Fales 2007b, 295; Arnold 2012). Yet, such a distinction can obscure the fact that components of many of the tribal groups, whether Arameans or (especially) Chaldeans, were urban. The population complexity in the region is interconnected to some of the regional environmental factors (fig. 10.1).

#### 10.2.1.1. Environmental Factors: Hydrology and Settlement

Both the Euphrates and Tigris Rivers have shifted their courses throughout history—the Euphrates more so, the Tigris less. These changes have impacted human settlement patterns. This can be seen in the archaeological sites themselves, as well as in the settlement patterns. Thus the size of

61. SAA 15:114, 167.4′–7′.
62. SAA 15:113–14, text 166.
63. Perhaps a work contingent which was typically ten men.
64. SAA 17:18, 17, esp. lines 8 and r.4.
65. SAA 19:169, 167, esp. line r.6; Saggs 2001, 224–25 and pl. 37.
66. SAA 15:149–50, 231.9′, 12′.
67. See Zadok 1985a, 425; Lipiński 2000a, 427 n. 98.

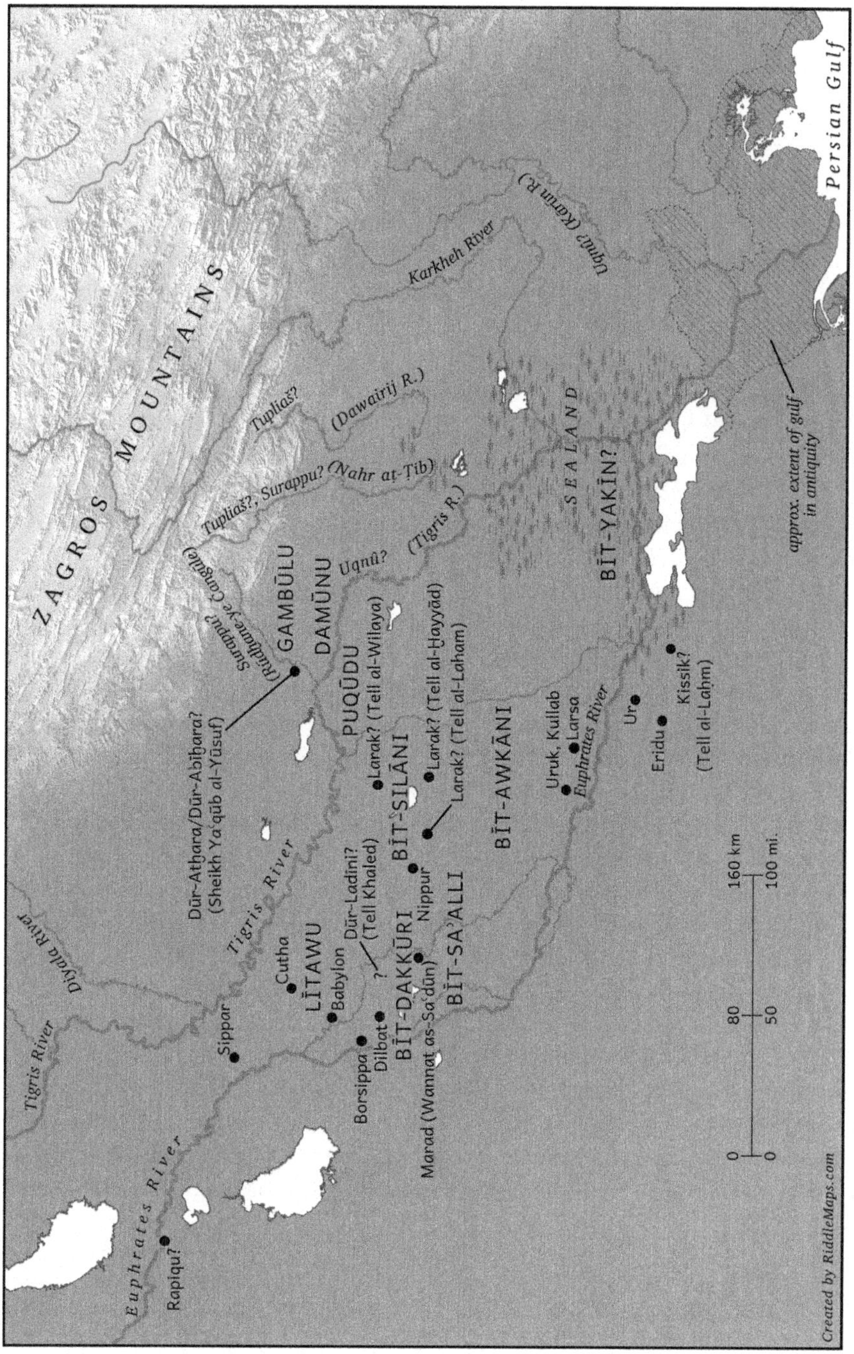


Fig. 10.1. Southern Mesopotamia

sites and the layout of the network of canals, revealed by regional and local surveys, and especially by aerial and satellite photography, demonstrate the complexity of these patterns. The study of the hydrology of the alluvium has also provided important insights for this period.[68] From all of these data, it is clear that the trend between the twelfth and the late eighth centuries BCE in the lower Euphrates region and in the Diyala is marked by a general decline in population levels through extensive abandonment and by a diminution of urbanism, with a corresponding increase of economic ruralization.[69]

However, it is difficult to assess whether this trend was the result of the shifting of river courses which might be linked to climatic change toward aridity (Neumann and Parpola 1987), or rather the result of social and political disruptions due to internal and/or external causes. It may be that both were critical factors. The textual witness indicates that certain parts of these regions were occupied by Aramean groups, most of whom were mobile tribal units. The low level of urbanization may be partly responsible for the scarce traces of settlements detectable through extensive regional survey techniques (Fales 2007b, 292).

However, there were some areas of the alluvium that, due to their proximity to the watercourses and canals, had significant urban development. The inscriptions of various Sargonid kings attest to this through their declarations of widespread destructions of walled cities belonging to the Chaldeans (Frame 2013, 100–14). There is evidence that all the main branches of the Euphrates had shifted westward, and an abundance of water characterized the entire western sector of the alluvium from the eighth to the seventh centuries BCE onward (Fales 2007b, 292). Hence, Borsippa was progressively surrounded by marshes and crossed by a "swollen" river, as a particular Neo-Assyrian letter indicates (Fales 1995, 209). But the eastern cities, like Nippur, were plagued by a serious lack of water (Brinkman 1995).

In light of this fact, it is not surprising that the territories of the three main Chaldean tribes (Bīt-Dakkūri, Bīt-Awkāni, Bīt-Yakīn) extended in a sort of arc, along the "living" branches of the Euphrates from the Borsippa region to the Uruk countryside to the southernmost reaches of the Euphrates around Ur and into the marshlands to the east (Fales 2007b, 293). This is in contrast to the more economically modest status of the Aramean tribes who were located in areas of progressive aridification. Thus the issue of water was no small reason for tensions between the Aramean pastoralists and the local

68. Adams 1965, 1981; Adams and Nissen 1972; Gibson 1972; Cole and Gasche 1999; 2007; in addition, see the contributions of Fales 2007b, 290–92 and Frame 2013, 89.

69. Fales 2007b, 291–92; Brinkman 1984, 8–11.

"population, who sometimes had to fight to remove Aramean squatters from their richly watered fields" (Brinkman 1995, 24).

There are two further complications. First, there is a degree of uncertainty as to where exactly the head of the Persian Gulf was, and how far did the southern marshes extend. Second, the precise location of some of the important rivers in the Transtigridian region is not known: the Surappu, Tupliaš (or Tubliyaš) and Uqnû Rivers. These rivers are sometimes mentioned in connection with the location of particular Aramean tribes (see below). Fuchs (1994, 459, 466–67) suggested that the Surappu was the modern Rūdḫane-ye Čangūle; the Tupliaš was the modern Nahr aṭ-Ṭib; and the Uqnû was the modern course of the eastern branch of the Tigris. A number of scholars have accepted these identifications.[70] Alternatively, Cole and Gasche have proposed identifying the Surappu with the Nahr aṭ-Ṭib, the Tupliaš with the Dawairij, and the Uqnû with the ancient course of the Kārūn, in particular the lower Kārūn, which they argue entered the Shatt el-Arab or marshes about 80 km northwest of where it currently does.[71] All this impacts our understanding of the exact geographical distribution of the Arameans.

10.2.1.2. Akkadians/Babylonians

One group has been designated "the Akkadians" (Frame 1992, 32–36) or "the Babylonians" (Arnold 2004; 2011), though in reality this group was actually an amalgam of several older groups (Sumerians, Akkadians, Amorites, and Kassites) who had completely merged their distinctive identities by this time.[72] They were sedentary, primarily distinguishable as the residents of the ancient urban cult centers (Babylon, Borsippa, Cutha, Dilbat, Sippar, Ur and Uruk). They were the bearers of the long tradition of Babylonian culture. Since most of the hinterland was given over to various tribal groups, the "Akkadians/Babylonians" should perhaps be considered to have more sociocultural implications than specifically ethnic ones (Frame 1992, 34). They and their cities formed the core of the Babylonian state.

70. Parpola and Porter 2001, map 16; Frahm 2003, 151–52; and Lipiński 2000a, 413, fig. 16.

71. Cole and Gasche 2007, 30, 32 fig. 71, and 35. See the earlier study of Cole and Gasche 1999; also Frame (forthcoming) who follows Cole and Gasche with regard to the identification of the Uqnû with Kārūn.

72. The term *Akkadian* is used in the contemporary sources for this group (Frame 1992, 32 n. 3). However, the term *Babylonian* may be less confusing with the much earlier group encountered in Mesopotamian history.

### 10.2.1.3. Chaldeans

A second group were the Chaldeans,[73] a tribal group that had both mobile and sedentary elements. Some Sutû/Aḫlamû may have been the ancestors of the Chaldeans (Zadok 2012, 576). Unlike the migrations of the Arameans into the alluvium from the Jezirah, there is no record of the process of the penetration of Chaldeans into Babylonia (Zadok 2013, 264). Their place of origin and the process of their settlement history cannot be established, because of the complete lack of Chaldean linguistic material. The first occurrence of the name Kaldu in Neo-Assyrian sources[74] comes from the time of Aššurnaṣirpal II's campaign of 878 BCE in the land of Sūḫu, which states:

> I established my victory and strength over the land Sūḫu. The fearsomeness of my lordship reached as far as Karduniaš (KUR *Kar-du-ni-aš*; i.e., Babylonia). The awe of my weapons overwhelmed Chaldea (KUR.*Kal-du*).[75]

Kaldu and Karduniaš are here synonyms for Babylonia (Streck 2014, 298). The first Assyrian campaigns against the Chaldeans are attributed to Shalmaneser III.[76]

The Assyrian documents often refer to the Chaldeans and Arameans in parallel, though it is clear that they are, in some ways, distinct from one another. There is some evidence to indicate that the Chaldeans were West Semites. Their place names, and especially those of their vast territorial and political enclaves, were characterized by the *bītu*-formula, which is followed by the linguistically West Semitic personal name of an eponymic ancestor or power figure. The gentilic form is *mār*, "son" of the eponymic ancestor. These forms are exactly like the contemporary Aramean states of the Jezirah

73. For the Chaldeans, see Brinkman 1968, 260–67; Cole 1996b, 30–34; Dietrich 1970; Edzard 1976–80b; Frame 1992, 36–43; 2013, 97–116; Rivaroli and Verderame 2005, 295–301; Zadok 1985c, 49–63; 2013, 265–71.

74. Zadok (2013, 264) states: "It cannot be proven that the isolated MA occurrence of KUR.*Kal-da-ie-e* has anything to do with the Chaldeans who appeared several hundred years later (see Nashef 1982, 147, *s.v.* *Kaldāju)."

Nashef (1982, 147, s.v. **Kaldāju*) states: "Nisbe: KASKAL[ni] *ša* KUR.*kal-da-ie-e*.MEŠ (VS 19,10,13) [VAS 19 = Freydank 1976]. According to the context, this is more likely to be interpreted as 'land of Chaldea.' Thus 'Babylon' is probably not meant by it because otherwise Karduniaš would be used. For the relationship of the later 'Chaldeans' to the 'Arameans' or 'Arabs,' see Brinkman 1968, 266 n. 1715. Zadok (1985:82) had earlier stated: "The Chaldeans are also mentioned as early as Tiglath-pileser I's time (in the Assyrian economic document VS 19, 10), but their abodes then cannot be established."

75. RIMA 2:213–14, A.0.101.1 iii.16b–25, esp. iii.24.

76. RIMA 3:31–32, A.0.102.5, vi.5b–7 and passim. See Frame 2013, 97–116; Brinkman 1968, 197–99.

and Trans-Euphrates.[77] The Chaldeans appear as tribal confederations[78] with significant sedentary components (Brinkman 1984; Cole 1996a).

The leader of each tribal confederation was indicated in the Assyrian texts as *ra'asu* "chief."[79] Such chieftains were all mutually recognized within a wider territorial-political complex, which ideally united the different Chaldean confederations. This is manifest by a letter from Nimrud/ Kalḫu from the time of Tiglath-pileser III (SAA 19:90–92, 87.4′–6′; Saggs 2001, 25–26, 4′–6′), in which the young Merodach-Baladan is described as "one of the chieftains of the land of Chaldea" (*ina* ŠÀ LÚ*.*re-e'-sa-ni ša* KUR.*Kal-di*).

The use of this *bītu*-formula also permits the postulation of a connection between the Chaldeans and the northern and western Arameans. However, no direct evidence exists for a specific link and this and other minor evidences are by no means sufficient to make any definite statement on the matter (Brinkman 1968, 265–67; Edzard 1976–80b, 291–92; Frame 2013, 97). They were located primarily in southern and western Babylonia and are mentioned as both a people (LÚ.*Kaldu*/*Kaldayu*) and a land (KUR.*Kaldu*). There was also a province named after them (*pīḫat* URU.*Kaldu*), possibly in the area of Babylon.[80]

In general, the Chaldeans, in contrast to the Arameans, seem to have embraced Babylonian ways with both Chaldean leaders and commoners mentioned in the texts often bearing fully Babylonian personal names,[81] with devotional reference to the traditional Sumero-Akkadian pantheon of the region (Fales 2007b, 290). The settlement pattern for the Chaldeans (as recorded in the Assyrian texts and palace reliefs) is located in the large tracts of land within the more well-watered areas in western and southern Babylonia, where they practiced agriculture (including date-palm cultivation) and breeding of horses and cattle. There were numerous Chaldean walled cities. Thus, Sennacherib, in his description of his first campaign into Babylonia (703 BCE), proclaims to have besieged and conquered 33 walled cities and 250 townships of Bīt-Dakkūri; 8 walled cities and 120 townships of Bīt-

77. See the discussion in chapter 2.

78. Fales (2007b, 296) states: "it would be more precise to state that such tribal units, in fact, represented tribal confederations which must have undergone—similarly to the Aramean tribal "households" of the northern Jezirah and Inner Syria—a relatively long process of social coalescence, although no trace of the latter is preserved in the written record."

79. See pp. 50–57 above.

80. McEwan 1984, 400:2 (time of Sîn-šumu-līšir). Frame (1992, 37 n. 26) notes that the location is suggested by the fact that the text is dated at Babylon.

81. In fact, only a handful of explicit Chaldeans bore non-Babylonian names, making the Chaldean onomasticon residual. See Zadok 2013, 266–71.

Ša'alli; 39 walled cities and 350 townships of Bīt-Awkāni; 8 walled cities and 100 townships of Bīt-Yakīn—a grand total of 88 major urban sites with defensive structures and 820 smaller settlements of mainly rural character in their environs (see Frame 2013, 102; Luckenbill 1924, 54–56, 36–50; Frahm 1997, 9). Putting aside all the rhetoric, it is clear that some of these Chaldean fortified cities represented a challenge for even the best Assyrian armies with all their sophisticated siege-technologies.[82]

However, being located in the western and southern regions of the Babylonian alluvium, the Chaldeans held a strategic position for the control of trade routes and other commercial interests as demonstrated in the tribute listed in the Assyrian royal inscriptions (Brinkman 1968, 198–99; Frame 1992, 37; Fales 2007b, 296).

Five Chaldean tribes are attested, three major tribes: Bīt-Awkāni (Bīt-Amukāni), Bīt-Dakkūri, and Bīt-Yakīn; and two lesser tribes (about which little is known): Bīt-Sa'alli/Bīt-Ša'alli, and Bīt-Silāni/Bīt-Šilāni/Ašilāni.

#### 10.2.1.3.1. Bīt-Awkāni (Bīt-Amukāni)

Importantly, this tribe is attested in the Aramaic Assur Ostracon where it is spelled *ʾwkn*. Zadok (2013, 69) notes that "the Aramaic spelling disproves the derivation from *ʿmq* (suggested by Lipiński 2000a, 419–20)." This may have been the largest Chaldean tribe. The city of Larak (likely located east or northeast of Nippur) is listed as belonging to Bīt-Awkāni, and Uruk is noted as an area where this tribe was quite active during the Šamaš-šuma-ukīn revolt. Thus Bīt-Awkāni may have stretched between these two cities. According to Assyrian inscriptions, Sapiya (likely Babylonian Šapiya) had been the capital of Nabû-mukīn-zēri of Bīt-Awkāni (731–729 BCE).[83] In Sennacherib's inscriptions, this tribe is attributed with thirty-nine walled cities and 350 villages.

#### 10.2.1.3.2. Bīt-Dakkūri

Bīt-Dakkūri was situated south of Babylon, along the Euphrates River from Borsippa to at least Marad (see Frame 2013, 102; Zadok 1985c, 54–57).

---

82. A letter to Tiglath-pileser III from a high-ranking Assyrian military officer reports about the significant effort required to overcome the city of Šapi'a, where the Chaldean rebel (Nabû)-mukīn-zēri and his son, Šumu-ukin had taken refuge (SAA 19:84, text 80; Saggs 2001, 45–46). My interpretation of the letter follows Fales 2005b, 171–87, esp. p. 185 (understanding the technique of the letter writer to indicate significant effort).

83. Tiglath-pileser III: Summary 7, RINAP 1:116–25, 47, lines 19–23 (= Tadmor 1994, 162); Summary 11, RINAP 1:134–37, 51, line 16 (= Tadmor 1994, 196).

Marad (likely modern Wannat as-Saʿdūn, located about 55 km southeast of Babylon) and Dūr-Ladīni (possibly Tell Khaled, located several km southeast of Hilla) were important cities of Bīt-Dakkūri. This territory or part of it bore the ephemeral name Bīt-Adīni[84] after its ruler of the mid-ninth century (Zadok 2013, 265; Brinkman 1984, 15 n. 59; 43 n. 211). This tribe provided two rulers over Babylonia: Nabû-šuma-iškun (760–748), Mušēzib-Yakīn (692–689). Another of the tribe's rulers (Šamaš-ibni) was termed a king by Esarhaddon. Sennacherib attributes thirty-three walled cities and 250 villages to this tribe.

10.2.1.3.3. Bīt-Yakīn

This was the most important Chaldean tribe. The tribal name and the toponym often appear to have been applied interchangeably (Frame 1992, 40–42). It was closely connected with the Sealand, the area of swamp-marsh around the lower courses of the Tigris and Euphrates Rivers at the head of the Persian Gulf.[85] In fact, during the ninth and eighth centuries, the Sealand was dominated by the Bīt-Yakīn tribe. This was the case until about the end of the eighth century when the Assyrians (especially Sargon II and Sennacherib) greatly weakened the tribe through mass deportations. After Sennacherib, the tribe is not mentioned very often. The walled cities included: Larsa, Eridu, Kissik, Kullab, and Dūr-Yakīn. Until its destruction in 707 BCE, Dūr-Yakīn served as the tribe's major center. Sennacherib attributed this tribe with eight walled cities and one hundred villages.

84. Not to be confused with the Aramean entity in Upper Mesopotamia (see chapter 5).

85. Frame (1992, 41–42) lists seven considerations for the identification of Bīt-Yakīn with the Sealand, or at least part of it: (1) The Sealand appears to have been at least partially coextensive with what has been described as Bīt-Yakīn territory; (2) In his inscriptions, Sargon II consistently separates Bīt-Yakīn from the other Chaldean tribes when mentioning them by name; he terms these other tribes "all of Chaldea"; (3) One Yakīn (or [*mār*] *Yakīn*), presumably the ruler of Bīt-Yakīn, was called king of the Sealand by Shalmaneser III; (4) Erība-Marduk, leader of the Bīt-Yakīn and ruler of Babylonia at some point in the first half of the eighth century, was later said to have been of a Sealand dynasty; (5) Merodach-Baladan II of Bīt-Yakīn was called king of the Sea(land) in an Assyrian inscription describing Tiglath-pileser III's campaign in 729; (6) The leaders of the Sealand whose affiliation is clear during this period were all members of the Bīt-Yakīn tribe (Nabû-zēr-kitti-līšir, Na'id-Marduk; and Nabû-bēl-šumāti); and (7) The Bīt-Yakīn are rarely mentioned by name during the years 689–627 and it is unlikely that they vanished totally.

### 10.2.1.3.4. Bīt-Sa'alli

Bīt-Sa'alli[86] appears to have been located just south of Bīt-Dakkūri (Zadok 1985c, 58). Although Sennacherib deported a large number of this tribe from Babylonia, which led scholars to conclude its disappearance since it was not mentioned after the time of Sennacherib, an unpublished fragmentary inscription of the Babylonian king Nebuchadnezzar II (604–562) in the Metropolitan Museum of Art mentions the land of Silāni (KUR.*Si-la-a-ni*$_7$) in connection with Bīt-Dakkūri and likely Bīt-Awkāni (Frame 2013, 99), indicating that at least the name of the tribal territory continued in usage for some period beyond Sennacherib.

### 10.2.1.3.5. Bīt-Silāni

This tribe was located near Larak and Nippur.[87] It is not mentioned after the reign of Sargon II (Fuchs 1994, 429). Part of its territory (namely its royal city of Sarrabānu/Šarrabānu) was apparently annexed by Bīt-Awkāni in the time of Sennacherib (Zadok 2013, 266; Frame 2013, 103).

There was a significant sedentary element to the Chaldean tribes (they are known to have had their own walled cities).[88] Some of these urban Chaldeans became "Babylonianized," taking Babylonian names and becoming involved in Babylonian political life. Even so, most Chaldeans maintained their tribal structure and distinct identity. Tribes were referred to as the "House of PN/GrN" (e.g., Bīt-Yakīn), with PN in this usage standing for the eponymous ancestor of the clan or tribe (Frame 1992, 37). They formed semi-autonomous units within the state, and at times could prove to be a disruptive element within Babylonia. It was very difficult for the Assyrian leaders to maintain authority over the Chaldean tribes who frequently rebelled.

Each of the three major Chaldean tribes provided at least one king of Babylonia: Bīt-Awkāni: (Nabû)-mukīn-zēri; Bīt-Dakkūri: Nabû-šuma-iškun, Mušēzib-Yakīn; Bīt-Yakīn: Erība-Marduk, Marduk-apla-iddina (Merodach-Baladan II) (721–703 reign in Babylon, died 700). The earliest Chaldean ruler of Babylonia was Marduk-apla-uṣur (ca. 775) whose tribal affiliation is unknown. There is no evidence of anti-Chaldean sentiment on the part

86. Tiglath-pileser III: Summary 2; RINAP 1:99–101, 40.

87. Tiglath-pileser III: Summary 2; RINAP 1:99–101, 40.

88. For the early attestation of which can be seen in the Balawat Gates of Shalmaneser III: Band XI of door C, upper register (see Schachner 2007, 303, taf. 11); Band XI of door C, lower register (see Schachner 2007, 303, pl. 11); and Band O of door C, lower register (see Schachner 2007, 307, pl. 15).

of the Akkadians, although the two could occasionally be in conflict. The Chaldeans were generally both important and accepted members of the Babylonian community.

10.2.1.4. Arabians

A third group were the Arabian tribal entities. There can be little doubt that Arabian tribal groups penetrated the region. In the first place, the arrival of an Arabian caravan (belonging to the Temanites and Sabeans) at Ḫindānu is attested in the mid-eighth-century inscriptions of Ninurta-kudurrī-uṣur, the governor of Sūḫu.[89] This demonstrates trade interconnections. In a hieroglyphic Luwian inscription from Karkamiš, Yariri claims to know among three other scripts "the Taimani script" (*taimaniti tupalaliti*, i.e., the *tymn* "southern" script).[90] This is most likely the North Arabian script, but possibly the South Arabian script and his knowledge of this came through "wayfaring" (see Younger 2014a).

Moreover, it appears that Arabian groups have penetrated the Nippur region by the middle of the eighth century according to letters from the Governor's Archive at Nippur (Cole 1996b, 34–42). An Arab raid on Sippar is mentioned in the time of Sargon II.[91] Soldiers under the command of Basqānu, the brother of Yati'e, queen of the Arabs, came to the aid of Merodach-Baladan II (Marduk-apla-iddina) against Sennacherib.[92] Later, a Qedarite confederation of Arabians led by Abī-yate' and Aya-ammu, joined by troops of Uaite', were allies of Šamaš-šuma-ukīn in the war against Aššurbanipal.[93] Apparently this confederation was not too far from the western border of Babylonia, but not within the country itself (Zadok 2013, 317).

Frame (2013, 117) notes that *ABL* 1404 records that the king of Babylonia had been visited by a merchant from Teima and a letter found at Ur (Figulla 1949, 167) may report that two families from Teima had fled from Eridu. Dispersed Oasis North Arabian inscriptions have been found throughout Mesopotamia and the Levant,[94] including on the Middle Euphrates.[95] Brinkman (1984, 28) has suggested that a number of new small settlements to the south of Ur may have been Arabian settlements. Thus the evidence

89. RIMB 2:300, S.0.1002.2, iv.27: LÚ.*te-ma-ʾa-a-a* LÚ.*šá-ba-ʾ-a-a*. See *COS* 2.115B:281–82.

90. Hawkins 2000, 130–33 pls. 36–37: KARKAMIŠ A15b.

91. SAA 1:75, 84.r.2–5. For a discussion, see Eph'al 1982, 115–16.

92. RINAP 3.1:34, 1, line 28.

93. Prism A vii.97–106; viii.30–41 (Borger 1996, 61, 63). See Frame 1992, 151–52.

94. Sass 1991, 38–102, figs. 8–41; Frame 1992, 50; Brinkman 1984, 28.

95. Kepinski 2006, 338, fig. 8. See also Robin 1994.

clearly indicates that Arabs were active in Babylonia, although there may have been a distinction. It seems that the Arabians on the periphery (i.e., the border region between the Babylonian alluvium and the Syro-Arabian desert) kept their separate identity, while in the alluvium they came under Babylonian and Aramean cultural influence and as a result were in various stages of assimilation to the Arameans.[96]

There were a number of Arabian tribes that did not have a residential component in Babylonia, for example, Qedar. Those Arabian tribes that may have had residence in Babylonia[97] are the following: Gurasimmu,[98] Tamdu (or Uddu), Isūqu, LÚ.*B/Pu-ú-sa-li*, LÚ.*Ú-a-sa-ḫa-nu,* Ubayānāt, D/Ṭaḫḫā, and Qalqalu.

### 10.2.1.5. Tribal Groups of Uncertain Affiliation

A fourth group were tribal groups whose affiliation cannot be determined (forty-five tribes of uncertain affiliation).[99]

### 10.2.2. The Explicitly Aramean Groups

The Assyrian lists identify the tribal entities explicitly as Aramean (see table 10.1). One of the main contentions in Lipiński's work[100] is that the Assyrian identifications cannot be accepted. Rather, a number of these entities were, in fact, North-Arabian tribes living in the region. In his opinion, the Assyrians did not consistently distinguish the two groups. Thus Lipiński (2003, 348) concludes: "the majority of the so-called 'Aramaean' tribes of southern and southeastern Babylonia are demonstrably of Arab descent, as can be shown by an etymological and morphological analysis of their names. They were all called 'Aramaeans' because their way of life was similar to that of better known Aramaean semi-nomads." This identification is, in turn, undergirded by his analysis of their tribal names as Arabian, usually as "broken plurals" (Lipiński 2000a, 409–89).

---

96. This is a distinction that has been observed by Zadok (2013, 264). Also Fales (2007b, 289–90) notes that camel-raising tribes of "Arabs" (*Arubu*) in the Central Mesopotamian steppe "intermingled" with the southern Arameans. Zadok's very careful study, however, clarifies the Arab/Aramean distinction.

97. For discussion see Zadok 2013, 317–18.

98. Frame (2013, 92 n. 23) notes: "I have tentatively suggested elsewhere that the Gurasimmu were also Arameans (Frame 1992, 47), but Lipiński (2000a, 482–3) and Zadok (2013, 317) have presented evidence to suggest that they were instead of Arabian origin."

99. For discussion, see Zadok 1985c, 74; 2013, 320–22.

100. Lipiński 2000a, 485–6.

However, the argument that many of the tribes that are identified as Aramean in the contemporary Assyro-Babylonian sources bore Arabian names is clearly contradicted by the historical-linguistic evidence: (1) Mesopotamia eventually becomes part of the vast Aramaic-speaking continuum of the ancient Near East, not the Arabic-speaking continuum[101]; (2) almost all the West Semitic loanwords in first-millennium Akkadian and other indications of linguistic interference are Aramaic, not Arabic[102]; and (3) the rich West Semitic onomasticon from first-millennium Mesopotamia is largely Aramaic (while the Arabian material has an impressive geographical distribution, but is clearly a small minority).[103] Finally, as Stockhusen (2013, 237) notes, the entire edifice stands or falls on the question of whether a broken plural is detectable in Old Aramaic, and this is extremely doubtful.[104]

Therefore, it is most reasonable to accept the Assyrian and Babylonian sources labeling of these groups as Aramean.[105] In addition to those tribes explicitly called Aramean in Assyrian royal inscriptions, there are a number of tribes that were probably also Aramean (see the "Highly Likely Aramean Tribes" enumerated in §10.2.3 below).

#### 10.2.2.1. First Occurrences in Babylonia until the Time of Tiglath-pileser III

While Tiglath-pileser I (1114–1076) and Aššur-bēl-kala (1073–1056) were attempting to deal with the Aramean incursions into Assyrian territory in the Jezirah,[106] there is still uncertainty as to what was exactly transpiring in Babylonia at this time. Assyrian Chronicle 4 gives evidence that the Aramean incursions were significant, dating to 1082/1081, the time of transition of power between Marduk-nādin-aḫḫē (1099–1082 BCE) and his son Marduk-šāpik-zēri (1081–1069 BCE). The Aramean penetrations to Rapiqu on the Babylonian border and their plundering of Īdu (Sātu Qala), well to the east

101. I.e., if the tribes in southern Mesopotamia were predominantly Arabian, how does one explain the Aramaic language's rise to dominance?

102. In short, why are there so few Arabic loanwords in Akkadian?

103. Zadok 2013, 273. He also observes: "Likewise, the Aramean tribal names which have exclusive Arabian etymologies without Aramaic interference (Ubūlu, Ḫagarānu, Lītawu) or parallels (Raḫīḫu and Ḫindaru) are a minority and only one tribe of the list of explicitly Aramean tribes (*Nabātu*) is probably identical with a Kedarite one (*Nbyt*, OT *Nbywt*). Taken together, tribes of non-Aramean extraction form just 14.28% of the explicit Aramean tribal composite list."

104. See the discussion of "broken plurals," pp. 39–40.

105. In my opinion, Zadok's study (2013) is quite compelling. See also Fales 2007b; Fales 2011d; Frame 2013; Arnold 2004; 2011.

106. See §3.2.3.2 above.

of the Tigris, emphasize the fact that Babylonia could hardly have been unaffected. It is simply that the evidence has not been preserved or discovered.

Nevertheless, in the eleventh and tenth centuries, official Babylonian texts indicate that tribal groups variously labeled as Arameans or Suteans carried out raids on a number of cities in the northern alluvial plain (Fales 2007, 289). Starting with Adad-apla-iddina (1068–1047), Babylonian kings mention Aramean incursions. According to an earlier understanding of Babylonian Chronicle 24, Adad-apla-iddina was himself an Aramean usurper.[107] However, this has been shown to be incorrect.[108] The Chronicle states:

> The Arameans (KUR.*a-ra-mu*) and a usurper (LUGAL.IM.GI) revolted against Adad-apla-iddina, son of Itti-Marduk-balāṭu, and [prof]aned the sanctuaries, as many as there were in the land. They demolished Dēr, Nippur, Sippar, and Parsa (Dūr-Kurigalzu). The Suteans uprooted and carried off the booty of Sumer and Akkad into their land.[109]

The little evidence there is suggests that relations between Arameans and the older settled population of Babylonia did not improve over time (Frame 2013, 92). Many of the cities of central Babylonia began to experience the presence of the Arameans in the tenth century, and evidence suggests they began to control the trade route along the Euphrates at this time. According to the Religious Chronicle, in 972 and 971, during the reign of Nabû-mukīn-apli (978–943), hostile actions by Arameans prevented the New Year's festival from taking place:

> In the month of Nisan, in the seventh year, the Arameans were hostile, the king did not go up to Babylon; Nabû did not venture forth, nor did Bēl [go out].
>
> In the month of Nisan, in the eighth year of king Nabû-mukīn-apli, the Arameans were hostile and seized the ford of Kār-bēl-mātāti. (Thus) the king could not cross; Nabû did not venture forth, nor did Bēl go out.[110]

About one hundred and fifty years later, in 814, Šamšī-Adad V of Assyria (823–811) claimed that Marduk-balāssu-iqbi, the Babylonian king, trusted in his muster of the lands of Chaldea, Elam, Namri, and Aram (KUR.*a-ru-mu*) in a battle that took place at Dūr-Papsukkal from which the Assyrians merged

107. See Grayson 1975, 65, 180.

108. Walker 1982, 414–15. Grayson read KUR.*A-ra-mu-u šarru ḫammâ'u* and understood this as "an Aramean usurper"; but it should be read as KUR.*A-ra-mu u šarru ḫammâ'u* "the Arameans and a usurper."

109. See now Glassner 2004, 284–85, text 47, 6′–9′.

110. Grayson 1975, 137, no. 17 iii.4′b–9′; Glassner 2004, 300–01.

victorious.[111] In the eighth century, Chaldean kings of Babylonia such as Erība-Marduk (ca. 765)[112] and Nabû-šuma-iškun (ca. 760—latest possible date for his accession—to 748 BCE)[113] had problems with Arameans usurping fields from city dwellers. These appear to be the earliest instances of substantial Aramean settlement in Babylonian territory, and they occur just before the widespread attestation of Aramean tribes all around Babylonia in the time of Tiglath-pileser III (Brinkman 1968, 280). Many of the cities of central Babylonia began to experience the presence of the Arameans in the tenth century, and evidence suggests they began to control the trade route along the Euphrates at this time. All this only indicates an Aramean presence in Babylonia proper (≈ Akkad). This may be due to the nature of the sources or it may indicate a pattern of penetrations.[114] In any case, by the time of Tiglath-pileser III over forty Aramean tribes are attested, distributed throughout Babylonia (table 10.1 above). They generally resisted sedentarization and assimilation into Babylonian life.

### 10.2.2.2. The Origins of the Arameans in Eastern Babylonia

The origins of the Arameans in eastern Babylonia (especially east of the Tigris) are still unknown. There are three different theories.[115]

(1) The Arameans in eastern Babylonia are the remote descendants of the Amurrites who had been established in almost the same territories one thousand years earlier in Syria, the middle Euphrates, and southeastern Babylonia. There is no evidence of a population displacement of the older Babylonian or Amurrite population. But this is due to the lack of sources. Since the occurrence of the *ia-* prefix and *-ān(um)* suffix in some Aramean personal names is similar to the same elements in Amurrite names, some scholars have interpreted this as evidence for a link. However, this is hardly more than circumstantial, and is the least likely of the three theories.[116]

(2) The Arameans migrated to eastern Babylonia and settled there at the beginning of the eleventh century (i.e., more or less contemporary with the attestations of Arameans in Babylonia Proper, even though these Babylonian

111. RIMA 3:188, A.0.103.1, iv.37–45.

112. Eclectic Chronicle: Grayson 1975, 182–83, no. 24, rev. 11–13.

113. RIMB 2:124, B.6.14.2001, i.15′–21′.

114. Caution is important, since this evidence does not necessarily mean that the Arameans had not already spread; it only really indicates the limitations of the sources telling us about their distribution.

115. For an earlier discussion, see Brinkman 1968, 281–85. See also Lipiński 2000a, 412–16.

116. See the discussion in chapter 2 (p. 87) above and Edzard 1964.

attestations do not mention or delineate Transtigridian areas). The migrations east of the Tigris may have begun earlier; certainly they did further north, if the Assyrian Chronicle 4's evidence (especially the location of Īdu) is correctly understood in light of recent archaeological information (see chapter 3). Thus penetrations may have progressed from the Lower Zab southward into the Transtigridian region.

(3) The Arameans were not present in eastern Babylonia until around 800 or slightly later. This theory is based on the lack of evidence for their presence in the region before Tiglath-pileser III. With the military activities of this Assyrian king, the Aramean tribes crossed the northern alluvium and the Tigris and spread southeastward along both banks of the river as far as the Elamite plain.[117]

Recently, Zadok (2013, 278) has asserted that the individual Aramean tribes migrated along the various watercourses in southeastern Babylonia as a result of "their migration from the Middle Euphrates to the Transtigridian region of Babylonia," which was "followed by constant incursions from the Transtigridian region into the western section of the alluvium," a region irrigated by the arms of the Euphrates and their canal system. He feels that

> This model of migration and penetration generally resembles that of the Amorites in the first quarter of the second millennium. Like the migrations of the Amorites, the Aramean tribal movements were an important incentive for the creation of the "toponymie en mirroir," i.e., that certain toponyms referring to locales in Upper Mesopotamia are paralleled by names of places situated in the Transtigridian region. Thus such toponyms are generally in east-west direction in first-millennium Babylonia echoing migrations (for the second millennium, see Charpin 2003b, 19 who coined this fitting expression). Therefore Lipiński's doubts concerning the relationship between the Aramean tribes and the homonymous toponyms are not justified (Zadok 2013, 278).

A good of example of this "toponymie en mirroir" can be seen in the fact that more than one settlement in the western alluvium was named after the people of the Middle Euphrates city of Ḫindānu: (1) the site of *Ḫi-in-da-i-na* in Bīt-Awkāni (Parpola 1970, 162) (2) the site of *Ḫindāyu* near Nippur (Zadok 1985a, 161). Moreover, a number of settlements of other groups in eastern Babylonia are paralleled by toponyms in western Babylonia. For example, a number of Gambūlean fortified towns on the Uqnû are paralleled by towns

117. See Cole 1996b, 25–26. This theory is, unfortunately, primarily based on an argument from silence.

near Sippar, Uruk, and Nippur (Zadok 2013, 279). These constitute further evidence of "toponymie en mirroir."

In my opinion, Zadok's suggestion has great merit. However, it is very likely that the military activities of a number of Assyrian kings in the southern Jezirah were also contributing factors.[118] The campaign of Aššur-dān II was perhaps the initial "push factor"; the campaigns of Aššurnaṣirpal II against Laqē, Ḫindānu and Sūḫu were a sure stimulus for the migration of other Aramean units to the south[119]; Shalmaneser III's campaign against Chaldea was another possible push factor; and most certainly, the campaigns of Tiglath-pileser III provided further motivations for movement to the south of a number of Aramean entities. In addition, it must be remembered that "pull factors" were likely also causes for Aramean migration to Babylonia, namely what may have appeared to them as available water sources due to the lack of strong central government in the region to deter their movement. Therefore, the migrations of Aramean tribes and clans into both western and eastern Babylonia was a complex process over many years, from many directions and with many causes or factors.

Thus it would seem that some time in the eleventh century the Arameans began to move into Babylonia. In Babylonia Proper this is well-attested. For the Transtigridian region, there were progressive penetrations at this time, with some later movements westward. This helps to adequately explain the diverse groups' presence. Moreover, these movements were greatly enhanced by the Assyrian military forays. Consequently, by the mid-to-late eighth century, the Arameans in the lower Tigris catchment area are clearly attested with over forty medium- to small-sized tribal entities, some of which were further fragmented into various sub-tribes or clans under the leadership of different "sheikhs" (*nasīku*).

After the reign of Tiglath-pileser III, there are three additional reasons for Aramean presence in Babylonia. First, there was "the stationing of auxiliaries of various tribes there (Itū'eans, Puqūdeans, Ḫamarāneans, Rehiqeans, Damūneans, Yadaqqeans, Lihuteans as well as other West Semites, viz. Hallateans, Ruqāḫeans and Aradateans)" (Zadok 2013, 278). There is, of course, direct evidence of this in the annals of Sargon II from 710 where he states that he recruited a third of the defeated tribesmen in Gambūlu.[120] Second, there were deportations of various Aramean groups, not all of which are known, especially the details. Third, continued Assyrian military activities during the period of the Sargonids.

118. Fales 2007, 289; Brinkman 1968, 268–72; Lipiński (2000a, 415) states: "the beginnings of this Aramaean immigration should be updated to the 9th century B.C."

119. As suggested by Fales 2011d, 213 n. 5.

120. Fuchs 1994, 142–43 n. 278. See the discussion in Fales 1991b.

### 10.2.2.3. Geographical Distribution

The watercourses where the Arameans dwelt must be reconstructed from various sources. The geographical information about the Arameans of Babylonia in the inscriptions of Tiglath-pileser III is insufficient to locate most of the tribal entities.[121] There is only the summary statement that these Arameans groups are dwelling "on the banks of the Tigris, Euphrates, and Surappu Rivers as far as the Uqnû River which is on the shore of the Lower Sea." In later Assyrian inscriptions there is more detailed information. It is important to note that the association of tribes and rivers is not consistent in the different inscriptions, which means that the tribes were either migrating or were divided into several branches with different dwelling places (Frahm 2003, 151).

The arrangements of lists of Sargon II and Sennacherib differ from those of Tiglath-pileser III, since they were dictated by the need to specify the tribes by watercourses.[122] Sargon's catalogue of Aramean polities is found in his "Great Display Inscription,"[123] the "Pavement Inscription 4,"[124] and the Tangi Var Inscription.[125] His lists distinguish between two groups of Arameans, those living "along the Tigris," and those whose dwelling places are "along the Surappu and the Uqnû":

Sargon II's Order

| | |
|---|---|
| on the Tigris: | Itū', Rupū', Ḫaṭallu, Labdūdu, Ḫamarānu, Ubūlu, Ru'a, Lītawu |
| on the Surappu and Uqnû: | Gambūlu, Ḫindaru, Puqūdu. |

Sennacherib's inscriptions (see note e to table 10.1) clearly repeat the order of the Aramean entities, but only the so-called "First Campaign Cylinder"[126] divides up the list according to the watercourse where the Aramean entities were located:

---

121. Zadok (1985c, 64–65) suggested that the list of tribes follows a north-south delineation. See the comments of Frahm 2003, 151.

122. For a discussion of the identifications of the watercourses, see above under hydrology §10.2.1.1.

123. Fuchs 1994, 195, lines 18–19.

124. Fuchs 1994, 265, lines 70–76.

125. Frame 1999, 37, lines 31–32.

126. Text edition: RINAP 3.1:32–33, 1, lines 12–14. Two versions of the text are known: one written on cylinders discovered at Assur and Nineveh, the other on cylinders from Tarbiṣu. Also one should consult Frahm 2003, 134–44, esp. p. 140. Since the names of the rivers associated with the tribes were incorrectly restored by Luckenbill in his edition

| | |
|---|---|
| Sennacherib's Order on the Tigris: | Tu'mūna, Raḫīḫu, Yādaqqu, Kib/prē and Mala/iḫu |
| on the Surappu: | Gurūmu, Ubūlu, Damūnu, Gambūlu, Ḫindaru, Ru'a and Puqūdu |
| on the Euphrates: | Ḫamarānu, Ḫagarānu, Nabātu and Lītawu. |

Normally, in Sennacherib's lists, one encounters the Ubūdu tribe in between Yādaqqu and Kib/prē, and thus it would seem best to locate this tribe also on the Tigris (Zadok 2013, 275).

However, it would appear that the Lītawu lived on the Tigris, along with the Ubūlu and Ru'a, according to Sargon II; yet the Lītawu are found on the Euphrates and the Ubūlu and Ru'a on the Surappu, according to Sennacherib. Furthermore, the Ḫamarānu were on the Tigris in Sargon II's day, but on the Euphrates in Sennacherib's.[127] Thus within a generation some of these tribes migrated from one location to another, undoubtedly the result of Assyrian aggression against them. Nevertheless, some of the larger tribal groups, like the Gambūlu, seem to have remained in their location.

#### 10.2.2.4. Social and Cultural Distinction

One of the very interesting facts about the Aramean entities in southern Mesopotamia is that, for the most part, they resisted the attractiveness of indigenous Babylonian culture with its prestigious ancient array of beliefs and lore. This social and cultural "separateness," as Fales (2007b, 293) notes, is all the more noteworthy in that many of the Aramean tribes were in close contact with the Babylonian settlements for everyday matters (see e.g., Cole 1996a; 1996b). It is even more noteworthy because of the tremendous propensity of the Arameans in all other regions to adapt quite readily to the cultures in which they found themselves.[128] Thus the Babylonian region is unique for the Arameans. For one possible exception, see the discussion concerning Nergal-šarru-uṣur below (p. 691).

---

of this text, there has been a lot of confusion regarding this passage. Fortunately, Frahm's study and the new RINAP 3.1 edition have clarified the text. For all of Sennacherib's lists of Arameans, see table 10.1 n. f.

127. Ḫamarānu dwelt in the Sippar region near the Euphrates (cf. Zadok 1985c, 66–67; Zadok 2013, 275).

128. While this observation holds true, it must be recognized that, at present, there is no identifiable archaeological evidence of Aramean material culture from the Mesopotamian region.

The Arameans also rejected unified leadership, preferring the complexities of socially constructed entities.[129] This is demonstrated by the geographically ubiquitous Puqūdu who segmented into various sub-groups, yet retained their common tribal organization. The social and political leadership of each unit rested in a *nasīku* sheikh (or in some cases sheikhs).[130] The multiplicity of these *nasīku*s would seem to indicate an ongoing segmentation within the tribal units themselves. There are no Aramean entities in southern Mesopotamia designated by the Assyrians with the *bītu*-formula. This is in contrast to the Upper Mesopotamian and Levantine situation where a number of Aramean polities were designated with the *bītu*-formula.[131]

### 10.2.2.5. Enumeration of Tribes

#### 6. Puqūdu

Lipiński argues at length that the name "Puqūdu should be considered as a grammatical 'broken' plural of *pāqidu*," which "must mean 'herdsmen.'"[132] Zadok (2013, 285) has correctly observed: "Since it has a suitable Aramaic denotation, there is no need to fit it into the scheme of Arabic 'broken' plurals as advocated by Lipiński." The root is *pqd* which is clearly attested in Aramaic. It had been suggested that *Puqūdu* was a secondary form (the outcome of Neo-Assyrian vowel harmony of *Piqūdu*); however, this is not the case since the original form is evidenced in the earliest Neo-Babylonian texts.[133] Lipiński (2000a, 430) explains the form Piqūdu as reflecting the weakening of the short *u* > *šewa* (the sign PI also has the phonetic value PE). Hence the Masoretic form Pekod (Jer 50:21; Ezek 23:23).

The earliest mention of the tribe is around 755–732 BCE in the so-called governor's archive from Nippur.[134] At this time, the whole tribe was participant in the local festival (*isinnu*) during the month of Ululu at Nippur (Cole 1996a, 88–90, text 27, lines 8b–13). From this same text, it is clear that there were numerous sheikhs of this Aramean tribe who were expected to make restitution at this time for the money or material that had been advanced to one of their tribesmen, a smith, in the event that he had embezzled it (Cole

129. See §2.3.2.
130. Brinkman 1968, 274–5.
131. See §2.3.1 above.
132. Lipiński 2000a, 429–31, esp. 430.
133. Zadok (1977, 131, 185) originally argued for the vowel harmony but now rejects it (Zadok 2013, 285) in light of Cole 1996a, 443.
134. See Cole 1996b, 27; Lipiński 2000a, 429–37; Radner 2006–8b, 115.

1996b, 89, text 27, lines 19–30). In another letter from the Nippur archive,[135] there is an interesting contrast in the quality of wool:

> The wool of the Puqūdu (LÚ.*Pu-qu-du*) is not good, and its price is not good; the wool of the people of Laḫīru (LÚ.*La-ḫe-e-ri*)[136] is good, and its price is good. Of the wool valued at five minas of silver received from the Puqūdu—when I sheared (it), it(?) did not amount(?) to five minas. They were each short one-third mina. When I found out, I wrote to my lord.

Thus Puqūdean wool had a rather low reputation!

Puqūdu was one of the strongest Aramean tribes between 745 and 626 with several coeval sheikhs.[137] The inscriptions of Tiglath-pileser III, Sargon II, and Sennacherib indicate that the Puqūdu were active along the Babylonian-Elamite frontier, although the correspondence of Esarhaddon and Aššurbanipal places them as far west as Bīt-Awkāni and Uruk (Brinkman 1984, 13 and n. 49). In one of his inscriptions, Tiglath-pileser III declares:

> I overwhelmed the Puqūdu like a net; I inflicted a decisive defeat on them; and I carried off much of their booty. I annexed that Puqūdu, the city of Laḫīru of Idibirīna, (and) the cities of Ḫilimmu (and) Pillatu, which are on the border of the land of Elam. I placed (them) under the authority of my eunuch, the provincial governor of the city of Arrapḫa.[138]

It is clear, however, that such "annexation" was hardly the end of Puqūdu independence. Thus Sargon II also claims that he subjugated the Puqūdu and Damūnu tribes as far as the town of Laḫīru.[139] Yet, it is very clear that during the period of Sargon II the Puqūdu were a sizeable confederation of tribes (or less likely, that these tribes were under its rule as dependents). A passage from Sargon's Annals lists five sheikhs that are designated as "five sheikhs of the Puqūdu":

> Yanuqu the sheikh of the "town" of Zamê, Nabû-uṣalla of the "town" of Aburē, Paššunu (and) Ḫaukanu of the town of Nuḫāni, Sa'-ilu of the town of Ibuli (= Ubūlu):[140] 5 sheikhs (LÚ.*na-si-ka-a-ti*) of the Puqūdu tribe, Abḫatā of the Rū'a tribe, (and) Ḫuninu, Same'u, Sapḫaru (and) Rāpiu of the

135. Cole 1996a, 23, text 46:10, 16b–29.
136. Concerning the city of Laḫīru, see the discussion below.
137. Fuchs 1994, 454. For further discussion see below.
138. RINAP 1:118–19, 47, lines 13b–14a; Tadmor 1994, 160, Summary 7.
139. Fuchs 1994, 65, Bull Inscription, lines 29b–30a.
140. Zadok 1985c, 40 n. 76. See discussion under Ubūlu below.

> Ḫindaru tribe, brought horses, cattle and sheep to me, their heavy tribute, to the city of Dūr-Abīhara. They kissed my feet.[141]

This passage is also important for demonstrating that there was a significant sedentary element to this tribal confederation by its attribution of "town of" GN to these sheikhs. In fact, the town of *Ú-bu-lu* of the Puqūdu is mentioned in a letter to Sargon II.[142]

According to Sargon II's inscriptions, the tribe dwelt on the Surappu and Uqnû Rivers; according to Sennacherib, they lived along the Surappu. Yet they had a much wider geographical distribution. Their lengthy and massive presence near Nippur left its mark on the local toponymy, seeing that an important canal was named after them (see below). When Sargon II established the province of Gambūlu in 710, the region of Yadburu, the territory of the Puqūdu and their confederates were included within the provincial administration zone.[143] From this period, it is evident that some Puqūdu lived in Bīt-Awkāni and feared deportation.[144] This was a well-founded fear since another letter, in this case from Uruk, reported that the Puqūdu who live in the Qatannu marsh (AMBAR.*qa-tan-nu*) report on a daily basis with the Babylonian leader Merodach-Baladan, who is designated the *mār-Yakīni*.[145]

The Puqūdu joined Merodach-Baladan's uprising but were defeated by Sennacherib in 704 with the other rebels.[146] They fought again against Sennacherib on the side of Elam in 691 at the battle of Ḫalulê.[147]

From the late Neo-Assyrian period, a letter (the time of Esarhaddon) about provisions of royal functionaries in Nippur includes a complaint that the Puqūdu have carried off all the dates.[148] In another complaint from the time of Esarhaddon or Aššurbanipal, it is reported that Nabû-zēra-iddina, a Borsippean, allied himself with Ṣillāya, and that together they caused Nabû-ušēzib of the Puqūdu tribe to become an enemy of Assyria.[149]

Nevertheless, Puqūdean (LÚ.*Pu-qud-a-a*) soldiers were part of the Assyrian army (presumably auxiliaries). They are enumerated together with other Arameans and West Semites in a fragmentary letter to Aššurbanipal.[150]

---

141. Fuchs 1994, 146–47, Annals, lines 284–286.

142. SAA 15:120, 179.11–16.

143. Fuchs 1994, 433; Radner 2006–8a, 65. Later in the seventh century, the province Gambulu was apparently allocated to the provinces Dēru and Dūr-Šarrukku.

144. SAA 15:144, 221.r.3–9 (= *ABL* 1434).

145. SAA 17:122, 142.7–r.4 (= *ABL* 1052).

146. RINAP 3.1, 32–34, 1 i.5–33, esp. i.13.

147. RINAP 3.1, 182–84, 22 v.43–vi.35, esp. v.48.

148. SAA 18:58, 76.2′–11′ (= Dietrich 1979, 495); Cole 1996b, 29 n. 44.

149. SAA 18:146, 176.10–r.3 (= *ABL* 808).

150. Zadok 2013, 285. See *ABL* 1009.

A tablet of Inurta-ila'i to the palace scribe mentions Puqūdeans (KUR.*Pu-qud-a-a*) under Assyrian military command.[151] In a letter from the time of Esarhaddon, the "officials" (*šaknūte*)[152] of the city of Puqūdu (URU.*Pu-q*[*u-du*]) are mentioned in a broken context.[153] Yet, loyalties could be conflicting. A segment of the tribe supported Šamaš-šuma-ukīn (see Frame 1992, 167–68).

Finally, there is clear evidence that Puqūdu retained its status as a region at least as late as the early part of the reign of Nebuchadnezzar II.[154] According to Zadok (1985a, 250, 351, 379), a town of *Pi-qu-du* was possibly situated on an important canal named after the tribe (*Nār-* or *Ḫarri-Piqūdu*).

In the biblical texts, the tribe is called "Pekod" in Jer 50:21[155] and Ezek 23:23. A recently identified tablet, however, may give additional insight in the singling out of this tribe's name. In Jer 39:3, translations have generally understood the passage to be listing the names of four Babylonian officials: Nergal-sharezer; Samgar-nebo (סַמְגַּר־נְבוּ); Sarsechim, the Rabsaris; Nergal-sharezer, the Rab-mag (NRSV). Thus Samgar-Nebo is taken as a personal name and Sarsechim as either a personal name or a title. However, a tablet in the British Museum dated to the reign of Nebuchadnezzar lists a certain Nabû-šarrūssu-ukīn with the function of Rab-ša-rēši, indicating that the biblical text, though later misunderstood, preserved in this case accurate data (Jursa 2008; 2010). The word Samgar must therefore be the title borne for the first person in the list,[156] Nergal-sharezer, which means that he can be identified without doubt with Nergal-šarru-uṣur the Simmagir in the *Hofkalender*.[157]

The identity of Nergal-sharezer the *simmagir* with the future king Nergal-šarru-uṣur (Neriglissar) (559–556) is now generally accepted. As Nergal-šarru-uṣur claims in his official inscriptions to be the son of one Bēl-šumu-iškun, it has also been proposed that the Bēl-šumu-iškun who appears as head of the Aramean tribe of Puqūdu in the *Hofkalender* should be iden-

151. SAA 19:62, text 56 (= ND 2470); Saggs 2001, 84–85, and pl. 13.

152. See *CAD* 17.1:188–89, s.v. *šaknu*, 3.

153. SAA 18:154, 187.r.11′ (= *ABL* 1365).

154. For the documentation, see Beaulieu 2013, 45–47; Zadok 2013, 285.

155. Here clearly there is a wordplay between פְּקוֹד "visitation" and the Aramean tribe Puqūdu.

156. Jer 50:21 should be understood as "When Jerusalem was taken, all the officials of the king of Babylon came and sat in the middle gate: Nergal-sharezer, the Samgar (= *Nergal-šarru-uṣur simmagir*); Nebu-sarsechim the Rabsaris "chief eunuch" (*Nabû-šarrūssu-ukīn rab ša-rēši*); Nergal-sharezer the Rabmag, with all the rest of the officials of the king of Babylon."

157. Hofkalender iv.34 (Unger 1931, 282–94; Beaulieu 2013, 34). For discussion, see Becking 2009; Jursa 2010, 85; Beaulieu 2013, 35.

tified as his father (Beaulieu 2013, 35). Additional circumstantial evidence from contemporary cuneiform documents can be adduced to support that hypothesis. Thus, the evidence appears to suggest that at least one ruler of the Babylonian Empire stemmed from an Aramean background and that, prior to ascending the throne, that future ruler participated in the capture of Jerusalem. This may mean that the biblical writers in the two passages that mention the Puqūdu were more purposeful in their choice than simply making a wordplay; that is, there was a real connection between the Puqūdu and the Babylonian Empire.

### 7. Ubūlu

Although *Ubūlu* is primarily an Arabian name (*ʾibil* "camel[s]," see Lipiński 2000a, 460–61), Zadok states: "it cannot be excluded that the word was borrowed in Northwest Semitic."

The earliest occurrences are in the so-called governor's archive from Nippur from the mid-eighth century. In a fragmentary letter from the archive, it appears that the Ubūlu have plundered the camels of the people of Uruk (Cole 1996a, 96, text 32:8). In another fragmentary letter, there seems to be a dispute between the sender of the letter and an unnamed sheikh of the Ubūlu over a parcel of land (Cole 1996a, 206, text 98:17). Cole (1996a, 206) suggests that this parcel was perhaps traditional Ubūlu pastureland that had attracted the *šandabakku*'s cultivators after a canal had been extended into the area. The inscriptions of Tiglath-pileser III, Sargon II, and Sennacherib all mention the Ubūlu as one of the Aramean tribes of Babylonia (table 10.1 above).

The tribe dwelt on the Uqnû River, according to the inscriptions of Sennacherib.

The fact that a man named Sa'-ilu, one of the sheikhs of the Puqūdu, was in charge of the town of Ibuli (Ubūlu)[158] probably means that the Ubūlu were an important clan of the Puqūdu or that the Ubūlu were part of a confederation known as the Puqūdu.

In a text from Ur (Figulla 1949, 140:8), Ubūlu (LÚ.*ú-bu-lu*$_4$) appears to be a member of the Aramean tribe Amatu. Zadok (2013, 286) observes that "the lack of attenuation *u* > *i* may be an indication that it is early Neo-Babylonian. The earliest attenuated form is URU.*i-bu-li* from Sargon II's time." Zadok also feels that the gentilic LÚ.*i-bu-la-a-a* is based on the same form found in a undatable letter where it refers to Ibulean(s) in Arrapḫa (Saggs 2001, 246–47). However, Luukko has recently reedited this document and

158. Fuchs 1994, 146–47, Annals, lines 284–286. See translation in the section on the Puqūdu above.

read this gentilic as: LÚ*.⸢*gan*⸣-*bu-la-a-a*, "the Gambūleans" (SAA 19:121–22, 119.4). Since the form with an initial I-sign occurs, and since Gambūlu is apparently not spelled with the GAN-sign, the reading here of *Ibūlāya* (as Zadok) seems more likely to be correct.

**8.** Ḫamarānu

Zadok (2013, 286) suggests that the name is based on the root *ḥmr* that ends in *-ān*.[159] He notes that "it is explicable in Aramaic terms ('to roar, foam' > *ḥmr* 'wine') ... There is no need to look for an Arabic etymology as is done by Moritz 1926, 188–89 and Lipiński 2000a, 442." Apparently, based on a number of the spellings of the tribe's name, the *-ān* element could be dropped (note some of the attestations below).

The tribe is first mentioned by Tiglath-pileser III (see table 10.1). Sargon II had issues with this tribe. According to his annals, because the Ḫamarānu (LÚ.*ḫa-mar-a-na-a-a*) had been "constantly robbing Babylonian caravans," and had now fled and taken refuge in the city of Sippar, Sargon initiated a campaign against them in which he claims:

> I sent my eunuchs, the provincial governors, against them; and they besieged them, (so that no one) whether small nor great could escape; wherever they could reach them with the weapon, they slaughtered them.[160]

In another instance, in a letter from the time of Sargon II (SAA 1:78, 90.11), it appears that some members of this tribe ([KUR].*ḫa-mar-a-na-a-a*) kidnapped an Assyrian messenger and released him in the city of Munu' (URU.*Mu-nu-*ʾ).

A settlement (*Ḫa-am-ra-nu*) is to be sought near Sippar.[161] Another settlement named after them (*Ḫa-am-ra-nu*) existed in Rāši on the Babylonian–Elamite frontier during the early Sargonid period.[162]

Some members of this tribe, like many of their Aramean tribal contemporaries, served in the Assyrian army. In an administrative text, fifteen Ḫamarānean soldiers and donkeys (KUR.*ḫa-mar-*⸢*a.e*?⸣) are listed after eighteen Itū'ean soldiers and donkeys (⸢KUR⸣.*ú-tu-u-a-*⸢e⸣).[163] According to a fragmentary letter, the chiefs (LÚ.GAL.[MEŠ]) of the Ḫamarāneans

159. See Zadok 1978a, 186.

160. Fuchs 1994, 155–156, Ann. 318–320a.

161. See Zadok 1985a, 425.

162. See Zadok 1985c, 45; Fuchs 1994, 436.

163. SAA 19:176–77, 177.12′–13′. Saggs (2001, 241–42) read: $^{\text{māt}}$*ú-tu-a-*⸢*ú*⸣ and $^{\text{māt}}$*ḫa-mar-*⸢*a*⸣*-n*[*a?-a?-a?*] respectively.

([L]Ú.*ḫa-mu-ru*) may have been stationed near Borsippa in the late Sargonid period write to the king.[164]

9. Li/uḫuātu

The name of this tribe appears to be spelled with or without the *-āt* ending (LÚ.*lu-ḫu-ú-a-tu* or LÚ.*lu-ḫu-ú-a-a*) according to Zadok (1995a, 229; 2013, 287).[165] Thus the tribe is first mentioned in the inscriptions of Ninurta-kudurrī-uṣur of Sūḫu (mid-eighth century), where it is spelled Luḫūya.[166] These inscriptions would locate the tribe in the Wadi Tharthar region. The first occurrence with the spelling Luḫu'ātu is in the inscriptions of Tiglath-pileser III (see table 10.1). A form [L]Ú.*Li-ḫu-a-ta-a-a* is found in a Neo-Babylonian letter from the time of Sargon II.[167] According to this letter, they lived in the Sippar region together with the Rabilu, the Ḫaṭallu and perhaps the Ḫamarānu. A very fragmentary letter also from the time of Sargon II lists the LÚ*.*Lu-ḫu-ta-a-a* along with the Ḫaṭallu and Awkaneans.[168] In another letter written at the time that Sargon abandoned Dēr in 710 BCE,[169] the tribe ([LÚ.*l*]*u-ḫa-a-a-a-t*[*i*] started hostilities with the Yašumeans (*iá-a-šu-ba-a-a*), attacking the wall and burning all the fortresses of the king. They also attacked the troops of the governor of Zamua. Interestingly in contrast, a fully functioning Assyrian fort was named "the fort of the Luḫūtāya" (URU.*bir-ti* ⸢*ša* LÚ**Lu*⸣-*ḫu-ú-t*[*a-a-a*]).[170]

10. Rubbū

Rubbū, which ends in *-ū*, is based on **rubb*.[171] This tribe is recorded only in the inscriptions of Tiglath-pileser III (see table 10.1). Zadok suggests that there was a homonymous canal that is mentioned in a document from late "Chaldean" Uruk.[172]

---

164. SAA 17:72–73, 81.1–2.

165. See also Lipiński 2000a, 444, who suggests that it is based on an Arabic "broken" plural. If true, then *Li/uḫuātu* would have a double plural.

166. RIMB 2:295, S.0.1002.2, i.9–10.

167. SAA 17:12, 7.11.

168. SAA 15:149–50, 231.8′.

169. SAA 17:152, 172.7′–r.6a.

170. SAA 15:113–14, 166.9.

171. Zadok 2013, 287; 1977, 186, 312 n. 7; see also Lipiński 2000a, 445.

172. Zadok 2013, 287: *Nār-Ru-ub-bu* (see Dougherty 1920, 14:3). He locates this canal in the western section of the Babylonian alluvium (Zadok 1985a, 380).

11. Rāpiqu

This tribe's name may be reflected in the town Rapiqu on the Euphrates River on the border between Sūḫu and Babylonia that is mentioned in the inscriptions of Tiglath-pileser III and Sennacherib.[173] The city is known from the Old Babylonian period,[174] and is mentioned in Tiglath-pileser I's texts where he claims: "I crossed the Euphrates [...] times, twice in one year, in pursuit of the Aramean-*aḫlamû* to the land of Ḫatti. I inflicted on them a decisive defeat from the foot of Mount Lebanon, the city of Tadmor of the land of Amurru, Anat of the land of Sūḫu, as far as Rapiqu of Karduniaš (Babylonia)."[175]

In Tiglath-pileser III's Summary Inscription 7,[176] Rāpiqu is the only name in the list not prefixed with a LÚ determinative (see table 10.1). On the basis of this and the fact that it is a city name, Lipiński (2000a, 445) does not consider it an Aramean tribal name and suggests that "the tribalization of the town and of some other cities may have been a fabrication of an Assyrian scribe." However, an annalistic text of Tiglath-pileser III discovered in 1976 through Polish excavations at Nimrud does have the LÚ determinative before the tribal name (LÚ.*ra-pi-qi*).[177] Like other instances,[178] here the tribal name and the city name are homonymic. Therefore, there is no reason to posit an Assyrian scribal fabrication.[179]

12. Ḫīrānu

The tribal name may derive from Aramaic *ḥyr* "to see" with an *-ān*. Lipiński (2000a, 46) explains *Ḫīrān* as deriving "from a personal name with the suffix *-ān* added to the Aramaic noun **ḫīr* > **ḫiʾar*, "noble," hence "free," still attested in Syriac by *bar-ḥiʾ-rē* ... The city name must derive from the tribal name."

This may be one of the oldest Aramean tribes. There was a tribal group known as Ḫīrānu[180] in the Kassite period. Some of its members were serving as guards in Nippur, though they are identified later in the text as "Aḫlamû."[181] In a ration text,[182] two individuals are described as *mār*

173. Zadok 2013, 287; 1985c, 78; 1977, 185; Brinkman 1968, 271 with n. 1742.

174. Groneberg 1980, 193, s.v. Rabiqum, Rapiqum.

175. RIMA 2: 37; A.0.87.3, lines 29–35.

176. RINAP 1:118, 47, lines 5–8 = Tadmor 1994, summary 7.

177. RINAP 1:25, 4, lines 3–7. Brinkman 1968, 271 n. 1742, was written before this text's discovery.

178. E.g., Sarūgu.

179. For the Elamite *Bi-it Ra-ap-i-qú*, see Zadok's comment (2013, 287).

180. See §2.5.1.1, discussion of Aḫlamû.

181. Clay 1912b, 114:10, 16, and pl. 53.

182. BE 15, text 198, lines 50 and 105.

$^{m}$*Ḫīrāni*. In a letter found at Dūr-Kurigalzu,[183] *ḫurād Ḫīrāna*, "troops of (the) Ḫīrānu," are described as stationed in territory normally belonging to Assyria and in the regions of Sūḫu and Mari on the Middle Euphrates.

While Tiglath-pileser III's inscriptions in the eighth century (table 10.1, columns 3–4) clearly identify the tribe as Aramean, there appear to be at least three cities named Ḫīrānu.

(1) There was a city of Ḫīrānu (URU.*ḫi-ra-nu*) in Aššurnaṣirpal II's annals (ninth century).[184] Based on the context of the annals, this city was unquestionably located in the land of Adanu and within the area of Mount Amadanu.[185]

(2) There was a city of Ḫīrānu (URU.*ḫi-ra-nu*),[186] along with an homonymous canal (*Ḫi-ra-nu*), located in the western section of the Babylonian alluvium near Sippar in the middle of the sixth century.[187]

(3) There appears to have been a city of Ḫīrānu in the Transtigridian region. In a contract for a purchase of a female slave in which the penalty clause states that the one who lodges a complaint, breaks the contract, and seeks litigation shall place three minas of silver and one mina of gold in the lap of the god "Bēlānu who dwells in the city of Ḫīrāna" ($^{d}$*Be-la-nu a-šib-bi* URU.*Ḫi-ra-na*).[188] The deity's name in Aramaic (*bʿln*) would mean "our lord."[189] The seller, Remanni-ilu, appears to be a priest of this deity ([LÚ.]SANGA *šá* $^{d}$E[N$^{?}$-*a-nu*] (line 2). The first seven witnesses are said to all be from Ḫīrā[na] (URU. *ḫi-ra-*[*na*](line r. 16); all the remaining witnesses are from the city of Diqūqīna (URU.[*di*]-*qu-qi-na-*⸢*a*⸣) (s. 3).[190] From this, it would seem that this city of Ḫīrānu was close to the city of Diqūqīna that is identified with modern Ṭa'ūq/Ṭawūq (Arabic: Daqūq or Daqūqā).[191]

---

183. Gurney 1949: 139, no. 10:4, 21. See also Nashef 1982, 128.

184. RIMA 2:219, A.0.101.1, iii.97.

185. For the general location of this city, see Liverani 1992a, 83 n. 404; Lipiński 2000a, 147.

186. Pinches 1982, no. 239, 3′; Strassmaier 1889, no. 505, 3. Zadok 1977, 284–85.

187. Zadok 1985a, 162; Jursa 1998, 95–96.

188. SAA 14:134, 162.r.6–7 (= *ARU* 204:20–21).

189. As pointed out by Lipiński (2000a, 49), though he places the location of Ḥīrānu east of the Tigris River, in an area situated south of the modern city of Kirkuk. Zadok (2013, 288) states: "It cannot be proven that it was identical with a homonymous settlement, NA *Ḫi-ra-na*, which is mentioned together with Diqūqīna (Parpola 1979, 164). The latter is to be sought near Arrapha which had connections with Sippar in the 'Chaldean' period."

190. Note also one of the witnesses from Diquqina is named "Abdi-Bēlānu, [scribe, keeper of the c]ontract" $^{m}$*ab-di*–$^{d}$[E]N$^{!}$-⸢*a*$^{!}$⸣-⸢*nu*$^{!}$⸣ [A.BA *ṣa-bit d*]*an-ni-te* (line s.2).

191. Lipiński 2000a, 46 n. 128; Astour 1981, 51 n. 363.

Whether these are to be associated with the tribe or not is debated. The text of *ABL* 1468 rev. 7 appears to read LÚ.*Ḫi-i-ra-*[*a-nu*]. Brinkman (1968, 271 n. 1743) has doubted the restoration since "Ḫirānu elsewhere is never written with a long first syllable." However, Zadok (1985a, 162) accepts the restoration and gives the vocalization: Ḫīrānu. The publication of an Old Aramaic contract provides additional evidence. In a sale of two slaves (ca. 700 BCE), the contract stipulates in the penalty clauses:

> Whoever against the other will be overturned will bring a pair of white horses (*'wrh . swsyn . ḥwrn*) to Baʿal Ḥīrān (*bʿlḥyrn*); (and) [will give?] a mina of gold to Baʿal Ḥarrān (*bʿlḥrn*); or whoever litigates, [ ], strikes the hand, will bring their substitutes.[192]

The deity to which the horses must be brought is clearly written *bʿlḥyrn*, and the presence of *y*[193] prevents confusing it with the more well-known deity *bʿlḥrn*, "Baʿal of Ḥarrān," mentioned in the very next line (Lemaire 2001c, 19; 2010, 211; Lipiński 2000a, 46 n. 125).

This must be a reference to the city of URU.*ḫi-ra-nu* in Aššurnaṣirpal II's annals (located in northern Mesopotamia), since the context of the Old Aramaic contract would hardly demand a payment of a pair of white horses to a deity located in a city in the Babylonian alluvium near Sippar or a Transtigridian location because they also demand the payment of a mina of gold to the deity of the city of Ḥarran (i.e., the moon god Sîn; Aramean: Śahr). Thus this city is located in the region close to Ḥarran[194] and should be vocalized

192. Lemaire 2001c, 14–24, text 1: lines 6b–13; (= Kwasman 2000, 274–80). In Schwiderski's volume (2004, 25), his version of L:1 and L:2 are the same as L:*35 and L:36 (text and line numbers given per Fales 1986). For a translation of the full contract, see Younger 2007c, 142.

193. It is clearly a *y* and not a *z*, which might have caused one to think of the well-known toponym "Ḫuzirīna," located north-northwest of Ḥarrān (modern Sultantepe). Lemaire (2001c, 20) correctly notes that this city cannot be understood to be the city of Ḫaūrina because in Aramaic one would expect *Ḥwrn* rather than *Ḥyrn*. However, Kwasman (2000, 278–79) argued: "*bʿlḥyrn* : *ḥyrn* in *bʿlhyrn* corresponds to [UR]U.*Ḫi-ra-na* in a sales document belonging to Šumma-ilāni (Kwasman 1988, 432–33, no. 378: lines 19–21 = SAA 14:135, text 163). Menzel appears to identify Ḫirrānu with Ḫarrānu (cf. AT T 215 no. 302). The *y* indicates the phonetic change of /a/ > /i/ in closed unaccented syllables (see S. Segert, *Altaramäische Grammatik*, Leipzig, 1990 3.9.1.). Thus Ḫirrānu is a phonetic variant of Ḫarrānu. See also *RlA*, 4 124b–25a, §§8, 9." This explanation is highly problematic: why separate the items to be paid if it is the same deity and why spell the same place name differently, literally three words later in the text? Moreover, in Segert's documenting of the vowel change in Biblical Aramaic that involves short vowels, none of the examples demonstrates a *yod* being used to mark this!

194. The exact identification of this toponym remains uncertain.

as Ḫīrānu, even though it is not always written with the additional I-sign in cuneiform texts.

Returning to the text of *ABL* 1468, it would seem that Brinkman's objection does not have the same force. Because the fragment *ABL* 1468 also mentions the people of Larak (r. 6′), the Rū'a (r.6′), the Puqūdu (r.7′), along with the cities of Uruk and Ur (r.8′), it seems very likely that the restoration in r.7′ should be LÚ.*ḫi-i-ra-*[*a-nu*], and the spelling with a long *ī* actually preserves the tribal name's vocalization. Whether the city in the far north (*ḥyrn* / URU.*ḫi-ra-nu*) should be linked with this Aramean tribe or not, it is impossible at this time to sure, but it cannot be ruled out.

However, a problem remains. The Old Aramaic contracts and the contract from Nineveh[195] both seem to reference the same deity: "Ba'al of Ḥīrān" and "Bēlānu who dwells in the city of Ḫīrāna."

13. Rabb-ilu

This tribal name was originally a personal name.[196] It is homonymous with the Nabatean royal name *Rb'l*, but this does not mean that the name is typically Arabian as implied by Moritz (1926, 189:9). There are Neo-Assyrian examples. It denotes "El is great" (Aram. *rb*).

The tribe is mentioned in the inscriptions of Tiglath-pileser III (see table 10.1). They lived in the Sippar region as early as Sargon II's time together with the Ḫaṭallu, Luḫu'ātu, and perhaps Ḫamarānu.[197] There was also a settlement of the same name: URU.*rab-bi-i-li*, URU.*rab-bi-lu* located in the western section of the Babylonian alluvium near Sippar in the "Chaldean" and early Achaemenid periods.[198] The tribe might have existed as late as the fifth century ([LÚ].*rab-bil-lu(?)* in the Murašû archive.[199]

14. Naṣīru

The name may derive from Aramaic *nṣr*.[200] It is not necessary to posit an Arabic derivation as Lipiński (2000a, 447) does. The Naṣīru tribe is mentioned in Tiglath-pileser III's inscriptions (see table 10.1). A homonymous settlement (NB/LB *Na-ṣir*) was located in the western section of the Babylonian alluvium, not far from Sippar (see Zadok 1985a, 236).

195. SAA 14:134, 162.r.6–7 (= *ARU* 204:20–21).

196. Zadok 1977, 32–33, 185, 295; 2013, 288. Lipiński 2000a, 446 erroneously connects it with Neo-Assyrian *Rab-ba*-AN /*Rabbān*/ and claims that the tribe is of Arabic origin.

197. SAA 17:12, 7.12 [LÚ].*ra-bi-la-a-a* (= Dietrich 1979, 42).

198. Zadok 1985a, 257, 425.

199. BE 9, 101, 3.

200. See Zadok 1977a, 186; 312 n. 5; Healey 1976.

15. Gulūsu

This tribal name is most likely based on a personal name, being a *qutūl* formation. It is explicable in Aramaic terms; therefore, there is no need to regard it as "broken" plural with an Arabic etymology as argued by Lipiński (2000a, 447–48), whose dissociation of the Neo-Babylonian settlement from the tribe is unconvincing (Zadok 2013, 288).[201] The Neo-Babylonian/Late Babylonian *Gi-lu-šú* ("Chaldean" and early Achaemenid) is with attenuation *u* > *i*.[202]

The tribe is mentioned in the inscriptions of Tiglath-pileser III (see table 10.1). The personal name occurs in Neo-Assyrian as Gulūsu, specifically a governor of the Itū': ᵐ*gu-lu-su* LÚ.GAR-*nu i-tu-ʾu*.[203] The name, spelled ᵐ*Gu-lu-šú*, occurs in the governor's archive from Nippur.[204] The homonymous settlement Neo-Babylonian *Gi-lu-(ú)-šú* was located in the western section of the Babylonian alluvium, not far from Sippar,[205] where several other settlements named after Aramean tribes were located.

16. Nabātu

This tribe's name occurs in the inscriptions of Tiglath-pileser III and Sennacherib (see table 10.1). Its name has been linked with the Nebaioth (נבי[ו]ת) in the Bible[206] and, in turn, understood by a number of scholars as being the Nabateans, most recently Lipiński (2000a, 448–50).[207] His argument (2000a, 449) is based on the fact that the LÚ.*na-ba-tu* appear in Sennacherib's inscription (see table 10.1) listed "between two North-Arabian tribes." He feels that this favors the Nabātu being North Arabians rather than Arameans and should be identified with the tribe which was later called *Nbyt*/*Nabayatu*, which is the "'broken' plural of *nabī* for *nabī'u*, 'distinguished man.'" Lipiński (2000a, 448) rejects the distinction between the *nabatu*/*nabayatu* and the Nabateans (*nbṭw*).[208]

201. The root *glš* is found in Biblical Hebrew (*HALOT*, 195), Jewish Aramaic (Sokoloff 2002b, 131a; Jastrow 1950, 251), and Arabic.

202. See Zadok 2013, 288; see earlier 1976, 118; 1977, 131.

203. SAA 7:9, 5.ii.11; and 7:18, 9.r.i.25.

204. See Cole 1996a, 97, text 33:1.

205. Zadok 1985a, 139; 2003, 260 (1.2.9, with seven individuals bearing Aramaic names).

206. Gen 25:13; 28:9; 36:3; Isa 60:7; 1 Chr 1:29.

207. For discussion and earlier bibliography, see Eph'al 1982, 222 and n. 30.

208. The spelling of the gentilic form in the Nabateans' own inscriptions! See Healey 2009, 52, text 1:7, etc.

The two tribes mentioned before and after the Nabātu are the Ḫagarānu and the Lītawu,[209] neither of which must be Arabian and therefore, the force of Lipiński's argument is lost. Moreover, both of these appear under the label "Arameans." Interestingly, in a fragmentary text from Nimrud, the tribes of Lītawu and Ḫagarānu are mentioned together in the context of Arameans.[210]

In the case of the link with the Nabateans (*nbṭw*), Lipiński does not account for the difficult shift from *t* (*nbt*/*nbyt*) to *ṭ* (*nbṭw*).[211] Therefore, as a number of scholars have pointed out, the root (*nbṭ*) from which the gentilic Nabateans is derived is different than the one from which Nabātu is derived,[212] though determining precisely this root is less certain. In any case, the Nabateans should be distinguished from the Nabātu.

Zadok suggests that Nabātu is a contracted form based on the root *nbʾ* and with the ending *-āt* (an ending found in a number of the other Aramean tribal names).[213] He also believes that the Nabātu is identical with the Ishmaelite tribe of *Nbyt*/*Nabayātu* since the latter is also spelled *Né-ba-ʾ-a-ti*, with *-ya-* > *-ʾ-* which is common in Neo-Babylonian/Late Babylonian. While this is certainly a possible explanation, it cannot be ruled out that the spelling with *-ya-* indicates a different derivation, and hence a different tribe (Knauf 1998–2001b). Hence, Nabātu may derive from *nbʾ* (or *nbt*? in which case the /t/ is part of the root and not an *-at* suffixal ending) and Nabayāt/Nebaioth derived from the root *nby* "proclaim."

In the inscriptions of Aššurbanipal and in a letter from the period of his reign, there is clear evidence of a person known as "Natnu, king of the Nabayatians" ([m]*na-at-nu* LUGAL KUR.*na-ba-a-a-ti*). He is mentioned in the context of Aššurbanipal's reprisals against Arab tribes following the rebellion of Šamaš-šuma-ukīn. This Natnu,[214] who lived in a remote region (*ašaršu rūqu*) and who never had any previous diplomatic contact with an Assyrian king, sent his emissary to Aššurbanipal and became a vassal.[215] However, Natnu did this only after Yauṯa' king of Arabia ([m]*ia-u-ta-aʾ* LUGAL KUR.*a-*

209. See below.

210. SAA 19:131, 128.8′–r.1 (Saggs 2001, 66): LÚ.*li-iʾ-ta-mu* (8′); [LÚ.*li-iʾ*]-*ta-mu* (12′); [L]Ú.*a-ru-mu* (edge 13′); [L]Ú.*ḫa-ga-ra-a-nu* (r.1).

211. See Dion 2002, 59. Eph'al (1982, 222–23) states: "However, it is difficult to identify נביות, *Nabayati*, with *Nbṭ*(*w*) (Arabic *ʾAnbaṭ*) because of the extensive spelling changes required: the shift from Assyrian and Hebrew *t* to Nabatean *ṭ*, and the elimination of the consonantal *y* from the earlier form.... This ... justifies the rejection of the *Nbyt* (Nebaioth)-*Nbṭ*(*w*) identity."

212. Eph'al 1976–80, 422; 1982, 222; Knauf 1998–2001a; 1998b; Zadok 2013, 288.

213. See Zadok 1977, 185; 2013, 288. He notes that the short unstressed first *-a-* shifted to *-ə*.

214. For a discussion of this name, see Zadok 2013, 289; Tinney 2001.

215. Prism B, viii.51 (Borger 1996 116).

*ri-bi*)[216] had fled to him in the land of Nabayati seeking asylum, which created fear in Natnu prompting him to send his messenger.[217] Later, having been loyal to Aššurbanipal, Natnu withheld his tribute and joined together with Abī-yate' (m*a-bi-ia-te-e*') in order to fight against Aššurbanipal. He was defeated by the Assyrian king who destroyed his cities, and deported him, his wife, his sons, and his daughters along with considerable booty to Assyria. Aššurbanipal then installed Nuḫūru, his (Natnu's) son, as king.[218]

In an undated letter, which nevertheless dates to the reign of Aššurbanipal, [Nabû-šumu-li]šir reports to the king that after envoys of Natnu, the Nabayatian (m*na-at-nu* LÚ.*na-ba-a-tu-ú-a*) had come to Babylon and met with the king (Šamaš-šuma-ukīn), Šamaš-šuma-ukīn sent one hundred men of Birtu and five Assyrian prisoners (described as subjects of the Assyrian king who had been held prisoner in Cutha) to Natnu.[219]

In another letter,[220] Nabû-šumu-lišir responds to Aššurbanipal's orders to give him whatever information about the Arabs (LÚ.*ar-a-bi*) that he hears. This official then reports:

> When that caravan had left (the territory of) the Nabayatians (LÚ.*né-ba-'a-a-ti*), Aya-kabar, son of Ammi-yata', the Massa'ean (m*a-a–ka-ba*!*-ru* DUMU-*šú šá* m*am-me–'a-ta-a*' LÚ.*mas-'a-a-a*),[221] attacked them, killed men and took booty. One of them, having escaped, entered the city of the king (lines 12–r.8).

It seems clear from these texts that this tribe spelled consistently with a *y*, *Nabayatu*, is Arabian and is the Nebaioth (נבי[ו]ת) of the Bible.[222] Thus it seems that the Aramean tribe Nabātu should be considered separate.

216. This man is described elsewhere as Yauṯa' son of Ḫazael, king of the Qedarites (m*ia-u-ta-a* DUMU m*ḫa-za-a*-DINGIR LUGAL KUR.*qa-ad-ri*) who was defeated on the Moabite border and fled to Natnu, king of Nabayatu. See Prism B, vii.93–94 (Borger 1996, 113).

217. Prism B, viii.29–31 (Borger 1996, 114); Prism C, x.63–78 (Borger 1996, 116); Göttesbrief, ii.50–iii.4 (Borger 1996, 79); Prism A viii.56 (Borger 1996, 63).

218. Prism A, viii.69 (Borger 1996, 64); Ištar Temple Inscription, 123 (Fuchs apud Borger 1996, 281). See also Eph'al 1982, 51, 143–45, 150, 154, 156–60, 164–65, 169 n. 156.

219. SAA 18:120, 147.1–14 (= *ABL* 1117).

220. SAA 18:122, text 149 (= *ABL* 260).

221. For this Arabian tribe, see Eph'al 1982, 218–19.

222. Eph'al 1982, 221–23; Reynolds in SAA 18:205, s.v. Nabaiāti. The sixth-century Taymanite inscriptions from Jebel Ghunaym mention a war between the people of Taymā' and the people of Nebaioth (*Nbyt*). See Winnett and Reed 1970, 99–101, nos. 11, 13, 15; pl. 19. They (1970, 99) comment: "Since the Assyrian inscriptions mention a North Arabian people called *Nabaiati*, and the Old Testament mentions a North Arabian *Nᵉbāyôt* (Nebaioth), there can be little doubt that the NBYT of the Jabal Ghunaym inscriptions are

Sargon II wrote a letter to a governor named Ašīpâ instructing him that the LÚ.*na-bat-a-a* of whom he had written the king were now at his disposal.[223] Although the exact place that this Ašīpâ was serving is nowhere stated in the correspondence, it is apparent that it was somewhere in the northern part of the empire, possibly the city of Tīdu (Radner 1998d). Thus these Nabātu must have been a cohort assigned to the northern frontier and provide no information on the tribe itself.

A city URU.*na-ba-tu*$_4$/*na-bu-tú*/*i* is documented in the later post-Assyrian sources, located not too far from Babylon (Zadok 1985a, 232). It may owe its name to the Aramean tribe of Nabātu.

## 17. Raḫīqu

*Raḫīqu* < *Reḥīqu* is a perfect rendering of Aramaic *rḥyq* "far, distant" (see Zadok 1977, 185; 2013, 289). Lipiński (2000a, 450) argues that this meaning "is not fit for a place name, tribal name or personal name." He suggests instead an etymology from *raḥīṣ*/*raḥīḍ* "washed, bathed"[224] which suggests that the tribal region was "bathed" in swamps. Dion (2002, 59) points to this argument as an example of etymology "dwarfing the topographical and historical information derived from Akkadian sources." Zadok reiterated this understanding noting that the adjective *rḥyq* "describes a distant relative in Jewish Aramaic, and in this sense it could have designated a tribal group."[225]

The first time that the Raḫīqu tribe is mentioned is in the inscriptions of Tiglath-pileser III (see table 10.1). Members of this tribe (LÚ.*Re-ḫi-qu-a-a*), along with two other Aramean tribes (the Itū' and the Yādaqqu), were part of the Assyrian army used as guards in Borsippa due to a Borsippean rebellion in 710 BCE.[226] In another instance, the leader of a contingent serving to guard pastureland on the Euphrates (from Dume-il to *Šadirtu*) writes the king stating that something (unfortunately the object is not preserved) is in the

to be identified with them. The discovery of the Arabic spelling of Nebaioth administers the coup de grâce to the old theory that the Nebaioth were the same people as the Nabateans (Ar. *Nabaṭ*, *'Anbaṭ*), for it is highly improbable that an original *Nabayat* (attested by the Assyrian transcription) would both lose the *y* and alter *t* to *ṭ*."

223. SAA 1:9, 5.3 (= *ABL* 305).

224. Thus Lipiński posits that the references to the Raḫīqu and the Raḫīḫu are to the same tribe, that etymological *ḍ* is rendered sometimes *q* and other times *ḫ*. See next note.

225. Zadok 2013, 289. He adds: "Furthermore, its physical identity with *Raḫīḫu* (anticipated by Streck 1906b, 68), which is not supported by the meager textual evidence (the fact that both tribes do not occur in the same inscriptions is at best circumstantial) is made by Lipiński under the assumption of <*q*> (/*ḍ*/) > <*ḫ*> (/*ġ*/), a shift which is exclusively Aramaic."

226. SAA 17:69–70, 75.r.5 (*ABL* 349); for the date, see SAA 17:xxxv; Frame 1992, 242.

city of Raḫīqu (*ina* URU.*ra*-⌜*ḫi*?⌝-*q*[*u*?]).[227] Finally, Raḫīqean (LÚ.*Ra-ḫi-qu-a-a*) soldiers in the Assyrian army (presumably auxiliaries) are enumerated together with other Arameans and West Semites in a fragmentary letter to Aššurbanipal.[228]

**18.** Raḫīḫu[229]

The first time that this tribe is mentioned is in a Neo-Assyrian letter (an intelligence report from the period of Sargon II) in which the movement of certain Aramean tribes is made known, namely that the Itū', the Rupū', and the Lītawu have crossed the river at the town of Apallâ, but "the Raḫīḫu (KUR.*Ra-ḫi-ḫa*) [*are spen*]*ding the night* at the town of Nunak."[230] At this time, the Raḫīḫu appear to be allies of Merodach-Baladan.[231] Later this tribe is listed in the inscriptions of Sennacherib (see table 10.1) where it is located on the Tigris in southeastern Babylonia. In addition, a settlement called *Bīt-Ra-ḫi-ḫa-e* in Bīt-Dakkūri during the early Achaemenid period was apparently named after them (see Zadok 2013, 289).

19. Kapīru

This tribe (LÚ.*ka-pi-ri*) is mentioned only by Tiglath-pileser III (see table 10.1). The most likely derivation for Kapīru is *kpyr* "young lion."[232] A *Nār-Ka-pi-ri*, located not far from Sippar, is mentioned in later times and may have been named after the tribe (Zadok 1985a, 374; 2013, 289).

20. Rummulūtu

The tribe is also only mentioned by Tiglath-pileser III (see table 10.1). The name may derive from Arabic *raml*, "sand" (Zadok, 1977, 186, 196; Lipiński 2000a, 451).

21. Adelê

This tribe is only mentioned by Tiglath-pileser III (see table 10.1). The name appears to derive from the root *ʿdl*, in Arabic "to be just, equitable," with the Aramaic plural suffix -*ê*.(Zadok 2013, 290; Lipiński 2000a, 452). It is found

227. SAA 18:162–63, 196.r.15 (= Dietrich 1979, 141).
228. *ABL* 1009.
229. See n. 225. The root is apparently *rḥḥ* "to widen, to add space" (Palmyrene: Hillers and Cussini 1996, 1624:1.9).
230. SAA 15:124–25, 186.r.4 (= *ABL* 830).
231. SAA 15:xv; Lipiński 2000a, 450–51.
232. As attested in a number of the Semitic languages; see Lipiński 2000a, 451, 510.

in personal names from North Arabia,[233] as well as in the Hebrew Bible (1 Chr 27:29) where the overseer of the cattle in the valleys was Shaphat, son of Adlai (ʿ*dly*).[234]

22. Kib/prē

The precise rendering of the tribal name is not known. It might derive from either *kbr* "to be great" or *kpr*, both explicable in Aramaic terms.[235] The reading *Gíb-re-e* suggested by Lipiński (2000a, 452) could also be based on a Northwest Semitic, including Aramaic, root: *gbr*. Thus, Zadok (2013, 290) correctly notes that Lipiński's conclusion that "the allegedly(!) Aramaean tribe would be an Arab one" contradicts the Assyrian sources and is unnecessary.

The Kib/prē tribe is listed in the inscriptions of Tiglath-pileser III (see table 10.1). According to the inscriptions of Sennacherib, the tribe lived on the Tigris (Lipiński 2000a, 452–53). In a fragmentary letter, perhaps from the time of Sargon II, the tribe (⌜LÚ⌝.*kip/b-re-e*) is mentioned, apparently as part of a group of Babylonians being settled in Gūzāna.[236]

23. Ubūdu

It appears that the tribal name Ubūdu derives from ʿ*bd* "to make," a common root in Aramaic.[237] The tribe's name is listed in the inscriptions of Tiglath-pileser III (see table 10.1). In another text of Tiglath-pileser III one encounters the reading KUR.*bu-ú-du*.[238] Frahm (1997–98, 401) questions whether this should be linked with the Ubūdu. However, the rendering may be the result of either apheresis or a scribal mistake (metathesis of *bu-ú* for *ú-bu*). In any case, following after Adelê, along with other entities in central or southeastern Babylonia, the probability is good that this is the tribe Ubūdu. According to the inscriptions of Sennacherib, the Ubūdu lived on the Tigris.

24. Gurūmu

The name of this tribe is clearly based on the Aramaic root *grm* (Zadok 1977, 341 and n. 9).[239] The tribe appears to be located near the Lower Zab in

233. Harding 1971, 410.

234. The place name Adullam (ʿ*dlm*) may also come from the root, though Akkadian *edēlu* has also been proposed (*HALOT*, 792a).

235. See Zadok 1978a, 173, 185; 2013, 290.

236. SAA 15:161, 257.3′.

237. See Zadok 2013, 290; contra Lipiński 2000a, 452–53.

238. RINAP 1:26–28, 5, line 7; Tadmor 1994, 42, Ann. 9:7.

239. Lipiński's argument (2000a, 454–55) that "the absence of the element *grm* in

Tiglath-pileser III's reign (see table 10.1).[240] However, at the time of Sargon II's 710 campaign, the tribe was located further south in Yadburu on the Babylonian-Elamite border when he deported many of its population.[241] In his annals, Sargon II relates:

> The cities of Samūna (and) Bāb-dūri, fortresses that Šutur-Naḫundi, the Elamite, had installed over the land of Yadburu, I overwhelmed [like] a thunderstorm; and I brought forth (as plunder) Sa-...-nu (and) Singamšibu, the (two) fortress commanders, together with 7,520 Elamites who were with them, and 12,062 people of the tribe of Gurūmu (L[Ú.*g*]*u-ru-mu*), (Elamite) wagons, horses, mules, donkeys (and) dromedary camels, together with much booty. I restored the city of Samūna; changed its name; and called it Enlil-iqīša.[242]

Yet, the Gurūmu were still living on the Uqnû River at the time of Sennacherib. Later, the official writing a letter to Esarhaddon claims that certain Gurūmu (LÚ.*Gu-ru-ma-a-a*) who had collaborated with a Tabalean criminal were impaled, even though the Tabalean escaped to the city of Babylon.[243] In the same letter,[244] the official states that he[245] did not enter the Gurūmu (territory) (LÚ.*Gu-ru-ma*). Finally, there was a homonymous settlement *Gi-ru-mu*[246] in the western section of the Babylonian alluvium.[247]

## 25. Ḫudādu

The tribal name seems to be derived from Aramaic *ḥdd* "to be sharp, pointed."[248] The only occurrence is in the inscriptions of Tiglath-pileser III (see table 10.1); however, there was a city of Ḫudādu, known in the Middle

---

Aramaean onomastics proves that the LÚ.*gu-ru-mu* are a North-Arabian tribe" and that the name is a broken plural is not convincing. See Zadok 2013, 290.

240. Ptolemy locates the Γαραμαῖοι to the south of Erbil, near the Lower Zab and this agrees with Old Syriac sources, which refer to *Byt Grmy'* in the same area. See Lipiński 2000a, 453–54; Zadok 2013, 290.

241. The tribe is not mentioned in Sargon II's list (see table 10.1).

242. Fuchs 1994, 150–51, Ann. 295–298a.

243. SAA 18:139–40, 170.3′–11′ (= *ABL* 967).

244. SAA 18:139–40, 170.r.6b–8a.

245. The antecedent for the verb [*u*]*l i-ru-ba* (line r.8) is not clear.

246. With attenuation *u* > *i*, see Zadok 1985a, 141.

247. In 1 Chr 4:19, one encounters "Keilah, the Garmite" (קְעִילָה הַגַּרְמִי); possibly "Garmite" should be connected with "the tribe of *Grm*" attested in a Thamudic inscription from the upper Wadi Sirḥan (Winnett and Reed 1971, 135, 211, No. 84, line 2. See Lipiński 2000a, 453 n. 352. However, the exact relationship, if any, to the Garūmu in lower Mesopotamia is unclear.

248. See Zadok 1977, 335, 338; 2013, 290.

and Neo-Babylonian periods, located somewhere between Sippar and the Tigris.[249] It is possible that the name of the town was the origin of the tribal name (Zadok 2013, 290) and a personal name (Röllig 1972–75).

26. Ḫinda/eru

The Aramean tribe of Ḫindaru[250] is attested in Assyrian royal inscriptions (see table 10.1), at Nippur, and in at least five letters from Nineveh. In these texts, the Ḫindaru are often mentioned in association with the Aramean groups known as the Gambūlu, the Ru'a and the Puqūdu (Lipiński 2000a, 457). The tribe is first attested in a Neo-Babylonian letter from Nippur sometime between 755 and 732. At this time, according to the letter,[251] the tribesmen of the Ḫindaru had either established permanent settlements in eastern Babylonia (near the territories of the Gambūlu and Ru'a), or their migratory orbits, which were determined by the grazing needs of their herds, were drawing them there seasonally (Cole 1996a, 63). The letter reports that "the Ḫindaru (LÚ.*Ḫi-in-da-ri*) have put an end to all good(will)," in other words, they have ended any good relations that had existed.

They occur in the inscriptions of Tiglath-pileser III, where the name is twice spelled LÚ.*ḫi-in-di-ru*[252] (see table 10.1). Later in the reign of Sargon II, the Ḫindaru tribe was one of the closest allies of Marduk-apla-iddina and was involved in his ascent to kingship. In Sargon's twelfth *palû*, the Annals (Fuchs 146, Annals 281–284a) read:

> The Rū'a, Ḫindaru, Yadburu, (and) [Pu]qūdu heard the capture of Gambūlu, and at nighttime they fled and took to the inaccessible Uqnû River. I blocked up the Tubliyaš, the river of their trust, with heaps of earth and reeds. I built two fortresses on each side, and I brought upon them hunger. From the midst of the Uqnû they came and seized my feet.

Thus having fled into the swamps along the Uqnû River, the Ḫindaru were forced to surrender because of starvation.[253] Four of the sheikhs of the

249. Brinkman 1968, 271 n. 1745; Nashef 1982, 129–30. Also a homonymous town may have existed Uruk (Zadok 1985a, 164). See also Röllig 1972–75; and Groneberg 1980, 100. This is clear a tribe in Tiglath-pileser's list (contra Lipiński 2000a, 455).

250. For the name, see Zadok 1976, 117 n. 42; 1977, 186; followed by Lipiński. See Minean *Ḥndr* (Harding 1971, 205.

251. Cole 1996a, 62–63, text 13:6.

252. Zadok (2013, 291) argues that "the variant with *-de-* precludes his (Lipiński's) normalization Ḫindāru (with *-ā-*)." See Lipiński 2000a, 455.

253. Fuchs (1994, 148, note to 283) suggests that the reading might better be *kallaptu* ≈ *galgaltu* (*CAD* 5).

Ḫindaru (4! LÚ.*na-sik-ka-a-ti ša* KUR.*Ḫi-in-da-ri*) paid their heavy tribute to Sargon II (Fuchs 1994, 147, Ann 285–286a).

The tribe dwelt on the Uqnû according to the inscriptions of Sennacherib. In another Neo-Babylonian letter,[254] an official named Lanšê (who was based in Gambūlu) writes Sennacherib who was inquiring about the murderers of some Babylonians. Lanšê declares that the Ḫindaru "speak lies" (*pír*!*-ṣa-a-ti i-dab-bu-bu*). This may imply that they were not reliable allies of the Assyrians, though it may, of course, simply speak to a generalization of the Arameans of this tribe. In any case, Lanšê reports to the king that he has delivered two Ḫindaru, instead of the murderers. In a second letter of the official, Lanšê, there is a report on his treatment of "hostages of the Ḫindareans" ([LÚ.*maš-k*]*a-na-ti šá* [L]Ú.*ḫi-i*[*n*]*-dar* and LÚ.*maš-ka-na-ti šá* LÚ.*ḫi-in-dar-a-a*).[255] The tribe is mentioned in broken context where a message was sent to the king "from GN? in Ḫindaru" (*ul-tu* [GN] *i-na* LÚ.*ḫi-in-dar*), apparently in central Babylonia.[256]

As with numerous other Aramean tribes, Ḫindareans served as soldiers in the Assyrian army (see a letter to Aššurbanipal, *ABL* 1009). Ḫindareans (KUR.*Ḫi-in-dar-a-a*), presumably auxilaries, are also mentioned before Ḫaṭallu troops in a fragmentary and undatable Neo-Assyrian letter.[257] Finally, in the "Chaldean or early Achaemenid period, there was a canal in the Nippur region named after this tribe (*Nār-Ḫi-in-da-ri*) (Zadok 1977, 17).

27. Damūnu

The name, which ends in *-ōn* (Zadok 1978a, 186), may be based on *dam* "blood" (cf. Zadok 1976b, 308a ad 195), which is not exclusively Arabian,[258] but common West Semitic.

The Damūnu are attributed to the Aramean tribes of Babylonia according to the inscriptions of Tiglath-pileser III and Sargon II (see table 10.1). Lipiński (2000a, 463) is probably correct to recognize that the Damūnu were one of the more powerful tribes in Babylonia. This is borne out by the fact that after numerous deportations, the tribal identity was not extinguished (Stockhusen 2013, 238).

Tiglath-pileser III purports to have deported and settled "600 captives of the town of Amlātu of the Damūnu" (6 ME *šal-la-at* URU.*am-la-te ša* LÚ.*da-*

254. SAA 17:84, text 92 (= *ABL* 848).

255. SAA 17:84–85, 93.7–8, 13–14 (= Dietrich 1979, 174).

256. SAA 17:127, 146.4′–5′.

257. See n. 65 above.

258. According to Lipiński (2000a, 463) there is a strong probability that the Damūnu are in truth a North Arabian tribe. But as in all cases, this is based on his alleged "broken" plural evidence.

*mu-ni*).[259] See discussion concerning Amlātu below. Interestingly, in the very extensive royal correspondence of Tiglath-pileser III,[260] there is no relevant material found so far concerning the Damūnu.

In 710, Sargon II was involved in a campaign to Babylonia against Marduk-apla-iddina II. During this campaign, the Damūnu (LÚ.*damunu*) are listed next to the Gambūlu, Puqūdu, Ru'a and Ḫindaru as auxiliary troops participating in the defense of Dūr-Yakīn.[261] The Damūnu are also mentioned next to the Puqūdu in Sargon's Cylinder Inscription,[262] the Bull Inscription,[263] and the Great Display Inscription.[264] From this, one might conclude that the Damūnu were a very prominent tribe among the southern Mesopotamian Arameans. However, the tribe is not named in three important lists of subjugated Aramean tribes: the Display Inscription, the Threshold Inscription 4, and the Tangi Var Inscription.[265] The available geographic lists seem to locate the tribe of the Damūnu in the territory of the province Gambūlu. This also fits with the finding that they are often mentioned along with the Puqūdu. A very fragmentary letter[266] could possibly come from the time of Sargon II and may mention the [L]Ú.*da-m*[*u*?-*na-a-a*], but little can be gleaned from this text.

When, after the death of Sargon II, Sennacherib's "first" campaign in Babylonia was against a renewed Marduk-apla-iddina II, the Damūnu were among the Aramean tribes fighting against Sennacherib.[267] While Babylon and the Babylonian population seems to have come off lightly,[268] a later inscription of Sennacherib, after listing the unsubmissive Arameans tribes, states: "I carried off into Assyria a substantial booty: 208,000 people, young (and) old, male and female, horses, mules, donkeys, camels, oxen, and sheep

259. RINAP 1:46, 14, line 3; Tadmor 1994, 66, Ann. 13:3. See also Stockhusen 2013, 225.

260. See now SAA 19; also Saggs 2001.

261. The Display Inscription, line 126 (Fuchs 1994, 227).

262. Cylinder Inscription, line 12 (Fuchs 1994, 33). A parallel text is the so-called Borowski Stela (Hawkins 2004, 154); the tribe would have been mentioned in the break in line 6.

263. Bull Inscription, line 29 (Fuchs 1994, 65).

264. The Great Display Inscription (ND 3411), line 10 (Gadd 1954, 199 pl. LI). The ductus of ND 3411 appears to be similar to the recent publication of the Moussaieff Fragment. See Abraham and Klein 2007.

265. The Display Inscription, lines 18–23 (Fuchs 1994, 195–96), Threshold Inscription 4, lines 70–90 (Fuchs 1994, 265–67) and the rock inscription of Tangi Var, lines 31–32 (Frame 1999, 37).

266. SAA 15:102, 153.8′ (= Parpola 1979, 673).

267. RINAP 3.1:36, 1, line 55.

268. Grayson 1975, 77, line 19; Glassner 2004, 196–99.

and goats, which were without number."[269] This is the largest number mentioned in the context of a single deportation in an Assyrian royal inscription.[270]

However, this was not the end of the Arameans in southern Mesopotamia. In 691 during Sennacherib's "eighth campaign," a large host of Arameans, including the Damūnu, joined in confederation with Šūzubu (Mušēzib-Marduk), king of Babylonia, and fought at the battle of Ḫalulê against the Assyrian king.[271] According to Sennacherib's inscriptions, the tribe dwelt on the Surappu River.[272]

In the dossier of letters assigned to the Assyrian official named Lanšê, there are numerous mentions of the Damūnu tribe.[273] Although Lanšê seems to have been stationed in the western region of Gambūlu (where he controlled the access road to Babylon and was able to report on potential troop movements in the Elamite border region), the dating of his dossier is fraught with difficulties, with some scholars favoring the reign of Sargon II and others the early reign of Sennacherib.[274]

In one letter,[275] the Assyrian king had ordered Lanšê to return to Zēru-ibni his servants. However, Lanšê refused to do this on the grounds that "there are no servants of Zēru-ibni in (my) presence (ARAD.MEŠ *šá* ᵐNUMUN–*ib-ni ina pa-ni* [*ia*]-*a-nu*). Truly, the two men, they are Damūnu, 'military commanders' of the king my lord (2 ERIM.MEŠ LÚ.*da-mu-na-a-a a-lik pa*?-*nu-ta*? *šá* LUGAL *be-lí-iá šú-nu*; lines 10–14a)." These two anonymous Damūnu were "the military commanders" (lit. "the one who goes before"), perhaps leaders of units of Damūnu in the service of the Assyrian king.[276] Because of the fragmentary nature of the next six lines of the letter, it is difficult to know whether the last lines continue to have the Damūnu as the subject. In any case, Lanšê sent people (perhaps these Damūnu?) to the governor of Damascus and then closes the letter with two suggestions for compensation for Zēru-ibni.

The Damūnu tribe is mentioned in some other letters in Lanšê's dossier. A very poorly preserved document seems to mention that the LÚ.*da-m*[*u*-

269. Chicago/Taylor Prisms. RINAP 3.1:173, 22, i.43–53.

270. Zehnder 2002, 128.

271. Chicago/Taylor Prisms. RINAP 3.1:182, 22, v.51.

272. RINAP 3.1:32–33, 1, line 13. See pp. 686–87 above for discussion of the lists.

273. SAA 17:84–91, texts 92–100. For this official, see Parpola and Pruzsinszky 2001.

274. For Sargon II, see Parpola and Pruzsinszky 2001; for Sennacherib, see Dietrich 2003, XIX–XX, XXVI–XXVII, and XXXVII.

275. SAA 17:88, 96.12 (= *ABL* 849).

276. See SAA 17:17, 15.8′, which mentions an *ālik pāni*, perhaps in connection with the tribe of Ru'a. See also SAA 12:62, 63.4 (written LÚ.DU.IGI).

*na-a-a*] rose up (in rebellion?) against Assyrian authority (*it-bu-ni*).[277] They are also apparently mentioned in another fragmentary letter where "the Damūneans ([LÚ.*d*]*a-mu-na-a-a*) sent (him, 'the son of Tabnea?') on the road (and) [help]ed (him) to flee." There is also a mention of Dēr in the broken context.[278]

In a letter from early in Sennacherib's reign,[279] Nabû-šuma-līšir and Aqār-Bēl-lūmur, fortress commanders stationed in the provincial capital city of Dūr-Atḫara/Dūr-Abīḫara, list the "city" of the Damūnu (URU.*da-mu-na-a-a*) after the city of Urḫulu (URU.*ur-ḫu-la-a-a*) and before the city of Aradātu (URU.*A-ra-da-ta-a-a*) in a letter concerning an Elamite attack, which was reported by the inspector (*qīpu*) of Dēr, Šamaš-bēlu-uṣur.

In the reign of Esarhaddon, an official named Šumāya writes the king stating that he has successfully executed the king's order: he has brought the deity-(images) to the city of Zanāki and there initiated a gathering of three thousand people. After a short break in the text, there is a passage about a dispute over marriage involving people of the city of Zanāki and the Damūnu.[280] Unfortunately, the context is not well preserved, but it appears that there is a guard (LÚ.*na-ṣi-*[*ru*?])[281] who has married a woman from among the Ruṣapu tribe (LÚ.*Ru-ṣa-pi*).[282] This man is a Damūnean ([L]Ú.*da-mu-na-a-a šú-ú*; r. 4′). This man had married a woman from the city of Zanāki thirty years previous, though now he is claiming her; so Šumāya is sending this Damūnu to the king. At this point the letter is clear: Šumāya makes a general declaration that the inhabitants of this city of Zanāki marry wives from the tribes of Damūnu and Gambūlu, and they are all regularly making claims (r.8′a–10′). Stockhusen's thorough analysis (2013, 232) leads rightly to the conclusion

277. SAA 17:89, text 97:4′–5′.

278. SAA 17:90, text 99:16′–17′, and e.22.

279. SAA 17:106–7, text 120:33e (= *ABL* 1335+).

280. SAA 18:91, 113.r.2′–12′, esp. r.4′, 9′ (= *ABL* 846).

281. Some interpreters interpret this as a reference to the Aramean tribe Naṣīru. See Lipiński 2000a, 447; Streck 1998–2001c. While possible, it seems more likely that this is a common noun *nāṣiru* "guard" (see Reynolds in SAA 18:91), since he appears to be identified in the text through the independent personal pronoun. Such an understanding interprets the verbal forms in r.3′ ([*i*]*-ba-áš-šú* and *iḫ-*[*ḫa-zu*]) as subordinate. However, if the writer is only enumerating some examples of the marriage customs of different Aramean tribes, this statement might be understood as "There are Naṣīru who take women from among the Ruṣapu as wives." The problem with this interpretation is one is left with the hanging statement: "He is a Damūnean" ([L]Ú.*da-mu-na-a-a šú-ú*) (r. 4′), i.e., to whom does the "he" (*šū*) refer?

282. Lipiński (2000a, 464) asserts that the LÚ.*Ru-ṣa-pi* were an Arabian tribe (based on a proposed Arabic etymology). However, Zadok (1985c, 73; 2013, 291) points out that the root *rṣp* is amply recorded in Northwest Semitic, including Aramaic; therefore, an Arabic derivation is unnecessary.

that the text is making a clear distinction between the townspeople of the city of Zanāki, the tribes of the Ruṣapu, the Damūnu and the Gambūlu.

Finally, the tribe may be mentioned in Aššurbanipal's time (Zadok 2013, 292). One of the Assyrian officials during this period was Bēl-ibni, who was involved in the civil war (651–648) and in the Elamite wars (647 and 646). One of his first duties was to campaign against the Aramean tribes in southern Babylonia. A fragment of a letter[283] is assigned to him. In this letter to the king, Bēl-ibni mentions the Puqūdu and the land of the Gurasimmu. Although in line 3 of the letter, the text reads: LÚ.*da*-[ ], it is uncertain what the restoration should be.[284]

28. Dunānu

The name is considered to be derived from Akkadian (Lipiński 2000a, 458–59).[285] In the mid-eighth century, this tribe (LÚ.*Du-na-a-nu*) is mentioned in the so-called governor's archive from Nippur (Cole 1996a, 142, text 61:8) and in Tiglath-pileser III's inscriptions (see table 10.1). At this time, the city of Paṣītu of the Dunānu (URU.*pa-ṣi-tú šá* LÚ.*du-na*-[*ni*])[286] is mentioned along with other Aramean tribes (Itū' and Rupū') in the central Babylonia area (Zadok 1985c, 64).

29. Nilqu

The tribe of Nilqu is only listed in Tiglath-pileser III's Summary Inscription 7 (see table 10.1). Lipiński (2000a, 459) suggests that the form Nilqu is a broken plural of *naqīy* (i.e., the root *nqy*) "pure." Zadok (2013, 292) prefers to derive Nilqu from the root *nqq* with dissimilation of the *l*.[287] Both scholars[288] suggest that the place name *Niqqu* of Tupliyaš[289] may be the origin for the tribal name, in which case it would be similar to Rāpiqu and Ḫudādu (see above). It would seem that a second city named *Ni-iq-qu* not far from Sippar

283. See de Vaan 1995, 334–35 (Dietrich 1979, 122).

284. Dietrich (1970, 102) and Stockhusen (2013, 233) feel that what remains is not sufficient for a sure restoration.

285. Zadok (2013, 291) questions: "Is the real West Semitic form masked here by an *interpretatio Akkadica*?"

286. RINAP 1:95–98, 39, line 4); Tadmor 1994, 122, Summary 1:4.

287. Cf. Hebrew *nqyq* "cleft of rock." See Zadok 1984, 44.

288. Lipiński 2000a, 459; Zadok 2013, 292.

289. In the inscriptions of Tiglath-pileser III. Iran Stela: RINAP 1:85, 35, ii.3′: *a-di* KUR.*ni-qi šá* KUR.⌜*tup*⌝-[*li-áš*], "as far as the land of Tup[liaš]." Summary 1: RINAP 1:97, 39, line 17: URU.*ni-qi šá* KUR.*tup-li-áš* "as far as the city of Tup[liaš]." Summary 3: RINAP 1:102, 41, line 5′; Summary 7: RINAP 1:120, 47, lines 29, 35 (URU.*niq-qu ša* KUR.*tup-li-ia-áš*); and Annals 15, RINAP 1:51, 16, line 12.

in the western section of the alluvium was named after the tribe in the early Achaemenid period.[290]

30. Radê

The tribe is only mentioned by Tiglath-pileser III (see table 10.1). It appears to derive from the root *rdy*.[291] There may have been a homonymous settlement in the Sargonid period: URU.*Ra-de-e*.[292]

31. Da-⸢i⸣-[x]-⸢nu⸣

Unfortunately, this tribe is only mentioned in Tiglath-pileser III's Summary Inscription 7 where the reading appears as: LÚ.*da-⸢i⸣-*[*x*]-⸢*nu*⸣.[293]

32. Karmâ

This tribe (LÚ.*kar-ma-ʾu*) only occurs in Tiglath-pileser III's Summary Inscription 7 (see table 10.1). Zadok (1977, 186, 312 n. 1) sees this as a *qatl* formation of the root *krm*, a well-attested Aramaic root (Zadok 2013, 292). Lipiński's lengthy argument (2000a, 461–62) for a derivation from a North Arabian "broken plural" that demonstrates that "the allegedly Aramaean tribe of Karmā' is in fact a North-Arabian group" is completely unnecessary.[294]

33. Amlātu

This entity (LÚ.*am-la-tu*) only occurs in Tiglath-pileser III's Summary Inscription 7 (see table 10.1). The name ends in *-āt* (Zadok 1977, 185) and likely has a derivation from the Aramaic root *ʿml* "work."[295] This group might have been a clan or subtribe of the Damūnu tribe, since there was a town named "Amlātu of the Damūnu" (URU.*am-la-te ša* LÚ.*da-mu-ni*).[296] Lipiński (2000a, 463) concludes that "It appears therefore that *ʾamlātu* was no tribe at all and probably not even a town in the territory of the Damūnu, but the site of the 'popular assemblies' of the tribe whose members have been

290. See Zadok 1985a, 243; Jursa 1998, 109: 8, 12.

291. Lipiński 2000a, 459–60; Zadok 1977, 185.

292. Zadok 1985a, 257 (*ABL* 281:r.16; 1464:6). See Brinkman 1968, 271 n. 1746.

293. RINAP 1:118, 47, line 7.

294. Zadok (2013, 292) argues also for a possibly related toponym opposite Tikrīt (contra Lipiński 2000a, 461).

295. Zadok 2013, 293. Such a derivation is more likely than an Arabic root *ʾml* (Lipiński 2000a, 462–63).

296. RINAP 1:46, 14, line 3; Tadmor 1994, 66, Ann. 13:3.

dragged into captivity by the Assyrians."[297] However, like the other entities listed by Tiglath-pileser III, it seems best to understand Amlātu was an Aramean socially constructed group (Stockhusen 2013, 236). Zadok suggests that there was a later town (URU.*Im-ma-lat*) attested in the Neo-Babylonian period, possibly in the Nippur region; however, this may not be correct.[298]

34. Ru'a[299]

The name of the tribe is frequently written with the gentilic ending: *ru-u-ʾ-a-a*, *ru-ú-a-a* (Zadok 1985a, 261–62), *ru-ʾ-a-a*, *ru-ʾ-a*, *ru-ʾ-u-a*, *ru-ʾ-ú-a*, *ru-ʾ-u*$_8$*-a*, *ru-u-a-a*, *ru-ú-a-a*, *ru-u*$_8$*-a*, *ru-u-a-a-a* (Streck 2006–8b, 470); but see one possible exception below. Lipiński (2000a, 464) argues that it "exactly corresponds to the Arabic 'broken' plural *ruʿāʾ*, 'shepherds,' which is formed on the rarely used pattern *fuʿāl*." However, Zadok has recently concluded "None of the 28 occurrences of Ru'a shows an interchange <ø/ḫ> which one would expect of a form deriving from R-ʿ-Y).[300] This does not necessarily exclude such a derivation, but a form of R-W/Y-Y 'to drink abundantly, be saturated' (Aram., Heb., Arab., Eth.) suits better the numerous spellings." Although Lipiński understands the tribe to be "North-Arabian," it is designated "Aramean" by Tiglath-pileser III and Sennacherib.[301]

The tribe is first encountered in the inscriptions of Tiglath-pileser III (see table 10.1). In a report of Šamaš-bunāya about Itū'eans protecting the Tigris in Babylonia during the reign of Tiglath-pileser III, the LÚ*.*r*[*u*]-⸢*ú*⸣-*ʾu* appear to be mentioned in a broken context, perhaps as protecting the road to Kār-Šamaš.[302] If this spelling—which is exceptional (see above writings of

297. He argues that "Since *ʾamlātu* seems to be an Arabic word, there is a strong probability that the Damūnu were a North Arabian tribe, despite their classification as 'Aramaeans' in Tiglath-pileser III's list." Such an argument is methodologically problematic: it explicates the better attested (Damūnu) by the lesser attested (Amlātu)! See above for discussion of the Damūnu.

298. Zadok (1985a, 180) cites BE 8, 17, 14. However, while the index to volume 8 (p. 70) lists a "[ālu]*Im-ma-kur*, 17 : 14," the actual text 17 (p. 29) does not contain this reading, and I cannot find this reading anywhere in the volume. Parpola (1970, 15) lists an URU.⸢*am*⸣*-lat-ti* that occurs in the White Obelisk (RIMA 2:256, A.0.101.18, line 30′ = MAOG 6, 12, line 31); however, this must be a different city, being located in the land of Dannuna in the region of Mount Kašiyāri.

299. Streck (2006–8b, 470) normalizes the tribal name as Ru'ūja.

300. Akkadian *rēʾû*, *rāʾû* "shepherd."

301. The personal names borne by members of this tribe are either Aramaic or Akkadian in derivation (see Streck 2006–8b, 470, contra Lipiński 2000a, 465: "the North Arabian extraction of the tribe is corroborated by personal names." See *ABL* 287 discussed here.

302. SAA 19:106, 100.12; Saggs 2001, 26–27 (= ND 2663). See Villard 1998 who suggests translating "the Ru'ua tribe [will protect?] the road to Kar-Šamaš."

the name)—actually refers to the tribe of the Ru'a, then it may be their earliest occurrence in the epistolary corpus.

Sargon II characterizes all the Aramean groups in his list as LÚ.*su-te-e ṣa-ab* EDIN (*ṣēri*) "Suteans, steppe people," drawing particular attention to their nomadic way of life.[303] According to Sargon II's annals,[304] the Ru'a were led by a *nasīku* "Sheikh."

In this regard, the Ru'a tribe seems to have been particularly mobile. There are various "homelands" scattered over large parts of Babylonia. Thus, on the one hand, according to Sargon II's Great Display Inscription,[305] the Ru'a lived together with other Aramean tribes on the banks of the Tigris. On the other hand, according *ABL* 268:810, the herds of the Puqūdu and the temple of Eanna graze together freely in URU.*ru'u-a*. This could refer to a town inhabited by members of the Ru'a or the settlement area of Ru'a; in any case, probably in the vicinity of Uruk.[306] Then, in Sennacherib's inscriptions, the tribe is said to dwell on the Uqnû River.

The majority of this Aramean tribe were consistent opponents of the Assyrians. Tiglath-pileser III (r. 745–727) defeated the Ru'a, deported segments of the tribe, and incorporated them into the Assyrian provincial system.[307] However, in the year 710, the Ru'a joined the side of Marduk-apla-iddina (Merodach-Baladan) against Sargon II. It seems clear that an Assyrian attempt to persuade the Ru'a to change sides failed. The attitude of the Ru'a leadership toward Assyria is well reflected in a letter[308] which tells of a certain "Nabû-zēru-ibni, the Ru'[aean] eunuch" (LÚ*.SAG KUR.*ru-*'[*u-a-a*]) who was recalled to his homeland from service in Damascus by Sargon II in order to get this tribe to defect to the Assyrian side. The letter notes that although Marduk-apla-iddina (Merodach-Baladan) was concerned about this, the leaders of the Ru'a tribe were not persuaded, stating "(This) brother of ours (i.e., Nabû-zēru-ibni) who has come is on the other side (i.e., the Assyrians). He came, but he will go back again" (i.e., they are not committing to Assyria). The letter goes on to report that the Ru'a, in fact, have not yet assembled and have not yet sent their messenger and intentions to him (i.e., Marduk-apla-iddina) because they are considering: "what (if) we sen[t (a commitment)] and the (Assyrian) king (then) defeated Marduk-apla-iddina,

---

303. Fuchs 1994, Annal, line 258; Great Display Inscription, line 19; Bull 4, line 77.

304. Fuchs 1994, Annals, line 284.

305. Fuchs 1994, 195, Prunk. line 19.

306. Streck 2006–8b, 471. Da Riva (2002, 378 n. 862) states: "Die aramäische Siedlung von Ru'a liegt in der Nähe von Babylon."

307. RINAP 1:118, 47.

308. SAA 15:4, 1.4, 9 (= *ABL* 158).

and [what (if)] these words [came to the attention of the (Assyrian) king, then the Ru'a would suffer]."[309]

In another letter, there is a report on Marduk-apla-iddina in which the LÚ*.*ru*-[*ú-a-a*] are mentioned.[310] Nevertheless, when Sargon attacked, the tribe was on Marduk-apla-iddina's side. Though they escaped before Sargon's army to the Uqnû, they were starved into submission.[311] The Tang-i Var inscription of Sargon II apparently mentions the tribe ([LÚ.*ru-ʾu*]-*x-a*).[312] Yet, Sennacherib also fought them in his first campaign (704–702) and in his eighth campaign (692–691).[313]

In a letter of Aššurbanipal, the king commends the people of Nippur for arresting three men of the Ru'a tribe named: Rēmūt (ᵐ*re-mut*), Ḫannanā (ᵐ*ḫa-an-na-na*), and Aia-ilā'ī (ᵐ*a-a*-DINGIR-*a-ʾi*).[314] The name of the first man is Akkadian; the second could be either Aramaic or Arabic; and the third is either Akkadian or West Semitic.[315]

A number of the occurrences of the tribal name are found in fragmentary contexts.[316] Finally, although the recent edition of a letter reads and translates: [LÚ].*ru-ú-a a-lik pa-ni* "*my companion*, the leader," in my opinion, this may be a reference to the Ru'a tribe, as well as to its *ālik pāni*, "commander."[317]

### 35. Qabi'

The name of the tribe (LÚ.*qa-bi-ʾu*), which only occurs in Tiglath-pileser III's Summary Inscription 7 (see table 10.1), has two possible Aramaic derivations. It could originate from *qbʿ*, "to fix, establish";[318] or it could come from *qbyʾ*, "reservoir."[319]

---

309. Ibid., lines 21–23 (my translation).

310. SAA 15:133, 202.2′.

311. Fuchs 1994, 136, 143, 147, Annals, lines 258, 281, 286.

312. Frame 1999, 37, line 31.

313. RINAP 3.1:36, 1, lines 55–56; 3.1:182, 22, v.43b–52a.

314. *ABL* 287:4–5, see Lipiński 2000a, 464–65.

315. Lipiński (2000a, 466) analyzes the third name as "North Arabian *ḥayy(a)-ʾilāhī* 'as my god liveth!'" However, it is more likely that the writing of the first component of the name (*a-a*) should be understood as the deity Ea (see all of the *Aia-* names listed in *PNA* 1.1:89–94).

316. Some examples are: "I have heard … the Ru'a tribe" (KU[R].*ru-u-a-a-a*) (SAA 10:292, 354.r.4); the Ru'a tribe is mentioned in a letter concerned with Elam (SAA 15:99, 146.1′); [LÚ*].⌜*ru-ʾu*⌝-*ú-a* (SAA 15:117, 172.2′); LÚ.*ru-*⌜*ʾu*⌝-[*a-a*] (SAA 17:166, 204:9′).

317. SAA 17:17, 15.8′. Or alternatively, the *ālik pāni* is the commander of another tribe missing in the break.

318. This is the preferred etymology of Lipiński 2000a, 467.

319. Zadok 1977, 186 n. 3; 1985c, 78.

## 36. Lītawu

The writing of the tribal name (LÚ.*li-iʾ-ta-a-ú*, LÚ.*li-iʾ-ta-ú*, LÚ.*li-iʾ-ta-a-a*, LÚ.*li-iʾ-it-ta-a-a*, LÚ.*li-ta-a-a*, LÚ.*li-ta-mu*, along with URU.*li-ta-mu*[320] and the personal name ᵐ*li-ta-me*) indicates a normalization Lītawu (Zadok 2013, 293–94). Most likely Lītawu is based on *layt* "lion" (found in Aramaic and Arabic; Blazhek 2005). Lipiński (2000a, 467–68), however, argues that the root is *liʾt*, since he considers the *-aw* ending as typically Arabian. In contrast, Zadok (2013, 294) asserts that the Neo-Assyrian form LÚ.*li-iʾ-ta-a-a* is without this suffix[321] and that "its identity with LÚ.*la-ʾ-tu-ú-a* or LÚ.URU. *la-ʾ-it-ta-a-ʾ* in the Neo-Babylonian documents from Uruk[322] is thus very probable."

Although this tribe is mentioned in the royal inscriptions of Tiglath-pileser III, Sargon II and Senacherib (see table 10.1), the earliest occurrence may be found in a deed dated to the ninth year of Erība-Marduk (i.e., 761 BCE), where a Kābitu, *mār* ᵐ*Li-ta-me*, is recorded.[323] While Lipiński (2000a, 468) suggests that this deed is from Nippur, there does not appear to be any clear evidence of this, and "in view of the later occurrences of this tribe, a location not far from Babylon would not seem far off the mark" (Zadok 2013, 293).

Like a number of the Aramean tribes, a portion of the Lītawu seems to be located in the Transtigridian area (at least in the context of the time of Tiglath-pileser III; Röllig 1987–90). Yet, also like their tribal counterparts, they had some element of the tribe located in the Babylonian alluvium (hence, the homonymic town of Lītamu near Babylon.[324] As in the other instances, the doubts of Lipiński (2000, 468) are unjustified.

While tribes like the Tūʾmānu and Ḫaṭallu may appear in the Sūḫu texts[325] to be very mobile—raiding sedentary regions, other groups like the Lītawu had sedentary elements. This can be seen in a text like BM 40548

320. For a complete listing of the occurrences, most of which come from the period of Darius I, see Zadok 1985a, 213. The *w* > *m* is demonstrated in the Neo- and Late Babylonian.

321. Fuchs 1994, 195, Great Display, line 19. Note the variant spelling: LÚ.*li-iʾ-it-ta-a-a*.

322. Zadok 1985a, 207, s.v. *La'etu.

323. Brinkman 1989, 38–40 (= BM 40548). Zadok (2013, 294) states: "It is noteworthy that already the earliest recorded sheikh (761 at the latest), *Kābitu*, bore an Akkadian name."

324. See Zadok 1985a, 213.

325. See Younger 2015a.

which indicates that these Arameans are engaged in agricultural work, owning their own fields.[326]

In a letter from the time of Tiglath-pileser III concerned with the revolt of Mukīn-zēri, it is reported that the Lītawu (⸢LÚ.*li*⸣-*ta-ma-a-a*) wrote to two Assyrian officials, Šamaš-bunāya and Nabû-nammir, declaring their loyalty to the king of Assyria.[327] Proximity to Babylon is implied in this letter (Zadok 2013, 293).

According to a letter from the time of Sargon II concerning the activities of "*mār*-Yakīn" (i.e., Marduk-apla-iddina), who was in Babylon at that time, an official named Nabû-ḫamātū'a, who had troops with him seems to have marched downstream as far as the Lītawu (*a-di* LÚ.*li-ta-mu*).[328] In the next part of the letter, the Lītawu seem to say "Why do the Assyrians constantly attack our cities? We shall go and attack the cities of Bīt-Dakkūri."[329]

In a fragmentary text from Nimrud, the tribes of Lītawu and Ḫagarānu are mentioned together in the context of other Aramean groups.[330] Finally, in a very fragmentary letter, it seems reasonable to restore "Lītawu" (LÚ.*li-t*[*a-mu*]).[331]

### 37. Marūsu

The name of the tribe appears to be a *maqtul* of the Aramaic root *ʿrs*, "bed."[332] Lipiński (2000a, 468) links it with Arabic *ʿarīš*, "hut," but since the root is extant in Northwest Semitic,[333] there is no reason to posit an Arabic derivation when an Aramaic one is available. The Marūsu tribe is mentioned only in Tiglath-pileser III's inscriptions (see table 10.1). The settlement *Su-qa-*$^{m}$*Ma-ru-si* in Bīt-Dakkūri, that is, in the western section of the Babylonian alluvium, was presumably named after this tribe (Zadok 2013, 294).

---

326. Brinkman 1989, 40–41, BM 40548, lines 7–12 (note the collective ownership of the property). See Lipiński 2000a, 423–24; Brinkman 1968, 270–71 n. 1738. Dated to the ninth year of king Erība-Marduk (ca. 775).

327. SAA 19:104, 98.r.9. See Saggs 2001, 10 (= ND 2632 = NL 1).

328. SAA 17:94, 106.9 (= *ABL* 436).

329. SAA 17:94, 106.10b–15a. Bīt-Dakkūri was located near Babylon and Borsippa. The rationale in this letter is not clear.

330. SAA 19:131, 128.8′–r.1: LÚ.*li-iʾ-ta-mu* (8′); [LÚ.*li-i*]*ʾ-ta-mu* (12′); [L]Ú.*a-ru-mu* (e. 13′); [L]Ú.*ḫa-ga-ra-a-nu* (r.1). See also Saggs 2001, 66–67 (= ND 2779 = NL 9).

331. SAA 17:162, 195.7′.

332. Zadok 1977, 186; 2013, 294.

333. Sokoloff 2002b, 420a; Jastrow 1950, 1121; *DNWSI*, 890; cf. Hebrew עֶרֶשׂ "couch, divan" (*HALOT*, 889).

38. Amatu

The derivation of the tribal name is, according to Lipiński (2000a, 469–70), *ʿ*Ammat* "clan, family, community" (written *ʿmt* extant in Palmyrene and Hismaic). It is based on *ʿamm* "ancestor" plus the suffix *-at* which means that it belongs to common West Semitic including Aramaic (as its occurrence in Palmyrene suggests; Zadok 2013, 294).

The tribe is first mentioned in the inscriptions of Ninurta-kudurrī-uṣur, the governor of Sūḫu and Mari (770–760), where it is part of the Ḫaṭallu confederation (see no. 5 above). The Ḫaṭallu confederation had two leaders: (1) "Šamaʾgamni, the herald (*nāgiru*) of the Sarūgu," and (2) Yāʾe, the son of Balammu, the Amatite" ($^{m}$*ia-a-ʾ-e* DUMU $^{m}$*ba-la-am-mu* LÚ.*a-mat-a-a* and $^{m}$*ia-a-a-e* DUMU $^{m}$*ba-li-am-mu* LÚ.*a-mat-a-a*).[334] In the case of Yāʾe, one can compare the Hebrew personal name יְעוּאֵל.[335] This man's patronymic has been likened to the biblical name Balaam.[336] It is also clearly the same as the Aramean ruler of Bīt-Zamāni, Amme-Baʿal.[337]

In 745, the tribe is mentioned in the inscriptions of Tiglath-pileser III (see table 10.1). In the time of Sargon II (710), a homonymous settlement Amate (URU.*a-ma-te*) is mentioned together with Nuḫāni (URU.*nu-ḫa-a-ni*) and Amâ (URU.*A-ma-a*) on the Uqnû River.[338] These are part of the Assyrian province of Gambūlu (Zadok 1977, 185). Interestingly, a person belonging to the Amatu tribe is found together with members of other Aramean tribes, the Nūḫānu and the Ubūlu, in a document from Ur.[339]

There seems to have been a homonymic settlement (URU.*A-ma-tu*$_4$),[340] named after the tribe, located in the Chaldean territory of Bīt-Dakkūri (western alluvium), where it is followed by another city (URU.*ḫa-ú-a-e*),[341] which is presumably homonymic with URU.*A-ú-a*[342] (possibly the Neo-Assyrian URU.*a-ma-a*), located, just like URU.*a-ma-te*, on the Uqnû River (Transti-

334. RIMB 2:295, S.0.1002.2, i.16b–18; 2:301, S.0.1002.3, i.7′–8′.

335. Note the *qere*: יְעִיאֵל and Old Greek: Ιιηλ. See further, *HALOT*, 419. Harding (1971, 646) gives *wʿy* "strong" (attested in Safaitic).

336. Dion 1995b, 68–69. Lipiński (2000a, 428, and n. 116) argues that the spelling of the name as $^{m}$*ba-li-am-mu* means that the name "can be interpreted confidently as *Baʿlī-ʿammu*, 'the Ancestor is my lord'" and has nothing to do with the name Balaam, son of Beor. However, given that one of the proposed etymologies for the name Balaam is Amma-baʿli (*HALOT*, 135, s.v. I בִּלְעָם), it seems possible that there is a connection with the biblical name.

337. See discussion §4.6.2.

338. Fuchs 1994, 149, Annals, line 292.

339. Figulla 1949, 140.

340. Pohl 1933, text 14:27–28.

341. Zadok 2013, 294.

342. BE 8, text 28:15; see Zadok 1985a, 36.

gridian region).[343] In other words, there appears to have been a pair of cities named Amatu/e and Amâ/Auâ on the Uqnû and a pair, Amatu/e and Amâ/Auâ, in Bīt-Dakkūri. Zadok (2013, 294) points out that it is possible that URU.*a-ma-tu* of Bīt-Dakkūri is the same city as URU.*ḫa-me-te*[344] mentioned earlier in a fragmentary letter about the revolt of Mukīn-zēri (time of Tiglath-pileser III),[345] together with Borsippa, which was very close to Bīt-Dakkūri.

This may be another indication of the movement of Arameans from eastern Babylonia to the western section of the Babylonian alluvium (Zadok 2013, 294). The homonymic settlement (Neo-Babylonian: *Am-mat*), which is mentioned in documents from "Chaldean" Nippur,[346] may be the same place as the eastern or western Amatu or another place near Nippur.[347]

Finally, there is good likelihood that Sargon II's references to Amate and Amâ on the Uqnû River are reflected in the biblical references to Avva (עַוָּא) and Hamath (חֲמָת) in 2 Kgs 17:24, 30–31; Isa 36:19; 37:13.[348]

39. Ḫagarānu

It is listed in the inscriptions of Tiglath-pileser III (LÚ.*ḫa-ga-ra-a-nu*) and Sennacherib (LÚ.*ḫa-ga-ra-nu*) (see table 10.1). In a fragmentary letter,[349] the [L]Ú.*ḫa-ga-ra-a-nu* are mentioned where the tribe appears to occur after the Lītawu ([LÚ.*li-i*]*ʾ-ta-mu*) and other unspecified Arameans ([L]Ú.*a-ru-mu*) in the conflict with Merodach-Baladan. The end of the letter (lines r.4–6) states: "… their heralds ([L]Ú.NIGÍR.MEŠ-*te-šú-nu*) [came] to me; I encouraged them: 'Fear [no]t, come out!'" This appears to be a reference to the Aramean, possibly even specifically the Ḫagarānu, leaders who were being encouraged by the Assyrian official to be loyal to the king.

Clearly, the tribal name has the *-ān* ending (Zadok 1977, 186). The fact that it is spelled twice with *-a-* indicates a long *ā*. Lipiński (2000a, 470) argues that the name is derived from Arabic *ḥajar* "stone" and that it should be normalized Haggarānu with *-gg-* based on Arabic *hajjār* "stone mason," "stone cutter." Zadok (2013, 295) argues that "this etymology hardly suits an

343. Fuchs 1994, 149, Annals 292. See Zadok 1976, 120–21.

344. With Neo-Assyrian vowel harmony.

345. SAA 19:129, 127.7′; Saggs 2001, 56–57 (= ND 2360).

346. Zadok 1985a, 22–23. Zadok (2013, 294) states: "<*mm*> is non-phonematic, but purely orthographic in order to preclude a reading -/*w*/-."

347. Zadok (2013, 294–95) notes that "Neo-Babylonian URU.*Am-mat* in the Neirab documentation is to be sought not far from Nippur." See also Zadok 1985a, 23.

348. Na'aman and Zadok 1988, 44–45; Younger 2004, 264–72.

349. SAA 19:131, 128.r.1; Saggs 2001, 66–67 (= ND 2779).

originally semi-nomadic tribe, and is at best an alternative, as the old derivation from *hgr* (south Sem. 'to forsake, retire') is quite plausible."

40. Gambūlu

The name Gambūlu is perhaps best analyzed as a *qattūl* formation (with dissimilation of *-m-*) from the root *gbl* "to create, fashion, form," which is found in the noun form *gbwl* "creator."[350] The Gambūlu tribe was one of the most important Aramean tribes in southern Mesopotamia, having no less than eight sheikhs. It is mentioned in the texts of Sargon II in 710, as well as throughout the texts of the next Sargonid kings. It also occurs in the inscriptions of the Neo-Babylonian monarch Nebuchadnezzar II.[351]

The Gambūlu had a large territory in southern and southeastern Babylonia, centered on the Surappu and Uqnû Rivers. Although this tribe was undoubtedly very important, it is not mentioned in the Assyrian records until Sargon II's reign, and even then only in his twelfth *palû*. Thus, a natural question is why it is not mentioned before. This is likely due to its remoteness from Assyria, not unlike the Puqūdu, who were not included in Tiglath-pileser III's list, only added into the main narrative. The Gambūlu were apparently largely marsh dwellers on the Elamite border, who were initially under Elamite political influence.

According to the inscriptions of Sargon II, the tribe lived on the banks of the Surappu and Uqnû Rivers near the Elamite border. During his 710 campaign (twelfth *palû*), Sargon declares that Marduk-apla-iddina brought the Gambūlu tribe into the city of Dūr-Atḫara/Dūr-Abīḫara,[352] situated on the Surappu, for the expressed purpose of strengthening its defenses against the Assyrian advance. However, Sargon captured the city in spite of the great efforts expended on various obstacles, deported many from the city, and renamed it Dūr-Nabû.[353] Other elements of the tribe fled to the swamps of the Uqnû, but then the eight sheikhs of the Gambūlu submitted to Sargon. Sargon incorporated the territory of the Gambūlu into a new province (see further below). Upon hearing of the Gambūlu defeat, the Ru'a, Ḫindaru, Yadburu, and Puqūdu tribes fled to the difficult marsh regions of the Uqnû. But

---

350. Zadok 2013, 299; 1977, 173, 189; Lipiński 2000a, 472.

351. Parpola 1970, 128–29; Zadok 1985a, 137.

352. The name of the city has been read as Dūr-Atḫara. However, a number of scholars have read the name BÀD-AD-*ḫa-ra* (*Dūr-Abi-Ḫara*). See Streck 1906a, 220–21; Zadok 1977, 53, 84 and 427; 1985c, 38; Lipiński 2000a, 472; Parpola 2002, 567; Stockhusen 2013, 213 n. 57.

353. Fuchs 1994, 138–43, Annals lines 266b–280.

Sargon built a dam with forts on either side of the river and forced them to surrender.[354]

In the inscriptions of Sennacherib, the Gambūlu lived on the Surappu.[355] The Gambūleans were engaged in anti-Assyrian hostilities and collaborated with Elam, Merodach-Baladan, and Šamaš-šuma-ukīn.

During the reign of Esarhaddon, the Gambūlu played a significant role. Esarhaddon was desirous to have peaceful relations with Elam and chose to entrust Bēl-iqīša (son of Bunanu), the submissive sheikh of Gambūlu, to guard Assyria's interests in the region. He built up Bēl-iqīša's stronghold, Ša-pī-Bēl, the indigenous capital of the Gambūlu. He also provided other support.[356] In a sense, Bēl-iqīša became practically independent.[357] It seems that the land became a breeding ground for plot and intrigue. A communication to king Esarhaddon[358] takes the form of a quotation of words spoken by Ṣillāya, in which he proposes killing Iḫiru, the Gambūlean, which seems to be in Babylonia's interest, and also proposes writing deceitfully to Chaldean chiefs. Another letter from Ninurta-aḫu-[...] to Esarhaddon informs the king that Bēl-iqīša is systematically creating marriage alliances by arranging for his daughters to wed within prominent families in Babylon, Borsippa, and Bīt-Dakkūri, hardly the right people as far as Assyrian interests go.[359]

Consequently, Esarhaddon's efforts soon backfired in the time of Aššurbanipal, when the Gambūlu, led by Bēl-iqīša's son, Dunānu, became an ally of Elam.[360] Aššurbanipal was required to expend much military effort in pacifying the region in 653 BCE (Frame 1992, 47, 118–20). This meant first of all defeating the Elamite king Teumman and placing Ḫumbannikaš II on the throne of Susa and Madaktu, and Tammaritu on the throne of Ḫidalu. Next, Aššurbanipal was able to direct his troops toward the Gambūleans.[361] After conquering the fortress city of Ša-pī-Bēl, Aššurbanipal placed Dunānu

354. Fuchs 1994, 143–46, lines 281b–284a. See above in the entries for Ru'a, Ḫindaru, Yadburu, and Puqūdu.

355. RINAP 3.1:33, 1, line 13; but note Frahm 2003, 135, line 13. Note esp. the Tarbiṣu manuscripts, which clearly preserve the entire line.

356. RINAP 4:18–19, 1, iii.71–83. "Bēl-iqīša, son of Bunnannū, a Gambulian whose residence is located twelve leagues distance in water and canebrakes.... I strengthened the city of Ša-pī-Bēl, the city (which is) his strong fortress."

357. See Baker 1999a, 7. Though it seems that Esarhaddon did remove the entire harem of Gambūlu to Assyria. See Parpola 2012, 604–5.

358. SAA 18:52–53, 69.2.

359. SAA 18:41–46, 56.14–r.5. See Barjamovic 2004, 82 n. 83.

360. Borger 1996, 105, Prism B vi.17–38. For Dunānu, see Baker 1999c.

361. Aššurbanipal's queries to Šamaš concerning the Gambūlu can be seen in SAA 4:247, 270.r.8; 4:248, 271.4, 5, 7, r.5, 9; and 4:250, 272.5.

and his younger brother, Šama'gunu/Samgunu,[362] in chains and fetters to transport to Assyria. He then destroyed Ša-pī-Bēl.[363]

Having brought the two Gambūlu to Nineveh, Aššurbanipal hung the severed head of Teumman, the king of Elam, around the neck of Dunānu.[364] Around the neck of Šama'gunu he hung the head of the Elamite Ištarnandi/ Šutu(r)-naḫundi.[365] A relief from the Southwest Palace (Room XXXIII, slab 5) probably depicts Dunānu and Šama'gunu since both men wear fetters and each has a head hanging from his neck.[366] In due course, Aššurbanipal threw Dunānu on a slaughtering bench and slaughtered him like a lamb.[367] Šama'gunu was also killed, along with some others, his flesh being cut off and carried around for all the lands to see.[368]

In an apparently later letter to Aššurbanipal, the Gambūleans asked for Rēmūtu and Šama'gunu (${}^{m}$*šá-ma-gu-nu*) to be installed as their sheikhs.[369] In another letter, the king's response is recorded where he consented to the appointment of Rēmūtu, but makes no mention of Šama'gunu.[370] This seems to indicate that at the time of their request either Šama'gunu had not yet been executed or the defeated Gambūleans did not know that he was already dead. Aššurbanipal appeared willing to grant the request partially, but was unwilling or unable to reinstate Šama'gunu (Frame 2006–8; Baker 2011).

The province of Gambūlu was established by Sargon II in 710. It did not necessarily overlap just with the Gambūlu tribal territory proper, but was expanded and thus also included the land of the Yadburu, and other Aramean tribal regions, extending from the Surappu and Uqnû to Elam (Radner 2006–8a, 65, no. 74). The new province was divided into six districts (*nagû*)[371] with forty-four fortified settlements, according to a list in Sargon II's annals[372] (forty-one of these names are partially or fully preserved). Zadok (2013, 296) suggests that the missing three may be restored from another list of fourteen Gambūlu fortified settlements in Sargon's annals,[373] of which one, *Pat-ti-a-nu*, is clearly identical with *Pa-ti-ia-a-an* (Zadok 1985c, 78, 207). The

362. See Frame 2006–8; Baker 2011.
363. Borger 1996, 39, Prism A iii.57 ‖ Prism F ii.79.
364. Borger 1996, 106, Prism B vi.51 ‖ Prism C vii.48.
365. Borger 1996, 106, Prism C vii.49–50.
366. See Russell 1999, 180–81; Frame 2006–8; Barnett, Bleibtreu, and Turner 1998 pls. 305–6.
367. Borger 1996, 108, Prism C vii.89.
368. Borger 1996, 108, Prism B vi.90 ‖ Prism C vii.108.
369. *ABL* 915, r.11.
370. *ABL* 293.
371. These were: Ḫubaqanu, Tarbugati, Timassunu, Pašur, Ḫirutu, and Ḫilmu.
372. Fuchs 1994, 144–45, Annals 279a–n.
373. Fuchs 1994, 149–50, Annals 291–292.

residence of the governor of the province was the city of Dūr-Nabû (originally called Dūr-Atḫara/Dūr-Abīḫara). Sargon formed the province in order to ensure a more effective control of the Arameans within the border region. However, it was rather ineffective and thus short lived. In the seventh century, the province of Gambūlu was no longer extant, its territory having been allocated to the provinces of Dēru and Dūr-Šarrukku.

Zadok (2013, 295–98) has recently studied the names of the fortified settlements and has noted some important points.

(1) All fourteen of Sargon's list of fortified settlements in Gambūlu bear West Semitic names, except for *Ma-ḫi-ṣu* and *Kalkal/Dan-dan*, which are Akkadian/Aramaic.[374]

(2) Regarding the long list, twelve out of forty-one (29.26%) are broken or damaged beyond recognition of their linguistic character, but half of the broken/damaged toponyms are of the type Ālu-ša-[PN] (assuming that the last component is a personal name.

(3) Of the remaining twenty-nine, most names (20 = 68.96%) are ultimately West Semitic, all explicable in Aramaic terms: fourteen are Akkadian genitival compound forms followed by Aramaic personal names (all follow the pattern Ālu-ša-PN, except for Bīrtu-ša-PN). Zadok believes that this construction may follow an Aramaic pattern, with the Akkadian *Ālu-ša*-PN perhaps translating the Aramaic genitive compound Qarat-PN (as preserved in the very first city in the forty-four-name list).

(4) Five toponyms are purely West Semitic. Of the remaining nine toponyms, one is an Aramaic genitive compound. In four cases, the personal names might be Akkadian or Aramaic, though in context, more likely Aramaic. Two toponyms are purely Akkadian but are named after contemporary Gambūlean sheikhs. Only two toponyms seem to be devoid of an Aramean connection.

(5) No fewer than eight settlements are named after contemporary Aramean sheikhs: five after Gambūleans, two after Puqūdeans, and one after a Hindarean.

Some Assyrian reports and census data track Gambūleans: "New Gambuleans" ([UR]U?*gam-bul-a-a* GIBIL.MEŠ), in other words, recent Gambūlean deportees or settlers, are recorded in one document from the Sargonid period.[375] Two others give totals of deportees in the region of Gambūlu or a

374. See also Zadok 1985c, 76–77, 81, 186.

375. SAA 11:60, 96.4′ (= *ABL* 716).

grand total of Gambūleans.[376] A number of other fragmentary letters mention Gambūleans.[377]

Finally, Gambūlu retained its status as a tribal (Aramean) region (presumably smaller than the Assyrian province) at least as late as the early reign of Nebuchadnezzar II,[378] when Marduk-šarra-uṣur is described in the so-called "Hofkalender" as "of (*ša*) KUR.*ga-am-bu-lu*$_4$."[379] A settlement of *Ga-am-bu-la-a-a,* "Gambūleans" was located near Nippur (Zadok 1985a, 137), that is, in the western section of the Babylonian alluvium, in the late-Achaemenid period.

41. Yādaqqu

Yādaqqu derives from the root *dqq*, "to grind, crush, be fine" (Zadok 2013, 299; Lipiński 2000a, 472). The tribe dwelt on the Tigris in the days of Sennacherib.[380] Early in 710 BCE during Sargon II's reign, some members of this tribe (LÚ.*ia-a-da-qu-a-a*) along with their fellow Arameans (Itū' and Raḫīqu) served as guards with the official Nabû-šar-aḫḫēšu in Borsippa.[381] There was apparently a homonymous settlement Yādaqqu was situated near Uruk.[382]

42. Malaḫu

At present, the only occurrences of this tribe[383] are in the inscriptions of Sennacherib where it is written as Malaḫu and Maliḫu.[384] Zadok (2013, 299) notes that "the second *a* is short in view of the interchange *Ma-la/li-ḫu*. The

376. SAA 11:132–33, 207.r.iii.4′; and 11:141–44, 219.ii.26′–27′.

377. SAA 1:18, 15.3′; SAA 10:286, 350 r.7; SAA 15:99, 145.6′; SAA 16:122, 136.r.4 (in a report on deserters, the servants of Yairu, the Gambūlean, are mentioned); SAA 17:154, 176.8′; SAA 18:55, 71.r.8, 11; 18:89–90, 111.r.4, 6 (a letter reports on Kunâ and the Gambūleans); 18:90–91, 113.r.9′ (a letter about marriages and claims among the Damūnu, Ruṣapu and Gambūlu, see above under 27. Damūnu).

378. For the references to the later contexts, see Jursa 2010, 95 n. 508.

379. Unger 1931, 285: 26, iv.27.

380. RINAP 3.1:32 and 36, 1, lines 12 and 55; 3.1:42, 2, line 14; 3.1:51, 3, line 14; 3.1:61, 4, line 12; 3.1:76, 8, line 12; 3.1:80, 9, line 12; 3.1:93, 15, i.22′; 3.1:112, 16, i.61; 3.1:129, 17, i.52; 3.1:173, 22, i.44; 3.1:190, 23, i.39.

381. SAA 17:69–70, 75.r.3–5 (= *ABL* 349).

382. URU.*ia-daq-qu* (Weisberg 1980, 203:3); and URU.*ia-daq-qa* (Weisberg 1980, 278:8). See Zadok 1985a, 185.

383. *ABL* 701, r.1 read a gentilic form of the name, but the most recent edition of this letter does not read the form (SAA 1:153, 195.r.1).

384. RINAP 3.1:32 and 36, 1, lines 12 and 55; 3.1:42, 2, line 14; 3.1:51, 3, line 14; 3.1:61, 4, line 12; 3.1:76, 8, line 12; 3.1:80, 9, line 12; 3.1:93, 15, i.24′; 3.1:112, 16, i.62; 3.1:129, 17, i.53; 3.1:173 and 182, 22, i.45 and v.50; 3.1:192, 23 i.40 and v.41.

tribe was located on the Tigris at that time. Since the root is obviously *mlḥ*, the name may denote "salt land" (Lipiński 2000a, 482) or "salt marsh," which would support Lipiński's location near the Persian Gulf. If the name was coined in the Sargonid period when the tribe dwelt there, this makes good sense. On the other hand, this root is productive of toponyms elsewhere,[385] for example, the city of Malaḫa in Aram-Damascus (home of a temple of the moon god Śahr).[386]

### 10.2.3. Highly Likely Aramean Tribes

The following tribes all have Aramaic etymologies as well as strong connections with explicitly Aramean tribes.[387] In fact, in a number of cases, there can be little doubt that they were Aramean. For some, the evidence is greater than others, but all can be considered to be Aramean tribes.

#### 43. Nūḫānu

The name of this group is derived from the root *nw/yḥ* "to rest" with an ending in *-ān*.[388] Since Sargon II states that five sheikhs of the Puqūdu among whom are Paššunu (and) Ḫaukanu of the settlement of Nūḫānu (URU.*nu-ḫa-a-ni*),[389] there are sufficient grounds for understanding this group as Aramean (Zadok 1985c, 66). It appears that at this time it was a subtribe or clan of the Puqūdu (Lipiński 2000a, 434). Thus the settlement would be named after the entity. This "city" was apparently located on the Uqnû River.

Later there was apparently segmentation with the Nūḫānu becoming a full-fledged tribe. In a Neo-Babylonian text from Ur, a member of the Nūḫānu tribe (LÚ.*nu-ḫa-a-*[*nu*]) is mentioned together with members of two other Aramean tribes (the Ubūlu and Amatu).[390] Moreover, in this period, there was a settlement with the same name *Nu-ḫa-*(*a*)*-nu* near Uruk.[391]

#### 44. Zamê

The tribal name appears to derive from *zmy*, a by-form of *zmm*, "to bind" attested in Aramaic (Lipiński 2000a, 434, with n. 172; Zadok 1977, 185).

385. See Zadok 1984, 44.
386. See §9.2 on Aram-Damascus.
387. See Zadok 2013, 304–10, and esp. 323.
388. Zadok 1977, 143, 160; 2013, 304; Lipiński 2000a, 434.
389. Fuchs 1994, 146–47, Annals 285–286.
390. Figulla 1949, 140:11.
391. Pohl 1933, text 62:7; *BIN* 1, 43:16; Dougherty1933, 342:13; Clay 1919, 156:25; see Zadok 1985a, 243–44.

One of the five sheikhs of the Puqūdu was Yanuqu, the sheikh of the town of Zamê (^m*Ya-nu-qu* LÚ.[*n*]*a-sik-ku*[392] *ša* URU.*Za-a-me-e*).[393] Thus, like the Nūḫānu, the Zamê seem to be a clan of the Puqūdu at this time, but later a separate tribe in the early reign of Nebuchadnezzar II, when it appears as a region in the so-called "Hofkalender" where Rēmūtu is called "the righteous governor of the land of Zamê (*ša-ak-nu ke-nu ša* KUR.*za-mé-é*).[394] A member of the tribal entity LÚ.*za-me*^!-*e* is mentioned in a text from the Uruk area.[395] There was a town of Zamê near Uruk,[396] that is, in the western section of the alluvium. A homonymous canal, Nār-Zamê ($I_7$-*za*^?-*mé*^?-*e*), was found in the same section near Nippur, if the reading is correct.[397] According to Zadok (2013, 305), their relationship to the homonymous settlement on the Uqnû River is another example of the "toponymie en mirroir."

45. Minū'

The name of this tribal entity may be derived from *mnʿ* "to withhold."[398] This Aramean group (LÚ.*mi-nu-ʾ-i*) is first recorded as a clan of the Ḫaṭallu confederation in the Sūḫu Annals of Ninurta-kudurrī-uṣur in the mid-eighth century.[399] According to a letter from Sargon II's reign,[400] there was a fort/settlement of Minu' (URU.*bi*[*rtú*] URU.*mi-nu-u*ʾ) located in northern Babylonia that the magnates had supplied with barley from the fort of the Luḫu'ātu (URU.*birti* ⸢*ša* LÚ*.*lu*⸣-*ḫu-ú-t*[*a-a-a*], another clan of the Ḫaṭallu according to the Sūḫu Annals). From this text, it is clear that this settlement was near the mouth of the Patti-Illil canal (*ša* ÍD.*pa-a-ti*-^dBE). Associations with the Ḫaṭallu can still be seen in a fragmentary letter where URU.*mi-nu*-[*u*ʾ] is mentioned along with five Ḫaṭallu tribesmen (LÚ*.*ḫa-ṭal*-[*la-a-a*]).[401] Another letter from the period documents that some members of the Ḫamarānu tribe ([KUR].*ḫa-mar-a-na-a-a*) kidnapped an Assyrian messenger and released him in the city of Munu' (URU.*mu-nu-u*ʾ),[402] which, on

392. Note one variant reads: "⸢*a*⸣-*lik pa-ni* of (the city of Zamê)."
393. Fuchs 1994, 146, Annals 284b.
394. Unger 1931, 286, 26 iv.31.
395. Dietrich 1979, 20:9.
396. Dougherty1933, 15:2; Weisberg 1980, 122:5; see Zadok 1985a, 333.
397. Clay 1912a, 182:2; Zadok 1985a, 394.
398. *DNWSI*, 661; Sokoloff 2002b, 318b; Sokoloff 2002a, 687b; and Jastrow 1950, 801.
399. RIMB 2:292, S.0.1002.1, line 20. They are a clan like the LÚ.*sa-ru-gu* and the LÚ.*lu-ḫu-ú-a-a*. See RIMB 2:295, S.0.1002.2, i.10.
400. SAA 15:113–14, 166.6–r.15 (= *ABL* 883).
401. SAA 15:114, 167.4′–6′.
402. SAA 1:78, 90.r.10′, 13e.

account of Neo-Assyrian vowel harmony is a secondary form of the tribal name.[403]

46. Ḫallatu

This tribal name is derived from the root *ḥll*.[404] In Sennacherib's list of the confederation that Marduk-apla-iddina (Merodach-Baladan) had assembled against him, he names nine tribes: Puqūdu, Gambūlu, Ḫallatu (LÚ.*ḫa-la-tu/tu₄*), Ru'a, Ubūlu, Malaḫu, Rāpiqu, Ḫindaru, and Damūnu.[405] Elsewhere the other eight tribes are defined as explicitly Aramean. Being listed third right after the Puqūdu and the Gambūlu, the two most important Aramean tribes is perhaps not insignificant. In a letter of Ṭāb-ṣill-Ešarra, the governor of Assur, to Sargon II, troops of the Ḫallatu (KUR.*ḫal-lat-a-a*) are mentioned alongside men of the Aramean tribe, Ruqāḫu, who are serving in the Assyrian army.[406] In the mid-seventh century, a sheikh of *Ḫal-lat* is recorded together with the sheikh of the region of *Ma-na-nu,* the *Na-ḫal* (region and canal), the Sealand, Pillatu, and Elam.[407]

47. Yašumu

In one of his letters to Sargon II, Bēl-iqīša informed the king that Marduk-apla-iddina (Merodach-baladan) was doing repair work in Larak and was settling in its midst "Ḫasinu, the Yašumean" ([m]*ḫ[a-s]i-ni* DUMU [m]*ia-a-šu-mu*), together with his clan (*qinnu*), and his Arameans (LÚ.*A-ra-mi-šú*).[408] The pattern $PN_1$ *mār* $PN_2$ here can be a parallel of $PN_1$ *mār Li-ta-me* (see Lī'tawu above). There was a region of Yašumu (Neo-Assyrian KUR/URU.*ia-su-me*) near Ṭūr-'Abdīn.[409] Perhaps this is the area from which the tribe originated.[410]

Zadok (2013, 306) suggests that there may be some additional occurrences of the gentilic form in which the syllable BA might better be read MA. For example, in a letter to Sargon II "after the king retreated from Dēr," an

403. Zadok (2013, 305) notes that this homonymic town is additional evidence for migration of tribesmen from Sūḫu to Babylonia.

404. However, while this root appears in Sam'alian Aramaic (Panamuwa, line 3, Tropper 1993, 107), since there are homonymic roots, the precise meaning must remain uncertain. See *DNWSI*, 375; Sokoloff 2002a, 464b; Jastrow 1950, 470.

405. RINAP 3.1:182, 22, v.48b–51a; 3.1:199, 23, v.40–42a.

406. SAA 1:79, 91.r.1–2 (= *ABL* 94). See Lipiński 2000a, 479. See chapter 4 on the Jezirah.

407. *ABL* 520, 13–14. See de Vaan 1995, 265–66.

408. SAA 17:25, 22.r.5–8 (= *ABL* 542).

409. See Fales 1973, 6, 44, 96–97, 128; OSyr. *'(y)šwm'*, see Zadok 1998, 2.

410. Zadok 2013, 306.

official states that the [L]uḫu'ātu started hostilities with another tribe. Dietrich read the name as *iá-a-šu-ba-a-a*,[411] but Zadok (2013, 306) suggests that since Neo-Babylonian has the same shape as Middle Assyrian, the reading *Iá-a-šu-ma-a-a* is preferable. Also in a document from the Sargonid period that lists items issued to visiting delegations, "[A]ḫi-lid[i], the Yasub[ean]" ([P]AP)-*li-d*[*i*? (x) LÚ?].*ia-su-b*[*a-a-a*] received small gold rings.[412] If the personal name is read correctly, it is an Aramaic name, and the gentilic might also be understood as referencing the tribe (again reading *ma* for *ba*). This may likewise be the case in an earlier document concerned with the revolt of Mukīn-zēri against Tiglath-pileser III where this gentilic is used as a personal name: m*Ia-su-ba-a-a*.[413] Zadok (2013, 306) argues that "the bearer of this name served in all probability in the Assyrian intelligence trying to persuade the inhabitants of Aramean and Chaldean tribal areas not to join the rebels. One expects that such a task was fulfilled by an Aramean rather than by a native of the Zagros who did not speak the local language."[414] The Neo-Babylonian LÚ.URU.*ia-šu-ba*/*ma-a-a* (Zadok 1985a, 189) may be a gentilic of either Yašubu or Yašumu.

### 48. Tēšu

The name of this tribe may derive from Aramaic *tyš*ʾ "he-goat."[415] The Tēšu appear to be an Aramean group in the northern Babylonia region. The gentilic forms, LÚ.KUR.*te-sa-a-a*[416] and LÚ.*te-šá-a-a*,[417] occur in the inscriptions of Sargon II. The tribe is mentioned together with the Aramean tribe of Tu'mūna as being deported.

### 49. Tanê

The tribal name may derive from Aramaic *tny*, "to repeat."[418] The Tanê are first mentioned in the so-called governor's archive from Nippur (mid-eighth

411. SAA 17:152, 172.8′–r.3, esp. edge 10′.

412. SAA 7:76 58.r.iii.2–3 (K 8787+ = *ADD* 1110+).

413. SAA 19:126–28, 125.9′, 16′, 18′; Saggs 2001, 22–23 (= ND 2717).

414. Zadok (2013, 306) tentatively suggests that the Neo-Assyrian spelling with <*s*> may support a differentiation of this gentilic from the non-Semitic (possibly Kassite) tribe of Yašūbu in the Zagros. He cites two examples: KUR.*ia-su-pi* (SAA 15:86, 123.4′; and text 151); and KUR.*ia-šu-bu* (SAA 10:127, 165, r.10′).

415. Sokoloff 2002b, 580b; Jastrow 1950, 1667; see Zadok 1985c, 79.

416. Fuchs 1994, 34, Cylinder, line 18.

417. Gadd 1954, 199, line 16.

418. *DNWSI*, 1223; Sokoloff 2002b, 585a; 2002a, 1218a; Jastrow 1950, 1680; see Zadok 1985c, 78–79. Lipiński (2000a, 471–72) argues that *tny* appears to be a variant of Akkadian *tamû* "to swear" with an *m*/*n* interchange. This seems unnecessary and unlikely.

century). Baḫiāni,[419] the servant of Nippur's governor writes that the situation with the Aramean tribe Ḫindaru has deteriorated. In addition, the Naqari (LÚ.*na-qa-ri*) and Tanê (LÚ.*ta-né-*⌜*e*⌝ tribes have gone over to the side of a man named Nūru and the Ḫalapi tribe (LÚ.*ḫa-la-pi*), apparently identical with the Aramean tribe called Bīt-Ḫalupē.[420] Cole (1996a, 63) observes that the Tanê and Naqari tribes ranged as far east as the Diyala and the Lower Zab.

In 745, Tiglath-pileser III claimed "I ruled over ... the Nasikku ([LÚ].⌜*na*⌝*-sik-ki*), Naqru (LÚ.*na-aq-ri*), (and) Tanê (LÚ.*ta-né-e*), ..."[421] A text from the Governor's Palace Archive[422] provides a list of eleven criminals who had undertaken a raid and had stolen seventy sheep. One group among these criminals was seven men of the Ruqāḫu tribe (LÚ.*ru-qa-ḫa-a*).[423] The man who was in charge of these thieves is designated as Yada-'ilu, the sheikh of "the Naqari" (LÚ.*na-si-ku ša* LÚ.*na-qi-ra-a-a*) and was actually caught red handed with the stolen sheep, yet is not included in the total of "11 criminals." Yada-'ilu has a clear Aramaic name.[424]

Lipiński (2000a, 472) dissociates Dūr-Tanê[425] of the Chaldean territory of Bīt-Sa'alli from Sennacherib's time as having any connection with this tribe. However, Zadok (2013, 306) argues that this is just another typical case of the "toponymie en mirroir" and cannot be discarded due to the many analogies.

### 50. Ḫamdānu

The derivation of this tribal name[426] should be taken from the Aramaic root *ḥmd*, "to desire."[427] The tribe is only mentioned in a report from the so-called governor's archive from Nippur (mid-eighth century). Text 14 describes the formation of an alliance between the Aramean tribe of the Puqūdu[428] and the Chaldean tribe of Bīt-Awkāni, and the fact that the LÚ.*ḫa-*⌜*am-da-an*⌝ have

---

419. The name is the same as that of the Aramean tribe that ruled Gūzāna/Gōzān (see §4.3).

420. Cole 1996a, 62–3, text 13, esp. lines 19–20. See Lipiński 2000a, 471–72.

421. RINAP 1:26–27, 5, line 6; Tadmor 1994, 42, Ann. 9:6; see also RINAP 1:114, 46, line 8; Tadmor 1994, 150, Summary 6:8. See Nasikku below.

422. Postgate 1973, 143–44, text 119.

423. See the discussion of this text at §4.1.1.2.

424. Lipiński (2000a, 471) states that Yada-'ilu "bears a perfectly Aramaic name, which is not common in North-Arabian."

425. RINAP 3.1:35, 1, line 40.

426. Compare the name חֶמְדָּן in Gen 36:26.

427. Lipiński 2000a, 431–32; Zadok 2013, 307.

428. Interestingly, the Puqūdu leaders are designated LÚ.SAG.KAL.⌜MEŠ⌝ *šá* LÚ.*pu-qu-du* (line 5).

now gone over to the side of this alliance.[429] This alliance did not last. The Puqūdu and Bīt-Awkāni became bitter rivals.

Cole (1996a, 65) compares the tribal name with the Yemenite (Sabean-Himyarite) tribe Ḫamdān. However, since the name is explicable in Aramaic terms, and since there was an Aramean (Gambūlu) sheikh named Ḫamdānu ($^{m}$*ḫa-am-da-nu*),[430] there are excellent grounds for concluding that the tribe is Aramean.[431]

51. Gāmu

This tribe is mentioned, at present in only two texts from Nippur (both from the eighth century), the most important of which states: So I have hea[rd]: "In Nippur, many of the […] tribe(?) and all the Gāmu tribe (LÚ.*Ga-a-mu*) have gone ov[er](?) to the Rupū' tribe" (*a-na m*[*uḫ-ḫi*] LÚ.*ru-pu-u*ʾ *it-*⸢*tal*⸣*-ku*).[432]

Lipiński (2000a, 439–40) suggests that this tribe aggregated to the Rupū' tribe. He also understands the reading of the tribe's name (*Ga-a-mu/me*) to be derived from Aramaic *qām* "betyl", arguing that there is ample evidence for Semitic voiced *qāf* and for a shift *q* > *g*. However, Zadok (2013, 307) argues that the alternative reading with *Qá-* is against the Neo-Babylonian syllabary. He concludes that "the name may render an Old Aramaic forerunner of Old Syriac *gw*ʾ "clan" as Neo-Babylonian <*VmV*> can stand for intervocalic /*w*/."

52. Ḫalapu

The tribe's name seems to be derived from the root *ḥlp* "to replace, pass away, succeed." In a letter from a servant of the governor of Nippur (mid-eighth century), an opposition group has been formed from a man named Nūru and the Ḫalapi tribe (LÚ.*ḫa-la-pi*) apparently identical with the Aramean tribe called Bīt-Ḫalupē.[433] Sargon II mentions a URU.*ḫi-li-pa-nu* on the Uqnû River in Gambūlu whose name appears to be based on the root *ḥlp*, perhaps on the tribal name.

429. Cole 1996a, 64–65, text 14:18.

430. Fuchs 1994, 141, Annals 272a.

431. Lipiński (2000a, 431–32) concludes that the tribe, being an ally of Puqūdu, is Aramean.

432. Cole 1996a, 177–79, text 83:4b–7a. For the other text, see Cole 1996a, 53–55, text 9:20: LÚ.*Ga-a-me*.

433. Cole 1996a, 62–63, text 13. See the entry for Tanê above. See also §4.5.

53. Ḫabi'

In the governor's archive from Nippur (mid-eighth century), there is a mention of the Ḫabi' (LÚ.*ḫa-bi-*ʾ).[434] Cole (1996a, 169) suggests that the name "may be related to Safaitic *Ḫb*ʾ." Zadok (2013, 307) has suggested Aramaic *ḫb*ʾ (sic: *ḥby*), "to withdraw, hide."[435]

54. Naqru

The tribal name is Aramaic derived from *nqr*.[436] A letter from the Governor's archive from Nippur narrates that the Naqru (LÚ.*na-qa-ri*) and Tanê (LÚ.*ta-né-*⸢*e*⸣ tribes have gone over to the side of Nūru and the Ḫalapi tribe (LÚ.*ḫa-la-pi*).[437] Cole (1996a, 63) observes that the Naqari tribe ranged as far east as the Diyala and the Lower Zab. Moreover, a text from the Governor's Palace Archive[438] (dating roughly to the first half of the eighth century) gives a list of eleven sheep-stealing criminals and their leader designated as Yada-ʾilu, the sheikh of the Naqru (LÚ.*na-si-ku ša* LÚ.*na-qi-ra-a-a*), who has an Aramean personal name.[439] The annals of Tiglath-pileser III mention the tribe together with the Nasikku and the Tanê.[440]

55. Nasikku

Obviously, the name of the tribe comes from **nasīk*, "sheikh." The tribe occurs only twice in the inscriptions of Tiglath-pileser III: once in the annals: [LÚ].⸢*na*⸣-*sik-ki*, where it is juxtaposed with the Naqru and the Tanê tribes;[441] and once in a summary inscription: [LÚ].⸢*na*⸣-*si-ku*, where it is juxtaposed with only the Naqru tribe.[442]

56. Yadburu

Zadok (2013, 308) analyzes Yadburu as a *yaqtul*-formation of the Aramaic root *dbr*, "to lead."[443] Moreover, he observes that the writing of the name with initial *ia-a-* does not render a long vowel (*yā-*). Rather the *-a-* is

434. Cole 1996a, 168–69, text 78:12, 16.
435. Sokoloff 2002a, 425a; Jastrow 1950, 418.
436. See Zadok 1979, 13 with n. 11; Lipiński 2000a, 470–71
437. Cole 1996a, 62–63, text 13, esp. lines 19–20. See Lipiński 2000a, 471–72.
438. Postgate 1973, 143–44, text 119.
439. See the full discussion under the entry for Tanê above.
440. RINAP 1:26–27, 5, line 6. See also Tadmor 1994, 42, Ann. 9:6.
441. RINAP 1:26–27, 5, line 6. See also Tadmor 1994, 42, Ann. 9:6.
442. RINAP 1:114, 46, line 8; Tadmor 1994, 150, Summary 6:8.
443. *DNWSI*, 239; Sokoloff 2002b, 138b; 2002a, 313a; Jastrow 1950, 278. By-forms are *Ia-a-di-bi-ri* (Fuchs 1994, 440–1) and (*I-*)*di-bi-ri-na* (region, cf. Zadok 1985c, 71).

inserted in order to retain the reading */ya/* since the sign IA can stand for *y* + any vowel. The original form of the name was *Yadbur* and with attenuation **Yadbir*. The latter with anaptyxis (vowel insertion) resulted in *Yadibir*, which is the base of *Idibirīna* (with *ya-* > *i-* and an Aramaic plural suffix *-īn*), i.e., "the (district) of the Yadbireans."[444]

In Sargon II's inscriptions Yadburu appears as an Aramean district. Although this is not explicitly stated anywhere, it is clearly implied. In Sargon's twelfth *palû*, the Ru'a, Ḫindaru, Yadburu (LÚ.KUR.*ia-ad-bu-ru*), (and) Puqūdu, all the Suteans, the steppe people, allied themselves with Marduk-apla-iddina (Merodach-Baladan).[445] However, after the capture of Gambūlu, these same four tribes are listed (there written: LÚ.*ia-ad-bu-ru*) as having fled into the swamps of the Uqnû, but Sargon forced them to submit.[446] In the Great Display inscription, Sargon lists eleven explicitly Aramean entities: on the bank of the Tigris: Itū', Rupū', Ḫaṭallu, Labdūdu, Ḫamarānu, Ubūlu, Ru'a, Lītawu; on the bank of the Surappu River (and) the Uqnû River: Gambūlu, Ḫindaru, (and) Puqūdu—Sūteans, steppe people of the land of Yadburu, as many as there were."[447] Yadburu is likely to be considered the twelfth conventional member in the list of Aramean tribes. At any rate, the district of Yadburu was comprised of Arameans.[448]

Finally, in Sargon II's annals,[449] there is a list of the sheikhs of the land of Yadburu who brought tribute and submitted to Sargon which reads:

> [$^{m}$]*mu-še-zi-bu* $^{m}$*na-at-nu* $^{m}$*a-a-lu-nu* $^{m}$*da-iṣ-ṣa-nu šá* KUR.*la-ḫi-ri* $^{m}$*a-a-ri-im-mu* (299) $^{m}$EN-URU *ša* URU.*su-la-*[*i*]*a* 6 (var. 5) LÚ.[*na*]-*si-ka-a-te ša* KUR.*ia-ad-bu-ri*

The first four are clearly designated as the sheikhs of the land of Laḫīru (see below). However, with the following signs, there seems to be an issue in the text: are there five or six sheikhs of Yadburu? It seems that $^{m}$EN-URU might best be understood as a title *bēl-āli*, "city-lord" and not as a personal name. This would yield "Ayarimmu ($^{m}$*a-a-ri-im-mu*), the 'city lord' of the

444. Zadok 2013, 308; 1977, 156, 253, 256. *Di-bi-ri-i-na* (/**Dibirīn*/) is the same form with omission of the first, unstressed, syllable. "The identification of Neo-Assyrian *Di-bi-ri-i-na* with OT *Sprwym* by Lipiński 2000a, 432 n. 150 *in fine* is totally unacceptable" (Zadok 2013, 308).

445. Fuchs 1994, 136, Annals 258.

446. Fuchs 1994, 146, Annals 281–284a. See Ḫindaru above.

447. Fuchs 1994, 195, Prunk. 18b–20; also Fuchs 1994, 265, Stier 4:70.

448. The Arameans (no tribal delineation) are said to dwell in the land of Yadburu (Fuchs 1994, 233 Prunk. 150–51).

449. Fuchs 1994, 151, Annals 298b–299.

city of Sūlāya, '5' sheikhs of the land of Yadburu."[450] Since the chiefs of Aramean tribes were invariably designated *nasīku* (pl. *nasīkāti*) "sheikhs" in the Assyro-Babylonian sources,[451] this appears to be the best option.

57. Laḫīru

Laḫīru is an Aramaic name. Zadok has analyzed *La-ḫi-ri* as a *laqtil* formation (*lʿyr*) of *ia-ḫi-ri*, both of which are causative forms of *ǵwr* "awake, rouse oneself" (*ʿwr* in Aramaic and Hebrew).[452]

The tribe Laḫīru is mentioned twice in a mid-eighth century letter from the governor's archive from Nippur: line 5, LÚ.⌜*la-ḫi-ru*⌝; line 25, ⌜LÚ.*la-ḫi*⌝-*ri*.[453] From this letter, it appears that they conducted caravan trade with Elam via Dēr. According to another letter,[454] Laḫīru was one of the destinations to which Nippur's textile traders dispatched their agents to buy wool because of its quality: "The wool of the Puqūdu (LÚ.*Pu-qu-du*) is not good, and its price is not good; the wool of the people of Laḫīru (LÚ.*La-ḫe-e-ri*) is good, and its price is good."[455] Not many years later, "the city of Laḫīru of Idibirīna" (URU.*la-ḫi-ru ša i-di-bi-ri-i-na*) is mentioned together with the Aramean tribe of Puqūdu in Tiglath-pileser III's inscriptions.[456]

It seems clear from the sources that there were two cities of Laḫīru that were very likely named after the tribe. One was located on the Turna (i.e., the Diyala River), the other in the district of Yadburu on the Babylonian–Elamite frontier southeast of Dēr and west of Susa. However, there are scholars who understand the data to indicate only one location. Although Brinkman (1968, 178 n. 1093) considers the possibility of two towns named Laḫīru, he ultimately assesses that this is "somewhat less likely." Joannès (2005, 187 n. 14) sees only a southern location and doubts the existence of a northern city; and Lipiński also considers only one location, in the south in the Elamite border region. However, the evidence, in my opinion, points to two separate towns.[457]

---

450. Fuchs 1994, 411, s.v. Janzū; 1998–99.

451. The only possible exception appears to be the one-time usage of LÚ.SAG.KAL.MEŠ in reference to the leaders the Puqūdu in the governor's archive from Nippur. See Cole 1996a, 65, text 14:5. See above under Puqūdu.

452. Zadok 1976, 114, with n. 9; 1977, 93; 2013, 308–10; Lipiński 2000a, 432. For Aramaic, see Sokoloff 2002b, 400b; 2002a, 849a; Jastrow 1950, 1057; for Hebrew, see *HALOT*, 802–3.

453. Cole 1996a, 116–17, text 43.

454. Cole 1996a:122–23, text 46:10, 16b–22a.

455. For further comment on the Puqūdean wool, see 6. Puqūdu above (p. 688).

456. RINAP 1:118, 47, line 13; Tadmor 1994, 160, Summary 7:13.

457. Parpola and Porter 2001, 12 and maps 10, 11.

The earliest occurrence of a URU.*La-ḫi-ri* is found in the inscriptions of Adad-nērārī II (911–891) where the Assyrian king claims to have defeated the Babylonian king, Šamaš-mudammiq, from Mount Yalman (in Jebel Ḥamrīn) to the Turna River (ÍD.*túr-an*) and to have annexed Babylonian territory from Laḫīru to Ugār-sallu.[458] In 851, Shalmaneser III conquered Meturnat[459] and URU.*La-ḫi-ru*.[460] In the following year (850) Shalmaneser captured Gannānāte and Ḫalman.[461] Thus, this city of Laḫīru was located on the Turna (Diyala) River. It was the location of a temple to Adad and served as the provincial capital. The earliest clear evidence of the province of Laḫīru is found in a letter to Sargon II.[462] The province of Laḫīru occupied the area east of the Tigris River, south of the Nahr al-'Uzaim and north of Diyala River (Radner 2006–8a, 57). In a letter to Aššurbanipal, Nabû-balāssu-iqbi and Nadin-Aya inform the king that Aššur-nāṣir has sent a royal bodyguard to the governors of Laḫīru (URU.*La-ḫi-ri*) and of Dūr-Šarrukku concerning a transport order that the governor of Laḫīru has obeyed and the governor of Dūr-Šarrukku has not.[463] Since Dūr-Šarrukku was in northern Babylonia not far from the confluence of the Diyala into the Tigris, it makes sense that this northern city of Laḫīru is the provincial capital[464] in view (not the city in Yadburu). Apparently, the Ebabbarra temple of Sippar in northern Babylonia had land and other economic interests in this city of Laḫīru.[465]

A second city of Laḫīru (URU.*la-ḫi-ri*), which belonged to the land of Yadburu[466] in the time of Sargon II, must be a different city with the same name, because it makes little sense to qualify it as *šá* KUR.*ia-ad-bu-ri* if the precise location has been known for over 170 years before Tiglath-pileser III. Zadok rightly observes that

458. RIMA 2:148, A.0.99.2, lines 26b–29.

459. Possibly modern Tall Haddād on the Diyala (Zadok 2013, 307).

460. RIMA 3:37, A.0.102.6, line 44; 3:46, A.0.102.8, line 23′; 3:53, A.0.102.10, line 34.

461. Modern Ḥolwān. See Brinkman 1968, 194–95.

462. SAA 5:178–79, 250.r.13′b–14′: *ša* URU.MEŠ-*šú-nu ina* ⌜NAM⌝ URU.*la-ḫ*[*i-ri*], "their cities in the province of Laḫ[īru]."

463. SAA 13:96, 124.12–r.11 (= *ABL* 558).

464. The governor of Laḫīru acted under Esarhaddon in 673 as eponym. The province is mentioned in letters to Esarhaddon (SAA 13:84, 104.r.4) and Aššurbanipal (*ABL* 543, 1108, 1244). In the year 670, the governor of Laḫīru, his deputy and two other subordinates sold a village to a eunuch of the crown prince of Babylon, i.e., Šamaš-šuma-ukīn (SAA 6:231, 287.1–5); and another subordinate of the governor of Laḫīru is mentioned in a document from the eponym of Nabû-da''inanni (under Aššurbanipal after 648). The province is also mentioned in a list of estates from the seventh century (SAA 11:151, 225.8′).

465. See Da Riva 2002, 82.

466. Fuchs 1994, 65 Stier, line 30.

> this special definition is in order to distinguish Laḫīru of Yadburu in the Babylonian-Elamite frontier southeast of Dēr and west of Susa from the homonymous provincial capital somewhere between Arrapḫa and the Diyala. This is another case of "toponymie en mirroir," but contrary to most cases it is not on an east-west axis but on a north-south one. The motivation of this phenomenon is understandable if one assumes that Laḫīru (Aram. *Lʿyr*) was originally a tribe which gave its name to the towns.[467]

In addition to the possibility of two cities of same name, Frame suggested that "it is also possible that the term (URU) was used loosely and referred simply to the tribe by that name."[468]

Thus, on the one hand, the tribe's existence in the northern location is explicitly demonstrated in the so-called governor's archive; on the other hand, the fact that in 710 BCE there were four sheikhs of Laḫīru in Yadburu (three of whom bear Aramaic names)[469] evinces the tribe's presence in the southern location. Since the sheikhs of Laḫīru and Nugu' (LÚ.*na-si-ka-a-ti šá* URU.*la-ḫi-ru ù* LÚ.*nu-gu-ú-ʾ*)[470] are mentioned together in the time of Aššurbanipal in the Babylonian-Elamite border region only further demonstrates the southern location. Laḫīru and other entities in eastern Babylonia submitted to Aššurbanipal in 647 BCE when he conducted his campaign against Elam (Da Riva 2002, 80–82). The evidence as presented demonstrates two cities of Laḫīru named after the tribal name.[471] Finally, the city of Laḫīru—probably the southern Babylonian location is intended—is referenced in 2 Kgs 19:13 and Isa 37:13.

467. Zadok 2013, 309. See also Fuchs 1994, 444 who states: "Von Lahiru am Diyala wohl doch zu trennen ... eben deshalb Lahiru mit dem Zusatz *ša māt Yadibiri* oder *ša Idibirina,* um eine Verwechslung der beiden gleichnamigen Orten zu vermeiden."

468. Frame 1992, 204, 224 n. 68. Contra Brinkman 1968 n. 1093.

469. The first-named sheikh, Mušezibu, has an Akkadian name. The other three, Natnu, Ayalunu, (and) Daiṣṣanu (ᵐ*na-at-nu* ᵐ*a-a-lu-nu* ᵐ*da-iṣ-ṣa-nu*) have Aramaic names (Zadok 2013, 311).

470. *ABL* 280, 19–20. See de Vaan 1995, 239–43; Oppenheim 1965, no. 120.

471. As an American, an analogy quickly comes to mind. There are many east-coast cities whose names reappear again and again in other states as immigration moved west, e.g., Richmond, VA, Richmond, IN, Richmond, IA, Richmond, CA, etc. All of these are ultimately named after the Richmond, England. The town of Richemont in Normandy was the origin of the name Richmond. This Richmond was the eponymous honor of the Earls of Richmond (or comtes de Richemont).

### 58. Nuguḫu

The tribal name perhaps derives from Aramaic *ngh* "to shine at dawn,"[472] *ngh*ʾ, "brightness," "lightness."[473] The formation is *qutl* with anaptyxis (insertion of a short vowel between consonants). Zadok (2013, 310) comments: "there is no need to regard it as an Arabic 'broken' plural (despite Lipiński 2000a, 430, 436–37)." The personal name *ngh*⌜*y*⌝ occurs in a text from Tell Shiukh Fawqani,[474] and the name *nsḥnghy* in a text in the Louvre.[475]

The sheikhs of LÚ.*Nu-gu-*ʾ and Laḫīru are mentioned together in the time of Aššurbanipal.[476] According to a letter from this period, Nabû-bēl-šumāti hired[477] members of various tribes on the Babylonian-Elamite border, including the people of the Ḫilimmu, Pillatu, LÚ.*Nu-gu-ḫu*, Yaši-il, and Lakabru tribes.[478] Frame observes that it is possible that the LÚ.*nu-gu-ú-*ʾ are to be identifed with the LÚ.*Nu-gu-ḫu* tribe[479] who had aided Nabû-bēl-šumāti against Bēl-ibni.[480]

## 10.2.4. Possible Aramean Tribes

In his comprehensive study, Zadok lists nine tribes that are explicable in Aramaic terms and may therefore be Aramean.[481] Only these will be discussed. There were other tribes that appear to be West Semitic, but cannot safely be suggested as Aramean or are now clearly not to be considered Aramean.[482] These will not be discussed here.

472. *DNWSI*, 714; Sokoloff 2002b, 340b; 2002a, 728b; Jastrow 1950, 872.

473. See Zadok 1985a, xxi.

474. Fales and Attardo 2005, 652, text 45, r.2′. Note the cuneiform attestation Nagaḫî and Nagaḫānu, see Pearce 2001a–b.

475. AO 25.341; Fales 1986, no. 58.

476. *ABL* 280, 19–20. See de Vaan 1995, 239–43; Oppenheim 1965, no. 120.

477. For the verb, see the comments of Frame 1992, 181 n. 257.

478. *ABL* 1000:6′, 11′–16′.

479. See also Dietrich 1979, 120:5: LÚ.*nu-g*[*u*?-ʾ/*ḫu*?]; and 282:9: LÚ.*nu-g*[*u-*ʾ].

480. Frame 1992, 206 n. 68; see also Dietrich 1970, 105, 107.

481. Zadok 2013, 311–16, 323.

482. While the Gurru/Qurru tribe has connections with the Itū' and with the Ḫamarānu, both Lipiński (2000a, 484–85) and Zadok (2013, 313–14) argue that they are not an Aramean group. Zadok (2013, 311–15) considers some tribes to be West Semitic, but their linguistic affiliation is not transparently Aramaic: Aḫēnna, Marsinu, Aradātu, Rasītu, Laḫitu, Riqtu, and Ḫamqadu. Zadok (2013, 312, 323) considers the Ruqāḫu to be Arabian; however, see the discussion at §4.1.1.2.

1. Yaši'-il

This tribe (LÚ.*ia-as-ìl*)[483] is mentioned in the annals of Sennacherib,[484] being located in southeastern Babylonia. It is also mentioned in letters from the time of Aššurbanipal. Bēl-ibni wrote Aššurbanipal informing the king that when Assyrian troops attacked the city of Irgidu they killed Ammaladin, the sheikh of the Yaši'-il tribe (m*am-ma-la-din* LÚ.*na-si-ku šá* LÚ.*ia-a-ši-ìl*) along with two of his brothers, three uncles, two of his nephews, Dalâ-il (m*da-la-a*-DINGIR), son of Abi-yadi' (mAD-*ia-di-i'*) and 200 notables of the city.[485] The names Ammaladin ("may the ancestor judge"),[486] Dalâ-il ("The god has saved)[487] and Abi-yadi' ("the father is knowing")[488] are Aramaic. In another letter from Bēl-ibni, there is a report of a famine that struck the tribe of Yaši-il (LÚ.*i-ši-ìl* / LÚ.*ia-ši-ìl*), along with other groups in the region.[489] Its name may derive from *'w/yš* "to grant"; hence, "God has granted."[490]

2. Lakabru

The Lakabru (LÚ.*la-kab-ra*) is mentioned, along with the Yaši'-il, in the annals of Sennacherib as an ally of Elam.[491] The tribe (LÚ.*la-kab-ru*) is also mentioned, along with the tribe of Yaši'-il, in the letter of Bēl-ibni to Aššurbanipal that reports of the severe famine.[492] Thus, it is also located in southeastern Babylonia. The name is explicable in Aramaic terms.[493]

3. Ḫarzūnu

The Ḫarzūnu tribe (LÚ.*ḫa-ar-zu-nu*) is mentioned in Sennacherib's annals[494] following the Yaši-il and Lakabru and before the Dummuqu[495] tribes. Thus

483. For earlier discussion, see Edzard 1976–80a.

484. RINAP 3.1:182, 22, v.44; 3.1:199, 23, v.36.

485. De Vaan 1995, 239–43 (= *ABL* 280) lines 13–17.

486. Lipiński 2000a, 480; Zadok 2013, 316.

487. Pearce 1999, 372; Zadok 1977, 85; 2013, 316

488. Zadok 1977, 53, 104, 352; Lipiński 2000a, 481.

489. De Vaan 1995, 292–96 (= *ABL* 1000), lines 6, 13 (respectively); cf. also de Vaan 1995, 318–22 (= *ABL* 1342), line r.2.

490. Lipiński 2000a, 480; Zadok 2013, 311, who notes; "The alternative **Yašiān* (based on the same verbal root with a compond suff. *-i-ān*) seems less likely but cannot be excluded as such a name is extant in the settlement NA [Ālu] ša *Ia-áš-ia?-nu* in Gambūlu."

491. RINAP 3.1:182, 22, v.45; 3.1:199, 23, v.36.

492. De Vaan 1995, 292–96 (= *ABL* 1000), lines 7, 14.

493. Zadok 1985a, xx: (*la-* + *qatl* of *kbr*). See also Dietrich 1970, 11, 105.

494. RINAP 3.1:182, 22, v.45; 3.1:199, 23, v.36.

495. Zadok (2013, 312) speculates concerning the Dummuqu that perhaps this is a West Semitic tribe in spite of the Akkadian name.

it was also located in southeastern Babylonia on the Babylonian-Elamite border. The tribal name is a *qatl* formation of *ḥrz* ("to pierce" in the G-stem; "to be strung together" in the Gt-stem)[496] with an *-ōn* < *-ān* suffix.[497]

4. Yaqīmānu

The Yaqīmānu (KUR.*ia-qí-ma-nu*) tribe is mentioned in a letter of Bēl-ušēzib to Esarhaddon that is concerned with political matters in the land of Mannea in the Zagros (adjacent to Zamua). Zadok (2013, 312) rightly points out that the Yaqīmānu is not a Mannean tribe.[498] The text states that "… the sheikh Yadi' and all the sheikhs of Yaqīmānu testified for him before the chief eunuch in Mannea" (LÚ.*na-si-ku* m*ia-di-i'* LÚ.*na-si-ku ù* LÚ.*na-si-ka-tu šá* KUR.*ia-qi-ma-nu gab-bi ina* IGI LÚ.GAL.SAG *ina* KUR.*ma-nu-a-a uk-tin-nu-šú*).[499] Its main sheikh (*nasīku*), Yadi', bore an exclusively Aramaic name (Zadok 2013, 312). Finally, there was a homonymic settlement URU.*ia-qi-mu-na* in Bīt-Dakkūri.[500]

5. Ḫamūru

The name of this tribe is from the same root as the Ḫamarānu tribe above.[501] The tribe seems to have been located near Borsippa and Bīt-Dakkūri. In a letter reporting on matters in Bīt-Dakkūri, the LÚ.*ḫa-mur-ra-a-*[*a*] are mentioned, though in a fragmentary context.[502] A letter was sent by the chiefs (LÚ.GAL.[MEŠ]) of the Ḫamūru tribe ([L]Ú.*ḫa-mu-ru*) to the Assyrian king (probably Sennacherib).[503] From the reign of Esarhaddon, a letter[504] reports that no bread has been provided for people who are identified as LÚ.PI.2.LÁ. MEŠ.[505] One of these persons, "a Ḫamurean LÚ.PI.2.LÁ,"[506] is quoted as stating: "Aššur-balassu-iqbi has not been present (but) has reduced my bread

496. Sokoloff 2002b, 214b; 2002a, 482a; Jastrow 1950, 500.

497. Zadok 2013, 312.

498. Contra Parpola SAA 10:index s.v. Yakimanu; followed by Lipiński 2000a, 485.

499. SAA 10:94, text 113.r.7b–r.10a (= *ABL* 1109+).

500. RINAP 3.1:35, 1, line 38. The Neo-Assyrian spelling with *ā* > *ō* is Aramaic. See Zadok 1977, 138, 267; Lipiński 2000a, 484–85.

501. Zadok 2013, 312. See 8. Ḫamarānu above (p. 693).

502. SAA 17:65–66, 69.r.23 (= Dietrich 1979, 19). See Brinkman 1968, 230 n. 1446.

503. SAA 17:72–73, 81.2.

504. SAA 18:96–97, 123.8.

505. Reynolds understands LÚ.PI.2.LÁ as the word *sukkuku* "deaf" (SAA 18:96–97, text 174, Logograms and Their Readings). In addition to this letter (SAA 18, text 123), letters (texts 121 and 122) are also about the rations of bread to the LÚ.PI.2.LÁ.MEŠ.

506. LÚ.PI.2.LÁ LÚ.*ḫa-mu-ra-a-a*.

(allowance)." A homonymic settlement (URU.*ḫa-mu-ru*) was perhaps not far from Sippar.[507]

6. Kib/prītu

The tribal name ends with the *-īt* suffix on the root *kpyr* "young lion," the same as *Kib/prē* above. The Kib/prītu (*Kib/p-ri-ta-a-a*) are mentioned together with Ḫindareans as both were incorporated into the Assyrian army in the time of Aššurbanipal.[508]

7. Magullu

The name of this tribe is clearly derived from *gll* with a *ma-* preformative.[509] The tribe (LÚ.*ma-gul-la-a-a*) is mentioned in the Murašû archive from late Achaemenid Nippur.[510]

8. Ḫaūnu

The tribal name may be derived from the root *ḥwy* (G-stem "to see"; D-stem "to show, announce").[511] In a letter to Aššurbanipal,[512] Bēl-ibni reports that the Elamite, Umḫuluma', sent his herald to various cities and peoples in the southern Babylonian-Elamite border region (apparently in order to secure their support); but they seized the herald and killed him. The Ḫaūnu (LÚ.*ḫa-ú-nu*) were one of the tribal entities mentioned in the text, along with the LÚ.*ki-par-a-ti*.[513]

9. Šarab/pu

This tribe's name may derive from either *šrb*$_1$ "to be dry, warm";[514] or *šrb*$_2$ D-stem "to propagate," Gt-stem "to be enrolled."[515] The two occurrences are found in an astrological report concerning the eclipse of the moon written by Munnabitu, a Babylonian astrologer, to the king (Esarhaddon) who mentions the LÚ.*Šar-ra-b/pu*.[516] It is possible that the tribe is also mentioned in a frag-

507. Zadok 1985a, 151. Camb. 394, 4.

508. *ABL* 1009, 12.

509. Zadok 2013, 314–15. For Aramaic *gll*, see Sokoloff 2002b, 130b; Jastrow 1950, 249; Payne-Smith 1902, 69. For Hebrew, see *HALOT*, 193–94.

510. BE 10, text 81:3, 8 (*šak-nu šá* LÚ.*ma-gul-la-a-a*). See Zadok 1985a, 216.

511. *DNWSI*, 353; Sokoloff 2002b, 190; Sokoloff 2002a, 437; Jastrow 1950, 432.

512. De Vaan 1995, 311–17 (= *ABL* 1311 + 1464), lines 6–10.

513. Note *Kib/p-ri-ta-a-a* above.

514. Jastrow 1950, 1627.

515. Payne-Smith 1902, 596–97.

516. SAA 8:178–79, 316.16 and r. 8.

mentary hemerology ([x x x] [(4)]*šar-ra-b*[*u* x x x]).[517] Nothing is known about this entity, though based on documents in which the name occurs, the tribe was probably located in Babylonia.

517. SAA 8:304, 565.4.

# CONCLUSION

THIS BOOK HAS DOCUMENTED WHAT IS KNOWN ABOUT THE GREAT COMPLEXITY concerning the Aramean socially constructed units throughout the ancient Near East, from the first appearance of these groups to the end of their identifiable polities. This complexity was due, in part, to the fluidity of their tribal structures, as well as their various movements over the course of their existences. The Aramean units' migrations were necessitated or stimulated by multiple factors throughout the period of their history. In the case of the development of the Aramean polities, geographic/environmental factors played a vital role, and this book has paid attention to the manifold regional issues encountered in the Jezirah, north Syria, south Syria, and southern Mesopotamia.

The prime markers for these groups were twofold. First and foremost—wherever it is evidenced—was the Aramaic language. The second marker was the abundant use of ethnicons by many peoples, including the Arameans themselves, that gives clear testimony to their identity. Much of their complexity is known from the Arameans' interactions with these other peoples, particularly the Assyrians and the Hebrew kingdoms. Yet some of the richest insights derive, of course, from their own inscriptions. These markers are very important. The consistent, incredible ability of these Aramean groups to acculturate is a hallmark of their willingness to adapt to the diverse regional influences. This tendency to acculturate obscures other possible markers. The only exception to this acculturation was in the case of the Aramean entities of southern Mesopotamia. Here they evince an apparent social and cultural separateness from the indigenous Babylonian culture.

Perhaps no other people group in the ancient Near East was impacted as greatly by the Assyrians and their imperial expansion as were the Arameans. The Aramean polities that were the more distanced from the Assyrian heartland and the earliest Assyrian expansions had the opportunity to develop tribal kingdoms that preserve some of the best indigenous knowledge concerning this people (e.g., Aram-Damascus, Arpad, Hamath and Luǵath, and

Sam'al). Unfortunately, as they blossomed and came to maturity, they were cut down by the Assyrian sickle.

While the Assyrians heavily impacted the Arameans, there are two ironies. First, it was the Arameans who impacted the Middle Assyrian kingdom, playing an important role in its demise[1] and thus in the creation of the Neo-Assyrian kingdom. Second, while subdued and absorbed by the expansion of the Assyrians, the Aramaic language gradually became the lingua franca of the late Neo-Assyrian Empire. Thus, while during the period of the existence of the Aramean entities the Aramaic language served as a prime marker of the Aramean groups, after the disappearance of these entities it became their greatest legacy.

1. Their impact on southern Mesopotamia was undoubtedly an important factor in that region, too.

# WORKS CITED


Abbadi, S. 1983. *Die Personennamen der Inschriften aus Hatra*. TSO 1. Hildesheim: Olms.

Abd el-Kader, D. 1949. Un orthostate du temple de Hadad à Damas. *Syria* 26:191–95, pl. 8.

Abel, F. M. 1933–38. *Géographie de la Palestine*. 2 vols. Paris: Gabalda.

Abou-Assaf, A. 1968. Tell ʿAschtara in Südsyrien: Erste Kampagne 1966. *AAAS* 18:103–6.

———. 1969. A. Tell Aschtara: Zweite Kampagne 1967. *AAAS* 19:101–2.

———. 1990. *Der Tempel von ʿAin Dara*. DaF 3. Mainz: von Zabern.

Abou-Assaf, A., P. Bordreuil, and A. R. Millard. 1982. *La statue de Tell Fekherye et son inscription bilingue assyro-araméenne*. Études Assyriologiques 7. Paris: Éditions Recherche sur les Civilisations.

Abraham, K., and J. Klein. 2007. A New Sargon II Cylinder Fragment from an Unknown Provenance. *ZA* 97:252–61.

Abu Taleb, M. 1973. Investigations in the History of North Syria 1115–717 B.C. Ph.D. diss., University of Pennsylvania.

Adam, K.-P. 2010. Warfare and Treaty Formulas in the Background of Kings. Pages 35–68 in *Soundings in Kings: Perspective and Methods in Contemporary Scholarship*. Edited by M. Leuchter and K.-P. Adam. Minneapolis: Fortress.

Adams, R. McC. 1965. *Land behind Baghdad: A History of Settlement on the Diyala Plains*. Chicago: University of Chicago Press.

———. 1981. *Heartland of Cities: Surveys of Ancient Settlement and Land Use on the Central Floodplain of the Euphrates*. Chicago: University of Chicago Press.

Adams, R. McC., and H.-J. Nissen. 1972. *The Uruk Countryside: The Natural Setting of Urban Societies*. Chicago: University of Chicago Press.

Adams, W. Y., D. P. Van Gerven, and R. S. Levy. 1978. The Retreat from Migrationism. *Annual Review of Anthropology* 7:483–532.

Adamthwaite, M. R. 1996. Ethnic Movements in the Thirteenth Century B.C. as Discernible from the Emar Texts. Pages 91–112 in *Cultural Interaction in the Ancient Near East: Papers Read at a Symposium Held at the University of Melbourne, Department of Classics and Archaeology (29–30 September 1994)*. Edited by G. Bunnens. AbrNSup 5. Leuven: Peeters.

———. 2001. *Late Hittite Emar: The Chronology, Synchronisms, and Socio-political Aspects of a Late Bronze Age Fortress Town*. ANESSup 8. Leuven: Peeters.

Aharoni, Y. 1979. *The Land of the Bible. A Historical Geography*. Translated by A. F. Rainey. Philadelphia: Westminster.

Aḥituv, S. 1984. *Canaanite Toponyms in Ancient Egyptian Documents.* Jerusalem: Magnes.
Ahlstrom, G. W. 1993. *The History of Ancient Palestine from the Paleolithic Period to Alexander's Conquest.* JSOTSup 146. Sheffield: Sheffield Academic.
Ahmad, A. Y. 1996. The Archive of Aššur-mātu-taqqin Found in the New Town of Assur and Dated Mainly by Post-canonical Eponyms. *Al-Rāfidān* 17:207–88.
Åkerman, K., and K. Radner. 1998. Ammi-Ba'al. *PNA* 1.1:103.
Akkermans, P. M. M. G. 2006. The Fortress of Ilipada: Middle Assyrian Architecture at Tell Sabi Abyad, Syria. Pages 201–11 in *Les espaces syro-mésopotamiens: Dimensions de l'expérience humaine au Proche-Orient ancien.* Edited by P. Butterlin, M. Lebeau, J.-Y. Monchambert, J. L. Montero Fenollos and B. Müller. Subartu 17. Turnhout: Brepols.
Akkermans, P. M. M. G., and I. Rossmeisl. 1990. Excavations at Tell Sabi Abyad, Northern Syria: A Regional Centre on the Assyrian Frontier. *Akkadica* 66:13–60.
Akkermans, P. M. M. G., and G. M. Schwartz. 2003. *The Archaeology of Syria: From Complex Hunter-Gatherers to Early Urban Societies (ca. 16,000–300 BC).* Cambridge World Archaeology. Cambridge: Cambridge University Press.
Akurgal, E. 1979. Analyse iconographique, stylistique et structural de l'architecture et de la sculpture de Tell Halaf. Pages 9–28 in *Florilegium Anatolicum: Mélanges offerts à Emmanuel Laroche.* Edited by E. Akurgal, F. Josephson, and E. Laroche. Paris: de Boccard.
Albenda, P. 1986. *The Palace of Sargon, King of Assyria: Monumental Wall Reliefs at Dur-Sharrukin, from the Original Drawings Made at the Time of Their Discovery in 1843–1844 by Botta and Flandin.* Editions Recherche sur les Civilisations, Synthèse 22. Paris: Editions Recherche sur les Civilisations.
Albright, W. F. 1924–25. The Jordan Valley in the Bronze Age. *AASOR* 6:13–74.
———. 1942. A Votive Stele Erected by Ben-Hadad I of Damascus to the God Melcarth. *BASOR* 87:23–29.
———. 1953. Syrien, Phönizien und Palästina. Pages 370–71 in *Historia mundi* 2. Edited by F. Kern. Munich: Lehnen.
———. 1956a. The Biblical Tribe of Massa' and Some Congeners. Pages 1–14 in *Studi Orientalistici in Onore di Giorgio Levi Della Vida.* Edited by R. Ciasca. Pubblicazioni dell'Istituto per l'Oriente 52. Rome: Istituto per l'Oriente.
———. 1956b. The Date of the Kapara Period at Gozan (Tell Halaf). *AnSt* 6:75–85.
———. 1975. Syria, the Philistines, and Phoenicia. Pages 507–36 in *History of the Middle East and Aegean Region c. 1380–1000 B.C.* Edited by I. E. S. Edwards, et al. CAH 2.1. Cambridge: Cambridge University Press.
Alkim, U. B. 1957. Steinbruch und Skulpturatelier von Yesemek. *Belleten* 21:377–94.
Alt, A. 1934. Die syrische Staatenwelt vor dem Einbruch der Assyrer. *ZDMG* 88:233–58 Repr. as pages 214–32 in vol. 3 of Alt, *Kleine Schriften zur Geschichte des Volkes Israel.* Munich: Beck 1959.
Altaweel, M. 2004. The Land of Ashur: A Study of Landscape and Settlement in the Assyrian Heartland. 2 vols. Ph.D. diss. University of Chicago.
Amadasi Guzzo, M. G. 1996. Le harnais des chevaux du roi Hazaël. Pages 329–38 in vol. 1 of *Scritti di antichità in memoria di Sandro Stucchi.* Edited by L. Bacchielli and M. Bonanno Aravantinos. 2 vols. Studi miscellanei 29. Rome: L'Erma di Bretschneider.

———. 2005. Area 1: Il frammento di stele in basalto con iscrizione. Pages 21–23 and fig. 18 in Mazzoni et al. 2005.
———. 2009. Un fragment de stèle araméenne de Tell Afis. *Or* 78:336–47.
———. 2014. Tell Afis in the Iron Age: The Aramaic Inscriptions. *NEA* 77:54–57.
Ambos, C. 2000a. Ḫabīnu. *PNA* 2.1:437.
———. 2000b. Ḫadi-libbušu. *PNA* 2.1:438–9.
———. 2002. Šamaš-aḫu-iddina. *PNA* 3.2:1189.
Ambos, C., and A. Fuchs. 2000. Ḫaiānu. *PNA* 2.1:440.
Anbar, M. 1991. *Les Tribus amurrites de Mari.* OBO 108. Fribourg: Universitätsverlag; Göttingen: Vandenhoeck & Ruprecht.
Andersen, F. I., and D. N. Freedman, 1989. *Amos*. AB 24A. New York: Doubleday.
Andrae, W. 1913. *Die Stelenreihen in Assur.* WVDOG 24. Leipzig: Nedruck der Ausgabe.
Annus, A. 2002. *The God Ninurta in the Mythology and Royal Ideology of Ancient Mesopotamia.* SAAS 14. Helsinki: Neo-Assyrian Text Corpus Project.
Anthony, D. 1997. Prehistoric Migration as Social Process. Pages 21–32 in *Migrations and Invasions in Archaeological Explanation.* Edited by J. Chapman and H. Hamerow. BARI 664. Oxford: Oxford University Press.
Arav, R. 1995a. Bethsaida Excavations: Preliminary Report, 1987–1993. Pages 3–63 in Arav and Freund 1995.
———. 1995b. Bethsaida, Tzer, and the Fortified Cities of Naphtali. Pages 193–201 in Arav and Freund 1995.
———. 1999. Bethsaida Excavation: Preliminary Report, 1994–1996. Pages 3–113 in Arav and Freund 1999.
———. 2004. Toward a Comprehensive History of Geshur. Pages 1–48 in Arav and Freund 2004.
———. 2008. Bethsaida (et-Tell). Pages 1611–16 in vol. 5 of *The New Encyclopedia of Archaeological Excavations in the Holy Land.* Edited by E. Stern. Jerusalem: Israel Exploration Society; Carta.
———. 2009. Final Report on Area A, Stratum V: The City Gate. Pages 1–122 in Arav and Freund 2009.
———. 2013. Geshur: The Southwesternmost Aramean Kingdom. Pages 1–29 in Berlejung and Streck 2013.
Arav, R., and R. A. Freund, eds. 1995. *Bethsaida: A City by the Northern Shore of the Sea of Galilee.* Vol. 1. Kirksville, MO: Truman State University Press.
———, eds. 1999. *Bethsaida: A City by the Northern Shore of the Sea of Galilee.* Vol. 2. Kirksville, MO: Truman State University Press.
———, eds. 2004. *Bethsaida: A City by the Northern Shore of the Sea of Galilee.* Vol. 3. Kirksville, MO: Truman State University Press.
———, eds. 2009. *Bethsaida: A City by the Northern Shore of the Sea of Galilee.* Vol. 4. Kirksville, MO: Truman State University Press.
Arav, R., and J. Rousseau. 1993. Bethsäida ville perdue et retrouvée. *RB* 100:415–28.
Arbach, M. 2002. *Les noms propres du Corpus inscriptionum Semiticarum.* Part 4: *Inscriptiones himyariticas et sabæas continens.* Inventaire des inscriptions sudarabiques 7. Paris: de Boccard.
Arbeitman, Y., and G. Rendsburg. 1981. Adana Revised [*sic*: Revisited]: Thirty Years Later. *ArOr* 49:145–57.

Archi, A. 1998. A Biconvex Seal from Tell Afis. Pages 367–69 in Cecchini and Mazzoni 1998.

Archi, A., P. E. Pecorella, and M. Salvini. 1971. *Gaziantep e la sua regione: Uno studio storico e topografico degli insediamenti preclassici*. Incunabula Graeca 48. Rome: Edizioni dell'Ateneo.

Archi, A., and F. Venturi. 2012. Hittites at Tell Afis (Syria). *Or* 81:1–55, pls. I–X.

Arie, E. 2008. Reconsidering the Iron Age II Strata at Tel Dan: Archaeological and Historical Implications. *TA* 35:6–64.

Arnaud, D. 1985–86. *Recherches au pays d'Aštata, Emar 6: Textes sumériens et akkadiens*. 3 vols. Paris: Édition Recherche sur les civilisations.

———. 1987. Les Hittites sur le Moyen Euphrate: Protecteurs et indigènes. *Hethitica* 8:9–27.

———. 1993. Lettre de Beya. Pages 248–49 in *Syrie: Mémoire d'une civilization*. Edited by M. Fortin. Institut du Monde Arabe Exhibition Catalogue 222. Paris: Institut du Monde Arabe.

———. 1999. Prolégomènes à la rédaction d'une histoire d'Ougarit II: Les bordereaux de rois divinisés. *SMEA* 41.2:153–73.

Arnold, B. T. 2004. *Who Were the Babylonians?* ABS 10. Atlanta: Society of Biblical Literature.

———. 2011. Aramean Origins: The Evidence from Babylonia. *AfO* 52:179–85.

Aro, S. 2003. Art and Architecture. Pages 281–337 in Melchert 2003.

———. 2010. Luwians in Aleppo? Pages 1–9 in Singer 2010.

———. 2013. Carchemish before and after 1200 BC. Pages 233–76 in *Luwian Identities: Culture, Language and Religion between Anatolia and the Aegean*. Edited by A. Mouton, I. Rutherford, and I. Yakubovich. Leiden: Brill.

Astour, M. C. 1963. Place-Names from the Kingdom of Alalaḫ in the North Syrian List of Thutmose III: A Study in Historical Topography. *JNES* 22:220–41.

———. 1969. The Partition of the Confederacy of Mukiš-Nuḫašše-Nii by Šuppiluliuma: A Study in Political Geography of the Amarna Age. *Or* 38:381–414.

———. 1971. 841 B.C.: The First Assyrian Invasion of Israel. *JAOS* 91:383–89.

———. 1975. Place Names. Pages 249–369 in vol. 2 of *Ras Shamra Parallels: The Texts from Ugarit and the Hebrew Bible*. Edited by L. R. Fisher. AnOr 50. Rome: Pontifical Biblical Institute.

———. 1977a. Continuite et changement dans la toponymie de la Syrie du nord. Pages 117–41 in *La toponymie antique: Actes du Colloque de Strasbourg, 12–14 Juin 1975*. Edited by T. Fahd. Travaux du Centre de recherche sur le Proche-Orient et la Grèce antiques 4. Leiden: Brill.

———. 1977b. Tunip-Hamath and Its Region: A Contribution to the Historical Geography of Central Syria. *Or* 46:51–64.

———. 1981. Semites and Hurrians in Northern Transtigris. Pages 3–68 in *In Honor of Ernest R. Lacheman on His Seventy-Fifth Birthday, April 29, 1981*. Edited by M. A. Morrison and D. I. Owen. SCCNH 1. Winona Lake, IN: Eisenbrauns.

———. 1995. Overland Trade Routes in Ancient Western Asia. *CANE* 3:1401–20.

———. 1996. Who Was the King of the Hurrian Troops at the Siege of Emar? Pages 25–56 in *Emar: The History, Religion, and Culture of a Syrian Town in the Late Bronze Age*. Edited by M. W. Chavalas. Bethesda, MD: CDL.

Athas, G. 2003. *The Tel Dan Inscription: A Reappraisal and a New Interpretation.* JSOTSup 360. Sheffield: Sheffield Academic.
Aufrecht, W. F. 2001. A Legacy of Syria: The Aramaic Language. Pages 145–55 in Fortin 2001b.
Avigad, N. 1968. An Inscribed Bowl from Tel Dan. *PEQ* 100:42–44.
Avigad, N., and B. Sass. 1997. *Corpus of West Semitic Stamp Seals*. Jerusalem: Israel Academy of Sciences and Humanities.
Avishur, Y., and R. Deutsch, eds. 1999. *Michael: Historical, Epigraphical and Biblical Studies in Honor of Prof. Michael Heltzer*. Tel Aviv-Jaffa: Archaeological Center Publications.
Bachelot, L., and F. M. Fales, eds. 2005. *Tell Shiukh Fawqani 1994–1998*. 2 vols. History of the Ancient Near East, Monographs 6.2. Padova: SARGON.
Badre, L. 1997. Arwad. *OEANE* 1:218–19.
Bagg, A. M. 2000. *Assyrische Wasserbauten: Landwirtschaftliche Wasserbauten im Kernland Assyriens zwischen der 2. Hälfte des 2. und der 1. Hälfte des 1. Jahrtausends v. Chr.* Mainz: von Zabern.
———. 2007. *Die Levante*. Part 1 of *Die Orts und Gewässernamen der neuassyrischen Zeit*. RGTC 7.1. BTAVO B/7. Wiesbaden: Reichert.
———. 2011. *Die Assyrer und das Westland: Studien zur historischen und Geographie und Herrschaftspraxis in der Levante im 1. Jt. v.u. Z.* OLA 216. Leuven: Peeters.
———. 2013. Palestine under Assyrian Rule: A New Look at the Assyrian Imperial Policy in the West. *JAOS* 133:119–44.
Baghdo, A. el-M. H., et al. 2009. *Vorberichte über die erste und zweite syrisch-deutsche Grabungskampagne auf dem Tell Halaf.* Ausgrabungen auf dem Tell Halaf in Nordost-Syrien 1. Vorderasiatische Forschungen Der Max Freiherr von Oppenheim-Stiftung 4. Wiesbaden: Harrassowitz.
Baker, H. D., et al. 1995. Kilise Tepe 1994: The Seventh Preliminary Report. *AnSt* 45:139–91.
Baker, H. D. 1999a. Bēl-iqīša. *PNA* 1.2:7.
———. 1999b. Bur-Rammān. *PNA* 1.2:354.
———. 1999c. Dunānu. *PNA* 1.2:388.
———. 2000a. Ḫadiānu. *PNA* 2.1:438.
———. 2000b. Katî. *PNA* 2.1:609.
———. 2000c. Ḫārānu. *PNA* 2.1:459.
———. 2000d. Mudadi. *PNA* 2.1:759.
———. 2000e. Ḫamatāiu, *PNA* 2.1:446.
———. 2000f. Kudurru. *PNA* 2.1:632–4.
———. 2000g. Inūrta-bēlu-uṣur. *PNA* 2.1:548.
———. 2001a. Mannu-kī-māt-Aššur. *PNA* 2.2:693–94.
———. 2001b. Māri'. *PNA* 2.2:737.
———. 2002a. Sangara. *PNA* 3.1:1088–89.
———. 2002b. Sapalulme. *PNA* 3.1:1091.
———. 2002c. Samuḫa-šar-ilāni, *PNA* 3.1:1085.
———. 2006–8. Šamšī-ilu. *RlA* 11:639–40.
———. 2011a. Šama'gunu, Samgunu. *PNA* 3.2:1187–88.
———. 2011b. Zāzâ, Zāzāia. *PNA* 3.2:1439–40.
Baker, H. D., and A. Berlejung. 2000. Kapara. *PNA* 2.1:604–5.

Baker, H. D., and A. Fuchs. 2000. Ḫūlāiu. *PNA* 2.1:476.

Baker, H. D., K. Kaniuth, and A. Otto, eds. 2012. *Stories of Long Ago: Festschrift für Michael D. Roaf.* AOAT 397. Münster: Ugarit Verlag.

Baker, H. D., and M. P. Streck. 2000. Idrūnu. *PNA* 2.1:507.

Baker, H. D., and G. Van Buylaere. 2000. Irḫulena. *PNA* 2.1:564.

Balkan, K. 1957. *Letter of King Anum-Hirbi of Mama to King Warshama of Kanish.* Turk Tarih Kurumu yayinlarindan 7. Ankara: Türk Tarih Kurumu Basimevi.

Balty, J., J. Ch. Balty, and M. Dewez. 1970. *Belgian Archaeological Research on a Site in Syria: Apamea on the Orontes.* Brussels: Ministry of Foreign Affairs and External Trade.

Bär, J. 1996. *Der assyrische Tribut und seine Darstellung: Eine Untersuchung zur imperialen Ideologie im neuassyrischen Reich.* AOAT 243. Neukirchen-Vluyn: Neukirchener Verlag.

Barjamovic, G. 2004. Civic Institutions and Self-Government in Southern Mesopotamia in the Mid-First Millennium. Pages 47–98 in Dercksen 2004.

Bar-Yosef, O., and A. Khazanov, eds. 1992. *Pastoralism in the Levant: Archaeological Materials in Anthropological Perspectives.* Monographs in World Archaeology 10. Madison, WI: Prehistory Press.

Barnett, R. D. 1963. Hamath and Nimrud. Shell Fragments from Hamath and the Provenance of the Nimrud Ivories. *Iraq* 25:81–85.

———. 1967. Layard's Nimrud Bronzes and Their Inscriptions. Pages 1*–7* in *E. L. Sukenik Memorial Volume (1889–1953).* ErIsr 8. Jerusalem: Israel Exploration Society.

———. 1972. More Gates from Balawat: Preliminary Report. *Qad* 17:29–32.

———. 1973. More Balawat Gates: A Preliminary Report. Pages 19–22 in *Symbolae biblicae et Mesopotamicae: Francisco Mario Theodoro de Liagre Böhl dedicatae.* Edited by M. A. Beek. Leiden: Brill.

Barnett, R. D., E. Bleibtreu, and G. Turner. 1998. *Sculptures from the Southwest Palace of Sennacherib at Nineveh.* 2 vols. London: British Museum Press.

Barr, J. 1978. Some Notes on *Ben* 'Between' in Classical Hebrew. *JSS* 23:1–24.

Barthélemy, D. 1982. *Josué, Juges, Ruth, Samuel, Rois, Chroniques, Esdras, Néhémie, Esther.* Vol. 1 of *Critique textuelle de l'Ancien Testament.* OBO 50.1. Fribourg: Universitätsverlag; Göttingen: Vandenhoeck & Ruprecht.

Bartl, K. 1989. Zur Datierung der altmonochromen Ware vom Tall Halaf. Pages 257–74 in *To the Euphrates and Beyond: Archaeological Studies in Honour of Maurits N. van Loon.* Edited by O. M. C. Haex, H. H. Curvers, and P. M. M. G. Akkermans. Rotterdam: Balkema.

———. 1990. Soundings at Khirbet esh-Shenef, a Late Bronze Age Settlement in the Balikh Valley, Northern Syria. *Akkadica* 67:10–32.

———. 2001. Eastern Anatolia in the Early Iron Age. Pages 383–410 in Eichmann and Parzinger 2001.

Bartl, P. V. 2011. "Middle Assyrian Occupation at Tell Fekheriye." http://www.fecheriye.de/pdf/2010_C_MiddleAssyrian_report.pdf.

Barton, G. A. 1940. Danel: A Pre-Israelite Hero of Galilee. Pages 29–37 in *Mémorial Lagrange: Cinquantenaire de l'École biblique et archéologique française de Jérusalem.* Paris: Gabalda.

———. 1941. Danel, a Pre-Israelite Hero of Galilee. *JBL* 60:213–25.

Beal, R. H. 1992. *The Organisation of the Hittite Military*. Texte der Hethiter 20. Heidelberg: Winter.
Beaulieu, P.-A. 2006. Official and Vernacular Languages: The Shifting Sands of Imperial and Cultural Identities in First-Millennium B.C. Mesopotamia. Pages 187–216 in Sanders 2006.
———. 2011–13. Sūḫi/u. *RlA* 13:639–40.
———. 2013. Arameans, Chaldeans, and Arabs in Cuneiform Sources from the Late Babylonian Period. Pages 31–55 in Berlejung and Streck 2013.
Becking, B. 1992. *The Fall of Samaria: An Historical and Archaeological Study*. SHANE 2. Leiden: Brill.
———. 2009. The Identity of Nabu-sharrussu-ukin, the Chamberlain: An Epigraphic Note on Jeremiah 39, 3. With an Appendix on the Nebu(!)sarsekim Tablet. *BN* 140:35–46.
Beckman, G. 1996. *Hittite Diplomatic Texts*. SBLWAW 7. Atlanta: Scholars Press.
Beek, M. A. 1950. Das Problem des aramäischen Stammvaters (Deut. XXVI 5). *OtSt* 8:193–212.
Bellino, C. 2008. The Stele of Tell Ashara: The Neo-Syrian Perspective. Pages 273–83 in vol. 1 of Córdoba et al. 2008.
Belmonte Marín, J. A. 2001. *Die Orts und Gewässernamen der Texte aus Syrien im 2. Jt. v. Chr.* RGTC 12.2. BTAVO B/7. Wiesbaden: Reichert.
Ben-Ami, D. 2012. The Early Iron Age II (Strata X–IX). Pages 52–153 in Ben-Tor, Ben-Ami, and Sandhaus 2012.
Ben-Ami, D., and N. Wazana. 2013. Enemy at the Gates: The Phenomenon of Fortifications in Israel Reexamined. *VT* 63:368–82.
Bendor, S. 1996. *The Social Structure of Ancient Israel: The Institution of the Family (Beit ʾAb) from the Settlement to the End of the Monarchy*. Jerusalem Biblical Studies 7. Jerusalem: Simor.
Ben-Tor, A. 2000. Hazor and the Chronology of Northern Israel: A Reply to Israel Finkelstein. *BASOR* 317:9–15.
Ben-Tor, A., D. Ben-Ami, and D. Sandhaus. 2012. *Hazor VI: The 1990–2009 Excavations, the Iron Age*. Jerusalem: Israel Exploration Society; Hebrew University of Jerusalem.
Benz, F. L. 1972. *Personal Names in the Phoenician and Punic Inscriptions*. StPohl 8. Rome: Biblical Institute Press.
Berlejung, A. 2013. Nachbarn, Verwandte, Feinde und Gefährten: Die "Aramäer" im Alten Testament. Pages 57–86 in Berlejung and Streck 2013.
———. 2014. Outlook: Aramaeans outside of Syria: 5. Palestine. Pages 339–65 in Niehr 2014.
Berlejung, A., and M. P. Streck, eds. 2013. *Arameans, Chaldeans, and Arabs in Babylonia and Palestine in the First Millennium B.C.* Leipziger Altorientalistische Studien 3. Wiesbaden: Harrassowitz.
Bernbeck, R. 2008. Sex/Gender/Power and Šammuramat: A View from the Syrian Steppe. Pages 351–69 in Bonatz, Czichon, and Janoscha Kreppner 2008.
Bernett, M., and O. Keel. 1998. *Mond, Stier und Kult am Stadttor: Die Stele von Beth-saida (et Tell)*. OBO 161. Fribourg: Universitätsverlag; Göttingen: Vanderhoeck & Ruprecht.

Beyer, W. 1986. *The Aramaic Language: Its Distribution and Subdivisions*. Translated by J. F. Healey. Göttingen: Vandenhoeck & Ruprecht.

Beyerle, St. 2009. Aram und Israel im 9./8. Jh. v. Chr. aus der Perspective der aramäischen und assyrischen Inschriften. Pages 47–76 in *Israel zwischen den Mächten: Festschrift für Stefan Timm zum 65. Geburtstag*. Edited by M. Pietsch and F. Hartenstein. AOAT 364. Münster: Ugarit-Verlag.

Bienkowski, P. 2009. "Tribalism" and "Segmentary Society" in Iron Age Transjordan. Pages 7–26 in *Studies on Iron Age Moab and Neighbouring Areas in Honour of Michele Daviau*. Edited by P. Bienkowski. ANESSup 29. Leuven: Peeters.

Bienkowski, P., C. Mee, and E. Slater, eds. 2005. *Writing and Ancient Near Eastern Society: Papers in Honour of Alan R. Millard*. LHBOTS 426. New York: T&T Clark.

Billerbeck, A., and F. Delitzsch. 1908. *Die Palasttore Salmanassars II. von Balawat Erklärung ihrer Bilder und Inschriften*. Beiträge zur Assyriologie und semitischen Sprachwissenschaft 6.1. Leipzig: Hinrichs.

Bin-Nun, S. 1968. Formulas from Royal Records of Israel and Judah. *VT* 18:414–32.

Biran, A., and J. Naveh. 1993. An Aramaic Stele Fragment from Tel Dan. *IEJ* 43:81–98.

———. 1995. The Tel Dan Inscription: A New Fragment. *IEJ* 45:1–18.

Black, J., and A. Green. 1992. *Gods, Demons and Symbols of Ancient Mesopotamia: An Illustrated Dictionary*. Austin: University of Texas.

Blazhek, V. 2005. Hic Erant Leones: Indo-European "Lion" et alii. *Journal of Indo-European Studies* 33:63.

Bloch, Y. 2008. The Order of Eponyms in the Reign of Shalmaneser I. *UF* 40:143–78.

———. 2010a. The Order of Eponyms in the Reign of Tukultī-Ninurta I. *Or* 79:1–35.

———. 2010b. The Period of Activity of the Scribal Family of the Sons of Ninurta-uballissu in Aššur. *NABU* 2010.2:43–44, no. 36. http://sepoa.fr/wp/wp-content/uploads/2012/06/2010-2.pdf.

———. 2010c. Setting the Dates: Re-evaluation of the Chronology of Babylonia in the Fourteenth–Eleventh Centuries B.C.E. and Its Implications for the Reigns of Ramesses II and Ḫattušili III. *UF* 41:41–95.

———. 2010d. Solving the Problems of the Assyrian King List: Toward a Precise Reconstruction of the Middle Assyrian Chronology. *Journal of Ancient Civilizations* 25:21–87.

———. 2012a. Assyro-Babylonian Conflicts in the Reign of Aššur-rēša-iši I: The Contribution of Administrative Documents to History-Writing. Pages 53–78 in Galil et al. 2012.

———. 2012b. Middle Assyrian Lunar Calendar and Chronology. Pages 19–61 in *Living the Lunar Calendar*. Edited by J. Ben-Dov, W. Horowitz, and J. Steele. Oxford; Oakville, CT: Oxbow.

Blocher, F. 2001. Assyrische Würdenträger und Gouverneure des 9. und 8. Jh.: Eine Neubewertung ihrer Rolle. *AoF* 28:298–324.

Block, D. I. 2005. What Has Delphi to Do with Samaria? Ambiguity and Delusion in Israelite Prophecy. Pages 189–216 in Bienkowski, Mee, and Slater 2005.

Blum, H., and B. Faist. 2002. *Brückenland Anatolien? Ursachen, Extensität und Modi des Kulturasutausches zwischen Anatolien und seinen Nachbarn*. Tübingen: Attempto.

Bonacossi, D. M. 2007. Qatna and Its Hinterland during the Bronze and Iron Ages: A Preliminary Reconstruction of Urbanism and Settlement in the Mishrifeh Region. Pages 65–91 in *Urban and Naural Landscapes of an Ancient Syrian Capital: Settlement and Environment at Tell Mishrifeh/Qatna and in Central-Western Syria*. Edited by D. M. Bonacossi. Studi Archaeologici su Qatna 1. Udinese: Forum Editrice Universitaria.

Bonatz, D. 1993. Some Considerations on the Material Culture of Coastal Syria in the Iron Age. *EVO* 16:123–57.

———. 2000a. *Das syrohethitische Grabdenkmal: Untersuchungen zur Entstehung einer neuen Bildgattung in der Eisenzeit im nordsyrischsüdostanatolischen Raum*. Mainz: von Zabern.

———. 2000b. Syro-Hittite Funerary Monuments: A Phenomenon of Tradition or Innovation? Pages 189–210 in Bunnens 2000c.

———. 2014. Katumuwa's Banquet Scene. Pages 39–44 in Herrmann and Schloen 2014.

Bonatz, D., P. Bartl, A. Gilibert, and C. Jauss. 2008. Bericht über die erste und zweite Grabungskampagne in Tell Feḫerīye 2006 und 2007. *MDOG* 140:89–135.

Bonatz, A. D., R. M. Czichon, and F. Janoscha Kreppner, eds. 2008. *Fundstellen: Gesammelte Schriften zur Archäologie und Geschichte Altvorderasiens ad honorem Hartmut Kühne*. Wiesbaden: Harrassowitz.

Bonechi, M. 1993. *I nomi geografici dei testi di Ebla*. RGTC 12.1. Wiesbaden: Reichert.

Bonnet, C., and H. Niehr. 2010. *Religionen in der Umwelt des Alten Testaments* II. *Phönizier, Punier, Aramäer*. Kohlhammer Studienbücher Theologie 4.2. Stuttgart: W. Kohlhammer.

Bordreuil, P. 1983. Poids inscrit de Hamat représentant un sphinx. Pages 219–300 in *Au pays de Baal et d'Astarté: 10.000 ans d'art en Syrie*. Paris: Ministère des relations extérieures, Association française d'action artistique.

———. 1986. *Catalogue des sceaux ouest-sémitiques inscrits de la Bibliothèque Nationale, du Musée du Louvre, et du Musée biblique de Bible et Terre Sainte*. Paris: Bibliothèque Nationale.

———. 1993a. Le répertoire iconographique des sceaux araméens inscrits et son évolution. Pages 74–100 in *Studies in the Iconography of Northwest Semitic Inscribed Seals: Proceedings of a Symposium Held in Fribourg on April 17–20, 1991*. Edited by B. Sass and Ch. Uehlinger. OBO 125. Fribourg: Universitätsverlag; Göttingen: Vandenhoeck & Ruprecht.

———. 1993b. Les royaumes araméens de Syrie. Pages 250–57 in Cluzan, Delpont, and Mouliérac 1993.

———. 1993c. Poids Syriens. Pages 266–67 in Cluzan, Delpont, and Mouliérac 1993.

———. 1998. Amos 1:5. La Beqaʿ septentrional de l'Eden au Paradis. *Syria* 75:55–59.

———. 2012. Encore HADADYISAʿY! Pages 87–94 in Lanfranchi et al. 2012.

———. 2013. Ḥamat la Grande. *Semitica et Classica* 6:285–90.

Bordreuil, P. and D. Pardee. 1993. Le combat de Baʿlu aves Yammu d'après les textes ougraitiques. *MARI* 7:63–70.

Borger, R. 1967. *Die Inschriften Asarhaddons, Königs von Assyrien*. AfO 9. Osnabrück: Biblio-Verlag.
———. 1979. *Babylonisch-assyrische Lesestücke*. 2nd ed. AnOr 54. Rome: Pontifical Biblical Institute.
———. 1984. Aus der Monolith-Inschrift Salmanassars III. *TUAT* 1.4:361.
———. 1996. *Beiträge zum Inschriftenwerk Assurbanipals. Die Prismenklassen A, B, C = K, D, E, F, G, H, J und T sowie andere Inschriften*. Wiesbaden: Harrassowitz.
Börker-Klähn, J. 1982. *Altvorderasiatische Bildstelen und vergleichbare Felsreliefs*. BaF 4. Mainz: von Zabern.
Bossert, H. Th. 1951–53. Zu dn Tafeln V–XVI. *Jahrbuch für kleinasiatische Forschung* 2:106–12 and pls. V–XVI.
———. 1958. Neues von Zencirli und Maraş. *Or* 27:399–406, pl. LVII, figs. 1–4.
Botha, P. J. 1996. The Textual Strategy and Intent of the BarRakib Inscription. *Journal for Semitics* 8:1–11.
Botta, P. E., and M. E. Flandin. 1849–50. *Monument de Ninive*. 5 vol. Paris: Imprimerie Nationale.
Bounni, A., E., and J. Lagarce, and N. Saliby. 1976. Rapport préliminaire sur la première campagne de fouilles (1975) à Ibn Hani (Syrie). *Syria* 55:233–79.
———. 1978. Rapport préliminaire sur la deuxième campagne de fouilles (1976) à Ibn Hani (Syrie). *Syria* 56:218–91.
———. 1979. Rapport préliminaire sur la troisième campagne de fouilles (1977) à Ibn Hani (Syrie). *Syria* 57:217–91.
Bounni, A., and M. al-Maqdissi. 1992. Tell Sianu: Un nouveau chantier syrien. Pages 129–40 in *Studies in Honour of Vassos Karageorghis*. Edited by G. C. Ioannidès. Nicosia: Society of Cypriot Studies.
Braun-Holzinger, E. A., and H. Matthäus, eds. 2002. *Die nahöstlichen Kulturen und Griechenland an der Wende vom 2. zum 1. Jahrtausend v. Chr.: Kontinuität und Wandel von Strukturen und Mechanismen kultureller Interaktion*. Möhnesee: Bibliopolis.
Breasted, J. H., ed. and trans. 1906–7. *Ancient Records of Egypt: Historical Documents from the Earliest Times to the Persian Conquest*. 5 vols. Chicago: University of Chicago Press.
Brew, G., J. Best, M. Barazangi, and T. Sawaf. 2003. Tectonic Evolution of the NE Palmyride Mountain Belt, Syria: The Bishri Crustal Block. *Journal of the Geological Society* 160:677–85.
Brichto, H. C. 1973. Kin, Cult, Land, and Afterlife: A Biblical Complex. *HUCA* 44:1–54.
Bright, J. 1981. *A History of Israel*. 3rd ed. Philadelphia: Westminster.
Brinkman, J. A. 1964. Merodach-Baladan II. Pages 6–53 in *Studies Presented to A. Leo Oppenheim, June 7, 1964*. Edited by R. D. Biggs and J. A. Brinkman. Chicago: Oriental Institute of the University of Chicago.
———. 1968. *A Political History of Post-Kassite Babylonia, 1158–722 B.C.* AnOr 43. Rome: Pontifical Biblical Institute.
———. 1977. Appendix: Mesopotamian Chronology of the Historical Period. Pages 335–48 in A. L. Oppenheim, *Ancient Mesopotamia. Portrait of a Dead Civilization*. Chicago: University of Chicago Press.

———. 1984. *Prelude to Empire: Babylonian Society and Politics, 747–626 B.C.* Occasional Publications of the Babylonian Fund 7. Philadelphia: University Museum.

———. 1987–90a. Marduk-nādin-aḫḫē. 7:377.

———. 1987–90b. Marduk-šāpik-zēri. *RlA* 7:378.

———. 1989. A Legal Text from the Reign of Erība-Marduk (c. 775 B.C.). Pages 37–47 in *DUMU-E$_2$-DUB-BA-A: Studies in Honor of Åke W. Sjöberg*. Edited by H. Behrens, D. Loding, and M. T. Roth. Occasional Publications of the Samuel Noah Kramer Fund 11. Philadelphia: Samuel Noah Kramer Fund, University Museum.

———. 1997. Unfolding the Drama of the Assyrian Empire. Pages 1–16 in Parpola and Whiting 1997.

———. 1998a. Abi-salamu or Abī-Salāmu. *PNA* 1.1:14.

———. 1998b. Aḫi-iababa. *PNA* 1.1:63.

———. 1998c. Amēl-Bēl. *PNA* 1.1:100.

———. 1998d. Azi-il. *PNA* 1.1:239.

———. 1999. Būr-Sagalê. *PNA* 1.2:355.

———. 2001a. Muqquru. *PNA* 2.2:770.

———. 2001b. Nūr-Adad. *PNA* 2.2:967.

———. 2001c. Nabû-apla-iddina. *PNA* 2.2:804–5.

———. 2004. Administration and Society in Kassite Babylonia. *JAOS* 124:283–304.

Brinkman, J. A., and D. Schwemer. 1999. Iāū(a) (Jehu). *PNA* 2.1:496–97.

British Museum. 1904. *Cuneiform Texts from Babylonian Tablets in the British Museum*. CT 18. London: Trustees of the British Museum.

Briquel-Chatonnet, F. 1992. *Les relations entre les cités de la côte phénicienne et les royaumes d'Israël et de Juda*. OLA 46. Leuven: Peeters.

———. 2004. *Les Araméens et les premiers Arabes: Des royaumes araméens du IX$^e$ siècle à la chute du royaume nabatéen*. Encyclopédie de la Méditerranée, Série Histoire. Aix-en-Provence: Édisud.

Bron, F., and A. Lemaire. 1989. Les inscriptions araméennes de Hazaël. *RA* 83:35–44.

———. 1991. Poids inscrits phénico-araméens du VIII$^e$ siècle av. J.-C. Pages 763–70 in vol. 3 of *Atti del II Congresso internazionale di studi fenici e punici: Roma, 9–14 novembre 1987*. Edited by E. Acquaro. Collezione di studi fenici 30. 3 vols. Rome: Consiglio nazionale delle ricerche.

Brown, B. A. 2008. The Kilamuwa Relief: Ethnicity, Class and Power in Iron Age North Syria. Pages 339–55 in vol. 1 of Córdoba et al.

———. 2013. The Structure and Decline of the Middle Assyrian State: The Role of Autonomous and Nonstate Actors. *JCS* 65:97–126.

Brown, D. R. 1999. Ēnī-il. *PNA* 1.2:397.

Brugnatelli, V. 1991. The "Feminine" Plurals in Old Aramaic: New Light from Tell Fekherye. Pages 167–84 in *Cushitic, Egyptian, Omotic, Semitic*. Vol. 2 of *Proceedings of the Fifth International Hamito-semitic Congress*. Edited by H. G. Mukarovsky. Veröffentlichungen der Institute für Afrikanistik und Ägyptologie der Universität Wien 57. Beiträge zur Afrikanistik 41. Vienna: Afro-Pub.

Bryce, T. R. 2003. History. Pages 27–127 in Melchert 2003.

———. 2005. *The Kingdom of the Hittites*. 2nd ed. Oxford: Oxford University Press.

———. 2012. *The World of the Neo-Hittite Kingdoms: A Political and Military History*. Oxford: Oxford University Press.

Buccellati, G. 1990a. "River Bank," "High Country," and "Pasture Land": The Growth of Nomadism on the Middle Euphrates and the Khabur. Pages 87–118 in *Tall al-Ḥamīdīya 2: Symposion; Recent Excavations in the Upper Khabur Region*. Edited by S. Eichler, M. Wäfler, and D. Warburton. OBO Series Archaeologica 6. Fribourg: Universitätsverlag; Göttingen: Vandenhoeck & Ruprecht.

———. 1990b. From Khana to Laqê: The End of Syro-Mesopotamia. Pages 229–53 in *De la Babylonie à la Syrie, en passant par Mari: Mélanges offerts à Monseur J.-R. Kupper à l'occasion de son 70e anniversaire*. Edited by Ö. Tunca. Liège: Université de Liège.

———. 1992. Ebla and the Amorites. Pages 83–104 in vol. 3 of *Eblaitica: Essays on the Ebla Archives and the Eblaite Language*. Edited by C. H. Gordon and G. A. Rendsburg. Winona Lake, IN: Eisenbrauns.

Bulakh, M. 2012. Review of Gzella and Folmer 2008. *Babel und Bibel* 6:545–64.

Bunnens, G. 1989. Tell Ahmar on the Euphrates: A New Research Project of the University of Melbourne. *Akkadica* 63:1–11.

———. 1990. *Tell Ahmar 1988 Season*. AbrNSup 2. Leuven: Peeters.

———. 1992. Melbourne University Excavations at Tell Ahmar on the Euphrates: Short Report on the 1989–1992 Seasons. *Akkadica* 79–80:1–13.

———. 1993. Tell Ahmar–Til Barsip. Pages 219–22 in *L'Eufrate e il tempo*. Edited by O. Rouault and M. G. Rouault. Milan: Electa.

———. 1993-94. Tall Ahmar/Til Barsip 1988–1992. *AfO* 40–41:221–25.

———. 1994. Ahmar. *AJA* 98:149–51.

———. 1995. Hittites and Aramaeans at Til Barsip: A Reappraisal. Pages 19–27 in van Lerberghe and Schoors 1995.

———. 1996. Syro-Anatolian Influence on Neo-Assyrian Town Planning. Pages 113–28 in *Cultural Interaction in the Ancient Near East: Papers Read at a Symposium Held at the University of Melbourne, Department of Classics and Archaeology (29–30 September 1994)*. Edited by G. Bunnens. AbrNSup 5. Leuven: Peeters.

———. 1996–97. The Archaeological Context. *AbrN* 34:61–65.

———. 1997a. Carved Ivories from Til-Barsib. *AJA* 101:435–50.

———. 1997b. Til Barsib under Assyrian Domination. Pages 17–28 in Parpola and Whiting 1997.

———. 1999. Aramaeans, Hittites and Assyrians in the Upper Euphrates Valley. Pages 605–24 in Olmo Lete and Montero Fenollós 1999.

———. 2000a. Géographie historique de la région du barrage de Tishrin. Pages 299–308 in Rouault and Wäfler 2000.

———. 2000b. Syria in the Iron Age. Pages 3–19 in Bunnens 2000c.

———, ed. 2000c. *Essays on Syria in the Iron Age*. ANESSup 7. Leuven: Peeters.

———. 2001. Tell Ahmar/Til Barsip, the Eleventh, Twelfth and Thirteenth Seasons (1988–2000). *Orient-Express* 65–68.

———. 2004. The Storm-God in Northern Syria and Southern Anatolia from Hadad of Aleppo to Jupiter Dolichenus. Pages 57–81 in Hutter and Hutter-Braunsar 2004.

———. 2006. *A New Luwian Stele and the Cult of the Storm-God at Til Barsib-Masuwari*. Tel Ahmar 2. Publications de la Mission archéologique de l'Université de Liège en Syrie. Leuven: Peeters.

———. 2009. Assyrian Empire Building and Aramization of Culture as seen from Tell Ahmar/Til Barsib. *Syria* 86:67–82.

———. 2013. Looking for Luwians, Aramaeans and Assyrians in the Tell Ahmar Stratigraphy. Pages 177–98 in *Syrian Archaeology in Perspective: Celebrating Twenty Years of Excavations at Tell Afis; Proceedings of the International Meeting Percorsi di Archeologia Siriana, giornate di studio, Pisa, 27–28 Novembre 2006*. Edited by S. Mazzoni and S. Soldi. Ricerche di archeologia del Vicino Oriente 4. Pisa: ETS.

———. 2014–16. Til-Barsib. B. Archäologisch. *RlA* 14:38–42.

———. 2015. On Upper and Lower Aram Again. *UF* 46:39–48.

Burney, C. F. 1903. *Notes on the Hebrew Text of the Books of Kings, with an Introduction and Appendix*. Oxford: Clarendon.

Burns, R. 2007. *Damascus: A History*. London Routledge.

Cancik, H. 2002. "Das ganze Land Ḥet": "Hethiter" und die luwischen Staaten der Bibel. Pages 30–33 in *Die Hethiter und ihr Reich: Das volk der 1000 Götter*. Edited by W. Jacob. Bonn: Kunst- und Ausstellungshalle der Bundesrepublik Deutschland.

Cancik-Kirschbaum, E. C. 1996. *Die mittelassyrischen Briefe aus Tall Šēḫ Ḥamad*. BATSH 4.1. Berlin: Reimer.

Cancik-Kirschbaum, E. C., N. M. Brisch, and J. Eidem, eds. 2014. *Constituent, Confederate, and Conquered Space: The Emergence of the Mittani State*. Topoi 17. Berlin: de Gruyter.

Cantineau, J. 1931. La stèle araméenne de Sefiré-Sourdjun. *RA* 28:167–78.

Capet, E. 2005. Les installations de la fin du Bronze récent et du début du Fer. Pages 379–407 in Bachelot and Fales 2005.

Caquot, A. 1962. L'onomastique religieuse. *Syria* 39:231–56.

Casana, J. 2009. Alalakh and the Archaeological Landscape of Mukish: The Political Geography and Population of a Late Bronze Age Kingdom. *BASOR* 353:7–37.

Casana, J., and J. T. Herrmann. 2010. Settlement History and Urban Planning at Zincirli Höyük, Southern Turkey. *Journal of Mediterranean Archaeology* 23:55–80.

Caubet, A. 1992. Reoccupation of the Syrian Coast after the Destruction of the "Crisis Years." Pages 123–31 in Ward and Joukowsky 1992.

———. 2002. Animals in Syro-Palestinian Art. Pages 211–34 in *A History of the Animal World in the Ancient Near East*. Edited by B. J. Collins. HdO 64. Leiden: Brill.

———. 2003. The Case of Ugarit and Carchemish: A Contrast. Pages 17–21 in Dever and Gitin 2003.

Cavigneaux, A., and B. Kh. Ismail. 1990. Die Statthalter von Suḫu und Mari im 8. Jh. v. Chr. *BaM* 21:343–57, 412–17.

Cavigneaux, A., and D. Beyer. 2006. Une orpheline d'Emar. Pages 497–503 in *Les espaces syro-mésopotamiens: Dimensions de l'expérience humaine au Proche-Orient ancien*. Edited by P. Butterlin, M. Lebeau, J.-Y. Monchambert, J. L. Montero Fenollos, and B. Müller. Subartu 17. Turnhout: Brepols.

Cecchini, S. M. 1998. Area G: The Iron I-III Levels; Architecture, Pottery and Finds. Pages 273–365 in Cecchini and Mazzoni 1998.

———. 2000a. Area G: Cronologia e presentazione. *EVO* 22–23:19–22.

———. 2000b. Un bâtiment mistérieux sur l'acropole de Tell Afis. Pages 199–204 in

*Proceedings of the First International Congress on the Archaeology of the Ancient Near East, Rome, May 18th–23rd 1998*. Edited by P. Matthiae et al. Rome: Università degli Studi di Roma "La Sapienza."

———. 2009. Les ivories de Arslan Tash. Pages 87–105 in *Syrian and Phoenician Ivories of the Early First Millennium BCE: Chronology, Regional Styles and Iconographic Repertories, Patterns or Inter-regional Distributions*. Edited by S. M. Cecchini, S. Mazzoni, and E. Sciglizzo. Acts of the International Workshop, Pisa, December 9–11, 2004. Pisa: Edizioni ETS.

———. 2013. La stele di Melqart. Pages 275–83 in *Fenícios e Púnicos por terra e mar: Actas do VI Congresso Internacional de Estudos Fenícios e Púnicos, Lisboa 2005*. Edited by A. M. Arruda. Lisboa: Centro de Arqueologia da Universidade de Lisboa.

Cecchini, S., and S. Mazzoni, eds. 1998. *Tell Afis (Siria): Scavi sull'acropoli 1988–1992; The 1988–1992 Excavations on the Acropolis*. Pisa: Edizioni ETS.

Chapman, J. 1997. The Impact of Modern Invasion and Migrations on Archaeological Explantions. Pages 11–20 in *Migrations and Invasions in Archaeological Explanation*. Edited by J. Chapman and H. Hamerow. BARI 664. Oxford: Oxford University Press.

Chapman, J., and H. Hamerow. 1997. Introduction: On the Move Again—Migrations and Invasions in Archaeological Explanation. Pages 1–10 in *Migrations and Invasions in Archaeological Explanation*. Edited by J. Chapman and H. Hamerow. BARI 664. Oxford: Oxford University Press.

Charbonnet, A. 1986. Le dieu au lions d'Erétrie. *AION* 8:117–56.

Charpin, D. 1988. *Archives Épistolaires de Mari I/2*. ARM 26.2. Paris: Éditions Recherche sur les Civilisations.

———. 1992. De la vallée du Tigre au "triangle du Habur": Un engrenage géopolitique? Pages 98–103 in *Recherches en Haute Mésopotamie: Tell Mohammed Diyab campagnes 1990 et 1991*. Edited by J.-M. Durand. Mémoires de NABU 2. Paris: Société pour l'étude du Proche-Orient ancien.

———. 1998. Toponymie amorrite de toponymie biblique: La ville de Ṣîbat/Ṣobah. *RA* 92:79–92.

———. 2003a. "Ein umherziehende Aramäer war mein Vater": Abraham im Lichte der Quellen aus Mari. Pages 40–52 in *"Abraham unser Vater": Die gemeinsamen Wurzeln von Judentum, Christentum und Islam*. Edited by R. G. Kratz and T. Nagel. Göttingen: Wallstein.

———. 2003b. La "toponymie en mirroir" à l'époque amorrite. *RA* 97:3–34.

Charpin, D., and M. Durand. 1986. Fils de Sim'al. *RA* 80:141–83.

Charpin, D., and F. Joannès, eds. 1991. *Marchands, diplomates et empereurs: Études sur la civilisation mésopotamienne offertes à Paul Garelli*. Paris: Éditions Recherche sur les Civilisations.

———. 1992. *La circulation des biens, des personnes et des idées dans le proche-orient ancien: Actes de la 38e Rencontre Assyriologique Internationale, Paris, 8–10 juillet 1991*. Paris: Editions Recherche sur les civilisations.

Charpin, D., and N. Ziegler. 2003. *Mari et le Proche-Orient à l'époque amorrite: Essai d'histoire politique*. Mémoires de NABU 6. Florilegium marianum 5. Paris: SEPOA.

Chavalas, M. W. 1996. Terqa and the Kingdom of Khana. *BA* 59:90–103.

Chavalas, M. W., and K. L. Younger Jr., eds. 2002. *Mesopotamia and the Bible. Comparative Explorations*. JSOTSup 341; Sheffield: Sheffield Academic; Grand Rapids: Baker.
Cholidis, N. 2010. Obere Hälfte einer Männerstatue (Nr. 42). Pages 250–51 in Cholidis and Martin 2010.
Cholidis, N., and L. Martin. 2002. *Kopf hoch! Mut hoch! und Humor hoch! Der Tell Halaf und sein Ausgräber Max Freiherr von Oppenheim*. Vorderasiatisches Museum, Staatliche Museen zu Berlin. Mainz: von Zabern.
———, eds. 2010. *Tell Halaf: Im Krieg zerstörte Denkmaler und ihre Restaurierung*. Tell Halaf 5. Berlin: de Gruyter.
———. 2011. *Die geretteten Götter aus dem Palast vom Tell Halaf: Begleitbuch zur Sonderausstellung des Vorderasiatischen Museums "Die geretteten Götter aus dem Palast vom Tell Halaf" vom 28.1.–14.8.2011 im Pergamonmuseum*. Regensburg: Schnell & Steiner.
Cifola, B. 1997–98. Ashurnasirpal II's Ninth Campaign: Seizing the Grain Bowl of the Phoenician Cities. *AfO* 44–45:156–58.
Clancier, P. 2006. Le moyen Euphrate de l'implantion des Arameens à la periode romaine. Pages 247–89 in Kepinski, Lecomte and Tenu 2006b.
Clay, A. T. 1912a. Business Documents of Murashu Sons of Nippur Dated in the Reign of Darius II. PBS 2.1. Philadelphia: University Museum.
———. 1912b. *Documents from the Temple Archives of Nippur Dated in the Reigns of Cassite Rulers*. PBS 2.2. Philadelphia: University Museum.
———. 1919. *Neo-Babylonian Letters from Erech*. Yale Oriental Series. Babylonian Texts 3. New Haven: Yale University Press.
Clermont-Ganneau, C. 1897. Les stèles araméennes de Naîrab. *Études d'archéologie orientale* 2:182–223.
Clines, D. J. A. 1979. *The Theme of the Pentateuch*. 2nd ed. JSOTSup 10. Sheffield: JSOT Press.
Cluzan, S., E. Delpont, and J. Mouliérac, eds. 1993. *Syrie: Mémoire et civilisation*. Paris: Institut du monde arabe: Flammarion.
Cochavi-Rainey, Z. 2011. *The Akkadian Dialect of Egyptian Scribes in the Fourteenth and Thirteenth Centuries BCE*. AOAT 374. Münster: Ugarit-Verlag.
Cody, A. 1970. New Inscription from Tell āl-Rimah and King Jehoash of Israel. *CBQ* 32:325–40.
Cogan, M. 1984. From the Peak of Amanah. *IEJ* 34:255–59.
———. 2001. *1 Kings: A New Translation with Introduction and Commentary*. AB 10. New York: Doubleday.
Cogan, M., and I. Eph'al, eds. 1991. *Ah, Assyria ...: Studies in Assyrian History and Ancient Near Eastern Historiography Presented to Hayim Tadmor*. ScrHier 33. Jerusalem: Magnes.
Cogan, M. and H. Tadmor. 1988. *II Kings: A New Translation with Introduction and Commentary*. AB 11. Garden City, NY: Doubleday.
Cole, S. W. 1996a. *Nippur IV: The Early NeoBabylonian Governor's Archive from Nippur*. OIP 114. Chicago: Oriental Institute.
———. 1996b. *Nippur in Late Assyrian Times c. 755–612 BC*. SAAS 4. Helsinki: Neo-Assyrian Text Corpus Project.
———. 1998. Azri-Iāu. *PNA* 1.1:240.

Cole S. W., and H. Gasche. 1999. Levees, Floods, and the River Network of Northern Babylonia: 2000–1500 and 1000–500 BC—A Preliminary Report. Pages 87–110 in *Babylon: Focus mesopotamischer Geschichte, Wiege früher Gelehrsamkeit, Mythos in der Moderne; 2. Internationales Colloquium der Deutschen Orient-Gesellschaft 24.–26. März 1998 in Berlin*. Edited by J. Renger. Colloquien der Deutschen Orient-Gesellschaft 2. Saarbrücken: SDV.

———. 2007. Documentary and Other Archaeological and Environmental Evidence Bearing on the Identification and Location of the Rivers of Lower Khuzestan and the Position of the Head of the Persian Gulf ca. 1200 BC–200 AD. *Akkadica* 128:1–72.

Collins, B. J. 2007. *The Hittites and their World*. ABS 7. Atlanta: Society of Biblical Literature.

Comfort, A., C. Abadie-Reynal, and R. Ergeç. 2000. Crossing the Euphrates in Antiquity: Zeugma Seen from Space. *AnSt* 50:99–126.

Comfort, A., and R. Ergeç. 2001. Following the Euphrates in Antiquity: North–South Routes around Zeugma. *AnSt* 51:19–49.

Contenau, G. 1957. La cryptographie chez les Mésopotamiens. Pages 17–21 in *Mélanges bibliques, rédigés en l'honneur de André Robert*. Travaux de l'Institut catholique de Paris 4. Paris: Bloud & Gay.

Coogan, M. D. 1976. *West Semitic Personal Names in the Murašû Documents*. HSM 7. Missoula, MT: Scholars Press.

Cook, E. M. 1997. Aramaic Language and Literature. *OEANE* 1:178–84.

Cooke, G. A. 1903. *A Textbook of North-Semitic Inscriptions. Moabite, Hebrew, Phoenician, Aramaic, Nabataean, Palmyrene, Jewish*. Oxford: Clarendon.

Cooper, E. and M. Fortin. 2004. Tell ʿAcharneh in the Middle Orontes Valley and the Assyrian Presence in Syria. Pages 17–56 in Frame and Wilding 2004.

Coqueugniot, E. 1999. Tell Djaʿde el Mughara. Pages 41–55 in Olmo Lete and Montero Fenollós 1999.

Córdoba, J. M., M. Molist, M. C. Pérez, I. Rubio, and S. Martinez, eds. 2008. *Proceedings of the Fifth International Congress on the Archaeology of the Ancient Near East (ICAANE). Madrid, April 3–8 2006*. 3 vols. Madrid: Universidad Autónoma de Madrid, Centro Superior de Estudios sobre el Oriente Próximo y Egipto.

Cornwall, P. B. 1952. Two Letters from Dilmun. *JCS* 6:137–45.

Corral, M. A. 2002. *Ezekiel's Oracles against Tyre: Historical Reality and Motivations*. BibOr 46. Rome: Biblical Institute Press.

Courtois, J. C. 1973. Prospection archéologique dans la moyenne vallée de l'Oronte (El Ghab et Er Roudj—Syrie du nord-ouest). *Syria* 50:53–99.

Couturier, G. 2001. Quelques observations sur le *bytdwd* de la stèle araméenne de Tel Dan. Pages 72–98 in vol. 2 of Daviau, Wevers, and Weigl 2001.

Craig, J. A. 1887. *The Monolith Inscription of Salmaneser II (860–824 B.C.): Collated, Transcribed, Translated and Explained Together with Text, Transcription, Translation and Explanation of the Throne-Inscription of Salmaneser II*. New Haven: Tuttle, Morehouse & Taylor.

Creason, S. 2004. Aramaic. Pages 391–426 in Woodward 2004.

Cribb, R. 1991. *Nomads in Archaeology*. New Studies in Archaeology. Cambridge: Cambridge University Press.

Cross, F. M. 1972. The Stele Dedicated to Melcarth by Ben-Hadad of Damascus. *BASOR* 205:36–42.
———. 1995. Paleography and the Date of the Tell Fakhariyeh Bilingual Inscription. Pages 393–409 in Zevit, Gitin, and Sokoloff 1995.
———. 2003. The Stele Dedicated to Melqart by Ben-Hadad of Damascus. Pages 173–77 in *Leaves from an Epigrapher's Notebook: Collected Papers in Hebrew and West Semitic Palaeography and Epigraphy*. Winona Lake, IN: Eisenbrauns.
Curtis, J. E., and J. E. Reade, eds. 1995. *Art and Empire: Treasures from Assyria in the British Museum*. London: British Museum Press.
Curtis, J. E., and N. Tallis, eds. 2008. *The Balawat Gates of Ashurnasirpal II*. London: British Museum Press.
D'Agostino, A. 2008. Between Mitannians and MiddleAssyrians: Changes and Links in Ceramic Culture at Tell Barri and in Syrian Jazirah During the End of the Second Millennium BC. Pages 525–47 in vol. 1 of Córdoba et al.
———. 2009. The Assyrian-Aramaean Interaction in the Upper Khabur: The Archaeological Evidence from Tell Barri Iron Age Layers. *Syria* 86:14–41.
Dalley, S. M. 1985. Foreign Chariotry and Cavalry in the Armies of Tiglath-pileser III and Sargon II. *Iraq* 47:31–48.
———. 1990. Yahweh in Hamath in the Eighth Century BC: Cuneiform Material and Historical Deductions. *VT* 40:21–32.
———. 1996–97. Neo-Assyrian Tablets from Til Barsib. *AbrN* 34:66–99.
———. 2000. Shamshi-ilu, Language and Power in the Western Assyrian Empire. Pages 79–88 in Bunnens 2000c.
Dalley, S. M., and J. N. Postgate. 1984. *The Tablets from Fort Shalmaneser*. CTN 3. London: British School of Archaeology in Iraq.
Daniels, D. R. 1990. The Creed of Deuteronomy XXVI Revisited. Pages 231–42 in *Studies in the Pentateuch*. Edited by J. A. Emerton. VTSup 41. Leiden: Brill.
Dankwarth, G., and Ch. Müller. 1988. Zur altaramäischen "Altar"-Inschrift vom Tell Halaf. *AfO* 35:73–78.
Darga, A. Muhibbe. 1992. *Hitit sanati*. Akbank kültür ve sanat kitaplari 56. Istanbul: Akbank.
Dassow, E. von. 1999. On Writing the History of Southern Mesopotamia. *ZA* 89:227–46.
Daviau, P. M. M., J. W. Wevers, and M. Weigl, eds. 2001. *The World of the Aramaeans*. 3 vols. JSOTSup 324–326. Sheffield: Sheffield Academic.
Dbiyat, M. al-. 1995. *Homs et Hama en Syrie centrale: Concurrence urbaine et développement régional*. Damascus: Institut français de Damas.
De Martino, S. 2004. A Tentative Chronology of the Kingdom of Mittani from Its Rise to the Reign of Tušratta. Pages 35–42 in *Mesopotamian Dark Age Revisited: Proceedings of an International Conference of SCIEM 2000 (Vienna 8th–9th November 2002*. Edited by H. Hunger and R. Pruzsinsky. Vienna: Verlag der Österreichischen Akademie der Wissenschaften.
Dearman, J. A., and M. P. Graham, eds. 2001. *The Land That I Will Show You: Essays on the History and Archaeology of the Ancient Near East in Honor of J. Maxwell Miller*. JSOTSup 343. Sheffield: Sheffield Academic.
Degen, R. 1967–68. Zur Schreibung des Kaška-Namens in ägyptischen, ugaritischen

und altaramäischen Quellen: Kritische Anmerkungen zu einer Monographie über die Kaškäer. *WO* 4:48–60.

———. 1969. *Altaramäische Grammatik der Inschriften des 10.–8. Jh. v. Chr.* Abhandlungen für die Kunde des Morgenlandes 38.3. Wiesbaden: Steiner.

Delaporte, L. 1939. La troisième campagne de fouilles à Malatya. *RHA* 5:43–56.

———. 1940. *Malatya I: Fouilles de la mission archéologique française; Arslantepe, La Porte des Lions*. Mémoires de l'Institut français d'archéologie de Stanboul 5. Paris: de Boccard.

Delitzsch, F. 1885. Assyriologisches Notizen zum Alten Testament. I. Das Land Uz. *ZK* 2:87–98.

Deller, K. 1992. Neuassyrische Rituale für den Einsatz der Götterstreitwagen. *BaM* 23:341–46.

Deller, K., and A. R. Millard. 1985. Zwei Rechtsurkunden aus Aššur im British Museum. *AfO* 32:38–52.

Del Monte, G. F., and J. Tischler. 1978. *Die Orts- und Gewässernamen der hethitischen Texte*. RGTC 6. Wiesbaden: Harrassowitz.

Delpech, A. 1997. *Les norias de l'Oronte: Analyse technologique d'un élément du patrimoine syrien*. Damacus: Institut français de Damas.

Dercksen, J. G., ed. 2004. *Assyria and Beyond: Studies Presented to Mogens Trolle Larsen*. PIHANS 100. Leiden: Nederlands Instituut voor het Nabije Oosten.

Deshayes, J., M. Sznycer, and P. Garelli. 1981. Remarques sur les monuments de Karatepe. *RA* 75:31–60.

Desideri, P., and A. M. Jasink. 1990. *Cilicia, dall' età di Kizzuwatna alla conquista macedone*. Turin.

Deutsch, R., and M. Heltzer. 1995. *New Epigraphic Evidence from the Biblical Period*. Tel Aviv-Jaffa: Archaeological Center Publication.

Dever, W. G. 1986. Abel-Beth-Ma'acah: "Northern Gateway of Ancient Israel." Pages 207–22 in *The Archaeology of Jordan and Other Studies*. Edited by L. T. Geraty and L. G. Herr. Berrien Springs, MI: Andrews University Press.

———. 1992. The Late Bronze–Early Iron I Horizon in Syria-Palestine: Egyptians, Canaanites, "Sea Peoples," and ProtoIsraelites. Pages 99–110 in Ward and Joukowsky 1992.

Dever, W. G., and S. Gitin, eds. 2003. *Symbiosis, Symbolism, and the Power of the Past: Canaan, Ancient Israel, and Their Neighbors from the Late Bronze Age through Roman Palestina; Proceedings of the Centennial Symposium W. F. Albright Institute of Archaeological Research and American Schools of Oriental Research Jerusalem, May 29–31, 2000*. Winona Lake, IN: Eisenbrauns.

DeVries, S. J. 1978. *Prophet against Prophet. The Role of the Micaiah Narrative (1 Kings 22) in the Development of Early Prophetic Tradition*. Grand Rapids: Eerdmans.

———. 2003. *1 Kings*. 2nd ed. WBC 12. Nashville: Thomas Nelson.

D'Hont, O. 1994. *Vie quotidienne des 'Agedat: Techniques et occupation de l'espace sur le moyen Euphrate*. Publications de l'Institut français de Damas 147. Damas: Institut français de Damas.

Diakonoff, I. M. 1992. The Naval Power and Trade of Tyre. *IEJ* 42:168–93.

Dietrich, M. 1970. *Die Aramäer Südbabyloniens in der Sargonidenzeit (700–648)*. AOAT 7. Kevelaer: Butzon & Bercker; Neukirchen-Vluyn: Neukirchener Verlag.

———. 1979. *Neo-Babylonian Letters from the Kuyunjik Collection*. CT 54. London: British Museum.

———. 1990. Die akkadischen Texte der Archive und Bibliotheken von Emar. *UF* 22:33–35.

Dillard, R. 1987. *2 Chronicles*. WBC 15. Waco, TX: Word.

Dinçol, B. 1992. New Archaeological and Epigraphical Finds from Ivriz: A Preliminary Report. *TA* 21:117–28.

Dinçol, A., B. Dinçol, J. D. Hawkins, and H. Peker. 2012. A New Inscribed Stela from Karkemish: At the Origins of the Suhi-Katuwa Dynasty. *NEA* 75:145.

Dion, P.-E. 1974. *La langue de Ya'udi: Description et classement de l'ancien parler de Zenčirli dans le cadre des langues sémitiques du nord-ouest*. Waterloo, ON: La Corporation pour la Publication des Études Académiques en Religion au Canada.

———. 1995a. Aramaean Tribes and Nations of First-Millennium Western Asia. *CANE* 2:1281–94.

———. 1995b. Les Araméens du moyen-euphrate au VIIIe siècle à la lumière des inscriptions des maîtres de Suḫu et Mari. Pages 53–73 in *Congress Volume: Paris, 1992*. Edited by J. A. Emerton. VTSup 61. Leiden: Brill.

———. 1995c. The Syro-Mesopotamian Border in the VIIIth Century BC: The Aramaeans and the Establishment. *BCSMS* 30:5–10.

———. 1995d. Syro-Palestinian Resistance to Shalmaneser III in the Light of New Documents. *ZAW* 107:482–89.

———. 1997. *Les Araméens à l'âge du fer: Histoire politique et structures sociales*. EBib NS 34. Paris: Gabalda.

———. 1999. The Tel Dan Stele and Its Historical Significance. Pages 145–56 in Avishur and Deutsch 1999.

———. 2000. L'incursion d'Aššurnaṣirpal II au Luḫutu. *Or* 29:133–38.

———. 2001. Les langues utilisées en Syrie vers 800 av. J.-C. Pages 157–62 in Fortin 2001b.

———. 2002. Review of Lipiński 2000a. *BASOR* 327:55–61.

———. 2006. Tell ʿAšarneh in the Kingdom of Ḥamath. Pages 43–48 in Fortin 2006.

Donbaz, V., and S. Parpola. 2001. *Neo-Assyrian Legal Texts in Istanbul*. Studien zu den Assur-Texten 2. Saarbrücken: SDV, Saarbrücker Druckerei und Verlag.

Donner, H. 1970. Adadnirari III. und die Vasallen des Westens. Pages 49–59 in *Archäologie und Altes Testament: Festschrift für Kurt Galling zum 8. Jan. 1970*. Edited by A. Kuschke and E. Kutsch. Tübingen: Mohr Siebeck.

———. 1977. The Separate States of Israel and Judah. Pages 381–434 in *Israelite and Judean History*. Edited by J. H. Hayes and J. M. Miller. Philadelphia: Westminster.

Donner, H., and W. Röllig. 1968. *Kommentar*. Vol. 2 of *Kanaanäische und aramäische Inschriften*. 2nd ed. Wiesbaden: Harrassowitz.

Dornauer, A. A. 2010. Die Geschichte von Gūzāna im Lichte der schriftlichen Zeugnisse. Pages 47–66 in Cholidis and Martin 2010.

Dornemann, R. H. 1997a. Tell Qarqur. *AJA* 101:134–37.

———. 1997b. Qarqur, Tell. *OEANE* 4:370–71.

———. 2000. The Iron Age Remains at Tell Qarqur in the Orontes Valley. Pages 459–85 in Bunnens 2000c.

———. 2003. Seven Seasons of ASOR Excavations at Tell Qarqur, Syria, 1993–1999. Pages 1–141 in *Preliminary Excavation Reports and Other Archaeological Investigations: Tell Qarqur, Iron I Sites in the North-Central Highlands of Palestine*. Edited by N. L. LaPages AASOR 56. Boston: American Schools of Oriental Research.

———. 2012. The Qarqur Challenge: Middle Islamic through Iron Age. *NEA* 75:162–77.

Dossin, G. 1930. Une inscription cunéiforme de Haute Syrie. *RA* 27:85–91.

———. 1944. BRG'YH, roi de KTK. *Le Muséon* 57:147–55.

———. 1959. Les bedouins dans les textes de Mari. Pages 35–51 in *L'antica società Beduina*. Edited by F. Gabrieli and W. Dostal. Studi semitici 2. Rome: Centro di studi semitici, Instituto di studi orientali, Università.

———. 1967. *La correspondance féminine*. ARM 10. Paris: Geuthner.

Dothan, M. 1993. Ashdod. *NEAHL* 1:93–102.

Dougherty, R. P. 1920. *Records from Erech, Time of Nabonidus (555–538 B.C.)*. Yale Oriental Series. Babylonian Texts 6. New Haven: Yale University Press.

———. 1933. *Archives from Erech: Neo Babylonian and Persian Periods*. Goucher College Cuneiform Inscriptions 2. New Haven: Yale University Press.

Driel, G. van. 2001. On Villages. Pages 103–18 in *Veenhof Anniversary Volume: Studies Presented to Klaas R. Veenhof on the Occasion of His Sixty-Fifth Birthday*. Edited by W. H. Van Soldt, J. G. Dercksen, N. J. C. Kouwenberg, and Th. J. H. Krispijn. Uitgaven van het Nederlands Instituut voor het Nabije Oosten te Leiden 89. Leiden: Nederlands Instituut voor het Nabije Oosten.

———. 2005. Ethnicity, How to Cope with the Subject. Pages 1–10 in van Soldt, Kalvelagen, and Katz 2005.

Driver, S. R. 1902. *Deuteronomy*. ICC. Edinburgh: T&T Clark.

———. 1913. *Notes on the Hebrew Text and the Topography of the Books of Samuel, with an Introduction on Hebrew Palaeography and the Ancient Versions and Facsimiles of Inscriptions and Maps*. 2nd ed. Oxford: Clarendon,

Dubovský, P. 2006. Tiglath-pileser III's Campaigns in 734–732 B.C.: Historical Background of Isa 7, 2 K 15–16 and 2 Chr 27–28. *Bib* 87:153–70.

Duistermaat, K. 2008. *The Pots and Potters of Assyria: Technology and Organisation of Production, Ceramic Sequence and Vessel Function at Late Bronze Age Tell Sabi Abyad, Syria*. Papers on Archaeology of the Leiden Museum of Antiquities 4. Turnhout: Brepols.

Dupont-Sommer, A. 1949. *Les Araméens*. Paris: Maisonneuve.

———. 1950. Deux nouvelles inscriptions sémitiques trouvées en Cilicie. *Jahrbuch für Kleinasiatische Forschung* 1:43–47.

Dupont-Sommer, A., and J. Starcky. 1956. Une inscription araméenne inédite de Sfiré. *Bulletin du Musée de Beyrouth* 13:23–41, pls. I–VI.

———. 1958. *Les inscriptions araméennes de Sfiré (stèles I et II)*. Mémoires présentées par divers savants à l'Académie des inscriptions et belles-lettres 15. Paris: Imprimerie Nationale.

Durand, J.-M., and L. Marti. 2005. Chroniques du moyen-euphrate 5: Une attaque de Qaṭna par le Sûhum et la question du "pays de Mari." *RA* 99:123–32.

Durand, J.-M. 1989a. "Roi de Kiri" fantôme à Emar? *NABU* 1989.3:34–35, no. 53. http://sepoa.fr/wp/wp-content/uploads/2012/05/1989-3.pdf.

———. 1989b. Review of Arnaud 1985–86. *RA* 83:163–91.

———. 1992. Unité et diversités au Proche-Orient à l'époque amorrite. Pages 97–128 in Charpin and Joannès 1992.

———. 1998. *Documents épistolaries du palais de Mari.* Volume 2. LAPO 17. Paris: Cerf.

———. 2004. Peuplement et sociétés à l'époque amorrite: (I) Les clans Bensim'alites. Pages 111–97 in Gatier, Geyer, and Rousset 2010.

Duru, R. 2004. *Yesemek: The Largest Sculpture Workshop of the Ancient Near East.* Istanbul: Türsab.

Dussaud, R. 1922. Le temple de Jupiter damaseenien et ses transformations aux époques chrétienne et musulmane. *Syria* 3:219–50.

———. 1927. *Topographie historique de la Syrie antique et médiévale.* BAH 4. Paris: Librairie Orientaliste Paul Geuthner.

———. 1928. Torse de statuette de Sefiré. *Syria* 9:170–71.

Ebeling, E. 1928. Ahi-iababa. *RlA* 1:57.

Edel, E. 1966. *Die Ortsnamenlisten aus dem Totentempel Amenophis III.* BBB 25. Bonn: Hanstein.

———. 1983. Kleinasiatische und semitische Namen und Wörter aus den Texten der Qadešchlacht in hieroglyphischer Umschrift. Pages 90–105 in *Fontes atque Pontes: Festgabe Hellmut Brunner.* Edited by M. Görg. ÄAT 5. Wiesbaden: Harrassowitz.

Edel, E., and M. Görg. 2005. *Die Ortsnamenlisten im nördlichen Säulenhof des Totentempels Amenophis' III.* 2nd ed. ÄAT 50. Wiesbaden: Harrassowitz.

Edelman, D. 1984. Saul's Rescue of Jabesh-Gilead (I Sam 11 1–11): Sorting Story from History. *ZAW* 96:195–209.

Edenburg, C. 2010. David, the Great King, King of the Four Quarters: Structure and Signification in the Catalogue of David's Conquests (2 Samuel 8:1–4, 1 Chronicles 18:1–13). Pages 159–75 in *Raising Up a Faithful Exegete: Essays in Honor of Richard D. Nelson.* Edited by K. L. Noll and B. Schramm. Winona Lake, IN: Eisenbrauns.

Edgell, H. S. 2006. *Arabian Deserts: Nature, Origin, and Evolution.* Dordrecht: Springer.

Edzard, D. O. 1964. Mari und Aramäer? *ZA* 56:142–49.

———. 1970. Die Tontafeln von Kāmid el-Lōz. Pages 50–62 in *Kamid el-Loz—Kumidi: Schriftdokumente aus Kamid el-Loz.* Edited by D. O. Edzard, R. Hachmann, P. Maiberger, and G. Mansfeld. Bonn: Habelt.

———. 1976–80a. Jaši'an, Jas'an, Iši'an. *RlA* 5:268–69.

———. 1976–80b. Kaldu (Chaldäer). *RlA* 5:291–97.

———. 1987–90. Mamli. *RlA* 7:329.

Edzard, D. O., and G. Farber. 1974. *Die Orts- und Gewässernamen der Zeit der 3. Dynastie von Ur.* RGTC 2. Wiesbaden: Harrassowitz.

Effendi, H. R. A. 1854. *The Thistle and the Cedar of Lebanon.* 2nd ed. London: Madden.

Ehrlich, C. S. 1991. Coalition Politics in Eighth Century B.C.E. Palestine: The Philistines and the Syro-Ephraimite War. *ZDPV* 107:48–58.

———. 2001. The *bytdwd*-Inscriptions and Israelite Historiography: Taking Stock

after Half a Decade of Research. Pages 57–71 in vol. 2 of Daviau, Wevers, and Weigl 2001.
———. 2002. Die Suche nach Gat und die neuen Ausgrabungen auf Tell eṣ-Ṣāfī. Pages 56–69 in Hübner and Knauf 2002.
Eichler, S., et al. 1985. *Tall Al-Hamidiya 1, Vorbericht 1984*. OBO Series archaeologica 4. Fribourg: Universitätsverlag; Göttingen: Vandenhoeck & Ruprecht.
Eichmann, R., and H. Parzinger, eds. 2001. *Migration und Kulturtransfer: Der Wandel vorder- und zentralasiatischer Kulturen im Umbruch vom 2. zum 1. vorchristlichen Jahrtausend; Akten des Internationalen Kollquiums Berlin, 23. bis 26. November 1999*. Kolloquien zur Vor- und Frühgeschichte 6. Bonn: Habelt.
Eickelman, D. F. 2002. *The Middle East and Central Asia: An Anthropological Approach*. 4th ed. Upper Saddle River, NJ: Prentice Hall.
Eidem, J., and K. Pütt. 2001. Iron Age Sites on the Upper Euphrates. *AAAS* 44:83–96.
Einwag, B. 2000. Die West-Ǧazira in Der Eisenzeit. Pages 307–25 in Bunnens 2000c.
Eissfeldt, O. 1964. *Einleitung in das Alte Testament, unter Einschluss der Apokryphen und Pseudepigraphen sowie der apokryphen und pseudepigraphenartigen Qumran-Schriften; Entstehungsgeschichte des Alten Testaments*. 3rd ed. Tübingen, Mohr.
Elat, M. 1975. The Campaign of Shalmaneser III Against Aram and Israel. *IEJ* 25:25–35.
Elayi, J. 1984. Terminlogie de la Mer Méditerranée dans le annales assyriennes. *OrAnt* 23:75–93.
———. 1993. L'ordre de succession des derniers rois de Byblos. *Syria* 10:109–15.
Elgavish, D. 2000. Objective of Baasha's War against Asa. Pages 141–9 in Galil and Weinfeld 2000.
El-Hakim, M., and M. Bakalowicz. 2007. Significance and Origin of Very Large Regulating Power of Some Karst Aquifers in the Middle East: Implication on Karst Aquifer Classification. *Journal of Hydrology* 333.2-4:329–39.
Elitzur, Y. 2004. *Ancient Place Names in the Holy Land: Preservation and History*. Jerusalem: Magnes; Winona Lake, IN: Eisenbrauns.
———. 2012. Qīr of the Aramaeans: A New Approach [Hebrew]. *Shnaton* 21:141–52.
Elliger, K. 1947. Samʾal und Hamat in ihrem Verhältnis zu Hattina, Unqi und Arpad: Ein Beitrag zur Territorialgeschichte der nordsyrischen Staaten im 9. und 8. Jahrhundert v. Chr. Pages 69–108 in *Festschrift Otto Eissfeldt zum 60. Geburtstage 1. September 1947*. Edited by J. Fück. Halle an der Saale: Niemeyer.
Emerton, J. A. 1969. Some Linguistic and Historical Problems in Isaiah 8:23. *JSS* 14:151–75.
Ephʿal, I. 1976–80. Karawane C. *RlA* 5:421–22.
———. 1982. *The Ancient Arabs. Nomads on the Borders of the Fertile Crescent Ninth–Fifth Centuries B.C.* Jerusalem: Magnes.
Ephʿal, I., and J. Naveh. 1989. Hazael's Booty Inscriptions. *IEJ* 39:192–200.
Epstein, C. 1993. The Cities of the Land of Ga-ru Geshur Mentioned in EA 256 Reconsidered [Hebrew]. Pages 83–90 in *Studies in the Archaeology and History of Ancient Israel in Honor of Moshe Dothan*. Edited by M. Heltzer, A. Segal, and D. Kaufman. Haifa: Haifa University Press. English summary, 19*–20*.
Epstein, C., and S. Gutman. 1972. The Golan [Hebrew]. Pages 243–95 in *Judaea,*

*Samaria and the Golan: Archaeological Survey 1967–1968*. Edited by M. Kochavi. Jerusalem: Archaeological Survey of Israel.

Eshel, H. 1984. An Allusion to the War Asa–Baasha in a Prophecy to Ahaz [Hebrew]. *Shnaton* 7–8:250–53.

———. 1990. Isaiah viii 23: An Historical-Geographical Analogy. *VT* 40:104–9.

Eyre, Christopher J. 1995. The Agricultural Cycle, Farming, and Water Management in the Ancient Near East. *CANE* 1:175–89.

Fabbro, R. del. 2012. The Roads from and to Aleppo: Some Historical-geographical Considerations in Light of New Archaeological Data. Pages 201–22 in Lanfranchi et al. 2012.

Fabritius, K. 1999. Gindibu'. *PNA* 1.2:424.

Fadhil, A., and K. Radner. 1996. Äste, Gras und Esel: Ein neuassyrischer Privatbrief aus Nimrud im Iraq Museum. *BaM* 27:419–28.

Faist, B. I. 2001. *Der Fernhandel des assyrischen Reiches zwischen dem 14. und 11. Jh. v. Chr.* AOAT 265. Münster: Ugarit-Verlag.

———. 2006. Itineraries and Travellers in the Middle Assyrian Period. *SAAB* 15:147–60.

Fales, F. M. 1973. *Censimenti e catasti di epoca neoassira*. Studi economici e technologici 2. Rome: Centro per le antichità e la storia dell'arte del Vicino Oriente.

———. 1977. On Aramaic Onomastics in the Neo-Assyrian Period. *OrAnt* 16:41–68.

———. 1980. New Assyrian Letters from the Kuyunjik Collection. *AfO* 27:136–53.

———. 1986. *Aramaic Epigraphs on Clay Tablets of the Neo-Assyrian Period.* Studi Semitici NS 2. Rome: Università degli Studi "La Sapienza."

———. 1990. Istituzioni a confronto tra mondo semitico occidentale e Assiria nel I millennio a.C: Il trattato di Sefire. Pages 149–73 in *I trattati nel mondo antico: Forma, ideologia, funzione*. Edited by L. Canfora, M. Liverani, and C. Zaccagnini. Saggi di storia antica 2. Rome: L'Erma di Bretschneider.

———. 1991a. Notes on the Royal Family of Emar. Pages 81–90 in Charpin and Joannès 1991.

———. 1991b. West Semitic Names in the Assyrian Empire: Diffusion and Social Relevance. *SEL* 8:99–117.

———. 1992. Mari: an Additional Note on Raṣappu and Hatallu. *SAAB* 6:105–107.

———. 1996a. Most Ancient Aramaic Texts and Linguistics: A Review of Recent Studies. *Incontri Linguistici* 19:33–57.

———. 1996b. An Aramaic Tablet from Tell Shioukh Fawqani, Syria. *Sem* 46:81–121, pls. 9, 10.

———. 1998. Abdi-ilīm. *PNA* 1.1:5–6.

———. 1999. Bar-rakkūb. *PNA* 1.2:271.

———. 2000a. The Use and Function of Aramaic Tablets. Pages 89–124 in Bunnens 2000c.

———. 2000b. Preparing for War in Assyria. Pages 35–59 in *Économie antique: la guerre dans les économies antiques*. Edited by J. Andreau, P. Briant and R. Descat. Entretiens d'archéologie et d'histoire 5. Saint-Bertrand-de-Comminges: Musée archéologique départemental.

———. 2001. *L'impero assiro. Storia e amministrazione (IX–VII sec. a.C.)*. Rome: Laterza.

———. 2002a. The Djezireh in Neo-Assyrian Sources. Pages 181–99 in *The Syrian*

*Jezira. Cultural Heritage and Interrelations*. Edited by M. al-Maqdissi, et al. Damascus: République arabe syrienne, Ministère de la culture.

———. 2002b. Central Syria in the Letters to Sargon II. Pages 134–52 in Hübner and Knauf 2002.

———. 2003. Evidence for West–East Contacts in the 8th Century BC: the Bukan Stele. Pages 131–47 in Lanfranchi, Roaf, and Rollinger 2003.

———. 2005a. The Assyrian and Aramaic Texts from Tell Shiukh Fawqani. Pages 595–623, 650–667 in Bachelot and Fales 2005.

———. 2005b. Tiglat-Pileser III tra annalistica reale ed epistolografia quotidiana. Pages 163–91 in *Narrare gli eventi: atti del convegno degli egittologi e degli orientalisti italiani in margine alla mostra "La battaglia di Qadesh."* Edited by F. Pecchioli Daddi and M. C. Guidotti. Studia Asiana 3. Rome: Herder.

———. 2007a. Between Archaeology and Linguistics: the Use of Aramaic Writing in Painted Characters on Clay Tablets of the 7th Century BC. Pages 139–160 in *XII Incontro italiano di linguistica camito-semitica (afroasiatica)*. Edited by M. Moriggi. Medioevo romanzo e orientale. Colloqui 9. Soveria Mannelli: Rubbettino.

———. 2007b. Arameans and Chaldeans. Environment and Society. Pages 288–98 in *The Babylonian World*. Edited by G. Leick. New York and London: Routledge.

———. 2008a. Canals in the Neo-Assyrian Rural Landscape: A View from the Ḫābūr and Middle Euphrates. Pages 181–187 in *Umwelt und Subsistenz der Assyrischen Stadt Dūr-Katlimmu am Unteren Ḫābūr*. Edited by H. Kühne. Berichte der Ausgrabund Tell Šēḫ Ḥamad / Dūr-Katlimmu 8. Wiesbaden: Harrassowitz.

———. 2008b. On *Pax Assyriaca* in the Eighth–Seventh Centuries BCE and Its Implications. Pages 17–35 in *Isaiah's Vision of Peace in Biblical and Modern International Relations: Swords into Plowshares*. Edited by R. Cohen and R. Westbrook. New York: Palgrave Macmillan.

———. 2010a. New Light on Assyro-Aramaic Interference: The Assur Ostracon. Pages 189–204 in *Camsemud 2007. Proceedings of the 13th Italian Meeting of Afro-Asiatic Linguistics held in Udine, May 21st–24th, 2007*. Edited by F. M. Fales and G. F. Grassi. HANE 10. Padova: S.A.R.G.O.N.

———. 2010b. *Guerre et paix en Assyrie: religion et impérialisme*. Les conférences de l'École pratique des hautes études 2. Paris. Edition du Cerf.

———. 2011a. Die Ausbreitung Assyriens gegen Westen und seine fortschreitende Verwurzelung: Der Fall der nordwestlichen Jezira. Pages 211–37 in Renger 2011.

———. 2011b. Transition: the Assyrians at the Euphrates Between the 13th and the 12th Century BC. Pages 9–59 in *Empires after the empire: Anatolia, Syria and Assyria after Suppiluliuma II, ca. 1200/800–700 B.C.* Edited by K. Strobel. Eothen 17. Firenze: LoGisma.

———. 2011c. Old Aramaic. Pages 555–573 in *The Semitic Languages: An International Handbook*. Edited by S. Weninger, G. Khan, M. P. Streck, and J. C. E. Watson. Handbücher zur Sprach und Kommunikationswissenschaft 36. Berlin: de Gruyter Mouton.

———. 2011d. Moving around Babylon: On the Aramean and Chaldean Presence in Southern Mesopotamia. Pages 91–111 in *Babylon. Wissenkultur in Orient und*

*Okzident*. Edited by E. Cancik-Kirschbaum, M. van Ess, and J. Marzahn. Topoi. Berlin Studies of the Ancient World. Berlin: de Gruyter.
———. 2012a. "Ḫanigalbat" in Early Neo-Assyrian Royal Inscriptions. A Retrospective View. Pages 99–119 in Galil et al. 2012.
———. 2012b. The Eighth-Century Governors of Kalhu: A Reappraisal in Context. Pages 117–39 in Baker, Kaniuth and Otto 2012.
———. 2013. Ethnicity in the Assyrian Empire: A View from the *Nisbe*. (I): Foreigners and "Special" Inner Communities. Pages 47–73 in *Literature as Politics, Politics as Literature. Essays on the Ancient Near East in Honor of Peter Machinist*. Edited by D. S. Vanderhooft and A. Winitzer. Winona Lake, IN: Eisenbrauns.
———. 2014a. Hamlets and Farmsteads in the Balīḫ River Valley: The Middle Assyrian and the Neo-Assyrian Evidence. Pages 227–41 in *Settlement Dynamics and Human-Landscape Interaction in the Dry Steppes of Syria*. Edited by D. Morandi Bonacossi. Studia Chaburensia 4. Wiesbaden: Harrassowitz.
———. 2014–16a. Til-Abnâ. *RlA* 14:32–33.
———. 2014–16b. Til-Barsib. A. Philologisch. *RlA* 14:34–37.
———. 2014–16c. Til-Bašerê. *RlA* 14:42.
———. Forthcoming. Ethnicity in the Assyrian Empire: A View from the Nisbe, (III): "Arameans" and Related Tribalists. Pages 133–77 in *At the Dawn of History: Ancient Near Eastern Studies in Honour of J. N. Postgate*. Edited by Y. Heffron, A. N. Stone, and M. Worthington. Winona Lake, IN: Eisenbrauns.
Fales, F. M., and E. Attardo. 2005. Tablets in Aramaic Alphabetic Script. Pages 650–66 in Bachelot and Fales 2005.
Fales, F. M., and S. Mazzoni. 2009–11. Sefire. *RlA* 12:342–45.
Fales, F. M., and J. N. Postgate. 1995. *Imperial Administrative Records, Part II*. SAA 11. Helsinki: Helsinki University Press.
Fales, F. M., and K. Radner. 1998. Attār-šumkī. *PNA* 1.1:236.
Fassberg, S. 2007. Collective Nouns in Old Aramaic [Hebrew]. Pages 426–34 in *Rabbinic Hebrew and Aramaic*. Vol. 2 of *Sha'arei Lashon: Studies in Hebrew, Aramaic, and Jewish Languages in Honor of Moshe Bar-Asher*. Edited by A. Maman, S. E. Fassberg, and Y. Breuer. Jerusalem: Bialik Institute.
Faust, A., and J. Lev-Tov. 2011. The Constitution of Philistine Identity: Ethnic Dynamics in Twelfth to Tenth Century Philistia. *OJA* 30:13–31.
Feldman, M. H. 2014. *Communities of Style: Portable Luxury Arts, Identity, and Collective Memory in the Iron Age Levant*. Chicago: University of Chicago Press.
Fernández Marcos, N. 2001. On the Borderline of Translation Greek Lexicography: The Proper Names. *JNSL* 27:1–22.
Figulla, H. H. 1949. *Business Documents of the New Babylonian Period*. Ur Excavations, Texts 4. London: Trustees of the Two Museums.
Filippi, W. de. 1977. The Royal Inscriptions of Aššur-Nasir-Apli II (883–859 B.C.). *Assur* 1.7:123–69.
Fincke, A. 2001. *The Samuel Scroll from Qumran: 4QSam$^a$ Restored and Compared to the Septuagint and 4QSam$^c$*. Leiden: Brill.
Finkel, I. L., and J. E. Reade. 1998. Assyrian Eponyms, 873–649 BC. *Or* 67:248–54.
Finkelstein, I. 1999. Hazor and the North in the Iron Age: A Low Chronology Perspective. *BASOR* 314:55–70.
———. 2009. Destructions: Megiddo as a Case Study. Pages 113–26 in Schloen 2009.

———. 2013. *The Forgotten Kingdom: The Archaeology and History of Northern Israel*. ANEM 5. Atlanta: Society of Biblical Literature.
Finkelstein, I., and A. Mazar. 2007. *The Quest for the Historical Israel: Debating Archaeology and the History of Early Israel*. Edited by B. B. Schmidt. ABS 17. Atlanta: Society of Biblical Literature.
Finkelstein, I., and N. Na'aman, eds. 2011. *The Fire Signals of Lachish: Studies in the Archaeology and History of Israel in the Late Bronze Age, Iron Age, and Persian Period in Honor of David Ussishkin*. Winona Lake, IN: Eisenbrauns.
Finkelstein, I., and L. Singer-Avitz. 2001. Ashdod Revisited. *TA* 28:231–59.
Finkelstein, J. J. 1953. Cuneiform Texts from Tell Billa. *JCS* 7:111–76.
———. 1962. Mesopotamia. *JNES* 21:73–92.
Fishbane, M. 1975. Composition and Structure in the Jacob Cycle (Gen. 25:19–35:22). *JJS* 26:15–38.
Fitzmyer, J. A. 1967. *The Aramaic Inscriptions of Sefire*. BibOr 19 Rome: Pontifical Biblical Institute.
———. 1995. *The Aramaic Inscriptions of Sefire*. Revised ed. BibOr 19A. Rome: Pontifical Biblical Institute.
Fleming, D. E. 1998. Mari and the Possibilities of Biblical Memory. *RA* 92:41–78.
———. 2002. Emar: On the Road from Harran to Hebron. Pages 222–50 in Chavalas and Younger 2002.
———. 2004a. *Democracy's Ancient Ancestors: Mari and Early Collective Governance*. Cambridge: Cambridge University Press.
———. 2004b. The Sim'alite *Gayum* and the Yaminite *Li'mum* in the Mari Archives. Pages 199–212 in Nicolle 2004.
———. 2012. *The Legacy of Israel in Judah's Bible: History, Politics, and the Reinscribing of Tradition*. New York: Cambridge University Press.
Fokkelman, J. P. 1981–90. *Narrative Art and Poetry in the Books of Samuel: A Full Interpretation Based on Stylistic and Structural Analyses*. 3 vols. SSN 20, 23, 27. Assen: Van Gorcum.
Folmer, M. L. 1995. *The Aramaic Language in the Achaemenid Period: A Study of Linguistic Variation*. OLA 68. Leuven: Peeters.
———. 2009. Alt- und Reichsaramäisch. Pages 105–31 in *Sprachen aus der Welt des Alten Testaments*. Darmstadt: Wiseenschaftliche Buchgesellschaft.
———. 2012. Old and Imperial Aramaic. Pages 128–59 in Gzella 2012.
Forrer, E. 1920. *Die Provinzeinteilung des assyrischen Reiches*. Leipzig: Hinrichs.
———. 1928. Ba'asa. *RlA* 1:328.
Fortin, M. 2001a. Hama et Tell ʿAcharneh: Deux sites comparables de la vallée de l'oronte. *BCSMS* 36:87–105.
———, ed. 2001b. *Recherches canadiennes sur la Syrie antique/Canadian Research on Ancient Syria*. Actes du colloque annuel de la Société canadienne des études mésopotamiennes. Toronto: Canadian Society for Mesopotamian Studies.
———, ed. 2006. *Tell ʿAcharneh 1998–2004: Rapports préliminaires sur les campagnes de fouilles et saison d'études*. Subartu 18. Turnhout: Brepols.
Fortin, M., and L. Cooper. 2013. Shedding New Light on the Elusive Late Bronze and Early Iron Ages at Tell ʿAcharneh (Syria). Pages 147–71 in Yener 2013.
Foster, B. R. 1992. A Sargonic Itinerary. Pages 73–76 in Charpin and Joannès 1992.

———. 2005. *Before the Muses. An Anthology of Akkadian Literature*. 3rd ed. Bethesda, MD: CDL.
Frahm, E. 1998. Adīnu. *PNA* 1.1:53.
———. 2003. New Sources for Sennacherib's "First Campaign." *Isimu* 6:129–64.
———. 2009. *Keilschrifttexte aus Assur literarischen Inhalts III: Historische und historisch-literarische Texte*. WVDOG 121. Wiesbaden: Harrassowitz.
———. 2013. A Sculpted Slab with an Inscription of Sargon II Mentioning the Rebellion of Yau-biʾdi of Hamath. *AoF* 40:42–54.
Frahm, E., and R. Zadok. 1998. Adānu. *PNA* 1.1:42.
Frame, G. 1992. *Babylonia 689–627 B.C.: A Political History*. PIHANS 69. Leiden: Nederlands Historisch-Archaeologische Instituut te Istanbul.
———. 1999. The Inscription of Sargon II at Tang-i Var. *Or* 68:31–57 and pls. i–xviii.
———. 2006. The Tell Acharneh Stela of Sargon II of Assyria. Pages 49–68 in Fortin 2006.
———. 2006–8. Samgunu. *RlA* 11:624–25.
———. 2011. Assyrian Royal Inscriptions. Pages 127–34 in *Cuneiform Royal Inscriptions and Related Texts in the Schøyen Collection*. Edited by A. R. George. Cornell University Studies in Assyriology and Sumerology 17. Bethesda: CDL.
———. 2013. The Political History and Historical Geography of the Aramean, Chaldean, and Arab Tribes in Babylonia in the Neo-Assyrian Period. Pages 87–121 in Berlejung and Streck 2013.
———. Forthcoming. Uqnû. *RlA*.
Frame, G., with L. S. Wilding, eds. 2004. *From the Upper Sea to the Lower Sea: Studies on the History of Assyria and Babylonia in Honour of A. K. Grayson*. Uitgaven van het Nederlands Instituut voor het Nabije Oosten te Leiden 101. Leiden: Nederlands Instituut voor het Nabije Oosten.
Frangipane, M., and A. Palmieri. 1983. Perspectives of Protourbanization in Eastern Anatolia: Arslantepe (Malatya); An Interim Report on 1975–1983 Campaigns. *Origini* 12:285–668.
Frangipane, M. 1993–97. Melid B. Archäologisch. *RlA* 8:42–52.
———, ed. 2004. *Alle origini del potere: Arslantepe, la collina dei leoni*. Centri e monumenti dell'antichità. Milano: Electa.
Frangipane, M., and M. Liverani. 2013. Neo-Hittite Melid: Continuity or Discontinuity? Pages 349–71 in Yener 2013.
Frankena, R. 1972. Some Remarks on the Semitic Background of Chapters XXIX–XXXI of the Book of Genesis. Pages 53–64 in *The Witness of Tradition: Papers Read at the Joint British-Dutch Old Testament Conference Held at Woudschoten, 1970*. Edited by M. A. Beek et al. OTS 17. Leiden: Brill.
Frese, D. A., and T. E. Levy. 2010. The Four Pillars of the Iron Age Low Chronology. Pages 187–202 in *Historical Biblical Archaeology and the Future: The New Pragmatism*. Edited by T. E. Levy. London: Equinox.
Freyberger, K. S. 1989. Untersuchungen zur Baugeschichte des JupiterHeiligtums in Damaskus. *DaM* 4:61–86.
Freydank, H. 1991. *Beiträge zur mittelassyrischen Chronologie und Geschichte*. Schriften zur Geschichte und Kultur des Alten Orients 21. Berlin: Akademie.
———. 1997. Mittelassyrische Opferlisten aus Assur. Pages 47–52 in Waetzoldt and Hauptmann 1997.

———. 2006. Anmerkungen zu mittelassyrischen Texten. 5. *AoF* 33:215–22.
———. 2007. "Honig"-Lieferungen für den Gott Assur. *AoF* 34:70–77.
———. 2009. Kār-Tukultī-Ninurta als Agrarprovinz. *AoF* 36:44–48.
———. 2011. Aus dem Opferarchiv des Assurtempels. Pages 431–40 in Renger 2011.
Friedrich, J. 1932. *Kleinasiatische Sprachdenkmäler*. Kleine Texte für Vorlesungen und Ubungen 163. Berlin: de Gruyter.
———. 1951. *Phönizischpunische Grammatik*. AnOr 32. Rome: Pontifical Biblical Institute.
———. 1957. Das Bildhethitische Siegel des BrRkb von Sam'al. *Or* 26:345–47.
———. 1966. Zu der altaramäischen Stele des ZKR von Hamat. *AfO* 21:83.
Friedrich, J., G. R. Meyer, A. Ungnad, and E. F. Weidner. 1940. *Die Inschriften vom Tell Ḥalaf: Keilschrifttexte und aramaische Urkunden aus einer assyrischen Provinzhauptstadt*. AfO 6. Berlin: n.p.
Fritz, V. 2003. *1 and 2 Kings: A Continental Commentary*. Translated by A. Hagedorn. Minneapolis: Fortress.
Fritz, V., and P. R. Davies, eds. 1996. *The Origins of the Ancient Israelite States*. JSOTSup 228. Sheffield: Sheffield Academic.
Fuchs, A. 1994. *Die Inschriften Sargons II. aus Khorsabad*. Göttingen: Cuvillier Verlag.
———. 1998a. *Die Annalen des Jahres 711 v. Chr*. SAAS 8. Helsinki: Neo-Assyrian Text Corpus Project.
———. 1998b. *BO* 55/1-2: cols. 191–92.
———. 1999. Bur-Anate. *PNA* 1.2:353.
———. 2000a. Ḫemti-ili. *PNA* 2.1:471.
———. 2000b. Itti'. *PNA* 2.1:587.
———. 2001a. Labṭuri. *PNA* 2.2:649.
———. 2001b. Lubarna. *PNA* 2.2:667.
———. 2002. Panammû. *PNA* 3.1:983.
———. 2008a. Der Turtān Šamšī-ilu und die große Zeit der assyrischen Großen (830–746). *WO* 38:61–145.
———. 2008b. Über den Wert von Befestigungsanlagen. *ZA* 98:45–99.
———. 2009–11. Sargon II. *RlA* 12:51–61.
———. 2011. Zur Geschichte von Gūzāna. Pages 353–58 in Cholidis and Martin 2011.
———. 2012. Urarṭu in der Zeit. Pages 135–61 in Kroll et al. 2012b.
Fuchs, A., and H. Hunger. 2002. Raḫiānu, *PNA* 3.1:1028.
Fuchs, A., and S. Parpola. 2000. Iau-bi'di. *PNA* 2.1:497.
Fugmann, E. 1958. *L'architecture des périodes préhellénistiques*. Hama 2.1. Copenhagen: Fondation Carlsberg.
Gadd, C. J. 1954. Inscribed Prisms of Sargon II from Nimrud. *Iraq* 16:173–202.
Gailani Werr, L. al-, J. Custis, H. Martin, A. McMahon, J. Oates, and J. Reade, eds. 2002. *Of Pots and Plans: Papers on the Archaeology and History of Mesopotamia and Syria Presented to David Oates in Honour of His Seventy-Fifth Birthday*. London: NABU.
Galil, G. 1992. Conflicts between Assyrian Vassals. *SAAB* 6:55–63.
———. 1996. *The Chronology of the Kings of Israel and Judah*. SHANE 9. Leiden: Brill.

———. 2000. The Boundaries of Aram-Damascus in the 9th–8th Centuries BCE. Pages 35–41 in Galil and Weinfeld 2000.

———. 2001. A Re-arrangement of the Fragments of the Tel Dan Inscription and the Relations between Israel and Aram. *PEQ* 133:16–21.

———. 2002. Shalmaneser III in the West. *RB* 109:40–56.

Galil, G., A. Gilboa, A. M. Maeir, and D. Kahn, eds. 2012. *The Ancient Near East in the Twelfth–Tenth Centuries BCE: Culture and History; Proceedings of the International Conference Held at the University of Haifa, 2–5 May, 2010*. AOAT 392. Münster: Ugarit-Verlag.

Galil, G., and M. Weinfeld, eds. 2000. *Studies in Historical Geography and Biblical Historiography Presented to Zecharia Kallai*. VTSup 81. Leiden: Brill.

Galling, K. 1941. Beschriftete Bildsiegel des 1. Jahrtausends v. Chr. *ZDPV* 64:122–79.

———. 1950. The Scepter of Wisdom: Notes on the Gold Sheath of Zendjirli and Ecclesiastes 12:11. *BASOR* 119:15–18.

Galter, H. Galter, H. 1988. 28.800 Hethiter. *JCS* 40:217–35.

———. 2004a. Militärgrenze und Euphrathandel: Der sozio-ökonomische Hintergrund der Trilinguen von Arslan Tash. Pages 444–460 in *Commerce and Monetary Systems in the Ancient World: Means of Transmission and Cultural Interaction*. Edited by R. Rollinger and Ch. Ulf. Melammu Symposia 5. Stuttgart: Steiner.

———. 2004b. Der Himmel über Hadattu: Das religiöse Umfeld der Inschriften von Arslan Tash. Pages 173–88 in Hutter and Hutter-Braunsar 2004.

———. 2007. Die Torlöwen von Arslan Tash Pages 193–211 in *Festschrift für Hermann Hunger zum 65. Geburtstag gewidmet von seinen Freunden, Kollegen und Schülern*. Edited by M. Köhbach, S. Procházka, G. J. Selz, and R. Lohlker. Wiener Zeitschrift für die Kunde des Morgenlandes 97. Vienna: Selbstverlag des Instituts für Orientalistik.

Garbini, G. 1976. La lingua di Ya'udi. *AION* 38 NS 26:123–32.

———. 1988. *Il Semitico nordoccidentale: Studi di storia linguistica*. StSem NS 5. Rome: Università degli Studi "La Sapienza."

Gardiner, A. H. 1937. *LateEgyptian Miscellanies*. Bibliotheca aegyptiaca 7. Brussels: Édition de la Fondation égyptologique Reine Élisabeth.

———. 1947. *Ancient Egyptian Onomastica*. 3 vols. London: Oxford University Press.

Garfinkle, S. J. 2007. The Assyrians: A New Look at an Ancient Power. Pages 53–96 in *Current Issues in the History of the Ancient Near East*. Edited by M. W. Chavalas. Publications of the Association of Ancient Historians 8. Claremont, CA: Regina.

Garrone, D., and F. Israel, eds. 1991. *Storia e tradizioni di Israele: Scitti in onore di J. Alberto Soggin*. Brescia: Paideia.

Garr, W. G. 1985. *Dialect Geography of Syria-Palestine, 1000–586 B.C.E.* Philadelphia: University of Pennsylvania Press.

Garstang, J. 1908. Excavations at Sakje-Geuzi, in North Syria: Preliminary Report for 1908. *AAA* 1:97–110.

———. 1913. Second Interim Report on the Excavations at Sakje-Geuzi, in North Syria. *AAA* 5:63–72.

———. 1929. *The Hittite Empire: Being a Survey of the History, Geography and Monuments of Hittite Asia Minor and Syria*. London: Constable.

Gaspa, S. 2005. Schemi narrativi nelle Summary Inscriptions di Tiglatpileser III: Il resoconto delle campagne babilonesi come caso di studio. *KASKAL* 2:159–98.

Gaß, E. 2009. *Die Moabiter: Geschichte und Kultur eines ostjordanischen Volkes im 1. Jahrtausend v. Chr.* ADPV 38. Wiesbaden: Harrassowitz.

Gatier, P.-L., B. Geyer, and M.-O. Rousset, eds. 2010. *Entre nomades et sédentaires: Prospections en Syrie du nord et en Jordanie du sud.* Travaux de la Maison de l'Orient et de la Méditerranée 55. Conquête de la steppe 3. Lyon: Maison de l'Orient et de la Mediterranee.

Gehman, H. S., ed. 1970. *The New Westminster Dictionary of the Bible*. Philadelphia: Westminster.

Gelb, I. J. 1980. *Computer-Aided Analysis of Amorite*. AS 21. Chicago: Oriental Institute of the University of Chicago.

Gellner, E. 1990. Tribalism and the State in the Middle East. Pages 109–26 in *Tribes and State Formation in the Middle East*. Edited by P. S. Khoury and J. Kostiner. Berkeley: University of California Press.

Genge, H. 1979. *Nordsyrisch-südanatolische Reliefs: Eine archäologisch-historische Untersuchung, Datierung und Bestimmung*. Historisk-filosofiske Meddelelser 49.1–2. Copenhagen: Munksgarrd.

Genz, H. 2013. 'No Land Could Stand before Their Arms, from Hatti … on …'? New Light on the End of the Hittite Empire and the Early Iron Age in Central Anatolia. Pages 469–77 in Killebrew and Lehmann 2013.

Gerardi, P. 1988. Epigraphs and Assyrian Palace Reliefs: The Development of the Epigraphic Text. *JCS* 40:1–35.

Gerlach, I. 2000. Tradition–Adaption–Innovation: Zur Reliefkunst Nordsyriens/Südostanatoliens in neuassyrischer Zeit. Pages 189–210 in Bunnens 2000c.

Gesche, P. D. 1999. Bēl-liqbi. *PNA* 1.2:322.

Geyer, B., J.-Y. Monchambert, J. Besançon, and E. Coqueugniot. 2003. *La basse vallée de l'Euphrate syrien: Du Néolithique à l'avènement de l'islam; Géographie, archéologie et histoire*. Mission archéologique de Mari 6. Beruit: Institut Français d'Archéologie du Proche-Orient.

Ghantous, H. 2013. *The Elisha-Hazael Paradigm and the Kingdom of Israel: The Politics of God in Ancient Syria-Palestine*. Durham: Acumen.

Gibson, J. C. L. 1975. *Aramaic Inscriptions Including Inscriptions in the Dialect of Zenjirli*. Vol. 2 of *Textbook of Syrian Semitic Inscriptions*. Oxford: Clarendon.

Gibson, McG. 1972. *The City and Area of Kish*. Miami: Field Research Projects.

Gilibert, A. 2011. *Syro-Hittite Monumental Art and the Archaeology of Performance: The Stone Reliefs at Carchemish and Zincirli in the Earlier First Millennium BCE*. Berlin Studies of the Ancient World 2. Berlin: de Gruyter.

———. 2013. Death, Amusement and the City: Civic Spectacles and the Theatre Palace of Kapara, King of Gūzāna. *KASKAL* 10:35–68.

Giorgieri, M. 2011. Das Verhältnis Assyriens zum Hethiterreich. Pages 169–90 in Renger 2011.

Giron, M. N. 1925. Cachet hébraïque. *JA* 19:63–65.

Glassner, J.-J. 2004. *Mesopotamian Chronicles*. SBLWAW 19. Atlanta: Society of Biblical Literature.

Glatt, D. A. 1993. *Chronological Displacement in Biblical and Related Literatures*. SBLDS 139. Atlanta: Scholars Press.

Goetze, A. 1939. Cuneiform Inscriptions from Tarsus. *JAOS* 59:1–16.

Gonnella, J., W. Khayyata, and K. Kohlmeyer. 2005. *Die Zitadelle von Aleppo und der Tempel des Wettergottes: Neue Forschungen und Entdeckungen*. Münster: Rhema.

Gonnet, H. 2010. Une stèle hiéroglyphique louvite à Tall Šṭīb. Pages 97–99 in Gatier, Geyer, and Rousset 2010.

Good, R. M. 2001. 2 Samuel 8. *TynBul* 52:129–38.

Gooding, D. W. 1964. Ahab according to the Septuagint. *ZAW* 3:269–80.

Gordon, E. I. 1967. The Meaning of the Ideogram $^{d}$KASKAL.KUR "Underground Water Course" and Its Significance for Bronze Age Historical Geography. *JCS* 21:70–88.

Goren, Y., I. Finkelstein, and N. Na'aman. 2003. The Expansion of the Kingdom of Amurru according to the Petrographic Investigation of the Amarna Tablets. *BASOR* 329:1–11.

Goren, Y., I. Finkelstein, N. Na'aman, and M. Artzy. 2004. *Inscribed in Clay: Provenance Study of the Amarna Tablets and Other Ancient Near Eastern Texts*. SMNIA 23. Tel Aviv: Emery and Claire Yass Publications in Archaeology.

Görg, M. 1976. Aram und Israel. *VT* 26:499–500.

———. 1979. Namenstudien III: Zum Problem einer Frühbezeugung von Aram. *BN* 9:7–10.

———. 1989. *Beiträge zur Zeitgeschichte der Anfänge Israels: Dokumente-Materialien-Notizen*. ÄAT 2. Wiesbaden: Harrassowitz.

Gosse, B. 1996. Isaiah 8.23b and the Three Great Parts of the Book of Isaiah. *JSOT* 70:57–62.

Grabbe, L. L. 2007. *Ancient Israel: What Do We Know and How Do We Know It?* London: T&T Clark.

Grabbe, L. L., ed. 2008. *The Archaeology*. Vol. 1. of *Israel in Transition: From Late Bronze II to Iron IIa (c. 1250–850 BCE)*. London: T&T Clark.

Grandet, P. 1994–99. *Le papyrus Harris I (BM 9999)*. 3 vols. Bibliothèque d'étude 109/12. Cairo: Institut franscais d'archéologie orientale.

Gray, J. 1970. *1 and 2 Kings*. 2nd ed. OTL. Philadelphia: Westminster.

Grayson, A. K. 1972–76. *Assyrian Royal Inscriptions*. 2 vols. Wiesbaden: Harrassowitz.

———. 1975. *Assyrian and Babylonian Chronicles*. Texts from Cuneiform Sources. Locust Valley, NY: Augustin.

———. 1976. Studies in Neo-Assyrian History: The Ninth Century B.C. *BO* 33:134–45.

———. 1980–83. Königlisten und Chroniken B. Akkadisch. *RlA* 6:86–135.

———. 1982. Assyria: Ashur-Dan II to Ashur-Nirari V (934–745 B.C.). Pages 238–81, 930–41 in vol. 3, part 1 of *The Cambridge Ancient History*. Edited by J. Broadman et al. 2nd ed. Cambridge: Cambridge University Press.

———. 1992. Mesopotamia, History of (Assyria). *ABD* 4:740–44,

———. 1993. Assyrian Officials and Power in the Ninth and Eighth Centuries. *SAAB* 7:19–52.

———. 1994. Studies in Neo-Assyrian History II: The Eighth Century B.C. Pages 73–84 in *Corolla Torontonensis: Festschrift Ronald Morton Smith*. Edited by E. Robbins and S. Sandahl. Toronto: TSAR.

———. 1995. Eunuchs in Power: Their Role in the Assyrian Bureaucracy. Pages

85–98 in *Vom Alten Orient zum Alten Testament: Festschrift für Wolfram Freiherrn von Soden zum 85. Geburtstag am 19. Juni 1993*. Edited by M. Dietrich and O. Loretz. AOAT 240. Kevelaer: Butzon & Bercker; Neukirchen-Vluyn: Neukirchener Verlag.

———. 1996. *Assyrian Rulers of the Early First Millennium BC II (858–745 BC)*. RIMA 3. Toronto: University of Toronto.

———. 1999. The Struggle for Power in Assyria: Challenge to Absolute Monarchy in the Ninth and Eighth Centuries B.C. Pages 253–70 in Watanabe 1999.

———. 2001. Assyria and the Orontes Valley. *BCSMS* 36:185–87.

———. 2004. Shalmaneser III and the Levantine States. *Journal of Hebrew Scriptures* 5:1–9. http://www.jhsonline.org/Articles/article_34.pdf.

Green, D. J. 2010. *"I Undertook Great Works": The Ideology of Domestic Achievements in West Semitic Royal Inscriptions*. FAT 2/41. Tübingen: Mohr Siebeck.

Greene, J. T. 2004. Tiglath-pileser III's War against the City of Tzer. Pages 63–82 in Arav and Freund 2004.

Greenfield, J. C. 1968. Dialect Traits in Early Aramaic [Hebrew]. *Leshonénu* 32:359–68.

———. 1976. The Aramaean God Rammân/Rimmôn. *IEJ* 26:195–198.

———. 1978. The Dialects of Early Aramaic. *JNES* 37:93–99.

———. 1998. Arameans and Aramaic in Anatolia. Pages 199–207 in *XXIVème Rencontre assyriologique internationale/XXXIV Uluslararası Assiriyoloji Kongresi, 6–10/VII/1987*. Ankara: Türk Tarih Kurumu Basımevi.

Greenspahn, F. 2002. Aramaic. Pages 93–108 in *Beyond Babel: A Handbook for Biblical Hebrew and Related Languages*. Edited by J. Kaltner and S. L. McKenzie. SBLRBS 42. Atlanta: Society of Biblical Literature.

Greener, J. S. 2013. *Dinner at Dan: Biblical and Archaeological Evidence for Sacred Feasts at Iron Age II Tel Dan and Their Significance*. CHANE 66. Leiden: Brill.

Grimme, H. 1904. *Mohammed: Die weltgeschichtliche Bedeutung Arabiens*. Munich: Kirchheim'sche Verlagsbuchhandlung.

Gröndahl, F. 1967. *Die Personennamen der Texte aus Ugarit*. StPohl 1. Rome: Päpstliches Bibelinstitut.

Groneberg, B. 1980. *Die Orts und Gewässernamen der altbabylonischen Zeit*. RGTC 3. BTAVO B/7. Wiesbaden: Reichert.

Gropp, D. M., and T. J. Lewis. 1985. Some Problems in the Aramaic Text of the Hadd-Yithʿi Bilingual. *BASOR* 259:45–61.

Grosby, S. 2002a. Borders, Territory and Nationality in the Ancient Near East and Armenia. Pages 120–49 in *Biblical Ideas of Nationality*. Edited by S. Grosby. Winona Lake, IN: Eisenbrauns.

———. 2002b. *ʾAram Kulloh* and the Worship of Hadad: A Nation of Aram? Pages 150–65 in *Biblical Ideas of Nationality*. Edited by S. Grosby. Winona Lake, IN: Eisenbrauns.

Gubel, E. 2012. Episème de bouclier ou égide (sam'alite?) à inscription ouest sémitique. Pages 253–68 in *The Ancient Near East, a Life! Festschrift Karel Van Lerberghe*. Edited by T. Boiy et al. OLA 220. Leuven: Peeters.

Guisfredi, F. 2010. *Sources for a Socio-economic History of the Neo-Hittite States*. THeth. 28. Heidelberg: Winter.

Gurney, O. R. 1949. Texts from Dur-Kurigalzu. *Iraq* 11:131–49.

Güterbock, H. G. 1957. A Note on the Stela of Tukulti-Ninurta II Found Near Tell Ashara. *JNES* 16:123.
———. 1958. Middle Assyrian Tablets. Pages 86–90 and pls. 81–85 in McEwan et al. 1958.
———. 1961. When Was the Late Hittite Palace at Sakçagözü Built? *BASOR* 162:49–50.
Gzella, H., ed. 2012. *Languages from the World of the Bible*. Boston: de Gruyter.
———. 2014. Language and Script. Pages 71–107 in Niehr 2014.
———. 2015. *A Cultural History of Aramaic: From the Beginnings to the Advent of Islam*. HdO 111. Leiden: Brill.
Gzella, H., and M. L. Folmer, eds. 2008. *Aramaic in Its Historical and Linguistic Setting*. Veröffentlichungen der Orientalischen Kommission 50. Wiesbaden: Harrassowitz.
Hachmann, R. 2012. *Kāmid el-Lōz 20: Die Keilschriftbriefe und der Horizont von el-Amarna*. Saarbrücker Beiträge zur Altertumskunde 87. Bonn: Habelt.
Hafþórsson, S. 2006. *A Passing Power: An Examination of the Sources for the History of Aram-Damascus in the Second Half of the Ninth Century B.C.* ConBOT 54. Stockholm: Almqvist & Wiksell.
Hagelia, H. 2006. *The Tel Dan Inscription: A Critical Investigation of Recent Research on Its Palaeography and Philology*. Studia Semitica Uppsaliensia 22. Uppsala: Uppsala University Library.
———. 2009. *The Dan Debate: The Tel Dan Inscription in Recent Research*. Recent Research in Biblical Studies 4. Sheffield: Sheffield Phoenix.
Haines, R. 1971. *The Structural Remains of the Later Phases: Chatal Hüyük, Tell AlJudaidah, and Tell Taʿyinat*. Vol. 2 of *Excavations in the Plain of Antioch*. OIP 95. Chicago: University of Chicago Press.
Hallo, W. W. 1960. From Qarqar to Carchemish: Assyria and Israel in the Light of New Discoveries. *BA* 23:34–61.
———. 1964. The Road to Emar. *JCS* 18:57–88.
———. 1992. From Bronze Age to Iron Age in Western Asia: Defining the Problem. Pages 1–9 in Ward and Joukowsky 1992.
Hallo, W. W., and W. Simpson. 1998. *The Ancient Near East. A History*. 2nd ed. Fort Worth: Harcourt Brace College.
Halpern, B. 1994. The Stela from Dan: Epigraphic and Historical Considerations. *BASOR* 296:63–80.
———. 1996. The Construction of the Davidic State: An Exercise in Historiography. Pages 44–75 in Fritz and Davies 1996.
———. 2001. *David's Secret Demons*. Grand Rapids: Eerdmans.
Halpern, B., and D. S. Vanderhooft. 1991. The Editions of Kings in the Seventh–Sixth Centuries B.C.E. *HUCA* 62:179–244.
Hämeen-Anttila, J. 2000. *A Sketch of Neo-Assyrian Grammar*. SAAS 13. Helinski: Neo-Assyrian Text Corpus Project.
Hamilton, M. W. 1998. The Past as Destiny: Historical Visions in Samʾal and Judah under Assyrian Hegomony. *HTR* 91:215–50.
Hammond, P. C. 1960. An Ammonite Stamp Seal from ʿAmman. *BASOR* 160:38–41.
Hanfmann, G. M. A. 1960. On the Date of the Late Hittite Palace at Sakçagözü. *BASOR* 160:43–45.

Hansen, C. K., and J. N. Postgate. 1999. The Bronze to Iron Age Transition at Kilise Tepe. *AnSt* 49:111–21.
Haran, M. 1967. Rise and Decline of the Empire of Jeroboam ben Joash. *VT* 17:266–97.
Harding, G. L. 1971. *An Index and Concordance of Pre-Islamic Arabian Names and Inscriptions*. Toronto: University of Toronto Press.
Harrak, A. 1987. *Assyria and Hanigalbat*. Hildesheim: Olms.
———. 1988. À propos de la poignée de sceptre au nom d'Aššur-šar-uṣur. *NABU* 1988.1:4, no. 4. http://sepoa.fr/wp/wp-content/uploads/2012/05/1988-1.pdf.
———. 1992. Des noms d'année en araméen? *WO* 23:68–73.
Harrison, T. P. 2001a. Tell Taʿyinat and the Kingdom of Unqi. Pages 115–44 in vol. 2 of Daviau, Wevers, and Weigl 2001.
———. 2001b. The Evidence for Aramaean Cultural Expansion in the Amuq Plain. Pages 135–44 in Fortin 2001b.
———, ed. 2007. Cyprus, The Sea Peoples and the Eastern Mediterranean: Regional Perspectives of Continuity and Change. *Scripta Mediterranea* 27–28. Toronto: Canadian Institute for Mediterranean Studies.
———. 2009a. Neo-Hittites in the "Land of Palistin": Renewed Investigations at Tell Taʿyinat on the Plain of Antioch. *NEA* 72:174–89.
———. 2009b. Lifting the Veil on a "Dark Age": Taʿyinat and the North Orontes Valley during the Early Iron Age. Pages 171–84 in Schloen 2009.
———. 2010. The Late Bronze/Early Iron Age Transition in the North Orontes Valley. Pages 83–102 in *Societies in Transition: Evolutionary Processes in the Northern Levant between Late Bronze II and Early Iron Age*. Edited by F. Venturi. Studi e testi orientali. Collana diretta da Giorgio Renato Franci 9. Bologna: CLUEB.
———. 2013. Tayinat in the Early Iron Age. Pages 61–87 in Yener 2013.
Harzig, C., and D. Hoerder, with D. R. Gabaccia. 2009. *What Is Migration History?* Cambridge: Polity.
Hasegawa, S. 2008. Adad-nērārī III's Fifth Year in the Saba'a Stela: Historiographical Background. *RA* 102:89–98.
———. 2010. Historical and Historiographical Notes on the Pazacık Stela. *Akkadica* 131:1–9.
———. 2011. The Historiographical Background for Jehu's Claim as the Murderer of Joram and Ahaziah. *AJBI* 37:5–17.
———. 2012. *Aram and Israel during the Jehuite Dynasty*. BZAW 434. Berlin: de Gruyter.
Hawkins, J. D. 1972–75a. Ḫalab, the First Millennium. *RlA* 4:53.
———. 1972–75b. Hamath. *RlA* 4:67–70.
———. 1972–75c. Hazazu. *RlA* 4:240.
———. 1974. Assyrians and Hittites. *Iraq* 36:67–83.
———. 1976–80a. Jaudu. RlA 5:273.
———. 1976–80b. Jaḫan. *RlA* 5:238–39.
———. 1976–80c. Karkamiš. *RlA* 5:426–46.
———. 1980–83. KTK. *RlA* 6:254–56.
———. 1982. The Neo-Hittite States in Syria and Anatolia. Pages 372–441 in vol. 3, part 1 of *The Cambridge Ancient History*. Edited by J. Broadman et al. 2nd ed. Cambridge: Cambridge University Press.

———. 1983. The Hittite Name of Til Barsip: Evidence from a New Hieroglyphic Fragment from Tell Ahmar. *AnSt* 33:131–36.
———. 1984. The Syro-Hittite States. Pages 65–92 in *The Cambridge Ancient History: Plates to Volume III*. Edited by J. Broadman. 2nd ed. Cambridge: Cambridge University Press.
———. 1986. Royal Statements of Ideal Prices: Assyrian, Babylonian, and Hittite. Pages 93–102 in *Ancient Anatolia, Aspects of Change and Cultural Development: Essays in Honor of Machteld J. Mellink*. Edited by J. V. Canby et al. Madison: University of Wisconsin Press.
———. 1987–90a. Luḫuti. *RlA* 7:159–61.
———. 1987–90b. Manṣuate. *RlA* 7:342–43.
———. 1988. Kuzi-Tesub and the "Great Kings" of Karkamiš. *AnSt* 38:99–108.
———. 1992. What Does the Hittite Storm-God Hold? Pages 53–82 in *Natural Phenomena: Their Meaning, Depiction and Description in the Ancient Near East*. Edited by D. J. W. Meijer. Koninklijke Nederlandse Akademie van Wetenschappen. Verhandelingen, Afd. Letterkunde; nieuwe reeks 152. Amsterdam: Royal Netherlands Academy of Arts and Sciences.
———. 1993. The New Inscription from the Südburg of Bogazköy Hattusa. *Archäologischer Anzeiger* 3:305–14.
———. 1993–97. Melid A. Historisch. *RlA* 8:35–41.
———. 1995a. Karkamish and Karatepe: Neo-Hittite City-States in North Syria. *CANE* 4:1295–1307.
———. 1995b. "Great Kings" and "Country Lords" at Malatya and Karkamiš. Pages 73–85 in *Studio Historiae Ardens: Ancient Near Eastern Studies Presented to Philo H. J. Houwink ten Cate on the Occasion of His Sixty-Fifth Birthday*. Edited by T. P. J. van den Hout and J. de Roos. Uitgaven van het Nederlands Historisch-Archaeologisch Instituut te Istanbul 74. Istanbul: Nederlands Historisch-Archaeologisch Instituut te Istanbul.
———. 1995c. The Political Geography of North Syria and South-East Anatolia in the Neo-Assyrian Period. Pages 87–101 in Liverani 1995.
———. 1995d. *The Hieroglyphic Inscription of the Sacred Pool Complex at Hattusa (Südburg)*. StBoT 3. Wiesbaden: Harassowitz.
———. 1996–97. A New Luwian Inscription of Hamiyatas, King of Masuwari. *AbrN* 34:108–17.
———. 1999. Tarkasnawa King of Mira "Tarkondemos," Boğazköy Sealings and Karabel. *AnSt* 48:1–31.
———. 2000. *Inscriptions of the Iron Age*. Vol. 1 of *Corpus of Hieroglyphic Luwian Inscriptions*. Berlin: de Gruyter.
———. 2002. Anatolia: The End of the Hittite Empire and After. Pages 143–51 in Braun-Holzinger and Matthäus 2002.
———. 2003. Scripts and Texts. Pages 128–69 in Melchert 2003.
———. 2004. The New Sargon Stele from Hama. Pages 151–64 in Frame and Wilding 2004.
———. 2005. Cilicia, the Amuq, and Aleppo: New Light on the Neo-Hittite Period. Lecture at the Oriental Institute of the University of Chicago, March 5, 2005.
———. 2006. The Inscription. Pages 11–31 in Bunnens 2006.
———. 2006–8. Samʾal. A. Philologisch. *RlA* 11:600–605.

———. 2009. Cilicia, the Amuq, and Aleppo: New Light in a Dark Age. *NEA* 72:164–73.
———. 2011. The Inscriptions of the Aleppo Temple. *AnSt* 61:35–54.
———. 2013. The Luwian Inscriptions from the Temple of the Storm-God of Aleppo. Pages 493–500 in Yener 2013.
Hayes, J. H. 1988. *Amos: The Eighth-Century Prophet: His Times and His Preaching*. Nashville: Abingdon.
Hayes, J. H., and P. K. Hooker. 1988. *A New Chronology for the Kings of Israel and Judah and Its Implications for Biblical History and Literature*. Atlanta: John Knox.
Healey, J. F. 1976. Syriac NṢR, Ugaritic NṢR, Hebrew NṢR II, Akkadian NṢR II. *VT* 26:429–37.
Heard, R. C. 2001. *Dynamics of Diselection: Ambiguity in Genesis 12–36 and Ethnic Boundaries in Post-exilic Judah*. SemeiaSt 39. Atlanta: Society of Biblical Literature.
Heimpel, W. 2003. *Letters to the King of Mari: A New Translation, with Historical Introduction, Notes, and Commentary*. MC 12. Winona Lake, IN: Eisenbrauns.
Helck, W. 1971. *Die Beziehungen Ägyptens zu Vorderasien im 3. und 2. Jahrtausend v. Chr*. 2nd ed. ÄgAbh 5. Wiesbaden: Harrassowitz.
Heltzer, M. 1981. *The Suteans*. Istituto universitario orientale: Seminario di studi asiatici, Series Minor 13. Naples: Istituto universitario orientale.
———. 1983. An Old-Aramean Seal-Impression and Some Problems of the History of the Kingdom of Damascus. Pages 9–13 in Sokoloff 1983.
———. 1995. Phoenician Trade and Phoenicians in Hamath. Pages 101–5 in van Lerberghe and Schoors 1995.
Hendel, R. 2005. *Remembering Abraham: Culture, Memory, and History in the Hebrew Bible*. Oxford: Oxford University Press.
———. 2010. Cultural Memory. Pages 28–46 in *Reading Genesis: Ten Methods*. Edited by R. Hendel. Cambridge: Cambridge University Press.
Herles, M. 2007a. Assyrische Präsenz an Euphrat und Balīḫ: Grenzkontrolle gegen Feinde des Reiches und nomadische Gruppierungen. *UF* 39:413–49.
———. 2007b. Zur geographischen Einordnung der *aḫlamû*: Eine Bestandsaufnahme*. *AoF* 34:319–41.
Herr, L. G. 1978. *The Scripts of Ancient Northwest Semitic Seals*. HSM 18. Missoula, MT: Scholars Press.
Herrmann, G., S. Laidlaw, and H. Coffey. 2009. *Ivories from the North West Palace (1845–1992)*. Ivories from Nimrud 6. London: British Institute for the Study of Iraq.
Herrmann, V. R., T. van den Hout, and A. Beyazlar. 2016. A New Hieroglyphic Luwian Inscription from Pancarlı Höyük: Language and Power in Early Iron Age Sam'al-Y'DY. *JNES* 75:53–70.
Herrmann, V. R., and J. D. Schloen, eds. 2014. *In Remembrance of Me: Feasting with the Dead in the Ancient Middle East*. OIP 37. Chicago: Oriental Institute of the University of Chicago.
Hertel, T. 2004. The Balawat Gate Narratives of Shalmaneser III. Pages 299–315 in Dercksen 2004.

———. 2012. Review of *The Balawat Gates of Ashurnasirpal II*, edited by J. E. Curtis and N. Tallis. *JNES* 71:118–20.
Hertzberg, H. W. 1964. *I and II Samuel: A Commentary*. OTL. Philadelphia: Westminster.
Herzog, Z., and L. Singer-Avitz. 2011. Iron Age IIA: Occupational Phases in the Coastal Plain of Israel. Pages 159–74 in Finkelstein and Na'aman 2011.
Hess, R. S. 1993. *Amarna Personal Names*. ASORDS 9. Winona Lake, IN: Eisenbrauns.
———. 2004. "Geshurite" Onomastica of the Bronze and Iron Ages. Pages 49–62 in Arav and Freund 2004.
Hetzron, R. ed. 1997. *The Semitic Languages*. London: Routledge.
Hillers, D. R., and E. Cussini. 1996. *Palmyrene Aramaic Texts*. Baltimore: Johns Hopkins University Press.
Hodge, C. T., and G. Janssens. 1975. *The Nominal Sentence in Semitic*. Monographic Journals of the Near East. Afroasiatic Linguistics 2. Malibu, CA: Undena.
Hoffner, H. A., Jr. 1992. The Last Days of Khattusha. Pages 46–52 in Ward and Joukowsky 1992.
———. 2009. *Letters front the Hittite Kingdom*. SBLWAW 15. Atlanta: Society of Biblical Literature.
Holloway, S. W. 2002. *Aššur Is King! Aššur Is King! Religion in the Exercise of Power in the Neo-Assyrian Empire*. CHANE 10. Leiden: Brill.
———. 2003. Use of Assyriology in Chronological Apologetics in *David's Secret Demons*. *SJOT* 17:245–67.
Honigmann, E. 1924. Historische Topographie von Nordsyrien im Altertum (Schluß). *ZDPV* 47:1–64.
———. 1928. Argana. *RlA* 1:143–44.
———. 1932. Syria. PW 4A.2:1549–1727.
———. 1938. Danabi. *RlA* 2:116.
Horn, S. 1922. Zur Geographie Mesopotamiens. *ZA* 34:123–56.
Horowitz, W. 1998. *Mesopotamian Cosmic Geography*. Winona Lake, IN: Eisenbrauns.
Hout, Th. P. J. van den. 1994. Death as Privilege: The Hittite Royal Funerary Ritual. Pages 37–75 in *Hidden Futures, Death and Immortality in Ancient Egypt, Anatolia, the Classical, Biblical and Arabic-Islamic World*. Edited by J. Bremer, Th. P. J. van den Hout and R. Peters. Amsterdam: Amsterdam University Press.
———. 1995. An Image of the Dead? Pages 195–211 in *Atti del II Congresso Internazionale di Hittitologia*. Edited by O. Carruba et al. Studi Mediterranea 9. Pavia: Gianni Iuculano Editore.
———. 2002. Self, Soul and Portrait in Hieroglyphic Luwian. Pages 171–86 in Taracha 2002.
———. 2006. Institutions, Vernaculars, Publics: The Case of Second-Millennium Anatolia. Pages 217–56 in Sanders 2006.
Houwink ten Cate, Th. H. J. 1961. *The Luwian Population Groups of Lycia and Cilicia Aspera during Hellenistic Period*. DMOA 10. Leiden: Brill.
Hrouda, B. 1962. *Tell Halaf IV: Die Kleinfunde aus historischer Zeit*. Berlin: de Gruyter.
———. 1972–75. Ḥalāf, Tell. *RlA* 4:54.

Hübner, U. 1992. *Die Ammoniter. Untersuchungen zur Geschichte, Kultur und Religion eines transjordanischen Volkes im 1. Jahrtausend v. Chr.* ADPV 16. Wiesbaden: Harrassowitz.

Hübner, U., and E. A. Knauf, eds. 2002. *Kein Land für sich allein: Studien zum Kulturkontakt in Kanaan, Israel/Palästina und Ebirnâri für Manfred Weippert zum 65. Geburtstag*. OBO 186. Fribourg: Universitätsverlag; Göttingen: Vandenhoeck & Ruprecht.

Huehnergard, J. 1995. What Is Aramaic? *ARAM* 7:265–86.

Hutter, M., and S. Hutter-Braunsar, eds. 2004. *Offizielle Religion, lokale Kulte und individuelle Religiosität: Akten des religionsgeschichtlichen Symposiums "Kleinasien und angrenzende Gebiete vom Beginn des 2. bis zur Mitte des 1. Jahrtausends v. Chr." (Bonn, 20.–22. Februar 2003)*. AOAT 318. Münster: Ugarit-Verlag.

Ikeda, Y. 1979. Royal Cities and Fortified Cities. *Iraq* 41:75–87.

———. 1984. Hittites and Aramaeans in the Land of Bīt-Adini. Pages 27–35 in *Monarchies and Socio-religious Traditions in the Ancient Near East*. Edited by Prince Mikasa. Wiesbaden: Harrassowitz.

———. 1984–85. Assyrian Kings and the Mediterranean Sea: The Twelfth to Ninth Centuries B.C. *AbrN* 23:22–31.

———. 1993. Once Again *KTK* in the Sefire Inscriptions. Pages 104*–8* in *Avraham Malamat Volume*. Edited by S. Aḥituv et al. ErIsr 24. Jerusalem: Israel Exploration Society.

———. 1999. Looking from Til Barsip on the Euphrates: Assyria and the West in Ninth and Eighth Centuries B.C. Pages 271–302 in Watanabe 1999.

———. 2003. "They Divided the Orontes River between Them": Arpad and Its Borders with Hamath and Patin/Unqi in the Eighth Century BCE. Pages 91*–99* in *Hayim and Miriam Tadmor Volume*. Edited by I. Eph'al, A. Ben-Tor, and P. Machinist. ErIsr 27. Jerusalem: Israel Exploration Society.

Ilan, D. Forthcoming. *Dan IV: The Early Iron Age Levels*. Annual of the Nelson Glueck School of Biblical Archaeology, Jerusalem: Hebrew Union College.

Ingholt, H. 1934. *Rapport préliminaire sur la première campagne des fouilles de Hama*. Copenhagen: Munksgaard.

———. 1940. *Rapport préliminaire sur sept campagnes de fouilles à Hama en Syrie (1932–1938)*. Copenhagen: Munksgaard.

Ionides, M. G. 1937. *The Régime of the Rivers, Euphrates and Tigris: A General Hydraulic Survey of Their Basins, Including the River Karun, Having Particular Reference to Their Lower Reaches Within Iraq, with Information for the Use of Irrigation Engineers, Etc*. London: Spon.

Irvine, S. A. 1990. *Isaiah, Ahaz, and the Syro-Ephraimitic Crisis*. SBLDS 123. Atlanta: Scholars Press.

———. 1994. The Southern Border of Syria Reconstructed. *CBQ* 56:21–41.

———. 2001. The Rise of the House of Jehu. Pages 114–18 in Dearman and Graham 2001.

———. 2005. The Last Battle of Hadadezer. *JBL* 124:341–47.

Ismail, B. Kh., and J. N. Postgate. 2008. A Middle Assyrian Flock-Master's Archive from Tell Ali. *Iraq* 70:147–78.

Ismail, B. Kh., M. Roaf, and J. Black. 1983. 'Ana in the Cuneiform Sources. *Sumer* 39:191–94.

Iwasaki, T. 2009. *Tell Mastuma: An Iron Age Settlement in Northwest Syria*. Memoirs of the Ancient Orient Museum 3. Tokyo: Ancient Orient Museum.

Jakob, S. 2003. *Mittelassyrische Verwaltung und Sozialstruktur: Untersuchungen*. CM 29. Leiden: Styx.

Jakob, S., and D. I. Janisch-Jakob. 2009. *Die mittelassyrischen Texte aus Tell Chuēra in Nordost-Syrien*. Vorderasiatische Forschungen der Max Freiherr von Oppenheim-Stiftung 2. Ausgrabungen in Tell Chēra in Nordost-Syrien 3. Wiesbaden: Harrassowitz.

Janeway, B. 2008. The Nature and Extent of Aegean Contact at Tell Taʿyinat and Vicinity in the Early Iron Age: Evidence of Sea Peoples? *Scripta Mediterranea* 27–28:123–46.

Janzen, J. G. 1994. The "Wandering" Aramaean Reconsidered. *VT* 44:359–75.

Japhet, S. 1993. *1 and 2 Chronicles: A Commentary*. OTL. Louisville: Westminster John Knox.

Jasink, A. M. 1995. *Gli stati neoittiti: Analisi delle fonti scritte e sintesi storica*. Studia Mediterranea 10. Pavia: Iuculano.

Jastrow, M. 1950. *A Dictionary of the Targumim, the Talmud Babli and Yerushalmi, and the Midrashic Literature*. New York: Pardes.

Jean, C-F. 1950. *Lettres Diverses*. ARM 2.Paris: Imprimerie Nationale.

Jeffers, J. A. 2013. Tiglath-pileser I: A Light in a "Dark Age." Ph.D. diss. University of Pennsylvania.

Jepsen, A. 1941–44. Israel und Damaskus. *AfO* 14:153–72.

Joannès, F. 1993. Histoire de Ḫarādum à l'époque paléo-babylonienne. Pages 30–36 in *Ḫaradum I: Une ville nouvelle sur le Moyen Euprate (XVIIIe–XVIIe siècles av. J.-C.)*. Edited by C. Kepinski-Lecomte. Paris: Éditions recherche sur les civilisations.

———. 2004. *The Age of Empires: Mesopotamia in the First Millennium B.C.*. Translated by A. Nevill. Edinburgh: Edinburgh University Press.

———. 2005. Les relations entre Babylonie et Iran au debut de la période achéménide: Quelques rémarques. Pages 183–96 in *Approaching the Babylonian Economy: Proceedings of the START Project Symposium Held in Vienna, 1–3 July 2004*. Edited by H. D. Baker and M. Jursa. AOAT 330. Veröffentlichungen zur Wirtschaftsgeschichte Babyloniens im 1. Jahrtausend v. Chr. 2. Münster: Ugarit-Verlag.

———. 2006. *Haradum II: Les textes de la période paléobabylonienne tardive (Samsu-iluna–Ammisaduqa)*. Paris: Éditions recherche sur les civilisations.

Jones, G. H. 1984. *1 and 2 Kings*. NCBC. Grand Rapids: Eerdmans.

Joüon, P. 1965. *Grammaire de l'hébreu biblique*. Corrected ed. Rome: Institut Biblique Pontifical. Orig. 1923.

Jursa, M. 1998. *Der Tempelzehnt in Babylonien: Vom siebenten bis zum dritten Jahrhundert v. Chr.* AOAT 254. Münster: Ugarit-Verlag.

———. 2001a. Mannu-kī-Aššur-lēʾi. *PNA* 2.2:690.

———. 2001b. Matiʾ-il. *PNA* 2.2:745.

———. 2008. Nabû-šarrūssu-ukīn, rab ša-rēši, und Nebusarsekim (Jer 39:3). *NABU* 2008.1:9–19, no. 5. http://sepoa.fr/wp/wp-content/uploads/2012/06/2008-1.pdf.

———. 2010. Der neubabylonische Hof. Pages 67–106 in *Der Achämenidenhof = The Achaemenid Court: Akten des 2. Internationalen Kolloquiums zum Thema "Vorderasien im Spannungsfeld klassischer und altorientalischer Uberlieferungen," Landgut Castelen bei Basel, 23.–25. Mai 2007*. Edited by B. Jacobs and R. Rollinger. Classica et Orientalia 2. Wiesbaden: Harrassowitz.

Kahn, D. 2007. The Kingdom of Arpad (Bīt Agūsi) and "All Aram": International Relations in Northern Syria in the Ninth and Eighth Centuries BCE. *ANES* 44:66–89.

———. 2011. The Campaign of Ramesses III against Philistia. *JAEI* 3:1–11.

Kalaç, M. 1975. Einige Stelen mit hieroglyphisch-luwischen Inschriften oder ohne sie. Pages 183–89 and pls. XL–XLIII in *Le temple et le culte: Compte rendu de la vingtième Rencontre assyriologique internationale; organisée à Leiden du 3 au 7 juillet 1972 sous les auspices du Nederlands Instituut voor het Nabije Oosten*. RAI 20. Publications de l'Institut historique et archéologique néerlandais de Stamboul 37. Istambul: Nederlands Historisch-Archeologisch Instituut te Istambul.

Kalimi, I. 2005. *The Reshaping of Ancient Israelite History in Chronicles*. Winona Lake, IN: Eisenbrauns.

Kamlah, J., ed. 2012. *Temple Building and Temple Cult: Architecture and Cultic Paraphernalia of Temples in the Levant (2.–1. Mill. B.C.E.)*. ADPV 41. Wiesbaden: Harrassowitz.

Kärger, B., and S. Minx. 2011–13. Sutäer. *RlA* 13:365–69.

Kaufman, S. A. 1974. *The Akkadian Influences on Aramaic*. AS 19. Chicago: University of Chicago Press.

———. 1982. Reflections on the Assyrian-Aramaic Bilingual from Tell-Fakhariyeh. *Maarav* 3:137–75.

———. 1996. Semitics: Directions and Re-directions. Pages 273–82 in *The Study of the Ancient Near East in the Twenty-First Century: The William Foxwell Albright Centennial Conference*. Edited by J. S. Cooper and G. M. Schwartz. Winona Lake, IN: Eisenbrauns.

———. 1997. Aramaic. Pages 114–30 in Hetzron 1997.

———. 2007. The Phoenician Inscription of the Incirli Trilingual: A Tentative Reconstruction and Translation. *Maarav* 14:7–26.

Keil, C. F., and F. Delitsch. 1900. *Biblical Commentary on the Old Testament*. Grand Rapids: Eerdmans.

Kepinski, Chr. 2005. Tilbeshar—A Bronze Age City in the Sajur Valley (Southeast Anatolia). *Anatolica* 31:145–60.

———. 2006. Haradu: A General Outline of the Middle- and Neo-Assyrian Fortress, with a Brief History of the French Excavations at Khirbet ed-Diniyeh. Pages 329–38 in Kepinski, Lecomte, and Tenu 2006b.

———. 2009. Conflict, Territory and Culture: The Case of Haradu, a Fortress on the Iraqi Middle Euphrates (11th to 7th Centuries BC). *Syria* 86:149–58.

Kepinski, Chr., et al. 2006. Travaux menés à Tilbeshar en 2005 (Sud-Est anatolien). *AnAnt* 14:251–60.

Kepinski, Ch., O. Lecomte, and A. Tenu. 2006a. Introduction. Pages 9–19 in Kepinski, Lecomte, and Tenu 2006b.

Kepinski, Ch., O. Lecomte, and A. Tenu, eds. 2006b. *Studia Euphratica: Le moyen*

*Euphrate iraquien révélé par les fouilles préventives de Haditha*. Travaux de la Maison René-Ginouvès 3. Paris: de Boccard.

Kepinski-Lecomte, Chr., F. Gérard, E. Jean, and R. Vallet. 1996. Tilbeshar 1994, 1995. *AnAnt* 4:291–301.

Kepinski-Lecomte, Chr., and R. Ergeç. 1997. Tilbeshar 1996. *AnAnt* 5:337–41.

Kessler, K. 1980. *Untersuchungen zur historischen Topographie Nordmesopotamiens: Nach keilschriftlichen Quellen d. 1. Jahrtausends v. Chr.* BTAVO B/26. Wiesbaden: Reichert.

———. 1986. Zu den Beziehungen zwischen Urartu und Mesopotamien. Pages 59–86 in *Das Reich Urartu: Ein altorientalischer Staat im 1. Jahrtausend v. Chr.* Edited by V. Haas. Konstanzer altorientalische Symposien 1. Xenia 17. Konstanz: Universitätsverlag Konstanz.

———. 1993–97. Muquru. *RlA* 8:426.

Kessler, K., and C. Müller-Kessler. 1995. Zum Kult des Wettergottes von Guzana. Pages 239–44 in *Eski Yakın Doğu Kültürleri Üzerin İncelemeler*. Edited by A. Erkanal et al. Istanbul: Arkeoloji ve Sanat Yayınları.

Kestemont, G. 1972. Le commerce phénicien et l'expansion assyrienne du Ix[e]–VIIIe s. *OrAnt* 11:137–44.

———. 1983. Tyr et les Assyriens. Pages 57–78 in *Studia Phoenicia I–II*. Edited by E. Gubel et al. OLA 15. Leuven: Peeters.

Khayyata, W., and K. Kohlmeyer. 1998. Die Zitadelle von Aleppo: Vorläufiger Bericht über die Untersuchungen 1996 und 1997. *DaM* 10:19–95.

Khazanov, A. M. 1994. *Nomads and the Outside World*. 2nd ed. Translated by J. Crookenden. Madison: University of Wisconson Press.

Killebrew, A. E. 2005. *Biblical Peoples and Ethnicity*. ABS 9. Atlanta: Society of Biblical Literature.

Killebrew, A. E. and G. Lehmann, eds. 2013. *The Philistines and Other "Sea Peoples" in Text and Archaeology*. ABS 15. Atlanta: Society of Biblical Literature.

King, L. W. 1902. *Annals of the Kings of Assyria*. Volume 1. London: Harrison.

———. 1915. *Bronze Reliefs from the Gate of Shalmaneser, King of Assyria, B.C. 860–825*. London: British Museum.

Kirleis, W., and M. Herles. 2007. Climatic Change as a Reason for Assyro-Aramean Conflicts? Pollen Evidence for Drought at the End of the Second Millennium BC. *SAAB* 16:7–38.

Kitchen, K. A. 1983. *Ramesside Inscriptions: Historical and Biographical*. Vol. 5. Monumenta Hannach Sheen Decicata 3. Oxford: Blackwell.

———. 1986. *The Third Intermediate Period*. 2nd ed. Warminster: Aris & Phillips.

———. 1996–99. *Ramesses II Royal Inscriptions*. Vol. 2 of *Ramesside Inscriptions Translated and Annotated*. Oxford: Oxbow.

———. 1997. A Possible Mention of David in the Late Tenth Century BCE and Deity *Dod as Dead as the Dodo? *JSOT* 76:29–44.

———. 2003. *Merenptah and the Late Nineteenth Dynasty*. Vol. 4 of *Ramesside Inscriptions*. Oxford: Oxbow.

———. 2008. *Setnakht, Ramses III, and Contemporaries*. Vol. 5 of *Ramesside Inscriptions*. Oxford: Oxbow.

Kitchen, K. A., and P. J. N. Lawrence. 2012. *Treaty, Law and Covenant in the Ancient Near East*. 3 vols. Wiesbaden: Harrassowitz.

Klein, R. W. 2006. *1 Chronicles: A Commentary*. Hermeneia; Minneapolis: Fortress.

Klengel, H. 1963. Der Schiedsspruch des Muršili II. hinsichtlich Barga und seine Übereinkungt mit Duppi-Tešup von Amurru (KBo III 3). *Or* 32:32–55.

———. 1982. Das mittlere Orontes-Tal (Ghāb) in der Geschichte des vorhellenistischen Syrien. *AoF* 9:67–80.

———. 1992. *Syria 3000 to 300 B.C. A Handbook of Political History*. Berlin: Akademie.

———. 1995. Tunip und andere Probleme der historischen Geographie Mittelsyriens. Pages 125–34 in van Lerberghe and Schoors 1995.

———. 2000. The Crisis Years and the New Political System in Early Iron Age Syria. Some Introductory Remarks. Pages 21–30 in Bunnens 2000c.

Kloekhorst, A. 2008. *Etymological Dictionary of the Hittite Inherited Lexicon*. Leiden Indo-European Etymological Dictionary Series 5. Leiden: Brill.

Knapp, A. 2012. Royal Apologetic in the Ancient Near East. Ph.D. diss. Johns Hopkins University.

———. 2014. The Dispute over the Land of Qedem at the Onset of the Aram-Israel Conflict: A Reanalysis of Lines 3–4 of the Tel Dan Inscription. *JNES* 73:105–16.

Knauf, E. A. 1988. Supplementa Ismaelitica. *BN* 45:62–81.

———. 1990. Edomiter. *NBL* 3:468–71.

———. 1998–2001a. Nabatäer. *RlA* 9:2–5.

———. 1998–2001b. Nabatu. *RlA* 9:5.

Knoppers, G. N. 1999. Treasures Won and Lost: Royal (Mis)appropriations in Kings and Chronicles. Pages 181–208 in *The Chronicler as Author: Studies in Text and Texture*. Edited by M. P. Graham and S. L. McKenzie. JSOTSup 263. Sheffield: Sheffield Academic.

———. 2003. *I Chronicles 1–9*. AB 12. New York: Doubleday.

———. 2004. *I Chronicles 10–29*. AB 12A. New York: Doubleday.

Kochavi, M., et al. 1992. Rediscovered: The Land of Geshur. *BAR* 18.4:30–44, 84–85.

Kochavi, M. 1989. The Land of Geshur Project. Regional Archaeology of the Southern Golan (1987–1988 Seasons). *IEJ* 39:1–17.

———. 1991. The Land of Geshur Project, 1989–1990. *IEJ* 41:180–84.

———. 1993. The Land of Geshur Project, 1992. *IEJ* 43:185–90.

———. 1994. The Land of Geshur Project, 1993. *IEJ* 44:136–41.

———. 1996. The Land of Geshur: History of a Region in the Biblical Period. Pages 184–201 in *Joseph Aviram Volume*. Edited by A. Biran. ErIsr 25. Jerusalem: Israel Exploration Society.

———. 1999. Tripartite Buildings: Divided Structures Divide Scholars. *BAR* 25.3:44–50.

Kochavi, M., and A. Tsukimoto. 2008. ʿEn Gev. *NEAEHL* 5:1724–26.

Köroğlu, K. 1998. *Üçtepe 1: Yeni Kazı ve Yüzey Bulgulari Işğında Diyarbakır/Üçtepe ve Çevresinin Yeni Assur Dönemi Tarihi Coğrafyası*. Atatürk Kültür, Dil ve Tarih Yüksek Kurumu. Türk Tarih Kurumu yayınları 45. Ankara: Türk Tarih Kurumu Basımevi.

Kohlmeyer, K. 2000. *Der Tempel des Wettergottes von Aleppo*. Münster: Rhema-Verlag.

———. 2008. Zur Datierung der Skulpturen von ʿAin Dārā. Pages 119–30 in Bonatz, Czichon, and Janoscha Kreppner.

———. 2009. The Temple of the Storm God in Aleppo during the Late Bronze and Early Iron Ages. *NEA* 72:190–202.

———. 2011. Building Activities and Architectural Decoration in the Eleventh Century BC: The Temples of Taita, King of Padasatini/Palistin in Aleppo and ʿAin Dārāʾ. Pages 255–80 in *Empires after the Empire: Anatolia, Syria and Assyria after Suppiluliuma II, ca. 1200–800/700 B.C.* Edited by K. Strobel. Eothen 17. Firenze: LoGisma.

Kottsieper, I. 1998. Die Inschrift vom Tell Dan und die politischen Beziehungen zwischen Aram-Damaskus und Israel in der 1. Hälfte des 1. Jahrtausends vor Christus. Pages 475–500 in *"Und Moses schrieb dieses Lied auf": Studien zum Alten Testament und zum Alten Orient; Festschrift für Oswald Loretz zur Vollendung seines 70. Lebensjahres mit Beiträgen von Freunden, Schülern und Kollegen.* Edited by M. Dietrich and I. Kottsieper. AOAT 250. Münster: Ugarit-Verlag.

———. 2007. The Tel Dan Inscription (*KAI* 310) and the Political Relations between Aram-Damascus and Israel in the First Half of the First Millennium BCE. Pages 104–34 in *Ahab Agonistes: The Rise and Fall of the Omri Dynasty.* Edited by Lester L. Grabbe. LHBOTS 421. New York: T&T Clark.

———. 2009. Aramaic Literature. Pages 393–492 in *From an Antique Land: An Introduction to Ancient Near Eastern Literature.* Edited by C. S. Ehrlich. Lanham, MD: Rowman & Littlefield.

Kraeling, E. G. H. 1918. *Aram and Israel.* Columbia University Oriental Studies 13. New York: Columbia University Press.

Krebernik, M., and V. Seidl. 1997. Ein Schildbeschlag mit Bukranion und alphabetischer Inschrift. *ZA* 87:101–11.

Kreuzer, S. 1996. Die Religion der Aramäer auf dem Hintergrund der frühen aramäischen Staaten. Pages 101–15 in *Religionsgeschichte Syriens: Von der Frühzeit bis zur Gegenwart.* Stuttgart: Kohlhammer.

Kroll, S. 2012. Salmanassar III. und das frühe Urartu. Pages 163–68 in Kroll et al. 2012b.

Kroll, S., C. Gruber, U. Hellwag, M. Roaf, and P. E. Zimansky. 2012a. Introduction. Pages 1–38 in Kroll et al. 2012b.

Kroll, S., C. Gruber, U. Hellwag, M. Roaf, and P. E. Zimansky, eds. 2012b. *Biainili-Urartu: The Proceedings of the Symposium Held in Munich 12–14 October 2007.* Acta Iranica 51. Leuven: Peeters.

Kuan, J. K. 1995. *Neo-Assyrian Historical Inscriptions and Syria-Palestine.* Jian Dao Dissertation Series 1. Hong Kong: Alliance Bible Seminary.

———. 2001. Šamši-ilu and the *Realpolitik* of Israel and Aram-Damascus in the Eighth Century BCE. Pages 135–51 in Dearman and Graham 2001.

Kühne, H. 1980. Zur Rekonstruktion der Feldzüge Adad-Nīrāri II, Tukulti-Ninurta II und Aššurnaṣirpal II im Ḫābūr-Gebiet. *BaM* 11:44–70.

———. 1983–84. Tall Šeh Hamad/Dur-Katlimmu 1981–83. *AfO* 31:166–78.

———. 1995. The Assyrians on the Middle Euphrates and the Ḫābūr. Pages 69–85 in Liverani 1995.

———. 1998. Tall Šēḫ Ḥamad—The Assyrian City of Dūr-Katlimmu: A Historic-Geographical Approach. Pages 279–307 in *Essays on Ancient Anatolia in the Second Millennium B.C.* Edited by T. Mikasa. Bulletin of the Middle Eastern Culture Center in Japan 10. Wiesbaden: Harrassowitz.

———. 1999. Imperial Mittani: An Attempt at Historical Reconstruction. Pages 203–21 in *Nuzi at Seventy-Five*. Edited by D. I. Owen and G. Wilhelm. SCCNH 10. Bethesda, MD: CDL.

———. 2000. Dūr-katlimmu and the Middle-Assyrian Empire. Pages 271–9 in Rouault and Wäfler 2000.

———. 2009. Interaction of Aramaeans and Assyrians on the Lower Khabur. *Syria* 86:43–54.

———. 2010. The Rural Hinterland of Dūr-Katlimmu. Pages 115–28 in *Dūr-Katlimmu 2008 and Beyond*. Edited by H. Kühne. Studia Chaburensia 1. Wiesbaden: Harrassowitz.

Kühne, H., R. M. Czichon, and F. Janoscha Kreppner, eds. 2008. *The Reconstruction of Environment: Natural Resources and Human Interrelations through Time. Art History: Visual Communication*. Vol. 1 of *Proceedings of the 4th International Congress of the Archaeology of the Ancient Near East 29 March–3 April 2004, Freie Universität Berlin*. Wiesbaden: Harrassowitz.

Kühne, H., and K. Radner. 2008. Das Siegel des Išme-ilū, Eunuch des Nergal-ēreš, aus Dūr-Katlimmu. *ZA* 98:26–44.

Kuhrt, A. 1995. *The Ancient Near East c. 3000–330 BC*. 2 vols. Routledge History of the Ancient World. London: Routledge.

Kupper, J.-R. 1957. *Les nomades en Mésopotamie au temps des rois de Mari*. Bibliothèque de la Faculté de philosophie et lettres de l'Université de Liège 142. Paris: Belles Lettres.

———. 1959. Le rôle des nomades dans l'histoire de la mésopotamie ancienne. *JESHO* 2:113–27.

———. 1998. *Lettres royales du temps de Zimri-Lim*. ARM 28. Paris: Éditions Recherche sur les Civilisations.

———. 1998–2001. Naḫur. *RlA* 9:86–87.

Kuschke, A. 1954. Beiträge zur Siedlungschichte der Bikāʿ. *ZDPV* 70:104–29.

———. 1958. Beiträge zur Siedlungschichte der Bikāʿ. *ZDPV* 74:81–120.

Kwasman, T. 1988. *Neo-Assyrian Legal Documents in the Kouyunjik Collection of the British Museum*. StPohlSM 14. Rome: Pontifical Biblical Institute.

———. 2000. Two Aramaic Legal Documents. *BSOAS* 63:274–83.

Kyreleis, H. 1988. Ein altorientalischer Pferdeschmuck aus dem Heraion von Samos. *MDAI* 103:37–61.

LaBianca, Ø. S. 1990. *Sedentarization and Nomadization: Food System Cycles at Hesban and Vicinity in Transjordan*. Hesban 1. Berrien Springs, MI: Andrews University Press.

———. 1997. Indigenous Hardiness Structures and State Formation in Jordan: Towards a History of Jordan's Resident Arab Population. Pages 143–57 in *Ethnic Encounter and Culture Change*. Edited by M. Sabour and K. Vikør. London: Hurst.

———. 1999. Salient Features of Iron Age Tribal Kingdoms. Pages 19–23 in *Ancient Ammon*. Edited by B. MacDonald and R. W. Younker. SHANE 17. Leiden: Brill.

Laessøe, J. 1959. A Statue of Shalmaneser III from Nimrud. *Iraq* 21:147–57 and pls. xl–xlii.

Lamb, D. T. 2007. *Righteous Jehu and His Evil Heirs: The Deuteronomist's Negative*

*Perspective on Dynastic Succession*. Oxford Theological Monographs. Oxford: Oxford University Press.
Lambert, W. G. 1968. Another Look at Hammurabi's Ancestors. *JCS* 22:1–2.
———. 1981. Portion of Inscribed Stela of Sargon II, King of Assyria. Page 125 in *Ladders to Heaven: Art Treasures from Lands of the Bible*. Edited by O. W. Muscarella. Toronto: McCelland & Stewart.
———. 1985. The Pantheon of Mari. *MARI* 4:525–39.
———. 1991. An Unknown King in an Unknown City. Pages 314–19 in Cogan and Eph'al 1991.
———. 1994. When Did Jehu Pay Tribute? Pages 51–56 in *Crossing the Boundaries: Essays in Biblical Interpretation in Honour of Michael D. Goulder*. Edited by S. E. Porter, P. Joyce, and D. Orton. BibInt 8. Leiden: Brill.
———. 2004a. Exiles and Deportees: A Third Category. Pages 213–16 in Nicolle 2004.
———. 2004b. Mesopotamian Sources and Pre-exilic Israel. Pages 353–65 in *In Search of Pre-exilic Israel: Proceedings of the Oxford Old Testament Seminar*. Edited by J. Day. JSOTSup 406. London: Continuum.
———. 2007. *Babylonian Oracle Questions*. MC 13. Winona Lake, IN: Eisenbrauns.
Landsberger, B. 1948. *Sam'al: Studien zur Entdeckung der Ruinenstätte Karatepe*. Ankara: Türkische historische Gesellschaft.
Lanfranchi, G. B. 2002. Chronology in the Inscriptions of Shalmaneser III and in the Eponym Chronicle: The Number of the Campaigns against Que. Pages 453–69 in *Anatolia Antica: Studi in memoria de Fiorella Imparati*. Edited by S. de Martino and F. Pecchioli Daddi. Eothen 11. Firenze: LoGisma editore.
———. 2003. The Assyrian Expansion in the Zagros and the Local Ruling Elites. Pages 79–118 in Lanfranchi, Roaf, and Rollinger 2003.
———. 2012. An Empire Names Its Periphery: the Neo-Assyrian Toponym for Damascus. Pages 399–434 in Lanfranchi et al. 2012.
Lanfranchi, G. B., D. Morandi Bonacossi, C. Pappi, and S. Ponchia, eds. 2012. *Leggo! Studies Presented to Frederick Mario Fales on the Occasion of His Sixty-Fifth Birthday*. Wiesbaden: Harrassowitz.
Lanfranchi, G. B., M. Roaf, and R. Rollinger, eds. 2003. *Continuity of Empire (?): Assyria, Media, Persia*. HANEM 5. Padova: S.a.r.g.o.n.
Langdon, S. 1912. *Die neubabylonischen Königsinschriften*. Vorderasiatische Bibliothek 4. Leipzig: Hinrichs.
Langenegger, F. 1950. Die Bauten und Schichten des Burghügels. Pages 3–324 in Naumann 1950.
Lapinkivi, P., and K. Radner. 1999. Gē-ammu. *PNA* 2.1:422.
Laroche, E. 1956. Documents hiéroglyphiques hittites provenant du palais d'Ugarit. Pages 97–106 in *Ugaritica III*. Edited by C. F. A. Schaeffer. Paris.
———. 1966. *Les noms des Hittites*. Études linguistiques 4. Paris: Klincksieck.
Lauinger, J. 2012. Esarhaddon's Succession Treaty at Tell Tayinat: Text and Commentary. *JCS* 64:87–123.
Layton, S. C. 1990. *Archaic Features of Canaanite Personal Names in the Hebrew Bible*. HSM 47. Atlanta: Scholars Press.
Lehmann, G. 1994. Zu den Zerstörungen in Zincirli während des frühen 7. Jahrhunderts v. Chr. *MDOG* 126:105–22.

———. 1996. *Untersuchungen zur Späten Eisenzeit in Syrien und Libanon: Stratigraphie und Keramikformen zwischen ca. 720 bis 300 v. Chr.* Münster: Ugarit-Verlag.
———. 1998. Trends in the Local Pottery Development of the Late Iron Age and Persian Period in Syria and Lebanon, ca. 700 to 300 B.C. *BASOR* 311:7–38.
———. 2002. *Bibliographie der archäologischen Fundstellen und Surveys in Syrien und Libanon.* Orient-Archäologie 9. Rahden/Westf.: Leidorf.
Lemaire, A. 1977a. *Les Ostraca.* Vol. 1 of *Inscriptions hébraïques.* LAPO 9. Paris: Cerf.
———. 1977b. Essai sur cinq sceaux phéniciens. *Sem* 27:29–40.
———. 1981. Le pays d'Eden et le Bit-Adini aux origines d'un mythe. *Syria* 58:313–30.
———. 1983. L'inscription phénicienne de Hassan-Beyli reconsiderée. *RSF* 11:9–19.
———. 1984. La stèle araméenne de Barhadad. *Or* 53:337–49.
———. 1987. Aššur-šar-uṣur, gouverneur de Que. *NABU* 1987.1:5–6, n. 10. http://sepoa .fr/wp/wp-content/uploads/2012/05/1987-1.pdf.
———. 1988. Hadad l'Edomite ou Hadad l'Araméen? *BN* 43:14–18.
———. 1989a. Remarques à propos du monnayage cilicien d'epoque perse et ses légendes araméennes. *REA* 91:141–56.
———. 1989b. Une inscription phénicienne découverte récemment et le mariage de Ruth la Moabite. Pages 124*–29* in *Yigael Yadin Memorial Volume.* Edited by A. Ben-Tor, J. C. Greenfield, and A. Malamat. ErIsr 20. Jerusalem: Israel Exploration Society.
———. 1990. SMR dans la petite inscription de Kilamuwa (Zencirli). *Syria* 67:323–27.
———. 1991a. Hazaël de Damas, roi d'Aram. Pages 91–108 in Charpin and Joannès 1991.
———. 1991b. La stèle de Mésha et l'histoire de l'ancien Israël. Pages 143–69 in Garrone and Israel 1991.
———. 1993. Joas de Samarie, Barhadad de Damas, Zakkur de Hamat: La Syrie-Palestine vers 800 av. J.-C. Pages 148*–57* in *Abraham Malamat Volume.* Edited by S. Ahituv et al. ErIsr 24. Jerusalem: Israel Exploration Society.
———. 1997. D'Edom à l'Idumée et à Rome. Pages 81–103 in *Des Sumeriens aux Romains: La perception geographique du monde.* Antiquites semitiques 2. Paris: Maisonneuve.
———. 1998a. The Tel Dan Stela as a Piece of Royal Historiography. *JSOT* 81:3–14.
———. 1998b. Une inscription araméenne du VIII^e^ s. av. J.-C. trouvée à Bukân. *Studia Iranica* 27:15–30.
———. 1998c. L'inscription araméenne de Bukân et son intérêt historique. *CRAI* 142:293–299.
———. 1999. La stele araméenne de Bukân: Mise au point épigraphique. *NABU* 1999.3:57–58, no. 57. http://sepoa.fr/wp/wp-content/uploads/2012/05/1999-3.pdf.
———. 2001a. Les langues du royaume de Samʾal aux IX^e^-VIII^e^ s. av. J.-C. et leurs relations avec le royaume de Qué. Pages 185–93 in *La Cilicie: Espaces et pouvoirs locaux (2^e^ millénaire av. J.-C. - 4^e^ siècle ap. J.-C.).* Edited by E. Jean, A. M. Dinçol, and S. Durugönül. Paris: Institut Français d'Études Anatoliennes.
———. 2001b. Les premiers rois araméens dan la tradition biblique. Pages 113–43 in vol. 1 of Daviau, Wevers, and Weigl 2001.

———. 2001c. *Nouvelles tablettes araméennes*. Hautes études orientales 34. Geneva: Droz.
———. 2006. Aramaic Script and Its Role in Creating Cultural Links. Pages 73–96 in *History of Script and Writing: Collected Essays of International Seminar of Tablet to Tablet (From Clay Tablet to Electronic Compact Disk)*. Ministry of Culture and Islamic Guidance. Tehran: Chameh.
———. 2007a. אב, "père" ou "maison paternelle" en 1 Rois 15,19a? Pages *46–*51 in *Biblical Hebrew, Masorah, and Medieval Hebrew*. Vol. 1 of *Sha'arei Lashon: Studies in Hebrew, Aramaic, and Jewish Languages in Honor of Moshe Bar-Asher*. Edited by A. Maman, S. E. Fassberg, and Y. Breuer. Jerusalem: Bialik Institute.
———. 2007b. West Semitic Inscriptions and Ninth-Century BCE Ancient Israel. Pages 279–303 in Williamson 2007.
———. 2010a. Les formulaires juridiques des tablettes araméennes. Pages 187–219 in *Trois millénaires de formulaires juridiques*. Edited by S. Démare-Lafont and A. Lemaire. Hautes études orientales 48. Hautes études orientales. Moyen et Proche-Orient 4. Geneva: Droz.
———. 2010b. Hazor in the Second Half of the Tenth Century B.C.E.: Historiography, Archaeology and History. Pages 55–72 in *The Historian and the Bible: Essays in Honour of Lester L. Grabbe*. Edited by P. R. Davies and D. V. Edelman. LHBOTS 530. New York: T&T Clark.
———. 2013. Le dialecte araméen de l'inscription de Kuttamuwa (Zencirli, VIII$^{e}$ s. av. n. è.). Pages 145–50 in *In the Shadow of Bezalel: Aramaic, Biblical, and Ancient Near Eastern Studies in Honor of Bezalel Porten*. Edited by A. F. Botta. CHANE 60. Leiden: Brill.
Lemaire, A., and J.-M. Durand. 1984. *Les inscriptions araméennes de Sfiré et l'Assyrie de Shamshiilu*. Hautes études orientales 20. Geneva: Droz.
Lemaire, A., and B. Sass. 2012. La stèle d'Ördekburnu: Vers la solution d'une énigme de l'épigraphie ouest-sémitique. *CRAI* 156:227–40.
———. 2013. The Mortuary Stele with Sam'alian Inscription from Ördekburnu Near Zincirli. *BASOR* 369:57–136.
Lemche, N. P. 1998. *The Israelites in History and Tradition*. Louisville: Westminster John Knox.
Lerberghe, K. van, and A. Schoors, eds. 1995. *Immigration and Emigration in the Ancient Near East*. Edited by K. van Lerberghe and A. Schoors. OLA 65. Leuven: Peeters.
Lerberghe, K. van, and G. Voet. 1991. *Sippar-Amnānum: The Ur-Utu Archive I*. Mesopotamian History and Environment, Texts 1. Ghent: University of Ghent.
Levenson, J. D. and B. Halpern. 1980. The Political Import of David's Marriages. *JBL* 99:507–18.
Levine, L. D. 1976–80. Kirruiri, Kirriuri (Ḫabr(i)uri?). *RlA* 5:606–7.
Levine, B. A. 1995. The Semantics of Loss: Two Exercises in Biblical Hebrew Lexicography. Pages 137–58 in Zevit, Gitin, and Sokoloff 1995.
———. 2008. The *CAD* and Biblical Hebrew Lexicography. Pages 111–18 in *Proceedings of the 51st Rencontre Assyriologique Internationale: Held at the Oriental Institute of the University of Chicago, July 18–22, 2005*. Edited by R. D. Biggs, J. Myers, and M. T. Roth. SAOC 62. Chicago: Oriental Institute of the University of Chicago.

Lewy, J. 1944. The Old West Semitic Sun-God Ḥammu. *HUCA* 18:429–88.
———. 1952. Studies in the Historic Geography of the Ancient Near East. *Or* 21:1–12, 265–92, 393–425.
———. 1961. Amurritica. *HUCA* 32:31–74.
Lidzbarski, M. 1898. *Handbuch der nordsemitischen Epigraphik nebst ausgewählten Inschriften*. 2 vols. Weimar: Felber.
———. 1915. *Ephemeris für semitische Epigraphik III*. Giessen: Ricker.
Linville, J. R. 1998. *Israel in the Book of Kings: The Past as a Project of Social Identity*. JSOTSup 272. Sheffield: Sheffield Academic.
Lipiński, E. 1969a. Le Ben-hadad II de la bible et l'histoire. Pages 157–73 in *Proceedings of the Fifth World Congress of Jewish Studies I*. Jerusalem: World Union of Jewish Studies.
———. 1969b. Trois hébraïsmes oubliés ou méconnus. *RSO* 44:83–101.
———. 1971. The Assyrian Campaign to Manṣuate in 796 B.C., and the Zakir Stele. *AION* 31:393–99.
———. 1974. From Karatepe to Pyrgi: Middle Phoenician Miscellanea. *RSF* 2:45–61.
———. 1979. Aram et Israël du X^e^ au VIII^e^ siècle av. n. è. *Acta Antiqua* 27:49–102.
———. 1981. Review of Gelb 1980. *JSS* 26:277–80.
———. 1983. The God ʾArqû-Rashap in the Samallian Hadad Inscription. Pages 15–21 in Sokoloff 1983.
———. 1985. Phoenicians in Anatolia and Assyria, 9th–6th Centuries B.C. *OLP* 16:81–90.
———. 1989. "Mon père était un Araméen errant": L'histoire, carrefour des sciences bibliques et orientales. *OLP* 20:23-47.
———. 1991. Jéroboam II et la Syrie. Pages 171–76 in *Storia e tradizioni di Israel*. Edited by D. Garrone and F. Israel. Brescia: Paideia Editrice.
———. 1993. Les Sémites selon Gen 10, 21–30 et I Chr 1, 723. *ZAH* 6:193–215.
———. 1994. *Studies in Aramaic Inscriptions and Onomastics II*. OLA 57. Leuven: Peeters.
———. 1999a. Ba'sa. *PNA* 1.2:275.
———. 1999b. Ba'alu. *PNA* 1.2:242.
———. 1999c. Baḫiānu, *PNA* 1.2:252.
———. 2000a. *The Aramaeans: Their Ancient History, Culture, Religion*. OLA 100. Leuven: Peeters.
———. 2000b. The Linguistic Geography of Syria in the Iron Age II (ca. 1000–600 B.C.). Pages 124–42 in Bunnens 2000c.
———. 2001. *Semitic Languages: Outline of a Comparative Grammar*. OLA 80. Leuven: Peeters.
———. 2002. Diyarbakır: An Aramaean Capital of the Ninth Century B.C. and Its Territory. Pages 225–39 in Taracha 2002.
———. 2003. "Broken" Plural in "Aramaic" Tribal Names. Pages 336–49 in *Semitic and Assyriological Studies Presented to Pelio Fronzaroli*. Edited by P. Marrassini. Wiesbaden: Harrassowitz.
———. 2006. *On the Skirts of Canaan in the Iron Age: Historical and Topographical Researches*. OLA 153. Leuven: Peeters.
———. 2008. Aramaic Broken Plurals in the Wider Semitic Context. Pages 27–40 in Gzella and Folmer 2008.

———. 2010. *Studies in Aramaic Inscriptions and Onomastics III*. OLA 200. Leuven: Peeters.
———. 2011. Zammānu. *PNA* 3.2:1433.
———. 2013. The Aramaeans in the West (13th–8th Centuries). Pages 123–47 in Berlejung and Streck 2013.
Litke, R. L. 1998. *A Reconstruction of the Assyro-Babylonian God-Lists An: $^{d}$A-nu-um and AN: An ša ameli*. Texts from the Babylonian Collection 3. New Haven: Yale Babylonian Collection.
Liverani, M. 1961. Bar-Gusi e Bar-Rakib. *RSO* 36:185–87.
———. 1973. Memorandum on the Approach to Historiographic Texts. *Or* 42:178–94.
———. 1987. The Collapse of the Near Eastern Regional System at the End of the Bronze Age: The Case of Syria. Pages 66–73 in *Centre and Periphery in the Ancient World*. Edited by M. Rowlands, M. Larsen, and K. Kristiansen. Cambridge: Cambridge University Press.
———. 1988a. The Growth of the Assyrian Empire in the Habur/Middle Euphrates Area: A New Paradigm. *SAAB* 2:81–98.
———. 1988b. *Antico Oriente: Storia società econontia*. Rome: Bari.
———. 1990. *Prestige and Interest: International Relations in the Near East ca. 1600–1100 B.C.* HANEM 1. Padova: Sargon.
———. 1991. Kilamuwa 7–8 e II Re 7. Pages 177–84 in Garrone and Israel 1991.
———. 1992a. *Topographical Analysis*. Vol. 2 of *Studies on the Annals of Ashurnasirpal II*. Quaderni di Geografica Storica 4. Rome: Università di Roma "La Sapienza."
———. 1992b. Raṣappa and Hatallu. *SAAB* 6:35–40.
———, ed. 1995. *Neo-Assyrian Geography*. Quaderni di Geografia Storica 5. Rome: Università di Roma "La Sapienza."
———. 1997. Ancient Near Eastern Cities and Modern Ideologies. Pages 85–107 in *Die orientalische Stadt: Kontinuität, Wandel, Bruch; 1. Internationales Colloquium der Deutschen Orient-Gesellschaft, 9.–10. Mai 1996 in Halle/Saale*. Edited by G. Wilhelm. Colloquien der Deutschen Orient-Gesellschaft 1. Saarbrücken: Saarbrücker Druckerei und Verlag.
———. 2000. Once Again on MLK KTK in the Sefire Stelas. *NABU* 2000.3:60, no. 53. http://sepoa.fr/wp/wp-content/uploads/2012/05/2000-3.pdf.
———. 2001. *International Relations in the Ancient Near East, 1600–1100 B.C.* Studies in Diplomacy. Houndmills: Palgrave.
———. 2004a. The Fate of Ashur-Uballit's Messengers in EA 16. Pages 117–20 in *Von Sumer nach Ebla und züruck: Festschrift G. Pettinato zum 27. September 1999 gewidmet von Freunden, Kollegen und Schülern*. Edited by H. Waetzoldt. HSAO 9. Heidelberg: Heidelberger Orientverlag.
———. 2004b. Assyria in the Ninth Century: Continuity or Change? Pages 213–26 in Frame and Wilding 2004.
———. 2005. *Israel's History and the History of Israel*. Translated by C. Peri and P. R. Davies. London: Equinox.
———. 2012. Melid in the Early and Middle Iron Age. Pages 327–44 in Galil et al. 2012.

———. 2014. *The Ancient Near East: History, Society and Economy*. London: Routledge.

Livingstone, A. 1986. *Mystical and Mythological Explanatory Works of Assyrian and Babylonian Scholars*. Oxford: Oxford University Press.

———. 1989. *Court Poetry and Literary Miscellanea*. SAA 3. Helsinki: Helsinki University Press.

Llop-Raduà, J. 2008. MARV 6, 2 und die Eponymenfolgen des 12. Jahrhunderts. *ZA* 98:20–25.

———. 2011a. The Boundary between Assyria and Babylonia in the East Tigris Region during the Reign of Tukultī-Ninurta I (1233–1197 BC). Pages 209–15 in *Between the Cultures: The Central Tigris Region from the Third to the First Millennium BC; Conference at Heidelberg January 22nd–24th, 2009*. Edited by P. A. Miglus and S. Mühl. HSAO 14. Heidelberg: Heidelberger Orientverlag.

———. 2011b. The Creation of the Middle Assyrian Provinces. *JAOS* 131:591–603.

———. 2012a. Did the Assyrians Occupy the Euphrates-Elbow in the Middle Assyrian Period (Late Bronze Age)? Pages 203–25 in *Broadening Horizons 3: Conference of Young Researchers Working in the Ancient Near East*. Edited by F. Borrell, M. Bouso, A. Gómez, C. Tornero, and O. Vicente. Congressos 8. Universitat Autònoma de Barcelona. Bellaterra: Servei de Publicacions.

———. 2012b. The Development of the Middle Assyrian Provinces. *AoF* 39:87–111.

Llop, J., and A. R. George. 2001–2. Die baylonisch-assyrischen Beziehungen und die innere Lage Assyriens in der Zeit der Auseinandersetzung zwischen Ninurta-tukulti-Aššur und Mutakkil-Nušku nach neuen keilschriftlichen Quellen. *AfO* 48–49:1–23.

Lombard, P. 1995. Contexte archéologique et données épigraphiques: Quelques reflexions sur l'interpretation du gisement de 1973–1992. Pages 227–37 in *Le pays d'Ougarit autour de 1200 av. J.-C.: Histoire et archéologie*. Edited by Marguerite Yon, Maurice Sznycer, and Pierre Bordreuil. RSOu 11. Paris: Editions Recherche sur les civilisations.

Long, B. O. 1984. *1 Kings*. FOTL. Grand Rapids: Eerdmans.

———. 1985. Historical Narrative and the Fictionalizing Imagination. *VT* 35:405–16.

———. 1987. Framing Repetitions in Biblical Historiography. *JBL* 106:385–99.

Lönnqvist, M. A. 2000. Between Nomadism and Sedentism: Amorites from the Perspective of a Contextual Archaeology. Ph.D. diss. University of Helsinki.

———. 2008. Were Nomadic Amorites on the Move? Migration, Invasion and Gradual Infiltration as Mechanisms for Cultural Transitions. Pages 195–214 in Kühne, Czichon, and Janoscha Kreppner 2008.

———. 2011. Outlooks to Cuneiform Texts and the Mesopotamian Lore. Pages 197–212 in Lönnqvist, Törmä, Lönnqvist and Nuñez 2011.

Lönnqvist, M. A., ed. 2008. *Jebel Bishri in Context: Introduction to the Archaeological Studies and the Neighbourhood of Jebel Bishri in Central Syria: Proceedings of a Nordic Research Training Seminar in Syria, May 2004*. BARI 1817. Oxford: Archaeopress.

Lönnqvist, M., M. Törmä, K. Lönnqvist and M. Nuñez. 2011. *Jebel Bishri in Focus: Remote Sensing, Archaeological Surveying, Mapping and GIS Studies of Jebel Bishri in Central Syria by the Finnish Project SYGIS*. BARI 2230. Oxford: Archaeopress.

Loretz, O. 1978. Die ASĪRUM-texte (I). *UF* 10:121–60.

Loretz, O., K. A. Metzler, and H. Schaudig, eds. 2002. *Ex Mesopotamia et Syria Lux: Festschrift für Manfred Dietrich zu seinem 65. Geburtstag*. AOAT 281. Münster: Ugarit-Verlag.

Lozachmeur, H.-A., and A. Lemaire. 1996. Nouveaux ostraca araméens d'Idumee (Collection Sh. Moussaleft). *Sem* 46:123–42.

Luciani, M. 1999. Zur Lage Terqas in schriftlichen Quellen. *ZA* 89:1–23.

———. 1999-2001. On Assyrian Frontiers and the Middle Euphrates. *SAAB* 13:87–114.

———. 2000. Iron Age Graves in Northern Syria: The Tell Shiukh Fawqani Evidence. Pages 803–13 in vol. 1 of *Proceedings of the First International Congress on the Archaeology of the Ancient Near East, Rome, May 18th–23rd 1998*. Edited by P. Matthiae et al. 2 vols. Rome: Università degli studi di Roma "La Sapienza."

Luckenbill, D. D. 1920. The "Wandering Aramaean." *AJSL* 36:244–45.

———. 1924–25. Azariah of Judah. *AJSL* 41:217–32.

———. 1926–27. *Ancient Records of Assyria and Babylonia*. 2 vols. Chicago: University of Chicago Press.

Luukko, M. 1998. Agūsu. *PNA* 1.1:56.

Lyon, J. D. 2000. Middle Assyrian Expansion and Settlement Development in the Syrian Jazira: The View from the Balikh Valley. Pages 89–126 in *Rainfall and Agriculture in Northern Mesopotamia*. Edited by R. M. Jas. MOS Studies 3. Istanbul: Nederlands Historisch-Archaeologisch Instituut.

Lyonnet, B. 2004. Le nomadisme et l'archéologie: Problèmes d'identification; le cas de la partie occidentale de la Djéziré au 3e et début du 2e millénaire avant notre ére. Pages 25–50 in Nicolle 2004.

Macdonald, M. C. A. 2000. Reflections on the Linguistic Map of PreIslamic Arabia. *Arabian Archaeology and Epigraphy* 11.1:28–79.

MacGinnis, J. 2011. Cuneiform Tablet ZTT 30. Pages 73–74 in T. Matney et al. Excavations at Ziyaret Tepe, Diyarbakir Province, Turkey, 2009–2010 Seasons. *Anatolica* 37:67–114.

———. 2012. Evidence for a Peripheral Language in a Neo-Assyrian Tablet from the Governor's Palace in Tušḫan. *JNES* 71:13–20.

MacLaurin, E. C. B. 1978. QRT-'ABLM. *PEQ* 110:113–14.

Machinist, P. 1982. Provincial Governance in Middle Assyria and Some New Texts from Yale. *Assur* 3.2:65–101.

———. 1986. On Self-Consciousness in Mesopotamia. Pages 183–202, 511–18 in *The Origins and Diversity of Axial Age Civilizations*. Edited by S. N. Eisenstadt. Albany: State University of New York Press.

———. 1994. Outsiders or Insiders: The Biblical View of Emergent Israel and Its Contexts. Pages 35–60 in *The Other in Jewish Thought and History: Constructions of Jewish Culture and Identity*. Edited by L. J. Silberstein and R. L. Cohn. New York: New York University Press.

Maeir, A. M. 2003–5. Philister-Keramik (Philistine Ceramics). *RlA* 10:528–36.

———. 2009a. Fragments of Stone Reliefs from Bliss and Macalister's Excavations at Tell eṣ-Ṣafi. Pp. 270–76, 291* in *Ephraim Stern Volume*. Edited by J. Aviram et al. ErIsr 29. Jerusalem: Israel Exploration Society.

———. 2009b. Hazael, Birhadad, and the ḤRṢ. Pp. 273–77 in Schloen 2009.

Maeir, A. M., O. Ackermann, and H. J. Bruins. 2006. The Ecological Consequences of a Siege: A Marginal Note on Deuteronomy 20:19–20. Pages 238–43 in *Confronting the Past: Archaeological and Historical Essays on Ancient Israel in Honor of William G. Dever*. Edited by S. Gitin, J. E. Wright, and J. P. Dessel. Winona Lake, IN: Eisenbrauns.

Maeir, A. M. and C. S. Ehrlich. 2001. Excavating Philistine Gath: Have We Found Goliath's Hometown? *BAR* 27/6:22–31.

Maeir, A. M., and S. Gur-Arieh. 2011. Comparative Aspects of the Aramean Siege System at Tell eṣ-Ṣāfi/Gath. Pp 227–44 in Finkelstein and Na'aman 2011.

Maeir, A. M., and J. Uziel. 2007. A Tale of Two Tells: A Comparative Perspective on Tel Miqne-Ekron and Tell eṣ-Ṣāfī/Gath in Light of Recent Archaeological Research. Pages 29–42 in *"Up to the Gates of Ekron": Essays on the Archaeology and History of the Eastern Mediterranean in Honor of Seymour Gitin*. Edited by S. White Crawford and A. BenTor. Jerusalem: W. F. Albright Institute of Archaeological Research; Israel Exploration Society.

Mahmoud, A. 2008. Fruchtbare Kooperation. Pages 389–92 in Bonatz, Czichon, and Janoscha Kreppner 2008.

Mahmud, M., and J. Black. 1985–86. Recent Work in the Nabu Temple, Nimrud. *Sumer* 44:135–55.

Maisler (Mazar), B. 1929. Die Landschaft Bašan im 2. vorchristl. Jahrt. *JPOS* 9:80–87.

Makinson, M. 2002–5. Muṣru, Maṣuwari and *MṢR*: From Middle Assyrian Frontier to Iron Age City. *SAAB* 14:33–62.

———. 2009. Mansuâte (Emesa?) porte d'Aram-Damas. *Studia Orontica* 6:24–32.

Malamat, A. 1953. Amos 1:5 in the Light of the Til Barsip Inscriptions. *BASOR* 129:25–26.

———. 1963. Aspects of Foreign Policies of David and Solomon. *JNES* 22:1–17.

———. 1973. Aramaeans. Pages 134–155 in *Peoples of Old Testament Times*. Edited by D. J. Wiseman. Oxford: Oxford University Press.

———. 1976. A New Proposal for the Identification of KTK in the Sefire Inscriptions [Hebrew]. Pages 7–11 in *Census Lists and Genealogies and Their Historial Implications*. Edited by M. Razin and S. Bendor. Haifa: University of Haifa.

———. 1983. Das davidische und salomonische Konigreich und seine Beziehungen zu Agypt und Syrien: Zur Entstehung eines Großreichs. *Österreichische Akademie der Wissenschaften Philosophisch-historische Klasse. Sitzungsberichte* 407:37–39.

Mallowan, M. E. L. 1966. *Nimrud and Its Remains*. 2 vols. London: John Murray.

Manning, P. 2013. *Migration in World History*. 2nd ed. Themes in World History. London: Routledge.

Manuelli, F. 2009. Assyria and the Provinces. Survival of Local Features and Imposition of New Patterns in the Peripheral Regions of the Empire. *Mesopotamia* 49:61–112.

———. 2013. Pottery as an Indicator of Changing Interregional Relations in the Upper Euphrates Valley: The Case of the Late Bronze-Iron Age Assemblages from Arslantepe/Malatya. Pages 373–91 in Yener 2013.

Ma'oz, Z. U. 1992. Geshur. *ABD* 2:996.

Maqdissi, M. al-. 1996. La reprise des fouilles à Mishirfeh en 1994. *Akkadica* 99–100:1–14.

———. 1997. Mishrifeh/Qatna. *AJA* 101:132–33.

———. 2011. Notes d'Archéologie Levantine, XXII: Le bas relief de Jisr el-Shughur. Pages 91–97 in *Archaeology for Cooperation: Afis, Deinit and the Museum of Idlib; Activities in the Frame of the MEDA Project*. Edited by M. Rossi. Studi di Archeologia Siriana 1. Naples: Tilapia.

Maqdissi, M. al-, M. Luciani, D. Morandi Bonacossi, M. Novák, and P. Pfälzner, eds. 2002. *Preliminary Report on the 1999 and 2000 Campaigns of the Joint Syrian-Italian-German Archaeological Research Project at Tell Mishrifeh*. Vol. 1 of *Excavating Qatna*. Documents d'archáologie syrienne 4. Damascus: Direction Général des Antiquités et des Musées de Syrie; Udine: University of Udine; Tübingen: University of Tübingen.

Maraqten, M. 1988. *Die semitischen Personennamen in den alt- und reichsaramäischen Inschriften aus Vorderasien*. TSO 5. Hildesheim: Olms.

Marchesi, G., H. Peker, and D. Hawkins. 2012. The "Quay of Kamis": A Crossroads of Peoples and Civilizations. *NEA* 75:143–44, 146–47.

Marchetti, N., et al. 2012. Karkemish on the Euphrates: Excavating a City's History. *NEA* 75:132–47.

Marchetti, N. 2006. Middle Bronze Age Public Architecture at Tilmen Höyük and the Architectural Tradition of Old Syrian Palaces. Pages 275–308 in *Ina kibrāt erbetti: Studi di Archeologia orientale dedicati a Paolo Matthiae*. Edited by F. Baffi, R. Dolce, S. Mazzoni, and F. Pinnock. Rome: Università di Roma "La Sapienza."

———. 2007. A Late Old Syrian Stela from Temple M at Tilmen Höyük. Pages 153–67 in *Refik Duru'ya Armağan/Studies in Honour of Refik Duru*. Edited by G. Dumurtak, S. Donmez, and A. Yurtsever. İstanbul: Ege Yayınları.

Marcus, M. I. 1987. Geography as an Organizing Principle in the Imperial Art of Shalmaneser III. *Iraq* 49:77–90.

Marcus, R. 1937. *Josephus with an English Translation*. 9 volus. London: Heinemann; Cambridge: Harvard University Press.

Mare, W. H. 1993. Abila of the Decapolis Excavations. *Syria* 70:208–14.

Margalit, B. 1976. Studia Ugaritica II: Studies in *Krt* and *Aqht*. *UF* 8:137–92.

———. 1981. John Day and the "Kennereth Hypothesis." *VT* 31:373–75.

———. 1989. *The Ugaritic Poem of Aqht*. BZAW 182. Berlin: de Gruyter.

———. 1994a. Studies in NW Semitic Inscriptions, III, Samaliana. *UF* 26:303–15.

———. 1994b. Exit Panamuwa II. *NABU* 1994.1:6–7, no. 5. http://sepoa.fr/wp/wp-content/uploads/2012/05/1994-1.pdf.

———. 1994c. Parricidal Panamuwa: The Sequel. *NABU* 1994.1:12, no. 12. http://sepoa.fr/wp/wp-content/uploads/2012/05/1994-1.pdf

———. 1995. Studies in NW Semitic Inscriptions, III, Samaliana. *UF* 27:177–214.

Margalith, O. 1992. A Note on *šālišîm*. *VT* 42:266.

Martin, L., and M. Fakhru. 2009. West-Palast und Lehmziegelmassiv. Pages 13–26 in *Vorberichte über die erste und zweite syrisch-deutsche Grabungskampagne auf dem Tell Halaf*. Edited by A. el-M. H. Baghdo et al. Ausgrabungen auf dem Tell Halaf in Nordost-Syrien 1. Vorderasiatische Forschungen Der Max Freiherr von Oppenheim-Stiftung 4. Wiesbaden: Harrassowitz.

Martínez Borobio, E. 2003. *Arameo antiguo: Gramática y textos comentados*. Barcelona: Universitat de Barcelona, Àrea d'Estudis Hebreus i Arameus.

———. 2008. Les dieux des états araméens antiques. Pages 379–415 in *Émar, Ougarit, Israël, Phénicie, Aram, Arabie*. Vol. 2 of *Mythologie et religion des sémites occidentaux*. Edited by G. del Olmo Lete. OLA 162. Leuven: Peeters.

Masetti-Rouault, M. G. 2001. *Cultures locales du moyen-Euphrate: Modèles et événements, IIe–Ier mill. av. J.-C.* Subartu 8. Turnhout: Brepols.

———. 2004. Rapporto preliminaire sui lavori della missione nel sito di Tell Masaikh nel 2003. Pages 536–44 in Progetto "Terqa e la sua regione." Rapporto Preliminaire 2003. Edited by O. Rouault and C. Mora. *Athenaeum* 92:536–44.

———. 2007. Mari et le Moyen-Euphrate au bronze récent et à l'âge du fer. problèmes historiques. Pages 281–300 in *Akh Purattim 1*. Edited by J.-C. Margueron, O. Rouault, and P. Lombard. Lyon: Maison de l'Orient et de la Méditerranée.

———. 2009. Cultures in Contact in the Syrian Lower Middle Euphrates Valley: Aspects of the Local Cults in the Iron Age II. *Syria* 86:141–47.

Maspero, G. 1900. *The Passing of the Empires 850 B.C. to 330 B.C.* London: Society for Promoting Christian Knowledge.

Matilla Séiquir, G. 1999. Tell Khamis. Pages 205–225 in Olmo Lete and Montero Fenollós 1999.

Matney, T. et al. 2011. Excavations at Ziyaret Tepe, Diyarbakir Province, Turkey, 2009–2010 Seasons. *Anatolica* 37:67–117.

Matthers, J., and D. Collon. 1981. *The River Qoueiq, Northern Syria, and Its Catchment: Studies Arising from the Tell Rifaʿat Survey 1977–79*. 2 vols. BARI 98. Oxford: B.A.R.

Matthers, J. and et al. 1978. Tell Rifaʿat 1977: Preliminary Report of an Archaeological Survey. *Iraq* 40:119–62.

Matthiae, P. 2008. Une note sur l'architecture araméenne de Hama et le probleme de ses origines. Pages 207–13 in Bonatz, Czichon, and Janoscha Kreppner 2008.

Mattila, R. 1999. Bēlu-lū-balaṭ. *PNA* 1.2:335–6.

———. 2000a. *The King's Magnates: A Study of the Highest Officials of the Neo-Assyrian Empire*. SAAS 11. Helsinki: Neo-Assyrian Text Corpus Project.

———. 2000b. Inūrta-kibsī-uṣur. *PNA* 2.1:552–3.

———. 2001. Nabû-mār-šarri-uṣur. *PNA* 2.2:845–46.

———. 2002a. *Legal Transactions of the Royal Court of Nineveh, Part II: Assurbanipal through Sin-šarru-iškun*. SAA 14. Helsinki: Helsinki University Press.

———. 2002b. Šamšī-ilu. *PNA* 3.2:1226.

Mattila, R., and K. Radner. 1998. Abi-rāmu or A(b)-rāmu. *PNA* 1.1:12–14.

Maul, S. M. 1992. *Die Inschriften von Tall Bderi*. Die Ausgrabungen von Tall Bderi 1. BBVO, Texte 2. Berlin: Reimer.

———. 2006. *Die Inschriften von Tall Taban (Grabungskampagnen 1997-1999): Die Könige von Ṭābētu und das Land Mari in mittelassyrischer Zeit*. ActSumSup 2. Tokyo: Institute for Cultural Studies on Ancient Iraq.

May, N. N. 2012. Triumph as an Aspect of the Neo-Assyrian Decorative Program. Pages 461–88 in Wilhelm 2012.

Mayer, W. 1995a. *Politik und Kriegskunst der Assyrer*. ALASP 9. Münster: Ugarit-Verlag.

———. 1995b. Anmerkungen zu den ZencirliInschriften. *UF* 27:351–354.

Mazar, A. 1997. Palestine in the Iron Age. *OEANE* 4:217–22.

Mazar, B. 1961. Geshur and Maacah. *JBL* 80:16–28.

———. 1962. The Aramean Empire and Its Relations with Israel. *BA* 25:98–120.
Mazar, B., A. Biran, M. Dothan, and I. Dunayevsky. 1964. ʿEn Gev: Excavations in 1961. *IEJ* 14:1–49.
Mazzoni, S. 1984. L'insediamento persiano-ellenistico di Tell Mardikh. *Studi Eblaiti* 7:87–132.
———. 1990a. Tell Afis and the Chronology of Iron Age in Syria. *AAAS* 40:76–92.
———. 1990b. La periode perse à Tell Mardikh et dans le cadre de l'évolution l'âge du Fer en Syrie. *Transeu* 2:187–99.
———. 1991–92. Lo sviluppo degli insediamenti in Siria in età persiana. *EVO* 14-15:55–72.
———. 1994. Aramaean and Luwian New Foundations. Pages 319–40 in *Nuove fondazioni nel Vicino Oriente antico: Realtà e ideologia; Atti del colloquio 4–6 dicembre 1991, Dipartimento di Scienze Storiche del Mondo Antico, Sezione di Egittologia e Scienze Storiche del Vicino Oriente, Universita degli Studi di Pisa.* Edited by S. Mazzoni. Seminari di orientalistica 4. Pisa: Giardini.
———. 1995. Settlement Pattern and New Urbanization in Syria at the Time of the Assyrian Conquest. Pages 181–91 in Liverani 1995.
———. 1997a. The Gate and the City: Change and Continuity in Syro-Hittite Urban Ideology. Pages 307–38 in *Die orientalische Stadt: Kontinuität, Wandel, Bruch.* Edited by G. Wilhelm. Saarbrücken: Saarbrücker Druckerei und Verlag.
———. 1997b. L'arte siro-ittita nel suo contesto archeologico. *Contributi e Materiali di Archeologia Orientale* 7:287–327.
———. 1998. The Late Iron I and Early Iron II Levels (Area E1). Pages 163–99 in *Tell Afis, Siria: Scavi Sull'acropoli 1988–1992*. Edited by S. M. Cecchini and S. Mazzoni. Pisa: Edizion ETS.
———. 2000a. Syria and the Periodisation of the Iron Age: A Cross-Cultural Perspective. Pages 31–60 in Bunnens 2000c.
———. 2000b. Pots, People and Cultural Borders in Syria. Pages 139–52 in *Landscapes: Territories, Frontiers and Horizons in the Ancient Near East III/2*. Edited by L. Milano, S. de Martino, F. M. Fales, and G. B. Lanfranchi. Padova: Sargon.
———. 2001a. Tell Afis and the Luʿash in the Aramaean Period. Pages 99–114 in vol. 2 of Daviau, Wevers, and Weigl 2001.
———. 2001b. Temples in the City and the Countryside: New Trends in Iron Age Syria. *DaM* 13:89–99.
———. 2005. Tell Afis, the Survey and the Regional Sequence. Pages 5–14 in Mazzoni et al. 2005.
———. 2008. Assyrian-Style Seals at Tell Afis. Pages 155–62 in Bonatz, Czichon, and Janoscha Kreppner 2008.
———. 2010. Syro-Hittite Temples and the Traditional *in antis* Plan. Pages 359–76 in *Kulturlandschaft Syrien: Zentrum und Peripherie; Festschrift für Jan-Waalke Meyer*. Edited by J. Becker, R. Hempelmann, and E. Rehm. AOAT 371. Münster: Ugarit-Verlag.
———. 2012. Temples at *Tell ʿĀfīṣ* in Iron Age I–III. Pages 23–40 in Kamlah 2012.
———. 2013. The Aramean States during the Iron Age II–III Periods. Pages 683–705 in *The Oxford Handbook of the Archaeology of the Levant c. 8000–332 BCE.* Edited by A. E. Killebrew and M. Steiner. Oxford: Oxford University Press.
———. 2014. Tell Afis in the Iron Age: The Temple on the Acropolis. *NEA* 77:44–52.

Mazzoni, S., et al., eds. 2005. *Tell Afis (Siria) 2002–2004*. Pisa: Università di Pisa.
McAnany, P. A., and N. Yoffee, eds. 2010. *Questioning Collapse: Human Resilience, Ecological Vulnerability, and the Aftermath of Empire*. Cambridge: Cambridge University Press.
McCarter, P. K., Jr. 1984. *II Samuel: A New Translation with Introduction, Notes and Commentary*. AB 9. New York: Doubleday.
———. 2008. Paleographic Notes on the Tel Zayit Abecedary. Pages 45–59 in *Literate Culture and Tenth-Century Canaan: The Tel Zayit Abecedary in Context*. Edited by R. E. Tappy and P. K. McCarter Jr. Winona Lake, IN: Eisenbrauns.
McClellan, T. L. 1992. Twelfth Century B.C. Syria: Comments on H. Sader's Paper. Pages 164–73 in Ward and Joukowsky 1992.
———. 2004. Funerary Monuments and Pastoralism. Pages 63–67 in Nicolle 2004.
McConville, J. G. 2002. *Deuteronomy*. Apollos Old Testament Commentary 5. Leicester: Apollos; Downers Grove, IL: InterVarsity Press.
McDaniel, T. F 1968. Philological Studies in Lamentations. *Bib* 49:27–53.
McEwan, C. W., L. S. Braidwood, H. Frankfort, H. G. Güterbock, R. C. Haines, H. J. Kantor, and C. H. Kraeling. 1958. *Soundings at Tell Fakhariyah*. OIP 79. Chicago: University of Chicago Press.
McEwan, G. J. P. 1984. *Late Babylonian Texts in the Ashmolean Museum*. OECT 10. Oxford: Clarendon.
McKenzie, S. L. 1991. *The Trouble with Kings: The Composition of the Book of Kings in the Deuteronomistic History*. VTSup 42. Leiden: Brill.
Meissner, B. 1933. Die Keilschrifttexte auf den steinernen Orthostaten und Statuen aus dem Tell Halaf. Pages 71–79 in *Aus fünf Jahrtausenden morgenländischer Kultur: Festschrift Max Freiherrn von Oppenheim zum 70. Geburtstage gewidmet von Freunden und Mitarbeitern*. Edited by E. F Weidner. AfOB 1. Berlin: Weidner.
Melchert, H. C., ed. 2003. *The Luwians*. HdO 28. Leiden: Brill.
———. 2004. Luvian. Pages 576–584 in Woodward 2004.
———. 2010. Spelling of Initial /A-/ in Hieroglyphic Luwian. Pages 147–58 in Singer 2010.
Melville, S. C. 2009. A New Look at the End of the Assyrian Empire. Pages 179–202 in *Homeland and Exile: Biblical and Ancient Near Eastern Studies in Honour of Bustenay Oded*. Edited by G. Galil, M. J. Geller, and A. R. Millard. VTSup 130. Leiden: Brill.
Menzel, B. 1981. *Assyrische Tempel*. StPohlSM 10. Rome: Pontifical Biblical Institute.
Meriggi, P. 1962. *Hieroglyphisch-Hethitisches Glossar*. 2nd ed. Wiesbaden: Harrassowitz.
———. 1975. *Tavole*. Vol. 2 of *Manuale di eteo geroglifico*. Rome: Edizioni dell'Ateneo.
Meshen, B., and E. A. Knauf. 1988. From Gadar to *Umm Qais*. *ZDPV* 104:128–45.
Michel, E. 1947. Die Assur-Texte Salmanassars III. (858–824). *WO* 1:5–20, 57–71.
———. 1954. Die Assur-Texte Salmanassars III. (858–824) 6. Fortsetzung. *WO* 2.1:27–45.
Mieroop, M. van de. 2007. *The Eastern Mediterranean in the Age of Ramesses II*. Malden, MA: Blackwell.
Miglio, A. 2014a. *Tribe and State: The Dynamics of International Politics and the*

*Reign of Zimri-Lim*. Gorgias Studies in the Ancient Near East 8. Piscataway, NJ: Gorgias.
———. 2014b. A Comparative Political History: Israel, Geshur and the "Amurrite Age." *JSOT* 38: 441–44.
Millard, A. R. 1962. Alphabetic Inscriptions on Ivories from Nimrud. *Iraq* 24:41–51 and pl. XXII.
———. 1966. Number 582. Pages 598–99 in vol. 2 of Mallowan 1966.
———. 1970. Fragments of Historical Texts from Nineveh: Middle Assyrian and Later Kings. *Iraq* 32:167–76 and pls. xxxiii–xxxvii.
———. 1973. Adad-Nirari III, Aram and Arpad. *PEQ* 105:161–64.
———. 1980a. A Wandering Aramean. *JNES* 39:153–55.
———. 1980b. Review of *From Tiglath-pileser I to Ashur-nasir-apli II*. Part 2 of *Assyrian Royal Inscriptions*, by A. K. Grayson. *JAOS* 100:368–69.
———. 1983. Assyrians and Arameans. *Iraq* 45:105–8.
———. 1987–90. Mariʾ. *RlA* 7:418–19.
———. 1990. The Homeland of Zakkur. *Sem* 39:47–52.
———. 1991. Large Numbers in the Assyrian Royal Inscriptions. Pages 213–22 in Cogan and Ephʿal 1991.
———. 1992a. Aramaeans. *ABD* 1:345–50.
———. 1992b. Assyrian Involvement in Edom. Pages 35–39 in *Early Edom and Moab: The Beginning of the Iron Age in Southern Jordan*. Edited by P. Bienkowski. Sheffield: Collis.
———. 1993. Eden, Bit Adini, and Bet Eden. Pages 173–77 in *Avraham Malamat Volume*. Edited by S. Ahituv et al. ErIsr 24. Jerusalem: Israel Exploration Society.
———. 1994. *The Eponyms of the Assyrian Empire 910–612 BC*. SAAS 2. Helsinki: Neo-Assyrian Text Corpus Project.
———. 1997. Assyrian King Lists. *COS* 1.135:463–65.
———. 2000a. The Inscription of Zakkur, King of Hamath *COS* 2.35:155.
———. 2000b. The Tell Dan Stele. *COS* 2.39:161–62.
———. 2000c. The Hazael Booty Inscriptions. *COS* 2.40:162–63.
———. 2003. Aramaic Documents of the Assyrian and Achaemenid Periods. Pages 230–40 in *Ancient Archives and Archival Traditions: Concepts of Record-Keeping in the Ancient World*. Edited by M. Brosius. Oxford: Oxford University Press.
———. 2007. Early Aramaic. Pages 85–94 in *Languages of Iraq, Ancient and Modern*. Edited by J. N. Postgate. Cambridge: British School of Archaeology in Iraq.
———. 2009. Assyria, Aramaeans and Aramaic. Pages 203–14 in *Homeland and Exile: Biblical and Ancient Near Eastern Studies in Honour of Bustenay Oded*. Edited by G. Galil, M. Geller, and A. R. Millard. VTSup 130. Leiden: Brill.
Millard, A. R., and H. Tadmor. 1973. Adad-nirari III in Syria: Another Stele Fragment and the Dates of His Campaigns. *Iraq* 35:57–64.
Miller, J. M. 1966. The Elisha Cycle and the Accounts of the Omride Wars. *JBL* 85:441–54.
———. 1967a. Another Look at the Chronology of the Early Divided Monarchy. *JBL* 86:276–88.
———. 1967b. The Fall of the House of Ahab. *VT* 17:307–24.
———. 1968. The Rest of the Acts of Jehoahaz (1 Kings 20, 22:1–38). *ZAW* 80:337–42.

———. 1999. Reading the Bible Historically: The Historian's Approach. Pages 356–72 in *Israel's Past in Present Research*. Edited by V. P. Long. Winona Lake, IN: Eisenbrauns.

Miller, J. M., and J. H. Hayes. 1986. *A History of Ancient Israel and Judah*. Philadelphia: Westminster.

———. 2006. *A History of Ancient Israel and Judah*. 2nd ed. Louisville: Westminster John Knox.

Mitchell, T. C. 1971–72. A Review of Acquisitions 1963–70 of Western Asiatic Antiquities (I). *The British Museum Quarterly* 36:131–46.

———. 1982. Israel and Judah until the Revolt of Jehu (931–841 B.C.). Pages 442–87 in vol. 3, part 1 of *The Cambridge Ancient History*. Edited by J. Broadman et al. 2nd ed. Cambridge: Cambridge University Press

———. 1996. Appendix: The Aramaic Inscription on the British Museum Pyxis, WA 118179. Page 165 in *The Furniture of Western Asia, Ancient and Traditional: Papers of the Conference Held at the Institute of Archaeology, University College London, June 28 to 30, 1993*. Edited by G. Herrmann and N. Parker. Mainz: von Zabern.

Mittmann, S. 1970. *Beiträge zur Siedlungs und Territorialgeschichte des nördlichen Ostjordanlandes*. ADPV. Wiesbaden: Harrassowitz.

Mittmann, S., and G. Schmitt, eds. 2001. *Tübinger Bibelatlas: Auf der Grundlage des Tübinger Atlas des Vorderen Orients*. Stuttgart: Deutsche Bibelgesellschaft.

Mohamed, B. 1988. L'utilisation de la cartographie dans la planification économique en Syrie. *al-Majalla al-joughrafia* (*Revue géographique syrienne*) 11–13:65–77.

Monte, G. F del, and J. Tischler. 1978. *Die Orts- und Gewässernamen der hethitischen Texte*. RGTC 6.1. BTAVO B/7. Wiesbaden: Reichert.

Montero Fenollós, J. L. 2010. Tell Qubr Abu al-ʿAtiq: From Early Dynastic City to a Middle Assyrian Fort. *AuOr* 28:73–84.

Montero Fenollós, J. L., and F Caramelo. 2012. New Data on the Middle Assyrian Expansion in the Valley of the Euphrates. Pages 51–62 in *The Perfumes of Seven Tamarisks: Studies in Honour of Wilfred G. E. Watson*. Edited by G. del Olmo Lete, J. Vidal and N. Wyatt. AOAT 394. Münster: Ugarit-Verlag.

Montgomery, J. A., and H. S. Gehman. 1951. *A Critical and Exegetical Commentary on the Books of Kings*. ICC. New York: Scribner's.

Moortgat, A. 1955. *Die Bildwerke, unter Verwendung der Bildeschreibungen*. Tell Halaf 3. Berlin: de Gruyter.

———. 1956. Vorläufige Berichte über eine Grabung auf dem Tell Fecherije 1955. *AAS* 6:39–50.

———. 1957. Archäologische Forschungen der Max Freiherr von Oppenheim-Stiftung im nordlichen Mesopotamien 1956. *AAS* 7:17–30.

———. 1959. Archäologische Forschungen der Max Freiherr von Oppenheim-Stiftung im nordlichen Mesopotamien 1956. *Wissenschaftliche Abhandlungen der Arbeitsgemeinschaft für Forschung des Landes Nordrhein-Westfalen* 7:6–13.

Moran, W. 1992. *The Amarna Letters*. Baltimore: Johns Hopkins University Press.

Morandi, D. 1988. Stele e statue reali assire: Localizzazione, diffusione e implicazioni ideologiche. *Mesopotamia* 23:105–55.

Morandi Bonacossi, D. 1996. "Landscapes of Power." The Political Organisation of Space in the Lower Habur Valley in the Neo-Assyrian Period. *SAAB* 10:15–49.

———. 2000. The Syrian Jezireh in the Late Assyrian Period: A View from the Countryside. Pages 349–96 in Bunnens 2000c.

———. 2008. Betrachtungen zur Siedlungs-und Bevölkerungsstruktur des Unteren Ḫābūr-Gebietes in der neuassyrischen Zeit. Pages 189–214 in *Umwelt und Subsistenz der Assyrischen Stadt Dūr-Katlimmu am unteren Ḫābūr*. Edited by H. Kühne. BATSH 8. Wiesbaden: Harrassowitz.

Moritz B. 1926. Die Nationalität der Arumu-Stämme in Südost-Babylonien. Pages 184–211 in *Oriental Studies Published in Commemoration of the Fortieth Anniversary (1883–1923) of Paul Haupt as Director of the Oriental Seminary of the Johns Hopkins University*. Edited by C. Adler and A. Ember. Baltimore: Johns Hopkins University Press.

Morrow, W. 2001. The Sefire Treaty Stipulations and the Mesopotamian Treaty Tradition. Pages 83–99 in vol. 3 of Daviau, Wevers, and Weigl 2001.

Mosca, P. G., and J. Russell. 1987. A Phoenician Inscription from Cebel Ires Daği in Rough Cilicia. *Epigraphica Anatolica* 9:1–28.

Moscati, S. 1959a. The Aramaean Ahlamu. *JSS* 4:303–7.

———. 1959b. *The Semites in Ancient History: An Inquiry into the Settlement of the Beduin and Their Political Establishment*. Cardiff: University of Wales Press.

Mouterde, R., and A. Poidebard. 1945. *Le limes de Chalcis: Organisation de la steppe en haute Syrie romaine*. Bibliothèque archéologique et historique 38. Paris: Geuthner.

Muhly, J. D. 2003. Greece and Anatolia in the Early Iron Age: The Archaeological Evidence and the Literary Tradition. Pages 23–35 in Dever and Gitin 2003.

Musil, A. 1927. *The Middle Euphrates: A Topographical Itinerary*. American Geographical Society of New York. Oriental Explorations and Studies 3. New York: American Geographical Society.

Mykytiuk, L. J. 2009. Corrections and Updates to "Identifying Biblical Persons in Northwest Semitic Inscriptions of 1200–539 B.C.E." *Maarav* 16:49–132.

Na'aman, N. 1974. Sennacherib's "Letter to God" on His Campaign to Judah. *BASOR* 214:25–39.

———. 1976. Two Notes on the Monolith Inscription of Shalmaneser III from Kurkh. *TA* 3:89–106.

———. 1978. Looking for KTK. *WO* 9:220–39.

———. 1988a. The List of David's Officers (*šālîšîm*). *VT* 38:71–79.

———. 1988b. Biryawaza of Damascus and the Date of the Kāmid El-Lōz ʿApiru Letters. *UF* 20:179–93.

———. 1991. Forced Participation in Alliances in the Course of the Assyrian Campaigns to the West. Pages 80–98 in Cogan and Ephʿal 1991.

———. 1992. Israel, Edom and Egypt in the 10th Century B.C.E. *TA* 19:71–93.

———. 1993a. Population Changes in Palestine Following the Assyrian Deportations. *TA* 20:104–24.

———. 1993b. Azariah of Judah and Jeroboam II of Israel. *VT* 43:227–34.

———. 1994. Assyrian Chronicle Fragment 4 and the Location of Idu. *RA* 88:33–35.

———. 1995a. Hazael of ʿAmqi and Hadadezer of Beth-rehob. *UF* 27:381–94.

———. 1995b. Province System and Settlement Pattern in Southern Syria and Palestine in the Neo-Assyrian Period. Pages 103–15 in Liverani 1995.

———. 1995c. Rezin of Damascus and the Land of Gilead. *ZDPV* 111:105–17.

———. 1995d. Tiglath-Pileser III's Campaigns against Tyre and Israel (734–732 B.C.E.). *TA* 22:268–78.
———. 1996. Sources and Composition in the History of David. Pages 170–86 in Fritz and Davies 1996.
———. 1998a. Jehu Son of Omri: Legitimizing a Loyal Vassal by his Overlord. *IEJ* 48:236–38.
———. 1998b. Siruatti the Me'unite in a Second Inscription of Tiglath-pileser III. *NABU* 1998.1:7, no. 6. http://sepoa.fr/wp/wp-content/uploads/2012/05/1998-1.pdf.
———. 1999a. The Historical Background of the Aramaic Inscription from Tel Dan [Hebrew]. Pages 112–18 in *Frank Moore Cross Volume*. Edited by B. A. Levine et al. ErIsr 26. Jerusalem: Israel Exploration Society. (English summary, 232*)
———. 1999b. The Contribution of Royal Inscriptions for a Re-evaluation of the Book of Kings as a Historical Source. *JSOT* 82:3–17.
———. 1999c. Lebo-Hamath, Ṣubat-Hamath, and the Northern Boundary of the Land of Canaan. *UF* 31:417–41.
———. 1999d. Qarqar 'Tell Asharneh? *NABU* 1999.4:89–90, no. 89. http://sepoa.fr/wp/wp-content/uploads/2012/05/1999-4.pdf.
———. 2000. Three Notes on the Aramaic Inscription from Tel Dan. *IEJ* 50:92–104.
———. 2002a. In Search of Reality behind the Account of David's Wars with Israel's Neighbours. *IEJ* 52:200–24.
———. 2002b. Aribua and the Patina-Hamath Border. *Or* 71:291–95.
———. 2004. Death Formulae and the Burial Place of the Kings of the House of David. *Bib* 85:245–54.
———. 2007. The Northern Kingdom in the Late Tenth–Ninth Centuries BCE. Pages 399–418 in Williamson 2007.
———. 2008. Let Other Kingdoms Struggle with the Great Powers—You, Judah, Pay the Tribute and Hope for the Best: The Foreign Policy of the Kings of Judah in the Ninth–Eighth Centuries BCE. Pages 55–71 in *Isaiah's Vision of Peace in Biblical and Modern International Relations: Swords into Plowshares*. Edited by R. Cohen and R. Westbrook. New York: Palgrave Macmillan.
———. 2012. The Kingdom of Geshur in History and Memory. *SJOT* 26:88–101.
Na'aman, N., and R. Zadok. 1988. Sargon II's Deportations to Israel and Philistia (716–708 B.C.). *JCS* 40:36–46.
Nashef, Kh. 1982. *Die Orts und Gewässernamen der mittelbabylonischen und mittelassyrischen Zeit*. RGTC 5. BTAVO B/7.5. Wiesbaden: Reichert.
———. 1987. *Rekonstruktion der Reiserouten zur Zeit der altassyrischen Handelsniederlassungen*. BTAVO G/83. Wiesbaden: Reichert.
———. 1991. *Die Orts- und Gewässernamen der altassyrischen Zeit*. RGTC 4. BTAVO B/7. Wiesbaden: Harrassowitz.
Naumann, R. 1950. *Tell Halaf II: Die Bauwerke*. Berlin: de Gruyter.
———. 1971. *Architektur Kleinasiens von ihren Anfängen bis zum Ende der hethitischen Zeit*. 2nd ed. Tübingen: Wasmuth.
Naveh, J. 1973. PḤLṢ in a Recently Found Aramaic Ostracon [Hebrew]. *Lešonénu* 37:270–74.
———. 1999. Marginalia on the Inscriptions from Dan and Ekron [Hebrew]. Pages 119–22 in *Frank Moore Cross Volume*. Edited by B. A. Levine et al. ErIsr 26. Jerusalem: Israel Exploration Society.

———. 2002. Epigraphic Miscellanea. *IEJ* 52:240–53.
Nelson, R. D. 2002. *Deuteronomy*. OTL. Louisville: Westminster John Knox.
Neumann, G., and K. Strobel. 2003–5. Phrygien, Phryger. B. Geschichte und Religion. *RlA* 10:546–49.
Neumann, J., and S. Parpola. 1987. Climatic Change and the Eleventh–Tenth Century Eclipse of Assyria and Babylonia. *JNES* 46:161–82.
Nicolle, C., ed. 2004. *Nomades et sédentaires dans le Proche-Orient ancien: Compte rendu de la XLVI*[e] *Rencontre assyriologique internationale, Paris, 10–13 juillet 2000*. Amurru 3. Paris: Éditions Recherche sur les civilisations.
Niehr, H. 1994. Zum Totenkult der Könige von Sam'al im 9. und 8. Jh. v. Chr. *SEL* 11:57–73.
———. 2003. *Baʿalšamem: Studien zur Herfkunft, Geschichte und Rezeptionsgechichte eines phönizischen Gottes*. OLA 123. Leuven: Peeters.
———. 2006. Bestattung und Ahnenkult in den Königshäusernvon *Sam'al* (Zincirli) und *Guzāna* (Tell Ḥalāf) in Nordsyrien. *ZDPV* 122:111–39.
———. 2010. Aramäer. Pp. 187–324 in C. Bonnet and H. Niehr, *Phönizier, Punier, Aramäer*. Vol. 2 of *Religionen in der Umwelt des Alten Testaments*. Studienbücher Theologie 4.2. Stuttgart: Kohlhammer.
———. 2011. König Hazael von Damaskus im Licht neuer Funde und Interpretationen. Pages 339–56 in *"Ich werde meinen Bund mit euch niemals brechen!" (Ri 2,1): Festschrift für Walter Groß zum 70. Geburtstag*. Edited by E. Gaß. Herders Biblische Studien 62. Freiburg im Breisgau: Herder.
———. 2013. The Religion of the Aramaeans in the West: The Case of Samʾal. Pages 183–221 in Berlejung and Streck 2013.
———. 2014a. The Katumuwa Stele in the Context of Royal Mortuary Cult at Samʾal. Pages 57–60 in Herrmann and Schloen 2014.
———. 2014b. Religion. Pages 127–203 in Niehr 2014c.
———, ed. 2014c. *The Aramaeans in Ancient Syria*. HdO 106. Leiden: Brill.
Nielsen, J. P. 2011. *Sons and Descendants: A Social History of Kin Groups and Family Names in the Early Neo-Babylonian Period 747–626 B.C.* CHANE 43. Leiden: Brill.
Nilhamn, B. 2008. Nomadic Life in Central and Eastern Syria: A Perspective from the Present Life on Badiya to the Amorite Nomadism in the Bronze Age. Pages 15–30 in *Jebel Bishri in Context: Introduction to the Archaeological Studies and the Neighbourhood of Jebel Bishri in Central Syria; Proceedings of a Nordic Research Training Seminar in Syria, May 2004*. Edited by M. Lönnqvist. BARI 1817. Oxford: Archaeopress.
Nöldeke, T. 1915–16. Glossen zu H. Bauer's Semitischen Sprachproblemen. *ZA* 30:163–70.
Noorlander, P. 2012. Samʾalian in Its Northwest Semitic Setting: A Historical-Comparative Approach. *Or* 81:202–38.
Norin, S. 1994. Ein Aramäer, dem Umkommen nahe—ein Kerntext der Forschung und Tradition. *SJOT* 8:87–104.
Noth, M. 1928. *Die israelitischen personennamen im Rahmen der gemeinseitischen Namengebung*. Stuttgart: Kohlhammer.
———. 1929. Laʿasch und Hazrak. *ZDPV* 52:124–41.
———. 1939. Zur Geschichte des Namens Palastina. *ZDPV* 62:125–44.

———. 1943. *Überlieferungsgeschichtliche Studien: Die sammelnden und bearbeitenden Geschichtswerke im Alten Testament*. Schriften der königsberger Gelehrten Gesellschaft, Geisteswissenschaftliche Klasse 18. Tübingen: Niemeyer.
———. 1955. Das Deutsche Evangelische Institut für Altertumswissenschaft des Heiligen Landes Lehrkursus 1954. *ZDPV* 71:1–59.
———. 1960. *History of Israel*. 2nd ed. Translated by P. R. Ackroyd. New York: Harper & Row.
———. 1961a. *Die Ursprünge des alten Israel im Lichte neuer Quellen*. Arbeitsgemeinschaft für Forschung des Landes Nordrhein-Westfalen, Geisteswissenschaften 94. Köln: Westdeutscher Verlag.
———. 1961b. Der historische Hintergrund der Inschriften von Sefîre. *ZDPV* 77:118–72.
———. 1966. *Die israelitischen Personennamen im Rahmen der gemeinsemitischen Namengebung*. BWANT 3/10. Hildesheim: Olms. (Orig. 1928)
———. 1968. *Könige*. BKAT 9.1. Neukirchen-Vluyn: Neukirchener Verlag.
Novák, M., and P. Pfälzner. 2000. Ausgrabungen in Tall Misrife-Qatna 1999: Vorbericht der deutschen Komponente des internationalen Kooperationsprojektes. *MDOG* 132:253–96.
Novák, M. 2002. Akkulturation von Aramäern und Luwiern und der Austausch von ikonographischer Konzepte in der späthethitischen Kunst. Pages 147–71 in *Brückenland Anatolien? Ursachen, Extensität und Modi des Kulturaustausches zwischen Anatolien und seinen Nachbarn*. Edited by H. Blum, B. Faist, P. Pfälzner, and A.-M. Wittke. Tübingen: Attempto.
———. 2004. Die Religionspolitik der aramäischen Fürstentümer im 1. Jahrtausend v. Chr. Pages 319–46 in Hutter and Hutter-Braunsar 2004.
———. 2005. Arameans and Luwians—Processes of an Acculturation. Pages 252–66 in van Soldt, Kalvelagen, and Katz 2005.
———. 2009. Zur Geschichte der aramäisch-assyrischen Stadt Gūzāna. Pages 93–98 in *Ausgrabungen auf dem Tell Halaf 2006 und 2007: Vorbericht über die 1. und 2. Syrisch-Deutsche Grabungskampagne*. Edited by A. el-M. H. Baghdo et al. Vorderasiatische Forschungen Der Max Freiherr von Oppenheim-Stiftung 4. Wiesbaden: Harrassowitz.
———. 2012. The Temple of *ʿAin Dāra* in the Context of Imperial and Neo-Hittite Architecture and Art. Pages 41–54 in Kamlah 2012.
———. 2013. Between the Mušku and the Aramaeans: The Early History of Guzana/Tell Halaf. Pages 293–309 in Yener 2013.
Novotny, J. R., and R. Zadok. 2011. Tutammû. *PNA* 3.2:1337.
Nuccetelli, S. 2004. Reference and Ethnic Group Terms. *Inquiry* 47:1–17.
O'Callaghan, R. T. 1948. *Aram Naharaim: A Contribution to the History of Upper Mesopotamia in the Second Millennium B.C.* AnOr 26. Rome: Pontifical Biblical Institute.
Oates, D., and J. Oates. 1976. Early Irrigation Agriculture in Mesopotamia. Pages 109–135 in *Problems in Economic and Social Archaeology*. Edited by G. de Sieveking, I. H. Longworth, and K. E. Wilson. London: Duckworth.
Oates, D., J. Oates, and H. MacDonald. 1997. *The Mitanni and Old Babylonian Periods*. Vol. 1 of *Excavations at Tell Brak*. Cambridge: McDonald Institute of Archaeological Research.

Oates, J. 1983. Balawat: Recent Excavations and a New Gate. Pages 40–47 in *Essays on Near Eastern Art and Archaeology in Honor of Charles Kyrle Wilkinson*. Edited by P. O. Harper and H. Pittman. New York: Metropolitan Museum of Art.
Oates, J., and D. Oates. 2001. *Nimrud: An Assyrian Imperial City Revealed*. London: British School of Archaeology in Iraq.
Oded, B. 1979. *Mass Deportations and Deportees in the Neo-Assyrian Empire*. Wiesbaden: Harrassowitz.
———. 1992. *War, Peace and Empire: Justifications for War in Assyrian Royal Inscriptions*. Wiesbaden: Harrassowitz.
———. 1998. Adad-nērārī. *PNA* 1.1:30–34.
Ohnuma, K., H. Numoto, and Y. Okada 1999. Excavation at Tell Taban, Hassake, Syria: Report of the 1997 Season of Work. *al-Rafidan* 20:1–48.
Olmo Lete, G. del, and J.-L. Montero Fenollós, eds. 1999. *Archaeology of the Upper Syrian Euphrates, the Tishrin Dam Area: Proceedings of the International Symposium Held at Barcelona, January 28–30, 1998*. AuOrSup 15. Barcelona: Ausa.
Olmo Lete, G. del, and J. Sanmartín. 2003. *A Dictionary of the Ugaritic Language in the Alphabetic Tradition*. Translated by W. G. E. Watson. HdO 67. Leiden: Brill, .
Olmstead, A. T. 1915. The Assyrian Chronicles. *JAOS* 34:344–68.
———. 1918. The Calculated Frightfulness of Ashur Nasir Apal. *JAOS* 38:209–63.
———. 1921. Shalmaneser III and the Establishment of the Assyrian Power. *JAOS* 41:345–82.
Opitz, D. 1927. Die Lage von Waššuganni. *ZA* 37:299–301.
Oppenheim, A. L. 1939. Une glose ḫurrite dans les Annales de Téglath-Phalasar I. *RHA* 5:111–12.
Oppenheim, M. von. 1931. *Der Tell Halaf: Eine neue Kultur im ältesten Mesopotamien*. Leipzig: Brockhaus.
———. 1933. *Tell Halaf: A New Culture in Oldest Mesopotamia*. Translated by G. C. Wheeler. London: Putnam's.
Odorico, M. de. 1995. *The Use of Numbers and Quantifications in the Assyrian Royal Inscriptions*. SAAS 3. Helinski: Neo-Assyrian Text Corpus Project.
Oren, E. D. 2000. *The Sea Peoples and Their World: A Reassessment*. University Museum Monograph 108. University Museum Symposium Series 11. Philadelphia: University Museum, University of Pennsylvania.
Ornan, T. 2007. Who Is Holding the Lead Rope? The Relief of the Broken Obelisk. *Iraq* 69:59–72.
Ornan, T., S. Ortiz, and S. Wolff. 2013. A Newly Discovered Neo-Assyrian Cylinder Seal from Gezer in Context. *IEJ* 63:6–25.
Orthmann, W. 1971. *Untersuchungen zur späthethitischen Kunst*. Saarbrücker Beiträge zur Altertumskunde 8. Bonn: Habelt.
———. 1993. Zur Datierung des Ištar-Reliefs aus Tell ʿAin Dara. *Istanbuler Mitteilungen* 43:245–51 and pl. 25, 1.
———. 2002. *Die aramäische-assyrische Stadt Guzana: Ein Rückblick auf die Ausgrabungen Max von Oppenheims in Tell Halaf*. Schriften der Max Freiherr von Oppenheim-Stiftung 15. Saarbrücken: Saarbrücken Druckerei und Verlag.
———. 2006–8. Sakçagözü. *RlA* 11:557–59.
Osborne, J. F 2012. Communicating Power in the Bīt-Ḫilāni Palace. *BASOR* 368:29–66.

Osten, H. von der. 1956. *Die Grabung von Tell es-Salihiyeh*. Vol. 1 of *Svenska Syrien-expeditionen 1952–1953*. Lund: Gleerup.
Otzen, B. 1974. אָבַד. *TDOT* 1:19–23.
———. 1990. Appendix 2: The Aramaic Inscriptions. Pages 266–318 in Riis and Buhl 1990.
Owen, D. 1993. Some New Evidence on Yaḫmadiu = Aḫlamû. Pages 181–84 in *The Tablet and the Scroll: Near Eastern Studies in Honor of William W. Hallo*. Edited by M. E. Cohen, D. C. Snell, and D. B. Weisberg. Bethseda, MD: CDL.
Page, S. 1968. A Stela of Adad-nirari III and Nergal-ereš from Tell al Rimah. *Iraq* 30:139–53.
Pakkala, J. 2010. What Do We Know about Geshur? *SJOT* 24:155–73.
Panitz-Cohen, N., R. A. Mullins, and R. Bonfil. 2013. Northern Exposure: Launching Excavations at Tell Abil el-Qameḥ (Abel Beth Maacah). *BAIAS* 31:27–42.
Pappi, C. 2006. The Jebel Bišri in the Physical and Cultural Landscape of the Ancient Near East. *KASKAL* 3:241–56.
———. 2012. Assyrians at the Lower Zab. Pages 597–611 in Lanfranchi et al. 2012.
Pardee, D. 1989–90. Ugaritic Proper Nouns. *AfO* 36–37:390–513.
———. 2009. A New Aramaic Inscription from Zincirli. *BASOR* 356:51–71.
Parker, B. 1961. Administrative Tablets from the North-West Palace, Nimrud. *Iraq* 23:15–67.
Parker, B. J. 2001. *The Mechanics of Empire: The Northern Frontier of Assyria as a Case Study in Imperial Dynamics*. Helsinki: Neo-Assyrian Text Corpus Project.
———. 2002. At the Edge of the Empire: Conceptualizing Assyria's Anatolian Frontier ca. 700 BC. *Journal of Anthropological Archaeology* 21:371–95.
Parker, S. B. 1996. Appeals for Military Intervention: Stories from Zenjirli and the Bible. *BA* 59:213–24.
———. 1997. *Stories in Scripture and Inscriptions: Comparative Studies in Northwest Semitic Inscriptions and the Hebrew Bible*. New York: Oxford University Press.
Parpola, S. 1970. *Neo-Assyrian Toponyms*. AOAT 6. Kevelaer: Butzon & Bercker; Neukirchen-Vluyn: Neukirchener Verlag.
———. 1979. *Neo-Assyrian Letters from the Kuyunjik Collection*. CT 53. London: British Museum Publications.
———. 1987. *Correspondence of Sargon II, Part 1: Letters from Assyria and the West*. SAA 1. Helsinki: Helsinki University Press.
———. 1990. A Letter from Marduk-apla-uṣur of Anah to Rudamu/Urtamis, King of Hamath. Pages 257–65 in Riis and Buhl 1990.
———. 2002. A Letter to Sennacherib Referring to the Conquest of Bit-Ha'iri and Other Events of the Year 693. Pages 559–80 in Loretz, Metzler, and Schaudig 2002.
———. 2008. Cuneiform Texts from Ziyaret Tepe (Tušḫan), 2002–2003. *SAAB* 17:1–114 and pls. i–xxv.
———. 2012. The Neo-Assyrian Royal Harem. Pages 598–605 in Lanfranchi et al. 2012.
Parpola, S., and M. Porter. 2001. *The Helsinki Atlas of the Near East in the Neo-Assyrian Period*. Helsinki: The Casco Bay Assyriological Institute and the Neo-Assyrian Text Corpus Project.
Parpola, S., and R. Pruzsinszky. 2001. Lanšê. *PNA* 2.2:652.

Parpola, S., and R. M. Whiting, eds. 1997. *Assyria 1995: Proceedings of the Tenth Anniversary Symposium of the Neo-Assyrian Text Corpus Project Helsinki, September 7–11, 1995*. Helsinki: Neo-Assyrian Text Corpus Project.

Paul, S. M. 1991. *Amos*. Minneapolis: Fortress.

Payne, A. 2006. Multilingual Inscriptions and Their Audiences: Cilicia and Lycia. Pages 121–36 in Sanders 2006.

———. 2008. Writing Systems and Identity. Pages 117–22 in *Anatolian Interfaces: Hittites, Greeks and Their Neighbours; Proceedings of an International Conference on Cross-Cultural Interaction, September 17–19, 2004, Emory University, Atlanta, GA*. Edited by B. J. Collins, M. R. Bachvarova, and I. C. Rutherford. Oxford: Oxbow.

———. 2010. "Writing" in Hieroglyphic Luwian. Pages 182–87 in Singer 2010.

———. 2012. *Iron Age Hieroglyphic Luwian Inscriptions*. SBLWAW 29. Atlanta: Society of Biblical Literature.

Payne-Smith, J., ed. 1902. *A Compendious Syriac Dictionary*. Oxford: Oxford University Press.

Pearce, L. 2001a. Nagaḫānu. *PNA* 2.2:921.

———. 2001b. Nagaḫî. *PNA* 2.2:921–22.

Pecorella, P. E. 1975. *Malatya III: Rapporto preliminare delle campagne 1963–1968; Il livello eteo imperiale e quelli neoetei*. Orientis antique collection 12. Rome: Centro per le antichità e la storia dell'arte del Vicino Oriente.

Pedersén, O. 1986. *Archives and Libraries in the City of Assur: A Survey of the Material from the German Excavations*. Vol. 2. Acta Universitatis Upsaliensis. Studia Semitica Upsaliensia 8. Uppsala: Almqvist & Wiksell.

———. 2005. *Archive und Bibliotheken in Babylon: Die Tontafeln der Grabung Robert Koldeweys 1899–1917*. ADOG 25. Saarbrücken: Saarländische Druckerei und Verlag.

Pfälzner, P. 1990. Tell Bderi: The Development of a Bronze Age Town. Pages 63–79 in *The Near East in Antiquity: German Contributions to the Archaeology of Jordan, Palestine, Syria, Lebanon, and Egypt*. Edited by S. Kerner. Amman: Goethe-Institute; Al Kutba.

———. 1995. *Mittanische und mittelassyrische Keramik: Eine chronologische, funktionale und produktionsökonomische Analyse*. BATSH 3. Berlin: Riemer.

———. 1997. Keramikproduktion und Provinzverwaltung im mittelassyrischen Reich. Pages 337–45 in Waetzoldt and Hauptmann 1997.

Pinches, T. G. 1982. *Neo-Babylonian and Achaemenid Economic Texts*. *CT* 56. London: British Museum.

Pitard, W. T. 1987. *Ancient Damascus: A Historical Study of the Syrian City-State from Earliest Times until Its Fall to the Assyrians in 732 B.C.E.* Winona Lake, IN: Eisenbrauns.

———. 1992a. Aram-Naharaim. *ABD* 1:341.

———. 1992b. Ben-Hadad. *ABD* 1:663–65.

———. 1994a. Arameans. Pages 207–30 in *Peoples of the Old Testament World*. Edited by A. Hoerth, G. Mattingly, and E. Yamauchi. Grand Rapids: Baker.

———. 1994b. The Reading of KTU 1.19:111:41: The Burial of Aqhat. *BASOR* 293:31–38.

———. 1996. An Historical Overview of Pastoral Nomadism in the Central Euphra-

tes Valley. Pages 293–308 in *Go to the land I Will Show You: Studies in Honor of Dwight W. Young*. Edited by J. Coleson and V. Matthews. Winona Lake, IN: Eisenbrauns.
———. 1997. Damascus. *OEANE* 2:103–6.
Plat Taylor, J. du, M. V. Seton Williams, and J. Waechter. 1950. The Excavations at Sakçe Gözü. *Iraq* 12:53–138.
Podany, A. H. 2002. *The Land of Hana: Kings, Chronology, and Scribal Tradition*. Bethesda, MD: CDL.
Pognon, H. 1907. *Inscriptions sémitiques de la Syrie, de la Mésopotamie et de la région de Mossoul*. Paris: Imprimerie nationale.
Pohl, A. 1933. *Neubabylonische Rechtsurkunden aus den Berliner Staatlichen Museen 1*. AnOr 8. Rome: Pontifical Biblical Institute.
Ponchia, S. 2003. Review of Donbaz and Parpola 2001. *Or* 72:274–82.
———. 2004. Mountain Routes in Assyrian Royal Inscriptions. *KASKAL* 1:139–78.
Pongratz-Leisten, B. 1997. Toponyms als Ausdruck assyrischen Herrschaftsanspruchs. Pages 325–343 in *Ana šadî Labnāni lū allik: Beiträge zu altorientalischen und mittelmeerischen Kulturen; Festschrift for Wolfgang Röllig*. Edited by B. Pongratz-Leisten, H. Kühne, and P. Xella. AOAT 247. Neukirchen-Vluyn: Neukirchener Verlag; Kevelaer: Butzon & Bercker.
———. 2011. Assyrian Royal Discourse between Local and Imperial Traditions at the Ḫābūr. *RA* 105:109–28.
Pongratz-Leisten, B., K. Deller, and E. Bleibtreu. 1992. Götterstreitwagen und Götterstandarten: Götter auf dem Feldzug und ihr Kult im Feldlager. *BaM* 23:291–356 and pls. 49–69.
Porten, B., and A. Yardeni. 1986–99. *Textbook of Aramaic Documents from Ancient Egypt*. 4 vols. Jerusalem: Hebrew University.
Porter, A. 2002. The Dynamics of Death: Ancestors, Pastoralism, and the Origins of a Third-Millennium City in Syria. *BASOR* 325:1–36.
———. 2004. The Urban Nomad: Countering the Old Clichés. Pages 69–74 in Nicolle 2004.
———. 2009. Beyond Dimorphism: Ideologies and Materialities of Kinship as Time-Space Distantiation. Pages 199–223 in Szuchman 2009d.
———. 2012. *Mobile Pastoralism and the Formation of Near Eastern Civilizations. Weaving Together Society*. Cambridge: Cambridge University Press.
Porter, B. N. 1995. Language, Audience and Impact in Imperial Assyria. *IOS* 15:51–72.
———. 2004. Ritual and Politics in Assyria: Neo-Assyrian Canephoric Stelae for Babylonia. Pages 259–74 in ΧΑΡΙΣ: *Essays in Honor of Sara A. Immerwahr*. Edited by A. P. Chapin. Hesperia Supplements 33. Athens: American School of Classical Studies at Athens.
———. 2005. *Ritual and Politics in Ancient Mesopotamia*. AOS Series 38. New Haven, CT: American Oriental Society.
Posener, G. 1940. *Princes et pays d'Asie et de Nubie*. Brussels: Fondation égyptologique rein Élisabeth.
Postgate, J. N. 1972–75a. Ḫarran. *RlA* 4:122–25.
———. 1972–75b. Ḫuzirīna. *RlA* 4:535–36.

———. 1973. *The Governor's Palace Archive*. CTN 2. London: British School of Archaeology in Iraq.
———. 1974. Some Remarks on Conditions in the Assyrian Countryside. *JESHO* 17:225–43.
———. 1976–80a. Itu'. *RlA* 5:221–22.
———. 1976–80b. Kilizu. *RlA* 5:591–93.
———. 1976–80c. Izalla (Aṣ/zalla, Ṣ/Zallu). *RlA* 5:225–26.
———. 1980–83. Laqê. *RlA* 6:492–94.
———. 1983–84a. Review of Machinist 1982. *Mesopotamia* 18–19:229–33.
———. 1983–84b. The Columns of Kapara. *AfO* 29–30:55.
———. 1985. Review of Nashef 1982. *AfO* 32:95–101.
———. 1992a. The Land of Aššur and the Yoke of Aššur. *World Archaeology* 23:247–63.
———. 1992b. *Early Mesopotamia: Society and Economy at the Dawn of History*. London: Routledge,
———. 1995. Assyria: The Home Provinces. Pages 1–17 in Liverani 1995.
———. 1998. Between the Plateau and the Sea: Kilise Tepe 1994–97. Pages 127–41 in *Ancient Anatolia: Fifty Years' Work by the British Institute of Archaeology at Ankara*. Edited by R. Matthews. Ankara: British Institute of Archaeology.
———. 1998–2001. Nappigi, Nanpigi, Nampigi. *RlA* 9:164.
———. 2000. The Assyrian Army in Zamua. *Iraq* 62:89–108.
———. 2007. *The Land of Assur and the Yoke of Assur: Studies on Assyria 1971–2005*. Oxford: Oxbow.
———. 2010. The Debris of Government: Reconstructing the Middle Assyrian State Apparatus from Tablets and Potsherds. *Iraq* 72:19–37.
———. 2013. *Bronze Age Bureaucracy: Writing and the Practice of Government in Assyria*. Cambridge: Cambridge University Press.
Postgate, J. N., and R. A. Mattila. 2004. Il-yada' and Sargon's Southeast Frontier. Pages 235–54 in Frame and Wilding 2004.
Provan, I. W. 1995. *1 and 2 Kings*. NIBC. Peabody, MA: Hendrickson.
———. 1997. *1 and 2 Kings*. OTG. Sheffield: Sheffield Academic.
Provan, I., V. P. Long, and T. Longman III. 2003. *A Biblical History of Israel*. Louisville: Westminster John Knox.
Pruß, A. 2002. Ein Licht in der Nacht? Die Amuq-Ebene während der Dark Ages. Pages 161–76 in Braun-Holzinger and Matthäus 2002.
Pruß, A., and 'Abd al-Masiḥ Bagdo. 2002. Tell Fecheriye: Bericht über die erste Kampagne der deutsch-syrischen Ausgrabungen 2001. *MDOG* 134:311–29.
Pucci, M. 2008a. *Functional Analysis of Space in Syro-Hittite Architecture*. BARI 1738. Oxford: Archaeopress.
———. 2008b. Visual Communication of Architecture: The Syro-Hittite Town of Zincirli. Pages 545–55 in Kühne, Czichon, and Janoscha Kreppner 2008.
Puech, É. 1978. Un ivoire de Bît-Guši (Arpad) à Nimrud. *Syria* 55:163–69.
———. 1981. L'ivoire inscrit d'Arslan-Tash et les rois de Damas. *RB* 88:544–62.
———. 1992. La stèle de Bar-Hadad à Melqart et les rois d'Arpad. *RB* 99:311–34.
Puglisi, S., and P. Meriggi. 1964. *Malatya I: Rapporto preliminare delle campagne 1961 e 1962*. Orientis antique collection 3. Rome: Centro per le antichità e la storia dell'arte del Vicino Oriente.

Pury, A. de. 2006. The Jacob Story and the Beginning of the Formation of the Pentateuch. Pages 51–72 in *A Farewell to the Yahwist? The Composition of the Pentateuch in Recent European Interpretation*. Edited by T. B. Dozeman and K. Schmid. SBLSymS 34. Atlanta: Society of Biblical Literature.

Quack, J. F. 1993. Eine ägyptische Parallele zu KAI 214,32f. *ZDPV* 109:37–38.

Radcliffe, R. R. 1998a. Defining Morphological Isoglosses: The "Broken" Plural and Semitic Subclassification. *JNES* 57:81–123.

———. 1998b. *The Broken Plural Problem in Arabic and Comparative Semitic: Allomorphy and Analogy in Nonconcatenative Morphology.* Amsterdam Studies in the Theory and History of Linguistic Science 168. Amsterdam: Benjamins.

Radner, K. 1998a. Der Gott Salmānu ('Šulmānu') und seine Beziehung zur Stadt Dūr-Katlimmu. *WO* 29:33–51.

———. 1998b. Aḫūnu. *PNA* 1.1:84–86.

———. 1998c. Arrāmu. *PNA* 1.1:132–33.

———. 1998d. Ašīpâ. *PNA* 1.1:142.

———. 2002. *Die Neuassyrischen Texte aus Tall Šēḫ Ḥamad: Mit Beiträgen von W. Röllig zu den aramäischen Beischriften.* BATSH 6. Berlin: Reimer.

———. 2003. An Assyrian View on the Medes. Pages 37–64 in Lanfranchi, Roaf, and Rollinger 2003.

———. 2003–4. Salmanassar V. in den *Nimrud Letters*. *AfO* 50:95–104.

———. 2003–5a. Pargâ. *RlA* 10:336–37.

———. 2003–5b. Pitru. *RlA* 10:585–86.

———. 2004a. *Das mittelassyrische Tontafelarchiv von Giricano/DunnušaUzibi: Ausgrabungen in Giricano = Excavations at Giricano = Giricano Kazilari.* Subartu 14. Turnhout: Brepols.

———. 2004b. A Neo-Assyrian Tablet from Til Barsib. *NABU* 2004.1:25–27, no. 26 and 2004.3:83, no. 82. http://sepoa.fr/wp/wp-content/uploads/2012/06/2004-1.pdf and http://sepoa.fr/wp/wp-content/uploads/2012/06/2004-3.pdf.

———. 2006. How to Reach the Upper Tigris: The Route through the Ṭūr ʿAbdin. *SAAB* 15:274–305.

———. 2006–8a. Provinz C. *RlA* 11:42–68.

———. 2006–8b. Puqūdu. *RlA* 11:111–15.

———. 2006–8c. Qipānu. *RlA* 11:179.

———. 2006–8d. Ru(g)ulitu, Rug(g)ulutu. *RlA* 11:448–49.

———. 2012a. The Stele of Adad-nērārī III and Nergal-ēreš from Dūr-Katlimmu (Tell Šaiḫ Ḥamad). *AoF* 39:265–77.

———. 2012b. Between a Rock and a Hard Place: Muṣaṣir, Kumme, Ukku, and Šubria—the Buffer States between Assyria and Urarṭu. Pages 243–64 in Kroll et al. 2012b.

Radner, K., and A. Schachner. 2001. From Tušhan to Amedi: Topographical Questions concerning the Upper Tigris Region in the Assyrian Period. Pages 729–76 in *Salvage Project of the Archaeological Heritage of the Ilisu and Carchemish Dam Reservoirs: Activities in 1999*. Edited by N. Tuna, J. Öztürk, and J. Velibeyoğlu. Ankara: Middle East Technical University/TAÇDAM.

Rahmstorf, L. 2003. Clay Spools from Tiryns and Other Contemporary Sites: An Indication of Foreign Influence in LH IIIC? Pages 397–415 in *The Periphery of the Mycenaean World: Second International Interdisciplinary Colloquium, 26–30*

*September, Lamia 1999*. Edited by N. Kyparissi-Apostolika and M. Papakonstantinou. Athens: Aohna.
Rainey, A. F. 1975. The Identification of Philistine Gath: A Problem in Source Analysis for Historical Geography. Pages 63*–76* in *Nelson Glueck Memorial Volume*. Edited by B. Mazar. ErIsr 12. Jerusalem: Israel Exploration Society.
———. 1996. *Orthography, Phonology*. Vol. 1 of *Canaanite in the Amarna Tablets: A Linguistic Analysis of the Mixed Dialect Used by the Scribes from Canaan*. HdO 25. Leiden: Brill.
———. 2001. Stones for Bread: Archaeology versus History. *NEA* 64:140–49.
———. 2003. Who Killed Joram and Ahaziah? *ANES* 40:3–42.
Rainey, A. F., and R. S. Notley. 2006. *The Sacred Bridge: Carta's Atlas of the Biblical World*. Jerusalem: Carta.
Reade, J. E. 1975. Aššurnaṣirpal I and the While Obelisk. *Iraq* 37:129–50.
———. 1978. Assyrian Campaigns, 840–811 BC, and the Babylonian Frontier. *ZA* 68:251–60.
———. 1979a. Ideology and Propaganda in Assyrian Art. Pages 329–44 in *Power and Propaganda: A Symposium on Ancient Empires*. Edited by M. T. Larsen. Mesopotamia 7. Copenhagen: Akademisk Forlag.
———. 1979b. Narrative Composition in Assyrian Sculpture. *BaM* 10:52–110.
———. 1981. Fragments of Assyrian Monuments. *Iraq* 43:145–56 and pls. VI–XXI.
———. 1989. Shalmaneser or Ashurnasirpal in Ararat? *SAAB* 3:93–97.
Redford, D. B. 1992. *Egypt, Canaan, and Israel in Ancient Times*. Princeton: Princeton University Press.
Reiner, E. 1970. *Ana nalban*. *AfO* 23:89–91.
———. 2006. The Reddling of Valerian. *Classical Quarterly* 56:325–29.
Reinhold, G. G. G. 1986. The Bir-Hadad Stele and the Biblical Kings of Aram. *AUSS* 24:115–126.
———. 1989. *Die Beziehungen Altisraels zu aramäischen Staaten in der israelitisch-judäischen Königszeit*. Europäische Hochschulschriften 23/368. Frankfurt am Main: Lang.
———. 2003. Zu den Stelenbruchstücken der altaramäischen Inschrift von Têl Dân, Israel. Pages 121–29 in *Bei Sonnenaufgang auf dem Tell = At Sunrise on the Tell: Essays about Decades researches in the Field of Near Eastern Archaeology*. Edited by G. G. G. Reinhold. Remshalden: Greiner.
Reisner, G. A., et al. 1924. *Harvard Excavations at Samaria*. 2 vols. Cambridge: Harvard University Press.
Rendsburg, G. A. 1986. *The Redaction of Genesis*. Winona Lake, IN: Eisenbrauns.
———. 1991. Baasha of Ammon. *JANESCU* 20:57–61.
———. 2002. Some False Leads in the Identification of Late Biblical Hebrew Texts: The Cases of Genesis 24 and 1 Samuel 2:27–36. *JBL* 121:23–46.
Renger, J., ed. 2011. *Assur—Gott, Stadt und Land: 5. Internationales Colloquium der Deutschen Orient-Gesellschaft, 18.–21. Februar 2004 in Berlin*. Colloquien der Deutschen Orient-Gesellschaft 5. Wiesbaden: Harrassowitz.
Reviv, H. 1989. *The Elders in Ancient Israel: A Study of a Biblical Institution*. Translated by L. Plitmann. Jerusalem: Magnes.
Reynolds, F. S. 1999. Ga'ūnu. *PNA* 1.2:422.

Richelle, M. 2010. Les conquêtes de Hazaël selon la recension lucianique en 4 Règnes 13,22. *BN* 146:19–25.
Rieken, E. 2010. Das Zeichen <sà> im Hieroglyphen Luwischen. Pages 651–60 in *Acts of the VII International Congress of Hittitology, Çorum, 25–31 August 2008*. Edited by A. Süel. Ankara: Çorum.
Riis, P. J. 1948. *Les cimetières à crémation*. Hama 2/3. Copenhagen: Fondation Carlsberg.
Riis, P. J., and M.-L. Buhl, eds. 1990. *Les objets de la période dite syro-hittite (Âge du Fer)*. Hama 2/2. Copenhagen: Fondation Carlsberg.
Río Sánchez, F. del. 2006. Diglosia en Arameo Antiguo. Pages 173–81 in *Šapal tibnim mû illakū: Studies Presented to Joaquin Sanmartín on the Occasion of His Sixty-Fifth Birthday*. Edited by G. del Olmo Lete, L. Feliu, and A. M. Albà. AuOrSup 22. Barcelona: AUSA.
Ritner, R. K. 2009. *The Libyan Anarchy. Inscriptions from Egypt's Third Intermediate Period*. SBLWAW 21. Atlanta: Society of Biblical Literature.
Rivaroli, M., and L. Vererame. 2005. To Be a Non-Assyrian. Pages 290–305 in van Soldt, Kalvelagen, and Katz 2005.
Roaf, M. 2001. Continuity and Change from the Middle to the Late Assyrian Period. Pages 357–69 in Eichmann and Parzinger 2001.
Roaf, M., and A. Schachner. 2005. The Bronze Age to Iron Age Transition in the Upper Tigris Region: New Information from Ziyaret Tepe and Giricano. Pages 115–23 in *Anatolian Iron Ages 5: Proceedings of the Fifth Anatolian Iron Ages Colloquium Held at Van, 6–10 August 2001*. Edited by A. Çilingiroğlu and G. Darbyshire. British Institute at Ankara Monograph 31. London: British Institute of Archaeology at Ankara.
Roberts, J. J. M. 1985. Amos 6.1–7. Pages 155–66 in *Understanding the Word: Essays in Honour of Bernhard W. Anderson*. Edited by J. T. Butler, E. W. Conrad, and B. C. Ollenburger. JSOTSup 37. Sheffield: JSOT Press.
Robin, C. 1994. Documents de l'Arabie antique III. *Raydân* 6:69–87, 179–90.
Rofé, A. 1990. An Enquiry into the Betrothal of Rebekah. Pages 27–39 in *Die Hebräische Bibel und ihre zweifache Nachgeschichte: Festschrift für Rolf Rendtorff zum 65. Geburtstag*. Edited by E. Blum, C. Macholz, and E. W. Stegemann. Neukirchen: Neukirchener Verlag.
Röllig, W. 1972–75. Ḫudādum. *RlA* 4:479–80.
———. 1976–80a. Jarqani. *RlA* 5:267.
———. 1976–80b. Kapara. *RlA* 5:391.
———. 1978. Dūr-katlimmu. *Or* 47:419–30.
———. 1980–83. Lallar. *RlA* 6:438.
———. 1983. Ein Itinerar aus Dur-Katlimmu. *DaM* 1:279–84.
———. 1987–90. Li'ta'u. *RlA* 7:33.
———. 1988. Die aramäische Inschrift für Haza'el und ihr Duplikat. *MDAI* 103:62–75.
———. 1992. Asia Minor as a Bridge between East and West: The Role of the Phoenicians and Aramaeans in the Transfer of Culture. Pages 93–102 in *Greece between East and West: Tenth–Eighth Centuries B.C.* Edited by G. Kopeke and I. Tokumaru. Mainz: von Zabern.
———. 1997. Aspects of the Historical Geography of Northeastern Syria from

Middle Assyrian to Neo-Assyrian Times. Pages 281–93 in Parpola and Whiting 1997.

———. 1999. Appendix 1: The Phoenician Inscriptions. Pages 50–81 in Halet Çambel, *Karatepe-Aslantaş: The Inscriptions*. Vol. 2 of *Corpus of Hieroglyphic Luwian Inscriptions*. Berlin: de Gruyter.

———. 2000. Aramäer und Assyrer: Der Schriftzeugnisse bis zum Ende des Assyrerreiches. Pages 177–86 in Bunnens 2000c.

———. 2001. Phönizisches aus Nordsyrien und der Gott Kurra. Pages 41–52 in *Punica, Libyca, Ptolemaica: Festschrift für Werner Huss zum 65. Geburtstag dargebracht von Schülern, Freunden und Kollegen*. Edited by K. Geus and K. Zimmermann. OLA 104. Studia Phoenicia 16. Leuven: Peeters.

———. 2002. Aus der Kleiderkammer einer mittelassyrischen Palastverwaltung *mašḫuru*-Kleider. Pages 581–94 in Loretz, Metzler, and Schaudig 2002.

———. 2003. Das Sitzbild des Kammaki vom Tell Halaf. Pages 421–32 in *Altertumswissenschaften im Dialog: Festschrift für Wolfram Nagel zur Vollendung seines 80. Lebensjahres*. Edited by R. Dittmann, C. Eder, and B. Jacobs. AOAT 306. Münster: Ugarit-Verlag.

———. 2008a. *Land- und Viehwirtschaft am Unteren Ḫābūr in mittelassyrischer Zeit*. BATSH 9, Texte 3. Wiesbaden: Harrassowitz.

———. 2008b. Duara—die Satellitenstadt zu Dūr-Kalimmu. Pages 189–96 in Bonatz, Czichon, and Janoscha Kreppner 2008.

———. 2009. Inschriften des Ninurta-bēlu-uṣur, Statthalters von Kār-Salmānu-ašared, Teil 1. Pages 265–78 in *Of God(s), Trees, Kings, and Scholars: Neo-Assyrian and Related Studies in Honour of Simo Parpola*. Edited by M. Luukko, S. Svärd, and R. Mattila. StOr 106. Helsinki: Finnish Oriental Society.

Rollinger, R. 2009–11. Semiramis. *RlA* 12:383–86.

Rollinger, R., and J. Wiesehöfer. 2012. Kaiser Valerian und Ilu-bi'di von Hamat: Über das Schicksal besiegter Feinde, persische Grausamkeit und die Persistenz altorientalischer Traditionen. Pages 497–515 in Baker, Kaniuth, and Otto 2012.

Rollston, C. A. 2000. Kir. *EDB*, 773–74.

Rom-Shiloni, D. 2012. When an Explicit Polemic Initiates a Hidden One: Jacob's Aramaean Identity. Pages 206–35 in *Words, Ideas, Worlds: Biblical Essays in Honour of Yairah Amit*. Edited by A. Brenner and F. H. Polak. Sheffield: Sheffield Phoenix.

Rosa, D. F. 2010. Middle Assyrian *Ginā'ū* Offerings Lists: Geographical Implications. Pages 327–42 in *Ana turri gimilli: Studi dedicati al Padre Werner R. Mayer, S. J. da amici e allievi*. Edited by M. G. Biga and M. Liverani. Quaderni di Vicino Oriente 5. Rome: Università Degli Studi Di Roma "La Sapienza."

Roskop, A. R. 2011. *The Wilderness Itineraries: Genre, Geography, and the Growth of Torah*. HACL 3. Winona Lake, IN: Eisenbrauns.

Rost, P. 1893. *Die Keilschrifttexte Tiglat-Pilesers III*. Leipzig: Pfeiffer.

Rouault, O., and M. G. Masetti-Rouault, eds. 1993. *L'Eufrate e il tempo: Le civiltà del medio Eufrate e della Gezire siriana*. Milano: Electa.

Rouault, O., and M. Wäfler, eds. 2000. *La Djéziré et l'Euphrate Syriens de la Protohistoire à la Fin du II^e Millénaire av. J.-C.* Subartu 7. Turnhout: Brepols.

Rouault, O., and M. G. Masetti Rouault. 2013. La mission 2013 à Qasr Shemamok–Kilizu (Kurdistan irakien). *ArchéOrient-Le Blog*. http://archeorient.hypotheses.org/1302.

Rousset, M.-O. 2010. Note sur le site de Tall Šṭīb. Pages 101–3 in Gatier, Geyer, and Rousset 2010.

Rousset, M.-O., and R. Ergeç. 1997. Tell Bāšir 1996. *AnAnt* 5:343–48.

Rova, E. 2008. Mirror, Distaff, Pomegranate, and Poppy Capsule: On the Ambiguity of Some Attributes of Women and Goddesses. Pages 557–570 in Kühne, Czichon, and Janoscha Kreppner 2008.

Rowton, M. B. 1967. The Physical Environment and the Problem of the Nomads. Pages109–22 in *La Civilisation de Mari*. Edited by J.-R. Kupper. RAI 15. Paris: Belles Lettres.

———. 1973a. Autonomy and Nomadism in Western Asia. *Or* 42:247–58.

———. 1973b. Urban Autonomy in a Nomadic Environment. *JNES* 32:201–15.

———. 1976a. Dimorphic Structure and the Tribal Elite. *Studia Instituti Anthropos* 28:219–57.

———. 1976b. Dimorphic Structure and Topology. *OrAnt* 15:17–31.

———. 1977. Dimorphic Structure and the Parasocial Element. *JNES* 36:181–98.

Rudolph, W. 1951. Zum Text der Konigsbücher. *ZAW* 63:201–15.

Russell, H. F. 1985. The Historical Geography of the Euphrates and Habur according to the Middle- and Neo-Assyrian Sources. *Iraq* 47:57–74.

Russell, J. M. 1991. *Sennacherib's "Palace without Rival" at Nineveh*. Chicago: University of Chicago Press.

———. 1999. *The Writing on the Wall: Studies in the Architectural Context of Late Assyrian Palace Inscriptions*. Winona Lake, IN: Eisenbrauns.

———. 2003–5. Obelisk. *RlA* 10:4–6.

Sader, H. 1985. Les colonnes ou les statues de Kapara? *RA* 79:61–63.

———. 1986. Quel était l'ancien nom de Hama-sur-l'Orontes? *Berytus* 34:129–33.

———. 1987. *Les états araméens de Syrie depuis leur fondation jusqu'à leur transformation en provinces assyriennes*. Beiruter Texte und Studien 36. Wiesbaden: Steiner.

———. 1992. The Twelfth Century B.C. in Syria. Pages 157–63 in Ward and Joukowsky 1992.

———. 2000. The Aramaean Kingdoms of Syria: Origin and Formation Processes. Pages 61–76 in Bunnens 2000c.

———. 2010. The Aramaeans of Syria: Some Considerations on their Origin and Material Culture. Pages 273–300 in *The Books of Kings: Sources, Composition, Historiography and Reception*. Edited by A. Lemaire and B. Halpern. VTSup 129. Leiden: Brill.

———. 2014. History. Pages 11–36 in Niehr 2014.

Saggs, H. W. F. 1955. The Nimrud Letters, 1952—Part II. *Iraq* 17:126–54.

———. 1963. The Nimrud Letters, 1952—Part VI. *Iraq* 25:69–80.

———. 1975. Historical Texts and Fragments of Sargon II of Assyria. I. The "Aššur Charter." *Iraq* 37:11–20 and pl. ix.

———. 1984. *The Might That Was Assyria*. London: Sidgwick & Jackson.

———. 2001. *The Nimrud Letters, 1952*. CTN 5. London: British School of Archaeology in Iraq.

Salam, A. A. 1990. *Les régions géographiques syriennes*. Damascus: University of Damascus.

Salvini, M. 1982. Forschungen in Azerbaidjan: Ein Beitrag zur Geschichte Urartus.

Pages 384–94 in *Vorträge gehalten auf der 28. Rencontre Assyriologique Internationale in Wien, 6.–10. Juli 1981*. AfOB 19. Horn, Austria: Berger.
———. 1984. Sui documenti scritti di Hasanlu. Pages 55–56 in *Tra lo Zagros e l'Urmia: Ricerche storiche ed archeologische nell'Azerbaigian Iraniano*. Edited by P. E. Pecorella and M. Salvini. Roma: Edizioni Dell'Ateneo.
———. 1987–90. Lutipri. *RlA* 7:180.
———. 1995a. *Geschichte und Kultur der Urartäer*. Darmstadt: Wissenschaftliche Buchgesellschaft.
———. 1995b. Some Historic-Geographical Problems concerning Assyria and Urartu. Pages 43–53 in Liverani 1995.
———. 1998–2001. Nairi, Na'iri. *RlA* 9:87–91.
———. 2008. *Le iscrizioni su pietra e roccia: I testi*. Vol. 1 of *Corpus dei testi urartei: Le iscrizioni su pietra e roccia*. Documenta Asiana 8.1. Rome: Istituto di studi sulle civiltà dell'Egeo e del Vicino Oriente.
Šanda, A. 1911–12. *Die Bücher der Könige übersetzt und erklärt*. 2 vols. EHAT 9. Münster: Aschendorff.
Sanders, S. L., ed. 2006. *Margins of Writing, Origins of Cultures*. OIS 2. Chicago: University of Chicago Press.
———. 2013. The Appetites of the Dead: West Semitic Linguistic and Ritual Aspects of the Katumuwa Stele. *BASOR* 369:35–55.
Sanlaville, P. 1985. *Holocene Settlement in North Syria: Résultats de deux prospections archéologiques effectuées dans la région du nahr Sajour et sur le haut Euphrate syrien*. BARI 238. Oxford: B.A.R.
Saporetti, C. 1979. *Gli eponimi medio-assiri*. Bibliotheca Mesopotamica 9. Malibu, CA: Undena.
Sass, B. 1991. *Studia Alphabetica: On the Origin and Early History of the Northwest Semitic, South Semitic and Greek Alphabets*. OBO 102. Fribourg: Universitätsverlag; Göttingen: Vandenhoeck & Ruprecht.
———. 2005. *The Alphabet at the Turn of the Millennium: The West Semitic Alphabet ca. 1150–850 BCE: The Antiquity of the Arabian, Greek and Phrygian Alphabets*. Tel Aviv Occasional Publications 4. Tel Aviv: Emery and Claire Yass Publications in Archaeology.
———. 2010a. Taita, King of Palastin: ca. 950–900 BCE? http://tinyurl.com/SBL1713.
———. 2010b. Four Notes on Taita King of Palastin with an Excursus on King Solomon's Empire. *TA* 37:169–74.
Sassmannhausen, L. 1995. Funktion und Stellung der Herolde (Nimgir/*nāgiru*) im Alten Orient. *BaM* 26:85–194.
———. 2001. *Beiträge zur Verwaltung und Gesellschaft Babyloniens in der Kassitenzeit*. BaF 21. Mainz: von Zabern.
Sauvaget, J. 1934. Esquisse d'une histoire de la ville de Damas. *Revue des études islamiques* 8:421–80.
Savage, C. 2009. The leshem Inscription. Pages 123–24 in Arav and Freund 2009.
Schachner, A. 2007. *Bilder eines Weltreichs: Kunst und kulturgeschichtliche Untersuchungen zu den Verzierungen eines Tores aus Balawat (ImgurEnlil) aus der Zeit von Salmanassar III, König von Assyrien*. Subartu 20. Turnhout: Brepols.
———. 2009. *Assyriens Könige an einer der Quellen des Tigris: Archäologische*

*Forschungen im Höhlensystem von Birkleyn und am sogenannten Tigris-Tunnel.* Istanbuler Forschungen 51. Tübingen: Wasmuth.
Schachner, A., Ş. Schachner, and H. Karabulut. 2002. Vier Sitzbilder aus Bīt-Baḫiani. *ZA* 92:106–23.
Schaeffer, C. 1948. Fouilles à Enkomi et à Arslan-Tépé. *CRAI* 92:338–45.
Schaudig, H. 2011. Die Zerstörung des West-Palastes von Guzana. Pages 359–63 in Cholidis and Martin 2011.
Scheil, V. 1909. *Annales de Tukulti Ninip, roi d'Assyrie 889–884.* Paris: Champion.
Schenker, A. 2000. *Septante et Texte Massorétique dans l'Histoire la Plus Ancienne du Texte de 1 Rois 2–14.* CahRB 48. Paris: Gabalda.
———. 2004. *Älteste Textgeschichte der Königsbücher: Die hebräische Vorlage der ursprünglichen Septuaginta als älteste Textform der Königsbücher.* OBO 199. Fribourg: Academic Press; Göttingen: Vandenhoeck & Ruprecht.
Schiffer, S. 1911. *Die Aramäer: Historisch-geographische Untersuchungen.* Leipzig: Hinrichs.
Schley, D. 1992. The *šālišîm*: Officers or Special Three-Man Squads? *VT* 40:321–6.
Schloen, J. D., and A. S. Fink. 2009a. New Excavations at Zincirli Höyük in Turkey (Ancient Sam'al) and the Discovery of an Inscribed Mortuary Stele. *BASOR* 356:1–13.
———. 2009b. Searching for Ancient Samʾal: New Excavations at Zincirli in Turkey. *NEA* 72:203–19.
Schloen, J. D. 2001. *The House of the Father as Fact and Symbol: Patrimonialism in Ugarit and the Ancient Near East.* Studies in the Archaeology and History of the Levant 2. Winona Lake, IN: Eisenbrauns.
———, ed. 2009. *Exploring the Longue Durée: Essays in Honor of Lawrence E. Stager.* Winona Lake, IN: Eisenbrauns.
———. 2014. The City of Katumuwa: The Iron Age Kingdom of Samʾal and the Excavation of Zincirli. Pages 27–38 in Herrmann and Schloen 2014.
Schmidt, H. 1943. *Tell Halaf I: Die prähistorischen Funde.* Berlin: de Gruyter.
Schmitt, H. C. 1972. *Elisa: Traditionsgeschichtliche Untersuchungen zur vorklassischen nordisraelitischen Prophetie.* Gütersloh: Gütersloher Verlagshaus.
Schmitt, R. 2007. Volksetymologische Umdeutung iranischer Namen in griechischer Überlieferung. Pages 363–80 in *Getrennte Wege? Kommunikation, Raum und Wahrnehmung in der alten Welt.* Edited by R. Rollinger, A. Luther, and J. Wiesehöfer. Oikumene 2. Frankfurt: Antike.
Schmitz, P. C. 2009. Phoenician KRNTRYŠ, Archaic Greek *ΚΟΡΥΝΗΤΗΡΙΟΣ, and the Storm God of Aleppo. *KUSATU* 11:119–60 and plate 1.
———. 2013. The Phoenician Words *mškb* and *ʿrr* in the Royal Inscription of Kulamuwa (KAI 24.14–15) and the Body Language of Peripheral Politics. Pages 68–83 in *Linguistic Studies in Phoenician: In Memory of J. Brian Peckham.* Edited by R. Holmstedt and A. Schade. Winona Lake, IN: Eisenbrauns.
Schniedewind, W. M. 1996. Tel Dan Stela: New Light on Aramaic and Jehu's Revolt. *BASOR* 302:75–90.
———. 1998. The Geopolitical History of Philistine Gath. *BASOR* 309:69–77.
———. 2002. The Rise of the Aramean States. Pages 276–87 in Chavalas and Younger 2002.

———. 2006. Aramaic, the Death of Written Hebrew, and Language Shift in the Persian Period. Pages 137–47 in Sanders 2006.

Schniedewind, W. M., and B. Zuckerman. 2001. A Possible Reconstruction of the Name of Haza'el's Father in the Tel Dan Inscription. *IEJ* 51:88–91.

Schrader, H. 1893. Inschrift Asarhaddon's Königs von Assyrien. Pages 31–43 in von Luschan 1893.

Schrader, E., H. Zimmern, and H. Winckler. 1903. *Die Keilinschriften und das Alte Testament.* 3rd ed. Berlin: Reuther & Reichard.

Schramm, W. 1973. *Einleitung in die assyrischen Königsinschriften: Zweiter Teil 934–722 v. Chr.* HdO 5. Leiden: Brill.

———. 1983. Usa = Sam'al. *Or* 52:458–60.

Schwartz, G. M. 1989. The Origins of the Aramaeans in Syria and Northern Mesopotamia: Research Problems and Potential Strategies. Pages 275–91 in *To the Euphrates and Beyond: Archaeological Studies in Honour of M. N. van Loon.* Edited by O. Haex et al. Rotterdam: Balkema.

———. 1995. Pastoral Nomadism in Ancient Western Asia. *CANE* 1:249–58.

Schwartz, G. M., H. H. Curvers, F. A. Gerritsen, J. A. MacCormack, N. F. Miller, and J. A. Weber. 2000. Excavation and Survey in the Gabbul Plain, Western Syria: The Umm el-Marra Project 1996–1997. *AJA* 104:419–62.

Schwartz, G. M., and J. J. Nichols, eds. 2006. *After Collapse: The Regeneration of Complex Societies.* Tucson: University of Arizona Press.

Schwemer, D. 1998a. Adda-idrī. *PNA* 1.1:46–47.

———. 1998b. Adda-immē. *PNA* 1.1:47.

———. 1998c. Adda-it'i. *PNA* 1.1:47.

———. 1998d. Adda-iata'. *PNA* 1.1:46.

———. 2000a. Gīr-Adda. *PNA* 2.1:424.

———. 2000b. Gīr-Dādi. *PNA* 2.1:425.

———. 2001. *Die Wettergottgestalten Mesopotamiens und Nordsyriens im Zeitalter der Keilschriftkulturen: Materialien und Studien nach den schriftlichen Quellen.* Wiesbaden: Harrassowitz.

Schwiderski, D. 2004. *Texte und Bibliographie.* Vol. 2 of *Die alt- und reichsaramäischen Inschriften.* Berlin: de Gruyter.

———. 2008. *Konkordanz.* Vol. 1 of *Die alt- und reichsaramäischen Inschriften.* Berlin: de Gruyter.

Seebass, H. 1971. Zu 1 Reg XXII, 35–38. *VT* 21:380–83.

Seeher, J. 2001. Die Zerstörung der Stadt Ḫattuša. Pages 623–34 in *Akten des IV. Internationalen Kongresses für Hethitologie: Würzburg, 4.–8. Oktober 1999.* Edited by G. Wilhelm. StBoT 45. Wiesbaden: Harrassowitz.

Segert, S. 1975. *Altaramäische Grammatik mit Bibliographie, Chrestomathie und Glossar.* Leipzig: Verlag Enzyklopädie.

———. 1997. Phoenician and the Eastern Canaanite Languages. Pages 174–86 in Hetzron 1997.

Seidmann, J. 1935. Die Inschriften Adadniraris II. *MAOG* 9.3:36–41.

Selz, G. J. 1998. Aḫzi-Iāu. *PNA* 1.1:88–89.

Sethe, K. 1907. *Urkunden der 18. Dynastie: Historisch-biographische Urkunden aus der Zeit Thutmosis' III.* Urkunden des Aegyptischen Altertums 4/11. Leipzig: Hinrichs.

———. 1926. *Die Ächtung feindlicher Fürsten, Völker und Dinge auf altägyptischen Tongefäßscherben des Mittleren Reiches*. Berlin: Verlag der Akademie der Wissenschaften.

Seton Williams, M. V. 1961. Preliminary Report on the Excavations at Tell Rifa'at. *Iraq* 23:68–87 and pls. XXXI–XLI.

———. 1967. The Excavations at Tell Rifa'at—1964: Second Preliminary Report. *Iraq* 29:16–33 and pls. V–X.

Seux, M.-J. 1980–83. Königtum B. II. und I. Jahrtausend. *RlA* 6:140–73.

Shaath, S. 1981–82. Tel Denit. *AfO* 28:215–17.

Shea, W. H. 1978. Adad-nirari III and Jehoash of Israel. *JCS* 30:101–13.

Sherratt, S. 2003. The Mediterranean Economy: "Globalization" at the End of the Second Millennium B.C.E. Pages 37–62 in Dever and Gitin 2003.

———. 2013. The Ceramic Phenomenon of the "Sea-Peoples": An Overview. Pages 619–44 in Killebrew and Lehmann 2013.

Shibata, D. 2007. Middle Assyrian Administrative and Legal Texts from the 2005 Excavation at Tell Taban: A Preliminary Report. *Al-Rāfidān* 28:63–74.

———. 2010. Continuity of Local Tradition in the Middle Habur Region in the Second Millennium B.C.: The Local Calendar of Ṭābetu in the Middle Assyrian Period. Pages 217–39 in *Dur-Katlimmu 2008 and Beyond*. Edited by H. Kühne. Studia Chaburensia 1. Wiesbaden: Harrassowitz.

———. 2011. The Origin of the Dynasty of the Land of Māri and the City-God of Ṭābetu. *RA* 105:165–86.

———. 2012. Local Power in the Middle Assyrian Period: The "Kings of the Land of Māri" in the Middle Habur Region. Pages 489–505 in Wilhelm 2012.

Shibata, D., and S. Yamada. 2009. The Cuneiform Texts from the 2007 Excavations at Tell Taban: A Preliminary Report. Pages 87–109 in *Excavations at Tell Taban, Hassake, Syria: Preliminary Report on the 2007 Season of Excavations, and the Study of Old Babylonian and Middle Assyrian Texts*. Edited by H. Numoto. Tokyo: Hirotoshi Numoto.

Shor, R. Joseph Bekhor. 1994. פירושי רבי יוסף בכור שור על התורה. Edited by Y. Nevo. Jerusalem: Mosad ha-Rav Kuk.

Short, J. R. 2010. *The Surprising Election and Confirmation of King David*. HTS 63. Cambridge: Harvard University Press.

Shukri, S. J. al-. 1988. Archaeological Survey of Ancient Settlements and Irrigation Systems in the Middle Euphrates Region of Mesopotamia. Ph.D. diss. University of Chicago.

———. 1997. Assyrian Frontier Sites on the Middle Euphrates, New Evidence from the al-Qadisiya (Haditha) Dam Region in the Western Desert of Iraq. Pages 219–21 in Waetzoldt and Hauptmann 1997.

Siddall, L. R. 2009. Tiglathpileser III's Aid to Ahaz: A New Look at the Problems of the Biblical Accounts in Light of the Assyrian Sources. *ANES* 46:93–106.

———. 2013. *The Reign of Adad-nīrārī III: An Historical and Ideological Analysis of An Assyrian King and His Times*. CM 45. Leiden: Brill.

Sigrist, M. 1982. Miscellanea. *JCS* 34:242–52.

Sima, A. 2002. Zu Formular und Syntax der alt-Aramäischen Inschrift aus Bukān (um 700 v. Chr.). *Mediterranean Language Review* 14:113–24.

Simon, Z. 2010. Das Problem des luwischen Nomadismus. Pages 545–56 in vol. 1 of *Proceedings of the Sixth International Congress on the Archaeology of the Ancient Near East, 5 May–10 May 2009, "Sapienza", Università di Roma*. Edited by P. Matthiae, F. Pinnock, L. Nigro, and N. Marchetti. 3 vols. Wiesbaden: Harrassowitz.

———. 2012. Where Is the Land of Sura of the Hieroglyphic Luwian Inscription KARKAMIŠ A4b and Why Were Cappadocians Called Syrians by Greeks? *AoF* 39:160–80.

Simons, J. 1937. *Handbook for the Study of Egyptian Topographical Lists Relating to Western Asia*. Leiden: Brill.

Singer, I. 1989. A New Stele of Hamiyatas, King of Masuwari. *TA* 16:184–92.

———. 1999. A Political History of Ugarit. Pages 603–733 in *Handbook of Ugaritic Studies*. Edited by W. G. E. Watson and N. Wyatt. Leiden: Brill.

———. 2000. New Evidence on the End of the Hittite Empire. Pages 21–34 in *The Sea Peoples and Their World: A Reassessment*. Edited by E. D. Oren. Philadelphia: University Museum, University of Pennsylvania.

———. 2006. On Luwians and Hittites. *BO* 62:430–51.

———, ed. 2010. *Ipamati kistamati pari tumatimis: Luwian and Hittite Studies Presented to J. David Hawkins on the Occasion of His Seventieth Birthday*. Monograph Series of the Institute of Archaeology Tel Aviv University 28. Tel Aviv: Tel Aviv University.

———. 2012. The Philistines in the North and the Kingdom of Taita. Pages 451–71 in Galil et al. 2012.

Smith, A., and N. D. Munro. 2009. A Holistic Approach to Examining Ancient Agriculture: A Case Study from the Bronze and Iron Age Near East. *Current Anthropology* 50:925–36.

Smith, G. 1875. *Assyrian Discoveries*. London: Scribner, Armstrong.

Smith, M. S. 2002. *The Early History of God: Yahweh and the Other Deities in Ancient Israel*. Grand Rapids: Eerdmans.

Soden, W. von. 1977. Aramäische Wörter in neuassyrischen und neu- und spätbabylonischen Texten: Ein Vorbericht. III. *Or* 46:183–97.

Soden, W. von, and W. Röllig. 1991. *Das akkadische Syllabar*. 4th ed. Rome: Pontifical Biblical Institute.

Soggin, J. A. 1970. Ein ausserbiblisches Zeugnis für die Chronologie des Jĕhô'āš/Jô'āš. *VT* 20:366–68.

Sokoloff, M., ed. 1983. *Arameans, Aramaic, and the Aramaic Literary Tradition*. Ramat-Gan: Bar-Ilan University Press.

———. 2002a. *A Dictionary of Jewish Babylonian Aramaic*. Dictionaries of Talmud, Midrash and Targum 3. Ramat Gan: Bar Ilan University Press; Baltimore: Johns Hopkins University Press.

———. 2002b. *A Dictionary of Jewish Palestinian Aramaic of the Byzantine Period*. 2nd ed. Dictionaries of Talmud, Midrash and Targum 2. Ramat Gan: Bar Ilan University Press; Baltimore: Johns Hopkins University Press.

Soldi, S. 2009. Aramaeans and Assyrians in North-Western Syria: Material Evidence from Tell Afis. *Syria* 86:97–118.

Soldt, W. H. van. 1994. *Letters in the British Museum*. Altbabylonische Briefe in Umschrift und Übersetzung 13. Leiden: Brill.

———. 1997. Studies in the Topography of Ugarit. 2. The Borders of Ugarit. *UF* 29:683–704.

———. 2008. The Location of Idu. *NABU* 2008.3:72–74, no. 55. http://sepoa.fr/wp/wp-content/uploads/2012/06/2008-3.pdf.

Soldt, W. H. van, R. Kalvelagen, and D. Katz, eds. 2005. *Ethnicity in Ancient Mesopotamia: Papers Read at the 48th Rencontre Assyriologique Internationale, Leiden, 1–4 July 2002*. Uitgaven van het Nederlands Instituut voor het Nabije Oosten te Leiden 102. Leiden: Nederlands Instituut voor het Nabije Oosten.

Soldt, W. H. van, C. Pappi, A. Wossink, C. W. Hess, and K. M. Ahmed. 2013. Satu Qala: A Preliminary Report on the Seasons 2010–2011. *Anatolica* 39:197–239.

Stacky, J. 1965. Nouvelle épitaphe nabatéenne donnant le nom sémitique de Pétra. *RB* 72:95–97.

Stadel, C. 2011. Syntagmen mit Nachgestelltem KL im Alt-, Reichs- und Mittelaramäisch. *JSS* 56:37–70.

Stark, J. K. 1971. *Personal Names in Palmyrene Inscriptions*. Oxford: Clarendon.

Starke, F. 1990. *Untersuchung zur Stammbildung des keilschrift-luwischen Nomens*. StBoT 31. Wiesbaden: Harrassowitz.

———. 1997a. Troia im Kontext des historisch-politischen und sprachlichen Umfeldes Kleinasiens im 2. Jahrtausend. *Studia Troica* 7:447–87.

———. 1997b. Sprachen und Schriften in Karkamis. Pages 381–95 in *Ana šadî Labnāni lū allik: Beiträge zu altorientalischen und mittelmeerischen Kulturen; Festschrift für Wolfgang Röllig*. Edited by B. Pongratz-Leisten, H. Kuhne, and P. Xella. AOAT 247. Münster: Ugarit-Verlag.

———. 1999. Kleinasien B. Hethitische Nachfolgestaaten. *DNP* 5:518–33.

———. 2003. Asia Minor, III. History, C. Hittite Successor States. *BNP* 2:117–29.

Staubli, T. 2003. Sin von Harran und seine Verbreitung im Westen. Pages 65–89 in *Werbung für die Götter: Heilsbringer aus 4000 Jahren; Eine Ausstellung in den Museen für Kommunikation von Bern 28.2.03–25.1.04 und Frankfurt 26.2.04–13.6.04*. Fribourg: Universitätsverlag.

Steen, E. J. van der. 1999. Survival and Adaptation: Life East of the Jordan in the Transition from the Late Bronze Age to the Early Iron Age. *PEQ* 131:176–92.

———. 2006. Tribes and Power Structures in Palestine and the Transjordan. *NEA* 69:27–36.

Steiner, R. C. 1997. The "Aramean" of Deuteronomy 26:5: *Peshat* and *Derash*. Pages 127–38 in *Tehillah le-Moshe: Biblical and Judaic Studies in Honor of Moshe Greenberg*. Edited by M. Cogan, B. L. Eichler, and J. H. Tigay. Winona Lake, IN: Eisenbrauns.

Steitler, C. 2010. The Biblical King Toi of Hamath and the Late Hittite State of "P/Walas(a)tin." *BN* 146:81–99.

Stevens, D. F. 1991. *Origins of Instability in Early Republican Mexico*. Durham, NC: Duke University Press.

Stith, D. M. 2008. *The Coups of Hazael and Jehu: Building an Historical Narrative*. Gorgias Dissertations 37. Piscataway, NJ: Gorgias.

Stoebe, H. J. 1994. *Das zweite Buch Samuelis*. KAT 8.2. Gütersloh: Gütersloher Verlag.

Stone, E. C., and P. E. Zimansky. 1999. *The Iron Age Settlement at 'Ain Dara, Syria. Survey and Soundings*. BARI 786. Oxford: Hedges.

Strassmaier, J. N. 1889. *Inschriften von Nabonidus, König von Babylon (555–538 v. Chr.) von den Thontafeln des Britischen Museums*. Leipzig: Pfeiffer.
Streck, M. 1905–6. Bemerkungen zu den "Annals of the Kings of Assyria, I." *ZA* 19:234–60.
———. 1906a. Über die älteste Geschichte der Aramäer. *Klio* 6:185–225.
———. 1906b. *Keilinschriftliche Beiträge zur Geographie Vorderasiens*. MVAG 11. Berlin: Peiser.
———. 1918. *Assurbanipal und die letzten assyrischen könige bis zum untergange Niniveh's*. 3 vols. Vorderasiatische Bibliothek 7. Leipzig: Hinrichs.
Streck, M. P. 1998–2001a. Name, Namengebung, F. Westsemitisch in Keilschrifttexten des 1. Jt. *RlA* 9:131–34.
———. 1998–2001b. Naṣībīna. *RlA* 9:185–86.
———. 1998–2001c. Nomaden. *RlA* 9:591–95.
———. 2000. *Die Amurriter, die onomastische Forschung, Orthographie und Phonologie, Nominalmorphologie*. Vol. 1 of *Das amurritische Onomastikon der altbabylonischen Zeit*. AOAT 271. Münster: Ugarit-Verlag.
———. 2002. Zwischen Weide, Dorf und Stadt: Sozio-ökonomische Strukturen des amurritischen Nomadismus am Mittleren Euphrat. *BaM* 33:155–209.
———. 2003–5. Orontes. *RlA* 10:131–32.
———. 2006–8a. Rupū'u. *RlA* 11:463–64.
———. 2006–8b. Ru'uja, Ru'āja. *RlA* 11:470–71.
———. 2014. Outlook: Aramaeans outside Syria. 2. Babylonia. Pages 297–318 in Niehr 2014.
Strobel, K. 2013. Qadesh, Sea Peoples, and Anatolian-Levantine Interactions. Pages 501–38 in Yener 2013.
Struble, E. J., and V. R. Herrmann. 2009. An Eternal Feast at Sam'al: The New Iron Age Mortuary Stele from Zincirli in Context. *BASOR* 356:15–49.
Summers, G. 1994. Grey Ware and the Eastern Limits of Phrygia. Pages 241–52 in *Anatolian Iron Ages 3*. Edited by A. Çilingiroğlu and D. H. French. British Institute of Archaeology at Ankara Monograph 16. Ankara: British Institute of Archaeology.
Suriano, M. J. 2007. The Apology of Hazael: A Literary and Historical Analysis of the Tel Dan Inscription. *JNES* 66:163–76.
———. 2010a. *The Politics of Dead Kings: Dynastic Ancestors in the Book of Kings and Ancient Israel*. FAT 2/48. Tübingen: Mohr Siebeck.
———. 2010b. The Tel Dan Inscription: A Critical Investigation of Recent Research on Its Palaeography and Philology. *JNES* 69:251–52.
Sweeney, M. A. 2007. *I and II Kings: A Commentary*. OTL. Louisville: Westminster John Knox.
Swiggers, P. 1981. Notes on the Phoenician Inscription of Kilamuwa. *RSO* 55:1–4.
———. 1982. The Aramaic Inscription of Kilamuwa. *Or* 51:249–53.
———. 1983. Commentaire philogique sur l'inscription phénicienne du roi Kilamuwa. *RSF* 11:133–47.
Symington, D. 1991. Late Bronze Age Writing-Boards and Their Uses: Textual Evidence from Anatolia and Syria. *AnSt* 41:111–23.
Szuchman, J. J. 2007. Prelude to Empire: Middle Assyrian Hanigalbat and the Rise of the Arameans. Ph.D. diss. University of California–Los Angeles.

———. 2009a. Bit Zamani and Assyria. *Syria* 86:55–65.
———. 2009b. Revisiting Hanigalbat: Settlement in the Western Provinces of the Middle Assyrian Kingdom. Pages 531–44 in *General Studies and Excavations at Nuzi in Honor of David I. Owen on the Occasion of His Sixty-Fifth Birthday October 28, 2005*. SCCNH 18. Bethesda, MD: CDL.
———. 2009c. Integrating Approaches to Nomads, Tribes, and the State in the Ancient Near East. Pages 1–9 in Szuchman 2009d.
———, ed. 2009d. *Pastoral Nomads, Tribes, and the State in the Ancient Near East: Cross-Disciplinary Perspectives*. OIS 5. Chicago: Oriental Institute.
Tadmor, H. 1958. The Historical Implications of the Correct Rendering of Akkadian *dâku*. *JNES* 17:129–41.
———. 1961a. Que and Muṣri. *IEJ* 11:143–50.
———. 1961b. Azriyau of Yaudi. Pages 232–71 in *Studies in the Bible: Edited on Behalf of the Institute of Jewish Studies in the Faculty of Humanities*. Edited by C. Rabin. ScrHier 8. Jerusalem: Magnes.
———. 1979. The Decline of Empires in Western Asia ca 1200 BCE. Pages 11–14 in *Symposia Celebrating the Seventy-Fifth Anniversary of the Founding of the American Schools of Oriental Research*. Edited by F. M. Cross. Cambridge: American Schools of Oriental Research.
———. 1981. History and Ideology in the Assyrian Royal Inscriptions. Pages 13–34 in *Assyrian Royal Inscriptions: New Horizons in Literary, Ideological and Historical Analysis*. Edited by F. M. Fales. Orientis Antiqvi Collectio 17. Rome: Istituto per l'Oriente.
———. 1985. Sennacherib's Campaign to Judah: Historical and Historiographical Considerations [Hebrew]. *Zion* 50:65–80.
———. 1994. *The Inscriptions of Tiglath-Pileser III King of Assyria*. Jerusalem: Israel Academy of Sciences and Humanities.
Tal, A. 2000. *A Dictionary of Samaritan Aramaic*. Leiden: Brill.
Talshir, D. 2003. The Relativity of Geographic Terms: A Re-investigation of the Problem of Upper and Lower Aram. *JSS* 48:259–85.
Taracha, P., ed. 2002. *Silva Anataolica: Anatolian Studies Presented to Maciej Popko*. Warsaw: Agade.
Taraqji, A. 1999. Nouvelles découvertes sur les relations avec l'Egypte a Tell Sakka et à Keswé, dans la région de Damas. *Bulletin de la Societé Française d'Egyptologie* 144:27–43.
Taşyürek, O. A. 1975. Some New Assyrian Rock-Reliefs in Turkey. *AnSt* 25:169–80.
———. 1979. A Rock Relief of Shalmaneser III on the Euphrates. *Iraq* 41:47–53 and pls. xv–xvi.
Tekoğlu, R., and A. Lemaire. 2000. La bilingue royale louvito-phénicienne de Çineköy. *CRAI* 144:961–1006.
Tinney, J. S. 2001. Natnu. *PNA* 2.2:938–39.
Tenu, A. 2003. L'expansion médio-assyrienne. *Orient Express*, 45–48.
———. 2006a. Le moyen Euphrate à la'époque médio-assyrienne. Pages 217–45 in Kepinski, Lecomte, and Tenu 2006b.
———. 2006b. Du Tigre à l'Euphrate: La frontiere occidentale de l'empire médio-assyrienne. *SAAB* 15:161–81.

———. 2008. Les fortresses assyriennes de la vallee du moyen Euphrate. Pages 151–75 in *Les armées du Proche-Orient ancien (IIe–Ier mill. av. J.-C.): Actes du colloque international organisé à Lyons les 1er et 2 décembre 2006, Maison de l'Orient et de la Méditerranée*. Edited by P. Abrahami and L. Battini. BARI 1855. Oxford: Hedges.

———. 2009. *L'expansion médioassyrienne: Approche archéologique*. BARI 1906. Oxford: John and Erica Hedges, British Archaeological Reports.

Tenu, A., and L. Bachelot. 2005. Tell Siukh Fawqani (Syrie): La campgne de sondages 2003 dans la nécrole à incinération. *Akkadica* 126:159–68.

Testen, D. 1985. The Significance of Aramaic r<*n. *JNES* 44:143–46.

Thalmann, J.-P. 1991. L'âge du Bronze à Tell ʿArqa (Liban): Bilan et perspectives (1981–1991). *Berytus* 39:21–38.

Thiele, E. R. 1983. *The Mysterious Numbers of the Hebrew Kings*. Grand Rapids: Zondervan.

Thompson, H. O. 1992. Kir. *ADB* 4:83–84.

Thompson, R. C. 1937. *Iraq* 4:43–6 and figs. 1–2.

Thompson, T. L. 1992. *Early History of the Israelite People: From the Written and the Archaeological Sources*. Leiden: Brill.

———. 1999. *The Mythic Past: Biblical Archaeology and the Myth of Israel*. New York: Basic Books.

Thureau-Dangin, F. 1933. La stèle d'Asharné. *RA* 30:53–56 and pl. I.

Thureau-Dangin, F., and M. Dunand. 1936. *Til-Barsib*. Paris: Geuthner.

Tigay, J. H. 1996. *Deuteronomy: The Traditional Hebrew Text with the New JPS Translation*. JPS Torah Commentary. Philadelphia: Jewish Publication Society.

Tilly, C. 1978. Migration in Modern European History. Pages 48–74 in *Human Migration: Patterns and Policies*. Edited by W. McNeill and R. Adams. Bloomington: Indiana University Press.

Timm, S. 1982. *Die Dynastie Omri: Quellen und Untersuchungen zur Geschichte Israels im 9. Jahrhundert vor Christus*. FRLANT 124. Göttingen: Vandenhoeck & Ruprecht.

———. 1989. *Moab zwischen den Mächten: Studien zu historischen Denkmälern und Texten*. ÄAT 17. Wiesbaden: Harrassowitz.

Tomes, R. 1993. The Reasons for the Syro-Ephraimite War. *JSOT* 59:55–71.

Toorn, K. van der. 1996. *Family Religion in Babylonia, Syria, and Israel: Continuity and Changes in the Forms of Religious Life*. SHANE 7. Leiden: Brill.

Tournay, R.-J. 1997. La stèle du roi Tukulti-Ninurta II: Nouvelle interprétation. *Subartu* 4:273–78.

Tournay, R.-J., and S. Saouaf. 1952. Stèle de Tukulti-Ninurta II. *AAAS* 2:169–90 and pls. 1–3.

Trilsbach, A. 1987. Environmental Changes and Village Societies West of the White Nile: Central Sudan. Pages 37–39 in *The Middle Eastern Village, Changing Economic and Social Relations*. Edited by Richard Lawless. London: Croom Helm.

Trokay, M. 1986. Le bas-relief au sphinx de Damas. Pages 99–118 in *Religio Phoenicia: Acta colloquii Namurcensis habiti diebus 14 et 15 mensis Decembris anni 1984*. Edited by C. Bonnet, E. Lipiński, and P. Marchetti. Collection d'études classiques 1. Studia Phoenicia 4. Namur: Société des études classiques.

Tropper, J. 1993. *Die Inschriften von Zincirli: Neue Edition und vergleichende Grammatik des phönischen, sam'alischen und aramäischen Textkorpus*. ALASP 6. Münster: Ugarit-Verlag.

———. 1994. "Sie knurrten wie Hunde." Psalm 59,16, Kilamuwa: 10 und die Semantik der Wurzel *lwn*. *ZAW* 106:87–95.

———. 1998. Orthographische und Linguistische Anmerkungen zur aramäischen Inschrift von Bukān. *NABU* 1998.4: 97–98, no. 107. http://sepoa.fr/wp/wp-content/uploads/2012/05/1998-4.pdf.

———. 2001. Dialektvielfalt und Sprachwandel im frühen aramäischen soziolinguistische Überlegungen. Pages 213–22 in vol. 3 of Daviau, Wevers, and Weigl 2001.

Tsukimoto, A. 1990. Akkadian Texts in the Hirayama Collection. *ActSum* 12:177–227.

———. 1992. Aus einer japanischer Privatsammlung: Drei Verwaltungstexte und ein Brief aus mittelassyrischer Zeit. *WO* 29:21–38.

Turkanik, A. S. 2008. *Of Kings and Reigns: A Study of Translation Technique in the Gamma/Gamma Section of 3 Reigns (1 Kings)*. FAT 2/30. Tübingen: Mohr Siebeck.

Unger, E. 1931. *Babylon, die heilige Stadt nach der Beschreibung der Babylonier*. Berlin: de Gruyter.

Unger, M. F. 1957. *Israel and the Aramaeans of Damascus*. Grand Rapids: Zondervan.

Ur, J. 2005. Sennacherib's Northern Assyrian Canals: New Insights from Satellite Imagery and Aerial Photography. *Iraq* 67:317–45.

Ussishkin, D. 1966. The Date of the Neo-Hittite Enclosure at Sakçagözü. *BASOR* 181:15–23.

———. 1971. Was Bit-Adini a Neo-Hittite or Aramean State? *Or* 40:431–37.

———. 1975. Hollows, "Cup-Marks," and Hittite Stone Monuments. *AnSt* 25:85–103.

———. 2009. On the So-called Aramaean "Siege Trench" in Tell eṣ-Ṣafi, Ancient Gath. *IEJ* 59:137–57.

Vaan, J. M. C. T. de. 1995. *"Ich bin eine Schwertklinge des Königs": Die Sprache des Bēl-ibni*. AOAT 242. Kevelaer: Butzon & Bercker; Neukirchen-Vluyn: Neukirchener Verlag.

Van Seters, J. 1975. *Abraham in History and Tradition*. New Haven: Yale University Press.

———. 1983. *In Search of History: Historiography in the Ancient World and the Origins of Biblical History*. New Haven: Yale University Press.

Vannesse, M. 2011. La mise en valeur de la plaine du Ghâb dans l'antiquité: Étude du paysage rural d'Apamée de syrie. *Syria* 88:285–300.

Vattioni, T. 1971. I sigilli aramaici. *Augustinianum* 11:31, No. 15.

Vaux, R. de. 1978. *The Early History of Israel*. Translated by D. Smith. Philadelphia: Westminster.

Venturi, F. 2007. *La Siria nell'età delle trasformazioni (XIII–X sec. a.C.): Nuovi contribute dallo scavo di Tell Afis*. Bologna: CLUEB.

———. 2010. Cultural Breakdown or Evolution? The Impact of Changes in Twelfth Century BC Tell Afis. Pages 1–16 in *Societies in Transition: Evolutionary Processes in the Northern Levant between Late Bronze II and Early Iron Age*. Edited by F. Venturi. Studi e testi orientali. Collana diretta da Giorgio Renato Franci 9. Bologna: CLUEB.

———. 2013. The Transition from the Late Bronze Age to the Early Iron Age at Tell Afis, Syria (Phases VII–III). Pages 227–59 in Yener 2013.
Verstraete, J., and T. J. Wilkenson. 2000. The Amuq Regional Archaeological Survey. *AJA* 104:179–92.
Vidal, J. 2006. La participación de tribus nómadas en el comercio internacional del Levant Mederráneo durante el Bronce Reciente. *AuOr* 24:127–33.
———. 2010. Sutean Warfare in the Amarna Letters. Pages 95–103 in *Studies on War in the Ancient Near East: Collected Essays on Military History*. Edited by J. Vidal. AOAT 372. Münster: Ugarit-Verlag.
Villard, P. 1998. Amūdāni. *PNA* 1.1:107.
Voos, J. 1986. Studien zur Rolle von Statuen und Reliefs im syrohethitischen Totenkult während der frühen Eisenzeit (ca. 10.–7. Jh. v.u.Z.). Ph.D. diss. Zentralinstitut für Alte Geschichte und Archäologie, Akademie der Wissenschaften der DDR, Berlin.
Waetzoldt, H., and H. Hauptmann, eds. 1997. *Assyrien im Wandel der Zeiten: XXXIXe Rencontre Assyriologique Internationale Heidelberg 6.–10. Juli 1992*. HSAO 6. Heidelberg: Heidelberger Orientverlag.
Wagner, W. 2011. *Groundwater in the Arab Middle East*. Heidelberg: Springer.
Wakita, S., H. Wada, and S. Nishiyama. 1995. Tell Mastuma: A Preliminary Report of the Excavations at Idlib, Syria, 1994 and 1995. *Bulletin of the Ancient Orient Museum* 14:1–73.
———. 2000. Tell Mastuma: Change in Settlement Plans and Historical Context during the First Quarter of the First Millennium B.C. Pages 537–57 in Bunnens 2000c.
Waldbaum, J. 1999. The Coming of Iron in the Eastern Mediterranean: Thirty Years of Archaeological and Technological Research. Pages 27–58 in *The Archaeometallurgy of the Asian Old World*. Edited by V. Pigott. Philadelphia: University Museum, University of Pennsylvania.
Walker, C. B. F. 1982. Babylonian Chronicle 25: A Chronicle of the Kassite and Isin II Dynasties. Pages 398–417 in *Zikir Šumim: Assyriological Studies Presented to F. R. Kraus on the Occasion of His Seventieth Birthday*. Edited by G. van Driel, Th. J. H. Krispijn, M. Stol, and K. R. Veenhof. Nederlands Instituut voor het Nabije Oosten Studia Francisci Scholten Memoriae Dicata 5. Leiden: Brill.
Walsh, J. T. 2006. *Ahab: The Construction of a King*. Interfaces. Collegeville, MN: Liturgical Press.
Ward, W. A., and M. S. Joukowsky, eds. 1992. *The Crisis Years: The Twelfth Century B.C. from Beyond the Danube to the Tigris*. Dubuque, IA: Kendall Hunt.
Warmenbol, E. 1985. La statuette égyptisante de Sfiré en Syrie du Nord: Une image d'orant de la première moitré du Ier millenaire av. J.-C. Pages 163–80 in *Phoenicia and Its Neighbours*. Edited by E. Gubel and E. Lipiński. Studia Phoenicia 3. Leuven: Peeters.
Wartke, R.-B. 2005. *Sam'al: Ein aramäischer Stadtstaat des 10. bis 8. Jhs. v. Chr. und die Geschichte seiner Erforschung*. Mainz: von Zabern.
———. 2006–8. Sam'al. B. Archäologisch. *RlA* 11:605–7.
Watanabe, K., ed. 1999. *Priests and Officials in the Ancient Near East: Papers of the Second Colloquium on the Ancient Near East—The City and Its Life Held at the Middle Eastern Culture Center in Japan (Mitaka, Tokyo)*. Heidelberg: Winter.

Watson, W. G. E. 2001. The Lexical Aspect of Ugaritic Toponyms. *AuOr* 19:109–23.
Wazana, N. 1996. Water Division in Border Agreements. *SAAB* 10:55–66.
———. 2008. From Biqʿat to KTK: "All Aram" in the Sefire Inscription in the Light of Amos 1:5. Pages 713–32 in vol. 2 of *Birkat Shalom: Studies in the Bible, Ancient Near Eastern Literature, and Postbiblical Judaism Presented to Shalom M. Paul on the Occasion of His Seventieth Birthday*. Edited by C. Cohen, V. A. Hurowitz, A. Hurvitz, Y. Muffs, B. J. Schwartz, and J. H. Tigay. Winona Lake, IN: Eisenbrauns.
Wee, J. Z. 2005. Maacah and Ish-tob. *JSOT* 30:191–99.
Weeden, M. 2013. After the Hittites: The Kingdoms of Karkamish and Palistin in Northern Syria. *Bulletin of the Institute of Classical Studies* 56.2:1–20.
Wegner, P. D. 1991. Another Look at Isaiah 8:23b. *VT* 41:481–84.
Weidner, E. F., A. Ungnad, and J. Friedrich. 1940. *Die Inschriften vom Tell Halaf*. AfOB 6. Berlin: n.p.
Weidner, E. F. 1923. *Politische Dokumente aus Kleinasien: Die Staatsverträge in akkadischer Sprache aus dem Archiv von Boghazköi*. Boghazköi-Studien 8–9. Hildesheim: Olms.
———. 1926. Die Annalen des Königs Aššurdân II. von Assyrien. *AfO* 3:151–61.
———. 1939–40. Die assyrischen Eponymen. *AfO* 13:308–18.
———. 1952–53. Ausgrabungen in Arslan Tepe. *AfO* 16:151–52.
———. 1957–71. Gari. *RlA* 3:146–47.
Weinstein, J. 1992. The Collapse of the Egyptian Empire in the Southern Levant. Pages 142–50 in Ward and Joukowsky 1992.
———. 1998. Egyptian Relations with the Eastern Mediterranean World at the End of the Second Millennium BCE. Pages 188–96 in *Mediterranean Peoples in Transition: Thirteenth to Early Tenth Centuries BCE*. Edited by S. Gitin, A. Mazar, and E. Stern. Jerusalem: Israel Exploration Society.
Weippert, H. 1988. Ahab el campeador? Redatktionsgeschichtliche Untersuchungen zu 1 Kön 22. *Bib* 69:457–79.
Weippert, M. 1966. Archäologischer Jahres bericht. *ZDPV* 82:296–99.
———. 1972. Review of Parpola 1970. *Göttingische gelehrte Anzeigen*. 224:150–61.
———. 1973. Menahem von Israel und seine Zeitgenossen in einer Steleninschrift des assyrischen Königs Tiglathpileser III. aus dem Iran. *ZDPV* 89:26–53.
———. 1973–74. Die Kämpfe des assyrischen Königs Assurbanipal gegen die Araber. *WO* 7:39–85.
———. 1976–80. Israel und Juda. *RlA* 5:200–208.
———. 1982. Zur Syrienpolitik Tiglathpilesers III. Pages 395–408 in vol. 2 of *Mesopotamien und seine Nachbarn: Politische und kulturelle Wechselbeziehungen im alten Vorderasien vom 4. bis 1. Jahrtausend v. Chr.* Edited by H. J. Nissen and J. Renger. RAI 25. Berliner Beiträge zum Vorderen Orient 1. Berlin: Reimer.
———. 1992. Die Feldzüge Adadniraris III. nach Syrien: Voraussetzungen, Verlauf, Folgen. *ZDPV* 108:42–67.
———. 1997. Israélites, araméens et Assyriens dans la Transjordanie septentrionale. *ZDPV* 113:19–38.
———. 2003. Berggötter, Löwen-, Stier- und Vogelmenschen: Rekonstruktion des Sockels G1 aus dem Tempel von ʿAin Dārā in Nordsyrien. Pages 227–56 in *Saxa Loquentur: Studien zur Archäologie Palästinas/Israels; Festschrift für Volkmar*

*Fritz zum 65. Geburtstag*. Edited by C. G. den Hertog, U. Hübner, and S. Münger. AOAT 302. Münster: Ugarit-Verlag.
Weisberg, D. B. 1980. *Texts from the Time of Nebuchadnezzar*. Yale Oriental Series. Babylonian Texts 17. New Haven: Yale University Press.
Weissbach, F. H. 1928. Assyrien (Geschichte). *RlA* 1:228–303.
Weissert, E. 1998. Aššur-būnā-uṣur. *PNA* 1.1:177.
Westermann, C. 1985. *Genesis 12–36: A Commentary*. Minneapolis: Augsburg.
Weszeli, M. 2002. Piḫirim. *PNA* 3.1:993.
———. 2003–5. Panamuwa I. und II. *RlA* 10:293–94.
Weulersse, J. 1940. *L'Oronte. étude de fleuve*. Tours: Maîtres Imprimeurs.
Whincop, M. R. 2007. The Iron Age II at Tell Nebi Mend: Towards an Explanation of Ceramic Regions. *Levant* 39:185–212.
———. 2009. *Pots, People, and Politics: A Reconsideration of the Role of Ceramics in Reconstructions of the Iron Age Northern Levant*. BARI 1902. Oxford: Archaeopress.
———. 2010. The Complexity of Ceramic Regions in the Iron Age Northern Levant: The Application of Correspondence Analysis to Near Eastern Ceramic Data. *Levant* 42:30–47.
Whitley, C. F. 1952. The Deuteronomic Presentation of the House of Omri. *VT* 2:137–52.
Wiggermann, F. A. M. 2000. Agriculture in the Northern Balikh Valley: The Case of Middle Assyrian Tell Sabi Abyad. Pages 171–231 in *Rainfall and Agriculture in Northern Mesopotamia: Proceedings of the Third MOS Symposium (Leiden 1999)*. Edited by R. Jas. Uitgaven van het Nederlands Historisch-Archaeologisch Instituut te Istanbul 88. Leiden: Nederlands Instituut voor het Nabije Oosten.
———. 2008. Appendix E: Cuneiform Texts from Tell Sabi Abyad Related to Pottery. Pages 558–64 in Duistermaat 2008.
———. 2010. Wein, Weib und Gesang in een midden-assyrische nederzetting aan de Balikh. *Phoenix* 56:18–60.
Wilhelm, G. 1982. *Grundzüge der Geschichte und Kultur der Hurriter*. Darmstadt: Wissenschaftliche Buchgesellschaft.
———. 1993–97. Mittan(n)i. A. *RlA* 8:286–96.
———. 1998–2001. Name, Namengebung. D. Bei den Hurritern. *RlA* 9:121–27.
———. 2009–11. Sauštatar. *RlA* 12:106–7.
———, ed. 2012. *Organization, Representation, and Symbols of Power in the Ancient Near East: Proceedings of the 54th Rencontre Assyriologique Internationale at Würzburg 20–25 July 2008*. Winona Lake, IN: Eisenbrauns.
Wilkinson, T. J., E. B. Wilkinson, J. Ur, and M. Altaweel. 2005. Landscape and Settlement in the Neo-Assyrian Empire. *BASOR* 340:23–56.
Wilkinson, T. J., and D. J. Tucker. 1995. *Settlement Development in the North Jazira, Iraq: A Study of the Archaeological Landscape*. Iraq Archaeological Reports 3. Baghdad: British School of Archaeology in Iraq.
Williamson, H. G. M. 1982. *1 and 2 Chronicles*. NCBC. Grand Rapids: Eerdmans.
———. 1993. First and Last in Isaiah. Pages 95–108 in *Of Prophets' Visions and the Wisdom of Sages: Essays in Honour of R.N. Whybray on His Seventieth Birthday*. Edited by H. A. McKay and D. J. A. Clines. JSOTSup 162. Sheffield: JSOT Press.

———, ed. 2007. *Understanding the History of Ancient Israel*. Proceedings of the British Academy 143. Oxford: Oxford University Press.

Winckler, H. 1893. *Altorientalische Forschungen*. Leipzig: Pfeiffer.

———. 1892. Das elfte Capitel des ersten Königsbüches, seine geschichtlichen Nachrichten und seine Bedeutung für die Quellenscheidung. Pages 1–15 in *Alttestamentliche Untersuchungen*. Leipzig: Pfeiffer.

———. 1900. *Geschichte Israels*. Vol. 2. Leipzig: Pfeiffer.

———. 1903. In Schrader, Zimmern, and Winckler 1903.

———. 1905. *Auszug aus der vorderasiatischen Geschichte*. Hilfsbücher zur Kunde des Alten Orients 2. Leipzig: Hinrichs.

———. 1909. *Keilschriftlichen Textbuch zum Alten Testament*. Leipzig: Hinrichs.

Winter, I. J. 1981. Is There a South Syrian Style of Ivory Carving in the Early First Millennium B.C.? *Iraq* 43:101–30.

———. 1983. Carchemish *ša kišad puratti*. *AnSt* 33:177–97.

———. 1989. North Syrian Ivories and Tell Halaf Reliefs: The Impact of Luxury Goods upon "Major" Arts. Pages 321–332 in *Essays in Ancient Civilization Presented to Helene J. Kantor*. Edited by A. Leonard and B. B. Williams. SAOC 47. Chicago: University of Chicago Press.

———. 1992. "Idols of the King": Royal Images as Recipients of Ritual Action in Ancient Mesopotamia. *Journal of Ritual Studies* 6:13–42.

Wirth, E. 1971. *Syrien, eine geographische Landeskunde*. Wissenschaftliche Länderkunden 4/5. Darmstadt: Wissenschaftliche Buchgesellschaft.

Wiseman, D. J. 1968. The Tell al-Rimah Tablets, 1966. *Iraq* 30:175–205.

———. 1972–75. Hadadezer. *RlA* 4:38.

———. 1993. *1 and 2 Kings*. TOTC. Downers Grove, IL: InterVarsity Press.

Wittke, A.-M. 2004. *Musker und Phryger: Ein Beitrag zur Geschichte Anatoliens vom 12. bis zum 7. Jh. v. Chr.* Kommentar zur TAVO Karte B IV 8. "Östlicher Mittelmeerraum und Mesopotamien um 700 v. Chr." BTAVO B/99. Wiesbaden: Reichert.

Wolff, S. R. 1998. Archaeology in Israel. *AJA* 102:757–807.

———. 2012. Review of Arav and Freund 2009. *BASOR* 368:116–18.

Woodward, R. D., ed. 2004. *The Cambridge Encyclopedia of the World's Ancient Languages*. Cambridge: Cambridge University Press.

Yadin, Y. 1955. Some Aspects of the Strategy of Ahab and David (1 Kings 20; II Sam 11). *Bib* 36:332–51.

———. 1972. *Hazor, the Head of All Those Kingdoms: Joshua 11:10; With a Chapter on Israelite Megiddo*. Schweich Lectures of the British Academy. London: Oxford University Press.

Yakubovich, I. 2010. The West Semitic God El in Anatolian Hieroglyphic Transmission. Pages 385–98 in *Pax Hethitica: Studies on the Hittites and Their Neighbours in Honour of Itamar Singer*. Edited by Y. Cohen, A. Gilan, and J. L. Miller. StBOT 51. Wiesbaden: Harrassowitz.

Yamada, S. 1994. The Editorial History of the Assyrian King List. *ZA* 84:11–37.

———. 1995. Aram-Israel Relations as Reflected in the Aramaic Inscription from Tel Dan. *UF* 27:611–25.

———. 2000a. *The Construction of the Assyrian Empire: A Historical Study of the*

*Inscriptions of Shalmaneser III (859–824 BC) Relating to His Campaigns to the West*. SHANE 3. Leiden: Brill.

———. 2000b. Peter Hulin's Hand Copies of Shalmaneser III's Inscriptions. *Iraq* 62:65–87.

———. 2008. A Preliminary Report on the Old Babylonian Texts from the Excavations of Tell Taban in the 2005 and 2006 Seasons: The Middle Euphrates and Habur Areas in the Post Hammurabi Period. Pages 153–68 in *Excavations at Tell Taban, Hassake Syria: Preliminary Report on the 2005 and 2006 Seasons of Excavations and the Study of Old Babylonian and Middle Assyrian Texts*. Edited by H. Numoto. Tokyo: Kokushikan University.

Yamazaki, Y. 1999. Excavations at Tell al-ʿAbr. Pages 83–96 in Olmo Lete and Montero Fenollós 1999.

Yasur-Landau, A. 2007. Let's Do the Time Warp Again: Migration Processes and the Absolute Chronology of the Philistine Settlement. Pages 609–20 in *The Synchronisation of Civilisations in the Eastern Mediterranean in the Second Millennium B.C. III: Proceedings of the SCIEM 2000–2nd Euroconference, Vienna, 28th of May–1st of June 2003*. Edited by M. Bietak and E. Czerny. Contributions to the Chronology of the Eastern Mediterranean 9. Vienna: Verlag der Österreichischen Akademie der Wissenschaften.

———. 2010. *The Philistines and Aegean Migration at the End of the Late Bronze Age*. Cambridge: Cambridge University Press.

Yener, K. A. 2005. *The Amuq Valley Regional Projects: Surveys in the Plain of Antioch and Orontes Delta, Turkey, 1995–2002*. Vol. 1. OIP 131. Chicago: Oriental Institute of the University of Chicago.

———, ed. 2013. *Across the Border: Late Bronze–Iron Age Relations between Syria and Anatolia; Proceedings of a Symposium Held at the Research Center of Anatolian Studies, Koç University, Istanbul, May 31–June 1, 2010*. ANESSup 42. Leuven: Peeters.

Yener, K.A., C. Edens, T. P. Harrison, J. Verstraete, and T. J. Wilkinson. 2000. The Amuq Valley Regional Project, 1995–1998. *AJA* 104:163–220.

Yoffee, N., and G. L. Cowgill, eds. 1988. *The Collapse of Ancient States and Civilizations*. Tucson: University of Arizona Press.

Young, I. 1993. KLMW BR TML. *Syria* 70:95–98.

———. 2002. The Languages of Ancient Samʾal. *Maarav* 9:93–105.

Younger, K. L., Jr. 1986. Panammuwa and Bar-Rakib: Two Structural Analyses. *JANESCU* 18:91–103.

———. 1990. *Ancient Conquest Accounts: A Study of Ancient Near Eastern and Biblical History Writing*. JSOTSup 98. Sheffield: JSOT Press.

———. 1998. The Deportations of the Israelites. *JBL* 117:201–27.

———. 1999. The Fall of Samaria in Light of Recent Research. *CBQ* 61:461–82.

———. 2002a. Yahweh at Ashkelon and Calaḫ? Yahwistic Names in Neo-Assyrian. *VT* 52:207–18.

———. 2002b. Recent Study on the Inscriptions of Sargon II: Implications for Biblical Studies. Pages 288–329 in Chavalas and Younger 2002.

———. 2002c. The "Contextual Method": Some West Semitic Reflections. *COS* 3:xxxv–xlii.

———. 2003a. Assyrian Involvement in the Southern Levant at the End of the Eighth

Century BCE. Pages 235–63 in *Jerusalem in Bible and Archaeology: The First Temple Period*. Edited by A. G. Vaughan and A. E. Killebrew. SBLSymS 18. Atlanta: Society of Biblical Literature.
———. 2003b. Joshua. Pages 174–89 in *Eerdmans Commentary on the Bible*. Edited by J. D. G. Dunn and J. W. Rogerson. Grand Rapids: Eerdmans.
———. 2004. The Repopulation of Samaria (2 Kings 17:24, 27–31) in Light of Recent Study. Pages 242–68 in *The Future of Biblical Archaeology*. Edited by J. K. Hoffmeier and A. R. Millard. Grand Rapids: Eerdmans.
———. 2005. "Haza'el, Son of a Nobody": Some Reflections in Light of Recent Study. Pages 245–70 in Bienkowski, Mee, and Slater 2005.
———. 2007a. The Late Bronze Age/Iron Age Transition and the Origins of the Arameans. Pages 131–174 in *Ugarit at Seventy-Five: Its Environs and the Bible*. Edited by K. L. Younger Jr. Winona Lake, IN: Eisenbrauns.
———. 2007b. Neo-Assyrian and Israelite History in the Ninth Century: The Role of Shalmaneser III. Pages 237–71 in Williamson 2007.
———. 2007c. Some of What's New in Old Aramaic Epigraphy. *NEA* 70:138–46.
———. 2009. Two Epigraphic Notes on the New Katumuwa Inscription from Zincirli. *Maarav* 16:159–79.
———. 2012a. Another Look at an Aramaic Astral Bowl. *JNES* 71:209–30.
———. 2013. Aram-Damascus. *OEBA* 1:42–49.
———. 2014a. The Scripts of North Syria in the Early First Millennium: The Inscription of Yariri (KARKAMIŠ A15b) Once Again. *Transeu* 46:155–67 (= *Volume d'hommages pour André Lemaire*. Edited by J. M. Durand and J. Elayi. Paris: Gabalda).
———. 2014b. "War and Peace" in the Origins of the Arameans. Pages 861–74 in *Krieg und Frieden im Alten Vorderasien: 52e Rencontre Assyriologique Internationale, International Congress of Assyriology and Near Eastern Archaeology, Münster, 17.–21. Juli 2006*. Edited by H. Neumann, R. Dittmann, S. Paulus, G. Neumann, and A. Schuster-Brandis. AOAT 401. Münster: Ugarit-Verlag.
———. 2015a. Another Look at the Nomadic Tribal Arameans in the Inscriptions of Ninurta-kudurrī-uṣur of Suḫu. Pages 603–29 in *Marbeh Ḥokmah: Essays in Memory of Victor Avigdor Hurowitz*. Edited by Shamir Yonah, E. Greenstein, M. Gruber, P. Machinist, and S. Paul. Winona Lake, IN: Eisenbrauns.
———. 2015b. The Assyrian Impact on the West: The Assyriological Perspective. *IEJ* 65:179–204.
———. Forthcoming. Tiglath-pileser I and the Initial Conflict with the Arameans. In *Wandering Arameans: Arameans outside Syria; Textual and Archaeological Perspectives*. Edited by A. Berlejung and A. Meier. Leipziger Altorientalische Studien. Wiesbaden: Harrassowitz.
Younker, R. W. 2000. Ramoth-Gilead. *EDB*, 1110.
Yun, I. A. 2006. A Case of Linguistic Transition: The Nerab Inscriptions. *JSS* 51:19–43.
Zaccagnini, C. 1990. Golden Cups Offered to the Gods at Emar. *Or* 59:518–20.
Zadok, R. 1976a. Geographical and Onomastic Notes. *JANESCU* 8:113–26.
———. 1976b. *The Jews in Babylonia in the Chaldean and Achaemenian Periods in the Light of the Babylonian Sources*. Tel-Aviv: Mifal Hashichpul.

———. 1977. *On West Semites in Babylonia during the Chaldean and Achaemenian Periods: An Onomastic Study*. Jerusalem: Wanaata and Tel Aviv University.
———. 1978. Historical and Onomastic Notes. *WO* 9:35–56, 240–41.
———. 1979. On Some Foreign Population Groups in First-Millennium Babylonia. *TA* 6:164–81.
———. 1981. The Toponymy of the Nippur Region within the General Framework of the Mesopotamian Toponymy. *WO* 12:39–69.
———. 1982. Remarks on the Inscription of *Hdysʿy* from Tall Fakhariya. *TA* 9:117–29.
———. 1984a. Assyro-Babylonian Lexical and Onomastic Notes. *BO* 41:33–46.
———. 1984b. On the Historical Background of the Sefire Treaty. *AION* 44:529–38.
———. 1985a. *Geographical Names according to New- and Late-Babylonian Texts*. RGTC 8. Wiesbaden: Reichert.
———. 1985b. Some Problems in Early Aramean History. Pages 81–85 in *XXII Deutscher Orientalistentag vom 21. bis 25. Marz 1983 in Tübingen*. Edited by W. Röllig. ZDMGSup 6. Wiesbaden: Steiner.
———. 1985c. Zur Geographie Babyloniens während des sargonidischen, chaldäischen, achämenidischen und hellenistischen Zeitalters. *WO* 16:19–79.
———. 1988. *The Pre-Hellenistic Israelite Anthroponymy and Prosopography*. OLA 28. Leuven: Peeters.
———. 1991. Elements of Aramean Pre-history. Pages 104–17 in Cogan and Ephʿal 1991.
———. 1995. The Ethno-Linguistic Character of the Jezireh and Adjacent Regions in the Ninth–Seventh Centuries (Assyria Proper vs. Periphery). Pages 217–82 in Liverani 1995.
———. 1996a. Geographical and Onomastics Remarks on H. Tadmor, *The Inscriptions of Tiglath-Pileser III King of Assyria* (Jerusalem: Israel Academy of Sciences and Humanities, 1994). *NABU* 1996.1:11–13, no. 17. http://sepoa.fr/wp/wp-content/uploads/2012/05/1996-1.pdf.
———. 1996b. Notes on Syro-Palestinian History, Toponymy and Anthroponymy. *UF* 28:721–49.
———. 1997. Historical and Ethno-Linguistic Notes. *UF* 29:797–814.
———. 1999. The Ethno-Linguistic Character of the Semitic-Speaking Population (Excluding Judeo-Samaritans) of Syria in the Hellenistic, Roman and Byzantine Periods: A Preliminary and Tentative Survey of the Onomastic Evidence. Pages 267–301 in Avishur and Deutsch 1999.
———. 2002a. *The Ethno-Linguistic Character of Northwestern Iran and Kurdistan in the Neo-Assyrian Period*. Tel Aviv-Jaffa: Archaeological Center.
———. 2002b. The Ethno-Linguistic Character of Northwestern Iran and Kurdistan in the Neo-Assyrian Period. *Iran* 40:89–151.
———. 2003. West Semites in Administrative and Epistolary Documents from Northern and Central Babylonia. Pages 255–71 in *Shlomo: Studies in Epigraphy, Iconography, History and Archaeology in Honor of Shlomo Mousaieff*. Edited by R. Deutsch. Tel Aviv: Archaeological Center Publication.
———. 2008. Neo-Assyrian Notes. Pages 312–30 in *Treasures on Camel's Humps: Historical and Literary Studies from the Ancient Near East to Israel Ephʿal*. Edited by M. Cogan and D. Kahn. Jerusalem: Magnes.

———. 2009. Philistian Notes I. *UF* 41:660–79.

———. 2012. The Aramean Infiltration and Diffusion in the Upper Jazira, ca. 1150–930 BCE. Pages 569–79 in Galil et al. 2012.

———. 2013. The Onomastics of the Chaldean, Aramean, and Arabian Tribes in Babylonia during the First Millennium. Pages 263–336 in Berlejung and Streck 2013.

Zarins, J. 1992. Archaeological and Chronological Problems within the Great Southwest Asian Arid Zone, 8500–1850 B.C. Pages 42–62 in *Chronologies in Old World Archaeology*. Edited by Robert W. Ehrich. 3rd ed. 2 vols. Chicago: University of Chicago Press.

Zeeb, F. 1998. Die Ortsnamen und geographischen Beziehungen der Texte aus Alalaḫ. *UF* 30:829–86.

Zehnder, T. 2010. *Die hethitischen Frauennamen: Katalog und Interpretation*. Dresdner Beiträge zur Hethitologie 29. Wiesbaden: Harrassowitz.

Zevit, Z. 1991. Yahweh Worship and Worshippers in Eighth-Century Syria. *VT* 41:363–66.

Zevit, Z., S. Gitin, and M. Sokoloff, eds. 1995. *Solving Riddles and Untying Knots: Biblical, Epigraphic, and Semitic Studies in Honor of Jonas C. Greenfield*. Winona Lake, IN: Eisenbrauns.

Zimansky, P. 2006. Writing, Writers, and Reading in the Kingdom of Van. Pages 257–76 in Sanders 2006.

Zwickel, W. 1990. *Eisenzeitliche Ortslagen im Ostjordanland*. BTAVO B/81. Wiesbaden: Harrassowitz.

# SCRIPTURE INDEX

Hebrew Bible/Old Testament

# GENERAL INDEX